HISTORICAL BRITAIN

Other books by Eric S Wood

COLLINS FIELD GUIDE TO ARCHAEOLOGY IN BRITAIN

Eric S Wood

HISTORICAL BRITAIN

A comprehensive account of the development
of rural and urban life and landscape
from prehistory to the present day

ILLUSTRATED BY REX NICHOLLS

THE HARVILL PRESS

LONDON

First published in Great Britain 1995 by
The Harvill Press
84 Thornhill Road
London N1 1RD

Text and captions copyright © Eric Wood 1995
Illustrations copyright © Rex Nicholls 1995

The author has asserted his moral right
to be identified as the author of this work

A CIP catalogue record for this title is available from the British Library

ISBN 1 86046 031 3

Designed and typeset in Photina by
The Libanus Press, Marlborough

Printed and bound in Great Britain by
Butler & Tanner, Frome and London

TO

PAM

WITH LOVE

Acknowledgements

During the long and laborious writing of this book I have of course drawn heavily on the work of others, and have been greatly and willingly helped by all those of whom I have asked questions. The lists of books for "Further Reading" record the books I have found most useful, and are intended to acknowledge my debt to their authors. Mistakes, misunderstandings, and ignorance of recent discoveries or interpretations are of course entirely mine. Collins, who suggested the book in the first place, as a kind of continuation of my *Collins Field Guide to Archaeology in Britain*, and Harvill, who finally saw it through, have been towers of strength, support, skill, and patience, and I offer them – Michael Walter at the beginning, and Christopher MacLehose, Bill Swainson, Candida Hall, and all at Harvill and the Libanus Press who have worked on the book – my warmest thanks.

The draft was typed by Mrs Joanna Kilmartin – a mammoth task – and I am full of admiration for her skill in unravelling my frequently chaotic text and often near-illegible handwriting. The illustrations, which are so conspicuous a feature of the book, and in a real sense make it what it is, are the work of Rex Nicholls. His grasp of the subjects, his artistry in conveying their essence, and his enthusiasm take the book into a different dimension.

My wife Pam has spent years under the shadow of the work, and has also contributed towards the indexes – a vastly bigger job than either of us anticipated; she has accepted considerable disruption to her life. The dedication to her is a quite inadequate acknowledgement of what she has done.

The copy editor, Mrs Valerie Horsler, has made a notable and sensitive contribution in tidying up and improving the text, and I am deeply indebted to her for this.

Those who answered questions so helpfully include the librarians of the Society of Antiquaries, the Athenaeum, the British Museum (later British Library), the University of London, the Surrey Archaeological Society (Mrs Janette White, Mrs Maureen Roberts and Mrs Susan Janaway), the Sussex Archaeological Society, the Guildhall Library; the reference or local studies libraries at Winchester, Southampton, Guildford, Farnham, Alton, Petersfield, Ealing, Oxford, Halifax and Norwich; the Museum of English Rural Life (Mrs Barbara Holden); the Weald and Downland Open Air Museum, the Science Museum (Mr B McWilliam, Mr John Lissin), the London Transport Museum, Guildford Museum (Mr Matthew Alexander); the Institution of Civil Engineers; the Royal Institute of British Architects; the Society for the Protection of Ancient Buildings; the Ancient Monuments Society (Mr Matthew Saunders); the tourist information centres at Winchester and Wallingford. I must mention also Mr David Howitt (Mull), Mr Alan Hewitt (Warlingham), Mr E L Walters (Bucklers Hard), Mrs Anne Mallinson (Selborne), Professor E M Yates (Selborne); and the Curator, Old Basing House, Mr David Brown (Oxbow Books), Henry Venables Ltd (Stafford). I hope those I have forgotten to record will forgive me. I am deeply grateful to them all.

O fortunatos nimium ...

ESW
September 1995

Contents

The Church

The Styles of Architecture

Castles and Military Works

Public Buildings

Introduction

This book was originally conceived as a continuation of the author's *Collins Field Guide to Archaeology in Britain* (1963 and later editions). But the writing was interrupted several times, and when the book was finally resumed, the author's interests had widened and shifted. He now finds himself involved in the exploration of the physical evidences for historical Britain generally. This entails less emphasis on prehistoric periods, which are only mentioned if they directly underlie or influence later remains, as well as less concern with the techniques and results of archaeology proper. Thus it emerges as not so much a sequel to the *Field Guide* as a quite different book.

The book begins in earnest when the Romans left Britain, except for backward glances at relevant Roman and pre-Roman material, and ends today, with Industrial Archaeology. This is a vast span of time, incorporating a vast spectrum of material. The technical developments of 15 centuries are so multifarious as to preclude detailed coverage. What I have attempted to do, while following a broad chronological development within each major section, is to give some answers to the questions which come to mind on seeing what remains of the past in country or town in Britain, questions such as: Who built or made it? What was its function in the context of its time? Why was it made the way it was? How has it changed and developed?

The writing of *Historical Britain* has been dogged by destruction. No sooner was a building selected to illustrate a point than it was knocked down to make way for a road, car park, or block of flats. This is scarcely an exaggeration. Progress, particularly technological, but also in personal and social attitudes, brings about a continual acceleration of change in our way of life, social structure and habits, and in buildings, planning, and environment generally. The rate of this change is now so fast that we are in serious danger of getting out of touch with the past. G M Trevelyan, some forty years ago, could rightly say that "our world has changed more in the last hundred years than it did in the previous thousand. Yet much still lives on, and helps to shape the world we live in." He might now have added that there has been more change in the last twenty years than in the previous hundred. Yet the present, and the future, grow inevitably out of the past, and a society unmindful of its past is likely to have an impoverished future. We live, in the sharpest sense, on the swiftly advancing frontier between two worlds, and the new generations are finding it increasingly difficult to visualise and understand the conditions in which even their parents were brought up, let alone those in which the towns and villages of this country developed over historical time.

But this in no way implies that the roots of our society are not still there, or are not important. Without a recognition of them there will be a growing and dangerous risk of floating at a superficial level along the currents of the modern world, with impoverishment at a profound level which will, by removing a dimension from life, make it much less satisfying and full, and may even have psychological repercussions.

It is of course easier to understand our roots if some of them are still showing. But they are not merely being pushed underground; their stumps are being cut out and replaced, so that they cannot be seen. Former townscapes and even town plans are becoming unrecognisable, and before long few major town centres will show much of their past or of their development. The rate of change is in fact so rapid that any account of our towns will be out of date before it reaches the reader, and the historical process will be observable in fewer, and usually smaller and more remote, places as time goes on. Unless something is said now the moment will have passed when what is significant in the past can be pointed out and described with any sense of meaning or reality. Old buildings and features are also increasingly hard to understand; they are often isolated and out of context among a mass of new buildings and roads on a different scale, and their original setting is very hard to visualise and reconstruct.

On this question of scale and character, a classic instance used to be St Patrick's Roman Catholic cathedral in New York, USA, which now crouches incongruously among a towering forest of skyscrapers. But examples nearer home are ubiquitous. The centre of Birmingham is now very difficult to recognise or recall. In London, much of the Georgian, and still more the Victorian, townscape is irreversibly gone. St Paul's, once a dominant feature of the City, is now only one of a group of tall buildings, and from some viewpoints is overshadowed. The New Zealand building clashes uneasily with the scale of Trafalgar Square. The University of London developments in Bloomsbury have left only Bedford Square (in spite of its change to professional use), the east side of Gordon Square, and perhaps Bedford Place to hint at the former character of the area. Victoria Street was not so long ago an interesting, if uninspiring, example of a major Victorian commercial and professional thoroughfare. It has nearly all changed in scale and character, and even the Army and Navy Stores, with its architectural reminders of Woolwich or Chatham, has been rebuilt as a standardised block. And so on.

RESCUE, the Trust for British Archaeology, set up in 1971, whose objects are to save what should be saved and record what cannot be, has publicised facts on the rate of destruction. Motorways now cover 30,000 acres (12,000 ha) of Britain; 60,000 acres (24,000 ha) of land are being submerged under suburban and industrial development every year, or the equivalent of a medium-sized county every seven years. Over much of lowland Britain, some 100 archaeological sites disappear every week, and we are down to the last few in some categories. Of 450 recorded barrows in Gloucestershire, only one group remains intact. In Wiltshire, out of 640 scheduled sites, 250 had been completely destroyed and a further 150 damaged by 1964. Between 1500 and 1950 about 300 medieval village sites were destroyed; between 1950 and 1970 another 300 sites were destroyed, and they are disappearing at the rate of 20 to 30 a year. In Gloucester, of 603 historic buildings listed in 1949, only 459 remained in 1971; in Poole, more than 150 out of 329 monuments in the central area were demolished between 1950 and 1972; and the process is far from complete. London has suffered some spectacular losses in recent years, such as the Shot Tower, the Euston Arch and Greek Hall, the Coal Exchange, Carlton Mews, and the early railway station at Nine Elms. Out of 70 major buildings described in Pevsner's *London: Cities of London and Westminster* (1972), 27 had gone by the second edition (1973). Such glaring losses stimulated the setting up of conservationist bodies such as the Civic Trust.

In 1984 it was calculated that there were about 635,000 known archaeological sites and monuments in England, whatever significance is to be attached to such a figure (an analysis was published in *Proceedings of the Prehistoric Society*, 50, 1984). Listing of buildings has been slow but in the last few years a national resurvey was put in hand and the final list may reach some 500,000 buildings.

Of the sites and buildings eligible for scheduling or listing, a certain number are always at risk and some are destroyed, but no reliable figures are available to gauge the full extent of the loss. But an idea can be gained from a recognisable class of buildings, the country houses,

of which 500 were demolished between 1945 and 1980. Twenty thousand or so round barrows and some 900 stone circles still exist, but the original number cannot be calculated.

The scale and weight of much modern building necessitates deep and specially prepared foundations. Whereas the cellars and foundations of Victorian buildings often cut through to Roman levels, current methods of ground stabilisation – compaction, vibration, and dynamic piling – totally destroy all ancient remains for some two metres beyond the area stabilised, and go far deeper than any 19th-century cellars. Traditional piling is less destructive, because its effects are confined to a more limited area, but within that area destruction is complete.

Roads, car parks, and services also take their toll, as do major works like factories and warehouses, public buildings, and even housing estates. The density of archaeological sites is not always appreciated. Surveys of the land ahead of motorways have consistently revealed several to the mile, and this must be envisaged in every direction over most of the country.

In the countryside a different, but no less destructive, set of causes operates. Besides urban and industrial building, there is opencast mining, gravel- and sand-working (eg the Thames and Trent valleys), drilling for oil, and flooding for reservoirs (eg Cow Green, Teesdale), to name a few. The important hillfort of Sutton Walls (He) was destroyed many years ago for a rubbish tip. As an example, some 3,500 acres (1,400ha) of sand, gravel, and other minerals are stripped and quarried annually. Archaeological surveys of gravel terraces suggest an average density of one settlement site every 50–250 acres (20–100ha). Thus mineral extraction may well destroy up to 70 archaeological sites and their associated landscapes every year. Leisure takes its toll too – not only cars and motorcycles driven destructively on ancient trackways, in woodland, and on hillsides, but the sheer number of quite legitimate and orderly visitors to sites or areas of scenic beauty, such as Stonehenge or the South Downs, causing in some places quite serious damage to grass, banks, and approaches. Users of metal detectors do untold harm, in an archaeological sense, by following up the clues given by their machines.

The biggest cause of damage to the natural environment is farming itself: deep ploughing for forestry and intensive cultivation (often subsidised); removal of hedges; drainage of wetlands; conversion of ancient broadleaved woodland to conifers or arable. The Nature

Conservancy Council's report *Nature Conservation in Great Britain* (1984) estimates the losses from these causes from 1949 to 1983 as follows:

- lowland neutral grasslands, including herb-rich hay meadows: 95% now lacking significant wild-life interest, 3% only left undamaged
- lowland grassland or sheepwalk on chalk or limestone: 80% loss or significant damage
- lowland heaths on acidic soils: 40% loss
- limestone pavements in northern England: 45% damaged or destroyed, 3% only untouched
- ancient lowland woods composed of native, broadleaved trees: 30–50% loss; against this some 25% of new planting of broadleaves has taken place, but coniferous woodland has increased by two and a half times
- hedges in England and Wales: 28% loss, or 140,000 miles (224,000km) (80 miles (128km) a week); figures vary, but in 1986 a total of some 190,000 miles (304,000km) was put forward
- lowland fens etc: some 50% loss or significant damage
- lowland raised mires: 60% loss or significant change
- upland grasslands, heaths, and bogs: 30% loss or significant damage

This almost unbelievable list could be extended.

And these figures are only part of a long-term trend, which is largely a function of steadily increasing population. For instance, 80% of heaths have been lost since 1800 in Britain (for Europe as a whole the figure is 95%). Thus, in Surrey and north-east Hampshire, heaths now cover 6,000 acres (2,400ha), against some 11,000 (4,400ha) in 1750. Deforestation has gone on for 5,000–6,000 years, and now only some 8% of Britain is covered by woodland. There is, for example, evidence round York for deforestation in the Roman period, followed by increased run-off and loss of soil (and silting and flooding of rivers); this is not unlike the effects of recent ploughing, removal of hedges, and agricultural intensification. Not all losses of trees are due to human activity, however. Climatic changes in the long term have altered the composition of British woodlands, and the losses of elms due to the Dutch elm disease in the 1960s, when 30 million trees were lost, will long be remembered. Several authorities think the elm decline in the Neolithic had a similar cause.

There are signs that the wholesale destruction of hedges in recent years is slowing up, and even that new field boundaries are being laid down. In 1983 the rate of loss was some 2,000 miles (3,200 km), although some estimates are as high as 4,000 (6,400 km). But unfortunately a former hedge is usually replaced not by a new hedge but by a wire fence, which is aesthetically and ecologically much less satisfying. Thus, from 1978 to 1984, 17,500 miles (28,000km) of hedges were removed, but 30,250 miles (48,400km) of wire fencing were installed (mostly in the Midlands and south). Only 2,187 miles (3,500km) of new hedges were planted in those years.

To set against this gloomy picture there is a growing consciousness of the issues, and of the urgent need to stem the tide of destruction. Archaeologists and conservationists are equally active in bringing the issues before the public, and in taking what steps they can to prevent further destruction, including seeking to increase the statutory protection of sites, finds, and the environment. Developers and farmers have become more responsive, the public are more aware, and the situation is not all black. But much remains to be done, and in some areas it is too late already. Thus, although the proportion of farming land in England and Wales altered little from 1947 to 1980, the area in cultivation increased from 37% to 48%. This figure, owing to changes in EU farming policy and the effects of produce quotas in an attempt to reduce surpluses, is now seen to be more than is required. In response to this the Government, in 1986 and 1987, proposed that surplus farmland outside designated areas should be "set-aside" for development – building, light industry, leisure facilities, etc. This will inevitably bring about a further change in the countryside, and have an incalculable effect on rural life and conditions.

What these statistics show, in short, is a complex panorama of widespread and rapid change. It underlies, and frequently colours, the approach to many of the topics covered in this book.

I have, of course, had to rely heavily on the original researches of others, scattered not only in books but in periodicals. Any comments or views on the facts presented are my own. The treatment of subjects is as objective as possible, but personal views necessarily come in from time to time. The stress throughout is on the explanation of the physical remains, but this cannot always be rigidly adhered to, and there are occasional forays into traditional history when this is essential. The structure of the book is straightforward: the broadly coherent subject groups, each as complete in itself as possible, are organised chronologically. Another author might have grouped some subjects differently, but if one collects so many often loosely related subjects together within one fence, like an uncaged zoo of different animals, it should not be surprising if the lion and the lamb find themselves to be neighbours.

It is a truism that W G Hoskins' *The Making of the English Landscape*, first published in 1955, and his later books, revolutionised our understanding of the subject, and put it irrevocably on a new path. There have been a few other seminal books in recent years of which much the same could be said. Among these are Oliver Rackham's *The History of the Countryside* (1986) – a classic already – and Richard Fortey's *The Hidden Landscape* (1993), which presents the geology of Britain in a fresh and exciting way. There are also significant studies or more limited subjects, such as Margaret Wood's *The English Medieval House* (1965), and Richard Morris' *Churches in the Landscape* (1989). These, and other similar studies, go into greater depth in defined fields. The present book – which is not of course primarily concerned with the natural world, as are Rackham's and Fortey's – has a wider scope (perhaps rashly), and is therefore more discursive and less specialised. It might indeed best be taken as an introduction to the topics it covers. But introductions have their place, and may well not only provide key information, but a spur to the reader to go deeper into the subject; the "Museums and Sites" and "Further Reading" lists are designed to point the way. Thus, *Historical Britain* does not set out to compete with the scholarly work of others, but stands as an overall guide in its own right, which I hope will give pleasure as well as information.

Abbreviations of County Names

The local government reorganisation of 1974 (England and Wales) and 1975 (Scotland) made several changes to boundaries and authorities which have by now passed into local usage, even though the former areas have not been wholly effaced, in certain contexts, in the minds of at least some of the older generations. For England, the relatively compact size of the new administrative divisions (most of which coincide with the old counties anyway) means that no great distortion of geographical or historical identity is involved by using the new names. This is generally followed in this book, unless for some reason it is desirable to pinpoint a site, or perpetuate its former location. For Wales and Scotland, however, many of the new divisions or regions cover wide areas and include several old counties. Here there are often grounds for continuing to name the old county, while adding the present region of which it forms part.

In the interests of brevity and consistency a set of two-letter abbreviations was devised by the author for his *Collins Field Guide to Archaeology in Britain* (5th ed, 1979), and it seems convenient to use these in this book, in the absence of any generally accepted national system (although the English Place-Name Society has devised a somewhat similar list).

The abbreviations for the pre-1974 and 1975 counties are:

ENGLAND

Bc	Buckinghamshire
Bd	Bedfordshire
Bk	Berkshire
Ca	Cambridgeshire and Isle of Ely
Ch	Cheshire
Co	Cornwall
Cu	Cumberland
Db	Derbyshire
Do	Dorset
Du	Durham
Dv	Devonshire
Ex	Essex
Gl	Gloucestershire
Ha	Hampshire
He	Herefordshire He

HP	Huntingdonshire & The Soke of Peterborough
Ht	Hertfordshire Ht
IW	Wight, Isle of
Kt	Kent
La	Lancashire
Le	Leicestershire
Li	Lincolnshire
	LH Holland
	LK Kesteven
	LL Lindsey
Ln	Greater London
Mx	Middlesex
Nd	Northumberland
Nf	Norfolk
Nh	Northamptonshire

No	Nottinghamshire
Ox	Oxfordshire
Ru	Rutland
So	Somerset
Sp	Shropshire
St	Staffordshire
Su	Suffolk (East & West)
Sx	Sussex (East & West)
Sy	Surrey
Wd	Westmorland
Ww	Warwickshire
Wo	Worcestershire
Yk	Yorkshire
	YE East Riding
	YN North Riding
	YW West Riding

WALES

An	Anglesey
Br	Breconshire
Cd	Cardiganshire
Cm	Carmarthenshire
Cn	Caernarvonshire
Dh	Denbighshire
Ft	Flintshire
Gm	Glamorgan
Me	Merioneth
Mg	Montgomeryshire
Mo	Monmouthshire
Pb	Pembrokeshire
Ra	Radnorshire

SCOTLAND

Ab	Aberdeenshire
Ag	Angus
Ar	Argyll
Ay	Ayrshire
Ba	Banffshire
Be	Berwickshire
Bu	Bute
Cs	Caithness
Ck	Clackmannanshire
Df	Dumfriesshire
Dn	Dumbartonshire
EL	East Lothian
Fi	Fife
In	Inverness-shire
Kb	Kirkcudbrightshire
Kc	Kincardineshire
Kr	Kinross-shire
Lk	Lanarkshire
ML	Midlothian
My	Moray

Nn	Nairnshire
Or	Orkney
Pe	Perthshire
Ps	Peebleshire
RC	Ross & Cromarty
Rf	Renfrewshire
Rx	Roxburghshire
Sd	Sutherland
Sg	Stirlingshire
Sk	Selkirkshire
Wg	Wigtownshire
WL	West Lothian
Zd	Zetland

IM ISLE OF MAN

CI CHANNEL ISLANDS

CA	Alderney
CG	Guernsey
CJ	Jersey
CS	Sark

The changes of 1974 and 1975 will be common knowledge locally or will be provided by any public library; they would take up too much space to detail here. The abbreviations for the new counties (and regions in Scotland) are:

ENGLAND

Av	Avon
Cb	Cumbria
Cl	Cleveland
GM	Greater Manchester
Hu	Humberside
MS	Merseyside
NY	North Yorkshire
SI	Scilly Isles
SY	South Yorkshire
TW	Tyne & Wear
WM	West Midlands
WY	West Yorkshire

SCOTLAND

Bo	Borders
Ce	Central
DG	Dumfries & Galloway
Fi	Fife
Gr	Grampian
Hi	Highland
Lo	Lothian
Or	Orkney
Sc	Strathclyde
Sh	Shetland
Ta	Tayside
WI	Western Isles

WALES

Cw	Clwyd
Dy	Dyfed
Gd	Gwynedd
Gw	Gwent
MG	Mid-Glamorgan
Pw	Powys
SG	South Glamorgan
WG	West Glamorgan

Places affected by boundary changes may have two abbreviations, for the old and the new counties: thus, Beverley, YE (Hu); Wantage, Bk (Ox). The abolition of the GLC and Metropolitan authorities in 1986 need not affect the relevant symbols.

Glossary

aisle lateral extension of a nave or choir, divided from these by an arcade or rows of columns; also found in an aisled hall

alluvium earth, sand, etc deposited by flooding in a river valley

angel roof with carved angels on the ends of hammer beams

anticline a geological ridge or fold

apse rounded extension of a church, chancel, or chapel; found also in major Roman buildings

arcade (1) row of arches; (2) covered walk between shops

archaeomagnetism technique of dating clay objects, eg pottery or glass furnaces. The iron oxides in the clay are magnetic, and the direction of the magnetism is fixed when the object is fired. If the object is reheated and cooled, it carries the present-day magnetic direction; the difference between the two readings gives the date of the previous firing

ard light, primitive plough, consisting of a pole with separate blade or point, drawn by man or animal; an ard did not produce a furrow, but merely scratched the soil

ashlar square-cut stones

assart land taken in for private farming from common land (woodland, heath, fen, etc)

atrium courtyard of a Roman building **aumbry** small cupboard in north wall of the chancel of a church, for keeping the communion vessels in

bailey the inner or outer courtyard of a castle, walled

ball-flower a motif of decoration consisting of a globular three-petalled flower enclosing a ball

baluster a short post or pillar supporting a rail or coping, or in a Saxon window

barbican outwork in front of gate of castle or town, consisting of outer gate joined by side walls to the inner gate

barrel vault simple roof of semicircular section

barrow burial mound

basilica the public hall of a Roman town

bastion forward projection from a defensive work

bastle a defensible farmhouse, with dwelling on the first floor and cattle on the ground floor

bay (1) division of building between two trusses; (2) dam of ironworking pond

bays (baize) cloth made from worsted warp and woollen weft fulled

bell pit excavation for mining iron ore, consisting of a circular pit wider at the bottom than the top

blind arcading a range of arches attached to a wall

blockhouse a small timber or concrete fort or defensive post

bloomery a simple clay iron-smelting furnace, producing a "bloom" or lump of iron

bocage countryside of small, irregular fields and scattered farms (see **severalty**)

Borough English inheritance by the youngest son or daughter

boss an ornamental knob covering or filling the intersection of ribs in a vault or ceiling

Boulder Clay debris left in a sheet by a receding glacier, consisting of mud and stones

bovate see Oxgang

brace a diagonal timber, either straight or curved, in the angle of a roof-frame, at tie-beam or collar level, or in a wall under the wall plate, to strengthen the structure

broach spire a usually octagonal spire rising from a square tower with no parapet; the four corners of the tower are filled by pyramidal masonry (broaches) built into the base of the spire

broadcloth fine twilled woollen or worsted cloth

Bronze Age the first metal-using period in Britain (*c* 2200–*c* 650 BC)

burgh a chartered town (Scotland)

burh a Saxon planted town, usually defended

buttress support built against a wall (a flying buttress leaps from the outside aisle wall to the navel wall)

butts (1) shooting-points on a grouse moor, marshes, etc; (2) military shooting range

canton Roman administrative division, representing the territory of a pre-Roman tribe (hence cantonal capital); see civitas

caschrom stick with bent and pointed end (digging-stick), pushed by a man

cashel see rath

cashmere fine wool from Kashmiri goats

celtic fields small, squarish, prehistoric fields, the result of cross-ploughing with an ard, and defined by banks and lynchets; groups of these are still visible in many areas

centuriation Roman allocation of land to veterans, settlers etc, laid out in a regular square or rectangular grid, fed by lanes, and linked to a road

champion (champaign) open field country – broadly, the arable zone of England

chancel the section of a church at the east end, continuing the nave and containing the altar

chantry chapel endowed for a chantry priest to sing masses for the founder's soul

chapter body of canons and other dignitaries of a cathedral or collegiate church, presided over by a dean or provost

chert a siliceous rock, having many of the properties of flint

Chi-Rho symbol of Christ, made up of the first two letters of his name in Greek

civitas Roman regional division, based on pre-Roman tribal territories, with considerable local autonomy, local capital, and system of smaller towns

clerestory upper storey of the nave wall of a church, with windows (above the *triforium* in a large church)

close-studding ornamental use of upright timbers set close together in the wall of a timber-framed house

clunch hard chalk used as building stone

clustered shaft one of several slender columns attached to a pillar or pier, door jamb or window surround

Coade stone artificial (composition) stone used for statuary and architectural ornament from 1769 to *c* 1840

cob walling material of clay mixed with straw

collar purlin purlin supporting the collars

collar short transverse member high up in a roof

colonial a Roman town set up to provide for retired soldiers or officials; later, an honorific title

constable the military governor of a castle

coppicing the cutting down, every few years, of small trees, to encourage the growth of fresh poles

corbel block of stone projecting from a wall, to support a beam etc

cornice the projecting ornamental moulding along the top of a building or wall

cottage orné a Romantic and picturesque style of building small houses in the late 18th and early 19th centuries

coulter vertical blade in front of ploughshare to open up the soil

countryside, ancient and planned broadly, the distinction between bocage and champion

crenellate to provide (eg a castle) with battlements or loopholes

crinkle-crankle a wavy wall, to protect fruit trees etc

croft (1) the area of a peasant's plot ("toft and croft") furthest from the house; (2) a smallholding, mainly in the Scottish Highlands

croglofft space within the roof and over the parlour or store, in a Welsh single-storey cottage

crown post central post in roof, from the tie-beam to a collar purlin (which supports the collar (*qv*)

crucks paired curved timbers (in a house) from the ground to the roof ridge (or the upper parts of these)

Dark Ages the period from the departure of the Romans to the late Saxon period – say AD 400–1000; but the phrase should be used with caution, as more evidence comes to light

delft tin-enamelled earthenware with Chinese-inspired decoration (17th–18th centuries)

demesne that part of an estate worked directly for the owner – the home farm

Dissolution the abolition, by Henry VIII, of the medieval monastic system and the takeover of the monastic houses and property (1536–40)

donjon castle keep

doocot dovecote (in Scotland)

double-pile house a house having four rooms of equal height on each of two floors; in larger houses there are often two parallel and equal roofs (late 17th to mid 19th centuries)

double splay a chamfered surface in a window or door opening

drugget coarse woven fabric

drumlin a pocket of morainic debris left by a glacier, in the form of rounded, often oval, hillock

dyke (1) drainage ditch; (2) bank, stone, or turf wall

einkorn a species of wheat (*Triticum monococcum*)

emmer a species of wheat (*Triticum dicoccum*)

enceinte the circuit of walls and bastions defending a castle or town

enclosure the reorganisation by landowners of open fields and common land for large-scale, centralised agriculture, sheep pasture, etc, at first by agreement or individual action, later by Act of Parliament

entablature in classical architecture, the upper part of an order consisting of architrave, frieze, and cornice

esker a long, winding bank of fine mud and pebbles, carried by a stream from under a glacier

Eustatic response of sea level to glaciation

fan vaulting vaulting with numerous ribs springing from one centre in equal diverging curves, giving the effect of a fan, and sometimes highly complex, with panels and minor ribs

fank shelter for sheep

felloe section of the rim of a wheel

felspar a mineral containing aluminium and other silicates

felt non-woven material made by compression, heat and moisture

foederati Continental tribesmen brought into Britain by the Romans (late 3rd to early 5th centuries) to discourage raiding or resettlement from their homelands

fogou prehistoric underground chamber, passage, store, etc

forest tract of land, not always entirely wooded, subject to medieval forest law

forum the market and assembly place of a Roman town

frieze coarse woollen cloth with nap on one side only

frit the first phase in glassmaking – the partial fusion of the basic ingredients, sand and fluxes

frog the indentation in the surface of a brick

furlong blocks of strips in a medieval open field

fustian cloth from linen warp and cotton weft

gablet small opening at the apex of a gable of a timber-framed house to let smoke out

galleting (garneting) the insertion of small pieces of ironstone etc in the mortar of a wall for ornament, strengthening, or magical protection

garderobe a medieval privy

gavelkind *partible inheritance* among sons, in Kent

geo narrow cleft or inlet in a cliff

gin a rotary device for driving a machine for grinding, crushing, hoisting, etc, worked by human or animal power

gneiss a metamorphic rock, usually with pink and black banding

gore a triangular or irregular piece of land

grange an outlying farm or estate centre, particularly one belonging to a monastery

granite an igneous intrusive rock consisting largely of quartz, felspar and mica

green man medieval representation of a human head with vegetation growing from his face or head, symbolising the union of Man and Nature

greenstone a green intrusive rock containing felspar and hornblende

greywacke a conglomerate rock

grit rock like a coarse sandstone, consisting mainly of angular grains of quartz

groin vault a vault produced by the intersection at right angles of two barrel vaults

grubenhaus Anglo-Saxon building with a sunken floor

haematite rock consisting of ferric oxide

hafod upland summer pasture (Wales)

hammer beam beam projecting horizontally from wall, at wall plate level, supported by a brace, and carrying roof members (braces and struts)

Harrying of the North punitive expedition by William I in the north of England (1069–70), causing extensive destruction

head heap of soil at the end of a furrow (in a medieval field) left when the plough was turned

henge a late Neolithic and early Bronze Age monument consisting of a circle or circles of stone or wood, set within a bank and ditch, with one or more entrances; used for religious and social purposes

herringbone masonry stone, brick or tile work, laid diagonally and not horizontally; alternate courses are laid in opposite directions, giving a zigzag effect

hide medieval measure of land, enough to support one free family (40–120 acres, 15–50ha)

Highland Zone one of two geographical zones into which Britain is conveniently divided for archaeological purposes

hollow way road on slope, sunken by traffic and weathering

hood moulding a projecting moulding above a door or window to throw off the rain

hudd portable shelter for clergy conducting a funeral outdoors

hundred a medieval land division originally containing a hundred hides, but with local variations; a hundred had a court deriving from an ancient popular mooty or assembly

hypocaust Roman central heating system, using heated air under floors and in walls

igneous (rock) produced by volcanic agency

index indicates the relative level of prices or wages compared with that at a date taken as standard

intervallum street road close inside the walls of a Roman fort

intrusive (igneous rock) which has penetrated overlying strata

Iron Age the last prehistoric phase before the Roman conquest (c 650 BC to AD 43); an age of tribal kingdoms and considerable social, economic, and artistic achievement

isostatic rise and fall of land relative to sea, particularly in response to glaciation or its absence

jetty projection of an upper floor of a house relative to the floor below

jowl thickening at the top of an upright post, eg a door jamb

Jurassic Ridge the limestone belt which crosses England from Dorset to Yorkshire, providing a corridor for communication, and building stone

kame winding gravel ridge laid down along the nose of a glacier

keep the principal tower of a castle

kersey coarse narrow cloth woven from long staple wool, and fulled

king post central post in roof, from the tie beam to the roof ridge

knapping trimming nodules of flint to produce core, flake, and blade implements

laithe house a dwelling house and cowhouse or barn in a single block, but with separate entrances

lathe a field barn

ledger a flat gravestone

lehr annealing furnace for glass (may be tubular, through which the glass is slowly moved)

lierne vault ribbed vault with liernes, decorative ribs not springing from the principal boss or springers (the stones from which the arch "springs")

light window opening in a church

lobby entrance a type of 17th- and early 18th-century house with a central chimney and fireplaces and a central door on the front; this door opened closely against the fireplaces, leaving a small lobby for access to the rooms

long and short work a Saxon quoin, consisting of long stones set vertically, between stones set horizontally

longhouse a dwelling house and cowhouse in one building, both reached through a single cross passage between the parts

Lowland Zone one of two geographical zones into which Britain is conveniently divided for archaeological purposes

lynchet a bank accumulated on a slope, owing to creep of soil loosened by ploughing

magma molten rock deep in the Earth's crust, which forms igneous rocks

magnesian limestone containing a high proportion of magnesium carbonate

maiolica tin-enamelled earthenware, richly painted, of Islamic and Mediterranean origin (16th century)

majestas a statue or picture of Christ in Majesty

manor a political and administrative unit which had rights over its tenants and the land; there could be one or more to a vill

mansio a Roman inn or hostel for official or military travellers

manufacture (medieval) the making of goods by physical labour, not usually using powered devices, often at home, and on a small scale

marl an earthy chalk used for liming the fields

mass-clock see scratch-dial

mathematical tiles tiles so shaped as to look like bricks when laid

medleys cloth made from mixed fibres

mercat market (in Scotland)

Mesolithic the Middle Stone Age, the last phase of hunting and food-gathering cultures, from the early post-glacial period to the coming of the first farmers (c 8000 to c 4000 BC)

metamorphic (rock) altered (eg limestone to marble) by pressure of overlying rocks or by heat

mistal a cow-house

moot Anglo-Saxon shire or hundred assembly, or site where this took place

moraine rock and earth material deposited by a glacier, terminally or laterally

motte defensive hillock (Norman), usually moated, with palisaded watch-tower or other structure on top

mouldboard curved board behind a ploughshare which turns the soil to form a forrow1

mound earthen hillock in garden, usually as base for an ornamental clump of trees

mount formal ornamental hillock in garden, with steps or structures, or path, to belvedere etc on the top

mungo wool from felt, used in poor quality cloth

nave (1) the main body of a church; (2) hub of wheel

Neolithic the New Stone Age, that of the first farmers, using pottery but no metal (c 4400 to 2200 BC in Britain)

nogging infilling of wall panel of a timber-framed house, usually in brick, often laid decoratively

non-juror clergyman refusing oath of allegiance in 1689

Ogam alphabet of Irish origin (1st millennium AD), consisting of lines or groups of lines incised along the edge of an upright stone

ogee arch pointed arch whose upper part is double-curved in the form of a shallow S and reversed S

oolite limestone rocks consisting of rounded grains

open fields the arable land of a medieval village, laid out in two, three, or more fields, each divided into strips; each villager was allocated a number of strips scattered among the fields to equalise conditions; the village also had meadow, pasture, woodland, and waste

oppidum a large, Iron Age, high status town, usually defended by ramparts of hillfort type, or by linear banks

order a column, with base (if any), capital, and entablature, in classical architecture; each order (Doric, Ionic, Corinthian, etc) had its own distinctive decorative scheme and proportions

oxgang medieval land division equal to 16 (strips) of 1 acre (0.4 ha) each

Palaeolithic the Old Stone Age, the first million years (or more) of human life on earth (until *c* 8000 BC in Britain)

pannage (1) the right to pasture pigs; (2) acorns, mast, etc as pig-food

pargeting plasterwork with raised decoration

parish an area of land presided over by a church, originally the area from which the church derived its tithes; usually contained one or more townships

partible inheritance equal division of an intestate's property between sons (or daughters if no sons)

pediment triangular gable above a door or window

peneplain land reduced by weathering to being almost a plain

penistone coarse woollen cloth

Piano nobile the principal rooms of a house of the classical tradition, higher than the other storeys, and usually on the first floor

pig oblong block of iron or lead from smelting furnace

pilaster an engaged column, or feature appearing as a flattened column, projecting from a wall but not detached from it

pillbox a small concrete defensive post

pingo circular or oval mound of melt material – an ice-lens – left by a glacier

piscina a basin set in the south wall of a chancel for washing the communion vessels

pisé rammed clay or earth as walling material

ploughshare the pointed blade of a plough which cuts and breaks up the soil

plush silk or cotton cloth with long nap

pollarding cutting a tree to some 10ft (3m) above the ground, to encourage growth of fresh poles

potarching preheating a glassmaking crucible to prevent it failing in the melting furnace

potin (speculum) a mixture of tin and bronze, used for some Iron Age coins

primogeniture inheritance by the eldest child (under feudal law the eldest son)

purlin a major longitudinal member in a roof

quartz a crystalline form of silica

queen post one of two posts from the tie beam to the collar

quern stone for grinding grain (by hand)

quintain a medieval exercise post for tilting at, with swinging sandbag to encourage agility

quoin the corner of a building, often marked by a contrasting material (eg stone against a brick wall, or brick against soft stone), for strength or decoration)

rath a prehistoric dwelling, farmstead etc, surrounded by a circular bank and ditch (if there is a massive stone wall instead of the bank and ditch, this is a cashel)

reave prehistoric land boundary (wall or bank) on Dartmoor and other open areas

redoubt small detached stronghold without provision for flank defence

reredorter privy of monastic dormitory

reredos screen behind altar

revetment wall etc supporting a mass of earth

Rhenish helm a Saxon tower roof with trapezoidal faces, formed by the spaces between four gables, whose spaces are centrally above the tower walls, and whose lower corners meet the tower quoins

rib projecting band on a ceiling or vault, separating the cells of the vault

ridge and furrow parallel banks in a once arable field, representing the strips of an open field

rift valley a valley with steep parallel sides caused by subsidence

ringwork an early Norman fortified enclosure, consisting of a circular bank, ditch and palisade, and often containing a motte

roll moulding moulding of semicircular section

rood a cross or crucifix; a statuary group of Christ on the Cross between the Virgin Mary and St John stood on a beam below the chancel arch, above a rood loft, which surmounted the rood screen. The scene was sometimes painted above the chancel arch.

run-rig the "infield-outfield" system of agriculture (north-west England and Scotland), the field nearest the village being cultivated more intensively than the other

rustication ornamentation of stonework by means of deeply cut joints or roughened surface

sceat Anglo-Saxon silver coin

schist a metamorphic rock containing mica

sconce detached fort with bastions

scratch dial a sundial (or part of one) incised in the wall or door jamb of a church, to indicate the time of Mass (also known as mass-clock)

sedilia seats for the priests in the south chancel wall of a church

sedimentary (rock) formed by the settlement of particles in water, or borne by wind

selion medieval strip or land

serf medieval unfree tenant, subject entirely to the manorial lord

serge cloth from worsted warp and woollen weft, twilled

sett brick-shaped block of stone used for paving

severalty individual ownership, eg of farms, as against the communal management of open fields

shale a sedimentary rock made of mud or silt

shalloon light twilled woollen cloth

shaw strip of woodland left after clearance of field

sheela-na-gig a medieval carving on a church, sexually explicit

sheiling upland pasture used in summer, with house or hut

shippon cow-house

shoddy fibre made from old cloth, shredded

silage green fodder pressed and kept in silo or pit for fermentation

sill (or sole-plate) the lowest member of a wall frame, which carries the posts and studs of the frame

sleeper beam horizontal beam supporting wall posts or floor joists, either at ground level, or at first floor level

soke right or area of local jurisdiction (hence sokeman)

solar upper room in medieval house, usually reserved to the family

sole-plate see sill

solifluction movement of wet soil down a slope, particularly over frozen subsoil

souterrain see fogou

spandrel triangular space between the shoulder of an arch and its rectangular frame

spelt a species of wheat (*Triticum spelta*)

splay an angled wall surface, so that a window or doorway is narrower than the face of the wall; a double splay has this feature on both sides of the wall

squint an opening through a pier or wall in a church to allow a priest officiating at a side altar to see the main altar

staple the quality of wool (or cotton) as determined by its fibre

stell shelter for sheep (also fank)

strapwork 16th-century decoration, of bands and forms resembling cut leather

stringcourse a projecting horizontal band in an exterior or interior wall

strip divisions of a medieval open field, first about a quarter or half an acre, later often averaging about 8 x 200yd (7 x 180m) or a third of an acre (also called lands or selions)

strut a timber either upright, from the tie-beam to a rafter, or diagonal, from the foot of a king or queen post to a rafter

stud a vertical timber in a wall or cross-frame, not a main load-bearing post (hence close-studding, studs set close together, for decorative effect)

sun-division (solskifte) a method (of Scandinavian origin) of laying out an open field village in which the tofts, counting clockwise (sunwise), are allocated the same relative strip furlong of the open fields; eg toft 1 has strip 1 in each furlong, toft 2 strip 2, etc

syas fine cloth like serge

syncline a geological trough

tammy plain woven often glazed woollen, made of fine worsted and cotton

temenos the sacred enclosure round an ancient temple

terrace (1) a bank of gravel etc left along the sides of a river valley as a result of the river cutting down in a cold phase into a sheet of gravel built up by the river in a warm phase between two glaciations; (2) a row of contiguous identical houses

thing people's assembly (in areas settled by Scandinavians)

through long stone linking the two faces of a drystone wall

tie beam horizontal beam joining two walls, usually at the level of the top of the wall

tithe a proportion (normally one-tenth) of the produce of the farms of a parish, payable in kind to the parish priest

toft the land immediately round a medieval peasant's house

township a complete, self-contained farming system; a township was the smallest taxable unit in the countryside

transept transverse arm of a cruciform church

transhumance the moving of livestock to upland pastures in summer and lowland in winter

triforium arcaded passage, or blank arcading, above the *nave* arcades, at the height of the aisle roof

Truck Act law allowing employers to pay wages in goods instead of money, or in money for use only in the employers' shops

tuff rock formed by the consolidation of volcanic ash

tundra arctic or periglacial open land with frozen subsoil

turnwrist plough a plough with two mouldboards, curved in opposite directions; one turns the soil to the right, going up the furrow; when the headland is reached and the plough turned, the other mouldboard is brought into play, and turns the soil in the next furrow to the left, thus maintaining furrow regularity

tuyère pipe through which air is blown into a furnace

tympanum area between the lintel of a doorway and a surmounting arch

vault (1) arched ceiling, often with a supporting system of ribs; (2) tomb, often below ground level

velvet closely woven cloth with thick short pile on one side

vernacular houses etc built in the styles and materials of the locality, and not designed by architects

vicus a small Roman town, originally a settlement associated with a fort

vill a medieval settlement

villa (1) a Roman high-status house, usually on a rural estate; (2) detached or semidetached house in residential district (Georgian and later)

villein feudal serf, tied to a manor, and totally subject to the manorial lord

virgate medieval land measure, *c* 25–30 acres (10–12ha); see yardland

wall plate beam along the top of a wall on which the roof rests

wapentake division of shire into the parts of England colonised by Danes, corresponding to the hundred of Anglo-Saxon England (the name implies that voting was done by the brandishing of weapons)

wattle and daub a method of infilling between wall members of a timber-framed house, consisting of wattle fencing plastered with a clay and straw mixture (lath and plaster is similar, but uses thin laths instead of wattle)

wic (and **emporium**) pre-Viking (middle Saxon in England *c* AD 600–850) trading centre

wind-brace a wooden member (in a timber-framed house) across the corner space between a vertical and a horizontal member, for stability or decoration

woollen cloth made from short staple wool

worsted smooth cloth made from fine combed long staple wool

yardland a medieval farm, averaging some 25 acres (10ha), scattered in strips throughout the open fields of the township

HISTORICAL BRITAIN

Abbreviations

A-S	Anglo-Saxon
AONB	Area of Natural Beauty
BA	Bronze Age
BAR	British Archaeological Reports
BM	British Museum
Cadw	Welsh Historical Monuments
CBA	Council for British Archaeology
CC	County Council
CPRE	Council for the Protection of Rural England
CUP	Cambridge University Press
DoE	Department of the Environment
DMV	Deserted Medieval Village
EBA	Early Bronze Age
EH	English Heritage
GLC	Greater London Council
HBMCE	Historic Buildings and Monuments Committee for England
HMSO	Her Majesty's Stationery Office
HS	Historic Scotland
IA	Iron Age
IFA	Institute of Field Archaeologists
LBA	Late Bronze Age
LCC	London County Council
MBA	Middle Bronze Age
MERL	Museum of English Rural Life
MSC	Manpower Services Commission
NCC	Nature Conservancy Council
NT	National Trust
OS	Ordnance Survey
OUP	Oxford University Press
PPG16	(DoE) Planning Policy Guidance Note no 16
RB	Romano-British
RCHME	Royal Commission on the Historical Monuments of England
RKP	Routledge and Kegan Paul (Publishers)
SM	Science Museum
V&A	Victoria and Albert Museum
W&D	Weald and Downland Open Air Museum
WFM	Welsh Folk Museum
WYAS	West Yorkshire Archaeological Service

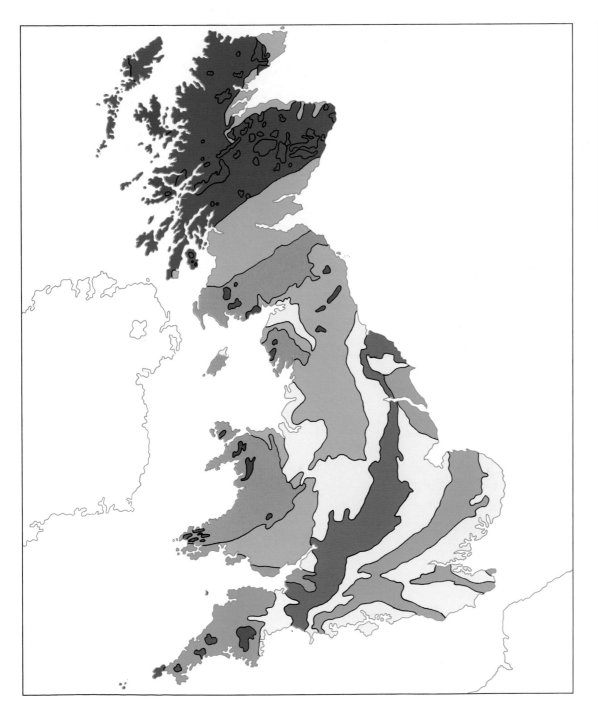

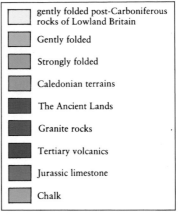

	gently folded post-Carboniferous rocks of Lowland Britain
	Gently folded
	Strongly folded
	Caledonian terrains
	The Ancient Lands
	Granite rocks
	Tertiary volcanics
	Jurassic limestone
	Chalk

Map 1 *The geological structure of Britain, showing the four main rock complexes:*

1, the ancient lands of the north of Scotland;

2, the Caledonian rocks of the southern uplands, the Lake District and most of Wales;

3, the sandstones and grits of central Scotland and western England, from Northumberland and the Pennines to east Wales and south-west England (1, 2 and 3 are the Highland Zone);

4, the limestones and chalk of all of England east of the Pennines and east of Wales to east Devon (the Lowland Zone). The limestone belt crossing the Lowland Zone has been emphasised.

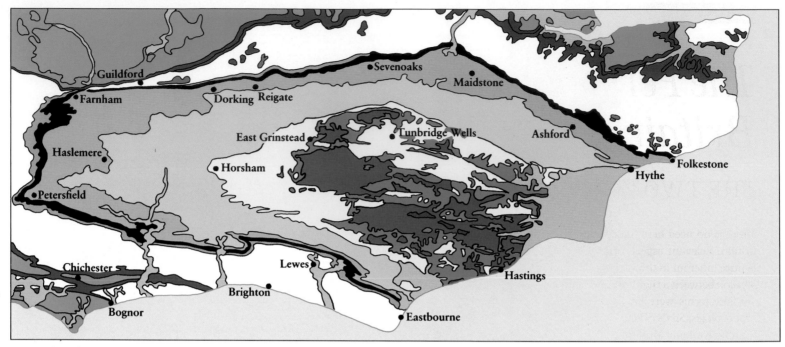

Map 2 *The geology of the Weald. This map gives a simplified overview of one of the most complex areas of Britain. The Weald is an area of sands and clays, heavy soils and dense woodland, and difficult for settlement, but yet was a centre of iron production from before Roman times to c 1830, and of glass making from the 13th century to the 17th. The North Downs, although having damp tree cover, were a thoroughfare from Mesolithic times, and the South Downs have been densely occupied for half a million years.*

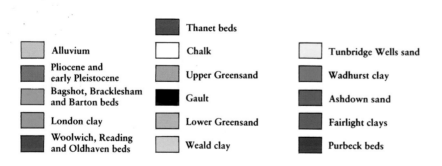

Alluvium	Thanet beds	Tunbridge Wells sand
Pliocene and early Pleistocene	Chalk	Wadhurst clay
Bagshot, Bracklesham and Barton beds	Upper Greensand	Ashdown sand
London clay	Gault	Fairlight clays
Woolwich, Reading and Oldhaven beds	Lower Greensand	Purbeck beds
	Weald clay	

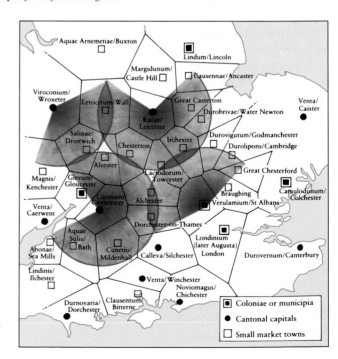

Map 9 *Roman towns in southern Britain in Thiessen polygons. Thiessen polygons are figures resulting from lines drawn at right-angles midway along lines joining two points (eg towns on a map), and define the immediate spheres of influence of the towns in question. Here they show the regularity of distribution of towns, and the radial relation of small (market) towns to the cantonal capitals.*

The Personality of Britain

THE TWO ZONES

There is no need here to describe, even in outline, the geography of Britain. Relevant aspects will necessarily occur in the text. But one feature inherent in the structure of the land must be pointed out – its division between a Highland Zone and a Lowland Zone.

These terms were brought effectively to public attention by the archaeologist Sir Cyril Fox, in his pioneer work *The Personality of Britain* (Cardiff: National Museum of Wales, 1932, 4th ed, 1943 (1959)), in which the relationship between the geography and the human settlement of Britain is investigated. Fox elaborated the significance of the division of Britain into two very distinct zones. The Lowland Zone is broadly all of England east of a line from the mouth of the Tees to the mouth of the Exe, with the addition of Cheshire and coastal Lancashire. It consists of the more recent rocks and deposits, and has no great heights; it contains land easy to settle and cultivate (chalk, gravels, sandstones, soft limestones, clay, and alluvium). The Highland (Upland) Zone is the rest: the south-west of England (with the Mendips and the Malverns as "islands"); Wales except the Vale of Glamorgan; the Pennines, the Lake District, and the north-east of England (the North York Moors are a borderland with features of both zones); and all Scotland (although the east coast has some of the characteristics of the Lowland Zone). In this zone the rocks are old and hard, the climate is wetter and windier than in the Lowland Zone, and much of the area is bleak moorland and mountain difficult to settle. This last generalisation may be modified by climatic fluctuations. Thus, for example, the warm, dry climate in the Bronze Age made the highlands more usable than the wet, cooler climate of the Iron Age, which led to a valleyward movement of people.

Cyril Fox linked the recognition of the two zones with a somewhat sweeping theory. As the Lowland Zone faces, and is readily open to, the Continent, many of the movements of people from Europe have entered Britain this way, rapidly occupying it, and spreading less rapidly into the north and west. (In fact, the western seaways have been important too, and many movements of people have entered Britain in the Highland Zone.) Fox deduced that in the Lowland Zone new cultures tended to be imposed on the earlier ones and to replace them; in the Highland Zone they tended to be absorbed by the older culture and to create new patterns of fusion. More recent archaeological work has shown, however, that the facts are not so clear-cut, and indeed that many phenomena are due to local initiative rather than importation from outside. But apart from this caveat, the concept of the two zones retains its validity and usefulness, and may be safely used in a wide range of contexts.

THE STRUCTURE OF BRITAIN

It is a commonplace that Britain's scenery is determined by her geology, which, in association with the climate, in turn determines the vegetation. A combination of all three governs the areas where human beings could settle, and from where they could extend their living area when circumstances demanded. Thus, to a very significant extent, the bulk of the population is still concentrated in the Lowland Zone, and in the central valley of Scotland – that is, away from the regions of the older rocks, which are in general mountainous and still difficult of access and communication.

Broadly, as the geological map (see **Map 1**, facing page 2) clearly shows, the older and harder rocks of Britain are in the north and west, the newer and softer in the east and south. The standard and classic Geological Map, that published by the Ordnance Survey, although of great value and interest (and a joy to look at), should be used with caution, as it does not give a true picture of what one sees in much of the country. This map shows only the "solid" geology, the underlying rock formations of which the land consists. These, however, may be obscured by "drift", soils left by the glaciers, which may be very different from the solid rocks beneath. This drift – much of it alluvium and boulder clay – covers most of northern England east of the Pennines, and much of Lincolnshire, the east Midlands, and East Anglia; there is also a patch in north Cumbria, a larger area in Lancashire and Cheshire, and a few small pockets on the coasts. There are also boulder clays in Scotland, as in the Lothians.

The geology of Scotland is extremely complex, being a jumble of ancient, mostly igneous or metamorphic rocks. A very simplified description, ignoring much local detail and variety, follows.

The Shetlands are complex, with a central spine of schists, with granite intrusions, and granite and Old Red Sandstone blocks in the western peninsulas. The Orkneys and much of Caithness, by contrast, are a uniform region of Old Red Sandstone. This has been an area of easy landfall and settlement since Neolithic times. This Old Red Sandstone continues down the north-east coast and into the Moray Firth.

The greater part of the Highlands consists of an extensive block of schist, from the north coast of Sutherland, and covering most of Ross and Cromarty and Inverness-shire, stretching east as far as Moray. This is punctuated by blocks of granite, which continue into Aberdeenshire. The west coast, with its sea-lochs (fjords and drowned valleys), has gneiss in Sutherland and Torridonian Sandstone in Wester Ross. The Outer Hebrides are largely gneiss, with some granite. Skye and Mull are basalt; Jura is mostly quartzite.

East of this very mountainous region, and down to the English border, are bands of rocks, running north-east–south-west. Perthshire and Argyll to Kintyre is a belt of schists and grits; south of this, from the Kincardine and Angus coasts to the Clyde estuary, is a band of Old Red Sandstone. The Ochils of Kinross and north Fife are volcanic of Devonian age. Much of Stirlingshire and Renfrewshire are also volcanic, but of Lower Carboniferous age.

The Central Valley and southern Fife is a rift valley between the Highland Line scarp and the Southern Uplands. It mostly consists of Carboniferous rocks – mountain limestone – surrounding a block of Coal Measures in Clackmannan, West Lothian, and Lanarkshire.

The Southern Uplands are a wide, largely homogeneous band of mainly volcanic rocks, Ordovician from East Lothian south-west to north Wigtownshire, Silurian south of this from Berwickshire through Selkirk, Dumfries, and Kirkcudbright to southern Wigtownshire. There is an area of Coal Measures in Ayrshire, and several masses of granite in the north-east and south-west. The Cheviots, in Roxburghshire and Northumberland, are volcanic rock of Old Red Sandstone age, with granite near Wooler.

Even this drastically over-simplified account gives a hint at the complexity of the events and phases of volcanic and mountain-building activity, and of marine deposition, which have contributed to the dramatic character of Scotland. This geological history should be sought in the relevant books (see "Further Reading" page 580). Certainly this history, together with a fairly severe climate, has led to much of Scotland still being inhospitable to human settlement.

Geologically speaking (and in other ways also), the English–Scottish border is real and valid, and mostly quite sharply defined. North of it, the Southern Uplands stretch from east to west (or rather north-east to south-west); south of it, Northumberland and then (south of the South Tyne) the Pennines lie north and south, right down to just north of Derby. The rocks of this large tract are essentially of Carboniferous age, except for the Lake District, which is a jumble of older rocks, slates, granites, and various volcanic rocks, giving scenery not unlike parts of the Scottish Highlands.

Most of Northumberland and the northern Pennines consists of Carboniferous (mountain) limestone, except for a block of Coal Measures in south-east Northumberland and most of Durham (there is also a small coalfield in west Cumberland). The southern Pennines and north Lancashire consist of Millstone Grit, flanked by considerable areas of Coal Measures, in central Lancashire and north Staffordshire on the west, and from Leeds-Bradford to between Nottingham and Derby on the east. The limestone occurs again in central Derbyshire. The contrast between the limestone and the grit is a conspicuous and familiar feature of the Pennines. The Highland Zone of northern England is completed by a narrow band of magnesian limestone which runs along the eastern edge of the features just described, from the coast between Tyne and Tees down to just east of Nottingham.

It is convenient here to continue the description of the Highland Zone, before entering the very different world of the Lowland Zone.

The oldest part of Wales is Anglesey, much of which is of pre-Cambrian age – gneisses and schists, with granite, slate, and limestone in great complexity. These ancient rocks continue south of the Menai Strait into Caernarvonshire. Snowdonia itself is largely composed of volcanic lava and ash, as is Cader Idris (both, like the Lake District, deeply sculpted by glaciation). These old rocks run in a narrow belt between the two mountain blocks, enclosing an area of slates and grits of Cambrian age between Harlech and Barmouth (Ardudwy and the Rhinogs). (The Isle of Man, except for the low-lying northern tip, is a similar formation.) Most of the rest of Wales, except for complex ancient rocks in Pembrokeshire, is a somewhat uniform upland of Ordovician and Silurian slates, sandstones, mudstones, and shales. This extends eastwards into south Shropshire and north Herefordshire; the Malverns are an outlier of Wales, with a pre-Cambrian core and other old rocks. South-east Shropshire is a complex area of basalt, dolerite, and Old Red Sandstone. South-east Wales – Brecknockshire, Monmouthshire, and most of Herefordshire and south Shropshire, with a narrow band running into Pembrokeshire – is Old Red Sandstone. There is Carboniferous Limestone in Flintshire, and in south Pembrokeshire, Gower, and south Glamorgan. This is part of a narrow band enclosing the syncline in Glamorgan which is filled by the Coal Measures. The coast of Glamorgan, between Cardiff and Bridgend, and outside this syncline, is Lias limestone. Glamorgan is thus part of the Lowland Zone.

The remainder of the Highland Zone is the peninsula of south-west England – Cornwall, much of Devon, and Exmoor. Much of Cornwall and south Devon consists of slates and grits; these are punctuated by several blocks of granite – Penwith, south of Redruth, south of Bodmin, Bodmin Moor itself, and Dartmoor. The Lizard and Start Point are of serpentine. Central Devon is Carboniferous grit, with New Red Sandstone on the east. North Devon, Exmoor, and the Quantocks are Old Red Sandstone. The Highland Zone ends in a more or less straight line from Watchet to Exmouth (except for the Quantocks just east of this).

The Lowland Zone is the whole of the east and south of England, east of an irregular line from the mouth of the Tees to the mouth of the Exe, and taking in also the low-lying land between the Pennines and Wales – the Cheshire Gap, ie most of Staffordshire, north Shropshire, Cheshire, and south and west Lancashire. The zone consists of the younger and softer sedimentary rocks, which, in its eastern parts, are overlain with drift. The (solid) geological map 1 reveals a striking pattern: the various rocks lie in roughly parallel bands, except for the formations in the south-east.

Starting from the east side of the Highland Zone, the first belt is one of Bunter sandstone, which hugs the magnesian limestone from Teesmouth to just south of Nottingham, broken only by the alluvium of the south Yorkshire rivers between York and Gainsborough (and on along the Trent). At the other end of the zone, there is a narrow band of Bunter sandstone along the highland edge in east Devon. East of the northern Bunter lies the major feature of the New Red Sandstone – sandstone and Keuper clays and marls. This begins at Middlesbrough and follows the Bunter (broken only by the Humber); beyond that it broadens out into the rolling country of the west Midlands – south Derbyshire, west Leicestershire, Warwickshire, and Worcestershire,

with scattered patches as far south as east Devon. In the centre of this long belt it covers Staffordshire, Cheshire, and west Lancashire, but in these counties it is interspersed with areas of Bunter. There are also Coal Measures in this central area – a narrow belt hugging the eastern edge of the Welsh massif, from Flintshire and Denbighshire through Shropshire, then with a gap until the Forest of Dean and Somerset are reached, and larger areas in east Staffordshire, Warwickshire, and west Leicestershire.

East of this is the great Jurassic Ridge which occupies much of the middle of England like a sort of hinge. It is in two parts: Lias limestones, shales, and clays on the west side, and oolitic limestones on the east, which give rise to the conspicuous scarps of the Hambletons, the Lincoln Edge, the Northamptonshire uplands, and the Cotswolds. This belt also includes the North York Moors at the northern end, and the hilly country of west Wiltshire, east Somerset, and west Dorset, reaching the sea between Lyme Regis and Bridport (Lias). and Bridport and Portland (oolite).

East of the Jurassic belt lies the Chalk, an equally conspicuous feature, and of central importance in the early settlement of the country. This begins with the Wolds of east Yorkshire and Lincolnshire (punctuated by the alluvium of Ryedale, the Humber estuary and the Lincolnshire coast, and the Fens). The chalk continues in west Norfolk, west Suffolk, Hertfordshire, the Chilterns, the Berkshire Downs, and the great block of Wessex – east Wiltshire, central Dorset, and most of Hampshire. From Hampshire run the two eastward prolongations of the North and South Downs. Much of the chalk is capped with deposits of clay-with-flints, representing the residues of formerly overlying rocks. The Lincolnshire Wolds are flanked on the west by a narrow band of Lower Greensand. This resumes in Norfolk, and continues to Buckinghamshire. From Norfolk along the entire rest of the Chalk, and overlapping into east Devon, the Lower Greensand is accompanied or replaced by a line of gault and Upper Greensand. The south half of the Isle of Wight shows similar features.

The geological interest of the south-east of England is concentrated in the Weald, the area between the North and South Downs, once a dome, but weathered down to expose the rocks between the chalk ridges (see **Map 2**, facing page 3). These ridges are therefore fringed, all round the Weald except on the Channel coast (the formation continues in France), by the Upper Greensand, the gault, and the Lower Greensand. The centre of the Weald (south Surrey, most of Sussex, and southern Kent) is made up of sands and clays. The Wealden landscape has a strong individuality, in spite of its low altitude.

East Norfolk and Suffolk are made up of glacial loams and boulder clays. Between the two arms of the chalk – on either side of the Thames valley – are clays, gravels, and sands: from the heavy clays of London and west Essex to river terrace gravels, and the mid Bagshot and Thanet sands. Similar sands occur in south Hampshire (with the New Forest).

Romney Marsh is a former bay, filled with alluvial material.

It is necessary here only to refer, without going into detail, to the long and complex geological processes which have given rise to the state now reached by the land of Britain. These include periods of volcanic activity, mountain-building movements, metamorphosis of rocks, the recurrent presence of seas, warm or cold, with resulting sedimentation, and the effects of glaciation (these, being more recent, are described below). All the time the slow relentless forces of weathering – wind, rain, frost – have been reducing mountains or domes, creating peneplains, and smoothing contours. Rivers too have changed their courses and carved new valleys, either by being deflected by a natural obstacle such as an ice front, or by cutting back in soft material and "capturing" another river.

But even this over-simplified account hints at, and largely explains, the astonishing variety of scenery in so small a space – as varied in Britain as in any country in the world. Each county has its distinctive character, and some have more than one type of scenery. The climate, interacting with the geology, completes the natural setting for human activity.

NATURAL RESOURCES

Such a varied geology finds its expression in a rich variety of minerals and materials, unusual for so small a country (see **Map 3**). The minerals include coal, which is widespread from the Central Valley of Scotland to the English Midlands and south Wales. In Scotland there are four main coalfields – Lanarkshire and Clackmannan, Ayrshire, Fife, and Midlothian. There is some coal in Cumbria, and a large and important field in Northumberland and Durham, which has been exploited for centuries. Another great field extends in and beside the southern Pennines from Leeds to Nottingham and Derby. This field surfaces again, after a gap, in Lancashire. There are small areas in north-east

Wales, and in north Staffordshire, and an important field running from south Staffordshire and Shropshire to Warwickshire and into Leicestershire. The other major field is in south Wales, with outliers in the Forest of Dean and in Somerset. There is a small pocket in east Kent.

Of the metals the most important is iron. This is found in the Coal Measures (in Scotland in the Millstone Grit and the Carboniferous Limestone as well); this source is no longer worked. The ironstones of the Jurassic belt are of great importance, particularly those of Cleveland, north Lincolnshire (Frodingham, Scunthorpe), and the area of Rutland, Northamptonshire, Leicestershire, and south Lincolnshire (Kettering and Corby being main centres). The Jurassic iron of the Banbury district is no longer worked. The other important sources are the haematite ores of west Cumbria (Egremont) and Llanharry (Glamorgan). The ores of Furness, the Forest of Dean, and east Kent are no longer worked. The main source of iron for many centuries was the Weald of Kent and Sussex, with outliers in the western Weald. The clay ironstones and the ferruginous rocks of this area were worked from pre-Roman times until 1830, and many traces of this industry survive.

Copper is found with tin in Cornwall, and in north Wales (Great Orme), and has been worked since the Bronze Age. Tin also occurs on Dartmoor. Lead was worked from pre-Roman times in the north Pennines and in Derbyshire, and also in the Mendips, Flintshire, Shropshire, and Leadhills (La). The Romans extracted silver from lead ore. Gold was mined by the Romans at Dolaucothi (Cm) and Dolgellau (Me), and is found in streams in southern Scotland.

Many of the raw materials used by the metal industries are now imported, the original sources having been exhausted or become uneconomical.

Britain also possesses a wide range of non-metallic materials: gravel is worked particularly in the river valleys of the Thames, Trent, etc; clay (for bricks) is widespread; fireclay is dug in the Coal Measures. Sand for concrete comes from the gravel-pits; for foundry use, from Trias deposits in the west and east Midlands; for glassmaking, from St Helens, Leighton Buzzard, King's Lynn, and Lochaline (Ar): the Forest glass industry got sand from the Weald, and 17th–19th-century glassmakers from Maidstone, Woolwich, Alum Bay (IW), Chelford (Ch), and Oakmoor (St). Gypsum comes from Nottinghamshire, Staffordshire, Appleby (Cu), and Battle (Sx); alabaster from Chellaston (Db). China clay is found in

Map **3** *Mineral resources in Britain. This map shows the wide distribution and the variety of minerals in Britain, which, with coal, stone, clay, and timber, have underpinned the life of the nation.*

Cornwall (St Austell) and south-west Dartmoor; alum and potash come from north-east Yorkshire, fluorspar from Derbyshire. Abandoned lead mines have in recent years been reworked to extract residuary chemicals from waste-tips. Salt was extracted until the 19th century in coastal salterns (eg Lymington (Ha) and, from pre-Roman times, the "Red Hills" of Essex); it was also mined (as rock-salt) in Cheshire, and pumped (as brine) at Droitwich (Wo), Stafford, Fleetwood (La), Middlesborough (Cl), and Cheshire.

Oil is now got from the North Sea, and from a growing number of inland fields, such as Arne (Do), Herriard (Ha), and Nottinghamshire. Natural gas also comes from the North Sea.

Further details of the above will be found in the relevant sections on Industries and Public Utilities below.

Building materials have, until this century, been taken from whatever was available in each locality, and are therefore intimately related to the geology. Thus, in stone districts, buildings are made of the local stone; where stone is lacking (as in Essex), the vernacular builders used wood, brick, clay, etc, and thatch for roofing.

Walling materials include stone: millstone grit and carboniferous (mountain) limestone in the Pennines and Northumberland; magnesian limestone in a narrow belt east of the Pennines; lias limestone in a long narrow belt from Cleveland through Lincolnshire and Northamptonshire to the Cotswolds and on to east Devon; oolitic limestone in a broader belt to the east of the latter, from north-east Yorkshire to Dorset. Much of the Midlands has various sandstones. The chalk, which yields clunch and flints, runs from the east

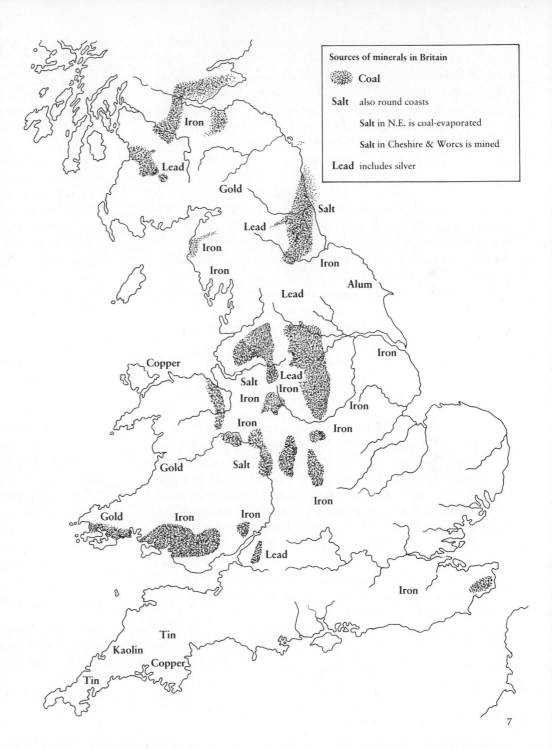

Sources of minerals in Britain

Coal

Salt also round coasts

Salt in N.E. is coal-evaporated

Salt in Cheshire & Worcs is mined

Lead includes silver

Yorkshire and Lincolnshire wolds to Norfolk, Suffolk, the Chilterns, Wessex, and the North and South Downs. Lining this belt is a narrow band of greensand. The Weald has various stones (Bargate, Rag, Malmstone, etc). Devon and Cornwall have a variety of sandstones and grit, and the Lake District a variety of ancient rocks, including slatey stone, also found in north and south-west Wales, and in east Cornwall and south Devon. Most of the rest of the Lowland Zone (the eastern parts of East Anglia, Essex, and Berkshire) uses brick or timber. Timber is also normal in the south-west Midlands, the Welsh Borders, parts of Hampshire, and much of eastern England south of the Wash. Cob or clay is found in north-west Cumbria, Leicestershire, mid-west Wales, Suffolk and Cambridgeshire, Wiltshire and Dorset, and north and east Devon. Pebbles or cobbles are used on the south and east coasts.

Roofing materials include slate in Cumbria and north Lancashire, Wales, Cornwall, and Leicestershire; stone slates in the Pennines, the limestone belt (eg Stonesfield "slates"), the Weald ("Horsham stone"), and the south Welsh borders. Plain tiles are used in the Lowland Zone, except in the pantile area and the south-western thatch area. Pantiles occur down the east coast from Northumberland to Essex, and in Somerset. Thatch, once widespread, is used in the south Midlands, Essex except on the coast, and southern England from Devon to West Sussex.

Scotland has its own complexion. For walling, sandstone is the commonest material, particularly on the east coast as far as Banff, from Kincardine to Roxburgh, and Renfrew and Ayr. Whinstone is found in Selkirk, Peebles and the Borders, the Lothians, Fife, Stirling, Dumfriesshire, the south-west, the west, and the Western Isles. Granite is characteristic of Aberdeenshire, Kincardine and Banff, and also Kirkcudbrightshire. North-east Caithness and Orkney use flagstone. Other stones include greywacke in the Borders and the south-west, and limestone in the east and Midlothian. Brick is not a first choice, but is used in the Lothians and from Angus to Dumbarton. Roofing is mainly slate, but stone slabs occur in the north-east and Orkney, and in Angus. Pantiles are used in Berwickshire and the Lothians, and in Stirlingshire, Clackmannan, and Fife. Thatch was universal before 1750. (See sections on "Houses" below.)

CLIMATE

The British have never found it easy to distinguish the climate from the weather, which plays a disproportionate part in our conversation, if not in our lives. Climate is the broad pattern which underlies the weather. Its slow fluctuations, as H H Lamb and others have pointed out, have not infrequently had a profound effect on human history. The weather can be a more local and temporary inconvenience.

Britain is a long narrow island, lying between latitudes 50° and 61° N – latitudes where the climate ranges from temperate to relatively cool, with rainfall spread throughout the year, but with no great extremes. We are in the zone of the westerly winds, and vulnerably exposed by our position as an offshore island. (Wind circulation is caused by unequal heating of different zones of the Earth. The Gulf Stream helps to moderate the effects of our exposed position.) The weather is bound to be capricious, and we have no high mountain barriers to compartmentalise it effectively, although there is a gradation from a wetter west to a drier east.

Britain is in fact centrally situated between three main pressure systems, and our weather is largely determined by their relative strengths. In winter there is a low pressure system over Iceland, a high over the Azores, and a large area of high pressure over East Europe. In summer there is still the low over Iceland and the high over the Azores, but the high pressure area over eastern Europe is now an area of low pressure. The Mediterranean and north Africa are high in both seasons, although the actual position of the various systems differs slightly between the seasons. In both cases Britain is in the path of depressions coming out of the Atlantic.

Historically speaking, there have been climatic changes pronounced enough to exert a recognisable effect on the land itself, its vegetation, and its inhabitants. The following outline can only be brief.

Glaciations and their effects

For the last million years or so – the whole of the Pleistocene period – the climate has been dominated by cold phases lasting thousands of years each. Early humans lived through the whole of their Palaeolithic phase in the shadow of this Ice Age, although of course the climatic events moved too slowly for them to be conscious of anything untoward.

There is no complete consensus on the causes of these glaciations, particularly as previous geological periods were not affected in this way. But one major cause seems to be cyclical variation in the ellipticity of the Earth's orbit and in the tilt of the polar axis relative to the plane of the orbit, both factors which affect the amount of radiation reaching the Earth. A summary of present knowledge is given by H H Lamb in *Climate History and the Modern World* (Methuen 1982).

Ten cold phases have been detected during the 1.6 or so million years of the Pleistocene, of which eight or nine have occurred in the last 700,000 years. Not all of these affected Britain. Glaciations usually contained warmer spells called interstadials, and were separated by longer mild phases called interglacials. The former were mild enough to allow the growth of conifer forest; the latter were warmer than these, and allowed mixed-oak forest.

We are mainly concerned, in Britain, with the last three glaciations (each of which had more than one cold peak). These are:

Beestonian glaciation –	Günz in the Alpine series
Cromerian interglacial	over 500,000 years ago
Anglian glaciation	c 450–400,000 years ago
Hoxnian interglacial	c 400–350,000 years ago
Wolstonian glaciation	c 350–125,000 years ago
Ipswichian interglacial	c 125–70,000 years ago
Devensian glaciation	c 70–10,000 years ago
Flandrian interglacial	c 10,000 years ago to the present

These are named after sites in which significant geological evidence has been found. The glaciations correspond broadly to the last three Alpine glaciations – Mindel, Riss, and Würm – which have been studied in detail, and whose names were used by British geologists until recently. We are now living in an interglacial which will no doubt last for several thousand years. Human beings first visited Britain in a mild phase of the Anglian glaciation, or possibly just before.

The Anglian glaciation reached as far south as the Thames valley; the southernmost extent of the Wolstonian is not clearly established, but probably ran from about Malvern to about Ipswich; the Devensian at its peak extended to a line roughly from Swansea to Yorkshire. Individual ice caps formed, at the height of the glaciations, over Sutherland, the Grampians, Galloway, the Lake District, south of the Isle of Man, Snowdonia, Cader Idris, and the Peak District.

The Thames flowed along the ice front (north of its present valley), along the Essex coast to the Naze area, and joined the Rhine on its way to its mouth west of the Dogger Bank (which was dry land).

It is not the intention here to enter into the archaeological aspects of the glaciations; books such as those by John G Evans or John Wymer should be consulted for this. The archaeology – and the geology – is greatly complicated by the fact that each glaciation disturbed, or even destroyed, much of the evidence left by humans before it, and the landscape was scoured clean each time.

The greater part of the land of Britain, down to the Thames valley, was physically affected, to a greater or lesser extent, by the passage or the proximity of glaciers. As the retreat of the glaciers began only some 12,000 years ago, most of these effects can still be seen. Being outside the experience of most of us, the sheer weight of a major ice sheet is hard to envisage. Yet, at the height of the glaciations, the ice above the site of Edinburgh was some 2,000ft (600m) thick.

Such immense volumes of ice, covering vast areas, had two effects: they locked up so much water from the sea that the sea level fell; and their weight over land depressed the land surface. As each glaciation came to an end, a eustatic rise in sea level took place, and the land recovered its former density in an isostatic rise. These two movements were not necessarily exactly synchronous or equally distributed. Indeed, for reasons not understood, each successive eustatic movement has been lower than the previous one. Thus, taking the present, Flandrian, level as 0m, the Ipswichian (last interglacial) level was 5–8m above the present level, and the Hoxnian interglacial was 30–32m higher. The present sea level has been rising, with fluctuations, since before 15,000 BC, from a low of some –70m. It reached its present level about AD 400, with later fluctuations. In Scotland at least, the isostatic recovery of the land exceeds the eustatic rise of the sea. These movements, particularly that of the land, are still going on.

The successive changes in sea level have given rise to flooded lands, as in the Fens or Cardigan Bay, and also to raised beaches, of which examples can be seen, for example, along the coast between Brighton and Portsmouth. On a rocky coast the sea may eat into the cliffs and form notches. A similar effect may take place along the shores of a lake. Thus, the "Parallel Roads of Glenroy" (In) (see **1**) are not roads, but show the successive lake levels as the lake responded to glacial phases. Inland, the rivers react to the changes in sea level

1 *The "Parallel Roads of Glenroy" (In). These level terraces along the mountainside are not roads, but the successive shorelines of a glacial lake.*

by building up terraces along their lower courses. During the warm phases the sea rises and the river flows more slowly, depositing sheets of gravel up to the new sea level. Then, in the cold phases, the sea falls and the river cuts down into this gravel, leaving a terrace on either side. This channel may be buried under a new sheet of gravel at the next fluctuation. As the sea levels are lower than their previous height in each successive warm phase, the terraces form a series of which the highest is the earliest. The Thames shows a complete series.

In its upper reaches a river reacts differently. In the warm phases it has enough water to cut down into its bed; in the cold phases it runs more slowly, and builds up an aggradation terrace (see **2**) from the material coming down the valley sides as a result of hillwash and solifluction (upper soil creeping down a slope over a frozen subsoil). When ice masses move horizontally across country, the effects are of a different order.

A glacier moving along a valley has the effect of smoothing the sides and rounding the bottom, leaving a distinctive U-profile. There are many such valleys in the Highland Zone, such as Glen Coe in Scotland, Wasdale in the Lake District, and the Llanberis Pass in Wales. The glaciated valleys in the Lake District lie roughly radially to the high centre, thus indicating the presence of a local glacier.

10

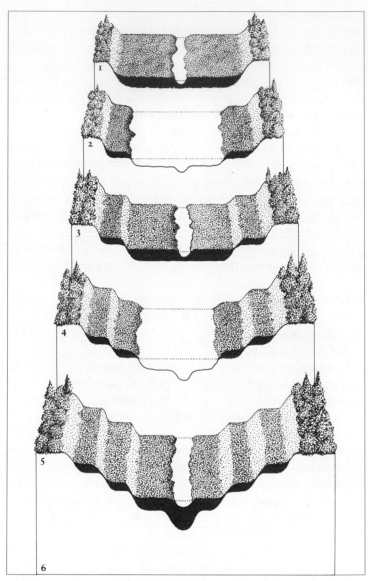

2 *The effect of glaciations on the lower course of a river leading to the formation of terraces: 1, the pre-glaciation river and its flood plain; 2, cold phase: the sea falls, the river cuts down, leaving terraces at the sides; 3, warm phase: sea level rises, river aggrades and forms new gravel sheet; 4, cold phase: sea level falls, rivers cuts down into the gravel sheet of phase 3, leaving second terraces and deep channels; 5, warm phase: sea level rises, river aggrades, forming new gravel sheet, which now buries the channel of phase 4; 6, the process continues for as long as the climate fluctuates.*

In Scotland the tilt of the land in relation to the Atlantic, coupled with the effects of eustasy, has produced a series of drowned valleys – sea-lochs or fjords – along the west coast, and classical examples inland such as Loch Ness.

The head of a glaciated valley, particularly in mountainous country, often takes the form of a corrie or cwm (cirque). This is a horseshoe-shaped basin where the snow consolidates to form the glacier, which is forced out into the valley as the ice accumulates. In leaving the upper side of the corrie, the ice tears away the rock-face with it, producing vertical cliffs. When the glacier finally melts, a circular lake is left. There are many corries in the Scottish Highlands, including spectacular examples in the Cuillins in Skye; Snowdon and Cader Idris also have good examples.

Glaciers are constantly, if very slowly, on the move, and they scrape up and carry along with them vast quantities of earth, rock waste, and stones, which are held in suspension in the ice. In addition, their upper surface may be littered with blocks of rock which have become detached by frost action from the valley sides and fallen on to the glacier. When the temperature rises the glacier starts melting, and its nose stops moving forward; but the ice still flows on behind, and at the now stationary nose its load of rock and earth is piled up into a bank (a moraine) across the end of the glacier (a terminal moraine). If the ice front recedes, debris will be spread back along the path of the glacier. Material at the sides is deposited in long lines along the valley sides (lateral moraines). If two glaciers meet and run alongside each other they form medial moraines.

Terminal moraines can be seen in large numbers in the Highland Zone, and many still retain a dammed-up lake. The Highlands of Scotland have a very large number of such lakes, of all sizes; Wastwater and Tal-y-Llyn are good examples in England and Wales. The terminal moraines across the Vale of York, at Escrick and York, a few miles apart, represent successive halts in the recession of the ice sheet. They enabled the vale to be crossed conveniently, and York itself is built on one of them. Lateral moraines can be seen, for example in the Yorkshire dales, sometimes, as in Nidderdale, complicated by hillwash on top of them, earth which has come down the hillsides in different conditions. In the Lowland Zone, where there were vast sheets of ice instead of valley glaciers, the ice fronts ponded up large lakes. Thus, the flat floor of Ryedale (NY) represents Lake Pickering, blocked in by an ice front along the coast; Lake Eskdale, behind Whitby, overflowed into Lake Pickering through a channel which is now Newtondale. The rivers of this area, such as the Derwent, still do not reach the sea direct, but turn back inland and flow into the Ouse. Lake Humber stretched from the Escrick moraine, south of York, to Nottingham; Lake Fenland spread from Goole to near Cambridge. Lake Lapworth, in Shropshire and Cheshire, cut the Ironbridge Gorge as one of its outflows. The presence of these lakes is still marked by expanses of flat land.

If, instead of a terminal moraine, recession was so fast that a sheet of debris was deposited, this takes the form of a mixture of mud and stones called boulder clay. Much of eastern England, as far south as Finchley, London, is covered by this "drift". Boulder clay includes stones carried by the ice over long distances: thus, that in North Wales contains stones from Scotland, and that on the east coast stones from Scandinavia. Even quite large rocks may be carried many miles on the ice, and left stranded. The Yorkshire dales have many such erratics. When the ice passed over a rock in its path, it might striate it with scratches made by stones embedded in the ice. Or it might smooth it, leaving *roches moutonnées* (like sheep), which are common in Scotland and North Wales. Sometimes pockets of debris are deposited as rounded hillocks (ground moraines). These are often conical, and may resemble barrows or mottes. But often they are oval and occur in groups, all pointing one way, showing the direction of the ice (sometimes a later glacier) which finally moulded them. Such drumlins are common in Yorkshire (eg in Craven), in the Vale of Eden (Cu), and in south and central Scotland.

A rarer but interesting phenomenon of glaciation is crag-and-tail, where a prominent volcanic plug in the path of a moving glacier has protected a "tail" of material. The classic example is the Rock of Edinburgh, where the Castle stands (the plug), with the long slope of the Royal Mile (the tail) – the burgh of Canongate – down to Holyrood House. Stirling is another such case. Similarly, the flat northern tip of the Isle of Man is a tail left as a glacier moved north past the island.

Under many glaciers flowed a stream formed of meltwaters, which ran out from a hole or cave in the nose of the glacier; this carried a great deal of fine mud and pebbles, which could be deposited in an outwash fan, and, as the nose receded, in a long winding bank called an esker. There are good examples on the north Norfolk coast between Blakeney and Morston, and in the Brampton area of Cumbria. (The winding gravel ridges of central Ireland, although known as eskers, are really kames, having been laid down parallel to the ice fronts and not at right angles to them.)

Other minor effects of glaciation include pingoes (circular or oval mounds of melt material (ice-lenses)), frost-wedges and frost-cracks. Solifluction is the creep of hardened snow, ice, and stones down a hill, leaving a deposit called "head" or "coombe-rock". The country for many miles round a glaciated area was a tundra, with frozen subsoil and carrying a specialised vegetation. A few tracts in Britain have survived with tundra-like vegetation – "relict wastes"; thus Caithness, Orkney, Shetland, and the Outer Hebrides have natural moorland (ex-tundra) which has never had trees. Parts of the northern Pennines, eg upper Teesdale, have similar features.

All in all, the scenery of a surprising amount of Britain is that of a country only recently vacated by moving ice, or by the accompanying tundra.

Post-glacial climatic changes

Some 15,000 years ago the glaciers began to recede, and for some 4000 years a period called the Late-glacial spanned the interval between the widespread presence of the ice, with its periglacial tundra, and the Post-glacial or Flandrian phase – generally accepted as an interglacial – in which we still live, and which will be with us for several thousand years yet. By about 12,000 BC all of southern Britain was again available for settlement, and this phase is characterised by the late Palaeolithic culture known as the Creswellian.

But the retreat of the ice was not uniform, and there were three re-advances. The long progress to the full vegetation cover of post-glacial times had, however, begun. This has been established by a century of analysis of pollen from a variety of environments, which has enabled a framework of climatic zones to be set up. The late-glacial sequence is summarised in Table 1.

Table 1: The late-glacial sequence

date BC	pollen zone	climate phase	climate	vegetation
c 14,000	Ia	Oldest Dryas	cold	tundra
	Ib	Bølling interstadial	warmer	
	Ic	Older Dryas	cold readvances of ice	
c 12,000	II	Allerød interstadial	warmer	birch & pine woodland
c 10,000	III	Younger Dryas		tundra

The Bølling and Allerød interstadials, named after sites in Denmark, used to be known as "oscillations". The Allerød phase was actually warmer than some later periods. Dryas is a tundra plant.

From c 10,000 BC the glaciation-ridden Pleistocene period is left behind, and the Flandrian period begins. The surviving late Palaeolithic cultures give way to the Mesolithic period of human prehistory about 8500 BC.

The climatic fluctuations of the Flandrian are broadly outlined in Table 2 (based largely on John G Evans (1975)).

Table 2: The Flandrian

date BC	pollen zone	climate phase	climate	vegetation and cultures
c 9500	IV	pre-Boreal	general amelioration	birch & pine
			increasing warmth	(final Palaeolithic)
c 8500	V	Boreal	warm and dry	mixed oak forest with hazel and pine
c 6500	VI	Boreal	climatic optimum warm and wet (English Channel opened c 6000 BC)	(Mesolithic) increase of alder
c 4000	VIIa	Atlantic	general deterioration	(first farmers c 4500) Early Neolithic forest clearance – elm decline
c 2900	VIIb	Early sub-Boreal	dry	increase of ash & birch (late Neolithic – early Bronze Age)
c 1400	VII–VIII	Late sub-Boreal	wet	increase of ash, birch, hornbeam & beech; decline of lime (middle & late Bronze Age)
c 600	VIII	sub-Atlantic	sudden deterioration cool and wet	(Iron Age) birch & beech more prominent

H H Lamb (*Climate History and the Modern World*, Methuen 1982), however, would put the climatic optimum rather later, at c 4000 to 1500 BC, with a peak at c 2500 BC. Lamb sees later recurrences of warmth at 1100–800 BC, the 4th century AD, and AD 900 to a peak in the 13th century. Cultivation on Dartmoor and Northumberland at these peaks rose to over 1500ft (450m), against the absolute limit of 975ft (300m) today.

In the Neolithic climatic optimum both summer and winter temperatures were 2–3°C higher than now. Dudley Stamp has pointed out that the opening of the Channel, by allowing free circulation of water round the island of Britain, caused the abrupt change from a cold or Boreal climate to the milder, damper Atlantic climate, by altering the oceanic circulation and its effects on air movements. The sharp climatic deterioration in the first millennium BC caused a massive increase in peat formation, which has benefited archaeology by preserving organic materials, including human bodies, here and on the Continent, such as the well-known Tollund and Lindow men.

There was a recovery of warmth throughout Roman times (c AD 50–400), but with more moisture than today. Vine-growing was introduced by the Romans into Britain, which was self-sufficient in wine by AD 300. There were dry summers in Britain round AD 400, and in the 8th, late 10th, early 12th, and late 13th centuries. Cooler and wetter conditions followed the Roman mildness, in the 6th century, and again from AD 750 to 900. Storms and sea-floods round the North Sea from AD 400–450, and again in the 6th century, caused coastal changes in the south of England; about 520 a whole area (Cantre'r Gwaelod) in Cardigan Bay was lost. Marsh encroached in eastern England throughout the Saxon period.

There was a renewal of warmth in the late 10th–12th centuries, with a peak from 1100–1300 (a second climatic optimum). The tree-line and the limits of cultivation rose, and vine-growing became feasible again south-east of a line from Hereford to the Wash. The early 14th century was a very wet phase, followed by droughts (eg there was a famine in 1315), but the temperature was still higher than today's. There were severe storms and sea-floods in the North Sea area from 1200 on, with great loss of life; the late 16th century was very severe also. The east coast towns of Dunwich and Ravensburgh were lost to the sea, as were the ports of Harlech and Forvie (Ab), and much damage was done by blown sand (eg the Culbin Sands in Moray). The climate became cooler and wetter after 1300, with wide variations between wet and dry summers. There were also severe winters in the 1430s – the worst on record since AD 1000 except for the 1690s. In general the 14th and 15th centuries were wet and unhealthy, and subject to plague, ergotism, etc; malnutrition and disease reduced the expectation of life by about 10 years from 1300 (when it was c 48 years) to 1400. This was a period of desertion of villages (see **Graphs 1–4**).

It was warmer in the first half of the 16th century than in the 15th, but with some cold winters. There was a sharp change after 1550, and it continued colder than today until 1700. This period has been called the Little Ice Age, although some authorities would give this description to the whole span between 1190, or certainly 1420, to 1850 or 1900. There were great storms in 1570, 1588 (when the Armada was blown off course), 1694, 1697, and 1703 (when the Eddystone lighthouse

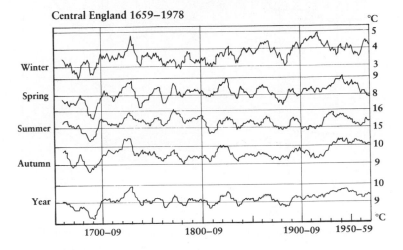

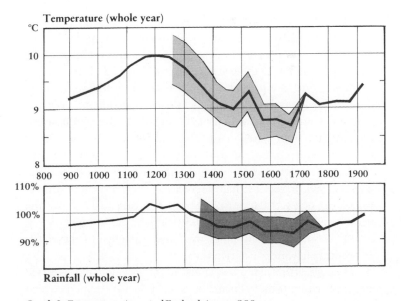

Graph 2 *Temperatures in central England since AD 800.*

13

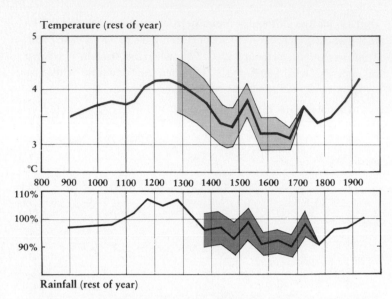

Temperature (rest of year)

Rainfall (rest of year)

Graph 3 *Rainfall in England and Wales since AD 800.*

was blown down, much damage done to houses and trees, and 8000 people killed). There were several years of famine in Scotland from 1560 to 1700, particularly 1674 and 1693–1700 (when between a third and two-thirds of the Scottish population died). England had bad harvests in the 1550s, and several outbreaks of plague (until 1665). Only after the 1780s did births exceed deaths substantially. The Thames was frozen over in London at least eleven times in the 17th century (see **3**), and in all 20–22 times between 1564/5 and 1813/14.

Around 1700 the temperatures all over the world were below 20th-century levels. But there was a sharp change to much warmer conditions for a decade or two after 1700, and the 1730s were as warm as recently. But there were fluctuations, and not until the late 19th or early 20th century was a more lasting warmth established. The 18th and 19th centuries were very variable, with some very cold winters and very hot summers. Yet 1725 had the coldest summer on record – a mean temperature of 13.1 °C in June, July, and August; and 1740 was the coldest year since records began in 1659 – a mean for the year of 6.8 °C (44 °F). Yet overall the weather was good enough to support the 18th-century advances in agriculture.

Lamb suggests that many, if not most, of the variations of this period may have been due to the frequency of violent volcanic eruptions, which threw dust high up into the atmosphere, from 1752 to the 1840s. Does

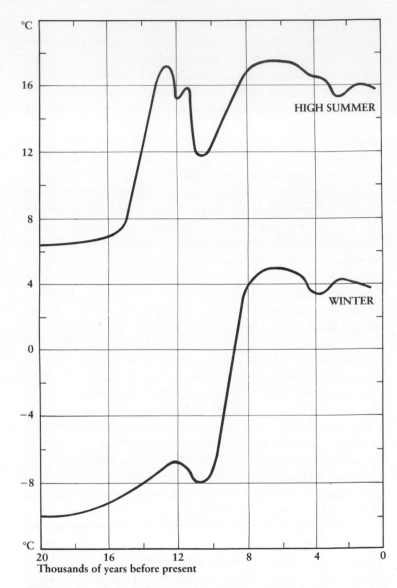

HIGH SUMMER

WINTER

Thousands of years before present

Graph 4 *Generalised graph of temperatures in central England over the last 20,000 years.*

this in part account for Turner's sunset colours? One particularly bad year was 1816 – "the year without a summer" – which led to the typhus epidemic of 1816–19, to the plague in south-east Europe and the east Mediterranean, to the first cholera epidemic of 1816–17,

3 *A fair on the frozen Thames, 1683–84 (from an old print).*

and to the famines of 1816–17 – similar effects to the bad years of 1315–50. In fact the years 1810–19 were the coldest in England since the 1690s, and had the interesting social side-effect of introducing warm underwear, which brought to an end the thin post-1789 fashions.

The 1820s and 1830s saw a return to greater warmth; 1826 was the warmest year on record, not excepting 1976. But great variability remained. Thus, 1829 was cold in Scotland, and there was much rain and flooding in the north-east of England. The 1820s, 30s, and 40s were wet, to the point of making irrigation on farms unnecessary. 1846 was very hot, but humid, allowing the potato blight fungus to take hold in Ireland, causing the Irish potato famine and a typhus epidemic, with 1 million deaths (the Irish population of 8.5m in 1845 was 6.5m in 1851 and only 4m in 1900, owing to continuing emigration).

1878 and 1879 were cold and wet, after difficult seasons since 1875, which contributed to the Great Agricultural Depression and led to emigration from the country to the towns and overseas. Other cold years were 1894–5, 1916–17, 1928–9, 1940, and 1962–3. But warming took place in the 1910s and 1920s, with peaks in the 1940s; the growing season was lengthened by two weeks, and open hilltop sites were favoured for expensive houses in the 1930s.

Since 1950 there has been an increase in variability, and the occurrence of extreme seasons – for temperature and rainfall – has increased. Thus, 1962–3 was the coldest winter in England since 1740; 1963–4 the driest winter since 1743; 1974–5 the mildest winter since 1834; 1975–6 saw the greatest drought since 1698. There have been sharp heat waves in 1975, 1976, and 1990. The frequency of gales has increased since the 1960s (the highest since the 1880s and 1890s), and some, like those of 1987 and 1990, were destructive.

The peak warm years of this century were those of 1933–52. Since then there has been a decline; thus there has been no average warm spring from 1965–80, but some warm autumns, eg 1969, the warmest for 320 years. The growing season has become shorter and summer later (as the past few years have shown). The glaciers are advancing again, after their lowest position, in the early 20th century, since the Little Ice Age. Sea level rose from 1895 to 1960, but has levelled off since then, unless a slight rise resumed in the 1980s.

Climate, as well as volcanic and human activity, has a direct effect on populations in marginal areas, crops, health, insects, and bacteria. Human-made pollutions since the Industrial Revolution began have created the "greenhouse effect", and disturbed the ozone layer; the overall temperature is already rising. But the natural climate is cooling, and the present interglacial could end, according to Lamb and others, round 3–7,000 years ahead. There could be recovery about 15,000 years hence, but return to today's temperature is not expected until after a full glacial climax about 6–8,000 years hence. The effects of the present pollutions (which may peak a century or so from now) are, in the long term, offset by this underlying trend. Meanwhile, the cooling since 1950 will continue for some decades.

It is not of course practicable here to give a detailed year-by-year analysis of the fluctuations of climate, taking into account temperatures, rainfall, winds, seasonal changes, etc. Nor is it always easy to discern trends, which often seem to be contradictory in detail. But the crucial role of climate in human history is undeniable, having a direct relationship to food supplies, disease, demography, and population movements. The detail should be read in the works of, for example, Gordon Manley and H H Lamb (who has been heavily drawn on here).

VEGETATION

It is often said that in prehistoric times a squirrel could have travelled the whole length of the country without once having to descend to the ground. This may be fanciful, but it conjures up a picture of a country entirely covered by forest, which is not far from the truth.

By about 12,000 BC the ice of the last glaciation had receded far enough for the recolonisation of Britain by trees and other plants to begin. This process took several thousand years. The periglacial tundra had extended from the Thames valley as far south as Bordeaux; and before the process of reafforestation was finished, Britain had become an island (c 6000 BC), and many species of both fauna and flora were left behind on the Continent.

The most recent account of the sequence of advance is that by Oliver Rackham in *History of the Countryside* (Dent 1986). He distinguishes five provinces of the "wildwood" (as he calls the primeval forest), in order of arrival:

1 Pine, in the eastern Scottish Highlands, with outliers in south-west Scotland and the Lake District (though there is some evidence to suggest that two groups of Scots pines, in the north-west and the south-west of Scotland, may have originated in trees which somehow survived glaciation and recolonised the restricted are as where they are now found (see *Forest Life*, 1990 (Forestry Commission))

2 Birch, in the western Scottish Highlands

3 Oak-hazel, in south and east Scotland, highland England, most of Wales

4 Hazel-elm, probably in south-west Wales and Cornwall

5 Lime, in lowland England

Tree cover did not extend to the northern coastal strip of Caithness and Sutherland, nor to the Northern Isles or the Outer Hebrides. This list reflects the situation up to about 4000 BC but, in the Lowland Zone particularly, a greater variety of trees developed in each area. In southern Britain there was a patchwork, and elm, ash, beech, hornbeam, maple, and holly appear, each commonest in certain areas (all these may predate 4000 BC).

The earliest human colonists when the ice receded – the final Palaeolithic Creswellians and others – had little or no effect on the forests. But their successors, the Mesolithic peoples from c 8000 to c 4000 BC, deliberately burnt off the forest to encourage the concentration of grazing animals in the clearings (as the Australian aborigines and the Canadian Indians still do). The Neolithic peoples – the first farmers – who began to arrive about 4500 BC continued this "slash and burn" clearance on a large scale, this time not only for animals but for cultivation. Add to this the so-called "elm decline" in the centuries round 4000 BC – partly due to Neolithic activity but perhaps also partly to a widespread epidemic of elm disease – and the extent of the wildwood became seriously reduced. By c 500 BC half of England had been cleared, and at least by Roman times the wildwood was severely restricted. The Roman landscape of villa estates, farms, towns and villages, and roads had a character recognisably akin to that of modern times. Clearance continued throughout the post-Roman centuries. By Domesday (1086) only some 15% of the land recorded was woodland and wood-pasture (modern France still has 20%). This figure, however, conceals some unusually wooded areas; thus, 70% of the Weald was woodland in 1086, and this area is still thickly wooded. From 1840 until 1870 about a quarter of the surviving ancient woods were destroyed for agriculture. After that there was little change until 1939, and then there was a 4% loss to airfields etc. From 1950 to 1973 a third was lost to forestry and agriculture.

Today only 1% of the wildwood remains, and even this is not primeval but has been affected by management. Rackham believes that the last of the natural wildwood was in the Forest of Dean, and was felled in the 13th century.

Stumps of trees from former forests may still be seen in, for example, the Fens, Glamorgan, and the Pennines. Far from the moorlands of the Highland Zone being primeval, they were in fact created by man, for hunting, shooting, or keeping sheep. By the Bronze Age most of the lowland heaths had been created: the New Forest and much of Surrey are good examples. Once created, heaths are self-sustaining.

Ancient woodland, defined as woodland known to have been so in 1600, is in most cases very probably derived from the original wildwood; but in most, if not all, cases it has been managed at some time. Good examples include Glen Trool (Kb); Bow Hill (Sx) (yew); Ebernoe Common (Sx); Binswood (Ha) (wood-pasture); Groton Wood (Sf) (lime). It has certain characteristic indicators, plants which will not readily colonise new sites, such as wood anemone, bluebell, herb paris, or dog's mercury. But it is unsafe to deduce the presence of ancient woodland, or former ancient woodland, from one species only. This is not the place for a complete list of such plants; G F Peterken (*Biological Conservation* 6, 1974) has identified 50 plants more or less confined to ancient woodland in Lincolnshire, and there are similar lists for indicators of old meadowland, old chalk grassland, and other habitats.

Secondary woodland is woodland arising on land which has at some time in the past not been woodland. Thus it might have colonised an abandoned field or part of a down, heath, or fen. There are examples where such a wood contains the ridge and furrow of medieval cultivation. Secondary woodland may date from any period since Roman times.

Woods have been managed since Neolithic times, and since the 13th century probably none has been untouched. Some have been used as pastures, others as sources of valuable and varied materials. Large trees were felled to provide timber for house- or ship-building. Underwood – hazels, ash, and willow – was coppiced, that is cut down to within inches of the ground regularly from 5 to 15 years (see **4**), to produce poles or material for fencing, wattles, or woodland crafts. A variant of coppicing is suckering, which relies on the habit of aspens and elms to throw up suckers from their roots. The wider use of coppicing would benefit many neglected copses. If there was a risk from grazing animals, a tree would be pollarded (see **5**), or cut to about 6ft (1.85m) from the ground; there are fine pollarded oaks and other trees in Epping Forest, for example. Underwood and branches also provided wood for charcoal-burning, and fuel not only for domestic use but for industry, such as (medieval) glassmaking. All parts of the tree could be used – twigs, leaves, bark. Bracken and other plants were gathered for litter and to make potash. The trees and grass were grazed, and the fallen nuts and mast were pannage for pigs.

All these features can be seen to perfection in Hatfield Forest, near Dunmow (Ex). This is a unique survival in England, and possibly

4 *Coppicing: before cutting, after cutting, and one year later.*

5 *Pollarding: before cutting, after cutting, and one year later.*

(in Rackham's view) in the world. It still contains deer, cattle, coppice woods, seven species of pollards, scrub, timber trees, grassland, fen, and a 17th-century lodge and rabbit warren.

Useful indicators of the presence of wildwood in Anglo-Saxon times are certain place-names. Names containing the element -*ley*, -*hurst*, or -*field* signify a settlement in a clearing in, or next to, a wood. *Roding* and *stocking* also imply forest clearings, as does *thwaite* in the Danish-settled north. *Lund*, *frith*, and *bere*, and some of the -*leys*, mean the woods themselves.

Of the two million hectares of British woodland, some half a million are broad-leaved. During the 1970s and 1980s most planting, both by the Forestry Commission and by private interests, was of conifers, but opinion is now favouring a more balanced planting policy. In 1990, 9% of Britain's land area was covered by trees, but only 2% by native species. In 1989 the Countryside Commission and the Forestry Commission launched a scheme for the planting of "urban forests", areas of land close to major cities which would be planted with trees. These would modify the green belt concept, and provide not only recreational lungs but the benefit of woodland as well. Sites have already been considered near London, in the Midlands, and in the north-east. But at the same time large areas of state forest in other areas are being sold off.

LAND USE

The use of land is conditioned by soil, climate, and accessibility to centres of population, as well as by the history of human interference in the landscape.

The total area of Britain is some 56 million acres or 93,000 square miles (23 million hectares); this is divided between England, 32m acres, Wales 5m acres, and Scotland 19m acres. According to 1989 figures (see *Britain 1991* (HMSO for COI, 1991), 77% of the land area is used for agriculture, the rest being mountain, forest, or urban, industrial, etc. Thirty million acres (12m hectares) are under crops and grass, and 15m acres (6m hectares) are rough grazing. In 1989, 573,000 people were engaged in agriculture, or 2.2% of the working population. They used some 500,000 tractors and 53,000 combine harvesters. There were 257,000 farm holdings, of which 75% in the east, south, and west were wholly or mainly owner-occupied; tenant farmers are normal in the Highland Zone of England and Glamorgan, and are preponderant in the east Midlands. The average area of farms (full-time businesses) was 265 acres (107.3 ha); the average farm size in the EU is some 40 acres. The 12% in the largest size group (over 300 acres) accounted for 57% of activity; the smallest size group (45% of farms) accounted for only 2.6% of activity. There are 5,800 statutory smallholdings in England, and 950 in Wales; in Scotland there are 1,525 crofts and holdings.

The size of farms has increased and the labour force employed has decreased, quite significantly since 1938, and even since 1960 (by some 35–40%). In 1989 cereals were grown on 9.6m acres (3.9m ha); in addition potatoes, beet, vegetables, etc were grown. Horticulture and market gardening took up 497,000 acres (201,000 ha). The arable land is mainly in eastern and central southern England and eastern Scotland. Three-fifths of full-time farms are devoted mainly to dairying or beef cattle and sheep; most of the cattle and sheep are in the Highland Zone.

Woodland covers 5.88m acres (2.38m ha), or 7.3% of England, 13% of Scotland, and 12% of Wales. Most planting is of conifers in upland areas, but the planting of broadleaved trees is being encouraged.

Urban and industrial land covered 4.4m acres in 1961 (9.9% of England and Wales and 2.6% of Scotland); by 1984 the figure had increased to some 12.5% of the total. The loss of agricultural land was some 42,000 acres (17,000 ha) a year during the 1960s and 1970s, but the rate of loss has declined since 1975.

Statistics older than the last few years divided the acreage between woods and plantations, rough grazing (including moors, deer forests, etc), permanent pasture, arable, and other. As a final detail, in 1965, in England and Wales, 60,800 farms were dairy, 24,700 livestock, 9,600 pigs and poultry, 26,600 cropping, 15,000 horticulture, and 19,500 mixed; the pattern in Scotland was different.

POPULATION AND DEMOGRAPHY

Population

There is considerable uncertainty in the calculation of populations before censuses began in 1801. For the prehistoric periods almost nothing certain is known, and the evidence of burial places and dwellings is hazardous in the extreme. For the Roman period figures can be deduced for the towns, but knowledge of the thousands of rural sites is very sketchy. The first conscious survey of population is Domesday Book (1086), which is very valuable but not comprehensive. The Poll Tax returns of 1377 give another, very valuable, fixed point. There are other official surveys – hearth tax returns etc – in the succeeding centuries, but not until Gregory King's analysis of the population by categories (1688) was a broadly acceptable overview available.

The current best guesses for the pre-census period, for what they are worth (the authorities vary very widely), are:

Late Neolithic *c* 10,000

Late Bronze Age *c* 100,000

Early Iron Age ?2 million

Roman (3rd century AD) 2–4 million, of which London had about 30,000, and Colchester and Verulamium some 15,000 each

Population declined in the 5th and 6th centuries perhaps as low as half a million, and by 1086 had only reached about 1.5 million. By 1340 the figure stood at about 5 million, but a decline had already set in (see below), which was accelerated by the Black Death (1348–9). Population took some time to recover, and by 1450 was only some 3 million. Recovery accelerated from the late 15th century, and in 1500 the figure stood at around 4 million. In the 1530s a start was made on the registration of births, deaths, and marriages, which, although completeness took many years to reach, put the assessment of population on a sounder basis. So, in 1570 the population of England was 4.1m; 4.8m in 1600; 5.6m in 1630; 5.7m in 1670; 6m in 1700 (as against Gregory King's figure of 5.5m); and 6.5m in 1750.

After this the rise was rapid until the present day. The United Kingdom census of 1801 (which was probably some 5% understated) gave figures for England and Wales of 8.9m, and Scotland 1.6m, out of a total of 11.9m. (Scotland had been growing from 1m in 1700 to 1.6m in 1801.) The figures then rose to: 1851 22.25m (total, of which England and Wales 17.9m, Scotland 2.9m); 1901 38.2m (England and Wales 32.5m, Scotland 4.5m); 1951 50.2m (England and Wales 43.7m, Scotland 5m); 1991 56.5m (England and Wales 50m, Scotland).

Within this framework it is interesting to see the changing pattern of towns. In England, London has always had an unchallengeable preponderance, and still has about a seventh of the population. The growth of London is phenomenal. In the 1st century AD its population was perhaps 30,000, reaching 45–50,000 in the 3rd century. By 1086 it was 14–18,000, by 1199 20–25,000, and by 1340 nearly 50,000. The Black Death and other epidemics and economic depression reduced this to 35,000 in 1377; the decrease continued into the 15th century, followed by a rapid increase in the 16th century, reaching 200,000 by 1600. By 1650 the figure had reached 350–400,000, and by 1700 575–600,000, one-tenth of the national total, and 20 times bigger than the next largest town. London was then the biggest city in western Europe. By 1750 the population was 650,000, and 959,310 by 1801 (county area), or 1,096,784 (Greater London area) – 11 times larger than Liverpool and twice as large as Paris. The increase continued: 2,363,341 in 1851 (2,651,939 in the Greater London area); 4,536,267, in 1901 or 6,506,889 in Greater London – a decline in the county area, and growth in Greater London. The peak was reached in 1939, at an estimated 4,013,400 (8,615,050). Decline set in, and the 1951 figures are 3,347,982 (8,193,921), and 1971 3,031,935 (7,452,356). 1981 saw a provisional 2,497,978 (6,713,165), the former 10% below 1971, the latter 17% below (see Ben Weinreb and Christopher Hibbert: *The London Encyclopaedia* (Macmillan 1983)).

Outside London, towns before industrialisation were small by modern standards; indeed, most of the 609 medieval boroughs listed by Beresford and Finberg (*English Medieval Boroughs: a handlist* (David & Charles 1973)) were no bigger than villages. The list of the ten or so major towns after London changes through the centuries, but reflects the varying fortunes of regional industries like cloth, or of long-distance trade.

In 1086 the list is: London 18,000, Winchester 6,000, Norwich 4,400, York 4,100, Lincoln 3,500, Thetford 2,300, Bristol 2,300, Gloucester 2,100, Cambridge 1,900, Chester 1,900. By 1377 this had changed to: London 60,000 (some authorities prefer 35,000 for 1377, 60,000 for 1520), York 18,100, Bristol 16,000, Norwich 13,000, Plymouth 12,100, Coventry 12,000, Lincoln 8,900, Salisbury 8,100, King's Lynn 7,800, Colchester 7,400, Boston 7,200. By the 17th century London had drawn well clear of the rest. In 1700, London had 5–600,000, while the next largest, Bristol, had 29,000. Norwich was the next largest, but was now followed by the growing new industrial cities, on their way to being conurbations – Manchester, Liverpool,

Birmingham, and Leeds. In 1801 industry led the field: London 864,000, Manchester 84,000, Liverpool 78,000, Birmingham 74,000, Bristol 64,000, Leeds 53,000; Norwich now had 37,000 and York 30,000. Since then this pattern has only been reinforced.

It must be said that there is considerable variation among the authorities over medieval populations; for instance, Barbara Green and Rachel Young, in *Norwich, the Growth of a City* (Norwich Museums 1972), only allow a figure of 6,000 for 1348 and 10,000 for 1523. Against this, a recent study of Winchester (T B James in *Hampshire Field Club, Local History Newsletter*, ns 1988) finds evidence for both low and high estimates before the 1801 census; thus for 1057 5,500 and 8,000; for 1300 8,000 and 11,625. From then to 1801 (6,194) the town was in decline, and in 1603 a low of 3,120 is possible. But subject to this caution the broad view is reliable.

The increases in the urban populations were caused not only, or mainly, by natural increase but also by migration from country to town and by immigration from abroad (eg the Flemish in East Anglia, the Huguenots, the Irish in Glasgow and Liverpool). Until the 16th century the bulk of the people, at least 90%, lived in the country or were dependent on agriculture. Soon after 1850 this proportion had declined to a point where over 50% of the people were urban; by 1901 77% were urban, by 1951 81%, and by 1981 87%, an almost complete reversal from the medieval position, although only some 10% of the country's land surface is covered by houses or other urban structures. In 1991 some 33 million people lived in the metropolitan areas, 6% of the national territory; the rural areas, more than a third of the land area, contained only 5% of the population.

The density of population has changed radically since medieval times. Using J C Russell's data, A H A Hogg (in Margaret Jesson and David Hill: *The Iron Age and its Hillforts* (Southampton University 1971)) has shown that the highest density in 1100, up to 17.9 per sq km, was reached in Suffolk; values over 10 per sq km are found in East Anglia and eastern England (except the Fens), and in Dorset, Somerset, and east Devon. Values in the 8s and 9s occur in a belt from Kent to Wiltshire and north-east to the Humber. West and north of this belt the values decline to 1.4. This pattern has much to do with the wool and cloth industry. In our day the pattern is totally different, the highest density being in a belt from south Lancashire through the West Midlands to London and the south-east.

Demography

Infant mortality was very high until the mid-19th century. Expectation of life was low: J C Russell estimates no more than 30–35 years for men during normal times in the 13th–15th centuries. If they survived childhood, and reached that age, they could expect a further 20–25 years. This appears to be the normal pattern until recent times. But there are local variations and class distinctions. For instance, in Bath in the late 18th century, a worker could expect to live only 25 years, and even this was better than in other large towns. A survey for 1840 showed that in rural Rutland the gentry and professionals could expect 52 years, tradesmen, farmers, and shopkeepers 41, and mechanics and labourers 38. At the same time, things were not so good in the industrial cities. In Whitechapel the corresponding figures were 45, 27, and 22, in Liverpool 35, 22, 15, while Manchester was a little better at 38, 20, and 17. In 1960 the expectation at birth was 68.3 for men and 74.1 for women, or, at age 70, 9.5 for men and 11.5 for women. These figures continue to improve.

Family (household) size in pre-industrial times averaged 4.5–5 persons, but this figure covers a range up to over 20 for households of the nobility, which included considerable numbers of servants. In 1982 the figure was 1.75, below the 2.1 needed to replace the population.

The age of marriage (following P Laslett's studies) in the 16th/17th centuries was on average 28 for men and 24 for women. The gentry married younger: the mean for men was 26.18 and for women 21.75. The nobility married earlier still, usually for reasons of inheritance or ownership of property: the mean age for 1600–25 was 24.28 for men and 19.39 for women, and for 1625–50 it was 25.99 for men and 20.67 for women. Today the mean is 28 or 29 for men and 25 or 26 for women. Medieval marriage age was affected by changes in the onset of puberty.

Stature is another variable factor. A recent study of skeletons in Denmark (Pia Bennike: *Paleopathology of Danish Skeletons* (Copenhagen, Akademisk Forlag, 1985)) shows – if its results are also valid for Britain – that stature was lowest in the Mesolithic and was on average several centimetres higher in the Bronze and Iron Ages, falling unexpectedly in the Viking period, recovering somewhat in the Middle Ages, and, even more surprisingly, lowest at about 1850.

Conditions of life

All these matters are strongly influenced by the way people had to live. Obvious factors in the question of life expectancy are housing, sanitation, hygiene, and pollution (animal and human waste, coal smoke, industrial effluents and vapours, etc), which are still to some extent with us; diet and disease were also influential. In times of good harvests more children were born; when harvests were bad the death rate went up. This was due largely to poor diet (although starvation would play its part), which made people more susceptible to disease. The declining population in the early 14th century was due to climatic fluctuations leading to bad harvests (famine in 1315–17), high corn prices, malnutrition, and the onset of a series of epidemics of bubonic plague and other diseases, culminating in the Black Death of 1348–9. Plague was endemic until the late 17th century (see page 25), but there were other killer diseases too – typhoid, anthrax (which some authorities see as the epidemic of 1348 instead of bubonic plague (*Current Archaeology* 93 (1984)), though this view is not generally accepted), and cholera, which was rife in the 18th and 19th centuries. The cholera outbreaks of 1849 and 1854, in which 40,000 people died, led to drastic improvements in public sanitation. Actual starvation could also occur, as at the end of the 17th century in the north of England and Scotland, and the Irish potato famine of the 1840s, caused by diseases of the crops.

There are other relevant factors, such as the state of medical skill, the removal of cemeteries from overcrowded areas, even improvements in clothing. But for the pre-industrial age at least (perhaps for all periods) the vital element is food. There does seem to be a direct link between food prices and fluctuations in population levels.

The peoples of Britain

Britain cannot be thought of as a simple trilogy of English, Scots, and Welsh. Far from it. If one looks below the surface one sees a quite astonishing mosaic and palimpsest of peoples, building up over half a million years. Not all of these strains have merged, and some may have died out. But the genetic patterns of the present British, and the prospect of future admixtures, remain of the greatest complexity.

For the long prehistoric periods it is clearly impossible to know with certainty who came in from where, and in what numbers. Moreover,

there is no exact equation between the cultural remains and the origins of the people who left them.

As long ago as 1933, in a classic book *The Horse and the Sword*, Harold Peake and H J Fleure felt able to say that "The old division of prehistoric times into the Stone, Bronze and Iron Ages,* though it has been of inestimable value during the last century in bringing a measure of order out of chaos, is now revealing signs of failure to meet the needs of today." Peake and Fleure saw culture change as a long process of diffusion of ideas and fashions in artefacts and processes across Europe from centres in the Middle East, only partly powered by actual invasions or mass migrations of peoples. The influential prehistorian V Gordon Childe, who died in 1957, also saw much merit in this concept. But even in Childe's day the invasion theory was still in fashion, in reaction against diffusion. Since the 1960s a modified diffusionism, based on the continuity of populations, has come to be seen as providing the most likely explanation of culture change. This current view sees the sequence of archaeological phases as being due only partly (and then not always) to actual movements of people, but more often to the arrival of new ideas, styles, practices, and artefacts, by way of tribal contacts, war, trade, gifts, or the occasional local invention. But in some cases actual immigrations, even on a small scale, must still be postulated, and in more recent periods can be substantiated historically.

During the long Ice Age, with its successive glaciations, small bands of hunter-gatherers wandered across Europe, and a few of these penetrated onto the southern parts of Britain (when it was still an integral part of the Continent) as the ice-fronts receded, in pursuit of game and seasonal vegetable foods. These people used implements clearly ascribable to specific Paleolithic cultures, but these cultures cannot always be attributed exclusively to particular human species. Moreover, physical remains of early humans are rare. But those which have survived indicate the human forms which reached Britain.

The significant remains are:

> Boxgrove (Sx): *Homo erectus cf heidelbergensis, c* 500,000 years ago (this is in fact the earliest human form in Europe); Swanscombe (Kt): probably a type transitional between *H erectus* and *H sapiens neanderthalensis*, some 250,000 years ago;

* devised by C J Thomsen in Copenhagen in 1816, and published in 1836

Paviland, Gower (WG): *H sapiens sapiens*, some 18,500 years ago (the earliest modern human remains in Britain); also Sun Hole, Mendips (So), some 12,500 years ago; Creswell (Db), some 10,400 years ago; Gough's Cave, Cheddar (So), some 9000 years ago; Thatcham (Bk), some 8000 years ago. Of these the last three date from after the final recession of the last (Devensian) glaciation; Thatcham is Early Mesolithic.

About 4400 BC farming was introduced into Britain, and this enables the principle of continuity to be scrutinised more closely. While it seems certain that the Mesolithic hunter-gatherers who then inhabited Britain adopted farming and Early Neolithic culture, including pottery, yet this culture must also have involved some degree of immigration of people from across the Channel (Britain became separated from the Continent about 7–8000 years ago) – sheep and goats, for example, which first occur here in the Neolithic, are not native to Britain, and imply some movement of people.

The later prehistoric periods from the Neolithic to the Iron Age (both inclusive) are thickly studded with new ideas – structures, practices, and artefacts, such as religious/social centres, tombs and barrows of various types, pottery, metallurgy, tools, weapons, ornaments, hillforts, *oppida*, and coinage. Most of these were of Continental origin, but some (such as henges and Severn-Cotswold tombs) were local inventions. Some foreign ideas were modified on arrival. These introductions did not all involve movement of people, or even of objects (as R J Harrison has said, of Early Bronze Age Beakers: "The pots did not move, the ideas did"). As there can be no certainty, in most cases, that these introductions were accompanied by fresh immigrants, all that need be said is that from time to time settlers arrived in Britain, mainly from western or central Europe.

Likely occasions for this are the Early Neolithic, the late Bronze Age, and the Iron Age (eg the Parisi in East Yorkshire and the Belgae in Hampshire). Otherwise, increase in population and prosperity can account for most phenomena (such as the Early Bronze Age Wessex culture).

When the Romans arrived in AD 43, Iron Age Britain was divided among a mosaic of native (mostly Celtic) states or tribes. But this did not mean that, even where a tribal name (eg Atrebates) coincided with one on the Continent, the tribe had migrated wholesale. This may have happened in rare cases, but generally the name could imply the arrival of a small dominant element, perhaps members of a royal house, ruling over a substantial substratum of indigenous people.

It appears probable that most of the inhabitants of Britain since the Neolithic spoke Indo-European languages. The Picts are an exception to this – their language was not Indo-European, and their origins are obscure. (A few other pockets of non-Indo-European languages and peoples survived in western Europe into more recent times, such as the Etruscans, the Iberians, and the Basques – the latter being still a distinct group. The "Mediterranean-looking" Silures of South Wales, still a recognisable type, and a group in Bedfordshire, may also be elements in the mosaic of early settlers.) The rest of the prehistoric settlers from Neolithic times may well have been proto-Indo-European speakers, whose languages crystallised during the Bronze and Iron Ages into the Celtic languages, which, in Britain, fall into two groups – Goidelic (Erse, Scottish Gaelic, and Manx), and Brythonic (Welsh, Cornish, and Breton). The differences between the two Celtic groups may be due more to local habits of speech than to racial origin.

From the Romans on we are on historical ground, and can recognise the settlers. These may be summarised as follows:

AD 43 — The Romans organised Britain as a province (later as several provinces) up to Hadrian's Wall; their hold was looser up to the Antonine Wall, and minimal in eastern Scotland; their occupation of Wales and the south-west of England was also limited. The Celtic states had a degree of autonomy within the Roman system. The Roman army, civil service professionals, merchants, etc came from all parts of the Empire, and many of these no doubt settled in Britain on retirement or on the withdrawal of Roman power in AD 410. Sub-Roman organisation continued during most of the 5th century.

410 — The Romans withdrew their military and civil power from Britain. The British continued to run the country on Roman lines until the late 5th century; native (Celtic) states began to form meanwhile. The British kingdom of Elmet in south-west Yorkshire survived until the 7th century.

mid 5th c — Anglo-Saxon raids intensify, and settlement well under way by the end of the century. (There had been raiding by

Angles, Saxons, and Frisians as early as the 3rd century, and a Germanic presence, sponsored by the Romans, at strategic points, to provide a warning of raids, at least.) The settlers included Saxons in the south, from the coast, and along the Thames (Essex, Middlesex, Sussex, Wessex), Angles in East Anglia, much of the Midlands and the North, as far as the Forth, a few Frisians in East Anglia and Lancashire, Jutes in Kent, south Hampshire, and the Isle of Wight, and Franks in Kent. There were Scandanavian elements in pre-Viking Anglian England. The settlement continued throughout the 6th and 7th centuries, and later in some areas (see **Map 4**, page 24).

5th/6th c — Irish raids, and some settlement, in south and west Wales.

In Scotland the situation was different. South of the Forth-Clyde line (the Antonine Wall) were British-speaking tribes; north of this line were Gaelic-speakers in the west (Dalriada), and Picts in the east. The Picts are first referred to in 297, but of course had been there since time immemorial; their kingdom ended in 843, when it was united with Dalriada. Scots (Scotti) from Ulster crossed to Argyll (Dalriada) in the 5th century, after raids from 297; their capital was transferred from Ireland to Scotland (Dunadd) by 500. (Columba reached Iona in 563.) Anglians from Northumbria entered the south-eastern lowlands in the second quarter of the 7th century, and Rheged later. Norse settled in the Northern Isles and northern Scotland (the Norse earldom of Orkney was under Norwegian rule until 1468), and in the Western Isles, Man, and Ireland (the kingdom of Dublin).

6th/7th c — Welsh and Cornish settlement in Brittany.

(793 — Vikings destroy Lindisfarne.)

835 on — Danes raid, then settle, in eastern England (with a small colony in south-east Lancashire). Danish armies operate from Five Boroughs – Stamford, Lincoln, Leicester, Nottingham, and Derby (from 851). Danish control of eastern England is recognised as the Danelaw (877).

9th/10th c — Irish/Norse from Ireland settle in north-west England and northern Pennines; Viking kingdom of York, 867–954.

late 9th/ early 10th c — Alfred, Aethelflaed, and Edward the Elder defeat the Danes.

980 — Fresh Danish raids; Danish kings reign in England (Cnut, Harthacnut) from 1016 to 1035 and 1040 to 1042.

1066 — Norman conquest of England. A relatively small number of Normans and French actually settled in England. Their leaders (including William I's relations, friends, and major supporters) were granted lands and positions of power, as territorial nobility, bishops, etc. French colonies were established in key towns (eg Nottingham), in separate areas from the Anglo-Saxons.

1070s — Jews, as financiers, were brought in, eg at York and Lincoln; they were expelled in 1290.

late 15th c — Gypsies reached England at the end of their long migration from India, and continued their nomadic life.

16th/17th c — Craftsmen of many kinds came in from Germany and the Low Countries, mainly Protestants fleeing persecution; many settled round the City of London, eg in Southwark. From the 1570s French Huguenots also arrived; the Revocation of the Edict of Nantes in 1672 brought another wave of Huguenots from France – these included silk weavers in Spitalfields (London). 6000 Dutch ("Strangers") came to Norwich in the 1560s and 1580s, as weavers of the "New Draperies". An influential Dutch element came in the 1690s, with William III. Jews (Sephardim) were allowed back in England in 1655.

18th/19th c — Significant numbers of Irish came to Britain during the 18th century, and very large numbers as a result of the potato famine of the 1840s. Major concentrations grew up in London, Liverpool, and Glasgow. Large numbers of Welsh came to England, notably London. Scottish farmers settled in eastern England, as far south as Romney Marsh (Kt).

late 19th/ early 20th c — Jews (Ashkenazim from eastern Europe) came in, and settled particularly in east (later north) London, Manchester, and Leeds.

20th c — A century of massive folk movements. The early part of the century saw the immigration of Jews from

23

eastern Europe, and in the 1930s from Germany. Since the Second World War people came in from many parts of the world. These include Caribbeans, who settled widely, but in significant numbers in London (Notting Hill, Brixton); Italians (Bedford); Pakistanis (Bradford); Indians (Leicester); Bangladeshis (Southall and succeeding Jews in east London). Chinese, Japanese, Thais, and Indians run restaurants all over the country, and the Japanese have a substantial business colony. Arabs have bought properties here. Cardiff has a large multiracial community at Tiger Bay. This varied population (and the above are only some of the nationalities involved) follow many religions. There are over 1 million Moslems in Britain, and significant numbers of Hindus, with lesser numbers of Buddhists, Sikhs, Jains, Ba'hais, etc; there are some quarter of a million Jews.

Map 4 *Anglo-Saxon and Celtic kingdoms and peoples in the 6th century AD. This map shows the position when the Anglo-Saxon settlement had reached some stability. Celtic kingdoms remain in the west of the country – the south-west peninsula, Wales, the north-west of England, and Scotland.*

The Black Death and its effects

"Plague is a disease of wild and peri-domestic rodents caused by a bacillus, *Yersinia pestis*. In nature the organism is transmitted among rodents and from rodents to man by the bite of infected fleas" (*The Pest Anatomized* (Wellcome Institute, 1985)). The disease has two main forms – bubonic plague and pneumonic plague. Mortality from untreated pneumonic plague is almost total, while from untreated bubonic plague it is more than 50%, though specific treatment can lower it to 15%. Over 30 species of flea are proven vectors, but in most countries the rat flea *Xenopsylla cheopis* is the most important. At least 220 different rodents can harbour bubonic plague; the black rat (*Rattus rattus*) was the main vector in England. When animals die from plague their fleas leave the body and seek another host, animal or human. In rural areas plague can be caught while hunting, trapping, or skinning, while in urban areas it is a disease of poor hygienic conditions. The incidence is higher in summer and autumn.

There are regions where plague is endemic, such as eastern Asia and parts of Africa and South America. The disease can be spread by migrations of rats or by transmission in ships, etc. This is by no means uncommon, and Europe has been affected many times.

The presence of the black rat has now been established in Roman Britain, probably reaching us from India along the trade routes of the Empire. It has been found in London (3rd–4th century), York (at least by the 4th century), and Wroxeter (5th century), as well as in the late Saxon period, long before its apparent peak in the 11th–15th centuries. There is thus a strong possibility that some of the obscure and ill-documented epidemics of Roman and Saxon Britain may have been bubonic plague, including the 7th century pestilence mentioned by Bede. This might even have been a contributory cause in the decline in the population of Roman London from AD 150–250.

A great pandemic in 542 seriously weakened the late Roman Empire; there was another in 664. In England, the main outbreaks were in 1258, 1348–50 (see below), 1361–2, 1369, 1407 (when 30,000 people died in London), 1426, 1433, 1437, 1439, 1450–4, 1474, 1499, 1517, 1531, 1535–48, 1563, 1593, 1603, 1625 (35,000 dead in London), and 1665 (when some 100,000 died); after that the plague all but died out in western Europe.

In southern Europe it lasted longer: there were outbreaks in Venice and Milan in 1575–8 and 1630–1 (when one in three died), 1720–1 in Marseilles, 1743 in Messina, 1771 in Moscow, 1813 in Malta, and 1815 in Corfu. In 1894 it struck Hong Kong, and reached India in 1896; by 1903 over a million had died in India, and by 1910 there were ten million deaths all over the world, including some in Suffolk. From 1964 to 1974 100,000 cases were recorded. But these are only some of the major outbreaks; smaller epidemics occur in the affected areas every few years, as the rats multiply and move. The rodent cycle of 3–8 years is a determining factor here.

The two outbreaks which have stayed in the consciousness of the English are the Black Death of 1348–50 and the Great Plague of 1664–5, in which nearly 100,000 people died in London out of a population of some 400,000. But the effects of the 1664–5 plague were not so serious as those of the Black Death, which was a landmark and turning point in English history.

The plague entered England from a ship at Weymouth (Do), and soon spread all over the country, reaching London in September 1348. It reached its peak in 1349, and died out in 1350. By then it had killed about a third of the entire population, and nearly half that of London (some 40,000). The effects were catastrophic. The population did not regain its 1350 level until the 16th century, and every aspect of national life was affected. The natural growth, development, and prosperity of the country were cut short, and absolutism – centralised royal dictatorship – was enabled to develop.

The feudal system itself collapsed: contracts of fealty and obligation could not be, or were not, fulfilled. Even the methods of sharing the cultivation of the open fields were largely abandoned. Instead of pressure on land due to over-population, land was going derelict for lack of labourers to cultivate it. The survivors shared the vacant land, and did this in blocks – compact farms – instead of in strips. The nucleated farmstead and hedged farm had arrived, and with it the wage earner, who was not tied to his manorial land. Rent became a substitute for service. Some manorial lords ceased to be farmers in consequence, and became country landowners, living on their rents. The serfs and labourers found employment with the new farmers, or moved to the towns. Some became vagrants, and this problem increased thereafter. Village life was disrupted. Many landlords went further, and enclosed the whole manor for sheep, and many villages were deserted for this reason also. Trade was interrupted, crime increased.

There were also effects on education and social life. High mortality among clerics (47%) eliminated a vast number of learned men on whom the country depended not only for religious guidance but also for much of the local and national government. The incidence among doctors was naturally high also. Schools, hospitals, and charitable help for the poor were all affected. To repair the losses of doctors and clerics new schools were founded, and new colleges at Oxford and Cambridge. London benefited by attempts to clean it up, and for example to move butchery outside the city. Perpendicular architecture took root after the Black Death, and the Gothic died with the masons skilled enough to build it.

Foreign contributions to British life

There have been immigrations into Britain from the earliest times, some of them quite small infiltrations, some major colonisations. Such events are important landmarks in prehistory and history. Since Roman rule in Britain faded away, there have been the familiar examples of the Angles, Saxons, Frisians, and Jutes, and later of the Danes and Norse; Scots came from Ireland into Scotland, Irish into Wales, and, in reverse, British Celts to Brittany. And the Normans made a lasting impact out of all proportion to their numbers (see pages 651–2 and 361–6).

But apart from these major folk movements, there have been a number of small but significant immigrations which it is worth while recalling. The contributions made by these people to the life of the country, economically, culturally, and socially, cannot be overempasised.

MEDIEVAL

There was a strong colony of Frisian merchants in York in the 8th century. They imported glass and wine, millstones, whetstones, and pottery, and exported wool, lead, and other things, including perhaps the greyhounds for which York was famous. The Normans settled colonies of French or Flemish burghers in many of their newly created boroughs, like Norwich and Nottingham. These were sometimes so numerous and cohesive that they formed what was virtually one half of a twin town with the other part inhabited by Saxons.

The Jews arrived in England after the Norman conquest, in the years round 1100. They settled in small numbers in London and York, but there was no sizeable influx until the reign of Henry II (from 1154), who was favourable to them. By 1159 there were Jewish colonies in nine or ten places. In York the colony was not considerable until the 1170s,

and then it only had some 20–40 households, or some 150 people in all. This colony may have grown out of a branch or agency of the great financial house of Aaron of Lincoln. (The sources are scattered, and recent research has been led by R B Dobson, who is pulling the medieval threads together.)

The colonies in London, Lincoln, and York were among the largest. They were very prosperous, and had a high standard of living. They were pioneers in stone domestic architecture, but stone houses, like those at Lincoln, were not all necessarily inhabited by Jews. They were principally engaged in commerce, and in public and private financing. They incurred popular and royal displeasure, and many false accusations about their way of life, and there were various persecutions. The colony at York was wiped out by massacre and mass suicide on 16 March 1190. Within five years they began to return to York, becoming even more prosperous than before, and were prominent in many spheres of life. Their wealth was conspicuous in the period 1210–1260; thereafter they declined, and were finally expelled in 1290, taking their treasures with them. It is not a pleasant page of English history. There were probably never more than 5,000 or so Jews in medieval England at any time, and under 3,000 in 1290.

Names like Old Jewry indicate where they lived. In York their main concentration was in the central section of Coney Street, near its junction with Jubbergate. The synagogue was in this area. They had their own cemetery at Jewbury, just north-east of the city, outside the wall. Excavation by the York Archaeological Trust suggests that this 13th century cemetery was used by the jews of Lincoln as well. Nine other medieval Jewish cemeteries are recorded in England, but little excavation has been done on them; one was where the Oxford Botanic Garden is now, and the one in London was just outside Cripplegate. The excavations at Jewbury (which remains the only such in Europe) are reported in J M Lilley, G Stroud, D R Brothwell and M H Williamson: *The Jewish Burial Ground at Jewbury* (*The Archaeology of York* 12/13, CBA/YAT 1994). (For the medieval Jews generally see eg M Adler: *Jews of Medieval England* (1939), and R B Dobson: *The Jews of Medieval York* (York, Borthwick Papers no 45, 1974).)

Archaeological effort to find remains of the medieval Jews in England is overdue, but the circumstances of history and of the sites probably mean that the full story will mainly depend on documentary sources.

Flemish weavers settled in Norfolk in the 14th century, and gave a strong impetus to the cloth industry of East Anglia. Hanseatic

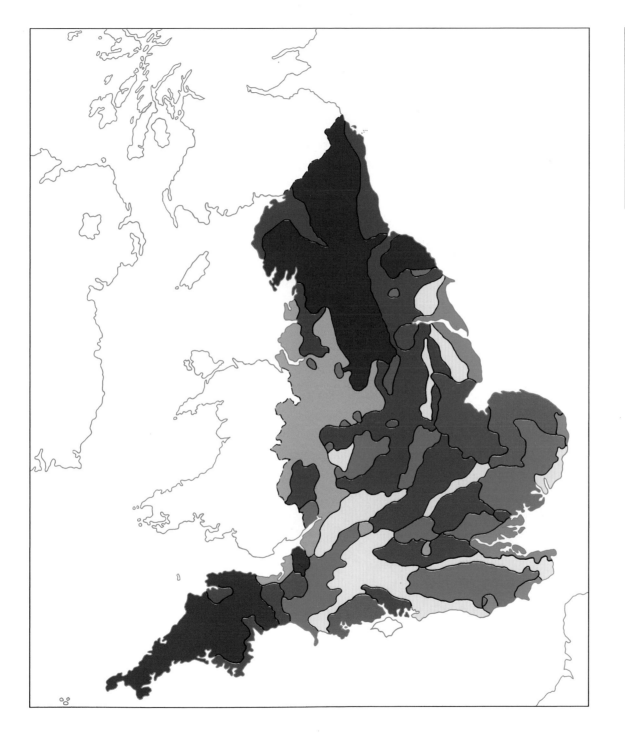

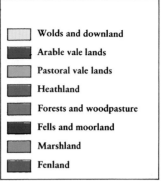

Wolds and downland

Arable vale lands

Pastoral vale lands

Heathland

Forests and woodpasture

Fells and moorland

Marshland

Fenland

Map 6 *English farming regions, 1640–1750. This map, based on the work of Joan Thirsk, shows in broad outline the different types of terrain in England in the early years of modern farming.*

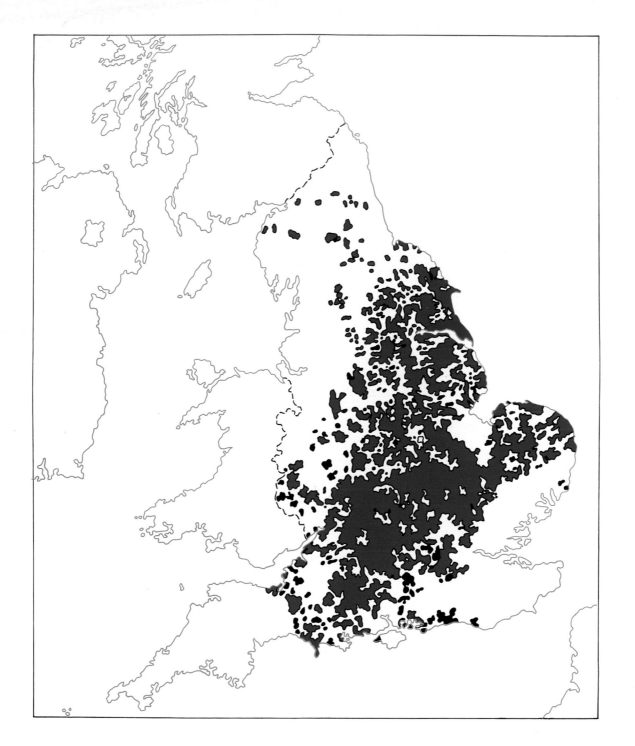

Map 7 *This map shows the extent of the enclosure of open fields and commons by Act of Parliament in the later 18th and earlier 19th centuries. The enclosure covered most of the central arable belt – the area of "planned countryside". The black symbols represent the residual common lands remaining after the main enclosure, and included in the General Enclosure Act of 1845.*

merchants, trading with northern Europe, were allowed in 1250 to keep permanent colonies in this country (rather like the "factories" of the East India Company in the 18th century along the coasts of India, which were harbours, collecting centres, and warehouses). They had these enclaves in London, Southampton, King's Lynn, Boston, and Hull principally; in London they lived round the Steelyard in Dowgate. They ran into commercial opposition, and their rights were finally terminated in 1580.

16TH TO 18TH CENTURIES

The arts and crafts were at times strongly influenced by foreigners or foreign sources. One has only to think of Holbein, Van Dyck, or Handel, or the tradition of pottery begun by Spanish, Italian, and Islamic faience in the 16th century, the tin-glazed earthenware (delft) which swept the country from 1570 to 1800, or the Rhenish salt-glazed stoneware in the 16th and 17th centuries. The blue-and-white delft had Chinese roots, and Chinese pottery was imported here from the mid 16th century, though delft made here or in Holland bore mostly European motifs. Oriental influence continued in many fields (see **6**): Chippendale imitated Chinese themes in his furniture and interiors, and Japanese art had a strong impact on English (and French) life from the mid 19th century. Of course, the Chinese invented gunpowder, which was used in Europe by 1250, and in cannon by the second quarter of the 14th century. The East also gave us spices, silk, tea, printed fabrics, and paper. Arab influences were strong in the Middle Ages in mathematics, science, and philosophy, as well as in pottery.

The 16th century saw the arrival here of people of many nationalities, mostly refugees from the wars of religion. They were mainly Dutch and Flemish, Walloon, French, and Italian. Germans came from 1568 to 1689 to improve the technology of the copper and brass industries. The Society of Mines Royal and other companies brought over in the late 16th century skilled men from Saxony to improve techniques of mining and smelting lead in Yorkshire, Derbyshire, etc. Frenchmen were engaged in the iron industry of the Weald. The relationship of the French to the English glass industry is a special one. Glass began to be made in England on a regular basis and sizeable scale from the mid 13th century (potash glass of the "Forest" kind, as opposed to the soda glass used by the Saxons and made in southern Europe). The technology of Forest glass was developed in Normandy and Lorraine,

6 *Oriental porcelain adapted for the European market. This famille-rose Chinese saucer of the 1730s bears a heraldic crest to meet the requirements of the European purchaser.*

and glassmakers from there came to England, with some men from further east (the Low Countries or west Germany) from that time on. They settled in the Weald and merged with the locals. In the 16th century techniques were improving, and from the 1550s Frenchmen again began to come over, bringing new ideas for furnaces and processes. A group was brought over in 1567 by Jean Carré, a merchant of Arras who saw an opportunity in the sharply increasing demand for glass to set up glasshouses with more efficient furnaces. Carré also brought over Italians to make glass of Venetian type in London, including such distinguished craftsmen as Verzelini and Ognibene. After the massacre of St Bartholomew in 1572 a large number of French glassmakers came here, including members of the great glass families of Normandy and Lorraine, who were mostly Protestants. They settled at first mainly in the Weald, but soon moved on to Hampshire, Staffordshire, and Gloucestershire. When coal-firing was applied to glassmaking in 1611 they took the industry to the coalfields, and it finally left the Weald for Stourbridge, Bristol, Newcastle, and elsewhere. Some of the French makers, like the Tysacks, went into other industries (in this case cutlery at Sheffield) as well. The French immigrants in the 1570s were also involved in a variety of other trades and industries.

The most numerous group at this period were the Dutch, who began to leave the Low Countries in large numbers as a result of Alva's persecution of Protestants in 1567. But they had been coming before then; the church of Austin Friars in London was assigned to the Dutch colony as early as 1550 (the French got their own church in London, St Anthony's Hospital Chapel, soon after). Austin Friars is still used by the Dutch, as is the corresponding English church in Amsterdam by the English. This soon became, and remained, the centre of the colony's life. The dates show that religious difficulties were not the only reason for coming; jobs were scarce in the Low Countries at this time, and many came to seek work.

The Dutch and Flemish newcomers spread widely over southern England, mostly in small groups, and to places as far north as Manchester and Bolton, and, in the far north, Carlisle and Newcastle. The main settlements and the earliest churches were in London (church 1550), Sandwich (1561), Colchester and Norwich (1565), Yarmouth (1569), Halstead and Maidstone (1576). Other centres were Dover, Canterbury (where the French Huguenots had a chapel), and Southampton. Records became more accurate after 1567, and allow an assessment of numbers. Thus in 1577 the membership of the Dutch church in London was 2,300, of the French church 1,850, of the Italian 100, of no church 650, and alien members of the English church 1,550, a total of 6,450. The figures were of this order during the rest of the century. The Dutch community shrank during the 17th century, and stood at around 700 in the 1680s and 1690s.

The foreigners had to live and work outside the City of London because of the restrictions imposed by the guilds (City Livery Companies); this rebounded in the end on the guilds. They settled mainly in Southwark and Bermondsey, Shoreditch and Whitechapel. They engaged in a wide variety of trades, of which the most important were clothing, trade and transport, textiles, and leather; these were followed by fine arts and liberal professions, metallurgy and jewellery, food and lodgings, wood-working, and a number of miscellaneous trades. Silk was woven in the later 16th century by the Flemish at Cripplegate, and in the early 17th century by the French at Spitalfields, but on a small scale. Dutch and

Flemish weavers had settled in East Anglia in Henry VIII's time, and continued to come. They introduced worsted to Norwich and "new draperies" (baize and serge) to the Suffolk-Essex borders. They worked in London and other places also at this trade. The Dutch made advances in dyeing cloth. A Flemish craft was tapestry, and the Mortlake factory (c 1619) was one of theirs. They went in for gloves, shoes, saddlery (all in leather), and felt hats. Brewing was a major activity in Southwark, and there was a small glassworks here in the 1540s. Delft pottery was made in Norwich in 1567 and in London in 1570, but not on a large scale until the early 17th century. It began in Southwark, and spread later to Lambeth and Vauxhall. The Dutch also did engraving, map-making, printing, publishing, and bookselling. They produced some distinguished sculptors, such as the Cure family of Southwark. The drainage of the Fens and the Thames estuary was carried out by Cornelius Vermuyden and others. Foreign bankers, mainly Flemish and Italian, were of great importance in England in this period. The fall of Antwerp as a financial centre about 1600 left the field clear for London, which was maintained thereafter, except for Dutch challenges as the 17th century went on.

During the 16th century the Dutch contribution had been mainly economic; in the 17th it became largely cultural, and in the 18th financial. By the Restoration the Dutch were well settled in, and of course under William III were in high favour. Holland itself was at the height of its influence in the later 17th century, and there was a flow of visitors in both directions. An obvious impact of the Dutch was in the building and allied trades – brick building, ornamental gables, sash windows, and woodcarving. Skilled interior workers were redundant when Amsterdam Town Hall was finished in the late 1660s, and many came here, particularly after the French invasion of 1672. Horticulture too benefited. Pendulum clocks were invented and made here by the Dutch, as were scientific instruments. In the arts, Dutch painters were active in the court of Charles I, and Dutch landscape and flower painting remained popular into the 18th century.

But the Dutch were greatly outnumbered after the Revocation of the Edict of Nantes (1685) by the French Huguenots. This was an unparalleled disaster for France: up to half a million Protestants left the country; even Vauban estimated the figure at over 200,000 merchants, skilled workers, and soldiers. The number who came to England is not precisely known, but must run into several thousand (estimates of up to 100,000 have been made). They settled mainly in

London (a figure of 15,000 has been suggested), Norwich, Canterbury, Bristol, and Southampton. A large number went to Spitalfields and east London and founded a thriving silk industry (this also happened in Norwich and Coventry); some made woollen cloth in the Cotswolds. Many went to Soho and west London, where they furthered the development of the linen and glass industries and the manufacture of satin, velvet, and brocade. Many became tutors, and some were musicians. The first gardening societies in England were founded by the French, and they and the Dutch greatly improved horticulture and introduced new plants. With the Dutch, Italians, and Jews also, they played a great part in the growth of London as a centre of banking and underwriting. The Huguenots are a very well-documented group, thanks to the Huguenot Society.

Elizabeth I had complained at the number of negroes taking jobs in England since the wars with Spain; but negro house-servants (or slaves) continued to be employed throughout the 17th and 18th centuries. A colonisation of the west of Scotland by the Irish took place in James I's reign. The Jews were allowed back in England in 1656 (they got their own synagogue, at Bevis Marks). They have never ceased since then to enrich the country, in commerce, science, politics, finance, and thought. There are now nearly 400,000, mostly in London (at first in the East End, later in Golders Green, and now spread generally), Manchester, and Leeds. Their place in Whitechapel has now largely been taken up by Bangladeshis.

A small, but very interesting and influential immigration was that of a few German craftsmen who came to England under the Hanoverians. These included the unusually talented family of Wyon, one of whom came to England under George II and settled in Birmingham. He was a silver chaser, medallist, and engraver. From then until the end of the 19th century the Wyons designed the coinage of the UK and its dependencies, as Chief Engravers at the Royal Mint. They also produced a vast number of commemorative medals for all kinds of occasions and bodies, as well as sculpture, and this tradition continued well into the 20th century, over 200 years.

19TH AND 20TH CENTURIES

The immigrations now are often much larger, and some are almost folk movements. Irish came to Britain from the 18th century, and by the potato famine of 1846 there were about 400,000. They were mostly engaged in constructional work. They formed the greater part of the workers who dug the canals (the "navigators" or navvies) and, when these were finished, turned to railways and then to house building, where many of them still work. They are our largest minority group, and form a major part of the population of cities like Glasgow and Liverpool. In the 19th century, West Indians settled in dock areas, and a large colony, mixed with other nationalities, formed Tiger Bay in Cardiff. Since the war there has been a large influx of West Indians and other blacks. They live mainly in certain parts of London (eg Notting Hill and Brixton) and the West Midlands, and are employed in transport, nursing, etc. Pakistanis have also come, and their work ranges from textiles in Bradford to medicine. The woollen trade in Bradford was also stimulated by an influx of Germans after the Franco-Prussian war of 1870. Poles formed a valuable group during the war. Cypriots, Maltese, and Chinese are also significant groups (Chinese, Indian, Thai, and Italian restaurants are a new feature of British life). The bulb industry of the Fens is a recent example of Dutch influence. Another mark of Holland, whose passing is regretted, is the Dutch eel boats which, from the 16th century until the last war, tied up by the Custom House in London.

The presence of business, diplomatic, or cultural communities of foreigners living in this country must not be overlooked. Although most of these people only stay a few years, some stay longer and few have no impact on British life, even if they tend to cling together, perpetuate their customs, and go home for holidays. Thus there are some 50,000 French people in the London area (where there are two French churches, a cultural Institute, a Lycée, and a primary school), and perhaps 15,000 in the rest of the country, with a large concentration in Liverpool and Manchester. There are several thousand Americans, in the defence services as well as in business, and 4–5,000 Japanese, not to mention others from Europe and all over the world. We should be poorer without them. Many people of foreign origin have made conspicuous contributions to our cultural life: one thinks of such names as Disraeli, Brunel, Rossetti, Du Maurier, Rothschild, Lutyens, Delius, Holst, and Pevsner.

Mention might be made here of movements of British people within the country. Such is the trickle of Scots, and to a lesser extent Welsh, to London, who work in administration, etc; there were also massive movements of Scots to London, and Welsh to London, Liverpool, etc, during the 19th century, who worked in a variety of occupations. There is strong English influence in South Wales, following the growth of the iron, coal, and tinplate industries. There was a flow of Scots sheep farmers to Romney Marsh.

In reverse, it is quite impossible to assess the effect on Britain of the constant emigration, since the early 17th century, of British people to the former colonies and dominions and to the United States, or smaller emigrations, such as the Welsh to Patagonia.

Large masses of immigrants are never easy to absorb (there can be reluctance on both sides, for a generation or two), whether in a large city like Bradford with its Pakistanis or a small one like Bedford with its Italians and other Europeans. But foreign incomers in the past, however numerous and disparate at first, have finished by being merged without distinction into our incredibly complex racial inheritance. The Dutch and Huguenots have long since been absorbed, the Poles are nearly so already. No doubt this will continue to happen in the future also, but it may take many generations before the Asian and West Indian inhabitants of Britain form part of a genuinely multi-racial society.

THE "NEW GEOGRAPHY"

Geography has suffered in the past from the lack of an integrated view of its functions; it has been regarded, according to the "Arts" or "Science" background of the beholder, as an earth science, a social science, or even a geometrical science. Some geographers have concentrated on the traditional approach: mapping, recording, describing, and interpreting the data to be seen on the ground. But the landscape is either "natural" or "cultural" (influenced by human activities); in this latter light geography can be seen as "human ecology". A third view is that geography is essentially a distributional science, and here locational theory and analysis have developed.

Whether or not there is a conflict between the classificatory and the functional viewpoints (as has been the case in economics), it is clearly important to identify the areas of overlap between the various "sets", and to study these in depth, if full understanding is to be achieved. The use of theoretical models and quantitative techniques of analysis, as tools of integration and deeper understanding, is now widespread. The brilliant synthesis by Peter Haggett (*Locational Analysis in Human Geography*, 1965) is a landmark; it summarises the various models and methods, and applies them to the understanding of the geometrical

symmetry detectable within regional systems. This twofold approach of the "new" geographers (as represented in Haggett's book) has been a powerful stimulus to the even more recent "new archaeologists" and their successors, who have found that much of the apparatus built up by the geographers can be used with little modification to solve the problems of archaeology. Recent syntheses such as *Man, Settlement and Urbanism* (ed Peter J Ucko, Ruth Tringham, and G W Dimbleby) and *Models in Archaeology* (ed David L Clarke), both 1972, and *The Explanation of Culture Change* (ed Colin Renfrew, 1973) show the usefulness of this approach in dealing with such matters as settlement patterns, the origins of urbanism, or the growth of towns.

Some of the main geographical concepts which have influenced current archaeological thinking in the areas with which this book is concerned are now briefly summarised.

FUNCTIONAL HIERARCHIES

It is not enough to grade settlements according to size. The real distinction between places is that of function. Towns can be graded in terms of the number of functions they perform (political-administrative, social-cultural-religious, and commercial-industrial), or, which is partly the same thing, the number of services they provide. Thus the capital (London) has an unparalleled range of functions and services: everything which the nation does is done, managed, or can be got there. Then there are the second order centres, the regional capitals (Manchester, Leeds, etc), which carry for instance daily newspapers and department stores; then the larger towns, often county towns, which have a hospital and a wide range of services (Chichester, Rugby); then small towns with only limited facilities (Thame, Uppingham); finally the villages, which only supply the immediate essentials to the population of a small area. Other things being equal, there is a broad correlation between the number of functions and services and the size of a place. But things are not always equal, and distortions can arise: a mining "village" may be larger than the higher-order small town where it does much of its shopping, and a one-industry manufacturing centre may be larger than the county town. A regional capital has its own hierarchy of local foci within it; London has a large number of centres of local government, and a whole series of shopping centres of different importance.

Hierarchies of towns are not a modern phenomenon, but a constant feature of settled life. In Britain they can be seen clearly by the Iron Age, although there are indications also in the Bronze Age. In the Iron Age there is a pattern of large hillforts ("tribal capitals"), smaller hillforts (subordinate centres), undefended settlements (villages), and isolated farms or hamlets. A similar pattern exists in Roman Britain where, apart from the few major places like London and the *coloniae*, there are cantonal capitals (eg Cirencester), market towns (eg Dorchester-on-Thames), villages (*vici*), down to villas and "native" farms. A somewhat similar system developed in post-Roman times down to the present day.

Locational analysis

In real life the pattern of settlement is rarely quite regular; there are always local factors to distort it. But geographers have found it helpful in understanding the evolution of the present situation to analyse it in terms of its fundamental geometry. For this it is necessary to postulate an undifferentiated plain (a tract of land either flat or only gently undulating, with no serious natural obstacles, good easy-to-work soils, and an equable climate), settled evenly. This sounds extreme, but actually much of Midland England is not unlike this, and the pattern of Saxon settlement is often surprisingly regular. In such a region settlement points (eg villages) would tend to be equally spaced and to form a triangular lattice. Each village would be at the centre of a circular area of land (the "site catchment area"), which contains all the land regularly utilised by the community. This area, which in England is about 2.5 miles (4km) in radius from the village, is itself arranged in "land use rings", concentric rings where the land of most immediate use to the villagers (gardens and vegetable plots) is closest to the village, arable is next, pasture and meadow next, and lastly waste or woodland. The concept of land use rings was elaborated by the German J H von Thünen in 1826; a recent key study is M Chisholm: *Rural Settlement and Land Use* (1962). These ideas were applied to medieval England by M W Beresford and J K St Joseph in *Medieval England: an Aerial Survey* (1958), and to wider archaeological problems by C Vita-Finzi and E S Higgs in papers since 1969. But contiguous circles leave unused pieces of land between them, and pressure of neighbouring communities means

that the ideal arrangement is adapted to a solid lattice of hexagons, where no land is left out.

In practice, of course, this pattern is often distorted. Apart from irregular spacing or clustering, for social or other, non-geographical, reasons, the commonest form of distortion in southern England is the long parish running from downland to weald (or similar types of situation), where the best soils for arable, pasture, or woodland are not in circular belts round the village but spread out one after the other in a long strip. Places on the sea, or a large river, or even a political frontier may be distorted in other ways. And of course some villages are larger than others. But it remains the case that in many areas (eg the Vale of the White Horse) the Saxon villages are regularly spaced at about a mile and a half apart.

Central place theory

An advanced society cannot, however, be organised entirely on the basis of simple villages; service centres, where the more complicated needs of the villages can be concentrated for convenience, soon become essential. The more specialised the services, the more segregated these are in higher centres in the hierarchy. As with the pattern of villages, that of hierarchies can also be studied by reference to the basic geometry. The higher order centres are also seen to lie in a regular pattern and the areas of influence round them can be defined by drawing "Thiessen polygons". These are made by joining the centres by straight lines and bisecting these by lines at right angles, which will result in hexagons or other figures according to the spacing of the centres. Thiessen polygons have been used by Barry Cunliffe and others to define the territories and hierarchies of Iron Age hillforts, and recently by Keith Branigan in postulating the possible territories of the *vici* (small towns) in the *civitas* of the Catuvellauni in Roman Britain (K Branigan: *The Catuvellauni* (Alan Sutton 1986)).

The application of this is due to W Christaller (in *Die zentralen Orte in Süddeutschland* (1933)), who took southern Germany as the test area. Each polygon round a major centre contains lower order centres, with their own polygons, nesting within it. The total number of settlements served by each central place is termed its K-value. This can vary according to whether the settlements on the borders of the hexagons are shared between two or more central places, ie the orientation of the hexagon net. Christaller assumed that the K-values in any region, once adopted, would be fixed; that is, they would apply equally to the relationship between all grades of the hierarchy, between farms and villages, villages and towns, towns and cities, etc. He postulated three alternative structures. The first is based on a "market principle", in which the supply of goods from central places is as near as possible to the places supplied. A higher order place will serve two of its lower order neighbours (although their location in regard to regional boundaries may complicate the relationships); this results in a K=3 system. The second structure is based on a "transport principle", where the number of central places located on major transport routes is maximised, which results in a nesting of centres on a rule of four (K=4). The third is based on an "administrative principle", where clear-cut control by the central place of all six of its nearest dependent places is important (K=7). The actual distances involved in these concepts are, for medieval England, about 4–6 miles between the smallest service centres (small market towns), 8–10 miles between lower order centres, and 21 miles between higher order centres.

Christaller's theory was found to be too rigid as a general rule, even in his own test area of southern Germany, in fact to be one choice only out of the many possibilities in real life. It was developed by A Lösch, in *The Economics of Location* (1954). Lösch used all the various hexagonal solutions and rotated the hexagonal nets round a single centre (the metropolis). By so doing he evolved a hierarchy consisting of a nearly continuous sequence of centres rather than distinct tiers. In this arrangement cities of the same size do not inevitably exercise the same functions, and the functions of larger central places do not necessarily subsume all those of smaller central places. In fact, useful and flexible as this solution is, it is probably more fitted to explain the spatial distribution of market-oriented manufacturing, while Christaller's pattern applies more to the distribution of retail and service business. Both viewpoints have sparked off much creative thinking in relation to the study of actual situations.

There are several factors which can cause distortion of the basic patterns. The main ones include large-scale industry and its accompanying agglomeration; resource localisation, where certain specialised centres remain in "eccentric" locations outside the general pattern of population; the draw of alternative markets; the effect of political or economic boundaries; and, particularly in simpler societies, but still to some extent operative today, irregularities of topography. A pattern may be broken by a major river, by soil differences, or by mountains (for instance, if the Pennines did not exist, the pattern of settlement of northern England would be quite different). Patterns can change with changes in social structure and priorities, or in planning policy. The future trend towards dispersion will have its effect. It has been pointed out that central place theory assumes that humans have an inbuilt drive for more material goods and greater economic complexity, when in fact this is a drive engendered only by a particular form of social system.

Central place functions may be periodic: a rural centre might only function as a K=3 central place on market days, and a group of towns may be central places cyclically, as traders move from market to market on different days. Central place functions, at least before the late Saxon period, may also be divided between places; thus, in the middle Saxon period, the trading centre of the kingdom was not usually also the centre of administration; Winchester and Hamwi (Southampton), for example, were complementary (see page 156), Martin Millett has pointed out a somewhat similar dichotomy in Roman Britain, where there were two central place networks, one (the *civitas* capitals) political and administrative, the other (the lesser towns) economic (see Eric Grant: *Central Places, Archaeology and History* (Sheffield University 1986)).

The potential value of Christaller's theory was not recognised until the 1950s, when it had a seminal and explosive effect. In the last decade the difficulties in applying it universally have stimulated a variety of proposals, and it is now only one of the instruments of modern geography (see Peter Haggett: *Geography: A Modern Synthesis* (Harper and Row, New York, 3rd ed, 1983)). But in spite of its limitations in complex contemporary situations, central place theory retains its usefulness in elucidating archaeological problems. It may be that the simpler organisation of earlier societies, which are the concern of archaeology, and the more direct relationships between demand, supply, and distance in these (pre-industrial) societies, enable central place theory to be used with fewer reservations. It has certainly stimulated much productive reappraisal, and seems likely to continue to be a suggestive and useful tool in the future as well.

Another aid to the description of regions and their components is mathematical "set theory". As applied to geography, this involves the drawing of "Venn diagrams", closed lines representing the distribution of something, which can be superimposed to account for the high or low incidence of the object under study, eg rainfall, temperature, soils, a particular crop, or the relation between tropical location and underdevelopment. This method has been applied to anthropology, eg to show the incidence of culture traits, and now to archaeology, eg to pottery types, building materials, house forms, settlement and farming patterns. At present it is in the experimental stage for archaeology, but could turn out to be a useful auxiliary tool.

There are several modern techniques used in geography, such as mapping and statistical and computer methods, which can be applied to settlement study and archaeology; indeed, the two fields overlap. The use of models of all kinds, ecological, demographical, ethnological, locational, etc, is rapidly taking hold in all these fields.

It is one thing to plot the situation at any given time; it is another, equally important, to trace the development, and if possible determine the causes of change, over time. The New Archaeology and its successors are trying to formulate models, or explanations, of historical changes. Much attention is being given to the origins of farming, domestication, and urbanism, and to the problems of settlement generally. The role of the social structure, the type of authority and government, and the influence of law and religion have all been studied. One field which merges into the realm of geography is population. Here a seminal idea (even when challenged) has been put forward by Ester Boserup (in *The Conditions of Agricultural Growth* (1965)). She suggests that population pressure leads to more intensive exploitation of the land, the use of irrigation and more advanced methods of farming, the use of bulky and hence permanent plant or devices, all of which can lead to the need for trading centres. And so we are back to hierarchies.

ENGLAND AS A MEDIEVAL REGION

A valuable contribution of the "New Geography" to our understanding of the urban pattern in the Middle Ages is the concept of regions. Here the work of Josiah Cox Russell is central, and his book *Medieval Regions and their Cities* (1972) is highly illuminating. Regionalism is an important factor or condition of society, and explains many of its characteristics. People, ideas, and institutions circulated within a region.

By 1300, population had "reached the limit of effective use of available lands in large parts of Europe, and began in some places to approach overpopulation". 85–90% of the people lived in agricultural villages. Cities and towns existed to house "basic factors", markets, castles, manufactures, monasteries, etc, which brought in money from outside. They tended to be arranged in a definite order, a "rank-size series". Everyone had to have a function, or a living, and there was no depressed mass urban proletariat, "poverty-stricken but prolific", as happened in the 19th century.

Certain geographic areas have common dialects, social customs, building patterns, and eating habits. Nations grew by accretion from germinal areas ("core areas"); France is a good example of this. But equally important are the economic factors: size and spacing of cities and the functioning of demographic factors like migration and differing economic groups.

The distribution pattern of villages, towns, and cities has long been recognised, but it has only recently been seen that within great areas cities are in a definite relationship to each other – that is, the population of the main city divided by the rank order of the others is regular: if city A has 1 million people, city B will have half, city C one-third, etc. This is roughly true today, but was not so in the Middle Ages, when the lesser cities were relatively larger, probably because the pre-industrial society had no means of keeping up the size of city A. There are also local variations which need to be explained. In any area which had a circulation of trade, some goods were very specialised, so only a small number of people could pay for them or wanted them; these would go to the city to buy them, or an agent would circulate and sell them. If there was room for only one agent in a region, he would either sell in one place or circulate from his home. If he sold more in a larger place, he would tend to live in that place. If there was room for two men, one would tend to settle in a smaller place, and so on. But the largest place would attract more of these agents of specialised wares and would thus grow faster than the others. The second largest city would grow in the second most populous or wealthy area. This tended to scatter the location of cities. Against this a basic factor (manufacturing, mining, etc) might appear, and could attract a larger number to a particular place, thus producing a city outside the normal rank-size series.

Some major cities were not in the centre of their regions but, like Dublin or New York, were "portal cities", the gates to regions. An agricultural society had small cities, about a day's journey apart (35–60km);

large cities were an indication of the industrial-commercial status of regions. In the Middle Ages cities were more evenly spread than now, and specialised centres tended to be still small. So distance was the determining feature of the pattern. Hamlets and villages were within walking distance of the fields; pastures were further away than gardens. Market towns were within easy walking range, say every 6.25 miles (10km) or so; cities were a day's journey away.

Remote areas, like parts of Scandinavia or north Scotland, were hardly regions at all in this sense. Southern Scotland was really part of England for many purposes. Edinburgh and Glasgow were sizeable, but hardly capitals of regions; Glasgow's situation was also complicated by its relationship with Ireland. Northern England was part of the region of London, but specialised in producing manpower, wool, hides, and meat for the cities of the region.

Migration patterns are important in the development of a rank-size pattern. There was migration from one city to another (eg a craftsman or tradesman sending a member of his family or group to start up in another town), and from the countryside to the towns. Local migration tended to build up local customs, ideas, dialects, etc in the cities, and to set up cultural areas say 35–60km in diameter. Local colonies developed in more distant cities (colonisation was the third kind of movement).

Regions so constituted developed rapidly between 1000 and 1348, partly because the population increased two to three times in that period. Cities had more women than men and a low marriage rate, so most of their growth came from the countryside. A quarter to a half of the population of cities came from this source.

Cities had two kinds of functional factor: basic, positions produced by outside income, and non-basic, those supported by the needs of the first group. Today a factory will increase a city's population by 6–7 times the number of its employees (each worker represents a family of 3–3.5, plus a non-basic worker and family to support him). In the Middle Ages the division was not between production and service personnel; but a castle, say, would have a village attached to it, not necessarily for protection, but merely to supply its economic needs. The basic elements were the king, bishop, monastery, cathedral, duke, earl, county officials, basic merchants, basic guildsmen, and small farms in the city. The presence of a royal court made a vast difference to a city, and no doubt accounts for the preeminence of London. The court, with several hundred members, plus their families, etc, was supplemented by many other people drawn there for political (eg foreigners), social (nobles),

and financial reasons. The textile industry is also important. Paper was important too from late 13th century/early 14th century; and wine. The average region had about 5% of its people in towns, of which about 1.5% were in the largest city or capital. The normal pattern took full shape in the 13th century.

London was both a portal city and a central city. It had direct sea commerce as well as capital status and functions. Roman roads were an important factor in city location, and London was a hub of them.

The European regions had a median area of 102,400km². The London region was sixth in size, with 131,800km². The average family or household had nearer four than five persons. The London region had a population of *c* 3.7 million, with a density of 28.1 per sq km; this gave it second place in Europe (below Paris with 5.25 million and above Toulouse with 3.4 million). Populations like these could normally be adequately fed. The density of the London region (28.1) was not far behind those of Paris (31.8), Florence (30), and Venice (29); Ireland and parts of Spain were only 8–10. London and probably Paris saw the urban and rural populations increase at about the same rate. London's urban index (populations of the ten largest cities as a percentage of the total) was low at 4.4; Florence was 26, but Paris was comparable at 4.9. Paris and London were larger than the standard for regional capitals.

Regionalism as a base for culture reached its peak in the period 1250–1348. Before then, units based on feudal land holdings, although often very large, showed little demographic organisation comparable to the rank-size series. The later nations were usually a group of regions, except England, which was a region-nation. The Industrial Revolution has produced a different world. Regions had characteristics of physical type, food, clothes, social customs, etc, and local patriotism. England and some others produced semi-democracies. The natural growth, development, and prosperity was cut short by the plagues, and absolutism developed.

The region of London was mostly England, but could include Wales and southern Scotland (unless there was in fact a region of Edinburgh – research has not gone far enough to determine this). London was always the largest city, and had consolidated its position over the centuries. It is a great sea port on which converge the great roads of the island. In 1086 England had 1.1 million people, in 1347 3.7 million. In 1086 only eight cities were over 2,000, while 22 had between 1,000 and 2,000. The top ten had 4.4% of the total population, a low figure; London had 1.5%, an average. The most populous area was

East Anglia, where the civic function was shared between Norwich (4,400), Thetford (2,700), Dunwich (1,600), and Colchester (1,400). This reduces Winchester (6,000) with its access to a harbour and the rich south coast lands, and a kind of capital, to third place. The fourth place is Gloucester (2,100)/Bristol (2,300)/Shaftesbury (1,100). York (4,100) is then fifth and Lincoln (3,500) sixth. Ekwall has studied the origins of the inhabitants of London; most, of course, came from within 40km, but an increasing number came from the east Midlands and the North. This, and the universities of Oxford and Cambridge, which also drew mainly from their neighbourhoods, helped to make the Midland dialect the official English language.

London maintained its supremacy easily. York was well placed to be the second city, but the north was smaller and less fertile than the south. Bristol was a good port, but had a more limited field of trade which it had to share with Plymouth and other ports. Norwich was limited by the odd shape of East Anglia. Coventry had potential, except that west of it the country was sparsely inhabited. London had the court, the bureaucracy and central government, and a rich social, political, and economic life. Its control of the other cities prevented them from gaining independence and power, as happened in Italy, and as York might have done. Moreover, the other cities failed to be magnets for the nobility and gentry, and the demands of the royal government on local effort prevented local leaders from developing their own centres of power. So the upper classes lived partly on their estates and partly in London.

According to the poll tax returns of 1377, villages with 200–400 people made up 16.5% of the total; 153, more than the expected average, were in Cornwall, Essex, Kent, Northamptonshire, Nottinghamshire, and the East Riding. Since these counties had 4/11ths of the villages of England, there were about 421 more villages in England with 200–400 than normal in England. These villages, which included the manufacturing places, prevented the growth of the cities, in spite of the modest 13th-century "industrial revolution". The population of the ten largest cities just before the plague was *c* 163,400, about 4.4% of the total of 3.7m (just below the average of 5%). So no relative growth had taken place since 1086. Further, the villages were smaller than the European average, perhaps reflecting greater security and better conditions.

The low urban average in England indicates that England was primarily agricultural. The density was 28.1, a relatively high figure (in the mid 13th century, on 2.5m, it would have been 19 per sq km).

Was England already overpopulated by 1300? England had 5000 watermills in 1086, which gave it a strong basis for later industrial developments. The food supply was good, with pasture land in the north and west and fish everywhere. Food was exported. The base of subsistence was some four acres a head, probably three times the area necessary to sustain life. The yield increased from 3.7 in 1200–1250 to 4.7 by 1350. It was higher in 1250–1300, because of a climatic amelioration. Climate worsened after 1300, and there was a famine in 1315–17. All in all, the population was adequately fed and indeed very prosperous in the 13th century. In 1350 the rank-size order was 1 London (over 40,000), 2 York (over 10,000), 3 Bristol, 4 Norwich, 5 Plymouth, and 6 Coventry; under 10,000 were 7 Lincoln, 8 Salisbury, 9 King's Lynn, 10 Colchester, and 11 Boston.

But a medieval region was not monolithic, and England is no exception. Derek Keene has pointed out (1986) that London had many regions of differing extent according to time and circumstances. Not only was London the principal market place for luxury and fashionable commodities, but was a centre for the exchange of ideas, from which innovations could be diffused, either directly or through provincial centres. Norwich might therefore be more subject to London's influence than somewhere in the depths of the Essex countryside, geographically much closer to the capital. But this efficiency as a disseminator may also mislead, by causing us to attribute a London origin to ideas which arose elsewhere but which became obvious or spread rapidly only via the city.

London's power of attraction in fact led to what amounted to a new region in the home counties; a ring of market towns handled London's corn supplies (eg Henley), and there were similar centres for other goods (fuel, metals, fish, etc), with colonies of Londoners in these places (Boston, Yarmouth, etc). Londoners moved into the home counties, for health and prestige. The influence of London ways affected provincial towns such as York or Winchester, although the latter had been a capital, and York might have been one.

Thus, a region was not just a simple function of distance round a centre. In any case London was a node in a network of contacts, not a centre of origination.

SETTLEMENTS AND LAND DIVISIONS

At this point it will help to clear the ground further if the terms for settlements and land divisions are defined.

Village

As appeared from the account of basic factors, a village is the focal point of a parish which otherwise contains only separated farms, houses, or hamlets. It meets the basic needs for the exchange of goods and services at an immediate level, and also provides centres for the social life of the parish. Thus it normally contains a general shop, often a basic craftsman such as a blacksmith, a church, a village hall, perhaps simple facilities for sport, and a pub. The point is that it aims to provide services only for the inhabitants of its own parish.

Town

This is not as easy to define as it may seem, as towns vary widely in the features they have in common. A study by the Council for British Archaeology (C Heighway: *The Erosion of History* (1972)) has identified a number of criteria for determining whether a place can rank as a town. These are:

> *defences*   at some time in its history a town might have a wall, a bank and ditch, or bank and ditch with wooden defences
>
> *internal street plan*   a town may be planned at any time in its history, or part of it may be planned, in a grid or other pattern; a street plan which integrally includes a market place is also the mark of a town
>
> *market*   this is perhaps the essential feature, although a market alone does not distinguish a town; the date of the market charter is a useful guide to when a place became a town mint
>
> *legal existence*   earlier studies of towns were usually based on the charters granting borough status or other

privileges, but the economic aspects are now regarded as at least equally important, and many places were towns before they had charters

> *position*   such as a focal point in a network of roads or rivers, or some role as a central place
>
> *population*   high density or size of population compared with surrounding places
>
> *diversified economic base*   various crafts, and long-distance trade
>
> *house plot and house type*   the town plan may show long narrow "burgage-type" plots (see pages 163–4); surviving houses will be urban rather than rural in form (see page 211)
>
> *social differentiation*   a wide range of social classes, and particularly a middle class
>
> *complex religious organisation*   more than one church, chapels, chantries, monastic houses, hospitals, etc
>
> *judicial centre*   courts of local or national status

It is obvious that far from all towns have more than a few of these criteria, but no place should be regarded as a town unless it has more than one of them, and preferably three or four. Moreover, many places have gone up or down in the world, and, although towns once, are so no longer. In Devon and Cornwall, for instance, and in Wales, there were many boroughs which never achieved administrative independence, or even a market; some, like North Elmham (Nf), were thriving places dependent on a cathedral or abbey, but reverted to villages when changes occurred; in that case the see was moved to Thetford in 1072.

Towns with most or all of seven characteristics have been called "primary towns" by Alan Everitt (1975). These are: a settlement of pagan Saxon or earlier date; association with early routes; the presence of a minster church; an early administrative centre (royal or church); an unusually large parish; the presence of a pre-conquest trading centre (a prescriptive market); and possibly a better capacity in medieval times to survive economic stress. Such towns, of which examples are Banbury and Maidstone, also made a distinctive contribution to the Industrial Revolution.

There are of course many such lists of characteristics, and few historians would agree in every detail. Size is a commonly posited criterion, but this varies so enormously that it ceases to carry conviction. Thus, in Scandinavia, a settlement of 200 people is classed as a town, but in Greece the figure is 10,000, and there is a great variety of figures in between. Density is important, but so is function: the inhabitants of a town or city are not primarily food producers, whereas those of a village are (or used to be). The nature of the local government is very important, but not overriding. The United Nations take 5,000 as the population figure which marks the point of change from village to town, but even at this point the distinctions of government and character are blurred. Perhaps one has to fall back on what the local people themselves call a place.

City

The other end of the scale is the line between town and city. Here clearly complexity and variety of functions and activities play a major part, but again the line is not absolutely fast. In Britain it is customary to think of a city as a place having a cathedral; but no one would call St David's or St Asaph cities, and even a place as big as Guildford, with a cathedral, a university, a military presence, and a major shopping centre, together with some 60,000 people, is called a town by its inhabitants. There is a subtle element of atmosphere here. No one would mistake the centres of Manchester or Leeds for towns, while the centre of Guildford has a different "feel". There is then no unanimity among the experts as to which of the characters in the lists above are more essential than others to the definition of a town or city. Some lay stress on one thing, others on another. A decision in any one case may have to be a matter of judgment, "unscientific" as this may sometimes appear (see Emrys Jones: *Towns and Cities* (OUP 1966) for a useful discussion of this).

Shire, hundred, etc

One of the lasting legacies of the Saxons to later generations is the organisation of local government into shires. Except for the four most northerly counties, and Lancashire and Rutland, all the present English counties (before the boundary changes of 1974 and recent years) were in existence, substantially within their present boundaries, before the Norman conquest. Those south of the Thames existed certainly by 850, and perhaps by 800. In this area Kent and Sussex represent old kingdoms absorbed into Wessex, and Devon and Cornwall were similarly independent Celtic kingdoms. The shire administration was headed by an *ealdorman*, who also had the job of leading the local fighting men when occasion arose. The West Saxon shires seem to have grown from land divisions representing the areas of settlement of the original settlers, and usually have recognisable natural boundaries like rivers or hills. The Midland shires, however, have more artificial boundaries, which obscure whatever earlier divisions there may have been. The shires of Gloucester, Worcester, and Warwick correspond with the old diocese of Worcester, and may represent the old kingdom of the Hwicce. But in the west Midlands generally the old groups of settlers have not left their names to the later counties, which are usually called after their county town. This may have arisen from the need to fortify and defend each centre against the Danes. Thus Hertfordshire has no natural cohesion, and was originally in two or three parts belonging to the neighbouring kingdoms; and the frontier of the Danelaw cut right through it, implying that in 886 it was not there. But when Hertford was fortified in 912 a county to back it up had to be created.

The east Midland shires are of Danish origin, and represent the division of the conquered parts of Mercia by the various Danish armies which settled there. Rutland formed part of Northamptonshire in Edward the Confessor's time, but as it was part of the traditional dowry of the English queen it came to have its own separate existence. The shires of Leicester, Derby, Nottingham, and Lincoln are the territories of four of the Five Boroughs of the Danelaw (see pages 161–2). Possible reasons why the fifth, Stamford, never became the centre of a Stamfordshire are mentioned later. North of the Humber the counties are of more recent origin, except Yorkshire, which represents the lands settled by the Danes in 876. Lancashire only emerged in the 13th century, and Westmorland probably not before the 11th. Durham was largely an ecclesiastical unit. Cumberland represents part of the Celtic kingdom of Strathclyde, and Northumberland is part of Anglian Northumbria.

The Welsh counties have a later origin. In 1284, when Welsh independence came to an end, Edward I divided Gwynedd Uchaf into Anglesey, Caernarvon, and Merioneth, created Flint as a buffer opposite Cheshire, and reorganised the provinces of Cardigan and Carmarthen. Pembroke was already an English-speaking colony planted by the Normans, and Glamorgan represented part of the old kingdom of Morgannwg. Gower was also a Norman colony, later taken into

Glamorgan. Monmouth was mostly the old Gwent. Henry VIII, to tidy up the border, created four more counties out of marcher lordships: Radnor, Brecknock, Montgomery, and Denbigh. The Welsh units were subdivided into *cantrefs*, like the English hundreds.

In Scotland David I (1124–53) set up sheriffdoms at suitably placed royal castles, and royal burghs grew up at these places; the areas under their control eventually became shires. This was done first in the Lothians, the Midland valley, and the eastern coastal plain, and then in the south-west. The sheriffdoms, and the modern counties in these areas, are called after the castle towns (Peebles, Roxburgh, Banff, etc). Kirkcudbright was a stewartry, under a royal nominee. Selkirkshire represents a royal hunting forest. The other counties, in the highlands but including Fife, were earldoms; most represented the territories of a clan, eg Argyll, which ultimately was the old kingdom of Dalriada. Sheriffdoms in Skye, Lorne, and Kintyre failed to survive as counties. Sutherland was the southern part of the Norse territories. Orkney and Shetland were ruled by Norse earls until 1469, when they became a county, separated into Orkney and Zetland in 1891 when Ross and Cromarty were combined. County councils were set up in 1889.

Smaller divisions

The English shires south of the Tees were, by the early 11th century, subdivided into units called *hundreds* or *wapentakes*. Most of the country used the word hundred, while wapentakes are found in the former Danish lands, particularly in the territories of the Five Boroughs, and in the north and west Ridings of Yorkshire; the functioning of both was identical. The word wapentake derives from the Scandinavian custom of those present at an assembly brandishing their weapons to convey approval of a measure. The hundred emerged as a unit of government in the 10th century. Meetings of those inhabitants entitled to take part in local government took place every four weeks, and were mainly concerned with thieves and stray cattle. Wapentakes had rudimentary juries to help the course of justice. These meetings were subordinate to the less frequent shire courts.

Hundreds vary widely in size – Staffordshire had five, but Sussex, about the same size, came to have over 60. A hundred, in the Midlands, was assessed for tax at 100 hides of land, which reinforces the somewhat artificial creation of the Midland counties referred to above. Hundreds in other areas could vary in their number of hides from 20 to 150.

The shire and hundred meetings, or *moots*, were held at traditional sites, which can be identified by their names or by some physical feature. These can be mounds, often flat-topped, on which the officials stood; some of these are adapted prehistoric barrows, eg Mutlow, Wendens Ambo (Ex), or Cuckhamsley (Bk). They can be natural hills, eg the morainic Claro Hill, Allerton Mauleverer (NY). Sometimes they are where roads or parish boundaries meet, as at Nassaborough (Nh), or Rosemary Hill, Blackheath (Sy). They can be in ancient hillforts, like Badbury Rings or Eggardon (Do), or at a prominent tree, stone, or post (Maidstone; Whitstable, a post; Copthorne (Sy), a tree; Skyrack (WY), the "shire oak"). Some of these places were also used for dancing etc at popular festivals, eg the flat mound with earth rim at Kings Caple (He). At Stirling the Motehill was also used for games. The most splendid is the highly formalised Tynwald Hill in the Isle of Man, where the parliament met; this is a mound with four steps or tiers at the end of a ceremonial way. Moots can often be tracked down by the presence of a place-name element such as *moot*, *thing* (Thingwall (Ch); Tynwald (IOM)), *toot* (Tothill, London), and sometimes *how* or *bury*, though these may refer to barrows. An interesting one is *shamble* or a similar word (eg Sample Oak, Shamley Green), from *sceamol*, a bench, referring to the seats on which the members of the court sat. However, field names can have these elements.

In the four northern counties the corresponding unit is the *ward*, which dates to the 13th century. The only exception is the wapentake of Sadbergh in Co Durham. In some parts there is a division between the shire and the hundred. There is also the *riding*, which usually means a third of the county, but not always. These occur in Yorkshire, Lindsey, and Orkney, ie, in Scandinavian areas. The word may in fact have come to mean merely a group of hundreds smaller than a shire. In Lincolnshire, Kesteven and Holland may have gone with territory dependent on Stamford, but the evidence for this is insecure. Sussex also had an intermediate division, the *rape*, derived from a space for the court being marked off by stakes and ropes. There were six rapes in Sussex, eg Pevensey, which may be of Saxon origin, but were affected by the redistribution of lordships after the conquest. Indeed, the rape of Bramber is a later creation still, consolidating the lands of William de Braose at the expense of his (Norman) neighbours. Chichester rape was carved out of that of Arundel in the 12th century. Hastings rape however looks older, and may represent an early Saxon territory. The hundreds in the rapes are mostly very small.

Some areas had relics of older systems. Thus, Northumbria never had shires, but "regions" or districts, such as the liberty of Hexham. A *soke*, such as that of Peterborough or the Soken east of Colchester, may be a similar unit. The word *-ge* in a name also means district, as at Ely, the eel-district (el-ge), which had 600 households. This also occurs in Essex (Vange), Surrey (the southern district), and Eastry, one of the old divisions of Kent (*lathes*). Lathes in Kent are parallel to hundreds elsewhere, and may well be older. They seem to perpetuate local government divisions under the kings of Kent; thus Canterbury, Faversham, and Rochester are all centres of lathes. There are hints that they may be older still; Lyminge lathe, the lathe of the *Limenewara*, reflects the Roman name *Lemanis*, so this could be a Roman land division.

Much in the origin and development of the lathes and rapes is obscure; one may have to look back to the Roman units of organisation of the Saxon Shore in the 3rd and 4th centuries, or even perhaps to pre-Roman times.

The 1974 local government changes

The traditional names of counties and smaller local government subdivisions have been used for locating places throughout this book. This is partly because they are familiar, and will no doubt continue to be so for many years, but also because they represent a continuous historical context within which the places have existed and developed, and which is meaningful for them. Thus, while there may be a case, apart from administrative convenience, for detaching the Vale of the White Horse from Berkshire, a village south of Selby, say, has never thought of itself as belonging to North Yorkshire.

But with effect from 1 April 1974 a new structure came into being, in the interests of economy and efficiency, which has meant a large number of changes to the map. To reduce confusion in using this book, a rough guide is given below of the main changes.

England was divided into Greater London, six Metropolitan Counties, and 39 non-metropolitan counties, the latter divided into 296 districts. Previously, England had 953 separate county boroughs, boroughs, urban districts, and rural districts. Greater London (reorganised shortly before the rest) takes in Middlesex and parts of Hertfordshire (Barnet), parts of Essex (Havering, Redbridge, Barking, Waltham Forest), parts of Surrey (Richmond, Kingston, Sutton, Merton, Croydon), and parts of Kent (Bromley, Bexley). The City of London remains separate. The six metropolitan counties were: Greater Manchester (which includes Bolton, Bury, Manchester, Rochdale, Salford, Stockport, Tameside, Trafford, Wigan); Merseyside (Knowsley, Liverpool, St Helens, Sefton, Wirral); South Yorkshire (Barnsley, Doncaster, Rotherham, Sheffield); Tyne and Wear (Gateshead, Newcastle, North Tyneside, South Tyneside, Sunderland); West Midlands (Birmingham, Coventry, Dudley, Sandwell, Solihull, Walsall, Wolverhampton); West Yorkshire (Bradford, Calderdale, Halifax, etc, Kirklees (Huddersfield etc), Leeds, Wakefield). Each of these subdivisions ranks as a metropolitan district. But then in 1986 the Greater London Council and the other six metropolitan counties were abolished, and their functions and powers distributed among the London boroughs and the metropolitan districts.

The new non-metropolitan counties include some unfamiliar groupings: Avon includes Bristol and Bath and the adjacent areas of north Somerset and south Gloucestershire; Cleveland is Hartlepool, Stockton, Middlesbrough, and the north-east end of the old North Riding; Humberside is Hull, and those parts of the East Riding and Lindsey which border the Humber. All these major groupings involve alterations in the old counties round them, and there are some other changes as well: Berkshire takes part of Buckinghamshire, but loses its north-west part to Oxfordshire; Cambridgeshire is now the old Cambs, plus the Isle of Ely, Huntingdonshire, and the Soke of Peterborough; Cheshire loses much, but gains parts of Lancashire; Cumbria is Cumberland, Westmorland, Lancashire north of the sands, and part of the West Riding; Derbyshire takes part of Cheshire; Durham loses to Tyne and Wear and Cleveland, but takes the part of the North Riding south of Barnard Castle; Dorset now includes Bournemouth and Christchurch; Herefordshire and Worcestershire are combined; Lancashire takes part of the West Riding (west of Skipton); Lincolnshire loses to Humberside; Leicestershire takes in Rutland; Norfolk takes part of East Suffolk; North Yorkshire is York, what is left of the North Riding, the north part of the East Riding, and the rest of the West Riding, including the area south of Selby; Suffolk, except the bit gone to Norfolk, is recombined; West

Sussex takes in the Horley and Charlwood part of Surrey. The Isle of Wight is a separate county, and the Scilly Islands are separate from Cornwall.

Wales has eight new counties, containing 37 districts. These are Clwyd (part of Denbigh, Flintshire, part of Merioneth); Dyfed (Cardiganshire, Carmarthenshire, Pembrokeshire); Gwent (Newport, part of Brecon, most of Monmouthshire); Gwynedd (Anglesey, Caernarvonshire, part of Denbighshire, most of Merioneth); Mid-Glamorgan (Merthyr Tydfil, part of Brecon, part of Glamorgan, part of Monmouthshire); Powys (Montgomeryshire, Radnorshire, most of Brecon); South Glamorgan (Cardiff, part of Glamorgan, part of Monmouth); West Glamorgan (Swansea, part of Glamorgan).

A new structure for Scotland was created by the Local Government (Scotland) Act 1973. From 16 May 1975 Scotland was divided into regions, each with districts: Highland (comprising Caithness, Sutherland, Nairn, Inverness (except its Western Isles), Argyll (Ardnamurchan, Ballachulish, Kinlochleven), Moray (Grantown, Cromdale), and Ross & Cromarty (except its Western Isles); Grampian (Aberdeen, city and county, Kincardine, Banff, Moray (except Grantown and Cromdale)); Tayside (Dundee, Angus, Kinross, Perthshire (except Callander, Doune, Dunblane, the Western District except Ardoch, and Muckhart)); Fife (Fife); Lothian (Edinburgh, East Lothian, Midlothian except Heriot and Stow, West Lothian except Bo'nessburgh and district); Borders (Berwickshire, Peeblesshire, Roxburghshire, Selkirkshire, Midlothian (Heriot and Stow)); Central (Clackmannan, Perthshire (Callander, Doune, Dunblane, the Western district except Ardoch, Muckhart); Stirling except Kilsyth, Western no 3 district, Kilsyth West, Kilsyth East (Barton), West Lothian (Bo'ness); Strathclyde (Glasgow, Bute, Dunbarton, Lanarkshire, Renfrewshire, Argyll except Ardnamurchan, Ballachulish, Kinlochleven, Ayrshire, Stirling (Kilsyth etc)); Dumfries and Galloway (Dumfriesshire, Kirkcudbrightshire, Wigtownshire). In addition there are separate authorities for Orkney, Shetland, and the Western Isles (Stornoway, Lewis, Barra, Harris, North and South Uist).

A fresh revision of local government was under consideration in 1992. This is likely to result in a reduction in the number of tiers (either county councils or district councils would be retained, but not both, depending on local circumstances), the abolition of some (locally unpopular) 1974 counties, eg Avon, Cleveland, and Humberside, and the reinstatement of some pre-1974 units, such as Rutland and Hereford.

In Wales, from April 1996 21 unitary authorities will replace 37 district councils and eight county councils. Cardiff, Swansea, Newport, and Wrexham will have unitary councils, as will most of the old (pre-1974) counties. Thus Clwyd, Dyfed, Gwynedd, and Gwent will disappear. Powys will remain, unless local pressure secures the reinstatement, in some form, of the pre-1974 counties of Brecon, Montgomery, and Radnor.

The Land

THE COUNTRYSIDE

There is a romantic fascination in seeking primeval or "virgin" landscape, a tract of country which has been untouched by human interference and still looks as it did before humans reached Britain. This is an illusion. Climatic changes and the work of animals have altered the landscape since prehistoric times, let alone since pre-human times. The trees and other vegetation one sees from a viewpoint in the Weald, for example, have changed with the passing of time, as ash and beech succeed lime, and so on. And a view from a mountain in Scotland or in the Pennines onto treeless or rocky expanses merely reveals the combined effect of man and climate on elm, pine, or birch. Views are contemporary, not retrospective.

There is in fact little, if any, genuinely virgin country in Britain. Humans have affected all of it.

P J Reynolds has pointed out that Neolithic people were already in control of their environment and engaged in managing even the timber, with the result that today there is probably no primeval forest. Much of our woodland was planted quite recently. Indeed, most of our landscape is less than 200 years old, and much only 20 years old.

In looking at a landscape it is also necessary to consider in unity the two aspects, physical and cultural. W G Hoskins, while not over-looking the natural component, took the perhaps over-simplistic view that man's continual and successive effects on the landscape were the dominant keys to unravelling its history (see, for example, *The Making of the English Landscape*, 1951). But natural changes, independent of human intervention, have been equally important. Andrew King (in Hampshire Field Club, *Newsletter*, 7, 1987) points out that it is not enough to see nature as providing the bare bones of the landscape which mankind clothes in a succession of alterations. Humans are in fact inextricably bound into the ecosystem. The forces of change, some natural, some human, are interrelated, "and many will be natural processes exaggerated, diminished, or in some way altered by the action of mankind". The interrelated nature of these processes, King concludes, means that most will be both causes and effects.

This intricate situation demands a painstaking, interdisciplinary approach if the true history of any landscape is to be unravelled, and the reasons for its being precisely as it is, and not otherwise, are to be determined. But at least the chances of success are thereby enhanced.

Ancient countryside and planned countryside

Oliver Rackham (in S R J Woodell (ed), *The English Landscape* (OUP 1985), and elaborated in O Rackham, *The History of the English Countryside* (Dent 1986)), has observed – and this is a very useful and enlightening concept – that the Lowland Zone of England can itself be divided into two zones, which he calls the "ancient countryside" and the "planned countryside". The ancient countryside is, in Rackham's words, "the England of hamlets and lonely medieval farmsteads, of winding lanes, dark hollow-ways, and intricate footpaths, of thick mixed hedges and many small woods — a land of surprises and still a land of mystery." Planned countryside has large regular fields with flimsy hawthorn hedges, few, often straight, roads, clumps of trees in field corners, few ponds, Georgian farmsteads, and a large village every two miles. In ancient countryside open fields are either absent or of limited extent; planned countryside is the area of open fields, and hence of the 18th- and 19th-century enclosures and replanning. Ancient countryside is the piecemeal growth of centuries, and some of it goes back well beyond the Saxons. The distinction is not confined to England – it is that between the *bocage* and the *champagne* in France. The Tudor agronomists called it *several* and *champion*. The concept is thus well known, but Rackham has sharpened it up.

Broadly, the Lowland Zone is split into three. The ancient countryside lies in a belt from east Devon and Somerset to the coastal strip of south-east Wales, the Welsh borders, and west Midlands, Cheshire, and most of Lancashire, with a narrow band along the magnesian limestone, east of the Pennines, to the mouth of the Tees; it also has an outlier in the Fens. Its other belt is in east Norfolk, Suffolk, most of Essex, the Home Counties and the south-east, down to the Hampshire-Dorset border. The planned countryside lies between these two belts, covering Dorset, most of Wessex, the south and east Midlands, Cambridgeshire, west Suffolk, west and north Norfolk, Lincolnshire, Nottinghamshire, east Yorkshire, and the Vale of York (but not the North York Moors). The division fundamentally reflects the difference in the farming – planned countryside is the zone of mixed farming, ancient countryside that of lowland pasture farming. It agrees well with the situation in, say, the 16th and early 17th centuries, as a map of the farming at that date will show (eg fig 1 in Joan Thirsk (ed), *The Agrarian History of England and Wales*, vol 4 (1500–1640) (CUP 1967)). Indeed, the ancient countryside has scarcely changed since *c* 1700, and some features antedate 1500.

In fact, the distinction between the two landscapes was well established by Anglo-Saxon times, even without the replanning due to the enclosures, and pre-Saxon (and pre-Roman) fields may still be in use in some areas (eg south Essex or Herefordshire). It is not, however, clear whether the hedges represent enclosure of earlier, almost hedgeless, open landscape. The Anglo-Saxons may have taken over a partly hedged landscape, out of which the open fields were made. The planned countryside in the Midlands is thus medieval and later de-enclosure; but east and west of this the open field traditions were weak, and soon disappeared – indeed, some areas were not reached at all.

Rackham also suggests that the planned and ancient countrysides reflect areas of little or much woodland at the end of the Roman period. The planned countryside area was suitable for the open fields, and later for the enclosures; the wooded belts were less so. The present countryside is not, on this view, the result of agricultural changes, so much as of growth, decline, and alteration of occupation patterns.

Field names

Field names are useful indicators of former conditions in the countryside. Most parishes have names going back to the 13th or 14th century (some even to the 12th), even if most are not actually recorded until the 16th. Many date from the 18th- and 19th-century enclosures of the common lands and the redistribution of the open fields. They give information on the shape and size of old fields or plots, on the use and condition of the land, the distance from the farm or village, local events, owners, or practices. They are thus of great value to archaeologists and local historians.

The meaning of the word "field" itself has changed since it was first used by the Saxon settlers to mean an area cleared of trees, and thus "open country" (as in Hatfield or Sheffield). Cultivation of such land altered the meaning of the word to "unenclosed land used for agriculture". In areas where open fields were the practice, each of the two, three, or four divisions of the village agricultural land became known as fields. Subdivisions of the open fields were themselves given names, as were enclosed pieces of land (what today we think of as "fields").

John Field in *English Field Names* (1972) – which also has a valuable dictionary of names – classifies field names into 26 categories, each illuminating an aspect of farming and its development and variety. These are, in bald summary:

size of the field	Great Acre, Nine Acres, The Bit
distance from the village	Far Close
direction	Above Town
order	Middle Acres, New Berry Field
shape	The Harp
type of soil	Pudding Acre
infertility	Pickpocket – derogatory name for unprofitable land
topography	Brook Close
type of cultivation	The Meadow
crops	Maize Acre
wild plants	Nettlebed
farm animals	Bull Acre
wild animals	Doe Croft
buildings	Gin House Bank
roads	Ford Mead
owner's name	Bacon Close
owner's trade	Millers Butts
person maintained from the land	Vicar Ing
value of the land	Halfpence
archaeology	Barrow Field
folklore	Holy Well
arbitrary names	Plato, Nelson, Balaclava
land on a boundary	Mark Field
legal terms	Copyhold
industrial use	Coal Pit Close
games	Plaistow – sport place

This is a useful and suggestive classification, which not only helps one to understand the nature of the land, but also the thought processes of its occupiers.

Field names can be got from old estate maps or from farmers themselves. But the most complete and accessible comprehensive source is the Tithe Award maps made for each parish about 1840. Many of these are kept in local record offices. The standard books on place-names, such as K Cameron: *English Place-names* (1961), and the county volumes of the English Place-name Society usually deal with field names as well as town, village, and other place-names.

The names of the old open fields may still remain as North, South, East, or West Field, even if these are sometimes subdivided into, for example, Far North Field. The open fields may also still be reflected in the name of a farm, eg Westfield Farm. Several names show old divisions of fields, such as Acre, Furlong, or Shot (a strip of land on a boundary). Broad can mean a wide strip, Butt a strip running to a boundary or to another strip, and Balk is the unploughed bank between two strips. Head is where the plough turned; Land and Ridge or Rigg are also found. Breck is land broken up for cultivation. Intake is land taken in from moor in highland areas settled by the Scandinavians, Ing a meadow in these areas. Lea, pasture, and Rod, a clearing, are common. Close and Croft, small enclosures, are met with, as are Lot, Piece, Yard, and Fold. There are names showing that a field was wet or stony; America, Lands End, and the like mean that the farmer thought the field a long walk away; poor land may be called Starveall, Poverty Close, etc. Names like Hundred Acre Field may be ironical descriptions of very small pieces. Some names refer to relations with the church, such as Lamplands, land whose rent was used for the upkeep of a lamp in the church; Amen Corner may refer to a halt in the beating of the bounds. Some names refer to old events, such as one in Essex, Deadmansland. These are only hints at the infinite variety.

Some names point to actual archaeological remains. Blacklands may reveal, by a patch of dark occupation soil, the former presence of a house, bloomery, or forge. Kiln Field could point to a lime, brick, or pottery kiln; Glasshouse Field, Copse, etc are found in the glassmaking areas of the Weald. In the parish of Egham (Sy) one field is called Many Crofts, another Warrens, where rabbits may have been bred. Puttenham (Sy) has a Norman church at the end of the village street, yet on a hill to the south is a field called Church Croft: could this represent a late Saxon chapel or preaching post, or a pagan shrine converted to Christianity and preceding the present church, or merely a piece of land belonging to the church? This is the kind of hint which can enlarge knowledge of a place.

Field names are used by archaeologists to help pinpoint possible sites for investigation on the line of new roads and other building. This was done, for instance, when the M5 was driven through Somerset and Gloucestershire in 1969–71. Field names giving significant archaeological hints numbered 226 in a stretch of 66 miles, or nearly four a mile; of these, as many as 130 were of direct value. After analysis it appeared that, in lowland Gloucestershire, about one name in six of the potentially significant ones indicated an archaeological site. This is of course only one of several methods of finding sites, but its value, hitherto hardly appreciated, is beyond doubt.

Changes in the countryside

In the areas of "planned countryside" changes can be both numerous and speedy. In the "ancient countryside" change is slower and much of the present pattern of roads, woods, and fields can be shown to have remained largely as it was before 1700. In some areas the pattern has persisted since pre-Roman times.

But in the broad belt of "champion" country lying between the Highland Zone and south-east England, several important changes have taken place. Knowledge of prehistoric and Romano-British farming patterns is necessarily sketchy and uneven, but the evidence points to loose nucleations associated with "native" fields as representing the Celtic kinship system. This was altered, under Roman rule, by the great villa estates linked to the cantonal capitals and, in some places, vast imperial farming enterprises and centuriated areas.

This landscape declined during the 5th century and was replaced, over several centuries, as a result of the Anglo-Saxon and Danish settlers and their communal approach to the use of land. Each village evolved a system of two, three, or more arable fields, divided into furlongs and strips, distributed by agreement among the cultivators and farmed on the basis of simple rotation of crops. There were also common meadows and grazing areas, and common woodlands and waste. This system developed over centuries, and was not finally in place until the mid 11th century. Its origins and the course of its development have been the subject of much research and long debate. Traces, almost ghosts, of the open field system and surrounding woodland can still be seen in some areas, such as

43

south Oxfordshire, north Devon, and the lower Trent valley. The system necessitated the farms being in the village, and examples of this can be seen also.

By the 13th century population increase began to break this pattern, and in some areas individual farmers colonised the waste land, creating *assarts*, or farms cleared from the woodlands or waste, and owned in *severalty* – individually and not communally. This created a pattern of dispersed settlement of a different kind from that in the highland or "ancient" zones. Attempts to control or limit this assarting – the Statutes of Merton, 1235, and of Westminster, 1285 – had little success.

In the later Middle Ages, notably after the Black Death, much of the land of the depopulated or deserted villages was enclosed by the manorial lords and used for pasturing sheep (which needed less labour and yielded more profit than arable farming). This was mainly in the Midland counties, but some small enclosures were made in the south-west as well. Enclosure for pasture changed the landscape at a stroke, leaving only the ridge and furrow of the former arable strips showing in the grass. Much of this late medieval enclosure was done high-handedly, taking advantage of the rural depopulation.

Enclosure, largely still for sheep but also to create private – prestige – parks, continued during the 16th century and into the mid 17th. These enclosures were done by agreement between the manorial lord and the lesser landholders, formalised by Chancery or Exchequer decrees. But much ill-feeling was caused by the frequent enclosure of commons and wastes as well as the open fields.

The Agricultural Revolution made a small beginning during the 17th century, with better equipment, land drainage, and the growing of new crops such as clover and roots. The open fields were not suited to these developments. Enclosure now had an increasingly economic base, and also reflected changes in the social structure. Its objectives (as W E Tate has shown) were twofold: to reclaim the still extensive waste land, and to rationalise the old open field agriculture and change to individual ownership and cultivation. The Tudor method of enclosure by agreement and Chancery decree gave way to the use of private Acts of Parliament. The first of these seems to be that for Radipole (Do) in 1603, but only a handful were passed during the 17th century. In the first half of the 18th century they became not only more frequent but also standard. After the middle of the century there was an explosion of these Acts. Before 1760 there were 259 Acts, more than half of them relating to parishes in Warwickshire, Northamptonshire,

and Gloucestershire, and in the North and West Ridings of Yorkshire. But from 1760 to 1844 there were some 5,400 enclosures, covering almost seven million acres, or about a fifth of the area of England, under nearly 4,200 Acts and several General Acts (1801, 1836, 1840, 1845, etc). Some enclosure took place after this until the end of the 19th century.

Enclosure on this scale profoundly altered the structure and appearance of the countryside. In many cases the modern village itself took its present form from its enclosure. The farms no longer had to be in the village, but could now be scattered over the land. Large regular fields were created, hedged or walled, and straight roads with wide verges were laid among them. Woodland and waste declined. About a half of the hedged and walled landscape of England dates from after 1700.

This changed landscape, in the area of "planned countryside", has persisted until the 1950s or 1960s, when a new change in these areas has taken place as a result of the "Second Agricultural Revolution" – the phase of mechanised and chemical farming ("agribusiness"). Changes due to this have been accompanied by profound social changes in the villages themselves.

Of course, this account is grossly simplified. The changes, although very real, are not consistently spread, even in the "planned country-side". But it remains true that we today would not recognise the countryside of AD 300, 1100, 1600, 1800, or even, in some areas, 1950.

Urbanisation of the countryside

This is a phenomenon of our time, which has been greatly accelerating in recent years. Many ancient civilisations, including the Roman, were urban in spirit, and the Roman model continued to dominate the former provinces in Italy and France. But the vast majority of the people of western Europe, including Britain, continued to live in, and depend on, the countryside. Not until the Industrial Revolution began (about 1750 in England) did this balance alter. But once started, the trend became a landslide. Not only were more and more people concentrated where the factories were, and in the fast-growing industrial towns, but they produced goods, and built up an environment, to which they became addicted and adapted, even if they could not escape them. And, for 200 years, country people continued to migrate into the industrial towns.

Changes in rural life have of course been noticed, and described, from at least the 17th century. Many writers have described life and conditions in their childhood (such as Gertrude Jekyll's *Old West Surrey* (1904) or Flora Thompson's *Lark Rise to Candleford* (1939)). Most of these books, absorbing as they are, do little more than enable change to be measured; they scarcely touch on urbanisation as such, except of course by implication (although Flora Thompson notes the coming of new villas and urban people to her village). Reading them, one is conscious of looking into another world and of the finality of its passing.

A few unusually percipient writers have realised the implications of this backward look, and help us to appreciate the qualitative nature of the change, as well as its extent and the reasons for it. Such is George Bourne, in *Change in the Village* (1912). And the impact of industrialisation on the craftsman, both rural and urban, was recognised and deplored by 19th-century sociologists like Ruskin and William Morris.

But urbanisation is now worldwide, and apparently irreversible; one can only try to save what can and should be saved.

As towns grow and spread, their pull on the countryside increases and the villages experience a growing dependence on urban culture. The standardisation of consumer goods, food, entertainment, social life, clothes, holidays, etc is hard to resist, indeed virtually impossible to evade. This affects the living standards and ways of the village people, not always for the better. And rural incomes and purchasing power are not normally as high as in towns.

Villages in what has been called the "accessible countryside" have become, in effect, "discontinuous suburbs", and in the "inaccessible countryside" – too far from towns for convenient, easy, and cheap access – villages have been seriously affected by a spiral of decline in services and facilities.

Villages in certain areas are on one hand invaded by tourism (with its accompaniment of cafés, souvenir shops, antique dealers, and car parks), and on the other have seen their atmosphere altered by commuting and incoming residents. Second or holiday homes not only freeze houses which village people could still live in but put their price up beyond the villagers' means. This is an increasingly serious problem in areas like rural Wales, and causes deep resentment, sometimes resulting in vandalism or even arson. Available houses are also snapped up as permanent homes by retired people and other "incomers". In some places demand for houses is so great that developers and speculators are attracted, and infilling takes place, often with houses or bungalows of quite unsuitable and incongruous design. The new residents can accentuate any unbalance in the social structure of the population.

Those who spent all their working lives in towns or in industry and retire to the country carry their urban or suburban habits, tastes, and attitudes with them. They furnish and equip their houses and plant their gardens in suburban ways. Their activities continue in the ways they have been used to. They tend to mix with similar people. This may not only create a division in the village, but in the long run the village people will be influenced, however unconsciously, to emulate them.

Frequently, even normally, the social life of a village is divided between that of the original villagers and that of the incomers. Both these elements will mix in the Women's Institute and in the annual dramatic show, summer fête, bonfire, and Christmas Fair. The pensioners' club is usually used by villagers only; the gardening club perhaps mainly by the incomers, and the local history and amenity society almost entirely so. The recreation ground is used essentially by the villagers, but supported by the incomers also. The church itself may be mostly attended and supported by incomers, although the villagers use it for baptisms, weddings, and funerals. If there is a chapel, the balance is reversed in the direction of the villagers. There may be a generation distinction also; the village youth have their discos and motorbikes.

This appraisal is not based on any particular village, but illustrates various situations that may well exist. This "us and them" mentality is very resistant to change, and in too many cases results practically in socially dual communities. Only the shopkeepers, milkmen, postmen, etc are entirely neutral, however much goodwill there may be. Mixing on a purely social level, outside certain organisations, is almost unknown.

Paradoxically, urbanisation goes with impoverishment of village life and a reduction of the quality of living for many. Rationalisation of rural patterns, eg consolidation of farms and changed farming methods, means fewer jobs on the land. This happens at the same time as fewer demands for craftsmen in the village (eg blacksmiths, carpenters, potters, millers, bakers, etc), as more and more goods and services can be got from the market town or city. So the number of jobs in the village declines, and the young people have either to commute to the towns or leave the village for good. One could almost say that only those who have one or two cars and a freezer can afford to live in the country; the young who need public services and schools go to the towns (they could not afford the price of village houses anyway).

Many rural areas are now seriously depopulated or socially maimed. The children are affected by urbanisation also. John Higgs could say as long ago as 1964 (in *The Land*): "The extent to which the future of the countryside lies away from the land may be judged from the fact that in one Oxfordshire village at least the children at the local school have to be taken to a farm during school hours to see what animals and crops look like."

The reduction in village amenities – less public transport, fewer services, the closing of village shops, post offices, and schools – has been matched by increased private car ownership and mobility, but the poorer inhabitants tend to be overlooked and economically depressed, and some of their centres of social contact are removed, thus adding to the difficulty of living a full life in the village. In some areas, even, the number of key centres has been reduced as a matter of local government policy (as in East Anglia and Northumberland), with reduction of transport services and the closing of post offices and schools.

There is also a deterioration in the visual environment. Power is taken across country by overhead wires, roads are widened, straightened, or otherwise "improved"; urban or industrial features creep in everywhere. Even most of the ever faster traffic on the country roads, and through the villages, is urban or industry-orientated.

The spread and growth, not only of towns but of industrial installations of all kinds – roads, airfields, power stations, even holiday and recreational facilities – in general completely ignore and override the existing amenities and nature of the countryside as such, but are intruded upon it, sometimes quite insensitively, without a thought for the interests or wishes of the local country people. Conservation is not everywhere a welcome idea, and the quality of the diminishing countryside has to be fought for every inch of the way. The nation itself is impoverished if our natural environment is damaged, and also if rural communities are prevented from being vigorous, working, and reasonably serviced settlements, making their own distinctive contribution to society as a whole.

PLACE-NAMES AND THE SETTLEMENT OF ENGLAND

It used to be taken for granted that place-names containing the element *-ingas* or *-ingaham* (like Hastings, Reading, or Gillingham) represented the earliest Anglo-Saxon settlement. The element means "people of (some personal name)" and "home of the people of ...". Many standard books on place-names still carry quite specific statements that this hypothesis is true. But since the late 1960s it has been undermined, and it is now accepted by the authorities that the real facts must have been different.

This is so important for our understanding of the nature and location of settlement that it is worth elaborating. The two main sources of evidence are archaeological (mostly from burials) and from place-names. J McNeill Dodgson (*Medieval Archaeology* 10, 1966) plotted the pagan burials in the south-east of England against the *-ingas* and *-ingaham* names, and showed conclusively that there is no agreement between the two. The names are just not where the burials are. So striking is this utter disagreement that Margaret Gelling could say (in *The Local Historian* 11/1, 1974) that "if we must regard them as contemporary, there was a law in operation from AD 400 to AD 600 which said that people of English descent might either have a pagan burial or live in a place with an *-ingas* name, but were to be strongly discouraged from doing both." The conclusion must be that the names represent a second stage of colonisation, after the initial settlement – sometimes on less good land.

This breakthrough was followed in 1973 by a study by Barrie Cox (*Journal of the English Place-name Society* 5), who gave evidence to show that the earliest element was *hām* (home of). There is a close relationship in the Midlands and East Anglia between *ham* and the sites of Romano-British settlement and villas, Romano-British and pagan Anglo-Saxon cemeteries, Roman roads and ancient trackways, and soils desirable to the earliest settlers. At the end of the *ham* phase names in *-ingaham* appear, and *-ingas* and *-inga* names are later still. Still later are names with *-tun* (farmstead, hamlet) and *-ingtun*. (*Tun* was very common in Old English. There are 554 in Yorkshire, including the Grimston hybrids; they are not as old as *ham*, but some are early.) Although this pattern is subject to further studies, the primacy of *-ingas* is no longer acceptable. There are also good reasons for thinking that topographical names share the primacy with *ham*.

In areas where *ham* is absent, such as north-west Berkshire (an area of early pagan burials), there is a concentration of names ending in *ford* and *eg* (ey, an island, dry ground in marsh). It may be that such topographical names are the original ones in some areas; in any case they give clues to the scenery and appearance of the land at that time. Barrie Cox's work has been taken further for the east Midlands by Joost Kuurman (*Journal of the English Place-name Society* 7, 1975). He has shown that *-ingaham* names, commoner here than in south-east England, mostly occur on attractive sites near Roman roads or main rivers; they may even be renamed extant settlements. *-ingas* and *-inga* names are upland and inland from these, and must be secondary (and, as Cox showed, they are rarely if ever associated with pagan cemeteries). Margaret Gelling, looking for middle-period settlements in the west Midlands, finds (*The Local Historian* 11/1, 1974) that the *-tons* and *-leys* are commonest in a crescent from Derbyshire through Warwickshire, Worcestershire, and Gloucestershire to Wiltshire. They are separate, but possibly contemporary. Her studies have also confirmed the close relation of the early names to the drift geology.

In the Danish parts of England the problem is a different one, and here the main evidence comes from place-names. The pioneer work was a study of the names of the Danelaw by Professor Kenneth Cameron in 1965. This compared the sites of Danish-named villages with English-named ones, from the point of view of situation, soils, and agricultural potential. The result was to show that the Danish villages were not previous English ones taken over by victorious Danes after 865, but were Danish settlements made by colonists, under army protection, who accepted second-best land not occupied on any scale by the English.

A profound study of the Scandinavian settlement of Yorkshire, following Cameron's lead, was made by Gillian Fellows Jensen (*Scandinavian Settlement Names in Yorkshire*, (Copenhagen 1972)), which shows the vital part place-name studies can play in unravelling a historical problem. Danish settlement in Yorkshire began in 876. In 919 Norse from Ireland settled in York (where Scandinavian rule did not end till 954). There was possibly some renewed Scandinavian settlement after Canute's conquest of England. The strong Scandinavian element led Harald Hardrada to attempt his conquest from Yorkshire, and was a major factor leading to William I's devastations of the north in 1069–70 and 1085.

The actual course and location of these settlements has to be deduced mainly from place-names, and reliance has to be placed on Domesday (1086), which gives the earliest forms of most of the names. But the Domesday Book has gaps, as it only names places through which obligations were due to the king or a lord, and omits subsidiary places.

There are 210 names in Yorkshire ending in *by* (village); of these 119 have a personal name as first element, and 72 have an appellative (eg Danby, village of the Danes). These proportions are the reverse of those in Denmark itself, but presumably reflect the conditions of a migration. *Thorp* (an enclosure, hence a village), which spread from Frankish lands into Germany and Denmark and was given to places up to about 1100, occurs 155 times. Of these, 85 have personal names as the first element, and 41 are simplex (that is, just thorp(e) by itself). These names indicate secondary settlements. There are also 30 Scandinavian habitative names (eg Lofthouse), and 104 topographical names. Then there is the important group of hybrids. These are names with the English *tun*, preceded by a Scandinavian or Scandinavianised first element. The 42 Grimston hybrids have a Scandinavian personal name as first element. These are on the fringes of areas where *by* and *thorp* are thickest. They may be English vills taken over by Danes, replacing an original English first element with a Danish personal name. Or they may mark the movement of Danes away from areas where they were numerous enough to dominate the local population linguistically as well as politically. Then there are 58 hybrids where the first element is an appellative, some understood by both peoples (eg Carlton, the village of free peasants). Of the Grimston type, some could represent Englishmen with Danish names but many must represent Scandinavian settlers. Finally, there are 145 Scandinavianised or other hybrid names.

The English names in Yorkshire have a different pattern from further south. Neither *ham* nor *-ingas* are common, but both are comparatively early, earlier than *-ingaleah* (the clearing of the people of . . .), *-ingahalh* (the watermeadow of the people of . . .), etc. *Hams* correlate with Roman roads, but are further removed from immigration areas than *ingas*. The scarcity of early names in the West Riding may be due to the survival of the Celtic kingdom of Elmet into the 7th century. Still later are the names in *tun* and *ingtun*, which are very common (about 30% of Yorkshire names), and show the spread of settlement; they are evenly spread, except in the North York Moors and the Pennines (apart from the Aire Gap).

The distribution of the names shows that settlement was densest in the East Riding. *Bys* (farmstead, village – Old Norse) are thickest in the Vale of York and the North York Moors foothills, otherwise fairly evenly scattered. *Thorps* (farm, hamlet – Old Danish and Old English) are found in the northern Wolds and Howardian Hills and in the south-east foothills of the Wolds, with a scatter elsewhere. *Thorps* are mostly in areas where there are also *bys*, in the North and West Ridings, but in the East Riding 32 of the 68 *thorps* are in areas where *bys* are not found. Some of these, eg in Holderness, are in areas already settled by the English. Habitative names often indicate summer settlements, so are absent from the main *by* and *thorp* areas (eg the southern Vale of York). Topographical names are evenly spread in the North Riding, but most are in the Vale of York. A large proportion are in river valleys, many where Roman roads cross the rivers. The Grimston hybrids are well spread in the Vale of York. In east Yorkshire there are five along the Roman road from Malton to Filey. There are none in the Wolds, but some in Holderness. In west Yorkshire they are on the limestone hills, but not over 800ft. They mark prosperous and fertile areas. Other *tun* hybrids are often in Grimston areas. The North York Moors foothills were neglected by the English, and first settled intensively by the Danes. Many hybrids represent less favourable locations.

There is no marked correlation between this settlement and Roman roads or river valleys, except for three examples north of York and the Grimston hybrids in the East Riding. In the West Riding the Norse settled along the Roman roads over the Pennines and in the dales. Names like Normanby and west Scandinavian personal names represent Norwegians from the north-west, Irby the Irish, Danby the Danes, and Birkby the Britons (Irish Norse). The Norse are thickest in the North Riding, while the Danes are all over Yorkshire.

The vills along the north Wold edge (Folkton, Garton, etc) have lands on carr (waste) to the north, arable on the sand and gravel, and wold (for pasture) to the south. Grimston hybrids were mostly Anglian vills already, and hence had balanced lands; new settlement, eg Flotmanby, is often on less favourable land. So the age of settlement can often be detected by the type of land, the extent of gravel etc, and the nearness to rivers. Eleven of the Grimston hybrids are in inferior positions, and here the Grim may not be a personal name but a by-name of the god, when it equated with the devil.

Where names are in pairs (eg Great and Little Ribston) one is often secondary to the other. *Thorps* are normally secondary, and later than the *bys*. *Bys* tend to be in valleys and yet not on the alluvium. Other names are usually in poorer situations. Hybrid and Scandinavianised names are often Anglian settlements taken over by Danes. Places with purely Scandinavian names are usually new settlements, but not in all cases; Anglian crosses are sometimes at *bys*, eg Whitby. Where the names remain English, Scandinavians could have settled without altering the names; this is pointed up by the numerous crosses in Scandinavian styles whose distribution is in areas where Scandinavian place-names are rare, but hybrid or Scandinavianised names common (so the latter represent actual Scandinavian settlement). *Kir(k)by* names are either replacements, where the church is pre-Viking (eg Kirkby Overblow), or true *by* names, with Viking churches.

In Domesday, the North and East Ridings were divided into wapentakes, the East Riding into hundreds (replaced in the 12th century by wapentakes). It is likely that these units were based on early Anglian units, but many of their names are Scandinavian or Scandinavianised. Some have elements like *haugr* or *berg*, implying the use of mounds as meeting places. Double villages exist (eg Halperby/Brafferton, Askham Bryan and Richard, West and East Ayton), some of which have hybrid or Scandinavianised names. Many *thorps* are lost villages, implying a poor position and decline. Indeed, a high proportion of deserted villages have Scandinavian names, reflecting minor or poor settlements. There is no certain evidence that any names were given when the Vikings were still heathen. Names denoting secondary settlements include those where the first element is an older place-name, eg Deightonby, Meltonby. Austhorpe lies east of Whitkirk, to which parish it belongs; Eastorpe lies east of Londesborough, Northorpe north of Kilnsea. Upleatham has a better position than Kirkleatham, which was probably secondary to it. Upsall and Upsland may be high, or just higher, than another place they depended on. The 41 simplex *thorps* show small minor settlements; some later added a prefix, to distinguish one from another. *By* names are stable, *thorps* are not.

To sum all this up, most hybrid and Scandinavianised names are older English vills occupied by Scandinavians; most *bys* mark occupation by

Danes of the best available vacant land, sometimes in virgin areas, sometimes edged in between English villages; the third stage, the occupation of poorer land, is shown by *thorp*s and Scandinavian names denoting temporary settlements (plus a few hybrids); *thorp*s have a high proportion of deserted vills. Scandinavians also settled in English villages without changing their names, and a few villages with Scandinavian names were originally established and settled by Englishmen. Most *by*s and *thorp*s were established at a fairly early date: the *by*s mark the first colonisation in the strict sense, the *thorp*s its second stage. Many Scandinavian topographical names were adaptations of older English names, but others were given by the Scandinavians to a natural feature and later transferred to the settlement which arose on the site.

Thus for the first time the real course of events can be seen, however broadly. Gillian Fellows Jensen's work has pointed the way to equally illuminating studies, and has demonstrated the great value of place-names when used properly and to the full.

Place-name evidence is often fluid and obscure, and caution is necessary before conclusions are drawn. Not only is the evidence – the record – normally much later than the original first giving of the name, but names can themselves change. One Anglo-Saxon element can be replaced by another, later, Anglo-Saxon element, or by a Scandinavian element (see above). Or a whole Anglo-Saxon name may be replaced by a Scandinavian one. Even a medieval deserted village can be reoccupied under a new name, and the original one forgotten. P H Sawyer has pointed out (in *Kings and Vikings: Scandinavia and Europe AD 700–1100* (Methuen 1982)) that place-name patterns may tell us more of the status of the estate than its novelty; in some areas change of names may betoken fragmentation of tenure rather than colonisation. The patient studies mentioned above have amply repaid the effort in terms of understanding of the sequence of events.

Romano-British elements in Old English

The early Anglo-Saxon settlers, or perhaps the descendants of the 4th-century *foederati* brought in by the Romans to help in the defence of Britain, acquired a few words of Latin origin which became interesting place-name elements. These include: *ceaster*, from *castar*, used by the Saxons for a Roman walled town or fortress which later became a Saxon town (see pages 155 and 159), eg Winchester; *eccles* (*ecclesia*), denoting a Romano-British church (see page 264); *funta* (*fontana*), a spring, well, etc, which occurs in several names hybridised with Saxon roots, such as Bedfont, Cheshunt (*ceaster-font*), Fovant, Havant, Boarhunt (*burh-font*), Fonthill (*font-ial*: Celtic for fertile upland), Fontmell; and *wic*, from *vicus*. *Vicus* meant the smallest unit of Roman local administration – a large village or small town, the civil settlement outside a fort, or the local divisions of a large town. When combined with *ham*, as in Wicham, Wickham, it can indicate the presence of a Romano-British settlement surviving into the early phase of Saxon settlement. Wickham has a wide distribution in England, but its greatest concentration is in areas where early Germanic settlement is mostly absent, and where the likelihood of sub-Roman survival is real. *Wic* later acquired other meanings, such as a town, port, or harbour, saltworks, street, dwelling, or dependent farm; in literature it means village, camp, and dairy farm as well! *Wick* or *Wich* as an element in a coastal or riverine name (eg Sandwich) is now seen to point to the presence of a trading port of the middle Saxon period (see page 156). *Port* (*portus*) indicates a Roman harbour, as in Portsmouth, Portchester, Portland; this later became a town or market (Milborne Port). *Foss*, a ditch (*fossa*), was a prominent feature which named the Roman Fosse Way. *Aust* perpetuates *Augusta*. Lincoln is *Lindum Colonia*. Faversham is the *ham* of a smith (*faber*). Kent has several survivals of Celtic names, largely geographical, such as the Saxon Shore names of Dover (*Dubris*, waters), Reculver (*Regulbium*, great headland), and Lympne (*Lemanis*, place of elms). London is Londonis' town (Celtic). A few names reveal the presence of Britons living among the Saxons; eg Chertsey is "Cerot's island" (Cerot is a British name).

FARMING

Farming was, until quite recently, the *raison d'être* of the countryside and of the village, and a brief outline of its development in Britain must be given here. The successive changes in agricultural structures and methods have had a direct effect on the nature and form of rural settlement.

Traces of field and farm patterns of all periods from the first (Neolithic) farmers about 4500 BC can still be seen in areas where later farming or building has not obliterated them – particularly from the air. For the prehistoric and Roman periods these traces survive most plentifully

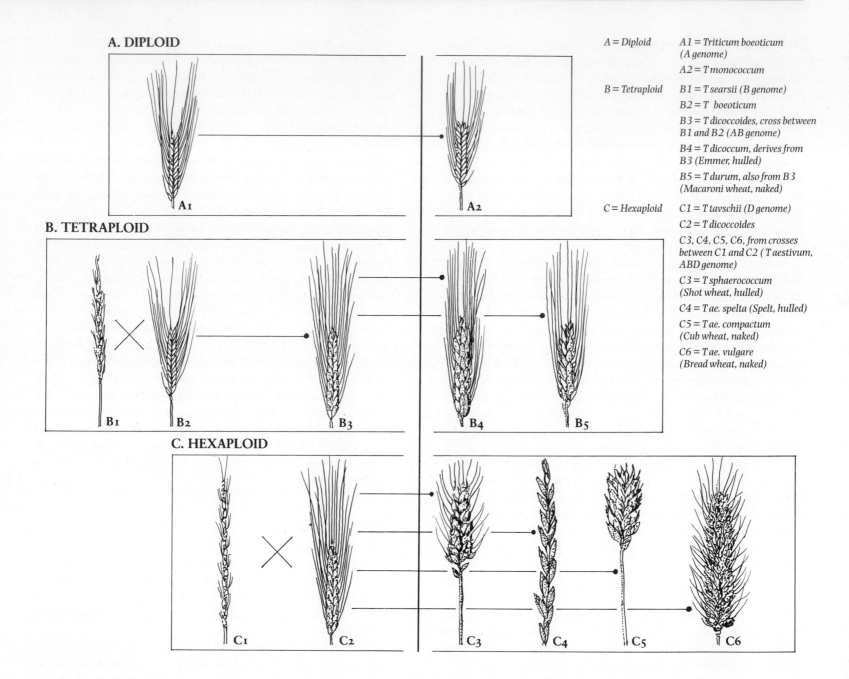

A. DIPLOID

A₁ **A₂**

B. TETRAPLOID

B₁ **B₂** **B₃** **B₄** **B₅**

C. HEXAPLOID

C₁ **C₂** **C₃** **C₄** **C₅** **C₆**

A = Diploid

B = Tetraploid

C = Hexaploid

A1 = *Triticum boeoticum*
   (A genome)

A2 = *T monococcum*

B1 = *T searsii* (B genome)

B2 = *T boeoticum*

B3 = *T dicoccoides, cross between
B1 and B2 (AB genome)*

B4 = *T dicoccum, derives from
B3 (Emmer, hulled)*

B5 = *T durum, also from B 3
(Macaroni wheat, naked)*

C1 = *T tavschii (D genome)*

C2 = *T dicoccoides*

C3, C4, C5, C6, from crosses
between C1 and C2 (T aestivum,
ABD genome)

C3 = *T sphaerococcum
(Shot wheat, hulled)*

C4 = *T ae. spelta (Spelt, hulled)*

C5 = *T ae. compactum
(Cub wheat, naked)*

C6 = *T ae. vulgare
(Bread wheat, naked)*

7 *The origins of cultivated wheat. The types to the left of the line are wild varieties, those to the right are the cultivated derivatives from these.*

on the chalk downlands; for the Middle Ages the ridge and furrow and the old lanes and tracks are still conspicuous in the "planned countryside" of the Midlands, and in certain areas elsewhere. The patterns of the fields and farmsteads themselves also reveal the sequence of colonisation and enclosure.

Prehistoric

Neolithic farming was at a subsistence level, based on the cultivation of small, often irregular, and sometimes unfenced plots. There was much woodland, waste, and ill-drained land. Cattle predominated over sheep and pigs. Sheep needed open grassland, and pigs woodland. Pigs were accordingly less common in the north. Arable crops included primitive wheats (*emmer* and some *einkorn*) (see 7) and barley, of which more was grown in the north. Many plants were collected, for food, flavouring, or medicine, and of course fruits, nuts, berries, and seeds were collected in season.

This pattern continued throughout the Bronze Age, but now population was increasing and fields were more regular. Early in the 1st millennium BC there is evidence for a greater variety of crops: *spelt* now replaces emmer, and some bread or club wheat is grown; rye, beans, and roots appear. The barley is hulled and six-row.

The Iron Age site at Ashville (Ox) gave evidence for four crop species and over 60 other plants, of which some (like vetch, cress, corn gromwell, and onion couch) may have been collected. But many were consciously grown, even if some were cornfield weeds harvested with the corn and used for food.

Iron Age farming was surprisingly efficient, given its limitations, as the researches and experiments of the Butser Ancient Farm Trust (led by Dr Peter Reynolds) have shown. At Butser, near Petersfield (Ha) in chalk downland, farming methods of c 300 BC have been meticulously reconstructed, and much has been learnt. Crop yields were high – at Butser yields of over 2.5 tonnes to the hectare have been achieved, a figure not again reached until recent times. In good years there was sufficient surplus for grain and leather to be exported to Europe. But in the absence of artificial fertilisers and pesticides, crops were subject to the full range of pests and weeds as well as being totally exposed to climatic variations, and in some years the people must have been brought near to starvation. Manure was used. The plough was the simple ard (see 8),

which could make a furrow on suitable soils 6 in (15 cm) deep. The evidence of seeds and pollen on occupation sites shows that Bronze Age, Iron Age, and Romano-British farmers grew some ten cereals, including einkorn (soon superseded by emmer), spelt, club wheat, old bread wheat, naked and hulled two-row and six-row barley, rye, and possibly oats. There were also peas and beans, and vegetables such as fat-hen; other plants included woad, poppy, buckwheat, vetch, hemp, and flax. Calamine was grown for oil, and a large variety of herbs was grown.

Livestock consisted of Celtic Shorthorn cattle (similar to modern Dexters), Soay sheep, goats, and pigs, of which the nearest to the ancient breed is a cross between the European wild boar and the Tamworth pig. Horses like the Exmoor were kept. The greylag and the mallard are the most likely geese and ducks to have been kept, and chickens could have been Indian Red Jungle Fowls or Old English Game Fowls. Grain was stored, not only in above-ground granaries ("four-posters"), but in pits, large enough to take the yield of half to three-quarters of a hectare. Bees were kept.

Roman

Roman farming largely continued that of the Iron Age, in that "native" farms and hamlets remained in being, and indeed are often hard to distinguish from pre-Roman farms. Two new types of farm, however, appeared: the holdings allocated by the state to retired veterans, sometimes in large blocks of land divided (*centuriated*) into regular

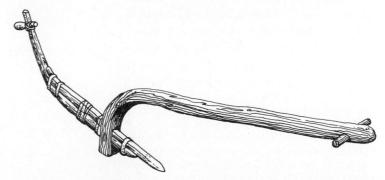

8 *A bow-ard. A wooden digging-stick with a bar handle enabling it to be pulled instead of pushed, the ard was the earliest form of plough. The bow-ard shown here was the type most commonly used in Britain.*

plots; and the villas. Villas were country houses or large farmsteads, sometimes owned by local British notables, sometimes by property magnates or speculators who might reside elsewhere in the Empire. They were the centres of estates partly run on slave labour. They were largely self-sufficient, and produced surpluses for sale or to pay taxes; often, particularly in later centuries, they had industrial components as well as agriculture. In addition there were imperial estates which might cover large tracts of land. Villas of the 1st and 2nd centuries have been likened to colonial plantations; those of the 3rd and 4th centuries to medieval manorial and feudal estates.

Some new animals and plants were introduced, and commodities such as olive oil, wine, and fish sauce (*garum* or *liquamen*) were imported.

The Butser Ancient Farm Project in 1985–7 ran a research programme at the Roman palace at Fishbourne (Sx) to reconstruct the cultivation and stockbreeding of the mid 1st century AD. Dexter cattle and Old English goats and Soay and Shetland sheep continued to be kept, and the Cotswold sheep were introduced. Gardens were more elaborate, if not new, and the Romans introduced a wide variety of vegetables, herbs, fruit trees, and vines. These included shallots, a pea (*Lathyrus sativus*), cabbage, celery, lentil, millet, anise, mulberry, and fig. The vine introduced by the Romans is that represented today by the Wrotham Pinot. A Roman ornamental garden has been

Map **5** *The midland system of open fields. This was the commonest form of field system across a wide swathe of central England – the "planned countryside". Each village had three open fields, shared between the cultivators. The fields were used in rotation: thus when Field 1 was used to grow wheat and barley, Field 2 would be fallow, and used for pasture, while Field 3 grew oats, peas, and beans. In the following two years these uses changed until the original order came round again in year 4.*

The area of the Midland system of open fields in the late 16th century. This was a broad belt across much of the lowland zone of England.

reconstructed, from archaeological and literary evidence, at the palace of Fishbourne itself.

Medieval

By the late Saxon period the central belt of lowland England became organised into "planned countryside", with villages and open fields practising arable and mixed farming (**Map 5**). Outside this belt lay the "ancient countryside" of small fields, scattered farms and hamlets, pasture, and mixed farming. In parts of the north, and in Scotland, the two-field or runrig system grew up. Here the infield, nearest the village, was continuously cropped; the outfield was the common pasture. The open field system of the "planned" zone was normally arranged in three fields (although two occur, as well as larger numbers). Within the fields and meadow the villagers held strips, distributed so as to give each man a fair share of the land and its good and bad qualities, and a share in each of the rotations each year. In the three-field system a typical rotation of use would be:

YEAR 1
> *Field 1* wheat and barley
> *Field 2* fallow (cattle grazing, and manuring, on last year's barley stubble; in autumn winter wheat sown)
> *Field 3* oats, peas, and beans

YEAR 2
> *Field 1* oats, peas, and beans
> *Field 2* wheat
> *Field 3* fallow

YEAR 3
> *Field 1* fallow
> *Field 2* peas and beans
> *Field 3* wheat

A simpler sequence might be: field 1, fallow; field 2, wheat and rye; field 3, barley.

Besides these fields, there would be a watermeadow, for hay for winter feed, though there was never enough for all the animals, and some had to be slaughtered in the late autumn; a common pasture; and woodland and waste, for fuel, timber, and pigs. Geese, ducks, and poultry were also kept, and a few sheep and goats. There were local variations in the use of the fields, as in East Anglia and Kent (see pages 67–73). In the 12th and 13th centuries in waste or marginal lands, as population increased, enabled independent farms to coexist with the open fields. The peasants grew vegetables and herbs, and kept poultry, pigs, and a cow, in their crofts. A wider variety of crops began to be grown in the later Middle Ages.

This pattern was violently disrupted by the Black Death of 1349 and later epidemics. It is hard now to visualise the profound and lasting impact of this disaster. At a time when 95% or so of the population lived in the countryside, between a third and a half of the people died. Some villages lost most or all of their inhabitants. The population in fact did not return to its pre-1348 level until the 16th century.

An immediate effect was that the tied peasantry now found themselves able to resist feudal obligations and dictate their own terms; many left the country for the towns. The landowners could consolidate their estates and enclose the open fields and the commons, using the undivided land principally for sheep; the cloth industry burgeoned. Feudal tenure began to be replaced by rent for tenants. Hundreds of villages shrank, or were deserted.

In many places the organisation of the open fields could not be maintained, and they were either emparked or occupied by scattered farms. This enclosure continued during the 16th and 17th centuries and was stimulated also by the dissolution of the monasteries in 1538, which led to former religious houses being converted to new estates, parks, and farms.

Scotland, in the 15th and 16th centuries and into the 19th, continued to rear cattle for the English market, and still farmed on the infield/outfield system.

The growth of London and other towns encouraged food production and certain areas began to specialise, within the limits of their soils and climate. Thus, Suffolk turned to butter and cheese, Sussex to wheat, Essex to oats, Norfolk to malt, the southern Midlands and Lincolnshire to cattle (for Smithfield), the Fens to grazing (the Fens only changed to arable in the 20th century), and Kent and Surrey to market gardening.

The 16th and 17th centuries

In the early 16th century the dominant crops were still wheat, oats, barley and rye, with oats, peas, and vetches for animal feed. By the end of the century variety increased greatly (see below).

In the 16th century, some two-thirds of the population were in farming, many of these at subsistence level, so the produce varied accordingly. Dairying was suitable for small family farmers, cattle rearing and fattening for larger farms in regions with gentry and yeomen, and grain for large farms – gentry or yeomen with many wage labourers. The 16th-century enclosure increased the number of medium and large farms, which led to increased arable.

After the Black Death, farmers had turned from grain to wool, but the increasing population in the 16th and 17th centuries raised the demand for grain again. However, in the first half of the 17th century population growth slowed down, and grain prices fell after 1650. Farmers then turned to meat and dairy, fruit and vegetables. Local demands, such as for cheese, butter, pork, or cider, were met in particular areas. Wool prices fell in the 17th century, owing to cheap imports and to the increasing use of linen and cotton. Prohibition of Irish cattle imports in the 1660s encouraged farmers in the north and west to rear cattle for fattening in the south and east, eg on the coastal marshlands of Yorkshire and Lincolnshire, and Romney Marsh.

It is illuminating, when considering the nature and components of a village, to see it in terms of the physical, social, economic, and political aspects of its regional background. Much attention has been given by geographers to defining the agrarian regions of Britain. This is not made easier by the very wide variety of geology and climate, and the differences in even quite small adjacent areas. Rural industries and social structures exert their influences also.

Joan Thirsk, in *The Agrarian History of England and Wales*, vols IV and V (Cambridge University Press, 1967 and 1984), used three broad divisions as the basis for detailed subdivision: mixed farming types, wood-pasture types, and open pasture types. These were broken down by farming practice, soils, location, and so on. The pioneer scheme of E Kerridge (*The Agricultural Revolution*, 1967), which defined 41 farming "countries" in England and Wales, was not only complex, but in some respects controversial. Thirsk's scheme had 12 types. Alan Everitt (*Landscape and Community in England*, 1985) reduces these to 8:

1 downland
2 wold
3 fielden or champion (vale lands, arable, or pastoral)
4 marshlands
5 heathlands
6 forest and woodpasture
7 fell or moorland
8 fenland

1 and 2 are grain regions, 6 and 7 are pastoral; the others vacillated in the 16th and 17th centuries from pastoral to arable, according to prices, draining, and (for 5) new crops, such as buckwheat, clover, sainfoin, lucerne, trefoil, rye grass, rape, etc (see **Map 6**, facing page 26).

Thirsk has further refined this (in *England's Agricultural Regions and Agrarian History, 1500–1750* (Macmillan 1987)) to:

1 wold and downland
2 arable vale lands (fielden or champion)
3 pastoral vale lands
4 heathland
5 forests and woodpasture
6 fells and moorland
7 marshland
8 fenland

The period from 1550 to 1750 was one of considerable agricultural innovation. This included "up and down husbandry" (rotation for up to 9 years, followed by grass leys up to 12 years – the dung from pasture restored fertility), fen drainage, watermeadows, new crops (rape for oil; fodder crops like clover, lucerne, and turnips; vegetables like potatoes and carrots (and peas and beans were now used as vegetables)); dye crops like woad and madder; saffron and teazels; hemp and flax; and new systems to accommodate the new crops in arable rotations.

There was a similar burgeoning on the livestock side: new breeds of cattle and sheep, and old stock improved by better feeding and selection. Cattle were developed for specialised purposes – milk, beef, or draught – and had sharp regional characteristics (eg red short-horns in the south-west, black longhorns in Yorkshire and the north Midlands, black and white in Lincolnshire). The milk yield increased, but still had far to go – in medieval times the average annual yield (and that in summer only) was 120–150 gallons, as against 2,000 gallons today. Sheep were housed in winter and fed on hay, pea-haulms, and straw. Their milk was made into cheese and butter. Sheep kept outside, eg the Dorset Horn, lambed earlier, which was useful for meat. As with cattle, regional breeds developed, short or long-woolled. Fleeces averaged 4–6lb by the late 16th century as against 2–3lb in the 14th. There were some 12 million sheep at both periods. The "improvements" of livestock were sometimes carried to excess, and 18th-century pictures show grotesque cattle and pigs.

Horses were used, often with oxen, for farm work from the 12th century on, and their breeds were improved in the 16th; heavy horses appear in Elizabeth's reign. Poultry, bred since Norman times, became an industry in Norfolk in the later 16th century, and buckwheat was introduced as a poultry food. Geese, ducks, and turkeys (introduced from Mexico in the 1530s) were kept. Swans and peacocks were reared for the table, and wading birds in the Fens. Pigeons provided meat, eggs, and saltpetre; rabbits provided meat and fur. Goats were kept on marginal land.

The 16th century also saw increasing prosperity and an improvement in standards of housing, domestic equipment and furnishing, food, and clothing. Gardens, which had hitherto concentrated on herbs mainly for culinary and medicinal use, now allowed flowers for pleasure.

Many of the advances which used to be associated with the period 1750–1850 were in fact under way in the 16th century. Kerridge indeed sees these 16th- and 17th-century advances as the Agricultural Revolution which was formerly placed in 1750–1850. Some geographers (eg G E Mingay in *The Agricultural Revolution* (1977)) in fact see the "revolution" as spreading from 1550 to 1950, while keeping the term for the century 1750–1850.

At this point caution may seem justified. Joan Thirsk (*op cit*, 1987) and Mark Overton (in A R H Baker and D Gregory (eds), *Explorations in Historical Geography* (Cambridge 1984)) prefer to see the advances as a continuum, part of the normal development of agriculture, while recognising some periods as changing faster than others. Pressures and emphases changed; at each phase some progress was made in the details of management or in the geographical spread. Every new farming method proceeded in well-defined stages. Experiments were made, and some failed. Labour requirements varied. Changes were tentative and irregular, and "revolution" is hardly the word for them. The time seems to have to come to abandon it.

If some value is seen in retaining the word, perhaps it might be more appropriately applied to the rapid and radical changes since the 1950s, the age of "agribusiness" (see below). This would match the Electronic Revolution, as the earlier Agricultural Revolution matched the Industrial.

The late 17th century

From the 1660s, agriculture became transformed from a way of life to an industry. There were new methods, systems, and machines, and increasing rationalisation of land (enclosure, reorganisation of farms), particularly in much of the Lowland Zone of England, which reached full momentum in the closing years of the 18th century and the beginning of the 19th (see pages 84–5). Manorial lords ceased to be farmers and became landowners with tenant farmers. The old peasantry had become wage earners, and subsistence economy was a thing of the past.

The changes included increased mechanisation and better equipment. During the 17th century regional varieties of ploughs came into use; the Kentish turnwrest two-wheel plough, for example, enabled the depth of furrow to be adjusted. Harrows were used. Oxen were still used on heavy soils, horses on lighter. Seed was broadcast or sown in furrows. Wheat was cut by sickle, barley, oats, and grass by scythe. Grass was improved. Watermeadows extended grazing time. Ley farming and the use of fodder crops like clover and turnips greatly increased.

Population increased from the four million of the 16th century to some five and a half million by 1700, and more farm produce was required. Land became a good investment. One result of this was the drainage and reclamation of a million acres of fens and marshes (sometimes against local opposition) in the Fens, east Yorkshire, Lancashire/Cheshire, and Somerset.

The 18th century

This was characterised by a steady increase in enclosure, reflecting the demands and opportunities begun in the previous century. Enclosure by private agreement had already been going on, mainly in the pastoral areas of the west and north, but the 18th century was the age of enclosure by Act of Parliament, which affected mostly the open field areas in the east, east Midlands, and south.

The 18th century opened with the first of a long line of new or improved machines, eg Jethro Tull's seed-drill (1701, but not widely used till later) and his horse-hoe (1714) (see pages 84–5). Conspicuous developments took place in farming systems led by the great landowners, of which the best known is Lord ("Turnip") Townshend's *Norfolk four-course rotation* (1730s). This consisted of alternate straw crops with root or seed crops, eg first year roots, second year barley, third year seeds, fourth year wheat. Townshend used turnips as the roots, which were eaten by sheep or, on heavy soils, fed to stock in yards, the dung being returned to the fields. The barley was undersown with red clover and rye-grass, or red clover alone, or sainfoin and trefoil with clover and grass. The seeds would yield hay next year, then the land was grazed before ploughing in autumn for wheat in the fourth year.

Thomas Coke, later Earl of Leicester, used Townshend's four-course rotation at Holkham (Nf) (1776), but reinforced by heavy marling. He grew large quantities of swedes and fed them to Southdown sheep and Devon cattle. His tenancies were based on using his methods, and he gave long leases and built fine farmhouses and buildings. This proved commercially very successful, and many independent farmers sold out to the local landowner and ran their farms as tenants with capital.

Many "model" farms were built in this century and the 19th, such as the two in Windsor Great Park by George III.

New crops included mangolds, grown for cattle food in southern England, cabbages, from the 1660s, kohl rabi, 1767, rape for oil and fodder, and hops in the south-east; potatoes were now grown for human consumption. Wheat yields increased.

Much effort was devoted to improving the breeds of livestock, such as Robert Bakewell's very fat Dishley sheep, developed from the Leicester (1760–95), cattle – shorthorns, Devons, Herefords, and Jerseys, pigs, eg the Essex Saddleback (by *c* 1830) and the Yorkshire (Large White), by 1835, horses – Suffolks, poultry – Dorkings and Hamburgs, and ducks – Muscovy and Aylesbury.

Arthur Young wrote in the late 18th century of new ideas in all areas. Communication of these ideas between farmers was furthered by the foundation of agricultural societies, trials, and shows.

Agriculture and the Industrial Revolution

Here it may be mentioned that several economic historians, including Paul Bairoch and E L Jones, consider that England's priority in the Industrial Revolution was largely, if not mainly, due to the advances in agriculture of the previous 50 years. Without this prior development the Industrial Revolution would not have happened as early as it did (*c* 1760), as the experience of other European countries and of America shows.

Paul Bairoch's brilliant analysis proceeds on the following lines. Agriculture was forced to develop, by the end of the 17th century, to meet the increase in population. That the level of production steadily increased is partly shown by the decrease in years of famine: there were twelve per century up to 1600, four in the 17th century, five in the 18th century, and one (1812) in the 19th century. By 1750 surpluses of agricultural products existed, and England became known as "the granary of Europe", even though population had increased by 5–7% since 1700. England, in its drive for new and improved methods, benefited from contacts with and actual immigration from the Low Countries. All this took place against a reduction in the population engaged in agriculture (75% in 1688, 26% in 1841).

There is in fact a direct relationship between the levels of productivity in agriculture and development in industry. A low level of agricultural productivity (such as that before the 1660s) was an obstacle to expansion in the industrial sector, for industrial expansion presupposes (at least in its early stages) an increase in its working population and an equivalent reduction in the agricultural working population. This latter would, however, have meant a fall in agricultural products and undernourishment and fewer resources in both sectors (and reduced sales of industrial products). The advantages of importing food in exchange for surplus industrial products would be nullified by the high cost of transport; indeed, before the 18th century less than 1% of cereal production went into international trade and it was not until after 1840 that England imported an appreciable part of her foodstuffs. A real network of exchange needed most of Europe to be industrial. So, if international trade were to solve the problem, there had to be a significant and permanent rise in agricultural activity. Thus the rise in agricultural productivity in England was the main cause of the impulse towards industrialisation; but it was also the main limiting factor for industrial progress. Until transport costs were significantly lowered, industrial productivity exceeded that of agricultural countries, and countries of recent European settlement developed their agriculture. English farmers met the demands of the growing industrial society by turning from the arable-livestock high farming in favour of grazing, dairying, and market gardening. So England moved from insignificant wheat imports in 1840 to almost total dependence on imports after 1880 (with a corresponding agricultural depression; see below). It was population pressures in England during the agricultural and industrial revolutions which produced the emigration to, and the pioneering development of, the USA which in turn enabled the USA to flood the UK with wheat after 1870, when transport costs were low enough. In one sense indeed, as Ralph Whitlock wryly remarks, the Great Depression can be seen as a direct result of the Corn Laws (see below).

Enormous increases in population took place while these events were going on: from 1630 to 1740 population in England increased by 8–10%; from 1740 to 1850 by over 150%. Medical advances after 1760 were one cause of this, but the main cause was the increase in food resources resulting from the agricultural changes in the first half of the 18th century, which overcame the risk of recurrent famines and also led to a greatly increased demand for manufactured goods. Production per agricultural worker rose by about 100% from 1700 to 1800; but one

can only eat so much, and in the event surpluses increased. Much of the profits were spent on clothing (with increased imports of cotton), which immensely stimulated the textile industry and with it the iron and steel industry, required to provide the machinery for the new (Blake's "dark satanic") mills which sprang up in the textile areas after 1760. Agriculture itself demanded more iron implements. As a footnote, the capital and entrepreneurs needed by these growing industries came largely from agriculture.

All in all, Paul Bairoch makes an overwhelming case for the thesis that agricultural development provided a crucial stimulus and a causal link for the Industrial Revolution.

The 19th century

THE CORN LAWS

From 1663 Acts were passed imposing duties on foreign wheat when the price fell below a stated amount, and providing for export bounties to encourage wheat exports. The Napoleonic Wars (1793–1815) interfered with the import of corn, and bad harvests made this worse. The price of wheat rose but farm wages did not. There was famine in 1812.

In 1815 a Corn Law was passed to protect British agriculture in this situation: the import of corn was prohibited until the price rose to an average of 80 shillings (£4) a quarter for wheat. In 1828 this was replaced by a sliding scale – as the price rose, duties increased.

The high corn prices benefited the landowners and large farmers, who consolidated their lands, but the labourers suffered. In 1795 (a famine year), at Speenhamland in Berkshire, the magistrates decided to supplement the wages paid by the local farmers out of the rates. The amount of the subsidy depended on the price of corn and the size of the labourer's family. This system was widely adopted by parishes all over the southern half of England – the Enclosure counties – but was not so common in the north. The farmers used the system to their advantage. Wages were kept low, and only key workers were retained all the year; the rest were employed seasonally and went on the rates in the winter, unless they could get work threshing (see 9). When threshing machines came in even this was denied them, one result

9 *Threshing with flails. This was seasonal work, which provided an occupation (a hard one) for many men in the winter. The introduction of threshing machines caused unemployment, and led to the farm workers' riots of 1830.*

being the riots of 1830. But many workers found the situation intolerable and left the countryside for the growing industrial towns, or emigrated. Their success overseas came to fruition in the 1870s.

The Irish famine of 1845–6, caused by the failure of the potato harvests, at last convinced the Government that corn must be imported without the burden of a heavy duty, and the Corn Laws were repealed in 1846. This action effectively ended the domination of the landed gentry, and was followed by 30 years of great prosperity for farming. By 1851, half the population lived in the towns, and only improvements in agricultural techniques and output enabled the urban population to be fed. But the countryside was overpopulated, and hardship was still general.

VICTORIAN HIGH FARMING

This is the period of Victorian High Farming, a period of high input of capital and labour and high returns. It was characterised by better breeds of stock and crops, the use of fertilisers, both natural and artificial, and much new machinery. Steam power came into its own. Mixed farming became general, and livestock were included in the rotations. Clay lands and wetter lands were drained, and deep ploughing was practised. The agricultural societies, national and local, were increasingly influential, and their annual and specialised shows were important foci of advance. The Bath and West of England was founded in 1777 and the Royal Agricultural Society in 1839, growing out of the Smithfield Club (1798) – the Royal Show is still held annually; in Scotland the Highland Agricultural Society was founded in 1784. A survey such as G E Fussell's *The Farmer's Tools* (1952) gives a good idea of the proliferation of trials and contests of machinery.

Science was now increasingly applied to agriculture and during the 20th century has become an essential part of the scene, under the aegis not only of the official Agricultural Research Council but also of industrial and commercial firms. The ARC runs institutions for research into, for example, animal diseases, animal genetics, poultry, weed, food, and meat; there are also grant-aided establishments (administered by the ARC in England and Wales, and the Department of Agriculture and Fisheries in Scotland), including distinguished centres such as Long Ashton, East Malling (apples), Pirbright (animal viruses), Rothamsted (soils, crops, etc), Shinfield (dairying), Wrest Park

(agricultural engineering), and Penicuik (hill farming). The Ministry of Agriculture also provides a veterinary research and inspection service and an agricultural development and advice service.

The demand for training has led to agriculture, horticulture, and forestry being taught at several universities, including Reading, Oxford, and Wye College (University of London). At a more practical level are colleges such as Cirencester, Harper Adams, Aberdeen, and Edinburgh, and the county colleges like Sparsholt (Ha) and Merrist Wood (Sy).

As has been said above, the landowners and farmers prospered in the mid 19th century; indeed, many of the yeoman farmers, and their wives, adopted social pretensions, such as a carriage, a piano, and a maid, and did little work themselves. The building of "model" cottages on many estates sometimes reflected a sense of guilt at the condition of the workers under all this conspicuous prosperity; these cottages – by no means universal – were indeed an improvement in living conditions for some, but did little to alleviate the grinding penury of most of the workers.

THE CONDITIONS OF THE WORKERS

Economic and social historians have laid much emphasis on the appalling conditions of the workers, both rural and urban, in the 19th century, which bring a lasting shame on the nation. A vivid first-hand account, charged with emotion, is that by Richard Heath in *The English Peasant* (edited by Keith Dockray as *The Victorian Peasant* (Alan Sutton, 1989)); and a balanced and well-nourished account is Pamela Horn's *Labouring Life in the Victorian Countryside* (Alan Sutton, 1976). It has to be accepted, as a report (by James Fraser) in 1867 says, that "the majority of cottages that exist in rural parishes are deficient in almost every requisite that should constitute a home for a Christian family in a civilised community." Diet, clothing, and sanitation were in general poor. The extremes of wealth and poverty were remarked on by many observers, including William Cobbett in his *Rural Rides* (1820s).

In the 1790s wages in Hampshire and Dorset were 7–9 shillings a week (one shilling = 5p, but no real comparison can be made). By the mid 19th century they were still only 7–8 shillings in the south, but 12–13 shillings in the north (Cheshire/Lancashire), the latter being influenced by the wages of urban workers, which for most of the century were more than twice those of rural workers. Wages rose, with the prosperity of High Farming, in the early 1850s and remained static until the early 1870s, when they rose again and stayed high till the disastrous harvest of 1879. They were low in the 1880s but then rose again, and by 1902 they stood at 50% above the level of 1850. In 1900 wages were 16–17 shillings per week in high wage areas, some 12 shillings a week in low wage counties, and about 14 shillings elsewhere. The worker could also count on about £5 extra, or even more, at harvest time, and his wife and children supplemented his income by other work – washing, mending, domestic crafts, bird-scaring, animal-minding, etc. But a family total of £1 a week could rarely be exceeded. Skilled men would earn a little more. Bad weather and illness meant loss of pay, and some farmers paid less in winter, when shorter hours were worked. Some farmers gave beer or cider instead of part of the normal wage, and some gave coal or food, to be paid for out of wages in instalments. These practices became illegal after the Truck Act of 1887. Prices were lower in the 1880s and 1890s, so more could be bought, and the use of friendly and benefit societies became more general. The classic account of cottage life in the 1880s, in north Oxfordshire, is Flora Thompson's *Lark Rise to Candleford*.

The standard of living of the artisans and shopkeepers, and of the vast numbers of domestic servants, was in general much higher than that of the farm labourers, although far below that of the farmers and minor gentry.

The relative isolation of the farm worker, together with the system of tied cottages, made it very difficult for concerted action to be taken to improve these conditions. An attempt to form a Union at Tolpuddle (Do) in 1833–4 was decisively suppressed. Fresh attempts were made in the mid 1860s but only succeeded, under the indefatigable efforts of Joseph Arch, in 1872. Now the National Farmers' Union is solidly established, and has great political influence.

THE GREAT DEPRESSION

After the prosperity of High Farming in the 1850s and 1860s, British farming took a sudden turn for the worse, a state which has become known as the Great Depression. It is difficult to overestimate the traumatic nature and effects of this phenomenon. It meant a major reorientation of British agriculture. Throughout the 1870s there were bad harvests, and 1879 was a disastrous year. The continued rise in population had led to a growing volume of corn imports in the 1860s,

but from about 1872 the trickle became a flood as the colonies – the USA, Canada, and Australia – found themselves able, with steam ships instead of sail and lower transport costs, to send to Britain huge quantities of grain and other farm products. From 1877 refrigeration enabled meat to be brought from Argentina as well. On top of all this, old and unprofitable farming methods and conservative habits of mind in the farming community combined to devastate the rural economy.

The full facts can be read in works such as P J Perry: *British Farming in the Great Depression 1870–1914* (David & Charles 1974), but it may be useful to fill out the picture a little here. Agriculture had accounted for 20% of the GNP in the late 1850s, but only 6% in the late 1890s; it employed over a fifth of the population in 1851 (over 1 million), but less than a tenth in 1901 (under 700,000). Between 1875 and 1882 there were no fewer than six bad years – cool summers in the 1870s, dry in the 1880s and 1890s. Cattle and sheep diseases were rife; in 1865–6 a cattle plague in urban dairies led to farmers sending liquid milk, as well as butter and cheese, by rail to the towns, a trade which continued until World War II. The cheap imports led to a sharp fall in wheat and wool prices – by a half from the early 1870s to the mid 1880s, and cattle and sheep prices by a quarter to a third. Farmers tried to maintain their standard of living; they reduced their arable and livestock in favour of grazing (fattening cattle), dairying, fruit and market gardening, and poultry. These changes led to modifications in buildings and equipment.

In general, lowland England was most affected. The Highland Zone bred the livestock to sell to the lowland feeder and fattener, and some Scots and Welsh migrated to south-east England for that purpose. Landlords also suffered, as their tenant farmers (nearly 90% of all farmers) could no longer pay an economic rent. Tenants left the land or emigrated. The class gap widened in these years.

Bad years continued; some wet years led to outbreaks of liver fluke (1885) and root failure (1887). The depression entered a second phase in the 1890s, with droughts in four years of that decade. The situation was only retrieved, and that only temporarily, by the demand for the maximum of home-grown food during the 1914–18 war.

The 20th century

THE TWO WORLD WARS AND THE INTERWAR PERIOD

World War I, of course, meant drastic changes in an agricultural industry unprepared for war. In 1914 Britain was only producing one-third of the food needed by the 45 million population. Although a great deal of food got through the submarine blockade, radical measures were essential at home. In 1916 War Agricultural Executive Committees were set up to organise the industry. Nearly three million extra acres were brought under the plough, much of this former pasture, waste, and marginal land. Cattle and sheep increased. A quarter of a million women were used on the land. "Digging for Victory" included large areas of allotments in urban areas. These efforts were backed up by a minimum price for wheat, no rent increases for farmers, and minimum wages for workers.

But after the war a rapid decline set in. From 1920 prices slumped and most of the new arable reverted to pasture. The Government adopted a *laisser-faire* policy. The Norfolk four-course High Farming system collapsed; sheep disappeared from central and southern England. Land prices fell drastically; rabbits infested everywhere.

Against this there was increasing mechanisation, some legislation to improve conditions (such as the encouragement of beet sugar production in eastern England in 1925), the revival of ley farming (pioneered by Sir George Stapledon in 1919) and alternate husbandry, and research and experiment into fertilisers, both organic and "artificial". But the decline continued, and reached its lowest ebb from 1929 to 1932. In 1932 the statutory farm wage was 10 pence (4 new pence) an hour, or about 40 shillings (£2) a week.

After 1931 Government encouragement became more active, with subsidies, grants, quotas and tariffs, and marketing boards (eg for eggs and milk). Imports were restricted (1933). An Agricultural Wages Board was set up, and the Ministry of Agriculture provided expert advice to farmers. Regional colleges of agriculture were established. Attention was given to animal health and nutrition. Friesian cattle gradually reached an ascendancy over other breeds.

In spite of all this, British farming entered World War II in 1939 derelict and under-capitalised. Again, only 30% of Britain's food was produced at home. There were 30% fewer agricultural workers than in 1914; arable acreage was less by 25%, or 4 million acres (1.6m ha);

the total agricultural area had fallen by 2.5 million acres (1m ha), mostly to urban growth. Somewhat similar steps were taken to those in 1914: grants and subsidies (for ploughing-up and draining), more guaranteed prices, more machinery and fertilisers, and the use of women on the land (a Women's Land Army of some 200,000).

During the war arable increased by 6.4 million acres, and food imports were cut by two-thirds. C S Orwin's farm economics were having a positive effect. The traditional methods, such as the use of horses, still prevalent in the 1930s, gave way to yet more mechanisation. Electricity and piped water spread throughout the countryside.

The years after 1945 were a turning point to a more solidly-based prosperity, and farming did not decline as it had in 1815 and 1920. Farmers were still encouraged to grow more crops, with assured markets and guaranteed prices, fixed under annual price reviews. New techniques became available, new machinery, pesticides and fertilisers, and new methods of mass production. New crops included comfrey and sunflowers, and oilseed rape was widely grown. "Agribusiness" involved monocultures, large machines, and genetic engineering, which changed the face of much of British farming. The number of owner-occupiers has been increasing since the 1920s, although institutional owners of large estates prefer tenants. The number of farm workers has declined, in line with increasing mechanisation.

POST-WAR DEVELOPMENTS – AGRIBUSINESS

Agriculture since the War has taken a new direction, of a magnitude and speed that may well justify the term "Agricultural Revolution", even if the first, in the 18th century, did not. In many areas the countryside has a new look. Indeed, in some areas the Enclosure landscape itself has been superseded, as hedges have been removed and the landscape has entered another phase.

This has come about as a result of a radical change in the methods and orientation of farming. Farming has now become almost wholly dependent on chemicals (pesticides and fertilisers), "factory" farming (called in the trade "controlled environment"), and monocultures. Food production, in fact, is now only one component in a chain, the other elements of which are finance, chemicals, machinery, processing, packaging, distribution, marketing, sales, and advertising. The products are standardised by means of additives. The farmer has to produce what is required, to a determined standard, set methods, and within a timescale. This food chain (a different thing from that in the natural world) is a continuous process, and one in which the farmer has lost much of his freedom of action. It also places the smaller farmers at a disadvantage: the cost of the modern computerised machinery, which includes milking equipment and battery ranges as well as combine harvesters, is very high, and needs a certain minimum turnover to make it viable. Scientific stock-breeding is also part of agribusiness; a dairy farmer frequently has a considerable trade in pedigree cattle, bred by artificial insemination. And during the 1980s advanced techniques such as biotechnology and genetic engineering were being developed. Irradiation of foods, to control bacteria and extend shelf-life, is now being allowed in the UK. The influence of agribusiness is very pervasive. The food production chain affects diet, consumer choice, and public accountability, and increases change in rural areas. Contracts with farmers enable agribusiness to avoid land purchases, employment of managers and labour, risks of weather and disease, etc. Non-agricultural factors control agriculture.

All this has had a marked effect on the land, and on rural life. The new farming methods require fewer men to operate them, and this, coupled with the "colonisation" of villages by urban incomers – commuters, the retired, and second home owners – has changed rural life beyond recall

All these factors, some of which predate the War, have led to a reduction of the agricultural work force and a reduction of land under farming. From 1945 to 1975 the net loss of land from farming was 39,250 acres (15,700 ha) per annum in England and Wales, and 5,000 acres (2,000) ha in Scotland. The demand for housing and other non-agricultural purposes has increased, and much of this will have to be met from greenfield sites, since the scope for infilling is limited. It has been estimated that by AD 2000 as much as 14% of the land area may be urbanised, as against c 10% in 1985. The average farm size in 1985 was three times what it was in 1946, but the labour force (175,000 full-time males) is only a third of what it was in 1946. As Howard Newby and others have pointed out, farming in the Second Agricultural Revolution is no longer tied to the seasons. A harvest that once could have taken weeks can now be gathered in hours by a computerised combine harvester. Agribusiness is geared to profit, not directly to the welfare and health of the consumer, and some of its methods

are short on ethics. Newby makes the point that the "improving" farming of the late 17th and early 18th centuries – the First Agricultural Revolution – was similarly geared to profit. What has changed is not the motivation but the tools.

The size of farm required for full agribusiness has doubled in each decade since the War. To maximise profits, production has been concentrated and mixed farming has given way to monoculture, though horticulture, dairying, and sheep are still within the reach of a small, family-run farm.

Agribusiness controls only 10% of the farms, but accounts for 50% of the production – arable and intensive livestock. There is, however, little direct competition between agribusiness and the small farmer, who may survive indefinitely, particularly in less favoured areas, in spite of official policy which favours the big interests. The European Common Agricultural Policy favours the small farmer, and seeks to develop rural life as well; thus opposition to the CAP will only favour agribusiness and further marginalise the small farmer.

THE CURRENT POSITION

Only 3% of the population is now engaged in farming. Mechanisation has greatly increased. In 1939 some 50,000 tractors were in use, in 1945 some 250,000, and by 1988 there were 518,000 (the latest figure available). Of the 60m (24m ha) acres total area of the UK (against France's 135m (54m ha)), 10m (4m ha) is urbanised and non-agricultural (France 10m), 5m (2m ha) forested (France 35m (14m ha)), 17m (6.8m ha) rough grazing (France 10m), and 30m (12m ha) agricultural (France 80m (32m ha)).

The nature of land tenure has changed over the centuries, and continues to do so. Up to 1750 the rural population consisted (broadly) of two classes: landlords and peasants. From 1750 to c 1900 there were three classes: landowners, tenant farmers, and landless labourers. Since about 1900 the pattern has been changing to owner-occupying farmers and farm workers, accelerated by the massive breaking up of estates after World War I. In 1939, 65% of the land was held on a landlord/tenant system, but in 1984 only 36%. Since 1945 there has also been the addition of ex-urban newcomers to the countryside.

In spite of, or perhaps partly because of, all this, organic farming is on the increase, responding to public pressures in favour of a "green" environment. European Union policy has also had a direct effect on

British farming. Various attempts to reduce over-production (the butter and beef "mountains" and the wine "lake") have led to the milk and beef quotas of 1984, which restricted output Europe-wide. This resulted in some farming land being unused, and this coincided with a growing demand for land for housing, industry, roads, and recreational amenities. In 1988 the Government launched its "setaside" scheme, under which a subsidy is paid to farmers for earmarking land for non-agricultural diversification, including the planting of broad-leaved trees. Some ten million acres (4m ha) are involved, or 1.5% of the total land farmed.

There have been increasing signs of downturn in agriculture since about 1979, and during the last few years (from *c* 1985) this has become a full recession, with bankruptcies and lay-offs.

FIELD SYSTEMS

Pre-Saxon field systems

By no means all the visible traces of early fields and farms are medieval; indeed, particularly in upland country, they are just as, if not more, likely to date from Roman times, the Iron Age, or even earlier. Here at the outset it is necessary to say that prehistoric peoples did not settle exclusively, or even mainly, on the higher or lighter soils, as was for so long assumed. They lived everywhere, and it may well be that the uplands were always marginal land. C C Taylor has pointed out that, whereas settlement on the uplands can often be traced, elsewhere, in valleys, plains, or heavier land, settlement has been largely or wholly destroyed by later occupation. He divides the country into a Zone of Survival and a Zone of Destruction, which are perhaps more important for the interpretation of the remains than Fox's old distinction between Highland and Lowland Zones. And even in the uplands, as Bowen and Fowler showed for Fyfield and Overton Downs (Wi), there is medieval cultivation overlying the Celtic and Romano-British fields and farms.

It has only recently been realised that the Iron Age and Roman patterns of settlement were very complete, from isolated farms and hamlets to villages, minor towns, and major towns. Yet the only area where a near-complete pattern can be seen is the Fens (eg at Cottenham (Ca)).

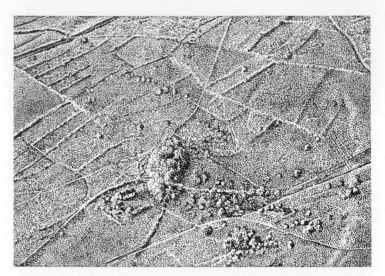

10 *Prehistoric and Romano-British fields. The squarish irregular fields (marked by banks and lynchets) on the right are prehistoric; the narrow rectangular ones on the left are Roman.*

All this said, it is the uplands which provide most of the evidence for pre-Saxon agriculture. The best-known remains are the networks of low banks, enclosing small squarish or rectangular areas, often broken by lanes between long banks and by clusters of mounds or enclosures of distinctive shape (eg the "banjo" enclosure, often associated with Roman villas). These are the so-called "Celtic" fields (see **10**), farm systems dating from the Neolithic to the end of the Roman period. Indeed, the Saxons saw them in use when they came. The banks are called *lynchets*, which are merely the effect of earth moving down a slope to the bottom of the field and piling up there. Side banks may have been made, and in rocky country the banks may represent stone walls or stone and turf, now decayed. The clusters of mounds are the ruins of the farm houses and buildings, often circular, timber-framed, and thatched. There may be ponds and special corrals for cattle in pastoral country. There are groups of these farms all over the chalklands of Wessex and Sussex and in the north of England (as at Grassington in Wharfedale (NY)). Among these, and sometimes at first glance associated with them, are the strip lynchets, but wherever these have been tested they are later than the Celtic fields and should as a general rule be regarded as medieval (they are described below). There are also linear earthworks, long banks with ditch alongside, which, if complete, could enclose larger areas than the fields, even vast tracts of country. These were the enclosures of cattle or sheep runs, and some may have been boundaries of farms, estates of Roman villas, imperial estates, or even land divisions.

Whereas pre-Roman fields are usually squarish, Roman fields are often rectangular as well. This reflects the use of a heavier plough. Derrick Riley (*Current Archaeology* 66, 1979) has noted through air photography groups of fields and settlements on the Bunter sandstone between Nottingham and Doncaster. These fields are in long strips, typically *c* 100m wide, running east–west. Short cross-ditches cut the strips into fields of up to 3 ha in size, forming a pattern resembling *brickwork* or *ladders*. Among the field boundaries are frequent rectangular enclosures, some isolated, others in groups of ten or more. They may have been used for some form of stock-rearing rather than for arable, but this point is undecided. They are dated by pottery to the middle or late Roman period. There are good examples between Blyth and Retford (No), eg Barnby Moor.

Intensive surveys by Andrew Fleming have elucidated extensive systems of field boundaries on Dartmoor, the *reaves* (see *Proceedings of the Prehistoric Society* 44, 1978 and 49, 1983). These date from the Bronze Age (*c* 1600–1300 BC), and reflect the territorial arrangements of several communities living round the edge of the moor. They are coherent enough to suggest distribution of the land by agreement. The reaves, originally stone walls, perhaps surmounted by hedges, but now in various stages of decay, are of three types: "watershed reaves", dividing each valley, presumably the territory of a community, from the next; "contour reaves", dividing lower-lying land from the high moors, which might have been common grazing; and "parallel reaves", typically about 100yd (90m) apart, within which were the actual farms, with the long strips between them subdivided irregularly by cross-reaves. There are extensive groups of such reaves; the Dartmeet system on Holne Moor is a good example. There are also pre-reave boundaries on Dartmoor, and indications that somewhat similar systems existed also in lowland areas. For instance, Oliver Rackham points to a system of small irregular fields divided into roughly equal blocks in "The Saints", a group of twelve villages in Suffolk, which could represent Bronze Age farming units (*The History of the Countryside*, 1986).

In Devon and Cornwall, Herefordshire, and other former Celtic lands, there are patterns of small irregular fields bounded by stone walls which may well represent Iron Age farms (eg Babeny, Dartmoor, and Bosigran,

Zennor). At Pendeen in Penwith (Co), some walls have been shown to form part of an Iron Age settlement; they were massive enough to contain a fogou, store-cupboards, and a storage pit datable to that period. Some of these farms may have been continuously occupied since the Iron Age, while some may have been abandoned and reoccupied in medieval times, it not being worth the trouble of removing the old walls. Another kind of case is shown at Cadbury (Dv); this parish is a fossilised territory of a Celtic (Dumnonian) hillfort, with its central shrine (replaced by a church dedicated to St Michael, a favourite saint for hilltops), five hamlets, twelve farmsteads, and a system of connecting lanes and irregular fields (see W G Hoskins: *Provincial England* (1963) and *Fieldwork in Local History* (1967)).

Traces of Roman land planning – grids of fields and access lanes, *centuriation* – survive in a few places, such as in the regular fields at Ripe (Sx), north-west Norfolk (Holme-next-the-Sea), or the Kentish "yokes". That other examples remain to be found is shown by a survey in 1975 of the Leatherhead–Ashtead area of Surrey, which revealed the apparent remains of a field system consisting of six roughly regular 2,300ft squares, avoided to a striking degree by the medieval roads, boundaries, and land units, and possibly connected with the Ashstead Roman villa. There is also a less rigorous form of centuriation. South-east Essex is covered with a close network of roads and hedges, unmistakably planned, which in some places antedate Roman roads. A very complete example is at Dengie, where there is an uninterrupted area of square and rectangular fields.

Most of the Roman villas had already fallen into ruin before the Saxons came; but it is not impossible that a few survived or that their fields and boundaries influenced later patterns. The recent aerial surveys in northern France by R Agache point to this, and there are suggestive cases in England like Woodchester (Gl), where the manor house, church, and a Roman villa lie close together. The villages and farms of humbler people seem to have survived better. Much native agriculture must have still been going on at the Saxon settlements, and much seems to have survived for a century or two. Good land was probably taken first, although even here there are pointers that the Saxons fitted into the earlier pattern in some areas. In the hills and marginal lands the natives could survive longer, until Saxon population pressure overtook them. At first this land would be shared, and whole villages survived to be assimilated later. A good example is Ashmore (Do), where the situation on a hill and the large round pond, which is the focus of the village (the church being secondary and off-centre), have all the marks of a Celtic origin (see H C Bowen: *Ancient Fields* (British Association, 1961) and Christopher Taylor: *Fields in the English Landscape* (Dent 1975); the subject is of course touched on in a large number of books on archaeology or air photography).

Pre-enclosure field systems

A traditional view of the agricultural systems of Britain up to the 18th century, which is still echoed in many textbooks, sees two contrasting systems, the *open fields* in the Lowland Zone, and particularly in the English Midlands, and the *infield-outfield* in the Highland Zone. This view largely derived from the important work of F Seebohm: *The English Village Community* (1883) and was reemphasised by C S and C S Orwin in *The Open Fields* (1938). The implication was that the open field system was introduced by the Anglo-Saxons, and replaced an earlier "Celtic" system. That the reality was not only more complicated than this but actually different was suggested by H L Gray in *English Field Systems* (1915) – although his view was contested by the Orwins – and modern research, led by students of agrarian history like Joan Thirsk, has in important aspects borne him out. The new concepts are set out in *Studies of Field Systems in the British Isles* (1973), edited by A R H Baker and R A Butlin.

But it is still necessary to visualise the two concepts in simple terms before local variations can be understood. It must be stressed that the following description is extremely schematic.

OPEN FIELD SYSTEM

Lowland Zone villages had near them mostly three very large fields, each about 600 acres; these were used for winter corn, spring corn, and fallow, in rotation. Where there were only two such fields, on slightly higher ground, one would be for winter corn and the other fallow. In other areas there could be four or even more fields. The rest of the village land was divided into meadow, along the stream, for hay for winter feeding of stock, common pasture, and woodland and waste, which provided timber for building, firewood, forage for pigs, game, berries and nuts, turf, manorial fishponds, etc. It was in the waste that colonisation of new land had to take place, and enclosed farms (assarts) came to be found in it.

The open fields were divided into *selions*, narrow bands of normally half an acre (220yd long by 11yd wide), but ranging from a quarter to half an acre in practice. These selions, separated by shallow trenches, give rise to the familiar *ridge and furrow* which can still be seen in former open field country. The selions were bunched in pairs (one acre) or larger numbers to give *strips*. An acre was in theory the amount of land which could be ploughed by an ox-team in one day; but in practice the amount which could be ploughed in a day varied with the nature of the land, and many strips were only about half an acre or even less. In any case the standard acre only became general in the 19th century. The strips were bundled together in groups called *furlongs*, and these bundles of strips can still be seen in many parts of the lowlands, particularly from the air. The selions in adjacent furlongs go in different directions, and the furlongs are obviously sub-units in the open fields. The selions often run in a sinuous line, a reversed S, which is due to the ox-team veering out to make its turn at the end. Odd-shaped bundles of selions could sometimes be left between furlongs, called *gores* or *butts*. The strips were divided by baulks of empty land. Baulks on the edges of furlongs have sometimes become lanes, which accounts for the zig-zag course of many country roads (a useful detailed description is given by Oliver Rackham in *The History of the Countryside* (Dent 1986)).

Each strip was cultivated by one farmer, and each man had several strips, scattered all over the fields, so that all had a share of good, bad, and indifferent land. The meadow was divided into temporary strips by fences; the pasture and waste were not divided, but all had specified rights in them. The farmers' animals were allowed to graze all the strips after every harvest and also in the fallow year. The number of strips in a furlong varied with the local farming pattern, the population of the village, the soil, and social reasons; the size and shape of the furlong could also vary if it was based on earlier land divisions such as Roman fields, which could be rectangular, long, or square, though there was a tendency towards compact, squarish parcels of land. The open fields were usually fenced or hedged, and sometimes the furlongs were also. The assarts, or intakes from the forest, were small and irregular, and averaged only about a quarter of a hectare.

Medieval strips

Medieval strips can be easily recognised as long, low, continuous parallel ridges across the modern fields; ploughing was done away from the neighbouring strip, so in the course of time the centre of each strip would stand some two feet or more higher than the outside. When the fields were enclosed (see below), the new hedges usually followed the edges of furlongs, so that the shape of the original field can still be seen. A good idea of this "ridge and furrow" landscape can be got from the London to Birmingham railway. There are still large areas of ridge and furrow, frequently punctuated by deserted villages, in Warwickshire, Leicestershire, and Northamptonshire. In some cases it is not always easy to make out whether the lanes, closes, house platforms, etc of a deserted village predate or postdate the surrounding ridge and furrow.

Robert F Hartley (in *The Medieval Earthworks of Rutland* (Leics Mus Service, Arch Rep 7, 1983)) points out that in early medieval times arable farming was still being expanded into surviving waste areas, whereas in late medieval times a contraction set in and pastoral

11 *Medieval cultivation terraces – Thorpe West Field, Wharfedale (NY). These broad horizontal terraces or lynchets on a hillside usually occur in flights of four or five. Some may have been made for Roman vine-growing, but most are medieval. Whether open field strips on a steep slope, or colonisation of marginal land, they usually have access ramps at the ends.*

farming became more important. The earthwork sites (eg deserted villages and ridge and furrow) owe their survival to a change of use, generally to pasture. Thus many of the surviving areas are likely to be anomalous, for it is in those areas best suited to arable cultivation that all evidence for medieval arable has been ploughed away. Recent deep ploughing has also destroyed a lot of ridge and furrow. There is another, narrower kind of ridge and furrow, caused by 19th-century ploughing of newly-enclosed land. This is of course in straight lines, and may, if superimposed on a medieval system, cut across the older strips and furlongs. In marginal areas in Scotland there are also spade ridges, the results of cultivation with hand tools.

Strip lynchets

Another very conspicuous relic of medieval agriculture is the strip lynchet or cultivation terrace (see 11). These are broad horizontal terraces on a hillside, often in flights of four or five; they can be well seen in Wessex, as at Bishopstone North (Wi), and in Wharfedale (NY). Although some may be for Romano-British vine-growing, most are medieval; they are either just open field strips on steep slopes or represent secondary colonisation of marginal land. A puzzling recent discovery is that of "long strips", up to 1,000yd (900m) long, apparently Saxon fields; their origin, reason, and use are poorly understood. Some of these were found at Wharram Percy.

Problems of studying medieval strip systems

As a result of the radical changes in farming practice in the last two or three centuries, very few medieval landscapes have survived. Perhaps the most famous survival is the open fields at Laxton (No), thanks partly to the detailed study of them by the Orwins. But here the strips have been reallocated so as to produce compact holdings, and only a few unaffected strips still remain. Braunton Great Field (Dv) again has been consolidated and partly enclosed, 85 owners "within living memory" having been reduced to 12 by 1954. On the Isle of Portland (Do) strips are in cultivation, but the original pattern has been altered by later building and quarries. Other open fields survive in some form at Axholme (Li), West Runton (Nf), and Westcote (Gl). In other places the once open fields have remained sufficiently unchanged (or at least unenclosed) as to give a good idea of what the medieval landscape was like. A particularly good area is that part of Oxfordshire between Oxford, Faringdon, and Wantage. Here villages like Cholsey or Charney Bassett are still nucleated centres in the middle of vast open stretches of field (often still called Northfield Farm etc), bounded on the horizon (up to a mile or so from the village) by belts of trees, the remains of once more extensive woodland. The whole atmosphere of this countryside is most evocative.

Study of the medieval layout of any particular place can most conveniently be begun from the Tithe Award maps of *c* 1840 or old estate maps where these exist. These usually show at least the outlines of the former open fields, if not smaller details like the furlongs or even strips, and the crofts and closes in the village itself. Another indispensable source is field names, many of which are given on the tithe maps.

INFIELD-OUTFIELD SYSTEM

Against this lowland system, the Highland Zone had one consisting of an infield, continuously cultivated land round the village, an outfield round that, in irregular patches cropped on a shifting system, pasture (land not good enough for arable), and moorland or waste (see further below).

Open fields are strictly fields with unenclosed parcels not cultivated or grazed in common; *common fields* are those over which common rules of cultivation or grazing operated. These two terms are often used indiscriminately, but this can be confusing.

There is a great variety, local and regional, in field systems. Even the "Midland" two- or three-field system is not homogeneous. Rotation was often based not on the field but on the furlong, so a three-course rotation was possible in a two-field township. Fallow and pasture could exist in arable fields. The two- or three-field system was not introduced by the Anglo-Saxons, but developed here. Regional differences are not ethnic, but are responses to local factors – soil, topography, social and economic conditions, climate, land tenure and inheritance systems, and even local decisions about who did what where. Gray saw that extensive waste (used for pasturage) could affect the two- or three-field system. Fertile valleys led to improvement, and hence to irregular field systems and early enclosure. Late reclamation of forest land, with sparse population and scattered hamlets, also gave rise to irregular field arrangements, usually a multiplicity of small open fields and numerous enclosures. The Orwins' assumption that strips were geared to a day's work by the ox-team, which led to fairly distributed strips, is not now

accepted; it implies that the whole system was imported by the Saxons ready-made, which is not now thought to be the case. The classic common field system seems in fact to represent an intensive system of farming for corn, characteristic of all well-populated villages in plains and valleys. The infield-outfield system, on the other hand, was necessarily geared to a pastoral economy. In pastoral areas, arable fields were a subsidiary element. Those fields parcelled into strips were sometimes worked in common, sometimes not.

PASTURE FARMING

Pasture farming was practised over much of highland England, and in all forests and fens in the lowlands. The open field system preceded, and was an immature stage in, the common field system, which matured in the mid 13th century, although a communal system was practised in Wessex as early as the end of the 7th century. In 12th-century Yorkshire some farms newly carved out of the waste were later divided into parcels and strips, and 200 years later emerged as villages with a common field system. Fields were partitioned among heirs, and inheritance customs were a major factor in change. As the population rose the management of a growing number of smallholdings became impracticable, and common operation developed.

ORIGINS OF STRIPS

It is no longer accepted that strips arose out of the custom of sharing ox-teams among neighbours, and that one ox contributed was repaid by one strip, allotted after ploughing. But it is agreed that newly-reclaimed land was divided into unenclosed parcels and shared among those who had joined in the clearance. This went on into the 17th century in some parts, eg Northumberland. Much assarting resulted in compact holdings also. Some of these were later subdivided into common field strips (eg in Yorkshire), as population increased and partible inheritance took effect. A third origin for strips is the fragmentation of demesne lands: eg in Kent demesne fields were directly cultivated by the lord or his agent, but frequently sown in sections with different crops. When the land ceased to be farmed by the lord, it could be leased out in parcels to different tenants; this happened in the Midlands by the late 14th century. In some areas the basis of crop rotations was the furlong (Midlands) rather than the field (Chilterns, East Anglia). Two- or three-course rotations were practised in strips from the 12th century; common pasturage may have developed later. There was much more or less complete reorganisation of field and settlement patterns in the 16th/17th centuries ("tidying up" of field arrangements and rearrangement of holdings) and such remodelling could also have taken place in the Middle Ages, and at any time from the 11th to the 18th centuries. Orderly arrangement of parcels may then derive from communal assarting, partitioning of holdings, or remodelling of holdings. Regional variations may be as much due to decisions about location or grouping of holdings, and about remodelling, as to population pressure or partible inheritance; eg in East Anglia, the Chilterns, and south-east England the holdings of individuals tended to be grouped in one part of the township rather than scattered all over.

EFFECTS OF POPULATION GROWTH ON FIELD SYSTEMS

There was a general tendency, with population growth, towards more intensive field systems. Growth was uneven, however, so local differences in farming practices arose. After, say, Domesday (1086) the rate of variety greatly increased. Before Domesday the system seems to have been based on the hamlet or small cluster of farmsteads of kinship groups, with an infield-outfield system. Near the cluster was a plot (in Baker and Butlin's words) "of intensively cultivated and manured arable, perhaps as undivided block fields or perhaps as subdivided strip fields." Other plots in the surrounding area could also be cultivated for short periods; considerable areas of pasture and woodland were also used. The importance of the arable infield has led to calling this a "one-field system", but this is misleading because of the temporarily cultivated outfields, and also because of rotations being used in the infield. The hamlets grew into villages, the infield area was enlarged, block fields were subdivided, and strip fields more intensively divided. Pasture areas were encroached on, so arable had to be used for pasture. Local solutions arose for local problems. A study in 1974 by Rex C Russell of 47 parishes in Lincolnshire, chosen from different farming regions, shows that each common field system was logically adapted to the geography of its parish, but that different parishes found different solutions. Enclosures of early date did not cross parish boundaries.

The infield-outfield system lasted in complete form until quite late in Scotland and highland England, and is now seen as the once universal system all over Britain, and in much of western and central Europe as well, from which other systems are deviant. In areas of high population pressure (lowland England) it evolved into more complex field systems by the end of the 13th century, although even in lowland England elements of the earlier system remained, such as the permanent cultivation of some plots and the intermittent cultivation of others.

Oliver Rackham associates open field with "planned countryside". It is widely associated with villages and with the larger areas of flat land, and occurs not only in Britain but in French, Germanic, Slavonic, and Greek lands as well. Rackham sees its origin in a "de-enclosure" movement in the Dark Ages, which replaced the original small-field landscape; the latter persists in the "ancient countryside", which was scarcely touched by the new movement.

REGIONAL VARIATIONS ON OPEN FIELD AND INFIELD-OUTFIELD SYSTEMS

North-west England: In the upland parts the pattern is infield-outfield-waste; in southern Lancashire and Cheshire it is likely that there was a three-field system. There was common arable in Cheshire, but less in Lancashire, Westmorland, and Cumberland. The frequency of place-names like Leasow and Ox Park denote the importance of pasture.

North-east England: Northumberland and Durham (both areas of Anglian settlement, except for Danish in the southern part of Co Durham) were a thinly populated frontier zone after the Harrying of the North in 1069, and a region of "Border tenure" under which part of the services of a tenant were military. Any extensive open and common fields had largely gone by the enclosures of 1750–1850, but were normal earlier, ie from *c* 1550. The system was a multiple-field one, having one to four fields or even more. In the upland parts of Northumberland settlements were small and arable small also; cattle, with transhumance, was the main farming, and this may have been based on a one-field system. Border tenure was abolished in the early 17th century, and rapid agrarian change followed. Medieval systems are difficult to establish, but may have grown from groups of furlongs into the 16th/17th-century pattern.

Yorkshire: The centre and east had open fields and the west, in spite of earlier views, is now seen to be not dissimilar. There were four elements: enclosures in the villages, common arable, common meadowland, and common pasture/waste. This was the standard pattern in the Wolds and the East Riding, but in the centre and west there was a large number of closes as well. Many villages, particularly in Holderness, were street or street-green, the crofts sometimes reaching the township boundaries. Several East Riding villages had a modified form of infield-outfield. There were regional differences in Yorkshire, mostly in the proportion of the township occupied by common land, in the ratios of arable, meadow, and pasture within the common land, and in the layout and mode of exploitation of the arable. An extreme form is the vast open moorland grazings (mostly for sheep) in the Pennines and the North York Moors, common to several townships. In the Middle Ages, land used in common was more widespread than in the 17th/18th century, except on monastic estates and in some remote dales like Littondale, upper Nidderdale, and Farndale. Many places had "foreland" or assarts beyond the common fields, divided into blocks (eg in the southern Vale of York). This indeed was the case over the whole of southern Yorkshire, and can be traced by place-names like *rydding, rudding, rod,* and *royd.* Three or more such names in one township are found in a solid block across the middle and south-west of the West Riding (where *royds* seem to be innumerable). This assarting took place before the 13th century; eg at Wheldrake (ER) assarts can be traced outside a turf dyke round the 350 acres of land immediately round the village, datable to 1154–1235. Ryddings were due to partible inheritance and division of the "Old Fields". Each was one or two oxgangs in size. The system is not so well attested in north and east Yorkshire. There were Old Fields at Spaunton and Appleton, but these were in the Forest of Pickering. In north and east Yorkshire extensive tracts were in cultivation in the 11th century. Many villages were reorganised after the Harrying, and regular (linear) plans and "sun division" ("solskifte") appear by the late 11th or early 12th century (eg Kilham or Southburn; but Wharram Percy and Wawne were replanned in the 14th century). So the regular field system of north-east Yorkshire looks post-conquest and may have grown up locally, as it seems earlier than the north European linear villages. This system seems to succeed a one-field system or a variant with outfield additions, which would have been obscured by the replanning. The name *scale* (*skali*) may denote summer grazing

pre-1200. The differences between these contrasts were blurred by late medieval and Tudor date, and by the 18th century there was, superficially, one system throughout Yorkshire.

West Midlands: There are two zones here, uplands in Staffordshire, north-east Warwickshire, and north-east Worcestershire, and valley/plain in the rest of the latter two counties. In this zone there are both regular and irregular "Midland" fields. This is also an area of widespread enclosure (1720–1880), which itself reflects the original extent of open arable and meadow. In the 18th century the four-field system was predominant; it can look like two-field on the ground or on maps, but field names can help here. There were even five, six, or more – up to fifteen – field units in the middle Avon valley in Warwickshire. In east Warwickshire there were mostly three fields. In Worcestershire the change from two to four fields took place before 1540, but two fields persisted in south Warwickshire till the early 18th century. By the mid 18th century four fields were dominant.

The rest of the area is a "woodland" area. In the champion (valley/plain) lands open fields occupied 70–80%, but in the woodlands the percentage was much smaller and enclosure was mostly from the waste (12th–18th centuries). The woodlands are divided into uplands ("core" systems, with little open arable, enclosed moated farmsteads, and great wastes) and lowlands, midway to the champion pattern. The basic two-field system in this area may go back to Romano-British times. H S A Fox has pointed out (1975) that there is a border zone from Somerset to Lancashire containing regular and irregular field systems coexisting well into the 14th century. South of this, in Devon, there is a flexibility contrasting strongly with the more rigid arrangements of the Midlands; and here the east Devon vales and the south Devon coastal strip show developmental and economic differences, for instance in the subdivided arable ("open") fields.

East Midlands: This area well illustrates the principle that farming develops *ad hoc* to meet local conditions; no permanent pattern was brought over by the Anglo-Saxons. Similarities are due to similar social or physical conditions. There are three groups: hill and vale, forest, and fen. The hill and vale system, 16th–18th centuries, resembles that in parts of Durham, Yorkshire, Wiltshire, and Buckinghamshire. The forest land is in well-defined patches – Sherwood, Charnwood/Leicester, Leighfield/Rockingham/Salcey/ Whittlewood. The fens are in the Isle of Axholme and in Holland/Soke.

The hill-vale country (the rest of this region) is the most densely settled, and has a uniform pattern: arable near the village; a few closes for vegetables, hemp, flax; meadows for winter hay; waste for common pasture, often with private rabbit warrens from the mid 13th century and fishponds. Breedon-on-the-Hill (Le) is typical, with four fields round the village, meadows along the river, waste and common further out (enclosed in a map of 1758); the demesne was scattered. Arable took up at least half the available land in this area, and meadow 8–15%. The average holding had one acre of meadow to 9 or 10 acres of arable (with local variations). In the Fens, in Holland, arable is small and mostly on the ridges where the villages were; the rest is in scattered parcels among the fen pastures. In Kesteven the parishes are long, narrow rectangles, with grazings and meadows at one end, arable in the middle, and heath common at the other. The forest areas had limited arable but abundant common pastures, with enclosed assarts.

Between Domesday and the 13th century some settlements came into existence while others were transformed. Fragmentation was stronger than amalgamation until the mid 14th century. The standard peasant tenement of freemen and villeins was the virgate (20–30 acres (8–12 ha) of arable and meadow) or the half-virgate, bovate, or oxgang (20 acres (8 ha) in Lincs), with common rights. Bovates varied in size, and could be altered or cut up. The Anglo-Saxons and Danes did not occupy virgin or empty land, but adapted existing estates and systems; even soke means a Celtic estate. The Celts had either single farmsteads or estates with central "mansio" and bond hamlets. Division and distribution began early, and by the end of the 12th century the two-field system was normal. After the Black Death open fields became managed in common, then in the 16th century the manor reasserted itself. Enclosure was the final answer to the continuing pressure on land, but common fields continued throughout the 16th and 17th centuries.

East Anglia: The systems here are different from the two- and three-field systems of the Midlands, except for west and central Cambridgeshire. South Cambridgeshire is transitional, and Norfolk and Suffolk are separate. These have distinctive soil divisions: the Fens in north Cambridgeshire and west Norfolk; the Broads; the sands and light loams of north Norfolk, Breckland and east Suffolk, and east Cambridgeshire – this is the "sheep-corn" country; and the strong loams in south-east

Norfolk and most of Suffolk – the "wood-pasture" country. The sheep-corn area had open arable fields and equally extensive heaths. The wood-pasture area had more wood and more enclosure, with cattle, not sheep. Enclosure of east and central Norfolk, and Suffolk, was largely completed by the 16th or early 17th century, but areas of open field survived in both counties until the Parliamentary enclosures. The system was the three-field, like the Midlands. Many medieval assarts, originally separately farmed, were brought into the common fields later. This process was most complete in the Midlands, but in East Anglia it only reached the stage of superimposing regular cropping shifts on to an irregular field pattern (by the 13th century). Breckland had infield, outfield, and brecks (heathland intakes). The tenement pattern and the lord's privileges over pasturage, which affected the land pattern, were ethnic.

Chilterns, south Midlands, and Essex: The Chilterns were a boundary between the Midland two- and three-field townships and the heavy lands to the east. The pattern in the Chilterns was linked to a gradual and piecemeal settlement. There was a preference in the whole area for intermixed strips which, later, were open to common grazing; the reason for this is not clear. The more prolonged the process of occupancy the more likely it is that new farmland was enclosed straight into individual ownership. Most of the area north of the chalk was settled by the 11th century, and arable there was held as strips in open fields. There are a few areas of late reclamation of woodland, with irregular fields. South of the chalk, early colonisation was greatest on river terraces and boulder clay plateaux in Hertfordshire and north-west Essex, by the 13th century common arable areas. The south-west Chilterns and south Essex were probably cleared directly into severalty (individual ownership). Whereas in the Midlands arable was generally in two fields, on the chalk and south of it strips were in a large number of small fields (from 12th/13th century on). It is difficult to create large unified common fields in hilly districts colonised in numerous small settlements.

The first major enclosures were made in the Midland two-field country, linked with late medieval conversion to pasture, and depopulation. South and east of the Chilterns enclosure only took place from the 16th century, and was finished off by the Parliamentary enclosures in the 19th century, for intensified farming to meet the demands of the London market. Parliamentary enclosure has redrawn much of the

Midland landscape, while on the chalk and east and south of it there has been growing uniformity of field patterns as enclosed landscapes have been opened up by the removal of hedges.

A parish conveying remarkable reminiscences of its medieval past is Charney Bassett (Bk, now Ox). This contains a small village on one side of a river crossing, with early Norman church, manor house close by (with 13th-century parts), and farms in the village streets and on the green. The rest of the parish has few houses; it consists of a wide stretch of open land, hardly interrupted by hedges, surrounded by a strip of woodland. A pre-enclosure map of the manor (of which a copy is kept at the manor house) shows three common fields surrounded by the woodland and waste; a post-enclosure map shows the new owners of the fields, but the outlines of the parish have not changed. This is still the case (although there is an isolated farm called Northfield with a fairly recent house), and one gets a clear sense of the continuity of a landscape. The whole of this rather remote countryside repays parish by parish study.

South-east England: This is a complex and diverse area, both in soils and settlement, although Kent is not seen as quite such an anomaly as it used to be. Proximity to the Continent no doubt played a part. The major contrast at Domesday in the distribution of plough-teams was between Wealden and non-Wealden areas. The eastern High Weald was densely settled, but the Low Weald, with stiff, ill-drained clay or loam, was wooded, with woods and swine pasture attached to settlements outside the Weald and with few centres of population. The South Downs and the coastal plain of Sussex were densely populated and villages were numerous, especially in the valleys and along the scarp-foot north of the Downs. The greensand was underdeveloped in 1086. There were frequent settlements in the Vale of Holmesdale and north and east of it. The Blackheath and Bagshot sands were poor, but the richer London clay had 7–11 people per square mile and about three plough-teams. The marshes were fairly well settled. The Lay Subsidy of 1334 shows several changes: the poorest areas were now the Bagshot sands and the central and western Weald, the richest north Kent from the Medway to Thanet; indeed, this was the richest part of south-east England, except for parts of the Sussex coastal plain and the Thames valley. Field systems varied greatly in all this region, often from place to place, but the pattern is only fully traceable in the 16th/17th century.

The evidence from Kent is rich for this period, with nearly 200 estate maps. There are regional variations in the size of fields, from over eleven acres in East Kent and Romney Marsh to under four acres on the Low Weald, with Holmesdale and the High Weald about halfway. The fields in the Weald are small and irregular, while those of East Kent are more rectangular. With the Kentish turn-wrest plough it was just as possible to plough squarish plots as rectangular strips. Wealden fields had strips of scrub and trees to edge them ("shaws" or "rews"), not hedges of single rows of bushes. Romney Marsh used ditches and post-rail fences. There were totally enclosed farms throughout the county. Open fields were largely confined to the north Kent lowlands and Holmesdale, often 15–20 acres (6–8 ha) only in size, and scattered among more numerous closes. These open fields were not common fields, but common meadows and pastures existed. In the Weald, ploughland was small (10 acres (4 ha)) per farm, and used mostly for fodder crops; cattle was the main emphasis. In Holmesdale the farming was mixed and based on sheep and barley. In Romney Marsh, beef and mutton were fattened and wool produced. By 1600, Kent was a county of largely enclosed, often compact, individually cultivated farms and smallholdings. Most farms were between 5 and 25 acres (2–10 ha), smaller in the Weald than in north and east Kent. Partible inheritance was abolished from 1538 to 1624.

The Kentish system of land tenure in the Middle Ages was peculiar, and was probably based on Roman centuriation. The land was divided into yokes (*juga*), rectangular areas which were fiscal units, assessed for services or rent and varying in size with the quality of the soil. There was another unit, the *logus*, with different services. Assarts (later than either) had no services, and may be identified by the names *-field*, *-land*, *-acre*, *-dene*, *-reede*, etc. The logus is of obscure origin and may be later than the yoke. Holdings were clustered, not scattered; Gillingham is a classic example of this system. Yokes were disintegrated through partitioning of holdings, subdivision of rents and services, and the ultimate commutation of the services. The yoke is a quarter of a *sulung*, and both may originally be related to plough-teams (eg a "yoke of two oxen"). The system goes back to the end of the 3rd century and is not particularly Jutish, although it has been so ascribed. It is a fiscal concept, not a given and fixed area of land and not a family holding. Gavelkind, with its associated partible inheritance, was widespread in Kent.

The Kentish systems extended, like its geography, westwards into Surrey and Sussex. The *-denn* names are almost confined to the Low Weald, and represent swine-herding in the forests, near the peripheral agricultural settlements. Although this has been assumed to be a reaction to local conditions, Jolliffe has suggested that it may be a general custom brought in by 5th-century settlers from the Rhineland. Some aspects of field systems may also be due to the integral management of the scattered estates of one owner (eg the Archbishop of Canterbury). The Archbishop's manors in Surrey are similar to those in Kent, but not, as it happens, to those in Sussex. Yokes are found in Surrey, as at Ewell. E M Yates' study of Holmesdale brings out the similarity of the parishes here to Kent: multiple open and enclosed fields associated with patterns of hamlets and isolated farmsteads, with wastes, woods, and heaths for common grazing. In the Weald, colonisation of the Low Weald was followed, early in the 13th century, by assarting of the High Weald. The mosaic of fields and farmsteads was similar to that in the Weald of Kent, as the classic study of Laughton (Sx) showed.

Gray regarded the Sussex Downs and coastal plain as the end of the Midland three-field system. But recent studies have shown this to be misleading. The three "leynes" of eg Alciston were not fields of fixed acreage but "seasons" of variable acreage. These central cores in the scarp-foot parishes were balanced by intermittently cultivated fields in the north end of the parish, like the "outfields" of Westerham etc. These outfields, for fodder crops, were part of the demesne, unlike the infields which were used for grains and sheep-folding. Common fields were not the basis of agriculture, but only one of its elements. Farms in severalty existed alongside them from the early 13th century. By the 16th century, extra-Wealden Kent and extra-Wealden Sussex had diverged; mature common fields had evolved in Sussex but not in Kent.

North Wales: The old Welsh laws, which predate the Edwardian conquest of 1283 and which no doubt go back at least to Hywel Dda (who died about 950), describe a hierarchy of land holdings, based mainly on multiples of four (eg four "acres" in a homestead, four homesteads in a "shareland", etc). The normal tenure was hereditary, and the fourth man became a proprietor. His share of the patrimony was often a personal holding of appropriated land and an undivided share of joint land. The appropriated land included a homestead and parcels of scattered land in one or more arable sharelands. The joint land was wood, pasture, and waste. Partible succession applied. There were detailed rules of inheritance, and each "lineage" had its recognised fund of land (*gwely*). "Reckoned land" was shared out among the bondmen of the township. There was also nucleal land, strips or gardens in a continuously cultivated infield. Common field cultivation can be inferred. The laws reveal a system of mixed farming organised in the main in open fields and with a degree of communal control. This began at least by the 6th century and perhaps much earlier; a customary law involving descent in nine generations came before the courts in Roman Britain in the 4th century, and must be Iron Age. There was certainly a settled Welsh organisation long before 1283.

The upland pastures were usually grazed only in summer (*hafod*), the common pastures within the townships being used in winter and Lent. At Dinorben (Dh) a multiple estate seems to represent the late Bronze Age territory of a hillfort. Bond hamlets often shrank into single home-steads; those dependent on large estates can often be identified, eg those round the old capital Aberffraw (An). The tithe maps of 1841 will often show the outlines of the old fields and estates, as at Llanynys (Dh). Enclosure was facilitated by the abolition of the traditional practices of land inheritance in the 16th century. Much of the land once cultivated is now under grass, and pasture is the main use of north Wales today.

South Wales: Before 1500 (enclosure began in the 16th century) most of the coastal lowlands of the Vale of Glamorgan, south of the Portway (A48) was champion, with common field patterns and farmsteads clustered in nucleated villages; they still are. The whole of south Wales had common arable fields divided into strips and common pasture on the hills. Strips and baulks can still be seen at Rhosili (Gower), Laugharne (Cm), and Llan-non (Cd); Breconshire has 151,000 acres of common rough grazing. But the common fields and settlements were on a smaller scale than in the English Midlands, and were also affected by the more broken landscape and by Welsh forms of land tenure. The mountain cores of the south Wales counties were largely pastoral, and only indirectly exploited by the Normans (who did affect the coastal strip, all round into Cardigan Bay and the river valleys; settlers and Anglo-Norman manorial tenure were introduced). The broken country gave rise to fields of different sizes, from large arable fields to small enclosed bundles of strips. Common arable and villages were widespread by the 13th century and, although small (as in Devon), contrast with the tenure and settlement patterns of the hilly hinterland. These go back before the Normans; eg Tidenham had common fields round its five hamlets in 956 and no doubt long before. The manorial system reached its peak in South Wales in the 13th century and declined in the 14th/15th century, but had displaced the old Welsh systems of tenure. The Marcher lordships had Englishries and Welshries, with contrasting patterns (eg at Hay and in Gower). In the hills the pattern was small arable plots and large common pastures. In the 14th century they were more densely populated than now. By the 15th century enclosed upland arable fields were more usual, farmed in severalty; by the 18th century these had mostly gone – enclosure had taken half of the common fields by the early 17th century and only a few survived (in Monmouthshire and Brecon) till the Parliamentary enclosures of the mid 19th century. Common meadows still exist at Laugharne and on Llanbethery Moor and existed until the 19th century in Cardiff itself (eg west of the Taff) and Llandaff. Hedged strips and small fields are still frequent everywhere in the south Wales lowlands. Early enclosure of meadowland can be seen from the irregular fields in the south-west parts of the Caldicot Level, near Newport, and the Wentlooge Level, near Cardiff.

Scotland: The infield-outfield system can be seen in its full development in Scotland. It is not "Celtic", as was once thought, but general in the whole of Atlantic Europe and ancestral to the two- and three-field systems. There were also survivals of archaic forms of agricultural organisation in remote parts well into the 19th, and even into the 20th century; but these are often local and late responses to conditions, and not representative of the mainland.

The infield (croft land, inbyland, mukked land) was permanently cultivated. Its area, layout, and method of cropping varied with time, place, and population density. It is not to be regarded as the core of the system but as a vital adjunct to the cattle-keeping sector. Manure for it was got from the byres and augmented by adding the thatch or turf roofs of the farmhouses and buildings, or even by humus from the hillsides. The infield was usually cropped in a one-third manured barley and two-thirds unmanured oats rotation.

The outfield varied greatly in size. Outfield lands lay in irregular patches round the settlement, and were broken up and cropped on a shifting system. The cattle were folded on them before ploughing (for oats). They were cropped for three or four years and rested for five. Infield crops were mainly food or brewing grains, and outfield crops were

primarily grown for straw, as the oats were usually poor. In some areas *haugh* or *laigh* land was also used to add to the arable (along rivers, kept in heart by silt in floods). *Brunt* land was also used – burnt-off heather. *Pasture* was just land not good enough for arable. All this (except brunt land) was often enclosed by a *head dyke*. Above or outside this were the *muir* lands, for pasture, either daily or in transhumance. The settlement was not a village in the English sense, except later in the lowlands, but a formless group of houses, a *clachan*, often on the upper edge of the infield.

The land was divided into a series of high-backed ridges, up to 6ft high and 20ft across, sinuous, with balks between and parallel to each other within any one unit of the infield or seeded outfield. Each man's ridges were dispersed, not grouped in a block. Gray's idea that the strips were fairly distributed over various types of land, and redistributed every year, cannot stand. In fact, *runrig* only means a system where any man's holding lies between those of others (tenants or owners (heritors)), though in Inverness, Arran, and the Outer Isles the strips were pooled and reallocated every three years. Much has been written about runrig, which has been assumed to be an essential part of the infield-outfield system. But recent research, by G Whittington and others, has shown that this is not the case. It is non-Celtic in origin, and since 1437 at least is associated with the Scottish Lowlands. It could there have meant simply a "run of ridges", and no periodic reallocation is inherently implied. The Scots did not need three fields: all grains were spring-sown, so two fields for grain were not needed and infield-outfield made a fallow field unnecessary. Runrig evolved in the period of the infield-outfield system; it first meant ridges running in parallel within the same agrarian unit, then it became associated with the sharing of the available land among the total number of cultivators involved, which may or may not have ensured fair distribution, and finally it also involved reallocation at regular – annual or longer – intervals.

Farm size varied greatly and several names for land units were in use, which, like the south-eastern ploughgate, could vary in size. The proportions of infield to outfield also varied on each farm, but one to three was common. There was a hierarchy of tenantry, from the proprietor to the tacksman to the tenant. Tenants could also hold from the proprietor, and subtenants from the tacksman, who developed during the 15th/16th centuries. As waste was taken in new classes developed (cottars etc), and there is much confusion in the literature. Cottars also did specialist work, like weaving, in the township. Mailers were the last class, often single men working on the estate. Infield-outfield existed over much of England also, but the divergence in Scotland seems to be due to the greater emphasis placed on arable in England, though the English system overspilled into adjacent areas of Scotland. The pattern in Scotland was flexible, as the study of the estate of Pitkellony (Pe) by B M W Third shows, though the increase in population did not call forth additions to the infield, but new settlement centres each with its own pattern. The landscape depended on the environment and on the policies of proprietors.

The *sheiling* was hill grazing used in summer only. It could be up to seven miles from the farm. The sheiling land was carefully demarcated and formed a unit complementary to the outer ring of the township's land, and as such was part of the overall pattern. The sheiling was often in two parts – good grass for milch cows and poor grazing for other animals. Not every settlement possessed a sheiling, but the system occurs throughout Scotland, not only in the Highlands but also in the Southern Uplands (especially the Lammermuirs) and the Cheviots. Transhumance, the moving of livestock to upland pastures in summer and lowland in winter, was killed not mainly by enclosure but by the introduction of potatoes and flax, which needed labour in the only period when the sheiling area could be used. The *burghs* also had infields and outfields. The infields got sold as building land, while the outfields survived as undivided common.

The early history of infield-outfield in Scotland, is obscure. It might have been accelerated by population growth in the 12th/13th centuries, by using the inner ring of land more intensively. Arable was also encouraged by the Crown at this period. In Moray, Fife, and the Lothians there are signs of only one field (developing into the two- and three-field system), and in any case there is a contrast between the arable east and the pastoral highlands (but this is not an ethnic matter). In the Lowlands the infield-outfield theme evolved into something nearer a modern concept of land use; in the Highlands and Islands the social environment led to the present *crofting* landscape pattern, with a change in the co-joint tenancy. The crofters, in occupying the transhumance and fishing sites, brought in a new field pattern – farms in a series of squared fields with dispersed settlement. This grew up during the 18th century, after the Act of 1695.

The enclosures resulted in small fields in the infield and larger ones in the outfield (Ayrshire, Galloway, Lothians, Merse, and the east coast). When enclosure was done by a landlord a more geometric

pattern emerges, and parks were laid out round the larger houses. There is no "Scottish field system", only a continually evolving pattern still being modified today.

The above account, which draws heavily on A R H Baker and R A Butlin, (eds): *Studies of Field Systems in the British Isles* (1973), shows how varied and local were the responses to the challenges of the open field system. But, in spite of the considerable effort which has been devoted to elucidating and dating its origins, there is still no general agreement on any major aspect of these. One can only say, tentatively, that although the open fields reached their "mature" form by the 13th century, it must have taken several centuries for this stage to have been reached. The process indeed could take place at any time, whenever and wherever there was sufficient population pressure.

For the discussion subsequent to Baker and Butlin (1973), see eg Robert A Dodgshon: *The Origin of British Field Systems: an Interpretation* (Academic Press 1980); Trevor Rowley in Leonard Cantor (ed): *The English Medieval Landscape* (Croom Helm 1982); Oliver Rackham: *The History of the Countryside* (Dent 1986). Much of the discussion appears in the specialist periodicals. For the field aspects, see Christopher Taylor: *Fields in the English Landscape* (Dent 1975).

The enclosures

The transition from the medieval pattern of open fields to the countryside which existed until the 1950s was brought about by the massive *enclosure* of the open fields. This took place in three stages:

1   In areas where open fields were not the normal pattern but existed as islands in the prevailing small hedged fields, they were transformed into enclosed country at an early date, eg in Devon in the 13th and 14th centuries.
2   In the open field country (particularly in the central Midlands) there was much enclosure of open fields and common pasture in the 15th and 16th centuries. This was mainly for pasture, particularly for sheep, and created many deserted villages. This enclosure was done by way of private agreements (registered in the Court of Chancery) between Lords of Manors and other owners of land, and in many cases the tenants also. The movement continued throughout the 17th century, and by 1700 half the former arable was enclosed.

3   The later 18th and early 19th century saw the final enclosure of the remaining five and a half million acres of open field land (nearly all that was left), this time by private Acts of Parliament. From 1702 to 1762, 246 Acts were passed, covering some 400,000 acres (160,000 ha). But the return to power of the Tories in 1761 and the attractions of the improved agricultural methods turned the movement into a flood, and from 1761 to 1801 over three million acres (1,200,000 ha) were enclosed, under some 2,000 Acts. From 1802 to 1844, nearly 2,000 more Acts covered a further two and a half million acres (1m ha). What was left, such as a few isolated parishes like Laxton (No) or Braunston (Dv), was swept up in a General Enclosure Act in 1845 (see **Map 7**. facing page 27).

The enclosures transformed the appearance of the country (see **12**), laying down the familiar pattern (in the areas affected) of straight ash or hawthorn hedges enclosing squarish fields, new straight roads, often with wide grassy verges, and new, usually brick-built farmsteads in the once open fields (such as Northfield Farm, Charney Bassett (Ox) or Westfield Farm, Hutton-le-Hole (NY)). In many areas the ridge and furrow of the open fields can still be seen, cut across by the enclosure field boundaries. The new consolidated estates could be organised as coherent units, with ornamental parks and tenant farms; great houses were built, and sometimes whole villages moved (eg Albury (Sy)).

Enclosure was usually done by parishes, so the field pattern and the roads may change at the parish boundary; eg fields may be at right angles to each other across the line, or roads may change width or direction or may go to the line and stop. Later medieval and 16th-century enclosure for sheep was by way of fairly large fields, of anything between 50 and 500 acres (20 to 200 ha). But these were found in the course of time to be too big and during the 17th century most were broken down into smaller units, averaging 10–20 acres (4–8 ha); a size of 16 acres (6.4 ha) is frequent. The 17th- to 19th-century enclosure

12 *Enclosure fields. These are in Yorkshires's stone wall country, an upland area of which field barns are a feature (see page 89).*

for arable or mixed farming demanded even smaller fields – 5–10 acres (2–4 ha) – on small farms, but up to 50–62 acres (20–25 ha) on large farms, broken into 10 acres (4 ha) parcels; there was a general evening up of size to 10 acres (4 ha). Contemporary farmers use fields of up to 100 acres (40 ha), but a square field of 50 acres (20 ha) is most economical to work, and the advantage of a larger size is marginal.

Enclosure deprived the peasants of their ancient rights and turned them into employees. It also speeded migration into the towns, and later into the industrial cities.

Enclosure is dealt with in most books on agricultural or economic history, but see W G Hoskins (ed): *Local History in England* (Longman 1972); Asa Briggs: *A Social History of England* (Weidenfeld & Nicolson 1994); or Ralph Whitlock: *The English Farm* (Dent 1983).

Field boundaries

Field boundaries vary according to the local material. In Britain the typical boundary in the Highland Zone is drystone walling, and in some parts stone slabs or wire or other kinds of fencing are used. The Lowland Zone is essentially a country of hedges.

The lengths of the field boundaries vary with the amount of improved farmland in each county; in Kirkcudbright there are some 7,000 miles (11,200km) of walls, while in Devon there were some 50–60,000 miles (80–96,000km) of hedges in the mid 19th century. Overall, in England and Wales, there are over three million kilometres of field boundaries for the 24.5 million acres (10m ha) of improved farmland. Of this some 65% is hedges, say 1.6 million kilometres or just under one million miles, but estimates vary and this has been regarded as too high. It would be safer to halve the figure and think of some 500,000 miles (800,000km) of hedges.

HEDGES

Hedges can originate in different ways: they may be woodland assarts, relics of old woodland vegetation managed as hedges, or hedges planted round woodland with shrubs from the wood; they may be formed from scrub growth along previously unhedged boundaries or open strips; they may have been planted as mixed hedges,

with 3–4 species or 5–6 species; or they may have been planted as single-species hedges. Some 500–600 plant species are found in hedges, but only half of these are classed as hedgerow plants. Most of these are herbs, but the important species are the trees and shrubs. These vary a lot, sometimes with the soil, sometimes with the region. Of the 20 commonest species in Warwickshire, over half are members of the *Rosaceae* (rose family); in Wiltshire, where the range of species is quite different, only a few are *Rosaceae*. The most common plant is the Common Hawthorn (*Crataegus monogyna*), which was planted as standard in enclosure hedges of the 18th and 19th centuries in the Midland and open field districts, sometimes together with trees, such as elm, oak, and ash (some 186,000 miles (300,000 km)). Hazel, unusual in these districts, is common in areas of old enclosure. South-west England has a lot of mixed hedges. Blackthorn is common on clay soils; brambles take the place of these species in the Highland Zone.

The enclosures of the 18th and 19th centuries saw huge mileages of hedges planted – some 200,000 miles (320,000km) from 1750 to 1850, as many as in the previous 500 years. This was also a period of building stone walls. Supplying the hawthorns etc for these hedges became a major industry. An enclosure hedge usually has its original row of hawthorns more or less intact. Older hedges may have coppice stools or pollard trees. Maple and dogwood may be found in Tudor hedges, but rarely in recent ones. Hazel and spindle indicate even older hedges. Hawthorn grows in most hedges except very early ones where it was not planted; elder occurs at random in hedges of any age. Trees and plants which normally grow in woodland indicate, if found in a hedge, that the hedge was once part of, or closely adjoined, an ancient wood. These include small-leaved lime, the Midland hawthorn, pimpernel, wood anemone, primrose, bluebell, and dog's mercury. Strips of woodland left along field boundaries after clearance of the rest of the wood can be seen in wooded areas such as the Weald of Sussex, where they are called shaws. Nearly all recent hedges have been planted; but hedges arise whenever land is left for a few years. Fences become hedges as a result of birds perching on them and dropping seeds.

Roman land boundaries seem to have been hedges, and some have been excavated, eg hedges of thorn at Farmoor (Ox). Anglo-Saxon hedges are recorded in the 10th century, and existed before then; some still survive. The boundaries of Saxon or medieval estates are

75

13 *Hedge-laying – the Midland method.*

less likely to be moved than those of the fields inside them, and can be very old. This applies even to the 18th/19th century enclosures, where the outside hedge had to be planted at once, leaving the hedges of the new fields to be laid down later; these could then be altered in the light of experience. Hedge management consists of *plashing* or *laying* (of which there are regional variants); slicing the stems low down, but not right through, and bending and fixing them diagonally or horizontally so that new growth rises up and fills the hedge (see **13**).

Up to about 30 years ago farming methods could be accommodated within existing field patterns. The use of large and expensive machinery, coupled with monocultures, involves, for maximum economy, much larger areas for manoeuvre. Farm enlargement has been one answer to this, and *dehedging* another. It is not easy to get a reliable figure of the extent of this; estimates vary between 10 and 20% loss in the past 30 years. But the effect is worst in the rich, level, arable lands of eastern England, where in some areas very few of the original hedges are left. Estimates have to be built up from detailed studies. Thus, in Huntingdonshire there were 71 miles (113km) of hedge in 1947, 46 miles (73km) in 1963, 20 (32) in 1965, 16 (25) in 1966,

10 (16) in 1970, and 15 (24) (a slight regeneration) in 1972. Over the country, this would represent 0.54 yards per acre, or 5,000 miles (8,000km) lost per annum for 1946–63. Another picture is set out below.

Date	Miles lost per annum	Total
1946–54	800 (1,280km)	7,200 (11,520km)
1954–62	2,400 (3,840km)	19,200 (30,720km)
1962–66	3,500 (5,600km)	14,000 (22,400km)
1966–70	2,000 (3,200km)	8,000 (12,800km)
Total	**48,400 (77,440km)**	**(10% of the total)**

Against this, in Devon, some 70% is estimated to have been lost in the past ten years.

These figures indicate that there is some slowing up in the rate of removal, and it may be that farming conditions are becoming stabilised at new levels. In other terms, the broad national picture is a 23% loss on arable land and an 8.4% loss on grassland, although in certain areas the reverse is the case; eg in Norfolk, by 1970, 7% was removed in the sheep-corn area (with an average field size of 53 acres (21.2 ha)), and 20% in the wood-pasture area (field size 10 acres (4 ha)). The ecological consequences of this process are hard to measure, but must be considerable, in terms both of the effect on wildlife and of erosion.

Hedges take up, at 6ft (2m) wide, 0.6% of a 100-acre (40 ha) field, 0.8% of such a field divided into two 50-acre fields, and 2.6% of this area divided into twenty 5-acre units. The cost and time saving with a field over 50 acres (20 ha) is marginal, and this may be a factor in the slowing down of hedge removal.

Dating hedges

It occurred to Professor W G Hoskins many years ago that an ancient boundary hedge ought to show considerable differences from modern hedges in the number of shrub species it contains, as a result of the chance intrusion of seeds carried by birds or wind or migration of trees from nearby woodland. The same idea also struck Dr M D Hooper, who made a systematic study of hedges of different known ages. When this idea was first published, in 1968, it looked as though a 100ft (30.7m) stretch of hedge carried an additional species for every 100 years of its life. But things are not quite so simple, and by 1971 Dr Hooper had evolved a more reliable formula:

age of hedge in years = 110 x number of species in a 30yd (27.6m) length
+ 30 ± 200

So a hedge with five species in a 30yd stretch is, on this basis, 580 years old, with a margin of error of 200 years, that is it dates from AD 1210 to 1610. The precise botanical explanation of this is still not entirely understood, but the correlation works and is clearly a very useful tool for the historian.

Work has continued to refine the formula. The wide variation possible may be due to climate, soil, differences in the management of hedges, or other regional factors. To test this a sample was taken in a limited area on clay on the Huntingdonshire/Northamptonshire border (see F Pollard, M D Hooper, and N W Moore: *Hedges* (Collins 1974). This gave a formula of:

age of hedge = (99 x number of species) –16, with a range of variation of 175

Thus the rule of thumb of one species for every 100 years is still near enough for practical purposes.

It is now possible to distinguish hedge boundaries of, say, Saxon estates from enclosures in the 13th-century agricultural expansion, or the latter from farming operations in the 15th- or 18th-century enclosures. In Devon over a quarter of the hedges are over 800 years old, and there was a further spate of enclosure some 700 years ago when a further quarter of the hedges were planted. Six-species hedges are infrequent, but five-species ones are again common, reflecting fluctuations in farming activity in those centuries. But of course anomalies occur; it is the general practice to plant hedges with one species only, say hawthorn or blackthorn, but on some occasions a hedge may incorporate existing trees, and there may be special practices in certain areas. Thus, when the waste areas of Shropshire were enclosed in the period from 1750 to 1850, it was the practice to plant hedges with three or four species, say hawthorn, holly, and blackthorn. Again, the date of a legal enclosure award may not be the date when the land was actually enclosed; in the Midlands an 18th-century award may merely be legalising an enclosure taken in and hedged 100 years before. Moreover, an encloser only had to plant his perimeter hedge when he got his award; he might not get around to planting the internal hedges on his land for years.

Hawthorns are useful indicators of another kind. Hedges, like houses, were made with local materials, so the species in them show what was at hand when they were laid. There are two species of hawthorn in Britain: the commonest is *Crataegus monogyna*, which has divided leaves, one style and one stone in its fruit, many small flowers, and tends to be more spiny; the other is a tree of heavy soils, *Crataegus laevigata* (the "Midland thorn"), which has entire leaves like a plum, with serrations, fewer, bigger flowers, and two or more styles and two stones to its fruits. *C monogyna* likes open country, while *C laevigata* is found mainly in woodlands on heavy clay soil. So the presence of the latter in a hedge is likely to denote the former proximity of woodland since cleared. And at some point its use was replaced by that of *C monogyna*. A clear example of this is along the Great North Road at Potterspury (Le); the old road, with its wide grass verges, was delimited by hedges containing *C laevigata*, but when the road was narrowed a new hedge was planted beside it, leaving a long-narrow strip field. The new hedge was *C monogyna*.

Recent work by Dr E Pollard at Monks Wood (Hu) has brought to light an interesting extension of Hooper's original hypothesis, the "assart hedge". Pollard suggests that if a hedge, besides containing several shrub species, also has ground plants of a woodland character (such as dog's mercury, wood anemone, or bluebell), it is a relic of a vanished wood edge, managed to form a hedge when the wood itself was assarted (cleared). This hypothesis is based on the discovery of a hedge which had been partly realigned between 1791 and 1835. In the original stretches the hedge, which contained eight, nine, and ten species in lengths taken at random (and so was some 900 years old) had such plants beneath it. The realigned sections did not have these plants. Assarting in this case, of part of Monks Wood, took place between 1612 and 1791, but the old hedge is referred to in a document of 1147 as being "put round the wood". It may be older than this, as it was a hundred boundary, and must have become assimilated into the wood in the course of time. Further examples to support Pollard's postulate are being sought, but there seems already little reason to doubt that dog's mercury in a hedge is an indicator of former woodland. Incidentally, there is documentary evidence that woods in which oxslip occurs are ancient woodlands. A very fine and easily accessible hedge, which well illustrates Hooper's principle (although it has been partly damaged and isolated by roadworks) is along the Hog's Back west of Guildford. This is the southern boundary of Guildford Manor park, itself part of the royal park of Windsor, and was probably planted in late

Saxon times. But there are anomalies, for instance in Shropshire, where a deliberate policy of planting mixed hedges means that the shrub counts and the documentary evidence for dates do not agree at all.

The number of hedge species thins out in the north and west, so the hedge rule only applies fully in lowland England. But in the Highland Zone brambles can be used instead. There are some 500 species of bramble (*Rubus*) in Britain, many not named and some still unknown. They grow not only in what hedges there are, but against walls and on banks which may represent tumbled walls (eg in the Isle of Man). Some of these banks are prehistoric. In Man the older stretches of the main roads have more species than modern bypasses, the secondary roads (once often the former main roads) have more still, and the lanes (often the ancient trackways, eg the old road from Kirkmichael to Tynwald, which is at least Iron Age) still more, including some less common species.

It is fair to add that Hooper's Rule, although undeniably attractive, has had its critics. While it has been applied with apparent success in many cases, the degree of uncertainty has tended to undermine confidence and induce a growing hesitation to use it. Richard and Nina Muir (1987) go further, and have presented arguments which in their view demolish the theory completely. They stress the fact that hedges were normally of mixed plantings – saplings and seedlings gathered from woods or waysides anywhere – before commercial nurseries sold hawthorns in bulk for the late 18th-century enclosures. Moreover, certain trees and shrubs will invade a hedge, spread along it, and depress the species count (these include elm and blackthorn, and less frequently holly and bird cherry). This extreme position is tempered by the work of C K Currie and A Scivier (see *The London Archaeologist* 5/10, 1987), who in 1985 made a detailed study of anomalies in Hampshire. They saw the need for a less rigid rule than Hooper's, to allow for multiple planting and for differing speeds of colonisation of different plants, while accepting as basic that older hedges contain more shrub species than younger ones. They recommend comparative studies in defined regions, where hedges of known date can be compared with those of unknown dates. Thus, Hooper's Rule should not be relied on wholly without supporting evidence from historical, documentary, or cartographical sources and from comparative studies (as indeed Hoskins hinted as long ago as 1971 (see *Hedges and Local History*)). But the problems should not be allowed to inhibit studies of hedges and banks all over the country, to extract what information they can give, before it is too late.

DRYSTONE WALLS

Drystone walls are characteristic of the Highland Zone, and to some extent other stone belts, such as the Cotswolds. The prehistoric land divisions – the reaves – of Dartmoor and elsewhere – are dealt with on page 63. The field pattern in much of Devon and Cornwall, particularly west Cornwall, has been shown to date from at least the Iron Age. Here the small irregular fields are bounded by banks based on large boulders, surmounted by smaller stones and earth. These banks wind about to take in boulders too big to move.

The Anglo-Saxons used hedges more than walls, reflecting the essentially lowland nature of their colonisation. Some medieval walls still exist, such as those built by monastic houses like Fountains, enclosing sheepruns in the Pennines (and the 12th-century "Monk Wall" surrounding the abbey itself). Over the centuries the mileage of walls became immense; for instance, in the Peak District there are some three miles of wall per farm, or 20 miles per square mile; Kirkcudbrightshire has some 7,000 miles (11,000km).

Walls were made from stones either collected from the neighbouring land or quarried from nearby outcrops or boulders. They can often be dated by the growth and species of lichen on them. The average life of a wall is about 200 years.

A typical wall might be about 1.4m high. It rests on a base of small flat stones in a shallow trench, and is slightly narrower than the base. The wall is built up with an inward batter, with larger stones on each side and a packing or hearting of small ones between. At about 60cm above ground level is a throughband of large flat stones laid horizontally right across the wall, and sometimes projecting from it; above this the

14 *Drystone walling – the normal field boundary in upland country. On the left is a section: the wall is built up with two outer skins of large stones, with a rubble filling between them; the wall tapers towards the top, and has a coping of larger stones (or stones set on edge). The "throughs", which bind the outer faces together, are shown in black. The finished appearance is seen on the right.*

wall continues to narrow. A cover band or top of flat stones surmounts the wall, and it is finished off with a coping of stones laid slanting or vertical along the top of the wall (see **14**). There are local variants of this general pattern, eg there may be two or three rows of throughs. The appearance of the wall is also affected by the nature of the stone; Cotswold stones are flat, Pennine grit lumpy and irregular; the limestones are white, while the grit is dark grey. Up a slope the stones are laid horizontally, not parallel to the slope; "heads" ("cheeks" in Scotland) are placed at intervals, on which the wall can lean.

The pattern of development of the walls can be well seen in the Pennines, where irregular and roughly-built walls on the lower slopes, enclosing small areas, represent the farms of the 16th century or earlier; higher up are larger enclosures, resulting from agreements between owners in the 16th and 17th centuries to enclose more land, and perhaps part of the waste (the "intakes"); above these still are the great common sheepruns on the high moors, fenced, or re-fenced, under the Enclosure Acts with walls of good quality which run for miles across the country, no matter how inhospitable.

Sheep-creeps, square openings, are made through the base of the walls. Cow-creeps can sometimes be found (eg at Grassington (NY)), which are openings right through the wall, wider at the top; these may be combined with a sheep-creep at the bottom, with loose stones in the space above which can be removed if cattle are to come through (see **15**).

15 *A sheep-creep – an opening in a drystone wall at ground level which a sheep can get through. The upper stones in this example of a Yorkshire field wall can be removed to make a gap wide enough for a cow, called a cow-creep.*

CONSUMPTION DYKES ETC

Consumption dykes were made as wide as necessary to use up all the stones on very stony land. One in Aberdeenshire (the West Dyke at Kingswell, of at least 1780) is 1.7m high, just over 8m wide at the top with a path of flat stones on it, and 475m long. In Scotland drystone dyking seems to have begun in Kirkcudbright about 1710, and spread rapidly all over the country. The best and tallest dykes were estate boundaries, and there seems to be a high standard of work after 1840. The Galloway hedge has thorns set through the wall into the slope the other side, which will grow up through the wall and make it impervious to sheep. The Galloway dyke consists of large single boulders placed on a base built as a conventional double wall. This enabled a wide range of stones to be used. In Aberdeenshire, as Robin Callander has shown, the walls were reorganised between 1770 and 1870; older ones were demolished and their stones reused in walls (the present "stane dykes") running in straight lines. A few of the older walls survive, but hardly any dating before 1730 except where agriculture retreated and left them alone.

OTHER FIELD BOUNDARIES

Other forms of boundary include *banks*, sometimes surmounted by hedges or trees. These can often be found in woodland which has encroached on formerly open land. In Devon there are double banks, with a lane between them, on major boundaries. *Pales* of deerparks were banks surmounted by a fence, with a ditch on the inside (eg Slindon (Sx)). *Walls* of turf or sods, planted with trees or hedges, are common in Devon and Cornwall. Turf walls are also found in Wales, the Isle of Man, and the Yorkshire Wolds. *Fences* include post and rail (popular for paddocks), or post and wire. Barbed wire was introduced into Britain in the 1870s, and has become almost standard for new boundaries. Movable electrified wire enclosures are used for cattle and sheep grazings. Fences may also be of split chestnut palings in woodland areas, wattle or woven laths, or planks (in Cornwall there is a type with upright separated slats). In East Anglia reed fences are used. Stone is used in areas where flat slabs are obtainable, such as slate in north Wales or flags in north-east Scotland.

16 *A watermeadow. These riverside fields in lowland England were provided with sluices and channels which enabled them to be flooded to encourage the growth of early grass for pasturage. The drawing shows the channels ("carriers") drowned ("floated") with water from the river.*

Watermeadows

Substantial increases in the numbers of sheep from the late 16th to the late 18th centuries intensified the problem of feeding them when the winter food ran out. The solution adopted generally in the southern half of England was the watermeadow (see **16**), which enabled the growth of early grass to be accelerated. A watermeadow is an area of grassland which can be flooded by a series of carefully planned sluices, earthworks, and channels. In areas of steep-sided valleys such as the west of England, and also in the Fens, a simple type was used, consisting of artificial channels or leats dug along the contours of the valley parallel with the stream; these were fed from a dam and side-leat, and the water released through hatches or sluices in the main leat back to the stream across the meadow. A very fine example at New Court Manor (He) has a Trench Royal three miles long, which could be used for transport; some 300 acres could be flooded by this system. A development of this was to dam the main stream and force the water to "float upwards" over the meadow. This was used in the Midlands and parts of Wessex.

In wide flat valleys more than these methods were needed, and watermeadows reached their peak along the valleys of Hampshire – the Avon, Test, Itchen, and Meon – where the water was made to "float down-wards". A main channel ("carrier") was dug across the land to be flooded, and the ground was built up into a series of ridges and furrows radiating from the carrier (these can look like ordinary medieval ridge and furrow). A shallow trench along the top of each ridge ("drowner") brought the water from the carrier, while drainage channels dug in the furrows returned the water to the river along the main drain. An even flow of water had to be maintained down the sides of the ridges ("panes"). The flow was controlled by weirs and hatches. Up to 50 acres (20 ha) could be "drowned" in this way.

Chalk country had the advantage of fairly constant and relatively warm (13°C) weather in winter and early spring, and of soluble nutrients from the land.

In Hampshire, the system was closely linked to the "sheep and corn" system of land management on the chalk downs. Sheep were folded on the downs to manure the arable land ready for spring sowing, and were fed on roots. By spring, roots were finished and fresh new grass could be got by flooding the lower lands. This enabled more sheep to be kept (hence better cereal yields), and produced earlier fattened lambs for the London market.

The drains and carriers were cleared and repaired in November, and the land drowned. Water was let in every few days till March. One acre of watermeadow could support 400 ewes and their lambs for one day. The sheep left in April, and the land was irrigated again for the hay harvest in June; two or even three hay crops might be got. Cattle were put on the meadows between hay harvest and November. The system paid handsomely, and greatly increased the value of the land.

Watermeadows began to be made soon after 1600, and gained momentum after 1650. By 1800 every parish along the Hampshire rivers had several acres of watermeadows. A fall in grain prices in the 19th century, caused by cheap imports, led to fewer sheep being required, and watermeadows declined. Some continued in use into the 20th century, but there are now only some five or six in operation. Most valley land has been drained since the War, and either ploughed or improved for grazing by fertilisers. The plant and animal ecology of the meadows has been seriously affected by this.

There has recently been a revival of interest in watermeadows and their place in farming history. For instance, the system along the Wey below Bramshott (Ha) has been investigated since 1985 by the River Wey Trust. Here the masonry of a "stop", which supported a hatch in one of the channels, was excavated; a three-span stone bridge at Passfield was shown to have slotted stones on the upstream side to hold hatches; at Hatch Farm, Standford, are the remains of an aqueduct which carried irrigation waters across the Wey until the 1930s; leats and control channels have been cleared; and the whole system can now be visualised and understood. This system was recorded as early as 1625.

Transhumance

Transhumance is the practice of pasturing sheep or cattle on low-lying ground in the winter, and moving them up to higher ground for the summer. This practice is ancient; it is most noticeable in highland areas, but it was used on a small scale even in southern England, eg on the chalklands of Wessex and the south-east. Sheep were subject to footrot and liver fluke if pastured on wet meadowland, and would in any case have damaged the grass in the course of its recovery and subsequent growth for hay.

Transhumance goes back to Neolithic times in Europe, is fully attested by the 13th century, and on the Continent still persists. In the Mediterranean area and in the Alps and Carpathians, it is still practised on a large scale and the routes may be traced over quite long distances (in Spain up to 800km; in France up to 100km). These routes are some 15m wide, and are well defined. In Britain it died out, in its original form, in the 18th century, but continued in Scotland long after it had been abandoned in England and Wales.

TRANSHUMANCE IN CONTINENTAL EUROPE

On the Continent three main types have been distinguished (Fernand Braudel in *The Mediterranean* has a convenient account): "normal", where sheep or cattle are taken to higher pastures in summer and the farmer lives in the lowlands – valley or plain – in winter and in the hills in summer (this type is the norm in southern France, eg in the maritime Alps, using Arles as the market); "inverse", where flocks come down from the highlands to market in winter (Spain and southern Italy); and a less firm category, "mixed", which combines both – dwelling and starting-point are halfway between summer and winter pastures (Corsica). The dwellings in these cases need not be fixed. There is a more primitive system underlying all these: nomadism, still practised in North Africa and the Middle East, where the family moves with the flocks and often takes its dwellings with it. Tented Bedouins, with sheep, goats, and camels, are a familiar sight in these areas.

The Massif Central of France has been studied by P F Fournier, who shows that transhumance went on from the 12th century to the early 19th, with both sheep and cattle. The keepers built pens and temporary huts, sometimes with sunken floors (called "burons"), which served as dwellings and for sheltering the animals in bad weather. If several herds were involved there could be groups or rows of burons. The requirements for dairy herds differed from those for fattening stock. Shepherds, on the other hand, often lived in movable huts, as sheep are more mobile than cattle.

TRANSHUMANCE IN BRITAIN

In Britain the "normal" type of transhumance was practised, but over much smaller distances. In the highland areas remains of houses occupied for the summer pasturing – sheilings in Scotland, *hafods* in Wales – and of cottages and huts can still be found; some of them are intact and still occupied. In Scotland whole families lived in the sheilings in the high pastures in the summer, with their cattle, and in the "ferm-touns" (or *clachans*) on the lower slopes in the winter. The practice lasted until the 19th century, but only Auchendrain (Ar) has survived to give an example of this way of life. Associated with the sheilings are the transhumance *tracks* along which the flocks and herds were taken. These can still be traced. An area which has been closely studied is Knoydart, between Loch Nevis and Loch Hourn, opposite Skye (see Christopher Taylor: *Roads and Tracks of Britain* (1979)). Here five settlements have been identified round the coast (ie on low pasture). From these a network of tracks leads up into the hills behind. The summer pastures might be up to six miles from their townships. In Wales the hafods sometimes became the houses or farms of new branches of the family, and some are still occupied.

In the north of England the sheep and cattle wintered in the dales and lived on the moors in summer. The upper lands of the villages were marked out by immensely long drystone walls into areas which were the common pastures of the villages. Each valley farmer was entitled to the use of a given number of *stints* (or "gates", "gaits"), units which specified the numbers of sheep allowed to be pastured; in the moorland or waste beyond the walls no limit was set. The summer dwellings are ruined now, but the stells and pens are still there. The access tracks can be traced, but there is no way of distinguishing transhumance tracks from drove roads, and of course they were in fact interchangeable.

Sheep farming in the north of England was greatly developed by the monasteries, which established *granges* or outlying farms in convenient places. Sheep and cattle wintered in the dales, and low-lying granges might concentrate on dairying or some other function; but granges on wold or moor edges were for sheep. A useful study of such granges is that by Bryan Waites: *Moorland and Vale-land Farming in North-East Yorkshire*.

In the south of England transhumance was carried out on a small scale, mostly on the chalklands and limestone hills, and sheep and cattle were brought to low pastures like Romney Marsh. The shepherds on these hills lived in movable huts, with a stove in one corner for heating and cooking. Examples can be seen at the Weald and Downland Museum, Singleton (Sx), or the Old Kiln Museum, Tilford (Sy). A form of transhumance still goes on, where lambs reared on upland farms are transported to the lowlands to be "finished" (fattened) in autumn or winter.

The practice of transhumance is revealed in place-names, particularly those of the Scandinavian settlement. The Old Norse term *saetr*, a summer pasture, was used by the Danes also, and is found widely in the north-east of England, and even further south. It occurs in names such as Appersett, Countersett, Gunnerside, Ambleside, Earl Seat, Simon's Seat; also in Somerset. The Irish-Norse entering the Lake District and the north-west Pennines brought a Gaelic element *erg* or *arg*, a sheiling, reflected in names such as Mansergh, Mosser, and those ending in *-airey*, *-ark*, or *-arrow*. Anglo-Saxon names revealing transhumance include Somerton (in Somerset and Lincolnshire), and the significant pair Somerton and Winterton in Norfolk.

FARMING EQUIPMENT

The first, Neolithic, farmers in Britain, in the later 5th millennium BC, were confronted with a sparsely-occupied land, covered with trees or scrub and not drained. This they cleared, at least on the drier and more easily worked soils, by a combination of means: "slash-and-burn", ring-

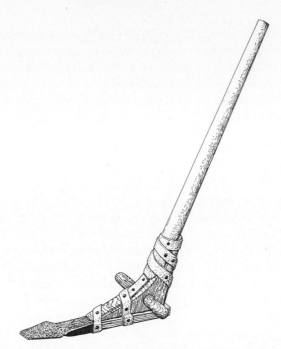

17   *A caschrom – a digging-stick, still used in Scotland in the 19th century.*

barking and felling of trees (with axes of polished stone), and grazing and rootling by cattle and pigs. The cleared ground was prepared for crops at first by *digging-sticks*, with hardened tips, pushed by the thighs. A digging-stick – the caschrom (see **17**) – was still used in the Highlands of Scotland in the 19th century. From these developed *hoes*, tipped with hardened wood, flint, or stone. The hoe, when pulled rather than pushed, was elaborated into a device which could be drawn, first by manpower and soon by harnessing an ox to it, and became a simple form of *plough*, an *ard*. The ard lasted in use from the late Neolithic, through the Bronze and Iron Ages, into Roman times, although there is some evidence for heavier ploughs, with mould-board for turning the sod on heavier soils, from late Iron Age and Roman times. The ard could not turn the soil, but only made a furrow; the field was therefore ploughed twice, the second time at right angles to the first, and the fields therefore tended to be square.

There were two types of ard: the *bow-ard* (see **8**, p 51), in which the main beam was curved at one end towards the ground, and the share, which was at one end of the stilt with its handles at the top, passed through a hole in the main beam, and the *crook-ard*, where the main

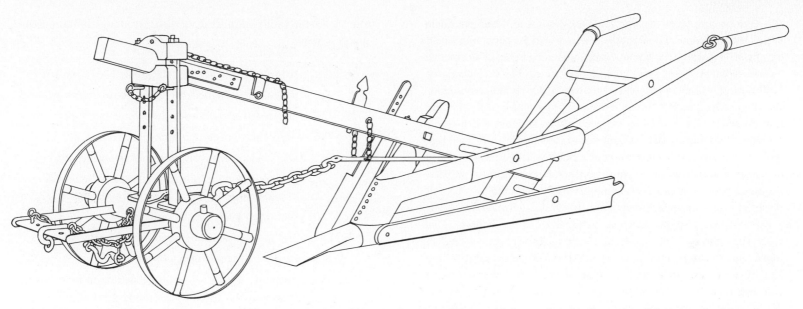

18 *A Kentish turn-wrist plough. This was an 18th-century innovation; its mould-board and coulter could be moved from one side to the other, so that all the furrows faced the same way, whether the plough was going up or down the field. This principle is still used today.*

beam was mortised into a share beam or sole, which had the *share* at one end and the stilt rising separately behind it. The crook-ard was used more in southern Europe, and both types were used in the north, the bow-ard being dominant in Britain. The share was progressively of hardened wood, flint or stone, bronze, and iron. Later (4th century AD) ards might have a *coulter* (a vertical blade in front of the share) as well, to open up the soil.

The *mould-board*, for turning the sod, which converted the ard into a true plough, came into use in the 3rd or 4th century AD, and enabled heavier soils to be tackled. As ploughs got heavier and needed up to eight oxen to pull them (although four was more usual), the last basic addition was a *wheel*, to steady the plough and help to keep it level in the soil. This seems to have been used in the 1st century AD, but was normal in Saxon times. It has indeed been suggested that the oxen-drawn wheel-plough was integral with the open field strip system. Even if this is not the case, it was used from the 12th century in many areas (eg Kent). Mixed teams of horses and oxen were also used in the 12th century, and remained in use until the early 19th century, although by then horses were the normal means of traction. Local varieties of plough began to emerge in the 16th century, and a double-furrow plough in

the 17th. Ploughs varied with county and type of soil, and reached a wide variety by the mid 17th century, such as the Kentish turn-wrist (see **18**), the Dutch disc coulter, swing ploughs, and wheel ploughs. In 1847 the firm of Wedlake was selling 40 types.

The other important tool for the preparation of the seedbed is the *harrow*. Its early form was a thorn-bush weighted with a log, but later (from the 16th century) harrows could be heavy wooden frames set with spikes, or flexible iron meshes, also spiked. There were also scufflers, drags, and spiked rollers.

Most of the other processes on the farm were carried out with *hand tools* before farming was mechanised in the 18th and 19th centuries; they have been almost entirely superseded by the machinery in use since World War II, except for some operations like hedge-laying. In prehistoric and Roman times the range consisted largely of hoes, spades, turfing tools, sickles, hooks, scythes, forks, rakes, flails and winnowing shovels, baskets, and sieves. These persisted practically unchanged until recent times, as have indeed tools used in carpentry and smithing.

By the late 19th and early 20th century the range of hand tools included breast-ploughs for turfing and paring; drainage tools and pipe-layers; watermeadow tools; hedging tools (billhooks, slashers);

drystone walling tools; seeding tools (seed boxes and baskets; fiddle broadcasters; broadcast barrows – horse-drawn for corn, hand-held for grass; seed-drills (the ancient Babylonians had one, of distinctive form)); dibblers; hoes, weed hooks, spuds, dock lifters; clappers for bird-scaring; sickles, hooks, and crooked sticks for reaping; scythes for mowing; rakes, iron for stubble, wooden for hay, and forks for turning hay; pitchforks, hay knives, straw rope twisters and throw-crooks, for stacking; flails, barley awners, and hummelers for threshing; riddles, baskets, shovels, and hand-powered machines for winnowing and dressing; chaffcutters and boxes; choppers, cutters, slicers, pulpers, bruisers, rollers, and crushers, for processing; and thatching tools. All these, and more, are described and their use illustrated in books such as C A Jewell (ed): *Victorian Farming*, or Roy Brigden: *Agricultural Hand Tools*. They may be seen in museums such as the Museum of English Rural Life (Reading), as can the obsolete relics of the earlier machine age. There is also an extensive range of specialised items used in dairying, cream- and cheese-making, and the management of sheep. Occasionally one can come across an old tool or machine rusting or decaying in an unused corner of a farm.

A fascinating insight into farming before mechanisation is provided by the 16th-century writer (of delightful doggerel) Thomas Tusser, in his book *Five Hundredth Goode Pointes of Husbandrie . . .* (1573).

Mechanisation and rationalisation came in with the 18th century, and revolutionised farming. The main landmarks, in what was a long, complex, and uneven development over two and a half centuries, with many false starts and blind alleys, but with continuous and cumulative progress, were:

1701	Jethro Tull's seed-drill (made public 1731) (see **19**)
1714	Jethro Tull introduces the horse-hoe from France
c 1720	James Meikle's winnowing machine
1730	the Rotherham plough (wood and iron)
1732	Michael Menzies' threshing machine (water-driven)
1760s	light plough, with triangular frame and iron-shod mould-board
c 1770	the first all-iron plough (John Brand)
1782	Tull's seed-drill and horse-hoe improved by gearing
1780s	Patrick Bell's reaping machine (pushed)
1784	Alexander Meikle's threshing machine and winnowing machine (later combined), worked by horse-gin
1789	Robert Ransome's cast-iron share

19 *A seed-drill. There are many types of seed-drill, following its invention by Jethro Tull in 1701. This is the heavy horse-drawn Suffolk type, with multiple nozzles – not popular with those who had to operate it.*

20 *A threshing machine. A Marshall box-type machine, belt-driven by a steam traction engine, a familiar sight in arable country until well into the 20th century.*

1790s	iron plough with replaceable standard parts
1802	Richard Trevithick's first agricultural steam engine (to drive a threshing machine) (see **20**)
by 1807	the horse-rake
1808	replaceable parts for ploughs
early 19th c	iron harrow; cultivator; iron roller
1833	O Hussey's reaping machine (pulled), replaced by C McCormick's 1834–48
1841	Crosskill's clod-crusher
mid 19th c	chopping and crushing machines
1840s	steam applied to chopping, crushing, threshing, winnowing
1850s	cultivating, reaping, and crop-processing machines
1856	hay-mower (American)
1858	steam ploughing (J Fowler system; there were several other systems)
1860s	stack elevators
c 1870	first concrete farm building (Buscot (Ox))
1880s	tank-type silos (tower silos 1920s); reaper-and-binder; gas engines
1888	petrol engines
1902	Ivel tractor, (the first "modern" tractor, superseding several earlier attempts which were not wholly satisfactory; in 1917 the Fordson (see **21**) swept the board, with some 6,000 imported during World War I; by 1939 some 60,000 were in use, in 1949, 260,000, and in 1956, 478,000
1920s	combine harvesters (fully developed in the 1950s)

This list, which is far from complete, gives an idea of the intense activity with which new labour-saving devices were sought and old ones improved, and it says nothing about the rate of adoption or the extent of use. The first major phase in the mechanisation of agriculture was from 1830–80, the age of iron implements, standardised products (with less reliance on local blacksmiths and carpenters), labour-saving machinery, and the use of steam power. "The harvest had become mechanised by 1891," as Fussell says.

Of course the nature of the farm still dictates the kind of machinery used. For instance, efficient tractors came in in 1902, but 50 years later many small farms, particularly in upland districts, where fields were small, steep, and stony, did not find them practicable (or indeed affordable), and still relied on horses. Major jobs on such farms were often done by cooperative effort between neighbours.

Power sources

The *power sources* to drive the machines have reflected those used in other industries. *Animal power* was used from the earliest times until well within living memory – oxen until the late 19th century, and horses from at least the 12th century. Much of the stationary machinery for threshing, chopping, etc permanently installed in farm buildings was driven by horses turning gins (see **22**, page 88) throughout the 19th century. This kind of machinery could also be worked by *water power* where conditions were suitable, such as in Wales. The use of *steam power* became fashionable for much of the 19th century, both to drive barn machinery (chimneys on "model" farms represent the engine-house), and, in movable traction engines, for ploughing and cultivating. The Fowler system used two engines to haul the plough between them. Steam was largely superseded by 1914, but was still in use in a few places even as late as 1960, and steam engines have been used even later for jobs like lake cleaning.

Power sources were used in combination, depending on the nature of the soil and the job to be done. A good example is that of Rider Haggard,

21 *The Fordson tractor, shown here drawing a seed-drill. These were imported from the USA in large numbers in 1917 to help the British war effort. They became very popular – indeed, almost standard – and half a million were still in service in the 1950s.*

far from an inefficient farmer, who had both light and heavy land on his farms in Suffolk. In 1898 his diaries reveal that he used scythes for barley, spades for draining, and spuds for weeding – and no doubt manpower also for innumerable odd jobs about the farm. On his lighter soils he used horses for ploughing, harrowing, cultivating, seed-drilling, hoeing, mowing, tossing, raking, reaping, and binding. On his heavier land he used steam for ploughing and cultivating, and his thresher was steam-driven. No doubt he would have gone over to petrol for most of these jobs a few years later.

The 20th century has been dominated by petrol and diesel, and by *electricity* for barn machinery, dairying, and other equipment.

FARM BUILDINGS

Farm buildings differ in time and place. They are designed for and adapted to the local type of farming and farming methods, and change when these alter. They also reflect the building methods, materials, and fashions of the time and place; apart from the "model" farms of the 18th and 19th centuries and 20th-century factory farms, traditional methods of construction were used in farm buildings until this century. Very few buildings survive above ground from before the 16th century apart from the tithe barns, and these are not typical. So for earlier centuries one has to rely on archaeology and on contemporary records and illustrations.

Although most farming in this country until recently was always mixed, the nature of the buildings in an old farmstead can give useful clues to the various activities of the farm, and to those that predominated. A succession of large-scale maps will show constant changes in the buildings and arrangement of farmsteads, and in local roads and other farm features; even ponds can be reshaped or even resited.

Prehistoric

Little is known about subsidiary buildings on prehistoric farms, although some of the smaller "houses", and many of the postholes, may well have had agricultural uses. But in the final centuries preceding the Roman conquest a type of building appears which is less equivocal – the ubiquitous "four-poster". Even on this opinion

is divided, since postholes are all the excavator has to go on, unless associated remains chance to point to a specific use.

A single posthole may represent a house with walls of turf, where the roof structure and the walls have disappeared; or it may represent a post to heap cut grass round (as Peter Reynolds suggests; and a single post in a shallow circular hollow certainly indicates a stack), or a tethering post (as Barry Cunliffe remarks), or any post on which to hang, or against which to support, anything at all. Two postholes (in evident relationship) may be for corn-drying racks, hide-stretching frames, looms, etc. Four-post arrangements are very common on Iron Age settlement sites (ie farmsteads) and in hillforts (eg Danebury, where they were numerous enough for Barry Cunliffe to use in his interpretation of the possible socio-economic status and function of hillforts of this type). There is broad general agreement that most of these settings supported small square buildings (with 2–4m sides on average) which may be called "granaries". But although some can be shown to have undoubtedly been granaries, others may have supported bases for haystacks; Reynolds points out that if there is a fifth, central post as well, this almost certainly would have been the post round which a circular stack was built. But some could be barns, byres, cart-sheds, stables, chicken-houses, shelters for smiths, potters, beehives, etc, watch-towers, or even platforms for exposing the dead before burial. There are larger "four-posters" with six posts, and Cunliffe points to a nine-post granary with 5m sides. A similar granary at the medieval motte and bailey castle of Hen Domen (Mg) was supported by 12 posts.

The other common feature of an Iron Age farm is the *storage pit*. Reynolds has shown, by experiments at Butser Ancient Farm (Ha), that grain and other foodstuffs can be quite successfully kept in pits dug in the ground, because of a build-up of carbon dioxide which inhibits bacterial growth. Meat can also be salted in such pits. This standard indicator of an Iron Age farm was first recognised by G Bersu at Little Woodbury (Wi) in 1938/9, (*Proceedings of the Prehistoric Society*, 1940) who exploded the then accepted idea that the pits were dwellings; the full implications of this adjunct to farming have in recent years been worked out at Butser. When no longer suitable for food storage the pits could be conveniently used as rubbish tips. Iron Age farms also had a variety of fenced enclosures for cattle, sheep, horses, poultry, etc.

Roman

Few excavations of Roman villas, or of "native" farms of Roman date, have been extensive enough to reveal the outbuildings of the farmsteads, but there is sufficient evidence for the presence of barns, stables, granaries (eg at Ditchley (Ox) or Lullingstone (Kt), *c* AD 280, later, *c* 380, used as a cart-standing), threshing-floors, and corn-drying or malting kilns. Bath houses, although integral parts of the domestic buildings, were often detached from the villa, for reasons of safety or to allow local people to use them. Some large buildings have a shelter for implements etc attached. Some villas take the form of an aisled hall, often with dwelling rooms at one end, sometimes for the family, sometimes, in detached buildings, for farm workers (eg Bignor (Sx) and Rivenhall (Ex)).

Villas in northern France may give a clue to the outbuildings in Britain. The aerial surveys of Roger Agache (eg see *Détection aérienne* (Amiens, *Bull Soc Préhistorique du Nord* 7, 1970)) have revealed huge villas consisting of a main house with a private courtyard or garden in front of it; in front of this, outside the courtyard wall, is a long rectangular courtyard, sometimes closed, sometimes open at the end away from the house, but which may have a separate building in the otherwise open end. This outer courtyard contains the steward's house and rows of farm buildings, usually separate, which may include houses for workers, barns (some very large), granaries, byres, and sheds. There are also dovecotes and ponds (eg Anthée, Belgium, and Estrées-sur-Noye, Somme, France; the villa at Brading (IW) seems to be of this type).

At Littlecote (Wi), which has been extensively excavated, there was a main house with a group of buildings adjacent, containing a workshop and workers' living quarters, and ranges on both sides forming the sides of a courtyard, which seems to have once had a fourth side. The range on the south contained domestic and farm buildings. But that on the north began as a large open-sided barn, containing corn-dryer and bread ovens (*c* AD 100); about AD 180 part was demolished to make way for a flint-built aisled barn, which was altered *c* 300 when a small bath suite was erected in one corner.

Anglo-Saxon

For the Anglo-Saxon period reliance has still to be placed on excavation. The commonest kind of subsidiary building is the *Grubenhaus*, the "sunken hut"; as these are not necessarily houses or huts, Philip Rahtz, who has analysed these structures (in David M Wilson (ed): *The Archaeology of Anglo-Saxon England* (Methuen 1976, CUP 1981)), prefers the term "sunken-featured building" (SFB). Some of these buildings are entirely sunk into the ground; others have floors mainly at ground level but part sunken. They average in size *c* 3m by 2m and the roof is supported on two, four, six, or even more posts. They are commonest in the early Saxon period, but continued in use into the Middle Ages, and even to quite recent times.

Many of these SFBs were single-cell dwellings, no doubt for domestic or farm workers, but some had been put to other uses, such as weaving-sheds or spinning-huts (eg at West Stow (Sf)), cheese-making, barns, byres, storehouses, bakehouses, and pottery or other craft workshops. At Mucking (Ex), excavation revealed some 50 posthole buildings, presumably substantial houses, and 211 SFBs; it seems highly likely that some of these were farm buildings. At Catholme (Sf), a small building next to a house was interpreted as a granary.

Medieval

In the Middle Ages the evidence for farm buildings in the usual sense becomes more recognisable. Villagers had *tofts* containing their dwellings and simple outbuildings, with *crofts* beyond for pasturing their animals etc. At Wharram Percy (NY) John Hurst has excavated a Grubenhaus like those of Saxon times, which was a workroom.

Farmyards began to develop in the 12th and particularly 13th centuries, open with irregularly-placed buildings at first, regular and closed later. Farmsteads had the dual function of lord's or steward's residence and farming (for the farmhouse see pages 94–6).

At West Cotton, near Raunds (Nh), excavations in 1985–6 revealed a 12th-century village of two or three large farms on a triangular green. Each farm had its own *malting-house* – a three-roomed unit with square malting oven at one end. This type continued until the site was deserted in the 15th century (see *Current Archaeology* 106, 1987). Nigel Harvey (in *A History of Farm Building in England and Wales* (1970)) illustrates an Oxfordshire farm of the early 14th century; this had the lord's house and subsidiary buildings, a barn for spring grain, a barn for straw, a granary for cereals, a granary for wheat, a byre, a shelter for cattle and carts, a piggery, dovecotes, and a fishpond. The Weald and Downland Museum has reconstructed Bayleaf, an early 15th-century farm of yeoman or lower gentry status, consisting of a Wealden hall house, garden, orchard, shaw, rickyard, barn, granary, byre, pighouse, and cartshed.

TITHE BARNS

The only surviving medieval farm buildings are the ecclesiastical or monastic *tithe barns*, and these are not typical. They were not only barns but central storehouses for monastic granges or church estates; that at Bradford-on-Avon (Wi) was indeed used until the 1940s for implements, feed, hay and straw, horses, even pigs, and in medieval times would have housed the tithes (produce) as well. Some, like that at Bredon (Wo) (See of Worcester), had a bailiff's office and lodging over one of the porches. Many were very large indeed; one at Cholsey (Ox) (demolished) was 303ft long, and Abbotsbury (Do), when complete, was 282ft. The largest still roofed is Frindsbury (Kt), 219ft long. Fine examples are those at Great Coxwell (Ox) (13th century, a grange of Beaulieu Abbey), 152ft long, Tisbury (Wi) (a grange of Shaftesbury nunnery), and Coggeshall (Ex) (see **166–8**, pages 289–90). These give a vivid idea of an aisled hall. Tithe barns were ubiquitous; there were between 2,000 and 3,000 belonging to the Cistercians alone. Rectorial barns, to house the produce of the parish glebe and the local tithes, are much smaller.

Early modern

From the mid 16th century the farmstead takes on its *early modern* (pre-"factory") form, although very few, if any, buildings survive from before the 17th century. Moreover, many of the surviving buildings have become obsolete or changed their use with the drastic changes in farming practice since the 1950s. But farms which are now regarded by most of us as "traditional" contained all or some of the following buildings (which were normally of vernacular construction):

BARNS AND GRANARIES

The principal *barn* was a place not only for storing cereals and other crops but for processing them. The building had doorways in the long sides, opposite each other, often with projecting porches. They were large enough to admit carts, and each pair was aligned into the prevailing wind. The grain was threshed across the barn in the space between the doors, where the winnowing was also done. Threshing was done by flail until well into the 19th century, but threshing machines were developed in the 18th century. One end of the barn was used for the new sheaves, the other to store the threshed straw.

The threshing barn had to be conveniently close to the straw and hay barns, if separate, the granary, and the buildings where the food and litter were to be used – the stables, byres, poultry houses, etc. This led to consciously planned farmyards.

The threshing machines were driven by wind or water power, but most commonly, until steam power took over in the second half of the 19th century, by horses. The machinery turned by the horses was contained in *gin-houses* (among other names) built onto the outside of the barn (see **22**). These were semicircular or angular when engaged into the barn wall, or circular just outside it; the roofs were of various construction, and there were several types of machine, either geared or rope-winding. The gin-houses were normally on the north side of

22 *A horse gin. A wide variety of farm machinery was powered by horses. This one is a crushing mill. The gin was often in a separate "gin-house", but this one is in an open shed (from Pyne's Microcosm, 1808).*

the barns, for ventilation. Up to four horses could be harnessed. The mill was used to operate cutting and crushing machines as well as threshing, churning, and pumping. Small cast-iron mills in the open air were cheaper than the engine houses and were used on small farms all over the country, becoming popular after the Great Exhibition of 1851. Travelling threshing mills were used in the later 19th century, using a steam engine pulled by horses, or later, particularly in south-east England, a mobile steam traction engine.

The horse-gins were used widely, but were most frequent in north-east England and eastern Scotland, and to a lesser extent in south-west England. The earliest in Scotland seems to be that at Phantassie (EL) in 1788; by 1800 there were 350 machines in use in East Lothian alone, and by 1845 386, of which 7 were powered by wind, 30 by water, 269 by horses, and 80 by steam. There were over 500 in Northumberland and over 200 in north-east Yorkshire. In Yorkshire they appeared in 1790 (at Nunnington), and were used until the 1930s. Most date from 1800 to 1830, but continued to be built throughout the 19th century. Many houses still survive, but are used for other purposes.

Horse-wheels were also used for raising water from wells or mines, and donkey or human power was also harnessed for a variety of purposes, such as driving a crane (eg Guildford and Harwich), or raising building materials (eg in Ely Cathedral). The earliest surviving horse-wheel is that at Carisbrooke Castle (IW). Animal power was replaced by steam from the 1750s for continuous water supply, but horses were more economical if only intermittent supply was required. Horse-wheels were still shown in the Exhibitions of 1851 and 1861. In 1972, 27 donkey-wheels still existed, and 24 more were recorded; 23 horse-wheels were then extant, and 31 others recorded (these are minimum figures). There are good examples at Greys Court, Henley (Ox), Patching (Sx), and Sawley Hall (NY).

Threshing barns were ventilated with small holes of different shape or in different patterns, and many had an *owl-hole* in the gable to encourage barn owls which would prey on vermin attracted by the corn.

A large farm might also have a separate barn for *hay*. In the 19th century the *Dutch barn* was adopted for storing hay and straw; it was introduced about 1780. This had an open side; after 1885 Dutch barns were merely roofs supported on iron frames, open on all sides, and these are still widely used.

In the Pennines a common feature is the field house, *field barn*, or lathe, isolated from the farmhouse to serve the lands newly enclosed

23 *A field barn. These barns are common features of upland farming in northern England. They were remote from the farmhouse, and were intended to serve the lands enclosed in the 17th to 19th centuries. They combined a cowhouse with storage for hay, and obviated the need to return constantly to the farmhouse, which could be a considerable distance away.*

in the 17th to mid 19th centuries. This is a small building, combining a cowhouse with storage for hay; it obviated the need to return constantly to the farmyard. A number of lathes dotted over the fields makes a very distinctive landscape, eg at Gunnerside, Swaledale (see **12**, page 74, and **23**). There are some 10,000 in the Pennines. A *bank barn* is a variety of barn commonest in north-west England and adapted to sloping sites. This has the barn on the first floor, with a cowhouse, stable, or cartshed below, entered from the other side.

A similar idea, but on level ground, is the *lean-to barn*, in which the barn is combined with a cowhouse etc in the same building; in this case the threshing area extends through the animal section. In Somerset there is a variant in which the threshing floor is above the cartshed on the ground floor. In Wiltshire there are barns with one or two threshing floors, built in a compact L-shape with a foldyard in the angle.

An *outfarm* is a more comprehensive unit consisting of a threshing barn, a shelter shed, and a foldyard, thus providing a convenient subsidiary centre in an outlying part of the farm. Sometimes a farm worker's cottage would also be built at the outfarm. These units can be found in most areas. New Barn Farm, Selborne (Ha) (note the name) is an 18th-century offshoot of Priory Farm, three quarters of a mile away; it was replanned and rebuilt in the mid 19th century, but was till recently used as a foldyard, cattle shelter, and equipment shed. Outlying threshing facilities became unnecessary in the mid 19th century when portable threshing machines could deal with ricks in the fields. On large 19th-century farms a fixed steam engine could power all the machines in one *mixing-house barn*, which combined threshing, straw store, and granary and was in close relation to the corn-stacks on one side and the cattle on the other (eg at Gilling, (NY)).

There is of course a certain fluidity in the design of farm buildings. The farmer will tend to improvise and make the most of his space. Thus, a barn might have outshuts for calf hulls or dog kennels, and pigeonholes in the porch.

25 *A wooden granary on staddles – Basing House (Ha).*

24 *Granaries on staddles. This type was in common use from the 16th to the 18th century, and used for many purposes since then. They were small, usually square, buildings, raised above the ground on staddles, mushroom-shaped stone, iron, or concrete pillars, which rats and mice could not surmount.*

A necessary accompaniment of the threshing barn is the *granary*. This consists of a room divided by low wooden partitions into bays in which the grain is stored, either along one wall or on two sides of a central gangway, with a door at one end; access is by movable steps, exterior stone steps, or interior stairs. The walls have to be stout and are often tile-hung or weather-boarded; the floor must be tightly tongued to keep rats and mice out. In the southern half of England a common type of granary is free-standing on staddles, mushroom-shaped supports of stone, concrete, or iron which vermin cannot climb (see **24** and **25**). Some of these are 17th-century. There is a granary on wooden posts at Peper Harow (Sy) and one on brick pillars at Slade's Farm, Bramley (Sy). Two-storey granaries of this type exist.

The other main type has the grain store above an open cartshed, supported on stone or brick piers or having a timber-framed front. In Hampshire the ground floor is commonly of stone and the upper floor of brick, but in other areas the whole building may be of brick or stone. Instead of a cartshed the ground floor may be a stable. Sometimes a granary could form part of a mixing-house barn and be adjacent to processing machinery. There could be a *drying-floor*, for grain, hops, or malt.

An accompaniment to the granary, particularly in damper areas and in the Highland Zone, is the *corn-drying kiln*. This might be a temporary stone-lined basin in the corner of a field or in a bank, through which hot air from a fire was drawn (the name Kiln Field may give a clue, although this name also referred to limekilns), or it might be permanent and built into the farmhouse (like a bread-oven) or at the corner of a barn. These square or round kilns are a familiar sight in northern Scotland (eg Stromness or Rackwick (Or)). Corn-dryers (grain dryers) have been used in Britain since Roman times, and are standard equipment on arable farms. Some were used for malting barley.

Animal houses

Provision had also to be made for the animals once they were no longer kept in one end of an aisled hall or longhouse. A separate *cowhouse* (byre, shippon, mistal, etc in regional terms) became a normal part of every farmyard. Most cowhouses before the 19th century had lofts above; until recent times farm servants (workers) often slept with or over the livestock. In Devon some first floor hall houses have byres on the ground floor (eg a farm building at Neadon, Manaton, once a house, *c* 1500). The yard in front could be used to collect manure for spreading on the fields; specially constructed *dung-pits* were developed in the 18th century. In some areas (eg Lincolnshire) dung was collected in specially dug hollows which, out of context, can look like quarry pits. On a large farm there could be a separate yard for loose cattle, and a *bull-pen*; in the late 19th century some larger farms had *covered yards*. There could also be open-fronted *shelter-sheds*, without the elaborate fittings of a permanent cowhouse; a *linhay* combines a shelter with a hay-loft above. *Calf-hulls* are also found, and *loose-boxes* for bulls or sick animals. Byres similar to cowhouses were also built for draught oxen, which were used until the end of the 19th century eg in the Cotswolds and Hampshire; a survivor can be seen at Cogges Farm Museum, Witney (Ox).

When a farmer was also a butcher a *slaughterhouse* was necessary. But the normal concomitant of cattle-keeping was the *dairy*, which was as much an adjunct of the house as part of the farmyard. Butter and cheese were made here; the cheese was normally kept in separate storerooms or *lofts*. The great houses often had elaborate ornamental dairies, such as that at Blaise Castle (Av) (1810–12). Liquid milk was not as a rule handled in bulk until the late 19th century, when it was sent to the towns by rail; the churns were stood on wooden *churn-stands* by the roadside for collection. In the 1920s the *milking-bail* enabled milking to be done in the fields, but this could only be used in dry, warm areas; elsewhere the *milking-parlour* on the farm was used. *Cream-ovens* are found, eg in Devon, for scalding cream to make it clot.

Cattle and sheep have from time to time to be rounded up on the farm for sorting, inspection, or treatment. This necessitates fenced enclosures, *pens*. Animals which strayed onto a road or into the village were detained in *pounds* by a *pindar*, a village official who charged a fee for handing them back to the owner. Pounds, round or square walled enclosures, survive in many places, eg Linton in Wharfedale (NY) or the somewhat stranded example on the A25 in the western outskirts of Dorking (Sy) (see **26**).

Sheep did not usually have buildings in the farmyard but needed structures elsewhere on the farm. These include the *buchts* of Northumberland, fenced enclosures against stone walls for milking ewes, the large 18th-century *sheepfolds* of Wales, and the *bields* or stells in the uplands, where the animals could shelter. These latter may be round or square walled enclosures, or have cross-shaped arrangements of walls, giving shelter as the wind changes. There are conspicuous stells in the Devil's Beef Tub, north of Moffat (Df), and they are common in the Highland Zone. There are also small stone pens in the corners of fields to gather sheep for shearing or other treatment, and hurdle pens have always been used. Shearing-houses and sheep-cotes were features of medieval and Tudor farms, but went out of use; the idea was not revived until recently, when special housing was developed in the 1960s on intensive sheep farms for shearing, lambing, and overwintering. (The "woolsheds"

26 *A pound. Somewhere in a village stood a pound, an enclosure, often circular, where stray animals could be kept until claimed. Most were round; this square one is at Dorking (Sy).*

of Australia have a longer history.) In Cumbria and other highland areas there were special *hog-houses*, to give shelter to yearling sheep ("hogs"). The other equipment for sheep-farming was the *wash*, usually a deep (*c* 3ft) place in a stream, controlled by a wooden dam and sluice; brick, stone, and concrete washes are also found. These are now obsolete, as sheep are now dipped in insecticide in pens or houses.

Pigsties were not universal until the 18th century; before that pigs were kept loose in the woods, foraging for themselves. There are, rarely, earth-banked enclosures in forest country giving shelter to pigs, such as Bat's Hogstye, near Chobham (Sy). Sties and boar-pens are normally small, cosy shelters with small, walled runs attached. They were found in cottage gardens as well as on farms; examples are preserved at Cogges Farm Museum, Witney (Ox) and Blist's Hill, Ironbridge (Sp). There are some 40 beehive-shaped corbelled stone pigsties in Wales, a type of very ancient origin; a similar tradition is found in the *potato cellars* of the Yorkshire Dales. Pigs kept in the open are provided with small movable shelters. A *pigwash* is sometimes found: a large stone trough lined with lead and fed from a millstream (eg at Shugborough (St)). The final end of pigkeeping is the *smoking chamber*, under the roof of a medieval house, where woodsmoke could pass among the sides of bacon (these are features of Devon hall houses), and the *bacon-loft*, for storing smoked sides and joints.

Horses were, and are, kept in *stables* (sometimes in a separate yard), with half-doors and wooden stalls. Some are open to the roof, necessitating hay being lifted into the feeding-racks on the wall from below, but some (eg at Cogges) have *hay-lofts* above with gaps along the wall through which the hay can be lowered into the racks from above. *Loose-boxes* are plain rooms, with door and window but little else, for sick or calving cows, sick or foaling mares, or young animals. A *hemmel* is a more elaborate loose-box, with yard attached, for a bull or fattening cattle. Adjoining the stables is the *harness-* or *tack-room*, where saddlery is kept and looked after. Nearby is the *cartshed*, for farm carts, and the *implement shed* for ploughs and other machinery. These are the province of the big farm horses – Suffolks etc – but the farmer also kept a pony or "nag" to draw his trap or "gig", and these might have a separate stable and shed. There is also a *toolshed*, and on larger farms or estate yards a *smithy*, not only for making and putting on horseshoes but where tools and parts of carts, gates, etc could be made and machines repaired. There would be a stone or galvanised *drinking-trough* in or near the farmyard.

27–29 *Bee boles. These were niches in garden walls where beehives could be kept. Their shapes varied:* **27** *pointed bee bole.*

28 *Round-headed bee bole.*

28 *Square-topped bee bole.*

30 *Probably the oldest grain silo in England was this open tank with shed roof, built in Herefordshire in 1885. This type was superseded by the towers which are a familiar sight today.*

Poultry, traditionally in the care of the farmer's wife, were kept in *hen-houses* or *roosts*, sometimes movable, or in *lofts*. The chickens usually roamed freely round the farmyard, but special runs were also provided. Small movable shelters were used in the fields. *Goose-houses* are found, eg in Norfolk. Bulk egg and broiler production is now, on specialised farms, carried out in large, specially equipped sheds.

Deer were protected on large estates from early medieval times (see deerparks, page 120); in some places, by the 18th century, this did not mean merely keeping them inside enclosed areas in a virtually wild state, but actively farming them. Thus, there is a specially built *deer-shelter* at Rousham (Ox), and a *deer-larder* at Chiswick (Ln). *Game-larders* and *icehouses* (see page 236) are also features of large estates. Fish-farming in specially constructed ponds (see page 123) also gave rise to special buildings for storage and processing, eg the fine monastic *fish-house* at Meare (So) (13th-century), and *eel-houses*.

Miscellaneous buildings, some of which were more extensions of the house than part of the farm, include: *middens*; *dovecotes* (see **35–7**, pages 100–2); *bee boles* in garden walls, to shelter hives (see **27**, **28** and **29**) (bee-houses also exist, as at Attingham Park (Sp)); *root and turnip houses*; *cider-houses*, which contained the *cider-press*; *boulting houses*, where flour was boulted or sieved through linen, to eliminate bits of grain, chaff, etc; *brewhouses*; *bakehouses* (with bread-oven); *washhouses* or laundries; sometime a separate *kitchen*; *horse-engine houses* (see **22**, page 88); *rickyards* (moated haystacks occur); *drying racks*; *pumps and wells*; *fieldwork* (gates, stiles, etc).

Silos were introduced into Britain in the 1880s. The earliest type was a brick or concrete rectangular tank (see **30**); one was in use in Herefordshire from 1885 to the 1960s. The tower type began in the 1930s. Silage is now made in the field, in combine machines.

Fertilising the fields necessitated *kilns* for marling and liming (see page 538), stores for chemicals, and *ash-houses* (in Devon), small buildings to store ash from domestic peat and wood fires on its way to the fields. At Dover there is a groove in the cliff where seaweed was hauled up from the beach to the land.

An essential concomitant of cattle and sheep farming is the *marketing* of the animals. Most country towns had markets with permanent pens, in the open, and many still have. The pens and showing ring have iron railings. An interesting case is that of the Iron Age hillfort of Yarnbury (Wi), which contains a late Bronze Age enclosure. Overlapping the latter is a rectangular block of low ridges representing long narrow parallel pens, part of the installation of a sheep-fair which ran from at least the early 17th century until it was discontinued in World War I (1916). Along the hillfort enclosure bank is a row of sheds connected with the fair. The block measures some 120m by 80m; the pens are arranged in two series of eight, once enclosed by hurdles and separated by access gangways. Each pen measures approximately 55m by 8m. Tracks leading to this fair can still be traced on the ground. This group is comparable to the still extant pens at Wilton sheep fair. Sheep fairs were held at longer intervals than local markets; those at Weyhill (Wi) and Lairg (Su) were exceptionally large. For cattle trysts and fairs (eg Falkirk or Mull), see the section on drove roads, pages 420–5.

From longhouse to farmhouse

Separate buildings for animals were uncommon in medieval times, the usual accommodation being at one end of a longhouse. This was the standard farmhouse below the hall level from at least the 13th century to the 16th and persisting until the mid 20th century in upland areas like Cumbria and north Yorkshire. It had its origin in the peasant's cottage which, unless it was a hovel of cob or wattle and daub, might be the bay formed by a pair of crucks, up to 18ft (5.4m) between the cruck feet and 12 to 16ft (3.6–4.7m) apart. This method of construction was introduced in Danish times in the north (A Raistrick: *Buildings in the Yorkshire Dales* (Clapham, Dalesman 1976)). It was found that a bay of this size was convenient for a pair of plough oxen, and the cottage was extended accordingly. This arrangement developed by the 11th or 12th century into a longhouse of several bays, of which one or two were the dwelling of the free tenant farmer – the "firehouse" – and one, two, or three were for the animals. There was often a separate barn. This form became standard in much of the country until the turn of the 16th/17th century, and several survive in the north and west. A possible remnant of the concept may be the *linear farms* of Northumberland (eg Whiteley Shield Farm, West Allendale).

The sequence of development from the longhouse to the modern farmstead in the Lowland Zone was clearly shown in the excavation of the deserted village of Gomeldon (Wi) (M Beresford and J G Hurst: *Deserted Medieval Villages* (Lutterworth 1971)). Here, in the 12th century, one farmstead consisted of one longhouse (known vividly in France as "maison mixte"), with oven in an annexe (building B2); in the 13th century this was demolished and replaced by two other longhouses (B1 and B4). Later in the 13th century a new longhouse (B3) appeared, with B1 being used either as another longhouse or as a stable or byre; B4 was partly demolished, leaving only part of its wall, with external oven attached.

At the end of the 13th century and during the 14th, longhouse B3 was altered to become a farmhouse; B1 was still a longhouse or byre, but now a yard was formed, with an oven enclosure on the site of B4, and a stretch of new wall, and a new barn closing the yard on the north side.

During the 16th century the prosperity of farmers led to the replacement of such longhouses by separate houses for the family, timber-framed or built of brick or stone according to the region, with separate buildings for the animals. A typical example is the (probably) late 17th-century farm built into the ruins of Bishop Waltham palace (Ha), which in 1806 is recorded as consisting of a farmhouse, a barn, a stable, a cartlodge, and a cowhouse. But the earlier pattern still survives in the far north: a blackhouse at Callanish, Lewis, has (or had in 1980) dwelling, byre, piggery, and barn all grouped under the same composite roof, in a tight cluster, for convenience in bad weather (this is a Scandinavian practice).

PLANNED FARMSTEADS

Farmyards in the modern sense of buildings grouped tightly and logically round a courtyard (see **31**), developed as a result of the rising prosperity and status of the yeoman in the period of the enclosures. Enclosure meant larger farms which could use the new methods. Arthur Young, in his *Six Months Tour in the North of England* (1770), thought that the farm should consist, as a minimum, of a good dwelling with a large barn, stables, cowhouse, and hogsties, preferably ranged round an enclosed yard. Raistrick sees the half century from the 1770s to the 1820s or 1830s as the time when farmyards surrounded by the buildings were adopted as the general farm plan, although farmhouses had been rebuilt or enlarged since the early 18th century.

The new fashion is reflected in the sharp increase in books on designs for farmsteads: some 30 from 1800 to 1837 as against 6 from 1750 to 1800 and 8 from 1837 to 1901. The authors included versatile architects of the stature of J C Loudon, but it must be said that some of these designs were more for effect than for practical farming (it was a Romantic age). Thus, John Plaw (in *Ferme ornée: or Rural Improvements* (1800)) proposed a design for "a Farmhouse and Offices, having the Appearance of a Monastery". In this the farmhouse was one of the buildings round a large square courtyard, in which stood a disproportionate octagonal dovecote. All conceivable styles were used, from Classical onwards, and farms were designed to look like castles or churches. Pugin built a "Gothic" barn at Oxenford Grange, Peper Harow (Sy) (1843). Joseph Gandy's designs in the "Classical" style are among the most successful.

The most important books are J C Loudon's *Encyclopaedia of Cottage, Farm and Villa Architecture* (1833) and Charles Waistell's *Designs for Farm Buildings* (1827). A useful summary of this interesting phase is in Martin S Briggs' *The English Farmhouse* (Batsford 1953).

In small farmsteads, Loudon and Waistell both think that the back kitchen should combine bakehouse, brewhouse, and washhouse, but prefer a detached building. A detached dairy (of 1795) can be seen

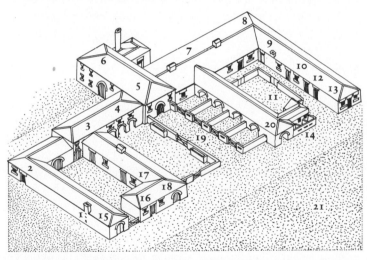

31 *Model farm. Model farms were developed in the 18th century in answer to the rationalisation of farming as a result of the use of new methods, the enclosures, and the rising prosperity and status of the farmers. Buildings were planned tightly and logically round a courtyard. A good example is this farm designed by Thomas Sturgess of Bedale in 1849. It continues the Hanoverian tradition, except that threshing is done by steam. 1, smithy; 2, fertilizer shed; 3, implement house; 4, turnip house; 5, straw barn; 6, threshing machine; 7, fattening house; 8, food store; 9, food preparation; 10, cow house; 11, manure yard; 12, loose boxes; 13, calf house; 14, piggery; 15, farmer's gig; 16, riding horses; 17, stable; 18, hay store; 19, cattle yards; 20, turnip house; 21, proposed site of dwelling house.*

at Kenwood, London. An icehouse was not usual in farms. Loudon suggests circular cowhouses, with the animals (which seen from above are wedge-shaped!) pointing into the centre. Stables should have their windows on one side only, to prevent draughts; upper haylofts, although convenient, are discouraged, as they bring dust and hayseeds into the horses' eyes. There should be separate houses for cows, calves, the bull, and sick animals. Sheep only need folds not houses, though Waistell advises houses. Henroosts can be built above pigsties to keep the hens warm and foxes away; an example is at Beamish Open Air Museum. Barns should incorporate threshing machines: Waistell favours horse-powered machines, Loudon water or steam. Granaries should be over a barn or cartshed, never over a cowhouse or stable. Malt and hop houses are provided as necessary. Room should also be provided for potato-steaming, roots, implements, rabbits, poultry, slaughter-house, turf and fuel, a privy (at least for women servants), the carpenter, and the smith. The farmhouse parlour should overlook the domestic offices and the granary, as exemplified at Cogges (Ox).

There is no doubt that these and similar ideas were very influential, and combinations of them can be seen up and down the country. A standard design was adopted, even for small farms, where the yard had an open side on the south and the buildings were as far as possible functionally arranged. The farmhouse might be in one of the south corners, either integral with the buildings of the yard or detached from it. A variant on the single farmyard is the multiple farmstead, with conjoined row of yards (eg Little Langford (Wi), *c* 1860).

Fine examples of planned farmyards are at Peper Harow (Sy), which has both a courtyard by the house (1760s) and a fine yard at the home farm, with a 17th/18th-century granary on posts. Holkham (Nf) was developed by the Cokes from the 1780s to the 1860s, and a series of model farms built, from Waterden (1784) to Egmere (1857). Local materials were used, and standard plans. An example of compact and very large buildings is at Eastwood Manor, East Harptree (Av) (1858). An elaborate farm was built for the Prince Consort at Windsor. Shugborough (St) has a model farm by Wyatt. Lainston House, near Winchester (Ha), has an octagonal farm of the 1930s. An exceptional assemblage is that at Erddig (Cw) (1770s). This has an estate yard furthest from the house, containing the joiner's shop and sawpit and the blacksmith's shop and wagon shed; next comes the lime yard and dog yard, with garden house and sawmill. An outer yard follows, then a stable yard. This is linked to the house by a range of domestic offices,

32 *The first concrete farm building was this cattle shed at Buscot (Ox), c 1870.*

once restricted to female staff – the laundry yard, with the bakehouse, scullery, and wet and dry laundries. The dovecote is beyond the estate yard and the drying green. The records of the staff and workers from the late 18th century combine to make this set of buildings unique.

Farm buildings with power sources embodied were not uncommon, besides the horse gin-houses dealt with above. These included water-wheels driving machinery, built-in steam engines, and even windmills. Evidence of water power can be seen, eg at Brownwhich Farm, Titchfield (Ha), using a fishpond of Titchfield Abbey, or at Abbotstone Farm (Ha).

The first concrete farm building in England was a barn at Buscot (Ox) (1870), which still exists (see **32**); the Holkham estate experimented with concrete in the 1870s and 1880s, eg at Egmere, but did not continue with it. The farming estate at Buscot was one of the most highly industrialised farms in 19th-century England, and foreshadows the factory farms of today. Buscot was an estate of over 3,500 acres, developed by Robert Campbell from 1859. It contained a 20-acre reservoir to drain the land (1863), a brick and tile works, a malthouse and a cheese wharf on the Thames, a canal from the Thames (Buscot Pill) with wharf, a gravel pit, and a distillery for extracting alcohol from sugar beet (on "Brandy Island") (1869). To collect the 10–12,000 tons of beet a year and other farm produce etc, a narrow-gauge railway (2' 8") was laid for six miles round the estate. Campbell also built on Brandy Island an oil cake mill, a gas works, artificial fertiliser works, and vitriol works. At Oldfield Farm was a water turbine-driven corn mill; the turbine also drove threshing and other machinery, and a dairy. A telegraph system connected the various units of the estate.

Cultivation was done by Fowler ploughing engines. Deep ploughing (up to 30in) was tried. The distillery was closed in 1879, and the estate was sold in 1887.

The huge cattle barn at Buscot continued in use, but its intensive fattening barn probably did not. The concrete unit next to it still exists. Cast-iron items, eg from the distillery, are to be found in buildings in nearby villages, and traces of the railway (small bridges etc, and rails used for other purposes) can be found. Oldfield Farm, at the end of the railway, contains the mill (largely destroyed), a barn (now replaced), the dairy, the blacksmiths', the cooperage, the wheelwrights', sawmills and other estate workshops, and also a 1940s' grain-dryer. The debris of the mill contains the turbine, a hoist, and some machinery. A full account is given by John R Gray in *Industrial Archaeology* 8, 1971. Capitalisation on this scale, exceptional even for Victorian high farming, may have been inspired by American or Australian experiences at a time of expansion in those countries (Campbell was an Australian), yet was symptomatic of what could be done, and, *mutatis mutandis*, has been done in recent years, given a sufficient agricultural prosperity.

Factory farms

Farming objectives and methods have changed radically since the 1950s, and many buildings and machines have become ill-adapted and obsolete. Many farms have replaced all their buildings to meet the new demands. The changes have included the monoculture of grain, root crops, potatoes, livestock, etc. The removal of hedges has created "economically"-sized fields for the massive combine harvesters and other machinery; a computerised combine of 1988 costing £100,000 requires huge fields for its economic employment, and the widespread use of costly machinery has led to a sharp reduction in farm labour. Often changes include the drainage of wetlands, deep ploughing, the greater use of fertilisers and pesticides, and the processing of arable crops, hay, etc in the field. Tristram Beresford quotes a farmer as saying "Farming is about money production, not food production", and there is no doubt that, given suitable soils and climate and access to the appropriate markets, much of British farming has been drastically reoriented and become "agribusiness".

The new buildings include not only massive tower silos and large

Dutch barns for hay and straw, but bulk grain stores and huge sheds ("intensive units") for the mass production of eggs, "broiler" chickens and ducks, calves, and pigs in "sweat-boxes". Vast milking parlours and overwintering sheds are required by the dairy industry and for beef cattle, and sometimes for sheep, with ancillary processing plant; and the sheep farmer needs a lambing shed. Fruit farms need large grading and packing sheds. The massive machinery needs capacious sheds, shelters, and parks. The result is to turn an old farmyard into a street of factory buildings. No less obtrusive are the greenhouses in market gardens for tomatoes, fruit, flowers, etc, and in nurseries for plant propagation and growing-on.

There are, however, modest signs of (belated) change in the late 1980s. Conservation and archaeological concern for the "heritage", coupled with growing public realisation of the damage done by chemicals to the environment and its wildlife and of the doubtful ethics of "intensive" rearing of animals, added to the economic effects of continent-wide overproduction of cereals and dairy produce and the social pressures for more land for housing and other uses, have caused a hesitation, however slight, in the onward march of factory farming. But the basic infrastructure exists, and this can be seen everywhere.

Power sources and farm buildings

The design and relationships of farm buildings have, over the centuries, been radically affected by changes in power sources, as John Weller has cogently shown in *History of the Farmstead* (Faber 1982). Weller identifies three types of farm building: for storage, for processing, and for production. The forms of all these relate directly to the type of power and its source used within them: natural energy; muscular effort (human or animal); indirect power; and fossil fuels. Thus, farm layout has evolved from the longhouse to the courtyard (mostly a product of lowland, mixed agriculture) to the linear (modern mechanised farm). The traditional farmyard and rickyard, the standard type from 1800 to 1950, is now as obsolete as the longhouse, although "model" farms reflected the advanced technology of their day. Modern farms are factories rather than dwellings; their buildings are either containers (cylinder or box), or long, low, insulated sheds for livestock, or wide-span, high-portal framed enclosures for machinery. In fact, the use of machinery had already by 1850 reached the point where a farm was more like a factory.

Weller traces the various sources of power and their influence on buildings. Only the briefest outline of the applications can be given here, to convey the interest of his analysis.

NATURAL ENERGY

Sun-power: orangeries, conservatories, glasshouses, frames etc. *Gravity power*: irrigation, watermeadows; effluent and feeding tanks; milk coolers; corn and feed mills; fertiliser handling, silage clamps. *Water power*: watermills; threshing and other barn machinery. *Wind power*: milling and draining; threshing; model farm layouts with central windmill for power (eg Arthur Young, 1799; Loudon 1833, etc); recent experiments for heating etc.

MUSCULAR POWER

Manual power: the perpetual search for more efficient, simpler, and mass-produced tools to ease labour; milking and dairying; seed-drills etc; barn machinery. *Ox power*: ploughing; haulage (the last ox-team was recorded in Britain in 1964). *Donkey power*: rotary mills; tread-wheels; transport of milk etc between outlying shippons and the farmstead. *Dogs* have also been used for light carts and treadwheels. *Horse power*: haulage; ploughing; rotary mills, gins, etc.

INDIRECT POWER

Warm air and solid fuel: corn-drying (without assistance in warm climates, and by kilns in northern countries); "Great Stoves" assisting fruit and vegetable growing; heat extracted in cooling milk used to warm the parlour or pens. *Steam power*: first used for threshing, later for ploughing. Andrew Meikle adapted steam for threshing in 1786, and by 1807 Arthur Young said that the barn for storing unthreshed corn had become redundant. Young it was who saw (in 1809) that the farm buildings had to be placed in a logical sequence of processes. By the 1860s corn was being threshed in the field or in the rickyard by portable steam-driven machines. Steam ploughing came into use in 1833, and several methods were devised. It was in wide use by the 1860s, but large fields were required. Steam had a direct effect on the buildings.

Lugar (in 1807) planned a piggery with central potato steaming boiler and the pigs kept radially round it. Many model farms in the period of prosperity, 1851–75, were planned round a steam engine – for example, H Stephens in *The Book of the Farm* (1871) illustrates a layout with central steam engine driving machinery by gearing and shafts. The chimney gave the impression of a factory. Steam ploughing continued until the 1930s, and even later in a few places. *Gas power*: gas engines arrived in the 1880s, but, along with steam, were quickly superseded by the internal combustion engine. Gas (compressed and liquefied – propane and butane) has been used since the late 1940s to heat broiler houses etc. Methane, from animal wastes, has been used for lighting since the 1890s, and recently for generating electricity. *Diesel power*: tractors were converted from steam engines in the USA in 1889, and designed from first principles in 1892. The Ivel (1902) was one of the first to have a power take-off to drive ploughs, threshers, or barn machinery, replacing the steam engine. Many makes followed, eg Sanderson, Ford (1908); by 1915 30 US firms were making tractors and 6,000 Fordsons were imported into the UK in 1917. The tractor then took off in this country, and by 1939 there were 60,000 here, accompanied by a decline in the use of horses. By 1949 there were 260,000 and by 1956 478,000. The forearm loader came in the 1950s, with a range of attachments. The tractor cabs of the 1970s made more headroom essential in farm buildings. The combine harvester appeared in 1928, but was not widely used until after World War II. The grass crop was mechanised in the 1960s. Stationary diesel engines were in use from 1895, and by 1950 there were some 200,000. They are still used as standby generators. *Electrical power* transformed the basis of farmstead design. This was foreshadowed before World War I, but did not become a reality until the 1950s. The prospect of radical change took root with the setting up of the National Grid in 1926, even though at first few farms were connected to it. Active encouragement to use electric power on farms began in 1928 with the increased use of telephones, wireless for weather forecasts, and electric motors for driving machinery; heated poultry brooders (1932) led to the broiler. Other applications were lit greenhouses for forcing plants, and rotary garden tools. Farm electrification did not however become significant until after World War II; some 30,000 farms were connected in 1938, 85,000 in 1949, and over 200,000 in 1959; over a quarter of a million (85% of all farms) were reached in the 1960s. There was an increasing variety of uses, both from mains electricity and from small, even portable, motors – "push-button farming". The 1970s saw electronic milking parlours, with automated feeding and cow identification. The design of buildings changed dramatically in the 1970s, and electronics, computers, and automated processes will dominate farming henceforth.

The structure and materials of farm buildings have always been closely related to other rural and village building – the vernacular – but this changed radically about 1950. Even this change was anticipated by the Dutch barn in the early 19th century and the concrete silo in the 1880s. But since 1950 farm buildings have used the general building technology employed for offices, schools, village halls, etc – framed and clad buildings and, for small buildings, prefabricated insulated timber-panel construction. The scale has increased and linearity has replaced the old enclosure pattern. Building innovations also reflect management changes. Farms are factories, and usually do little for the environment. John Weller sees the future as continuing standardisation, but including improvisation as costs rise and more organic crops are grown. In his estimation farming is likely to polarise between a core of high-technology factories and a substratum of more "life-style" farms; by 2000 the proportions may reach 4:1, with a 1:4 ratio of workers.

33 Oasts. These are kilns, either square or circular, for drying hops as an essential stage of brewing. They are familiar sights in traditional brewing counties, such as Kent and Hampshire.

As a footnote to Weller's thesis, it may be added that the field pattern of a farm, not only its buildings, also reflects changes in equipment and its power sources, and the methods of farming, as well as changes in social structure. There are useful insights on this in C T Smith: *An Historical Geography of Western Europe before 1800* (Longman 1967).

Oast houses and maltings

Not all drying kilns were for drying grain before storage or milling. Some were for *malting* – roasting barley to make malt – even in Roman times. Beer was made universally until the 19th century in houses, farms, and institutions of all kinds, and most inns brewed their own beer. Gilbert White built a brewhouse at Selborne in 1765, and Queen's College, Oxford, made its own beer from 1340 until World War II. Specialised breweries appeared by the late 17th century.

More distinctive indications of brewing are the *maltings* and the *oast houses* (see **33**) for drying *hops*. Although perhaps not strictly farm buildings, they are none the less specialised buildings for processing farm products. Making malt is the preliminary process of brewing. Barley is steeped in water, spread on floors to germinate, and, when sprouting begins, is dried in a kiln to stop further growth. The result is malt. Maltings therefore consist of a long building for spreading the

34 *Maltings. Malt is prepared from barley, and has to be dried and cured to stop germination; this is done in kilns. Large maltings, such as this one at Farnham (Sy), c 1880, contain all the processes in one complex.*

barley and a kiln or kilns, not unlike oasts, which are usually visible from outside. Many are still in use, and many others survive unused or converted to other uses, such as the spectacular and famous examples at Farnham (Sy) (see **34**) or Snape (Su).

The malt is then transferred to, or within, the brewery, which again can be small and local, or vast and national, like those at Burton-on-Trent or Alton. The malt is first crushed in a mill to make *grist*, then *mashed* (mixed) with water and put in a *tun*, where the starch is converted into sugar. The sugary liquid (*wort*) is drawn off into a collecting vessel, where more hot water is sprayed on the mash to remove the remaining sugar (*sparging*). (The spent grains are used for cattle feed.) The wort is transferred to a *copper*, where hops are added, and boiled; the length of boiling controls the colour, "nose", and strength of the beer. The spent hops are removed and used as fertiliser. The wort is cooled and run into a *fermenting* vessel, where yeast is added. The surplus yeast is used for food products. Finally, the beer is run off into tanks to mature for keg or bottled beers, or racked into casks for draught beer. More hops can be added at this stage and, at the end, isinglass to clear the liquid. Maurice Lovett's booklet (*Brewing and Breweries*, Shire, 1981) gives a useful account of these processes.

English *ale* was made from fermented malt, but did not contain hops. *Beer* (which does) was introduced to Winchelsea from the Low Countries in 1400, although hops had been grown in England in the 14th century, but only as herbs. Hops used in brewing in the 15th century were imported until the end of the century, when brewers settled in London, using hops grown in Kent. Kent was not only closest to the Low Countries, but the soils were right, the enclosed fields were suitable for hop growing, and there was wood for poles and casks and charcoal for drying the hops. Beer gained ground in the 16th century, and was encouraged by Edward VI. Hops were grown on a commercial scale by 1520, eg at Westbere (Kt).

By the 1550s there were 26 breweries in London, and many innkeeper brewers. In 1577 there were nearly 20,000 taverns, alehouses, and inns in England and Wales; there are now 75,000, of which 50,000 are tied (tied houses date from the late 18th century). In 1840 there were nearly 50,000 brewers, in 1880 under 25,000, in 1900 just over 3,000, and now about 200. Breweries replaced innkeeper brewing (except for a few) by the end of the 17th century.

By the mid 17th century hops were grown in 14 counties, but mainly in Kent (a third of the crop), the Weald, Surrey and Hampshire (particularly around Farnham and Alton), and Herefordshire and Worcestershire. A hop market was set up in London, at Little Eastcheap in the late 17th century and later in the Borough; this building still stands, but is put to other uses. Kentish and Wealden growers used the London market; Stourbridge Fair (Ca) covered hops as well as wool in the 18th century, but was superseded by Weyhill (Ha). By 1850 there were 50,000 acres of hops, and by 1870 hops were grown in 40 English, 8 Welsh, and 5 Scottish counties. The peak was in 1878, with over 70,000 acres, but this reverted to the 1850 figure by 1900. In recent years the acreage has sharply declined owing to increased imports, and former hop areas are studded with disused or converted oast houses.

A great many systems of poles, wires, and string (coir is the best) have been tried; Henry Butcher's wirework system of 1875 is still in use, as is Coley's vinery system of 1874. The old pole system was used until the 1970s in some areas, but permanent wirework systems are now well established. Hops were picked by hand until recent years, but the hop-picking machine introduced in 1934 brought this practice practically to an end after World War II. In the late 19th and early 20th century whole families, mainly from east or south London, and sometimes three generations at once, spent their holidays, usually in the same hop fields, year after year. Conditions were often bad, but gradually special housing was built for the pickers and even a hospital (Hopper's Hospital, Five Oaks Green (Kt), which existed from 1910 to 1969). Special missions worked among them (as they did among dockers, seamen, and coal-heavers). Some hop gardens were well organised, of course, such as the vast 300-acre (120 ha) farm of Whitbreads at Beltring (Kt), which has a spectacular row of oasts (see 33); here some 5,000 pickers were employed, handling half a million bushels of hops from half a million plants (*hills*). The hops were picked into a bin (or into baskets in east Kent), then put into sacks (*pokes* or *pockets*) and taken to the oast to be dried. The amounts picked were recorded by tokens or tally sticks.

The earliest surviving oast house is near Cranbrook (Kt), *c* 1750. It consists of three rooms, one with a drying floor on which the hops are spread and which is reached by the hot air from the kiln. When dry the hops are raked into the third room to cool. Wood was used for firing the kiln in the 16th and 17th centuries, but charcoal was standard from then to the 1930s. One hundred sacks of charcoal were required to dry a ton of hops. Oil heating is now general. (The development of the oast is conveniently sketched by Richard Filmer.) The 17th-century oasts were often just barns with a fireplace under a drying floor. During the

18th century, greater quantities of hops needed a pyramidal ceiling over the fire, to give more draught; these kilns were often inside the roof, with merely a cowl projecting. The familiar round kiln, with drying floor over the furnace, and adjacent cooling room, over a storage area for the filled pockets, began in the early 19th century. Square kilns were easier to build, and came in about 1900. Electric fans enabled the pointed cowls to be replaced by louvred openings by 1930.

The dried and cooled hops are tightly packed in the pockets under compression, at first by treading and then from *c* 1850 by means of

35 *Dovecotes. The keeping of pigeons, for meat, eggs, feathers, and saltpetre, was limited to manorial lords in medieval times. Pigeons were kept in lofts, or in special buildings, square or circular. Inside were nest boxes in the walls, reached by a revolving ladder (a potence). This one is at Kinwarton (Ww), 14th century.*

a press; the pocket is suspended in a cradle under an opening in the cooling room floor. The pockets take 1.5cwt (75kg), and are sewn up when filled. Each pocket is marked with the year, place of growth, and grower's name. Until 1980 sulphur was added to give colour. The hops are moved to the press with a *scuppet*, a broad shovel, which takes regional forms. The hops in the pocket are *sampled* for quality and graded. Since 1979 the hydraulic hop baler has been used, giving a rectangular bale.

36 *Interior of Kinwarton dovecote, showing the revolving ladder or potence.*

Whisky kilns

The kilns of the Scottish whisky distilleries are as distinctive as the English oasts. Brewing from malt was at least as important in the early 18th century as distilling, but whisky gained ground later. Much domestic brewing and distilling was done, but large breweries existed in Glasgow and Edinburgh by 1830, and were numerous after 1850. In 1835–6 there were 640 licensed brewers in Scotland, but only 217 in 1866, of which only 98 were selling wholesale; the larger breweries had come to dominate the industry. Private brewhouses continued, as that at Traquair House, Innerleithen (Ps), built about 1730 and still in production.

Whisky was distilled in the 18th century, publicly in the Lowlands and mostly illicitly in the Highlands. The trade was got under control, with difficulty, by the 1830s, but illicit stills are not unknown even today. Of the two main types of whisky, that *blended* from grain and malt became very popular in the 19th century. The unblended, or *malt*, whisky is made from barley soaked in water and spread on a malting floor, where it germinates, and its starch is converted into sugar. Germination is then halted by drying the barley over a peat fire in a kiln, which gives a distinctive flavour. The kiln usually has a pagoda-like roof, with square vent at the top, and this form marks the particular style of a distillery. The dried malt is crushed, soaked in hot water to dissolve the sugars, and this liquor, with added yeast, is transferred to a vat for fermentation. The alcoholic mash is twice distilled, in large spheroidal pot stills. The alcohol vapour condenses in a copper worm cooled in a tank of running water. The whisky end product is matured in oak casks for a minimum of three years, and sometimes up to twenty. The golden tint is achieved by using old sherry casks, or by adding caramelised sugar. The water used in these processes should come off granite and through peat. Thus the malt industry, although once spread wider, is largely concentrated in Speyside, but with outliers as far apart as Kirkwall (Or) and Campbeltown (Ar). In 1824 there were 120 malt-whisky distilleries; this number rose to over 200 in the 1830s and 1840s, but fell again to 122 in 1884, the largest centres being Glasgow, Campbeltown, Edinburgh, Linlithgow, and Speyside. Blending has since the 1820s been concentrated in the Central Lowlands and Fife, using imported maize. There are now about 100 malt distilleries in Scotland, and only 13 grain, yet the latter produce about half the total spirit. Many of the old buildings, both distilleries and warehouses, still remain.

Dovecotes

Dovecotes are a highly individual class of building in, or more often just outside, the farmyard. Pigeons were reared for their meat (squabs were mostly taken, as being less tough than adult birds), their feathers and down, for beds and pillows, and their dung. The latter was a highly-prized manure for barley, hops, vines, and other plants; it was also used in tanning and, from the 15th century, to make saltpetre for use in the manufacture of gunpowder. The keeping of pigeons was introduced by the Normans, and throughout the Middle Ages was restricted to barons, abbots, and lords of manors; later it was extended to parish priests, and by the 18th century every farm had a dovecote or a pigeon loft. Decline set in by 1800, and dovecotes went out of use during the 19th century. But in the 17th century there were said to be 26,000, each containing 500–1000 birds. In the Middle Ages the pigeons were legally allowed to gather food where they liked, and were a constant source of discontent to the peasantry who had to watch them eating their grain. A similar situation in France has been cited as one of the grievances which led to the Revolution.

Dovecotes occur in all building materials. They are often circular (see **35**), with a pyramidal roof with a cupola containing openings for the birds and providing a rain shelter; but they may be square, rectangular, octagonal, cruciform, or "lectern" (mainly in Scotland and the north of England, with a lean-to roof against a straight rear wall). Pigeons are also kept in the gables or the upper storeys of buildings, the lower floors of which are used for quite different purposes, and even in church towers. The inside walls of dovecotes are lined with rows of identical nest boxes, let into the wall or added to it; these are normally L-shaped, but may be rectangular. The circular dovecote lends itself to a "potence", a central post with bars projecting from it to which is fixed a ladder; this revolves on a pivot, to give the pigeon keeper access to any nest box (see **36**). Good examples are at Bisham Abbey (Bk) or Albury (Sy). Walls are thinner in 18th-century dovecotes, and doors larger from the 17th century.

The few Norman dovecotes to survive (eg Manorbier Castle (Pe), *c* 1150, or Dunster (So), 11th/12th century) have been largely rebuilt, but a fine intact early example is that at Garway (He) (1326). Other good examples follow, but there is a very wide variety to be seen: Bollitree Farm, Weston (He) rectangular, with iron rat-guards; Melcombe Bingham (Do) round, 15th-century; Henley Hall, Ludlow (Sp)

37 *A special Scottish type of "doocot" is a lean-to building against a back wall. This typical example is at Glamis.*

octagonal, potence, holes with left turn (unusual); Elmley Lovett (Wo), brick, square, but with potence, and alighting ledges; Bretforton (Wo), which once had six, and still has three, one medieval, one 17th-century, one 18th-century; Garsington (Ox) has two square ones, 17/18th-century.

At Maxstoke (Ww) an upper room in the castle gatehouse was fitted with nests in the 16th century; Warmington (Nh) has the nest holes built out from the wall on a wooden framework plastered over; Notley Abbey, Long Crendon (Bc) has projecting inner walls to carry more nests (it has between 4,000 and 5,000). Nest holes can be seen in the church towers at Sarnesfield (He), Llanwarne (late 14th-century; in ruins), Collingbourne Ducis (Wi), Monk Bretton (WY), and Elkstone (Gl); at Marlborough a room over the chancel was adapted for nests,and there are some in a mill at Manor Farm, Upper Swell (Gl). At Corby (Cu) is a cote in the form of a Doric temple, with potence (1813); the Halifax district has several "pigeon-hoils" in gables and porches. At Llanthony (Mo) is a circular one 2m or so below ground level with a beehive roof (once perhaps covered with earth); domed roofs are also found in Pembrokeshire and the south-west of England. At Buckland-tout-Saints (Dv) a thatched cote was adapted as a game larder, and at Stoke Rivers (Dv) a cote was converted for bees. At Wisbech (Ca) is a cast-iron cote with two boxes, set in a bricked-up window space of Queen Anne date. There are many cotes in the south-west (called culveries), and in some parts of the Midlands.

The Scottish "doocots", met with also just on the English side of the border, are usually round or oblong; some have two compart-ments, perhaps to avoid disturbing the birds too much or to foil thieves; nest boxes are usually rectangular, not L-shaped. Of the oblong types Nether Liberton, near Edinburgh, with its lean-to roof is typical (see **37**); of the circular or beehive Gilmerton (EL), and of the circular with sloping roof Phantassie, Preston Kirk (EL) are typical. A more southerly "lectern" dovecote is that at Willington (Bd) (c 1520). Some "architectural" examples verge on the folly.

The Village

A village is a rural agglomeration, usually quite small, providing the minimum essential amenities and services primarily, if not exclusively, for the inhabitants of its own parish. Features of a village, not shared with a town, are the irregular building and building line, trees and gardens in the streets, and the small scale.

There are some 10,000 villages in Britain, but only about a quarter of the population lives in them; fewer than 3% of village dwellers are engaged in agriculture, and the majority of them earn their living away from where they live or derive their income from sources elsewhere. In 1800 some three quarters of the people lived in villages, and over half worked on the land or in related occupations. This is a striking change, the causes and effects of which are outlined on page 44. Villages have gradually grown larger over the centuries, particularly in the Midlands and East Anglia, but before 1700 the average village population was under 200.

Villages certainly existed in the Roman period and the pre-Roman Iron Age, and perhaps, in some form, from the first days of farming in the Neolithic (5th millennium BC). Following the breakdown of Romano-British life after the Romans left Britain in the early 5th century AD, a fresh start was made by the Anglo-Saxons and related incomers, and villages, usually on new sites, again covered much of the country. They had several possible origins: they may have come into being by growth from a single place (shrine, church, farm, etc), or by a voluntary concentration of farms originally scattered as part of the first (post-Roman) settlement (thus Brian Roberts calls a late Saxon village a "linked farm cluster"), or by the agglomeration of two discrete settlements with the creation of a green between them from what was originally heath or meadowland, or, finally, by deliberate planting and planning.

THE SHAPE OF VILLAGES

With many possible origins and a wide variety of local circumstances, it is evident that villages can take many forms, and that the three or four basic shapes can merge into variants, and shift and change.

It has long been observed that the complex English village, on which so much lore and tradition has been based, is actually a characteristic of the Lowland Zone – the Midlands and eastern and southern England – while in the Highland Zone villages are smaller, hamlets (small settlements, usually grouped round a farmstead, and with no church, isolated from the nearest village) are more common, and the "typical" pattern can even be isolated farms scattered over the usable land. Thus it became customary to refer to a "Celtic" pattern of farming, as opposed to an Anglo-Saxon one, and to attribute the different types to the different backgrounds, customs, and temperaments of the two peoples. The origins of "green" and "street" villages were sought in the Anglo-Saxon homelands of north Germany, from where they were supposed to have been brought direct by the first Germanic settlers in England.

But recent researches have shown that this dichotomy is too simple, and can be not only misleading but actually false. While cultural and ethnic differences cannot be entirely overlooked, and may in certain cases still have substance, it is now clear that the guiding factors were not racial, but social and economic. Thus the Scandinavians, who settled in Britain long after the Celts or the Saxons, made no specific contribution to the shape of villages. Danish villages in eastern England are no different from Saxon ones, and the scattered pattern of Scandinavian farms in the Pennines and north-west England would not be out of place in Cornwall or Wales.

It is not absolutely clear why the normal basic pattern over most of the country is not the *nucleated* village (one based on three or more farmsteads and associated buildings, at a junction of roads) at all, but scattered farms and hamlets. Nucleated villages indeed are commonest in the former open field areas. Opinion leans towards the explanation being the result of a reorganisation carried out in the late Saxon period, or perhaps even continuing after the Norman conquest, within a pre-existing framework of much older estates. Nucleation may have arisen because of rising population, the development of open field farming, the parochialisation of the church, and the imposition of feudal authority. Certainly the formerly held theory that nucleated villages were brought to England with the first European settlers is now seen to be untenable. The "importation" theory of the origin of nucleated villages is set out, for example, in Harry Thorpe: "The green village in its European setting" (ed Alan Small): *The Fourth Viking Congress*, 1965.

The source of the difference must therefore be looked for in the way of life in the two zones. It is at once apparent that villages are an outcome of arable or mixed farming in the Lowland Zone, and scattered farms and hamlets of pastoral farming in the Highland Zone. Arable farming, particularly after the development of the open field system, demanded cooperation among the farmers of each parish; clearance of waste land and woodland for fields could best be done in common, and the heavy work of ploughing, drainage, etc often called for the sharing of equipment, tools, and oxen; stock also needed protection or management in mixed farming. Pastoral farming, on the other hand, could be carried on by a family without much help, and it was more convenient to live among the pasturages.

Another point to be borne in mind is that, while most villages were in existence before Domesday (1086), and many were much earlier, there is little evidence for their original shape. Records are almost wholly silent on this; although some villages may have continued substantially unaltered, others are known to have changed. Thus plots may be empty or back lanes deserted, which can alter the form of the village, or the church may now be some way from the village, one reason for which may be that the whole village has moved.

THE SITING OF VILLAGES

It goes without saying that villages were sited in the most convenient place, preferably on dry ground (an extreme case being the gravel "islands" in the Fens), with handy water supply, at focal points for local, if not main, roads, and with ready access to the fields, the meadowland, and the waste. These principles can be demonstrated from prehistoric times. Founders of villages had a sound, if instinctive, eye for geology, which sometimes determined the shape also. Thus Selborne (Ha) – Saxon, and not replanned – is a mile-long street lying along the junction of the Lower Chalk and the Upper Greensand, taking advantage of the spring line. Yet some villages are sited in apparently unsuitable positions. Thus the deserted part of Rockingham (Nh) was built on an unstable slope, Piddletrenthide (Do), was actually in a stream, and Whittlesford (Ca) was in a damp peat hollow. One suspects that in some cases good land was too valuable to build on!

Detailed study of a particular area may reveal the variety which siting produces. An illuminating survey by E M Yates of the villages between Dorking and Guildford in Surrey, along the southern edge of the North Downs, can serve to illustrate this. The type of village here depends on the space available and the water supply. There is an absence of springs, so most of the villages are along the streams; only Headley and Abinger are dependent on well water. Many of the villages are associated with strip parishes, ie long parishes running from downs through sand to the Weald, in order to benefit from as many types of soil and ecology as possible. Each settlement is very different: Wotton has no village as such and may have been a scatter (unless there was once a village by the church); Chilworth church is isolated but there is a village; many farms have old, Saxon names; Gomshall had a small number of large farms; Shere was a settlement, either of small farmsteads or industrial. The settlements are small, and some are mere hamlets. In Domesday Dorking had 55 people, Gomshall 44, Shere 31, and Chilworth 8. Similarly placed villages, with similar geology, in Berkshire were much larger. The pattern was like that of present-day Kent. The original Saxon-Jutish pattern was farms and hamlets. The growth was due to the adoption of the two- or three-field system, which encouraged the grouping of farms, but for its full development needed ample open land. Those villages, like Betchworth, which fulfilled these conditions show steady growth as villages. Where the strips were widely scattered, then the single farmstead remained the focal point.

Kent was relatively free from feudal dues, owing to its high proportion of large grazing lands; at Shere, Gomshall, and Dorking in Surrey, the demesne lord was the king, who was more remote than a resident lord, and, except for Betchworth, the villages had vast areas of poor grazing land. So growth was uneven and indeed industry, not farming, was the cause of the growth of Shere and Gomshall (cloth), Abinger Hammer (iron), and Chilworth (gunpowder). The influence of London also affected these places. Each village, in fact, has to be studied as a special case. Place-names often help to show the sequence of settlement – thus, in Surrey, early names of farms remote from the streams (Paddington, Sutton, Westcott) indicate secondary settlements. The influence of situation can also be seen here: most of these villages are not particularly well sited for modern conditions, and have not grown large; but one, Dorking, was in a gap in the downs, and thus could become a focal point and a market town. Another type of change is exemplified by Harting (Sx), which began as a scatter of farms, many of which have disappeared since the 17th century, being replaced by a village (see *Field Studies* I, 3 (1961)).

In open field land, villages are fairly uniformly spaced; B K Roberts (*Rural Settlement in Britain*, Folkestone, Dawson, 1977) finds an average distance of 2.4km from village centre to the furthest point on the perimeter of the open field land, and 2.5km to the township boundary.

TYPES OF VILLAGE PLAN

It is convenient to recognise three main types of plan, based fundamentally either on *rows* or *agglomeration (nucleation)*: *street plans* (see **38**), where rows of tofts (house plots) are located along one or both sides of a street or a long, narrow green; *green plans*, where the tofts stand round, or within, a spacious open green; *agglomerated plans* (see **39**), where the tofts line more than one street, with the streets lying at angles to each other; where the roads meet at one point, the village is radial eg Beaumont (Cu) (see **40**). In addition there are *scattered* villages and certain *planned* villages.

But although these may be the basic minima, villages are extremely varied and complex, and it is not always easy to place a village at once into one of the categories. Each category can be divided into regular and irregular forms eg one-row, irregular, Wasdale Head (Cu) (see **41**); regular nucleated, Braithwaite (Cu) (see **42**); irregular nucleated, Cardington (Sp) (see **43**). B K Roberts has recognised 11 variant

forms, and some of these shade into each other – and each plan type can occur either singly or as a component of a complex form. Regular forms are where the tofts are in clear rows or are in some standard and repeated shape or size along the street or round the green. Villages can vary in size from quite small hamlets to small towns, and this can sometimes make it harder to identify the basic form (see **44**). Archaeological investigation, not always practicable, is often the only way of determining the sequence.

Every village has two groups of elements: those where all members of the community have rights and those where the usage rights are restricted to individuals. The *common* elements are the church and churchyard, the common land or green, with pinfold or pound where stray animals could be kept until claimed, the smithy, the bakehouse, the stocks, and the routeways – the street, the back lane, the cattle drift to the common grazing (greens were also used for recreation, and as butts for archery or firearm practice). The *private* elements are the manor house and hall garth, with its dovecote and fishponds, and the tofts or garths themselves; the word toft originally meant the whole tenurial plot but later came to be restricted to the house site, while the associated enclosures, gardens, etc were called crofts; but the earlier usage is convenient.

Later common elements included a shop, an alehouse or inn, the school, the village hall, and a recreation ground if there was no green.

38 *Village plan elements: 1.*

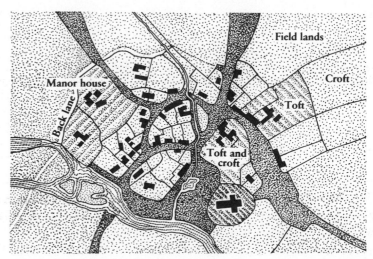

39 *Village plan elements: 2*

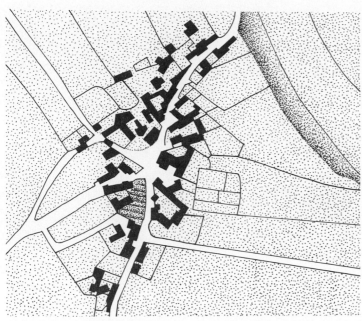

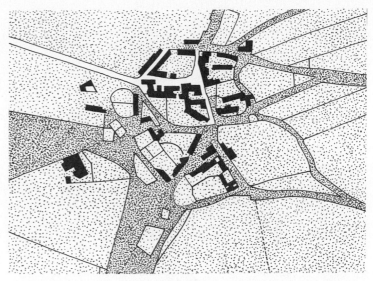

42–3 *An agglomerated village is a tight cluster of buildings at the meeting-point of several roads. This again may be regular, as 42 – Braithwaite (Cu) (from a map of 1866), or irregular, as 43 – Cardington (Sp) (from a map of 1883).*

40 *The radial type of village is an agglomeration where the roads meet at one point, which often forms a central space – Beaumont (Cu) (from a map of 1867).*

A large village might also have a lock-up, an almshouse, and a work-house. An "open" village might have a chapel. The mill was usually manorial at first, but served the needs of the villagers. (These elements are described in detail below.)

All these types are found in Europe, eg the German Rundling (see **45**), but the detailed reasons for their appearance in England are still not clear. The green, which some have thought might be a feature of

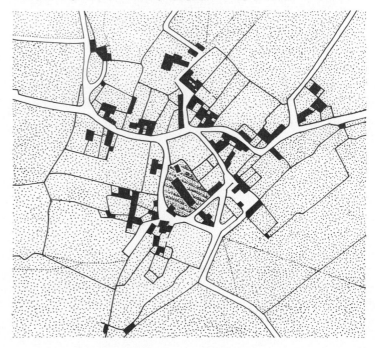

41 *A very basic form of village, the one-row type; this has houses along one side of a street, continuous or irregular, as here – Wasdale Head (Cu), from a map of 1862.*

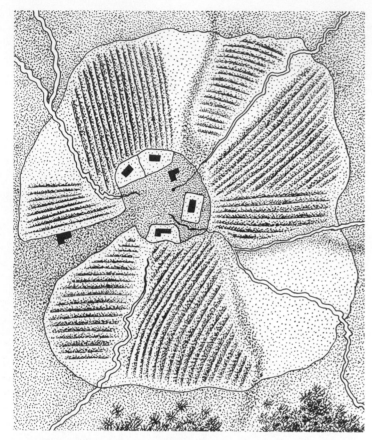

44 *A basic medieval village, with farms on a green, surrounded by open fields and meadows, with access track and ways into the woodland and waste.*

medieval replanning, may in fact be an original Anglo-Saxon feature.

In recent years the shape of villages has also been changed by the building of new houses, whether "council estates" or private houses or bungalows. Retired people have moved into villages as well as commuters working in nearby towns, which has also altered the balance of the social life of the village. Second or holiday homes or conversions of older cottages are a continuing problem for villages, and in some areas (eg Wales) have caused great upheaval and resentment, not only by disturbing the pattern of occupation but by sending up property values to levels beyond the reach of the local people (see "urbanisation", page 44).

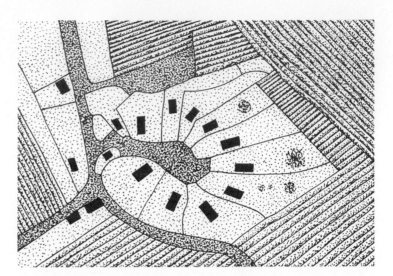

45 *A German Rundling, or round village. An archetypal village plan in the Anglo-Saxon homeland.*

Street villages usually consist of two long rows of houses, cottages, and farms along both sides of a road. Examples are numerous, such as Long Melford (Su), White Roding (Ex), Henley-in-Arden (Ww), or Appleton-le-Moors (NY) (see **46**); a regular two-row village without green. The presence of active farms in village streets is not uncommon even today, as at Thornton-le-Dale (NY). A broad street can sometimes look very like a narrow green. A very frequent form of this type is where the village is sited at a crossroads or where several roads meet. In this case it may be called *nucleated*. Shere (Sy) is a good example, and indeed some of the most typically "English" villages are of this type.

Green villages are distinctive and frequent in the Lowland Zone. The functions of a green were: the convenience of feeding, watering, and milking livestock close to the village farms; prevention of straying on to open arable fields (some village greens were banked, some gated); ease of collecting manure; the protection of livestock at night or in emergency; its function as a place for meeting and recreation. Greens carried rights of common pasture and of recreation as well. Middridge (Du) is a good example of a regular two-row village with green (see **47**).

In England only the farms facing directly onto the green normally had the right to graze cows, sheep, horses, and geese (not pigs), not those on the back lane. In Yorkshire only those fronting on the green had those rights, not those with gable ends only facing it. Buildings on the

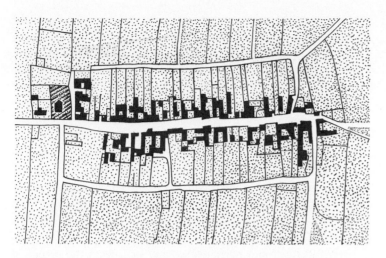

46 A regular two-row village without green – Appleton-le-Moors (NY) (from a map of 1895); tofts and crofts along a street, with church and manor house at the end.

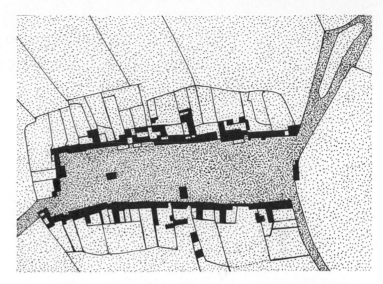

47 Some villages are built round a grassy open space, or green (some have more than one green), used for grazing and other commercial activities. This is a very good example of a regular two-row street green village – Middridge (Du) (from a map of c 1844).

green are usually only those of common use – church, chapel, smithy, pound, wellhouse, inn, and later the school and village hall. Squatters (landless people encroaching on commons, roadsides, etc) were not usually allowed, until farming changed from pastoral to arable, or the rise of artisans etc. Most greens had a pond or spring. The village road pattern was originally concentrated on the green; later, additional roads often related to the back lane. Green villages are associated with common systems, eg open fields, common pasture, etc.

All the activities of the village centred on the green. Leisure was provided for: maypoles survive in many places, such as Aldborough (NY); there is a quintain at Offham (Kt); cricket was later played there. Local law and order was enforced there (lock-ups, stocks, pillories). Markets and fairs were held on the green, if the village had them, and in due course the inn and shop were there too. As the village grew but could not expand into the open fields, encroachment took place on the green. At first this was restricted to the school, the smithy, and perhaps the chapel, but later ordinary houses were built (as at Airton (NY), and the green would begin to become irregular in appearance, if not in basic shape.

A study by H Thorpe of villages in County Durham shows that out of 232 villages in the county, 101 have greens, divided almost equally between street green, broad or regular greens, and indefinite or irregular greens. The street greens are in some sense an intermediate type between the street villages and the green villages. Before the time of metalled roads many villages had their houses set far enough back from each other to allow the road room for several tracks and for animals to graze; there might also be a pond for ducks and geese. This gives a wide main street, with farms and gardens at right angles to it, and back lanes; the plan resembles a bicycle pedal. This type is common in north-east England. Appleby (Cu) has all the appearance of having begun in this way, although it has now "hardened" into a town.

A variant of this form is an oval or spindle-shaped village, and triangular forms can grow at nodal points. Open or incomplete forms may be either inchoate or defective, perhaps because of depopulation. Some so-called street villages have front gardens along the street, but these may be the long green enclosed as front gardens (eg Alne (NY)). In southern and midland England there are "squatting settlements" on old heaths, roadsides, commons, and "greens" (green lanes).

The green proper is wider than the street green. The regular (sometimes also confusingly called "nucleated") is most frequent in the northern half of eastern England, and may be seen as the culmination of the village set in the middle of its open fields. The houses are close-set

109

round a rectangular space, often quite large. The church and manor house may be among, or close to, these buildings, but this is not always the case. The road usually passes through the green, and sometimes a stream also. There are usually back lanes dividing the crofts from the fields, and sometimes a bank also. Milburn (Cu) and East Witton (NY) are good examples. Thorpe showed that most such villages in Durham and adjacent counties were aligned roughly east–west. This is probably the effect of "solskifte", or sun division, a tradition brought from northern Europe, under which "the land rod used to measure village tofts was used to lay out the field strips, and furthermore the field strips follow the order of tofts in the village" in an east–west direction (to quote the convenient definition of B K Roberts). Solskifte is not confined to the north-east but is found throughout the country; eg there are 13 cases in Somerset. In Lincolnshire (eg Scotton) the size of regular greens suggested to Maurice Barley that they represented the first furlong of land cleared by the first settlers, and this may give a clue to the origins of many.

Provision for expansion varied with the form of the village and was most difficult with broad-green and circular forms. Back lanes were used, of course. The green itself could be extended, eg Heighington (Du), or converted, as the town grew, into a market square, eg Ripon (NY); Cottingham (Hu) has one called "Market Green", and compare Cross Green in Otley (WY) and Bull Green in Halifax. Or there might have been peripheral development or the actual filling-in of the green. The street green village could just lengthen unless blocked at one or both ends by a river, manor house, or church. In this case development could take place at the other end or along the back lanes or other roads. Both types could become agglomerated.

Some villages have marginal or peripheral greens – those with no central green today, eg Copt Hewick (NY). A need may have been seen for a green and it was made at one end. Former street green villages whose green became enclosed as gardens may have needed a green and made one at one end (Carleton (Hu)). Villages which had a central green but needed others also, perhaps for additional grazing or for recreation, could add more greens (Gargrave (NY) has three). Or a market town could move its market from the centre (once a village green) to a new green on the outskirts (eg Royston (Ht)).

The northern limit of green villages is about 57°N. In Britain, they exist in England (but not in the south-west or the Lakes), and in south-east Scotland to the Forth; they do not occur in Wales. The limit is related to the climatic basis of the economy involved. The ultimate focus is not known, but is probably north-central Europe.

The *irregular greens* can be of all sizes to very large indeed. They are not always closely built all round, and indeed the houses may be widely spaced. The church and manor house may be some way away, and not all the farms of the village are on the green. These greens in fact seem not to be planned as such, but probably represent relics of heathland which has been retained as meadow or open space after houses have grown up round about. They are therefore commonest in areas where there is much surviving heathland, such as the Weald, west Dorset, and parts of the Midlands; they occur also in Suffolk and Essex, where reclamation of land has been carried further. Good examples are Pirbright (Sy), Wisborough Green (Sx), Matching Green (Ex), and South Elmham All Saints (Su).

Greens in Essex and Hertfordshire are not always the greens of villages but separate growths, whose origins are not always clear; Sandon (Ht) has four greens in the parish, and three other medieval settlements without greens. ("Green" has another sense also, mainly in Essex, as a droveway or disused track between hedges, eg Epping Long Green.) Green villages too seem mostly to be a product of a relatively late extension or reorganisation; some, eg Baulking (Ox), are due to clearance of earlier buildings or crofts (see C J Bond in Della Hooke (ed): *Medieval Villages* (Oxford University Committee for Archaeology, Monograph 5, 1985)). But Chalton (Ha) was built round a green in the 7th century.

Polyfocal villages are those with two or more centres – greens or other focal points. They usually represent the addition of a unit to, or beside, an existing one; this addition may be planned by the sole lord or may be the creation of another manor, eg Bardolfeston (Do). A good example is Hook Norton (Ox), which has four contiguous units, Scotland End, Town End, Southrop, and East End. Reach (Ca) is both polyfocal and planned. An interesting variant of this is the *dual settlement*, where two hamlets next to each other, both present at an early date, remain in association. Such is Haselor (Ww), which formed three manors in 1086 and where a parish church is midway between the hamlets of Upton and Walcot (the latter meaning home(s) of the British). Whissendine (Le) is a double village, like Hildersham (Ca), made up of two separate manors; Thornton Dale (NY) has three sections. Goathland (NY), built round several greens, and Chilfrome (Do) or Swaffham Bulbeck (Ca) (see **48**) are hard to explain, and Sawston (Li) is almost too complex to unravel. The market town of Alton (Ha), although not strictly a village, consists of two manors, on each side of a stream, one with the church and the other with the market place.

The antithesis of the irregular greens is the *planned village*. As said above, villages have been changing their shape all through the centuries, and it is unlikely that the present plan of a village will be the same as that of its Anglo-Saxon predecessor. While some villages have expanded or declined, and yet preserved their original shape, others have changed from one type to another; such drastic changes can hardly have been other than planned by a landowner or agreed by

the villagers. Much light has been thrown on this process in the last 30 years by the excavations on the sites of deserted villages (see below). Planned villages postdate manors, and most were created by lords in the 12th or 13th centuries. It would be interesting to know how far the villagers shared in the planning, or how far it was entirely imposed.

Less is known about medieval Scottish villages than English ones, but four broad categories are recognised: irregular; regular with house gable ends at right angles to the coast (these are east coast sea towns, and may be of one row, eg Crovie (Ab) or several, eg Avoch (RC); regular linear villages or burghs, comprising two rows, eg Kinrossie (Pe); and regular, grouped round a central square, eg Gifford (EL) or green, eg Denholm (Rx); an elaborate example is Aberchirder (Ba) (see **49**).

In medieval Wales freemen held substantial homesteads which were sometimes grouped in *clusters*, but more frequently in *girdle-patterns* round the edges of open field arable sharelands, eg Hendre Gaerwys (Gw). The bond undertenants of such freemen lived in *hamlets*, eg Llan-non (Dy). Royal vills, such as Aberffraw (An), might consist of an enclosure containing the king's hall and chapel, adjoining which were a hamlet of bondmen and a cluster of homes of the king's officers, making a polyfocal village. For Scotland and Wales, see *Medieval Villages*, *op cit*.

Somewhat apart from the villages with formal shapes, there is yet another type, the *scattered* settlement. This, as has been said above, is linked to largely pastoral farming, which did not demand the sharing

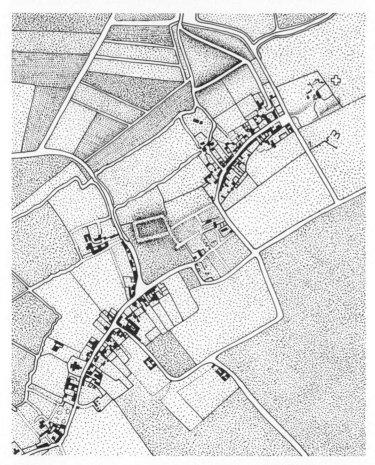

48 *Swaffham Bulbeck (Ca): the original village (bottom left) has shrunk at both ends, leaving a gap between it and a newer settlement outside the gates of the priory (top right).*

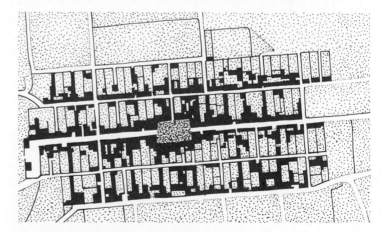

49 *A regular grid village with central square or green – Aberchirder (Ba) (from a map of 1868).*

111

and cooperation of arable farming, with the result that the farmer could live anywhere in the grazing lands if he had water and a sheltered site. The church and manor house (if any) might attract a hamlet, where small shops and services could later be centred, and isolated farms themselves might be in groups of two or three, perhaps for family convenience. But otherwise the parishes were dotted with isolated farms, and there was no nucleated village of the kind usual in the Lowland Zone. This is still the typical pattern in Cornwall and Wales. The studies of Devon in late Saxon times by W G Hoskins have shown that this was the original pattern there too; traces of it can still be seen in the distribution of the older farmhouses (including the "bartons", or medieval demesne farms) and the predominance of hamlets over villages. A Midland example of the fragmented village is Middle Barton (Ox).

Isolated farms could also be the result of medieval assarting – the colonisation of marginal or waste land under the increasing population pressure of the 12th and 13th centuries – though some isolated farms are not medieval assarts but relics of an earlier pattern of scattered farms, even in the Lowland Zone. But perhaps this category can only be called villages by stretching the definitions too far!

Secondary settlements, mostly 12th to 14th centuries, have had varying fortunes. Northchapel (Sx), a colony of Petworth, and Upton (Ha), an offshoot of Hurstbourne Tarrant, have remained villages (the latter no more than a few houses and an inn); but Overton (Ha), a colony of Whitchurch, being at the crossing of two major roads, has developed into a town. In some large parishes outlying settlements have become parishes on their own, eg the Burnham group in Norfolk, now six villages, including Burnham Norton and Burnham Sutton.

In Devon hamlets often grew up round the bartons, outlying manorial farms; sometimes these grew into full villages, with their own church, and the former large parish became split into smaller ones. This process can often be deduced from the boundaries shown on the maps. In many parts of England, as Hoskins has shown, similar divisions of large parishes took place, sometimes by the promotion of secondary settlements or hamlets, sometimes when the estates of sub-manors, or manors independent of that where the church stood, became viable villages in themselves. It is sometimes possible to deduce the existence, and persistence, of Saxon manors into the later Middle Ages, and these in turn may sometimes reflect the

former entities of Roman villa estates and even, beyond these, prehistoric land units.

Most secondary settlements are offshoots of existing villages, on outlying parts of their lands, or sometimes assarts on marginal land; but there are special cases. Hoskins (*The Making of the English Landscape*, Hodder & Stoughton, 1955) instances the case of the villages in Lincolnshire from Tetney to Cockerington; in the late Saxon period they built a sea dyke along the (then) coastline to reclaim the marshy land between them and it. Along the dyke they planted a row of daughter villages, from North Cotes to Saltfleet, to develop the situation.

There remain to be considered a few types of *specialised village*. There are villages – some of them now towns – which had early on a concentration of a cottage industry, such as weaving. In Suffolk and the Cotswolds many of these grew by the 15th century into small towns with a preponderance of "industrial" buildings, and large churches and market halls. Lavenham (Sf) is a good example. Industrial villages of the Industrial Revolution were usually planned as such. Industrialists built model villages for their workers near their mills. Outstanding early examples are New Lanark (Lk) (1784 onwards) and Styal (Ch), which has the owner's house by the mill and, a little way away, a spacious village of good terraces, a few older houses, two chapels, and an apprentices' hostel (1780s). But these are the beginnings of model industrial housing (see page 252), and are really urban in concept, not rural, in spite of their situations. Model *estate villages*, or at least extensive groups of rural housing, are dealt with later (see page 226).

Fishing villages are also individual, but of course the elements of rural life reflected in agricultural villages did not apply. Some consist basically of one street leading down to the harbour, such as Clovelly and Buck's Mill in Devon, or Robin Hood's Bay and Staithes in Yorkshire. Some cluster round the harbour, like the string of little ports in Fife (Elie, St Monance, Pittenweem, Anstruther; Crail is larger and has some features of a small town).

CHANGES IN VILLAGE PLANS

Until recently it was assumed by geographers that the various typical village plans (see above) were not only unchanging but went back to the original settlements. The earliest maps of villages (16th century), from which continuity could be shown to the present day, seemed to go a long way towards bearing this out. But the excavations which have been carried out during the last 30 years or so on the sites of deserted medieval villages have shown that in fact villages have been surprisingly fluid and mobile. The results have been synthesised by J G Hurst, who has played a leading part in the excavations.

There were three basic medieval peasant house types: the small cot of one or two rooms, the home of the landless worker; the longhouse of the villein, with living part at one end and byre at the other; and the farm, where the living house was separate from the byre or barn. The change from longhouse to farm was more a matter of prosperity than date or region, and in many areas longhouses survived into the 16th century or later. All Anglo-Saxon and early medieval houses were built of either timber or turf; after the late 12th century stone was used in stone areas and stone foundations in others. Whatever they were made of, most of the houses were poorly built, and were only intended to last for a generation (perhaps to allow a son to have the kind of house he wanted when he took over from his father). Excavation has shown not only that these houses were frequently rebuilt but that they were often not rebuilt on the same foundations but in a new position. This could be just to one side of the old house or on a quite different alignment, even at right angles to the old house. In some villages alignments slowly revolved. Even property boundaries were sometimes changed in this way.

One example, at Wharram Percy (NY), is a 12th-century manor house moved to another site in the 13th century; its site was occupied by two peasant houses set parallel to the street. In the 14th century their two tofts were combined and a single house built across the new plot on the same general alignment; finally, in the 15th century this house was replaced by one at right angles to it. The village itself expanded continuously. At Wharram Percy the latest tofts all date from the 15th century and were not fixed earlier; nor do they overlie the older ones. Two of the original tofts were thrown into three in the 13th century, on account of population increase, and reduced to two again in the 15th century owing to late medieval decay, until depopulation for sheep struck the village in the early 16th century. In the towns the tofts were stable; eg those at Lydford (Dv), of the 9th century, are still unchanged. So the practice in the towns differed from that in the country.

Whole villages show the same kind of movement. At Wawne (Hu), the village of the 14th century was a haphazard sprawl of houses round a rectangular green. In the 15th century this was completely abandoned and replaced by a linear street village to the south. By the 17th century this had gone and the village had shrunk to two farms. Other examples of the complicated residual plans left by such changes are Burwell and Cottenham (Ca) (see **50**).

This kind of change has evidently been going on widely. Several green villages have been shown to be quite recent in that form, and few seem to go back beyond the 13th century. In fact, in the 13th and 14th centuries, manorial lords were replanning their villages at the same time as towns were being laid out with regular plans. Generally, it is unlikely that a present village plan will be the same as in Anglo-Saxon times. The old idea that a Saxon village has stayed on the same site, and simply grown, is now untenable. Churches are fairly stable, but a manor house was often moved to a better site, which meant replanning the rest of the village. And villages were deserted, and new ones founded, even in the Saxon period. So the whole distribution pattern is fluid also; and these varied changes mean that village morphology may well not reflect its socio-economic basis. Few villages have, however, changed much since the 16th century (see **51** and **52**).

The rate of change could be slowed down or accelerated according to whether the village was "open" or "closed", that is whether there was little or no control over its development or whether it was controlled by a landowner or other authority. There were also periods of growth and decline which could alter the shape of the village. Broadly, there was decline in the early to middle Saxon period, following the disastrous outbreak of plague in AD 542 in which half the population died. The low population figure persisted throughout the 7th century, from 700–850 there was a rapid increase, and then a slow rise or static situation till the century from 950 to 1050. From 1050 to 1300 the population rose rapidly, but this rise was drastically checked by the Black Death in 1348–50, when a third of the people died. The effects of this lasted, with only slow recovery, until into the 16th century.

The main period of village planning was the 12th–13th centuries, after which the pattern begins to resemble that of today. A possible important exception to this was in the north of England, which was "harried", or devastated, by William I in 1069. This reduced the population to a point where the old farming systems from before the conquest could not continue to cope with the needs of the people, and so delayed the restructuring which took place elsewhere. In other parts of the country the increased population led to improved farming systems, which in turn affected the shape of the villages.

Further work has revealed regularity in planning in areas not devastated in the harrying, and it may be that the rise in the prosperity of York in the 10th and 11th centuries resulted in a more conscious organisation of the resources both in and round the city; research continues (see P V Addyman in *Archaeological Papers from York Presented to M W Barley* (York Archaeological Trust 1984)).

Villages may migrate, leaving their church isolated, as at Chalgrove (Ox). Theddingworth (Le) moved from a north–south street, now deserted, to an east–west street at its southern end. Longham (Nf) began as a small settlement round the church in the 6th–10th centuries; in the 11th–14th centuries another settlement grew up round South Hall Green; and 15th-century and later settlement developed to the east of this at Kirtling Common. Burwell (Ca) is an

example of a village whose present appearance is the result of movement, planning, and expansion. Colworth and Brime (Nh) were two villages under single management in the 13th century, joined, as a last stage, by a green inserted between them. Sawston (Ca) was on a south–west road, and had a north–south village added to it in the 13th century.

There are many cases of manor houses being built over earlier peasant houses which happened to occupy the best site, with the result that the rest of the village had to be replanned. Similar drastic action took place in towns, as at Norwich where the castle displaced a whole area of Saxon houses. But although few villages have changed their shape radically since the 16th century, there have been several new creations, mostly deliberately planned. The first wave of these was in the mid 16th century, when monastic estates were taken over by new landowners. These often built a new house

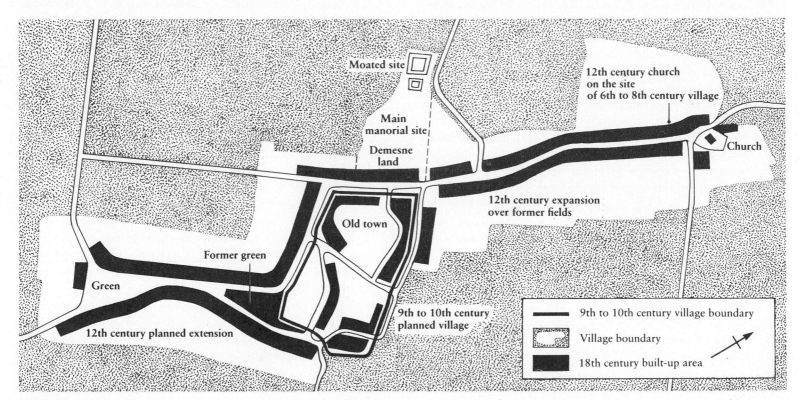

50 *Cottenham (Ca) is a village with a complex history, some of which is indicated here.*

out of the materials of the monastery – a fine example of this is Fountains Hall, next to Fountains Abbey – and sometimes rebuilt the village at the monastery gates as well. An example is Nun Monkton (NY), where the village lay round a large triangular green with the nunnery at its apex. The new owner in the 1540s built himself a new house on the site of the nunnery and rebuilt the village too, in this case keeping its distinctive shape. In the period of creation of landscaped parks, from about 1730 to 1850, many villages which had been close to the house were moved outside the park. Some of these were built in the best taste of the age, which of course enhanced both the estate and the owner's reputation, like Harewood (WY), by John Carr in 1760. Some reflected the whim of the owner, like Milton Abbas (Do), a "street" village of romantic semi-detached cottages (1787), or Albury (Sy), in Mock Tudor (1784 to *c* 1850, partly by Pugin). A Scottish example is Inveraray (Ar), where the village was rebuilt on a new site in the 1770s–90s to a cruciform design. But landowners could be expected to follow their own tastes when building or rebuilding their villages. Thus Eaglesham

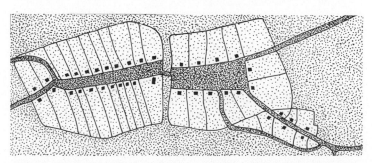

51–2 *Pockley (NY). 51 The early medieval village, showing two stages of planning – the original nucleus left and a later extension right; 52 the modern village, showing the abandonment of the green and the break-up of the tofts.*

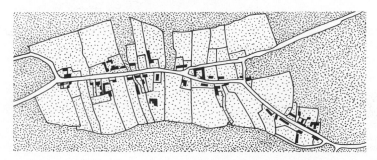

(Rf) is laid out in the shape of an A, the arms of which enclose a 15-acre (6 ha) common (1770s–90s); Denholm (Rx) has a large square green (Playfair, 1831).

SHRUNKEN, DESERTED, AND SHIFTED VILLAGES

Meanwhile other causes affecting village shape, and even existence, were in play throughout the Middle Ages. Epidemics, variations in population, or economic failure (bad harvests or changes in the prosperity of an industry) sometimes meant that a village became no longer viable and its remaining inhabitants went elsewhere, leaving a village shrunken to, say, a church and a farm (eg Priors Dean (Ha)), or even merely a site (see **53**). But the main reason for desertion was the enclosure of village lands for deerparks or sheep, when the village itself died or was moved (mainly from the 12th to the 15th or early 16th century).

Over 3,000 deserted villages are now known, most of them in England, particularly in the Lowland Zone. The highest density seems to be in the Isle of Wight, with some 30 sites. Up to the Black Death (1349) some 300 villages were cleared for the royal forests and the monastic farms, but as a result of the Black Death another 1,000 disappeared. The scarcity of labour led to a great increase in sheep-farming, for which open fields were enclosed. From about 1450 to 1550 the peak of the wool industry extended the areas affected by the enclosures; by 1500 there were three sheep to every human being. People reached the point of saying "the sheep eat men", and "where forty persons had their livings, now one man and his shepherd hath all". During this time also great private parks were created, both ornamental and for hunting, which altered villages and diverted roads.

Of villages cleared away by William I to make the New Forest, 21 village sites are known and 12 unknown. Villages cleared for sheep include Argam (NY) and Clopton (Ca). The monasteries cleared land too, and much of North Yorkshire was reshaped by the great Cistercian abbeys; villages affected include Cayton and Herleshaw. The Black Death led to the desertion of places like Tilgarsley (Ox). Emparking accounts for a large number, such as Ickworth (Su) and Great Childerley (Ca).

53 *A medieval deserted village from the air: the flat mounds, covering the houses, and the lanes and alleys of the village are surrounded by the ridge and furrow of the open fields – Barton Blount (Db).*

The earliest recorded seems to be Holdenby (Nh), in the 1570s. Other important examples are New Houghton (Nf), 1729, Nuneham Courtenay (Ox), 1760s, and New Wimpole (Ca), *c* 1845. The enclosures under the Enclosure Acts from the late 17th to the early 19th century, carried out for consolidation of estates and improved agriculture, although very extensive, did not in general affect the villages.

Another, later, example of enclosure for sheep is the Highland Clearances of the 1810s–20s, when whole tracts of land, including the villages, were depopulated and many people emigrated. Rossal, in Strathnaver (Sd), may be cited as an example of a village deserted at this time.

There are other reasons for desertion too: deterioration of climate (medieval to 18th century) led to some 30 villages dying in the Lammermuirs. Marginal land could be abandoned – St Kilda's became untenable and was evacuated in 1930. Leake (NY) and others were destroyed by the Scots; military training areas have absorbed places like Imber (Wi) and Stanford (Nf). Some villages have been inundated by reservoirs, such as West End and Timble in Yorkshire or Mardale by Haweswater. Some were submerged by the sea, such as Dunwich (Su) or Ravenserodd (Hu), or smothered by sand, like Skara Brae (Or) in the Neolithic period, or West Stow (Su) and Forvie (Ab) in the Dark Ages. Old Rattray (Ab) was sealed in by a sandbank. Villages may also be deserted on account of the decline or shifting of industry, for example the villages built for leadmining in the Pennines. Individual houses may also be abandoned for this reason.

Desertion is not always sudden, but can take place over centuries. Life does not stop when a village is deserted, and some have been overploughed. Much "shrinkage" is really enclosure next to part of the village. Some villages had monastic sheep-farms tacked on in the 12th century.

Deserted villages usually show on the ground as a group of low platforms (the remains of the houses) separated by troughs (the lanes). Larger mounds represent the church, the manor house, and the mill. A windmill mound and fishponds can often be seen as well. The ridges of the village's fields may stretch away round the site. Clear examples can be seen in most counties, eg Abbotstone (Ha).

Over 100 deserted medieval villages (DMVs) have been at least partially excavated, and much has been learnt about the houses and their contents. The Medieval Village Research Group continues to investigate them. This group merged in 1986 with the Moated Sites Research Group, to form the Medieval Settlements Research Group. The most extensive excavation, now classic, is that of Wharram Percy (Hu), where John Hurst worked for 40 years; this has transformed knowledge of the development of such a village. Conservation of the best 50 DMV sites has been proposed, but lack of resources makes this unlikely in the near future. Three are, however, in State care: Wharram Percy (Hu), Gainsthorpe (Li), and Hound Tor (Dv). Management agreements are being sought with the owners of the others. Sites which have yielded most information on excavation include Goltho (Li), Caldicote (Ht), Raunds (Nh), and Gomeldon (Wi).

DISPERSED SETTLEMENT

This is the converse of the village – a landscape of scattered farms and/or hamlets instead of a nucleated village with associated farms. Dispersed settlement is in fact the basic pattern over most of the country. Nucleated villages may actually be seen as exceptional, and the reasons why the village developed in parts of the country and not in others are not entirely clear.

Several factors can result in a pattern of dispersed settlement. It still survives in much of the Highland Zone, where it seems to be indigenous (for example the "Celtic" dispersal in Devon (eg the Hartland area) and Wales). A group of assarts could be promoted to become a separate parish. Partial dispersal may be due to partial abandonment, or the desertion of a village leaving scattered farms, or post-medieval dispersal of farms in a newly-enclosed landscape. In some cases a dispersed farm may represent a deserted village, eg Whiteparish (Ha), now a farm, but once a hamlet. Bletsoe (Bd) is a village with an isolated farm, North End; this is itself a planned village, not just a single assart, so this is a planned landscape of dispersal. Therleigh (Bd) has scattered farms all on the 12th–13th century open fields; this is a late dispersal on top of arable land so looks dispersed when the fields are abandoned. But in upland there can be dispersal from the beginning.

There is a different situation in the Weald of Kent and Sussex. Saxon manors round the fringes had outlying clearings for sheep, cattle, or pigs in the Wealden woodlands, sometimes up to 20 miles away. These later – from the 8th century – developed into separate farms and then into small independent manors. The place-names indicate some of these pastures – names like *-den* in Kent or *-fold* in Sussex. The resultant pattern is seen in parishes such as Shipley, West Grinstead, or Sheffield, which have scattered farms but no villages. This area is also crossed by a close network of drove roads, connecting the original manors with their pastures (although some of these tracks may have Roman origins). The small irregular fields, in a network of woods and shaws, still reflect the making of these farms.

THE FORM OF PARISHES

At the risk of oversimplification, the shape of rural parishes may be thought of in three ways: irregular, regular, and strip. Most of what later became parishes, townships, or estates were in existence in the early Anglo-Saxon period; the coming of Christianity to the Saxons (AD 597) led to the gradual establishment of parish churches and hence parishes. The basis of these parishes was normally an Anglo-Saxon estate – the Church found it convenient to collect tithes from an established and coherent unit of agriculture.

How far these early Anglo-Saxon estates continued the estates of Roman villas or other Roman land units is not universally agreed. But that this is a serious probability in some cases was postulated by H P R Finberg for Withington (Gl) (see *The Agrarian History of England and Wales*, vol I, ii (Cambridge 1972)), and other possible cases have been adduced. Peter Salway (in *Roman Britain* (Oxford 1981)) suggests that a gap in occupation for say 50 years inhibited incomers from occupying a particular piece of land, and necessitated a new pattern of settlement. Where there was no break, continuity of pattern is likely. So some early Saxon settlers could have adopted Roman occupational patterns while, after the upheavals of the second half of the 5th century and the Saxon conquests of the later 6th, quite new patterns emerged in many places. But not all authorities accept that pre-existing land units dictated the boundaries of Anglo-Saxon estates (eg Ann Goodier in *Medieval Archaeology* 28, 1984).

Anglo-Saxon parishes, particularly in upland or sparsely settled areas, were often very large and served by a mother or "minster" church, with dependent chapelries in centres of population. Such were the vast parishes in the north of England, like Danby or Clitheroe, or in the south-west, eg Lydford, which included most of Dartmoor. The pre-1811 parishes of Cheshire and the northern Welsh borders resemble those of the north of England, having several townships in a parish (over 30 in some), and an average area of over six square miles. In south-east England the average is under 1.75 townships and under four and a half square miles. The influences at work were the early settlement patterns, whether the church was Celtic or English, and the degree of Anglo-Saxon or Norman political control; but areas tended to have as many churches as they could afford to build or maintain. Diocesan policies also influenced social and economic developments.

In the Lowland Zone the process of division of these minster parishes into small but irregular parishes, each consisting of one or more manors, has been demonstrated (eg by Christopher Taylor, in *Dorset* (Hodder & Stoughton 1970)) from a careful study of maps and charters. Thus, the parish of Sturminster Marshall (Do) once included the present parishes of Corfe Mullen, Lytchett Matravers, Lytchett Minster, and Hamworthy; and curious extensions of the internal boundaries suggest that Henbury, Combe Almer, Dullar, and Slepe were once centres of old estates. Raunds (Nh) shows a similar pattern. Not all parishes containing several estates were subdivided into parishes; thus Legsby (Li) contained seven estates, each with its own settlement, of which only Legsby has survived as a village. This process went on into the 13th or 14th century. Secondary settlements or assarts could grow into hamlets, independent manors, or villages with churches, and become parishes of their own.

In the central Weald there is a type of parish where the outlying, peripheral settlements (eg Rotherfield) are older than the central nucleated village, which appears only in the 13th century. The Saxon settlement of the Weald indeed was as much by scattered pasture farms (folds, wicks, and dens) as by the main villages or manors. Shipley (Sx), for instance, still has this character; although it has a church, this was a Templar house, and the parish is one of scattered farms with no real centre. Conversely, some parishes are an aggregation of small manors, fixed by the 8th century; in Kent there are parishes made up of several Saxon estates or land units.

In the flatter lands of the Midlands and East Anglia, where the open fields developed by the 7th/8th century and the Anglo-Saxon settlement was more evenly distributed, the parishes tended to be roughly round and equal, with the villages spaced about one and a half miles apart.

Not all medieval manors were in one piece, and there are many instances of detached pieces of a manor/parish, of varying sizes, lying in other parishes. Certainly, a parish could have more than one manor, or sub-manors, and conversely a manor could be spread over more than one parish. In Surrey, manors, vills, and parishes were coterminous, but this was not the case in East Anglia, where manors were more split up. Manors could have detached or outlying specialised farms (cf the monastic granges), eg Vachery at Cranleigh (Sy), which was the dairy farm of the manor of Shere; many manors on or near the chalk had pig or sheep pastures in the Weald.

The third category of parish form is the *strip*. This was designed to give the inhabitants a selection of the soils in the district; thus, a downland strip parish would run from the woodlands of the Weald, through the good greensand arable, to the chalk pastures of the Downs. These parishes tend to run in groups along a geographical feature, such as a range of hills or a stream or spring line. They may be about a mile wide and three or four miles long, or even longer. There are well-known groups along the North Downs in Surrey and the South Downs in Sussex: here there are two lines of villages, one at crossings of the Rother, the other, parallel to it, on the spring line at the foot of the chalk escarpment (see Trevor Rowley: *Villages in the Landscape* (Dent 1978)). Many of these strips in the Weald and under the Downs were divided later into separate parishes, eg Dorking–Holmwood–Capel; Reigate–Newdigate; Blechingley – Horne – Outwood. Such subdivision breaks up the original "rectangular" form of the parish, as is seen eg at Abington, Hildersham, and Linton in Cambridgeshire.

There is another row along the Marlborough Downs, where Cobbett noted 11 churches in 15 miles; others occur on the edge of the Lincolnshire Wolds, on the Fen edge, between Boston and Spalding, and on the south side of the Tees. On the slopes of Dartmoor the parishes are long, running from low arable to high moorland grazing (eg Shaugh to Holne); these seem to represent early Saxon estates.

There are also rows of long parishes along rivers, such as the Nene in Northamptonshire, south of Oundle; west of this are contrasting large woodland parishes such as Benefield and Brigstock (John M Steane: *The Northamptonshire Landscape* (Hodder & Stoughton 1974)). An interesting case is that of Charminster (Do), where there was a line of ten narrow strips alone the Cerne, each centred on a village or hamlet; some of these have been deserted, which obscures the pattern.

There are of course many anomalies in this oversimplified scheme. Parishes have complicated histories, and each has to be studied on its merits. For instance, parish boundaries round Haverhill (Su) seem to be drawn round existing fields, in contrast to Cambridgeshire parishes north-west of them, eg West Wratting, drawn across uncultivated land or woodland. The parish of Gamlingay (Ca) has a curious promontory on the west projecting into Huntingdonshire and Bedfordshire, in which is the modern Woodbury Farm. This was once a separate medieval land unit included in Gamlingay for ecclesiastical convenience. There are parishes with two or more villages, and villages divided among two or more parishes; Willingale Spain and Willingale Doe (Ex) have two churches in one churchyard. New parishes continued to be formed in the 12th and 13th centuries, in response to local needs or in the interests of manorial lords. The Yorkshire Dales are one such area, as is the Lincolnshire coast, where lines of new villages grew up along the sea walls which enclosed reclaimed land.

Parish boundaries, from the earliest times, were regularly perambulated by the manorial agents and the priest, and details of the various landmarks along the route are recorded in Saxon and medieval charters. These include Roman roads, former river beds, ancient hedges, prominent trees, unusual hillocks, even prehistoric remains. Hundred moots are often where several parishes meet, on prominent features such as Five Lords' Burgh, a long barrow on the Downs north of Seaford (Sx). At one place, Rymer Point (Su), eleven parishes and ten roads once converged on a group of small meres on a Breckland heath; the villages are 2–3 miles away. There are now only nine parishes here, including Euston, Barnham, and Little Livermere (see Oliver Rackham: *The History of the Countryside* (Dent 1986)).

Early urban parishes usually include not only their towns but the towns' open fields and common lands as well, or lie along natural features or old roads (eg at Stamford (Li)). Later ones are purely urban, cut from extant parishes or based on property divisions, sometimes quite small, reflecting the large numbers of churches in the larger towns, like London, Norwich, or York. Some urban parishes may represent the precinct of a religious house; eg the parish of Holy Trinity, Aldgate, London (united with St Botolph Aldgate in 1899) was the precinct of the abbey of St Clare, the nuns' chapel being succeeded by a parish church in 1566. From the later 17th to the early 19th century, when the towns were expanding, new churches were built in the new estate developments, with new parishes (eg St James's, Piccadilly). In the 19th and 20th centuries churches have similarly been built where the social need for them demanded it. The new parishes were carved out of existing ones. Thus, in Guildford (Sy), Christ Church parish was carved out of Stoke in the 1860s, as the district was developed, and Burpham out of Worplesdon.

From the 1820s there have been many other changes of parish boundary, both ecclesiastical and civil, and many civil parishes are no longer coterminous with the ecclesiastical one of the same name. Thus, Selborne (Ha) civil parish includes the parish of Blackmoor and the chapelry of Oakhanger, now part of Kingsley.

Parks, Gardens, and Sports

HUNTING

Deerparks

In medieval Europe, wherever the feudal system prevailed, most of the land was divided into manors owned ("held") by lords of various degrees, or the Crown, or the Church. The manorial lords had achieved their dominance in exchange for protection during upheavals such as the Danish settlement of eastern England. A small manor might be just a village and its lands, on which the free tenants and the unfree peasants – the people of the village – had rights and obligations; a major lord might have a large number of manors scattered over a wide area, some in blocks. The lords were the beneficiaries of the Game Laws, which protected their rights to hunt; hunting provided not only a leisure activity, but skins and an important source of animal food. Therefore the early medieval (Anglo-Saxon) kings and their nobles enclosed areas of land – parks – to keep the deer in. These were surrounded by banks and ditches topped by a fence, hedge, or wall – boundaries which can still be traced. The ditch was usually outside the bank, eg John of Gaunt's park at King's Somborne (Ha) which still has a stretch 12ft (3.7m) high with ditch outside it.

An excellent example is at Slindon (Sx), a favourite retreat of the medieval archbishops of Canterbury. The deerpark is a roughly circular area, south-west of the village and over a mile across. It now consists of a broad belt of woodland within which the bank and ditch are quite clear, enclosing open land. Another untouched medieval deerpark is at Bradgate (Le). Binswood, Worldham (Ha) is a deerpark of similar size, which was once within Woolmer Forest and used by King John. Its roughly oval outline can be seen on the map; the northern part is now fields, but the southern is an area of unimproved woodland-pasture, still used for grazing, and as such virtually unique. It gives an unrivalled impression of a medieval scene. Binswood also retains its "common" outline, a series of curves broken by funnelled entrances where rights of way emerge. Another exceptionally complete working wood-pasture is Hatfield Forest (Ex).

Deerparks could also have internal works, such as banks and pits for driving animals to slaughter. Such, on first appearance, are those at Scamridge (NY) which were in an Anglian royal deerpark. However, the real function of these, and of similar banks and enclosures nearby (eg Levisham), is still not finally determined; they may after all be late Bronze Age farm or ranch boundaries, or used for driving cattle.

The distribution of Saxon parks in England is uneven, but even in the small county of Dorset some 50 certain cases are known and over 40 possibles. After the Norman conquest they are found everywhere. Most early parks were on the edge of the cultivated land, well away from settlement centres; 16th-century parks, in contrast, tended to swallow cultivated land. Parks were normally small, some 100–200 acres. The land was "unimproved", that is had natural grazing and woodland for covert. It was quite different in appearance from the later "amenity" parks. In Domesday (1086) 36 parks are recorded, mostly in the south-east. There was an expansion from 1200 to 1300, when most lords and bishops had parks (the Bishop of Winchester had 23). After the Black Death many were "disparked" or converted to amenity parks. Most of the 1900 or so parks in 1350 were in the south and Midlands, with the highest densities in Staffordshire (88), Warwickshire, Buckinghamshire, Hertfordshire, Essex (98), Surrey, and Sussex. They were convenient lands for fishponds also, and these may indicate where the parks once were. Even if the banks no longer exist, park boundaries can often be traced by careful study of maps and work on the ground on the alignments of later boundaries.

Forests and chases

The later medieval kings developed hunting *forests*. Thus, William I created the New Forest over a large tract of land in Hampshire, destroying villages and farms in doing so. By the time of Henry II royal forest (in a legal sense; see below) reached its greatest extent, covering no less than one-third of England, although only some 3% was actually woodland. Richard I and John raised money by releasing back to normal use a great deal of this land, thus giving impetus to colonisation of the waste. By the early 13th century 33 counties contained forests.

Forests were not normally covered with trees, but were tracts of country with all the local variety. A good example is Knaresborough Forest in Yorkshire, which runs from ordinary lowland farmlands up to the moors; another is Windsor Forest, which extends well south of Windsor Great Park to its southern boundary (an ancient hedge) on the Hog's Back west of Guildford. Forests were in fact merely tracts of land made subject to forest law, and thus for some purposes outside the common law of the land. Forest law was a system devised to preserve certain designated animals and the trees and pasture which provided food and shelter for them ("vert and venison"), for the king's pleasure and profit, not only on royal demesne lands, but in extensive areas elsewhere as well. Only about a fifth of legal forest was actually woodland, unless this estimate of Oliver Rackham's is too low.

The main animals preserved in forests were fallow deer (the favourite of the Norman kings), red deer, roe deer (till 1339), and wild boar. Clearing and farming were prohibited. The forests had special officials, workers, and courts assigned to them (like the Speech House in the Forest of Dean), and the law was strictly enforced. The keepers or wardens of the forests necessarily had wide local powers and high status, an idea of which can be got from the castle-like Barden Tower in Wharfedale (NY) (c 1485), one of six lodges for the keepers of the Forest of Barden.

Some monasteries had rights in royal forests, eg Chertsey Abbey in Windsor, which had rights of grazing and use of timber, and parts of forests could be given to nobles as chases. Sixty-nine forests have been identified, covering about a fifth of the country by the 13th century. Some were very large; one, for example, covered most of Essex. There were, however, none in East Anglia, Lincolnshire, Durham, the south-east, or the south-west (except for Dartmoor in the 14th century). The forests gave the king not only hunting but rents and goods of all kinds, as well as fines.

Forests were gradually encroached and assarted by the later Middle Ages, and their woodlands eroded. They became disforested – ie released from the forest laws – after the late 14th century. By the late 15th century few were left and after a revival by Charles I there was a rapid decline; the last, Delamere (Ch), went in 1812. Now only fragments remain to show what they were like, such as Epping Forest and the New Forest.

The medieval kings allowed certain nobles to have *chases*, or private forests, but these were subject to the common law, not the forest law. In some cases their rights were limited to certain types of hunting.

Some chases were detached from forests, eg Sutton Chase (Ww) from Cannock Chase (St) (1125), and Cannock Chase itself (1290). Cranborne Chase (Do) went in and out of royal hands. There were 26 chases all told.

Parks and chases, then, were the hunting preserves of private landowners, in which the forest laws which governed the royal forests did not apply. But the landowners still had exclusive rights to hunt, even under 18th- and 19th-century game laws. By then, however, hunting in its present sense had developed, outside the old parks. Forest officials continued to exist until 1817. From the 17th century, field hunting began to concentrate on foxes, for "sport", not food. When the countryside had become too open, *coverts*, small woods or patches of gorse, were planted to encourage the foxes; these are common in the Midlands. Artificial *fox earths* were also made, consisting of a pit with approach gullies with brick runs and chambers. One first recorded in 1765 was recently excavated at Bishop Burton (NY). Fox-hunting also entails special *stables* and *kennels*, often very large. An 18th-century example is at St Boswells (Rx).

Deer were kept inside the pales of the parks by means of *deer-leaps*, sloping laddered planks on a gate which the deer could negotiate one way only. Special *deer-houses*, or deer-larders, were often built to assemble the results of a hunt; a late example is at Chiswick (W Kent, 1730s). *Hunting lodges* were built in the forests and chases for the use of the manorial lord on his visits. Odiham Castle (Ha) grew out of a moated house, or minor castle, built by King John as a staging post between Windsor and Winchester, but used by him mainly as a hunting lodge, on land used for royal hunting since Harold's time. The keep is mid 13th century, but in the 14th and 15th centuries the castle reverted to being a hunting lodge. Most, of course, had no military overtones. Brimham Lodge, in Nidderdale (NY), was a hunting lodge of the abbots of Fountains; the present house was rebuilt in 1676. Hunting and shooting lodges are still a feature of the vast deer forests and grouse moors of the north and of Scotland.

Warrens

Apart from these major hunting rights, the Crown could also grant *rights of free warren* to manorial lords, permitting them to hunt small game on their own lands – fox, rabbit, hare, wild cat, badger, marten, otter, squirrel, pheasant, and partridge. The area over which this right was exercised was known as a *warren*, but this was not the same as the limited place where rabbits were enclosed and bred.

Rabbits were regarded as useful animals. They were introduced by the Normans in the late 12th century, but were not common until the mid 13th. They were reared in vast numbers, not only for food but for their fur, used widely for trimming and lining cloaks and dresses. The *rabbit warren* was an enclosed area, ranging in size from a small field to a square mile or more. Large warrens were under the control of a warrener, who usually lived on the spot. At Abbotstone (Ha) the entire hillside west of the deserted village, up to the drove road, was a warren, and the cottage on this now empty area is the successor of the warrener's lodge.

The warren at Thetford (Nf) was so important, and the risk of theft so great, that the warrener's lodge there is fortified, like a peel-tower. In the early 19th century Thetford was the rabbit centre of England, sending some 20,000 annually to London; on a good morning 200 could be caught with ferrets and lurchers. This warren had rabbit enclosures surrounded by banks of turf 1.2m high, with reeds growing on them; the rabbits were trapped in "tipes", pitfalls about 2.4m deep, lined with flints, and closed by a trapdoor.

A standard method of concentrating the rabbits was to provide them with artificial warrens called *pillow-mounds*. These are low, oblong mounds, usually 50–90ft (15–27m) long by 20–40ft (6–12m) across and 1.75–3.25ft (0.6–1m) high, often with a flat top; most have a shallow ditch round them. Rabbits might be left to burrow into these for themselves, but many mounds had grooves or trenches dug along or across them, or parallel ridges – some even have tunnels inside them – to encourage the rabbits. At Danebury (Ha) excavation has revealed two types of 17th/18th-century warrens, where the burrows were dug into the chalk rock and filled with soil or vegetation, and even possibly boarded over, before the topsoil was put back. One type had parallel trenches joined at intervals, or a single spine trench, with others joining at right angles; the other had a long trench in the bottom of a broader slot with, at intervals, rabbit-sized burrows bored through the chalk to the surface.

These mounds are found widely over most of southern England (eg Steeple Langford Cowdown (Wi)), with a few in the north (eg Hutton-le-Hole (NY)), and in Wales (eg Llanfihangel nant Melan (Ra) (Pw), over 30 on a slope). Some can be shown to be medieval, some

Napoleonic. R G Haynes, who has studied (1971) the rabbit warrens of Dartmoor, has identified 81 *vermin traps* associated with warrens, from the stone-built funnel walls; at 18 sites the traps are still in position at the convergence of the funnel. These traps are probably 18th century or earlier in date; in the 19th century guns and gin-traps were used. By the early 20th century a variety of ingenious fences was used to keep rabbits from straying. The sites of former warrens may sometimes be identified from field names like Coney Garth, Conegar, Coneycroft, or similar forms.

Special enclosures were also made in the great parks for *hares*; there was one in Bushey Park (Mx), and there is still a Hare Warren at Badminton (Gl).

Fowling

Certain *birds* were always bred for meat, eggs, and feathers, and geese and ducks were a regular feature of every village green. A more specialised case was that of swans, which on the Thames belonged to the Crown. The great swannery at Abbotsbury (Do), run by the local Benedictine abbey, still survives.

Wild ducks, and some other birds, were caught in the Middle Ages in nets of various types. Decoys are recorded from the 13th century consisting of v-shaped nets at one end of a pond into which the birds were driven, with the help of side nets. In the 1660s an improved form was introduced from Holland, of which one was made in St James's Park, London. This consisted of "pipes" or channels leading from the pond, covered with nets and screens (see **54**). Many such were made in the 18th and 19th centuries – there were 38 in the south Lincolnshire Fens – and can be found with the aid of a large-scale map. A specialised type of duckpond had concentric rings of banks, broken into short lengths; the wet spaces between these protected the nesting place on the central mound (eg the Ringlets on Hutton Moor, near Ripon (NY), 1770). Duck were shot on the mud-flats of East Anglia from "graves" dug in the mud.

The breeding of game birds such as pheasants, although widespread and intensive, leaves few archaeological traces. Grouse were shot on the northern moorlands from batteries, lines of butts, or low horseshoe-shaped shelters, open at the top and one side, and made of turf or stone. Special houses were built on the moors for the convenience of shooting and hunting parties (shooting boxes or hunting lodges).

The manorial lord also had the sole right to keep pigeons, and dovecotes appeared in England in Norman times. Pigeons provided meat and eggs, and their dung was used for manure and, from the 16th century, for making saltpetre for gunpowder. In the mid 17th century there are said to have been 26,000 dovecotes in England, one to every manor house or grange, each housing from 500 to 1,000 pairs of birds. The peasants were not allowed to interfere with them, and the vast quantities of grain they ate was a factor in the decline of the system, as well as causing deep resentment. See above (pages 102–3) for the forms of dovecotes.

Hawks or falcons were sometimes kept in cotes, or sometimes in mews, as at Farleigh Hungerford (So). Owlstones, or owlholes, pierced with a round or square hole to let owls in, can be found in gable ends of barns, eg Wycoller (La).

Fishing

Fish was a major part of the medieval diet, fresh or smoked. Sea-fishing will be dealt with under Ports (pages 561–3). Freshwater fish were either caught in rivers or bred in fishponds. Little needs to be said about river fishing; the methods used were much the same as today. Fish were guddled by hand, speared (with one-, two-, or three-pronged spears), netted, trapped, or angled. Special arrangements of posts and nets were, until very recently, used in the Severn, Wye, and Solway. On larger streams fishing was sometimes done by *fish-garths*, artificial channels diverting part of the river and fished with nets hung from stakes. Eels were popular and caught in large quantities, particularly in eastern England. One way to catch them in bulk was to dig a pool fed from a river, into which the eels could be diverted by a sluice. The pool emptied through another sluice into a small brick bay with parallel sides, floored with an iron grating set on a slope and closed off by another grating. The eels were checked by the gratings, and could only escape through openings in the brick wall leading to two other compartments, in the last of which they could be kept alive for a few days until required. Such a trap, dated 1818 but on the site of a monastic one, was excavated in 1976 at Newark Priory (Sy). Others are still in use on the river Test at Fullerton (Ha), and at Fiddleford and Sturminster Mills on the Stour in Dorset. Eels were also speared, and even caught by cormorants. A method still in use is "rayballing",

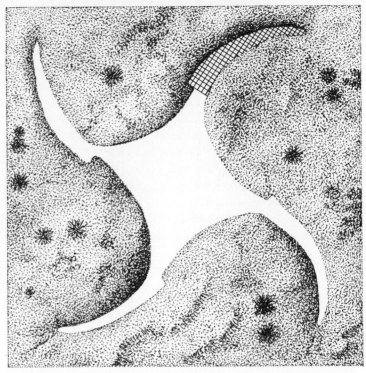

54 *A decoy pond. The lake has curving ditches (pipes) covered with netting; wild ducks are driven into the pipes and trapped under the netting.*

a ball of worms on the end of a line. Elvers are caught in fine nets and salmon in rows of narrow traps made of withies ("putchers" on the Severn).

Fish were also stored in small buildings called *fish-houses*; there is a monastic one at Meare (So) (15th century). Fish for consumption were widely kept in *fishponds* on manorial or monastic lands, not always close to the house but fed by a suitable stream. The fish bred in these *vivaria* were mostly pike (a great delicacy), bream, perch, and roach; carp were added in the late 15th century. Salmon and trout were caught in rivers, eels at mills and in river-traps, and only in ponds when these were drained; crayfish are also recorded. Fishponds began to be made in the mid 12th century, reflecting the rise in profitability of demesne farming. They were mostly long and narrow, made by damming a stream, but could be square, on flat land, in the form of a shallow basin surrounded by banks (eg Long Whitton (Le)). The banks could be strengthened with stone, and there would be a sluice to control flooding. A gentle flow of water was maintained, as in a watercress bed. The fish were caught by seine-netting from boats.

Complete small examples can be seen at St Cross, Winchester, or Glastonbury Abbey. Very large fishponds could be made on suitable streams by making a long dam, so forming a lake resembling a millpond or ironworking pond. Some of these are still in water and are very impressive. The Bishops of Winchester created such a pond at Alresford (Ha) *c* 1200, by damming a valley fed by two streams with a dam (The Great Weir) over 400yds (370m) long and some 20ft (6m) high; the water area was then some 60 acres (24ha), and is still 30 (12ha). Frensham Ponds (Sy) also belonged to the Bishops of Winchester; the Great Pond now covers over 100 acres (40ha). There were other large ones at Taunton and Byland Abbey (NY). Such ponds needed careful and constant management, and a system was evolved by 1250 which lasted until the 19th century. This involved sluices to control the dam and the various channels, and a feeder stream diverted round the pond by a bypass channel, which might have enlargements or *stews* for holding fish when the pond was drained. Draining and cleaning the pond and sorting the fish had to be done at least once a year, and the larger establishments employed special officials to manage the ponds.

By the later 15th century the demand for fresh fish grew to a point where many manorial lords took up production on a commercial scale and made additional fishponds to cope. Many ponds linked to moats, which can be confusing on the ground, may be of this kind; fish were sometimes kept in the moat itself. Fishponds are therefore sometimes in groups, either along a stream, or in rows parallel to each other divided by banks (eg Kirkstead Abbey (Le)). In such cases there may be a main pond with subsidiary ponds for breeding, or several main ponds for different kinds of fish. The monastic fishponds at Bury St Edmunds (Su) ("The Crankles") are a conjoined series of eleven parallel arms.

Swans were also kept on fishponds. A valuable account of the Bishops of Winchester's ponds is that by Edward Roberts in *Proceedings of the Hampshire Field Club*, 42, 1986.

Special boats have been developed for river fishing, such as the *coracles* of Wales, the Wye, and the Severn (see pages 475–6).

On the Bristol Channel coast, eg at Stolford (So), sledged barrows or "mud-horses" were made for use on the mud-flats. A useful conspectus of fishing methods and equipment – spears, nets, pots, boats, etc – is shown at the Welsh Folk Museum at St Fagans, near Cardiff.

55 *Part of the Roman garden at the palace of Fishbourne (Sx); this has ornamental box hedges along the paths, setting off seats and other features.*

GARDENS AND AMENITY PARKS

Gardens are a pleasant and distinctive feature of civilised life and reveal the tastes and artistic influences of their times as well as changing ideas on man's relationship with nature. The earliest recognisable gardens in Britain are Roman. Although the influence of Roman gardens on later British gardens can only have been indirect, it is worth seeing one as a historical basis. That in the great courtyard of the Roman palace at Fishbourne, near Chichester, has been reconstructed as a unique survival (see 55). It consisted of a wide central path dividing two symmetrical areas. The paths were lined with hedges, probably of box, planted in alternate rectangular and semicircular recesses, once containing either beds or statues, urns, seats, etc. The spaces had shrubs or, more probably, were grassed. There were well-placed trees, and conspicuous features like statues, basins, and fountains. The flowers have not left traces, but records exist of similar gardens in Roman Italy and what was planted there. South of the palace was a wide terrace sloping down to a quay along the inlet of the sea which gave access to the palace. This was laid out as a "natural" garden or small park, with trees and shrubs. A kitchen garden lay in the angle of the north and west wings, and the Butser Ancient Farm Trust began in 1985 to develop this area with the fruit, vegetables, herbs, and vines which the Romans would have had. It is probable that most villas in Roman Britain had similar, if smaller, arrangements.

After the Romans, gardens did not become regular or important features until well into the Middle Ages. Monasteries had gardens in their cloisters, usually grassed, with often a well, basin, or tree in the centre (eg Fountains); these were sometimes also the burial grounds of the monks. By the infirmary was a kitchen and herb garden, with simple beds, and there were also beds for the provision of altar flowers. Castles had ornamental gardens, where space allowed, in a courtyard, often small or irregular (see 56). These had networks of paths with raised beds of flowers and seats of turf with flowers growing in the grass. A mound was a common feature, to give a view over the walls. By the 14th century less fortified houses had larger, but still small, gardens by the private wing. These were enclosed by fences or hedges, inside an earthen bank. They might have flower beds, but more often were just grass with a few trees or arbours. Bowls and tennis were played on the lawn.

After the Wars of the Roses in England, a new class of landowner arose. Following the dissolution of the monasteries in the late 1530s, these "new men" took over the old estates of the Church and developed them in a different way. One result was the creation of private parks round the manor houses, not only for keeping deer, cattle, and sheep, and for timber, but also for amenity and prestige. Many of these were enclosed from common lands, or even the fields of the villages. Petworth and Hatfield, with their walls, show the extent of some of these. The wild or rural nature of the parks was contrasted with the formal, intimate, and sheltered gardens round the house, strongly influenced in the 16th and 17th centuries by Italian, French, and Dutch ideas.

Garden design began seriously with the Tudors, although the early ones continued the medieval tradition. Renaissance (Italian) ideas influenced gardening by the mid 16th century. These were the banishment of trees from the garden to the deerpark beyond, the disposal of beds about an axis related to the facade of the house, thus bringing garden and house into formal relationship for the first time, and the ornamentation of the raised walks and mounts with balustrades and timber garden houses. Statues and sundials were popular. A distinctive Tudor feature was the *knot garden*, which replaced the medieval raised beds, and which was intended to be

56 *A medieval garden (13th century) recreated by Sylvia Landsberg in 1986 at Winchester Castle: this has a formal path, an arbour, a fountain, and a turf alcove (not shown).*

57 *A garden in the style of c 1600, recreated at Basing House (Ha) by Elizabeth Banks, 1989. This has ornate parterres edged and patterned with low hedges of box.*

seen from the terrace or mount (see **57**). Knots were rectangular arrangements of beds, each compartment filled with complicated designs of low hedges, usually of box; the spaces were filled with low flowers, herbs, and shrubs. Knots are related to mazes of the low hedge type.

No actual Tudor or medieval garden has survived intact, but aspects remain in a few places. There is an early 19th-century reconstruction of a medieval garden at Ashridge (Ht). The gardens of deserted manor houses can often be made out from terraces or other earthworks; thus, those of the 15th-century manor house at Brearton (NY) can be distinguished from the other low mounds which represent the house, its moat, and its fishponds; at Harrington (Nh) (16th century) are five long, broad terraces descending the slope, linked by paths or steps, with below them a rectangular sunken garden or lawn. The role of the raised walk can be appreciated at several houses, such as Harrington (Li), and of the terrace at Albury (Sy) which, although laid out by John Evelyn in the late 17th century, dominates a partly Tudor garden; this terrace is a monumental one, being nearly a quarter of a mile (400m) long, with a grotto as a central feature. The flavour of Tudor gardens can be felt at Montacute (So), Haddon Hall (Db),

Wadham College, Oxford, and Hampton Court, to name only a few. The knot garden at Hampton Court, though well in spirit, was made in 1924. The famous maze here is of the high hedge type, laid out about 1700, but it succeeded one of the earlier kind. The 17th-century garden at Ham House, Richmond (Sy) has been reconstituted as it was.

Most of the 17th century was dominated by French ideas. French gardens developed in the wide, flat landscapes of the Paris basin and the Loire valley. They have great breadth and strict symmetry, laid out with rectangular beds (*parterres*) on both sides of an axis leading away from the house, and defined by masses of trees. The parterres were filled with designs in box or yew, rather like knot gardens. Formal expanses of water set them off. These concepts were exploited to the full by André Le Nôtre, gardener to Louis XIV, and Versailles became a model for all Europe. But in Britain the scale was more modest, partly because there are fewer flat expanses than in France, and partly because of the cost. The style was in full vogue after the Restoration; the chief designers were George London (died 1714) and Henry Wise (1653–1738), who set up a nursery and advisory service in 1681. Examples are Blickling Hall (Nf), Melbourne (Db), and Chatsworth

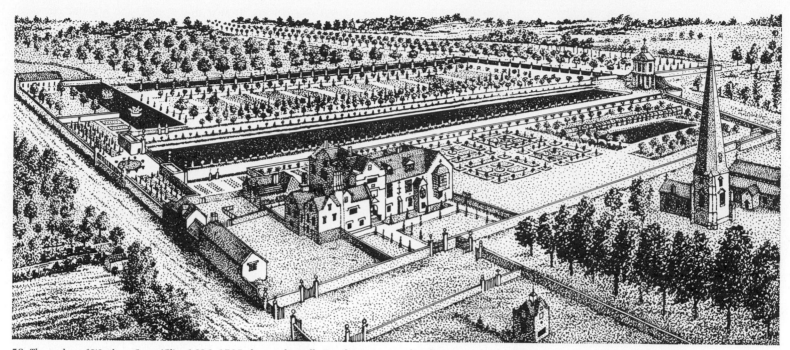

58 *The gardens of Westbury Court (Gl), c 1696–1705: these are basically French in inspiration, but show strong Dutch influence in the canals and other water features.*

(Db). The Versailles ideal culminated in England at Hackwood, near Basingstoke (Ha), where 70 acres of woodland were laid out before 1728, probably by James Gibbs, with radiating alleys, glades, an amphitheatre, a cockpit, and formal pavilions and water.

Dutch influence, important after 1688, is shown by the greater use of water, a profusion of lead statues and elaborate detail, trees in tubs, complicated parterre designs, the use of bulbs, and a great development of *topiary*, now more often in yew than in box or rosemary. Westbury Court (Gl) is a good example (see **58**).

The 18th century saw a swing back to "nature", although in a very subtle and sophisticated way. Literary and artistic influences were powerful here, such as the landscape paintings of Claude, as was the experience of visiting Italy during the Grand Tour of Europe which was part of the education of the landowning classes. A good early example of the new ideas is Chiswick, designed in the 1730s for Lord Burlington by William Kent (1685–1748). The layout is based on a series of vistas which look informal but are carefully planned. Temples, obelisks, etc provide focal points at the end of glades; pathways wander, lines are

no longer straight, and grass replaces some of the parterres. Kent later used the *ha-ha* (a ditch between the garden and the park, which gave the illusion of a continuous, unfenced sequence from one to the other and also prevented cattle straying into the garden) to great effect (see **59**) – the whole landscape was now the garden, a complete contrast to the medieval desire for a garden as a private refuge from hostile Nature outside. The formal canal became the "natural" lake. Trees were carefully positioned, singly or in clumps.

One of the earliest of these English-style *parks* and quite one of the best, is Painshill Park, Cobham (Sy), laid out by Charles Hamilton from 1738 to 1773, drawing on the ideas of Kent and others. This contained a lake, a vineyard, a bastion, a gothic temple, a ruined abbey, a Chinese bridge (see **60**), a Roman bath, a grotto, a cascade, a mausoleum in the form of a ruined triumphal arch, a Turkish tent, a Temple of Bacchus, a hermitage, and a gothic tower. Not all of these have survived, but a long-term restoration scheme is in progress. The only garden still as Kent left it (allowing for the passage of time) is Rousham (Ox), 1738, which uses the river Cherwell instead of a lake, but has separate ponds instead, and

127

59 *A ha-ha: a concealed ditch to keep cattle from getting into the garden from the park; the wall cannot be seen from the house, and a railing is unnecessary. This one at Stowe (Bc) (Charles Bridgeman, 1730s) is an early example.*

a number of pavilions, grottos, and statues, and a gothic cowshed. Charles Bridgeman (died 1738) was also a distinguished garden designer at this time, and his creation at Claremont, Esher (Sy) (1720s), with its lake, grotto, and huge terraced amphitheatre on the hillside, is notable.

It has been said that the landscaped park, or rather the whole contrived setting of the country house with its gardens and its relationship with the park and surrounding farmlands, was the most significant contribution of England to European culture – a claim only challenged by the Perpendicular style of architecture. The dominant figure in this movement was Launcelot "Capability" Brown (1716–83), who created or transformed a large number of the finest landscaped parks in England (see **61**); his work may be seen at Longleat, Burghley, and Petworth, but his masterpiece is Blenheim. Brown's lead was taken over by Humphrey Repton (1752–1818), who worked, on a smaller scale, from 1788. Brown brought grass right up to the house, but Repton used gravel paths and ornamental terraces as well, and reintroduced a separate flower garden. The focal buildings were now more romantic than classical – ruins, grottos, etc. Some of Repton's small layouts have great charm, such as at Betchworth House (Sy).

By the 1830s this impetus had faded, and 19th-century interest turned back to the garden itself. This looked back to Renaissance Italy, with geometric form and ornamental terraces. But taste moved to

60 *The "Chinese" Bridge, Painshill (Sy) – Charles Hamilton, 1760s. A style known as Chinese was very popular in the later 18th century and early 19th century in furniture, railings, etc, and is associated with designers like Chippendale and John Nash.*

flowers massed in beds (raised in greenhouses and planted out); designs and colours could be exotic. J C Loudon (1783–1843) was a pioneer of this style, although he designed few gardens himself. Another park designer was Joseph Paxton (1803–65), but he also made Italianate gardens, such as in the terraces at Chatsworth (Db). Massed flower beds, often with an educational slant, were a feature of the public parks of the period. There were also curiosities like floral clocks, of which that in Princes Street Gardens, Edinburgh, is probably the sole survivor. By the 1870s taste turned again, this time back to the wild or natural garden; the main exponent of this was William Robinson (1839–1935), whose ideas had a comeback

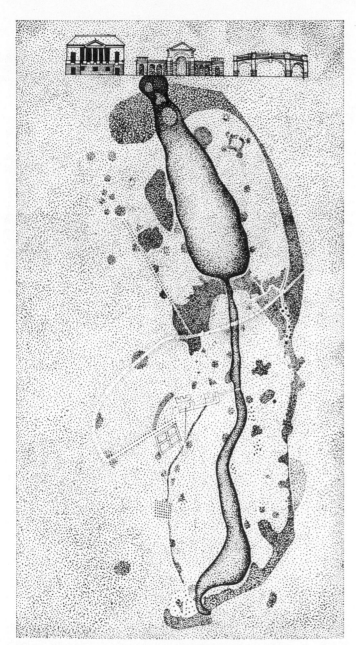

61 *"Capability" Brown's park layout for Packington (Ww), 1770s: the stream is widened into a lake, and the trees are carefully placed to look natural, but to create an artistic landscape inspired by the paintings of Claude Lorraine.*

62 *Greenhouse, Syon House – Charles Fowler, 1824: a massive piece of Victoriana in iron and glass.*

63 *People's Park, Halifax – Sir Joseph Paxton, 1856. A very Victorian conception, with terrace, statues, pavilion, bandstand (not in this picture), and close-set flowerbeds.*

in the present century after another revival of the formal garden by Reginald Blomfield (1865–1942).

The Victorians loved greenhouses (see **62**) and conservatories, rustic work, grottos, and ferneries, and cultivated the overgrown, secluded effect. Some of the best Victorian gardens are in public parks, like the People's Park, Halifax (see **63**), but private examples can be seen at Bodnant (Dh), Hever Castle (Kt), and Wilton (Wi). Rockeries and water gardens may also be mentioned here.

The 20th century opened with the wild garden and the formal garden both in vogue. It occurred to some that these could be combined as different parts of the same garden; Hidcote Manor (Gl) embodies this idea, as does Sissinghurst Castle (Kt), with their enclosed "rooms" divided off by walls or hedges, each with a uniform type or colour of flowers.

Gertrude Jekyll (1843–1932) developed the herbaceous border and colour planning; her own garden is at Orchards, Munstead (Sy) (a Lutyens house), and she had a wide influence. She drew some of her ideas from the traditional cottage garden. This appears to go back to the rebuilding of cottages and small houses which took place in the late 16th and early 17th century in the south, and the later 17th century in the north. It has a haphazard jumble of simple flowers wherever they can be grown, climbers on every wall and

on trellises, and a fruit tree or two. Here the influence of Margery Fish is noteworthy.

Gertrude Jekyll sometimes designed formal, often geometrical gardens, in relation to the house. She was also attracted to the water garden, of which she has left examples of various sizes and elaboration, including quite modest ones along a stream with a formal feature at one end, as at Vann, Hambledon (Sy). Gertrude Jekyll's other major contribution to garden history is that of the formal layout conceived as integral with the house, and ideally constructed with it and as a structural extension or annexe to it (see **64**); examples are at Hestercombe, Cheddar Fitzpaine (So) and Marsh Court, near Stockbridge (Ha), both Lutyens houses; she had a long and fruitful collaboration with Lutyens.

There are many good general 20th-century gardens to be seen, such as Nymans (Sx), Cotehele (Co), or Jenkyn Place, Bentley (Ha). Indeed, there is a very wide range of houses and gardens now open to the public, both owned by the National Trust and still in private hands. They are well worth visiting. Although the gardens of suburban houses tend to greater formality, the cottage garden idea is making headway in larger gardens, and evidently reflects current English taste. Eighty per cent of houses in Britain – 14.5m out of 18.1m – have private gardens, and they cover an area twice as large as Surrey.

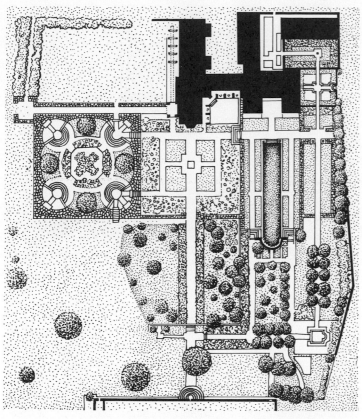

64 *Plan of an Edwin Lutyens–Gertrude Jekyll garden, Folly Farm, Sulhamstead (Bk), 1906–12: one of their last collaborations, with all their characteristic motifs of "rooms", formal and informal, and a water feature.*

Useful lists of parks by the great designers are given in Hugh Prince: *Parks in England* (1967).

Topiary, the cutting of trees into artificial shapes, needs a special section. The Romans used it, it was reintroduced by the Normans, and by the 12th century mazes and labyrinths were common. Under Italian influence in the Middle Ages it influenced the Tudor formal garden. The trees used were privet, box, juniper, and rosemary, with cypress also in the early 17th century. Yew became usual after the Restoration. Topiary declined in the 18th century as landscaping rose, but was revived in the 19th century (eg Compton Wynyates (Ww) 1895), and the 20th (at Lutyens houses).

Major schemes worth seeing are at Rockingham Castle (Le) (elephant hedge, early 16th century); Manor House, Keevil (Wi), 1580; Montacute (So), early Jacobean; Packwood House (Ww) (Sermon on the Mount group, 1650–70); Levens Hall (Wd) 1698, perhaps the finest of all; Chastleton House (Ox) *c* 1750; Melbourne Hall (Db), tunnel; Binghams Melcombe (Do), immense yew hedge round the bowling green; Painswick churchyard (Gl), 1792 to 19th century; Hidcote Manor (Gl), modern, with "tapestry" hedges. Topiary can be seen everywhere, in cottage and small house gardens as well. Pheasants, peacocks, squirrels, etc are common; some designs are more elaborate, like the destroyer Queen Elizabeth at Beckington near Frome (So), the Severn Bridge at St Awans (Mo), and a cottage at Westwood Manor (Wi). In some respects topiary reflects the English outlook which produced follies (see below).

The culmination, so far, of garden design is the creation by Sir Geoffrey Jellicoe at Sutton Place (Sy) (1980s). This is highly subtle and sophisticated, and is based on a comprehensive symbolism allegorising the journey through life. It uses water and stone as well as contrived wildness.

There are also specialised kinds of garden, such as the oriental, influenced by the taste for Chinese things in the late 18th century and for Japanese in the 19th; examples can be seen at Cannon Hill Park, Birmingham, or Tatton Park (Ch). Gardens of factories or institutions, or roof gardens at stores, are of course conditioned by their location.

Garden features

In describing gardens and parks mention has been made of various kinds of constructions or buildings for convenience or embellishment. These must be looked at more closely. Raised walks and terraces speak for themselves, as do statues, fountains, basins, stone seats, sundials, alcoves, arbours, pergolas, and the like. *Mounts* (see **65**) are conical hillocks with flat tops, rather like mottes; they can be merely to provide a view, either onto the outside of the garden, over the wall, or over some feature of the garden itself – in which case they have, or had, pavilions on top – or may be purely ornamental; the two categories overlap. New College, Oxford, has a good example, as has Little Moreton Hall (Ch). *Mounds* are low humps of earth, to add "scenery" to a flat expanse or

65 *A formal Elizabethan garden, with an elaborate ornamental mount – New College, Oxford.*

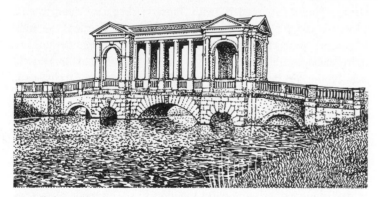

66 *Palladian Bridge, Stowe, c 1740: an adornment of a landscaped park, of Italian inspiration. Others are at Wilton and Prior Park, Bath; this one is beautifully proportioned.*

variety to a garden or park. The low rockeries at the south corners of Russell Square, London, are the remains of early 19th-century mounds, and there is an attractive one in the middle of the Circus at Bath; the Circus was originally, when laid out, paved, and the mound was added in the early 19th century, with the great plane trees which stand round it.

Buildings include *garden houses*, *summer houses*, *belvederes*, *gazebos*, *bridges* (including the Palladian bridges at Stowe (see **66**),

Wilton, and Prior Park, Bath), and *temples* and *pavilions* of all kinds. Garden houses on raised walks were usually wooden before the 16th century, and stone or brick thereafter; they shade off into the profusion of rustic summer houses which most Victorian gardens had. Belvederes gave views across the garden, park, or countryside; they could be in the classical, romantic, or gothic styles, according to the taste of the times. Gazebos were placed to command a view of the road, so that the ladies of the house could pass the time watching the passers-by (eg North Stainley, near Ripon). Temples, usually modelled on some classical building, served as retreats or picnic places, and might be in the garden or the park. If in the park, they had the additional function of providing a feature to embellish a view or vista. Most 18th-century parks had one, and some several. Stowe and Studley Royal have a large number, of all shapes and sizes, and very lovely and impressive they are. Those at Stourhead are quite magnificent, as is the Temple of the Four Winds at Castle Howard. Circular temples at viewpoints, open all round, are common.

Grottos come in here, although they verge on the folly (see below), because many of them were used as pavilions as well as ornaments to the garden. They are essentially artificial caves, though they are sometimes real caves adapted and sometimes just buildings above

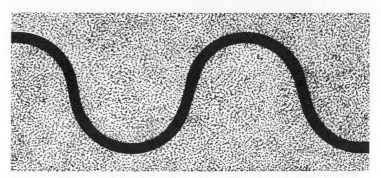

68–9 *A crinkle-crankle – a curved wall for sheltering fruit trees: most are in East Anglia, but this one is in Guildford – view and plan.*

67 *Gilbert White's ha-ha at The Wakes, Selborne (Ha), 1761.*

ground. They were usually open in front (often opening onto the lake, as at Stourhead or Painshill), and contained seats, statues, and sometimes a spring (St Ann's Well at Malvern is in a grotto). The walls and roof could be left as rock or could be encrusted with flints, rough rockwork, or shells; the grotto at Margate, 18th century, has rooms and passages, and is covered with shells in decorative and symbolic designs; Goodwood has one built by the Duchess of Richmond and her daughters with their own hands in 1740, and adorned with shells. They range from quite small ones, as at Moor Park, Farnham (Sy), to medium-sized ones as at Albury (Sy) (late 17th century), and to splendid complex ones as at Stourhead. Some, like that at Fonthill (Wi) (William Beckford's house, 1796–1807), had a paid hermit living in them. Some have baths, as at Downton. Pope's grotto at Twickenham was used as a study.

Water is a feature of many gardens and parks. The systems range from simple basins or groups of fountains to linked groups of ornamental ponds of various shapes and sizes, sometimes on the flat, but often sunk into complicated terracing (as at Studley Royal). Gardens in the French or Dutch styles (17th century) had long straight canals

(eg Wanstead or Hampton Court), but in the 18th century these were replaced by natural-looking lakes. These were in nearly every case dammed streams; those at Blenheim and Holkham (Nf) are fine examples. Sometimes the remains of one in the shape of a broken dam in a dry valley can be found. The earth removed in making an ornamental lake was sometimes heaped up to form "scenery", as in Battersea Park, London.

Ha-has (see above), so named by John James in 1712 and much used by Kent and Capability Brown, are ingenious ditches between a garden and a park; the garden side is a straight wall, and the ditch slopes up to the park (see 59). This not only gives the illusion that garden and park are continuous but keeps cattle and deer out of the garden. Most great houses have them (eg Burghley, Petworth, or Rousham), as well as some quite small houses, like Gilbert White's at Selborne (see 67); there is one in the churchyard at Thursley (Sy) and one round Gray's monument at Stoke Poges (Bc), which avoids the need for unsightly railings.

Crinkle-crankles, or ribbon walls, are brick orchard walls, wavy in plan (see 68–9); the curves give shelter to fruit trees. They were popular in

70 *Brighton Pavilion, 1815–22: the Prince Regent's (later George IV) "pleasure dome". It was developed in several stages from 1786, and brought to its present exotic form by John Nash, 1815–22 – internally chinoiserie, externally "Indian".*

17th and 18th century New England as a means of saving bricks. In Britain they are most numerous in Suffolk, where there are nearly 50, against about half that number in the rest of the country. One at West Horsley Place (Sy) was recorded in 1740; they date mostly from the early 19th century, but a few are late Victorian.

Views in parks were obtained in several ways. One was to make a hole in a hedge through which a prospect or a temple could be seen as in a picture frame (as at Studley Royal). The view of a house when approached along the drive could be enhanced by an *avenue* of trees, as at Clandon (Sy) or Traquair (Ps). The trees of some avenues were planted on low banks or mounds, and parallel banks may therefore be the remains of a vanished avenue. Avenues were also planted along roads, eg south of Wilton (Do), at Mellerstain (Be), half a mile long with six rows of trees each side, on a vast scale at Clumber (No), two miles long with 1,296 trees in double rows, or the one and a half mile avenue of beeches at Stansted (Sx), early 18th century, replanted 1820. There was also the walk among the trees, ending in a seat, statue, or other feature.

Vistas in parks were obtained either by straight rides among the trees, ending at a temple or obelisk, or by wide, irregular glades or series of clumps of trees, carefully positioned. There is a remarkable example of the use of rides, in reverse, at Rievaulx Abbey (NY) where a walk links a number of concentric gaps in the trees on a steep slope, focusing on the abbey. Interesting minor avenues can be seen in some churchyards, from lychgate to church door, as at Hatfield Broad Oak (Ex) or at Crondall (Ha). Trees were sometimes arranged in purposeful clumps, not only for scenic effect but to represent something. Thus at Blenheim the copses represent the line-up of the troops before the battle, and at Douthwaite Hall, near Kirbymoorside (NY), clumps of trees shaped like ships sail towards the hill from which they can best be seen (the whim of an admiral). Incidentally, on the Downs west of Lewes, an attempt was made to spell out the name Victoria in trees, a project which never got beyond the V.

Follies

Follies are probably commoner in England than anywhere else, and the English character can hardly be fully understood without taking them into account. What is more, the country would be poorer without them. The English in fact have a love, if often repressed, for the irrational, the grotesque, the extravagant, and even the useless. When this is combined with wealth, space, and a favourable cultural background, the folly may run rife. The mentality which could create an artificial landscape for a private park would not stop at a bizarre building.

The age of follies began in the late 16th century and reached its peak in the 18th and 19th, but the spirit behind it still persists. The Renaissance had opened up to the wealthy and the scholarly not only the classical world but also the Middle Ages, and these provided a rich vein for architectural experiment. The Grand Tour in the 18th century enabled rich young men to see antiquities for themselves, and what they saw was mostly ruins. Already a Romantic spirit was abroad, and by the time the gothic came into fashion the folly got out of hand and reality went by the board.

Architectural follies (unless one counts as a beacon the four-storey tower with one room on each storey at Bringham (Nf)) began with Sir Thomas Tresham's Rushton Lodge and Lyveden New House (Nh), built from 1595 to 1600 to express his views on the Passion, the Trinity, and symbolic numbers. Freston Tower (Su), *c* 1595, and Eyre's Folly

(Wi), early 17th century, are other early examples. But in the 18th century follies arrived with a rush. It is not always easy to separate a fantasy from a legitimate building – after all, follies had an element of surprise and the unexpected – and the ruin was coming into its own. The picture is necessarily confused. Thus, Stowe has a temple of Modern Virtue (a ruin) as opposed to a temple of Ancient Virtue (not a ruin); the "bridge" at Kenwood is a facade only; a lodge at Mereworth (Kt) is in the form of a Roman triumphal arch; Vanbrugh's castellated but otherwise faintly Baroque belvedere at Claremont (Sy), 1717, has a distinctly ambiguous air. Shugborough (St) has splendid classical buildings, like the triumphal arch called the Gates of Jerusalem, all over the park, yet has a gothic ruin in the private garden right in front of the house.

Tombs lent themselves to disguise, eg Dashwood's Mausoleum at High Wycombe, and the popular pyramid, such as those at Castle Howard, St Ives (Co), and Farley Mount (Ha) (to a horse). Cottages, cowsheds and hermitages were built as ruins, with carefully-placed cracks and well-trained ivy; facades are frequent and whole villages could be "picturesque". The *ferme ornée* at the Leasowes, Shenstone (St) and the Cottage at Mellerstain (Be) are of this latter type, as is the three-sided "Gothic" church tower added to the front of a group of cottages at Tattingstone (Su) to improve the squire's view. Whole houses may be considered follies, like the Brighton Pavilion (see **70**), or Fonthill (which fell down). Sham castles are not uncommon, as at Mow Cop (Ch); the Sham Castle at Bath is not strictly a folly; it was built in 1762 by Richard Jones for Ralph Allen, to try out an architectural principle used later in Allen's house at Prior Park. At Scotney Castle (Kt), the 17th-century part was deliberately "ruined" when the new house was built. Mixture of styles was no deterrent – by Colchester Castle is an imitation Roman temple combined with a sham gothic ruin. At Virginia Water is a temple built of genuine stones from Leptis Magna (1826). One of the most splendid and romantic follies is The Pineapple at Dunmore Park (Sg) (see **71**); this was put up in 1761 by John Murray, 4th Earl of Dunmore, for reasons now obscure.

Follies were sometimes built to relieve unemployment. Yorke's Folly, on the edge of Guy's Cliff, Nidderdale (NY), was intended as a picturesque ruin, but its exposed position has produced what may be called secondary ruination. The Colosseum at Oban is another example. The unfinished Parthenon on Calton Hill, Edinburgh, is not a folly – it was projected as a memorial to the Scottish dead in

71 *The Pineapple, Dunmore Park (Sg), 1761: this unlikely building, a folly par excellence, was put up by John Murray, 4th Earl of Dunmore.*

the Napoleonic Wars, but had to be abandoned when funds ran out.

Towers are perhaps the commonest form of folly, and went on being built until recent times. Examples are Perrott's Tower, Edgbaston, *c* 1760, now engulfed by urban development, and Wainhouse's Folly, Halifax (1871, 282ft (86.75m) high). Lord Berners built a tower at Faringdon (Ox) in 1935. Leith Hill Tower (Sy) was built (1766) to raise the sightseer from 965ft (297m) to 1,000 ft (308m). The list and the variety are endless. There is the hermitage built against standing tree-trunks at Halberton (Dv); the "Druids" Temple at Ilton, Masham (NY) imitates prehistoric remains; the vast series of underground rooms at Welbeck (No) may well count as a folly, as does the dining-room under the lake at Witley Park (Sy). They can be found everywhere. Many have odd or almost incredible stories attached to them. Thus the squire of Dallington (Sx) swore at a dinner-party that he could see the spire of the village church from the house, and when this proved to be untrue, built the pyramidal Sugar-Loaf out on his land to represent it (*c* 1815). One of the most incredible follies was the planting of dead trees in Kensington Gardens in the early 18th century, for the effect.

Follies are still close to the popular mind; one has only to see front gardens filled with gnomes fishing, windmills, and exotic shells. Folk art may, at this end of the scale, be just round the corner. A good introduction is Barbara Jones: *Follies and Grottoes*, 1974.

A not wholly unrelated topic is *secret passages*. Belief in these is curiously persistent, in spite of the evidence, and all kinds of tunnels have been described as secret. Passages are supposed to link old houses with monasteries or churches (eg St Martha's Church, near Guildford, to the former old house of Tyting, half a mile away, down a steep hillside in soft sand). Some are said to have been for getting persecuted priests and recusants away from hiding holes in the 16th and 17th centuries (and even many of the hiding holes have other explanations), some to get contraband from secluded coves or desolate but exposed beaches to secret storehouses, eg from Beer (Dv) to Bovey House, one and a half miles of very hilly country, and some for many other disreputable if romantic purposes. Few of these stories can be substantiated and most of the passages don't exist. In some cases there is a natural fissure in the ground into which animals or men have fallen, thus giving rise to the legend (eg St Guthlac's Priory, Hereford), or the cause may be, as in the case of Llanthony, the monastery sewer. Some passages are said to run for distances which rule them out of rational consideration, eg from the "Roman Well" at Ipsden (Ox) to Wallingford, four miles in hilly country, and some are said to run under rivers and other obstacles. Alfred Watkins, the author of *The Old Straight Track*, suggested that these legends may reflect the imaginary direct line between two prominent points linked by a track overground but which cannot be seen from each other because of an intervening hill, eg Danebury to Quarley Hill "camps" in Hampshire, which are four miles apart. But this cannot be proved, and there are no doubt many explanations of the passage.

Most passages, where they exist, seem to have been sewers or for water supply. A few appear to have genuinely been made for escape from castles or houses, as at Dover Castle, and these are probably medieval; those at St Andrews are a mine and counter-mine of 1546. Some are 16th- or 17th-century, like those at Shrewsbury (St Chads and Dogpole).

Mazes

These have a long history going back probably as far as the religious practices of the Neolithic. Some were in the open and some in special buildings, like the famous Egyptian and Cretan labyrinths. They were the scene of ritual dancing representing the convolutions of the soul's journey to the other world or the inward journey into the unconscious and back again – denoting rebirth, integration, initiation, fertility, etc. At the centre would have been a symbol of divinity or eternity.

There was a strange revival of mazes in medieval times, sanctioned by the Church, although the pagan origins were not forgotten as the association of the name of Troy with them indicates. Mazes were set in the floors of some cathedrals, like Chartres and Seville, and there is one on the Mappa Mundi in Hereford Cathedral. But most were in the open air, and were either made or restored at this time (13th–14th century).

72 *A maze of Chartres type, derived from a Roman form, probably in the 9th century; four symmetrical quarters emphasise a Christian cross symbol.*

There were a large number in Britain, made of turf walls a few inches high, usually circular but in other shapes as well; the designs were either spirals or segments of symmetrical figures. Some are near the sites of prehistoric villages or hillforts and are not related to medieval or modern ones; these may have been restored rather than newly made, unless they were put where they are because of the continuing tradition of sacredness in these places. Thus, the fine Mizmaze on Breamore Down (Ha), said to have a mile of windings, is in Celtic fields and near a long barrow (the name mizmaze or Troy-town may indicate the former existence of a maze). There are good ones at Alkborough (Li) and Wing (Ru), and there is one on the green at Saffron Walden (Ex), with "wings" at the corners. The one on St Catherine's Hill, Winchester, inside the hillfort, is square, and is 17th-century, not medieval. The terraces on Glastonbury Tor may be the remains of a three-dimensional maze.

The hedge mazes in gardens (see **72** and **73**) are only indirectly related to these, being made for ornamental and not religious reasons,

73 *Plan of a labyrinth. Unlike a maze (which derives from this prehistoric pattern), this has no dead ends or misleading pathways, but consists of a single pathway from the entrance to the centre.*

although they, and knot gardens, may carry a faint reminiscence of the earlier thing. They are features of the Italian style of garden in vogue here from the 16th century. The famous maze at Hampton Court was made about 1700, replacing an earlier one.

THE ROYAL PARKS

An important and unique feature of London is the *royal parks*, which provide thousands of acres of well-kept and high-quality open space in the heart of the built-up area. Some originated in the private gardens and grounds of royal residences (St James's, Greenwich, Richmond, Hampton Court, Kensington), while others are the remnants of a hunting forest enclosed by Henry VIII (Regent's, Hyde). They all have a strongly individual character. There are herds of deer in Richmond and Bushey.

St James's was opened to the public by James I, and was a favourite resort of Londoners from the beginning. Laid out at first in the French style, it was redesigned less formally by Nash. *Green Park* was added to it by Charles II. *Hyde Park* was part of Henry VIII's hunting forest, and up to the 1690s extended to Kensington. It was opened to the public by James I. The Serpentine was made by Queen Caroline (1730) by damming the Westbourne; the bridge is by Rennie. The Great Exhibition of 1851 was held along the south side in Paxton's great glasshouse, the Crystal Palace, moved later to Sydenham and destroyed by fire in 1936. *Kensington Gardens* were formalised and enclosed from Hyde Park by Queen Caroline. Its main features are the sunken garden by the palace, the Orangery (1704), the Round Pond, the Broad Walk (until recently an avenue of elms, now replaced by limes and maples), the Flower Walk, and that Victorian masterpiece the Albert Memorial.

Regent's Park, also part of Henry VIII's chase, was remodelled by Nash in 1811–12 as part of the Prince Regent's scheme. It contains the London Zoo, the Inner Circle (with the remnants of the former Royal Botanical Gardens), and St John's Gardens, and is surrounded by the very distinguished Nash terraces, with Park Village just behind them. *Primrose Hill*, to the north, is a fragment of open country. *Greenwich Park* was the grounds of a favourite medieval and Tudor palace; it was opened to the public by Charles II. It contains the Queen's House (Inigo Jones), the Royal Observatory (on the meridian), and Wren's Royal Naval College, besides the National Maritime Museum and remains of the old deerpark. *Richmond Park* is on the grand scale, being two and a half miles across. It was enclosed in 1637 to enlarge the grounds of Richmond Palace, but opened in 1639, although access was limited until the mid 18th century. The Pen Ponds are artificial, and the other small ponds are old gravel pits. Henry VIII's Mound is an artificial hillock on which the king could stand during game drives. Features of the park are the Isabella Plantation and Woodland Garden, and the Queen's Ride; the White Lodge is the headquarters of the Royal Ballet.

Hampton Court Park is the formal park round the palace, and *Bushey Park* is the adjacent deerpark. Round the palace are the Orangery, the Privy Garden (with iron screen by Tijou), the Tennis Court (Henry VIII–Charles II), the Maze (*c* 1700), the Knot Garden (1924), and the site of the Tilt-Yard; further away are the Long Water and the Ice House. The deerpark contains Wren's Diana Fountain and the Waterhouse Plantation. (A useful summary is Richard Church: *The Royal Parks of London* (1965).)

OPEN SPACES AND URBAN PARKS

A few tracts of land, still forming external lungs for London, were vested in the City Corporation in the 19th century and are known as the *City of London Open Spaces*. The largest of these is Epping Forest which, with outliers, forms a strip about a mile wide from Wanstead Flats to beyond Epping. It contains a variety of woodland scenery, has very pretty country on its edges, and has always been popular with those Londoners within reach of it. It was a royal hunting forest and covered some 60,000 acres (24,000ha) in the 17th century, most of this being agricultural land. But it was threatened by progressive enclosure, and by the mid 19th century seemed doomed to extinction. The woodland part of it was also threatened by the traditional lopping rights claimed by local people, and these were contested in the courts in the 1860s. The area was regulated under an Act of 1871, and finally vested in the City Corporation by an Act of 1878 as a permanent open space. By this time the woodland area covered some 6,000 (2,400ha) acres (see Georgina Green: *Epping Forest Through the Ages* (1982)). Similar wooded areas such as Hainault Forest and Burnham Beeches were also placed in

the care of the City, which also owns parks and commons in and around London (eg West Wickham Common, Highgate Woods), and over 80 small open spaces in the City itself.

London indeed has an unrivalled collection of parks and open spaces, which have a wide and instructive variety of origins. There are the Royal and City parks, just described. The inheritors of the Greater London Council maintain most of the others, and these grew, or were laid out, from open country or waste (Hampstead Heath, Blackheath), monastic lands (Abbey Wood), commons of former villages (Clapham), greens (Islington), otherwise unusable ground (Southwark), grounds of private houses (Kenwood, Waterlow, Springfield), marshes (Hackney), or just odd pieces of waste ground. There are even old plague pits at South Kensington and Charterhouse Square. Then there are the squares, which were the lungs of Georgian building estates, some now public, like Russell Square, some still private, like Bedford. Sometimes a former churchyard has been converted, such as the garden between the Foundling Hospital and Regent Square. And even this remarkable list is probably not exhaustive.

The creation of parks in towns was a world-wide movement in the late 18th and early 19th century, which reached Britain in the second quarter of the 19th century. Here it reflected the same sort of public concern which gave rise to urban cemeteries (see pages 325–7). The parliamentary reports on sanitary conditions in towns (1842), interment conditions (1843), and public health (1844) resulted in the Public Health Act of 1848 which, among other things, empowered local administrative bodies to establish "public walks" and "means of exercise or amusement to the middle or humbler classes".

London, in spite of its overcrowding, was in a special position and was able to get off to a good start; it had a chain of unrivalled open spaces in the central area already (see above). Victorian parks played a notable part in education; their horticultural standard was high and there was great public enthusiasm for gardening. Parks were usually accessible from all parts of the city. Many of them were intended to, or at least did, bring up the value of surrounding property (eg the gardens of the New Town of Edinburgh, Regent's Park, London, and Birkenhead Park (1845)). Their size was usually determined by land value, but they made use of a wide variety of land. There was in fact no system; each park was isolated and of individual and unrelated shape and size. Their layout reflected the tastes of the time, a vernacular version of an 18th-century gentleman's landscaped park. Many were designed by notable landscape gardeners, such as Paxton, Papworth, Kemp, and Loudon (who was also an expert in the design of cemeteries). They declined in quality at the end of the century, and massed carpet bedding tended to replace more skilful arrangements.

By no means all the best parks are in London. One of the finest in the country is Roundhay Park in Leeds, and a very choice Victorian specimen is the People's Park in Halifax (by Paxton, 1856), one of the benefactions to the town of the carpet manufacturing family of Crossley. Aston Park in Birmingham and Temple Newsam, Leeds, are good examples of grounds of former private houses adapted to the new use. Many of Birmingham's open spaces are not formal parks, but "islanded" pieces of natural country.

Parks are now evolving, under the influence of current ideas of town planning, into small rest gardens and pedestrian precincts, residential parks with playing fields in housing estates, regional parks, national parks, and forest parks. The last two categories contain footpath systems, picnic grounds, and riding and camping sites, and make use of rivers, beaches, and woodlands; an early example of a riverside park is at Buxton (Db).

SPECIALISED PARKS AND GARDENS

Botanic gardens

During the 17th century, people began to develop a keen interest in plants and trees for their own sake, and many new species were introduced. Botanic gardens were founded for the scientific study of botany, in which the Tradescants were pioneers. John Rose (1629–77) and John Evelyn (1620–1706) were leading figures.

Kew was a royal park before a botanical garden was founded there by Queen Caroline in 1759, and it became the state centre for botanical research in 1841; it combines this with an arboretum, and the greenhouses are very important, including the great Palm House (Richard Turner and Decimus Burton, 1844–8) (see **74**). Of these greenhouses, 26 have been replaced (1985) by one immense tropical

74 *Palm House, Kew – Richard Turner and Decimus Burton, 1844–8: a major example of Victorian iron and glass construction.*

conservatory, combining under one roof a wide range of growing conditions from desert to mangrove swamp. Kew in fact is a centre for botanical research of world-wide importance and authority. Kew has a branch garden at Wakehurst (Sx).

There are, of course, older private botanical gardens, such as the Chelsea Physic Garden (*c* 1670), and those at Oxford (1621) and Edinburgh (founded in 1670 on the site of Waverley Station and moved to its present site in 1823). Other notable ones are those at Glasgow and the delightful Victorian one at Sheffield. St Andrews has a beautiful new garden outside the town (1962), replacing that in the university (1889).

Evelyn's love of trees was revived by J Chardon in his book *Arboretum et Fruticetum Britannicum* (1838), and the *arboretum* became a favourite feature of the 19th-century estate. Westonbirt (Gl), 500 acres in size, is one of the best. The first municipal arboretum was that at Derby (1840). There is a National Pinetum at Bedgebury (Kt) (1924), and important private collections, such as Hillier's near Romsey (Ha).

Zoological gardens

The most famous is the London Zoo, still run by the Zoological Society of London in Regent's Park, which was part of the original plan for the park in 1828; it has a 20th-century offshoot at Whipsnade. Other important zoos are those at Edinburgh, Chester, Bristol, and Manchester, and they are proliferating in the form of wildlife or safari parks all over the country, including those at great houses such as Woburn and Longleat. Among the scores of private and other zoos are some of considerable distinction, such as Chessington (Sy), and Marwell (Ha). Some zoos are highly specialised, eg the Aquarium at Brighton, the

Wildfowl Trust aviaries at Slimbridge (Gl) and Arundel (Sx), Birdworld near Farnham (Sy), the New Forest Butterfly Farm at Ashurst, near Southampton (Ha), the Rare Breeds Survival Trust at Stoneleigh (Ww), and the rare breeds farm near Tonbridge (Kt).

Another specialised form of park, although it is properly a museum, is the *open air museum*, which is growing in number. These are indeed a valuable means of presenting a subject with bulky remains in an appropriate setting. Originating in Scandinavia, they have enabled much to be preserved and presented which might otherwise have been lost. Distinguished examples include: St Fagans (Gm), the Folk Museum branch of the National Museum of Wales; Beamish (Du) – industrial history of the north-east; Ironbridge Gorge (Sp) – early Industrial Revolution – iron, coal, pottery etc; Morwellham (Dv) – copper and arsenic port; Maritime Museum, Exeter (Dv) – boats; Gloucester – canal history; Amberley (Sx) – quarrying; Gladstone Museum, Longton (St) – pottery; Weald and Downland, Singleton (Sx) – vernacular buildings and country crafts; Ryedale Folk Museum, Hutton-le-Hole (NY); Avoncroft (Wo) – vernacular buildings; Old Kiln Museum, Tilford (Sy) – farm implements, old shops, etc.

Recently farms have been adapted, for educational purposes, as museums where stock and processes can be demonstrated; such are Manor Farm, Cogges (Ox) and Bursledon (Ha). Over 60 open areas in inner cities have a similar objective, eg Kentish Town City Farm, London.

Another kind of park was the amusement park. This was popular in the 17th and 18th centuries. Vauxhall ran from the reign of Charles II to that of George III, Ranelagh from 1733 to 1805, and there were many others. A pale idea can be got from what is left of the pleasure park in Bath, Sydney Gardens (1796), in which stands the hotel which is now the Holburn of Menstrie Museum. A great Victorian example is Belle Vue, Manchester. A faithful living survival of this fashion is Tivoli in Copenhagen, Denmark.

The Bear Pits in Cardigan Road, Leeds, are the last survivors of the zoos and amusement parks which were a feature of West Riding life in the late 19th and early 20th centuries. Only three remain out of a former twelve, and these three are untypical – Roundhay Park, Leeds, Lister Park, Bradford, and Shipley Glen (WY). Most had fairground features, roller skating, and a lake, and some had zoos. Notable parks were Sunny Vale, Hipperholme, Hope Bank, Honley, and Halifax Zoo. (See Douglas Taylor in *Yorkshire Archaeological Journal*, 58, 1986.)

COMMONS

Common land was an essential ingredient of the life of a medieval community, even of an urban one. The common was part of the land of the manor and belonged to the manorial lord, who might of course be the Crown or the Church or other corporation, if not an individual. But it was distinguished from other land in that certain people had (and still have) free access to it, and common rights to use it – eg pasture for their animals, estovers (collection of wood for fuel), turbary (digging of peat for fuel), piscary (fishing), and gathering of bracken for fuel or cattle bedding. Not all the villagers necessarily had rights over the common. These rights might well be confined to particular people, such as those living round the village green (or, as in Yorkshire, those whose houses fronted on the green, and were not built gable end to it), or an otherwise defined class of people. Such rights had existed from time immemorial, ie certainly from the early Saxon period, and who knows from how long before that. The popular belief that a common belongs to everybody indiscriminately, and that anyone, wherever they live and whoever they are, has the right to use it, is totally without foundation.

On the other side, the landowner must not obstruct the rights of the commoners – and must not build on the common, or even fence it. Such a situation must be of great antiquity, and deeply ingrained in the life of the community. The common rights in the New Forest, for example, were robust enough to survive William I's afforestation of the area, and were not granted by him in compensation for the people he displaced. The grazing on Dartmoor is certainly as old as Devon (mid 8th century), and may even reflect the prehistoric pastures delimited by the "reaves", the cross-country boundary banks which traverse the moor. Some lands are common to a whole county, eg the Somerset Levels, Andred's Weald to Kent, and Sherwood Forest to Nottinghamshire. Shirley, near Southampton, may have been common to Hampshire. Andred's Weald – the "Weald" – later became split into smaller pasture areas (some called "denns", eg Tenterden, Rolvenden, Biddenden) attached to manors or villages often many miles away. Thus Speldhurst near Tunbridge Wells was in the 8th century a swine pasture belonging to Halling on the Medway, 17 miles away.

Some towns had commons in late Saxon times, limited to burgesses, eg Port Meadow, Oxford, the Town Moor, Newcastle-upon-Tyne, and the still extensive commons of Southampton. Otmoor (Ox) looks like a prehistoric grazing tract, its 4,000 acres (1,600ha) common to seven villages. Some towns grew up on common land, such as Liverpool, Woodstock, and Petersfield (all *c* 1200). Some, like London, enveloped commons as they grew, and these commons still exist – such as Blackheath, Clapham, Streatham, Wimbledon (1,100 acres (44 ha)), or Hampstead (800 acres (320ha) with Kenwood). Epping Forest (6,000 acres (2,400ha)) is a special case. The Strays of York are also now absorbed in the city; Harrogate Stray is not strictly a common, although public land.

Village greens, the common property of the village, are dealt with above (pages 108–11).

There were several million acres of common land in 1086, but these were reduced by 1350, and then greatly by the Enclosures of the 18th and 19th centuries. Gregory King, in 1688, says that nearly a quarter of the total area of England and Wales was still waste land, of which some three million acres (1,200,000ha) were commons. Enclosure reduced this to the present figure of one and a half million acres (600,000ha) (1,055,000 in England, 450,000 in Wales). This is 4% of the total land surface, or nearly as much as land which has been built over. Two-thirds of English commons are in the seven (pre-1974) northern counties, and most of the rest are in Hampshire, Surrey, and Devon. In Westmorland one acre in four is common land, in North Yorkshire one in six. In Wales most commons are in Brecon, Radnor, and Glamorgan – in Brecon nearly 30% of the land is common. Some common land has of course survived as such because it is agriculturally poor and therefore escaped enclosure; thus the famous Surrey commons and heaths, eg Merrow, Thursley, Ranmore, Chobham, Hurtwood, Farley Heath/Blackheath, Frensham, and Witley, are mostly on Lower Greensands or Bagshot Sands.

The most useful study of commons is L Dudley Stamp and W G Hoskins: *The Common Lands of England and Wales* (Collins 1963). This draws on the findings of a Royal Commission set up to review the status and consider the future of the then remaining commons, and is thus comprehensive and authoritative. The Commission's Report was followed by the Commons Registration Act of 1965, under which owners of common lands had to register them if their future integrity was to be preserved. The result has been of great national benefit. But many commons were not registered or have been deregistered since, and few have any formal management structure, so are vulnerable to encroachment. There is now a movement to make common land open to the public and to stop unregistered commons being swallowed up by developers. The Countryside Commission reported on this to the Government in 1986, with a view to legislation. The report also seeks to give local residents a legal right to use their village greens for sport and pastimes, a right which is at present not clear in law.

NATIONAL PARKS

The National Parks and Access to the Countryside Act of 1949 had the intention of facilitating access to open countryside and to confer powers of development control in order to protect beautiful countryside from despoliation. Under it a number of areas receive special status as national parks; within these the park authority can preserve and enhance the particular quality of the landscapes and can provide for its enjoyment by the public in a way consonant with the other uses and values of the area. These parks are not parks in the sense of the royal or municipal parks; ownership of property within them is unaffected, and normal farming and industry go on. But the public has freer access than it had, and certain amenities and parking areas have been provided. In some parks, indeed, the inflow of visitors has created acute problems, but there is no doubt that the parks are and will remain valuable national assets.

The region most provided with national parks is the north of England, with its unrivalled stretches of bare upland. There are three in the Pennines: the Peak District, the Yorkshire Dales, and Northumberland (which adjoins a large forest park). There are also the Lake District and the North York Moors. Exmoor and Dartmoor complete the series. Together they cover a wide variety of geology, scenery, and human activity. Wales has the Snowdonia national park, which stretches as far south as Aberdovey and contains a small forest park as well, the Brecon Beacons, and the Pembrokeshire Coast. There are no national parks in Scotland, although the matter has been under consideration since 1988. Instead of Areas of Outstanding Natural Beauty, Scotland has National Scenic Areas, of which in 1994 there were 40, scattered across all regions, and covering 2,475,448 acres (1,001,800ha).

Forest parks, as their name implies, are specialised areas devoted to forestry but to which the public has certain access, subject to fire precautions. These include the Forest of Dean in England, and in

141

Scotland the large parks of Glen Trool (Kb), Argyll and Queen Elizabeth north-west of Glasgow, and a small one at Glen More in the Cairngorms.

The Act of 1949 also enabled certain areas to be designated *Areas of Outstanding Natural Beauty*. Although these do not have the full status of national parks, they enjoy certain protections from unsuitable development and certain freedoms for the public. The need for them is greatest in areas within easy reach of the great conurbations or in vulnerable parts of the coast. Thus in England they include long stretches of the Cornwall and Devon coasts, the coast from the Exe to Poole Harbour, with much of Dorset, much of the Isle of Wight, and the adjacent coast of Hampshire, the East Hampshire chalklands and greensand, the South Downs, the Surrey Hills, and the Kent Downs. Inland they include the Chilterns, the Cotswolds, the Quantocks, the Malvern Hills, the Shropshire Hills, and Cannock Chase, together with much of the coasts of Suffolk and Norfolk, and Dedham Vale. In the North, the Forest of Bowland, upper Nidderdale, the North Pennines (Upper Teesdale, Cross Fell, and the Alston area as far as the South Tyne), part of the southern Solway shores, and the Northumberland coast have been designated, together with, in Wales, the Wye Valley, Gower, and much of the coasts of Lleyn and Anglesey.

Finally, the National Parks Act enabled *continuous footpaths* to be created. These are now the North and South Downs Ways, the Pennine Way, from Derbyshire to the Border, the Cleveland Way, the South West Peninsula Coast Path, the Ridgeway Path (Berkshire Downs and Chilterns), the Pembrokeshire Coast Path, and Offa's Dyke Path (following the Anglian defensive line along the Welsh border).

The public desire for freer access to the countryside has also led to the maintenance of *traditional footpaths*. The Act of 1949 required paths and bridleways to be registered if they were to have the protection of the county authorities. A third category, "roads used as public paths", mostly former tracks or disused roads (sometimes spectacular hollow ways rich in wildlife), were reviewed and classified under the Countryside Act of 1968. A definitive map of all these was made under the Wildlife and Countryside Act of 1981.

The Countryside Act of 1968 enabled *country parks* to be set up, and about 100 have so far been designated; these include parks round stately homes, like Elvaston Castle (Db), stretches of woodland eg Kingsford (Wo), and almost any kind of terrain. The same Act also initiated *picnic areas*.

In parallel with this public desire for fuller access to and protection of the countryside, there has been in recent years a corresponding realisation of the need not only to conserve exceptional natural areas for their own sake but to protect the habitats of rare or distinctive species, both flora and fauna. Accordingly, under the Wildlife and Countryside Act 1981, National Nature Reserves have been set up (eg the Cairngorms and Wicken Fen (Ca)), and certain, usually fairly small, areas have been designated Sites of Special Scientific Interest; the statutory protection of these is being strengthened.

In addition, bodies such as the National Trust, the Woodland Trust, and the various county wildlife and conservation trusts are steadily buying up or acquiring land threatened by development. National bodies such as English Nature, Scottish Nature, the World Wildlife Fund UK, the Council for the Protection of Rural England, the Open Spaces Society, the Ramblers' Association, and the Royal Society for the Protection of Birds exercise constant vigilance.

As an appendix to this section may be added the relatively recent Leisure and Sports Centres, as some of them have features which touch on parks. These are tracts of country, often otherwise unusable, such as disused and converted gravel pits, which cater for a variety of sports or are specialised centres for boating, skiing, or games. They are usually supported by the Sports Council and the local authority. Examples are Holme Pierrepoint (No) or Thorpe (Sy), for water sports, smaller boating centres like Olney (Bc), or Thrapston (Nh); general centres include Wyndley, Sutton Coldfield, games areas like Bingham (No), which is linked to a school, skiing centres like Southampton, or local sports centres like those at Alton or Cranleigh. An important private club assisted by the Sports Council is Queen Mary Reservoir Sailing Club at Staines.

The first *Regional Park* to get off the ground was the Lea Valley Scheme. This is supported by no fewer than 28 local authorities. It consists of a long strip of land along the river Lea from east London into Hertfordshire; some of this is open, some industrialised, some derelict. The park has facilities for various sports and activities, as well as riverside walking, camping, boating, etc.

SPORTS AND GAMES

The village green was the natural place for sports and games, fairs, and other leisure and social activities of the village. What follows goes wider, into organised sport generally. Most popular sports and games took place on open sites or on traditional spots, which cannot now be recognised unless recorded. But some needed special grounds or places, or developed the need for these; remains of these can still be seen, or indeed have become conspicuous features of villages and towns today.

Bullbaiting is commemorated by the name bullring in many towns (eg Birmingham and Wakefield), but few have survived. At Northallerton (NY) the site of one is marked out in the market place. The bull was attached for baiting to a ring set in a stone or post; some of these have been preserved, as at Snitterton and Eyam (Db), Cellarhead (St), Brading (IW), Horsham (Sx), and Loppington (Sp). A bullpit, to keep the animals in when not being baited and to send dogs in with the bull, is at Buckland Dinham (So). Bears were kept in beargardens or pits for the same purpose. The bearpits in Cardigan Road, Leeds, were part of a zoo (1840–58). The famous bullring and bearpits in Southwark have not survived. Badgers were usually hunted with dogs but were baited as well, and a pit for this survives at Ipsden (Ox). Pits were also used by farmers to catch badgers, about 5ft deep and 4ft (1.5 x 1.2m) long, narrowed at top and bottom and wider in the middle.

Cockfighting was very popular in the 18th and early 19th century, and heavy bets were laid on the birds. When the sport was practised openly, cockpits were mostly either hollows in the ground or on the tops of low mounds. Examples can be seen at Aberavon (Gl), Llandwrog (Cn), and a walled one on the Boverton estate, Llantwit Major (Gl). That at Wycoller (La) is a sunk circle surrounded by a low raised bank. There is an early 18th-century example in the formal woodland garden at Hackwood (Ha). On Chislehurst Common (Kt) is a circular space marked by a shallow bank and ditch, inside an oval depression some 4.5ft deep and 125ft long, but this may be only an example of a sporting site taking advantage of a disused pond. There was a famous cockpit in St James's Park, London, from the early 18th century to 1816, replacing one built by Henry VIII in Whitehall Palace (the first). Sometimes cockpits were housed in special buildings, such as the roofed one from Denbigh which has been re-erected at St Fagans. Many towns had cockpits built into inns, remains or traces of which can often still be seen (eg at Saffron Walden (Ex)). Cockfighting was made illegal in public in 1849, and went underground. But many of the old sites continued to be used, and arenas were constructed in the basements of houses. Some of the old sites, particularly those in inns, were turned over to *ratting*, which replaced cockfighting in popularity in the later 19th century; here dogs competed to kill as many rats as possible in a given time.

Tournaments and *jousting* were a favourite pastime of the court and landowners throughout the Middle Ages and into the 16th century. Henry VII had a tiltyard wherever he lived. *Tilting* was carried out on rectangular fields, often surrounded by banks for wooden seating. There is a good example attached to a private house at Gawsworth (Ch). The only surviving quintain, or tilting post, is on the green at Offham (Kt), which is late medieval. Quintains were posts with a movable horizontal arm from which hung a sack of straw, or some such target, for tilting at with a long pole, or for practice.

Among quasi-military activities, mention should be made of *archery* and *shooting*, which have always verged on sports. Both were compulsory for men of military age (the latter from the 16th century) until after the Civil Wars. But they were normally done on open spaces outside the towns; Moorfields was used for archery practice by Londoners, and the Butts at Alton (Ha) still exists as a green, so have left no visible remains. Shooting was practised in Artillery Yards, like that on Horslydown in Bermondsey, London. In the 19th century rifle shooting became an organised sport, and is still carried out not only on private ranges but on military ranges such as Bisley. There are remains of butts on Puttenham Common (Sy).

Horse-racing was probably practised well before the conquest, and is recorded in the 12th century at Smithfield. It was organised from the 16th century, and horse-breeding began under James I. Racing stables were set up at Lambourn and Newmarket at this time or soon after. The first formal *racecourse* seems to have been at Chester (on the Roodeye), 1540. A track was laid at Doncaster in 1595, and at Lincoln in 1607. Newmarket was in operation at least by 1671, and Ascot was founded in 1711. By 1800 there were 72 racecourses in England, 15 in Ireland, and a few in Wales and Scotland. The Jockey Club was founded in 1750 to regulate racing, and the great races began soon after – the St Leger at Doncaster in 1776, the Oaks at Epsom in 1779, the Derby in 1780, though this had already been run in the Isle of Man in 1671. The first enclosed course was Sandown Park, Esher (Sy), 1875. A feature of horse-breeding is the *horse-breaking ring*; there is one in the form of a circular bank of earth with no ditch on Jullieberrie Down, Chilham (Kt), but one has recently come to light at the Roman fort at The Lunt, near Coventry.

Turning to games, *tennis* (now known as *real tennis*) was played at least in the 14th century, and became fashionable in the 16th and 17th. The court at Hampton Court was built in 1530, and there is a very fine 16th-century example at Falkland Palace, Fife. In 1615 there were 16 courts in London (against two in 1961); there are now 15 in England. There are older survivals at Bath and elsewhere. The attempt to play tennis out of doors in the late 18th century led to the development of *lawn tennis*. The game reached its modern form in 1874; the MCC drew up rules in 1875, which were revised in 1877 by the All-England Croquet (later Lawn Tennis and Croquet) Club of Wimbledon, which built its present famous ground in 1922. The Lawn Tennis Association was founded in 1888, and the game has been popular ever since, with courts everywhere. Grass courts are of course no longer universal; many courts have long been asphalt or clay, and these are standard in many parts of the world.

Cricket is the village green game *par excellence*. There has been a bat and ball game since at least the mid 13th century, and this could well have become cricket in the 15th. A recognisable cricket was certainly played in Tudor times, and is recorded at Guildford Grammar School before 1550. The game went through several stages, the first lasting till about 1750; in this there was no artificial preparation of the pitch, wickets were greater in width than in height, and the ball was bowled underarm at two stumps; it was because it so often passed between them without dislodging the bail that a third stump was eventually added. This was the next phase, when the present type of bat and wicket was developed; the pitch has always been the same length. The first code of laws dates from 1744.

The famous Hambledon club in Hampshire, formed about 1750, flourished for some 40 years, but gave way to the Marylebone Cricket Club (MCC). Matches were played first on Broadhalfpenny and later on Windmill Down. Hambledon's last recorded match was played in 1793 at Lord's, the MCC ground, named after its founder Thomas Lord. The MCC was founded in 1787, and the original Lord's ground was on the site of Dorset Square; the present ground dates from 1814. The MCC quickly became recognised as the central authority on the game. The first women's match, between XI Maids of Bromley and XI Maids of Hambledon, took place in 1745 at Gosden Common, Bramley (Sy).

The innovations which converted a fairly simple game into a highly sophisticated and tactical competition took place in the 19th century. Round-arm bowling was introduced in 1835 and dominated the third phase, which lasted until the present rules were fixed

in 1864. Overarm bowling, adopted by men in 1807, became official in 1862; wicket-keeping gloves, pads, and spliced bats were standard about 1850; and wickets began to be prepared and tended. All this coincided with the advent of W G Grace, who raised playing techniques to new heights. Most of the changes in practice have been due to the constant tension between batsman and bowler. The golden age of cricket was the period between 1890 and 1914, when technique was at a high level and the amateur had great influence. The distinction between amateur and professional was not abolished until after the last war, since when all players have been paid on a similar basis.

County matches have been played since the early 18th century – Kent v Surrey at Penshurst in 1725, Kent v Sussex in 1728, Middlesex v Surrey in 1730. The Gentlemen v Players series began in 1806. County clubs date from the 1830s, eg Sussex 1839, Surrey 1845. The Trent Bridge ground in Nottingham has been in use since 1837, Bramall Lane, Sheffield since 1855, and Old Trafford, Manchester since 1857. By 1870 tables were published giving the relative positions of the competing counties.

At the other end of the scale, cricket has continued to be a game played on village greens. It is so recorded at Mitcham by 1685, at Malling in 1705, and at Henfield in 1727. The present first-class game has been infiltrated, and to some extent distorted, by commercial sponsorship, in common with other games, like tennis and football, where big money is involved.

I am grateful to Mr A J M Hewitt for much of the information in this note on cricket.

Football has been played from time immemorial in local ways, and some folkloric games between two parts of a town still go on, eg at Ashbourne (Db), Jedburgh (Rx), Kirkwall (Or), and Chester-le-Street (Du). But it was not organised in its present form until the Football Association was founded in 1863 and the rules standardised in 1883. The grounds which are such conspicuous features of our towns are therefore all modern. *Rugby* was invented in 1823, at the school, and clubs were formed in the 1860s (Blackheath 1862, Richmond 1863 – they played each other on Richmond Green in 1863/4). The Rugby Union dates from 1871.

Golf is a Scottish game and was a national sport by the mid 15th century. At St Andrews play was allowed on the town links in 1553, and the club which later became the Royal and Ancient began in 1754.

Golf reached England with James I, and was played at Blackheath in 1604, but till the 19th century was almost confined to Scotland. Golf courses are almost works of art, with skilful planning and high scenic quality, eg Gleneagles, by James Braid, or Wentworth. There are some 1,500 in Great Britain, most of them built before World War I; they are greatly on the increase.

Bowls was a popular game at medieval houses, and bowling greens were a feature of gardens from at least the 15th century. Where not still preserved, their traces can often be made out in the form of a flat oblong piece of ground with a raised rim of earth round the edge. There are examples at castles, such as Guildford, and at houses, like Melcombe Bingham (Do) (16th-century – this house also has a 15th-century dovecote). Southampton claims the oldest (1299).

There is a *fives* court dating from 1760 at the Fleur-de-Lis inn at Stoke-under-Ham (So). The two kinds of fives, Eton and Rugby, are quite distinct; the latter is not unlike squash.

Counter and *board* games have left no archaeological traces, except a few from excavations, and games of the nine-men's-morris type. There is, for instance, a stone at the head of the Afon Glen-Sais, Llanfairfechan (Cn), incised with three concentric squares, which is probably of this family; and a "board" for whiling away the monks' time is scratched on a bench in the cloisters at Gloucester Cathedral.

Boxing and *wrestling*, although originally carried out in the open, and other indoor games like squash, did not have their own special buildings until well on in the 19th century. The great *sporting clubs* date from this time also, like Hurlingham 1869 and Queens 1886. Similarly, *ice-skating, curling*, and, later, *skiing* were pastimes of the northern winters; the first two were enabled, by the development of refrigeration techniques, to have their own indoor rinks, and the last now has extensive installations in several places in the mountains. Roller-skating is less expensive to provide for, and a Martello tower on the south coast was once adapted for this. *Swimming-baths* might come in here; many arose as adjuncts to the Victorian public baths and wash-houses (for people as well as clothes), but are now features in their own right. All towns of any size have them, some of Olympic proportions.

Since the mid 19th century sports and recreation grounds have been regular features of public parks everywhere, and there are many private ones also. Finally, mention has already been made of the general *amusement parks*, of which Bellevue at Manchester is the type. These developed out of fairgrounds, but some went on to include zoos and a variety of other things. This family includes the simple amusement arcades in most shopping centres, but culminates in very large centres such as Alton Towers (St).

The Evolution of Towns

BASIC FACTORS

As an aid to understanding the pattern of villages and towns in a given area, it is useful to have guidelines which will show, however roughly, how the pattern may have developed. No model can of course reflect precisely what actually happened in each place, human variety being inexhaustible; and the perfect model would have to take account of several factors, such as the political and administrative conditions of each period as well as the economic and demographic. But for practical purposes the situation can be fairly set out in terms of the economics alone, as these are the most important factors in the natural growth of a community.

Such a model has been constructed by B W Blouet, using the work of J C Hudson and other geographers. Blouet assumes the settlement of a plain of uniform relief and agricultural potential (not unlike the lowlands of Britain colonised by the Anglo-Saxons). He sees the following phases:

1 The initial settlement of subsistence farmers is spread out evenly over the land, to make the most efficient use of the resources available. This ignores any special needs such as defence, and any factor other than the economic.

2 If these farmers succeed in producing a surplus, they will wish to exchange this with neighbours who may have something to exchange which they need. Such exchanges are carried out most easily by using a centrally placed settlement. This will contain, as well as the facilities for exchange, a few specialised craftsmen and services for the convenience of the producers. These central points are the *villages*. The Anglo-Saxons planted many ready-made villages like this as part of their original colonisation. Again, the villages will tend to be equally spaced.

3 If general economic growth continues, trade in the surpluses will take place over wider areas. In any sizeable group of villages, one, near the edge of the group, will be best placed to funnel and handle the imports from the next group. Its links with the villages furthest away will be weaker than with those near at hand, but a village in the middle will become the centre for internal trading in the group. At this point these two places (let us call them A and B) will be appropriate points for a wider range of crafts and services than the villages can provide, and they then assume the status of *towns*. They have markets of their own to handle the growing trade, and their growth is self-generating. Some of the less well-placed villages in the group may decline.

4 The next phase is the introduction of new technologies which enable goods to be produced on a larger scale by mass production methods. Such methods depended on proximity to sources of power and raw materials. Water as a source of power has been widely distributed, but suppose a localised source like a coalfield is discovered near town B and several nearby villages. So long as the coal is near the surface and easily mined, any of the villages may develop as mining centres. But in practice those nearest to town B, with its financial resources, trades and services, and market potential, will develop most rapidly. New settlements might also grow up round B at mines sunk near the town. Industries will also congregate round the town – heavy ones to take advantage of the raw material sources, and light ones to be near the growing market and labour supplies. So B expands into a mining and manufacturing centre, and this function in its turn becomes a major basis of wealth creation and attracts more people to live there.

Meanwhile town A, though not well situated to become initially a manufacturing centre, will probably be contributing to the financial development of the coalfield. The new sources of wealth in its catchment area will also enable it to build up its importance as a transportation centre. With the improvement in communications (the first railway in the area will naturally join A and B), A can then set up as a manufacturing centre of its own. The improvement in communications breaks the dependence of industry on the mines and other raw material sources, and the materials can now be moved to the factories, which can remain at A or B, wherever the mines now are. At this point the old hierarchies of hamlet, village, and town are becoming blurred and, round A and B, the pattern is becoming a continuum.

5   If this process continues the advantages of living and working in or near A or B become overwhelming, and they then pass from being urban sprawls into conurbations. Ribbon development takes place along the railways and roads, and smaller places nearby are absorbed into the urban area. Residential, professional, and other specialised areas grow up. The range of goods and services greatly increases. The once rudimentary public and administrative services develop into a powerful system of local government, requiring town and county halls, law courts, and municipal departments. The old small buildings are replaced by multi-storey blocks in the central area, for shops, offices, and warehouses. The street plan developed in phase 3 is no longer adequate for the vastly increased flows of traffic, people, and goods, and is adjusted or replanned.

6   The problems raised by the conurbations are still very much with us, and the pattern of the future is not entirely clear. Land, labour, and congestion costs are high, and commuting is not an unmixed blessing. But better communications enable industries and other activities to be dispersed over wide areas, and urban satellites can be set up in places away from the conurbations. The ideal location for all aspects of the life of the community can be considered and planned, and this may lead to the stagnation or decline of towns based on the conditions of phase 4. This may also happen if the demand for certain commodities, like coal, declines with changing ways of life or technology.

All these trends involve increasing population and an increasingly high proportion of the population living in urban areas. It has been estimated that in phases 1 and 2 no more than 5% of the people live in urban or tribal centres, in phase 3 between 10% and 20%, and in phase 4 some 50%. But it should not be assumed that the creation of satellite towns is necessarily the final answer to our problems. It may even be that a whole tract of country (such as the "coffin" from London to Liverpool) should be replanned as a "neither-town-nor-country" zone, where the population increase till the end of the century can be housed and maintained, leaving the rest of the country much as it is now, or that Frank Lloyd Wright's concept of a "Broadacre City" should be tried, on the lines of, but going further than, the plan for Milton Keynes. In any case it is unwise to make life in the existing cities unbearable, or to destroy their character beyond recall, until a permanent and viable solution can be agreed on.

The pattern described here applies, of course, most to the Lowland Zone of Britain; the course of events in the upland areas has been influenced by different conditions.

THE FUNCTIONS OF TOWNS

These can broadly be classified as:

Commercial   This function centres round the buying and selling of goods and the storage of goods for sale. In the smaller towns this is served by a market and shops; the larger the town the greater the separation between the wholesale and retail aspects. Here there is usually a definite commercial centre, apart from the retail shopping area (a medieval shopping street, with central drainage runnel, survives in Cheap Street, Frome (So). The warehouses will tend to be grouped round the railways or docks. In such a town the commercial centre will contain the offices of merchants, and the banks, insurance, and financial houses.

Administrative This function includes local government – borough, city, or county – and specialised units like law courts. There will also be branches of civil service departments and the post office.

Industrial The presence of factories depends on the supply of suitable labour as well as on transport and/or sources of raw materials. They are often grouped in definite areas.

Social Most towns of any size have facilities for social life, apart from shops: hotels, where meetings can take place as well as contacts made, and where one can eat and stay, clubs for different groups of people, societies catering for cultural or sporting interests of all kinds, and entertainments. Some towns, notably the resorts and spas, have developed these aspects to a degree where they become specialised. Outdoor recreations and open spaces may be included here.

Residential Some towns are essentially residential or are dormitories for a large city or a conurbation; others have residential quarters or suburbs, or housing estates, public or private.

Others These functions could include education and religion, above the normal level of local schools and churches. Thus university towns and cathedral cities can have a distinctive character, and even some smaller towns where the main institution is a public school can find their social life centring round it.

One or two of these functions may overshadow the rest in a given town, and planning must take account of these local variations and of the need to strike the proper balance for each place. The degree of mixture of the functions varies also, and in many towns they are carried on in separate areas.

URBAN MORPHOLOGY

Towns can be looked at not only in terms of their functions but of the distribution of those functions. As Professor A E Smailes says: "Towns are themselves areas of appreciable size, and have an internal geography that is full of interest and significance." It is a common-

place that the west end of a large town is the more prosperous residential district, owing to the prevailing winds of this country. The exceptions to this only prove the general rule. But the matter goes much wider. Each town has its own history, which will often determine where the various functions will be concentrated.

The principles may be demonstrated from the example of St Albans, which has been the subject of a detailed study by Stewart Thurston. The Abbey, with its precincts, together with what is left of the adjacent medieval town, still form a compact unit. Most of the older houses are here, some refronted and altered in Georgian times. A new coaching road bypassed this in 1833 (Verulam Road, replacing Fishpool Street). The area just north-east of this, the city centre, contains a great variety of trades, shops, and services, and since 1918 has spread along St Peter's Street into a former residential area. East of the city centre is the central industrial area, with factories intermixed with small houses. This area is tending to become a warehouse area, where the factories have not been broken up into small units. Crowding here in the early 20th century led to a new factory area east of the main railway, along the Hatfield branch line, and this has caused large housing estates to grow up on the east side of the town. The railways also led to St Albans becoming a commuter town for London, and the area round the City Station was a good residential district (since rather broken up). The main residential belt was to the north; this has been added to, and similar districts opened up in the south and south-east. Finally, there are newer residential areas even further out. St Albans illustrates not only the east–west dichotomy, but that between higher and lower land as well.

This is a good example of the tendency for a town of some size to grow in homogeneous chunks, each with its own part to play in the whole. So, as a general rule, a town has a core, carrying the commercial and mercantile functions; as the town grows, the surrounding districts tend to be differentiated, one for industry, several for different classes of residential use. The inner parts, immediately round the old core, tend themselves to change and become mixed as the wealthier people move further out. The result is an onion of three or more layers or skins, and with each skin changing character as one goes round the circle. Residential decline is indicated by the division of houses into flats, or large premises into smaller ones.

Just as social classes tend to congregate, so do industries. Sometimes this is in order to be near a transport focus such as a goods station or docks, sometimes to take advantage of a common source of raw material (pottery clay or glass sand), and sometimes because of the power used (eg mills in woollen or cotton towns had to be strung along the local river). The workers' houses would be built near the factories, if there was room. But there are some specialised cases: Birmingham has its jewellery and gun quarters, the first round St Paul's church, the second further east (both are declining, but they still survive). Jewellers and gunsmiths congregated here partly no doubt because like attracts like, but also because of the particular structure of these industries. Birmingham's varied metal industry is divided between a very large number of small firms, often one-man or employing only a few people. These are traditionally carried on in rooms in the owner's house, or in a building added on at the back. These firms tend to specialise in one or two processes only, for lack of space to have more equipment and lack of capital to open up a full-scale factory. This division of processes has continued to be a feature of the jewellery and gun trades. A piece will be taken to another workshop for another process to be done or a part to be added, until the article is finished, in a different place from where it started. It is therefore convenient for all those who contribute to the manufacture of an article to be near each other.

Another type of zoning is exemplified, exceptionally clearly, by Oxford. There is here a very sharp division into the University quarter, the residential area north of it, and the more modern industrial area to the east.

The vast area over which London has spread (more than 700 square miles (1,813sq km)) has not reduced it to uniformity. London remains surprisingly differentiated, and in quite small units. Many of its residential districts have sharply defined borders, often between one street and another. Mayfair and Belgravia, although infiltrated by businesses, still have their upper-class flavour, and Hampstead its "intellectual" and "village" one. This is, of course, one of the keys – the absorption into London of a large number of small villages and towns, each providing a local focus and continuing to do so. Even the apparently indistinguishable suburbs differ in character to those who know them. There are bedsitter neighbourhoods, such as Earls Court, South Kensington, and Brompton; still mixed but rising districts like Barnsbury; almost rural enclaves like Dulwich Village. The City is still based on commerce and finance; the West End has the entertainments and the shopping.

But change is constant. Silk weavers settled in Spitalfields and Bethnal Green in the late 17th century, as potters had done in Southwark and Lambeth in the 16th and early 17th. Most of these have gone. Tanning is still carried on in Bermondsey, and brewing in Mile End. The east is heavily industrial, and new industrial areas have developed along the Great West Road and in the north-west suburbs. Clothing and furniture, once concentrated in Stepney and Whitechapel, have spread to Soho and parts of Mayfair and Marylebone. The art and antiques trade has collected both sides of Piccadilly. But London is well documented, and there is no need for more detail.

London illustrates two other principles: the development, sometimes quite rapid, along the railways, as new districts are opened up to commuters (such as the early 20th-century example of Metroland); and the irrational, but very real, boundaries created by natural features such as rivers (marshes can be understood as barriers, but rivers are less easy). The character of London is quite different north of the Thames to south of it, and this difference persists, both economically and socially – businesses are unwilling to go south, and the people from the two halves rarely mix. A symmetrical town is rare.

Important towns have spheres of influence in their countrysides or hinterlands. Thus certain kinds of shopping, or certain entertainments, can only be done in the county town, or in another large town nearer, if there is one. Even this is not always simple; people in Yorkshire tend to get some shopping in Leeds and some in Bradford, even those who habitually go to Leeds. There are several different spheres: the catchment area of the grammar school will not necessarily coincide with that of the hospital, or the commuters, or the shoppers, or the local newspaper. And in thickly populated areas there will be overlaps.

ROMAN TOWNS

The town as we know it began in Britain with the Romans, but the idea had shadowy beginnings before the conquest. Pre-Roman Britain had villages, some of them defended "hillforts". Defences, of course, do not make a village into a town; they merely indicate the use to which the place has been put, not its civic status. Few if any hillforts, even if they were the seat of a local chieftain or even a tribal king,

149

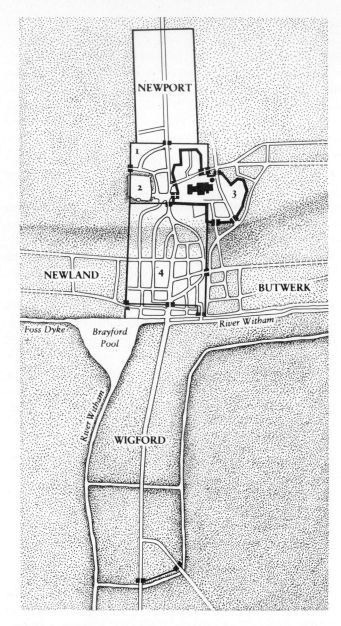

75 *Roman and medieval Lincoln. 1. The legionary fortress, later containing 2, the castle; 3, the minster and the close; 4, the colonia, which continued as the medieval city (with bishop's palace in NE corner). The four early suburbs are shown. The medieval city with its suburbs had 47 churches and eight other religious foundations.*

were more than villages in any meaningful sense. Only in the south-eastern part of Britain, in the century or so before the Roman conquest, did a few exceptional places show a real advance towards urbanisation, under the influence of ideas brought to Britain by tribes from northern France and the Low Countries. The idea spread up from the Mediterranean world – a place like Ensérune in Languedoc, for instance, was unquestionably a town – into western and central Europe.

These were the *oppida* described by Roman authors. Although still not towns in the full Roman sense, they yet had the germs of the idea – chief's residence, temple, market, crafts, and stores ("granaries" and pits). Some of them had the rudiments of street grids (Danebury (Ha) is a good example). They developed out of a certain level of centralised power in a sometimes dense population and in response to the increasingly varied economic demands, and complexity of social structure and organisation, which resulted. They were clearly collecting centres for produce, and they reflected a market and money economy, instead of an exchange or gift economy.

Oppida might be major hillforts, like Maiden Castle or Croft Ambrey; but a new type appears in the later 1st century BC. This consists of a large tract of country, usually low-lying, defended by long cross-country banks and ditches – good examples are Sheepen near Colchester, Stanwick in North Yorkshire, and Selsey near Chichester. Sometimes an *oppidum* enclosed and made use of an earlier hillfort, while sometimes it lay on fresh ground. The loose internal articulation and only partial planning are a world away from the tight Roman town. But *oppida* are towns all the same, with all the basic functions of a town, however inchoate.

The Romans did not recognise these sprawling places as towns at all. The Romans were essentially urban people, with deep roots in Greek, Asiatic, and Etruscan urbanism. They moved the tribal capitals to new centres of their own creation, which we would recognise as genuine towns today (eg Sheepen to Colchester, Selsey to Chichester; see Barry Cunliffe and Trevor Rowley: *Oppida in Barbarian Europe* (British Archaeological Report S11, 1976)).

Many of these new towns are on sites chosen for later towns and have been continuously occupied, except for the post-Roman gap, since Roman times. In these cases Roman influence can often still be seen in the street plan, and in many also there are actual remains of Roman walls or other buildings (eg Lincoln (see **75**)).

Map 8 *The territorial divisions of Roman Britain. The country was at first (from AD 43) governed as a single province, and later subdivided. This central control included military, legal, fiscal, and administrative aspects of government. But within this system the former native (Celtic) states were reformed into cantons (civitates), with some local autonomy. These had cantonal capitals, and networks of market and smaller towns. This map shows the cantons with their capitals, and the strategic towns (coloniae) and legionary fortresses retained by the central government.*

Towns were founded by the Romans in Britain not for any altruistic motive (such as to enable the natives to lead a more comfortable, satisfactory, or civilised life), but simply to make the conquest stick, and stick quickly. The Romans had to have administrative and military centres from which to govern the new province conveniently, and these centres were also conscious centres of Romanisation. The notables of the local native tribe were expected to take an active part in local government, and for this purpose to live in the new tribal capitals. The notables and much of the population could be concentrated in the new towns, and so under easy surveillance, and could be kept there by the amenities of Roman life. The towns were from the beginning the social and economic centres for their districts; they had the markets, industries, and crafts, and were the foci of communications. (see **Map 8**)

Towns were in fact an essential element of Roman civilisation. The Romans did not recognise the villages of the natives or the, to them, informal agglomerations of houses and buildings in the hillforts or the sprawling settlements within vast defensive banks as towns at all. The Roman town, on the other hand, was the permanent symbol of a religious, social, and political system which was the essence of Romanity. To the Romans, a human collectivity only became a town in so far as its inhabitants succeeded in creating the conditions and instruments for a

The cantons (civitates) of Roman Britain, with their principal towns.

■ Colonia or municipium

● Cantonal capital

⬛ Legionary fort or fortress

151

collective life. The Romans found themselves having to elaborate a doctrine of urbanism to enable them to solve all the practical problems of living in cities. The soil itself was consecrated to the gods, and constituted a sacred place in perpetuity. The towns of the provinces, particularly the *coloniae* (founded for Roman citizens detached from the metropolis) were an image of Rome. They reproduced as exactly as possible the institutions, monuments, and cults of the mother city, the Urbs *par excellence*.

A town like Verulamium, with 15,000 people and a range of civic buildings, was well on the way to being a real city in the classical sense. The Romans created some 25 planned towns in Britain (compared to more than 400 in Italy), and many low-status, smaller communities. The towns declined during the 3rd century, reaching a low level in the 4th; but against this the 4th century was the heyday of the villa (a large rural estate), which reflects a change in the pattern of social life.

The towns which did not possess the high status of a *colonia* tended to model themselves on these, and to imitate their institutions. A *colonia* was a town founded by the state for military and civilian veterans, like that at York; these towns soon became widely sought after as places of residence, and became important centres. In Britain the Romans found it necessary to found a number of new towns, which contained the standard elements of the Roman planned town (see below). In practice, particularly in the early days of the conquests, military or official planners and architects were employed.

A "regular" town was a microcosm, reflecting the structure of the universe. It was laid out in a square or rectangle with two major axes, the *cardo*, lying north–south, representing the hinge on which the heavens turned, and the *decumanus* running east–west, which was oriented on the sunrise on the day the city was laid out. The main gates were where these two axes crossed the limiting bank (or later wall). The quarters were divided by grids into *insulae* (blocks), and their roads were also *cardines* and *decumani*. This was, of course, only fully possible on open, flat, and unoccupied land. To found a city was a religious act before it was a social, economic, strategic, or administrative one. There was a specific ritual for doing so and for ensuring the protection of the appropriate gods – the sky gods Jupiter, Juno, and Minerva, who were worshipped in a joint, central, official temple, the *capitol* ("head of the city"), which stood on a hill or was raised on a podium or artificial terrace, usually on the edge of the central square (the *forum*), as is well seen at Ostia.

These doctrines and rites were inherited by the Romans from the Etruscans, who applied their religious theory to Greek practice, which they saw in the Greek cities in southern Italy and which came from Ionia and no doubt further east.

In Britain, as in other provinces, these principles were applied in a direct form in legionary fortresses, although here the internal arrangements were simplified and modified to meet the requirements of military life as against civilian, and many elements of civil towns were absent (eg Chesters (see **76**) and Vindolanda (see **77**)); minor forts were even more simplified. They were also applied in the *coloniae*, towns founded for army veterans and others, and strategically placed; the earliest in Britain were Colchester, Lincoln, and Gloucester, and, later, York. The new major towns also followed them – the cantonal capitals, which often only had the status of *vici*, like Chichester, Silchester, and Wroxeter, or other important centres with municipal status like London or Verulamium (a *vicus* was initially a small country town, or civil settlement to service a fort, but the term later became applied to any town of lower administrative status than *municipium*). Some of these could have more or less the full theoretical plan, while others had to be adapted to their sites, but the diversity was contained within a broad unity of concept.

The way in which a disused legionary fortress was incorporated into an extended and replanned city has been demonstrated at Colchester and Exeter. A similar process seems to have taken place at Lincoln and Gloucester, and other towns too have military origins. Chichester is an interesting example of a new foundation. It was built on a new site, replacing native settlements, and had all the proper features. It was in fact a demonstration model, in a "client kingdom", to impress the new province with the benefits of Roman urban civilisation. With it was linked the equally demonstrative palace at Fishbourne for the client king.

Although the archaeology of Roman Britain, as such, is no concern of this book, the standard elements of the Roman town must be briefly listed. In a central place was the *forum* (see **78**) usually a rectangular space, often colonnaded, in which were the temple to the gods of the city, and sometimes also to the emperor and his family, the *basilica* or administrative offices, law courts, exchange and public hall combined, and the *curia*, or local council chamber. Wroxeter has a good example of this standard Gaulish and British type. Temples to native gods or minor shrines were in other parts of the town. The forum's main

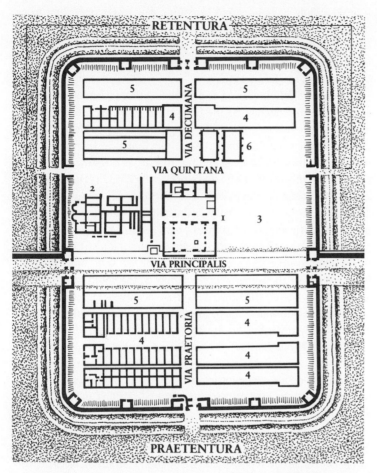

76 *A Roman auxiliary (cavalry) fort – Chesters, on Hadrian's Wall (Nd). Its form – of "playing-card" shape, rectangular with rounded corners – is similar to that of a legionary fortress, and the type was general. In the centre is 1, the principia, the headquarters building; to its left is 2, the commandant's house and baths; to its right 3, probably workshops and stores. The other buildings are 4, barracks; 5, stables; and 6, granaries. The fort is crossed by north–south and east–west roads. Hadrian's Wall can be seen meeting the fort at the main east–west road.*

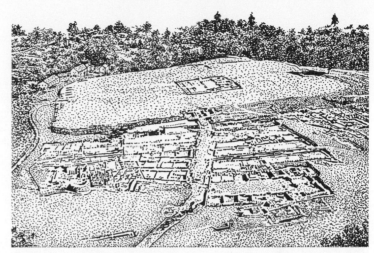

77 *The Roman fort at Vindolanda (Nd). This view shows the vicus, at the gate of the fort. The vici, which had local self-government, were civilian villages which grew up at the gates of forts, for shops supplying goods to the troops, for inns, and for families living outside the forts. Villages of similar status occur also along the roads in non-military areas of Roman Britain.*

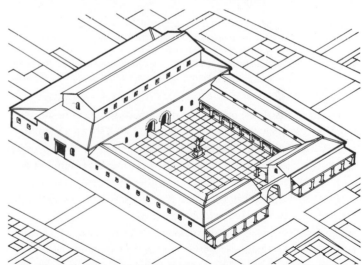

78 *A Roman basilica and forum: the basilica was a public or town hall, the forum a market place with shops and offices round.*

function was to centralise and give an image of the Roman way of life; as time went on its buildings were given or improved by local notables. It was also the centre of local life, where the market was held and (at first) public entertainments. Later in the 1st century the latter took place in *theatres*, *amphitheatres*, and *circuses*. The theatre was adapted to Roman usage from the Greek model and was used for tragedies and comedies, both of which had a religious base; the only visible example is at Verulamium. Amphitheatres, although elaborate stone buildings in Europe, were earthen in Britain, even if partly revetted; they were

153

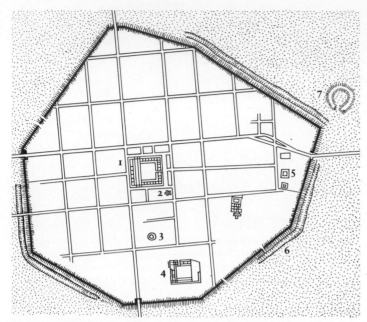

79 *Plan of Silchester (Ha). This was the chief town of the pre-Roman Atrebates, and was rebuilt by the Romans as a cantonal capital. Although irregular in shape and layout, it possessed the normal features of a Roman town – a crossing of main roads, 1, basilica and 2, forum (town centre and official buildings), 4, mansio (hostel for official travellers), baths, 3 & 5, temples (and 2, Christian church), and 7, amphitheatre outside 6, the walls.*

a piped supply to houses and buildings, but water often had to be brought in from outside the town, by way of leats (as at Dorchester (Do)) or aqueducts (as at Lincoln); pressure was ensured by cisterns and water towers. Water was also used for drainage, as the sewers found at York in 1972 testify.

Towns were delimited, and to a certain extent protected, at first by earth banks and ditches. At the turn of the 2nd/3rd centuries these were strengthened or replaced by stone walls; turrets were added in the 4th century. Some towns had walls only, and some had none. Gates went through several forms, ending in that with roadway and foot passages passing under arches with projecting flanking round towers, as at the Newport Arch in Lincoln and the Balkerne Gate in Colchester. Triumphal arches are a Roman invention – symbolic gates, though not in walls, through which a triumphant general could enter the city. Monuments, like that at Richborough, were also a feature of Roman towns, and statues were ubiquitous, some of gods or traditional figures, some of the emperor or his family. These could be of colossal size. The *insulae* of the town could be occupied either by public buildings or open spaces, or by small houses, shops, workshops, etc, or by wealthy town houses. In Britain the latter did not usually fill a whole block, but did have gardens; some were of the corridor type, some of the courtyard – ie they were rural houses adapted to urban life. Inns were also regular features, and an interesting example has come to light in the vicus attached to the fort of Vindolanda in Northumberland.

Martin Millett (in Eric Grant (ed): *Central Places, Archaeology and History* (Sheffield University 1986)) has pointed out that there seem to be two different types of centre fulfilling different roles in the province – the *"public"* towns, the *civitas* capitals, which were primarily political, administrative, and economic centres acting as major nodes, and the *small towns* in the intermediate areas which provided secondary services and industry. As time went on the economic importance of the major towns declined, in favour of the smaller ones. Thus two separate networks developed, one administrative and the other economic (see **Map 9**, facing page 3).

Many of the "small towns" (*vici*) were really nothing more than large villages and lacked many or most of the essential elements of the planned Roman town. They were country-based, and had markets; they were self-sufficient, as opposed to the towns which were parasitic on the countryside. Some had industries, such as pottery

military, as at Caerleon, or civil, as at Aldborough, Dorchester (Do) (Maumbury Rings), Cirencester, Silchester (see **79**), or Chichester. Circuses, like the Circus Maximus in Rome or the one that gives its shape to the Piazza Navona, have not been found in Britain, but one almost certainly existed at Lincoln, and there were no doubt others elsewhere. Amphitheatres were used for games, shows, combats, and executions, circuses for horse and chariot races.

Baths replaced *fora* as centres of social life by the later 1st century. They provided a sequence of baths at different temperatures, and for exercise or conversation. They were a feature of villas and wealthy town houses, and the public ones could be very large and ornate. They are ubiquitous, and a familiar feature of the excavation of Roman sites. Those at Bath are among the most accessible. Baths imply a regular water supply, which was another feature of Roman towns. Not only were wells and springs harnessed to public fountains and to provide or metalworking; some on the main roads had *mansiones* (inns or hostels) for official travellers; some were ports. Some small towns seem to have been centres of *pagi*, tribal subdivisions, as in Gaul, and had villages clustering round them. Some *vici* were civil communities attached to forts, such as Housesteads or Vindolanda; some of these succeeded forts, but many were built on new sites. Neatham, near Alton (Ha) (Vindomis), is a good example of a small town covering some 50 acres, and with some 2500 people, at the crossing of two major roads. This, as well as being a centre for the immediate countryside, was probably also a minor administrative post, with a *mansio* for official travellers. A somewhat unusual administrative centre was Stonea, in the Fens, which had a remarkable multi-storied forum.

All this elaborate, and indeed impressive, urbanism was an aspect of Romanity itself, and could not survive the removal of Roman rule from Britain in 410. The consciousness of being Roman did not of course die overnight, and town life went on in some form in many places till well into the second half of the 5th century. But the Anglo-Saxons who then came in were not urban people, as the Romans understood the term, and a break in continuity was inevitable.

In a few places, like York, where Germanic people had lived in the city since at least the 4th century, continuity may have been real, if non-Roman. But in most places the incomers ignored the gathering ruins, which they neither understood nor had the ability to reconstruct; in a few, where the site imposed itself, they eventually squatted among the ruins and at last a new, but quite different, town emerged. Some towns were abandoned in the countryside, like Silchester; elsewhere new towns grew up on adjacent sites, like St Albans by Verulamium; some, like Chichester, succeeded the Roman town on its old site. Where this happened, the Saxon town found itself conditioned by three things: the walls, which often stood more or less intact for centuries; the major streets, which led to the former gates, and which in any case were solidly laid and could be used as foundations for houses if no longer as routes; and the ruins of Roman buildings, which often stood high. Chichester (see **80**) gives an example of the use of walls and major streets, while the recent excavations in York have shown that the orientation of the first Anglian minster was determined by ruined Roman buildings.

But the idea of the Roman town survived on the Continent when

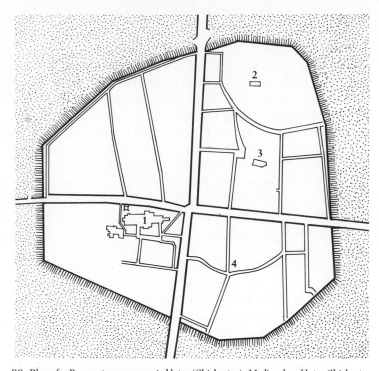

80 *Plan of a Roman town reoccupied later (Chichester). Medieval and later Chichester found it convenient to use the walled area of the Roman city, with its north–south and east–west roads as the basis of its growth and layout. 1, the cathedral and related buildings occupy the south-west quarter, and 2, the Priory and 3, St Mary's Hospital fill much of the northeast quarter. The north-west and south-east quarters, each containing local churches, are essentially residential. The shops are on the main streets, the market outside the walls. The town hall is in North Street, the modern District and County Halls in the south-east and north-west quarters respectively. The (Tudor) market cross is at the central cross-roads. The Archbishop of Canterbury owned much of the south-east quarter, and this area – 4, the Pallant – imitates the Roman layout of the town it formed part of.*

it died out in Britain, and eventually entered the consciousness of the Germanic peoples, as did the Romanesque style of architecture. By the 9th century towns were again being planned in England, and one like Cricklade (Wi) is strangely reminiscent of a Roman town of the 1st century; but by this time it lacked the internal features which expressed the distinctive doctrine of Roman urbanism.

THE ANGLO-SAXON TOWN

Apart from *wic*, an undefended coastal or riverine trading town (see below), Old English had three main words to describe a place larger than a *ham* or *tun* (a village, hamlet, or large farmstead); these were *burh*, *port*, and *ceaster*. A *burh* meant basically a fortified place – the modern form borough stresses its administrative aspects. A *burh* could be the protected house and farm of an individual, and it was the usual word for a prehistoric hillfort, such as Cadbury or Cissbury; it also meant a fully defended town. Some minor *burhs* still await identification. *Port* was the word for a sea port but was also commonly used of a town, especially one with a market and a mint, and never of an individual's house (eg Milborne Port (So)). *Ceaster*, in its modern form "chester", is familiar as the word for a town on the site of a Roman walled town or fort, like Chichester or Gloucester. It does not imply continuity of settlement from Roman times, although in a few cases this might be true in the sense that it harboured squatters, not consciously urban citizens; it merely recognises the presence of the old Roman walls. And it was sometimes, confusingly, applied also to non-Roman towns, particularly in northern England and south-east Scotland.

But the Anglo-Saxons, when they came to Britain, were essentially rural people, not community-minded, and took only slowly to the idea of living in towns at all. In some places, like York, the Romans had settled bodies of Germanic soldiers and their families in or close to Roman towns to help defend them in emergency, and in these places continuity when the Romans left is more probable; but these people were not the later settlers and the generalisation above is broadly true. In fact, there is no evidence for Anglo-Saxon towns in the real sense before the 9th century in or near places which had not been Roman centres; and, except for York and a few other places, the towns were in the south-east (the urban status of the middle Saxon trading centres (see below) is still questionable).

There were two great stimuli to the creation of towns – the growth of trade (which was surprisingly widespread) and the Danish invasions from 875, which necessitated strong organisation against them. So the mid 9th century was a kind of watershed, and the next 200 years saw one of the great periods for the creation and planning of towns in England.

As the country, after the initial settlement phase, became organised into kingdoms, the need arose for administrative and judicial centres, based on royal palaces or large royal estates; these centres in turn gathered round them supporting services, crafts, and markets. In the 7th and 8th centuries palaces and churches were in rural settings, and while some never reached urban status (such as Cheddar (So)) or even disappeared entirely (like Yeavering (Nd)), others gave rise to later towns, eg Canterbury, Winchester, Northampton, Tamworth, Malmesbury. These *royal centres* would not be recognisable as towns in any real sense. The only central places in England in the middle Saxon period (600–850) (and these only perhaps because of their size) were the *wics*, the trading centres (see below).

Northampton is a good example of a royal centre. Excavations in 1981 and 1982 revealed a large timber hall, probably of the 7th century, replaced in stone in the 8th, with a church and other buildings close by. Continuity of authority, secular and ecclesiastical, throughout the Saxon period seems to be an important factor in the location of late Saxon towns (see *Current Archaeology* 85, 1982). The stimulus towards urban status in Northampton's case may have been the Scandinavian presence in the 9th century (see John H Williams, Michael Shaw, and Varian Denham: *Middle Saxon Palaces at Northampton* (Northampton Development Corporation, *Archaeological Monograph* 4, 1985)). Royal centres on Roman sites, such as Canterbury, were divided, almost completely, into enclosed holdings (*haga* or *tun*), most having a share in the open fields and common meadows, woods, and marshes. The buildings had to be fitted in between what Roman ruins were still standing, and congestion led to spreading into suburbs by the early 9th century. These towns developed into market and trading centres, superseding the *wics*.

The wics

Recent excavations in middle Saxon trading towns (*wics*), such as Hamwih (Southampton), Ipswich, York, and London, have opened up a new appreciation of the economics of this period. It is now clear that such towns – coastal and riverine ports – were much more numerous than had been thought, and that any town with *wic* (wick, wich) in its name must be re-examined for its status in the 7th and 8th centuries. Thus, the following towns are now considered certainly to have been trading places: Hamwih (Southampton), Dover (Wyke below the western heights), Sandwich, Fordwich (by Canterbury), Lundenwic (Aldwych, London), Ipswich, Dunwich, Norwich, Lincoln (Wigford, below the Roman walled city), and York (Eoforwic, earlier than the Viking city of Jorvik). Harwich and Swanage (Swanawic), and possibly Greenwich, Woolwich, and Berwick, are also candidates. There may be others too, but it is interesting that all are either on the eastern Channel coast, or on the North Sea. There is also some evidence to suggest that these ports were under centralised control and may have been key elements in the economy of the Saxon kingdoms (eg Hamwih for Wessex, Ipswich for East Anglia).

The classic example, and the best known, of the Middle Saxon *wics* is Hamwih (or Hamwic), on the west bank of the Itchen, opposite the Roman town of Clausentum (Bitterne) and east of the medieval walled town of Southampton. Hamwih was the largest town in 8th-century England, and the first planned town in post-Roman Europe. More is known about it than about Viking York. The site has been excavated on and off since 1946. The town was founded about 700, probably by King Ine of Wessex, and operated under central control. It lay in the Six Dials area, and its centre was some distance from the river (a similar situation to that at Ipswich). Occupation was intensive; over 65 structures have been found, in an area of over 110 acres (45ha), on three north–south streets and two east–west streets. There was a ditch on the west side, and marshy areas north and south of the town. The houses are not the European longhouse type, as at Dorestad (Wijk bij Duurstede, the great emporium on the Rhine in Holland), or halls as at Chalton (Ha), but hybrid types, rectangular, with posts, slots, and stakes. The front walls were very substantial, the others less so; the walls were filled in with wattle and daub, and the roofs were thatched. Some of these houses had five or more rebuilds. They may have been sheds or warehouses rather than, or as well as, dwellings. There were pits and wells, and seven small cemeteries, one with a two-celled church (the later St Mary's). The waterfront is still enigmatic.

The very numerous finds give a full picture of the life and trade of these towns, and can be taken as typical of them. Crafts included boneworking (pins, combs, skates, spindle whorls, etc), metalworking (iron keys, axes etc, bronze pins etc), gilding (using the mercury-floating process for the first time in England), glassmaking (simple vessels), weaving, spinning and carding, and leatherworking.

The crafts were not zoned, but mixed up all over the town. Coins included sceattas, the standard middle Saxon unit; some 150 of these were found, more than anywhere else in England, of which some 50 were minted at Hamwih. Foreign coins were also found. Pottery was of poor quality, of which over 80% was of local manufacture, though there were also good quality, wheel-thrown, imported tablewares. The imports were mostly pottery from France and Germany (with its contents), hones and querns from the Rhineland, and ornamental glassware, also from Germany; there was internal trade also, into Mercia. The exports included wool and cloth, dogs, honey, and perhaps slaves. The animal bones found were of old animals – the diet was plentiful but dull. The people of Hamwih were urban, and bought in their food. Hamwih lasted from 700 to 875, and declined when other Saxon towns were just emerging. It was still occupied in the 10th century, but had shrunk to the waterfront, St Mary's church, and along the north–south street; but how urban it was by that time is hard to say.

Martin Biddle has pointed out (in David M. Wilson (ed): *The Archaeology of Anglo-Saxon England*, 1976) the close complementarity of Hamwih and Winchester, some 10 miles away. Winchester was a royal town, with king, bishop, and nobles; Hamwih had a mint, a regular plan, long-distance trade, intense industrial activity, and a relatively dense population. When Winchester was refounded by Alfred and became a planned town within the Roman walls, it took over the functions of a central place, and Hamwih declined. There remained in fact a late Saxon *burh* at Southampton (a Burghal Hidage fort – see below), but this may have been on the site and within the walls of the Roman town of Clausentum on the east side of the Itchen, so not a continuation of Hamwih.

London is a particularly interesting case, and one which fits perfectly into the pattern revealed by Hamwih and Ipswich. It had long been a puzzle why virtually all the Saxon finds in the walled city were late Saxon (Alfredan and later). Martin Biddle and Alan Vince hit on the idea, simultaneously but independently, in 1984, that the answer might lie in the name Aldwych (in the Strand), which could mean the "old *wic*". Reanalysis of Saxon finds and some new excavation by the Museum of London (eg in the Covent Garden area) showed beyond doubt that the middle Saxon trading centre was not in the walled city at all but along the river between Whitehall and the mouth of the Fleet. There seems to have been no formal waterfront – the traders' boats were drawn up on the Thames foreshore. Both Biddle and Vince see Lundenwic (Aldwych) as a new creation, possibly royal, with possible 6th-century origins, but certainly a *wic* by 640.

It was then Alfred who reactivated the walled area, as a measure of defence against the Danish threat in the 870s, and in fact founded a new town inside the Roman walls which were refurbished as necessary. Late Saxon London (within the walls) seems to have been laid out in three stages: mid 9th century, streets south of St Paul's and up to the Walbrook (south-west quarter); late 9th century, east of Walbrook, with new bridge (*c* 886–90) (south-east quarter); 10th century, north of St Paul's (north-west quarter). From the 9th to the 12th century trading in London was centred along the river bank; from the 13th century and on commerce moved north of Thames Street. (For Lundenwic see M Biddle in *Popular Archaeology*, July 1984; A Vince in *Current Archaeology* 93, August 1984; Tim Tatton-Brown: The Topography of Anglo-Saxon London, *Antiquity* 60, 1986.)

York is another case of recent reappraisal. Here too the location and nature of the pre-Viking city (Eoforwic) was not certain. But in 1985/86 the York Archaeological Trust, while excavating a 13th-century priory between the confluence of the Foss and Ouse and Fishergate, discovered Middle Anglian (8th century) remains below the monastic buildings. "Halls" along a lane – large wooden buildings, merchants' houses/warehouses – and rubbish pits containing typical trading and craft goods were found, and the whole site seems to have a carefully spaced layout between two north–south roads. The Anglian centre (Eoforwic) is in the Walmgate suburb east of the Foss, well away from the Viking city of which Coppergate is the best known excavation, and is outside the medieval walls (see Richard Kemp in *Interim* 10/4, 1985, 11/3, 1986, and 11/4, 1986/7).

Excavation is showing that the *wics* had similar features and similar patterns of crafts and trade. Ipswich, for instance, and Hamwih have many features in common. The precise details of their trade of course depended largely on their geographical situation; thus much of Hamwih's trade was with northern France, while most of Ipswich's was with the Low Countries. The English *wics* traded with similar places on the continent, which were emporia and trans-shipment centres with wide hinterlands. Thus Quentovic, by the mouth of the Canche near Etaples, was the great entry port into the Carolingian Empire; Domburg and Dorestad in Holland (8th/9th centuries) channelled the products of Germany and central Europe. Duisburg

on the Rhine, still the largest barge port in Europe, has only recently (1986) been recognised as a great trading port in the 9th century. Further north, controlling the Baltic trade, lay Helgö (300–800), Birka (800–1000), and Sigtuna (*c* 990 on) in Sweden, and Haithabu (Hedeby) with Schleswig in north Germany (804 on). Ribe (up to *c* 850) in Denmark and Kaupang, near Oslo, face the North Sea. There were many smaller places, as in England. (For details of the continental centres see M W Barley (ed): *European Towns* (Academic Press 1977).)

The Anglo-Saxon trading towns declined in the 9th century, and in areas occupied by the Vikings were superseded by Danish or Norse trading towns, such as those at Thetford, Lincoln (where the Flaxengate area, north of the river, succeeds Wigford), or York, where the centre shifted from Walmgate/Fishergate to Coppergate. In Scotland, at Whithorn, excavations in 1986 revealed a Norse trading and manufacturing town, with Irish connections, dating from 950–1100.

The classic example of a Viking trading centre is York (Jorvik), where the town was replanned in the early 10th century in and around Coppergate, half a mile from the Middle Anglian town of Eoforwic. New tenement boundaries were drawn up and fenced off (many of these plot boundaries have persisted to this day). The buildings were of post and wattle panels, coated with daub. They were occupied by craftsmen who worked in the rear and sold their goods at the front. The crafts included metalworking, glassmaking, minting, jewellery, amber and jet carving, bone- and antlerworking, leatherworking, and woodturning. There is evidence of world-wide trade, including silks from Byzantium (no doubt coming from further east, as is shown by finds of Chinese pottery at Lincoln). The excavations (by the York Archaeological Trust from 1976 to 1981) produced a great deal of evidence for diet, hygiene, parasites, and other aspects of daily life. Part of the town has been reconstructed in an extremely vivid way in the Jorvik Viking Centre, built on the site of the excavations, which was a milestone in museum presentation. York in the 10th century was one of the greatest trading centres of the Viking age, excelling Hedeby and Birka in size and possibly also in wealth (see Richard Hall: *The Viking Dig* (Bodley Head 1984)).

The burhs

The *wics* were succeeded by the fortified late Saxon *burhs*. Alfred and his son and successor, Edward the Elder, were faced from *c* 880 to

920 with the problem of the Danes, whose presence in eastern England threatened Wessex. Their solution was to plant a line of fortified towns round the coasts and frontiers of Wessex (the *Burghal Hidage* towns – see below). These were followed, from 910 to 916, by another series – a double line from Runcorn on the Mersey to Witham and Maldon in Essex, along Watling Street, the frontier with the Danes – built by Edward and his sister, Aethelflaed of Mercia; these include, behind the line, Bridgnorth, Stafford, and Tamworth. The *burhs* were more than just towns protected by earthen banks and ditches (the bank was often revetted in wood, and later by a wall as well); they were planned, usually in grids, under continental (Frankish) and ultimately Roman influence, and were something new. In fact Cricklade, within a rectangular bank very like the playing card form of a Roman fort, and with a cross of main streets and an intervallum street, is strangely reminiscent of a Roman model.

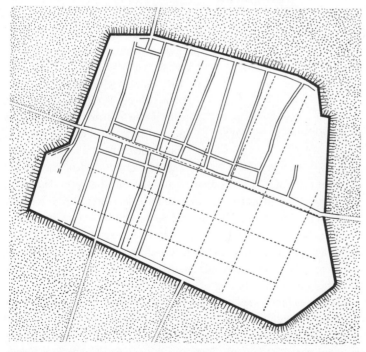

81 *Late Anglo-Saxon Winchester with the underlying Roman street grid. The street-grid of the Saxon (Alfredan) city, although it uses the Roman main street, does not coincide with the Roman minor streets, but is laid out just beside them.*

Some of these towns occupied the space inside the walls of former Roman towns. There – Winchester (see **81**) and Chichester are good examples – the main roads leading to the Roman gates (or gaps where the gates had been) could still be used. At Chichester the four main streets are on the Roman line (except that South Street has a few deviations). The grids in the four quarters however have no direct relation to the Roman streets; they were set out afresh, although in some cases the Saxon houses were built on the firm foundation of the Roman streets, causing the Saxon streets to be to one side of the Roman ones. The walls could be used as they stood, patched up as necessary. Inside the walls ran an "intervallum" street, to enable men and supplies to be got quickly to any point of the walls (a Roman idea, as in London Wall, London).

Of 34 *burhs* founded by the West Saxons from 840 to 925, 27 were associated with Roman roads, although ten sites were not Roman. As a result of his excavations at Winchester and his consequent study of Anglo-Saxon towns generally, Martin Biddle pointed out (in 1971) that a group of important Burghal Hidage towns have rectilinear plans not of Roman origin. This was part of a deliberate policy of urban foundation in response to a military situation – a change of emphasis from fortress to fortified town. The street plan provides for permanent urban settlement. Four of these towns are on the sites of former Roman towns: Winchester, Chichester, Exeter, and Bath; three are on non-Roman sites: Wareham, Wallingford, and Cricklade. These are Alfredan, but the rectilinear idea was successful and was followed in several large towns founded by Edward the Elder and Athelstan. There is a strong presumption of deliberate planning in these new towns, of which many, even those on new sites, have a pattern of a main axial street, back streets, side streets, and wall streets (these latter emphasising the initial military purpose of the *burhs*). Alfred's replanned Winchester had specific areas for administrative, commercial, and domestic activity, a degree of internal organisation with no continental parallel and one of the outstanding achievements of the Anglo-Saxon period.

The Burghal Hidage

This is a valuable document prepared under Edward the Elder probably between 914 and 918, which describes the arrangements for the defence of Wessex carried out by Edward and his father

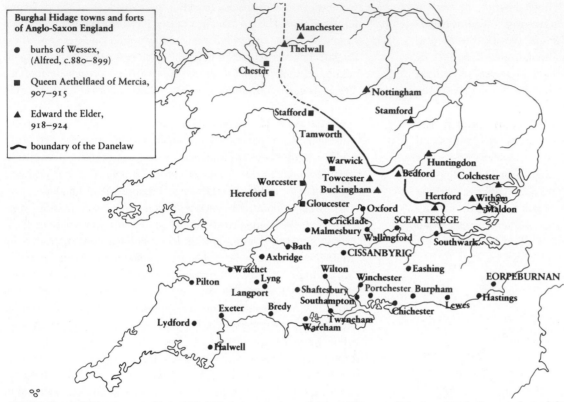

Map 10 *Burghal Hidage towns and forts, 890–930: these were set up as defences of Wessex and Mercia against the Danes, and recorded in a document giving the hides or land units providing the defence of the burhs (fortified places).*

there are discrepancies; Cricklade was allotted 1,400 hides, which would cover 1,925 yards of bank. But the actual bank is nearly 2,300 yards long, and the discrepancy is unexplained.

The towns vary greatly in size, as may be expected from their diverse origins. Winchester and Wallingford (see **82**) are the largest with 2,400 hides; Southwark is next with 1,800 (but little or nothing is known about it), Wareham and Buckingham have 1,600, Oxford and Chichester 1,500, Wilton and Cricklade 1,400, and Lewes and Malmesbury 1,200. At the other end of the scale, Portchester, Hastings, and Tisbury had 500 hides each, giving a defence circuit of 625 yards, while Lydford and Lyng, with only 150 hides each, must have been mere villages. The list therefore gives very useful information about some Saxon towns at a critical stage of their development.

Biddle draws a clear distinction between the Burghal Hidage *towns* and the Burghal *forts*. The latter are relatively small and do not seem to have been organised internally on regular lines. Burghal towns may be Roman walled towns reused, like Winchester, new towns on open sites with rectangular perimeter, like Wallingford, or new towns on promontory sites, with irregular perimeter, like Lewes. Burghal forts may be Iron Age or Roman forts, like Chisbury or Portchester, or new forts, like Burpham.

A more detailed subdivision may help to illuminate the strategic thinking of the time and the possible alternatives. Thus towns in *reused Roman fortifications*: pre-850 Canterbury, York, Rochester, Lincoln; post-850 London, Bitterne, Winchester, Chichester, Exeter, Bath, Gloucester, Portchester, Chester, Colchester, Dorchester (Do), Ilchester, and, later, Pevensey. *Large burhs on new sites*, or otherwise

Alfred (see **Map 10**). It gives a list of 30 fortified towns. Except for Buckingham, all of these places lay on or south of the Thames, and ranged from Pilton and Lydford in the west to Hastings and Southwark in the east. A specified area of land (calculated in "hides") was allotted to each stronghold; in time of need one man was to be sent from each hide, and every pole of defence work defended by four men. From the number of hides given in the Burghal Hidage it is possible to calculate the theoretical length of the defences of each place. Thus, Winchester is allotted 2,400 hides, which implies defences of 600 poles, or 3,300 yards (just under two miles). The medieval wall of Winchester was about 3,280 yards long, and is based on the Roman walls. Thus the *burh* of Winchester in the time of Edward the Elder coincided in area with Roman Winchester. But in other cases new foundations (all post-850): Cricklade (rectangular), Wareham and Wallingford (squarish), Oxford, Hereford, Worcester, Huntingdon, Wilton, Winchcombe, Warwick; *burhs* of Athelstan: Barnstaple, Totnes; monastic *burhs*: St Albans; ports: Bedwyn. *Promontory burhs* (spurs of land defended by a ditch and bank across them): pre-850 Bamburgh; post-850 Lewes, Burpham (Sx), Twineham (Christchurch), Lyng, Lydford, Langport, Buckingham, Stafford, Hertford, and, later, Durham. *Fortlets and fortified residences*: pre-850 Yeavering (Nd), possibly Kingsbury; post-850 Athelney, Pilton, Halwell, Liston. The *enclosed suburb* derives from these classes, except the reused Roman town. *Double burhs*, after 850 (one opposite another, to block a river): Southwark, Bedford, Stamford, Nottingham. *Reused Iron Age hillforts*: post-850 Badbury, Chiselbury, Eddisbury, and, later, South Cadbury, Old Sarum, and Cissbury. Some places come into two categories, for instance Buckingham and Hertford are also double *burhs*.

There is little to see of most of these Saxon towns. Stretches of defensive banks and ditches survive at Wareham, Wallingford, Maldon, Witham, and Cricklade, and in many towns the street plan is Saxon, such as Cricklade, Wallingford, Winchester, Chichester, and Gloucester where the wall road can be well seen. But most of our knowledge is the result of excavation. A fresh analysis of the establishment of the *burhs*, with some different emphases, has been made by Jeremy Haslam in *Early Medieval Towns in Britain* (Shire 1985).

Last phases

After the Danish problem was settled by the reconquest of the Danelaw and the creation of a unified England, the late Saxon (or Anglo-Danish) kingdom reached a high level of prosperity and culture. More towns were founded or replanned and much building done, right up till the Norman conquest. Much is known about the organisation of towns in the 11th century, and the rights of the burgesses and of the trade and craft guilds.

By the Norman conquest many places had grown well beyond the status of large villages, and can be regarded as genuine towns in the modern sense. London, York, and Winchester were pre-eminent, each having features of a capital. London may have had around 20,000 people, York at least 8,000. Other places were much smaller:

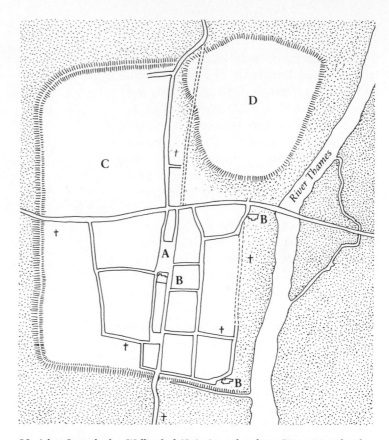

82 *A late Saxon burh – Wallingford (Ox): A, market place; B, surviving churches; †, former churches; C, site of priory; D, (Norman) castle. The street-grid is probably largely Saxon.*

Norwich and Lincoln had about 5,000 each, Thetford 4,000, Oxford 3,500, Colchester 2,000, Cambridge 1,600, Leicester 1,500, Ipswich 1,300. Most of the rest had only a few hundred.

THE DANELAW

Viking raids on northern and eastern England had taken place since the late 8th century, and the raid on the monastery of Lindisfarne in 793 was traumatic. But from 865 Danes landed in England to settle, and from 875 came in such numbers that it was in effect a folk migration (although scholars differ as to the actual number of people

Map 11 *Anglo-Saxon kingdoms in c AD 900, with the Danelaw.*

involved). The Danes settled in three groups or blocks: in Yorkshire (North and East Ridings), 875–6, in Lincolnshire, Nottinghamshire, and Leicestershire, 876, and in Norfolk and Suffolk, 879. Northumbria itself remained in Anglian hands. Yorkshire and East Anglia were regular kingdoms, but the area between them was controlled by separate Danish armies from "Five Boroughs": Lincoln, Stamford, Nottingham, Derby, and Leicester.

The Norwegians settled the Scottish islands, from Shetland and Orkney along the Hebrides, with Caithness and Sutherland, and also set up a kingdom at Dublin. From about 900 a reverse migration took place, of Irish Norse from this area across the Irish Sea to the Isle of Man, where a Norse kingdom was set up, and to the coasts of Cumbria, Lancashire, and Cheshire. Some of these immigrants crossed the Pennines into the north-western parts of Yorkshire, and by 919 a band of Irish Norse set up a kingdom in York itself, retaining links with Dublin. York was the seat of Danish and, later, Norse kingdoms from 867 to 954.

By 886 the situation was such that England was virtually divided into two nations (see **Map 11**), and Alfred of Wessex made a treaty with Guthrum of East Anglia to recognise a frontier. This ran along the Thames to the Lea (London remained in English hands), up the Lea to its source near Dunstable, then to Bedford, and up the Ouse to where Watling Street crossed it at Fenny Stratford, then along Watling Street into Staffordshire. A line of fortified places continued this line to the Mersey at Runcorn. North and east of this line, the Danelaw developed on its own course. It was not politically homogeneous, or even long independent (the Five Boroughs were reconquered in 942), but it kept

162

its different and distinctive character until after the Norman conquest. Danish law (including the beginnings of a jury system) and local government (a hierarchy of *things* or assemblies), had lasting influence, both immediately on Saxon institutions and through them on later English history. Indeed, the Norse assembly at Tynwald in the Isle of Man is still in being. Coins were struck in the Danish towns and their trade had its own patterns. The Danish language affected not only place-names but the later English dialects of eastern England. (See "Shires", page 37, and "Place-names", page 46.)

LATER MEDIEVAL TOWN FOUNDATION

As described above, Alfred and his successors established fortified towns (*burhs*) to facilitate the defence of Wessex and Mercia against the Danes. The Norman conquest saw the foundation of a large number of towns, but for a different reason. 256 new towns are recorded in the Middle Ages in England and Wales, of which over 90% came into existence between 1066 and 1350. The conquest had brought the country into the sphere of European trade, the population expanded rapidly, and the presence of a strong central government enabled urban institutions to flourish and markets and fairs to multiply. Not only the king but feudal lords also took advantage of the new conditions to set up towns on their lands, often on new sites between the existing market centres. There were therefore two classes of borough, not unlike the situation in Scotland (see page 175): royal demesne boroughs (most of the old English boroughs were in royal control), and seignorial or mesne boroughs (nearly all post-conquest trading centres modelled on French precedents). Although the burgesses of the new boroughs had advantages, such as rights to trade, tenure of their burgage plots, and protection, yet of course the lords had other advantages in setting up towns, not least the convenience of having concentrated sources of taxation and other dues. The life of the boroughs then depended on economic prosperity continuing, though in fact some 16% of the new boroughs failed; some were never really viable and others (the small ones and most of the seignorial ones) were unable to bear the heavier taxation imposed in the first half of the 14th century.

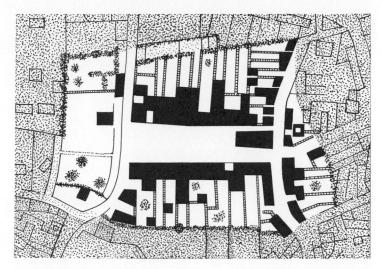

83 *Medieval planted town – Wickham (Ha), 1268. The market place is surrounded by shops and houses in long burgage plots (the church is just out of the picture at the south-east corner).*

There was still a valid distinction to be made between a town and a village, apart from size, density, etc. A village could have a market charter and remain a village; examples are Selborne (Ha), where the market place (The Plestor) survives but the market did not last, or Bampton (Ox). The borough charters of towns, which included the holding of a market, covered other functions as well.

Old towns given new borough charters were mostly towns of some importance anyway, and many were successors to Roman towns with advantages of siting. Most were set up in the 12th and 13th centuries, and most were fortified, either with earth ramparts sometimes later strengthened by walls, or immediately with walls. Some, like Devizes, were given a new castle. A notable example of baronial foundation of towns is the group along the Welsh border, in which Hereford, Shrewsbury, and Rhuddlan were dominant. Many of them were old towns made into new boroughs, with their constitutions modelled on the "laws and customs" of Breteuil in Normandy. There is no essential difference between a new borough created from an existing town and a new plantation on fresh ground. In some cases there is doubt which it is. Many towns had burgage tenements added to them; thus, at Leeds the new burgages are separate from the old centre round the parish church. So a town may have one part with a grid of streets

163

and another part with no planning at all. Saxon *burhs* normally had grids, and some confusion has arisen on this account. In fact the grid, usually associated with medieval planted towns (see 83), is not so common in England as it is in new towns in France. Most towns in England, even if planned, have a linear or oval form and not a grid. The new streets were adapted to the old.

It is convenient to recognise two phases of town creation: a general and very variable group from 1066 to the mid 13th century and the much more homogeneous group set up by Edward I (late 13th century). The first group contains many towns set up by barons, bishops, and abbots, as well as by the king. Bury St Edmunds was enlarged by the abbey to cater for expansion, and the grid then laid out is still conspicuous. A new port was laid out at Hedon in East Yorkshire in a corner of a rural parish, with three "havens"; all this is still visible. Launceston is an oval growth round the castle, all enclosed in walls, a typical seignorial plan. New Buckenham (Nf) is a castle and town on a new site, with a very clear grid. Brackley (Nh) has a long street widened to form the market place, and with the typical long burgage plots clearly visible along both sides of it. New Radnor is now a village, but was once a defended town, which has decayed.

Edward I had political problems on all sides, on the south coast, from Wales, and from Scotland. One of his responses was to create a series of new towns at strategic points, which were garrison towns (with castles) and trading posts at the same time. Earlier Norman kings had done something similar when they planted French or Flemish colonies by the castles in important centres like Norwich or Nottingham. His burgesses were also foci of English influence in Wales or on the Scottish border. Edward had many grid towns to copy in England, but he was familiar also with the *bastides* of south-west France, and drew heavily on French planning experience. The French bastide was a fortified market town, near the uneasy frontier of Aquitaine, based on a square or rectangular grid with central arcaded market place and burgage plots of uniform size; the church was usually near the square, and often fortified; the whole town had a rectangular shape, and was walled. Some were combined with castles. Excellent and accessible examples of bastides can be seen along the Dordogne, such as the English foundations of Libourne (by Edward's seneschal Roger Leyburn), 1269, Monpazier, 1284, or Beaumont, 1272; or the French ones, founded or refounded by Alphonse de Poitiers, brother of St Louis – Villefranche-de-Rouergue, 1252, Villeneuve-sur-Lot, 1253, or Villeréal, 1269 (note the names). Incidentally, where the grid is not square to the perimeter, the main axes can take the form of a St Andrew's cross rather than up and down lines, as at Villeréal.

Edward's towns in Wales are very reminiscent of the bastides. He planted ten towns, with castles and walls, but also markets. Three, Flint, Rhuddlan (a refoundation), and Aberystwyth, followed the end of the war of 1277; five, Conway, Caernarvon, Harlech, Criccieth, and Bere, followed the fall of Llewelyn in 1282; Beaumaris and Newborough were created after the rising of 1294; Caerwys seems to be a purely commercial plantation. The towns dominated the north and west coasts of Wales both militarily and economically. At Denbigh a new town succeeded the hilltop settlement which had been the centre of a Welsh barony; Welshpool and Llanfyllin were founded by Welsh lords. Edward's towns were mostly linked to their castles by walls, but even when they were not they still had borough status.

Edward also refounded Berwick-upon-Tweed in 1297, but here the plan grows out of the old town's and is not a grid. Kingston-on-Hull is a special case, being set up as a defended port. Newton, near Poole, never got off the ground. The most perfect example of these towns is probably New Winchelsea (see 84), which has been little altered, having decayed because of the recession of the sea in the 15th/16th centuries. It is a hilltop site, walled and gated, laid out in 39 large rectangular plots, some of which are now empty and some scarcely filled. The church is on one of the central squares, the market place further west. There are eight east–west streets, and concentrations round the harbour and market. The history of the town and its tenants is known in considerable detail, and the whole place is very instructive.

The new towns did not supplant the old towns (with a few exceptions like New Salisbury or Rhuddlan II), but they supplemented them. The pioneer study of medieval new towns by Maurice Beresford (*New Towns of the Middle Ages* (1967)) analyses the course of events. New plantations in England began in Saxon times, with St Albans (*c* 950), New Romney by 960, and Durham, 995–1006. Then over 120 were established after the conquest, from Richards Castle, 1066–86, to 1297. Another 50 were created up to the Black Death (New Eagle, 1345), when they stopped, except for Queenborough, 1368, and Falmouth by itself in 1613. Between 1066 and 1100 21

84 *New Winchelsea (Sx) as originally laid out, 1292. A–G, gates or posterns; H, Town Hall; I, St Thomas's church; J, St Giles's church; K, St Leonard's church, Iham; L, butcheries; M, Monday market; N, Greyfriars; O, St John's Hospital; P, Holy Cross Hospital; Q, St Bartholemew's Hospital. The town had decayed by the late 15th century, owing to French raids and the silting up of the river, but the grid remains.*

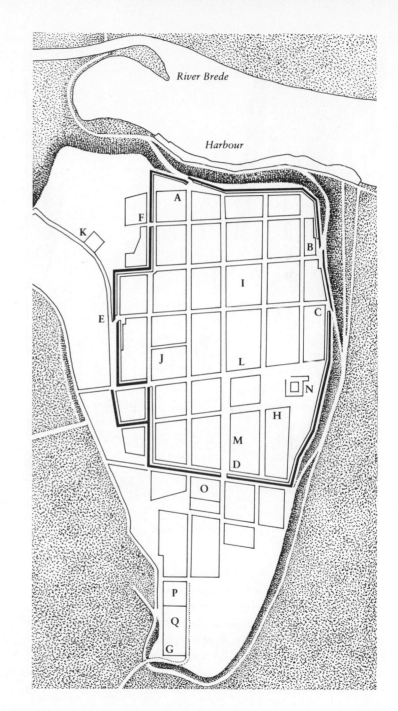

were set up, and 19 from 1100 to 1130. Of the total of 173, 21 were created by kings (12%), 77 by seigneurs (45%), 25 by bishops (15%), 31 by abbots (18%), with 18 (10%) unknown. In Wales there were 87 medieval boroughs, of which 84 were new plantations. Rhuddlan I (921) stands by itself, followed by 20 from 1066 to 1135, 26 from 1136 to 1274, and 37 after 1274. 29 were founded by kings (35%), the rest by lords and others – a very different situation from that in England, which shows the different pressures operating in Wales. The peak of new town creation in England lay between 1150 and 1230, in Wales from 1270 to 1300, and in Gascony from 1250 to 1330. After the Black Death no new towns were created in England until those of the industrial magnates (like New Lanark or Saltaire), the model suburbs of the late 19th and early 20th century, and the New Towns of today (see pages 252–6).

ASPECTS OF MEDIEVAL TOWN PLANS

J R Conzen, a pioneer in the study of medieval towns, has shown that there is no real opposition of "regular" and "irregular" plans, nor real equation of these with "planned" and "unplanned". In reality the medieval town reflected the kind of corporate organisation it had, and the stage of transport and power sources reached in its time. It was adapted to its natural site and pre-existing features, eg old routes, field boundaries, abbey, castle, etc. This was in contrast to Roman plans, and to those of Renaissance and modern times (see **85**).

Towns could have uni-nuclear or multi-nuclear origins. Thus, there was often a pre-existing urban nucleus, for instance a castle; this could be followed by the growth of a traders' and craftsmen's settlement outside the gate, with wedge-shaped market place and convergence of routes, and with burgages on each side (as at Alnwick or St Albans). These settlements tended to be about 12–15 miles apart, and often grew into boroughs. When they expanded, the additional areas could

85 *A good example of a medieval street – Low Petergate, York. The burgage houses and shops are built on narrow plots, and have their gable ends onto the street.*

main streets and a staggered-parallel street system. Tillicoultry (Ce) is triangular because it is built on an alluvial cone. And so on. In many towns there was almost total rebuilding in the 16th and early 17th centuries, which wiped out much of the medieval plan as well as the medieval buildings.

SPECIALISED TOWNS

These are places so exclusively dominated by one particular feature or activity that their amenities and buildings are devoted to it and their nature has become distorted. Medieval pilgrimage centres were of this kind. Some, like Canterbury or Glastonbury, had enormous churches to house the venerated relics and the throngs of people who visited them. Some, like Walsingham, were on a smaller scale. All had subsidiary churches and chapels clustering round the main shrine to spread the traffic, and all had inns and other accommodation for the people. Walsingham, for example, had little else.

A small town with a cathedral or abbey might also come into this category, like Ely or St David's. Here the point is the dominance, not the uniformity, of the towns themselves. A school can have a similar effect, such as Eton, and to a lesser extent places like Felsted or Marlborough. Oxford and Cambridge were once more dominated by their colleges than they are today, although both had castles and local market and administrative functions. Cambridge was more university-oriented perhaps than Oxford, its natural centre coinciding with the (geographical) centre of the university. Another type is the town devoted to a particular activity, as Newmarket is to horse-racing. (Ports and industrial towns are dealt with elsewhere.)

RESORT TOWNS

The early history of seaside resorts is closely linked with that of sea bathing. This was practised before 1700 on a small scale, and indeed was advised as a relief for gout in a treatise on Scarborough Spa in 1667 – Scarborough being the spa which happened to be by the sea – but became popular only after about 1750. Even then the accent was more on medicinal benefit than pleasure. A Dr Russell published a *Dissertation concerning the Uses of Sea Water in Diseases of the Glands*,

be in blocks or cells (as at Ludlow) or in concentric rings round the centre. The functions of streets were differentiated; the market place became infilled, as did burgage heads. A later stage was the alteration of the burgage pattern, and redevelopment. "Fringe belts" developed, such as urban friaries; road widening just inside or outside the town gates indicates the line of the old boundaries. Ludlow has a composite plan with five units, but a parallel street system; Conway is triangular, determined by the castle, the length of quay needed, and the flood-plain on the other side, so it only has three gates. The shape led to two in Latin in 1750 and in English in 1753, which had much influence. Dr Russell settled in Brighton in 1754, and Brighton grew from about this time. Pleasure gradually entered in. Ralph Allen demonstrated his bathing machine at Weymouth in 1763, and George III visited Weymouth regularly from 1789 to 1805, while his son (later the Prince Regent and George IV) visited Brighton from 1783 and held court there from 1788 to 1823. By 1780 Brighton already had some of the usual amenities. Sea bathing was now fashionable, and resorts grew up to provide it. There is a delightful engraving of bathing from machines in George Walker's *Costumes of Yorkshire* (1814).

The English resorts were well established by the time of the Napoleonic wars, and indeed were stimulated by them. As with the spas, people came to live in them as well as just visit them. All major resorts, in fact, have a Regency if not an 18th-century history. But, owing to the widespread enjoyment of sea bathing by all classes of people, their amenities were different from those of the spas. They often lacked the rooms and gardens designed for high social life, and concentrated, very naturally, on the enjoyment of the sea itself, by way of promenades (derived from the "walking-galleries" of 16th-century Buxton) and later of piers. The first pier was the Chain Pier at Brighton (1823), which suffered much from storms and was demolished in 1896. Piers had two objects, to provide a jetty for steamers to come right to the middle of the town's "front" and to make an extra promenade romantically over the sea itself. To add to the attractions, the pier had at its end a restaurant, a concert and dance hall, seats and deck-chairs (and a band), and fishing. On the way you could use slot machines to share in "What the Butler Saw". If the pier had to be a long one to enable the steamers to use it (as at Southend, $1\frac{1}{4}$ miles (2 km)), there was a railway too. The architecture and ironwork were fanciful, and as remote as possible from ordinary life.

Steamers and later railways were the traditional approach to seaside towns, and part of the trip or holiday. Margate and Ramsgate, until the 1850s, had an enormous steamer trade from London, mostly for day trippers, and were only eclipsed when the railways reached Southend. These resorts filled the place, for Londoners, of the 17th-century London spas and 18th-century pleasure gardens (just as did, later, Rothesay for Glasgow). As Colin and Rose Bell say (in *City Fathers* (1969)): "The seaside resort was the spa, and the riviera, of the poor, its Variety their theatre, its pier their Casino, its promenade their boulevard." Its rise also coincided with that of the industrial towns, which had few if any amenities and no place for fairs, festivals, romance, or holidays. By the end of the 19th century, the Wakes Weeks of the northern factory towns had made Blackpool and Scarborough very large, just as Brighton and Southend had to grow to cope with the throngs from London.

The railways benefited from these demands for mass transport, and took a hand in the creation of some resorts. Thus Cleethorpes was built by the railway to go with its station, which is on the promenade (1863), and Skegness was largely the creation of the Great Northern Railway (1873–81). But some towns were favoured by the railway at the expense of others; thus Beaumaris and Caernarvon were eclipsed by Rhyl, Colwyn Bay, and Llandudno, which were nearer to Liverpool. Oban has a typical history: founded as a port and store for the trade with the Western Isles in 1711, by the early 19th century it was a bathing place as well, and developed into a full-scale, if small, holiday centre after the railways and steamers arrived. Tenby is a similar case.

Resort towns can be divided into three groups: spas, catering for a highly formalised social life (eg Bath, Brighton); towns for picturesque retirement, ie towns as much like the country as possible with villas and gardens, like the wealthy (contemporary) residential suburbs of the big towns, only more so (Torquay, Bournemouth, Southport, Leamington, Cheltenham); and fairgrounds by the sea (Brighton, Southport, Blackpool). The categories overlap, sometimes in different quarters of the same town. There has been a tendency, as noted in the section on spas (see below), for pure spas, or the spa element of a seaside resort, to die out. Retirement is still very much a feature of some resorts; Douglas was an early example, and Worthing, Bexhill, and Clacton are today.

In Scotland the pattern of holiday traffic has not created large resorts, but there are a number of small ones, and Aberdeen and St Andrews have grafted sea bathing onto their other functions. (See Sarah Howell: *The Seaside* (Vista); Pat Hodgson: *The Changing Seaside* (Hove, Wayland 1979).)

SPAS

There is a widespread tradition, going back to prehistoric times and not only in Britain, of the curative and wish-answering properties of holy wells (see page 299). These were believed to cure a wide variety of diseases (including those of the emotions), and in some cases this belief had a certain amount of medical justification; but the actual curative constituents of the waters, if any, differed equally widely. A large number of these wells, particularly those with dedications to saints, were in the hands of the Church.

In two places towns had grown up round the springs at least as early as Roman times: the hot springs of Bath (Aquae Sulis) and the warm ones of Buxton (Aquae Arnemetae). The Romans also made use of the salt waters of Droitwich (Salinae), but their medicinal properties were only discovered around 1830 during a cholera epidemic. Bath and Buxton were well known during the Middle Ages, and were named in the Poor Law of 1572 as places to which the sick poor could legitimately travel without being returned as paupers to their own parishes. After the Dissolution the waters at Bath passed to the town, which improved and developed the baths. At Buxton the Earls of Shrewsbury promoted St Ann's Well, which had been a prosperous pilgrimage centre, and provided amusements for the visitors, including "walking-galleries", the origin of the seaside promenade. But apart from these two special cases, spas in the present sense began in the Tudor period when English doctors, who had visited foreign spas, studied the properties and effects of springs in England. The waters of Harrogate, discovered in 1571, were so like those of Spa in Belgium that Harrogate was called "the English Spa" and gave this name to all the others.

There were three main types of spa – chalybeate or "tart", sulphurous or "stinking", and saline or "salt". Some places had both hot and cold springs. Many, like Harrogate itself, had a large number of springs of different types. Spas, as they developed as fashionable resorts during the 17th century, all came to possess a standard range of features: a pump room, where the waters actually came up and were dealt out; a long room, for tea, cakes, and syllabub; an assembly room; an entertainments room for concerts and plays; and a gambling room. These were set if possible in pleasant gardens, preferably by a river or lake, with seats, arbours, and alcoves. Some spas also had racecourses and other sports. Later, some spas had specialised establishments where treatments could be taken in medical conditions, hydros, and hospitals for the local speciality, such as that for rheumatism at Harrogate.

By the end of the 17th century spas had a secure place in English social life. Over 100 springs were discovered between 1660 and 1714, and by 1800 several hundred spas existed. There are now only a handful, social and medical tastes having changed. In many of the former spas remains of the features mentioned above can still be found, even if only a fragment of stonework or a row of houses. Most of the wells or springs of course still flow, even if some are piped and out of sight.

The spa fashion first got under way with Tunbridge Wells, discovered in 1606, which soon had royal patronage. Epsom followed about 1620, Scarborough about 1626, and Leamington in 1688. London had quite a number of little wells, each with its modest amenities and its particular clientele. The most important were Islington (1680s to 1826), Sadler's Wells, Baggnigge Wells, near King's Cross, Hampstead (Well Walk, 1660s), Wanstead (by 1619), Bermondsey (Spa Road), Dulwich, and Streatham. Epsom itself attracted residents as well as visitors, but was killed by the rise of sea bathing in the 18th century.

The major spas, like Bath, rose during the 18th century to quite remarkable heights of architecture and town planning; details of some of them will be found in the section on Houses (see page 244). The spas were stimulated by the Napoleonic wars, but had by then really lost out to the seaside resorts. What kept them alive as social centres was as much the people who came to live in them as those who just visited. For most of the 19th century they were inhabited by retired officers, colonial merchants and administrators, and retired and independent people of all kinds. Cheltenham still retains something of this character. But the spa atmosphere was weakened and diversified by the end of the 19th century, and during the 20th it has died out. The larger spas have become important conference centres. Spas are essentially, in Britain, English; only a few have succeeded in Wales (such as Builth, Llandrindod, and Llanwrtyd) or Scotland (Moffat, Peebles, Strathpeffer), But this is partly due to the pattern of social travel. The public library in a former spa town will say where remains are to be seen.

THE CINQUE PORTS

The ports of Kent and East Sussex have a legal status unique in Britain, as the "Cinque Ports". When the kingdom was unified and conditions settled in the late Saxon period, the need to control the Channel became inescapable. Edward the Confessor rationalised this by granting the Kentish ports of Sandwich, Dover, and New Romney the profits of justice in their courts in return for the provision of ships and seamen for the royal service when required. Hastings and Hythe were added later, and made up the original "five ports". In the 13th century Rye and Winchelsea joined Hastings, and in the 14th century assumed full status as "Ancient Towns". But such was the need for defence, and such the advantages, that a number of other towns joined as "limbs" of one or other of these seven ports. Thus Tenterden, at the inland limits of the sea arms behind Rye, became a limb of Rye, and Seaford and Pevensey were attached to Hastings. No fewer than 42 towns formed the confederation at its height.

When not engaged in coastal defence the towns were of course devoted to trade and fishing. They even controlled the herring fisheries as far as the Norfolk banks, and at one point round 1300 Yarmouth and Rye were in a state of hostility bordering on civil war. The ports, as such, had varying fortunes. Where a secure harbour could be made, as at Dover, their prosperity continued. But where the sea receded, as in the area round and behind Rye and Winchelsea, the less favoured saw their rivers or sea access silted up. This process was complete by the end of the 16th century. Winchelsea and Tenterden thus declined into villages, with only the site of their ports surviving (The Strand and Smallhythe respectively). Rye struggled on on a river, no longer on the sea, and kept going as a port. The official residence of the Warden of the Cinque Ports is Walmer Castle.

TOWNS IN WALES

There are several factors making the history and development of Welsh towns different from those in England or Scotland. This subject has been studied very illuminatingly by Harold Carter (in *The Towns of Wales* (1965)). Some of his conclusions can indeed be applied beyond the borders of Wales.

The pre-existing nuclei round which towns could grow in the earlier periods were Roman *vici* (some *vici* were settlements providing services to Roman forts, and so located in relation to the Roman conquest of Wales as it developed; others were small market towns related to native hillforts – their pattern only touched Norman requirements coincidentally), monastic establishments, and native centres (Maerdrefi). In fact, continuity of site is the exception; these centres were adopted if convenient, but that is all. The Norman

policy was to carry towns into fringe areas – castles as military posts, protecting and supervising a native market centre or a Norman borough. These were placed on the lowland occupation routes from Chester, Shrewsbury, and Hereford. Castles came first, towns later, except for Edward I's bastide series (see page 164). Moreover, the Norman system was manorial; and more adapted to the conditions of lowland England than to those of upland Wales. Some sites were nodal points, like Carmarthen – the routes could precede the town, and the town could develop the routes. Sea access was a further advantage; thus Pwllheli was an early trading centre. Towns where existing nuclei were used include Cardiff, Denbigh, and Rhuddlan. Lines of towns tended to grow up along the valleys, commanding the upland blocks; this pattern was not necessarily planned. The sites of medieval towns fall into three main groups: promontory, eg Tenby (35%), riverine, eg Haverfordwest – quadrant, Carmarthen – terrace, Brecon – step (60%), and ridge, eg Montgomery (5%).

Some towns prospered, others decayed. The castle lost its point, and the future depended on the town's economic viability. Real stability was not reached until after the Tudor period. Wales was poor and divided throughout the Middle Ages, and seriously hit by the Black Death and the Glyndwr revolt of 1400–10. Roads, mostly on the Roman net, were mainly packhorse tracks; agriculture was on a subsistence level. There was little need for towns, and the country tended to lapse into its pre-Norman condition where towns were not needed. Without the military prop, the country was not strong enough economically to support the whole urban pattern. Full revival did not come until the 18th century; and not till the early 19th did shops, open daily, succeed weekly markets.

Under important Acts in the years from 1536 to 1543 Wales was incorporated with England and organised on English lines. The main Tudor towns, serving as regional capitals, had markets, assizes, a chancery, and an exchequer (Denbigh and Caernarvon); Brecon and Carmarthen had a grammar school as well. There were other towns in the hierarchy with fewer components: thriving local centres included Cardiff, Haverfordwest, Swansea, Abergavenny, Ruthin, and Wrexham; intermediate towns were Presteigne, Beaumaris, and Monmouth; small towns were Cowbridge, Montgomery, Bangor, Bala, Dolgellau, Machynlleth; declining towns included New Radnor, Newport (Gw), Cardigan, and Caerwys. Beaumaris failed as a centre for Anglesey because of its eccentric situation; Monmouth was ousted by Abergavenny, New Radnor by Presteigne (it was a good Norman forward base, but wrongly sited as a market), but Presteigne could not grow much either, because of the poverty and sparse population of Radnor. The small towns developed to a point because they had functions, such as administration, which however were out of keeping with their economic status. Montgomery was superseded by Welshpool, which was better situated; Newport (Gw) only rose with industry. Builth was a castle town in origin, later the centre for the upper Wye, but as such was smaller than towns nearer the sea. Aberystwyth replaced Cardigan, being better placed on the west coast. Aberavon declined because it was Welsh controlled, and had no Anglo-Norman burghers. Kidwelly declined through the silting up of its estuary, Newborough from sand dunes (which have obliterated the former borough of Kenfig). Declining towns kept their administrative status, and growing ones did not get this for some time.

There was a different hierarchy in the 18th and early 19th centuries, based on functions – market, trades, shops, banks, insurance, theatres, newspapers, grammar schools, professions, assizes or quarter sessions, Poor Law Union. At this time 11 towns were in the highest grade: the same ones as the first two categories above, minus Ruthin and Denbigh, and plus Aberystwyth, Monmouth, and Newport. Carmarthen was now a regional capital (and also a considerable coastal trade port), with smaller towns dependent on it. This kind of town developed a middle class and a distinctive atmosphere (having a theatre, a racecourse, and an agricultural society – the first of which was at Brecon). Seven of the eleven were ports, mostly with a population of 5–10,000, but Swansea had nearly 14,000, Newport nearly 11,000, while Cardiff had only 6,000. The rise of Swansea was based on metallurgy etc (centred at Neath in the 16th century); the rise of Newport was due to its iron port (iron was developed on the north-east rim of the coalfield). Denbigh was replaced by Wrexham, which was a better centre, and easier to get to England from; Wrexham became a coach and carrier centre, and after 1830 a coal town. Of the smaller centres, Bangor depended on slate, Pembroke on its docks; Welshpool was held back by Newtown and Llanidloes. Industry was growing at Neath, Merthyr, Pontypool, Newtown (Gw), and Holywell (wool, textiles, iron). Cardigan had declined, and Hay and Bala were very local in scope. Narberth was a town on the boundary of the spheres of influence of Carmarthen and Haverfordwest, and its rise led to the decline of Tenby; St Asaph was another such. Amlwch, Llanelly, Milford (a planned town), and

Holyhead depended on industry or transport. Finally, there were small market towns – Builth, Presteigne (its area was too small and it never developed), Knighton, and Lampeter.

This balance, reached by 1800, of regional centres, transitional towns, major local centres, and purely local towns, was soon upset by industry, which caused the disproportionate growth of certain towns, like Merthyr Tydfil. The Industrial Revolution in fact initiated a second phase of town formation:

1. the hinterland of an existing town was industrialised (Bridgend, Wrexham)
2. the town itself became industrialised as well as the hinterland (Cardiff, Newport, Flint)
3. new settlements were created by industry (a) round, or in relation to, a pre-urban nucleus (Merthyr, Holywell) or (b) with no pre-existent nucleus (Ruabon, the Rhondda towns); the sequence in the valleys was first the exploitation of iron along the northern outcrop of the coalfield, then coal down the valleys, leading to the formation of nodal points like Pontypridd)
4. new settlements were created by transport (Barry for coal docks, Neyland at the end of the railway)
5. new resort towns were created (Porthcawl).

Coming to the situation as it is now, Carter points out how the function of a town determines its character. All towns are multi-occupational, but a very large industry (say over 25% of the employment, like metallurgy and engineering at Llanelly) can *cause* the growth of a town. This can be seen by classifying the towns by main occupation: towns with balanced occupational structure (Cardiff); fishing towns with over 5% fishing, and, with water transport, more than double any other occupational group (Milford Haven); mining towns – over 20%, and at least twice any other group (Tredegar); quarrying towns (Ffestiniog); metallurgy and engineering – 15% and largest group (Port Talbot, Swansea); other industrial towns – 15% and largest group (Flint – chemicals/rayon) – some with several large groups, eg Pontypool, with mining and metallurgy/engineering; transport towns (15% and largest group) (Fishguard); resort towns and tourist centres (20% and largest group) (Llandudno,

New Quay); garrison towns (20% and double any other group) (Brecon); commercial towns (10%) (Bangor, Lampeter, Dolgellau). There are of course special cases and hybrids. Thus, Merthyr has mining but is a service centre as well. Some towns have industries unique to their areas, such as the tinplate of Llanelly, Neath, and Port Talbot. Ebbw Vale represents a revival of the steel industry, not a migration from the old iron belt. Tenby, with walls and old houses, developed into a resort with a unique character; Barmouth is an enlarged fishing village, Llandudno a planned resort. Some resorts, like Porthcawl, developed into residential towns.

The rules governing the hierarchies of towns and spheres of influence of course apply to Wales, but are greatly complicated by the difficult geography and the pattern of industry. Carter finds it necessary to adapt Smailes' scheme to Welsh conditions, and has evolved the following sequence:

> major city and national capital
> major towns dominating both industrial and
> outlying rural areas
> regional centres dominating large rural areas
> industrial centres dominating tributary areas
> which are intensively developed
> resorts of major importance
> major local centres (of rural areas)
> industrial centres with limited tributary areas
> local centres (small rural areas)
> industrial centres (small areas)
> resorts of minor importance
> ports
> sub-towns (can be industrial suburbs or
> "industrial villages")

Cardiff has supplanted all the regional centres; it dominates south Wales, but shares some of its functions with Swansea and Newport, whose development is stunted by being too close to Cardiff. A big city tends in fact to overshadow smaller centres, even those with genuine regional (C) status; thus Carmarthen, Haverfordwest, and Aberystwyth all have spheres within that of Swansea, and Wrexham, a similar centre for north Wales, is undermined by Chester and Liverpool. Spheres of influence can frequently overlap or be shared, as with Caerphilly and Bargoed.

Urban services need repetition about every 10 miles (16km) (or, for the Severn and Wye valleys, about 20 miles (32km)). Regional centres are about 17 miles (27km) from local centres, and are about 34 miles (54km) apart. If sub-towns are excluded, major county towns are about 30 miles (48km) apart while, when local centres are included, towns are about 10 miles (16km) apart. Population can be broadly linked to the classes of town: thus, a major city has over a quarter of a million, a major town 100,000–175,000, a regional centre 8,000–15,000, an industrial centre 30,000–40,000, a major resort about 20,000, local centres 3,500–7,500 and 1,800–1,500, and sub-towns under 1,800. Cardiff, Swansea, and Newport have all lost by migration (partly due to bombing and clearances); regional centres have all increased; industrial centres have decreased, except Port Talbot (coal and iron, but replaced by light industries). Wrexham is an exception, having increased; the resorts have increased also, especially in north Wales; small towns show a varied performance, but local centres and sub-towns have increased.

As in other countries, the origins and functions of towns influence their plans and growth. Most features of Welsh towns, allowing for the particular flavour of Wales, can be found in England and Scotland also; and urbanism is not a native Welsh product – it was introduced from outside, whether by Edward I or in the 18th century. But there are three main types of Welsh town: castle towns, sub-towns, and linear mining towns. (It might be added that Wales has produced one highly distinctive form of architecture, the chapel.) Castle towns can be either planned (eg Flint) or adapted to the site. In the former case the plan is rectilinear, based on Aigues Mortes or other French bastides; in the latter it may be enforced by a difficult site (as Pembroke or Newcastle Emlyn) or dominated by a major street (Welshpool). Development is often from the market place, or some intersection; this can end up as a regular plan, as at Llanidloes. Caerleon is on the general lines of the Roman fort, but a Roman plan forms no part of present towns. A few towns are T-shaped, like Cardiff or Cardigan. Some places consist of blocks round a central space, as at Carmarthen or Brecon.

Growth is often uneven, owing to stagnation, retarded growth, or unbalance by new functional areas; old kernels can be left intact, become a separate quarter, or be submerged. New Radnor, a retarded sub-town, is incompletely filled up; Cowbridge has continued in long streets either side of the old centre. Cardigan shows intermediate growth – expansion from the original street in districts, and a northward movement of the market and centre, with decay of the port area. Llanidloes shows incipient zoning, while Denbigh has developed zones where function relates to structure. The standard development of a castle town may be illustrated by Aberystwyth. From the 13th to the 18th century there is little change in the function of the old centre; in the 18th and 19th century came a market, port, and resort, each with its own effect on the town; with the coming of the railway the resort aspect grew. These changes are represented by (1) a planned walled town, (2) a grid on the north side, and (3) late 19th-century linear growth in the north valley. In the 20th century came the university, council estates, and the absorption of villages. The coming of industry, as at Neath, can have the effect of shifting the commercial core, and of creating zones of decay, and even slums. Cardiff and Swansea are particularly large and complex examples of these trends. Cardiff is not a natural capital – there isn't one – but is symbolic of Welsh links with England, centralisation, and urbanisation.

"Native" towns can be stunted, as St David's, retarded, as Tregaron, intermediate, as Llangefni, standard, as Bangor, or industrial (with transformation, as at Holywell, or submergence, as at Llanelly). There is no standard form of core for these towns. Another wave of planned towns emerged in the late 18th and early 19th century, like Milford, Aberaeron, or Tremadoc, followed by echoes of the garden cities, as at Llandudno or Colwyn Bay. Industrial towns, like Merthyr, grew up with early cottages and masters' houses, followed by later terraces, then inter-war semi-detached housing, and finally housing estates. Tredegar is a rare case of planning – most are strung out along the valleys and beside the mines and factories. In some a commercial core was built in the front gardens of early cottages (eg at Tonypandy), and the division can be seen. Finally, there are the ports and resorts. Holyhead and Fishguard are pure Irish seaports; Barry, Penarth, and Porthcawl are ports become resorts. Llandrindod and Llanwrtyd are inland spas.

It is evident that Carter's remarkable analysis greatly helps in visualising and understanding the distinctive nature of Welsh towns. Wales is a fairly manageable area to study, and has unique history and conditions, but similar studies for other parts of Britain would help to lay down a uniform base of information. (The development of 105 Welsh towns and villages, with plans, is usefully outlined in Ian Soulsby: *The Towns of Medieval Wales* (Phillimore 1983).)

172

THE GEOGRAPHY OF TOWNS IN SCOTLAND

The conclusions of the new geography (see page 30) are harder to apply directly to much of Scotland than they are to the Lowland Zone of England. Geology, and the distribution of easily-settled soils, loom larger in Scotland. Even today some four-fifths of the land of Scotland is uncultivable, and in the times of settlement the proportion of good land must have been quite minimal. Apart from the central valley, the good lands are confined to the valley bottoms (and not always there), and a few small areas near the sea. This is broadly where most of the towns are, unless there are other reasons for them. So the old-style geographical approach (as exemplified in the study by Grace Meiklejohn as long ago as 1927) can still be illuminating.

As in England, the burghs of Scotland (see page 175) had to have a reasonable defensibility and an adequate economic base; even so, many of them failed. The extreme of defensiveness is represented by Edinburgh and Stirling, the castles perched high on their volcanic plugs and the towns clinging, in the shelter of the castles, along the ridge of the glacial tails which slope away from the plugs. Of the more usual river and cliff sites, Old Roxburgh is a good example. Of trading sites, Glasgow is an outstanding case. Built at the lowest bridgeable place on the Clyde, with rich valleys and alluvial lands round it, it soon developed into a flourishing market and then into a trading centre and a port, through which were funnelled the produce and manufactured goods and raw materials of an increasingly rich and prosperous hinterland. This in turn made it a nexus of communications and a manufacturing centre in its own right. This sequence is very similar to that of London and is clearly a recipe for success and vast growth. For the ordinary run of towns, a few examples from each of the areas into which Grace Meiklejohn divides her survey will quickly illustrate the main principles.

The Northern Highlands (west of the Great Glen)

The population is denser on the east coast. The average density in Scotland (in 1927) was 1 person to 4 acres – only 8 of the 64 parishes in this area are above this, while 12 have more than 100 acres (40ha) per person. 23 have 20 acres (8ha) and below per person, all on the east coast and north Caithness; of these 17 have 10 acres (4ha) and under, and of these 12 are in east Ross & Cromarty, 2 in east Inverness, and 3 in Caithness. These 17 are the smallest in the region, 8 under 10,000 acres (4,000ha) and none over 50,000 (20,000ha). The exceptions are Loth, Dornoch, and Golspie, and these have lesser extents of Old Red Sandstone. The small and denser parishes are wholly or partly on the ORS. They include Dingwall, Logie Easter, and Alness; these parishes are long and narrow (like those near Devizes or round the Weald edge), and all have a water frontage. Places north along the coast to Helmsdale are somewhat similar. Only two parishes in the region are inland, Contin and Lairg. On the west and north coasts parishes are fan-shaped, with the broad edge on the sea (except Glenshiel, on lochs). They are all very large – Gairloch 200,000 acres (80,000ha), 72 per person, Lochbroom 261,000 acres (104,400ha), 113 per person.

Inverness to Dornoch Firth The population is mostly on the low ground; the 50ft beach (a beach raised 50ft (*c* 15m) above the present sea level, as a result of the recovery of the land level in relation to the sea at the end of the last glaciation) is good wheat land, with mixed farms and crofts on the higher and poorer soils.

Dornoch Firth to Helmsdale This is a poorer stretch – only 2% of Sutherland is under grass and crops, as against 7% of Ross & Cromarty.

Caithness This is a plateau on shelly boulder till, replacing raised beaches; there is much peat inland. But 24% is under grass and crops, of which four fifths is arable (on the coast from Reay to Berriedale, and inland at Thurso, Bower, and Olrig). Stock feeding is carried on, and flagstones quarried.

Most of this region is grouse moor and deer forest, with crofting in the north and west, supplemented by fishing. The sizes of the crofts decline sharply from east to west. Moraines or lochsides are used for some villages, eg Corston or Morefield. Most of the villages and towns are on the east coast. The villages tend to be just rows of houses on both sides of the road, with no nucleus (eg Keiss); towns are often the same, only bigger or with more streets (eg Eventon has expanded by repetition). At Invergordon the town spreads along both the main road and the shore. At road junctions the town thickens (Maryburgh, Cononbridge). Churches are often separated from the village (Eventon 1 mile, Dingwall on the edge); there are only three with concentration round the church – Fortrose, Dornoch, and

Thurso, all originally round ancient cathedrals, even if the centre has since shifted. The railway has influenced some places, such as Mallaig, where an old port had a new town added to it, and Wick, once built close round its harbour, then spread out to surround the station. Ullapool was built in 1758 for fishing, on raised beaches, but has been going over to crofting and tourism. Specific industries boil down largely to flagstones at Thurso, coal at Brora, the spa at Strathpeffer, and sheep at Lairg and Helmsdale.

The Central Highlands

The density is similar to that of the Northern Highlands, and highest round the coast. The average parish has one person to between 2 and 6 acres, but some are very sparse (Fortingall 1 to 142 acres, Laggan 1 to 229), and there are some very large parishes, like Crathie/Braemar with 182,000 acres. There is no regularity of form, but the smallest are all in the north and east. Aberdeenshire has the highest cattle count of any Scottish county (Ayr comes next), and a fifth of the whole turnip acreage in Scotland.

Stonehaven to Fraserburgh The 100ft (31m) raised beach carries the railway. Aberdeen is the primary centre for this region, for road, rail, river, and sea. Its main industries are granite and fish (and now oil); there are granite quarries also at eg Ballater and Kenmay. Monymusk has coal and sawmills. North of Aberdeen the coastal plain is wider and stockraising goes on. Fraserburgh is the largest centre of this plain, with a large fish-curing industry (and the necessary barrels and boxes); special houses have evolved for this, for curers in summer and storage in winter.

Fraserburgh to the Spey relies on agriculture (oats at Deer and Turriff). The buildings are of red sandstone. There is lime at Keith etc, bricks at Plaidy and Cullen, and fishing. The villages are on the raised beach and against the cliff, eg Findochty and Cullen (with the modern town above and behind). Macduff is on the slopes from the harbour. Buckie has curing. Houses are often built with gable ends towards the north-east winds, eg at Gardenstown, Crovie, and Peterlie. Banff, as the port, market, and county town, is more highly developed.

From the *Spey to Inverness* there is a low belt of rich land, where the average holding is larger (in Moray and Nairn) than in Banff or Aberdeenshire. Wheat is grown here. There is fishing at Lossiemouth, and with net and line at Burghead and Hopeman. Elgin is the city and market town (bricks); unlike Dornoch and Thurso, the cathedral is away from the market. Like Nairn, with the old town on the shore and the new towards the railway, Elgin has spread to the railway. Inverness is the nodal point of this area. The Spey valley has terraces, prosperous farms, and planned towns like Fochabers.

In the *Highland* area, towns are growing with the tourist trade – Pitlochry, Blair Atholl, Kingussie, Newtonmore. A narrow strip of alluvium runs just south of the Highland line, and on this is a long line of small towns like Crieff, Callender, and Aboyne. Crieff, Callender, and Dunkeld were once pass towns, commanding roads into the Highlands, but they have now lost this character, though Aberfoyle has kept it. There are local industries at Kinlochleven (a late industrial settlement), Ballachulish (slate), Bonaive (granite), Furnace (quartz, once iron); Lochgilphead and Ardrishaig are markets and local centres, and Tarbert is a fishing port. Apart from the special cases of Rothesay, Dunoon, and Oban, developed as holiday centres from their beginnings as little fishing centres, there is no sizeable town in the west, between Campbelltown and Stornoway, some 250 miles.

The Midland Valley

The density ranges from 1 person to 8 acres in Kincardine to over 2 per acre in Renfrew. Where conditions are rural, there is a high percentage of crops and grass; but there are only small numbers engaged in agriculture compared to industry – in Clackmannan, Lanark, Renfrew, and Dunbarton less than 5%. The major industries in Clackmannan are textiles; in Ayr, Stirling, Dunbarton, Renfrew, metals, manufacturing, and ship building; in Fife, Midlothian, Lanark, and west Lothian, mines and quarries. Local industries include linoleum at Kirkcaldy, flax and hemp at Arbroath and Montrose. Most of the population live in 107 burghs, of which 35 have over 10,000 people; 31 are south of the Ochil/Lennox hills, ie on the coalfield; 26 have markets, many medieval. Round Dunbar potatoes are grown, in what is possibly the most highly farmed area in the world, and also round Girvan. Round the large towns, economics override climate and soil; thus, round Edinburgh and Dundee, much land once arable is now used for cattle. The farming is mostly mixed, but there is fruit in upper Lanarkshire, round Crieff and Auchterarder, and in the Carse

of Gowrie. The 100ft (31m) beach at Prestonpans is used for market gardens. Oats are grown in the east, dairy produce in the west. Villages have grown up at crossroads or round a green (Gifford); there are some market towns, like Haddington.

In the industrial areas, mining villages are not round a green or space but in long terraces – eg Macmerry (EL), while some, like Leadhills, are more openly planned. Some older towns have been taken over by coalmining and developed round their old cores (eg Tranent (EL)). Special soils have special industries; clays carry potteries, as at Sinclairtown and Wemyss (using the port of Kirkcaldy), or brickworks. Iron and steel grew up at Carron, Falkirk, and Coatbridge, but now less local ores are used. Sheep are reared on the Ochils (Alva, Menstrie, Tillicoultry, built on alluvial fans, and so triangular in plan). New Lanark has rope, Edinburgh beer; Fife, Perth, and Forfar have linen, Dundee jute and flax (this has kept towns going when fishing declined, as shown by Bervie, flourishing while Crawton has decayed). The Edinburgh-Linlithgow area has oil shales and ammonia, and is dotted with "bings" of waste shale. The vast suburban growth of Edinburgh and Glasgow is an inescapable feature of the landscape. Coastal towns are also being developed, like Crail, St Andrews, North Berwick, Tarbert, and Arrochar. The Fife coast has a close line of fishing ports. From Montrose round to the Moray Firth the fishing town is separate from its new development, eg Ferryden and Montrose, Gourdon and Bervie, Stonehaven, Torry, and Aberdeen. The form of towns in this area is strongly influenced by the geography. Long towns are common on the east coast, on the lower beaches, eg Dundee, Bo'ness, Kirkcaldy (the "Long Town"), or in the west Girvan, Cove, and Skelmorlie. Towns on fans include Tillicoultry, Alva, Blairlogie, Menstrie, and Dollar. Old market places survive more in unindustrialised towns, like St Andrews or Pittenweem, than in others, like Dundee or Falkirk. Stirling and Perth are major road centres, Ladybank (Fife) a railway town; Carstairs has an old village and a new one a mile away round the junction.

The Southern Uplands

There is no great density in this region, with 1 person to 8/10 acres the average. Minnigaff is the largest parish, with 88,000 acres (1 to 100). The largest are in the hill country – Tweedsmuir,

Castleton, Teviothead, Roberton, Lauder, Longformacus, Collingham, Eskdalemuir (43,000 acres). Most people live in the valleys. Farming is general, with textiles in Selkirks, Roxburgh, and Peebles.

The *Lower Tweed* area is rich farmland (the Merse). Berwickshire holdings are larger than anywhere else in Scotland (211 acres). Fields (wheat) are large, and the roads tree-lined. Villages are often small (Chirnside is the largest); some, like Hume or Smailholm, have peels, relics of the Border past. Towns are at road junctions, with large market squares, eg Duns, Kelso. St Boswells is a local residential centre (ie largely for farmers' families or retired farmers). Lauder is a typical road town. Floors and St Boswells have old fairs. The *Dales* are sheep country, centred on Walkerburn, Galashiels, Selkirk, Hawick, and Jedburgh, all towns which have grown strongly. Hawick has a wide high street instead of a market square. Peebles and Melrose are resort towns (although Melrose, like Kelso, grew up round its abbey); Broughton is almost a commuting outlier of Edinburgh. Langholm grew up at the meeting place of several valleys. Sheep sales are held at Lanark, Biggar, Lockerbie, Peebles, and Moffat (the last two are also spa resorts). Lockerbie is also a milk collecting centre. The Clydesdale villages have shown sharp growth, eg Symington, Crawford, and Elvanfoot. The *Solway* area is pasture land. The centres are Dumfries (a county and market town, and a wool centre), Annan (oats, salmon fishing, with nets, red sandstone quarries), Kirkcudbright (on raised beach), Castle Douglas (a local centre), and Dalbeattie (granite). Wigtownshire is also dairy country, with ports at Stranraer (on 25 and 50ft beaches round its harbour; local transit trade, creameries) and Portpatrick (once the port for Ireland, now a resort). The *east coast* towns are separated from the Merse by a ridge on which Chirnside stands. The villages are road settlements (Reston, Grantshouse, Ayton, Coldingham, Cockburnspath). There are a few small bays in the cliffed coast. St Abbs is on the cliff, over the harbour, Eyemouth on an estuary, Burnfoot at the cliff foot, on ledges. The region also has mining at Leadhills and Wanlockhead (lead, zinc, etc) and coal at Sanquhar, Thornhill, and Kirkconnel.

This survey shows the overriding importance in Scotland of raised beaches, alluvium, and valleys as the sites of towns. The standard pattern is greatly distorted by the various industries of the Midland Valley and by fishing (the string of ports from Fife to Nairn speak for themselves). Few towns are built on hilltops – Crieff is a rare case, and there are special reasons for Leadhills and Wanlockhead.

THE BURGHS OF SCOTLAND

Every town has a history of its own, including those of Scotland; yet Scotland, with its distinctive burghs, has a unique urban organisation. Much research has gone into the origins and development of the burghs, and they are best seen in their wider European setting. The various alternative explanations have been summarised by W M Mackenzie. The term *burgus* first appears in charters of David I's reign. It is not certain how far organised towns with recognised rights existed before then (1119–24), although many must have been growing from hamlet to village to town to burgh. Yet there is little time for such growth between the introduction into Scotland of monasteries and castles and the appearance of burghs. David Murray suggests that burghs may precede towns clustered round a castle or abbey; and some abbeys, eg Inchcolm, did not have towns. In his view David I aimed at the creation of trade centres in places already based on agriculture and landholding. A charter was merely the "conferring of trade privileges on an existing burgh". The alternatives being discussed in this long controversy were:

1 "free towns" undefined and unaccounted for
2 village communities doing a little trade but in villeinage to their lords
3 agricultural communities municipally organised and directed to trade by the king or a lord

These views conflict, so there must in some cases have been a nucleus or root from which the burgh developed, while in other cases the burgh was a genuine new creation on vacant land (eg Canongate with the abbey, 1128–53, or Nairn with its castle, c 1190). The best modern view is that burghs were creations, not growths. Their charters might in some cases merely confirm an earlier royal act, even an oral one.

The "Laws and Customs of the Four Burghs" (Edinburgh, Roxburgh, Berwick, and Stirling) as models for the rest are not now credited, but they may have existed and been ratified by charter, and in any case these laws and customs did not run elsewhere. The Laws of Newcastle, often cited as models for the Four Burghs, are in fact later. In fact, any burgh could express its customs in terms of those of some other place, as in England. Hereford and other towns stated that their customs derived from those of Breteuil in Normandy.

Several burghs were founded by later kings – William and Alexander II, eg Glasgow 1175–8, Ayr 1202–7, Dumbarton 1222. They had markets, and freedom from toll and custom for the personal goods of the burgesses. These had to be settled in the place, and in any case the charter was often granted before the inhabitants arrived. Burgesses were exempt from *kirset* (payments) until they had built their house, with a limit of five years; this is similar to continental town creations, and was meant to encourage settlers. The new burgesses were often English or Flemings. This reinforces the view that these were new creations.

The word *burgh* implies defensibility. Edinburgh was a *burg* or defensible residence on the Rock before it became a burgh, a town. The usual defences were a rampart, palisade, and ditch; walls came later, if at all. Edinburgh had walls in the 13th century, while Berwick in 1296 had a rampart and ditch. Defences were normal but were not always walls.

Burghs had special privileges, based on resident merchants buying and selling. Burgesses were those occupying a burgage tenement, and had full rights of trade; others could pay for them. There were markets for purely local trade; fairs grew up to cater for longer-distance trade. Burghs had rights of export by land and sea. Some early burghs had freedom from tolls over the whole land, some later ones had restricted areas of such freedom (the "liberty"), such as a barony or sheriffdom. Foreign merchants were restricted correspondingly, and trading in other liberties could only be carried out by permission. Royal burghs had a specially advantageous position in the system, because of their liability to provide a share in any grant of money to the king.

Burghs of barony, founded by a landowner other than the king, were in Scotland as early as royal burghs. They gradually got similar rights, and by the mid 15th century burghs of barony and regality were equal to royal burghs; a lord of regality had the same jurisdiction over his lands as a king. Burghs were managed by a Provost and Town Council, with the active participation of the Merchant Guilds, which later became subordinate to the Town Councils. The Craft Guilds were in rivalry with the Merchant Guilds, and formed leagues with the Craft Guilds of other towns.

Clashes between the rights of the burghs and the national interest were inevitable. By the 16th century the creation of new burghs was opposed by the rest. Monopolies were set up to safeguard the interests of burghs. The power of the burghs gradually declined in the 17th and 18th centuries as burghal rights became an increasingly serious obstacle to national promotion and regulation of trade in the new conditions of the Union. The jurisdiction of a lord of regality was practically abolished in 1747. A Royal Commission in 1833–5 recommended the abolition of the whole system, and this took place in 1846, but by then the burghal rights were already obsolete.

There were 482 burghs. G S Pryde compiled an annotated list of them, divided into 81 burghs of the king and royal burghs (from Berwick and Roxburgh in 1119–24 to Dunkeld in 1704), 55 burghs not dependent on the king (from Annan, 12th century, perhaps 1124, and St Andrews by 1144, to Newton-upon-Ayr in 1450), and 346 burghs of barony and regality (from Strathaven in 1450 to Ardrossan in 1846).

There was a general establishment of new towns in the 12th and 13th centuries in England, Wales, Scotland, and France, and lords imitated kings in this. New towns were a political as well as an economic device. Where the economic basis was weak the town could fail – 19 out of 23 baronial foundations in Lancashire failed, and many did in Scotland (eg Fyvie, Auchterarder). The aim was intermunicipal and foreign trade, and political control. Towns were part of Norman garrison policy, together with castles, dioceses, and monasteries. The French or Flemish colonies in London, York, and other cities were part of the same plan.

New towns were regularly laid out. Early ones often had a straight street running from the castle, with back lanes and connecting streets, eg Forres, Elgin, or Inverness, where the streets followed the curve of the river on both banks. A rectangular market place was a later feature than a wide-street market; Perth is a rectangular block bastide town, but here the market square has been built over. Peebles is a double town, with the Old Town north-west of Peebles Water, with church, street leading to the bridge, and Old Market Place by the Hospitium of the Abbot of Arbroath; the New Town lies between the Peebles Water and the Tweed, with the Castle on the point, a wide street (Hie Gait) to the cross, then three streets, Bridgegait back to the bridge, Northgait, and East Port; the New Town was walled.

TOWN PLANS IN SCOTLAND

Although plans of some Scottish towns have been published and studies of individual places carried out, the systematic study of Scottish towns as a whole is still in its early days and cannot be said to be complete. A brief survey was made in 1969 by J W R Whitehand and K Alauddin, following the pioneer studies of M R G Conzen for England. More work is needed, since the history of Scottish towns differs from that in England.

In England there is a broad distinction between towns of medieval origin and those laid out in the Renaissance period. Medieval plans are characteristically based on a focally-placed street market widening at one end or point and usually flanked by strip-like, and often slightly curving, plots or burgages, running back to common boundaries or back lanes parallel to the sides of the main street. The whole plan is usually irregular, contrasting with the gridded plan already used for some new towns in the Middle Ages and standard from the 16th century. There is a gap of about 200 years between the two phases, and in the later period most new plans are additions to existing towns rather than creations on new sites. Scotland is somewhat different, in that while in most of Europe the majority of town nuclei had been laid out by the 15th century, in Scotland the laying out of new towns continued into the early 19th century. Renaissance ideas were not applied until well into the 18th century, and towns laid out up to the early 18th century were still on medieval lines. The medieval (in this sense) and later plans differ in distribution. Plans of medieval type are practically all in the Lowlands and the valleys of the Southern Uplands; in the central Lowlands they are more easterly than the later type. The latter are few in the Southern Uplands but occur in the Highlands as well as the western parts of the central Lowlands.

Medieval systems

The commonest form is the single-street. This can have subsidiary streets at angles, or the main street can end at a T. Haddington combines these, having its main street, widened to form the market (although now filled in), continuing only along one side by a street leading to the bridge. Lauder and Jedburgh are more simple examples. But few towns have precisely the same arrangement of their elements. Over half the single-street towns have back lanes, which are characteristic of the period before 1250 although not exclusively dating from before then. Early plans without back lanes are common in the west (eg Kilwinning). The parallel-street system has an east coast distribution, with a concentration of 12 round the firths of Forth and

Tay. A higher proportion dates from before 1250, and they are royal foundations, with the idea seeming to come from the Low Countries. In England such plans appear to be deliberate, but in Scotland many seem to have resulted from additions to an original single-street plan. Crail is a good example of this type. The third medieval form is the convergent-street system, where several streets meet at a focal point, usually the market place. It is not common, and most examples are in the east (eg Coupar Angus); Strathaven is a good one from further west. These towns show no evidence of deliberate planning, and all ten cases were late in reaching burgh status, 16th or 17th centuries.

With these types goes wide variation in the way building plots are laid out and built up. A considerable number of Scottish plans have no recognisable burgage pattern, particularly in the convergent type, but also generally in towns whose burgh status was late. Many early towns have regular width and length of plots, on the English model. It may be that in later creations plots were added and fitted in as the need arose. Some parallel-street plans may have arisen from back lanes being developed into full-scale streets. In such cases the pattern of plots will be different from one where the two streets were equal and original. High building coverage is characteristic of all larger towns, and arises from burgage plots being filled in with extensions, sheds, workshops, etc in the late 18th and 19th centuries. Edinburgh, with its high degree of building by the mid 17th century, is exceptional; population growth and pressure on limited land took place earlier in the capital city. Most intensive building-up is a product of 19th-century conditions. Another feature is the infilling of market places by buildings usually succeeding market stalls. This usually dates from at least the 17th century, and in many cases may be older. It occurs widely, but the densest examples are on the east coast (eg Haddington or Crail). In some towns, like Montrose, such concretions have been cleared again.

The plans in the east side of Scotland tend to be more fully developed than in the west. Such developments can take the form of additions to the plan, or of infilling or altering existing plots. These changes were accelerated in the east by the wealthier agriculture and the greater trade with Europe. The resultant pressures led to the infilling of plots and even the insertion of streets between the two old parallel streets (as at Anstruther Easter). The Industrial Revolution also exerted pressures which affected town plans, such as in some of the Border towns like Hawick. As well as a contrast between eastern and western

177

Scotland, the town plans of Scotland as a whole are markedly less developed than in England and elsewhere in Europe. One explanation is the relatively low population; the other is the Scottish practice of creating new towns instead of adding to old ones. Indeed, about half the town plans of Scotland are of entirely post-medieval character.

Later types

Inadequate study has been done in this area, but up to 1969 six main types had been recognised: the *gridiron*, with squarish or broad rectangular divisions (eg Lossiemouth); *regular rectilinear*, with long narrow rectangular sections, often with central back lane (Burghead); *irregular rectilinear*, where the axes are not parallel or the total area is irregular (Girvan); *regular single-street*, filled up both sides with plots of regular size and shape (Charlestown of Arelour); *irregular single-street*, where the street itself is not straight, or its filling incomplete or highly varied (Elie); and *convergent-street*, reminiscent of the medieval form but very variable (Stonehouse). Wide variations occur in the subsidiary streets and in the plot pattern and block plans, and a more detailed classification may be justified. Some regular single-street towns may be the first stages in laying out a larger, rectilinear town which was never justified by events. Most of these are away from the central Lowlands, where by contrast there is a high proportion of irregular plans, reflecting piecemeal accretions as demand arose, and no overall plan at all.

The Scottish 18th- and 19th-century new towns tend to be more spacious than English ones (and much more numerous) because of the greater amount of land available to the creator, usually a large landowner. English creations of this period were usually additions to, or quarters in, existing towns, and the overall space available may well have been strictly limited. Similarly, growth of medieval towns was often seriously impeded by surrounding common fields or other limitations (as in the notorious case of Nottingham).

There is an interesting town form in the former Scandinavian parts of Scotland. The main, once the only, streets are narrow and paved, with no roadway or pavements. They run parallel with the shore (these towns were all fishing and trading ports), with jetties behind the houses and alleys connecting these with the street. Stromness is the best example, but the feature can also be seen at Kirkwall, Lerwick, and Stornoway.

STREET NAMES

Street names are very useful indicators of social history. They show how occupations were distributed in a town and where important buildings were. They reflect the growth of new districts, and who developed them and when. They follow national events and movements of taste and public interests. They have been classified by Gillian Bebbington, using examples from London. London, of course, with its thousands of names, is an easy quarry of examples of every kind, but similar cases can be found in any old town. Further instances are given in the sections dealing with the growth of specific places.

Street names are descriptive, possessive, or topical. The earliest names were almost all descriptive, but with the expansion of towns after the late 17th century (after the Great Fire of 1666 in the case of London) possessive names became common. The 18th and 19th centuries liked topical names, and the 20th century advertising names (a kind of descriptive name).

Descriptive names arise naturally as a result of usage, not deliberate choice, and are very persistent. They represent people (Carter Lane, Old Jewry); trades (Haymarket, Seacoal Lane); animals (Cock Lane, Cowcross Street); plants grown locally (Vine Street, Saffron Hill); destinations (Great Tower Street, Hampstead Road); buildings (London Wall, Barbican, Whitehall); signboards, in common use before house numbers and general literacy (White Lion, Bell, Angel); rural descriptions, such as rivers (Fleet Street, Strand, Westbourne Terrace, Knightsbridge), fields (Long Acre, Farm Street, Smithfield), or pursuits (Riding House Street, Pall Mall, Birdcage Walk); or just plain description (Long Lane, Stoney Street).

Possessive names may denote noble landowners (Russell Square, Grafton Street, Southampton Row); institutions which owned or developed the land (Great College Street, Rugby Street, St Thomas's Street); or minor landlords, builders, obscure personages, or their wives (Goodge Street, Edith Road). The latter are often found given to mines, like Wheal Jane in Cornwall or Mary Kathleen in Australia (where is also Alice Springs).

Topical names commemorate events (Waterloo, Trafalgar, Blenheim, and the innumerable houses called Inkerman, Balaclava, Khartoum, etc); royalty (York, Cumberland, Regent Street) – an interesting case, for a different reason, are the Methodist chapels called eg

Hanover Chapel in the 1790s, to assert their loyalty at a time when Methodists were suspected of being revolutionaries); great men (Chatham, Nelson, Wellington, or Compton, Kemble, Faraday); minor obscurities.

Advertising names came in with new developments, particularly in the suburbs, to attract purchasers (Prospect Place, Belmont, Mountview).

The meaning of some names is not always immediately apparent, but these may include some which illuminate an otherwise lost or obscure aspect of the town's history. An example is the Shambles (York and elsewhere): a shamble was Old English for a shelf, where goods were displayed in the front of the shop; only later was the word specifically linked to butchery. Finsbury Pavement (London) was once the only firm path across the marshy area of Moorfields. Godliman Street was where *godelmynnes* were sold – shoes made from the skin of young animals, and named after Godalming in Surrey, a tanning centre. At Seven Dials once stood a column with seven faces, now at Weybridge. Pont Street commemorates a bridge over the Westbourne. Mare Street, Hackney, refers to a mere or marsh. In Gracechurch Street stood a church (St Benet's) close to the grass (hay) market; the Gracious Streets in eg Knaresborough and Selborne may also refer to grass. Mount Street refers to a Cromwellian siegework. Lammas Road and Lammas Lands (Godalming and elsewhere) recall land enclosed for crops between Lady Day (March 25th) and Lammas Day (August 1st), after which it reverted to pasture. The Pallants (Chichester) is an area with a cross of streets representing an enclave of the Archbishops of Canterbury (the "Palace" estate) – a city within a city. The likeliest explanation of Soho (London) is that this was the rallying cry of the Duke of Monmouth (who had a house in the Square) during his rebellion in 1685, and that this became attached to the whole district.

All old towns have illuminating street names, some, such as York, in great numbers. Indeed, York is rich in periods not so commonly represented elsewhere, the Anglian and Viking. This is an endless and fascinating study.

Street name signs affixed to the building at the end of a street, although becoming increasingly standardised, still exist in some variety. Many towns, such as Bath, Oxford, and Barnard Castle, have taken pride in individual styles. These are often in cast iron, with raised letters painted black, and sometimes with an ornamental border. Birmingham has an ornate style all its own, in cast iron mounted on short iron posts. In some towns signs are painted on wooden boards, some directly on to the wall. The practice began in the 17th century, with inscribed stone tablets. Several of these still exist in London, such as Devereux Court (1676), Stafford Street (1686), Marsham Street (1688), Great James Street (1721), Rathbone Place (1778). (See also John Whittich: *Discovering London Street Names* (1977); and Ben Weinreb and Christopher Hibbert: *The London Encyclopaedia* (1983).)

THE TOWNSCAPE

No study of towns would be complete if it overlooked the aesthetic aspect. A town is more than a collection of buildings, or even homes, factories, schools, churches, etc. It is the physical background to the lives of real people; if its visual appearance is satisfying (as its articulation is efficient) then their lives are that much richer. Towns are in many ways an expression of a civilisation. The growth of towns has produced ensembles often of great aesthetic interest and value, and not always or entirely by accident.

One might sometimes imagine that the site of a town was chosen partly for its visual effect. It is of course hard to prove without contemporary evidence, but it is also hard to believe that our ancestors' hearts were not lifted, as ours are, by the sight of Durham or Lincoln. It is of course commonplace that the earlier 18th century, before the Romantic movement changed attitudes, disliked mountains, which we now think beautiful (like the Lake District, or even Switzerland), and the sea, which later became an English fetish. Against this, scenes of industry, mills, factories, and mines moved the Victorians, but that was after they had been educated by the Romantic movement and may also have been because the mills were making money for someone, and enhancing his power, both, in their view, marks of divine approbation. People are complex. Yet Shakespeare's words about England, put into the mouth of Henry V, were evidently valid for the years round 1600, and there is no good reason to suppose that they were not equally valid for 1400, or 1200.

In the case of villages of whatever form (street, green, etc), it would appear to be psychologically and visually more satisfying for the vista to be closed, that is for the eye to be prevented from seeing right through the village to the country beyond, but to be involved in the group of buildings and rest there. This sense of being contained within the village, and thus sheltered from the emptiness outside, is got by irregular placing of buildings (often of course quite fortuitous), and by bends or turns in the road. These, as Thomas Sharp, the pioneer of this aspect of urban study, noticed (in *The Anatomy of the Village* (1946)) transform a village into a place from being "merely an incident on the roadside". Buildings may be so placed as to emphasise points of aesthetic interest (say the church) or to create foci of attention. In most square or green villages the roads in are staggered, thus also closing the view. Finchingfield (Ex) is a complex case, having a green with a pond in a hollow, giving rising ground up to the church, and with all views closed except one inward. The usual building to close a vista is the church, which thus becomes the climax of the village (often deliberately), but sometimes a castle does this, or even a big house (as at Tarvin (Ch) or Petworth (Sx)). Planned villages, even if regular and repetitive (like Milton Abbas (Do)), can be informal too. Some can have ingenious formal but subtly varied patterns, like the two open squares and the half-circus at Lowther (Wd). Streams can greatly beautify a village and give it a wandering focus – not only a dense village like Castle Combe (So) but a loose one like Hutton-le-Hole (NY) (even more so before its fords were bridged).

Towns introduce a different set of problems, or perhaps show up the crucial matter of scale. Closure of vistas is still important; a church at the end of a Georgian street, with its different but blending facades, is still the obvious case (eg Henley or Louth). Some places have a very intricate arrangement of jutting blocks, irregular vistas, and staggered streets, like Thaxted (Ex) (where the view is also dominated by the church). Many are focused on a castle, like Castle Street, Farnham (Sy), some on a group of church and castle (Skipton (NY)), and some with one at each end (Appleby (Wd)). A variety of heights in a row of houses, within some fairly narrow limit of style or overall scale, can be very satisfying (eg at Stamford), but another satisfaction is got from a deliberately formal unity, as in a Georgian terrace or crescent, or a set piece like Bedford Square in London. There can be a unity through the building materials used, as in the stone towns of the Cotswolds or Northamptonshire or the red tiles of the North Riding.

Whole towns can be visually satisfying, and so give an idea of the possible ideal or spirit of a town – Stamford, or King's Lynn, or Bath. Perhaps Oxford presents the most dramatic examples of townscape, as in the intimate but theatrical movement of Catte Street, with its Renaissance overtones. The majestic curving sweep of High Street is described by Sharp as "one of the finest pieces of sustained townscape in the world". This consists of dramatic focal points, such as Queen's and the two churches, which arrest the eye and lead it on to the next stretch, each stretch having its own variety and interest. The distant view of Oxford is perhaps the nearest thing in England to that of Florence.

The question of scale comes in here. One tower block, even if well placed, would irretrievably alter the proportions of such a view. This is a subjective area, and the developer and the conservationist, or even the ordinary appreciative person, are unlikely to agree. Large scale can sometimes be justified; a group of cooling towers could hardly be otherwise, but it is unfortunate when they are allowed to crush, by over-proximity, Ferrybridge or Coleshill or Rugeley. And large installations can swamp or distort even a countryside. Inside a town this situation can become acute. There will be differences of opinion on the merits in the townscape of Millbank Tower or the Bullring in Birmingham, but few could feel that New Zealand House does anything for the National Gallery. (As yet we have no Eiffel Tower (1889)!) A well-designed and well-placed tower block can enhance a townscape, eg the Library building of Glasgow University. But the problems come in a congested setting. Here siting is important – the view of St Paul's up Ludgate Hill is now irritatingly interfered with by a new block which juts into the roadway just too far. Scale is not only size but also style. There are too many cases of good groups of houses (eg at Chippenham) needlessly pulled down, or only partly pulled down, and replaced by something quite inappropriate. There are new buildings in any High Street which should never have been allowed.

Planning should preserve the visual satisfactions which increase the quality of urban life, and we should all be vigilant to see that it does. The exigencies of modern building techniques, and their relatively manageable cost, should not be allowed to impoverish our lives.

Houses

THE MEDIEVAL BUILDING INDUSTRY

It is far from easy to visualise the impact of the Norman conquest on the Anglo-Saxons. Apart from the political and organisational changes, there was a spate of building which must have bitten deeply into the resources of the natives. As the Norman armed bands moved into the country, estates and people were taken over, and strategic points fortified. Saxon labour must have been impressed on a large scale.

William envisaged about 5,000 knights' fees throughout the country, but many of the great nobles created more than their quota; there were some 170 baronies and around 50 higher nobles. Not all of the knights threw up mottes, and probably most of the mottes actually built had only timber watchtowers on top to take them above the trees, though some had stone buildings later. The higher nobility, on whom the broad management of the country rested, had stone castles, some very large; many of them had several, as their estates were scattered. The king built castles in the main towns and other sites of military importance.

From 1066 to 1071, 34 castles were built, and from 1071 to 1086, another 50. By 1216 there were some 700: 480 in England, 160 in Wales, 60 in Scotland, and two in the Isle of Man. By 1154 there were five baronial castles for every royal one. A similar or even greater number of mottes with only timber towers was built in the same period, some of which have disappeared (for further details see "Castles and Military Works", pages 361–8).

As soon as the network of castles was laid down, and even before it was finished, other building was undertaken – cathedrals, monasteries, churches, palaces. All the Saxon cathedrals, however large, were rebuilt (eg Winchester). By 1150 some 20 great churches had been built, and 140 Augustinian houses; from 1130 the Cistercians began to build their 40 houses, many in very remote places; by 1220 there were some 60 Dominican houses as well, and between 1224 and 1250, 57 Franciscan. In the 12th century from 400 to 500 large collegiate and monastic buildings were erected, and in nearly every parish the church was rebuilt. There were also royal and episcopal palaces, like Clarendon and Wolvesey. The Office of the King's Works was continuously active. The energy of the Normans was quite incredible.

This fantastic output, which changed the face of the country, required a relatively enormous labour force, both skilled and unskilled (see **86**). The population of England at the conquest was only something over two million, and this demand must have been a severe strain. It is not easy to estimate the labour actually required for any given building. A castle keep, if there was no hurry, rose at the rate of 10 to 12ft (3–3.7m) a year. But when Beaumaris castle had to be built in a great hurry, it absorbed, during the summer of 1295, 400 masons, 2,000 labourers, 30 smiths, several carpenters, 200 quarrymen, 100 two-wheeled carts, 60 four-wheeled carts, and 30 ships. A small motte could be thrown up in a few days.

E S Prior and John Harvey stress the vast size of the cathedrals – consider the castle and cathedral, next to each other, at Durham. The English cathedrals may be compared with the greater churches in Europe; Cluny covered 54,000 square feet (4,860 sq m) and Cologne 90,000 (8,100 sq m). Yet Winchester was intended to cover 66,000 (5,940 sq m), and Bury St Edmunds abbey was nearly 70,000 (6,300 sq m). Lincoln was also 70,000, and Old St Paul's nearly 100,000 (9,000 sq m). Prior also points out that the Norman piers in Durham choir (c 1093) are 17 times as big as those of Canterbury choir (Early English, 1175). In spite of considerable increases in technical mastery a relatively high proportion of Norman towers fell down (eg Winchester), compared with the durability, to our times, of most Gothic work. Cathedrals took longer to build than castles. This is partly explained by the military necessity of putting a castle up quickly and the consequent lavish use of labour, and partly to the relative lack of money for the cathedrals; there is also the more elaborate detail and finish to a cathedral. Harvey also suggests that people were reluctant to pull down, even to "improve", a church, like Durham, for which they had an affection.

All this building needed a large and highly organised industry. In Norman times many clerics and military clerks of works had architectural knowledge, but by the late 12th century there was a complete lay organisation. There were two ways of building a great church, for example: the earlier was the direct method, the later by placing contracts for the work. In the direct method the Chapter

86 *A medieval building scene, showing masons shaping stones, stones being hoisted by a crane worked by a manpowered wheel, and stones being laid.*

appointed a monk or canon to administer the work and to be responsible for the accounts. He delegated a great deal of the responsibility to a master mason (or architect), and in some cases (eg Exeter) these two acted jointly. The master mason managed the various craftsmen. In practice, certain craftsmen could be paid lump sums for doing a whole job, and this gradually led to the contract system.

The master mason at first lived on the job, but later (by the end of the 13th century) he became a supervising visitor, which implies that he had several jobs to look after and that at each job there was a resident deputy. A distinguished 12th-century master mason was William of Sens at Canterbury; later architects included Henry Yevele

in the 14th century. The working of the early system was described by Villard de Honnecourt, who worked in France in the 13th century.

The master mason had a group of masons under him, who cut their stone in "lodges", open huts or lean-tos. There were freemasons, who were qualified to cut and carve freestone (ungrained stone which could be worked in any direction), and rough-masons, who squared the stone and did straight mouldings (for masons' marks see below). There were also other specialists like carpenters, smiths, glaziers, and clerks, and a large number of labourers. Tools and equipment were primitive. Plans were diagrammatic, that is the builders were told what was required, but not how to do it in detail. So in some cathedrals, eg Lincoln, details of the front and in the side aisles, although aiming at the same result, are asymmetrical. The master mason had to visit local quarries and select his stone or arrange for its import, usually by water, from a source of his choice (eg Caen, Portland, or Barnack); sometimes old material could be reused, such as Roman bricks from a nearby villa. Half the cost of a building was materials, of which half was carriage; the other half was finishing and erecting. All this labour force was itinerant, moving from one job to another, except that some of the masons might stay at one place if the work took a long time; thus, in our day, there is a permanent masons' yard at Liverpool Anglican cathedral, where three generations of one family have worked. Many cathedrals, like Chichester, have found it necessary to set up their own masons' yard to deal with restoration as well as building work (see **88**). York has a special glaziers' workshop, to handle the vast area of stained glass in the Minster.

The actual erection of a major building was laborious in the extreme. Each stone had to be lifted into place on a rising web of wooden scaffolding, using windlasses, hoists, cranes, and pulleys. The vaulting of churches, and flying buttresses, were laid on pre-erected timber frames. Treadwheel cranes survive at Ely and Salisbury cathedrals, and a hoist at Beverley.

Timber-framed houses, on the other hand, were built by carpenters and their teams. The houses were always prefabricated; all joints were cut and fitted before the house was erected. The building was treated as a series of frames, which were assembled on the ground and fitted together – side-wall and cross-wall frames, floors, roof frames, and trusses. These frames were then raised into position, joined together like a box, and pegged. Infilling of the walls, and roof covering, could then be done.

(Details of the building industry, its organisation, materials, and economics, are given in eg L F Salzman: *Building in England Down to 1540* (Oxford 1952).)

Masons' marks

These are a familiar feature of the stonework of churches and old buildings, and tell much about former building practices. They are small incised signs, some geometric, some letters (often looking like those of primitive alphabets), some even using curved lines; there are a great variety of them, mostly about an inch high (see **87**). They are usually cut in the stone with chisel and punch (see **88** and **89**), or stone axe; some are scratched, but these need caution because many scratched marks may be mere doodles, and not masons' marks at all. The common mark of a circle cut into "petals" is most likely to be the result of trying out new compasses, and churches often have crosses on door jambs which may be pilgrims' marks, dedications, or in pursuit of vows; there is also a wide variety of graffiti to add to the confusion. Masons' marks are usually on jambs of doors or windows, but can be on any stone.

The mark not only identified a particular mason but was his sign of proficiency in his craft. Medieval masons travelled from job to job, and the mark identified them as they came to another lodge and helped them to get work in the new place. Another use was to certify the quality of a block of stone dressed at the quarry, which could then be regarded as good for immediate use in the building. Masons themselves called the signs "banker marks" – a mason's working bench is his "bank". Such marks are still used. A variant is the mark identifying not one mason but a whole lodge (compare the inscriptions recording the building of a stretch of Roman wall by a military unit). At Lincoln Cathedral these take the form of three-dimensional motifs, carved reliefs in the form of a closely fluted circle.

Masons' marks can be found freely on churches, particularly the greater ones – they are very common at Westminster Abbey, and a list of over 1,000 different signs has been compiled for Lincoln Cathedral by G T Hemsley. But they also appear on houses, where they are useful in identifying work by the same man at two houses (eg the same marks occur in two 16th-century houses a few miles from each other in Yorkshire: Tatefield Hall, Beckwithshaw, and

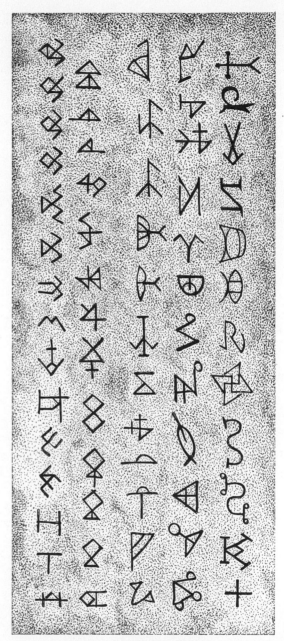

87 *Masons' marks: a selection from Salisbury Cathedral, Lincolnshire churches, and elsewhere, from a very great variety. Each mason carved a distinctive mark on his work, to show which mason had carried out the cutting or dressing of the stone.*

183

Padside Hall, Darley). But caution is needed here; a mark could be passed down from father to son. There is a fine and rather unexpected range of marks on Rennie's Dundas Aqueduct on the Kennet and Avon Canal near Bath (1800). Similar marks are found on old kerbstones.

Another type of craft mark is the *carpenter's mark* on old timbers. These are usually straight lines side by side, cut at the ends of beams for ease of assembling them together rightly. They can be seen in old houses, particularly on the roof timbers, but are most accessible on the timbers of old barns. Local or county studies of these marks (such as that for Lincolnshire churches by T B Parks) can be of great value in understanding the organisation and movement of builders in a given area.

88 *Stonemason at work in Lincoln Cathedral. The great cathedrals employ permanent staffs of craftsmen to deal with the constant maintenance required.*

Adze marks, showing how stone was dressed, can be seen on stonework up to about 1850, and also on some later "craftsman-built" houses, together with straight saw marks on woodwork. After that date, stone has normally been sawn and wood cut by circular saw (which leaves distinctive curving marks). Ashlar, for major buildings, has always been cut by straight (usually two-handed) saws, leaving finish and detail to be adzed or chiselled.

Medieval tiles

Tiles are a common feature of churches, monasteries, and castles, mostly for flooring but sometimes (as at Westminster Abbey) on walls as well. They are decorated in several techniques, all of which probably originated outside England. They have been exhaustively studied by Elizabeth Eames. Some decorated floor tiles seem to have been used in England before the 13th century, but were only used in large and increasing numbers from the second quarter of the 13th century (perhaps stimulated by Henry III's marriage to Eleanor of Provence in 1236). They passed into general use in middle-class houses during the 14th century. Changes in fashion killed the industry in the early 16th century, although medieval-type tiles continued to be made in the west of England up to the 18th century. The tiles closely imitating medieval designs used wholesale in Victorian church restorations can be easily distinguished, as they were mass produced from standardised clays and glazes, were uniformly fired, and have sharply impressed designs; the result lacks variation and the character of handwork.

On the other hand, no two medieval tiles are exactly alike; mixing of clays and glazes, and firing conditions, were haphazard by modern standards, with highly individual and homely results. No paints or enamels were used – the colours depended on the use of different clays and on the glazes. If a polychrome effect was wanted, it was got by juxtaposing tiles of different colours, and a polychrome pattern on a tile was made by using different coloured clays. The usual method was to inlay a design in white-firing clay into a red earthenware body (the Victorian term for this, "encaustic", is incorrect, as it implies the use of enamel). The glazes were all lead glazes, as used on contemporary pottery; when the normal clear lead glaze was fired it appeared brown over the red body and yellow over the white inlay.

The earliest datable tile pavements in England were made of mosaics of dark green and yellow pieces of different shapes, laid in panels of geometric designs. The colours imitated Italian black and white marble floors. These were mostly in Cistercian monasteries; some survive in the south transept at Byland Abbey (NY), but there are some in Canterbury Cathedral (1220). Birds, fleurs-de-lys, and gothic tracery were also used. These simple shapes were then elaborated, either by patterns impressed on the tiles with wooden blocks or by inlaying the patterns with white-firing clay. At this stage circular patterns were laid down, with the inlaid tiles combined with the simple shaped ones to form a composite mosaic.

This was a speciality of Chertsey Abbey, the most famous centre for 13th-century inlaid tiles in England. Square inlaid tiles soon became very popular, and are more numerous than any other type. These were introduced into the royal palaces and castles (eg Winchester) by Henry III, and from there spread to churches and abbeys, (eg Westminster). Most of these tiles were made in local kilns, and show minor variations; thus, the designs of the tiles at the royal palace of Clarendon (Wi) were copied for the new cathedral at Salisbury not far away (1258), but were made in different kilns. The tile industry of this area supplied buildings all over Wiltshire and Somerset, while another branch of this Wessex school (the Westminster-Chertsey branch), using different designs, operated in Hampshire and north of the Thames. The designs were very varied, and included popular stories like those of Tristram and Richard I, as well as floral and heraldic motifs and human figures.

The Westminster-Chertsey branch gave rise to two tile-producing centres in the Midlands in the 14th century, one at Coventry and Nuneaton and the other at Nottingham. Heraldic shields became very popular at this period. Another 14th-century group grew up in the Chilterns, round Penn, and spread from there down the Thames to beyond London. It used a "printing" technique, in which the design was stamped on the tile with a die dipped in white slip, thus printing the design on the surface in one operation. Repeating patterns were often used in this group. A variant of this, made in London, depressed the design below the surface of the tile, thus avoiding undue wear. The Coventry centre adopted printing in the later 15th century.

The earlier type of inlaid tile was revived in the mid 15th century in the Severn basin, and examples can be seen in Gloucester Cathedral and Malvern Priory; this spread as far west as St David's, and the trade may have been in the hands of itinerant craftsmen. Malvern designs are found in the Midlands into the 16th century.

During the whole of this long period, when inlaid or printed tiles were used, the east of England preferred tiles in relief or depressed counter-relief, either imported from the Rhineland or made here. St Albans Abbey had a wide range of designs replaced in the 19th century. A main centre for these, in the later 14th century, was at Bawsey near King's Lynn; its tiles, like the Chiltern ones, are small and thin, for ease in handling. Relief tiles of medieval type were made in Devon (Barnstaple) until the early 18th century. The East Midlands and East Anglia also remained attached to the early line-impressed type, some of which can be seen at Ely (c 1325). Other groups of this family were made in the late 14th and 15th centuries in Derbyshire and Staffordshire.

The use of medieval floor tiles is mainly confined to the Lowland Zone, but was there so common that few buildings of any standing did not have them; many can still be seen, *in situ* as well as in museums. The British Museum has a very extensive collection.

Delft and later tiles

The 16th century saw a fashion for tin-glazed (also called tin-enamelled) earthenware. This was a ware covered with a lead glaze

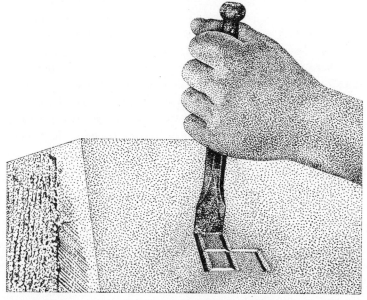

89 *Carving a mason's mark ("banker's mark"). A bank was the bench on which a mason worked.*

made white and opaque with tin oxide; designs were painted on this glaze or enamel before firing, in blue, purple, yellow, brown, green, or (less frequently) red. It was imported into England from Spain (as maiolica, whose decoration was inspired by Islamic and Persian motifs) and Italy (faience, with Chinese modes of decoration). The Dutch became major makers of faience, and Delft was the centre of this industry. "Delft" indeed became synonymous with blue and white ware, and large quantities were imported into England in the 16th and earlier 17th centuries.

Tiles, intended mainly for walls and fireplaces, were an important part of the Dutch output and certainly caught on in England, where many potters sought to join in the trade. Rhoda Edwards, in her exhaustive study of the London potters from c1570 to 1710 (*Journal of Ceramic History*, 6, 1974), shows that Dutch potters were working in England from about 1540, but these early migrants may have been making the ordinary Dutch earthenware. Tin-glazed pottery is, however, recorded as being made in Norwich in 1568; earlier manufacture of this, if it existed, is not recorded. In the 1570s delft was being made at Sandwich and King's Lynn, and possibly also at Maidstone and Colchester. The records become clearer in the 17th century. Tiles were being made in London from 1612/13, at least, and in Southwark from the same date. The Southwark potter Christian Wilhelm initiated a distinctive "bird on rock" style of decoration, on pieces dated from 1628 to 1644. Delft was being made in Lambeth from 1673. Elsewhere, Bristol and Liverpool were the main centres; the latter specialised in transfer-printed, not hand-painted, tiles during the 18th century. At first the decoration of Dutch tiles was complete on each tile, but in the 18th century tile pictures which needed four, six, or more to complete them became popular. The designs were mostly well painted; they consisted of figures (such as the well-known "popular games" series), urban or rural scenes (such as views of towns, or castles, or shipping), and floral or other natural motifs.

Earlier tiles were thick, often half an inch (1.25cm); by the 18th century they had become thinner, and 1/4 in (62mm) is common. Dimensions vary – early tiles could be 5 or 5 1/2 in (12.5 or 13.75cm) square, 18th-century tiles 5in or less. Hand-painted tiles largely ceased to be made after 1800, but delft tiles remained in vogue throughout the 19th century and tiled fireplaces can be found in very many Victorian houses.

In the late 19th century it became fashionable for the upmarket "craft" potters to make tiles. A leading exponent of this was William de Morgan (1839–1917), who made a large quantity of striking tiles, with lavish decoration, in lustre pigments, based on Islamic, Oriental, and William Morris-type designs. He mostly used tiles 6in square. Many 20th-century artists and potters have also made tiles, sometimes with the decoration covering large areas and hundreds of tiles (eg Arthur Boyd in Australia).

The use of tiles, both for floors and walls, is standard in 20th-century building. An interesting example from between the wars is that of the London Underground, which used coloured tiles to great effect in the stations; each station had its own combination of colours, which made identification certain and added an individual note.

Reuse of materials and buildings

Reuse in new buildings of material from old or disused buildings in the vicinity is by no means uncommon at all periods. Thus, recognition of older stones in a wall or house implies the presence of an older building, often one from near at hand. This may have been completely demolished and used up, or ruins may remain.

Some material which is incongruous in its setting is there by chance, such as a Neolithic or Iron Age quern in a stone field wall, collected with other stones when the field was cleared and walled; or pieces of Victorian china in a field, thrown away onto the farm midden and scattered with manure on the field. But most use of old stones by a farmer was deliberate (unless he did not appreciate that the source of his stone was an ancient monument). Stone circles and megalithic tombs are raided for stones, to be built into barns or used as gateposts. This still goes on; as recently as 1974 a megalithic tomb was discovered in the Black Mountains near Talgarth, which had been partly eaten into by the farmer for stone, a practice which continued after the tomb was excavated. The enormous tomb of Barnenez in Brittany has a sizable quarry in its side, revealing tomb chambers and seemingly inexhaustible.

The Romans often reused their own earlier material, eg a carved piece of cornice at the base of the south-west gate at Lincoln, carved slabs from a monumental arch reused as building material in the late Roman riverside wall in London, and several instances of 1st- or 2nd-century tombstones in 3rd-century bastions. Roman material was of course freely used in Saxon and medieval churches and buildings of all kinds.

The convenient and useful squared stones of which Hadrian's Wall was built have found their way into houses on both sides of the Border. A good example is the stretch near Gilsland (Nd), where there is a long gap in the Wall. This gap is represented by Thirlwall Castle; but this is not the end of the story, because Thirlwall Castle itself has found its way into the structure of many farmhouses round about.

So Roman stones or tiles reused can point to villas, towns, or other monuments nearby. Material from Verulamium is built into St Albans Abbey; Escomb church (Du) (7th century) draws on the neighbouring Roman fort. It should be borne in mind that, even as late as the Norman period, much Roman building was still standing several feet high. Thus, the Normans pulled down streets of ruined Roman houses in Colchester, not only to be able to lay out new streets but to get material for the castle.

This has gone on in recent times too. Medieval stones, often carved, can be seen in houses and garden walls in the vicinity of old monasteries. Loseley was built from the stones of Waverley Abbey in the 1560s, and Fountains Hall out of the fabric of Fountains Abbey in c 1611. Lacock Abbey church was converted into the stable block of the new house in the 1540s. The cathedral at Fortrose was used to build Fort George in 1784. The wall of St Mary Magdalene church at Lincoln, strengthened in the 19th century, contains, most incongruously, a piece of stone clearly inscribed APOTHECARY from a probably 18th-century grave. Slag from the Roman ironworks at Beauport Park (Sx) was used to metal a road in the 19th century. And these examples could be multiplied freely.

Older structures may be incorporated in later ones, particularly when the purpose of the two is the same. Thus, a Roman road may be embedded in the foundations of a more recent road on the same line; Roman town walls were frequently built up and refurbished in medieval times, with the Roman work as the lower portion and the medieval work higher up. Churches have many examples of this: the Norman west front at Lincoln is surrounded by the larger and more elaborate 12th-century facade, but is still visible as a small part of the whole.

Buildings themselves may be reused for another purpose, and this is of interest where the character of the earlier use shows through the later. Thus, monasteries were sometimes converted at the Dissolution into private houses (eg Lacock) or schools (Sherborne). Churches and chapels may become factories or warehouses, or cinemas, or even be turned into dwelling houses. Country houses become hotels, training or research centres, nursing homes, schools, or colleges; in some the original character has been successfully kept (as at Stowe School (Bc)). In Southwark a block of the early 19th-century buildings of St Thomas' Hospital is now occupied by the Post Office, but its strangeness in this use is very evident. In Lincoln the hospital built by Carr of York in the 1770s was converted into a theological college 100 years later, but the original use shows clearly through; for instance, the dining-room and library are unmistakably old wards.

Sites will obviously be reused, or continue in use, if they are suitable for their purpose, such as a town at a focal or strategic point (like London or York), or a fortified hilltop (such as the medieval castle inside the Iron Age fort at Castell Dinas in the Black Mountains, or the Norman motte in the Iron Age defences at Thetford). Sometimes the nature of the original use attracted other uses later: thus, Old Sarum (Wi) began as an Iron Age hillfort, continued with a Roman and Saxon village thus partially protected, and ended with a Norman town, castle, and cathedral. Similarly Portchester, a very strong Roman Saxon Shore fort, later contained a Saxon village, a Norman castle, and a priory, and much later was used to house French prisoners in the Napoleonic wars. Sometimes the thread is more tenuous, as when a sacred site was reused after a long interval, eg the church at Rudston (Hu) with a Bronze Age monolith in its churchyard, or the church at Knowlton (Do), inside a Neolithic henge. Churches on mounds, or with round churchyards, are often on ancient sacred sites, but there may be other reasons – a mound may merely serve to keep the church above wet ground. And some such associations may be quite fortuitous; thus it is doubtful whether the builders of the medieval priory of St Mary Overie in Southwark knew that under the site of the church was (possibly) once a temple of Isis. A conspicuous example of inconsequence is Maumbury Rings, Dorchester (Do); this was built as a Neolithic henge, was adapted by the Romans as an amphitheatre, and converted in the Civil Wars to a gunpost.

These examples, and the many like them, give an added dimension to the locality concerned.

Protective devices on buildings

Houses and their inhabitants, farm buildings and animals, bridges, etc were commonly protected against witchcraft, lightning, and other evil forces either by devices carved in or mounted on them, such as circles

90 *Sheela-na-gig – Kilpeck (He). A Sheela-na-gig is a female figure with explicit and usually ugly sexual display, carved on a church wall or a pillar, with the object of dissuading parishioners from irregular sexual activity, and/or of driving away evil from the church.*

of stones with a central stone, or objects incorporated in or buried under the building, usually under thresholds, hearths, or chimney-pieces, or on the doors or door posts of farm buildings. In Iron Age and Roman times a variety of foundation offerings could be made to protect the house – a number of different animals, some heads only, humans, or human heads, including babies, pots, coins, etc. In more recent times other objects have been used – Neolithic axes, holed stones, tanged and barbed arrowheads, acorns, or horseshoes (still to be seen in farm buildings); shoes, chickens, or cats were placed in niches and walled up, and horses' heads could be buried under the floor. Witch-bottles and pots (eg

Bellarmines) containing pins or thorns, hair, or model hearts are also found; some of these may have been meant to counter a specific threat, but the principle is the same. In North Yorkshire and Lancashire one of the supports of the fireplace might be carved with protective designs ("witch-posts"). These things are often described in books on folklore or country life, but the first comprehensive study is Ralph Merrifield: *The Archaeology of Ritual and Magic* (Batsford 1987).

Weathercocks on church spires and towers are dealt with on pages 297–8. The cock is a symbol of vigilance, and one of his functions on the top of the church may well have been to keep an eye open for hostile spirits approaching the church along the wind. Other devices aimed at keeping evil influences away from churches include *finials* on spires and pinnacles, which can take the form of a variety of animals and symbols, *crosses* (some richly ornamental) on gable ends, and *animal figures* on roofs (like those at Southwell Minster). *Gargoyles*, although their obvious function is to carry rainwater away from the wall, also have the job of frightening evil spirits. This is also one of the purposes of *grotesques*, fanciful, humorous, or ugly heads or other figures carved inside as well as outside the church; no doubt these were often created for fun or exuberance, or to represent a personage in caricature, but the magical purpose was there as well. They can often be seen in rows along the cornice of a Norman church (eg Kilpeck (He)), guarding a potentially vulnerable place in the architecture. These types, except the crosses, are found on houses, castles, and barns, as well as on churches, on the roof, gable, or over the door; for instance, there are animals on a barn at Highleadon (Gl).

A special form of grotesque is the *sheela-na-gig* (see **90**), which had a different purpose originally but by the 13th century had come to be used for magical purposes (for fuller details see pages 297–9). Sheela-na-gigs are figures of women displaying their sexual organs. The female sexual system was, from earliest times, thought to be the seat of uncanny powers, and great caution was necessary in dealing with it. If properly directed, it could repel evil spirits and was placed on churches with this in view (or perhaps existing figures became thought of in a new light). There are some 70 examples in Ireland and nearly 30 in Britain, of which one of the best is at Kilpeck. There are several types, depending on the position of the limbs. Some (as at Whittlesford (Ca)) are associated with male figures. The distribution is mainly in the Welsh borders, and south and south-west England, but there are a few in Essex and Yorkshire, and three in

Scotland, of which the best is at Rodil, Harris. Good examples are also at Oaksey (Wi) and Binstead (IW); the only one in Britain not in a church is in Royston Cave (Ht).

Another part of the body with magical powers is the head. The Iron Age Celts of Britain and Europe were head-hunters, not only to secure trophies or proof of military achievement but because for them power resided in the head, could be acquired by possession of the head, and could be used to protect the person and property of the possessor. At first actual skulls were used for these purposes, but later the custom grew up of carving stone heads which could be mounted in or on the house and last indefinitely. Many of these survive and can be seen on gables, built into the wall under the gable or over the door, or made part of the keystone of the door or porch arch. They should be distinguished from the purely commemorative or portrait heads in churches. Not all of them are Celtic, of course; the custom has persisted to very recent times, and many heads have been carved in living memory. The ancient, Celtic heads have a distinctive expression: the eyelids are joined to form a continuous oval, or there are no eyelids at all; the eyes can be bulbous, nostrils are usually absent, the mouth is often a mere slit; the face can be flat and pointed; the neck is either long or absent; there may be moustaches or beards; there may be a hollow in the top, for use as an altar or font. These heads seem to be most common in the former West Riding of Yorkshire, which may indicate either the strength of the belief among the Brigantes or more assiduous searching in that area. The pioneer student of these heads, the late Sidney Jackson, found over 400 in the West Riding alone, and there may well be substantial numbers in other parts of the north of England, with a scatter elsewhere. Many have been found in gardens or fields, but many still survive built into walls. Examples which are apparently early are in a barn gable at Hill Top Farm, Newsholme, Keighley, over the door at Mockbeggar Hall, Appletreewick, and in the back wall of Oakworth Hall, Keighley. Obviously recent heads are numerous; one is built into the parish hall at Ramsgill (NY), which may be 17th or 18th century but may be much earlier. Animals also appear among the more recent figures; for instance, there is a bird in a house wall at Kettlewell (NY). These may have had magical significance as well as being ornamental.

Another class of protective device is non-sculptural. These include the *crusaders' crosses*, small crosses with long uprights and pellets or dots at the ends of the arms, incised or scratched on the door jambs

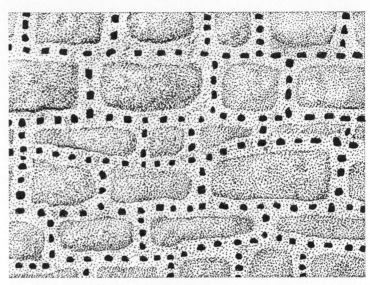

91 *Galleting (garneting) in a wall – Dunsfold church (Sy). The black spots are chips of ironstone set in the mortar, for strengthening, magic protection, or just decoration.*

of churches (there is a good set at Shere (Sy)). The evidence for these having actually been cut by returning crusaders or pilgrims in gratitude for safe return is inconclusive, and these crosses are more likely meant to protect the church.

The chips of ironstone pressed into the mortar between the stones or bricks of church or house walls mainly in the south-east of England (*galleting or garneting*) go back to a belief in the protective properties of iron, although many examples are Victorian or recent, and done for decorative effect, or to strengthen the mortar. A good example is at Dunsfold Church (Sy) (see **91**).

The best study of galleting is that by W R Trotter (*Trans Ancient Monuments Society* 33, 1989). Trotter points out that galleting (garreting, garneting) occurs in two well-defined areas only: the western Weald and the North and South Downs, and west Norfolk. There is no invariable association of materials: Trotter instances malmstone (upper greensand) galleted with carstone (ferruginous lower greensand), but also bargate with carstone, carstone with carstone, malmstone with malmstone, carstone with pebbles, carstone with brick, brick with carstone, sarsen with carstone, sandstones with flint, brick with flint, flint with flint, flint with carstone, and even flint with fragments of glass bottles.

The practice seems to have begun in the 17th century, peaked between 1800 and 1850, and died out in the early 20th century. Links with folk beliefs or with building necessity cannot be substantiated, and it seems to have been purely ornamental, and merely a fashion, originating in the two areas where it commonly occurs. There are a few instances elsewhere and at other times, such as with oyster shells at Eton in 1441.

Houses, particularly in the Highland Zone, may have *charms* set in the wall to keep the evil eye away or evil spirits out of the house. These can take the form of circles of small stones, sometimes with a central stone, set over a door or window (eg on a cottage at Rhiw (Cn)). Related protection against the evil eye is the painted eye on the prow of a ship (fishing boats in the Mediterranean still have them), whose function was not only to enable the ship to see its way through the pathless sea but to protect it as well.

Farmers used to keep in their barns or other buildings, and some still do, a variety of objects to protect the buildings and their contents, animals or other – not only horseshoes (representing the fertility goddess aspect of the horned moon), but flint arrowheads, stone axes, holed stones, acorns, etc. And St Columba was not the only man to carry holy stones in his pocket! A specialised protection for animals is the *horse brass*. The use of these goes back to prehistoric times, and depends on the idea that light is an antidote to the powers of darkness – the brasses glint and gleam as they move up and down. The devices depicted were at first the traditional religious and magical symbols, but their range has grown in the last two or three centuries to include any kind of object or commemorative design.

In the North York Moors the post supporting the smoke-hood beam in old houses is carved at the top, usually with devices which include a cross and with roll-mouldings whose meaning is unknown. Some still stand *in situ*, but some are now in museums (eg the Ryedale Folk Museum at Hutton-le-Hole and the Pitt-Rivers Museum, Oxford). Most come from Eskdale; one from Postgate Farm, Glaisdale, is dated 1664, and these *witch-posts* seem to be in 17th-century style, consonant with their function of keeping the evil power of witches at bay (see Marie Hartley and Joan Ingilby: *Life in the Moorlands of North-East Yorkshire* (1972)).

The remaining class of protectives is the ephemeral. *Stack ornaments* are the vaguely human-looking projections on the ends of the "gables" of a corn or straw stack. They are tied and bound, not plaited, and their ritual significance has been questioned; they are regarded by some as just convenient ways of finishing off the stack. But their human form, and all the analogies, suggest leaving the question open. *Corn dollies* are a different matter. These are serious folkloric objects. Both after sowing and after harvest symbolic figures made of straw were carried round the fields in procession. They represented the corn deities and fertility goddesses, and their object was to place the goddess, in effigy, in the control of the people, thus ensuring a good crop, and to acknowledge this crop after reaping. The effigies were also the focal points in the "Mell Supper" held after harvest, and of the similar but symbolic celebration in church. The name may derive from "idol". The dollies are plaited in a definite way, and traditional forms have developed in different regions. Thus there are the Cambridgeshire Bell, the Suffolk Horn and Whip, the Essex Terret, the Staffordshire Knot, the Suffolk Horseshoe, the Northamptonshire Horns, the Vale of Pickering Chalice, as well as the traditional and obviously ancient forms like the Horn of Plenty and Mother Earth.

BUILDING MATERIALS

Wall materials

Brickwork required a different range of skills, not of such a high order as masonry perhaps, but none the less exacting. The use of bricks is a fairly late phenomenon. Roman bricks and tiles had been reused in a few Saxon and Norman buildings. They can be seen in small quantities in many churches, and on a larger scale were used in the Saxon doorway of Trinity Church, Colchester, in the Norman tower and transepts of St Albans Cathedral, in the west front and nave arcades of St Botolph's Priory, Colchester, and in the arches and window heads at Brixworth (Nh), most of whose bricks are Roman. But these swallows do not make a summer. Brick was made again, for possibly the first time since the Romans left (although some of those at Brixworth may be Saxon), in East Anglia in the early 13th century (eg St Nicholas Chapel at Little Coggeshall Abbey, *c* 1220), under Flemish inspiration. These bricks were larger than those later imported from the Low Countries – $10^{1}/_{2}$–$12^{1}/_{2}$ in long, 5–6 in wide, and $1^{3}/_{4}$–$2^{3}/_{4}$ in thick (26.25–31.25 x 12.5–15 x 4.37–6.8 cm). By the later 13th century trade between the eastern parts of England and the Low Countries and the Baltic had increased to the point where the expanding ports needed warehouses, houses, churches, and public buildings, and these were built of bricks brought in from Europe. The parish church of Hull is an early example.

It is not easy to date buildings by the size of bricks. The large, locally made bricks were used until the early 15th century. The imported ones, and those made in eastern England to imitate them, were about 8–9³/₄ in long, 3³/₄–4³/₄ in wide, and 1³/₄–2¹/₂ in thick (20–24.3 x 9.3–11.8 x 4.4–6.25 cm). From the 15th century some Dutch bricks, 6–8¹/₄ in long, 3–5³/₄ in wide and 1³/₈–1³/₄ in thick (15–20.6 x 7.5–14.3 x 3.25–4.4 cm), were imported. Until the 16th century there was no recognised standard, and the so-called Tudor brick was in use until the 18th century. Attempts were made to regulate brick sizes, and to increase them: 1571, 9 x 4³/₄ x 2¹/₄ in (22.5 x 11.8 x 5.6 cm); 1625, 9 x 4³/₄ x 2¹/₄ in (22.5 x 11.8 x 5.6 cm); 1725, 10 x 4¹/₄ x 2⁵/₈ in (25 x 10.6 x 6.5 cm). But there are overlaps and variations, and no clear-cut sequence. In 1784 a brick tax led to bricks becoming larger, 10 x 5 x 3 in (25 x 12.5 x 7.5 cm) or so; but in 1803 a change in the tax led to the adoption of a smaller size, 9 x 4¹/₂ x 3 in (22.5 x 11.2 x 7.5 cm). This gradually become 8¹/₄ x 4¹/₈ x 2⁵/₈ in (20.6 x 10.3 x 6.5 cm). The standard metric size (1972) is 215 x 102.5 x 65mm.

Bricks were made by hand in wooden moulds until the mid 19th century, when mechanical methods were applied, one of which was to extrude a bar of stiff clay which could be cut into the required lengths. The striations caused by this process are visible on the bricks. "Frogs", moulded or pressed depressions to assist in keying-in the mortar, were used from c 1690. The variety of clay used and the degree of firing affect the colour of the brick, which can range from purple to red to brown, to buff, yellow, grey, or even white.

Bricks are laid in courses, with a regular arrangement, the "bond". The usual bond from the 15th century was the English Bond, alternate rows of headers (the ends showing) and stretchers (the sides showing). In the early 17th century the Flemish Bond (alternate headers and stretchers in the same course) was introduced (Kew Palace 1631), and became very popular in the late 17th and 18th centuries. There are in addition a number of other bonds – all headers, all stretchers, and combinations of these. Three bonds commonly met with, particularly in the south-east of England, are the English

Garden Wall Bond – three courses of stretchers to one of headers; the Flemish (or Sussex, or Surrey) Garden Wall Bond – three stretchers and one header, repeated, in each course; and the Rat-trap Bond, where the bricks are laid on edge with a cavity between the stretchers. This was in use in the early and mid 19th century; it used fewer bricks than the usual bonds, but had less strength. Twentieth-century brickwork commonly uses stretchers only. Pointing can be used decoratively (see **92**).

From the mid 15th to the late 17th century there was a fashion of ornamental brickwork: diaper and other patterns made by using different coloured bricks (eg Layer Marney (Ex) 1500–25; Hampton Court, 1515–30; Compton Wynyates, 1520), or patterns made from moulded or carved bricks (eg "Tudor" chimneys, or the ornate façades of two late 17th-century houses in High Street, Godalming (Sy) (see **93**)).

The brick tax of 1784 encouraged the use of tiles which, when hung on a wall, appeared to be ordinary brickwork. These "mathematical" tiles were in fact used, for cheapness, before 1784 (eg Lamb House, Rye (Sx), c 1755). They were adopted widely in the south-east of England – major centres are Canterbury (138 examples), Brighton (152), and

English

English Cross

Flemish

English Garden

Stretcher

Flemish Garden

Header

Monk

93 *17th-century ornamental brickwork – Godalming (Sy). Patterns of carved or moulded brickwork were popular in the 16th and 17th centuries.*

Lewes (87) – but they are found as far north as Althorp (Nh) (1787), Attingham Park (Sp) (*c* 1785), and Penrhyn, Bangor (Cn) (*c* 1800). An early example is West Hill House, Epsom (Sy), *c* 1690 (now demolished).

Stone is the natural material where it occurs locally and, because of its strength and good appearance, is used for churches, castles, and major buildings in every part of the country. The nature and colour of stone varies widely and produces a distinctive character in each region. Stone is used either in irregular lumps (or rubble) or, if it lends itself to shaping, in squared blocks (*hammer-dressed*). Rubble may be used random, or uncoursed; or random but coursed. If squared, it lends itself to a variety of coursing patterns. Intractable stones like granite or ragstone may be roughly dressed and assembled in random polygons. In Hampshire the soft malmstone was treated in this way from c 1870, which gives a useful dating point. A fine regular appearance can be got by the use of *ashlar*, slabs of stone dressed to a smooth finish and applied as a facing to a wall. In contrast, *rustication* was popular in the 18th century; this consisted of sharply separating each stone by means of a deep indentation, with the stones left smooth or roughened by tooling. This effect was often used on ground floors of great houses, to heighten the impact of the *piano nobile* on the first floor.

In chalk areas, *flint* is commonly used for building. In the Downlands and Chilterns it is usually left in irregular lumps and laid either random or roughly coursed. In East Anglia it is often knapped square; here too very fine regular squaring may be achieved, which lends itself to patterns in the wall such as chequers of flint and stone (common also in Wessex). "Flushwork", very popular in the later 15th century, consists of ashlar into which a pattern is cut and filled with flint (eg Long Melford Church (Su)). *Cobbles*, and the smaller *pebbles* (untrimmed stones from the beach), are used within a few miles of the sea on the coast of east Sussex and west Kent (eg Brighton) and in Norfolk, Holderness, north Lancashire, and north-west Cumberland.

Flint and the softer sandstones are often unsuitable for corners when first laid, and dressings (quoins, and door and window surrounds) are usually either of brick (as with the malmstone of Hampshire) or some harder stone. This may be laid proud for emphasis. But a mixture of materials – stone and brick, brick and stone, or even two kinds of stone – is sometimes used deliberately for effect. In Hampshire buildings are frequently of stone on the ground floor and brick above.

Unbaked earths were often used, in suitable areas, for cottages and farm buildings, or for free-standing walls. If laid on a plinth and protected by a roof, these could be very long-lasting. Mud mixed with lime or chalk and straw or dung (called *cob* in the south-west) is the most general, and may still be found in use. *Pisé* is stiff earth mixed with gravel (but not straw), and rammed between boards when nearly dry. A three-roomed house of this material, dating from the late 12th or early 13th century, has been excavated at Wallingford (Ox). *Clay lump*, used in East Anglia, is earth mixed with straw, moulded into blocks, and dried in the air.

Timber-framed houses needed to be infilled between the frame or studs. This was done with *wattle and daub* (hazel or withies covered with a mixture of crushed chalk (3/4) and clay (1/4), *lath and plaster*, or, later, brick "*nogging*", either laid straight or in a pattern such as herringbone (this was used from the 17th century, and in some urban houses may even be medieval). Many houses, mostly timber-framed, are, particularly in Kent and Essex, *weather-boarded* – faced with overlapping boards. Also mainly in the south-east *tile-hanging* is common. The tiles applied to the wall may be regular like a roof or patterned, and they may be of different shapes. Slate is also used to cover walls.

94 *Pargeting – Newport (Ex). Ornamental plasterwork on houses is distinctive particularly in Essex and Suffolk.*

Any house in any area may be rendered with *plaster* for extra protection. This may then be painted, coloured (eg the "Suffolk pink" at Bury St Edmunds), or limewashed. In Suffolk and north Essex particularly, plaster, or plaster panels in a timber frame, are often *pargeted* – decorated with moulded designs in wide variety (see **94**). *Terracotta* as a decorative facing material was popular for great houses in the 16th century (eg Sutton Place, near Guildford). *Stucco* was much used in the late 18th and early 19th century as a superior plaster. This could also be scored to look like stonework. *Coade stone* (see page 195) is a specialised kind of cement ornamentation of this period. *Roughcast* (*harling* in Scotland) is a more durable wall rendering than plaster; it consists of sand, gravel, or stone chippings mixed with slaked lime and now with some cement. It has been used since the 15th century (eg Westwood House, Bradford-on-Avon (Wi)).

Roofing materials

Primitive buildings in the Highland Zone might use *turf*. A few survivors can still be seen in Scotland. In some houses, eg blackhouses in the Outer Hebrides, turf was laid first on the roof timbers and then covered with thatch (eg Arnol, Lewis).

Thatch (see **95**) is the oldest and most general covering, and was used in prehistoric times (see eg the Iron Age replica at Butser Ancient

95 *Thatching with longstraw: the thatcher is finishing off a section just completed.*

Farm (Ha)). Although now largely superseded it is still surprisingly common, particularly in the south of England. A wide range of vegetable material was used, from heather in the Highland Zone to broom, sallow, flax, sedge, grass, and a variety of cereal straws. But the main materials are wheat straw (in southern England) and reeds (mainly in East Anglia, and grown specially for this purpose in Norfolk). The straw or reeds are laid in bundles, tied, and pegged in with hazel or withy rods. The ridge may be ornamented, and the slopes may be patterned with overlapping thatch or with arrangements of twigs. In Scotland thatch may be held down by a network of rope, tied on to stone pegs at the eaves or to stone weights. Much thatch has been replaced by tiles, but this fact may often be detected by the flow of the roof over dormer windows. Thatch is also good for following complex shapes on a cob building. The use of thatch was prohibited in London in 1212, in favour of tiles or slates.

A simpler form of roofing is *shingles*, slices of wood (normally oak, but recently cedar has been used) laid like tiles (on walls also). They were common from Roman times until the 12th century and beyond – Salisbury Cathedral was once roofed with them – but were superseded by clay tiles. Shingles are still used for church spires, particularly in the south-east and the Home Counties. Their life is limited, and no old shingles survive. Shingles are longer and narrower than tiles, and laid with a larger overlap.

Baked clay *tiles* were used by the Romans, but continuity was lost in the 5th century. They were made again certainly by the 12th century, but whether before this is not known (the effect of roofing on Scandinavian hogbacks may represent shingles). By the end of the 13th century tiles were made in at least 14 counties in east and south-east England. In 1477 the size of roof tiles (for floor tiles see pages 184–5) was standardised at $10^{1}/_{2}$ x $6^{1}/_{4}$ x $^{5}/_{8}$ in (26.25 x 15.6 x 1.5 cm), but many local variants persisted. In 1725 this standard was reaffirmed, as the average size had by then diminished a little. Today several other sizes are in common use. Like bricks, the colour of tiles depends on the clay used; in Cambridgeshire effects are obtained by blending tiles of different colours. Today a variety of other materials, mostly concrete-based, are in common use.

Tiles are either flat or curved. The *pantile* has a double curve, and each tile is fitted into the next. They have been made in England since the 18th century, in East Anglia, having since the 17th century been imported from Holland. They give a very distinctive, southern European, character to the areas where they are normally used (eastern England, from London to the Scottish border; and Bridgwater (So)); thus in North Yorkshire they are combined with stone walling, in East Yorkshire with brick. The *Spanish tile* has a single curve, and is fitted together alternately. County Hall, London, is roofed in this way. Flat tiles are also used for wall-hanging, and for floors.

In areas where stone is found in thin slabs, or is fissile, it is used for roofing. Suitable stones are found both of limestone and sandstone. Stone was a favourite roofing material, from the 16th century to the early 19th, in the north of England, the Welsh borders, the limestone belt from the Cotswolds to Stamford, Somerset, and Dorset, and the Weald. The main sources of limestone were Stonesfield (Ox), which supplied much of the Cotswold area, and Collyweston (Nh). Purbeck was also important. The most distinctive sandstones were the Horsham stone of the northern Weald and various stones from the Pennines. Stones were laid with the largest at the bottom. These could be from 16in (40cm) wide to as much as 30in (75cm). The small ones at the top were often only four or six inches wide. The weight of a Cotswold roof was nearly a ton for 100 square feet (9 m²); Purbeck

was heavier, and Horsham heavier still. The irregularity of the Cotswold stone required a steep roof (55° on average), to ensure run-off of water. But the heavier stones needed a lower pitch (45° for Horsham, and even as low as 24° in the North).

Slate, as an efficient alternative to tiles, has been used since the 12th century in areas away from its sources. Slate from Devon and Cornwall was shipped to the rest of southern and south-eastern England from about 1170. Welsh slate was used in Chester in the 14th century; but the canals, and later the railways, enabled it to be widely used in England from the late 18th century, and for a time in the mid 19th century it almost swept the board and nearly replaced thatch. London became a slate-roofed city by the early 19th century.

The main sources of slate were Cornwall and Devon, Leicestershire (Swithland), Westmorland (Furness) and Cumberland, the Isle of Man, and, very prolifically, north-west Wales (Penrhyn, Blaenau ffestiniog). There is a range of standard sizes of Welsh slates (called by names like Duchess and Countess), of which 24 x 12in (60 x 30cm) and 16 x 8in (40 x 20cm) are the most usual. Slates are not laid in graduated sizes, as is roofing stone, but can be monotonous and, on a wet day, even forbidding. But their effectiveness as a roof covering is undeniable. They are used also for wall-hanging and flooring.

Lead was used by the Saxons for roofing, and it again became popular in the 15th and 16th centuries. Most of the greater churches were roofed with sheet lead, and many smaller ones too; it was also used in castles and in great houses. Rainwater pipes, gutters, and cisterns were also frequently of lead in the 16th century. But it went out of fashion before the Civil Wars (although lead cisterns were still made into the 18th century). Lead had the advantage of being usable on flat or nearly flat roofs. Lead was also important as cames for holding small windowpanes in place.

Copper was used for roofing from the 19th century, but was never as popular as lead.

Other materials

Iron as a building material was, for most of the Middle Ages, confined to hinges, brackets, strapwork on doors and chests, locks, cramps, nails, and the like. Not till the later 18th century was it used for larger articles like balconies, railings (the Sussex iron railings of St Paul's are an exception), balustrades, and street furniture. This was wrought iron. After the Regency this was replaced by cast iron, and the aesthetic quality sharply declined (as in Victorian railings and rainwater goods). Corrugated and galvanised iron was found convenient for farm buildings, sheds, factories, and the like from the later 19th century, for walls as well as roofs. Now many corrugated materials are used.

Asbestos also came in in the 19th century. Concrete, used by the Romans for bath-houses and eg the Pantheon in Rome, was again used for buildings in the 19th century. The first major group of farm buildings in concrete was at Buscot (Ox), *c* 1879.

Coade stone

This is an ingenious artificial substance much used for statuary, reliefs, and house ornament in the late 18th and early 19th century. It is a kind of terracotta largely based on kaolin, but its precise formula has never been recovered. It could be moulded and painted, and was much cheaper than carved stone; it defied frost, and has kept its sharp forms to this day. With stucco, it contributed to altering the face of London from the 1770s. It appears as quoins and ornaments to doorways (see **96**), as figures and memorials, and was used on all kinds of buildings, important or private.

Artificial stone seems to have been invented by Richard Holt and others; Holt took out patents in 1722 and 1723, and wrote a book about it in 1730. An improved form was developed by Daniel Pincot about 1767; he also wrote a book on the subject in 1770. Pincot seems to have had a hand in setting up the Coade factory at Lambeth in 1769. The proprietor, Mrs Eleanor Coade, took her son-in-law, John Sealy, into partnership, until his death in 1813. The sculptor John Bacon was associated as designer and modeller from 1769 until his death in 1799, and put the products on a very competent artistic level. The firm later employed another sculptor, Frederick Woodington, but ran into competition by the 1830s and finally died out about 1840. Fashion changed after the Napoleonic Wars, and Coade stone was replaced by stucco, cast iron, and precast cement.

A conspicuous example of Coade production is the large lion which used to adorn a brewery on the South Bank and has been re-erected at the south end of Westminster Bridge (1837); others are the caryatids at St Pancras Church. But smaller items can be seen everywhere, such as the fine set which ornaments the houses in Bedford Square. An idea of the variety of products can be gauged

96 *Coade stone (an artificial stone based on kaolin) was much used for architectural ornament from the 1770s to 1840: this is a doorway in Bedford Square, London, 1776.*

from the firm's catalogue of 1784, which listed 778 items. A taste for terracotta revived in the 1870s (it was used, for example, by G F Watts), but the quality of this later material was not as good as the original Coade stone.

Wood

Wood was the major, indeed the chosen, element in building until superseded generally by brick in the 18th century; and even now it is standard for roof frames and floors. The wood normally used was oak. In the 15th and 16th centuries elm was sometimes used as a cheaper substitute, as were willow and sallow. Beech was used for laths. Pine and fir began to be imported from Scandinavia from the mid 18th century, although pine is found exceptionally in some earlier houses.

It has been pointed out, as a result of recent work, that the earlier idea of medieval England as a country of almost continuous woodland is incorrect. The destruction of the wildwood – the primeval, primary forest – began in the Neolithic and reached a climax in the Iron Age and Roman periods. With increasing population farmers wanted land, not trees, and by the late Saxon period the landscape, even in its details, was not unlike what it remained until the Enclosures, or in some areas even until the last 30 years. Oliver Rackham points out that the Anglo-Saxons did not colonise the whole landscape afresh, but merely continued a process that the Romans had already partly completed. The woodlands were in islands – the Weald, west Essex, the Chilterns, Dean, the New Forest, etc – much as they are today.

At Domesday (1086) only half of the 12,850 settlements recorded possessed woodland or wood-pasture, and this made up only 15% of the country. Much of the Midlands, Yorkshire, and the Fens had no woodland at all. Eleventh-century England was less wooded than most countries of 20th-century Europe. By 1350 woodland covered only 10% of the land, and remained thus until a further period of destruction from 1700 onwards.

This situation at once raises a question as to the sources and nature of the timber and other forest products used in medieval vernacular building. Rackham estimates that there are over 100,000 medieval houses, barns, and churches extant in England, most of which contain some original timber fabric; and the original figure would of course exceed this, perhaps considerably so. Much of this timber had therefore to be transported from more wooded areas, sometimes quite a long distance away. Thus, King's Lynn has medieval pine timbers which were presumably imported from across the North Sea. Rarely did a large town, like London, Cambridge, York, or Norwich, have adequate supplies of timber for building (as opposed to underwood for fuel etc) near at hand.

Most of the wood for timber-framing of houses etc was oak, although smaller and humbler houses might use elm or other woods. Usually each member was made (shaped by adze, not sawn – the adze marks can still be seen on many timbers) from a single log. The smallest oak that would provide the required beam was chosen and felled where possible. In most woods therefore there was a rapid turnover of small

oaks, felled at from 30 to 70 years of age, and constantly replaced. Timbers are rarely much more than 20ft long; over that length the tree begins to get crooked and knotty, and to branch out when it gets above the underwood. This normally maximum length thus determines the design of large buildings such as aisled barns – few ordinary houses have members as long. Very large buildings, such as castle halls or cathedrals, needed exceptional trees (30ft (9.2m) or so of usable timber), and these were often granted to the builders by the king from his own manors or forests, sometimes a long way away. Thus, William I provided timber for Winchester Cathedral (in 1079) from Hempage Wood, and Henry III sent timber from his manor of Kingswood near Colchester, 70 miles by sea, to Dover Castle. A contemporary case is provided as a result of the fire in the south transept of York Minster in 1984. Oaks for the restoration of the roof frame included massive trees felled in the New Forest and given by the Forestry Commission, which yielded usable beams 40ft (12.3m) long. Each beam was used to provide two members for the A-frames of the outer roof, with 12 x 6in (30 x 15 cm) section. Other trees, donated by estates across the country, form the ribs of the vaulted ceiling. (I am grateful to Henry Venables Ltd of Stafford for this information.)

It is interesting to count the number of trees used in a particular building. Rackham quotes a farmhouse at Stanton (Su), consisting of an open hall and seven other rooms, which was made from 333 timber trees, from 32 oaks less than 6in in basal diameter used for rafters to three oaks more than 18in in diameter for principal posts. Half the trees were less than 9in in diameter. On the basis of the probable numbers of suitable oaks, a wood of 50 acres could have produced such a house every six years, were there no other demand on its timber. The woods of west Suffolk, covering some 5.5% of the land, could probably have yielded just enough timber to meet the demands of rural housing in the county, but not of the urban housing as well.

Analysis of the wattle in medieval wattle and daub gives an interesting insight into the species growing in the local underwood. Thus (Rackham), a small house of c 1400 at Hartest (Su) had a frame of small oak trees. Its wattle rods, of 7 years' growth and about 1$\frac{1}{2}$ inches (3.75 cm) in diameter at the base, were a mixture of hazel, ash, maple, willow, and aspen, tied with clematis stems, strips of lime bark, and one-year willow rods. The source of these was most probably a local wood lost in the 17th century; the spread of species accords well with records from other places, and with the composition of surviving ancient woods in thisarea. (Oliver Rackham in Kathleen Biddick (ed): "Archaeological Approaches to Medieval Europe" (Kalamazoo, *Studies in Medieval Culture*, 18, 1985.))

Sources of building materials

BRICKS AND TILES

These were mostly from the non-stone areas of the Lowland Zone. In the Middle Ages bricks were made anywhere where suitable clay was to be had. Brickmaking was local and quite unstandardised; clay was often used *ad hoc* for a particular building. From about 1700 brick had become the predominant building material east and south-east of the limestone belt, and during the Industrial Revolution became standard also between this belt and the Welsh border. Since 1880, when machine-made and wire-cut bricks became standard, one-third of the production comes from the Oxford and Lias clays – Oxfordshire, Bedfordshire, Cambridgeshire (Fletton), to Lincolnshire, one third from Carboniferous beds, and, of the remaining third, a half is from recent glacial and alluvial deposits. Red bricks predominate in the west Midlands (within the triangle Tewkesbury–Grantham–Birkenhead), with an outlier at Bridgwater. A few small centres, eg Selborne (Ha), produce red bricks from gault clay. "White" bricks are made from calcareous sandstones, from Dorset and Wiltshire to Cambridgeshire. Midhurst (Sx) also produces white bricks, from gault. Blue bricks centre on Staffordshire. "Grey" (yellow) "stock" bricks, of which London is largely built, come from Thames Valley clays.

STONE FOR WALLING (see **Map 12**)

Limestones Stone from the Magnesian Limestone belt (Nottinghamshire and the west side of the Vale of York) was used by the Romans at York

Map 12 *The sources of building materials: walling*

and Tadcaster, and in great churches such as York, Ripon, Beverley, and Southwell Minsters and Selby Abbey. Roche Abbey's quarries were one of the main sources. Carboniferous limestones from the western Pennines were used for local buildings; the white field walls of this area are very distinctive.

Oolite from the Jurassic ridge, from the Lincoln Edge through Northamptonshire to the Cotswolds, with its southern extension to Dorset, was extensively used; it falls into several groups. The northern group, south of Stamford, is noted for several stones like Ancaster, Clipsham, Barnack, and Ketton (when the great Barnack quarries – the "hills and holes" – were worked out). The famous *Cotswold* stone, having an equally distinctive character, came from many quarries, of which Painswick and Taynton (Burford) are very important.

West of the Cotswolds is a small source of *Tufa*, round Tenbury and Dursley. South-east of the Cotswolds is the *Bath stone* area, with great sources at eg Corsham and Box. This is a beautiful stone, but it weathers badly; a great deal of restoration has been needed at Oxford in the past few years. Ham Hill, from this area, is a stone intermediate between limestone and sandstone. Wiltshire produced a good stone, at Tisbury and Chilmark (the stone in Salisbury Cathedral). In the south, *Portland* is a hard, well-wearing stone, used widely in London. *Beer* stone was used in Devon. West of the Jurassic ridge is the *Lias*, with marlstones.

Minor stones of these belts are the "*marble*" from Purbeck, used for its dramatic contrasting effects by the Normans, eg at Salisbury. Various other stones which take a polish are also called marble, such as Frosterley (Du), Bethersden (Kt), and a group in Derbyshire (used in Guildford Cathedral). *Alabaster* was got at Chellaston (Db) in the 15th and 16th centuries, and used for sculpture at Nottingham. Kentish Rag is also a limestone; it is intractable, but was used in many important buildings such as the Roman walls of London. The Maidstone area is the main source.

East of the Jurassic belt lies the *chalk*, from east Yorkshire through Lincolnshire to East Anglia, the Chilterns, the Wessex block, and the North and South Downs. This produces *clunch*, a hard chalk suitable for building. An important and high-quality source of this was Totternhoe in the Chilterns. Clunch was quarried and used *ad hoc* all over this belt, eg at Guildford for the Castle and St Mary's Church, and at Compton (Sy) for the church and local farmhouses. The chalklands

also produce *flint*, a concretion of silica in the chalk. This is used widely for buildings of all kinds. Flint occurs in several colours, such as black from the boulder clay on the Yorkshire coast to yellow-brown, grey or blue-grey, and white (when patinated). A minor stone of the Home Counties is *puddingstone*.

Sandstones In the north of England these are mainly from the *Millstone Grit* and the *Coal Measures*, along the central Pennines. The main stone sources are in Derbyshire (Darley Dale) and west Yorkshire. The famous *York stone*, used widely for paving, comes from the area Bradford–Halifax–Holmfirth.

The Jurassic rocks of north-east Yorkshire and Northampton produce a stone used locally.

The *New Red Sandstone* lies in a wide belt from Worcester to Chester, with an extension to Carlisle, and gives a very distinctive character to the cathedrals and very many other buildings of this area. The *Old Red Sandstone* occurs in south Devon and Cornwall, and also in south-east Wales and the southern end of the Welsh borders (ie Herefordshire and north to Ludlow).

The south-east of England is characterised by the *Greensands* and the *Wealden* beds. The *Upper Greensand* produces *malmstone*, a soft but usable calcareous rock, used widely in Surrey and east Hampshire (Winchester Castle is built of rock from Selborne); in east Surrey, round Reigate, *firestone* and *roadstone* were quarried. The *Lower Greensand* has several useful stones, like the ferruginous *Bargate* of the Godalming area. The Wealden beds have a variety of stones, in the Hastings beds. In Norfolk there is a ferruginous sandstone called *Carstone*.

Granite although not easy to work, is used for building both locally, as in Aberdeenshire, and more widely. Aberdeen granite was in fact used in London buildings. Other sources are north Wales, Cumberland, Cornwall (Penryn, Lamorna, St Austell, Bodmin Moor), Dartmoor, and Charnwood in Leicestershire. *Basalt* (called *whinstone*) also occurs in small outcrops in Devon and Cornwall. *Dolerite* (also called whinstone) occurs in Northumberland, and was used in the Roman wall.

Many quarries important in the Middle Ages are now worked out, such as Barnack, Selborne, Quarr, and Binstead. (Arundel Castle and Beaulieu Abbey were built from Quarr stone, and Winchester Cathedral from Binstead.) The Normans imported much stone from Caen and used Surrey malmstone (Reigate stone) as a cheaper substitute.

STONE FOR ROOFING (see **Map 13**)

Limestones The main stone used was Stonesfield (Ox), Collyweston (Nh), and Purbeck (Do).

Sandstones Mainly Horsham (Sx), and Pennant and Rossendale from the Coal Measures.

Slates These are mainly from Cumbria, Gwynedd (eg Penrhyn, Blaenau ffestiniog), and Cornwall.

Many of the stones mentioned above were used very early. E M Jope (in *Medieval Archaeology*, 6 (1964)) has analysed some 500 middle and late Saxon buildings (mostly churches, but including some stonework in timber buildings) in the Lowland Zone of England. He was able to identify a number of stones which were also used in medieval times: Ham Hill (local use); Bath/Box (used in Wessex buildings); Barnack (East Anglia, Cambridgeshire, northern Northamptonshire); Taynton (Upper Thames); other oolites (lower Severn valley, Lincolnshire, Cambridgeshire, Norfolk); Osmington (Dorset, Devon); Portland (west Wessex); Purbeck (local); Quarr (Hampshire, West Sussex). Other stones occur in Wales, the north Midlands, and a scatter in Essex and the south-east.

BUILDING FEATURES AND DETAILS

Floors

The ground floor of most houses until the 15th century was normally of beaten earth, sometimes mixed with a stiffener such as bull's blood, lime, or clay. Superior cottages and larger houses might use stone flags, bricks, or tiles. Upper floors were planked, wide planks being earlier.

Map 13 *The sources of building materials: roofing*

Windows

These were at first just openings in the wall, not always protected or covered up. Glass was used by the Romans in villas and major buildings, but before it again became within the reach of most people (in the late 16th century, and from the end of the 15th in richer houses), draught was excluded and (some) light admitted by a variety of materials – horn, oiled paper or cloth, linen canvas, thin slabs of mica, or alabaster. But even into the 17th century many windows merely had open grilles of wood, stone, metal, wicker, or even reeds; some had wooden shutters. In Scotland vertical slats covered with rabbit skins and shuttered were used (cf Pitt's Cottage, Westerham (Kt)).

Medieval great houses and castles normally had windows in the domestic rooms and halls with stone tracery in the current architectural styles. Halls could be given more light and sitting space by way of a projection to the building, called a *bay*. This could be square (as at Loseley (Sy), 1560s), splayed (18th century), or round (early 19th century). The bay was glazed as fully as possible. Round bays, some of which do not reach the ground, and some of which are on one floor only, are often called *bows*; these were often used as shop fronts in the 17th and 18th centuries, and came back into fashion in the Regency.

Narrower projections above ground level, particularly on upper floors, are called *oriels*. The famous example at Oriel College, Oxford, was rebuilt in 1637–42, and seems to replace a medieval one. First-floor oriels were common from the late 16th century, mainly in towns (eg Sparrowe's House, Ipswich), and were popular in seaside towns in the early 19th century. A fine, and early, oriel is that in the Abbot's Lodgings of St Osyth's Abbey (Ex) (1520s).

In the 16th and most of the 17th century, *casement* windows were popular. These might have stone mullions, with iron or wood frames, or, in later houses, no mullions. The ironwork, handles, etc could be ornate. The glass was in diamond panes set in lead cames; in the 17th century rectangular panes, up to 8 x 6 in, became popular. Surrey has a large number of examples. The *Suffolk window*, found in a belt from Lincolnshire to north Essex, and particularly in Cambridgeshire, has one casement section only in a larger window.

In the 1680s the *sliding sash* window came in, but was closely followed by the *vertical sash* (perhaps of Dutch origin), which swept the board, and indeed was a perfect match for the Palladian, classical, and Georgian architecture of the time; it has remained in vogue. It was first used at Chatsworth (1676–80), but the earliest surviving example seems to be at Churchill House, Alcester (Ww). These sash windows have wooden glazing bars, which become narrower, from 2in (5 cm) in Queen Anne's time to $1/2$ in (1.25 cm) by 1820. Most windows are three lights wide, with usually six or nine panes in each sash. After 1800, the bars can be of metal. Iron glazing bars are common in 19th-century mill and factory buildings, and also in small warehouses, being very durable. There is an example in Little Minster Street, Winchester. "Queen Anne" style windows (*c* 1690–1720) are taller and narrower than the full Georgian (eg Great James Street, London; Tadworth Court (Sy)). Most 18th-century panes were of crown glass (cut down from the big circular sheets), but by then the central "bull's eye" (revived in some "modernised" pubs) was not used. Crown glass replaced the other type, cylinder or "muff", by the mid 18th century. Blandford (Do), rebuilt after its fire in 1731, has many original windows.

Georgian houses all over the country can often be seen with one or more windows blocked up. These are mostly filled in with brick, but some with wooden planking; many of them are painted to look like windows, grey or black with white bars. Some apparently blocked-up window spaces never had windows in them at all. This is in most cases a result of the window tax. This tax was first imposed in 1696, on the number of openings in all houses worth over £5 a year, in an attempt to recoup the Exchequer for losses on clipped or defaced old coins being called in on the issue of a new silver coinage. In 1746 a heavy excise duty on glass was also levied. From then on windows were blocked out in large numbers. The tax was increased on six occasions between 1747 and 1808, notably by Pitt in 1784 and 1802. After the Napoleonic Wars it became so unpopular that it was reduced in 1825, but it was not abolished until 1851.

A style of sash window popular in the 17th and 18th centuries is the Palladian, Gibbs, or *Venetian window*. This uses an early 16th-century Italian design, the Serliana (because first published by Serlio in 1537, but probably invented by Bramante). It has three openings, the central one arched and wider than the others. It was enthusiastically adopted by Robert Adam, eg in the Royal Society of Arts, London, 1772–4, where it is contained in an arched recess, and is very diagnostic of his work.

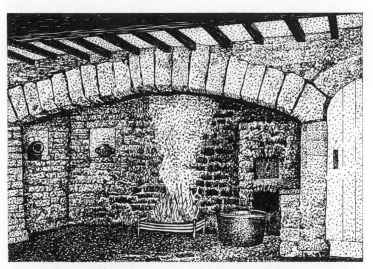

97 *A 17th-century open fireplace, with bread oven and salt-box – Longbridge, Bishopdale (NY). The bread or bake oven is the upper aperture on the right of the fire, closed by a wooden shutter; below it is an ash-oven, to make use of the heat from the ashes raked out of the bake-oven.*

The Victorians had the unhappy idea of replacing the small panes and the glazing bars of Georgian windows with plain glass, sometimes with a single vertical bar. This has continued into our own day, but the tendency is now being reversed. Plain glass totally ruins the graceful effect of the multi-paned windows.

Plate glass began to be made in England, under French licences, in 1773; in 1838 a commercial method of polishing it was discovered, and from then on the use of plate or sheet glass was universal, leading to the development of the modern float glass and its many specialised varieties. It made possible the familiar type of shop window.

French windows are long windows reaching to ground level and opening in two leaves like a pair of doors. They are found in a few houses in this country in the 17th and 18th centuries, eg York House, Twickenham (Ln) (*c* 1700). Single garden doors, popularly called French, became common at lower levels of housing in 19th-century suburbs.

Long rows of continuous windows, mullioned in stone districts, were used in the upper floors of weavers' cottages and terraces in the Pennines and north Midlands (eg Heptonstall (WY)); similar rows,

with wooden frames, were used to light workshops in the south (there are still a few left in Surrey).

Dormers were introduced (or multiplied) when floors were inserted in open halls (later 16th century), although they were used on the Continent earlier (in Belgium, Holland, and Germany they occur on medieval buildings). They became common in the 17th century in the garret floors of larger houses, and in the 18th century in terraced cottages. In Scotland they are still a very distinctive feature in single-storey (1^1/$_2$ storey) cottages, from the 18th century onwards. In the 16th and 17th centuries a more continental type was built into the tower houses and town houses; their use in such houses declined in Georgian town building, but was revived in the 19th century.

Gables

Gables lend themselves to becoming an ornamental feature of a house. Indeed, Alec Clifton-Taylor remarks on the profusion of gables in the Cotswolds, which form a central feature of the very distinctive architecture of that area. These are highlighted by a prominent coping, and may be surmounted by a ball or finial. In the 16th century, under Dutch influence, the *crow-stepped* gable was introduced. This has a series of steps up each side. It is common in eastern England, and is also very characteristic of eastern Scotland (eg Fife). In the early 17th century, also from Holland, came the so-called *Dutch gable*, whose sides are curvilinear, often in a complex manner. Mill House at Denham (Bc) has two crow-steps and two curved gables on a single front. Another type, common in south-east Scotland, is the gable carrying a chimney, which protrudes from the point.

Chimneys

In medieval vernacular houses (eg Wealden halls) heating was by way of open hearths, the smoke finding its own way out into the thatch or through the roof, sometimes by a hole or louvre. When a central hearth became inconvenient, it was moved against a fireback wall; the smoke then went up through a partitioned section of the roof (a *smoke-bay*) or into a timber and wattle and daub *smoke-hood* or hooded chimney. The smoke-bay was inefficient, and was soon replaced by a brick or stone *fireplace* (see **97**), with *flue* and *chimneystack*. The smoke-hood was better, and remained in use until the late 18th century in the Highland Zone, in conjunction with a peat fire against a fireback wall – superseded in the 19th century by a fireplace designed to burn coal. Smoke bays and hoods, and smoke-blackened areas, can still be found among the roof structures of old houses.

The Romans in Britain used chimneys on villas and major buildings. Some were of stone (usually Bath), and were "architectural" in design; many were of pottery, usually tall round pots with holes cut out of the sides, often ornamented with raised bands or incised patterns and surmounted by finials. They next occur in the 12th century (Christchurch Castle hall (Do) *c* 1160, has a plain tall round chimney; many early ones could be square or facetted). There is a wide range of designs: Woodstock (Ox), *c* 1290, has "architectural" chimneys; at Motcombe, late 13th century, they have wide openings and a finial, as has Woodlands Manor, Meare (So), early 15th century. The Vicars' Close at Wells (1348) has round stone chimneys with pierced octagonal tops. The Archbishop's Palace at Southwell, *c* 1360, has octagonal chimneys with "steeple" top, with openings. The 15th-century chimneys at St Cross Hospital, Winchester, are tall and octagonal with frilled tops (a variant of a battlemented type).

Small houses and cottages rarely had chimneys at all before the 16th century, having holes in the roof, if that. A royal decree of 1212 aimed at encouraging more fireproof chimneys, in London at least, but the effect of this was patchy. Many poorer houses everywhere, if they had chimneys at all, might have plaster ones, or timber; these have been noticed in recent years in north-west England and Cambridgeshire, and in remote parts of Scotland (eg Papil, Shetland); wicker and thatch were also used, and the latter survive in Carmarthenshire. Inclined slates are met with in slate areas, such as the Lake District.

Stone was not the only fireproof material in the Middle Ages. Pottery chimneypots were in fact in general use in large houses in southern England in the 13th century (the so-called "Sussex" type, subject of a study by Gerald Dunning in 1961). These are conical, with straight or bulging sides. They are open at the top, and may have holes in the sides as well. They are variously decorated. Of the 36 known examples, 24 are in Sussex (now in museums). Medieval pottery *roof ornaments* were also common, and often took the form of grotesque human heads or busts.

It was realised in the mid 15th century in East Anglia that brick gave better heat resistance than stone, and large houses went over to this. The fashion spread, and by the 16th and 17th centuries brick chimneystacks were being built into timber-framed houses. One is reminded of the early colonists' dwellings in Australia, wooden shacks with stone fireplaces at one end, with massive stone chimneys outside, to minimise fire risks.

In Henry VIII's time brick chimneys reached their peak of ornate decoration, and were tall and round, with prominent tops. The decoration was by way of moulded or carved brickwork, with striking

98 *A typical group of Tudor chimneys, made of moulded or carved bricks.*

effect. These chimneys are often set in rows or clusters (see **98**). Good examples are to be found at eg Hampton Court or Layer Marney (Ex). These so-called "Tudor" chimneys were imitated by the Victorians, as at Albury (Sy). From the 18th century onwards chimneypots have become smaller and plainer, and in the 19th century the plain round pot became universal (although in large or pretentious houses they could be octagonal, for example, and ornamental).

Chimneystacks are usually square or triangular, and flat-sided, but in areas where undressed stone is used, eg south-west Wales, north-west England, and Cornwall, they are round. (Medieval chimneys are well covered by Margaret Wood in *The English Medieval House* (1965).)

Secondary uses of a domestic fire include a salt box, a recess in the side of an open fireplace in which to keep salt and other commodities dry, and a bacon loft, a small room or partitioned area in the roof space, through which smoke was allowed to pass for curing hams and bacon. Bread ovens are sometimes found in open fireplaces, using heat from the fire. Another type is built into a wall (and usually protrudes through it), with its own chimney in front of the entrance, which is closed by a movable wooden lid when the oven is in use. Live coals are placed in the oven and raked out when the right heat is reached, when the bread can be put in. A fine example is at Old Tokefield, Cranleigh (Sy).

Doorways

Medieval doorways in great houses followed the architectural style of their times. The doors themselves were of planks, and often had ornate, wrought-iron straps to strengthen them, and heavy locks. These can be seen in churches all over the country (eg Selborne (Ha)). Vernacular houses of this period might have more or less ornate doorways in wood. A common type is the frameless door: the door was hung direct on the structure of the house, rather than on a door frame.

In stone areas in the 16th and 17th centuries, vernacular doorways became plain and simple, but often had decorated lintels. These could include fanciful shapes, carved heads, inscriptions (usually the initials of the couple who built or modernised the house), or the date. The Pennines and Lake counties are full of these.

Porches came in in the later 16th century (church porches are earlier, and have other functions besides giving shelter to the doorway; see page 316). They sometimes, in large houses, form part of a projection from the house, and may contain a room above the doorway.

17th- and 18th-century domestic building, in the Palladian and classical tradition, shows a rich proliferation of doorways and doorcases. Even at the vernacular level doorways could be quite architectural, with square head and often a cornice and ornamental keystone. Even in terraced cottages some elements of sophistication could creep in.

Most doorways had heads or pediments, square, triangular, semicircular, elliptical, scroll-like, reversed, or broken (with an urn or bust between lower portions of a triangle). All these contained the door itself, within a close frame. Later, arched types appear, and heads of heavy stonework. Features of this kind were not confined to the heads. Many doorways had classical side columns, applied fretwork or rosettes, or panelling at the sides of the porch. A porch effect could be adumbrated by, eg, a shell surmounting the doorway (as in a house in the South Bailey at Durham). There could be steps up to the door, and iron railings, foot-scrapers, torch extinguishers, etc.

The door itself usually had four or six raised panels. Light could be admitted to the passage or hall by a fanlight over the door. This could be a horizontal strip under a flat entablature or, quite often, a semicircular light with a more or less ornate pattern of glazing bars. Fanlights of this type are a signature of the Adam style (see **99**). If the width of the hall allowed, there could be a narrow light on each side of the door. A very fine, perhaps unrivalled, range of Georgian doorways can be seen in Chichester (see **100**).

VERNACULAR BUILDING

Vernacular is the term normally applied to buildings, usually simple and direct in style and construction, made by local people from local materials by methods using craft rather than mechanical processes (although large houses may be more elaborate). This of course gives rise to regional or even local styles. Such buildings may be dwelling houses, ancillary domestic or farm buildings, or industrial buildings such as mills or houses specially adapted for cottage industry. They may be rural or urban.

There are two main ways of constructing a house: *mass construction*, where the loads of roof, floors, and walls are conducted through the walls to a foundation which carries all the loads; and *frame construction*, where the loads are carried through the vertical elements of the frame. The former includes buildings with stone, brick, or cob walls; the latter can be divided into *box-frame* (see **101**) and *post-and-truss* construction, where the verticals form part of the walls, and *cruck* construction, in which the verticals are concealed and the wall can be of any material, stone, brick, or timber-frame. Timber-framing was normal for the whole country, but was replaced or succeeded by stone in certain areas. Brick came into use for whole houses in the 17th century. Cob and the like are very ancient.

Cruck construction

Crucks are pairs of inclined or inward-curving timbers at intervals along the length of the building, which collect the roof loads by way of side purlins and wall plates, and down to padstones or a continuous sill. Each cruck has a tie beam, collar, or yoke: the tie beam projects to carry the wall plates; the collar helps carry the side purlins; the yoke ties the crucks just below the ridge. The walls carry no load, and can be of either mass or frame construction (see **102**).

There are several variations of the full crucks, which rose from ground to roof ridge – curved trees of the required full length were not always available. The *base cruck* terminates below the upper part of the roof; it is joined by a heavy collar, above which is a separate roof construction (this form was used in late medieval large houses). The *raised cruck* rises from a solid wall. *Upper crucks* do not go down to ground level, but end at a beam carried by a mass wall. *Jointed crucks* (which have a western distribution) are in two pieces joined together. *Truncated crucks*, at collar level, enable thatch to flow over half-hipped roofs. A wall-post may rise from a cruck, not outside it. Stability was often secured by means of wind braces between purlins and the crucks.

The curious distribution of cruck buildings has led to a great deal of research into, and controversy about, the origins of crucks and the reasons for their distribution. These problems have still not been cleared up to the full satisfaction of all the authorities in this field. A notable step forward was taken in 1964 by J T Smith, with his paper, "Cruck Construction: a survey of the

99 *Adam style doorway, with side lights – Greyfriars, North Street, Chichester.*

100 *Georgian doorcase – High Petergate, York, c 1779: next to it is a torch extinguisher.*

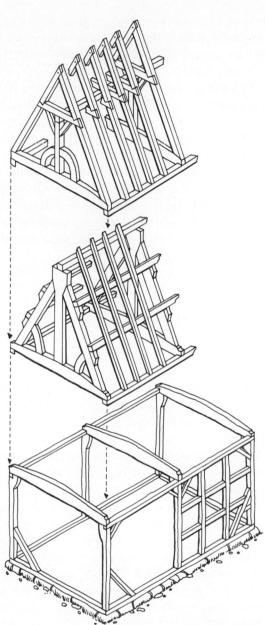

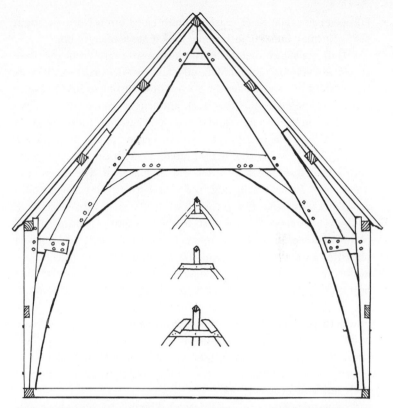

102 *Cruck construction. The crucks are the curved members, concealed within the walls and roof, and steadied by a collar. The walls carry no load.*

101 *Box-frame house construction. The posts form part of the walls, which are linked and steadied at the top by tie beams. The roof trusses contain various types of main support – here are shown a crown post based on a tie beam, and supporting a collar linking two rafters, and a king post rising to the roof ridge.*

problems", in *Medieval Archaeology* 6 (1964). In that year some 450 examples were known, nearly all in highland Britain, with outliers to the east. Most were in Yorkshire, Fylde (Lancashire), Leicestershire, and the south Welsh borders, with a scatter in other counties, but none in Lincolnshire, Cambridgeshire, Essex, East Anglia, Kent, Sussex, Surrey, Cornwall, or north of the Tyne-Solway line. Some 2,000 examples are now known, but this distribution essentially stands. There are also a few examples in north-east France, north Germany (Oldenburg and Hanover), and Venetia, and derivatives in Belgium, the Lower Rhine, and Périgord. Some of these examples date from the Iron Age.

Smith concluded that the British distribution argued a Celtic origin, and that the absence of crucks in the east and south-east ruled out an Anglo-Saxon derivation and hence a north-west

European one. For other reasons Smith ruled out a Norman origin also – Norman building techniques took quite a different line.

But the existence of local variations raises more problems. Base crucks are common in the Midlands, and two-tier crucks in Wessex (eg Glastonbury and Bradford-on-Avon tithe barns); in Herefordshire crucks are mainly in the hilly west, and trussed rafter and principal rafter roofs in the low areas and the towns. These may indeed be areas where Celtic elements were strong even after Anglo-Saxon colonisation. Another line is that buildings with central posts were once widely distributed, from the Iron Age at least. The function of crucks is to do away with ridge-posts, and create more space. Smith postulates a sequence of solutions to the problem of ridge-posts.

The cruck seems to come first, in the first four centuries AD, and perhaps earlier. The next development would have been the king post on a tie beam, still common in the north of England (except east Yorkshire). The third stage would have been nave and aisles with king post on a tie beam over the nave; aisled construction is common in Germany, to bring animals and crops under one roof, and succeeded crucks there. Finally would have come the triangular truss – tie beam and braces, with principals tenoned into the tie beam, and a ridge-piece; some examples have a collar as well. This form does not occur in south-east England and is rare on the Continent, so suggesting a likely link with crucks.

Smith also points out that there were different carpentry traditions in different strata of society; so relic techniques may be expected in humbler forms of building. Moreover, most English and Welsh crucks are late medieval – ie hall-type buildings which still suited the type of farming practised. And crucks are convenient for building longhouses.

This bald summary, omitting much interesting detail, hardly does Smith justice. But his ideas stimulated the experts for the next 20 years, and several alternatives or compromises have been suggested. One theory, for instance, seeks to explain local variations in crucks partly by the availability of pedunculate oak, which yields better and longer cruck blades than sessile oak. A recent suggestion, which challenges the Celtic origin of crucks and carries much plausibility, has been put forward by Jean Chapelot and Robert Fossier (in *Le Village et la Maison au Moyen-Age* (Paris, Hachette, 1980); English translation by Henry Cleere: *The Village and House in the Middle Ages*, 1985). Crucks, and the longhouses with which they are largely associated, have been identified with a pastoral or mixed economy as against an arable one, to explain the distribution. But Chapelot and Fossier favour a blend of economic and technical factors. The earliest cruck buildings in England are at Gomeldon (Wi), 13th century; there are few survivors before 1450, and the present distribution is therefore post-medieval. The disappearance of the cruck in the east and south-east can be linked to rising prosperity in these areas, with its growing demand for more rooms and higher living standards, and hence to the 15th-century spread of the two-storey house (which in fact began in a small way in the 13th century) and to the accompanying perfecting of the box-frame technique of construction. In these areas too the longhouse gave way to the farm with separate dwelling and outbuildings. The rising price of timber, coupled with the growing demand for naturally curved timbers for ship building in the 16th and 17th centuries, may be contributing factors.

The last word may of course still not have been said, but the question is of such interest as to justify the efforts which have been made to solve it.

Box-frame/post and truss

This entails the assembly of studs (verticals) and rails to form the frame of the wall, whose panels are then either infilled or covered with cladding. This frame is held rigid by wall plates and tie beams, and some diagonal members (braces). The roof is a separate item, held rigid by a collar purlin joining the collars. The joints at the head of the wall posts are complex, and arranged so as to hold post, wall plate, and tie beam rigid (see **103**).

Infilling may be wattle and daub or, later, stone or brick nogging (rarely, split oak pales woven round oak staves). Cladding may be weatherboarding, tile, slate, mathematical tile, or lath and plaster; the latter could be rendered and, in eastern England, pargetted.

Jetties became popular in the 15th, 16th, and 17th centuries. These were stud walls rising from a sole-plate carried on projecting joists. They gave more space to the upper floors, but may have been mainly for effect (see **104**).

In late medieval houses in Lincolnshire, Leicestershire, and coastal Lancashire, mud and stud walls were used; these had no stud and rail panels, and the posts may rest on the earth.

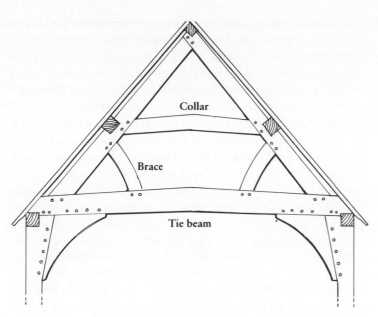

103 *The structure of a roof truss in box-frame construction. The walls are held rigid by a tie beam, which supports a frame into which are set the ridge and purlins on which the roof rests. This frame is strengthened by a transverse collar, and may be also braced (as here). There may also be a crown post or two queen posts between the tie beam and the collar.*

Roofing of solid-wall houses

Roofs may be single, having rafters only, or double, with rafters and purlins; in either case a ridge is unusual. The structure may be divided into *bays* by trusses, or run uninterrupted from end to end. Purlins may lie between trusses (butt purlins), or may rest on the trusses (through purlins). Roofs may end in *hips* or *gables*. A double rafter roof often has *crown post* and collar purlin; in a single roof there may be a boarded ceiling (barrel vault) under the collar. Purlins are usually found with crucks, but can also support rafters which are also supported by a ridge purlin and wall plates.

A common form is trussed rafters steadied by collar plate and crown post. Varieties of cruck construction were also used, such as raised or upper crucks. Some roof forms were more common with solid walls than with timber frame, particularly the king post truss, consisting of tie beam, king post, ridge purlin, and principal rafters which carry the side purlins. Struts and braces were often inserted

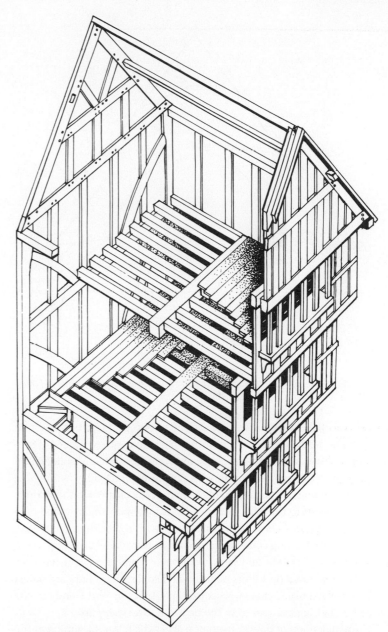

104 *The structure of jetties. The floor joists of first or higher floors are carried out beyond the wall plate of the floor below. The outer wall of the floor so extended consists of upright studs rising from a sole-plate at the ends of the joists. This can be repeated on higher floors, and projecting windows can also be fitted into the scheme.*

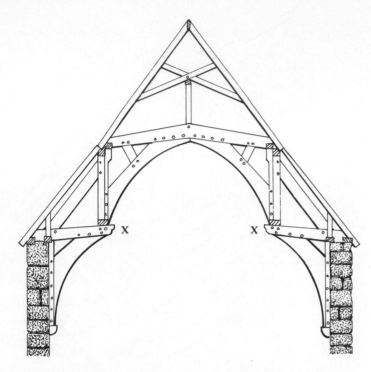

105 *A roof-truss of a large building – a hall or a church – showing hammer-beams (at X), and the system of braces up to the collar.*

between these members to steady the structure. Such construction continued from medieval times into the 19th century. Indeed, 18th- and 19th-century farm buildings, mills, etc were often as solidly built as medieval houses, although with pine or elm instead of oak. These had either king posts, with struts from the base of these to the purlins, or *queen posts* to the ends of the collar. Double-pile houses could now have an M roof (where the central gully was higher than the eaves), supported on a long collar with two supports from the tie beam. In the 19th century joints and pegs were often replaced by iron bolts or straps. (A crown post joins tie beam and collar; the collars are linked by a collar purlin. Queen posts join the tie beam to the ends of the collar. A king post rises from the tie beam to a ridge purlin.)

An indication of date is given by a *jowl*, which is a thickening at the top of a wall post running up behind the wall plate (which sits on the post) to meet the tie beam and give extra stability to it. This was not used in early work or in work after the first few years of the 17th century.

An open hall can dispense with tie beams by using *arch braces*, which rest on the principal rafters, or on a hammer-beam, and underpin the collar, fitting closely to both. *Hammer-beams* are used in halls and churches but rarely in ordinary houses; they are short members projecting at wall plate level (supported by a brace), and themselves supporting a queen post (or the upper arch brace) (see **105**).

Roofs with base crucks surmounted by short principals are a feature of a well-defined class of medieval house. They have been analysed by N W Alcock and M W Barley (1972), who identified over 90 such houses, west of a line from Selby to Chichester. Of these, 23 are barns; most were put up for the gentry, rather than for great houses, which only accounted for five, with a few for abbeys (eg Glastonbury, *c* 1180). Five are urban, mostly of religious guilds, but many of these may have been lost. They begin mostly in the 13th century; many date from 1250 to 1320, and many more were built by 1350. The base cruck probably originated as a compromise between the cruck tradition and the aisled hall tradition, which had higher social status. The base cruck was adapted from crucks to free large buildings from aisle-posts, when suitable timber could be had. In the 15th century local schools of base crucks developed (Kent/Sussex, Midlands, West Midlands and Wales, south-west England).

Another feature of vernacular architecture which needs explanation is the crown-post roof. The most detailed study of this is by J M Fletcher and P S Spokes (in *Medieval Archaeology* 6 (1964)). This form of roof structure originated in north-west Europe in the late 12th century, but had an independent development in England. The ridgeless roof with uniform rafters (the Romanesque form) had a longitudinal instability, which was relieved by means of a central purlin supported by a tie beam and crown post. There are good 13th-century examples at Charney Bassett Manor (Ox) and Old Soar, Plaxtol (Kt). The other early European form had principal rafters (or crucks) crossing at the apex and supporting a ridge-pole. This form was submerged in south and eastern England by the Romanesque form, under Norman influence, but re-emerged in later medieval times in the form of "double-framing"; it supplanted, except in the extreme south-east, the Romanesque form, by then anglicised.

The development sequence, useful for dating, is: Carolingian-Romanesque, by 950–1200 – vertical and horizontal braces; post-Romanesque, 1180–1270 – diagonal bracing and no purlin (scissors braces, eg at Ely nave, 1245), secondary rafters (eg Great

Coxwell barn, mid 13th century, which also has king post), and longitudinal braces; these led to, 1200 on, braced collars and collars with purlin, with king post (continental form) or crown post (English form).

King and crown posts were on the increase in France, with purlins, early in the 13th century, king posts being more usual, and were in use for several centuries. Crown posts have their own development, thus: 1220–1280, square or chamfered, braces straight, tie beam uncambered, almost square in section; 1280–1310, long and octagonal, with mouldings to cap and base, tie beam with slight camber and roll-mouldings; 1310–1360, short, braces often curved, tie beam well cambered, made of divided balks. Traditions froze for a generation or more after the Black Death, and when they resumed they followed local traditions of *c* 1350. Thus, crown-post roofs were built in the southeastern counties in the 15th century, because principal rafters had not reached there by 1350. By the second half of the 15th century there was general use of a crown post with no braces or central purlin, merely as a support to the collar. There was some overlap, but these forms form a useful dating sequence. The roof forms reinforce changes in window tracery and in mouldings.

Perhaps fewer than 1% of 13th-century roofs have survived, yet these show developments in France and England to be parallel. Southeast England copied France till about 1270. The developments that stand out as English are the Edwardian roof with principal rafters and the short, decorated crown posts in 14th-century halls and churches.

As well as chronological sequences, there are also regional differences in timber-framing details. J T Smith has analysed the various forms of brace and decoration, and has deduced the existence of three traditions of carpentry: eastern, close studding and tension bracing; western, square panelling and angle bracing (with a correlation with crucks); northern, the interrupted sill (ie the wall posts go into the ground between lengths of sill, as against the continuous sills of the Midlands and south (this has a correlation with king post roofs).

These findings of Smith's have met with general acceptance; there is thus no need to see an antithesis between cruck and box-frame traditions. They appear to be both aspects of the one tradition of building timber-framed houses, and the wide variety and endless detail spring from local circumstances.

It should be borne in mind, when looking at timber-framed buildings, that their appearance is not necessarily the same as in their early days. Highly ornamented houses were no doubt intended to be seen as such, and left black and white (or another colour); but most frames were functional. They were therefore either left as natural timber members and infilled (nogging could be decorative), or they might be completely clad, to protect them from the weather; the plaster might be limewashed or treated with another colour, such as "Suffolk pink". The Victorians, however, had a tendency to expose the beams, and to paint them black. This does nothing but shorten the life of the building. We are still largely at this point, although much contemporary restoration is sensitive enough to return to the colour of the natural wood.

It will be seen that this field is a highly complex one; the above account is a simplification. Many details have to be taken into account as one examines an old house. Moreover, few houses have not been altered, extended, split up, and recombined through the centuries, and their history can often be quite hard to unravel. Perseverance and practice are necessary; there are also Vernacular Architecture groups in most counties which will give support. A good introductory guide is R W Brunskill's *Houses* (Collins 1982); there are also books on the local houses, such as Brunskill's on those of the Lake Counties, or John L Baker's *A Picture of Surrey* (1980), or his book on Hampshire; or, in finer detail, K W E Gravett on the timber-framed houses of Kent, or Joan Harding on the old houses of Charlwood (Sy).

VERNACULAR HOUSES

R W Brunskill (*Illustrated Handbook of Vernacular Architecture* (Faber 1970) conveniently divides houses into *great houses*, which are not part of the vernacular tradition, and three vernacular classes, *large houses*, *small houses* and *cottages*. But there are many gradations and overlaps, and social movements through the centuries. Thus houses tend to decline – a manor house becomes a farmhouse, which is later divided into cottages, and finally becomes a farm building or workshop. (This trend can of course be reversed, and a pair of cottages can be converted into, or back into, a house – but this takes us away from the topic. There is also the deliberate Arts and Crafts "Vernacular" of the late 19th and early 20th centuries.)

The large house exceeds the ordinary vernacular in having, as well as size, a conscious aesthetic element; an architect or good materials may be employed, and the finish has style, not always only local style.

The cottage is of local materials, and may be built by the occupier. In the late 18th and 19th centuries the farmhouse too might have pretensions, and even the cottages of the late 19th century could be of national rather than local tradition. Today nearly every house has some element of the "polite" (derived partly or wholly from formal architecture), and the vernacular is at an end.

Brunskill also draws attention to the *vernacular threshold*: houses high in the social scale survive longest, those of middle level are more recent, and those at the bottom more recent still. Thus we can see the houses of medieval knights but not generally of medieval farmers, of 17th-century yeomen but not of cottagers, but of 19th-century artisans at the humblest level. The vernacular threshold is regional also. The *Great Rebuilding* (see below) took place from 1570 to 1620 in the lowlands of England, but from 1670 to 1720 in the north of England, and later still in Wales. The later the rebuilding, the further it extends down the social scale. Perishable materials, such as timber and cob, continued in use until the late 19th century. There is a *vernacular zone* between the two thresholds.

The social classes and types of house

A cardinal feature of English society is the fluidity of the social grades. There are very many examples of families who have risen, or fallen, in the social scale over the generations, and sometimes in one generation. Intermarriage and mobility are so common that Stenton could say, in noting the vagueness of the definitions of persons in Domesday, that these reflect "blurring of class distinctions and confusion of personal relationships". It is thus hazardous to attempt to equate a given social status with a particular type of house. Yet the attempt should be made, even at the risk of oversimplification.

Anglo-Saxon society had three broad divisions: the *unfree*, the *free*, and the *lords*. The unfree (*theow*), bound to the estates and providing major services on the land, consisted of *serfs* or slaves, *cottars* and *gebur* or smallholders who owed services, and *geneat* or the "followers" of the thane. The free *ceorls* might still owe some military or household services, but farmed their own land. Above these were the manorial lords, *thanes* or *gesith* (companions of kings or nobles). Broadly, the cottars lived in one-room huts or sunken huts (see below), the freemen in the larger square houses revealed by excavation, and the thanes in halls. But the reality might not be quite so clear-cut, and, in any case, manorial tenure did not run in the Danelaw, the far north, East Anglia, Kent, and the south-west. In these areas the life of the people was centred in the village, not the manor. Here the peasants moved direct from payments in kind to payments in coin. Indeed, in East Anglia and the Danelaw, there were large numbers of peasants both legally free and economically independent. In northern England and Scotland the peasants were still paid in kind.

The manorial system was most complete in the south Midlands and the south. Here in the late 13th century, out of some 650 villages studied, over half did not tally with manors; a manor could contain all or part of several villages, and one village could contain all or parts of several manors.

Slavery declined after the conquest, but cottars (or *bordars*) were still bound to the land. The *villeins* (the Anglo-Saxon *gebur*, higher peasants) were technically unfree in Domesday, but by 1100 the word meant just "villager", and carried no suggestion of unfree status; villeins normally owed feudal service, but held shares in the common fields. Villeins held village and manorial offices. The vast majority of the population were still unfree in certain respects until into the 14th century.

The freemen comprised the *sokemen* and *yeomen*, freeholders farming their own lands (but in some cases, eg in Kent, paying rent or giving some sort of service), and the *burgesses* in the towns – merchants and craftsmen. Above these were the manorial lords (*gentlemen* and *knights*) and the *nobles*. The gentlemen included the *serjeants* (esquires, stewards, etc), who performed some feudal service other than military.

In medieval Wales there were two systems: *bondmen* living in hamlets, and *freemen* living in dispersed homesteads.

In the post-medieval period (from the later 15th century) the classes settled down into *labourers* (cottagers – free by 1600 but very poor); *husbandmen* (smallholders – tenants, practising subsistence farming); *yeomen* (freeholders – often farming quite large farms, and sometimes richer than lower gentry); then the *gentry* and squirearchy, and the *nobility*.

In Scotland feudalism had decayed by the 17th century, when the lairds entered into tenancies with their retainers; the rents, however, were mostly in kind, under the prevailing clan system.

Types of house

It would be convenient to correlate Brunskill's classification of houses (see above) with these social grades. Thus, cottars or labourers would live in one- or two-roomed *cottages*; villeins, husbandmen, or lesser yeomen in three-roomed *small houses*; higher yeomen and gentry in *large houses*; and nobility in *great houses*. It is obvious that this scheme is too clear-cut, and is partly invalidated not only by the constant social mobility and blurred distinctions, but by differences in wealth in different parts of the country, each with its own traditions, climate, geology, and type of farming. But the distinction between the Lowland and Highland Zones, with an intermediate (hybrid) zone, does apply broadly to houses, and also reflects arable versus pastoral or mixed farming.

There are social sources of confusion too; for example, a cottage may have been occupied by a son or female relative of a higher grade farmer. Archaeological evidence is hardly available in such a case; the evidence may come from records or inventories. (In the 20th century it is quite acceptable for a gentleman to live in a "cottage".)

Few, if any, cottages, or indeed other peasant houses, survive before the 16th century. Not only were they of flimsy construction – wood, cob, etc – but villages were rebuilt or repaired in every generation, as tastes and requirements changed with new occupiers, and as the structures decayed. When this happened village centres could shift and houses be realigned or built on new sites. And many villages were replanned by their lords in the 12th century.

The Great Rebuilding

The percipience of W G Hoskins in recognising the phenomenon which he called *The Great Rebuilding* (first enunciated in "The Rebuilding of England, 1570–1640" (*Past and Present*, Nov 1953), and reprinted in *Provincial England* (1963)) shed a brilliant light on a phase of transition in architectural history, and explained much that seemed obscure. In many ways, the Great Rebuilding represents the culmination of the vernacular. After it there is only decline.

Hoskins dates the peak of this movement as 1575–1625. Its surviving evidence is more rural than urban now, but it took place in the towns too; there it is masked by the higher rate of replacement of buildings. What happened was the rebuilding or substantial modernisation of medieval houses, together with a great increase in furnishings and household equipment. This was sudden and very widespread (eg in Devon some 1,000 farmhouses were treated in this way). Houses were not usually completely rebuilt, but modernised. This comprised inserting a ceiling in the hall, so producing a living room and parlour on the ground floor and bedrooms above, and requiring a staircase; the partition of larger rooms, which meant more windows and fireplaces; plaster ceilings and perhaps wainscot in the main rooms; perhaps also a new porch and entry; glazed windows; the improvement of equipment, eg chairs instead of benches. Hoskins was able to trace this all over England, and recognised that rebuilding was later in the north of England, and even as late as the 18th century in the four northern counties.

A concomitant feature was the building of new houses on new sites, in fact almost entirely cottages and farm buildings. The activity in cottage building in the lowlands generally was greater than in any century since the 13th, and there was much conversion of barns etc to dwellings. This denoted an increase in rural population (eg at Brigstock (Nh) some 40 new houses were built from 1600 to 1637, and others enlarged or modernised; in the manor of Epworth and adjacent parishes, 100 new cottages were built in the 40 years to 1630). Not everyone had a new house, of course, but the general raising of living standards – comfort and equipment – is unmistakeable (except, as yet, in the four northern counties).

Most of the Great Rebuilding was the work of freeholders – the bigger husbandmen, the yeomen, and the lesser gentry. Since the 1540s these social groups had relatively fixed expenses against rising selling prices. Labour costs rose indeed, but wages lagged well behind prices and conversion of land to pasture farming saved more labour. So from the mid 16th century to the Civil Wars the yeomen could save money. At first they put it into their farms, but from the 1560s into their houses and domestic standards. (Suppliers of goods responded with satisfaction to this sudden rise in demand – witness the lively recrudescence of the glass industry in the 1570s.) After 1570 more and more could afford it.

Hoskins thought that the Great Rebuilding led to a rise in population, which in turn led to more improvements and much new building. Higher living standards include more privacy, hence more rooms, and also functional rooms instead of the hugger-mugger of the Middle Ages. So two floors were needed, and the servants

211

could be separated from the family. The higher gentry had begun to do this in the late 15th and early 16th century, adopting the new style developed in Italy in the 15th century. By the early 17th century most of the rural population above the cottager level had followed suit. Houses of wealthy merchants in the towns show the same multiplication of rooms. By the mid 17th century the typical farmer's house had three to six rooms, and the bigger yeoman's eight to ten.

The development of this is interesting. Greater use of coal and glass (giving more warmth, ventilation, and light), better and more varied food, and the greater use of herbs, led to less infant mortality, perhaps higher fertility, and a sharp rise in population (doubled in the towns). So by the mid 17th century congestion began again, the benefits of the Great Rebuilding were annulled, and, in Hoskins' words, "a century of endemic sickness set in".

This is a fascinating picture, but it may in fact be too sharply drawn (although its value in stimulating thought and research is unquestionable). R W Brunskill, in 1970, had already spaced the Great Rebuilding out, as 1570–1620 in southern England, 1670–1720 in northern England, and later still in Wales and the four northernmost counties. Recent research goes further. R Machin (in The Great Rebuilding: a Reassessment (*Past and Present* 77 (1977)) suggests that an 18th- rather than a 17th-century rebuilding was quite widespread. He questions a Great Rebuilding at a specific period, and thinks we should look rather at the successive rebuildings of vernacular houses from the late 16th to the early 18th century, and their eventual replacement, later in the 18th century, by copybook designs, allowing all along for regional variations in timing.

The end of the vernacular

Vernacular building and styles continued into the 17th century, and followed their traditional course well into the 18th. Houses of the early 17th century are indeed hard to distinguish from late Tudor ones, and much 18th-century rural building is very like much from the 17th century. At the upper end of the social scale of building, the vernacular was given a jolt by the introduction by Inigo Jones of Palladian architecture, which at once influenced great and even large houses, and which spread downwards gradually.

But a more immediate blow was struck by the Great Fire of London in 1666, which had traumatic repercussions throughout the country. The fire risk inherent in timber-framed buildings, particularly in the congested towns, was in fact recognised in Elizabeth's time. A proclamation in 1580, reinforced by an Act of 1592, laid down that there was to be no new building on new foundations within three miles of the City of London, and no subdivision of existing houses or letting rooms to lodgers. Similar proclamations followed up to 1630, when it was laid down that any new houses on old foundations were to be of brick and stone. But these measures were largely ignored.

The Great Fire introduced a note of urgency. The Act for the Rebuilding of the City of London (1667) provided that houses were to be built of brick and stone, with a minimum of external timberwork, and it regulated various details of materials and design. This Act, although applying strictly only to the London disaster, was taken as a model by other towns and spelt the end of the vernacular. It let in a new breed of architects, developers, and speculators, who proceeded to lay out the new squares and extensions of London in the new style, materials, and methods. Brick and stone were in, timber was out; standardised designs were in, informality was out.

But the risk of fire remained, and the 18th century was punctuated by attempts to reduce it. The Building Act of 1707 abolished the wooden eaves cornice; the Building Act of 1709 laid down that window frames were to be recessed at least four inches from the external face wall. These Acts were not however always obeyed, which complicates the dating of many houses. In 1774 all previous measures were consolidated in a single Act, under which most of the window frame was to be set within the brickwork of the reveals, so that only a thin strip of wood was showing. This did at last produce a diagnostic effect.

Later Acts dealt progressively more with planning than with building. Two relevant ones in this context are the Building Act of 1844, which regulated the width of new streets and the ratio between height of buildings and width of streets, and an instrument of 1894 which restricted the height of buildings to 80ft; the effect of this is shown dramatically by the buildings along the Albert Embankment west of Lambeth Bridge.

However, in rural areas, the vernacular trickled on, mostly in cottages; larger houses, in the main, increasingly adopted the new styles. Cottages rarely had fewer than two rooms by 1640. In the

18th and early 19th century cottages might be of one, 1¹/₂, or two storeys, with few windows, ladders instead of staircases, two rooms on the ground floor, perhaps an outshut, and not all rooms heated. Farmhouses and hall houses were often converted into cottages (and many converted back again in recent years!).

Christopher Powell (in *Discovering Cottage Architecture* (1984)) distinguishes three phases of the final decline of the vernacular: 1750–1815, the building of the pattern-book farm and estate cottages; 1815–1875, rural housing (by small builders and speculators); 1875–1914, cottages designed by architects and developers, under controlled standards. These phases represent in fact a steady departure from the vernacular, which was all but over by the 1870s. Estate cottages and workers' cottages, rural and urban, were more and more "polite" and/or standardised; by 1914 the vernacular was over, and after then no fresh country cottages were built. Powell points out that the old distinction between vernacular and polite cottages had gone, and was replaced by a distinction between "polite functional" and "polite ornamental". The world of Flora Thompson had passed away.

PRE-CONQUEST HOUSES

Prehistoric

The main thrust of this book being essentially post-Roman, there is no need to do more than adumbrate the houses of prehistoric times, and that only in so far as they have a possible bearing on later buildings.

The caves, rock shelters, and flimsy huts of skins and branches of the Palaeolithic and Mesolithic hunter-gatherers have no aftermath in this context; some Mesolithic features continued into the late Neolithic, but then ceased.

The first farmers to live in Britain arrived from western Europe about 4400 BC, and their period, the Neolithic, runs on till about 2200 BC. Their houses were altogether more substantial than those of the nomadic hunter-gatherers. The western European tradition, which they brought with them, favoured a circular house form. But round and rectangular traditions seem to coexist all over Europe, and

evidence for both forms is found in Britain, as well as a variety of small houses of nondescript or irregular shape. Large Neolithic houses were both round and rectangular, but as time went on, through the Bronze Age and into the Iron Age, the round form progressively predominated. The circle was in fact a powerful theme in prehistoric Britain: the henge monument and the stone circle seem indigenous in this country. Against this, there are whole villages of rectangular houses on the Continent, particularly east of the Rhine (eg Köln-Lindenthal). There are similar dichotomies in the shape of megalithic tombs, with passage graves of western European affinities under round barrows, and gallery graves with northern and eastern European connections under long, oval, or trapezoidal barrows; while Bronze Age and Iron Age barrows are round. Some areas contain both traditions. If these tombs represent houses (however distantly and symbolically) among other things, this may well indicate the mixture of peoples, origins, and traditions of the Neolithic population of Britain. It will be seen that the post-Roman Celts reverted to, or continued, the round houses of their Iron Age, and that the Anglo-Saxon immigrants brought with them the northern European idea of rectangular houses.

In fact very few domestic sites of the Neolithic or the early Bronze Age are known from excavations. It may be that the expectation that houses would be found near barrows or other monuments was ill-founded; the dead may have been buried away from the farmsteads, which may well have been on lower, richer land, now covered by soil movement downhill. Most excavated houses are rectangular, like those from the early Neolithic at Haldon or Fengate (Peterborough) or the late Neolithic house at Mount Pleasant (Gl) – 5.7 x 5.3m, with stone footings, posts, and pitched roof; that at Ronaldsway (IM) is similar. The famous village at Skara Brae (Or) (see **106**, and also **107** facing page 266) was preserved under blown sand, and because, the area being treeless, the houses were built of stone slabs, gives an unusually complete idea of the contents of such houses. The houses are rectangular with rounded corners, linked by narrow passages, and contain beds, cupboards, hearths, and other furniture; the average size is 4.5x6m. Many Neolithic houses are oval or irregular. In Shetland some 60 houses have survived which can be associated with the builders of chamber tombs; a fine example is at Stanydale, a large, oval, stone-walled house with rooms partitioned off round the inside walls; no doubt the roof was of branches and thatch. Some Neolithic barrows contain so-called "mortuary houses", which may reflect, or

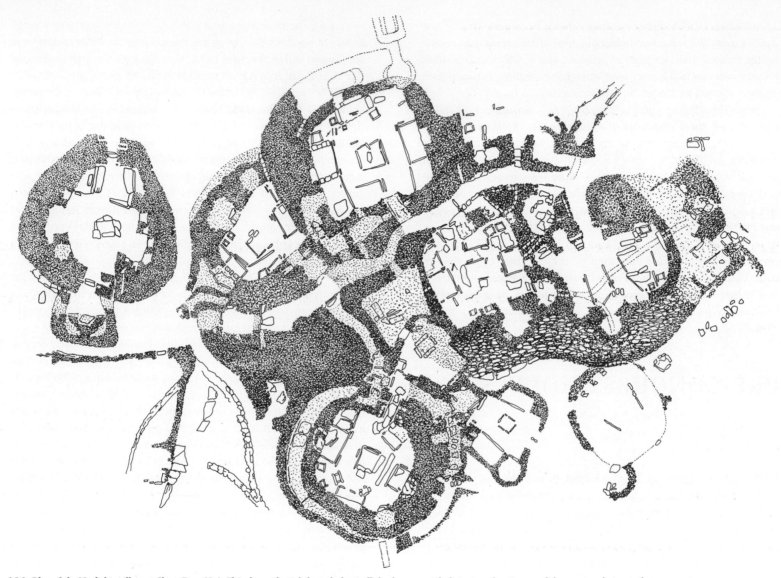

106 *Plan of the Neolithic village at Skara Brae (Or). This shows the tightly packed unicellular houses, with their stone furniture, and the passages between them.*

actually be, houses of the living given over to the dead; these are wooden square huts, with timber-framed walls and central post supporting a ridged roof (eg Fussells Lodge barrow (Wi)). Such structures continued into the Bronze Age (c 2200–700 BC). At Kemp Howe, a barrow at Cowlam (Hu), a long hut, sunk in the ground, had six posts and was roofed with timber covered with earth and stones. Such houses may reflect influences from northern Europe.

Several henge monuments have been found to contain circular settings of posts, which may have been roofed and were probably ceremonial buildings; such are Durrington Walls and Marden (Wi).

Few houses of the users of Beakers have been identified; but from then on, throughout the Bronze Age, rectangular houses seem to be superseded by round or oval ones. Round houses found at Downpatrick, Ireland, may give clues to their nature; these were 12ft 8in (3.9m) and 31ft 6in (9.7m) in diameter, and had posts and gulleys which were bedding trenches for close-set timbers. An oval house at Beacon Hill, Flamborough, had walls of wattle or turf. A round house at Gwithian (Co), 14ft 8in (4.5m) in diameter, had a central post and a post circle. At Northton, Harris, the walls were drystone. At Belle Tout (Sx) there were three circular houses, one rectangular, and one trapezoidal. Many earth circles or ring-ditches of the Bronze Age may be the remains of houses (eg Rams Hill (Bk)). The "palisaded farms" of the Iron Age in Northumberland, Roxburgh, and north Wales are a continuing Bronze Age form.

Several sites in southern England from the middle or late Bronze Age have yielded round houses, such as Thorny Down (Wi), Chalton (Ha), and Black Patch and Plumpton Plain (Sx); at Shearplace Hill (Do) a round hut was built of concentric posts, and was thatched. In the Highland Zone huts were commonly round and stone-built, such as those in the hillfort of Mam Tor (Db) or the spectacular enclosed village at Grimspound, Dartmoor (Dv).

Immigrants in the later Bronze Age from central Europe brought with them their tradition of rectangular houses, and these coexisted with the native round houses into the Iron Age (c 700 BC to AD 43). Thus at Crickley Hill (Gl), there were long rectangular and round houses, and also small buildings on four (sometimes six) posts called "granaries", though other uses are possible. These have been found at many sites, including large numbers at hillforts such as Croft Ambrey (He) or Danebury (Ha); one of their functions may have been to store local agricultural surpluses. Some round houses of this period have a single ring of posts, some with a central post (eg Maiden Castle (Do)), while some have a double ring – a Bronze Age type. A very large house at Little Woodbury (Wi) (a classic excavation at which storage pits were found, thus opening up a new appreciation of farming techniques) was 14m in diameter, and had a double ring of posts and four central posts as well (deduced from excavated post holes). A house with double ring of posts, entrance porch, and central hearth, found at Pimperne (Do), was reconstructed (see 108 and 109) at the Butser Ancient Farm, near Petersfield (Ha), where the farming processes of the Iron Age are being reassessed.

In the Highland Zone there are several types of round stone houses, from the irregular courtyard houses of Cornwall (eg Chysauster) to the duns, wheelhouses, and brochs (see 110, 111, and 112) of Scotland.

Iron Age types continued into the Roman period in less Romanised areas, and perhaps also, for some of this time, for natives in Romanised areas (cf the round stone huts in the hillfort of Tre'r Ceiri (Cn)).

Roman

In terms of houses, the Romans may be seen as introducing, encouraging, or even imposing a totally alien Mediterranean tradition on Britain, although Roman influences had certainly been reaching Gaul and, in a small measure, Britain before they arrived. It was a foreign interlude, which ignored the past and had little influence on the immediate future (the Celtic and Anglo-Saxon "Dark Ages"), but none the less, while it lasted, made profound changes in the way of life of the provincials. The Anglo-Saxons brought their own traditions with them, and in any case, by the time (mid 5th century) they began to arrive in appreciable numbers, Roman civilisation and buildings were things of the past. The Celts in the west survived with their own culture, and however Romanised they felt or tried to be, their buildings, even their palaces, were only sketchy reminiscences of the Roman grandeur.

Roman houses, including public buildings, were usually built with timber frames on sleeper beams or stone plinths in the early days of the province, and were often rebuilt in stone in the 2nd century. A

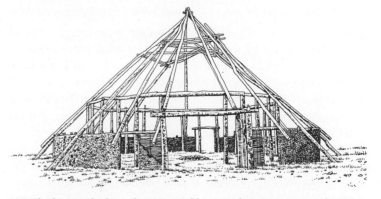

108 *The framework of a prehistoric round house, under construction at the Butser Ancient Farm (Ha) (based on an excavated Iron Age house at Pimperne (Do)).*

109 *The Pimperne house reconstructed. The walls below the thatched roof are of wattle and daub.*

good example is the Flavian timber basilica at Silchester, replaced in the 2nd century by a stone one. Detailed information exists on the whole range of buildings from the unique palace of Fishbourne (Sx) to villas (large country houses), and urban houses, shops, and workshops of all types. In Martin Biddle's words, urban houses were "thoroughly Romanised timber buildings with tiled roofs, painted walls, glazed windows, and the occasional mosaic floor" – one might add the occasional hypocaust also (see **113**). And of course what distinguishes totally a Roman town from the inchoate urbanism of the Iron Age *oppida* is the presence of public buildings – forum, basilica, civic temple, baths, theatre, amphitheatre – and town planning itself. The buildings of the forts – *principia*, barracks, stores, etc are

something else again. The entire scale had changed, as it did with the Norman conquest and again in the 20th century.

But such buildings had little or no aftermath, at least not for the next 500 years or so. They will not therefore be described in detail; ample accounts will be found in the many excellent books on Roman towns (eg John Wacher *The Towns of Roman Britain*, Batsford (1975), Guy de la Bédoyère *Roman Towns in Britain*, Batsford/English Heritage (1992)), and Roman villas (eg A L F Rivet (ed) *The Roman Villa in Britain*, Routledge & Kegan Paul (1969), or John Percival, *The Roman Villa*, Batsford (1976)).

But one thread must be followed, from the Iron Age (at least) through the Romans to the Saxons – the aisled hall, house, or barn.

An *aisled hall* is a rectangular building with two rows of posts along its length, supporting the roof and leaving spaces or aisles along each long wall. The average width of the nave or central space is about 20ft (6m), and of the aisles 8–10ft (2.5–3m); the posts are some 8–10ft apart. The length varies widely, from some 40–100ft (12.3–30.7m).

There are two basic types of Roman villa in Britain: (1) the *corridor* (see **114**), a series of rooms leading off a corridor, which develops by the 4th century into the *courtyard* (see **115**) type – not a Mediterranean house with a central *atrium* but a corridor house with wings developed into a courtyard; and (2) the *basilical* or barn type (see **116**). These two types interact, and some plans are difficult to unravel; indeed, very few plans of the thousand or so Roman villas

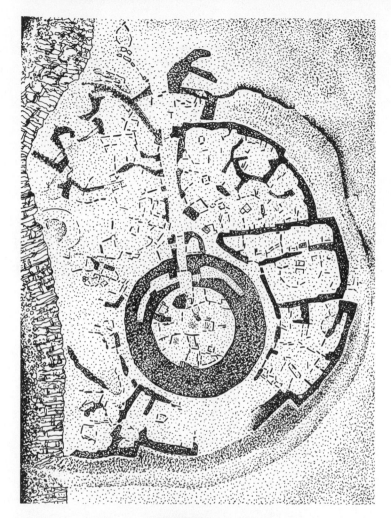

110–11 *A broch and its associated village – Gurness (Or). 110 plan; 111 view. The broch tower was once considerably higher; the village is enclosed in walls and ditches, and the whole is built on the edge of a geo (left), early centuries AD.*

112 *The very impressive broch of Mousa (Zd), with its encircling wall, and built, like so many, on the sea's edge.*

217

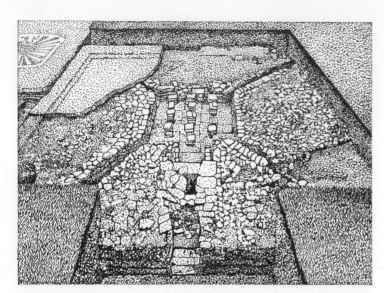

113 *Roman hypocaust system (Fishbourne): this consists of a furnace and flue to a central chamber with pillars (pilae) to support the floors of the room, and other channels taking hot air to the walls.*

in Britain are alike. Both types originate in the Iron Age of north-west Europe (northern Gaul, Belgium, the Rhineland, Frisia, Lower Saxony, and Denmark), and were presumably introduced into Roman Britain by immigrants from these areas or were built for British magnates by architects influenced by northern European traditions (see **117**).

One early (Iron Age) type of corridor house, exemplified in Britain at Iwerne (Do), consists of a single long room with a small room or rooms at one end. This is a native type, still found in derivatives in Celtic areas today. This two-roomed form is common in northern Gaul and Germany, in houses as well as outbuildings (cf Stroud (Gl), where the large room was used for livestock, the smaller as a granary). This type was thus originally a stall and dwelling, with variant use of each element. Some buildings of this type are aisled "halls" with a room outside the aisled part at one end (eg Spoonley Wood (Gl)). This villa is a case combining the two-roomed cottage with the basilical house. Both these elements have a common origin, or one may have evolved from the other; the latter is more probable, as Applebaum points out – the house at Ezinge Warf, Groningen, Holland (1st century BC) is an aisled hall subdivided. Some villas in Germany are two-roomed houses with wing rooms added at the corners,

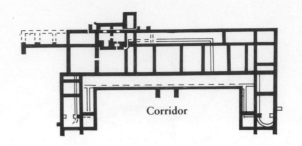

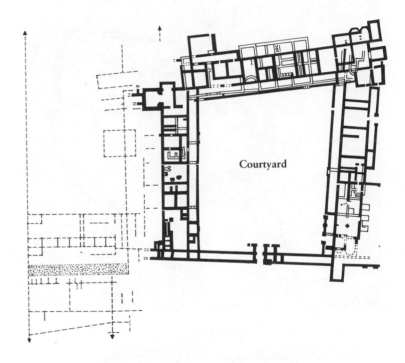

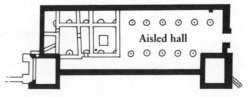

114–16 *Nearly all the Roman villas in Britain fall into one of three types – 114 corridor; 115 courtyard; 116 basilica or aisled hall – or combinations of these.*

and joined by a verandah (ie a corridor villa). In other cases the two-roomed building became an outbuilding with economic, not residential, functions.

Several villas in Britain also show these features – Titsey (Sy) is a hall with wing room at one end (with baths and other rooms added in the 2nd century); Camerton (So) has a large central hall with corridor and wing projections (AD 270–350); Colerne (Wi) has a central hall, surrounded by rooms, some leading off the corridor. The range of variations is wide. The corridor type reached Britain in a developed state; in the 1st century AD houses such as Ditchley and Hartlip had wing rooms integral with the corridor plan, and the hall shrunken and merged into a continuous range. Adaptations continued throughout the Roman period.

The "hall" type continued in use, but was relegated to buildings or outbuildings for farmhands or farm use. The basilical house can be classified as (after Applebaum): (1) the independent self-contained farm residence; (2) the same, wholly or partly readapted for residence, with agricultural functions in other buildings; (3) the purely economic building (for workers, livestock, and crops), subsidiary to the residence.

In Frisia the plan originated in a stock-rearing society, and the aisles were used for cattle stalls; but in some cases the workers also used the aisles, with the farmer's family at one end. The aisle subdivisions could also hold stores or have craft uses. A very wide variety of uses is possible. Most British basilical farmsteads belonged to a mixed economy, as did those in Lower Saxony.

Of course, the Roman villa in Britain far outstrips in variety, ingenuity, and complexity the relative simplicity and monotony of its continental antecedents, but it remains a curious fact that this notable contribution to Roman Britain is strictly an import and an interlude. When the Anglo-Saxons came to Britain it was as though Romanised buildings had never existed; they brought the traditions of their homelands with them, and ignored or avoided the meaningless remnants of the Empire.

Anglo-Saxon

This period covers the 5th to 11th centuries – early, 400–600; middle, 600–800; late, 800–1066.

The Anglo-Saxons were a people of lowland farmers, and settled essentially the Lowland Zone of Britain. They came from north

117　*The facade of a Roman aisled building – Meonstoke (Ha) (from excavated evidence).*

Germany and southern Denmark, and similar peoples from Jutland and Frisia also migrated to England, with a few pockets of Swedes and Wends. They had a more or less "heroic" society, consisting of nobles (kings and their warbands of noble companions, "thegns", whom they rewarded with lands), free peasants who worked the farms, and slaves, owned by both these classes.

Continental sites and villages, such as Wijster in Holland, Warendorf in Westphalia, and Feddersen Wierde in Friesland, contain a variety of house types, which is reflected in a similar variety here. Being a transference of whole peoples, not just a military invasion (although there was an element of raiding at the beginning and in the 4th century), the Anglo-Saxon way of life continued, as far as conditions permitted, the life they had lived in their homelands. Indeed, D M Wilson can say (1976): "The people who lived in an Anglo-Saxon village in 1050 probably lived a life little different from that of their predecessors 500 years earlier", apart from inevitable developments in material culture and institutions.

Broadly speaking, the house types correspond to the social classes: the thegns lived in halls, either aisled or with buttressed walls like those at Warendorf (kings had larger versions); the free farmers had longhouses or rectangular houses; the serfs had small squarish huts which may in some cases be the type of house occupied by junior members, and women, of higher classes. There were also "Gruben-häuser", sunken-featured buildings, single-room structures whose floor was two or three feet below the ground surface, and whose thatched roof, supported on two, four, six, or more posts, swept almost to the ground. Many of these seem to have been ancillary buildings, but some may have been inhabited or be cellars below a small wooden, cob, or turf house. There were also granaries and various buildings for stock etc. P V Addyman, in his masterly, and still cogent, survey in 1972 of the then archaeological knowledge of Anglo-Saxon houses, reminds us that as recently as 1950 virtually only sunken huts were known, giving a curiously distorted view of Saxon life. Since then important excavations such as those at Maxey, West Stow, Mucking, and Chalton have brought to light well over 150 secular timber buildings, and it is now possible, not only to have a much more balanced understanding of Anglo-Saxon life, but to realise clearly its roots on the Continent.

There was in fact a Germanic presence in England in the 4th century, of *laeti* – soldiers brought over by the Romans, with their families, to help in guarding the province (often against their own fellow-countrymen!). These were stationed at coastal sites like Bishopstone (Sx) and Highdown Hill (Sx). At the same time there seem to have been genuine immigrants, seeking land to farm in eastern England, not employed by the Romans. Important sites such as Mucking (Ex) and West Stow (Su) seem to fit into this category in their early phases. Mucking may have been a main port of entry, sanctioned at first by the Romans. The main immigration began in the mid 5th century. Some buildings in Roman towns, like Canterbury and Portchester, were put up in the 4th or 5th centuries. These were sunken huts, fitting between Roman buildings, which may have been ancillary buildings. At Dorchester-on-Thames simple rectangular buildings, perhaps half-timbered, on unmortared stone footings have been found. These small buildings in Roman towns may imply the continued use of Romano-British buildings as main dwellings.

The new Anglo-Saxon villages of the 5th century (the period of the main immigration) are closer to continental models. Large farmsteads consist of a large house, smaller ones, and ancillary sunken huts and granaries, in a fenced enclosure. West Stow (5th to 6th centuries) has some six halls, each with sunken huts nearby, and other buildings

also; part of this village has been reconstructed. Mucking had over 200 sunken huts, and over 50 halls or large houses. Over 100 villages possessing sunken huts are now known. The pattern seen at West Stow seems to have been long-lived; even London itself may have had a similar arrangement in the 9th century.

There is an intermediate type of house and all three types were found at Chalton (Ha). Some are square, some rectangular; some of the earlier ones have postholes, while others have slots, which did not hold sleeper-beams but close-set posts; the longhouses have opposing doorways in the middle of the long walls, and a separate compartment at one end. These seem to be the houses of free farmers. Similar houses have been found at Maxey (Nh), North Elmham (Nf), and St Neots (He).

The halls, houses of the thegns, were sometimes aisled and quite large; some were longhouses, and others two or three houses joined end to end. Some had buttressed walls and were not aisled. The latest phase of the royal hall at Yeavering (Nd) was over 80ft long and over 50ft wide. Other large halls are known from Thetford (Nf), North Elmham (Nf), and Sulgrave (Nh). Thetford's hall was 110ft long, the largest known building in Anglo-Saxon England; there was also here a composite building which eventually reached 135ft. At Alfred's vill at Cheddar (So), the hall and main buildings were of timber until the 12th century. But in late Saxon times stone might be expected for major buildings, as Asser, Alfred's biographer, suggests. A stone house in fact came to light in Winchester in 1971.

Some of these great halls are boat-shaped, ie the long walls are bowed outwards, perhaps to give more wind resistance. The type occurs in the later phase at Warendorf (8th century), and in several sites in England, eg Yeavering (6th–7th century), Thetford, Cheddar (late 9th century), and Westminster. It also occurs in Norse houses in Orkney (Birsay), Shetland (Jarlshof), and Man (The Braaid). The hogbacks (see page 321) represent houses like these. The well-known boat-shaped buildings at Trelleborg, Denmark, are as late as AD 1000. And Edward the Confessor's Westminster Hall, the largest hall in Europe for its date (as rebuilt by Rufus in the 1090s, 240ft (73m) long by 67ft 6in (20.5m) wide), also had slightly bowed sides. The 11th-century halls at Buckden and St Neots (Ca) derive from such predecessors.

Urban houses, in streets in fenced plots, have come to light at Hamwih (middle Saxon Southampton), Portchester, and Winchester. A feature of these towns is that in many cases the plot boundaries

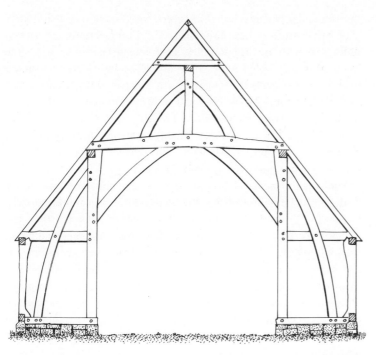

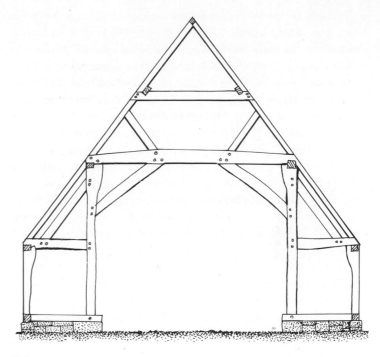

118–19 *Two forms of truss of an aisled hall or barn: 118 15th century; 119 17th–18th century*

119

persisted from the middle to the late Saxon period, and on into the post-conquest period. Some persist even into the present or at least recent times (as at Bergen or Amsterdam). Lydford (Dv), an Alfredan planned *burh*, is a case in point. Boundaries of Viking plots in Coppergate, York, were equally persistent before the recent rebuilding of the site.

Little evidence survives from the carpentry of the walls or roofs of these houses, but the Saxon royal mill at Tamworth (St) (8th century) provided a valuable insight into floor construction (where, that is, the floor was other than earth). This mill had a floor of close-fitting planks over joists, between the sills which supported the walls.

Many features once thought to be typically medieval (12th century on) are now seen to originate at least in late Saxon times, and in some cases much earlier. Such are the aisled halls themselves, which appear in Norman castles and palaces, and in later (13th-century) barns. The aisled hall in this form became obsolete in the 14th century, but had a revival in a new form in the 15th century, under the influence of

the great preaching churches of the Friars, eg Austin Friars, London, 1354. The earliest were the Merchant Adventurers' Hall and the Guildhall in York; the latter (1446) has timber posts. The aisled hall had died out by about 1500 (see **118** and **119**).

Ground sills and wattle and daub are other Saxon features. The origin of crucks and king posts is still obscure, but there are hints of quite early origin. An early cruck house has been found at Latimer (Bc) – sub-Roman, late 4th or early 5th century – eight centuries older than the earliest cruck building previously found in England (Gomeldon, near Salisbury, 13th century). In Holland crucks are found two centuries earlier still, so our example could be an import from Holland or north Germany, or the differences could imply independent invention. If so, the origins and date of British crucks are still obscure.

Recent excavations have shown that there grew up in Saxon England a distinctive type of house building. This was first recognised, and its implications assessed, by Martin Millett as a result of excavations at Cowdery's Down, near Basingstoke (Ha), in 1978–81 (see *Archaeological Journal* 140, 1983; 141, 1984). This settlement existed from the early Bronze Age to the post-medieval. The early to middle Saxon period (5th to 8th century) was characterised by large rectangular "halls", in three building phases, with a total of some 16 houses; each phase had one large building, with smaller ones nearby. The shapes of the timbers had survived in the ground, so exact plans could be drawn up. The walls consisted of squared timbers, either in pairs or "stepped" alternately; these held in place walling panels of horizontal planks or of wattle and daub. At the corners the posts were arranged to hold the panels tight. Outside each upright wall post was a rectangular baulk leaning in towards the top of the wall, which was 1¹/₂–2 m high. These were not buttresses for the wall itself, but appear to support a wall plate; so these external raking timbers were part of the roof structure, not of the walls. Inside the walls were, at longer intervals, large postholes which represented a framework of base crucks. These crucks would have supported king posts to a ridge piece, and the rafters would rise to this from the wall plates (Yeavering had aisle posts instead of crucks). Varying reconstructions of the probable actual roof are possible. For greater stability, a raised floor acted as a (reversed) tie beam.

This method of construction enabled very large houses to be built – house C12 at Cowdery's Down was 70ft (21m) long by 30ft (9m) wide. There were doors at one end and in the sides, and both ends were partitioned off.

This highly sophisticated tradition is comparable to the cruck and box-frame traditions of the later Middle Ages, though the later crucks carried the load, unlike these middle Saxon ones. It reaches its peak in the 6th to 8th centuries. Some 40 sites in Britain have houses built in this way, or with elements of it, including the royal halls of Yeavering, Cheddar, and Northampton, and other halls at Thirlings, Chalton, Mucking, Sprouston, and Foxley. Such sites have one or a few halls of this type, and several smaller buildings.

The origins of this distinctive tradition are to be sought in two directions. The halls of Germanic northern Europe are longhouses, frequently aisled or with central posts, with hearth at one end and byre at the other, eg Wijk bij Duurstede, Vreden, Warendorf, Ezinge, Feddersen Wierde. In Germany there was a tendency to reduce and then eliminate internal posts, and push the load on to the walls, presumably with crucks. There is thus a similarity to the English

houses, and probably a link. But several late Romano-British houses (3rd–4th centuries) show a similarity of ground plan; these are open halls, but with no free-standing roof supports, unlike the large Romano-British aisled halls. They are often based on a 2-square module, with doors in the long walls and end partitions, a feature also of the Saxon houses; some have end annexes, unknown on the Continent but occurring in the Saxon houses (eg at Cowdery's Down, Landwade, or Norton Disney). Raking external timbers and wall panels are common in Holland and Germany (eg at Wijk bij Duurstede), but unknown in Roman Britain.

These early medieval English houses therefore seem to derive from both Romano-British and continental Germanic models. Cowdery's Down is a blend of both. Millett asks whether the impetus for this blend was due to Germanic incomers adopting Romano-British ideas but still using their own construction techniques, or to native Britons building houses native in plan but in structure imitating the fashions of the, now dominant, incomers. He inclines towards the latter model. The tradition changed by about AD 800, and by the 9th century the picture is complicated by the Vikings, and later by the Normans. It had few survivals as late as this.

Recent excavations have shown that the Anglo-Saxons favoured nucleated villages; this was certainly the case in Germany. The process can be seen at work in the cattle-raising settlements of North Holland and Friesland, such as the classic case of Feddersen Wierde (1st century BC to 5th AD). This had small beginnings, but grew larger in successive phases as the sea encroached, and the land was raised into an artificial hill (a *Terp* or *Wurt*). By the 3rd century AD it was a large village of aisled halls, most with six-post granaries close by, radiating from the centre of the terp.

Viking

The Vikings (9th and 10th centuries), whether Danes or Norse, added little to the Anglo-Saxon picture described above. But the Norse, from Shetland (eg at Jarlshof) to Yorkshire (eg Braida Garth, Kingsdale), favoured the laithe-house or coit. This is a dwelling and farm buildings erected simultaneously, under the same roof and usually rectangular. Some coits are as much as 50ft long. They differ from the longhouse

120 *Footings of a Viking-age house – Birsay (Or).*

in that the latter has a cross passage between the two elements. Both types survive in Yorkshire, and reflect a pastoral economy (see **120** and **121**).

The Celtic west

The departure of the Romans in 410 left Britain as an essentially Celtic country, British (proto-Welsh and Cornish) up to the Clyde, Gaelic beyond that, with Picts in eastern and south-eastern Scotland. The Northern Isles, Caithness, Sutherland, the Hebrides, and Man became Norse in the 9th century. Celtic states reasserted themselves (those in Scotland had never been Romanised, except for superficial contacts), though their kings and nobles remained more or less Romanised for the rest of the 5th century. But this did not touch the mass of the people, whose hold on Latin was fairly sketchy. Celtic languages, culture, and institutions revived remarkably, as though the Iron Age peoples were merely waiting for the Romans to go away before resuming and developing their own life.

In the Highland Zone, where for a long time the Celts were outside the movements of peoples from over the North Sea, the Iron Age tradition of round houses persisted, in the form of duns in Scotland and rounds in Cornwall. Circular or oval stone huts also continued. The round embanked sites gradually gave way to open farmsteads, with longhouses or laithe-houses, sometimes inside the old boundaries (eg Mawgan Porth in Cornwall is a courtyard house of prehistoric type with a longhouse inside it). In some cases the courtyard house itself continued in occupation, as at Goldherring, Sancreed, or Helangy Down on St Mary's, Scilly, until the 5th or even 6th century.

The new open settlements were larger than these old houses, and had newly-cleared land round them. Their houses, as at Gwithian,

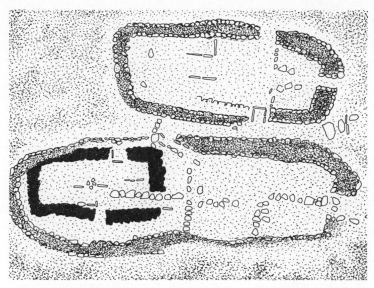

121 *Plan of two Viking-age houses, with a medieval house (shown in black) inside the larger one – Birsay (Or).*

were round huts with turf walls on a stone foundation, and some of this type were in use until the 11th century. The richer classes built large halls, such as the two inside the Iron Age fort of Castle Dore (Co) (6th century). Early Celtic laws show that such buildings were accompanied by several ancillary structures – a chamber, kitchen, chapel, barn, kiln-house, stable, dog kennel, and privy.

The situation in Devon is more complicated. Once Celtic, it was subject to Saxon settlement in the 6th century, and it is not always easy to distinguish the houses and farms of the Celts from those of the incomers. But by the 10th century a pattern of longhouses is established, as at Hound Tor near Manaton, where longhouses and laithe-houses were accompanied by smaller buildings; the walls of these were built with a double row of stakes.

It seems likely that the longhouse was introduced from English and Viking sources into the Celtic lands; but it took root there, and remained a living form in the Highland Zone until recent times. The longhouses were the dwellings of substantial farmers. The poorer people, however, from Cornwall to north-west Scotland, lived in hovels of various degrees of discomfort; many of these had walls of earth, clay, or turf, thatched roofs with no chimneys, no glazed windows, and few partitions; the beds were heaps of straw and a

122 *A Scottish blackhouse – Kilmuir, Skye. The thatch is held down by weighted ropes.*

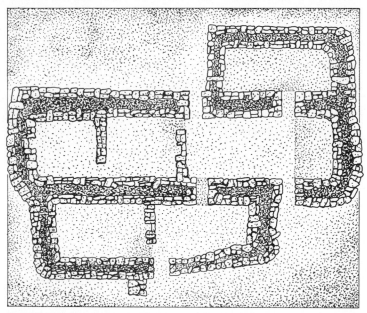

123 *Plan of a large Scottish blackhouse – Callanish, Lewis. This combines farm buildings with the living quarters.*

blanket. In parts of Wales, such as the borders and a few relatively prosperous towns, houses of English inspiration were found, but the generalisation broadly holds good. And the materials of the hovels ensure that little of them remains.

A specialised use for the small, single-roomed hut is represented by the cells of Celtic monks, from Cornwall to Scotland. Their background is sketched on page 261. Examples can be seen on Priestholm (Ynys Seiriol) (An), Lag ny Keilley (IM), and Kingarth (Bu).

In the Hebrides there was a unique development of the longhouse, the *blackhouse*, which remained in use into this century. This had a longhouse as core, with, built against it, a barn, stables, store, and porches. The walls could be 6ft thick. They were built, in the Outer Isles, of turf pressed down between two skins of stones. The roof of turf on brushwood was set on the inner skin of stones, so that rain could drip into the turf core and keep it wet and windproof. A similar construction occurs in the late 9th century Norse houses at Jarlshof. On Skye the roof, of thatch held down by a net of rope weighted with stones, covers the entire wall. Examples of these two types are preserved at Arnol on Lewis, and Kilmuir and Colbost on Skye (see **122** and **123**).

POST-CONQUEST HOUSES – RURAL

Cottages

The peasant's cot in the Middle Ages at first usually had but one room, of an average size around 5 x 3.5 m; two-roomed cots appeared by the 13th century, either in the original building or by addition. The one-roomed cot lasted longer in the Highland Zone. Cots of both sizes occur on Saxon sites (eg Chalton (Ha)), and appear again in the 12th century; but none older than *c* 1700 survives. Such houses were normally timber-built, at first with posts in slots, later on wooden sills, and finally on padstones. Infilling was commonly lath and plaster or wattle and daub. Even a single room was usually divided by furniture or partitions into a more "public" area and a more "private" area; two rooms, of course, made such a distinction easier.

From the 17th century on, cottages have usually been more substantial, and large numbers were built in the late 18th and 19th centuries. More permanent materials enabled the cottager, by the 18th century, to have four rooms, two up and two down, and this became a norm into the 20th century. Other variants include a one-unit cottage with loft; a one and a half unit with loft (the half unit being a small second room on the ground floor, for a pantry – cooking being done in the main living room; the loft is the bedroom), a type common in the west Midlands; a single-storey type with three rooms. Two-up two-down cottages are often in pairs, in which case the rooms on each floor are one behind the other, in a double-pile manner (see below).

There are regional variations in the materials used, in the standards of building, and in the position of the door and of the kitchen. Some cottages had store-sheds and privies out at the back. The highest standards are in the south-east, particularly in Kent. One region has been studied in detail by J M Proctor (*East Anglian Cottages* (1979)), but other regions no doubt have similar variety. Thus, Proctor contrasts the high thatch of Suffolk with the low-flowing ("blanket") thatch of Hampshire. Suffolk roofs are steeply pitched and have "peaks", projecting points at the gables. In Norfolk, gable walls rise above the level of the thatch. Essex, Cambridgeshire, and West Suffolk have half-hipped gables. Horizontally sliding windows are the norm in the east Midlands and from Lincolnshire to north Essex, with a centre in Cambridgeshire; Suffolk has a local style of window with a casement in part of the window only. Suffolk cottages are often tall in relation to their width. The Fens have "catslides", where the cottage has two storeys in front and one at the back, with a long roof extending over the upper storey to cover the outshut. Essex and Hertfordshire (and parts of the south-east) use weatherboarding. There are differences in bricks and other building materials also.

A variant in Wales is the *croglofft* cottage. This has two rooms on the ground floor, a main room with gable fireplace and the entrance door, and a parlour and/or service room; over this parlour is a loft for sleeping, reached by a ladder from the main room.

In Scotland the Highland crofters lived in turf or earth houses, with two or three rooms, arranged in longhouse manner with space for animals at one end. The animals' end was called the "but", the living end the "ben"; but if there were only two rooms at the living end, one was the "but", the other (inner) the "ben". In the western Highlands and the Islands the Gaelic blackhouse still occasionally survives (see above).

The single-storey tradition is strong in Scotland, and most rural cottages in the Lowlands are of this type. It is indeed this feature which strikes the visitor from south of the Border as distinctively Scottish.

One-room cottages continued to be used by squatters on roadsides etc into the 18th century. Temporary huts of branches and thatch were built by charcoal burners (one is reconstructed at the Weald and Downland Open Air Museum at Singleton (Sx)), and gypsies, until recently, lived in tents or caravans of several types (see specimens at the Romany Museum at Selborne (Ha)).

Larger houses were sometimes divided into two or more cottages, and recently this trend has been reversed, as cottages and farm buildings are converted into houses. There is another distinction to make – that between vernacular cottages and "polite" cottages, a topic usefully summarised by Christopher Powell (in *Discovering Cottage Architecture* (1984)). Polite cottages are those designed by architects, or at least taken from builders' pattern-books, and reflecting the taste of the time as fully expressed in the large and great houses. They were usually built by landowners for their estate workers, and therefore had to have a certain style or even pretension. Renaissance architectural ideas and motifs began to reach the smaller house in the 17th century, but the full impact of polite building did not take effect until the mid 18th century. Before then, from the end of the 17th century, a few planned groups of cottages had been built, but using vernacular materials and methods. Examples are at Chippenham (Ca) (1696), Houghton Hall (Nf) (1729), and a later but influential group at Nuneham Courtenay (Ox) (1761) – 20 semi-detached cottages along the road, with detached stores and privies.

The full polite style is reached in two major examples, one in a rural spirit – Milton Abbas (Do) (Chambers and Brown, 1773), rows of paired cottages with single entrance doors – and one in an urban spirit – Harewood (WY) (Carr of York 1760), including houses of different types and sizes reflecting the status of their occupants. By the end of the 18th century cottage architecture was influenced by the "Picturesque" taste, which included asymmetry, irregular building forms, details taken from the practice in larger houses, and a general attempt at the "rustic". Contrasting examples are the Umbrella House

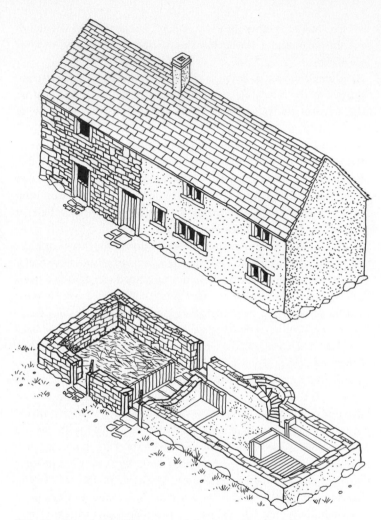

124 *A longhouse has dwelling accommodation at one end, separated by a cross-passage from a livestock area; the passage gives access to both parts. The roof is undivided.*

at Lyme Regis (Do) and the estate cottages at Blaise, near Bristol. Some of these are hard to distinguish from the "cottages ornés", intended for people of means (see page 251).

By the early 19th century the stock of vernacular cottages was in sharp decay, and many farm workers lived in damp, ill-equipped, and squalid conditions. Landlords began to replace these with well-built cottages, using less local materials than the vernacular builders had been able to – Welsh slates, imported pine, brick, sheet glass, better

doors, cast iron fireplaces, etc. Many of these cottages were two-up two-down, and many were in pairs. The trend at this period was towards more, larger rooms.

The more enlightened landlords were actuated by philanthropy as well as by a willingness to improve obviously defective buildings. They were helped by a growing number of pattern-books and periodicals, culminating in the works of John Loudon (1833), J Young McVicar (1849), and Henry Roberts (1850). Roberts and Thomas Postans (1830) advocated paired cottages, which were cheaper to build, and this was influential. Picturesque ideas continued, as at Selworthy (So) (1828). The farming prosperity of the 1850s and 1860s led to an upsurge in "model" estate cottages, and these can be seen widely (eg Holkham (Nf) 1860s, but begun in 1819 and 1831; Willington (Bd) (1849); Lockinge (Ox) (1860s); Charney Bassett (Ox)). From the 1860s the Picturesque declined and was replaced by the whole range of Victorian eclecticism – Gothic, Renaissance, Tudor, Chalet, etc (eg Chatsworth (Db), begun in 1838).

After 1870 the rural population began to decline and fewer cottages were built. Powell notes that by 1900 only one person in five lived in the countryside, and 100,000 labourers left the land every ten years. But the new cottages which were built were affected by new legislation to improve sanitation, light, ventilation, etc (the Picturesque had been deficient in such things), although some local builders were reluctant to comply. The best new cottages were strongly influenced by the Arts and Crafts Movement, the Garden Cities Movement (Letchworth 1905), and architects like Lutyens and Williams-Ellis. C R Ashbee applied himself to improving old cottages without spoiling them. New or better materials were used – concrete, cement roof tiles, urban-type plumbing, etc, even prefabrication of house sections. Designs were simple but effective. The typical cottage contained a living room/ kitchen, a scullery, a larder, and three bedrooms. A few had a parlour and a fourth bedroom as well – many families were large. Interestingly, some of the best designs for rural cottages had some influence in the towns, and not only in the Garden Cities.

By 1914 the old distinction between vernacular and polite had gone, but was replaced by a distinction between the polite functional and polite ornamental. Country cottage building never revived after 1914, but their influence continued in post-war "cottage estates", and much speculative housing in the suburbs.

Small houses

The medieval smallholder (villein or husbandman) and the lesser yeoman, lived in houses of three rooms. The commonest type of small farmhouse was the *longhouse*. This had two living rooms at one end, separated by a *cross-passage* from a compartment at the other end in which animals or other farm stores or produce could be kept. The cross-passage provided the entrance to both parts, by means of doors along it; in some cases it was also used as a feeding passage for animals (see **124**).

Longhouses seem originally to have been standard for the whole country and to be linked with cruck construction, which is a convenient basis for a longhouse. But, like crucks, they are now confined to the Highland Zone, having been replaced in the lowlands by other forms of building by the 16th century. They are still to be found in Cumbria and north Yorkshire, south Wales, south Devon, and Scotland, although most of them have been internally altered.

As with crucks, the origins of the longhouse are obscure, but they both appear together in the 12th century at Gomeldon (Wi), and were diffused in the 13th. The extant examples date from the mid 17th to the late 19th century (see **125**). But John Steane points out that the cruck-framed, multi-bayed longhouse is an expression of a rise in pastoral farming, a more prosperous peasantry, and the contracting size of rural settlements after the Black Death. The drier arable lands in eastern England produced more straw, and enabled cattle to lie out. In the west and north cattle had to be brought indoors. This may account for the odd and still unexplained distribution of cruck-framed longhouses: crucks may have solved the problem of keeping men and animals under the same roof. The surviving late medieval houses in the present longhouse areas are mostly evolved forms, now with chimneys and halls split into two levels.

The retreat of the longhouse to its present areas began with the increase in farming prosperity in the lowlands in the later 14th and 15th centuries. Prosperity gave rise to a demand for more, and differentiated, living rooms. When the sleeping room was separated from the living room, the stock was separated from the dwelling and put into specialised buildings. By the mid 16th century the farm replaced the longhouse in the Lowland Zone, and itself was caught up in the Great Rebuilding as farming wealth increased still further. By then the feudal peasantry was at an end, and the yeomanry was rising.

125 *A possible longhouse – Spout House, Bilsdale (NY). The single door opens onto the cross-passage, with the dwelling to the left and the byre to the right.*

In fact, examples can be found of separate farm buildings from the late 13th century. The farmstead at Gomeldon (Wi) shows a sequence from one longhouse (12th century) to two longhouses (early 13th century), three longhouses of which one could be a stable (mid 13th century), and finally house, yard, barn, and stable (late 13th century).

There is a specialised form of combined men/animals house in West Yorkshire (eg in the Halifax area), reminiscent of, but distinct from, the longhouse. This is the *laithe-house* (a term coined by C F Stell, using the dialect word laithe, a barn). It consists of a dwelling and farm buildings under the same roof, but with separate entrances to each part (not a cross-passage common to both). The dwelling part may have three or four rooms on the ground floor and bedrooms above, with a loft extending over the farm part. The latter often has a wide passage for threshing and cattle-feeding, with stalls on both sides. Laithe-houses appear about 1650, and were in their heyday from the late 18th to the late 19th century.

The most distinctive house of the more prosperous yeomen – and some of these were wealthier than some of the minor gentry – was the *open-hall* house. This has a central hall, open to the roof, with a two-storey part at each end, usually contained within a rectangular plan. Early examples had a central hearth, but this was later moved to the service end of the hall, with a smoke-bay, or replaced by a fireplace.

An important variant of this type is the *Wealden* house, normal for upper yeomen in the south-east of England but scattered widely, even in towns (eg there is one as far north as Goodramgate, York). They date mainly from the 1480s to the 1530s, and then of course shared in the Great Rebuilding. Some early ones may have been manor houses, but the type was heartily adopted by the more prosperous yeomen, particularly in Kent, where there are some 350 readily recognisable examples (eight in Marden parish alone), and many in adjacent counties.

The Wealden house had a central hall open to the roof, flanked by two-storey bays, of which the upper storeys are jettied out at the front or sides, and sometimes at the rear as well. The ground floor plan is rectangular, but H-shaped at first-floor level; the roof is rectangular, covering hall and wings and projecting over the central part in front. The hall was normally split into two levels in the later 16th century. There was an entrance and cross-passage at the service end of the hall (see **126** and **127**). There are good examples, out of very many, at

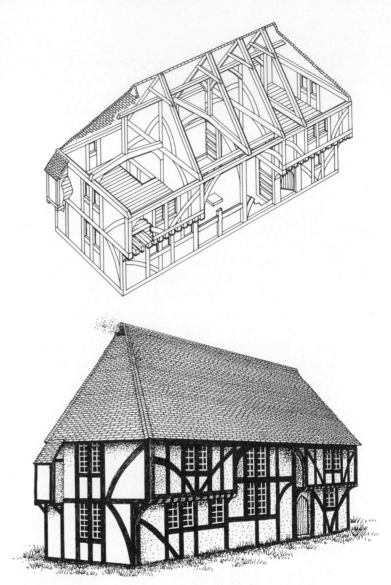

126–27 *A Wealden house, a type of yeoman's house from c 1480 to the mid 16th century, common in the south-east of England, but found as far north as York. It had a central hall, open to the roof (the "gablet" or opening for smoke can be seen at the end of the roof-ridge): at each end of the hall were rooms, domestic at one end, for the family at the other, the upper rooms of which projected in "jetties". One roof covered all. The projection at the left-hand corner is a privy. This example is Bayleaf, a farmhouse from Chiddingstone (Kt), re-erected at the Weald and Downland Open Air Museum, Singleton (Sx).*

Pattenden, Goudhurst (Kt), Smarden House, Smarden (Kt), Bayleaf, Chiddingstone (Kt), re-erected at the Weald and Downland Open Air Museum, at Singleton (Sx).

There are many variants of the hall house with end wings. North of the Thames a common type has the same plan as the Wealden house, but no jetties (Blue Gates Farm, Great Bromley (Ex)). A simpler version has a two-storey upper end and a single-storey service bay at the lower end (Upstreet Cottages, Lyminge (Kt)); an even simpler type has two equal bays (Winkhurst, Chiddingstone (Kt), re-erected at the Weald and Downland Museum); in this type the hall occupies one bay, to the roof, and the ground floor of the other bay, which has an upper storey. The smallest form has only two rooms, both open to the roof, and one heated by open hearth (St Mary's Grove Cottage, Tilmanstone (Kt)). In Essex there is a type with variants (the T and L plans) which have a hall and either one cross-wing or, more rarely, two. Where there is one wing this has two rooms on each floor, one larger than the other, and jettied at the front or on a long wall as well, with at the lower end a bay for service quarters. The hall and bay could be lower than the two-storeyed wing.

In south-west and north-east Wales, Somerset, and much of Devon, there is a type where the fireplace which replaced the open hearth in the hall was not moved to an inner wall but to a long side wall (the *lateral chimney* house). This creates a very distinctive feature, the chimney stack projecting from the front of the house (eg The Old Vicarage, Thorverton (Dv) and Plas-ucha, Llanfair DC (Cw)).

By the mid 16th century the Wealden house had been improved by jettying the full upper storey along the front. By the 1560s, in most of the Midlands, Lincolnshire, Cambridgeshire, Norfolk, and the south-east, the walls were flush and not jettied, and there was a *lobby entrance* against a chimney stack instead of a through passage (see **128**). By 1620 this type could have two storeys and attics, often used only for storage. This type is an important expression of the Great Rebuilding.

In other areas south of the Trent there are two- or three-cell houses influenced by the longhouse; these have chimney stacks backing on to the cross-passage, but never a buttery/pantry division in the room below the passage. Farmhouses built entirely as dwellings are of one build, but longhouse derivatives were rebuilt piecemeal, and this shows externally. They also ended up with an external differentiation of house and byre, as the living end was heightened. The kitchen could

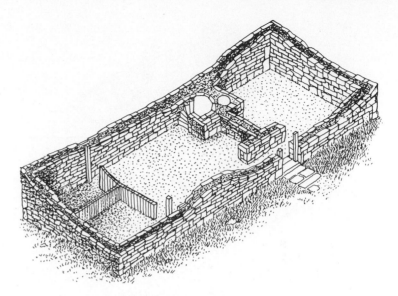

128 *Schematic view of a lobby-entrance house, showing the fireplace block just inside the door, and the staircase beyond.*

be added at the back, or in the former byre, which could be rebuilt next to it or across the yard. A dairy also might be added in the late 17th or early 18th century. Neither part of these rebuilt houses is complete in itself, unlike the houses of eastern and south-east England, where an old house was enlarged integrally.

The improved houses of the 16th and 17th centuries reflect the passing of the feudal peasant and the rise of the free yeoman. They announce the end of the medieval way of life. Another contributor was the introduction of the Renaissance concept of symmetry. The medieval house was lopsided, reflecting the cross-passage, which was not central. Symmetry was being sought by the 17th century, and the vernacular plan was largely killed by it by the early 18th century. The social implications of this trend are expressed by Maurice Barley as "the end of a way of life based on kinship and community, and its replacement by one of farmers and labourers, employers and employed".

In Northumberland and Durham few houses built before 1800, and almost none before 1700, survive. In the rest of the north of England, north of the Trent, among surviving houses of the 18th century or earlier, there is a distinctive type, in which the smoke was removed by a fire-hood (or smoke-hood), not a chimney stack. This affected

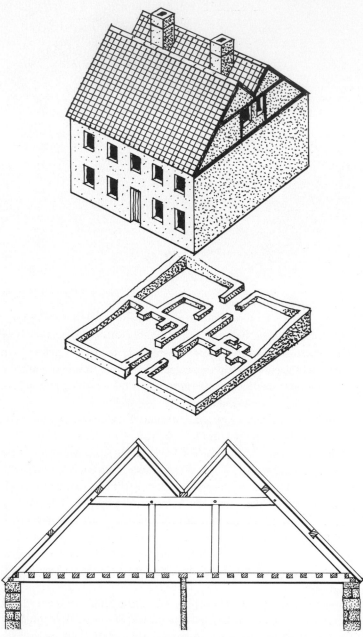

129–30 *The double-pile house began in the late 16th century, and was popular in the 17th. It had a symmetrical ground-floor plan, with four equal rooms and central passage. The roof could take several forms, of which this one is typical.*

the plan and the position of staircases, and eliminated a cross-passage. In the 18th and the first half of the 19th century a very common type over much of England was the *end-chimney* house. This derived from the two-room cottage, with hearth at one end. The door was next to the hearth, pushing it off-centre (but variants exist). These houses are small, commonly 11–13ft wide. In the Midlands they are mostly two-storeyed. They are common in broken or heathy terrain, and are often encroachments on greens, particularly in the west Midlands and Welsh borders; they were often craftsmen's houses. Half a million houses of this type were registered for hearth tax in 1685. In eastern England, from the mid 17th century, there was often a chimney at each end. By the end of the 17th century houses of this type sometimes had a central door and passage.

A small version of the *double-pile* house (a type which may be small, large, or urban – see below) is vernacular. The type began in the late 16th century, and was popular in the 17th (see **129** and **130**). By 1650 it had four equal rooms on the ground floor, two on each side of a passage from the front door (one behind the other), and rooms upstairs. There were various solutions to the roofing problem. This type may have originated in the Midlands. It could be extended at the back by outshuts and even hearths. (A useful summary of these small houses, with much detail, is contained in Peter Eden: *Small Houses in England, 1520–1820* (Historical Association 1969).)

In lowland England one-storey houses were rare by the end of the 17th century, since farmers needed more rooms for family and servants. But in the west of England the multi-storeyed house caught on, and in the north the house grew by adding rooms on the ground floor. But there was another type, developed in Saxon times and spread in Norman times for defence, in which the first floor was used for living and the ground floor for storage. The parsonage houses of south-west England are a special regional form, which may derive from a storeyed tradition with a first-floor hall. In parts of Wales and along the Scottish border a typical fortified house, the *bastle*, is found, with living rooms on the first floor. At a higher social level this idea is expressed in the *tower-house* or *peel*, built on the same principle, but square and not oblong, and usually with two storeys above the ground-floor storage area. These were often called *stonehouses*, implying that the Scottish peasant lived in single-storey, timber-built houses.

In England two storeys were a status symbol. But in France and Scotland single storeys continued into recent times, in parallel with living on upper floors, and hence in flats. This idea was carried, in Scotland, to the practice of buying flats, a practice only recently taken up in England. In great houses, living on the first floor, the *piano nobile*, was an idea borrowed from Renaissance Italy, and had no immediate reference to defence.

Large houses

These are the houses of the gentry and manorial lords, granges and estate management centres, and, mainly in post-medieval times, the houses of landowners, rich yeomen, merchants, and industrialists; they include "country houses". The line is often hard to draw between these and the larger "small houses", and, at the top end, between these and the Great Houses or Stately Homes. Yet there is enough generic similarity in the group to enable these lines to be drawn most of the time.

The medieval manor house grew out of the prehistoric and Anglo-Saxon aisled hall, the home and administration centre of the lord or thegn, and the hall remained the focus of the house throughout the Middle Ages. It housed the lord and his family who ate and slept at one end, with the retainers and servants at the other; at first there seem to have been no partitions or divisions into functional areas, but later some halls were divided into two unequal portions, the larger for the lord's public functions, the smaller for his private life, sometimes with service rooms on the ground floor and private rooms above them. Round the hall were smaller, secondary buildings, for farm and other purposes. (This is in contrast to the aisled halls of Germany, which were complete farmsteads under one roof.)

The aisled hall is commonest in the south-east of England, and at higher social levels in Suffolk, Essex, Kent, and Sussex (eg Fyfield Hall (Ex), *c* 1300). There is a late 14th-century group in the southern Pennines, particularly round Halifax (eg High Bentley, Shelf), the houses of wealthy farmers or wool magnates. The most conspicuous, and the largest, aisled halls are in castles (eg Oakham, *c* 1190, or Winchester, 1220s) and bishops' palaces (eg Lincoln, *c* 1224). Westminster Hall, late 11th century, is exceptionally large – 239ft 6in x 67ft 6in (73.5 x 21.7m) – most range from 35–85ft (10.7–26m) long, in proportions usually either 2:1 or 3:2, length to width. Haddon Hall (Db) is typical, at 42 x 27ft (13 x 8.3m). A rare

131 *A "first-floor hall". This description, although usual, is really a misnomer. A house of this type, common in the 12th and 13th centuries, was only the chamber block of a composite house, the hall and kitchen being in a separate block which has not survived. The chamber-block had stores on the ground floor, and private family rooms on the first floor. Eventually the two components were combined in a single building, which became the standard late medieval English house. This fine example is at Boothby Pagnell (Nh), c 1200.*

survival is the hall of St Mary's Hospital, Chichester, with a chapel at one end, and the aisles still used for dwellings. York has three 15th-century aisled halls in "public" buildings – the Guildhall, the Merchant Adventurers' Hall, and St Anthony's Hall. Aisled halls, having central hearths, were on the ground floor and open to the roof. By the late 13th century improved methods of carpentry enabled the aisle posts to be eliminated. (Margaret Wood lists 86 good examples of unaisled halls in *The English Medieval House* (1965).)

There is a group of houses seemingly having a hall on the first floor and a solar or bedroom on the same level; the ground floor could be a vaulted storeroom (most of the surviving examples are stone-built) and service area. These are mostly in castles, palaces, monasteries, and colleges, and the idea was convenient for town houses. They had side-wall fireplaces instead of the central hearth. They range from the 12th to the 14th centuries, eg Boothby Pagnell Manor House (Li) *c* 1200 (see **131**), Christchurch Castle (Do), *c* 1160, and Charleston Manor House (Sx). "First-floor halls" are often called "King John's Houses", but few had any connection with him. Margaret Wood lists 13 good examples, including The Gloriet, Corfe Castle (Do), Warnford Manor House (Ha), and Cranborne Manor (Do). The bastle (see above) is

132 *A typical peel, or fortified house, on the Scottish border. This 14th-century example, at Embleton (Nd), was the local vicarage.*

another form of this type of house. The idea was of course popular in areas subject to unrest, such as Wales and the north, eg Markenfield Hall, near Ripon (NY). Margaret Wood lists 58 examples (including some King John's Houses).

The *tower house* was another version of the "first-floor hall", but had higher storeys as well. It is common in Scotland, but is also found widely elsewhere. In some cases it crosses the line between the large house and the great house, as in the enormous keeps of the Tower of London, Colchester, and Castle Acre (Nf). In Scotland, Threave (Du), late 14th century, has five storeys. The larger Scottish towers were developed by the addition of wings into L- and Z-Shaped plans, or with parallel projecting wings like Borthwick (ML). The smaller ones remained simple border *peel-towers* (see **132**). The culmination in England is perhaps Tattershall (Li) (mid 15th century), which is an independent chamber block adjoining the hall.

The defensive nature of the tower house leads us to consider the status of castles generally, in relation to living quarters. The Norman castle was essentially a private house, the defended residence of its lord. It was also the place where the management of the manor was carried on, and any judicial or administrative functions allowed to or laid on the lord by the king. The larger castles, centres of royal or noble power, had garrisons as well. All had buildings for these purposes, which included homes for the lord or the constable. The very large castles, like Windsor, Arundel, Alnwick, or Warwick, have developed into Great Houses. The small motte and bailey castle was just a manor house with defences.

The lord's house, then, was similar to contemporary undefended (or perhaps moated) houses, but had to fit into an often cramped site. It usually had a hall, with the lord's chamber on the first floor over service rooms at one end of the hall. Or the hall could be on the first floor. In some cases the lord's house might be in the tower on the motte, or in the shell keep or tower keep which succeeded it; but these might come to be too small, and the house was then built in the bailey. Restormel (Co) has buildings in a shell keep (hall, chamber, kitchen, stores, chapel) rebuilt in stone in the 13th century; Castle Hedingham (Ex) and Odiham (Ha) are examples of tower keep houses. Rochester has two suites, one above the other, each with hall and chamber and one with chapel as well, for the lord above and the constable below. Tretower (Po), 12th–13th century, is a good example of a castle proving unsuitable for living in: a 14th/15th-century manor house has been built alongside. By the 13th century, indeed, the hall for formal purposes was often in the bailey, and the lord's house was in the keep.

Some castles are well developed in this sense. Goodrich (He) has the constable's rooms in the gatehouse, next to the lord's hall and rooms; next to these are the state hall and rooms, then the kitchen, then the keep; the remaining side is taken up with the guests' hall and rooms, and the circuit is closed by the gatehouse. An astonishing case is that of Bodiam (Sx) (1380s), which should perhaps be regarded as a Great House. Bodiam was the home of a knight, Sir Edward Dalyngrigge, who sought to build a romantic or dream castle, almost a folly. It is nearly square, with round towers at the corners and square ones on the sides and is set in a wide moat. One is reminded of the fantastic castles in French Books of Hours. Inside these walls were four separate ranges round a courtyard, with at least seven halls.

One range was Sir Edward's private house, on the first and second floors; the constable lived on the ground floor; another range was for ceremonial occasions; the other two ranges were for guests and their officials and servants.

The next development of the hall house was the movement of the solar to the upper (dais) end of the hall from its former place over the service end. By the 13th century this became a transverse, two-storey wing making a *T-shaped* or single-ended hall house. Margaret Wood suggests that the staircase to the solar, outside in a projecting turret, may have given rise to the later oriel, when the stairs were removed from the turret and a window put in. By the 14th century a typical large house consisted of a hall with a two-storey block at each end, the *H-plan*. One wing had a first-floor solar, with storeroom below; the other had service rooms. There is a good example of a solar wing, with vaulted store below and chapel leading off the solar, at Charney Manor, Charney Bassett (Ox) (13th century). Burton Agnes (Hu) has a good Norman undercroft. The H-plan facilitated the enlargement of the house on symmetrical lines when Renaissance ideas came in.

In the 15th century there was a demand for more rooms, not only for retainers and guests in the house but to enable family rooms to have specialised functions, eg to separate living from sleeping. A parlour was thus often made out of the storeroom under the great chamber. The greater use of the wall fireplace led to the decline of the lofty open hall and permitted the insertion of a floor in the hall, which then declined in central importance, until it finally became a mere entrance passage. By the 15th century, then, the house had become a compact block under a single roof, after its long development as a hall attaching to itself disparate units as separately roofed wings.

The medieval (or sub-medieval) tradition continued in the 16th century, but in its first half the H-shaped house began to be replaced by one with the main range built in two storeys. At the same time floors were being inserted in the halls of older houses (see The Great Rebuilding, page 211 above), so the newly-built examples are not easy to distinguish. Medieval front doors were off-centre, because of the cross-passage and the central hearth; but by the mid 17th century a central front door is general. The larger of these new houses sometimes had three-storey wings as well as two storeys in the central part; more rooms had fireplaces, so the roof had several chimneys, often ornamental ones. Gables were in fashion, and stone ornaments;

symmetry was the rule, or at least aimed at, and each side, as well as the front, was a formal unit. The house was shaking off the vernacular, and heading towards the architectural.

There is a small and anomalous group of houses of vaguely *cruciform* plan, consisting of a main block with two rooms on each floor, a projecting wing at the back of one room on each floor and a staircase, and a projecting porch with room over. Another form of this family has a main block with four rooms on each floor, projecting staircases on each side, and projecting porch. Cruciform houses were common in Wales in the 17th century, but occur also in England. They can be seen as transitional in the line of development, marking a step away from the medieval concept of the house as basically one room deep.

In the north, where the aisled hall tradition continued, enlarged by a row of outshuts in the rear, by 1700 new large farmhouses were square in plan and two rooms deep. In the south, the *double-pile* house emerged in the mid 17th century. These were conceived in a solid square or in rectangular solid blocks, with central front door opening onto a passage or small "hall", with a room on each side and two or three rooms behind these, a staircase, and sometimes attics as well. The distinction between the formal rooms in the front half and the service rooms behind is emphasised by a double roof, with its valley along the central line of the block, though there are examples where the valley ends over the front door, presenting two gables in the front of the house. The ground floor is now the principal floor, in contrast to the practice continued in Great Houses.

These square houses led into what became the normal form of *"country house"* or parsonage in the 18th and 19th centuries – square or oblong blocks with more and often larger rooms for the family than in previous centuries, with the servants pushed into the basement and the attics, and separate buildings for stables etc and outdoor staff. Most of these houses, particularly the Georgian ones, including the *"villas"* of the later 18th century, are modest and unpretentious, but have left the vernacular for the "polite"; they benefit from the symmetry, balance, and proportion which characterised the Palladian idea. By the early 19th century some of them had pretensions to being Great Houses, like Decimus Burton's villas in Regent's Park, London (Nuffield Lodge and The Holme, 1820s); they were finally swamped in the welter of Victorian taste. Villas have in any case a more or less urban character, even when they are in the country, and are best considered under Urban Houses below.

The study of houses is made more complicated and often uncertain by the changes they have undergone over the centuries – additions, alterations, reshaping, conversions, movement up and down the social scale. Helpful guides to unravelling these stages are to be found in R W Brunskill: *Houses* (1982), chapter on How Houses Develop; and J T Smith and E M Yates: *On the Dating of English Houses from External Evidence* (reprinted from *Field Studies* (1968)).

Great houses

With the last of Brunskill's four categories of house we enter the realm of the architect, leaving behind the vernacular, even if some features of some Great Houses were designed or constructed by local builders or craftsmen or by vernacular methods. We are also at a different social level.

The great house, in all periods, goes beyond being merely the dwelling place of a family. It is also the focus and power centre of the ruling class. It is the centre of administration, justice, military power, state display, and hospitality. Power was based on ownership of land as well as devolution from above (the crown or a great nobleman, tenant-in-chief). Land meant tenantry; the medieval landowner had people under his control who could fight for him, the post-medieval magnate had people to vote for him. He also entertained lavishly, and up till the 19th century ordinary travellers could ask to stay on their way in a country house. The lord was also a patron of artists and craftsmen.

The space and number of rooms required to meet all these functions meant an establishment of a different kind from the ordinary manor house or large farmhouse. Not only was the household itself served by a small army of staff of all kinds, but the senior officials had their own servants and staff as well, and guests and visitors brought theirs with them. A royal visit could tax the resources of a whole district. Food and accommodation on a relatively vast scale were essential. The house and its estate has been compared to a large employing firm of our time, and this is not a bad way of visualising the great house up to the beginning of this century.

Apart from the monasteries and bishops' palaces, up to the end of the 15th century (before the upheavals of the Wars of the Roses and the Renaissance) the great houses were mostly the larger castles, such as Windsor, Caerphilly, Kenilworth, Arundel, or Alnwick. Business and entertainment focused on the hall, and later on the state rooms; the rest of the premises carried as much private accommodation as could be got in. Major officials, such as constables and stewards, either had their own suites or separate houses within the complex or in the vicinity.

With the Tudors came the New Men and their new houses. Defence in the form of castles was no longer necessary, and ostentation could flourish in houses and their gardens and contents. Renaissance ideas coupled with the last phase of the Perpendicular gave a particular flavour to the Tudor style. Most of the old nobility had passed away, and the newly rising gentry and merchants who carried on Tudor administration either built new houses (like Sutton Place (Sy) *c* 1525), or adapted old ones. The Dissolution in the late 1530s gave much scope for this. Abbey buildings, such as Forde (So) or St Osyth's (Ex) were remodelled by their new owners, or new houses were built alongside, such as Fountains Hall (NY). Wolsey's already huge Hampton Court (he had a household of 600) was further enlarged by Henry VIII (and several more times during the 17th and 18th centuries).

Some Elizabethan houses were not excessively large by the standards of the competing New Men, eg Haddon Hall (Db), Loseley (Sy), 1560–69, Compton Wynyates (Ww), or Little Moreton Hall (Ch). But some certainly were so, and reflected a kind of megalomania. Such are Burghley (Ca) 1560–87, Longleat (Wi), Wollaton (No), or Montacute (So), 1590s – all quite breathtaking in their insolent exuberance. Hatfield (Ht), 1607–11, follows these closely, and Knole (Kt) reached its final form, with its 365 rooms, early in the 17th century.

The Elizabethan style involved the use of Renaissance detail: huge windows, symmetry, size, and height. Mark Girouard has said, with Montacute in mind, that "great Elizabethan houses were not meant to melt inconspicuously into the landscape, but to stand out from it, and to be as impressive and remarkable as possible".

The Classical styles which emerged with Inigo Jones in the 1610s, and which led on to the well-proportioned and often delightful Georgian houses, of which so many fortunately remain, gave rise to several good (but not particularly small) houses at the end of the 17th century, such as Melton Constable (Nf), Belton (Li), 1689, or Fenton House, Hampstead, 1693. It also produced vast show-pieces like Chatsworth, 1680s–1700, Castle Howard, 1700–37, and Blenheim, 1705–37. But one may well feel uncomfortable with these, and prefer the more modest scale of Clandon (Sy), *c* 1733, or Newby Hall (NY), or Palladian villas like Chiswick, *c* 1720–25, and Mereworth (Kt), 1720–23, with its ingenious arrangement of chimneys, the flues from different parts of the house all meeting in a central shaft. The landscaped grounds of these houses are of great importance and are one of the main English contributions to European culture (see pages 125–37).

The main living floor of these great houses was the first, the *piano nobile*. Growing desire for privacy, in the presence of continual guests, led in the 17th century to the inclusion, or insertion, of a corridor off which the bedrooms opened; this replaced the earlier arrangement en suite (as at Versailles), in which one had to pass through other rooms to reach one's own, even if they were occupied bedrooms. To this end at Montacute, in 1785–6, an entire new west front was added to the house to accommodate the corridors. During the 18th century also, the numbers, functions, and layouts of rooms were rationalised and stabilised, to meet the requirements of family life and work in conjunction with the constant hospitality and entertainment which the great house was designed for. This was developed, and brought to a fine art, in the 19th century.

The standard pattern, when even great houses were only two rooms deep, was a hall on the north front leading to a saloon, off which opened state apartments on the south front; other rooms could be located haphazardly on both floors. Blenheim (Ox) and Clandon (Sy) are examples. Clandon also typifies, as does Uppark, the tendency for kitchens and service rooms to be in the basement and servants' bedrooms in the attics. The best house from which to appreciate the servants' world is Erddig (Fl) (1680s, enlarged 1720s and 1770s). Here the kitchen is on the ground floor and the servants' hall, butler's pantry, agent's room, and other rooms are on the lower ground floor. Attached to the house are the laundry, bakehouse, stable yard, outer yard, lime yard and sawmill, blacksmith's shop and wagon shed, sawpit, joiner's shop, and estate yard. The importance of Erddig in this connection lies in the exceptionally complete records, pictures, photographs, and other material relating to the servants, who had an unusually significant place in the household.

The culmination of this process of assembling in one building all rooms necessary for a large centre for lavish and continual entertainment is found in the Victorian country house (admirably described by Mark Girouard in his book of that title). These houses were huge, ugly, rambling piles, whose irregularity was due not only to the eclectic welter of Victorian architecture, but to the collection under one roof of a large and disparate assemblage of rooms. A typical example (by no means the largest) is Bear Wood (Bk), 1865–74, which has about 40 rooms on each of the ground and first floors, and about 30 on the second. The ground floor contains the main family rooms – hall, dining-room, luncheon-room, children's dining-room, drawing-room, library; a separate group of "men's rooms" – billiard-room, smoking-room, study, morning-room, business-room, waiting-room, and various ancillary rooms such as gun-room and deed-room; some houses had chapel and picture gallery as well. On the same floor are the service rooms and kitchen, with a large number of ancillaries. The first floor contains the family bedrooms, dressing-rooms, boudoir, another drawing-room, nurseries, schoolroom, sick-room, and maids' rooms. Upstairs again are more bedrooms, with specialised groups for bachelors, young ladies, and guests' servants. There are no fewer than seven staircases, each reserved for a different category of people. Attached to the house is a conservatory, and there are ranges of "outside" buildings, such as stables, coach-houses, and workshops.

These vast establishments, where most tasks had to be done the hard way, were geared to the power and prestige of a class, and to the opulent, if often gracious, way of living which expressed it. Some houses, like Cliveden (Bc) or Polesden Lacey (Sy), became the pleasure grounds of "society" at the highest level, where life was a round of balls, garden parties, and house parties for shooting and hunting.

Great houses have been designed by an imposing succession of distinguished architects, from Wren, Hawksmoor, and Vanbrugh to Kent, Adam, and Carr, Pugin, Barry, and Salvin (earlier Victorian), Kerr, Ruskin, and Burges (High Victorian), Webb, Shaw, and Nesfield (transitional). There was a "nouveau riche" style in the 1870s, even more ostentatious, and a neo-Georgian in the early 20th century. Notable examples are Cragside (Nd), Bear Wood (Bk), Adcote (Sp), Highclere (Bk), Waddesdon (Bc), Eaton Hall (Ch). The final fling is perhaps Lutyens' Castle Drogo in Devon, 1910–30. Lutyens gave his clients what they wanted and could afford, and this house harks back rather oddly, and perhaps symbolically, to a castle-like solidity.

The great house went into decline between the wars, with the changing pattern of society and economic pressures, and collapsed catastrophically with the Second World War. Today some 30% of the 6,000 listed country houses (of which say 500 are great houses) are no longer owned by their ancestral families, and have been put to new uses. Some have been bought by companies as training or conference centres, or as offices and laboratories. Some are schools, colleges, or nursing homes (many served as hospitals in the two wars, or as military headquarters). Some have been converted into flats. Many are open to the public, with their gardens, to make ends meet, and some of the larger houses, such as Woburn, Longleat, or Beaulieu, have developed "attractions" like zoos, museums, or amusement parks. The fortunate ones have been acquired by the National Trust and their future is assured, to a high standard of maintenance, if perhaps fossilised. But the less fortunate have gone under, their contents dispersed, their parks under pressure from buildings and roads. From 1875 to 1975 over 1,300 major country houses have been wholly or partly destroyed. From 1945 to 1974, 712 houses were demolished, gutted, or have fallen into ruin (476 in England, 203 in Scotland, and 33 in Wales). Others are empty and disused. But they have had a brilliant day.

Ice storage

Ice and snow were used for keeping food fresh and for cooling drinks in the eastern Mediterranean area by 1000 BC, in Greece by the 4th century BC, and in the Roman Empire. This practice was reintroduced into France in the late 16th century, and the earliest ice house known in Britain was at Ormerod House (La) (1595). In France and England ice was an important commodity by the mid 17th century. In 1660 icehouses for storing ice cut from ponds were built in Upper St James's Park (later The Green Park) in London, and became widespread in large houses by the early 18th century.

In France the ice trade was well organised by 1648, and in Provence, for instance, this trade took two forms – free commerce (using ice from Dauphiné) and "fermage". The latter involved ice made in artificial ponds and stored in icehouses within easy reach of large towns, which gave contracts to "fermiers", eg Fontfrège, which supplied Toulon. These fermiers were ousted later by free traders and by the railways – the towns no longer bought from one source, eg Marseilles, which preferred free trading with ice merchants (see *Archéologia* 206, 1985 (Dijon)).

By the early 19th century the demand had gone beyond the needs of private houses, and become large enough for a commercial trade to develop. Ice was imported into Britain in large quantities from Norway from 1820, when a London merchant, William Leftwich, brought a sailing ship to Norway to collect a cargo of ice. The centre of supply was the area round Oslo fjord and the Skagerrak coast. The ice was collected in the winter from lakes and ponds, stored in wooden sheds on the shores of the fjords, and shipped across the North Sea in the spring and summer. At the turn of the century about 5,000 men were employed in cutting and moving the ice overland, and 1,000 seamen in over 100 ships transported it to Britain, France, Belgium, and the Netherlands. In 1901, 11,000 tons were landed at Shoreham in Sussex. It was used in iceboxes in larger households and restaurants, butchers and dairies, but most of it was supplied to fishermen for use in keeping fresh fish caught at sea, so much of it went to east coast ports (see note by Tom Cook in *Local History News*, 11 (1986)).

There was also a lively trade in and from North America in the 19th century; the ice of eg the St Lawrence, the Hudson, and other east coast rivers was sawn into blocks and shipped not only to other parts of America but to Europe and even Asia as well. F Yorke mentions a US ice merchant with a capacity of 13,000 tons in just one of his houses, the year's turnover being some 30,000 tons. The trade was hit by the manufacture of ice and the development of bulk refrigeration in Britain and elsewhere from the mid 19th century, but did not cease completely until *c* 1960.

Mechanical refrigeration was introduced in the mid 19th century; ice-making machines were patented in the 1830s, and became numerous in the 1850s. Frozen meat was being imported by sea by the late 1870s. But small refrigerators suitable for private houses were not widespread until well into this century, and ice itself was used in houses and shops even in the 1920s.

Before then the large houses used icehouses to store ice, for use in the house when required, and less often to store actual food. The idea was introduced from France on a large scale in the reign of Charles II, but a few English examples may be earlier than this, some even late medieval. During the 18th and much of the 19th century most large country houses had icehouses, but many still remain to be discovered (where they still exist) and little study has been made of them. Local ponds were used to collect the ice from, and in a few cases special ponds were made. After the railways, of course, ice could be sent to any house in bulk for storage.

There were two types of storage systems: *ice wells*, brick-lined pits, either wholly or partly below ground, and *icehouses*, wholly or mostly above ground but sometimes covered by a mound. They had to be dry as well as cool, and in this country were usually partly underground. In the icehouse type the chamber was approached by a passage with two stout doors; steps led down to the chamber. In the ice wells a rope ladder had to be used for access. There had to be a drain or soakaway under the ice level; if a drain was used, the floor was often of brick; if a sump or soakaway, it could be wooden slats, or a grid, or even sticks wrapped in straw. The walls were sometimes lined with straight straw thatchwise, held on by wires.

In the well type, the ice was crushed and rammed tightly in chopped straw, either piled up in the centre of the bottom part of the pit, or ranged round the walls at their base, up to ground level. The ice could slip down the walls and compact. In the icehouse type, the ice was in blocks, packed in bundles of straw. Sometimes straw alternated with layers of ice. Ice could be kept for a year like this. The food to be kept cold (where this was done) was either placed directly on the ice or on wooden trays on the ice; meat could be hung from hooks. The chamber could be of a variety of shapes; an egg-shape was common.

Interest in icehouses is growing and some county surveys have been published. The pioneer in this study was F W B Yorke, concentrating on Warwickshire (1955); *Country Life* carried several contributions, also mainly in 1955 and 1956; more recently a useful survey of those in Dorset was made by Alan Penny (1965). Penny gives examples of the four varieties in Dorset: well, wholly below ground, Melbury Park, partly underground, Frampton Park; icehouse, above ground, under mound, Bindon Park; no mound, Weymouth Quay. A typical icehouse is at Barrells Hall, Ullenhall (Ww); its dome is about 10ft (3m) high, covering a brick structure with an egg-shaped chamber 17ft 6in high and 13ft 8in in diameter (5.25x4.1m), entered by a short passage with an iron grille at the outer end and an oak door at the inner; the "box" once had steps down to it, and a drain. This dates from between 1845 and 1850. A near perfect example of this type, with a brick-paved yard in front, was rediscovered and investigated in 1976 in the grounds of Lythe Hill House, Haslemere, Surrey. At Parden Hill Farm, Bishops Cleeve (Gl), is a small stone icehouse in a bank, which may be

monastic; at Blakeshall, Wolverley (Wo) is one cut out of a sandstone cliff. In fact banks are a good place to look; that at Milton Abbas (Do) is another example. Rectangular and beehive chambers are also found. Of the free-standing ones, that at Croome Court (Wo) is a circular stone wall supporting a heavy polygonal timber and thatch roof, and at Morden Hall (south-west London) there is a concrete one, covered with wattle inside and out. At Swakeleys, Ickenham (Mx) an icehouse is built into the lower levels of a dovecote, which had a separate entrance reached by a ladder, on a platform round the top of the icehouse dome; nearly half the 750 or so nesting boxes were below this level. Some icehouses are indeed near the manorial dovecote, but others are anywhere in the park, often in a shrubbery.

Private icehouses are not all in the grounds of country houses. There are, for instance, several in London. Thus, a large one 12ft deep and 30ft in diameter, at the house of one Samuel Dash in Park Crescent (*c* 1818), was discovered during rebuilding in 1961. Under the hay-market at Cumberland Market (1830) was a large commercial icehouse holding 1,500 tons, built for the trade from Norway up the Regent's Canal. There is a small icehouse under a house in Downshire Hill, Hampstead, with its entrance in the small front garden.

Among the more spectacular are those at Petworth House (Sx) (three chambers, 1784), Dalkeith House (EL), Long Hall (Sp), rebuilt at the Avoncroft Museum of Buildings, and Spey Bay (My), part of the fishing trade, with three icehouses side by side, all split-level structures, with six chambers in all, built in 1830. The adjacent fish-house dates from 1783. This group was in use until 1940, and is now a museum of Spey salmon fisheries.

Most county or local surveys of industrial archaeology refer to icehouses, and county lists are still being drawn up. Thus in 1982, Monica Ellis published a history of the icehouse and the ice trade, with a gazetteer for Hampshire (*Ice and Icehouses through the Ages* (Southampton University Industrial Archaeology Group, 1982)). Seventy-three icehouses in Hampshire are located and described in this book, which is a very useful summary of the subject, and illustrates the main types. Of these 73, remains survive in 42 cases. A survey by R Martin of the 80 or so icehouses in Sussex was in progress in 1986. Of these some 30 belonged to commercial premises in Brighton. In recent years a group called The Ice-house Hunt, led by Sylvia Beamon and Susan Roaf, has been making a comprehensive survey of the whole country. They have identified 3,000 sites, many of which are ruinous or no longer exist. A brief account of this work has appeared in *Current Archaeology* 105 (1987), and a definitive book, *The Ice-Houses of Great Britain* has been published (Routledge, Kegan Paul (1988)).

POST-CONQUEST HOUSES – URBAN

Medieval

The medieval urban house differed from the rural house in that it had to be fitted into a very limited space, with little or usually no elbow room on either side. It also usually had to combine a dwelling with a shop, store, counting house, and perhaps a workshop. The streets of the medieval market town were closely lined with *burgage plots*, to be taken up by the burgesses, who were encouraged to come into the town and run their businesses; this benefited both the burgess and the lord who granted the town's charter. Very few, if any, market towns were unplanned, or grew haphazardly. The plots were usually of standard sizes, and as many as possible were got in.

133 *Jew's House and Jew's Court, Lincoln: a Norman town house, c 1180, occupied by Jewish merchants until the expulsion of the Jews in 1290, and a synagogue next door (altered later).*

Some plots appear to be determined by the previous use of the ground, eg furlongs of common fields. Thus, Stratford-on-Avon and Thame have plots 60ft (18m) wide by 200ft (60m) and 650–700ft (195–210m) long respectively. At Salisbury (laid out in 1220) are plots 50x115ft (15x34.5m). Other plots relate to the normal dimensions of a timber-framed house. At Alnwick (Nd) (scene of M R G Conzen's pioneer study of the medieval town layout (Alnwick, Northumberland, *A Study in Town Analysis* (Trans and publns of the Institute of British Geographers, 27, 1960)), nearly half the burgages had a width of 28ft (8.4m), and another third were 32ft (9.6m). Many of the rest were 14 or 16ft (4.2 or 4.8m) wide – the width of a bay. So the standard frontage was for a house of two bays, with eaves facing the street. In some towns the present-day plots are less wide than they were when laid out; they vary from 25ft (7.5m) to as little as 6ft (1.8m). There are in fact records of half or quarter burgages as early as the 13th century; the peak of subdivision, to maximise the number of trades in the town, was in the 16th and 17th centuries. This tendency gives us the long narrow plots we see today in most old towns. A consequence is that any expansion of the premises at the street end has to be by building back along the plot, with an entrance along an alley on one side, through a door or archway, often under the house, or from a back lane.

But, given the tendency to subdivide, many plot boundaries remained stable for centuries. Thus in York (Coppergate), the Danish boundaries of long narrow plots *c* 18ft wide did not change from the 9th to the 18th century, and some were found (in the recent excavations) to have influenced the layout of the factory which latterly occupied the site. And, for a surprising number of towns, a large-scale plan or an air photograph will show the persistence of the medieval plots, still running back from the main streets. Good examples are Devizes (Wi), Thame (Ox), and Pembroke (Dy); but most old towns have some.

Most houses were vernacular timber-framed until the 17th century, but in some places, eg Lincoln, Southampton, Canterbury, and York, there was a change to stone in the late 12th century. Some of these stone houses have survived, and are sometimes known as "Jews' Houses"; indeed, the Jewish financiers preferred the safety of stone houses to keep their gold, silver, and securities in. The best-known examples are the two in Steep Hill at Lincoln (see **133**), and Moyses' Hall in Bury St Edmunds. The Jew's House at Lincoln (1170–80) has two rooms on the ground floor and three on the first, with a possible one-room extension on two floors out at the back. The "Music House" in Norwich (late 12th century) has a first-floor hall, with a spectacular vaulted undercroft, and an entrance forebuilding.

John Steane points out that in Norwich there was a cycle of redevelopment every 150–200 years, when either buildings wore out or fashion dictated rebuilding. All the houses in an area might reach the end of their useful life at the same time, resulting in destruction of earlier phases. Steane also stresses that the standing buildings which have survived in towns are often atypical, being houses of wealthy burgesses, a very small proportion of the inhabitants. These are often on double plots.

Medieval urban houses seem to derive from the rural three-cell type, but from the 16th century there is a variety of types. The medieval side passage, if any, was replaced in the 18th century by doors each side of the shop – one for the shop, one for the dwelling. A double plot could contain a courtyard house or even a farm.

A W Pantin defined two main types of house – the *parallel*, where the hall lies along the street frontage, and the *right-angle*, which has the hall at right angles to the street, with sometimes a solar and other rooms parallel to the street. If the plot was narrow, the hall, solar, and service rooms were along the plot, with an alley at one side. This type got commoner as plots narrowed by subdivision. Another type is the *double-range*, where the dwelling house is set back, with a shop or courtyard in front. These types continued until well into the 17th century, after when many towns were radically altered. Medieval backs can still frequently be seen behind later fronts.

Examples of most of these types may be seen at York or Southampton, eg at Southampton, large merchants' houses such as the Norman House in Cuckoo Lane, on a plot 56ft 6in x 105 ft (16.95 x 31.5m), and 4 High Street, a "King John's House" – ground floor storage and sales, hall and chambers upstairs, and at York, the present Black Swan Inn, Peasholme Green, formerly a merchant's house. Plots in Southampton were normally *c* 19ft (5.7m) wide, and could be nearly 300ft (90m) long, eg those between the High Street and the town wall. Houses gable-ended onto the street can be seen on these narrow plots, particularly in York. The continued use of timber-framing until the 17th century indicates its advantages over stone, particularly for jettying and rising higher. Roofs were tiled or slated, not thatched, from the 12th century.

From the late 16th century the usual types are the large courtyard houses, the small two-storey house, with four or five rooms (both these types died out in London), and the three-storey (or even four), three rooms deep, after 1600; but smaller houses might only have one room on a floor.

Much valuable research has been done into the occupancy of blocks of houses in certain towns at different periods. London, for instance, had a good deal of open space even into the 17th century – gardens and yards for growing vegetables or keeping pigs or poultry – while the built-up parts became more and more congested as the population increased. We are fortunate to have a detailed survey, made by Ralph Treswell in 1612, of properties of Christ's Hospital and the Clothworkers' Company. The latter, in Fenchurch Street and Billiter Lane, was a warren of interlocking buildings, with shops along the streets and rooms of all sizes and uses behind. Some of the tenants occupied one room or houses with a one-room plan; some had quite large houses. There was a complete mixture of social and economic grades (see John Schofield: *The Building of London* (1984)).

In larger towns like London, buildings got taller in the 16th century, and in Glasgow and Edinburgh very tall. In Scotland, indeed, the middle and working classes preferred to live on one floor of these tenement blocks – "flats", often of only two rooms. Some of these blocks, eg those off the Royal Mile in Edinburgh, are six storeys high. (Useful detail will be found in eg M W Barley: *The House and Home* (1963); J M Steane: *The Archaeology of Medieval England and Wales* (1984); M Aston and J Bond: *The Landscape of Towns* (1976).)

The Chester Rows

An exceptional piece of medieval urban building is the *Rows* of Chester (see **134** and **135**). These may indeed be unique anywhere (with the possible exception of Thun, Switzerland). The Rows consist of continuous ranges of arcades or galleries along the central streets, at first-floor level, reached by stairways at intervals; the arcades are open to the street, and on the side away from the street are shops. Below the arcades, at street level, are shops, some with medieval cellars or undercrofts behind. The Rows occur along both sides of Watergate Street (from Cork Street) and Eastgate Street (to St Werburgh Street and Newgate Street), and on both sides of Bridge Street (as far as

134–5 *The Chester Rows: shops, workshops and living quarters etc on two levels. The section shows the relation of the Rows to the street and ground levels.*

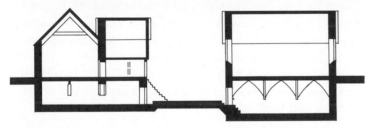

Whitefriars and Pepper Street). The area of the walled city east of Nicholas Street and north of Pepper Street is on the site of the Roman legionary fortress of Deva, and the line of its main thoroughfares is broadly followed by Northgate Street, and accurately followed by Watergate Street-Eastgate Street, and by Bridge Street. all of which lead to the gates of the fortress. The Rows therefore line the present streets which most closely supersede the Roman streets, and it is reasonable to see some significance in this.

The Rows reached their present form between 1500 and 1800, but seem to have been developing from the 12th century. The property strips along the streets were laid out in the late 11th/early 12th century, but the Rows as such are not recorded until 1330, at which date they were public thoroughfares.

The determining factor is that medieval building in these central streets was conditioned by the existence of banks of Roman ruins and building debris along both sides of the streets. Until the 10th century, at least, the legionary fortress area was only sparsely occupied, among the Roman ruins. Only after then did the population reach a level where a normal town could be built; but even then the Roman remains were not all cleared away. Meanwhile the Roman streets themselves continued in use, but the banks of debris remained.

The second factor is that in 1278 most of the walled area was totally devastated by fire. Whatever buildings preceded this had to be rebuilt, and this gives a reasonable beginning for the Rows as they later took shape. J T Smith suggests that the close links in trade between Chester and Gascony led to the rebuilt houses having arcades like those in the contemporary bastides in France (such as Monpazier), but on the first floor, not the ground. An alternative view is that the Rows developed from *c* 1100, piecemeal, from shops on first-floor hall/chamber level above an undercroft, at a time when regular street frontages were the rule. To have continuous shops on two levels was, on this view, a commercial development, stimulated by the fire of 1278. Smith's theory could fit in with this.

But the building on two levels still has to be more fully explained. The answer may be that the property strips may have stopped short before the slope of the debris, allowing a thoroughfare to connect the properties at the street end, at the level of the top of the bank, ie the first floor. The buildings then may have been enlarged by way of upper rooms built forward over this thoroughfare, thus forming the Rows beneath them. The overhanging rooms would have been on stilts, as cellars were dug into the bank beneath the thoroughfare (later also occupied by shops along the street). Perhaps a combination of all these theories is required (for details see B E Harris *et al*: "Galleries which they call, The Rows" (*Journal of the Chester Archaeological Society* 67, 1985).)

Post-medieval

The open hall went out of favour by 1500 or so, and houses built in the 16th century and later had two or more storeys, each with two rooms, connected by staircases, and with fireplaces instead of open hearths. Some replaced houses on the narrow plots in the old town centres, but most were built outside these, on wider plots. This type remained popular into the 19th century.

A house on a plot of limited width, even a wide one, could only be enlarged by adding to the height or by extending at the back. This was often done by adding a third room behind one of the two front ones, giving an L-plan, or, if added in the centre, a T-plan. Earlier houses usually had central chimneystacks, reflecting back-to-back fireplaces. Larger houses were frequently, by the 17th century, double-pile, with four rooms on each floor and chimneys at the gables. The front door of all these types was central, leading to a narrow hall or passage, and the frontage was symmetrical (see **136**). This, with variations of size, became the standard town house – from the tradesman's house with shop to the gentleman's "town house" – from the mid 17th century and throughout the 18th. Examples can still be found in any town of any size or distinction, such as Chichester, Bury St Edmunds, Stamford, or York. At the upper social levels these town houses were the expression of a social system under which the gentry lived in their country houses in the summer and came into the county town for the winter and the social "season". The county and similar towns had assembly rooms round which this way of life revolved, as at York or Bath.

Some of the gentry still preferred not to live right in the town centre, but to retain one foot in the country. Their houses – *villas*, an Italian

136 *A late Georgian house, West Street, Farnham (Sy): a simple yet very satisfying design.*

Renaissance legacy – were often on the scale and type of large country houses (see above, page 234). Such, in the London area, are Inigo Jones' Queen's House at Greenwich (*c* 1620), Lord Burlington's Palladian Chiswick House (1725–29), several at Richmond and Twickenham, such as Marble Hill (*c* 1725), Kenwood House, Highgate (Kent, rebuilt by Adam 1768), or Burton's Nuffield Lodge (1822–24) and The Holme in Regent's Park (*c* 1818).

The narrow frontage houses on the medieval town centre plots, which might be only 12ft wide, of necessity had to have the two rooms on each floor one behind the other, with longitudinal passage along one side. Some had separate kitchens etc across a yard at the back.

The terrace house

The terrace idea – houses of uniform plan, or broadly so, joined together in rows – took off in the 1670s, in housing schemes built in London by Nicholas Barbon, and has continued in popularity ever since. The English have a deep-seated preference for living in their own houses, entered at ground level, with if at all possible gardens, or at least yards. This is in contrast to the Scots or the French, who are content with flats in larger houses or blocks. The terrace idea proved to be convenient and well-adapted to general standards and ways of living, was cheaper to build, and was more economical of space. It therefore became the normal form of housing for workers in the Industrial Revolution, and in the 19th century became standard for the middle classes also.

The terrace was not in fact unknown in the Middle Ages. In St Pancras Lane, Winchester, Martin Biddle's excavations in the 1960s revealed a row of four cottages for clothworkers (14th century), each of two rooms (one room with hearth, entered from the lane, with partitioned-off sleeping room behind). York, at 64–72 Goodramgate, has a row of workers' houses (1316), two storeys of one room each. 54–60 Stonegate is a storey higher; each bay had three rooms – shop, hall, and chamber. There are similar houses in St Peter's Street, Northampton (15th century).

But the great expansion of the terrace idea began in London, where the Great Fire of 1666 necessitated vast rebuilding and where the population was increasing rapidly, with much migration from country to town. The terrace was the obvious answer to these demands. Not only were terraces cheaper to build than single houses, but they economised in space and also in road-making. The roads were therefore laid out with long strips running back from them, often with a garden or courtyard, and, in the richer areas, mews behind for coach-house and stables. All except the poorest had basements; but these were shallow excavations, as the roadway was partly raised above the level of the gardens.

John Summerson (in *Georgian London* (1945, rev 1962)) says that "Georgian London was a city made up almost entirely of these long narrow plots with their tall narrow houses and long gardens or courts. Practically the whole population lived in one version or another of such houses. A handful of aristocrats had their isolated palaces; and the unemployable and criminal classes had their centuries-old rookeries; but the remainder, from earls to artisans, had their narrow slices of building, now called, for no very good reason, 'terrace-houses'."

The builders of these houses found standardisation their most economical course, and there was indeed little scope for variety on a plot 12ft, or even 24ft wide. The individuality (and this very

limited) came by applying ornament and detail from the classical repertory. The public was ready for this; Inigo Jones had brought Renaissance ideas of symmetry and order, and classical detail, into England in 1615, and his Banqueting Hall in Whitehall (1619–22) must have given a lively shock to public taste, and heralded the end of the vernacular. The Covent Garden scheme of the 1630s, bringing the Italian piazza into England, showed what could be done on a scale within the reach of the people. On a less formal scale, Great Queen Street, also of the 1630s, must have been a revelation.

But the pre-fire city, with its medieval timber-framed buildings, still existed, and the political difficulties of the mid century (the Civil Wars and the Commonwealth) did not encourage much new building. The Restoration and the fire provided the impetus for a new start, a veritable revolution in housing and living conditions. After the Restoration two great landowners decided to capitalise on the potentialities of their estates: the Earl of Southampton, with Bloomsbury Square (the first London square to be so called), which he let out in 24 plots on building leases (1661), and the Earl of St Albans, who created St James's Square (1662 onwards). Both built houses for themselves in the squares. The scheme for St James's Square began with the idea of large town houses, but had to be changed to something more modest.

These schemes initiated the pattern of development of the great estates for the next hundred years. Each scheme consisted of the owner's own house, a complete unit of development, with square, secondary streets, market, and perhaps church, and a speculative builder as middleman and actual builder of the houses.

The new opportunities were fully exploited by an entrepreneur of genius, Nicholas Barbon, who from 1670 to 1700 bought up or leased vast areas of building land all over London, on which he built houses of very stereotyped design, or let land to speculators to build on. His work may still be seen, at its best, in Bedford Row (nos 36–43) and Great James Street. In Barbon's houses the front door was on one side, leading to a more or less narrow "hall" or passage, with staircase at its end. There were two rooms on each of three floors, and a basement. The ground floor had two windows, the others three. There might be a small room or closet opening off the back ground floor room. (Incidentally, Barbon did much to encourage house insurance.)

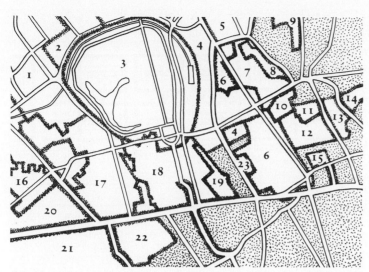

137 *The 18th-century development of part of west London. London, and other cities, expanded in the 17th and 18th centuries by way of the independent development of private estates. These were of course of different shapes and sizes – some had squares, churches, and shops, others just terraced streets. Each estate had its own character. The pattern in the West End of London, of which this map shows part, is very complex. The estates shown here are: 1, Eyre; 2, Portland; 3, Crown (Regent's Park and associated terraces); 4, Southampton; 5, Camden; 6, Bedford; 7, Somers; 8, Brewers' Company; 9, St Bartholomew's Hospital; 10, skinners' Company; 11, Harrison; 12, Foundling Hospital; 13, Galthorpe; 14, Lloyd Baker; 15, Bedford Charity; 16, Grand Junction Canal Company; 17, Portman; 18, Portland (Cavendish–Harley); 19, Berners; 20, Bishop of London; 21, Crown (Hyde Park–Kensington); 22, Grosvenor; 23, City of London.*

A 17th-century double-pile type of terrace house has a central staircase, in a space leading off the long passage, between the front rooms and the back rooms. This type was revived in the late 18th and early 19th century for some of the most elaborate town houses.

These trends continued throughout the 18th century, and culminated in some monumental schemes in the early 19th. After a few ornate and almost exotic terraces like Queen Anne's Gate (c 1704), most of the building was plain, in London yellow or grey brick, and sometimes quite drab. Better houses could have stone bands and cornice, and different colour dressings. The use of pattern-books by builders was universal. Variety was mostly in the internal arrangements and in the details. Houses on wider plots might have the front door between two rooms. On small plots the upper floors might show only two windows, and on the smallest the "front room" might only have one; indeed, on a 12ft plot the door might open straight into the front room.

138 *Cumberland Terrace, London – John Nash, 1826: an impressive part of Nash's "corridor" between St James's Park and Regent's Park.*

The large private estates to the west of the City were developed until building was continuous. The Cavendish-Harley (Portland) estate was one of the first (1717); later estates included the Portman, Bedford, Grosvenor (Mayfair and Belgravia), and Southampton (Fitzroy) (see 137). A large number of distinguished architects were involved with these, but the speculators were also present.

The culmination, almost the apotheosis, of the terrace is Nash's development of the Crown estates from the Mall (Carlton House Terrace), along Lower Regent Street, Regent Street, and Portland Place, to the stupendous terraces on both sides of Regent's Park (1811–35) (see 138). This provided a spine to the amorphous West End and, although not all the original plan was carried out, and

139 *The Circus, Bath – John Wood the Elder, 1754: one of the foci of Georgian Bath.*

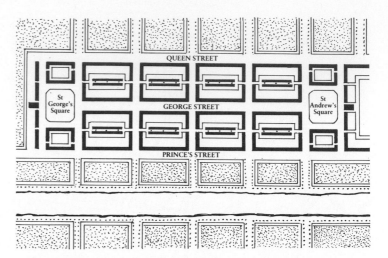

140 *James Craig's plan for part of the first New Town of Edinburgh, 1767. This, with its regular grid and its symmetry, was in complete contrast to the haphazard medieval city.*

Regent Street has been rebuilt, the effect remains (see John Summerson: *John Nash: Architect to King George IV* (1935 and 1949)).

Of course, such developments were not confined to London, although their full range can be studied there. Bath, although its development was piecemeal and somewhat haphazard (and perhaps partly because of this), conveys an unrivalled impression of the spirit of the 18th century – an impression enhanced in Bath's case by its magnificent hilly site. Bath was made suddenly popular by the long visit of Queen Anne in 1702–3. Before then it was largely confined within its medieval walls, although it had the apparatus of a spa on a modest scale – pump room, assembly rooms, infirmary, and places to promenade in. But now there was a change of scale. In 1715 8,000 visitors came, and not only did the life of the resort have to be more closely organised (a task which "Beau" Nash carried out from 1705 for 30 years), but there was a growing demand for houses for long stays or even permanent living. By 1720 several small streets had been laid out on the edge of the old town.

The later 1720s saw the beginnings of large-scale development. But, as said above, this was piecemeal. Some 5,000 houses were built between 1720 and 1800, but to no regular plan. The extraordinary unity of Bath is due, not to its planning, but to the classical uniformity and dignity of its architecture and to the mellow colour and soft texture of its stone – the "Bath Stone" quarried at Combe Down from the 1720s by Ralph Allen, whose villa, Prior Park, looks down over the town. In 1727–8 the Kings Mead-Avon Street area was built, and in 1729–36 the famous Queen Square and Gay Street (by John Wood the elder, who in 1740 built North and South Parades). There was another surge of activity from *c* 1755 to 1770; from 1754 John Wood

designed the (King's) Circus, the first modern (circular) circus, which was finished by his son, John Wood the younger (see **139**). The latter continued the scheme with the stupendous Royal Crescent (1767–74), and built the new Assembly Rooms in 1771. The last burst of 18th-century building was St James's Square higher up the hill, in no relation to the Wood schemes on the same estate (whereas Queen Square, Gay Street, the Circus, and Royal Crescent are all organically linked), and Lansdown Crescent beyond this. Also in the 1770s and 1780s the Bathwick estate was laid out, based on Great Pulteney Street (1785) and linked to the city by Adam's pretty bridge (1771); this is the only major area of Bath with a single coherent plan.

Part of the uniqueness of Bath is due to the architectural *facades* given to the major schemes, such as those of the Woods – ie a side of a square, or a whole crescent or terrace. These give more than mere unity; they create the illusion of being the frontages of great buildings in their own right. The idea was taken up to great effect elsewhere, as in The Crescent at Buxton, *c* 1780, Charlotte Square, Edinburgh, 1791, Bedford Square, London, and the Nash terraces in Regent's Park and the Mall, 1820s, The Promenade, Cheltenham, *c* 1823, and Adelaide Crescent, Hove, 1830, to name a few.

The terrace house reached a regular layout and usage by the later 18th century, in Bath and elsewhere. The norm was: kitchen and scullery in the basement; family rooms and dining-room on the ground floor; drawing rooms on the first floor; bedrooms on the second floor; garrets above. While the fronts were uniform, the backs could have bays or extensions. Importance was attached to uniformity of frontages; thus in Regency Square, Brighton (1818 onwards), the 70 plots were leased to different people with option to purchase. Each builder had to complete his facade to an approved pattern, with a balcony, area, and pavement.

The New Town of Edinburgh is another major Georgian townscape. The first part of this was laid out by James Craig in 1767, on a rather rigidly geometric plan (see **140**). Its central spine was George Street, linking St Andrew's Square with St George's (later called Charlotte) Square. Parallel on either side were Queen Street and Princes Street; these were planned to have houses on one side only, so as to face the view of the Forth and the gardens which replaced the Nor'Loch (where the railway now runs) respectively. This arrangement was broken by north–south cross streets – Castle, Frederick, Hanover, etc – and within each block so formed were mews and narrow lanes of small houses. The plots were feued to private developers, and houses had to be built along the lines of the plan; the maximum height, fixed in 1781, was 48ft. The standard house was of three bays, with door to one side. This formal scheme is saved by its excellent and airy site from being dull.

North of Queen Street is another grid, centred on Hanover Street (1809 onwards). At the west end this second New Town is broken and enlivened by Royal Crescent and Moray Place (c 1822–30); west of Charlotte Square, Melville Street opens up a third element of the New Town, while east of Calton Hill are Regent Terrace and Royal Terrace (1819), which began a link with Leith which was never completed.

The extent and cohesion of these successive phases make Edinburgh an extremely impressive summary of a century of architecture, in which the changes of style can be clearly followed. The detail too is of interest, eg the ironwork. The Edinburgh terraces were at first separate houses, as in London, but later became tenements or maisonettes, following the Scottish liking for living in flats. James Craig also worked in Glasgow from 1786, and the developments west and north of the old city centre (High Street) gave Glasgow a reputation for elegance.

The 18th century left its mark on a great many towns, and individual houses and terraces of merit can be seen everywhere. Particularly numerous or good examples – whole streets or even areas – are conspicuous in York, Chichester, Bury St Edmunds, Stamford, Blandford (rebuilt after a fire in 1731), and Haddington, to name a few. And many towns have exceptionally good single streets, such as Farnham (Sy); and Odiham and Alresford (Ha). Regency schemes are well seen in Cheltenham (The Promenade, 1818; Montpellier, 1809; Pittville and Lansdown, 1825) and Brighton, not only in the streets clustering round the Pavilion, but in the spectacular squares, open to the sea, in Kemp Town (Sussex Square, 1823) and Hove (Brunswick Square, 1825).

The rapidly growing industrial cities tended to be developed by estates, as in London; the plans and individual character of these have been studied by C W Chalklin (in *The Provincial Towns of Georgian England* (1974)). Those in Liverpool, Birmingham (Colmore, Gooch, etc), and Manchester (Byrom, Aytoun, Shepley, Stevenson, etc), from the 1770s on, and also Bath, were leasehold and built up by developers; in other towns, such as Nottingham, Hull, Plymouth, and Portsmouth, the land was freehold. These differences led to variations in the actual developments.

The Industrial Revolution – workers' houses

The workers in the burgeoning and increasingly congested industrial towns did not have the benefit of these "polite" developments. The rate of industrialisation was so rapid that houses were flung up round and among the factories and mills at the lowest cost and in the smallest space practicable. Some of these developments speedily became slums, while most never shook off an inherent drabness, accentuated by the soot and pollution which permeated the towns. Any description of this housing is bound to be depressing.

An interesting variety of industrial housing is the *back-to-back*. This is a house, normally one of a terrace, built immediately against another house at its back, with no space between them – ie sharing the same party wall. It has acquired an unfavourable reputation – not perhaps entirely justified – and has been rapidly replaced by modern forms of housing. But a number still survive. Back-to-backs are a feature of the industrial towns of the north of England: Manchester had 10,000 in the 1890s; Sheffield had over 16,000; Liverpool 20–30,000; Birmingham some 40,000; and they could be seen in most towns. Even London had a few (the earliest known was in Bermondsey, 1706), and Edinburgh still has (but so brightened up that

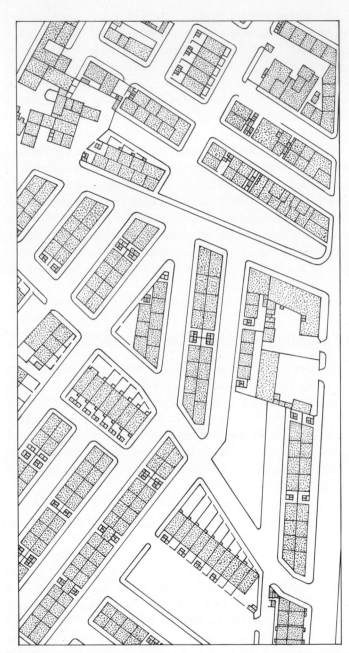

141 Back-to-back housing, Leeds: this shows development in irregular blocks, based on the ownership of small plots of land.

at first glance it is not easy to be sure what they really are). But the centre of the back-to-backs was Leeds, which built more of them than anywhere else, built them for longer, and kept them longest (see **141**). They have in fact no industrial function, and their frequency in the north is hard to explain (the particular conditions of Leeds did not apply everywhere), except on vaguely regional or "cultural" grounds. A recent study of this phenomenon has been made by Professor M W Beresford (1971).

In Leeds in 1801, of 11,500 houses in the city, fewer than 1,000 were back-to-back; in 1886, of 61,000, 49,000 (71%) were of this type, and in 1920, of 108,000, 78,000 (71%). Initially, a back-to-back had only one room down and one up; it reflected the search for the maximum rentable or saleable houses per acre. Even in the 1850s they measured 5x5yd only, but many rural cottages were no larger, nor were the working-class houses which crowded the innyards, burgage plots, and gardens of older houses in the centre of the town from the 1750s. Their real defect was the lack of ventilation and light; yet they were warm. The end houses, on large roads, could readily be made into shops.

The original development of industrial Leeds was the "fold-yard" type, infill of the yards of farmhouses and the like along the roads out of the city on the southern and eastern sides. The houses which filled the yards gave no straight frontages, like the middle-class squares and terraces, so even a main road like Marsh Lane was of irregular width. This Folds development (1750–1850) was accompanied by another type of urban cottage building, the filling in of any vacant space behind the houses in the old centre. This lined the interior walls of an innyard or garden with cottages, and thus may have begun the back-to-back. All this central area had yards suitable for this: Kirkgate had the crofts of the original village, Briggate the burgage plots laid out in 1207, and Headrow the new extensions of the early 17th century. By 1815 these were all filled solid with cottages, warehouses, and finishing shops.

Until 1781 the Folds and the infill could cope with demands for housing without creating new streets. A long block of houses east of Mabgate was not back-to-back, but rows on a long narrow field. This was the first of many. The main roads were being continuously built up, and new workers' housing would have to be in new streets opening off them into the fields and breaking through into the main roads. The first such was in 1787, between Vicar Lane and Sheepscar Beck

(Union, George, Ebenezer Streets, etc). The houses in these streets, now demolished, were back-to-back and were built by a building club. Most new central streets between 1787 and 1815, on the north, east, and south of Leeds, were back-to-back in the old fields.

The largest area of back-to-backs was that north of the river Aire, now largely cleared for blocks of flats. They went from Great Woodhouse to Carlton Hill, and high land values could not explain them all. In fact, they conveniently fitted the vacant spaces available for building, which were long narrow fields deriving from the strips of the open fields, enclosed in the late Middle Ages. These had been used for grazing, market gardens, or tenters. It was more profitable to fill these with two rows of back-to-backs, with a narrow alley between, than two rows of through houses with wide roadway. The other factor was the prevalence of smallholdings and small estates, so building grounds were often small. The largest estate had been taken up for west end houses – the Parks – in the 1780s and 1790s. So back-to-backs are often in small, unconnected parcels, blocked off by old field boundaries. The extreme is the "half-back", against a boundary.

These piecemeal streets were hard to service, and were often not maintained by the local authority. The streets of the 1870s and 1880s were longer and wider. This was due to a change in the size of the building unit, as the city spread north into larger estates (at Roundhay, Headingley, etc) which could be planned.

Back-to-backs were criticised from the 1830s, and were slowly improved or rebuilt, against opposition. By the 1860s some had kitchens on the ground floor. In 1910–14, when 1,946 houses were built in Leeds, a quarter were back-to-back. The last street was completed in 1937 (at a time when 150-year-old back-to-backs were being cleared for the new development at Quarry Hill). The later ones, like Luxor Avenue (1907–8), look like any other terrace of the period.

If Leeds was the capital of the back-to-back, Liverpool was the home of the *court*. This was a narrow alley 6–15ft wide, with facing rows of houses normally of three storeys – two rooms 10 or 11ft square, a garret, and often a cellar. The court was entered through a *tunnel* under the "front house" on the road; this had a better position, but was usually overcrowded. The court houses were often combined with *cellar* dwellings, a dark, damp room with access by stairs from the court. The court normally shared one water closet and one tap.

The great industrial cities underwent phenomenal population expansions from about 1770, which were met by the running up of houses as cheap and close as possible, fitted in between factories, mills, railways, etc, and using any available land. Most of this housing was for the lower grades of workers. In Liverpool, from 1780 to 1850, the poorer housing (in the central areas, Wapping, Exchange, Vauxhall, Lime Street) was of three types: cellar dwellings (12% of the population lived in these in 1790), built as such; back-to-backs (20%); terraces and tenements. All this housing was grossly overcrowded. From 1820 growth was more erratic, in a series of booms, which extended into the middle-class areas (Rodney Street and Abercromby wards) as the richer people moved out. From 1840 workers' housing spread to the suburbs (Toxteth, Everton, Scotland), round the new docks to the north. The Irish immigration in the 1840s accentuated the overcrowding, which by then well exceeded the national average. Vauxhall ward had 56.75% living in courts and cellars, as against 34.33% in Liverpool overall. Lodging houses appeared in the late 1840s, and the situation slowly improved from this time. But the effect of these conditions on public health was appalling; in 1843 the mean duration of life in Liverpool was 26 years, while for London it was 37, and for Surrey 45. The social effects can be gauged from eg Engels' celebrated study of Manchester (*The Condition of the Working Class in England* (1845)).

Birmingham had a somewhat different development, resulting from infilling rather than the building up of vacant plots. By 1731 there were already 150 courts and alleys, and building plots shown on a map of 1750 (in the Great Charles Street and Coleshill Street areas) were not related to the field system. In 1786 more than a third of the houses in the town were described as "back houses". By 1880 the area south of Great Charles Street was packed with some of the most congested small property in Birmingham, and this originated with the lining of paddocks and gardens with small houses. The canal links which broke the isolation of Birmingham led, from the 1760s, to solid brick and slate merchants' houses, of three or even four storeys, built to accommodate a warehouse and counting house as well as living quarters. These usually had gardens or "back land". The "shopping" – stables, pump, and later workshop – was at the back. The yard was surrounded by a high brick wall, against which workmen's cottages could be built. By the late 18th century houses were built in terraces, but still with embellished front, and yard and workshops in the rear. These were also developed.

By 1836 there were 2,030 courts in Birmingham, containing 12,254 tenants; but cellar dwellings were unknown. Even then the workers in the larger towns were better off than in small, obscure, industrial places; in the Black Country many lived in cob and thatched one-room huts. When the inner suburbs were built up in the 1860s and 1870s, the layouts preserved the workshop-court pattern, behind long terraces. But Birmingham was not relatively overcrowded, and the activities of friendly societies and building clubs greatly improved conditions for the upper working and lower middle classes.

Bad as Liverpool, Leeds, and Birmingham were, the blackest spot of the Industrial Revolution was Nottingham, up to 1750 an elegant, aristocratic, spacious town, but by 1840 having the worst slums in Britain, and second only to Bombay for slums in the entire British Empire. By 1835, 53,000 people occupied a site formerly housing 10,000. This population depended on hosiery (depressed in the early 19th century), cotton spinning after 1784, and lace (prosperous).

Nottingham's misfortune was to be hemmed in by a wide belt of ancient common land, which, as a consequence of long-drawn-out wrangles between the various interests involved, was not enclosed until as late as 1845. Incidentally, this enclosure gave an opportunity to regulate new housing and plan the layout of the new town, which determined the character of modern Nottingham. But before the enclosure, although some upper workers and small machine-owners migrated beyond the common lands to suburbs like Radford or Lenton, and although the lacemakers were able to live in good districts, the growing numbers of poor cotton-spinners and frame-knitters had nowhere to go. By the end of the 18th century shared houses were common, and families even lived, slept, and worked in one room. Nottingham then had good cottages on the outskirts, shared houses in the centre, rock dwellings in the north-east round Sneinton Hermitage and on Castle Rock, and very small cottages on the town margins. The poorest districts were the "Rookeries", north of Market Square, and Narrow and Broad Marsh. The Rookeries had back-to-backs by 1744; but the main housing boom began in the 1780s. This was mainly three-storey houses, for living (ground floor), sleeping (first floor), and working (second floor), with sometimes a loft for storage. The second floor had long workshop windows. There could also be a cellar. These houses were back-to-backs, in courts, with tunnel entrances.

The second boom, in the 1820s, brought in floods of migrants and slum houses multiplied, with serious overcrowding. A survey in 1832 (against a threat of cholera) revealed 11,000 houses of which nearly 8,000 were back-to-back, mostly in courts; 650 were classed as inferior in construction (excluding lean-tos and those exposed to severe contamination). The higher, better districts almost entirely escaped the cholera. The slum areas had 60% shorter life expectancy. Not till after 1845 did the pressure ease. The solid Victorian terraces date from the 1850s, but the first council housing was not built until 1877.

Glasgow made its own response to its population explosion. The elegant 18th-century city was disrupted by the Industrial Revolution and by the massive immigration of Highlanders and Irish in the 1820s and 1830s. Villages became suburbs, the "respectable" went west, and the centre became slums, complicated by railways, public buildings, and industries. Population density reached 1,000 an acre in some districts.

The character of Glasgow's workers' housing is largely set by the efforts to clean up this situation and rebuild the worst slums, after the City Improvement Act of 1866. The City Improvement Trust provided new housing, but not enough; municipal house building began in the Saltmarket in 1890, but again only 1% of the population was rehoused by 1914. Lodging houses indeed catered for more people than these efforts; by 1871, 23% of all Glasgow families had lodgers, mostly in one or two rooms. "Ticketed" houses were set up after the 1866 Act; houses of three rooms or less were measured and "ticketed" with the number of inhabitants allowed – 300 cu ft for everyone over 8 years of age. In 1881 some 75,000 people (14% of the population) lived in these (22,000 houses). But less than half of Glasgow's one-roomed houses were ticketed. Most of these were subdivisions of existing property, which became grossly overcrowded.

Private builders became active from the 1870s, and after 1901 middle-class tenements were converted into "made-down" houses. Company housing and artisans' building societies also played their part, as did "house-farmers" (furnished subtenancies). The social impact of the replacement of areas like the Gorbals by new tenements, and of massive suburban schemes like Easterhouse, still remains to be fully worked out. Glasgow housing was "built to last too long" (John Butt).

(For details of all this see Stanley D Chapman (ed): *The History of Working-class Housing* (1971), and Stefan Muthesius: *The English Terrace House* (1982).)

Muthesius describes a number of variants of the small worker's house. A feature of the north-east of England is the *single-storey miner's house*. In the 19th century this was two rooms deep, often with an added kitchen under a lean-to roof (catslide) at the back. Earlier miners' houses had shared water closets. Sunderland is distinguished for its single-storey "cottages" (as opposed to "houses", which have two storeys). These have their own water closets. The reason for these in Sunderland is not clear. Another type is the *single-pile*, one room deep on two floors; these have a wide distribution. Some of these are built up against walls, and some had backdoors and backyards, but no windows at the back (*blind-backs*).

There are many varieties of the *two-up two-down* type, a widespread type of terrace house in all areas. A common type of dwelling in the north-east is the *flat in terraces*, where each floor is self-contained, with its own front door. Well over half the dwellings built on Tyneside in 1900 were of this type. They occur in London also.

A specialised variant of the back-to-back is the *up and down house*, a type adapted to the very steep hillsides of West Yorkshire, from Halifax to Todmorden – they can be well seen at Hebden Bridge. These consist of vertical pairs of two-storey houses, in terraces. The lower house is built into the hillside, and is thus a blind-back. On top of it is built another similar house, its front facing the other way into an access road, its back vertically continuing the front of the house below.

Occupational houses

Weavers' houses had loom-shops, usually on the upper floor, with continuous or long windows. Power-spinning and weaving in mills was introduced in the late 18th century, but weaving woollen cloth, some cotton processes, lacemaking, and knitting continued as cottage industries until well into the 19th. Such cottages may be seen in many parts of Yorkshire, Lancashire, Nottinghamshire, Leicestershire, and elsewhere (eg Cromford (Db), used for weaving or framework knitting, or Heptonstall (WY) (see **142**)). Silk weaving was introduced by the Huguenots after 1685, and similar weavers' houses could be found until recently in Spitalfields and Bethnal Green, London. The industry moved to Macclesfield, Stockport, Leek, and Manchester

in the later 18th century, and long-light houses still exist there. Somewhat similar rows of lights are found in first-floor workshops above shops in south-east England (see **143**). In Cumbria spinning was carried out in *spinning galleries*, open verandahs on the first floor of farmhouses. Some of these still survive.

The *metal trades* were also based on cottage industry, such as nail making in the Black Country, in small one-man forges in backyards. Needles were made similarly at Redditch (Wo), and knitting needles at Hathersage (Db). In Birmingham small arms manufacture, and that of jewellery, were concentrated, owing to the organisation of these industries in specialised quarters, such as the jewellers' quarter round St Paul's Church.

Tollhouses on the turnpike roads were purpose built, often facetted or even round (the so-called Round House, now partially altered, on the Alton–Liss road (Ha), is in fact facetted). This was to enable windows to face both ways along the road, for the tollkeeper to see traffic coming and open the gate which adjoined the house. There are still good examples to be seen, such as those at Alresford (Ha), Dorchester (Ox), or east of Marlborough (Wi). A simple type,

142 *Woollen weavers' houses, Heptonstall (WY), with long lights in the upper floor workshops, early 19th century.*

143 *This shop with workshop over – weatherboarded and with a row of windows – is a type characteristic of the south-east of England, and once common there. This one was in Guildford (Sy); one has been preserved in the Weald and Downland Open Air Museum at Singleton (Sx).*

scarcely more elaborate than a hut (from Beeding (Sx), 1807), has been re-erected at the Weald and Downland Open Air Museum, Singleton (Sx), and a more elaborate cottage, with its gate, is now at the Ironbridge Gorge Museum. Turnpikes, that is roads kept up by contributions collected from users, began with the road from Wademill (Ht) to Stilton (Ca) in 1663, and by 1800 there were some 1,100 turnpike trusts controlling 23,000 miles of road.

Houses were provided for *lock-keepers* on the canals, normally designed consistently by the architect of the canal (as early railway stations were), and so of distinctive type for each canal. The more elaborate *agents' houses*, where tolls for cargoes carried on the canal were collected and accounted for, had special offices built onto the house. There are good examples at Kirk Hallam (Db) on the Nutbrook Canal (1793–6) and, not far away, at Trent Lock, Sawley (Db) on the Erewash Canal (1777). The cottages of *level-crossing* keepers are also of distinctive pattern for each railway.

Lodges at the gates of country house estates take a wide variety of forms, depending on the whim of the owners. Some are neat and Palladian, some are "cottages ornés", and some border on the folly, ranging from the "rustic" timber to the mock Gothic or the classical temple. A large number of these sacrifice the convenience of the occupants to appearance or to the prestige of the estate.

Marginally eligible as occupational houses are *Bothies* (*hafods* in Wales, *sheilings* in Scotland). These are small, often one-room houses on upland or moorland sheep-runs, where sheep were pastured in summer (see "Transhumance", page 81). The shepherd would live with the sheep or visit them when necessary. These may still be seen in the Highland Zone. Sometimes a movable *shepherd's hut* was used, a wooden hut on wheels, like a large bathing hut, which could be drawn by horse to where it was needed. It contained a bed and a stove.

Gypsies used *caravans* also, fully equipped for living, and usually lovingly and lavishly decorated, painted, and carved. There are now very few left, as most gypsies live in houses. Caravans have not always been used; they were preceded by low tents, which could later be used in conjunction with caravans.

Bargees and their families lived in cramped quarters on their boats. This can still be seen in this country, and is a commonplace on the Continent.

Charcoal-burners lived and brought up families in very small huts, as they needed to be with the burning kilns night and day. The huts were made of turf and sacking over a conical frame of poles. One such hut has been reconstructed at the Weald and Downland Open Air Museum.

Later 18th and 19th centuries

Workers' housing up to the Industrial Revolution normally took the form of cottages on individual plots (however close together), with consequent variations in size, form, and position. In Scotland the one- or two-room cottage persisted until 1940 at least; in 1914 nearly half the population lived in one or two rooms. The rapidly growing demand for housing in the emerging industrial towns after the 1750s led at once to mass production of standardised houses on building plots, and to the use of the terrace to save space and cost. The earliest stages of this process were necessarily somewhat piecemeal, as demand grew. But in some cases circumstances allowed a degree of planning, on the lines of the estate developments of the "better sort". Thus, the new iron town of Middlesbrough was laid out, from 1820–50, on a broad square of streets, divided into four quarters by wide streets converging on a market place. But as the industries grew, and the railway occupied a huge area to the west of this new town, Middlesbrough spread to the south by the continual addition of groups of straight terraced streets, each group on a different alignment from its neighbours, forming a vast amorphous sprawl of monotony and gloom. In some towns the houses on the wider, more main, streets might be larger. This kind of development is normal for the rest of the century. In towns not made lopsided by a river or major industrial or railway installation, as Middlesbrough was, the inner core, with its public buildings, courts, and "rookeries", was closely hemmed in all round by such areas of terraces, with better-class districts in more open and salubrious areas beyond (such as the "west ends" of many towns, on the side protected by the prevailing wind from the smoke and pollution of the city; Sheffield has an excellent example of this).

In the 18th century there was more mixing of social classes in the new housing developments, and in Scotland and on the Continent this has continued, even in blocks of flats. But during the 19th century in England the classes began to split off from each other, and the middle classes lived further out from the workers, or at least in well-defined districts of their own. But the terrace form of housing, roomier and more airy, was still the normal way of life for the lower- and middle-middle classes, and this largely still persists.

Meanwhile a new process was taking shape, to reach full fruition in the mid 20th century. Some enlightened landowners in the later 18th century, when providing new and better housing for farm and estate workers, adopted the *semi-detached* type of house (see page 226). The first example of this is at Milton Abbas (Do) (1773), and the practice spread widely from then on. The first scheme to adopt this form on a large scale was the Eyre Estate in St John's Wood (1794–1830). It became general after 1840, eg in Clifton, Bournemouth, Southport, and Edgbaston (Birmingham).

A logical further step, for people who could afford the larger plots, was the *detached* house. This was at first an application of the Picturesque style of architecture, and soon developed into the "cottage orné", whose broken rooflines and extravagant detail reflected the Gothic aspect of the Romantic Movement. Nash built a whole group of such little houses

144 *A "Picturesque" cottage in a "model village". This is one of a group built by John Nash in 1810–11 at Blaise Hamlet, near Bristol, for retired estate workers.*

in 1810 at Blaise Hamlet, Bristol, which had a wide influence (see **144**). He followed this up in Park Village East and West close to Regent's Park in 1824. (He regarded this as a kind of consolation for not being allowed to build the villas he planned in the park itself.) Good examples are Fountain House, Camberwell Grove, London, the Umbrella House at Lyme Regis, or the cottages at Stourhead.

For people of greater means the *villa* became sought after. This was a detached house, in a garden or sizeable plot, which could be thought of as a kind of miniature country house. It was adopted eagerly by the upper middle classes, and built not only singly but in whole suburban developments, such as Lansdown, Cheltenham (1825).

The influence of these two approaches to the detached house was so powerful that the terrace ceased to be fashionable as early as 1840. By the 1850s houses were being generally preferred by the upper middle class, and by the 1880s this had become the standard pattern. The model suburb of Bedford Park, west London (Godwin and Shaw, 1876), had no proper terraces at all, whereas Calverley Park, Tunbridge Wells (1827–52), contained a mixture of detached villas and Regency-type terraces. North Oxford was strongly developed with villas from 1853 onwards, as were the better-class London suburbs,

251

145 *New Lanark (Lk) is the most notable monument of the Industrial Revolution in Scotland. It consists of cotton mills along the Clyde, with a model village for the workers, containing 170 houses and communal buildings. It was founded in 1784 by David Dale and Richard Arkwright; from 1798 to 1825 it was the scene of the socialistic experiments of Robert Owen.*

such as Highgate, Dulwich, Blackheath, or Putney. (The houses in the London parks, such as Springfield, Clissold, and Waterlow, are really country houses in small estates.)

During this time the conditions in the working-class districts had got worse, and improvement schemes – flats replacing slum dwellings – were put in hand. Such schemes began in the 18th century, and became common in the mid 19th. Notable examples are the Albert Family Dwellings in Stepney, 1849 – flats of four rooms in five-storey blocks, the Metropolitan Association for Improving the Dwellings of the Poor, and the Peabody Trust, 1860s. Since 1880 flats became acceptable to the wealthier classes, such as those off Victoria Street. But by 1911 only some 3% of all dwellings in England and Wales were flats – a situation which has changed since. Up to 10% were detached or semi-detached; most houses were terraced.

Another mode of attack on inferior workers' housing was the *model village*. These began in the 1770s, as with Styal (Ch), where next to the cotton mill are rows of workers' houses, hostels for apprentices, and other amenities. The most influential early example is New Lanark (Lk), 1785–90 (built by David Dale, but taken over in 1799 by Robert Owen the economist-philanthropist cotton-master). There are four mills, and tenement housing along the valley. In the middle, opposite the mills, are three buildings: a four-storey block with three flats to each staircase (the ground floor being wash-rooms); the three-storey offices of the Lanark Provident Cooperative Society;

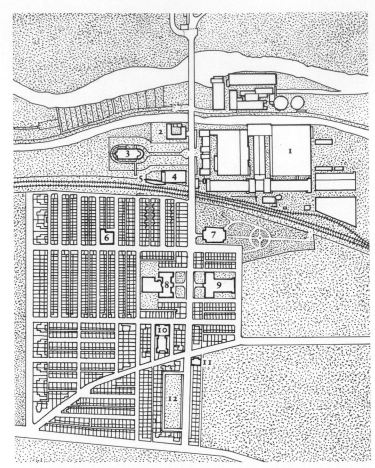

146 *Plan of Sir Titus Salt's model industrial "village", Saltaire (WY) (Lockwood and Mawson, 1853–1968) – a very comprehensive example. 1, Saltaire Mills; 2, stables etc; 3, Congregational church; 4, dining room; 5, railway station; 6, baths and wash-house; 7, Congregational Sunday School; 8, elementary school; 9, institute; 10, Weslyan chapel and Sunday School; 11, hospital; 12, almshouses.*

and a post office. Owen added to Dale's nucleus the "nursery buildings" for the pauper apprentices, the schoolhouse, the "Institution of the Formation of Character", and the village shop, bakery, slaughter-house, and vegetable market. The group encapsulates the whole Scottish tradition (see **145**).

The next major landmark (there are many less influential industrial villages throughout the 18th and 19th centuries) is Saltaire, near Bradford (1853–63). This was founded by Titus Salt to house the

148 *The Institute, Saltaire: another focus of this "model" village.*

147 *Congregational church, Saltaire: part of Titus Salt's scheme for his "village".*

employees of his mill. He laid out a considerable area on a grid, with a 9½-acre mill, 22 streets, 805 houses, 45 almshouses, five chapels, a Sunday School, baths and wash-house, assembly hall, hospital, and school, all in neo-Venetian Gothic style (see **146**, **147**, and **148**).

The next two major schemes, Bournville and Port Sunlight, aimed at a less urban character and incorporated trees and open spaces into their planning. Bournville, begun in 1879 and enlarged and altered

in 1894 and frequently since, provided good housing, with gardens, for the employees of the Cadbury cocoa and chocolate factory. It was always more than an industrial village, but a suburb as well; only some 40% of its inhabitants work at Cadbury's. Houses are both detached and in short terraces; it has schools, churches, almshouses, recreation grounds and social clubs, and its own station and shops. It now covers over 1,000 acres (400ha), and has some 4,000 dwellings and a population of 13,000.

Lord Lever's Port Sunlight (1887) is similar to Bournville, but more autocratic in conception and planning. An undulating and marshy site was levelled and landscaped, and a complete town erected, with houses and terraces of different sizes and architectural styles. There is a technical college, a hospital, an art gallery, gardens, churches, shops, library, social halls, even a pub.

Other 18th- and 19th-century special-purpose towns also used terrace housing as a norm, such as coastal ports like Whitehaven, canal ports like Stourport, industrial towns like Barrow or Middlesbrough, and railway towns like Swindon or Crewe.

The 20th century

In a real sense the growing suburbanisation which characterises the 20th century is a product of the consumer society, a consequence of a new phase of the Industrial Revolution. Colin and Rose Bell have well said (in *City Fathers*, 1969) that "until industrialisation had reached the level of sophistication – the production of much that is not essential – where it requires a growing middle class to operate it and to absorb its output, no one needed middle-class housing". By the end of the 19th century, new towns and suburbs were being planned not tied to one factory.

Commuting was made possible by the rapid development of public transport in the 1840s, and transformed by the motor car in the 20th century. Vigorous advertising has led to, or has reflected, a certain levelling off of taste and demand, helped by foreign travel and mass entertainment. Increased prosperity (although that has had its ups and downs!) has encouraged the desire for private house ownership.

These factors, among others, have all encouraged the wish to replace the terrace house, first by the semi-detached and then, if and when one could afford it, the detached, in suburbs ever further away from one's work. There has also been a desire for class separation, and for each family to have a house of its own (subletting is less common higher up the social scale, but in 1911 40% of all London families had to share a house). But terraces have proved very long-lived, not only because of standardisation of plans and building processes; there was, in the 19th century and beyond, almost no alternative to the terrace for the lower- and middle-middle classes, let alone the working class. But this led to unacceptably high densities – 60–200 houses per acre, with an average family of 4.5.

London, by reason of its extent and population, illustrates all the problems. These have been studied by many experts, and among these a convenient guide is A S Wohl in S D Chapman: *The History of Working Class Housing* (1971).

In 1800 London extended for two miles on each side of the river, and was five miles from east to west – one could comfortably walk right across it. By 1850 London had doubled its size, and by 1900 it was 18 miles across. The population grew by 50% in each decade from 1851 to 1891, and by 45% from 1891 to 1901. In 1801 it was under a million, in 1881 nearly four million, in 1911 over seven million. In 1970, inner London extended six or seven miles from the centre, outer London some seven miles beyond that; the Green Belt then took 10–12 miles, beyond which the Outer Metropolitan Area (with secondary centres such as Guildford or Reading, and long-distance commuting) stretched another 15 miles or so, to about 40 miles from the centre.

The growth of the early 19th-century city entailed the absorption of a large number of old villages, such as Chelsea, Hampstead, Islington, Hackney, Stoke Newington, Camberwell, and Dulwich; and new housing spread along the main roads. Some of the old villages have retained a surprising amount of their former identity and atmosphere. During the 19th century the central areas continued to grow, leading to gross overcrowding, made worse by public, street, commercial, and railway building. For example, Somers Town was pulled down by the Midland Railway in the 1870s, but few people were rehoused; wide new streets, like Kingsway, were cut through crowded districts – Farringdon Street displaced 40,000 people. The City was converted from residential to finance and commerce by the 1880s. And from 1902 to 1913 some 70,000 working-class rooms were destroyed for "improvements", and only 15,000 for new working-class dwellings. The result was not broad dispersion but increased over-crowding in adjoining areas. These conditions did nothing for sanitation and public health, as the incidence of cholera between 1831, when it reached Britain, and 1875, when Bazalgette completed his new drainage system, clearly shows.

Real movement to suburbs further out began in the 1850s, when cheap and rapid transport made this possible. The result was explosive, and vast areas were covered with houses, mostly terraces. In 1851 Willesden had 3,000 inhabitants, in 1891 114,000; West Ham rose from 19,000 to 267,000; Leyton from 5,000 to 98,000. The new suburbs developed identities of their own, and became largely self-sufficient communities. Growth was fastest in north and east London, owing to the cheap fares policy of the Great Eastern Railway. By 1907, 13,000 families a year were leaving the inner city; by then, the middle classes had already gone further out, leaving houses to be occupied by the working class. The new working-class suburbs declined in status by 1914, and the process was repeated further out.

These movements did not alter the social differences between inner and outer London, or improve the status of the south bank as against the traditional focus of activity on the north bank – in spite of the wealthy southern suburbs. Terraces amounted to 37% in both inner and outer London in 1966; flats totalled 48% in inner London,

20% in outer; recent building will have altered these proportions (for much useful information on this see M Ash: *A Guide to the Structure of London* (1972)).

The building of The Red House, Bexley Heath, London, by Philip Webb for William Morris (1859), was a turning-point in the history of the villa. This was a blend of "Gothic", Queen Anne, and cottage vernacular, with broken rooflines and fine details. It had a profound influence on subsequent house designs, both in the upmarket range, such as the private houses of Norman Shaw, Voysey, and Lutyens, and in the middle-range "garden city house". This influence appeared in Bedford Park (1876), and in the so-called "Domestic Revival" which began in the 1870s, in which pattern-books were used, and individually made details. This in turn was part, with the High Art, Aesthetic, and Arts and Crafts movements, of the general reaction against stereotyped Victorian values in the later 19th century, following the powerful stimulus of the ideas of William Morris.

Another landmark was Ebenezer Howard's book *Tomorrow: A Peaceful Path to Land Reform* (1898 – reissued in 1902 and again in 1946, as *Garden Cities of Tomorrow*), which led to the foundation of the *garden cities* of Letchworth and Welwyn, and their paler imitations, *garden suburbs*, like Hampstead. These drew inspiration from Bedford Park, Morris, and Norman Shaw, and foreshadowed not only the inter-war suburban developments but the post-war New Towns.

While these movements were fermenting, the terrace persisted as the normal housing in the inner cities, and even in London's outer suburbs. By this time there were considerable differences, both local and regional, in styles, materials, and decoration. Muthesius, in his far-reaching study *The English Terraced House* (1982), points out that there was a class distinction also, in details such as decoration, gables, roof furniture, and bay windows.

While working-class districts in the 20th century had straight roads, with terraces of identical houses and a few cul-de-sacs, council estates could have mixed houses and flats; more recent estates might have wide verges, but few trees. Middle-class, low-density housing in new suburbs (inter-war and just post-war) tended to curving roads and cul-de-sacs, with semi-detached houses set in gardens and trees. David C Thorns (*Suburbia* (1972)) describes the "reluctant suburb" of the 20th century. In this, a village is taken over by incomers, and grows by the addition of new small housing developments round the edge, creating a low-density unplanned suburb. These contain houses of many types built at different periods, mostly since 1945.

The inter-war period saw the expansion of the Metropolitan and Underground railway systems in London to well out on the west, north, and north-east of the central area. This made possible expensive suburbs (of which "Metroland", celebrated by Betjeman, is only one area), predominantly upper middle-class in character. These were based on detached houses, in curving roads and closes, with sizeable gardens, and verges. Similar roads were also created in the wealthier towns, such as those in the eastern districts of Guildford.

From the 1960s on, detached houses in closes remain popular, but have been accompanied by smaller houses in groups ("maisonettes" and "town houses"), and by small blocks of flats or bungalows. The latter were popular in the inter-war years at seaside resorts, of which Peacehaven is a notorious example. Infilling in the grounds of larger older houses is widespread, and the demand has in recent years been widened to include "sheltered" flats and other accommodation for the elderly.

The 1930s in the big cities saw another phenomenon – the *high-rise* blocks of flats, for which Le Corbusier has much to answer! Earlier examples include the spectacular working-class schemes in Leeds (Quarry Hill), Sheffield (Park Hill), and Coventry (Tile Hill), which at the time were regarded well beyond Britain as models. London had schemes like Roehampton (altering the skyline of Richmond Park), and the socially mixed project at the Barbican, in the City. Such building continued till about 1970, when not only constructional defects, due to hasty building methods and materials failures (as at Ronan Point, which partially collapsed) became apparent, but also the sometimes disastrous effect on the lives and social well-being of the inhabitants, with vandalism and other evils. There has since been a retreat from the high-rise principle, and a return to the terrace, or the small house. The inter-war years also saw the building of "cottage" estates for workers, eg Becontree, 1932, which has a population of 112,000. In the 1930s also, private developers provided a large number of three-bedroomed, semi-detached houses, aimed at young middle and lower middle-class couples; these extended up to 15 miles from the centre of London by 1939, at 12–14 houses to the acre.

In Scotland, national preferences have resulted in a different pattern: inner towns have blocks of flats, outer suburbs have widely-spaced, detached houses. The vast, largely terraced, rehousing schemes such as Easterhouse in Glasgow were not an instant success in social terms. The Scots make a sharper distinction between town and country than the English, and suburbs developed earlier in England.

Perhaps the most imaginative advance since the War has been the creation of the *New Towns*. These were set up under the New Towns Act of 1946 (extended by that of 1959). They embodied many of Howard's ideas for the Garden Cities (see above), being self-contained units of limited size, with separate residential, commercial, industrial, and civic zones, surrounded by a green belt. The residential units each had shops, schools, and playing fields.

The first batch of New Towns was a ring of eight round London, intended partly to meet a need for overspill of people affected by the disruption of the War. These were Stevenage (1946), Harlow and Hemel Hempstead (1947), Hatfield and Welwyn (1948), and Basildon, Crawley, and Bracknell (1949). Six were in the provinces – Aycliffe and East Kilbride (1947), Peterlee and Glenrothes (1948), Cwmbran (1949), and Corby (1950).

In the 1950s policy swung towards the expansion of existing towns by local authorities rather than the creation of New Towns by central government. The Town Development Act of 1952 set up overspill schemes for London at Bletchley, Haverhill, Swindon, King's Lynn, and Basingstoke. These schemes were influenced by the existing New Towns, and in turn influenced later ones, such as Cumbernauld (1955). Estates were laid out with vehicular and pedestrian traffic completely segregated, housing density was greater, and the complex civic centre incorporated shops, civic offices, and entertainment in one precinct.

More New Towns were set up in the 1960s: Skelmersdale (1961), Livingston (1962), Telford (1963), Redditch, Runcorn, and Washington (1964), Irvine (1966), Newtown (Mon) (1967), and Warrington (1968). London overspill was further catered for at Peterborough (1967) and Northampton (1968), with other schemes at Bury St Edmunds, Andover, and Ipswich; non-London overspill was catered for at Worcester and Erskine. Bletchley was absorbed in the New Town of Milton Keynes (1967), which in many ways represents the apogee of the system. Milton Keynes is planned on very spacious lines, with a large civic centre and local facilities in the neighbourhood units. Town and country are meant to stand in an integral relationship. It has nine types of housing, including two- and three-storey terraces (back in vogue!), low blocks round courtyards, low blocks of flats, semi-detached and detached houses, and single-storey semis and terraces. The total population of all these schemes is intended to be some 280,000. The demand for houses with gardens is partly met by private developers.

Apart from this major effort, public authorities, in conjunction with private interests, have had to face since the War the rebuilding of bombed city centres, such as Coventry, Plymouth, and Southampton, renewed centres as in Birmingham, new shopping precincts, as at Ealing, and the major transformation of the City of London. Such achievements will have far-reaching consequences for housing and social conditions.

(In addition to the books mentioned above, the following are also useful: Colin McWilliam: *Scottish Townscape* (1975); Robert J Naismith: *Buildings of the Scottish Countryside* (1985); A M Edwards: *The Design of Suburbia* (1981); J B Cullingworth: *Town and Country Planning in Britain* (1972) (up to the boundary changes of 1974–5).)

The break with the old

As a postscript it seems worth remarking that current methods of design and construction, as well as materials, have caused a sharp, if not total, break with all previous building. The enormously increased scale of building, if it is to be economical, has demanded new standardised techniques and new materials – one affects the other – and the abandonment of local sources. Innovations have of course been introduced over the past two centuries, starting with the Iron Bridge in Coalbrookdale in 1779, and the iron-framed mill at Shrewsbury, 1797, but their explosive and virtually exclusive use since the War has transformed our towns and cities beyond retraction.

As J G Ballard put it, in romantic terms, in *The Crystal World* (1968): "The architecture of the twentieth century, characteristically one of rectangular unornamented facades, of simple Euclidean space and time, [is] that of the New World, confident of its firm footing in the future and indifferent to those pangs of mortality which haunted the mind of old Europe."

The Church

RELIGIOUS PREHISTORY

Christianity did not appear in Britain in a religious vacuum. Far from it. Pagan religions permeated the life of the country from the earliest times until well into the first millennium AD, and their remains are ubiquitous. What follows is a brief and not at all exhaustive summary of some of the evidence.

The beliefs of Palaeolithic and Mesolithic peoples are, although obscure to us, reflected in burial customs such as the use of red ochre on the corpse as a sign of the afterlife, and simple grave-goods. The Neolithic peoples buried their dead in megalithic tombs, with stone chambers and forecourts for rituals (eg West Kennet); in lowland areas earthen long barrows (eg Fussell's Lodge) contained wooden "mortuary houses" (see 149); grave-goods were left with the dead, and the remains of ritual meals. The megalithic tombs, at least, were symbolic entrances to the other world, and to the Mother of all (see 150).

Late Neolithic and early Bronze Age people built stone circles, settings, avenues, and cursuses, and erected monoliths, some of which were memorials to the dead. The circles ranged from small simple ones to complex monuments like Avebury, Stonehenge, and Callanish (see 151 and 152, view and plan); these were religious and social centres, and many had astronomical functions also – to calculate eclipses and mark significant phases of sun, moon, and stars. Silbury, the largest artificial mound in Europe, has often been likened to a ziggurat, or Sumerian holy hill.

The Bronze Age people buried their dead under round barrows or cairns (see 153), with grave-goods, and many of these had features of symbolic significance. Cremations were often put in urns and deposited under barrows.

The Iron Age had formal temples and shrines, as well as sacred places in natural settings, like woods, glades, springs, and streams. The use of healing wells, beginning in prehistory, survived into Roman and much later times. Gods and nature spirits come into view now. Formal Celtic temples were of various shapes, like that found at Heathrow, a square chamber (*cella*) to contain statues and ritual objects,

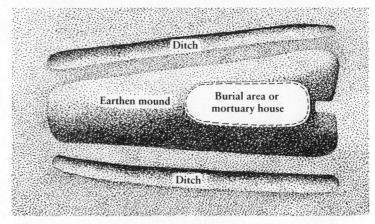

149 *Plan of an earthen long barrow.*

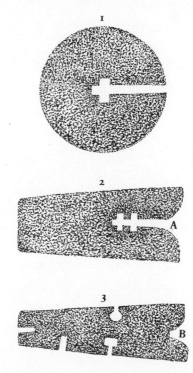

150 *Types of Megalithic tombs. 1, passage grave in round barrow or cairn; 2, gallery grave in long or trapezoidal barrow or cairn (A = forecourt); 3, Severn-Cotswold type with lateral chambers (B = forecourt with false entrance).*

257

151 *The important Late Neolithic stone circle at Callanish, Lewis (WI).*

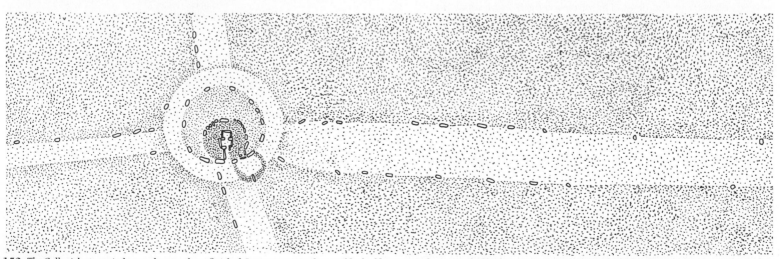

152 *The Callanish stone circle complex may be unfinished. It now consists of a possibly double stone circle, approached by four stone avenues, three of which are incomplete. Inside the circle is a later passage grave formerly under a round cairn.*

BRONZE AGE

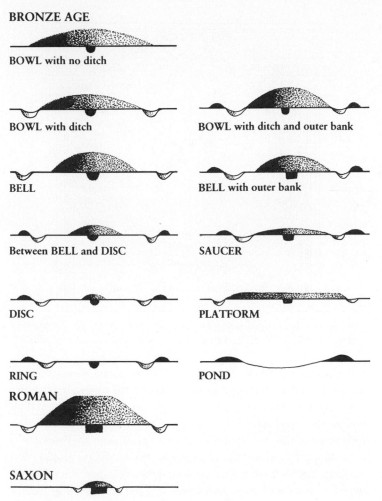

BOWL with no ditch

BOWL with ditch

BOWL with ditch and outer bank

BELL

BELL with outer bank

Between BELL and DISC

SAUCER

DISC

PLATFORM

RING

POND

ROMAN

SAXON

153 *Round barrows, main types (left), variants (right).*

surrounded by a verandah for memorials and public use, all set in a sacred enclosure or *temenos*. The *cella* seems to have originated as a covering for the sacred pit which provided communication with the underworld. The Celtic religions were practised well into the Roman period, and Romano-British temples and shrines were contemporary with the Roman temples of classical type, for the official religion of the Roman state (eg Colchester). The Romans also brought other religions, such as those of Mithras and Isis, and Christianity often had a difficult way to make.

CHRISTIANITY IN ROMAN BRITAIN

Little is known of Christians and their activities in Britain during the first three centuries of our era, although the work of Charles Thomas, Peter Salway, A H M Jones, and others has greatly deepened our understanding. Jocelyn Toynbee's pioneering summary of 1953 is still a very useful brief account. It can only be said that there are indications that the first missionaries came to Britain, and well-established Christian communities took root, before the end of the 2nd century. There were no doubt individual Christians even in the 1st century, though traditions like the presence of Joseph of Arimathea at Glastonbury should be regarded as unsubstantiated. The earliest martyrs – St Alban at Verulamium and Aaron and Julius at Chester – cannot be pinned down to any particular persecution (the mid 2nd century seems the most likely period), but their tombs or shrines must have been focal places of the cult between persecutions. But that for much of this time Christians had to be circumspect is shown by the famous word square found at Cirencester: ROTAS OPERA TENET AREPO SATOR "Arepo the sower holds the wheels with diligence", which can be rearranged in the form of a cross made up of the letters of PATERNOSTER A O, in each direction. This is very reminiscent of the sad subterfuges of symbolism and allusion found in other parts of the Empire, even in the catacombs of Rome.

The Peace of the Church in 313, when Constantine recognised Christianity as the official religion of the Empire, changed the atmosphere completely and enabled the Christians to come out into the open. Church institutions could now develop and play a full part in the life of the community. In fact, there is no doubt that Christians in Britain had already been organised on normal Catholic lines. In AD 314, three British bishops attended a Council at Arles; these were the bishops of York, London, and Lincoln, and Cirencester may also have been represented.

For the next century evidence for Christianity is more plentiful. Nothing is known of the cathedrals of the bishops before 312, but they were probably multi-cellular house-churches as in other parts of the Empire. After the Peace of the Church proper basilicas could be built, and the cantonal capitals, as in Gaul, were probably sees. A church

259

154 *Praying figure in painted plaster, Lullingstone (Kt).*

156 *Chi-Rho device (representing the name of Christ) – Roman wall-painting, Lullingstone villa. X (ch) and P (r) are the first two letters of the Greek word, Christos.*

was certainly built at Verulamium to commemorate St Alban, and there is known to have been one at Canterbury (St Pancras). A church has been excavated at Silchester, an apsidal building 42ft long by 33ft wide, and there are indications that similar buildings very probably existed at Lincoln (Flaxengate), Colchester (Butts Road) and Richborough, at least. House-churches probably continued to be the normal places of worship in the villas and the countryside. The well-known one at Lullingstone (Kt) had several rooms, and was decorated with painted plaster (with motifs such as praying figures) (see **154**). That many villa owners were Christian is indicated by mosaic pavements such as that at Hinton St Mary (Do) and Frampton (Do). At Hinton the central feature was a portrait of Christ (see **155**, facing page 266), and symbols such as the Chi-Rho (see **156**) and the Fish occur elsewhere. There is also a class of villa pavement with pagan motifs – such as that of Orpheus at Littlecote (Wi) – which may carry Christian allegorical overtones. The chapel at Littlecote containing this pavement is of early Christian form (it dates from *c* AD 360), but whether the villa owner was pagan or Christian is unclear.

It is possible that some chapels or house-churches may have been succeeded on the same sites by parish churches. There is evidence also for cemetery churches, sometimes based on *martyria*, *mausolea*, or *memoriae* – saints' tombs or shrines – outside the towns. Baptisteries have been found at Icklingham (Su), Richborough (Kt), Witham (Ex), and possibly Silchester (Ha). There are large numbers of Christian objects from the 4th century, widely spread over the country – tombstones, "gypsum burials", vessels, spoons, rings, graffiti, and symbols. The lead tanks from eg Icklingham (Su) and Walesby (Li), often decorated with baptismal scenes and the Chi-Rho, may well be portable fonts. There is no doubt that Christianity had found its feet, and was a significant element in society. The demise of the London Mithraeum has been plausibly ascribed to Christian opposition. Excavations in 1984/85 at St Martin's, Canterbury (Kt) showed no Roman cemetery round the church, as had been previously expected, so this may not be a *cella memoria* in a cemetery but a late Roman building, even part of a villa. Is this indeed the site of the 6th-century royal vill at Canterbury, the church being its (and Queen Bertha's) chapel?

Yet Christianity did not have it all its own way, particularly in the countryside. "Pagans", indeed, are the people of the *pagus*, the countryside, so are merely the "countrymen". The pagan comeback under Julian (360–3) met with a ready response in many quarters, and indeed the 4th century was a period with a multiplicity of cults, not only Mithraism, as M J T Lewis has shown. The restoration of the Giant Column at Cirencester, dedicated to Jupiter, is likely to have taken place at this time, and in 364, when Christianity had been officially restored, a great temple and centre of healing was built at Lydney in the Forest of Dean, dedicated to a Celtic god of healing, Nodens. Vast masses of coins and votive objects have been found at the wells and sacred places of the old cults. Temples of the Celtic type (square buildings with verandahs and inner cult-chamber) and rural shrines flourished. The evidence points to the conclusion that, while Christianity may have been conspicuous in the towns and practised in many villas, yet it had little or no hold over the general population. In the first half of the 5th century, when Roman rule had been withdrawn and the country was breaking up into numerous Celtic kingdoms, the episcopal organisation seems to have weakened and faded out. W H C Frend has suggested that perhaps it was too closely linked to the Roman regime and the official classes to survive in the new climate of independence, however much a Roman veneer was maintained. The Church therefore failed (in Frend's words) "to exert the unifying force in Britain vis-à-vis the invaders that it did elsewhere in the west." After a hiatus, or at least a very low level of activity (for instance, a basilica was excavated a few years ago at Lydd (Kt) which may have survived the Anglo-Saxon incursions to form part of a later church), Christianity was reintroduced into Britain from the west after c 475 by Celtic monks and missionaries. (A valuable recent summary of the evidence is in Richard Morris: *The Church in British Archaeology*, CBA Research Report 17 (1983).)

CELTIC CHRISTIANITY

The Christianity of Roman Britain, with its bishops in cities and cantonal capitals and its house-churches in villas, appears to have collapsed, with the social structure, during the upheavals of the first half of the 5th century. But there is some sparse evidence for the survival of individual Christians, and even of small communities, in the settlements and trading-posts of the Highland Zone, the south-west of England, the north-west, and Wales. In these areas Celtic

kingdoms formed, and these became the basis for bishoprics. The first of these dioceses for which there is good evidence was at Carlisle, from where it seems that Ninian set one up at Whithorn, both dating from the early 5th century. From this area, the kingdom of Rheged, Christianity spread slowly northward from c 450–600, to the other kingdoms of southern Scotland. These dioceses were based on Glasgow (for Strathclyde), perhaps Abercorn (for Gododdin), and perhaps Old Melrose for the Tweed valley (the later Bernicia). Further research might discover other centres.

In parallel with this there grew up what was to dominate and give distinctive character to the Celtic church – its special kind of monasticism. This seems to have arrived in Britain fully-blown from the centres of desert monasticism in the eastern Mediterranean in the latter part of the 5th century, and Charles Thomas has suggested a link with the imported eastern Mediterranean pottery (A and B ware) found in Dark Age sites in south-west England and south Wales. Tintagel, dating from about 480, with its un-British rectangular cells, may be one of the first of these monasteries. The distribution map of monastic sites and A and B pottery finds shows a close correlation. There were also movements from Ireland into north-west England by the late 6th century, and to Northumbria after 635; from there it spread to other parts.

The Celtic Church shared the same doctrine as the Roman, but differed in points of practice (eg the date of Easter and the shape of the tonsure), marriage discipline, and pastoral structure. The ritual differences were resolved in Britain by the Synod of Whitby (664), and during the 8th century in other countries; other differences continued till the 12th century. The bishop's role was essential, as in other parts of Christendom, but instead of the episcopal system being separate from the monastic, the latter was the basic structure. The bishops lived in monasteries as monks, but the abbots, not the bishops, were the heads of the monasteries. The people normally looked to a monastic house as their pastoral centre.

The *Canons*, attributed to St Patrick but probably later, describe a system in Ireland in which the bishop had a hierarchy of priests in his diocese, with local churches; the diocese seems to have been called a *parochia*, and what we know as a parish was called a *plebs*. It is possible that a similar system operated in Strathclyde; if Paisley derives from *basilica*, as is probable, its church would have been subordinate to the cathedral at Glasgow. The third element in this picture is the cemeteries of the church-going people, whether for families or communities. Burials were often in long stone cists, and several are known in southern Scotland. Important burials could be marked by memorial stones, of which a good group is that at Yarrow (Sk), one of which is inscribed (see below). Wooden oratories might be put up in such cemeteries, some of which would develop into full-blown churches. Glasgow cathedral itself may have grown from such an oratory in a cemetery consecrated by St Ninian.

During the 6th century the Celtic church developed into a church of monasteries under abbots who were priests rather than one of territorial dioceses under bishops. The organisation of a monastery is described in the life of St Samson of Dol (Brittany) (c 480–560), who was brought up in the monastery of St Illtud in south Wales (later Llantwit). Similarly, much is known about how the monastery of Iona worked, from Adomnan's *Life of St Columba* (Iona was founded in 563). The abbot (*abba*) was in complete control, assisted by senior monks called *seniores*; there was also an important monk, the scribe, in charge of the teaching, the keeping of annals, and the copying of the manuscripts. The founder's kin was of great importance in these houses, and daughter houses were often founded by them. At Iona there are echoes of the kin as late as Dr Johnson's visit in 1772, long after the monastery had ceased. Monks who had the right qualities could be made bishops, but continued to live as monks.

The monastery and its daughter houses, dependent hermitages, cells, oratories, etc together constituted a *parochia*. These little empires created great power for the abbots. Pastoral care of, and priestly service to, the people thus centred in the monastery or the local elements of its parochia. The monks travelled round this extended community, teaching, baptising, and celebrating on portable altars; that used by St Cuthbert when he was a monk at Melrose is preserved at Durham. Travellers and those in need were looked after in hospices.

Ireland was very rich in monasteries, and Irish monks played a major part in spreading Celtic monasticism in Britain and indeed over the whole north Atlantic area. Many of the most complete and spectacular examples are in Ireland, such as the monastic "town" of Clonmacnois, or Skellig Michael and Church Island (both islands off the Kerry coast). In Britain, most of the best-preserved sites are in Scotland, but there were also many monasteries in south-west England, Wales, and northern England. (In this field the researches of Ralegh Radford, Charles Thomas, and Rosemary Cramp have been

seminal.) In Cornwall, Tintagel has a cluster of rectangular cells, a type new to Britain at that time (late 6th century), if indeed they are monastic. Glastonbury was an important early monastery, but only small traces of its enclosure have been found beneath the later abbey. In Wales two of the greatest and most influential monasteries, Llantwit Major and St David's, have left few if any traces; but remains have been excavated at Burry Holms (Gm), Clynnog Fawr and Llandegai (Cn), and Penmon and Ynys Seiriol (An). The Anglian kingdom of Northumbria (which contained the old Celtic kingdoms of Bernicia, Deira, and Elmet, where there had been churches and dioceses) was Christianised by Irish monks in the early 7th century. Aidan was brought from Iona to found the great house of Lindisfarne in 635, Cedd founded one at Lastingham (NY), and Hilda the famous double house (men and women) at Whitby (657). Tynemouth and Jarrow also probably date from this time. There were once some 20 of these establishments. Irish monks also founded monasteries in East Anglia, such as Burgh Castle (Su) inside the Roman fort, and Cedd's church at Bradwell-on-Sea (Ex) (the present church here may not be Cedd's, but the second on the site). The monasteries in Scotland were at first mainly in the south (eg Old Melrose), but spread all round the coasts, up to the Northern Isles. The latter include great houses like Iona, Lismore, and Applecross, down to quite small ones like Deerness (Or). Place-names like Papa Westray (Or) or Papil (Zd) commemorate these monks.

A major monastery was surrounded by a bank or wall. Most of these were not really defensible, unless they were adaptations of an earlier fort, but more symbolic: they created the image of a fortress of the soldiers of God, an idea brought from the Near East (eg from St Catherine's in Sinai) where the idea of Celtic monasticism originated. In Ireland banks are called *lis* or *rath*, walls *cashel* or *dun*; but in Britain *vallum* was commonly used. The vallum at Iona has been partially traced, and many can be seen in stretches, eg St Helen's, Scilly, and Birsay (Or). In some cases the wall of a churchyard represents the line of a Celtic vallum; there are good examples in Cornwall (St Kew), and an outstanding one at Maughold (IM). On coastal sites use was sometimes made of a promontory fort, or a promontory could be cut off by a transverse bank (Coldingham (Be), Annait, Skye, Old Melrose). Islands or peninsulas were very popular (Deerness (Or), Kirkholm (Zd), Caergybi (An)), not to mention sites on larger islands like Iona or Canna; and the Farnes were used as retreats by the monks of Lindisfarne.

The buildings contained within the enclosure were a chapel, usually a small rectangular structure, small cells for the monks, round (Annait) or rectangular (Tintagel), and a graveyard. The Irish *cill* meant an enclosed cemetery, but in Man has become *keill*, now applied to the cells or oratories inside the cemeteries – there are three still visible at Maughold. (Some keills, however, are not cells but chapels related to land units, as in Orkney and Shetland (see below).) Graves could be marked by stones, sometimes inscribed, or crosses; and there could be a preaching cross. A large number, some 200, of Celtic memorial stones survive. They date from the 5th to the 7th centuries, and almost all of them are concentrated in Devon and Cornwall (*c* 50), south Wales (90), north Wales (55), and southern Scotland (12). Most of them are inscribed, some in Latin, some in Ogam, and over 60 in both. They commemorate a wide range of ecclesiastical and aristocratic notables. Burial was often, particularly in Scotland, in long stone cists. Cemeteries could also be unenclosed (Addinston, Lauder; Balladoole (IM), partly covered by a Viking cairn). Circular grave enclosures, each containing one grave, are known (eg the Catstane, Kirkliston).

Ardwall Island, near Gatchouse of Fleet (Kb), is a good example of a thoroughly excavated site (by Charles Thomas) showing a long historic sequence. It began as a rural lay cemetery, of dug graves, in the 6th or even the late 5th century; it was probably unenclosed. The graves clustered round a slab shrine, probably the grave of a local saint. Next a small chapel or oratory was built, with further graves and another shrine, or a second phase of the first one. Later still a stone church was built on the site of the timber one, but on a slightly different axis; more burials were aligned on this. Around AD 1000 more graves were inserted in the church, then in ruins, and in the 13th century the stones of the church were used in building a medieval hall house. A somewhat similar sequence has been found at Burry Holms (Gm). The cult of relics was in fact very strong, and many graveyards and later churches began as memorials to, or in the shelter of, a saint. A well-known shrine is that of St Ninian in Shetland, where a silver treasure was found in 1959. Many of these shrines were made with grooved stone posts with slotted-in panels, in woodworking technique. Carved crosses are common, not only on memorial stones (eg Ardwall) but on the walls of caves (eg Physgyll, Whithorn). Many of the Pictish symbol stones are Christian. Excavation at the Priest's House, Malham Tarn (NY), showed that it was probably a cell from the time of the Celtic church in this area; it closely resembles cells at Whitby.

The churches, as opposed to the small oratories, were sometimes single-celled buildings, but sometimes had two elements, a nave and a chancel; examples are Caldey, Birsay, Wyre, and St Ninian's. The famous "candida casa", the white house, at Whithorn, reputedly built by St Ninian or in his time (early 5th century), despite having small patches of cream mortar (and therefore at one time having been white), may well be of 7th-century date, although features have been found at Whithorn which may be contemporary with Ninian.

Lindisfarne was sacked by Viking raiders in 793, Jarrow in 794, and Iona in 795. The first period of the Celtic church was over. About 804 a new monastery was founded at Kells, as a refuge for the Iona monks, and Iona ceased to be the leading monastery in central Scotland. Its place was taken by houses such as Abernethy, Dunkeld, and St Andrews, and Irish influence in the church in Britain faded.

From the 9th century the practice became common of an abbot being a married layman from the family who had hereditary rights to the office (usually the founder's kin, and often members of ruling families, which could be an advantage in those times). Monasteries became bodies of married clerks in minor orders, and laymen; one member was a priest. The office of scribe tended to disappear, and his place was taken by the master of the schools (*rector scholarum*, lector or doctor).

In the late 8th century a movement for reform was initiated by St Maelruan at Tallaght, near Dublin, which influenced the Scottish monasteries in the 10th and 11th centuries. The monks concerned were a group within a monastery who tried to combine the eremitical life with that of a community under a superior. They were called *keledei*, companions of God (*culdees*). They were responsible for the services. In Scotland they are first mentioned at St Andrews in 940, and by the end of the 11th century they were found in most of the greater monasteries in the east of Scotland. At Abernethy at this time there were six priests, of whom two were culdees. They were found in England also, as at York.

The monastic buildings in the 10th and 11th centuries were now of stone, some of which have survived, like the round towers (used for bell ringing and storage, and sometimes for refuge) at Abernethy and Brechin, and tower-nave churches (where the nave is the ground floor of the tower – cf Earls Barton (Nf)), eg Dunfermline, Restennet, and St Regulus at St Andrews.

By the end of the 11th century the structure of the Celtic church was seen to be archaic and inefficient; priests were too few, pastoral care suffered, and the bishops were inadequate. During the 12th century the church was reorganised into territorial dioceses and parishes, as in parts of England, and brought into line with the rest of British Christendom. Tithes became obligatory, which helped to fix the parish as a unit. At first the dioceses were coterminous with the elements of the parochia when their cathedrals were Celtic monasteries, and thus St Andrews, Dunblane, and Dunkeld all had units in each other's territory. The cathedrals were staffed by secular canons.

The smaller monasteries and cells which happened to be in centres of population became parish churches; the rest remained as burial grounds or disappeared. At the same time new parish churches were built in the lowlands by the English and Normans who had come to Scotland in the 12th century (eg Ednam (Rx)). In certain Norse areas, after the Norse had been converted in the 11th century, a kind of parochial system grew up, based on the local land unit, the ursland or ounceland. Each unit had a chapel and burial ground, under the control of the owner. There were some 200 of these in Orkney, and similar systems occur in Kintyre and Man. Many of these chapels (or keills in Man) survive. Later parishes were formed by establishing the parish church on the site of the ounceland chapel nearest the hall of the local chiefly family. Thus the 40 ancient churches in Kintyre evolved into 10 parishes by the 15th century.

During the decay, the anchorites continued in vigour and carried on valuable pastoral work. But eventually the last relics of the Celtic church were the hereditary dewars or keepers of monastic insignia, the founder's staff and bell and the parcels of ground, some with private cemeteries, attached to the keepership. At Auchlyne (Ce) the croft of the dewar is a medieval chapel and burial ground surrounded by an earth and stone enclosure wall; this could also represent an ancient anchorite's settlement. The dewars went on into the 19th century.

An interesting feature of the Middle Ages was the *double monastery*, houses for both men and women, headed by an abbess. This gave great scope for a series of competent and cultured women to exert notable influence in their world. These monasteries originated in Egypt, and were introduced to western Europe in the 6th century; they reached Britain either from Ireland (Kildare) or Gaul. A celebrated example was that at Whitby, where St Hilda played a prominent part in the Synod of 664, which accepted the Roman form of Christianity instead of the Celtic Church in Britain.

The double monasteries were very popular, but disappeared during the Danish settlement of eastern England. The Roman Church tolerated them, but never encouraged them, although large numbers existed in France and Spain. The 12th century saw a revival of double monasteries and also of variant forms, in which royal and noble women could make their mark. Such were Fontevrault near Angers, France (1101), (the burial place of Henry II, Eleanor of Aquitaine, Richard I and John's queen, Isabella of Angoulême), and its daughter house at Amesbury (Wi). Distinguished women of this period include Héloïse (died 1163), who discussed with Abelard how to adapt the Benedictine Rule to women, when she was abbess of The Paraclete; and Hildegard of Bingen, mystic, author, composer, and many other things. Other notable religious women, not abbesses, include Julian of Norwich (14th century). A complex order was that of the Gilbertines, founded in 1131; this provided for both men and women – the men were Augustinian Canons, who acted as chaplains to the nuns, who lived under the Benedictine Rule; the lay brothers were Cistercian. The 13th century saw the important nunneries of Lacock (Wi) and Wherwell (Ha). A late revival in Britain was the house at Syon (Mx) (1415), under the rule of St Birgitta of Sweden. The abbeys of nuns as cultural centres were replaced by cathedral schools and universities in the 12th to 14th centuries.

The element eccles in place-names

An interesting footnote to this survey of the Celtic church is provided by a group of place-names containing the element *eccles*, which derives from a Primitive Welsh word *egles* (modern Welsh *eglwys*), adopted by the Anglo-Saxons as *ecles*. This has come down to us as *eccles*, and places with this element in their names go back to some sort of British population centre with organised worship. The Celts derived their word for church from (Greek) *ecclesia*, "the gathered people of Christ", the Saxons from *kyriakon*, "the Lord's place" (hence Anglo-Saxon *cirice*, church/kirk; both words carried either meaning). Place-names in, or derived from, *eccles* then are a very convenient index of Celtic presence.

There are 20 of these places in England, six of them consisting just of the word Eccles: in Lancashire, west of Manchester, in

Derbyshire, near Chapel-en-le-Frith and near Hope, in Norfolk, near Attleborough, and formerly on the coast near Hickling, and in Kent, near Aylesford. The other 14 have an Anglo-Saxon element added, and show that the Anglo-Saxons took over a Celtic place while its church was still in use or a living memory. Some have *tun*, a homestead or village – Eccleston (La), one near St Helens, one near Chorley, and Great and Little Eccleston near Poulton; Cheshire has one near Chester. *Halh*, a nook, corner of land, water meadow, occurs at Ecclesall, near Sheffield, Eccleshall, near Stone (St), and two Exhalls in Warwickshire, one near Alcester, one near Coventry. The others are Eccleshill (La), near Darwen; Eccleshill, near Bradford; Egglescliffe, near Stockton; Ecclesfield, near Sheffield; Exley, near Bradford (with *leah*, a wood or glade); and Eccleswall (He), near Ross, which may imply a well or spring. Over half of these names are in the north-west Midlands and south Lancashire, and there are eight in West Yorkshire, in the British kingdom of Elmet. All are situated close to rivers or streams, except the Norfolk one on the coast; three-quarters are not far from Roman roads, and a quarter close to Roman sites like Alcester (as Kenneth Cameron has pointed out).

There seem to be three in the old Primitive Welsh-speaking areas of southern Scotland: Eccles in Berwickshire, and Eccles and Ecclefechan in Dumfriesshire; the latter may be either St Fechan's church or little church. Their situation is similar to that of the English ones. There are many places in the rest of Scotland which might appear to have the same element, eg Eggleston, but these may derive from the Gaelic *eaglais*, church, and not imply anything so early. But some, like Egilsay (Or) – church island, where the *ay* is Norse for island – speak of a Celtic church being taken over by the Norse settlers.

Recent study by Faull (1979) suggests that the *eccles* places lie outside the areas of primary English colonisation, and that, when they were overtaken by the English and given compound names, the *eccles* element was retained because it represented something for which the English had no word – perhaps a Celtic Christian settlement of monastic type.

It is possible that Paisley derives from *basilica*, and certain that Dysart (Scotland) and Disserth (Wales) come from *desertum*, a remote place where Celtic monks could live in solitude.

THE DEVELOPMENT OF THE PARISH

Since the beginnings of the Christian Church, the primary unit through which it carries on its mission has been the *parochia* or parish. But in the Roman Empire this was a different concept from the territorial unit familiar to us today. The parochia was the community of Christians living in a city, not the geographical area they lived in. The chief resident clergyman of such a community was the *bishop*, not, as in a modern parish, the rector or vicar. The bishop was normally present at all services and performed all the ritual functions of the church himself; he had only a few priests and deacons to help him. Normally also there was only one church in a city; if there was more than one, only the bishop could send a priest to work in the other church. The *priests* assisted the bishop in the administration of baptism and the celebration of mass; the *deacons*, of whom the chief became known as the *archdeacon*, were concerned with the management of the parochial finances; below these were clergy in minor orders – subdeacons, acolytes, exorcists, readers, and doorkeepers – who all had specific functions in the whole organisation. The property of each church was administered by the bishop, who paid the clergy their stipends. In smaller cities the clergy might live with the bishop in one house (the *domus ecclesiae*), part of which might be the church or cathedral; a notable example has been excavated at Mérida in Spain, and the type was known as late as Merovingian France.

During the 4th century Christianity in western Europe began to establish itself in the countryside. The bishop either went out himself from the city into its dependent territory to convert the people and set up churches (like St Martin of Tours), or sent his priests. So the term parish came to be applied not only to the community in the city, but also to the new communities in the smaller towns and villages in the *civitas*. This area, the civitas, then came to be known as a *diocese*, of which the bishop in the city was still the head. A diocese was in fact an administrative area of the late Roman Empire, between a prefecture and a province. In 6th-century Gaul, diocese was often used for a country parish; in 7th-century Saxon England the whole area under a bishop was his parish. Only from the 9th century onwards did the two terms come to have their modern meanings.

265

In the 6th century a series of councils in Gaul laid down rules for standardising the organisation and work of the country parishes. Churches fell into three grades: churches in the episcopal city; country churches with a permanent staff of clergy, where the surrounding Christians regularly worshipped; and oratories on the estates of Christian landowners. The cities themselves continued to be worked as one unit under the bishop. The country churches might have quite large staffs, who could live in common; the church was more like a mission station than a modern parish church, and the parochia was often sprawling and ill-defined, covering several villages. The bishop visited these churches, and their clergy attended synods in the city. The oratories on the villa estates were private – the owner appointed whom he liked as priest, had him ordained by any bishop he chose, and paid him what he liked. The parishioners were the family of the villa, and the servants, workers, and slaves of the estate. Such churches began in the 4th century, and remains of one have been found at the villa at Lullingstone (Kt). By the 6th century in Gaul these oratories had very inferior status as churches, and very limited functions. But it is from them, and not from the regular country churches, that most later parish churches derived. An owner could endow his oratory so that it could have a permanent staff of clergy. When this happened, the people tended to look to this church for all the ministrations of the Church, and not to the church in the nearby town. The latter then declined. C W O Addleshaw records that, of the 37 parishes in the diocese of Auxerre in the 6th century, only 13 originated as mission stations in the larger villages; the other 24 grew out of oratories that had risen to parochial status.

Anglo-Saxon England was converted to Christianity by bishops who came from Iona, Gaul, or Rome. But for the first 80 years or so after Augustine's mission in 597, there were no dioceses but only missions, each under a bishop. England was divided into dioceses by Theodore of Tarsus, Archbishop of Canterbury from 668 to 690; his dioceses were either the Saxon kingdoms or tribal subdivisions where the kingdoms were too large. Within each diocese the pastoral work of the church was carried out from mission stations, called *minsters*, which corresponded to the country parish churches of contemporary Gaul. Later Anglo-Saxon law described these as the "old" minsters, or mother churches; one such minster, the "head" minster, was the bishop's headquarters.

The parish of a minster might be an estate belonging to its founder – a king, bishop, or monastery – or a tribal area. The minster would be in the village or place which was the administrative centre of the estate or area. Some minster parishes were very large, and most covered several towns or villages; there were no parish boundaries; a minster's area merged into the surrounding forest and waste. The word *minster* is the Latin *monasterium*, but minsters were not all staffed by monks. Their clergy, the *familia*, might be secular clerks, living a community life, or monks under Benedictine or Celtic Rule. The head was known as the *abbas* or *praepositus*. Some minsters were double monasteries, with nuns and attached clerks, under an abbess. Whether monks or clergy, the actual life and functions were much the same. Besides the services, the minster ran a school; teaching and mission were essential parts of their work. The revenues of a minster were derived from land, and dues from the local people.

The old organisation continued into the 12th century in many parts. In Kent in the 7th century there were few or no rural churches on the Gallic model, so the minsters, with their clerical families and ministering to the countryside, had a parochia or diocese. They were minsters of clerks, headed by clerical abbots. Canterbury and Rochester were cathedrals, and there were other minsters at Upminster, Reculver, Southminster, Dover, Folkestone, Lyminge, Sheppey, and Hoo. For Dorset, Christopher Taylor has pointed out that many of the minsters can be identified by their names – Beaminster, Iwerne Minster, Wimborne Minster, Charminster, Sturminster, etc; others, like Sherborne and Wareham, did not have minster in their names. Incidentally, the street system of Sherborne appears to be laid out inside the precinct of a Celtic monastery, Lanprobi – the later abbey is outside this. The monastery lands can be traced in the surrounding countryside. Beaminster and other towns in the south-west appear to have similar origins. In the middle Thames valley, Stenton has identified minsters at Aylesbury, Lambourn, Reading, Bampton, and Sonning; in the Avon valley in Worcestershire, there were minsters at Evesham, Fladbury, Pershore, and Bredon, as well as Hanbury, Kidderminster, Kempsey, and Worcester itself. In the north of England, where population was sparser, minsters could serve huge areas. Thus, Dewsbury covered Mirfield, Thornhill, Kirkburton, Almondbury, Huddersfield, Bradford, and all the country westward to the Pennine watershed. Even today the parishes in the Pennines and Lake District are very large, although only small parts of the original minster parishes.

107 *Interior of Hut 7, Skara Brae, showing the hearth, box beds, dresser, wall cupboard, and floor receptacle for keeping shellfish etc.*

155 *Mosaic from Hinton St Mary (Do) Roman villa. This head, with the Chi-Rho behind it, and the two pomegranates symbolising eternal life, is accepted as one of the earliest representations of Christ in the Roman Empire.*

202 *Wall paintings – Holy Sepulchre Chapel, Winchester Cathedral. These were executed in two stages, the Deposition and Entombment, c 1180, and Christ in Majesty, early 13th century.*

179b *Well-dressing – Tissington (Db). The well after dressing. See 179a, page 299, for an illustration of the same well before dressing.*

Besides the minster itself, there were local holy places (*loca sancta*) which grew into independent churches. When Christianity first came to the villages or great estates from the minsters, the priests would set up a wooden cross to preach from (later the cross was of stone, and some are masterpieces of art). The people would assemble here daily for prayer, and eventually a church would be built, first usually of wood, later of stone. Some of these crosses became centres of burial grounds, but usually for a long time burials would take place at the minster itself, and the funeral procession would have to travel long distances. There are "corpse roads" across the North York Moors leading to Danby church; and on some of these there are resting places, or coffin-stones, where the cortège could rest on the way. In due course these local churches would have a permanent priest, and ultimately achieve parish status. After the Danish raids this became the norm, and smaller parishes were set up everywhere. Thus in Yorkshire, Kirkdale church was originally a minster for the whole of Ryedale, but fell into ruin and had to be rebuilt (by Orm in 1060); it was then the church just of its neighbourhood, and the other villages in Ryedale had their own churches. Study of the local boundaries has unravelled the units into which the huge minster parishes were divided. Thus, in Dorset, Charminster had ten units, and Sturminster Marshall also several. Canford Magna, however, covering most of Poole and part of Bournemouth, remained vast until the 19th century. In general few churches, apart from the minsters, antedate the conquest by very much.

A similar system existed in Wales, the "clas" (mother) church system, and W Rees has identified most of them. Place-names containing the elements *lan* (Lanivet), *llan* (Llandaff), *church*(Whitchurch), *kirk* (Ormskirk), or *minster* (Beaminster) are good indicators of an early church.

From the days of Charlemagne (768–814) the movement began, which was to continue for the next 300 years, for every village to have its own church and priest. By the end of the 11th century every diocese north of the Alps was well on the way to achieving this end. The building of churches was made easier by the conversion in the 8th century of the old system of voluntary donations by the faithful into compulsory tithes. Together with the glebe, these became the normal income of the local church and its priest. The new village churches were founded mainly not by the king and the bishops but by the local lord (who was not always an individual, but could be an abbey). The lord had certain rights in the appointment of the priest and the management of the church endowments. Similar rights were of course known in Roman times, and in relation to pagan shrines. As a result the priest came more under the control of the lord than the Church as a whole, and popes like Urban II (1088–99) had to initiate reforms, which fixed the system for the succeeding centuries. The situation in England in late Saxon and early Norman times is given most fully in Domesday Book (1086). This shows that over large parts of England the old minster system had been replaced by the new parochial system. The new parishes were usually coterminous with villages or manors; in the towns they reflected administrative divisions or the ownership of property. Any church was now called a minster, as against the "old minster" of early Saxon times. The parochial system based on villages was more developed in the east than in the west of England, and was strongest in the Danish areas. Domesday records 345 village churches in Suffolk, 255 in Lincolnshire, and 217 in Norfolk; but in parts of the west and north the old minster system continued – whole hundreds were served from churches in their administrative centres, supplemented by a few manorial churches. The other churches often had a small community of priests. In the towns the proliferation of churches seems grotesque, but they served in fact as meeting places for all kinds of purposes (see The Parish Church, below).

Reorganisation in the eastern half of England was necessary when the country settled down after the Danish invasions and wars, which had a very disruptive effect on church and village life. The process can be seen in a document called the Domesday Monachorum of Christ Church, Canterbury, where the diocese is shown as divided into 12 groups of churches; each group had one church in a dominant position. These dominant churches were all either old minsters from pre-Viking times or places important in late Saxon times. The subordinate churches can be shown to have been founded mostly in the late 10th or 11th centuries. By the time of the document they had not reached full parochial status. The document thus shows one stage in the process by which village churches gradually emerged. The establishment of village churches began in the 9th century, but the majority date from the 10th or 11th, although many were rebuilt later, and have little to show from the Saxon period. By the mid 11th century, indeed, the existence of a church on an estate is one of the signs of the thanely status of the owner. Some churches in the north were rebuilt by the lord after the Norman devastations, thus following the earlier tradition (eg Weaverthorpe). The lord, in return for building the church, had the right of choosing the priest (an office which was sometimes hereditary*), and of receiving from him a small rent in money or kind. The glebe land, on which the priest largely lived, was on average about 15–30 acres (6–12ha). Tithes were obligatory. The lord could sell or transfer his rights, or bequeath them; rights in a church could be split into fractions. Under Edward the Confessor, lords began to grant their rights over churches to cathedrals or monasteries, a practice which affected the working of the parish system in the succeeding centuries.

The 11th century saw several codes of regulations relating to parochial practice. Three principles which are still in force date from this time: that a priest once in possession of a church cannot be deprived of it by the lord, but only by the bishop (in certain circumstances); that for all this independence the priest is still under the authority of the bishop; and that the parishioners must take their share in the upkeep of the church.

The parishes are of course the base of an ecclesiastical pyramid. The provinces of Canterbury and York (which were continued after the Reformation) are divided into dioceses, each under a diocesan bishop, who is usually assisted by suffragan bishops (bishops responsible for parts of a diocese, and also for assisting the diocesan bishop when required). The diocese is further divided into rural deaneries, in which the local clergy are grouped. The administration and finance are carried out by archdeacons, each having charge of a geographical division of the diocese. The Dissolution of the Monasteries resulted in much charitable and social work formerly done by the monasteries being thrown on the parishes, in the absence of a state system of social service. By 1700 there were some 9,000 parishes in England and Wales, almost all serving both ecclesiastical and civil purposes (various non-ecclesiastical functions were laid on the parish vestries in the 16th century (see below)). The numbers steadily increased by subdivision; as urban population grew, inner parishes would be split

up or new parishes formed at the expense of those outside the former town area. There were church building and parish forming schemes under Queen Anne, and again under George III. The Victorian growth of cities saw many such, and in addition at this time there was a wave of new churches of various complexions. The parishes as defined by law for civil purposes did not always coincide with the old ecclesiastical parishes (a system of civil parishes was formalised, and parish councils with defined functions set up, under the Local Government Act of 1894). In 1821 there were 10,693 ecclesiastical parishes, in 1835 15,635 civil parishes. There are now over 14,000 ecclesiastical and 11,000 rural civil parishes, with some overlap. Although attempts have been made in recent years to match the churches to the incidence of population, there is still a great deal of mismatch, both in the towns, where the new suburbs are not always adequately served, and in the country, where there are too many churches (which has led to grouping). There is a massive problem of redundancy of churches.

By the 17th/18th centuries there was considerable autonomy in the parishes, and a great variety of functions. Thus the parishes had churchwardens and sidesmen, but also overseers of the poor and of apprentices, a petty constable, a waywarden or surveyor of the highways, a parish clerk, and a sexton. There could also be a pinder (an impounder of stray animals), a dykereeve (to see that ditches were clean), a hayward (in charge of fences and enclosures), a headborough tithingman (the chief of a tithing, or group of ten householders under the frankpledge system, in which each member of a tithing was responsible for the conduct of, damage done, etc, by every other member – so, a petty constable). Oversight of the poor became the main burden on the parishes, till the Act of 1834 took it away. The vestry meeting still survives, but is now vestigial.

Until lately, the parish functions included oversight of pumps, paths, greens, lighting, watching, baths and wash-houses, burial and recreation grounds, allotments, and rights of way. The parish councils have been continued under the Local Government Act of 1972, but with modified powers. They should not be confused with the parochial church councils, which are concerned only with matters relating to the churches themselves.

In Scotland the churches are maintained by heritors, not by the parishioners, and there are no churchwardens, vestry meetings, parish councils, or parish meetings.

---

*Clerical celibacy had a chequered history in the Roman Church: since its institution in the early days, from at least the 4th century, practice had become lax, until the monastery of Cluny demanded its restoration in the 11th century; it was reimposed in 1074. But there was continued popular support for clerical marriage, resulting in a fresh campaign for celibacy in the 16th century. Great Reformers like Luther and Zwingli rejected celibacy, but it was reimposed by the Council of Trent (1545–63).

It may be added that in many places the churches have largely ceased to be the focus of the life of their neighbourhoods, which has left them on one side in favour of secular meeting places.

The decline of the rural churches has certainly impoverished life in the countryside; a report in 1985 sounded a very serious note on this. The problem is complex, and the various causes of the decline interlock. The grouping of parishes to match reduced populations, smaller congregations, and fewer priests has led to the group clergyman being overstretched, with a knock-on effect. The appeal of the Church and of its traditional services has fallen off, particularly among the young. Church schools have become steadily more secularised. House groups partially offset these trends, but do not meet the specific problems. The pull of urban culture and values seems irresistible. Nonconformists are in many areas even harder hit, while the Roman Catholics have suffered least. The churches in the towns, inner cities, and suburbs have their own problems, but the general outlook is not reassuring.

Since 1958, nearly 2,000 of the 16,000-odd parish churches in England have been made redundant, and of these a quarter have been demolished. In 1968 a Pastoral Measure dealt with this problem, and between then and 1983 1,043 churches were closed. Of these, 238 have been demolished and 187 vested in the Redundant Churches Fund. Some areas are more affected than others; since 1968 12 out of 25 redundant churches in Wakefield have been pulled down, and 16 out of 27 in Liverpool. But it is of course far from easy to find a suitable alternative use. It looks as though a further 1,000 churches may become redundant by the end of the century.

Parish priests were, and are, appointed under a system of *patronage*, which has gradually kept in step with changes in social outlook. The "advowson", or right to appoint a priest, lay with the manorial lord. This could be the Crown, a bishop, a monastery, and of course, in many cases, a layman. A bishop or abbot appointed a vicar, or deputy; the rest appointed a rector; both were of the same rank. Formerly a vicar or rector could himself, at his own expense, appoint a curate, if he had more than one parish, or a very populous one, or if he had to be away frequently. Many curates had little supervision, as well as little income. Where there was no provision for a full priest, as in a non-parochial church, the priest-in-charge could be a Perpetual Curate (a priest without institution or induction, a practice in use since 1404 – such a man was commonly known as a vicar).

Patronage by lay lords could have disadvantages, from blatant nepotism to the landowner who advertised for a new rector in *Horse and Hound*! But a more sinister aspect of patronage was the possibility of undue pressure, social or even political, on the parishioners. In fact the open association, until well into the 19th century, of the Church of England with the landowning and industrial classes caused popular distrust which still persists, and has contributed to the Church's irrelevance in the lives of large sections of the population.

The patronage system has been recently reviewed, and a Measure of 1986 now provides for a patron to register his patronage, for all patrons to be communicant members of the Church of England, or to nominate someone who is, and for all appointments to be made in consultation with the bishop and the Parochial Church Council.

The Establishment of the Church of England – its formal links with the Crown and State – has its own virtues and drawbacks, which will not be discussed here. It comes under fire from time to time, but has proved remarkably resilient. Public reaction to Establishment in Scotland has in the past been more positive. During the 18th and early 19th centuries state interference in the spiritual freedom of the Church of Scotland created much bitterness. This came to a head in the Non-intrusion controversy, which led in 1843 to the Disruption, in which those who would not tolerate the undesirable effects of the Church's alliance with the State seceded to found the Free Church of Scotland – this only reunited with the Church of Scotland in 1929, when the dangers had long since receded.

Parish records were at the discretion or whim of the priest until the 16th century, when the system was tightened up. In England, from 1538, detailed records had to be kept of baptisms, marriages, and burials. But they were still not always very religiously kept – in fact, many children never got registered at all. The system improved when from 1598 parish clerks had to send transcripts of their registers to the bishop's registrar each year. Other churches kept their own records in their own form; among these the Quakers have a high reputation for the quality of their records from the mid 17th century. Many records are now lodged in county archives or record offices, and in many cases transcripts have been published or are available. The remaining gaps were closed and the system finally standardised in England and Wales from 1 July 1837, from which date certificates of births, marriages, and deaths are kept at the General Register Office in London. In Scotland they are held at the New Register House,

Edinburgh (from 1855). Irish records run from 1864. These records may be searched, and copies obtained. Wills and inventories are not parish records, but formerly had to be lodged in the various diocesan registries, a practice which began in the 14th century. Since 1858 wills, after probate has been granted, are kept and indexed in the various probate registries, or in some county record offices, or in the Principal Probate Registry in London. All these may be freely consulted.

(There are of course vast numbers of other types of record of interest to local historians and genealogists; useful brief introductions are: David Iredale: *Discovering Your Family Tree* (Shire 1977), and, for local history, W G Hoskins: *Local History in England* (Longman 1972).)

THE PARISH AS RITUAL TERRITORY

The significance of the parish in medieval times was not exclusively a territorial one; it had a non-material aspect, which must be mentioned here to enable it to be understood in all its roundness. The church and parish in fact provided the emotional and social environment of the people, and were the centre and theatre of much of their lives and activities. Appreciation of this has been greatly furthered in recent years by what might be called the *new folklore*. The study of folk customs and beliefs has changed direction, and a fresh and truer perspective is emerging. The 19th-century approach, which culminated in *The Golden Bough*, Sir James Frazer's masterpiece (1890), consisted largely of collecting a vast mass of facts from all over the world and detecting relationships among them. The relationship was not in many cases actually so direct, and the assumption that, say, an English custom could be explained by a foreign one of apparently similar character or, even more, by one practised by a primitive community, has turned out to be unreal. And there is certainly no guarantee that a medieval custom will illuminate the practices and beliefs of prehistoric man. So, 50 years after Frazer, the study of folklore was flagging. But since the 1950s there has been a revival, on new lines. The emphasis is now on a contemporary functionalist explanation of customs, comparing them with cultural factors and in fact trying to see them in their own setting. There is caution in assuming long

continuity, and a care to understand the reasons for changes, let alone to unmask "revivals" or modern embellishments. The need to trace customs as far back as possible is accepted, and to link them with popular beliefs. A useful summary of these new attitudes has been given by Charles Phythian-Adams in *Local History and Folklore: a new framework* (1975).

Customs are social phenomena, and changes in them mean either shifts in popular opinion or interference from a superior social level (the regulation or suppression of a custom). National and local pressures need to be studied, and the part played by popular and Christian influences. Little is known before about AD 1200. The relationship between Romano-British (Celtic) religion and the beliefs and practices of the Anglo-Saxons has yet to be worked out. There was paganisation under the Scandinavians, but the nature of the Christian reaction cannot always be determined. It is at least certain that the Church took over, rather than suppressed, old beliefs and sites, such as holy wells, festivals, and agricultural rituals, and the Anglo-Saxon beings of evil, the elves and dwarfs, became the fiends of Christian lore. But innovations continued into the later Middle Ages, such as the firm establishment of the feast of Corpus Christi in 1311, the increasingly lavish processions in the towns, and the various Lords of Misrule, etc. The Reformation caused a sharp break in the continuity of many customs and in the balance between the sacred and the profane in the life of ordinary people. But a few customs survived, even if in a changed form, down to the 1914–18 war.

Phythian-Adams distinguishes four interrelated facets of ritualistic social customs: the context of popular beliefs, the physical location of the observances, their calendrical timing, and the social position of the participants. Popular beliefs have to be regarded strictly in their own particular setting; English customs cannot be compared to others without circumspection. English popular life had had little foreign influence for several centuries after the Norman conquest, and had diverged from it in many ways. Keith Thomas has pointed out the strong differences between witchcraft in England in the 16th century and witchcraft abroad.

In pre-Reformation England the village and parish were the focus and stage of the people's activities and beliefs, which were rooted in their local environment. Magic and religion were merged in the beliefs. There was also a parallelism between the festivals of the Church and the events of the natural year: birth, death, and rebirth (or resurrection) were reflected in them. Popular symbolism (such as mistletoe) was allowed in churches. The Church in fact recognised the non-natural essence of inanimate things. Popular cosmology supplemented the Christian hierarchy of the Trinity, the Blessed Virgin Mary, the saints and angels, and their counterparts the Devil, fiends, and demons. The air and sky were full of strange, evil, and terrifying beings, and crosses, incense, gargoyles, and bells were used to keep them away. Fire and smoke were also efficacious. The tapers used at Candlemas were blessed to ensure that they kept the Devil away. Bonfires, fires of bones or in which bones were thrown, caused a stench of great magic power. Leaping through or over fires stimulated fertility; fires were lit in fields and orchards; the Yule log protected the home.

The sacredness of trees in pagan religions survived in medieval times in the form of the protective or prophylactic power of certain trees, such as hawthorn, birch, rowan, or ash. The carved Jacks-in-the-Green on bosses or corbels in churches may have been personifications of such trees. The corn dolly made from the last sheaf of the harvest may have been not a personification of a corn goddess, but an attempt to carry over to the next year the last of the vital force behind the current harvest, or perhaps of the god who promoted the fertility of living things, the consort of the Earth Mother in prehistoric times. In some customs the dolly (John Barleycorn) was buried in the fields, and this could represent the sun and fertility god, the consort of the Goddess, who had to be ritually killed after each harvest so that he (and the crops) might rise again next year. These examples are of course only a minute selection of such beliefs. The separation of religion from magic at the Reformation must have been quite traumatic and bewildering for many ordinary people.

A custom has a close relationship to the place it is practised in. For most people this was the parish, or in towns sometimes a group of parishes. This was not only because the parish was the administrative unit of the Church, but was the physical environment where the natural and the supernatural overlapped. The ritual centre of all this was the church. This had different parts with differing sanctity and function. The chancel, where the altar was (and structurally the rector's responsibility), was the ritual powerhouse, where Mass was conducted and the sacrament reserved. The tower or bellcote did not just advertise the church and ring for services: the bells kept evil spirits away, and were particularly needed in *rites de passage*, to protect

a newly-baptised child, a married couple, or a departing soul, or to avert natural disasters like storms. The nave, the responsibility of the congregation, usually had no seating and was both a consecrated area and a village hall, where the people worshipped and were taught, but where also sacred plays were performed and church feasts held. The actual *rites de passage* took place here, with the people as witnesses.

The churchyard had its peculiar atmosphere of death, suspense, and unseen menace, and the power of its being consecrated ground. But the general absence of permanent tombstones (until the 17th century), and the reluctance to bury on the unlucky north side of the church (the Devil's side), left free ground which was used for a variety of secular purposes. Courts, musters, markets, plays, games, dancing, and feasting took place there. And church processions on special feast days (like Whitsun or Corpus Christi) went round the churchyard; indeed, if the church was built too close to the churchyard wall it might be pierced by a passage to let the processions through, as at Wrotham (Kt), or Lapworth (Ww). Processions also went out from the church into the parish outside, or vice versa, along set routes – "procession ways" – used for Rogation ceremonies and by weddings and funerals (like the "corpse roads" of Yorkshire and elsewhere). Houses were decorated at appropriate times – Christmas, Easter, May. The paths and ways of the parish were linked into the ritual structure, and the whole environment of the people was a meeting place of two worlds. The fields themselves were included in this, and certain spots were set aside for rituals at certain times – Easter egg ceremonies, bonfires, harvests, village games, or contests. The parish boundaries themselves were ceremoniously defined at regular intervals. The boundaries might run from holy well to a special tree, but even if not, processions would go round them ("beating the bounds"), stopping at stated places, often marked by crosses like the complete set on the boundary of the liberty of the collegiate church at Ripon. In towns, the walls had a similar significance as a ritual frontier against the unknown.

The changes at the Reformation destroyed much of this web of activities. It also altered the balance of the parts of the church itself. The chancel and nave were thrown into one, and the strong ritual function of the chancel diminished. Seating in the nave made it less capable of being used for secular purposes, and gravestones had the same effect in the churchyard. In fact, the use of the church and yard was progressively confined to religious functions of specific (and narrower) kinds, and church houses and halls were built for some of the old activities. Processions were discouraged, and only a few of the outdoor activities survived.

Medieval life was geared to a well-defined calendar of occasions, on which specific things were done. The absence of clocks, days and hours of uniform length, and a rigid secular calendar threw emphasis on feast days, which did not follow each other at regular intervals. The seasons and these festivals governed the medieval year, rather than our modern concept of undeviating time. The festivals themselves punctuated or expressed the seasons, and most of them had a basic agricultural significance. (Most of the people lived by, and all depended on, country pursuits.) Thus, Michaelmas ushered in the season of winter sowing, slaughter, threshing, and winnowing; Christmas, spring ploughing and sowing; Lady Day, fallow ploughing and shearing; and Midsummer, the harvesting of hay and corn. May Day, in the north, probably marked the time to put stock out to summer pasturage. The major days of the year also had pagan undertones. The first half of the year, from Christmas to Midsummer, had a more intense ritualistic content than the second half, and was in general more imbued with a sense of the supernatural. Christmas was merged with the pagan midwinter festival, Easter with the spring, St John's with midsummer, all using fire in their ceremonies. The Church in fact accompanied the events of the agricultural year with devices to protect the seedtime, the crops, the harvest, the fields, and the people themselves. The people seconded the efforts of the Church by the vigour with which they feasted, danced, and played at these times. Licence was accepted at these times as the obverse of high ritual. In one sense it was another way of ensuring the prosperity of the community; in another, it was just a normal way of expressing social solidarity – farmers and farmworkers sharing the harvest supper on equal terms – but also, by implication, reinforcing the divisions inherent in the social structure. Controlled licence, such as the Lords of Misrule, when the roles of master and servant were reversed, had the function of restating regularly and communally the position which each had reached. The custom of Boy Bishops fits into this pattern also. (A Boy Bishop was a chorister of a cathedral, collegiate church, and some parish churches appointed by his fellows to act as a bishop from St Nicholas' Day (6 December) to Holy Innocents' Day (28 December – St Nicholas was the patron saint of schoolboys). During this time he was allowed to perform the duties of a real bishop,

so far as he was able. He was treated with great respect and hospitality. The custom was abolished in 1541, revived by Mary I, and abolished again by Elizabeth I; it died out in Protestant countries, but continued elsewhere until the late 18th century. It has been revived in several parishes in this century.)

The agricultural cycle was echoed by a set of observances relating to the ages of man. Christmas was a feast of motherhood, birth, and childhood, with Candlemas and mid Lent; Shrove Tuesday was a holiday for schoolboys and apprentices; St Valentine's day, May Day, and Hock Monday were times of mating; midsummer was a feast of fertility. Autumn and early winter were concerned with ageing, death, and the afterlife – Michaelmas marked the victory over the powers of Hell, while All Souls' Day protected the living as well as the dead.

All these days were celebrated on two levels, public and private. Different symbols were used, special foods eaten, special clothes worn; verbal formulae were repeated, seasonal games played; traditional sites were used. Much research remains to be done in this area, but already an understanding is being reached of the customs and beliefs which were central to medieval life, and their place in the social setting.

(There are many books giving further information on these customs, of which Geoffrey Palmer and Noel Lloyd: *A Year of Festivals* (1972), may be found useful. Other aspects of the folklore of churches are dealt with in Dedications and Folklore below.)

THE GREATER CHURCHES

Origins and foundations of cathedrals

The ministry of the early Church was made uniform by St Ignatius about AD 110–117. He laid down that it should consist of bishops, presbyters, and deacons. The bishops ruled the cities and possibly also their dependent countrysides; French sees are still based on Gallo-Roman cities, and are therefore much more numerous than English ones. The bishops were assisted and advised by a council of presbyters. From the 3rd century, churches were built in each city to replace the house-churches of the early years. In these the bishop had his throne at the east end (the symbol of his authority) and his council of priests round him. When Christianity reached northern Europe, which had fewer cities in the southern sense, bishoprics covered much wider areas, usually those of a whole tribe or kingdom. But the church still had the bishop and priests at the east end, with the bishop's *cathedra* (chair). The area in which the bishop had his chair, and over which he exercised pastoral care and authority, was his *see* (seat).

The council of priests sometimes shared the bishop's house, or sometimes lived in communities under his control. If the latter they were *canons*, (either because they lived under a rule, or because their names were entered in the roll of the church. Canons were at first all clergy on the official staff of a diocese, and later the staff of a cathedral or collegiate church, responsible for specific duties, such as precentor, sacrist, etc. There are also non-stipendiary canons serving in parish churches. Each canon had a *prebend*, his source of income (money, lands, manors, parishes, etc).

Monasteries rose in power and influence from the 10th century, and took over from the secular canons in several cathedral churches where the latter were proving unsatisfactory (eg Worcester, founded for secular canons in 680, taken over by Benedictine monks from *c* 970 to 1539). So two types of cathedral bodies grew up, those composed of secular clergy and those composed of monks. In the latter case the bishop replaced the abbot, and the monastic community was ruled by a prior. The word "chapter" probably derives from the practice in monastic houses of reading a chapter of scripture etc before a meeting – the chapter is the totality of the canons of a cathedral or collegiate church, meeting for church business under the dean or provost.

Henry VIII replaced monastic chapters by secular clergy (the New Foundation, eg Gloucester, 1541). The old secular cathedrals retained their constitution and are the Old Foundation (eg York, 625, Lincoln, 1072). The cathedrals created more recently are all secular; some are in ancient monastic churches (eg Southwark, 1905), some in enlarged parish churches (Manchester, 1847).

The management functions of the chapter in the cathedral church and diocese had to be divided among several members. A pattern evolved under the influence of the churches of York, Lincoln, and Salisbury, and by the end of the 12th century it was standard to have four major dignitaries. These were the *dean*, who normally presided over the chapter; the *precentor*, responsible for the services; the *chancellor*, who among other duties taught the theological school; and the *treasurer*, who looked after the cathedral plate, vestments, etc. Other offices included those of *sub-dean*, *succentor* (deputy to the precentor), *vice-chancellor*, and *sacrist*. The *archdeacons* looked after other churches in the diocese. Every prebendary had to provide a substitute to take his place when he was absent. These were the *vicars choral*, some of whom were priests. They provided the master of the choristers and the organist. At Lincoln there were also *poor clerks*, who assisted the priest at Mass.

The *close* is a distinctive feature of English cathedrals. In the early years no official provision was made for housing the various members of the chapter, and they had to find their own accommodation as near the cathedral as possible. They were in fact not expected to reside in the cathedral city all the year round, and some, like the archdeacons, were habitually absent much of the time, either on church affairs or in the service of the king or even the pope. But by the end of the 13th century the chapters recognised the advantages of owning houses for the clergy to use, and from then on there would be, besides the bishop's palace, a regular deanery, chancellery, etc, and houses for the canons.

Most closes are fragmentary now, and few contain a comprehensive spread of houses for the different levels of the clergy. Many, like Salisbury and Winchester (see **157**), have very pleasant settings. But perhaps the only complete close, where the full articulation of the machinery of a cathedral can still be seen, is at Lincoln. This has been studied by Kathleen Major and Stanley Jones, and the houses have been identified and changes in their occupation worked out. Many have in fact changed hands; thus, the deanery was formerly (before 1195) the house of a canon; the dean lived there until 1960 when it became a choir school and the dean went to live in the house which had for centuries been the home of the precentor. The sub-deans have occupied the same house since *c* 1160.

The close was enclosed by a wall, which at Lincoln still stands high and nearly complete. It was begun in 1285, and by 1350 Minster Yard was surrounded by its wall with the gates locked and guarded at night. The wall was allowed to enclose land outside the city wall, where some of the canons were living. The city wall had in any case to be taken down to allow the cathedral to be extended at the east end in 1256. Three gates still remain at Lincoln: the impressive Exchequer Gate,

Pottergate, and Priory Gate. Gates into cathedral precincts also exist in other cities, such as Canterbury and Salisbury, but are the gates of monastic precincts rather than of closes proper; the "close wall" at Winchester is part of the monastery wall.

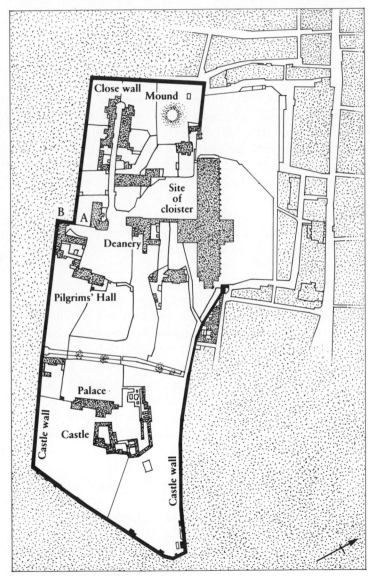

157 *Winchester Close, plan.*

The vicars choral normally lived together; at Wells (see **158**, and **159**) and Chichester they were along a street, with a chapel and hall at one end; at Lincoln their lodgings are round a quadrangle. Provision was also made for the choir school and for housing the choristers, as well as for the poor clerks and the theological school. Chantries grew up within the close.

The "Greater Churches"

These are the medieval churches built as cathedrals, and the churches of the larger abbeys. They are a distinctive group, not only on account of their size, but because they have features in common not shared by the parish churches. Architecturally and functionally they must be studied as a whole: Westminster Abbey ranks with the finest cathedrals on most counts, and the cathedrals themselves were sometimes built as secular churches, and some as abbey churches; some were sees for only a short time, and some changed from secular to monastic or vice versa. Over 100 churches come into this class, of which a quarter are now cathedrals, a quarter have been destroyed, and the remaining half are wholly or partially in use, or are more or less fragmentary ruins. A few large collegiate churches may also be considered with them, such as Ripon, now a cathedral, and with many of the cathedral features. A collegiate church like Ottery St Mary, however, although exceptional, and with the remains of a close, probably falls within the parish church class.

The greater churches have the following elements, subject to local variation and the passage of time, but all dictated by functional necessity: starting from the west end, there is a nave with side aisles, for the lay people; a crossing under the central tower, with transepts north and south of it to give a cruciform plan; a screen west of the choir, where are the stalls of the clergy and choir, and the bishop's throne; a retro-choir with chapels or saint's shrine (or ambulatory for processions); a lady chapel (unless this is elsewhere, as at Ely); chapels in transepts and retrochoir, and sometimes round the sides of the choir also (not usually along the nave walls, as in France). Externally there is usually a central tower, and two lower towers at the west end; the west front is emphasised and can be ornate; the main doors are sometimes, as in France, in the west front, but more usually in a lateral porch. There is also a chapter house (where the canons conduct their business), and in many cathedrals a cloister (a necessity for the life of a monastery, but only for show in a secular cathedral). Very long churches, such as Lincoln, Worcester, Beverley, or Salisbury, may have another pair of transepts east of the main ones. In elevation, a cathedral consists of an arcade of columns supporting the roof, separated by arches with above this a gallery or triforium providing access to all parts at "first floor" level, and above that a row of windows under the roof, the clerestory, to let light in to the nave and choir. Parish churches have no such gallery, and lack other elements also (see below).

"ENGLISHNESS"

The English cathedrals are a notable illustration of the particular characteristics and flavour of English art and architecture, which itself closely reflects elements in the English outlook. How the elements described above are put together, and how their details are treated, are in many ways quite unlike the corresponding features in the greater churches of France (whence the concept reached England). Pevsner and others have analysed what constitutes the "Englishness of English Art", and have drawn many of their examples from the greater churches. Certainly a knowledge of the principles helps in the understanding and appreciation of these often overwhelming buildings. What follows is of course in very general terms, and individual cases may well appear more complex.

158 *The Vicars' Close at Wells (So) – the houses of the vicars choral – is an early example (1348) of urban terrace housing. The street ended with a hall and chapel.*

English art is basically linear, not sculptural; it goes in for outlines, straight in some periods, curved at others, and flat surfaces. This may also be seen in drawing, illumination, and painting, from Saxon times

159 *One of the houses in the Vicars' Close at Wells; this has a hall to the right of the chimney, with a chamber over. The chimney is typical of the 14th century.*

to the present. The flat surfaces may bear surface ornament, but this is itself linear, like arcades in low relief, or designs of continuous mouldings, or interlaced arches. The west front at Lincoln is a good example. The summit of this English trait was the Perpendicular style of the 15th and 16th centuries, which had straight vertical lines in the windows and blind tracery on the walls. This architectural phase is absent in Europe, for complementary reasons – the people there preferred curves and three-dimensional figures. Another English tendency was towards more and more light, which again culminated in the Perpendicular, in which the windows took up most of the walls (made possible by the earlier invention of the flying buttress, which took the thrust of the roof and enabled the walls to be thinner and eventually less solid). One purpose of the great east windows (as at Gloucester) and the choir transepts (York) was to let more light onto the altar. There is a constant tension between the horizontal and the vertical. Horizontality is seen not only in a tendency to greater length, as at Norwich, but in long unbroken horizontal lines; eg at Lincoln the long roof along the roof vault is answered by that under the gallery, which counteracts the effect of height; while at Ely the verticals are stressed. French cathedrals, on the other hand, tend to be broad in proportion to their length, often with double aisles but very high, narrow naves; they gave up prominent galleries quite early. Purbeck columns, a feature of the 13th century, show up black and emphasise height, eg at Salisbury, and statues, as at Wells, may be elongated (as also in France). But the impression of compromise and fear of the extreme remains. For instance, a row of wide Perpendicular windows, with their flattened tops, filling a church wall (such as Fairford (Gl)), emphasises the horizontal; this is modified by the frequent vertical lines of the window uprights. Tudor houses, like Hardwick (Db), offer further examples. The idea recurs also, later, in Georgian terraces, which have long horizontal lines broken by innumerable verticals.

This leads to the question of proportions, again quite differently resolved from the practice in France. One problem was the relations of the three storeys of arcade, gallery, and clerestory. The ideal balance seems to be that at Durham and Lichfield, 2:1:1, while at Wells the ratio is 2:1:2, and at St David's and York the triforium and clerestory are combined. At York the great height is deliberately counterbalanced by great width. Exeter, the triumph of the 14th century, seems to be completely balanced. In most English cathedrals

the ratio of height to width is 2:1, while in France (and here at Norwich) it is 3:1. The west front is emphasised (eg Wells or Exeter), not as a frame for a main entrance (which was often on the side) but to finish off the church (or begin it!); here the lack of a prominent front at Winchester is conspicuous. The extreme is perhaps Lincoln, where the original Norman west end has been extended on both sides by an arcaded flat screen which dwarfs it but still lets it be seen. Asymmetry is a trait not so common in France. Masons

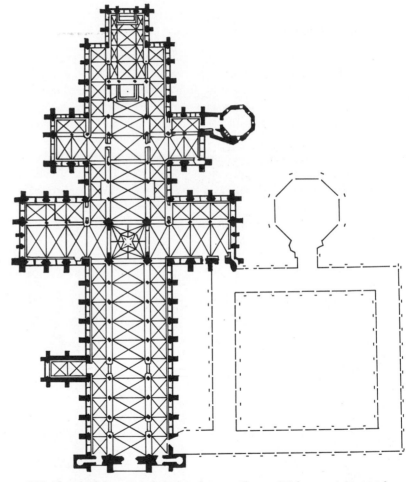

160 *Plan of Salisbury Cathedral, of similar age to Chartres (13th century), but a total contrast. This shows all the English emphasis on compartmentalism, height, length, and narrowness. The east end is squared. The lines combine the vertical and the horizontal.*

in England were told what to do but not how it was to be done, so followed their bent. The result can be seen in the aisle vaulting at Lincoln, and elsewhere there.

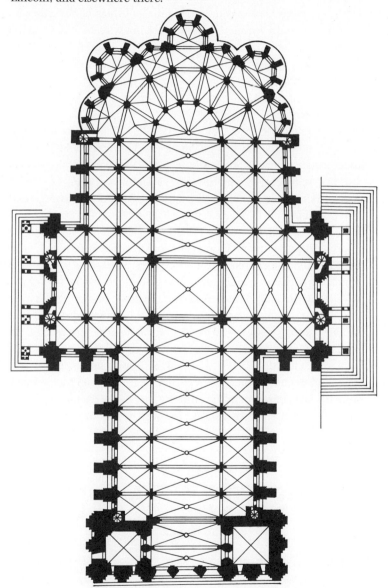

161 *Plan of Chartres Cathedral. A typical French plan, with unified volume and space, wide and low, with round east-end and apsidal chapels.*

In putting all the elements together the countries also differed. In England the feeling was for angularity, so the elements were designed as square or rectangular boxes and assembled one after the other. In France they could be curved, and were combined in a more integrated way; compare the plans of Salisbury and Chartres (see **160** and **161**). Incidentally France (eg Chartres and Amiens) have shorter naves than chancels, symbolising a different relation of priest to people. English angularity preferred, from Saxon times, the squared-off east end rather than the continental rounded apse with cluster (chevet) of chapels. Norwich has kept its chevet, and is in many ways the most French of our cathedrals (cf Westminster Abbey), but in many cases east ends were altered to the English style or were built squared in the first place. Round ends occur mostly in south-east England, nearest France, while straight ends are usual elsewhere. This equates with the flat-topped tower of Perpendicular churches (like Cawston in Norfolk). Throughout the centuries genuine vision and inspiration, so plentiful in the greater churches, has been tempered by a very English conservatism. Wren was made to give his new St Paul's a medieval plan, although he wanted a central plan; Liverpool (Anglican), Guildford, and even Coventry are fundamentally medieval, and in great contrast to Liverpool (Roman Catholic). One style merges imperceptibly into the next.

Dioceses

There are 43 dioceses, and hence cathedrals, in England – 29 in the province of Canterbury and 14 in York. Of these 27 are greater churches as described; 15 have always been cathedrals, 9 secular and 6 monastic. The secular cathedrals are York, London, Lichfield, Hereford, Wells, Lincoln, Chichester, Salisbury, and Exeter; the monastic are Canterbury, Durham, Winchester, Norwich, Worcester, and Rochester – Ely was made a cathedral in 1109 and Carlisle in 1133. This Norman pattern lasted until the New Foundation of Henry VIII, when 5 cathedrals were added, Gloucester, Bristol, Oxford, Peterborough, and Chester. Since 1836 4 medieval greater churches have been made cathedrals, to cope with increased population – Ripon, St Albans, Southwark, and Southwell – and 21 others, some former parish churches (Manchester, Newcastle, Wakefield, Birmingham, Chelmsford, Coventry, Blackburn, Bradford, Bury St Edmunds, Derby, Leicester, Portsmouth, Sheffield). Truro, Liverpool, and Guildford were designed from the outset as cathedrals, and Coventry has been rebuilt. There are a few secular greater churches which never became cathedrals, like Beverley, but these should on no account be overlooked in any study of the class.

Before the Norman pattern the Anglo-Saxon sees had been based largely on political divisions, but many changes took place and some sees were quite short-lived. In the 8th century the sees were:

Whithorn	Hereford	London
Lindisfarne	Worcester	Sherborne
Hexham	Leicester	Winchester
York	Dorchester	Selsey
Lichfield	Elmham	Rochester
Lindsey	Dunwich	Canterbury.

In the 10th century they were:

Chester-le-Street	Elmham	Ramsbury
York	London	Winchester
Lichfield	St Germans	Selsey
Dorchester	Crediton	Rochester
Hereford	Wells	Canterbury.
Worcester	Sherborne	

Most of the cathedrals were small country churches, and it was Norman policy to bring the bishops into the main centres of population, where they could be national administrators and spiritual powers, complemented by the military power of the local earl in his castle, instead of pastoral scholars.

In Wales there were four medieval (secular) cathedrals – St David's, Llandaff, St Asaph, and Bangor, with Newport and Brecon added in the 19th century. In Scotland there were twelve dioceses in the later Middle Ages: the Orkneys, with its cathedral at Kirkwall, subordinate to Trondheim until 1468, Caithness with Sutherland (Dornoch), Ross (Fortrose), Moray (Elgin), Aberdeen, Brechin, St Andrews, Dunblane, Dunkeld, Glasgow, Argyll (Lismore, then Iona from 1507), and Galloway (Whithorn). St Andrews was the seat of an archbishop from 1472, and Glasgow from 1500. Most of these churches were not large, or are fragmentary today; St Andrews and Elgin are major ruins, and only Glasgow and Kirkwall are greater churches in the European sense (like St David's in Wales). Elgin is a serious loss; it was very French in inspiration, and would have held its own with almost any cathedral south of it.

Anglo-Saxon cathedrals

Saxon cathedrals are by no means negligible as churches, and were often very large. Little is known about most of them because they are buried in or under Norman churches, but many seem to have got big by agglutination. Thus Augustine's church at Canterbury (St Peter and St Paul) is flanked to the west by a church or chapel of unknown dedication, and to the east by the church of St Mary (see **162**). In the 11th century St Peter and St Paul was linked to St Mary's by a great octagon.

Most is known, as a result of Martin Biddle's excavations from 1961 to 1969, of the Old Minster at Winchester. This was not built over by the Norman cathedral, and is thus available for study. The first church was begun about 648, and raised to cathedral status in the 660s. It was a rectangular building with square chancel and two *porticus* (lateral chambers), making a cruciform plan. West of it, but detached, was a tower dedicated to St Martin, probably built later than the church. Between these lay St Swithun's grave (862) and other monuments. The church and the tower were linked in 971–980 by a building with two lateral rounded "transepts", and from 974–980 a west front was added, incorporating the tower. From 980 to 994 the church was extended to the east by a long rounded apse with square eastern chapel, and two round lateral wings east of the original square ones. The whole composite building was some 230ft long by 110ft wide (70.7 x 33.8m). St Swithun's grave was replaced by a monumental shrine as a focus for pilgrimage, and his remains were housed elsewhere in the church. There are general parallels to this agglutinative process, and to the west work, on the Continent.

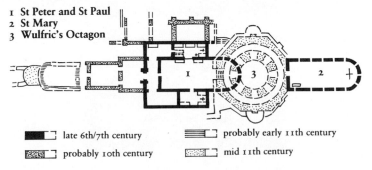

1 **St Peter and St Paul**
2 **St Mary**
3 **Wulfric's Octagon**

late 6th/7th century   probably early 11th century

probably 10th century   mid 11th century

162 *A major Saxon church – St Augustine's, Canterbury. Such churches grew by linear addition of parts.*

The Normans pulled all the Saxon cathedrals down and rebuilt them, sometimes but not always on the same spot. At Winchester the Old Minster was flanked on the north by the New Minster, an abbey founded in 903 and removed *c* 1110, and on the south by the present cathedral, built from 1079 to 1093, when the Old Minster was pulled down. But for a few years there were three huge churches side by side.

A list of the Saxon sees is given above. Their subsequent fate is varied. Dunwich and Selsey are under the sea. The first cathedral at York has been found under part of the present Minster but on a different alignment (fitting into Roman buildings still standing when it was built); some are under or within existing cathedrals (Worcester); at Hereford the first cathedral was probably to the south of the present one, but has not been found; some are under or within parish churches, like Stow (Li) – starkly cruciform – Ramsbury (Wi), or Dorchester-on-Thames. The crypt at Hexham survives. One, that at North Elmham (Nf), fell into ruins, and the present church was built nearby but not on the same site. This has therefore offered a valuable opportunity to find out what a small and remote country cathedral was like. It was excavated in the late 1950s by S E Rigold, and its remains have been preserved. The church offered a much more unitary appearance than Winchester or Canterbury, although there were several building phases. It was a long, narrow building, with nave only some 20ft (6.1m) wide internally. The east end consisted of a solid transverse block, with a small rounded apse projecting at the east and two small square rooms or chapels on each side where the nave began. The whole building was some 120ft (36m) long. Elmham was a see from 673 to 1075, (with a break during the Danish settlement from *c* 840 to the 950s, when it was moved to Thetford and soon after to Norwich.

Medieval cathedral architecture

The medieval cathedral churches are textbooks of architecture. Most of them show a wide variety of styles which usually blend happily, and most show a consistently high standard of inspiration and technical competence. There are a few which give the impression of homogeneity. Such are Durham for the Norman period (although this has a later east end), Salisbury and Lincoln for Early English, Exeter and Lichfield for Decorated, Bath for Perpendicular, St Paul's for Baroque, Liverpool Roman Catholic for contemporary (for an account of "The Styles of Architecture" see pages 347–60).

Sometimes the very evident contrast of styles is itself an essential feature, eg the fragment of the old Norman font at Lincoln and the Decorated spire of Salisbury. Sometimes a large fragment in one style dominates the rest, like the Norman naves at Southwell, Hereford, St Albans, or Peterborough, or the Perpendicular choir and east window at Gloucester. Most cathedrals have at least one outstanding feature, not equalled elsewhere, which it is worth a long journey to see. Such are the chapter house, wood carving, and general detail of Lincoln, the west front at Peterborough, the octagon at Ely, and the spire at Salisbury. Others are the galilee at Durham, the cloisters at Gloucester and Wells, the stalls at Ripon and Manchester, the detached bell tower at Chichester, the crypts at Ripon (*c* 660), Winchester, and Hereford, the bishop's throne at Exeter, the holy well at Glasgow, the shrines at Lincoln or St Albans, the chantries at Winchester, the wooden roof at St David's, the stone carving at Southwell and Lincoln, the east window and the earliest fan vaulting at Gloucester (1370), the Five Sisters window at York, the Bishop's Eye window at Lincoln, the chevet and bishop's throne beyond the High Altar at Norwich, the Wren Library at Lincoln, and the closes at Lincoln and Winchester. Each will have his preference, after seeing many. And no one building can have everything. But my own preference goes to Lincoln which, with its size, breadth of concept, detail, site, and close, stands comparison with Chartres itself, the Mother of them all (see **163**).

Bishops' palaces

As a footnote to this section, a byway of considerable fascination is the life style of the medieval bishop. A bishop was a major magnate, with multifarious duties, vast responsibilities, and unremitting activity. An archbishop had the comparative rank of a duke, a diocesan bishop of an earl, and they were expected to live accordingly. As well as being prelates of the Church, bishops were great feudal lords, having manors in many places and full judicial powers, including imprisonment and death. They were Fathers in God to clergy and people, administrators, advisers, upholders of the power and prestige of Church and State; the Lords Spiritual were also Lords Temporal. They counselled the King,

163 *Much of Lincoln Cathedral was destroyed in an earthquake in 1185, but the Norman west front and west towers survived. The west front (of 1072–92) was incorporated in a much larger Early English front by c 1240; the towers were raised c 1420. These changes can be seen in this picture.*

sat as peers in Parliament, and were given a wide variety of jobs, personal for the king, administrative and political for the state; they conferred with their fellow bishops, and attended the Archbishop's conferences. They kept an eye on their estates, and consulted and entertained on a vast scale. In doing all this they travelled incessantly, and hunted and feasted in their spare time.

They lived in palaces – domestic buildings on the scale of an Oxbridge college or a fair-sized monastery – geared not only to private living but also to lavish entertainment, constant guests, audiences, and

courts, and housing staffs of chaplains, financial and legal officials, advisers, secretaries, estate and farm stewards and bailiffs, personal servants, domestic functionaries and managers, officers of justice, and men-at-arms. They also housed leeches, barbers, musicians, artists, craftsmen, domestic servants, farm workers, grooms, and huntsmen. Vast quantities of food were required at all times.

Bishops were constantly on the move, within their (usually very large) dioceses or travelling to London or to wherever the king might need them. The Bishop of Hereford is recorded as never travelling with a train of fewer than 50 horsemen, and many bishops exceeded that. They stayed at monasteries on the way, or conveniently placed manor houses or castles.

A very interesting special case is that of Winchester in the 12th century. Henry de Blois, grandson of the Conqueror, brother of King Stephen, the Pope's legate, abbot of Glastonbury, and one of the wealthiest men in Europe, was bishop from 1129 to 1171. He was vigorous, ambitious, active, highly intelligent and cultivated, a patron of the arts, and a great builder. He enlarged his palace of Wolvesey in Winchester and built up well-situated manors and castles into palaces, so that he could travel to London and elsewhere in appropriate style and with adequate support. He found Wolvesey as a not very spacious hall and a range of private apartments. He added a new and very large great hall and audience chamber, and left the building as a large complex. (The present palace of Wolvesey was built in 1684.) He enlarged a manor house at Bishop's Sutton, near Alresford, and remodelled Farnham Castle and added domestic buildings round a courtyard below the keep (these were altered in the 15th and 17th centuries). At the London end, he rebuilt the old palace at Southwark, though the present great hall here is 13th century. He rebuilt Bishop's Waltham, the centre of a large manor; quite recently (1985) a hitherto unexcavated palace comparable to this has been investigated at Witney (Ox). He also had castles at Marden, Downton, and Taunton, and numbers of manors.

Palaces of other bishops are also of great interest, even if not forming such a spectacular series. The Archbishop of Canterbury had a large palace by the cathedral, of which the hall has recently been excavated. He had other palaces too, such as Croydon. His London house is Lambeth, a fine and remarkable building. The bishop of London had a palace in the City till the 19th century, and then settled in his nearest manor, Fulham (owned by the see since c 691 – the present house is early 16th century). Other bishops had London houses too, such as Ely, the chapel of whose palace survives in Ely Place and has reverted to Roman Catholic use. The Archbishops of York's palace was next to the Minster, and its chapel is now the Library; their seat is now Bishopthorpe, a manor house built in 1226 and rebuilt *c* 1769. Wells has an impressive palace, 1206, with 14th-century walls and moat. Many others have medieval houses adapted later, which are worth seeking out in every old cathedral city.

A special case is Durham, where the Prince-Bishops had Palatine powers – they were guardians of the Border. To carry out this not always easy function they lived in the great Norman castle just north of the Cathedral (1072, hall late 13th century). In 1832 Bishop van Mildert gave up this title and most of his vast revenues, founded the university, and went to live in an outlying manor, Bishop Auckland (12th century, rebuilt early 16th). Many Scottish bishops also lived in castles; there are good remains at St Andrews and Dornoch. St David's in Wales also has extensive remains of the bishops' palace.

MONASTIC HOUSES

The monastic aspects of the Celtic church are dealt with on pages 261–4 above. The conversion of the pagan Saxons, which began with the arrival of Augustine in Kent in 597, was by no means the first event in the history of Christianity in Britain, as the preceding pages show. But it was of the greatest importance, and from it flowed the establishment of bishoprics and monasteries of continental type in the Roman Catholic tradition, the gradual development of parishes, and the continuance of that tradition unbroken until the Reformation.

The orders

Augustine himself founded the first Benedictine monastery in England, that of St Peter and St Paul in Canterbury. The Roman monks took their missions to Wessex, where they took over the great monastery of Glastonbury, the only one which passed intact from the Celtic church to the Roman. The *Benedictines* were founded by St Benedict, once a hermit, who realised that a community could have more social impact than monks living separately as hermits or anchorites, as had been the early Christian tradition in the Near East,

and from there to the Celtic church. His first house, Monte Cassino, was founded in 529. In these houses the monks lived a life of prayer, hard work, self-discipline, and good deeds, under a Rule which involved vows of poverty, chastity, and obedience. The hours of the day were filled by a rigid timetable of prayer, services, and work. Scholarship was included, and the house sought to be as self-sufficient as possible. Each house was independent, under its own abbot. After the upheavals caused by the Danish raids and settlement, a number of Benedictine houses was set up, particularly by Dunstan, abbot of Glastonbury, after he became Archbishop of Canterbury in 960, and then by men inspired by him. These include the great houses of Bath, Winchcombe, Abingdon, Crowland, Peterborough, Ely, Bury St Edmunds, and Winchester. By the conquest there were 35 Benedictine monasteries and 9 nunneries.

By the later 11th century many of these houses had become wealthy and less austere, and in the late 11th and during the 12th century several orders were founded aimed at returning to Benedict's original simplicity. Most of these began in France. The *Cluniacs* were the first to reach England, at Lewes about 1078. They wore black like the Benedictines and they spent much of their time in church services, leaving farm and garden work to paid servants. By 1160 there were 36 Cluniac houses, mostly quite small; larger ones were Castle Acre, Thetford, and Much Wenlock. The Order of *Tiron*, 1115, was a branch of the Benedictines; it had major houses at Selkirk (later Kelso) and Arbroath. The Order of *Grandmont* (Bonshommes), *c* 1204, was claimed by the Benedictines, but its members were hermits under the rule of St Augustine.

The puritan reaction against the Benedictines culminated in the *Cistercian* order, developed by St Bernard of Clairvaux and Stephen Harding. The first house of these White Monks in England was Waverley (1128). In 1147 the order united with that of *Savigny*, founded *c* 1123. The Cistercians would not build their monasteries in towns, but chose places in remote spots in wild country, often far up the valleys of small rivers. The north of England and Wales offered many such sites, and vast areas of land to exploit. In their solitudes the monks had a severe rule based mainly on hard manual work, which had the not entirely intended result of making them very prosperous. They were not so scholarly as the Benedictines. Their churches and interiors were simple and unadorned; even towers were forbidden, although as the order grew richer they appeared, as at Fountains. They did not employ servants, but as their way of life attracted large numbers of uneducated men they divided themselves into two classes, the *choir monks*, who attended all the services and ran the monasteries, and the *conversi* or *lay brothers*, who did most of the heavy or outside work. Large houses, like Fountains (1132), Rievaulx (1131), or Byland (1147), could have 150 or so monks and up to 500 or 600 lay brothers. The movement spread rapidly; for instance, Rievaulx, within six years of its foundation in 1131, established houses at Melrose and Warden, and continued with Dundrennan in 1142, Revesby in 1143, and Rufford in 1148. By the 13th century there were 75 houses in Britain, and 26 nunneries.

The *Carthusians*, who under St Bruno broke away from the Cluniacs in 1084 at La Grande Chartreuse, had an even more austere rule. They lived solitary lives in separate cells, spending their days in prayer, meditation, and gardening, only meeting in church and rarely speaking to each other. They were in fact too severe to become popular, and had only nine houses in England (from 1178–9), of which the most complete remains are those of Mount Grace (NY) (1398).

Another type of monastery was that of the *Regular Canons*. The main order was the *Augustinians*, or Black Canons. They lived in communities like monks, but went out preaching. Their churches were often large (reflecting their popularity among the people), and they were generous of alms and hospitality. They followed the rule of St Augustine of Hippo. Their first house in England was Colchester (*c* 1100); other houses were at Bristol, Carlisle, Lanercost, Christchurch, and Southwark. They had 218 houses. They had three minor branches – Canons of Arrouaise (contemplatives, at Dorchester (Ox), *c* 1140, and Notley (Bc)), and Canons of St Victor and of the Holy Sepulchre. The *Premonstratensians*, the White Canons, founded their first English house at Newsham in 1143, and had 31 abbeys and two nunneries, including Alnwick and Egglestone; they were an austere order. The *Trinitarians*, called Red Friars, were not a mendicant order, but spent their revenues on relief of the poor and the ransom of captives. They had a house at Knaresborough (*c* 1200). The *Bonshommes* (not those of Grandmont) had two houses, Ashridge (1283) and Edington (1352).

The *military orders* had specialised functions. The *Knights Hospitallers of St John of Jerusalem* (*c* 1144) protected and provided for pilgrims to the Holy Land. The *Knights Templars* (*c* 1125) aimed to defend Jerusalem. Their churches were round, like the Holy Sepulchre in Jerusalem; the survivors are the Temple churches in London, Northampton, Cambridge, Little Maplestead (Ex); at Orphir (Or) there is a round church built after 1120 as a penance for the martyrdom of St Magnus. They had widespread branches – "commanderies" – on their lands, eg at Selborne (Ha). The Templars were suppressed in 1311–12, and their possessions granted to the Hospitallers. Other military orders served hospitals – those of *St Lazarus*, *St Thomas the Martyr of Acon*, and *St Mary of Bethlehem* (see below).

Double houses

In some orders certain houses contained monks or canons and lay brothers as well as nuns, but they became simple nunneries by the early 14th century. Some of these were Augustinian (Marton) or Benedictine (Moxby); the order of *Fontevrault* was a branch of the Benedictines. The *Gilbertines*, founded by Gilbert of Sempringham, was the only order founded by an Englishman (*c* 1131). It was, except for one or two houses, an order for nuns, lay sisters, canons, and lay brothers, and lasted till the Suppression. They had 26 houses; these had separate cloisters and living quarters, but one common church, divided down the middle by a wall (Watton (Hu) is a good example). A house for men only was excavated in York in 1986 (*c* 1200). The *Bridgettines* had one house in England, Twickenham (Mx) (*c* 1415), which moved to Syon in 1431; this was a nunnery with a large college of priests attached.

Several of these orders had *nunneries*, and there were finally over 100. The Benedictine houses began to be founded before the conquest; of these Romsey has the finest church. Lacock was Augustinian, Hinton Carthusian. *Sisters of Penitence* appear at Worcester in 1241–2, but are obscure. Franciscan nuns (1293–4), known as *Poor Clares* or *Minoresses*, had a house in London; Dominican nuns had only one house in England, Dartford (1346). In Scotland there is much the same spread of orders, but one, the *Valliscaulians*, is not found in England. They had three houses, Pluscarden, Beauly, and Ardchattan.

Mendicant orders

In the 13th century a new type of religious arose, the preaching *friars*. These were not monks or canons; they professed poverty and held no property – even their churches and convents were held in trust for them. They moved among the people, not only preaching but doing the kind of things the Salvation Army does in our own time. They lived on alms and made collections for their work. They became firmly fixed in the affections of the people. They encouraged learning also. There were several orders: the *Dominicans*, or Order of Preachers, the Black Friars, arrived in 1221, the *Franciscans*, or Grey Friars, in 1224, the *Carmelites*, or White Friars, in 1240–2, and the *Austin Friars*, or Hermit Friars of St Augustine, in 1248. In addition to these main orders there were the *Crutched Friars*, *c* 1250, under the rule of St Augustine, and three minor orders suppressed in 1274 – the Friars of the Sack, the Pied Friars, and de Ordine Martyrum. All these orders had houses in London, and most towns of any size in the Middle Ages can show names or traces of some or all of them (see also below, page 287).

In addition to these orders of monks and friars, there were other religious communities, such as the collegiate churches, who were *colleges* of secular priests. In this category fall the colleges at Oxford and Cambridge founded before the Reformation, which had similar organisations, with students attached. Finally, there were the *hospitals* (see pages 385–8). Most of these were secular but some were monastic, being run by a closed community of men or women. Most of the orders ran hospitals, especially the Augustinian canons and the Trinitarians. The military orders (see above) existed chiefly for hospital management, and with them the order of *St Anthony of Vienne*.

The dignitaries

The religious community living in a monastery or nunnery was a *convent*. It was presided over by an *abbot* (or *abbess*) if an independent house, or by a *prior* (or *prioress*) if a cell, or daughter house, of a larger monastery (such as Tynemouth, which, although large, was dependent on St Albans). Augustinian houses were usually called priories. At first the abbot lived with the rest, but later his status and duties increased and he had a separate house. The abbot's deputy was the prior, who had several *obedientaries* reporting to him for the various management functions. These were the *precentor* (whose deputy was the *succentor*), who was in charge of the services, the library, and the archives, and the *sacrist* (and subsacrist), who looked after the church and its contents (plate, vestments, etc); the subsacrist rang the bells

and kept the time, arranged funerals, and looked after the fabric and repairs. At St Albans is a watching loft from which the subsacrist could watch the relics during a pilgrimage. The *cellarer* and his assistant managed the food and stores of the house (the cellars in which these were kept could be enormous, as at Fountains); he was also responsible for the brewing and baking, the mills and granaries, the farms, granges, and lands and he managed the leases, sales, and purchases, and the overseers of the farms. In a large house he was second only to the head. The *kitchener* looked after the cooking, and the *fraterer* or refectorian saw to the serving of the food and the cleanliness and good order of the refectories and lavatories. The *chamberlain* had charge of the other buildings in the cloister, and the monks' clothing, washing, shaving, and heating. Foot washing might be once a week, baths once a quarter. The *infirmarian*, or master of the farmery (infirmary), cared for the old, infirm, or sick, who lived in a separate block (with its herb garden); this block also often contained the prison for offending monks. The *hosteller* ran the guest house, and sometimes maintained the roads leading to the monastery; the *almoner* fed the poor and wayfarers (as is still done at St Cross in Winchester). The *master of the novices* trained those who wished to join the community. There were also *bailiffs* to keep accounts and conduct legal affairs, and pay wages; and stewards or *graingers* in Augustinian houses for property management. Add the monks themselves, the lay brothers or servants, and the various permanent residents (living under corrody or pension, or in sanctuary), and the complexity and size of the communities will be appreciated.

The buildings

At the conquest there were fewer than 280 religious houses in England and Wales; by 1200 the figure had increased to over 1,300, largely owing to the introduction of new orders from France. By the Black Death in 1349 the numbers had increased to over 2,000, which now included the friaries, more hospitals, and other houses. At this time there may have been some 15,000 monks, nuns, and canons. The Black Death and the decline of the feudal system led to a fall, and in the 15th century there were under 1,700 houses.

The general arrangement of the monastic buildings was common to most of the orders, although it might differ in detail and had be

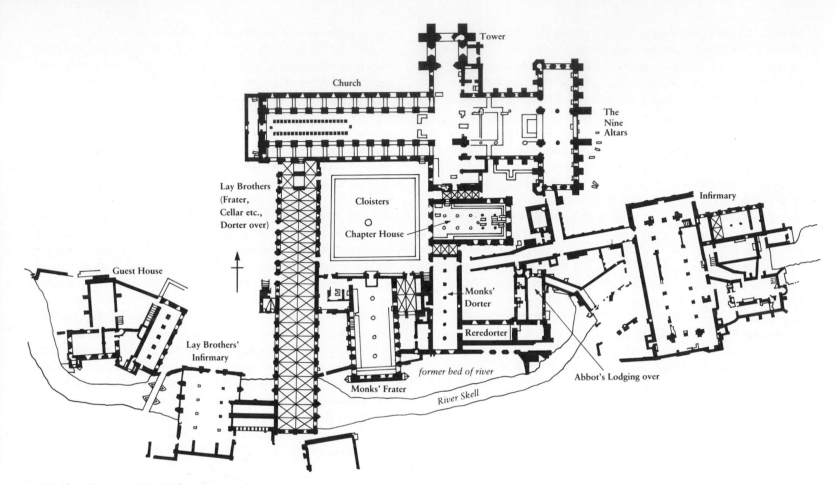

164 *Plan of Fountains Abbey (NY); the very complete remains of a major Cistercian monastery.*

standardised before the end of the 11th century. The focal point, and in most cases the most conspicuous architectural block, was the *church*, round which the life of the monastery turned. This followed the "greater church" concept described above (page 274), except in the smallest houses. The church was cruciform; from east to west it had a presbytery, a choir (for the monks), transepts, often with chapels, and a nave, for the lay brothers and the local people. Norman presbyteries, where the High Altar was and behind which was an ambulatory, were at first rounded, in the French manner; the Cistercians introduced the square end, which became the standard English type. There could be a Lady Chapel, usually on the end of the apse, but sometimes

elsewhere. The Cistercians dedicated all their churches to the Virgin Mary, so did not need a Lady Chapel. There is a good example of an ambulatory at Norwich, and of a Lady Chapel at Winchester. Even the Cistercian presbytery became more elaborate, and could then be aisled, as at Abbey Dore (the simple form can be seen at Kirkstall); Rievaulx had seven bays, and Fountains (imitated by Durham) added a spectacular eastern transept, the Chapel of the Nine Altars. The choir was separated from the nave by a screen called a *pulpitum*, from which the epistle and gospel were read, and which later had an organ above it. The nave could be very long, as at Winchester or Norwich. The west door was used for processional entrances and sometimes had an ornate porch, as at Malmesbury. The churches were high, with triforia and clerestories; there was usually a central tower, and one or two at the west end. Even the Cistercians took to towers in the end, and that at Fountains (*c* 1500) is a very fine one. If the abbey possessed a saint, whose relics could be the point of attraction for pilgrims, the relics were kept in a shrine, which could be very elaborate. This was usually behind the High Altar (Canterbury and Durham are good examples). Friary churches (see below) had large, wide naves for preaching, with narrow choirs.

The monastic buildings crowd up against the south side of the church, to which access was needed at all hours. Most abbeys are now fragmentary, if they are visible above ground at all, but many have a surprising amount to show. The most complete ruin is Fountains (near Ripon (NY) (see **164**), and this well repays detailed exploration. One difficulty in visualising what these buildings once looked like is that few of them have much standing above the ground floor, except in the few cases where perhaps one building is used, mostly for another purpose; a good example is the range at Sherborne, now part of the school. One of the best English examples is Battle (Sx). Here the eastern range of the cloisters, containing the chapter house and parlour, is fragmentary, but it is continued to the south by a range built on a steep slope, at its south end standing to its full height of two storeys. The ground floor is occupied by a large common room(?), a slype, a smaller room, and a large room perhaps for novices; the first floor is the monks' dorter, complete all but the roof. Traces of the reredorter can be seen at the south-east corner. Looked at from below (south) this range gives a magnificent idea of the mass and solidity of a monastic (13th-century) building. The abbey at Hambye in Normandy, where the buildings were long used as a farm, and some of which still stand to two storeys, has been skilfully and lovingly restored by Madame E Beck for the Département de la Manche; this gives a striking impression of the various buildings and rooms as they once were, and helps greatly in one's understanding of buildings less complete. But Hambye is a small house whereas Fountains takes up a very large area, and, with its enormously larger number of inmates, has many more components. It is thus useful to perambulate Fountains to identify these components.

The *cloister* here is in its usual position south of the nave of the church. Sometimes the lie of the land prevented this. The cloister is a square court, with covered walks all round (here the roofs have gone,

but the points on the walls from which they sprang can be seen). The walk against the church was the principal place for the monks to meditate, but all the walks were used for exercise or communication. The centre of the court was grassed, and could have a well or tree in the middle. There are many good cloisters, such as Gloucester; Westminster has two. Cleeve has an abbot's seat against the church wall, for when readings were given in the evenings. Some cloisters have stone benches to sit on, and one at Gloucester has a gaming board scratched on it. Glass was installed in cloisters in the late 13th century, when the climate deteriorated.

The eastern range of the cloister has several rooms, of which the most important is the *chapter house*. This is usually a rectangular room for business meetings with benches round the walls for the monks (the "chapter" may refer to the passage from St Benedict's Rule read on these occasions). Abbots were often buried here, and Rievaulx has a shrine, that of the first abbot. Between the church and the chapter house was the *slype*, a passage leading to the monks' cemetery. This was often used as a parlour, where monks could speak to each other, and sometimes as a library. There is a fine one at Gloucester. At Fountains there were book cupboards in the chapter house, and the parlour was beyond. Above this range was the monks' dorter, or dormitory. In some houses this was reached by stairs from the south transept, as at Hexham; in some the dorter is separated from the church, and the stairs are elsewhere. Beneath the dorter is an *undercroft*, a vaulted and pillared room used as a store. At the south end of this block is the *reredorter* or garderobe of the monks, latrines discharging (in the case of Fountains) into the river which runs below. Here also is a room, probably the day room of the novices, which forms the south side of a small court, of which the east side is the prison block. Beyond this are the buildings of the *infirmary*, with its own hall, chapel, kitchen, and dormitory. The *abbot's house* was in this area.

The south range of the cloisters contained the *refectory*, with kitchen on one side and warming room on the other. At Glastonbury the kitchens, monks' and abbot's, are detached buildings, as at Fontevrault. At Fountains the kitchen is between the refectory and the lay brothers' wing (the west range of the cloister), and served both; it could also draw on the great store below the lay brothers' dorter. The refectory had a pulpit for reading during meals. This *lay brothers' wing* is one of the finest and largest monastic buildings anywhere. At the

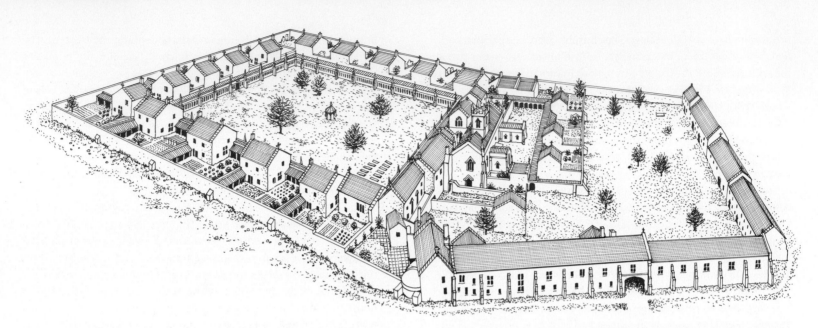

165 *Mount Grace Priory (NY) (Carthusian, 1398). This view of the priory, based on Alan Sorrell's reconstruction, shows the monks' cells and gardens (houses and plots), the church in the centre, the prior's house, guesthouse in the right foreground, and stabling, barn, etc on the right.*

south end of it was a reredorter, over the River Skell, and to the west of it another infirmary block, with kitchen. West of this again were three *guest house* blocks.

Another specialised room in a large monastery was the *misericorde*, where the monks ate who had been bled, or were on a diet on account of age and health. That at Westminster (located in 1921, but only excavated in 1975) was between the frater and the kitchen, southwest of the cloister. Originally, if the monks needed rest, say after the regular bleedings they had to undergo for their health's sake, or after illness, this had to be taken in the house itself. But later, such rests or holidays (called *seyneys*) came to be taken outside the house in "seyney-houses". These could be manor houses or granges belonging to the abbey, or sometimes subsidiary monastic houses. Thus, Spalding used Wickham Grange, Durham sent its monks to Finchale Priory, St Albans to Redbourn. The abbot of Bury was said in 1535 to "lay much forth in his granges". The abbot of Glastonbury rebuilt his manor house at Ashbury (Bk) in the late 15th century as a comfortable staging-post on his road to London.

The *gatehouse* was a separate building, as were the *bakehouse* and *malthouse*. There were also *mills* and other farm buildings (see below).

There are many minor details; Gloucester has a fine example of the wash-basins next to the refectory entrance where the monks washed their hands before meals, and a recess to hang their towels. Some houses, like Canterbury, had elaborate water supplies. Some houses have a detached dovecote, in others this is combined with one of the buildings. Patrons and founder's kin are often buried near the altar. The *outer court* contains not only the bakery and brewery but all kinds of farm buildings, stables, cartsheds, toolsheds, styes, cowsheds, henhouses, mason's shop, smithy, carpenter's shop, etc. Most of such buildings were made of wood, or timber-framed, and have not survived. The home farm also had kitchen gardens and fishponds (eg fine ones at Glastonbury, which also had a fishery at Meare with a house for the fisherman). Some houses had fishing rights on rivers or in the sea, as St Dogmael's or Chester. The house was usually surrounded by a wall, called the *paradise* or garden wall. eg Winchester (where Paradise was the cemetery of the Old Minster). At Fountains the Monk Wall runs far across country and encloses a large tract of land, probably the home farm. Crossraguel in Strathclyde, a Cluniac house, has a very rare 15th-century range of *corrodians' lodgings*, built to house the lay pensioners.

Monasteries also had to cater for pilgrims, often in large numbers, and while most of these no doubt camped where they could, some houses had *inns* for them, as at Glastonbury. Near this also is the building where the abbot's court was held. There were also wayside *chapels* for pilgrims, like the Slipper Chapel at Walsingham. Many houses built parish churches or chapels just outside their walls (Merevale), or hospitals (Bermondsey), or schools (Canterbury).

Double houses, like Watton in Yorkshire, had two blocks of buildings, each with cloister and essential elements round these, and a common church. A very different arrangement is that of a *Carthusian* house. Mount Grace is the finest example of these (see **165**). This had two courts. The outer court contained the gatehouse, the guest wing, stables, granary, and kitchen. The church was on the far side of this, surrounded by monks' cells. The inner court had the chapter house, the prior's cell, and was bounded by more monks' cells. Each monk had in effect a small house, with lobby, study, living room, and bedroom/oratory; upstairs was a workroom; he had also a small garden with privy. Meals were delivered to him through a hatch. The whole court was built at an angle, and the hatches were angled so that no monk could see another.

Friaries show many differences in their buildings from monasteries, owing to the nature of the friars' life, dependent on preaching and alms collecting and hence being essentially urban, in total contradistinction to, say, the Cistercians. The buildings were generally smaller, although some friaries, as in York, developed the housing and entertainment of royal and noble visitors into a major activity. The dorters were from the first subdivided by partitions into a series of open cells, cubicles, or study-bedrooms. The church was contained in a single rectangular cell, under a single unitary roof. It was in three parts: the east end, church of the brothers, the nave (aisled in later large urban churches), the church of the laity, and a walking place separating them, which led to the cloister (not used for study). A pale idea of a large urban friary church of the later Middle Ages can be had from the (modified) church of the Black Friars, now St Andrew's Hall, in Norwich. The west door opened directly onto the street, for the convenience of the townspeople.

The Friars depended on getting a foothold in the most populous and prosperous towns, and the number of friaries inside the walls of a town is a good indication of the town's importance. Thus, there were houses of the four main orders (Dominicans, Franciscans, Carmelites, and Augustinians) in London, Canterbury, Winchester, Bristol, Oxford, Cambridge, Northampton, Stamford, Kings Lynn, Norwich, Boston, Lincoln, York, Newcastle, and Berwick, and of three in Edinburgh, Perth, and Aberdeen. If there was no room inside the town (and sometimes the existing monasteries opposed the settlement of friars, quite apart from the availability of space), the friars got as close to it as possible, even accepting a damp or inconvenient place to do so. This is the case at Bury St Edmunds, Hereford, Nottingham, and Leicester. At Oxford the Greyfriars' house had to straddle the city wall, with much of the church and the graveyard outside it and the other buildings inside.

ORDER	ENGLAND & WALES		SCOTLAND	
	Before 1250	By 1500	Before 1250	By 1500
Franciscans (Grey Friars, Friars Minor)	41	60	4	8
Dominicans (Black Friars)	23	53	2	16
Carmelites (White Friars)	27 by 1300	29 by 1350	5 by 1300	9
Augustinians (Austin Friars)	25 by 1300	40 by 1534	–	–
Crutched Friars	9	9	–	–
Friars of the Sack	17	–	–	–
Pied Friars	3	–	–	–
Trinitarians (Red Friars)	5	–	8	7
Observantines (Reformed Franciscans)	–	–	9	9

Distribution

Monasteries are thickly distributed over most of the Lowland Zone of England, particularly in the Thames valley, East Anglia, Lincolnshire and Yorkshire, the Severn valley, and Somerset. The old towns are very rich in them, and most orders are represented in the larger towns. London had over 50 houses of various sizes and types, from major houses like St Bartholomew's, Westminster, Southwark, or Bermondsey, to hospitals and specialised houses and to the chapel on London Bridge. Benedictine and Augustinian houses are widespread; Cistercian houses tend to be in the less well populated areas. Thus the north of England, and particularly Yorkshire, has a large number. In Yorkshire, Roche, Kirkstall, and Meaux are major houses; but in the northern part of the county is the remarkable group of Fountains, Jervaulx, Rievaulx, and Byland, all with impressive ruins. Kirkham and Guisborough are Augustinian, Whitby Benedictine, and Mount Grace Carthusian. There are many smaller houses, but these alone make Yorkshire a place of pilgrimage for the understanding of the monastic spirit (as is Burgundy). Wales has the major houses of Strata Florida, Valle Crucis, and Llanthony, and several descendants of Celtic monasteries round the coast. Scotland also has many of the latter, including Iona and the secular college of Lismore. Among the most impressive remains are those at Whithorn, Sweetheart, Dundrennan, Dunfermline, Arbroath, Inchmahome, St Andrews, and the remarkable group on the middle Tweed – Melrose, Dryburgh, Kelso, and Jedburgh. The cathedrals which were formerly monastic (see page 274) usually have some remains of their former communities. Some of the older university colleges, like Magdalen or New College at Oxford, retain a certain semi-monastic atmosphere, even though their layout is specialised. But it is mostly the churches that have been preserved, and often these are all that remain of once extensive buildings.

Social and economic aspects

The major monasteries tried to be self-sufficient, and mention has been made of their home farms, breweries, bakehouses, mills, fishponds, dovecotes, etc. There was an enormous demand for food, not only for the monks and their servants or lay brothers. who could number several hundreds, but for the not inconsiderable numbers of guests, infirm, travellers, pensioners, etc who depended on the monastery. The monasteries were also the centres of learning, not only schools for boys or of theology, but the writing of histories and books on philosophy, theology, and secular subjects also, and the copying and illumination of manuscripts. Some houses had really extensive and important libraries. Music was also fostered. The monasteries provided rare facilities for the study of nature and scientific experiment. Many monks had laboratories in their cells, for alchemy or a more modern understanding of science. Retorts etc used for alchemy are indistinguishable from those used for the production of acids for assaying or for the distillation of essences or spirits (Chartreuse and Benedictine are well-known examples of this latter activity). Such retorts have been excavated at several monasteries (eg Selborne and Pontefract).

Nunneries had a special role to play among women, apart from their hospital and charitable work. Thus, Lacock not only ran a finishing school for girls but provided a home for women whose husbands were away or abroad, and for widows and unmarried women. Some continental nunneries restricted their inmates to women of proved aristocratic descent, but most English houses were not so rigid.

Monasteries were also great landowners, and it was part of the Cistercian ethos to colonise the waste. In the Lowland Zone these lands contained a high proportion of arable, and this is reflected in the huge *tithe barns* in the arable areas, where corn and other farm produce could be stored and distributed (see below). The monastic estates, which were as compact and manageable as could be achieved, were run from local farms called *granges*. But even in the lowlands a lot of land was given over to sheep, and in the great expanses in the north vast flocks were maintained, and the monasteries became major figures in the wool and later cloth trade. It is instructive to take a fairly small area, and analyse the variety of monastic activity in it.

Thus, upper Nidderdale in Yorkshire was controlled by two houses, Byland and Fountains. Byland owned the land at the head of the dale (Stonebeck Up and Stonebeck Down), formerly part of the Honour of Kirkby Malzeard, and Fountains had to allow them access to it through its own lands. Fountains then obtained a grant of land on the east side of the dale; in 1198 the boundary of this with Stonebeck Down was fixed and delimited by the Mere (or boundary) dike; this land became known as Fountains Earth. Fountains also acquired contiguous lands in Bewerley, Bishopside, Dacre, Brimham, and Ripley, and into the royal Forest of Knaresborough, thus making a large slice of good land. They also had large tracts in Malham, Littondale, and Bordley in Wharfedale, not far to the west. These lands were controlled directly from granges and lodges, except some outlying lands (as in Hartwith and Winsley) which continued to be farmed by tenants. Many of these granges survive, mostly as houses rebuilt in the 16th century. Those of Byland include Woodale, Ramsgill, and Gouthwaite (moved to its present position from nearer the river); those of Fountains include Covill Houses, Bewerley, Banger Houses, Dacre Grange, Brimham Grange, and Cayton Grange.

These large estates (and similar ones covered great tracts all over the country, not only in the north) not only carried sheep; the minerals were exploited as well. Both abbeys in Nidderdale mined for coal, lead, and iron. Old coal pits on Byland land can be seen near Scar; there are monastic iron workings and bloomeries at Bouthwaite, above Ramsgill, and some of the lead workings at Greenhow are monastic.

The large number of granges in this small area – 20 miles by 5 (32km by 8) – (Byland 19, Fountains 29) indicates the intensity with which the land was exploited.

Fountains had its own road system, separate from the public highway from Ripon into Craven, which crossed the dale at Pateley Bridge. There were no churches in these townships, but monastic chapels at Ramsgill, Bouthwaite, Bewerley, and Brimham, and parochial chapels at Middlesmoor and Pateley Bridge (these two depending on parish churches at Kirkby Malzeard and Ripon respectively, not on the ancient Nidderdale churches at Hampsthwaite, Ripley, and Nidd); this emphasises the relative isolation of the upper dale into recent times.

Other abbeys of course did the same: Durham had coalmines, Bolton worked lead, Kirkstall iron. Many houses had salt pits, in Cheshire, Salop, Staffs, and Flint. Vale Royal in Cheshire was making glass in the 13th century. Other industries were developed also. St Albans had a fulling mill, which it compelled all the weavers in the town to use; Meaux had a tannery; Abbotsbury, rather exceptionally, a swannery (but this could count as food supply); Repton, Malvern, and Chertsey made tiles; Tewkesbury and Glastonbury had vineyards. This list could be extended, but it may convey something of the enormous social and economic power of the monasteries.

Tithe barns

Tithes were originally a levy of a tenth of the produce of a manor towards the upkeep of the local church and priest. Some were partially converted into rents, but essentially they were paid in kind. Normally, the produce was stored by the priest in his own barn, but in the case of monastic lands or granges the volume was so great that special barns were built. Some of these barns are among the largest buildings of the Middle Ages. They can be of several bays, and up to 200ft (61.5m) long (that at Frindsbury (Kt) is 219ft (67.4m)). There are wagon doors, usually with porches, in the middle of the long sides. One of these porches may have an upper room or tallat loft, an office for the supervisor. The barns are open to the roof, and some have very impressive timber-framing. Notable examples are at Great Coxwell (Ox)

166 *The interior of the very large monastic tithe barn at Great Coxwell (Ox), at a former grange of Beaulieu Abbey (Ha). This is an aisled building, and one aisle is seen here.*

(on a former grange of Beaulieu Abbey (Ha)) (see **166**), 152ft (46.8m) long, mid 13th century, Tisbury (Wi) (on a former grange of Shaftesbury nunnery) (see **167** and **168**), 188ft (57.8m) long, and Bradford-on-Avon (Wi) (Barton Farm), early 14th century, 168ft (51.7m) long.

Monastic watermills

It is not always appreciated that a mill was a regular part of the supporting services of all but small monastic houses. A recent study by David Luckhurst has brought this out clearly. The food

167 *The 13th-century tithe barn at Tisbury (Wi), on a former grange of Shaftesbury nunnery (Do) (exterior).*

requirements of the larger houses were very considerable. In a Cistercian house like Rievaulx, in the late 12th century, there were 140 monks and no fewer than 600 lay brothers; in addition, the abbey distributed alms, ran a "hotel" for travellers, entertained a variety of visitors and special guests, and maintained an infirmary; it also had manorial rights over much of its lands, and the tenants would have to have their corn ground at the abbey mill; there could also have been a number of pensioners and others living in or out of the abbey, and dependent on it for food. Not only corn for bread was ground in the abbey mill, but barley also for beer, and so the brewhouse and malthouse, as well as the bakehouse, adjoined the mill. Traces of these buildings remain at Waverley and Fountains. It was also quite usual for the miller to sell fish and eels from the millpond, and supply poultry. Where the abbey had no mill of its own, it usually had rights of free user at the local manorial mill.

The standard layout of a Cistercian house grouped the ancillary buildings such as the mill, bakehouse, brewery, forge, workshops, and farm buildings round a "curia" or outer court, separated from the inner precinct by a gate, but still within the outer wall surrounding the monastery. Few English houses have coherent remains of these curiae, but at Hambye in Normandy (Benedictine) the outer court, containing stable, cartshed, cider press, and pigsty (but not mill), has been restored with the rest of the elements of the monastery, and gives a most vivid insight into what a living monastery looked like.

168 *Tisbury tithe barn (interior).*

In some cases, where clothmaking was one of the activities of the abbey (eg at Abingdon), there was a fulling mill also. All the mills usually used the same stream or water system, and in some cases the millrace was also used to clear the abbey drains (eg at Easby); in others, such as Fountains, the local river served these purposes. In some places the river was diverted, for convenience or other reasons. Thus at Rievaulx the river made two very sharp loops in front of the abbey, which had a difficult and narrow site anyway. The monks straightened out these bends, both to make the precincts more spacious and to cut another canal (still traceable) parallel with the river to drive the mill and flush the drains.

374 *Berkshire wagon.*

377 *Huntingdonshire wagon.*

375 *Devonshire wagon.*

379 *Sussex wagon.*

376 *Dorset wagon.*

380 *East Anglian wagon.*

382–3 *Romany (gypsy) caravans: 382 bow top type; 383 Reading type.*

Very few traces of monastic mills survive, so they can easily be overlooked. Only one, that at Fountains, is in a recognisable state. It was once some 100ft (30.7m) long, built across the millstream and with two wheels. The mill at Rievaulx has been much altered, and its water supply is different from the simple use of the river in monastic times. At Reading remains of the mill are incorporated in the 19th-century Abbey Mill. Durham had two mills, at each end of the weir on the Wear, but not much of medieval work in either. At St Albans the causeway built for the Roman road over the Ver may have been used as a dam for the abbey millpond. At Easby the mill itself has been rebuilt, but the original watercourses can be seen. Abingdon is of great interest as showing the probable appearance of the buildings associated with a monastic mill; these include the granary and bakehouse, the checker (where the accounts were kept), which has a 13th-century chimney and wine-cellar beneath, and a Tudor long gallery which housed the clerks. In some cases the site of the mill is known, but no trace remains. Such is Westminster, where the mill was at the end of the cellarer's wing, over the millstream which ran along the line of Great College Street; but its nature and appearance are not known. In a few other cases later mills survived until recently on monastic sites, and may well have succeeded the monastic mills. (For the machinery and operation of watermills see page 541.)

The later Middle Ages

The half-century or so after the Black Death was a time of acute upheaval in rural life and in the structure of society itself. Rural labour was scarce and wages escalated. Men were able to become more mobile as ties with their former lords weakened. Cereal prices collapsed in the 1370s. So monastic incomes ceased to keep up with costs, in particular with wages, and there was a general movement away from demesne farming to leasing out the demesne lands, a movement which continued into the 15th century.

Another aspect of this period was the growing unrest of the farm workers, which sometimes erupted into actual violence, as in the Rebellion of 1381. The monasteries barricaded themselves against this by building walls and moats round their houses, manors, and granges, and sometimes by even fortifying their barns, eg Buckland (Dv); a good Scottish example is Sweetheart (DG), early 14th century.

The walls and gatehouse at Battle had already been built in the 1330s, partly against French raids along the coast, and Bury had similar features at this time; Thornton (Li) built its imposing gatehouse in the 1380s. Michelham (Sx), perhaps the best English example, also dug its moat and put a tower to guard the bridge across it in response to the French threat. In the north some monasteries became virtually castles, eg Alnwick (Nd) and Crossraguel in Scotland, and tower houses appeared on both sides of the Border as raiding flared up from both directions.

The monasteries recovered their wealth and stability during the 15th century, and by the end of that century and in the early 16th, much luxurious rebuilding and enlargement took place. The great and very fine central tower at Canterbury (Bell Harry) was of this time, as was Abbot Huby's tower and abbot's lodging at Fountains; other notable rebuildings can be seen at Forde (Do), Muchelney (So), and Thame (Ox). All this is reminiscent of the great 18th-century blocks and abbots' houses at French abbeys such as St Wandrille or Fontenay during the Benedictine revival of the 1730s.

The Dissolution

All this wealth and influence came to an abrupt end when Henry VIII dissolved the monasteries and chantries in 1536–40. The reasons were largely political, although the monastic system was undoubtedly declining and some of the houses were not living up to their former ideals. Nevertheless, the hiatus was a serious blow to many people. Hospitals, schools, almshouses, inns, and all kinds of charitable work had to be replaced in the following decades by similar institutions under secular control, and a whole system of poor laws had to be passed to cope with the vagrants and the homeless. Many monastic churches passed to the parishes, and still survive; many were looted or destroyed. Some, and most of the monastic buildings, fell into ruin or were rebuilt as private houses and institutions of all kinds. Fragments can be seen built into houses and farms or used as barns (Latton (Ex)); some are private houses (Forde, Newstead); some were robbed of stone to build houses (Fountains); some became schools, or part of them (Sherborne, Battle); Orpington Priory has recently been restored for use as offices. In many cases the church has survived intact (Southwark, Romsey); in others only part remains (Waltham, nave only, St Bartholomew's, London, choir only). At Tilty (Ex) the lay chapel is now the parish church; at Beaulieu the Frater. Greyfriars, Lincoln, is a museum. Malling houses Anglican nuns; Aylesford has been rebuilt as a monastery. Iona has been restored for a centre of the Church of Scotland. At Melrose a Presbyterian church was awkwardly built in the choir (much less successfully than the Reformed church inside the vast Pieterkerk at Leiden).

Modern monasteries

Since Catholic Emancipation in 1829 the religious orders have established themselves again in Britain, and now include not only the old medieval orders – the Benedictines, Cistercians, Augustinians, etc – but a large number of new ones. The Roman Catholic hierarchy was reorganised in 1850. There were then four male and 20 female new and reformed orders and congregations (non-monastic communities); in 1967 there were 75 male and 209 female. These include the Salesians, the White Fathers, the Jesuits, Redemptionists, Passionists, Oratorians, etc, and the Ursulines, Carmelites, Sacred Heart, Notre Dame, Assumption, St Vincent de Paul, and Franciscan nuns. Not all these new orders are closed or contemplative; some run schools, hospitals, and other social works. To these may be added the colleges and seminaries, like Ware, Ushaw, or Wonersh. Noted houses are Mount St Bernard (1835), St Hugh's Charterhouse, Cowfold, Ampleforth, 1802, Buckfast, 1882, Douai, Downside, Prinknash, Quarr, Ramsgate, Worth. Farnborough is a daughter of Prinknash.

Monasteries have also become a feature of the Anglican church; important houses are the Community of the Resurrection at Mirfield, the Cowley Fathers at Oxford, the Society of the Sacred Mission at Milton Keynes (formerly Kelham), Nashdom, and the sisterhood at Wantage. Iona shares certain monastic ideals.

THE PARISH CHURCH

There are over 15,000 Anglican parish churches in Britain, of which some 14,000 are in England, with c 1,100 churches in Wales and c 300 Episcopal churches in Scotland. In addition there are large numbers of private chapels (of colleges, schools, almshouses,

hospitals, private houses, etc). Domesday Book (1086) records or indicates some 2,800 churches and chapels in England; but its coverage is uneven, and the real total may be in the region of 4,500 to 5,000, if not higher. R K Morris estimates a figure of between 9,000 and 11,000 parish churches and parochial chapels in England by the 16th century. In 1801 there were 11,379 parish churches in England.

Churches usually originated in the activity of a missionary priest or monk, who set up a wooden preaching cross by his cell or temporary home, or at some other spot convenient to the local people or to the manorial lord (see Siting, page 293). In some cases this spot was at the grave of a martyr or other holy man (as at St Albans or Wells), or by a holy well. Burials of the converted would soon be made round the cross, and a wooden burial chapel would be erected. As momentum grew a larger church would be needed, and this would also be of wood. The only survivor of this phase in this country is the nave at Greensted (Ex) (in a church otherwise much "restored" and altered), where the walls are built of longitudinally split tree-trunks set vertically side by side on a sleeper beam. Morris suggests (*The Church in British Archaeology*, CBA Research Report 47, 1983) that some of these wooden churches themselves may in fact be only the second churches in the area, the first, and original, church having been built on another site in a "pre-parochial" phase.

During the later Saxon period, particularly in the later 10th and 11th centuries, the church was rebuilt in stone (with local variations of building materials – see below). In this period also, with increasing population and wider settlement, most of the vast areas served by the original minsters were split up into smaller parishes, based mostly on new manors or estates and the new villages or hamlets on them. The new churches were usually built of stone from the first. By 1200 practically all the present parish pattern was established.

Lordship is the main key to this multiplication of churches, rather than new settlement. Many churches also were built on virgin sites in the 12th and 13th centuries. Some chapels were elevated to the status of churches (ie with rights of burial); others declined. So the age of the church is not necessarily a guide to the age of the settlement. Furthermore, a considerable number of churches and chapels have been abandoned owing to population shifts and changes, and many have been lost (in the northern part of the old East Riding of Yorkshire, for instance, some 33 lost churches have been identified, and this number may not be complete). The total of such desertions appears to be larger than was once suspected, and they occur at all periods. Former minsters, however, did tend to be in sizeable towns, which have continued in being. Indeed, the majority of medieval markets were in places with minsters, or churches of status above the basic.

A conspicuous feature of medieval cities is not only the large number of monastic houses of all kinds, but the close-set city churches. There was often a church serving every few streets, built by the landowner to serve his tenants as a meeting place and guild centre as well as a church; and some were built by groups of neighbours. London had 107 churches before the Reformation (indeed, Becket's biographer FitzStephen says that there were 136 parochial churches in the 12th-century City); York had over 50, Lincoln 47, and Norwich 59 (of which 28 survive). One – St Mary's, Tanner Street – was excavated at Winchester in its setting and in all its phases by Martin Biddle in the 1960s, and much was learnt from it. Even a small town like Dunwich, a trading and fishing port on the Suffolk coast (destroyed by marine encroachment in the 13th–16th centuries), which had in its heyday only perhaps some 3,000 inhabitants, had no fewer than eight churches, three chapels, and six chapels of monasteries or hospitals – 17 in all, or roughly one for every 170 people of all ages.

The 16th century saw the taking over as parish churches of some of the churches of former monastic houses. A few new churches were built during the 17th century, and thereafter new churches were built to cater for newly-developed districts in the growing cities and towns, eg those built as a result of the "Fifty New Churches" Act of 1711, for London and Westminster (see **169**). The Industrial Revolution from c 1750 accelerated this need, and the 19th and 20th centuries have seen the creation of hundreds of new urban churches. Yet changes in the population pattern, as always, have complicated the needs for churches. There is a serious redundancy problem in

169 *Christ Church, Spitalfields, London – Nicholas Hawksmoor, 1723–29: a very original design.*

the countryside and too few churches in the new urban districts – a situation made worse by an overall shortage of clergy.

THE SITING OF CHURCHES

We are here concerned mainly with the churches of the Roman Catholic tradition, introduced to Anglo-Saxon England by Augustine in 597. This was a missionary situation, and churches originated purely as preaching points, followed by burial grounds and by wooden structures; each point served a large area.

These preaching points were chosen for various reasons: an existing sacred place; the convenience of the local people, ie a focal point in a land division; proximity to the house of a manorial lord or other patron (which led to many churches being private chapels) – this was the commonest reason; or just the availability of suitable (often waste) land. The missionary or his successors might, but not always, live by the church.

Remoteness could be an attraction if local pagan hostility was strong, and a Christian missionary post could well be deliberately not by a pagan shrine – such shrines could not all be taken over and absorbed by the Christians at once.

Some early churches might use a more or less ruined Roman building, eg a forum, as at St Paul in the Bail, Lincoln, or St Peter-on-Cornhill, London; York Minster took advantage of the *principia* of the legionary fortress. Roman buildings seem to have been used in St Martin's and St Pancras' churches at Canterbury, among the first to be built after 597. Some churches are built on Roman roads, a firm, dry, and ready-made foundation, and churches were also built close to villas.

Sometimes a Roman cemetery was Christianised, as at St Bride's, London. At Wells a Roman mausoleum formed the focus of a Christian burial ground, with a burial chapel, later (10th century) incorporated

293

into St Mary's Chapel. The holy well of St Andrew was close by, and three liturgical wells were dug in the cemetery. The later Minster of St Andrew was built west of this complex, and succeeded it. In a few cases (eg Sancton, Hu) a pagan Saxon cemetery seems to have been taken over; but these may in fact have been separate.

Some churches probably took over earlier sacred sites, eg the church at Rudston (NY) with a monolith in the churchyard (see **170**) or that at Knowlton (Do) with a henge; some churches are built on barrows (see below). The absorption of a holy well is common. This may be under the church (as at Walsingham), in the churchyard, or outside it (Barton-upon-Humber (Hu); Holybourne (Ha); Dunsfold (Sy) – but here the well is on a low wet site, the church on a high dry one). Liturgical wells may be dug in the churchyard, as at Barton-upon-Humber. Some sites may reflect the use, or reuse, of ancient sacred places. Thus at Ilchester, the Anglo-Saxon mother church of St Andrew was located outside the town and in the vicinity of a Roman cemetery; at Great Dunmow the mother church of St Mary lies outside the town but on a Roman site with at least one Roman grave nearby. Martin Biddle has suggested that the churches of St Brides, Fleet Street, St Andrew, Holborn, and St Martin-in-the-Fields may mark a return to abandoned or "latent" Christian sites in the suburbs of early London. These are by no means isolated examples.

A large cruciform church standing isolated in the middle of a village is likely to be a minster. As the vast areas served by minsters grew too unwieldy (eg Lydford (Dv), 50,000 acres; Beaminster (Do); Halifax (WY)), they were divided into smaller parishes, each based on villages or hamlets detached, sometimes by miles, from the central place. Each of these acquired a new church, so most late Anglo-Saxon, Norman, and later medieval churches are built on new sites. These were chosen for purely local convenience or the convenience of the manorial lord, even if a few did occupy sites of earlier significance. But more and more churches were built on new sites as time went on.

It should not therefore be assumed that there is any intrinsic connection between churches and "ley-lines", or that there is any continuity of church sites with Neolithic times. There is in fact no evidence for this (apparent cases to the contrary, like Rudston, are extremely few), and it is normally coincidence if, very exceptionally, such connections or continuity appear likely.

Most churches, in fact, were built on convenient spots close to manor houses. A survey by Rodwell of the churches of the archdeaconry of Colchester showed that about 44% were coupled with halls (about 33% were an isolated church and hall), about 16% were in complete isolation, and about 29% were in villages.

Churches are sometimes built on mounds, but it is not usually easy to decide whether a particular mound is a prehistoric barrow or a mound thrown up *ad hoc* when the church was built. If a barrow, this need not mean the continuity of a sacred site but merely the use of a convenient mound. If *ad hoc*, it may have been to make the church more conspicuous (Wisborough Green (Sx)), or to raise it towards Heaven, or merely to take it above flood level (Chithurst (Sx); Corhampton (Ha); Middle Claydon (Bc); Romney Marsh).

The churchyard is sometimes circular, subcircular, or oval, and here again, continuity with a prehistoric circle of some kind is difficult to prove, though it may be true in a few cases. It might in some cases just be the most economical use of land.

An exceptional variant of siting is when two churches stand in the same churchyard, eg Heptonstall (WY), Westminster (St Margaret's and the Abbey), Willingale Doe and Willingale Spain (Ex), and Aylsham (Nf) (where there are three churches). This usually results from a village having two manors, with the lord of each founding his own church. This may once have been commoner than now appears the case.

170 *Rudston church (NY): this has a prehistoric monolith close by in the churchyard, and is a clear example of the continuity of use of a sacred site.*

ORIENTATION

Churches and graves are traditionally oriented east–west – east being the (notional) direction of Jerusalem. The church has its altar at the east end, the nearest point to Jerusalem, and the grave is so arranged that the body, with its head at the west end, may rise on the Last Day facing the east. There are, however, a few cases where, for unavoidable reasons of location, this orientation was not possible. A conspicuous, if far-flung, example, is the Anglican Cathedral of St Paul's in Melbourne, Australia, where the church lies north-west–south-east along Swanston Street, with its altar at the north-west end. Nearer home, Rievaulx Abbey church lies north–south, because of the site – a narrow piece of land between the river and the hill. Liverpool Anglican Cathedral is also set north–south, because of the lie of the limestone ridge it is built on. The Saxon church which preceded the present (Norman) York Minster lay on a different alignment, being deflected by the presence of a still largely standing Roman building. Winchester Cathedral is oriented east-south-east.

Variations in orientation may also be due to the direction of sunrise on the day the church was laid out – often on the patronal festival (see also "Churchyards", page 320). Gilbert White observed this phenomenon at Selborne, but offered a different explanation: in Letter IV of *The Antiquities of Selborne* (1788), he says, "In speaking of the church, I have all along talked of the east and west-end, as if the chancel stood exactly true to those points of the compass; but this is by no means the case, for the fabric bears so much to the north of the east that the four corners of the tower, and not the four sides, stand to the four cardinal points. The best method of accounting for this deviation seems to be, that the workmen, who probably were employed in the longest days, endeavoured to set the chancels to the rising of the sun."

Several instances exist where the chancel is not on the same line as the nave; thus at Lichfield the chancel lies at an angle of 10° north of the nave. This has been explained as representing the inclination of Jesus's head on the Cross. But in fact it is almost always due to chancel and nave being laid out at different times, and is quite accidental. Could this too be due to laying-out in relation to the sunrise or sunset?

DEDICATIONS

The siting tells us one thing about the church; the dedication tells us another. Dedications can be central or peripheral to the mainstream of Christianity, and they can reflect religious fashion or local preferences – although such are the changes, and the deficiencies of the records, that one cannot often pin down a particular class of dedication to a particular period. The plethora may however be somewhat simplified by dividing them into groups:

1 *Mainstream*: Christ (Christchurch (Do)), Holy Rood (Edinburgh), Holy Cross (Waltham Abbey), Holy Trinity, the Apostles, Our Lady (Walsingham (Nf), New College, Oxford), also St Mary, Blessed Virgin, etc, Anne, Joseph, John the Baptist, etc.

2 *Popular saints, national or local*: St Thomas of Canterbury (after 1170!), St Swithun (Winchester), St Cuthbert (Durham), St Wilfred (Ripon), St Olaf (London, York), St Magnus (Kirkwall, London), St David (Wales, early, and by 12th century in Yorkshire and Nottinghamshire), etc. This is a mixed bag, containing heroes, wonder-workers, missionaries, martyrs, founders of abbeys. Some saints, like Nicholas, can be of doubtful authenticity or none, but had their time of popularity. This class shades off into

3 *Local saints*, particularly frequent in the Celtic west: St Mungo (Glasgow), the Welsh and Cornish monks and missionaries (Cybi, Padarn, Enodoc, Fimbarrus, etc). These in turn shade off into

4 *Concealed pagan gods*: this is an interesting and important class. Pope Gregory, who sent Augustine to England in 597 to convert the Saxons, laid down that old shrines, festivals, customs, etc should, if too strong to neutralise quickly, be taken over by the Church. This led to a variety of dedications which conceal old gods, or to sites like sacred circles or enclosures, hilltops, wells, rivers, groves, etc continuing in use. Thus, the Welsh Elen, goddess of travellers and Roman roads, was easy to convert into Helena – St Helen – mother of Constantine and discoverer of the True Cross and the Holy Places of the Holy Land.

St Michael is frequently found at hilltop churches, eg Brentor (Dv), but he is an assimilated sun god. The All Angels often linked with him are his rays (his messengers). He is also, like St George, associated with killing a dragon, who represents darkness, winter, or evil being overcome by light, spring, and good. St George is a similar god; the Church accepted the allegory that George stood for Christ, the Dragon for the Devil, and the citizens of Silena (who became Christian when the dragon was killed) for the human race redeemed by Christ. But George and Michael are old light gods, associated with hills and horses – the white horse pulls the sun chariot through the skies. The White Horses, like that at Uffington (Ox), represent part of this annual enactment. St Martha's, near Guildford (Sy), although on a hilltop, is anomalous. The dedication is unique in Britain, but probably does not represent St Martha of Provence, who is associated with a dragon (or with defeating one). One tradition, which may well be true, derives St Martha from Sanctorum Martyrum, and the church (which is in any case on a hill with recurrent, if not continuous, sacred associations from the Bronze Age on, and which has at least one 6th-century Saxon burial) may be on the site of a martyrium, memoria, or mausoleum, commemorating Christian martyrs. It had a Good Friday fair, with fertility dancing, and the context of the martyrdoms could be the pagan Saxon Spring festival.

St Catherine is another hilltop "saint", who also has a wheel representing the turning sky; she is the pure one, the moon, like Margaret, the pearl, and the Welsh goddess Arianrhod, the silver wheel. Dedications to Our Lady, as at Chartres, may conceal earlier devotion to a Mother Goddess, and, in her form as Star of the Sea, to Isis or Astarte. Statues exist of Our Lady associated with a crescent moon (eg in the Church in the Attic, Amsterdam).

5   *Victorian dedications*: the new churches of the mid 19th century, particularly those of the High Church movement, were often dedicated to the lesser apostles, like Jude or Matthias, or to All Saints. Christ Church, or Christ the King, were also popular. Chalbury (Do) was rededicated to All Saints at this time, its original dedication being unknown.

6   *20th-century* churches have sometimes also sought out-of-the-way dedications, such as The Good Shepherd (Carshalton (Sy)), or The Wisdom of God (Lower Kingswood (Sy)). Guildford Cathedral is dedicated to the Holy Spirit.

7   Some dedications were *changed* at the Reformation, eg St Mary Overy, Southwark, changed to St Saviour's; and some are *multiple* (St Mary and St Hugh, Harlow (Ex); Winchester Cathedral, now dedicated to the Holy Trinity, St Peter, St Paul, and St Swithun, but begun as St Swithun's Priory, rededicated to the Blessed Trinity in 1541; Selby Abbey, dedicated to the Virgin and St Germanus). Richard Morris points out that double dedications may sometimes reflect the dedication of a redundant church being added to that of a church with which it is merged; thus St Peter, Stainton (Li) was united in the early 17th century with St Mary's, Wadingham, now called St Mary and St Peter.

Dedications can be used to trace the movements of missionary saints; it has recently been shown, from a study of dedications, that south-west England and parts of Brittany were evangelised from Wales. Thus St Samson of Dol, after being abbot of Caldey, travelled to

171   *The Abbots Bromley Horn Dance (St): this is performed in September, and is unique in Europe; the characters, beside six horn dancers, are a Fool, a Hobby-Horse (Robin Hood), Maid Marian the Man-Woman, a Bowman, and two musicians.*

Cornwall where churches are dedicated to him at Golant and St Kew (and to his followers elsewhere in Cornwall); St Sampson's on Guernsey may represent a stage on the journey to the Rance estuary, where many churches bear his name.

Founders too travelled widely. The northerner St Wilfred is recorded as founding the church at Warnford (Ha), and St Cedd that at Bradwell (Ex).

THE FOLKLORE OF CHURCHES

The link with pagan gods mentioned in (4) above suggests a note on the involvement of the Church generally with pagan beliefs, practices, and memories (see also above pages 270–2). The names of the days of the week, in English, derive from Anglo-Saxon gods, and even a festival as Christian as Easter takes its name from the Saxon goddess of Spring and light, Eostre. Christmas has never shaken off its old character as

172 *The carved image of a Green Man, a human head with leafy branches springing from his mouth, face, or hair, can be found in many churches. The Green Man symbolised the unity of human beings with the natural world, and also Spring and resurrection; it may also be an echo of the Celtic cult of the head, a symbol of power. This example is at Llangwm (Mo).*

a midwinter festival. A few churches had a fair on Good Friday, a very unsuitable day from the Christian point of view – St Martha's has already been mentioned. Painswick (Gl) still has Spring dancing in the churchyard.

The horn dance at Abbots Bromley (St) (see **171**) goes back well into prehistoric times, to the nature god Cernunnos, the Horned One. The horns are kept in the church and blessed before use. Cernunnos, as a stag, is represented in Christian times by St Hubert, who has a cross between his antlers. Horns are a very ancient symbol of natural power, and are also linked with the moon. Other fertility customs, such as the Helston Furry Dance, the hobby horse, morris dancing, pace-egging, cheese-rolling, etc, were sanctioned or at least tolerated by the Church. The prominent sexuality of the Cerne Abbas giant (Do) was not abolished by the nearby abbey, and is still honoured in local custom. Any book on folklore will provide further examples.

The Green Man, or Jack-in-the-Green, appears in sculpture in churches all over the country; some churches even have more than one – Ottery St Mary has three. This human head, with leafy branches springing from his mouth, eyes, ears, or nose, or growing among his hair, may represent the fundamental unity of man with the rest of nature, but may equally be a symbol of Spring and resurrection. It may also be an echo of the Celtic cult of the head (a symbol of power) – an acorn or a vine planted in a buried head – so also reinforcing the prophylactic power of certain trees (see **172**).

This, of course, is an excellent example of the ambivalence and ambiguity of ancient religion, and the multiple nature of its symbols. The Celtic cult of heads (see **173–7**) and the triple deity (the phases of the moon, and of life) are also represented by the three-faced head in Salisbury Cathedral. Diana and the witch cult, with Satan, are painted in a window at Fairford (Gl).

The Grail legend, formerly attached to Glastonbury and the Arthurian cycle, derives, in one of its many meanings, from a pre-Christian vessel or cauldron of rebirth. In spite of its links with the blood of Christ, it was never officially accepted by the Church.

Protective devices on churches are sometimes only marginally Christian and many of them apply equally to secular houses as well as to churches. They are dealt with on pages 187–90 above, but those more specifically used in churches are briefly mentioned here. They include gargoyles and grotesques (gods, giants, and folk figures to frighten off evil spirits), *sheela-na-gigs* (carved figures explicitly

173 *Celtic Head – Bon Marché, Gloucester.* 174 *Celtic Head – Wakefield, Criggiestone.*

175 *Celtic Head – Boston Spa, Wetherby.*

176 *Celtic Head – Halifax, Greetland.*

173–7 *The human head was a symbol of power among the Celtic peoples, and was the basis of a cult; carved stone heads have been found in all the Celtic lands. These examples are typical; they have almond eyes and thin lips. They come from Gloucester; Criggiestone, Wakefield; Boston Spa (WY); Greetland, Halifax – this one is triple, and represents the phases of life and of the moon. These are all ancient; that set in the wall of the village hall at Ramsgill (NY) may be relatively modern.*

showing the female sexual parts, as at Kilpeck (He) (see below)), and weathercocks (Ottery St Mary has one put up in the 1330s) which are vigilant for evil spirits, and crow to give warning of their approach; gable crosses are also protective. It is, however, not easy to distinguish the pure exuberance of local sculptors from unconscious paganism; how is one to interpret the carved animals at Southwell?

The carvings on capitals were not only decorative but could have a variety of meanings, including homely wisdom – good things on the south side, bad on the north – and had close links with folklore, nursery rhymes, etc. At Great Bedwyn (Wi) they seem to portray the qualities, good and bad, of specific local people!

In areas where iron-rich pebbles are found, such as the Lower Greensand country of the Weald, such pebbles are often pressed into the mortar of the walls of both churches and houses. This "galletting" or "garnetting" is usually regarded as strengthening for the mortar, or even as merely ornamental, but in one view is an Iron Age apotropaic use of a "magic" material (to turn away evil spirits).

Sexual imagery in churches

The tightening-up of the practice of celibacy for the clergy in the 11th and 12th centuries led to an over-reaction against sex, resulting in misogyny and overheated imagination. One result of this was the appearance in churches of sexually explicit carvings of women and men displaying their sexual organs, or copulating. These figures are made deliberately ugly and unattractive, and were no doubt used by the clergy to expound the moral dangers of irregular sex. They were not intended to be erotic – quite the contrary.

179a *Well-dressing – Tissington (Db). The well before dressing. See* **179b**, *facing page 267, for a colour illustration of the same well after dressing.*

178 *Holy Well of simple type – St Non's Well, St David's (Pb).*

The centre of these carvings is the south-west of France and northern Spain, with outliers in the Auvergne. This seems to indicate a connection with the pilgrim routes to Compostela, and to the Church preaching to the pilgrims in the special churches on the routes. There were close links between south-west France and England in the 11th and particularly the 12th centuries, and the carvings no doubt reached England from the Saintonge area (as did the beakhead as an ornamental motif).

The distribution in England is wide, but the greatest concentration is in Herefordshire and Shropshire. Some 26 are recorded in England (of all types), and about 70 in Ireland. A famous example (female, a sheela-na-gig) is at Kilpeck (He). Kilpeck also has a male mask with foliage emerging from its mouth, like the French masks with snakes; these masks may have symbolised blasphemy, heresy, scandal, or evil in general (the resemblance of this to the later Green Man is coincidental – see below). The "Kilpeck School" of sculpture is due to one Oliver de Merlimont, who went to Compostela *c* 1138 and brought home, in the 1150s, the motifs he saw on his journey.

Much research has gone into these sexual images, but the recent work of Anthony Weir and James Jerman (*Images of Lust*, 1986),

points strongly to a didactic explanation. The images do not appear to antedate the 11th century, and do not seem to be fertility figures, or ancient deities, or to represent Mother Church (as one theory has it), or mere "graffiti". But when the 11th/12th-century campaign against sin died down, there is no doubt that the carvings were left in the churches (few are defaced) as apotropaic objects (to turn away evil). Somewhat similarly, the Green Man motif succeeded the earlier head with foliage after the Romanesque period, but with changed significance.

Holy wells

Holy wells are not always Christian in origin, although some may be – St Mungo's in Glasgow only became holy after the saint had used an ordinary spring, and the Chalice Well at Glastonbury, although now embedded in the local traditions, has been shown to be a medieval well-house, built round a spring to safeguard the water supply of the abbey. But many were sacred to a pre-Christian water spirit, and have been Christianised. The "holiness" of many of them, in the sense that it would be wiser not to defile them, is still active, and some are still credited, however light-heartedly, with the power to heal or to grant wishes. Many carry names, often of Christian saints; and because many of the pre-Christian water deities were feminine, a high proportion of Christian dedications are to female "saints", as Anne, Agnes, Helen, Catherine, or Our Lady. Others are called after historical

299

or legendary personages (such as Talbot or Robin Hood), or non-human objects (Borage Well, Ripon). Healing wells were activated by the gift of a metal object such as a pin or coin, or a rag, ribbon, tape, handkerchief, etc, or just by putting the hand in – the object being to place oneself, by substitution, into the beneficent power of the spirit of the spring. "Rag wells", with scraps fluttering from the trees round them, or "wishing wells", containing coins, can still be seen.

Examples of wells with specific powers to heal are St Bede's, Jarrow (children), Fergan (Ba) (skin diseases), St Cynhafel's (Dh) (warts), St Keyne (Co) (fertility), and Mother Shipton's, Knaresborough (anything – still very much used!). Water worship is directly reflected by the use as baptismal wells of St Chad's, Lichfield, or St Milburga's, Much Wenlock. Some of the more potent wells were firmly attached to Christianity by the erection of a church over or close by them, eg St Andrews, Wells Cathedral, St Winifred's, Holywell (Ft), Holybourne, Alton (Ha), St Helen's, Kirkby Overblow (NY), and St Bride's, London. Some have medieval superstructures, others are quite modern.

Some wells are remote from churches, yet were equally treated as ritual sites, eg St Ann's, Malvern. St Cybi's, Llangybi (Cn), has a complete "establishment" built in 1750, with stone basin, seating, and custodian's cottage. St Non's (see **178**), near St David's (Pb), once had a walled forecourt; in the field with this well and St Non's chapel are several ancient standing stones which may, if they relate to the well, indicate its great antiquity as a sacred site.

The holy wells of Wales have been surveyed by Francis Jones (*The Holy Wells of Wales*, 1954, Univ Wales Press, 1992), who lists 1179, of which 62 are associated with megaliths. Scotland has over 600. Those in England still await detailed study. No published figures are complete, but the total number is very large.

A local manifestation of the cult of wells is the *well-dressing*, mainly of Derbyshire. This is a placation of water nymphs to ensure the next year's supply, given a Christian face. It consists of the making, by local teams of children and adults, of large pictures by the wells. Frames and figures of wood are covered with clay and moss, and the pictures made from petals, leaves, buds, and berries pressed into the clay. They usually represent a biblical scene, with suitable wording. Services, and processions from the churches to visit the dressings, make clear the involvement of the Church. Tissington (see **179a**, and **179b**, facing page 265) and Wirksworth are good examples out of nine or ten still active centres.

THE SHAPE OF THE CHURCH

This is of course determined by the liturgical and social requirements of each period, and by the rise and fall of the population. No two churches have quite the same history, but a certain amount of generalisation is legitimate. A helpful guide to a typical sequence is given by Cox and Ford in their classic *Parish Churches of England*. This may be summarised as follows:

11th and 12th century: a simple nave, rectangular and barn-like, with a rounded sanctuary, its roof lower than that of the nave, beyond a narrow chancel arch; door usually at west end of south nave wall

13th century: a north aisle is added to the nave, to cope with increased numbers, and a benefactor or guild has added a chapel in the south-east corner; the sanctuary has been enlarged to a square-ended chancel

14th century: the south-east chapel has been extended to a full south aisle, the north aisle has been widened, and a north porch added; the chancel arch has been enlarged, and a sacristy added in the south-east corner

early 15th century: the guild has enlarged its south aisle, and added a porch, with room over; the parish has built a tower at the west end; another guild has added a north chapel to the chancel; a rood screen and loft have been built against the chancel arch

late 15th century: a third guild has added a south chapel to the chancel, with the sacristy becoming a chantry at the south-east corner; the chancel roof is raised; the nave arcades might be rebuilt, and a clerestory inserted; the tower is raised to its full height, and bells installed; the north porch gets a chamber over.

A good extant example is that of St Peter's, Barton-upon-Humber (see **180–7**). An urban church, because of having to fit into a burgage plot or two, is limited for space and usually remains rectangular, with aisles only if there is room. It may have to depend for light on a clerestory. In any event, post-Reformation churches were adapted and simplified to meet the new emphasis on preaching.

These descriptions are basic, and a number of variants exists. Indeed, some churches went through a surprising number of building phases, eg 12 at Wharram Percy, 18 at St Paul-in-the-Bail, Lincoln.

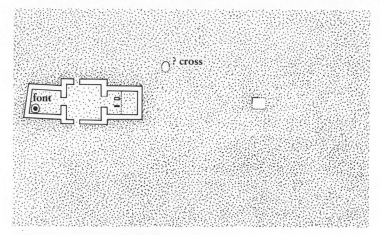

180 *St Peter's, Barton-upon-Humber – earliest stage*

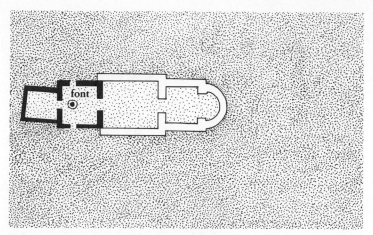

181 *St Peter's, Barton-upon-Humber – second stage*

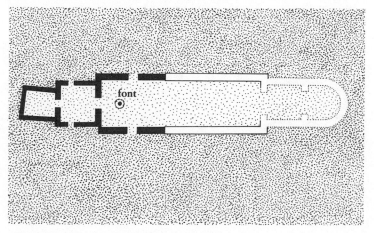

182 *St Peter's, Barton-upon-Humber – third stage*

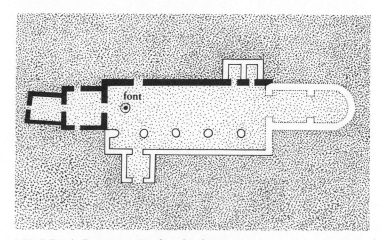

183 *St Peter's, Barton-upon-Humber – fourth stage*

180–7 *The development of an actual church, St Peter's, Barton-upon Humber. 180 The first stage was a small late 10th-century church. 181 Second stage: the chancel (with rounded apse) in the mid to late 11th century. 182 Third stage: the 11th-century nave was greatly extended, and a chancel with rounded end added, in the early to mid 12th century. 183 Fourth stage: in the mid to late 12th century the nave was widened on the south side, and a porch added; two chapels were built at the north-east end of the nave. 184 Fifth stage: the nave was widened on the north side in the late 12th century. 185 Sixth stage: the nave was again widened on the south side in the late 13th century, and a larger porch built to replace the earlier one. 186 Seventh stage: the north aisle was widened and a north porch added, in the mid 14th century. 187 Eighth and ninth stages: the east end was enlarged and remodelled with a square end in the late 15th century; a vestry was added to the north side of the chancel in the late 19th century.*

Early churches were sometimes built with square chancels, some with round apses (Worth (Sx)), some polygonal (Wing (Bc)). But another major type, the three-cell, has a central tower between nave and apse (Barton-upon-Humber; Stewkley (Bc)). The simple two-cell type is commonest in the east and south-east, eg Hales (Nf),

Nately Scures (Ha), Wisley and Pyrford (Sy), and the small Sussex downland churches. A few major churches have a cross plan, with opposing transepts on each side of a central tower, eg Old Shoreham (Sx), Patrington (Hu), St Mary Redcliffe, Bristol, Melton Mowbray (Le). In a few cases the bell tower is separate from the church,

301

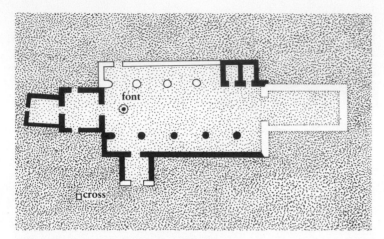

184 *St Peter's, Barton-upon-Humber – fifth stage*

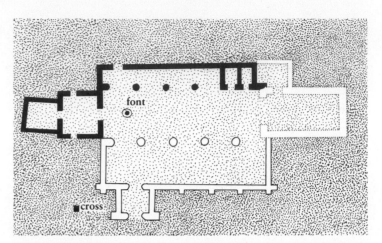

185 *St Peter's, Barton-upon-Humber – sixth stage*

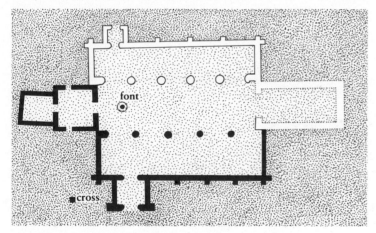

186 *St Peter's, Barton-upon-Humber – seventh stage*

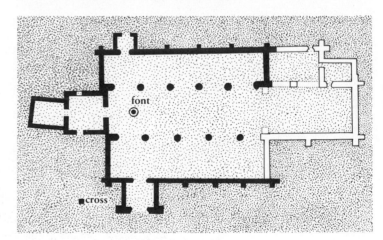

187 *St Peter's, Barton-upon-Humber – final stages*

eg Chichester Cathedral, Long Sutton (Li), Brookland (Kt), and Pembridge (He).

The Reformation brought with it changes in liturgical requirements which affected the layout and contents of churches. Moreover, the parish took over the responsibility for the chancel as well as the nave. The sedilia, piscina, and rood loft could be abandoned. Room had to be found for instrumentalists, and later for a larger organ. Preaching became more central to the services, and the pulpit assumed more importance. The need for pictorial windows and paintings declined as education spread.

New churches built in the 17th and 18th centuries (1660–1820), eg Staunton Harold (Le), 1653, St John's, Leeds, 1630s (a Laudian church), and Avington (Ha) (1768–71), could now be simplified into rectangular boxes, having wide windows with clear glass and prominent pulpits. Some medieval churches, eg Warminghurst (Sx), were transformed in the 18th century. Town churches (St Martin-in-the-Fields, London, 1720–26, St James, Piccadilly, London, 1676–84, Blandford, 1732) had galleries. The influence of nonconformist architecture was also felt. The apogee of this trend is St John's, Chichester, 1812, where the pulpit occupies a central place in front of the altar.

When the classical tradition died out with the Regency, the succeeding architectural taste led to a medievalist revival, and most new churches imitated or reinterpreted the Gothic styles, particularly the Early English. Even so, church building from 1820 to 1850 is distinguished by experiment in plan form and by an eclecticism in architectural style which makes it recognisable. But sometimes imitation of Gothic went too far, and features are included which are inappropriate to the ecclesiastical stage the church had reached in the 19th century.

Ecclesiastical reaction set in with the Tractarian Movement of the 1850s, and some Roman Catholic arrangement and ornateness was brought back. Butterfield's All Saints, Margaret Street (London) (1849–59) is a good example, as is Burges' Studley Royal (NY) (1871–8). In general, new Anglican churches of "middle" or "low" type built since 1870 or so looked very like new churches of other denominations. The "Gothic Revival", a reaction from the classical (Baroque, Palladian, and humbler Georgian), had its beginnings in the 18th century, swept England after the Regency, and lasted until well into the 20th century.

Churches built since World War II take full advantage of contemporary methods and materials – concrete, laminated wood, "chunky" glass, etc – and often have simple metal crosses and very plain furnishings. They may be square, octagonal, or circular (eg Gibberd's Roman Catholic Cathedral, Liverpool, 1962–67). They often have slender detached towers.

LOCAL STYLES OF THE ENGLISH PARISH CHURCH

Surprisingly few pre-Reformation churches in England are closely alike, except the very simplest. They were built to meet strictly local needs at the time, and changed when the needs changed. They reflect local materials, the standards of available craftsmanship, and religious and social requirements. They grow out of the local soil like the houses. They express the character and atmosphere of their county.

But as they change they also reflect the taste, wealth, and prestige of an individual or a group, who can afford, or who wish to afford, better materials and more expensive architects and craftsmen. It is now hard to recapture the small, simple churches which developed, or leapt, into the great wool churches of, say, East Anglia; and the latter are for ever distanced from their predecessors, and from those which were not transformed. They might be different species. The influence of cathedrals, abbeys, and magnates on churches founded or owned by them should not be overlooked (as Ottery St Mary was influenced by Exeter).

So it is possible to distinguish two levels of local styles: the native and evolutionary, and the polished jewels which often seem to be superimposed on the basic pattern, while indeed greatly enriching this pattern, and of course still speaking the common English language. But it is easy to be too simplistic here, and the distinction just drawn may well be largely subjective. In any case the former category can emulate the latter, and there is an element of overlap between them – an occasional reaching after higher things.

Post-Reformation churches are in a different category; here we are dealing with the homogeneous products of single architects – Wren, Gibbs, Butterfield, Woodyer, etc – whose technical lineage and aesthetic preferences we can study and unravel. Local style becomes personal achievement, which is not the same thing.

Many attempts have been made to sort out local styles, not all of them wholly satisfactory. Some concentrate on the topographical character of each county or subdivision of a county (Betjeman), some on architectural considerations (Pevsner), some on local building materials (Cox and Ford), some on the intrinsic merits of individual churches (Addison). It should be remembered also that local styles are often determined by only a few churches among the scores in each county; most churches are in fact more or less anonymous.

The local styles then are those which stand out from the run-of-the-mill churches, which, with little variation, are found all over the country. The generalised village church is usually a two-cell building, with chancel lower and smaller than the nave, and a simple, often low, tower or belfry; they may have one or more aisles. Town churches, like St Helen's, York, or St Lawrence, Winchester, are often plain rectangular halls, adapted to fit into a burgage plot. Greater town churches, like those in Hull or Melton Mowbray, although on a grand scale and redolent of wealth and prestige, tend also to be fairly uniform, and not particularly local.

Cox and Ford distinguish a "small stone" type, found generally in stone-producing areas, a "small stoneless" type, common in the Lowland Zone, and a "limestone belt" type, from the Cotswolds to Lincolnshire and south-east Yorkshire. In addition, they pick out areas with some specific individuality: the south-west, East Anglia, the north Midlands, the west Midlands, and the north. This is useful, but, with the large number of churches it is difficult to avoid over-generalising. For the present purpose it seems best to point to a few characteristics which are genuinely local, that is, found normally only in certain limited areas.

The chalk downlands have a series of very small rural churches, some, like Litlington (Sx), virtually only rooms, and many not much bigger. Masonry is largely determined by the local materials, and the effect of the use of flint is very different from that of squared stones. Beach pebbles are used instead of flint in churches close to the sea. East Anglia has developed finely knapped flint, with square faces, from which patterns can be made by inserting strips of stone (flushwork). Chequerboard flintwork is found in the south-west.

Essex, with an absence of stone, built in brick and timber (eg Sandon and Ingatestone). Timber-framing (black and white), as in contemporary houses, is found in the west Midlands, Cheshire, and the Welsh Borders (eg the tower at Pirton (Wo)). Essex excels in the use of timber for towers and belfries, of which there are over 100; some are free-standing, and spectacular examples are those at Margaretting and Blackmore. Surrey has a group of wooden belfries with frames inside the church (eg Alfold and Thursley).

Towers can be highly local. The finest are the Perpendicular ones of Somerset, which are usually of three storeys, with prominent corner buttresses, wide fenestration, and ornate parapet and pinnacles (Huish Episcopi, Isle Abbots, Bruton). There are several sub-groups. Devon has similar towers, but they are normally less grand (eg Widecombe); one Devon type has a stair turret in the middle of one side of the tower (eg Totnes). The Kentish tower is distinctive, built of ragstone, with battlemented parapet, external round or polygonal stair turret at one corner rising above the parapet, and buttresses ending below the top stage at a prominent string-course (late 14th to early 16th centuries). Maidstone All Saints is a good example, and there are two interesting outliers in London, at Lambeth, next to the Archbishop of Canterbury's palace, and Fulham, near that of the Bishop of London. There is an exceptionally fine detached bell-tower at West Walton (Nf) (1240s), of three stages, each with lights, and surmounted by pinnacles.

189 *Broach spire – Sleaford (Li), 14th century. The broaches are the pyramidal buttresses at the base of the spire, which has lights (lucarnes) as well.*

188 *The 15th-century spire at Louth (Li) is said to be the finest in the country – "the ultimate in spire construction" according to Sir William Addison.*

190 *A typical 14th-century broach spire – Olney (Bc).*

The magnificent tower at Boston (Li), although unique, may be classed as local, as it is surmounted by an octagon, of which Ely, not far away, is the best example. The ubiquitous towers of East Anglia (more than 1,000 in Norfolk and Suffolk) are plain, with straight parapets and usually no battlements or pinnacles (eg Lavenham); they are in four or five stages, often with openings called "Norfolk air-holes" in the stage below the bell chamber. There is a Henley (Ox) group of towers with octagonal corner buttresses. Cornwall has plain granite towers; granite is hard to work, so the churches often have low walls of cob.

A distinctive group of towers are the round flint towers of East Anglia. These may have been for (or at least used for) defence or refuge against sea- or river-borne raiders, as they do not occur all over the English chalklands. A case has been made for their being Anglo-Saxon, presumably for defence against the Danes. But their shape may equally well be dictated by the fact that irregular lumps of flint, or rounded pebbles, do not make satisfactory corners; the solution chosen locally was to do away with corners altogether. There are 112 in Norfolk, 41 in Suffolk, six in Essex, and only seven elsewhere (eg a group in and round Lewes (Sx)), out of some 200 originally.

There are 124 pre-conquest towers in England, of which 34 are in Lincolnshire.

The 19th-century towers of the former West Riding of Yorkshire have prominent pinnacles at each corner, eg Leeds, Kettlewell. Herefordshire has squat solid towers, with corner buttresses, eg St Weonards.

The small churches of central Wales usually have no towers at all; but some Welsh counties have local styles: Monmouthshire has plain thin towers, often with string-courses (Clodock); Radnor has two types, of low or medium height, the latter with battlements, and both with low spires; Brecon towers are of medium height, in good masonry, with battlements and one corner turret (Llywen); Cardiganshire has very thin, tall, plain towers, with battlements and low spires (Llanon); Pembrokeshire is similar, but without the spire (Manorbier). The towers of these coastal counties were used as look-out posts.

The spires of the limestone belt, mostly in Northamptonshire, are distinctive. Some are broached, some Decorated; all are landmarks. The finest spire in England is just north of this belt, at Louth in Lincolnshire (see **188**), and Grantham runs it close. Good examples of broach spires are Warboys (HP) and Sleaford (Li) (see **189**), and local groups in Gloucestershire and Oxfordshire (broaches are pyramidal buttresses built into the corners of a spire at its base on the tower) (see **190**);

of spires rising inside a parapet round the top of the tower, Uppingham is one of the best. Essex and Surrey have stumpy, almost pyramidal, spires, oak-shingled (eg Merstham). Hertfordshire and other home counties have thin spirelets in the centre of often squat towers (Hitchin).

Roofs differ in pitch, depending on the covering material. There are reed-thatched roofs in Suffolk (eg Iken) and Norfolk (eg Acle). Rough slabs of Horsham stone are used in the central Weald, and a variety of local stones in the limestone belt. The carpentry of roofs is often left exposed inside the church, although barrel and wagon vaults may be plastered over. Wagon roofs are universal in the West of England. King post roofs are characteristic of the south-east, as tie beams are of Somerset as well as Suffolk. The hammer-beam is almost confined to the eastern counties. The two latter types lend themselves to being decorated by carved and painted angels at the joints. In East Anglia (eg Blythburgh (Su) or Wymondham (Nf)) the angels usually have outspread wings; in the south-west they are more vertical and closed up (Bere Regis (Do)). Bere Regis has a minor angel roof in the chancel, but a unique and very splendid nave roof with apostles on the hammer-beams (*c* 1485). Both in Kent and Cornwall aisles often have separate roofs, giving a two- or three-gable form at the east ends; Shorwell (IW) is a particularly good example of a church with three gables (see **191**)

191 *Although aisles are normally lower than the nave, in some cases they are of equal height, as at this parish church at Shorwell (IW), which has what amounts to three naves.*

The elaborate carved wooden screens of Somerset, Devon, and Cornwall are typical of those counties, which also lack chancel arches. Local styles can also be recognised in bench-ends – poppy-headed in Suffolk, square-headed in the west of England. Fonts are octagonal in East Anglia, developing into "seven sacrament" fonts; Norfolk has 23, Suffolk 13. Aylesbury fonts are also local, Tournai marble fonts hardly so. Pulpits are of stone in Gloucestershire and Somerset.

The north has few local styles, but one could mention the Ripon school of wood-carvers in the 15th century, as in the stalls at Ripon and Manchester. The North Yorkshire Pennines have churches with no division between nave and chancel, eg Kildwick, the "Lang Kirk o' Craven".

An interesting regional style is the *crown spire* of the north-east – a slender spire supported above the tower on four flying buttresses. The best is the earliest, at Newcastle Cathedral (*c* 1442), and there are famous examples also at St Giles, Edinburgh (1495) and King's College, Aberdeen (*c* 1500, but rebuilt 1633) (see **192**).

More a fashion than a local style is the liking for Purbeck marble from the later 12th century (Canterbury) to the late 13th (Salisbury). It came in several colours and was used for polychrome effect; its use declined because of its unreliability. It was marketed through Corfe and Ower, and largely worked in London. Many small churches have it, such as Dunsfold (Sy). Purbeck fonts were at first restricted to south-eastern coastal and riverine areas, but later ones with Decorated panels are found in East Anglia.

FITTINGS AND FURNISHINGS

So far we have been considering churches as institutions or buildings. But of course there is more to them than that. They are centres of the religious life and practice of the parish or a wider area. Before the Reformation they were the social centres too, where all the communal activities of the parish took place, not only social, but business meetings, education, even commerce. Even after the Reformation some of these functions continued, until parish halls or other meeting places were provided.

The church contained a considerable number of furnishings, equipment, and fixtures to allow its religious purposes to be fulfilled. There are many excellent books giving full descriptions of these objects; what follows is a mere list of them, to bring the total picture into balance. Not all churches contain all these things, but some of the larger and more prosperous have a surprising number. There is also a wide difference between the "greater churches" and the small, remote, country church. But, of course, the basic message is identical. This account puts first the pre-Reformation church, many of whose features became obsolete and irrelevant at the Reformation, and were treated accordingly. A new ethos and ambience developed after the Reformation, and churches acquired a new atmosphere, distinctively Protestant. What we see now is a palimpsest, not only of objects but of ideas.

The *chancel* is the priest's domain. Here is the *altar*, in early or important churches a solid stone slab on a stone base or pillars, like a tomb; the slab (*mensa*) symbolises the body of Christ, and has a cross incised at each corner, and one in the middle, to represent the Wounds. A Saxon one at Cranleigh (Sy) was reused as a gravestone. In some churches it is of wood. Before the Reform movements it stood against the east wall, but more recently has sometimes become free-standing, and in large churches has moved out under the crossing, towards the nave.

Under Puritan and evangelical influence in the 16th–18th centuries, the altar was replaced in many churches by a *communion table*; this is standard in nonconformist churches. The altar has its own equipment: a cross or crucifix in the centre, with frequently a candle on each side of this. In addition, there are the altar cloth and frontal, the chalice, paten, and candlesticks, candles (including the large Paschal candle), censers, ewers, etc (the "church plate"). There is always a processional cross. Other portables include offertory plates and vessels for flowers. A *credence table* is a side table, shelf, or niche to put the elements on before consecration (eg Cranleigh (Sy)).

There is sometimes a *reredos*, an ornamental panel on the wall behind the altar, carved or painted; in some cases, eg Winchester or Southwark, this can be a tall ornate screen with statuary. In front of the altar, usually from wall to wall, is a *rail* of wood or metal, at which communion is taken. This was introduced in the late 16th century, and had close-set balusters to keep dogs away from the altar. "Laudian" rails, late 16th and early 17th century (encouraged but not invented by Archbishop Laud), envelop the altar on three sides.

Set into one wall is a cupboard for the communion vessels and elements, with a wooden door – the *aumbry*. In front of it hangs a white lamp. A red light sometimes hangs above the altar, and a blue light in front of a figure of the Virgin and Child. A candle burns before the altar cross, and on the rood beam. A circle of candles might be suspended in front of the altar, and remains of the pulley for this, and for the Lent veil, can still be seen (eg Ubbeston (Su)). The sacrament was reserved in a *pyx* (anything from a cloth-covered box to an

192 *The Crown of King's: the crown spire of King's College, Aberdeen (1500, rebuilt 1633), one of a distinctive northern type of spire; other early examples are at Edinburgh and Newcastle-upon-Tyne.*

307

elaborate metal and jewelled container) suspended in front of the high altar; a pulley socket for a pyx remains at West Grinstead (Sx).

In the sanctuary also is a chair for the priest, and set into the south wall a row of three seats, the *sedilia*, for the officiants and servers. In the wall also is a *piscina*, a basin with drain for washing the vessels after the Eucharist. Not all churches had separate vestries, and the vestments, parish records, and special collections (eg for the Crusades) were often kept in lockable wooden *chests*. There was often a separate door into the chancel for the priest's use.

Outside the sanctuary, but still in the chancel, are the *choir stalls*, usually facing each other along the side walls; in many churches, medieval as well as post-Reformation, the choir sat at the west end of the church, beneath a musicians' gallery, or sometimes in a gallery themselves. In the greater churches, where the music was more elaborate, the choir seats were made to tip up, with a projecting support for the singers (*misericords*) (see **193**). The underside of the seat was often carved with symbolic scenes, or even quite secular and fanciful ones (eg Beverley). The stalls themselves could be elaborately carved, as could the ends of the music stands. Ripon has a splendid set (15th century), and here the organ is placed on the screen at the crossing end of the choir; the organist has a movable hand projecting behind him into the choir to beat time with. Where a greater church has such stalls, they usually carry the titles of the canonries or other church dignitaries whose places they are.

The chancel is often divided from the nave by a screen of wood, stone, or ironwork, more or less elaborate. In a greater church this is

193 *Misericord – Exeter Cathedral, 13th century. Misericords are tip-up seats in choir stalls, for monks to rest against during the long services; they have free carvings underneath, which are seen when the seat is tipped up. There are innumerable designs, some fanciful like this, others showing human activities, animals, traditional stories, and religious motifs.*

called a *pulpitum* – the epistle and gospel were read to the congregation in the nave from here. It was usually surmounted by a *rood*, a cross or crucifix. If the latter, it was frequently flanked by a figure of Mary on Christ's right and John on his left. There might also be an angel on each side as well, or instead. The upper part of the screen sometimes contained a *rood loft*, a singing gallery; this was reached by a stairway against or inside one of the pillars of the arch. The doorway and remains of this are often to be seen. Above the rood could be a hole in the roof to let doves fly down into the church at Whitsun (eg Boxgrove (Sx)). The rood is sometimes on, or hanging from, a *rood beam* across the chancel arch, eg Shere (Sy).

Remarkable examples of 20th-century roods are those at St Mary, Wellingborough (Nh) (Comper, 1930s) and Willen Priory, Milton Keynes (Bc) (C S Jagger, 1929, formerly at Kelham (No)). The striking aluminium figure of Christ by Jacob Epstein (1950s) in Llandaff Cathedral is not a rood but a *majestas* (this symbolises Christ in glory, as opposed to crucified).

In the south wall of the chancel could be a *low-side window*, nearly to the ground, through which people outside could watch the Mass, and through which also (by way of a shutter or movable pane) the priest could bless or sprinkle them, or ring his bell. The chancel floor could be paved with stone, as in the Saxon church at Bradford-on-Avon), or with inlaid tiles (for these see page 184).

The *nave* was for the congregation who, until the 13th century, had to stand. There were, however, low stone benches along the walls, for the old or infirm ("the weakest goes to the wall"), eg at Arundel (Sx). *Pews* or benches in the body of the nave became general in the 13th century (eg Dunsfold (Sy)), and bench ends were often carved. The names of the farms or houses whose occupants had to maintain the churchyard fences were sometimes inscribed on the backs of the pews (eg West Grinstead (Sx)). The wives and daughters of these people sat elsewhere, and their servants or farm workers further away still. After the 17th century the pews were enclosed in high wooden partitions (*box pews*), with doors into the aisles; the lord of the manor had a larger, more comfortable one, often with a fireplace (eg Gatton (Sy)), placed near the *pulpit*, which, because of the box pews, was raised up high, with a lectern below and a seat below that for the parish clerk (a *three-decker pulpit* (see **194**); good examples are at Warminghurst (Sx), Avington (Ha), Fairfield (Kt), or Molland (Dv). Minstead (Ha) has box pews, private pews, galleries, three-decker pulpit, and many other features of interest. A pulpit often had a *tester*, a wooden sounding-board which magnified the voice of the preacher; many 17th- and 18th-century examples are ornately carved (eg Old Dilton (Wi), Shorwell (IW) (see **195**). Medieval pulpits in use after *c* 1340 are tall and narrow, often supported on a slender stem. Later pulpits may be barrel-shaped, and 17th- and 18th-century ones may have a sounding-board above. Pulpits are found in stone or wood, and may be on either side of the nave. In a simple church they may combine the functions of a *lectern*, but lecterns are often separate reading stands, on a more or less ornate pillar, and sometimes made to represent the symbolic eagle of St John. The pulpit usually had an *hourglass*.

Lighting was by candle or rushlight; a few country churches are still lit by candles (eg Colemore (Ha)) or oil lamps. *Cressets* are now rare – there are some at Blackmore (Ex). Many splendid 18th-century chandeliers survive, with ornate brasswork and Bristol or Waterford glass; Southwark Cathedral has a very fine one. Lamps might be placed on stone brackets projecting from the wall, as in the porch at Breamore (Ha). Candleholders, moveable or fixed, survive in a few places.

Heating is still very often by clumsy and primitive systems, using heavy pipes round the walls and under a grille along the aisle. Greater churches sometimes have stoves at intervals – Gurney "tortoise" stoves with fins and upright flues (eg Peterborough) (see **196**).

Clocks exist, but are rare. There is a spectacular one at Salisbury, and a group at Exeter, Wells, Wimborne, and Ottery St Mary (the only one with its original mechanism still working). Wells, Norwich, and

194 *A three-decker pulpit and box pews. The pulpit has a tester or sounding-board; below that is the reader's desk, and below that the parish clerks' seat – Old Dilton (Wi), 18th century.*

195 *A stone pulpit, c 1440, with a Jacobean wooden tester – Shorwell (IW).*

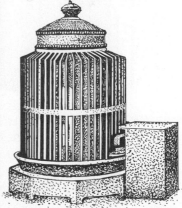

196 *A Gurney "tortoise" stove – Peterborough Cathedral.*

309

197 *An Easter sepulchre: the setting for a ritual reenactment of Christ's death and ressurrection. This example is at Crediton (Dv).*

officiant could follow the events at the main altar. One of these chapels is usually a Lady Chapel, with statue or emblems of the Virgin Mary, and set aside for private devotion. In large churches this is usually at the east end, beyond the high altar. Abbey churches and monastic cathedrals often have rows of chapels along the nave aisles (eg Chichester), in the transepts, and, if the apse is round, round the ambulatory. These became necessary when monks were encouraged to become priests in the 12th century, and proliferated later when more and more altars were required, as for chantries. Where the east end is square, there may be a retrochoir with chapels, as at Southwark, or a special extension, as at Durham or Fountains (the Chapel of the Nine Altars). Large transepts have chapels too (Winchester). Special cases are the aisle set aside for Roman Catholic use in the (Anglican) church at Tichborne (Ha), and the Orthodox chapel in the Anglican church at Walsingham (Nf). Chapels or chantries are separated from the body of the church by means of *parclose* screens.

Somewhere along the walls of nave or chancel is an *Easter sepulchre*, a long low recess cut into the foot of the wall and containing a slab where the emblems of the Resurrection could be displayed (see **197**). There are niches or brackets on the walls or pillars to contain or support *statues* of saints etc (mostly destroyed at the Reformation or by 17th-century Puritans). *Carved ornament* crept in everywhere in the Middle Ages: heads or grotesques on corbels (eg the "Cheshire Cat" at Cranleigh (Sy)) – often folkloric, like the foliate heads or "Green Man" – designs on string-courses or round arches, natural or allegorical scenes on capitals, etc. Bosses and other vantage points on the roof timbers or ceiling could be decorative or heraldic, and usually some of the heads were those of royal or noble founders or benefactors. Angels made good ends for hammer-beams!

Some churches were the homes of *anchorites*, who lived in small cells built out from the church wall (as at Compton or Shere in Surrey). These had squints into the church and openings onto the outside for food to be handed in.

There was a holy water *stoup* at the nave door and an *alms box* inside. Minor items of furniture were the stands on two pews for the churchwardens' staves, and, in city churches (eg London and York), sword or mace-rests for use at civic services. In York also the city churches have painted boards with names of parishioners who have become Lord Mayor. Staves and banners are kept in special long cupboards. Dole cupboards and vestment and embroidery chests can be found.

York have clock *jacks*, figures which struck the time before dials came into use in the 14th century. Medieval churches had to be cleaned out occasionally, and some made provision for swilling the floor by inserting *plugholes* at the base of the walls (as at Dunsfold (Sy)).

The east ends of the side aisles are usually occupied by *chapels*, each with its altar and piscina. From these, *squints* were cut diagonally through the pillars of the chancel arch, so that the

198 *Norman font, Castle Frome (He): an elaborately carved example.*

199 *Font of black Tournai marble, Winchester Cathedral (late 12th century): this is one of seven in England, imported probably from a single workshop; each is carved with scenes from the Bible or the lives of saints.*

Somewhere in the nave or tower room was found for the bier, pall, parish coffin, and hudd, for a ladder to deal with emergencies on the roof, and, where appropriate, forks or hooks for pulling burning thatch off the roof, and for sticks, whip, long tongs, or crooks for ejecting dogs ("whiping ye doggies" is recorded at Selborne).

Round the walls were consecration crosses and Stations of the Cross (still used in "higher" Anglican churches).

An important feature near the door (symbolically at the entrance to the church) was the *font*. This sometimes had a font cover which could be raised by a pulley or crane (eg Salle (Nf)). There is an unusual standing canopy at Trunch (Nf). Early fonts – Saxon and Norman – are usually solid barrels of stone, but later ones are often on feet or pillars and decorated in the styles of the period; some carry biblical or symbolic scenes. There is a superb Norman font, *c* 1140, at Castle

Frome (He & Wo), covered with deep interlace, out of which look the symbols of the four evangelists (see 198). There are a few special groups, such as the seven Norman fonts of black Tournai marble, square and closely carved; these are at Winchester (see 199) and Lincoln Cathedrals, Southampton St Michael's, East Meon (Ha), St Mary Bourne (Ha), Thornton Curtis (Li), and Ipswich St Peter's. Others are zodiac fonts (eg Brookland (Kt)), Norman lead fonts (over 30, eg Tidenham (Gl)), seven sacrament fonts (22 in Norfolk, 11 in Suffolk) (see 200), and an Aylesbury group. The font reached its peak in East Anglia in the 15th century. There are some surprising 17th- and 18th-century fonts, such as that at Lurgashall (Sx).

If the church possessed relics of a saint, these would be kept in *reliquaries*, ornate containers. Saints buried in the church were laid in *shrines* (eg St Thomas at Canterbury, St William at York, St Cuthbert at Durham, St Richard at Chichester); these could have openings through which the bones could be touched (see 201). They attracted a large, lucrative, pilgrim traffic. The shrine of St Alban at St Albans has a *watching loft* nearby for crowd control. Wealthy patrons endowed

311

chantries, which sometimes take the form of small chapels covering their tombs, in which Masses could be said for their souls (see below, Private Chapels, page 332).

Galleries became common in post-Reformation churches, and were usually built at the west end. They housed the musicians and sometimes the choir or the organ (but the organ is nowadays usually in the chancel). In 18th-century preaching churches, such as St Martin-in-the-Fields or St James, Piccadilly, and in nonconformist churches, a gallery usually extends round three sides of the church to accommodate more people to hear the sermons. Whitby (St Hilda's) has a fine array of small, separate galleries.

Organs were common in pre-Reformation churches, but the only one to survive is that at Old Radnor in Wales. From the 17th century, after

a century of Puritan rejection of music in church, organs came back into vogue. A few barrel-organs survive, as at Avington (Ha) or Wood Rising (Nf). Country churches retained small orchestras until the mid 19th century, with pipes, bassoons, serpents, trumpets, clarinets, and strings.

Stained glass: to avoid confusion of terms in this field, stained glass is synonymous with *painted glass*, in distinction to *coloured glass*, in

201 *A 12th-century shrine, for the relics of a saint (St Melangell), of architectural type – Pennant Melangell (Mg). This has an altar attached, at which masses or invocation to the saint could be said. The crosses incised in this altar represent the five wounds of the crucified Christ. This is the oldest shrine in Britain, and probably in northern Europe (1160–70). It has recently been restored, and once again contains the bones of the 7th-century saint.*

200 *A seven sacraments font, East Dereham (Nf), 15th century: these are confined to East Anglia; they depict the sacraments in seven panels, and the crucifixion or baptism of Christ in the eighth.*

which the colour is produced by additives or other methods in the making, and goes all through the glass. Coloured glass can be used by itself to form designs or pictures in a window, and may itself be painted. Coloured glass was not made in England until the late 16th century; before then it was imported from France. The glass of the "Forest" period, made in England from the early 13th to the early 17th century, of local sand and potash derived from forest products (oak wood and bracken ash mostly), contained many natural impurities and was pale yellow- or blue-green (see page 506). This glass could be coloured if, as in France, made with beech ash, by varying the oxidation in the furnace, or, as usually in England, by the addition of colourants, eg cobalt or copper oxides. Glass coloured in these ways was made in France in the 10th century, but was not used in England until the 12th. Another method of colouring was by coating one side of plain glass with a thin layer of coloured glass (a "flash"), which gave a lighter and more translucent effect. Both these methods were used to build up pictures or designs with pieces of glass in a mosaic, held together in a specially designed framework of lead ("cames"). Lines could be drawn in black oxide. There is little 12th-century glass in England; most of it is at Canterbury, but there is some at York, Dorchester (Ox), and Brabourne (Kt).

By the 13th century there was a vogue for "grisaille", windows filled with white (ie green) glass, painted finely with close-set geometric or foliage patterns, eg the Five Sisters window at York. In the 14th century yellow and green became more frequent than blue and red. Silver stain was introduced, to give yellow, which enabled heads to be more realistic; lines were now also scratched through flash. Grisaille became filled with foliage. Figures or subjects were often shown under (painted) architectural canopies.

The 15th century developed these trends in great profusion, and all can be studied in York. The Renaissance weakened the mystical atmosphere of the medieval mosaic glass, and the glass in 15th (eg Thornton's windows in York) and 16th centuries windows became essentially paintings, and comparable with contemporary canvases. By the mid 16th century such painting was done with enamels fused to the surface of the glass. The windows of the 17th and 18th centuries are frankly paintings (Oxford is a good place to study them).

The 19th century brought a renewed interest in the Gothic and in medieval craftsmanship. The windows of this period are crammed with detail and incident and, even when created by Burne Jones or Morris, usually lack life and a sense of religion. Unfortunately, they form the majority in most churches. Many are merely memorials to people, with little obviously religious relevance. Contemporary glass has reverted to early simplicity, and some of it consists of chunks of glass set in thick concrete, with brilliant colours. The effect can be striking, as at Coventry and Liverpool Roman Catholic Cathedral.

Bells are an essential feature of a church, with several functions – to signal significant occasions, such as national events (victories, disasters, accessions, jubilees, royal births), personal events (weddings, funerals), calling to services, and originally to drive away evil spirits when the elements of the Mass were exposed.

A single bell has limited expression. But more than one make possible greater variety, and a full peal of 12 is capable of a wide range. Most western countries have developed carillons, played by one person from a central keyboard. But the art of change ringing is an English invention, and has remained essentially English. Over 5,000 churches in England have rings of five or more bells.

From the 14th to the 16th century the method of hanging bells was improved, until in the end the bells were mounted on a whole wheel and could be controlled by means of a slider and stay. From the 17th century societies of bell-ringers were formed (eg the Ancient Society of College Youths, 1637), and the multiplicity of possible changes on various numbers of bells, from 3 to 12, was worked out by Fabian Stedman (1668 and 1677). Regular ringing is carried out today in nearly 6,000 churches. Call-changing is still popular in the south-west. "Cartwheeling", close-sequence bell-ringing, is a feature of west Yorkshire, and is also part of the change-ringing tradition in the south-west.

There are still a few medieval bells, as at Goring (1290, no longer rung) and Caversfield (Ox), *c* 1250. The earliest dated bell is at Claughton (La), 1296. Over 3,000 medieval bells are still in use; the oldest are long and narrow. A bell dated 1480 at Chiddingfold (Sy) is inscribed "Holy Trinity pray for us"(!). Most bells are mounted in the church tower, with ringing-chamber below; many are still rung from the floor of the tower. Small churches, and most nonconformist churches, usually have only one bell, mounted in a belfry or bellcote. In a few cases the bells are in a separate tower (eg Ledbury (He), Evesham (Wo), Chichester, Brookland (Kt); at East Bergholt (Su) the bells are in a wooden cage or "bell-house" in the churchyard.

Many bells have inscriptions cast into them, giving a date, a text or aphorism, a dedication, or a donor's name. The founding and tuning of bells is of course a highly specialised and skilled craft, in the hands of few firms (eg the Whitechapel Foundry, 1570, and John Taylor and Co, Loughborough, 1786).

Memorials are an ubiquitous feature, since one of the main social functions of the church was that of burial. ("Churchyards" are dealt with below, see pages 319–24.) Burial inside the church, either under the floor or in separate vaults dug close to the walls or under private chapels added on, was at first reserved for the clergy, nobility, gentry, and the more important parishioners, with founders and their families as near the altar as they could get. The great raised tombs as elaborate as they could afford (like the Percy tombs at Beverley); more ordinary people had ledger-slabs on the floor or tablets on the walls. (Katharine Esdaile's *English Church Monuments* (1946) is the best guide to these.)

Medieval tombs often took the form of recumbent *effigies*, earlier on low plinths or later on high altar-tombs. The men were often shown in armour. Most are stone, but wooden ones exist, eg ten in Essex and a row at Chester-le-Street (Du). Priests' tombs were usually cross-slabs. *Brasses* were popular from the 13th century; some 3,000 survive out of about 150,000. They are commonest in East Anglia, Oxfordshire, Kent, and Essex, then in the other home counties. The metal (latten) was made in the Low Countries and Germany, and engraved in England. Palimpsests (where a brass has been turned over and inscribed again on the other side) are known. Brasses give a valuable insight into costume. Cobham (Kt) has a large and coherent group described by Pevsner as "fabulous". *Alabaster*, mostly from the Nottingham area, was in vogue for effigies in the 15th and 16th centuries. *Cadavers* appealed to medieval and 17th-century taste (as at Winchester or Ewelme (Ox), or the shrouded effigy of John Donne in St Paul's).

The tombs of the 16th to the 18th centuries were often large and highly ornate, and some were frankly ostentatious. The 18th and early 19th century is the heyday of wall tablets, some of which are exquisite. Bath Abbey is very rich in them, and they give a fascinating insight into the life of the spa. Westminster Abbey and York Minister are veritable museums of them. In all periods great sculptors have worked on these monuments, and their names can often be found on the sides of the bases. Not all church guides mention that the church

has work by eg Evesham, Stone, Nollekens, Rysbrack, Flaxman, Bacon, Chantrey, or Westmacott, but such work is always worth seeking out.

Tombs are of course a major and valuable vehicle for *heraldry*. *Hatchments*, the painted boards carried before the coffin with the deceased's coat of arms, are hung on the walls after the funeral. Parade helmets, gauntlets, or banners are sometimes hung on brackets over the grave (eg Farnham (Sy) and Tenterden (Kt)). Spinsters were sometimes commemorated by a wreath of white flowers ("virgin crantz") and a pair of white gloves; a good row of these is at Abbots Ann (Ha).

Medieval churches were usually highly decorated with painted geometric or floral patterns, imitation stonework, etc, traces of which can often be found. The nave walls could have *paintings* (see **202**, facing page 267) of biblical events, scenes from the lives of saints (frequently St Christopher), etc. The space over the chancel arch might have a painting of the Crucifixion, or Christ in Majesty, or the Last Judgement. Similarly the windows, when stained or painted glass came into use in the 12th century, could be filled with scenes from the Old Testament (the precursors of Christ) on one side, and from the New Testament (the fulfilment of prophecy and the Redemption) on the other, culminating, in the east window, in Christ in Majesty or the like. These paintings were used by the priest in teaching the people. Later, when people could read, a board containing the Ten Commandments stood behind the altar. After the Reformation churches displayed the *Royal Arms*, high on the wall, to assert the people's loyalty to the regime, and this became compulsory after the Restoration. Other *boards* on the wall listed the incumbents, benefactions, and, in the tower or ringing-loft, the peal-board and rules for bell-ringers.

Sculpture was of course used as well for religious figures and scenes, from the Saxon roods, as at Romsey, Breamore, or Headbourne Worthy (all in Hampshire) and the Lazarus scenes at Chichester to the vast multiplication of statues of biblical figures, saints, and dignitaries inside churches, as well as outside, in porches and on west fronts, as at Wells or Exeter. The Norman doorway at Kilpeck (He) is unusually ornate (see **203**).

In recent years there has been a lively movement for beautifying churches with contemporary works of art. Windows include the Piper set at Coventry, the Piper and Reyntiens at Liverpool Roman Catholic Cathedral, the Hutton engraved glass at Guildford, the

Chagall window at Chichester, and the Prisoner of Conscience window at Salisbury; tapestry examples are the Sutherland at Coventry and the Piper at Chichester; painting includes the Sutherland at Chichester; sculptures are the Epstein at Llandaff, the Eric Gill at Guildford, the Frink Madonna at Salisbury, the Pietà group at York, the Henry Moore in St Matthew's, Northampton, and a great deal more. There are also Stations of the Cross, like the Brangwyns at Farnborough Abbey, and a great deal of excellent woodwork and metalwork. But of course the best contemporary art has always been put into churches, like Grinling Gibbons' wood-carving in Wren's London churches or the fine 17th-century woodwork at St John's, Leeds.

Miscellaneous features include libraries – many churches had a few, or at least one, book, some of them chained – and graffiti in large numbers, particularly where the stone is not too hard to carve; they represent a wide variety of things, some religious, some

203 *Norman doorway, with tympanum – Kilpeck (He), c 1140. This is a particularly ornate example of Norman sculpture, of varied artistic ancestry, including Scandinavian (Ringerike style).*

204 *Sanctuary knocker, Durham Cathedral. Using this entitled a person pursued by the law to claim refuge in the cathedral.*

315

secular. Ironwork is often of interest, from strapwork, tracery, even figures and ships, on doors, to screens, gates, railings, grilles, cages over tombs, and sanctuary knockers (eg Durham (see 204)). Acoustic devices, jars or pottery pipes sunk in floor or walls to improve resonance, can be found. Brookland (Kt) has shutters to protect the windows when fives was played against the church wall. *Wafer-ovens*, for baking communion bread, exist at Chichester Cathedral, Smarden (Kt), and Charney Manor (Ox), a grange of Abingdon Abbey, *c* 1260.

Other objects include the church Bible, with markers, prayer books, and hassocks; there has been in recent years a vogue for local people or bodies to embroider these with a variety of motifs – there are good sets in Guildford Cathedral and eg Steep (Ha). Sacred emblems or monograms, such as IHS or the Maria symbol, are often carved or painted, or embroidered into the altar frontal. The Victorian revival churches of the Oxford Movement, like All Saints, Margaret Street, London, have a profusion of such symbolism and emblems.

Crypts are not usual in parish churches, except sometimes where the ground slopes sharply, where they act as foundations for part of the church (eg Duntisbourne Rous (Gl)). Some Norman churches have crypt chapels, eg Lastingham (NY). The reverse of this is a two-storey chancel, as at Compton (Sy), with chapel above the main east end of the church. Greater churches often have extensive crypts, as at Winchester. There are a few Anglo-Saxon crypts, eg Repton, Brixworth, and Wing, and the spectacular ones at Hexham and Ripon, used to house relics and as centres of pilgrimage. From the 15th century, when burials increased and churches were enlarged, crypts (or just "bone-holes") were sometimes made (in some cases extending under the churchyard) to house bones cleared out when the graveyard was full (*charnel houses*). Examples are at St Bride's, London, Maldon (Ex), Witney (Ox), and Hythe (Kt). At Ripon (NY) it was formerly thought that a nearby natural mound, Ailsey (or Ailcy) Hill, was used for the reburial of surplus bones from the churchyard, but excavations in 1986 showed that the heaps of charnel are part of a close-laid cemetery of the 7th to 10th centuries.

Porches were not only to shelter the doorway, but places to rest in and even to be married or churched (ritually purified after childbirth) in. Many have benches. Some porches have an upper storey, usually reached from inside the church. These rooms had a variety of purposes: some were chapels or singing galleries for Palm Sunday processions; some were for a night watchman, and might have a fireplace and a squint or window into the church; some were used as libraries or schoolrooms, and some even for trade guilds; that at Cirencester even served for a time as the town hall. Christchurch (Do) Grammar School was housed in St Michael's loft, over the Lady Chapel, from 1662 to 1869; Atherstone Priory Church (Nh) was itself used as a grammar school.

The *masonry* and construction of churches, and *masons' marks*, are dealt with in "The Medieval Building Industry" (see page 181–6).

Outside the church are several features to note, including gable-crosses and decoration on the corbels. Mass-clocks (scratch-dials for showing the times of services (see **205**)) were placed by the south door or porch; early dials, including Saxon ones, have four parts, subdivided, with only the lower half operating, while medieval dials usually have 24 thin incised lines, marking the beginning of the hours, whereas Saxon dials mark the middle. Putlog holes in the tower walls were to support scaffolding for repairs (Cranleigh (Sy)). Other features include benches (Hawkshead (Cu)), tethering-posts for parishioners coming on horseback (Tongham (Sy)), mounting-blocks, stables (Wixford (Ww); Edrom, Scotland, has an early 19th-century row of stables 125ft (37.5m) long against the north wall). Carvings include crosses incised on the door jambs, probably to protect the church from evil, but perhaps also in expiation of a vow, weathercocks, and grotesques and gargoyles, including sheela-na-gigs (see pages 187–9), which were sometimes merely exuberant, but basically apotropaic (turning away evil). Lurgashall (Sx) has a shelter by the south doorway, used later as a schoolroom. There is an open-air pulpit at Holy Trinity, Marylebone Road, London. Miscellaneous buildings in churchyards, and the relics of body-snatching, are dealt with under Churchyards below.

The use of the church in the Middle Ages may leave signs of its presence. Before separate halls or other facilities were available, the church was the natural meeting place of the parish and the centre of its social life. Markets, fairs, and festivities were held in the church; trade and religious guilds and fraternities met there; schools were held there; judicial ordeals were carried out there. Some of these have left traces. Ovens are sometimes found, used either for baking eucharistic bread, or by guilds, or for some other now unknown purpose (eg Pontefract, and St Paul-in-the-Bail, Lincoln). Some features remain unexplained, such as channels round the interior, as at Ormesby (Cl), the tank-like structure at St Nicholas, Colchester, the vertical-sided pits at Burnham (Hu), and the pot buried in the middle of the first church at Raunds (Nh).

Next to, or near, the church stood the *rectory* or vicarage, which is a house of its period, with no special features relevant to its use. There is a very good medieval vicarage at Muchelney (So), 1308. A few priests' houses, for priests living elsewhere, and coming to the church occasionally, survive, as at Itchingham (Sx). In the northern counties disturbed conditions called for fortified rectories, as at Embleton (Nd), where a peel-tower forms part of the house.

205 *Scratch-dial (mass-clock) on a Norman doorway – Martyr Worthy (Ha). Simple sundials were set up at church doors to indicate the time of Mass.*

THE SYMBOLISM OF CHURCHES

The object of stained glass windows was as visual aids which could be used by the priest to teach the people the elements of the faith, and as permanent reminders of these elements. The small country church could, of course, only have fragments, but the greater churches could have carefully planned, if not complete, schemes. Ideally, a cathedral was a symbol of Christianity, in time as well as space. Every part was symbolic, and contributed to a whole. The concept was begun by Suger at St Denis, and was finally worked out at Chartres, by Bernard and his school, in the mid 12th and early 13th century. It spread across France, and reached England in the 13th century. The north side represents the past – the Old Testament; the south side the present – the New Testament; the west is the future – the Last Judgement and the New Jerusalem. These are joined by the Incarnation, the pivot of the Church's teaching – the chancel, with its leaning head of Christ on the Cross (although this is not always deliberate – see above). The windows give the stories appropriate to each side; Fairford (Gl), is a good example.

The nave (ship) represents the Ark of the Old Testament that saved all life from the Flood, and is transformed into the vessel which carries mankind through time. Also the Ark of the Covenant represents knowledge. The pillars are also trees, branching out like the creative energy of nature (as Capability Brown said of Exeter Cathedral). So the whole church is alive with carved leaves, buds, flowers, and fruits. The Cross was also a Tree – the World Tree. Southwell is full of leaves (see **206** and **207**); but the nature gods, the Green Man etc, have their place in this context. The plan is the Cross – the horizontal aspect being life on earth, the vertical eternity – or the physical and its aspirations to the spiritual. The spires and towers point up to heaven.

The *rose windows* are the stars that guide the ship. They represent the Logos, the Word itself, Christ; they symbolise the creation and the created universe, with earth at the centre of the spheres. They are mandalas, symbols of wholeness and integration. The rose is nature's ultimate purpose, love and sacrifice (also shown as flame), beauty and metamorphosis. Christ is the centre of the rose windows – as a child in the north, resurrected in the south, in majesty in the west. The north

206–7 *The "Leaves of Southwell"; the Chapter House area of the Minster is richly ornamented with carvings of leaves, flowers and fruit, and a few figures, including* **207**, *the Green Man.*

207 *The Green Man, c 1293–1300.*

also has the Virgin Mary at its centre – the sum of all the past, and the beginning of the new creation (north and south are the truth of the Old Testament revealed in the light of the New). The geometry of the tracery represents order (the plans and construction of cathedrals are based on elaborate symbolic geometry).

The radiating form of most rose windows indicates many paths to one centre. The wheel represents the sun, and also the means of escaping the cycles of fate; the wheel spins – the loom of creation. The rose is also light – the New Jerusalem – and carries all the varied symbolisms of the lotus, the union with God. Rose windows clearly reflected the group unconscious of the age, the desire for wholeness amid the confusion; and the above outline by no means exhausts all the lessons which were no doubt drawn from them (see the detailed studies of this subject by Painton Cowen and M D Anderson).

Chartres, and some other churches, possesses a *maze* inscribed on the floor. This echoes the west window and is a diagram of the "shells" of reality. It has a rose at its centre; union with Christ, love, at the centre enables the soul to brave the dangers of life on the way out. Prehistoric mazes may well have carried a somewhat analogous symbolism.

Rose windows developed from simple circular openings, or *oculi*, into the wheel windows of the Romanesque (oculi can be seen in the 8th-century Basse-oeuvre at Beauvais). The wheel became a rose at Mantes *c* 1180. By 1200 the symbolic scheme was in full swing. There are fewer roses in England: Lincoln has the best 13th-century ones, and those at York and Durham are later. Roses ceased to be made by the 16th century, but a few modern church architects have liked the idea of a circular window, eg at Guildford or in Lancing College Chapel.

CHURCHYARDS

The archaeology of these has been given attention lately, notably by Warwick Rodwell (eg *Church Archaeology*, Batsford/EH 1989), and the Council for British Archaeology and other bodies have issued booklets for the guidance of investigators. A great deal has been learnt from this work.

Rodwell points to the importance of interpreting the relations between the churchyard, the church, and the surrounding terrain; eg some graveyards do not contain their related churches, and some churchyards were not used for burial (eg the Norman church at Stoke Orchard (Gl) was only a chapel of ease of Bishops Cleeve, and no burials took place there until the mid 19th century). A churchyard boundary is likely to be ancient if there is a substantial and abrupt fall to the road or to the next property. A graveyard, in time, will slowly rise as more burials are inserted, and will eventually be higher than the floor of the church (eg Selborne (Ha)). A cemetery used for 1,000 years will contain remains of some 10,000 burials. This problem was even more acute in towns, where parish burial grounds became grossly over-used; this led to separate cemeteries by the late 18th century (see below), and eventually major institutions like the London Necropolis (1853). Some churchyards have been extended.

The problem of *continuity* of some churchyards with pre-Christian sacred sites is a vexed one, and it is usually very difficult to be sure. There are special cases, like the church inside a henge at Knowlton (Do) and the huge monolith and Iron Age cist in the churchyard at Rudston (NY). But more commonly, if a churchyard has a circular boundary (usually a bank, as at Stoughton (Sx)), a Saxon church, or a wall, or contains barrows (eg Taplow (Bk) or Wickham St Paul (Ex), where the church itself seems to be in secondary relation to a barrow), or where the church itself is built on an artificial mound (Barton-on-Humber), it is reasonable to infer continuity of some kind. Yet not all circular/oval churchyards are early; there are some in Wales, for instance, known to have been created in the 12th century. In Shropshire some 40% of medieval churchyards are circular or oval. This is a problem which awaits final solution. Some mounds are in fact natural, and it is sometimes hard to tell whether a mound is natural or not; and some artificial mounds may merely be to take the church above marshy ground or flood level. There may be a local tradition to give a clue in these cases.

Roman cemeteries outside towns were sometimes Christianised (eg St Bride's, London) and led to the building of a church. Some early Anglo-Saxon churches were built by or inside the forum of a Roman town (Silchester; Lincoln), and the churchyard used the courtyard of the forum. Some pagan rural cemeteries continued into Christian use or were very close to churchyards, as at Winnall, near Winchester. Roman mausolea sometimes gave rise to a church, as at Wells. And holy wells in churchyards give a strong presumption of ancient date and continuity. Churches were often built close to manor houses for the convenience of the founder or patron, so the churchyard is likely to be an enclosure round the church, and used for burial. If a Roman villa or early Saxon hall preceded the manor, presumption of continuity is again strong.

Many old churchyards contain *yew* trees. Some of these were planted to mark important graves, some on the line of an old boundary, and some for their religious symbolism (yew is symbolic of everlasting life). The age of a yew is far from easy to determine, and expert help is needed. The famous yew at Selborne (Ha) was generally regarded (before its loss in a storm in 1990) as some 1,000 years old, but Alan Mitchell, an authority on trees, re-estimated (1985) its age as perhaps 1,700–1,800 years. Records suggest at least 1,300, and this of course may not be the date of planting. Even 1,300 years suggests a Saxon church in 680 (the present church, probably the third on the site, was not built till 1180); 1,700–1,800 years would suggest a pre-Christian sacred site.

Medieval churchyards were not so cluttered with monuments as later ones, and were put to a variety of uses, secular as well as religious; thus, markets could spill over into them, and even into the church itself, and they were in fact public meeting places. It is not unknown for the fringes of churchyards to have been sold off and houses built on the consecrated ground, with the result that burials may be found beneath medieval houses. Ancillary buildings of many kinds occur in churchyards, such as the priest's house at Itchingham (Sx) or the timber bell-cage at East Bergholt (Su). The classic case is perhaps Rivenhall (Ex), where Rodwell records that the one-twentieth of the area which was excavated contained no fewer than 12 buildings: a Roman villa, a 6th-century post-built hall, a middle Saxon mausoleum/chapel, a late Saxon timber church, a possible 11th-century priest's house, three other successive priests' houses on another part of the site, a 14th-century bell-cage

319

foundation, a medieval latrine hut, a 17th-century herring shed, and other features. A post-medieval sexton's house (not excavated) and a chantry chapel (not located) are also recorded for this churchyard. Deskford, near Keith, Scotland, has a fine sacrament house of 1551.

Horses, sheep, and pigs were kept in many churchyards – sheep still graze the churchyards in Romney Marsh – and there are records of stables in them. Sheep-stiles keep the sheep in but allow people to enter (eg Mells (So)). Some churchyards have cages, grilles, or railings to keep sheep off the graves (eg Brookland (Kt)). Churchyard fences were kept up in lengths by local farmers etc, and the names of the farms responsible were sometimes painted on pews in the church (eg West Grinstead (Sx)). Entrances to churchyards and paths across them may indicate relationships with the former topography, and with buildings or foci now lost.

The main purpose of a churchyard has, since the Reformation, been for *burial*. As said above, burial inside the church was at first reserved for ecclesiastics and local dignitaries, and then extended to any who could pay. But from the 16th century on the churchyard itself was used by the rich as well as the poor, and the memorials thus throw light on all social classes. Even so there are favoured locations; period groups can be found in particular areas, and families or relations are often buried in groups. Richer graves are often seen lining the main paths. The north and west sides of the church (the Devil's side) were considered unlucky, and were filled up last; indeed from the 17th to the 19th century at least they were reserved for strangers, paupers, unbaptised infants, those who had died a violent death, and suicides.

Graves were normally oriented east–west, with the head at the west end (see page 295). But there are many anomalies here; at Barton-on-Humber graves predating the 10th-century church were aligned on a topographical feature as yet undiscovered, 8° different from the orientation of the church; at Wells, burials before 1200 are aligned with the Saxon cathedral, burials after that date with the present cathedral, 12° different. Graves may be deflected if close to a boundary or to the wall of an apse. Indeed, earlier features in the surrounding land may influence the shape or layout of the churchyard. Thus at Nazeingbury (Ex) a middle Saxon graveyard was arranged within the bounds of a Romano-British field.

A subtle variant of orientation was noticed by Calvin Wells when investigating the burials in two middle Saxon cemeteries in Norfolk (Burgh Castle and Caister-on-Sea – mid 7th to late 9th centuries). Here the graves were aligned on the bearing of sunrise on the day they were dug, and the alignments showed a marked clustering at the equinoxes. The reason for the latter is not entirely clear, but the likeliest explanation is that more people, particularly the young and the old, died in late winter/early spring and late summer/early autumn, mainly from respiratory infections and dysenteric diseases respectively. Alignment on sunrise might also apply to some early churches. It is fair to say that sunrise orientation of graves has been recently (1986) challenged, in favour of purely topographical considerations. Changes in orientation in a graveyard may be due to changes in fashion, or Christianisation, not the advent of new peoples.

Grave-goods are not customary in Christian burials, although coins, mugs of beer, and joints of meat still occasionally accompany burials in remote districts, and coronets still sometimes surmount coffins in aristocratic vaults. But the absence or presence of grave-goods is not an infallible indicator of Christianisation. There may be non-Christian burials in Christian graveyards, or non-Christian customs may be used by Christians. In general, however, the latest ("final phase") pagan Saxon burials have no grave-goods, and by fully Christian times (8th–9th century) their absence is the norm.

Vaults are often found under private chapels, or even under the body of the church or built out under or from it; from the 18th century they occur in churchyards. Bones cleared out to make room for new burials were kept in charnel-houses (see above).

Many of the numerous churches in cities, serving small areas which were the property of single landowners, were in such congested surroundings that there was no room for churchyards. In such cases burials had to be made in the church itself, and because airtight coffins – indeed, coffins of any kind – were the exception, the situation became intolerable. Rodwell quotes the case of Enon's Chapel, Clements Lane, London, where no fewer than 20,000 bodies were crammed beneath the floor, which led to the church being disused! With increasing populations in cities after the Industrial Revolution this situation could only get worse, and by the end of the 18th century separate cemeteries began to be set up outside the urban areas (see below, pages 325–6).

Coffins, made of stone, lead, tile, or wood, were used by the Romans; the Anglo-Saxons used wooden ones, and medieval priests and lords often used stone cists or shaped stone coffins. Poorer people did not use coffins, but some Roman burials are covered in gypsum or chalk (symbols of purity and immortality), and late Saxon or early medieval burials were laid in charcoal. Most were buried in a shroud or their clothes, but some in nothing. Lead was popular for richer burials in the 17th and 18th centuries, but coffins were in fact not general until the mid 19th century.

The *gravestones*, memorials, and monuments are perhaps the most immediately obvious features of a churchyard. (Memorials inside the

208–9 *Hogbacks: 208 Brompton (NY), with bear ends; 209 Gosforth (Cu). These Viking-age grave covers clearly represent timber-framed houses.*

church, some of which, like wall tablets, are in any case more appropriate inside than outside, are dealt with on page 324.) The best introduction to these is still Frederick Burgess: *English Churchyard Memorials* (1963). An excellent analysis of the graves in a graveyard (Llangar in Wales) was made by Ron Shoesmith (*Archaeologia Cambrensis* 129, 1980).

Monuments were not common before the Reformation, no doubt because those who could afford them were usually buried in the church. A few Anglo-Saxon memorial crosses survive, like that at Bewcastle (Cu) (see page 328). Before 1200 there are a few cross-slabs, mostly marking the graves of ecclesiastics, some head and foot stones accompanying coffin-slabs or ledgers (cf the hogbacks), and some house tombs or coped stones.

The *hogbacks* are a specialised class of funerary monument. They occur in the areas settled by Scandinavians, and seem to be Irish-Norse or Norwegian in origin; there are none in Ireland, Man, or Scotland except a few derivatives from England. They are solid long stones, usually with the upper surface raised in the middle, and often with tile or shingle decoration to represent a roof; they seem then to echo the boat-shaped houses of northern Europe, but are probably adaptations of stone shrines to serve a different purpose. They are not graves of saints, and indeed some are pagan. The house idea is sometimes reinforced by a biting beast at each end – animals are common on the roofs of northern European houses, perhaps apotropaic in function. Bailey has shown that they are most likely to be parts of composite monuments, fitting between head and foot stones. They date from after 920, mostly from the 10th century. Good examples are to be seen at Sockburn (Du), Brompton (NY) (see **208**), Gosforth (Cu) (see **209**), Lythe (NY), and Penrith (Cu).

Between *c* 1200 and 1550 the variety of monuments increases and includes coffin-slabs, headstones, and, from the 14th century on, coped stones, chest tombs, and half-effigies. Alabasters and brasses, mainly found inside the church, have already been dealt with. A few medieval tombstones (in churchyards) survive, but few are in their original position. The dozen or so at Limpley Stoke, near Bath, are an exceptional case.

From the mid 16th century, with prosperity extending down the social scale, grave monuments appear more widely, until in the 18th and 19th centuries the variety is bewildering. Headstones of stone, wood, and iron appear in the 16th century, wooden "bedboards"

210 *A bedboard grave. Bedboards are wooden planks with painted inscriptions mounted on short posts over a grave.*

211 *Multiple bedboard over a family grave – Yateley (Ha); such examples are rare.*

(see **210**) from the 17th (bedboards on a family grave may be multiple, eg at Yately (Ha) (see **211**)). The earliest stones tend to be thicker than later ones, and can be as thick as 4in (10cm). Local stones are of course used, until the marble and granite of the 19th century; for instance, slate gravestones are very characteristic of parts of Wales and Cumbria. Wooden "headstones" occur in Essex, and some Monmouthshire church-yards have painted stones. Five wooden grave-markers were dis-covered in 1973 in Leatherhead churchyard – these were mid 19th century, small posts, with painted inscriptions (not like bedboards), a common type before stone was introduced in the 17th century.

They are at the foot (east) end of the graves, and are not headstones; but many gravestones were, and still are, at the foot.

Cast iron is used in the Weald, at first in slabs rather like firebacks, but later in crosses. Other medieval forms continued after the Reformation include ledgers, coped stones, and chest tombs (see **212**). The latter reach a peak in the Cotswold area in the 17th century, and Painswick and Burford have remarkable ranges of them.

In the 17th century the variety becomes wider, and includes body-stones, coffin-stones, bale tombs (features of wool districts) (see **213**), and table tombs (in the north,

212

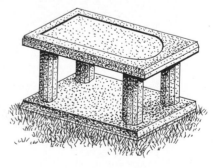

214

212–14 *Types of tomb: 212 chest tomb; 213 bale tomb; 214 table tomb.*

culminating perhaps at Elgin Cathedral, where the churchyard hardly contains anything else (see **214**)). By the 18th century the pedestal tomb comes in, with a base surmounted by a pyramid, an obelisk, a casket, or an urn; mausolea also occur. Local materials now include brick, and barrels in that material occur in the south, eg Brookland (Kt) or Froyle (Ha) (see **215**). Some poor graves have no stones at all, and are just mounds of earth or turf. The Quakers had a specialised type of their own – a small, simple stone with only a name, date, and age inscribed on it (eg Penn (Bc) or Wanstead (Ex), meeting houses). Quaker burial grounds are used less now, and many have disappeared. Some, in districts with fewer Quakers, are now in very remote places, eg Lowna in Farndale (NY).

Scotland has some distinctive types. Rough chips or lumps of rock are found, usually uninscribed – just marking a grave. A number of these together, as at Jarlshof, Shetland, can be very moving to see. At the other end of the scale are the urban churchyards and cemeteries crammed with huge monuments, like cities of the dead – Dumfries is a good example, but the apogee is perhaps the Necropolis in Glasgow. A peculiarly Scottish group is the Covenanters' graves, mostly in the south, usually with long and detailed inscriptions (eg Dalry (Kb), Lesmahagow (Lk)).

Inscriptions and carving on gravestones are extremely varied, and reflect the tastes and styles of their periods very closely. They are also a mine of genealogical, heraldic, and social information. Lettering is often very good indeed. Epitaphs range from the serious to the whimsical or even anecdotal. Occupations may be shown in word or image, like the tools of a craft. Carvings may be classical, biblical,

or symbolic; the 17th and 18th centuries used a range of symbols of death (skulls, urns, etc), resurrection and salvation (rocks, anchors), time (hourglasses, clocks, sundials, etc), eternity (angels), and religion (tree, cross, heart, book, etc). They may merely be purely decorative, like scrolls or arabesques, although even here symbols creep in, such as ivy leaves for protection against evil. The carvings on gravestones are not only religious symbols, but can sometimes be interpreted as references to the lives, or weaknesses, of those commemorated. The full range, as it was expressed in the 19th century, is concentrated, with strong aesthetic effect in Highgate Cemetery (see below, pages 325–6). Even into the present century by no means all burials were marked by gravestones or memorials. For instance at Wharram Percy (Hu) only 47 burials out of 318 between 1770 and 1878 had memorial stones. Wider research might show whether this is typical generally, or whether country differed from town in this respect, or region from region. There is clearly an economic factor here.

Other features of churchyards include: *lychgates* and coffin rests (see **216**), where the coffin was received by the priest at the church gate after its last journey, perhaps of many miles along a lyke-road (eg Chiddingfold (Sy); none survives in Scotland); *hudds*

216 *Lychgate with coffin rest – Chiddingford (Sy). The coffin was brought to the gate of the churchyard, where it was received and taken over by the priest.*

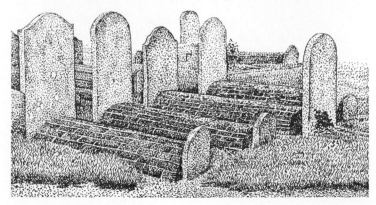

215 *Brick barrel graves – Froyle (Ha).*

(see **217**), portable shelters to protect the clergyman at the graveside, which were stored of course in the church, eg Ivychurch (Kt) and Friskney (Li); *dole-stones* or plague-stones, where money or food could be left (eg Eyam (Db) and Shipley (Sx)); alms basins and stools (Greyfriars, Edinburgh; St Andrews). Gatehouses for collecting alms occur in Scotland. There is a 17th-century *pest house* in the church-yard at Odiham (Ha) (see **218**) where people suffering from contagious diseases could be isolated.

Railings round churchyards and graves may be good of their kind and period. The *body-snatching* of the 18th and early 19th centuries gave rise to protective devices, such as watchmen's huts (eg Wanstead (Ex)), mortuary or watch houses, to keep the body in overnight (eg Crail (Fi)), or iron cages over the grave itself (eg Govan, Glasgow). Scotland also has some hearse houses (Saline (Fi) 1810, and Glenisla, 1821). Cranleigh (Sy) has a tomb used as a store by *smugglers* from the south coast, who met the "merchants" from London there and conducted the sale of the "merchandise" on the top of the tomb.

It goes without saying that the investigation of a burial ground, of any period, is not just a matter of recording the monuments but also of excavation. This is a very important element in archaeology, and the excavation of, say, a Saxon cemetery or a disused or redundant churchyard will produce otherwise unobtainable evidence for the demography and health of the population: the distribution of the sexes, age at death, physique, endemic diseases, (eg rickets), illnesses suffered during life (tooth abcesses, arthritis, etc), and cause of death. There is a growing volume of information

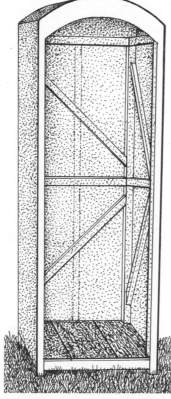

217 *Hudd – Odiham (Ha). A hudd is a portable shelter for a priest officiating at a graveside.*

on these matters, which is helping materially to understand the social conditions of the past. Where a complete assemblage – or at least a very large sample – can be investigated, as in the case of the churchyard of St Helen-on-the-Wall, York, a church which had been demolished in the 1550s and memory of which had been lost, the value is even greater. Here some 1,100 burials were analysed. Even more illuminating were the recent excavations in the crypt of Christ Church, Spitalfields (Lo). Some 1000 skeletons were excavated, including nearly 400 with coffin plates giving names, age, and date of death; they ranged from 1646 to 1852. Many of the individuals could be matched with documentary evidence for their lives, which made it possible to verify methods of analysing growth and ageing processes and has indeed cast doubt on traditional archeological methodology. Studies on this scale are rarely possible, but important evidence has been extracted from smaller groups, or even individuals, by palaeopathologists such as the late Calvin Wells.

218 *Pest house for isolating people with contagious diseases; a good 17th-century example – Odiham (Ha).*

CEMETERIES

Cemeteries, as distinct from churchyards, are features of all towns of any size. As we know them, they are the product of a 19th-century reform movement, and some of them are showpieces in their own right. They formed part of the Victorian cult of death and funerals, to which much display and expense was devoted by all classes. The larger cemeteries usually provided for Anglicans to be buried in consecrated ground and nonconformists in unconsecrated ground; each had their own chapels. Jews and Roman Catholics usually had their own burial grounds, as did Quakers.

Before the Industrial Revolution the churchyards could, in general, cope with the normal level of burials. But the Industrial Revolution brought an increase in deaths as well as in wealth. In 1842 the average age at death of a professional man and his family was 30, and of a working man 17 (these figures include a high rate of infant mortality). The population also sharply increased; in 1837 only five places in England and Wales outside London had a population over 100,000 – in 1800 there had been none – but in 1891 there were 23.

219 *Victorian funerary architecture – the Egyptian Avenue in Highgate Cemetery, London. This cemetery has notable examples of elaborate and extravagant monuments and features.*

The religious and moral revival after the Regency, the Romantic movement and the Gothic revival, and the popular affection for the dead, which demanded secure and dignified resting places, also played their part.

General burial inside the church and in the churchyard was standard from the 16th century, but the growing use of coffins took up a lot of room. By the 17th century town churchyards were grossly overcrowded, and the levels built up (many City of London churchyards are higher than street level). Ossuaries were resorted to to make more room (as at St Bride's, Fleet Street). Not till after the Plague of 1665 were proper regulations made, and burial districts set up. By the late 18th century a small, but real, start had been made to solve the problem.

There were no major reforms until the 19th century, in spite of the pioneer establishment of Bunhill Fields (before 1665) by the Dissenters (this was preserved as an open space, and because of its monuments, in the 1860s). Cemeteries outside city centres, for those who could pay, were established by private companies in Liverpool in 1825–9 and Glasgow in 1832. These, as well as being early, are still among the most interesting and spectacular outside London. St James' in Liverpool (1825), behind the Anglican cathedral, has ramps for access and catacombs, but has lost much of its character; the Necropolis in Glasgow (1831), modelled on Père Lachaise in Paris (with set layout but individual freedom to put up monuments), has Egyptian vaults and a Jews' sepulchre – it is a grand and exciting place.

The first great metropolitan cemetery was Kensal Green (1833). This had an Anglican and a nonconformist chapel, catacombs, and monumental entrance; it had a hydraulic lift to serve the catacombs from the chapel above. It soon became one of the sights of London, and displays the whole range of Victorian taste. Other cemeteries followed – Norwood (1837), Highgate (1839), Nunhead (1840, closed 1969), Abney Park (1840, with fine entrance gates), Tower Hamlets (1841). All these are of interest, but Highgate is the most romantic, with its vaguely Italian atmosphere and its remarkable Egyptian Avenue (see **219**) and Circle of Lebanon catacombs. Brompton (1840) was the first to be taken over by the government (the Board of Health), the company being in difficulties. The winding paths and the planted forest and ornamental trees greatly contribute to the charm of these cemeteries. The private joint-stock cemeteries were built in the Greek or Egyptian styles, not Gothic, because they were not church foundations. Many fine monuments lie neglected in cemeteries, such as that to Captain Charles Ricketts by Burges at Kensal Green or that to F R Leyland (1902), a masterpiece by Burne Jones.

Burials of the poor in churchyards still continued, and became a pressing problem, not helped by cholera and other epidemics. Conditions in these became indescribably hideous. In 1842 a Parliamentary committee reported that there were 218 acres of intramural burial grounds in London, and that over 44,000 burials were made in them every year. There was great opposition to change, usually on financial grounds, but in the end conditions forced the government to action; in 1850 a Metropolitan Burial District was formed, and the Board of Health was empowered to take over private cemeteries and provide others. Nevertheless the London Necropolis at Brookwood (1854) was a private venture; it had its own rail connection with Waterloo. A few more private cemeteries were founded, such as Plaistow and New Southgate, but most after 1850 were run by public Burial Boards. The first was at Finchley (1853). Two notable ones were Paddington and the City of London Cemetery at Ilford (1856).

The new cemeteries were also used for the reburial of people formerly buried in City churchyards now closed and cleared. The later cemeteries tend to be uniform and not so well landscaped and planted as the earlier ones. There were also a few small private grounds (eg Victoria Park, 1845–94), but many were closed after 1884 and converted into public gardens.

In 1951 municipal burial space covered over 25,000 acres in England and Wales, and churchyards and private cemeteries about 50,000. Burial takes up 0.13% of the land surface, and this increases by 400 acres every year. A hygienic alternative to this use of land was seen to be *cremation*, which was advocated generally from about 1875. The first crematorium was at St John's, Woking, in 1878, but the practice was not legalised until 1885. Golders Green was set up in the 1900s, and there are now crematoria all over the country; few are distinguished, but some, such as Guildford, are not unpleasing.

A specialised and limited kind of burial ground is worth noting. The great epidemics of the past brought with them the problem of hastily burying large numbers of people. Existing churchyards were used as far as possible, certainly for the plague of 1665, but in other outbreaks special pits were dug, mass graves where victims were thrown and covered with lime. Some of these, like Charterhouse Square in London (Black Death of 1349), have never been built over. The garden of New

College, Oxford, lies over a plague pit for the Black Death. The area was previously covered by houses, but was depopulated by the epidemic and cleared for use as a burial ground. The plague pit at Holywell Mount, Shoreditch (1665) continued in use as a burial ground. Plague pits were sometimes covered with a mound, as at Twyford (Ha). The same problem resulted from a battle, and there are many traditions that barrows are where the dead of a local battle are laid. In most cases mounds were probably not raised, but there is one at Enborne (Bk), containing dead from the first battle of Newbury (1643). Some other epidemics also had special burial grounds, like that outside York station for the victims of cholera in 1833–4.

Passing mention might be made of *animals' cemeteries*. Graves of favourite dogs or horses are to be found in the grounds of many

220 *Six types of cross. 1, Celtic; 2, Saxon (both 1 and 2 are richly decorated with sculpture); 3, village or market cross; 4, gable cross on church roof; 5, incised on church doorpost or pillar, by an individual, before or after a venture; 6, consecration cross, incised or painted on a church wall.*

country houses (eg Petworth), and there is a formal pets' graveyard on the northern edge of Hyde Park, in Bayswater.

CROSSES

Celtic, Anglo-Saxon, and Viking

A cross (see **220**), or at least the base of one, is still a common feature of an old churchyard. Few areas lack a representative range, although

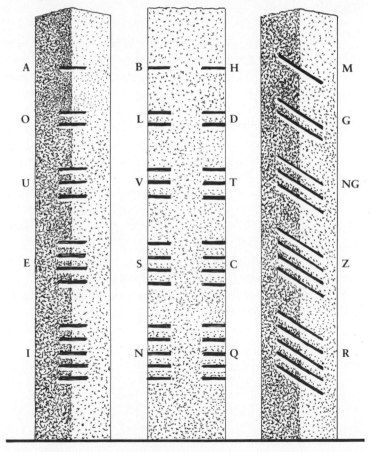

221 *The main letters of the Ogam alphabet (Irish, 5th–8th centuries AD). This consists of lines carved along the edge of a stone.*

many have fallen to time and Puritans, and in some areas most were made of wood and have disappeared. There may once have been some 5,000 crosses in England. The many problems raised by their art and its development have been illuminated, if not all entirely solved, by the work of scholars such as W G Collingwood, Baldwin Brown, T D Kendrick, and latterly Richard Bailey.

Crosses appear to derive from, or at least to continue the idea of, prehistoric monoliths (some of which seem to have been memorial stones and others waymarks or boundary marks, among other possible uses). They may have been introduced into this country by Irish missionaries in the 5th and 6th centuries. Many early ones are found along the west coasts of Britain. Some were prehistoric stones, Christianised by the addition of a carved cross or by actual reshaping of the head into the form of a cross. Many are carved also on their faces, either with abstract decoration or scenes containing human or animal figures, and some with inscriptions in Latin, Ogam (see **221**), or Runic. Crosses whose heads are enclosed in a ring are of Irish or west Scottish origin (as at Iona), and appear later in Viking times under the inspiration of these Celtic sources. In England and Man, on the contrary, only Viking crosses have wheel- or ring-heads – the Anglo-Saxon crosses which preceded them do not (as is exemplified at Irton (Cb)). Ring-knots, circle-heads (with groups in Cumbria and north-east Wales and Cheshire), and hammer-heads are Viking forms. The rings may represent a halo or symbolise the sun.

A type of cross of strictly limited origin and distribution is that of the *Pictish symbol stones*. These occur in the part of the Pictish area north and east of the Forth and probably orginated in the Moray Firth/Black Isle area. The southern Picts were converted to Christianity in the 5th century by St Ninian from Whithorn (Wg) (where incidentally the "Latinus" memorial stone dates from about 450). By the 7th century the Picts were making their very original symbol stones, carved with combinations of some 18 devices – crescent, V, Z, disc, snake, fish, comb, mirror, and animals (see **222**). These may well represent the tattoo designs, placing the dead person in his personal, functional, or tribal context or may record important marriage alliances. They are clearly not Christian, but some stones (Class II) have not only the symbols but crosses as well, and some were reused for later crosses. There are collections at Meigle and Glamis. In the 8th century the Picts produced *cross-slabs*, with horsemen and mythological scenes, but of broadly "Celtic" type (Rossie or Meigle).

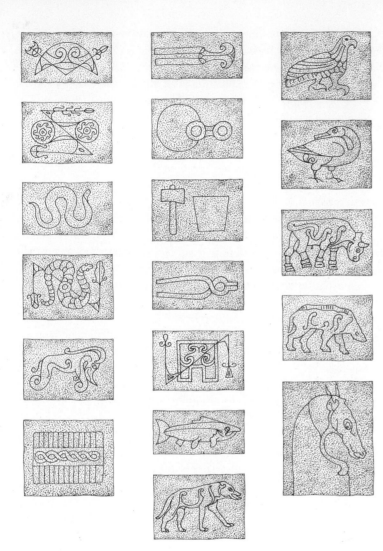

223–6 *Types of Viking-age sculpture: 223 Borre, mid 9th to late 10th century; 224 Jellinge, late 9th to late 10th century; 225 Mammen (an axe from Denmark), c 960 to 1020; 226Ringerike, c 980 to mid 11th century.*

224

222 *Devices on Pictish symbol stones. The meaning of these is not fully understood, but they may represent, on a memorial, the status, tribe, and sometimes the occupation or marriage alliances of the dead person.*

The early crosses, 6th to 11th centuries, have shafts either circular (ie pillars, as at Wolverhampton) or square/rectangular. Many never had bases. Dating these is often difficult, and must normally depend on study of the decoration. Anglo-Saxon crosses usually carry either a continuous vine scroll or panels of knotwork or interlace (eg Sandbach (Ch) and Bewcastle (Cb)). Some panels may contain figures,

eg of apostles or saints. Viking crosses may also have scenes with figures, but if these date from a phase transitional between paganism and full acceptance of Christianity (9th–10th century) the figures may represent legends of the Norse gods and heroes, sometimes combined with Christian themes. But the pagan scenes themselves may, as at Gosforth (Cb), actually be symbolic of Christian themes.

Scandinavian art styles relevant to English sculpture are:

Borre (mid 9th to end of the 10th century) – split ribbon-plait in hollow-sided lozenge (Gosforth) (see **223**);

Jellinge (end 9th to end 10th century) – ribbon animal, with spiral hips, tendril ("lappet") lips, and "pigtail" (York) (see **224**);

Mammen (c 960–1020) – thicker animal, more tendrils, pelleted infill (Workington; Levisham) (see **225**);

Ringerike (11th century) – long, curling tendrils, pear-shaped motif between leaf-like forms (London St Paul's; Otley) (see **226**);

Urnes (mid 11th to mid 12th century) – ribbon animals; subtle, rounded, flowing lines (Jevington).

Richard Bailey has found that similarities in design can sometimes be explained by the use of templates by professional sculptors (eg a warrior at Brompton (YN), Sockburn (Du), and Kirklevington (Cl)).

These art styles occur also in contemporary manuscripts and illumination.

Medieval

From Norman times on it is convenient to classify crosses into types, as was done by Aymer Vallance: those with shafts and heads, "spires",

225

226

and the crown type. Crosses of a particular function may not always be of the same type. In any case, many, perhaps most, crosses had more than one function.

The earliest crosses were *preaching* crosses, set up where a missionary had his station, or where a burial ground and church developed. A preaching cross could also be a *memorial* cross, if it were set up at a tomb or martyr's grave, or be a simple symbol of the faith (Hereford; Iron Acton (Gl)). Other crosses, perhaps almost as early, could be set up by the *wayside* or at crossroads (eg one on B3213, three miles west of Moretonhampstead (Dv)), or mark boundaries (eg one on Park Brow, Kettlewell (NY)). Some boundary crosses were stopping places for people beating the bounds of a parish or manor; but some could combine these functions with also being *sanctuary* crosses (as at Ripon), where the boundary was also that of a church liberty. Memorial crosses, which in the 13th to 15th centuries could be of elaborate "spire" type, might commemorate a person, such as the series of Eleanor crosses from Lincoln to London (1290) of which only those at Geddington (see **227**), Hardingstone, and Waltham survive, or an event, such as the battle of Boroughbridge (1322), now at Aldborough, or Neville's Cross (1346). *Village* crosses shade into *market* crosses (to encourage honest trading). Some are simple shafts on steps or bases, some are of spire or canopy (crown) type. Important examples of the latter class are

227 *Eleanor cross – Geddington (Nh). This is one of three original survivors of the crosses marking the funeral journey from Lincoln to London of Edward I's queen, Eleanor of Castile, in 1290; that at Charing Cross, London, is a replica.*

228 *The City Cross, Chichester (1501): the finest of its type.*

those at Malmesbury, Salisbury, and Chichester (see **228**). Some are simple domes on pillars (Swaffham (Nf)); some have rooms above, or at the side, and these develop into *market halls* (Wymondham; Witney; Ross). A special type is the *butter* cross (Winchester, Oakham, Bungay), which again may be a spire or crown. A preaching cross is sometimes in the form of a small open chamber sheltered under a spire (Iron Acton (Gl)).

A class of *weeping* crosses has sometimes been recognised, but it is unlikely that this is so – a funeral could after all halt at any cross, village, market, or wayside. But some puzzles remain – a few crosses have the step or base hollowed out: at Bishops Lydeard (So) this may be for alms to be left; at Ripley (NY) it could be for penitents to kneel at. But the purpose is not definitely established. Wansford (Nh) has a *bridge* cross. At Deeping St James (Ca), the base was used as a lock-up (1819), as was that at Bungay. Some shafts have niches cut in them, and these are thought to be to hold the pyx during the Palm Sunday procession. Cross heads can be simple crosses, but may be more ornate – gabled, to shelter a crucifix or statuary group (Tyberton (He)), hollowed for a lantern, or in the form of a sundial (Steeple Ashton (Wi)).

The variety is very large. There are also local or regional types, such as the mercat crosses of Scotland (see **229**), the domed canopies of East Anglia, the simple stones of the North York Moors. Celtic and Scandinavian sculpture is well represented in the Isle of Man.

CHURCHES IN THE LANDSCAPE

The church and manor house were the most substantial buildings in the village, and often the church was the only stone building. It dominated not only the village but the surrounding country as well, more so when towers reached their full height of two or three storeys by the 15th century, or when spires came into vogue in the 14th. No doubt this was partly a challenge to be taken up by the church, apart from the inherent function of the tower or spire. Salisbury, Norwich, and Chichester spires can be seen a long way off, and advertise the church as well as pointing travellers to the town, and everyone to heaven. This holds of course for places of any size, such as Grantham or Louth, as

well as for a small village. The village churches of Northamptonshire or Lincolnshire with their distinctive spires, or the slender towers of Somerset, form pleasant foci in their rolling countrysides, and add to their character.

In towns too the church dominated the scene, and ended every street – not only tight centres like Hull or Melton Mowbray, but small country towns like Thaxted. The view of St Andrews (Fi) from the south gives a very good impression of a medieval town. The

229 *A typical Scottish mercat cross – Culross (Fi).*

230 *Chantry chapels, Winchester Cathedral: left, Bishop William Waynflete, 1486; right, Cardinal Beaufort, 1447. Winchester Cathedral is very rich in chantry chapels, ornate buildings over a tomb, with an altar where a "chantry priest" could sing masses for the soul of the dead person.*

main cities like London, York, or Norwich, with their scores of churches, had a distinctive skyline which comes out clearly in late medieval and 16th-century paintings and engravings. Many of London's towers and spires, and the great cathedral of St Paul's itself, were destroyed in the Fire of 1666, but the rebuilding by Wren replaced them in the new Baroque style and continued the romantic effect; compare the panorama by Visscher (1616, but probably showing London as it was in the late 16th century) with that by Kip of *c* 1720. The City of London had 108 churches in 1666; 66 were

destroyed in the Great Fire, of which 51 were rebuilt by Wren; 26 were demolished in later years. In World War II 26 were destroyed or damaged, of which 18 were restored. The present total is 39.

The planned developments in newly-built districts in the 17th and 18th centuries made full use of the visual effect which churches could make. Look at St George's, Hanover Square, St Paul's, Covent Garden, or St James's, Piccadilly, which closes the vista up the hill from St James's Square. The spires of 19th-century churches and chapels also contributed much to the townscape.

The Normans took full advantage of bulk to impress and overawe the English, and castle and cathedral could stand together to emphasise the twin powers of State and Church. Durham is a classic example of this, and Old Sarum was so once. Modern cathedrals too can be sited to convey the message of the presence of religion in an urban setting, like the two cathedrals in Liverpool or that at Guildford, isolated on its hilltop. In York, the huge Minster and the great abbey church of St Mary's close by cannot have failed to impose their message.

A more minor, but useful, role of churches in the landscape was as beacons, waymarks, or mariners' sighting points. All Saints, Pavement, York has an openwork tower in which shone a beacon to guide travellers to the city through the Forest of Galtres. Churches round the coast are often near the cliff edge or the shore, for incoming ships to steer by, eg Rye (Sx), Cley (Nf), Blythburgh (Su), and, the supreme example, Boston Stump.

PRIVATE CHAPELS

A specialised category of churches is the chapels of great houses and institutions. For reasons of space, cost, and purpose, these are normally rectangular, small, and plain, with liturgical features reduced to the simplest terms. The royal chapel of St George at Windsor Castle is a conspicuous exception.

It was customary for the medieval nobility to maintain a private priest, who served the family and staff, taught the children, and acted as a confidant. This was continued by many great houses after the Reformation. Examples of private chapels are the castle chapels such as the Tower of London, bishops' palaces like Lambeth or Wolvesey

(Winchester), and great houses like Petworth, Knole, or Wardour. Smaller manor houses sometimes had small chapels or prayer rooms, often leading off the solar or bedrooms, as at Charney Manor (Ox), 13th century.

Institutions with similar chapels include colleges (eg New College, Oxford, King's College, Cambridge, both with lobbies at one end, and King's College, London, High Victorian)), and schools (Eton, Winchester, Lancing (very large and prominently sited), St Olave's, Orpington, has an octagonal chapel (1969) with movable communion table to adapt it to various uses and denominational practices. Almshouses usually have chapels, if space permits, eg Cawley's at Chichester (1626) and, also at Chichester, St Mary's (early 13th century), where the residents live along the sides of a great hall, one end of which is the chapel. On the other hand, St Cross at Winchester has a fully-fledged church. Hospitals also have chapels, of which a good example is at Guy's, London (1722), which has an important monument by Bacon; a pleasing modern example is that at Basingstoke.

Medieval trade and religious guilds usually had their own chapels, either a part of a church set aside for them or a separate building. Bridges, which were often maintained by guilds set up for the purpose, might have a chapel on or at the end of the bridge, where travellers could give thanks for safe passage, and to act as fund-raising points for the guild's work (as at Wakefield, or Bradford-on-Avon, later used as a lock-up).

There was also a variety of chapels owned by individuals, and served by paid priests, such as the *chantries* (memorial chapels) – not only those over the tombs of important people, as in Winchester Cathedral (see **230**), where their souls could be prayed for. In some cases an entire church is a chantry; thus the Woodville family took over the small monastery at Grafton (Nh) and converted it into a manor house; its chapel had already become a family chantry. The church at Fotheringhay (Nh) was a collegiate chantry for the Yorkists, associated with an almshouse, and there are many similar cases of hospitals whose chapels were family chantries (as at Arundel and Ewelme). Chantries were not always separate shrines or chapels; they could be founded at various altars in the church. For instance, York has hardly any chantry chapels or shrines, but there are records of some 60 altars, many with multiple dedications, and many of them used for several chantries.

There remains the small group of memorial chapels, ranging from those in cemeteries and crematoria to military chapels in churches, to war memorials (as at Edinburgh), and to chapels commemorating a single person, as the Sandford chapel at Burghclere (Bk) or the Watts chapel at Compton (Sy).

THE ARCHAEOLOGY OF CHURCHES

Out of some 14,000 parish churches in England, of which *c* 12,000 are pre-Reformation, a high proportion, perhaps as many as three-quarters, may be redundant, and at least 4,500 may be destroyed, by the end of the century. This presents an archaeological problem well beyond any likely resources.

To test the possibilities, a pilot scheme was set up in 1971 by the Society of Antiquaries round the important Saxon church of Deerhurst (Gl). Excavation had shown a former apse, and indicated that the church probably existed before the earliest historical records of it in the early 9th century. It was hoped to show the historical sequence and relations of doors, windows, chapels, and galleries on three levels. Much information on the history of churches by way of excavation and clearance both outside and inside churches is being obtained in Holland, Germany, and Scandinavia, but this is still only beginning to be general practice in this country. Deerhurst also had a monastic establishment attached to the church, about which little is known. It is at present surrounded only by a farm and a few houses, but there are traces of a medieval village in the adjoining fields.

Another source of information is the burials in the church and churchyard. At Deerhurst all the surviving inscriptions on monuments and gravestones have been recorded and analysed. There are 437 of these, dating from the late 17th century to the present day, and there is a medieval chest tomb with no inscription as well. The churchyard has burials for some five feet down, and Roman burial urns have been found in the church; this represents a total of some 20,000 burials. Many of the inscriptions record people not included in the parish registers, and they reveal much about the life of the village and the occupations and relationships of the people. If the actual skeletal remains could also be examined, they would show the physique, diseases, and diet of the people at different periods.

It is clear that if this kind of investigation could be made, and fully followed through, at selected churches all over the country, the history, not only of the churches themselves but of the people, could be greatly illuminated.

Another approach was that at Rivenhall (Ex), where a training school for archaeologists and architects was set up in 1972 to examine the apparently Victorian church (it was believed to have been rebuilt in 1839) from all points of view. It was discovered that the rebuilding had not destroyed the former church, but was only a face lift within which the Saxon and medieval churches were well preserved. Moreover, the site had been occupied, before the church, from Neolithic to Roman times. This kind of history could well occur elsewhere.

Until recently the excavation of a church was aimed at recovering an exact plan, rather than unravelling the development of the church in its changing social environment. Even after the war little or no record was made when clearing away bombed churches, and it was realised how little was known about the history of most churches. The breakthrough came with Martin Biddle's excavations at Winchester from 1961–71, and the projects at Deerhurst and Rivenhall. In fact, from 1955 to 1980, archaeological work took place in some 500 churches, from excavation to survey and observation, in various degrees. But more total investigations are needed. A list of all this work has been made by R K Morris (1983).

But only since 1972 has church archaeology been established as a specific branch of archaeology, and this may be said to date from the setting up by the Council for British Archaeology in 1972 of a Churches Committee. Since then earlier work at Brixworth has been reviewed and analysed, town churches in Winchester and York, and country ones like Wharram Percy (NY) have been investigated complete with their graveyards, and important work has been done at Repton.

Redundant churches can sometimes be thoroughly worked over, but excavation in a "living" church may have to be hurried, sketchy, or partial. Notable contributions to church archaeology have been made by Warwick and Kirsty Rodwell, and by Richard Morris, who have done much to put its practice on a detailed and systematic basis.

Plans have been got out for each stage in the growth of the church, and much learned from these. Saxon stone (Barton-on-Humber) and even wooden churches (Rivenhall) have been revealed inside or close by Norman or later churches. In some cases burials have been shown to predate even the first wooden church. H M Taylor evolved a method of investigation involving the stone-by-stone drawing of the inner and outer faces of the walls, and then analysing this. Building methods and materials are revealed, sequences and stages of building, alterations, and even hitherto unknown features (eg blocked Anglo-Saxon windows, medieval doors, etc).

Churches normally grow by enlargement and addition, but cases are known where they have shrunk – usually owing to decay of the village or decline of the local population, but sometimes to liturgical changes or to more unexpected causes such as the 14th- and 15th-century French raids along the south coast.

The results of excavation have vastly illuminated the growth and shrinkage of churches, as two or three examples will show. No two churches have quite the same history, but Rivenhall, Wharram Percy, and Barton-on-Humber (St Peter's) may be taken as reasonably typical. The variety of layout can be seen from these sketch plans, and it may almost be suggested that each century was, perhaps unconsciously(!), aiming at a distinctive shape (see **180–7**, pages 301–2). St Mary, Tanner Street, Winchester, was shown to have been a private church, adapted from an earlier dwelling house; Raunds (Nh) was a 10th-century stone church first enlarged and then converted into part of a medieval manor house.

Excavation of churchyards can not only elucidate the health and physique of the population, but the arrangement of graves over time, the development of the tombstone, and also the various uses, clerical and lay, to which churchyards have been put (see above, pages 319–24). Light may also be shed by church archaeology on interior features, such as liturgical arrangements, seating and other furnishings, screens, windows, wall paintings, sculpture, etc.

Note on redundancy Although a great many of the 8,000 or so parish churches in England likely to become redundant by the early 21st century will no doubt be destroyed or fall into ruin (as they have through the centuries – such ruins can still be seen, eg at Greatham (Ha) and large numbers in Scotland), yet uses can be found for many of them. These include conversion into houses (nonconformist chapels lend themselves particularly to this!), factories and warehouses (the Free Church in Wick is now a garage), guild centres (eg St Mary Woolnoth, London), other cultural or charitable centres (York, Norwich), museums (St Mary Castlegate, York; Priory, Chichester), archives (Winchester), libraries (Lincoln College, Oxford; York Minster Library in former palace chapel), bookstore (Holy Trinity, Marylebone, London), and architect's office (Sheffield). Use by other religions now has a good deal of support.

THE NONCONFORMIST CHAPEL

There are some 15,000 nonconformist chapels still in use in England and Wales, about as many as Anglican parish churches. Fewer, however, are of much intrinsic interest; only some 2,000 are potentially worthy of listing. They are being closed at an alarming rate, including some which should be saved, such as the cob-built Unitarian chapel at Crediton (1721) or Bold Street Methodist Church, Warrington (1850). Methodist chapels declined from 11,500 in use in 1960 to 8,500 in 1970 (and this figure includes new chapels replacing old ones). But several have been saved in recent years, and many new churches of considerable architectural merit have replaced chapels of little or no interest, to the advantage of the environment.

Nonconformity has played a great part in English life since the later 16th century, and for most of the 19th century was in many parts the dominant religious outlook. The "nonconformist conscience" reflected the principles of a wide section of the community, and influenced commercial, social, and political morality. The nonconformists had had to establish themselves and their rights in the face of long opposition, and emerged with a vigour and cohesion which was a real social force. All this found expression in the architecture of their churches, which ranged from the very simple to the highly sophisticated, but which had a distinctive flavour allied to popular art. It could be quiet and tasteful, but was more often plain, outspoken, rugged, even bizarre, or obtrusively ugly; it was rarely without individuality. England would be the poorer without its chapels.

Although the Church before the Reformation had had its rebels, like the Lollards, no chapels were built by them. With the Reformation and Henry VIII's break with the Pope, religion in England could find its own way. The newly-established Church of England did not satisfy everyone, and there were broadly two kinds of reaction to it; the puritan approach wanted to reform it from within, the separatists saw no alternative to leaving and starting again. The dissenting churches originated from this latter attitude. The Quakers – founded in 1652 – represent a third – the mystical – strand in Christianity.

By 1567 congregations were meeting in private for religious services. Such "Independent" units gave rise to the *Congregational* churches which, although later linked in a national association (Union), retained their individual autonomy. The *Baptists*, whose principles were similar, but who believed in adult baptism, are identifiable from 1603. The *Presbyterians*, who were moderate puritans within the Church of England, came to the fore in the Civil Wars. They formulated their characteristic system of church government, which had four tiers of assemblies, in 1644. But this failed to establish itself within the Church, and in 1662 they came out. Of the 2,000 clergy ejected in that year, all but 400 were Presbyterian. They continued to hope to influence the Church and to return to it, so no separate church was set up. After the Toleration Act of 1689 they faded out, and most of them became either Independent or *Unitarian*. A Presbyterian Church in England was founded in 1836, in connection with the Church of Scotland, and became the Presbyterian Church of England in 1876. In 1974 this church united with the Congregationalists to form the *United Reformed Church*. It had some distinctive churches, like Regent Square, London (bombed).

Before the Congregational Union was formed in 1832, the Independents had had some exchanges with the Unitarians and Presbyterians, and, from 1780, with a small group called the Countess of Huntingdon's Connexion. But their history is simple compared with that of the Baptists and Methodists. The Baptists, in the 17th century, had two main groups, the General Baptists who were Arminian (believers in free will) and the Particular Baptists who were Calvinists (believers in predestination). Both these groups themselves split and reunited several times in the 18th and 19th centuries, leaving small bodies behind at each reunion (very like what happened in the Church of Scotland – see below). The left-wing bodies are strongest in Yorkshire and East Anglia.

The *Methodists*, great chapel builders, were the result of the activities of John and Charles Wesley and their associates, from 1739. Their evangelism had an extraordinary impact on the industrial masses, whose conditions predisposed them to enthusiasm and utopianism. At first part of the Church of England, they set up bodies of their own. The death of John Wesley in 1791 led to a large number of separate groups and recombinations. In 1932 the three largest Methodist churches (the United, the Primitive, and the Wesleyan) joined to form the Methodist Church. The *Quakers* are dealt with below.

Apart from these major nonconformist bodies, there are a large number of small sects, such as Elim, the Plymouth Brethren, and the Bible Christians, whose chapels are small and simple. The *Salvation Army* (1873) citadels are *sui generis* (see below). The earliest nonconformist meeting places were private houses, cottages, barns, or the open air. The few chapels built before general toleration were therefore simple buildings, made to look like farms or houses from a distance, or actual converted or extended houses. Chapel building, with few exceptions, began about 1650 (particularly after 1662), and again after 1688. There was a decline in the first half of the 18th century, until the Wesleyan revival, then a spate throughout the 19th century. Puritan churches, although they can be very simple, have different requirements from nonconformist chapels (see below) – a "Chapel of Ease" is not a chapel (eg Bramhope, Leeds). But Low

231 *Methodist chapel, Heptonstall (WY); an early octagonal building, 1764.*

Anglican churches in the mid 18th century could be very like chapels, especially if the latter were built in the full Georgian idiom (Rivington (La)), and the early post-Wesley Anglican church can be essentially a preaching house – a good example is St John's at Chichester (James Eames, 1812). There are a few cases of medieval chapels being converted to meeting houses, such as Kirkstead Abbey chapel (Li), Deerhurst (Gl), or Langley (Sp). One church built for the Puritans within the Establishment – Toxteth, Liverpool, 1618 – was retained by the Presbyterians later.

The essential elements of a nonconformist chapel are simple, indeed minimal. All that is required is a "barn-like" structure (the word has sometimes been used pejoratively, but it is a simple fact), with windows on three sides and a pulpit in the middle of the fourth. In front of the pulpit is a plain communion table, which can be out in the middle. Later, there might be a lectern. There is a font somewhere, perhaps,or, in a Baptist chapel, a baptismal tank. The organ and choir may creep up behind the pulpit in bigger churches. By the 1770s there were often galleries round three sides. There are fixed pews, not chairs, and no central aisle, and there are no altar, chancel, or room for processions, as in even a simple church. The chapel was a *preaching house*.

The architecture of the barn-like structure has been divided by Betjeman into three phases, although it should be borne in mind that variety is the keynote of this essentially popular art-form. The first phase is the "theological style", including the first chapels after the disguise stage, later 17th and early 18th century. These have simple exteriors but often lavish interiors, like a Wren church. Good examples are Friars Street, Ipswich, 1700, Unitarian, Bury St Edmunds, early 18th century, Underbank, Stannington (WY), 1742. The second phase is the "architecture of enthusiasm"; these are larger and flimsier, and can have moulded decoration inside, though externally they continue to be Georgian. They are the early Methodist churches remote from the parish church, so aiming to seat as many as possible, and doing without the Anglican features of the parish church. The first of these is the first Methodist church, Horsefair, Bristol, 1739, though this was not then in Methodist use; the oldest in continuous use is Newbiggin (Du), 1760. They run until the very end of the Georgian tradition, as at Louth, 1835. The third phase is the Victorian, a profusion of churches of all styles and none, starting with classical and veering to the "Gothic" or the flamboyant. Everyone is familiar with these, and examples are not necessary.

There are a few exceptional forms, such as the "chapelles ornées", based on romanticised farm buildings (eg Roxton (Bd)); others include octagons, of which the pioneer was the Unitarian church in Norwich, 1754, followed by the Methodists at Yarm, 1763, Heptonstall, 1764 (see **231**), and others, and the round or oval, like St George's Congregational, Liverpool, 1841, Belvoir Street, Leicester (Unitarian), 1845, Bewdley (Roman Catholic in a Presbyterian chapel), or Saltaire, 1858. At Fressingfield (Su) is a Strict Baptist chapel shaped like a coffin (1835). By the later 19th century nonconformity was accepted as "respectable", and many chapels were built to look vaguely like Anglican churches, in Gothic style (at least externally), and with a prominent spire. The townscape of London is punctuated by these spires. By the later 19th century also, the great central churches were built, such as the City Temple (Congregational, 1874) and the vast Methodist Central Hall (1905–11). To these phases may be added a fourth – the contemporary building since the war. This is shared by all denominations, but there are several distinguished chapels among them. They are usually plain and simple, making full use of brick and concrete to get their effect. In these, pulpit, table, and lectern may be strung out along the east wall.

There are a few differences between the denominations. The few chapels built before 1662 are either Congregational or Baptist. The former have the oldest in the country, Horningsham in Wiltshire (see **232**), founded in 1566. The building, at first a farmhouse, was remodelled or rebuilt about 1700, and again altered in the 19th century.

Although much of its original impact is lost, it still has a high pulpit, and hat-pegs in rows (see 233). At Walpole (Su) is a 16th-century house converted to a Congregational chapel in 1647; it has box-pews, and is lit by candles and oil. The oldest Baptist church is at Tewkesbury, where a medieval house was converted some time between 1623 and 1655; it is near the river, no doubt deliberately – many Baptist churches are near water. Another early one is Cote, Bampton (Ox), 1664, which has a tank under the communion table. At Buckland, not far away, a 16th/17th-century house has been converted to a Baptist chapel.

Presbyterian chapels have bellcotes at the west end (eg Tunley, Risley (La)). Wesley's Chapel, City Road, London (1778) had a profound

232 *The oldest purpose-built nonconformist chapel (Independent, now Congregational, founded 1566) – Horningsham (Wi).*

233 *Old Meeting – Horningsham (Wi). The building has been altered c 1700 and in the 19th century. Note the central pulpit behind the communion table, and the hat-pegs in the gallery.*

influence on chapel architecture generally, and fixed the preaching house form for a century. Many Wesleyan chapels were named Brunswick or Hanover as a sign of loyalty to the Crown when, during the French Revolution, Methodists were suspected of being revolutionaries. In the 1840s the Unitarians experimented with near-Anglican forms. In 1847 the chapel at Gee Cross, Hyde (Ch) was the first nonconformist church to be Gothic inside and out, and to have an altar in the chancel and the pulpit moved to one side. In the same year the similar Mill Hill Chapel, Leeds, was the first to use stained glass. One unusual feature from the early days is an escape tunnel from Flowergate Unitarian Chapel, Whitby, to a shop.

Nonconformist burial grounds are sometimes round the church, sometimes separate (as Bunhill Fields, London, 1695–1852). The effect can be one of crowded headstones, deeply lettered, and often adorned with symbolism and folk art. Many bear biblical quotations. Some burial grounds were in use before the chapel was built. Memorial tablets inside the churches are not so common as in Anglican churches.

Chapels lend themselves, on redundancy, to reuse as warehouses, factories, or to conversion to private houses, and should be looked for under these guises.

Until nonconformity had grown to include a large proportion of the population, and until its legal and social position was secure, chapels were either in inconspicuous positions or were modest and unassuming buildings on the edge of villages or in the back streets of towns. Available funds may also have something to do with this. But by the late 18th century a village chapel could be a prominent feature of the village. In the towns, chapels are only central and prominent in towns newly or greatly developed in the 19th century, like Swindon or northern textile towns. In the older towns, the medieval parish churches took the central or focal point unquestioned. In Wales the reverse is true. There chapels, particularly in Glamorgan, seem to be dotted all over the countryside, and to sprout at every street corner. Chapels were central to Welsh life, in a way the episcopal church was not, and when most of them were built, in the 19th century, were quite confident and unselfconscious. But wherever they are, chapels have the knack of attracting notice and making a positive contribution to the landscape, whatever their architectural qualities.

Revivalist preaching places, by the wayside or in the country, can often be detected from their names, eg Gospel Ash (Do) and Gospel Oak, London.

FRIENDS' (QUAKER) MEETING HOUSES

These form a distinctive group, and can hardly be classed as chapels. The simplicity of a Quaker meeting is so absolute that theoretically all that is required is a room to meet in, the simpler and plainer the better, and benches (more recently chairs) to sit on. The smaller meeting houses reflect this simple need, and owe little or nothing to contemporary chapel or church architecture. Indeed, John Betjeman called the Quakers "The Cistercians of nonconformist builders".

The Religious Society of Friends was founded, by George Fox, in the early 1650s, and like other dissenters was harassed and persecuted till nearly the end of the century. The early communities therefore met in houses, barns, etc, and formal meeting houses were not built for several decades. The earliest, or at least the earliest still in use, is that at Hertford (1670), built in a very domestic style. The other 17th-century houses are also in vernacular styles, like Almeley Wootton (He), *c* 1672, timber-framed, Alton, 1672, Brigflatts, near Sedbergh, 1675, Jordans, near Rickmansworth, 1688, and Farfield, near Skipton, 1689. This tradition lasted well into the 18th century, as at Come to Good, Kea (Co) 1708 (see **234**), or The Pales, Radnor, 1716, both thatched. These are custom-built; many early meeting houses are either extensions of existing cottages, like Amersham (cottage 1635, meeting house added 1685, extended 1785), or converted from existing houses, like the Blue Idol, Thakeham (Sx) (a farmhouse of *c* 1600, with one end made into a meeting room in 1691). Later buildings, particularly in the towns, could be more pretentious and have a chapel flavour, at least externally. Good examples are Mount Street, Manchester, 1830, or Ackworth (SY), 1847 (part of quite a grandiose architectural scheme based on the school). Twentieth-century examples include Bournville, 1905, in the spirit of the model estates, and the central Friends House, London, 1927, which includes offices, library, and bookshop as well as meeting rooms, and is in a class by itself; it replaced the old haphazard collection of buildings at Devonshire House, in the City, 1791.

Recent research by David Butler (1985) shows that 90% of all meeting houses in the first century of the Society (1650–1750), 60% in the second, and 35% in the third were of the *cottage* type. London,

234 *A Quaker meeting house – Come to Good, Kea (Co), 1704. This is a good early example; it has a loft or upper room, for women's business meetings (no longer separate). Not shown are the raised benches along one wall, for ministers, elders, and overseers (ministers no longer exist, and elders and overseers no longer sit separately).*

but not the Home Counties, went over to the *chapel* type. In the third century (1850–1950), Somerset, Westmorland, and Essex kept to the cottage. The early nonconformist meeting house had two doors in a symmetrical long wall, and a pulpit in the centre of (usually) the opposite wall, with a gallery or loft on two or three sides; the whole interior had box pews, and the two doors followed from the need to have a large central block of seats in front of the pulpit. This

changed to the standard chapel form by the late 18th century, a process paralleled by the Quaker change from cottage to "chapel". The latter change was due to updating a former cottage to fit into closely-built urban areas (cf a "town" church), and to follow the example of other denominations' chapels.

To obviate any confusion, it needs to be clearly said that the use of the word "chapel" does not imply that a Quaker meeting house is actually a chapel; Quakers have never thought of or called their meeting houses anything other than meeting houses. "Chapel" here is an architectural term only, used to emphasise the direction of design evolution, mostly in relation to external features – proportions, windows, etc – but sometimes, in large urban meeting houses, after the vernacular or "cottage" stage, also internal.

In Cornwall four early 19th-century meeting houses are large granite boxes up to 60x30ft (18x9m), with central (cross) passage between sash shutters and three doors (eg Redruth, 1814). In North Yorkshire seven similar meeting houses were built between 1770 and 1840, and nearly as many in Essex. Height, 1677, and Swarthmoor, 1688, were altered to this form. In Norfolk there are square meeting houses with ministers' stand opposite the door and a loft along each side wall reached from stairs by the door; these had no separate room for women's business meetings. In Cumberland and Westmorland women's chambers were added to the main (men's) chamber, side by side, with doors onto a lobby or into the fresh air (Whitehaven, 1725, and others, Darlington, 1846, Wisbech, 1954). In London in the mid 19th century a type developed with side rooms (classrooms etc) linked by a colonnade (Stoke Newington, 1828, Peckham, 1826). These relate closely to the development of villages into London suburbs in the 1820s. Large meeting houses by Hubert Lidbetter took the form of a high square room with lobbies on three sides and lofts above them (Friends House, London, 1930, Bull Street, Birmingham, 1933, Liverpool, 1948).

There are a few peculiarly Quaker requirements. A normal feature of all but very modern meeting houses is the Ministers' Stand, a raised platform along one side of the meeting room, on which recorded ministers, elders, and overseers sat facing the rest of the members (ministers were abolished in the 1920s). There might be three tiers for these people, or only one for all. In some cases the stand was divided so that women could sit at one end and men at the other (see **235**). (Women normally had separate meetings, and in many houses had

235 *A Quaker meeting house – Come to Good (Co), 1704. This view shows the ministers' and elders' benches behind the table.*

a separate room to themselves.) There are three types of stand – centre of back wall; full width of wall; or no raised seat but only a platform. The first type was common in the early years in Norfolk and the Cotswolds, but declined fairly rapidly – elders were a late development, and affected types only from the mid 18th century. In Yorkshire there are eight cases of a central stand with raised seats in corners on both sides of it, enclosed by a low screen (1689 on). In the Pardshaw area of Lancashire, there are raised seats on either side of a fireplace, perhaps derived from a converted cottage (1710–40). Stands are no longer reserved for ministers, elders, or overseers – Friends normally sit round a table in the middle of the room, with no distinction of personal function. But the former exclusive occupancy of the stand by what used to be called "weighty Friends" – a breed now almost extinct! – is still remembered.

In most cases the women's room was merely divided by a movable partition from the men's, so that both parts could be thrown open into one (eg Esher (Sy), 1797). Another feature is the loft, usually once for overflow accommodation. This is often the women's room, and is usually closed off by a movable screen. An example can be seen at Guildford (1805). Lofts are mainly found in the south-west. Porches are unexpectedly uncommon, even in the north; they are mainly found in 19th-century meeting houses in the south-east. Ornamentation

is practically non-existent, although the bench ends at Godalming (Sy), 1715, are lightly carved and recall fowls! There is a pen for members' dogs at Brigflatts and stabling at several country meeting houses (eg Brant Broughton (Li), 1701).

Another distinctive feature of Quaker meeting houses is their burial grounds. Traditionally the Quakers have been buried in grounds apart from churchyards or cemeteries, either with no marker or with a plain small headstone with no ornament and usually only the name and date. There are a few exceptions to this, but not many. Sometimes the burial ground is attached to the meeting house, as at Alton, Godalming, Wanstead, or Jordans (where the Penn family are buried). Sometimes it is isolated, like the ground at Lands End, some 10 miles from the nearest meeting house at Marazion, or the remote plot at Lowna in Farndale (NY). But some remote burial grounds may once have been attached to a meeting house no longer in use, or even in existence. Occasionally there is a Quaker section of a nonconformist burial ground, as at Bunhill Fields, London (1685), where lie George Fox and "many thousands of Friends". Some grounds have been converted into public gardens, like the "Quaker acre" at Guildford.

As the membership of the Society has declined or shifted, meeting houses have been sold. Some of these are still recognisable, eg that at Darley in Nidderdale (NY); some are concealed in later rebuilding, and must be traced through records; some have disappeared. Friends' meeting houses are rarely conspicuous. Many early ones were built off the main routes to give them some protection from attacks by the authorities, and many in towns are in back streets. In some cases the burial grounds were created first, as Quakers could not, and would not, be buried in church graveyards.

THE WELSH CHAPEL

It would be hard to exaggerate the part played by the chapel in the life of Wales in the 19th century and well into this. Chapels were the centre of village life and the natural expression of popular taste. There was something flamboyant and defiant about them, as though they were the foci of national feeling in a hostile or at least indifferent world. Inside, the sermon rose to an emotional *hwyl*, and the architecture often made a fitting frame for this. It is emphatic, often over-emphatic, even violent. Betjeman remarks that "the chief characteristics of

Welsh chapels are a disregard of the established rules of proportion, very varied proportion for each building, though not much structural originality, and strong colour schemes". The contrast between chapels in England and in Wales demonstrates the reality of folk art, and reveals the differences between the two peoples, not only in temperament but in their religious and cultural history.

There are far more chapels in Wales and Cornwall than in the rest of Britain. They would dominate the villages by their mere size compared with the rows of small cottages, even if the steep hillsides did not allow them to stand out to a degree sometimes grotesque. This dominance, and their difference from ordinary buildings, is often marked by vertical lines – long narrow upright windows, with strong quoins or bands of raised stone surrounding them. Many are painted in contrasting colours, whites, greys, or yellows for the walls, purple for the woodwork. Even where stone walls are left unpainted, they may be broken up by bands of lighter material. Doors are often grained. Inscriptions are the rule. Designs may be vaguely classical, with a pediment or a suggestion of one, but even these may also have the exaggerated verticals and some unclassical ornament (eg Siloh Independent, Maesteg, 1876 (see **236**)). Yet symmetry is the rule, however unclassical the proportions. Windows can be numerous and their arrangement unusual (eg Zion, Cwmafon). Inside the emphasis is on the pulpit, which is often raised high. Pews and galleries may be simple, but may be garish yellow.

The graveyards are full of headstones made of local rocks. Thus in north Wales the close-set slabs of slate are very distinctive, and carry a rich folk art. There are coloured stones in Monmouthshire, eg Llanvetherine.

The first dissenting chapel in Wales was at Llanvaches (Mo), Congregational, 1638. Another early one is Maes yr Onnen, Glasbury (Ra), Congregational, 1696, which still has the appearance of a farmhouse and its 17th-century furnishings. After the Restoration the influence of the episcopal church began to decline, and nonconformist churches became the norm in Wales. The *Methodist* movement took firm root from the 1730s. The meeting house at Trefecca, near Talgarth (1768), now forms part of a Methodist college and has early relics. The Methodists separated from the established church in 1811, and were called Calvinistic Methodists, later to be known as the Presbyterian Church of Wales. There are a good many early 19th-century churches of the various Methodist branches. The *Baptists*

had a church as early as 1649 (Ilston (Gm)), and in the 19th century built a number of very large chapels. There is a chapel near Llanbedr (Me) (Salem) which has a strong 18th-century atmosphere and is by water, and a delightful one in the Black Mountains, Capel y Ffin (1762). There are several good *Congregational* chapels, like Capel Newydd at Llangian (Cn), 1769, or that at Ruthin (1820). The

236 *A typical Welsh chapel – Maesteg (MG). These often flamboyant buildings once dominated Welsh townscapes.*

Unitarians have a few, of which the interesting one at Rhydowen (1834) is now closed. The octagonal church in Margam (Beulah, 1838) is of architectural interest.

There are some 5,000 chapels in Wales, of which 4,000 were built in the 19th century, and this number is now greatly exceeding the demand. One village in north Wales, with fewer than 500 inhabitants, has ten chapels. Redundancy is therefore facing an increasing number of them, and they are being put to a variety of uses, some highly incongruous.

THE CHURCH IN SCOTLAND

The long period of Celtic Christianity in Scotland is dealt with above (pages 261–4). Compared with England, in Scotland relatively few churches have survived from the later Middle Ages. As in England, the monasteries are ruins, although some, like Melrose, Sweetheart, Jedburgh, or Dunfermline, are still impressive. Of the old cathedrals, the two greatest, Elgin and St Andrews, are ruins, and most of the others are either truncated or drastically altered – Dornoch, Fortrose, Dunkeld, Dunblane. The latter has the nearest to a close in the English sense. Only Glasgow and Kirkwall are still complete and functioning, and they are both important and impressive. In fact they, with Elgin and St Andrews, are major churches in a European context.

The little church of St Rule (Regulus) at St Andrews gives the best impression of a building of the Dark Ages, as does the Irish-inspired Reilig Oran at Iona. Leuchars has a fine Norman apse; Orphir (Or) is a circular church of Crusader inspiration. Urban expansion after the Norman episode led to the building of burgh churches, of which Crail (early 13th century) is the first. The second half of the 15th century saw great activity in the founding of both burgh churches and collegiate churches. A specialised form of the collegiate church

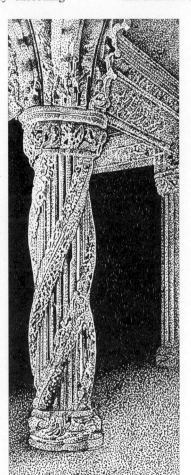

237 *The Apprentice Pillar, Rosslyn (Roslin) Chapel (ML), 15th century: a prominent feature of an incredibly elaborate ornamental scheme, using motifs and symbols from pagan, ancient Hebrew, Celtic, Nordic, Cathar, Templar, and Masonic sources; the chapel was built by William St Clair, 3rd Earl of Orkney.*

is the university church, such as King's College, Aberdeen, and St Salvator's at St Andrews. St Giles' in Edinburgh is a burgh church become collegiate. A few small chapels survive, such as St Margaret's in Edinburgh Castle, the Episcopalian church at Kirkcudbright, and the ornate 15th-century building at Roslin (collegiate 1521, restored 1862 for Episcopalian use) (see **237**). A distinctive feature of Scottish medieval churches, particularly in the east, is a tall narrow square tower surmounted by a squat stone spire (eg Crail (Ff)).

The Reformation (which may be seen as an aspect of the Renaissance) involved a complete break with medieval standards and outlook; the subsequent history of the churches has been greatly clarified by the work of George Hay, on which the following account leans heavily.

Post-Reformation churches were influenced by the liturgical requirements of Reformed worship, and by the ascetic Protestant attitude to art; there was a profound, often violent, reaction against popular Catholic imagery, including stained glass. Lack of money was another factor in the 16th-century situation. The medieval church owned a third to a half of the nation's wealth, and this passed into secular hands over the 16th and 17th centuries, not to the parishes or the Reformed church. Thus the few surviving medieval churches (many had been destroyed or were reused for other purposes) were adapted to Reformed use, and those new churches which were built in the late 16th and during the 17th century were perforce simple.

From the 13th century on, the most common plan (over two-thirds) was an aisleless rectangle, without chancel, transepts, or tower (eg Foulis Easter); many were thatched until the mid 18th century. The earliest post-Reformation churches followed these in design. Most of the larger medieval churches are still in use.

From 1560 (the Reformation) to 1603 (the union of the Crowns) it was usual to adapt medieval churches. The benefice holder was responsible for the chancel (one-third) and the heritors (owners of land in the parish) for the nave (two-thirds). The abbey churches of

Jedburgh, Kelso, and Melrose were adapted, the latter somewhat drastically by the insertion of a new church building. Chancels were often left to decay. The basic needs were facilities for the Reformed sacraments and for preaching, so that all could see, hear, and participate. Long communion tables replaced altars. The smaller kirks were adapted by putting a pulpit against the south wall, a basin bracketed to it, and a table along the long axis. Lofts were built at both ends, and sometimes a transeptal aisle on the north side, often containing a heritor's loft and vault. Thus developed the *T-plan*, typical for new kirks until the 19th century (eg Duddingston, Foulis Wester, Monymusk).

In large churches, the nave (kirk), cross-kirk, and choir were separate units (cf Glasgow cathedral or Aberdeen St Nicholas); 16th-century adaptations used the nave for preaching and daily services, the choir for communion. But the tendency was to bring all functions into one area; thus at Greyfriars, Edinburgh, screens and cross-walls have been progressively removed. In some cases (Kirkwall, Linlithgow, Dunkeld) where the nave was too large, the choir was adapted as the parish kirk; Dornoch survived whole until the nave was burnt in 1570, when the choir and transepts were adapted as a T-plan kirk. Some large churches were divided into two or more kirks; ie the building was shared between parishes (eg Perth, Dundee, Glasgow Cathedral). Aisles were sometimes added to medieval kirks in the 16th and 17th centuries, as family burial places, and often family pews and lofts as well (eg Gray aisle, Kinfauns (Pe), 1598; south aisle at Banff, 1580). New churches of this period were usually rectangular (Kibkell (Pe); Eassie (Ag), 1580s). Burntisland (Fi), 1592, is square, with central plan – an adventurous departure.

The 17th century (1603–1714) was a time of church building, despite the political difficulties; in 1712 lay patronage was reimposed. Presbyterian and Episcopal churches were very similar. Gothic was used in a few (Cawdor (Nn), 1619; Dairsie (Fi), 1621), and Dutch Renaissance in the Tron Kirk, Edinburgh. In form a few were rectangular (Anwoth, 1626; Dirleton, 1615; Dairsie, 1621). Greyfriars is the only large church in medieval form, aisled and arcaded, with western tower (1602). Most were of the typical Scottish T-plan (Anstruther Easter, 1636; Polwarth, 1703); Durisdeer, 1699, is a T with a burial aisle added, to house Nost's great monument of 1711. Fenwick, 1643, and Canongate, c 1690, are cruciform; Lauder, 1673, is a Greek cross.

1714–1800 was an age of secessions, mostly on the patronage issue – 1733, 1761, 1843 and many minor ones, with reunions in 1820, 1840, 1852, 1900, 1929, 1956, etc. The Gothic faded, and the classical (Palladian and Vitruvian) was the norm. Earlier churches are often rectangular (Livingston, 1732; Kilmany, 1786). The import of long timber scantlings from Scandinavia in the second half of the 18th century enabled wider spans and lofts (Farr (Sd), 1774; Inverarity (Ar), 1754; St Andrews, Dundee, 1774). Towers are more common, at one end (Dundee) or on one side (Currie (ML), 1785). Fochabers, 1798, is a good example of the wide classical type, with portico or formal front.

The T-plan is still popular (Golspie, 1738; Kirkmichael, 1787). The *central plan* has several variants – circular with four wings, as at Hamilton, 1732, or circle in T-plan with porch. Octagons are popular (Kelso 1773), as are circles (Kilarrow, Islay, 1769) or ovals (St Andrews, Edinburgh, 1785). *Galleried hall churches* occur, eg St Nicholas West, Aberdeen, 1755, and finally, the double church (English-Gaelic) at Inveraray, 1794.

1800–1843 saw the Industrial Revolution and population increase. The 1824 Act for 42 new churches in the Highlands and Islands gave scope to Telford. After the Greek revival (Aberdeen North, St Giles, Elgin, and much in Glasgow) the Gothic became supreme by the mid 19th century. Some churches early in the century had lateral rectangular plans (Comrie, 1805), as did Telford's (Iona and Ulva, 1824–30; Berriedale, 1826); Dingwall, 1801 and Kilmarnock Laigh Kirk, 1802 are others. The T-plan occurs still, eg at Ettrick, 1824, with original fittings. The central plan can be seen at Lochwinnoch, 1806, St Pauls, Perth, 1807, Glenorchy, 1811, and St Stephens, Edinburgh, 1828. There are a few aisled and arcaded churches, as at Criag (Ag), 1799 and Kincardine in Menteith, 1816, and hall churches at Lochbroom, 1817 (with double communion table), and Ceres (Fi), 1806, with table pews. Greyfriars, Glasgow, 1821, is a Secession hall kirk. Classical detail can be well seen at St George's, Glasgow, 1807, and North Leith, 1816, Greek revival at St Giles, Elgin, 1828, Aberdeen North, 1826, St Vincent, Glasgow, and Gothic spires at Melrose, 1834, and Edinburgh Tolbooth Kirk, 1844.

After the Disruption of 1843 the parish kirks were often reduced in size by partitions, and the new Free Church erected its own buildings; it was strong in the north. Free Churches and other separatist churches are usually simple and chapel-like, but there are a few imposing ones, like Belhaven-Westbourne Church, Glasgow, 1880. The Reunion of 1929 led to the abandonment of some churches, and depopulation also caused parishes to combine. After 1925 maintenance became the responsibility of the congregations, which again meant that many churches could not be kept up. New buildings from 1843 to 1929 were mostly "Gothic" in style, as in England. Since then new Scottish churches have mostly been in contemporary architectural and aesthetic styles, built in current materials and to current building methods (eg St Columba's, Glenrothes, 1960 and St Christopher's, Meikle Road, Glasgow, 1961–2). Some restorations have been carried out recently too, as at Iona.

There are also, as a separate group, the fishermen's mission halls in north-east Scottish ports and in Shetland.

In 1690 bishops in the Church of Scotland were replaced by Presbyterianism. *Episcopalians* were given freedom of worship in 1712, and chapels could then be built by them, though non jurors (ministers refusing the oath of allegiance in 1689) were not free until 1792. They were strong in the north-east. Their chapels are very simple (St Andrews, Glasgow, 1751; Cowgate, Edinburgh). Nonjuring chapels were in private houses or camouflaged.

The early post-1792 chapel of St George, Edinburgh, 1794, is centrally planned, but most were rectangular, as at Peterhead, 1814, or had shallow apses. A few pre-Reformation-built episcopal chapels survive, as at Kirkcudbright. St Mary's Episcopal Cathedral, Edinburgh, is conspicuously Gothic.

The *Roman Catholic* Mass was proscribed in 1560 but still continued, and Catholic families survived all over Scotland, apart from the Gaelic masses. Roman Catholics were persecuted from 1697 to 1745, and were free only in 1793, with full rights in 1829. Two chapels built before 1793 are still in use: Tynet (My), 1755, like a longhouse, and Preshame, three miles away, 1788, a wide rectangular church. After 1793 many priests designed their own churches. St Peter's, Aberdeen, 1804, is Gothic revival; St Mary's, Edinburgh, 1814, is rectangular with shallow apse and Gothic facade, a common type. St Andrew's, Glasgow, 1815, is a large Gothic church; Dumfries Roman Catholic Cathedral, 1814, is in the Greek style; St Thomas, Keith, 1831, is a Greek cross plan, with Italianate facade; Huntly, 1834, is octagonal with sanctuary.

ROMAN CATHOLIC CHURCHES

These deserve separate, if brief, treatment of their own, on account of the history of the Roman Catholic Church in England. The medieval parish churches, cathedrals, and abbeys were taken over by the new established church at the Reformation, and for the most part were simplified in accordance with the new attitudes. A very few have reverted to Roman Catholic uses, of which an interesting one is St Etheldreda's, Ely Place, London, once the chapel of the palace of the bishops of Ely. This was a typical private chapel, on two storeys, like St Stephen's, Westminster, or the Sainte Chapelle in Paris. It was built about 1290 and was bought back by the Roman Catholics in 1874.

A few private house chapels also survived, where the family was influential or innocuous enough to avoid attention from the State; such include Stonor, near Henley, or the Fitzalan chapel at Arundel (Sx) (1380). Arundel, indeed, may be termed a double church in a positive sense. Here the chancel, once collegiate, is separated from the nave by a screen, and has a separate entrance; it is a private Roman Catholic chapel, while the nave is the Anglican parish church. Tichborne (Ha) has an aisle reserved for Roman Catholic worship. Most of these private chapels, such as Petworth, came under Protestant ownership.

So the Roman Catholics had to begin afresh with church building after the Emancipation of 1829. The churches were mostly rather undistinguished architecturally. The larger ones are different from Anglican churches because of the greater elaboration, with chapels, shrines, processional aisles, and other features. A few cathedrals stand out, such as Pugin's at Southwark (1841) and of course the Byzantine Westminster (Bentley 1895–1903, and still unfinished).

The provincial ones, like Birmingham or Leeds, are modest. The vast St Philip Neri at Arundel (Hansom 1869–76) is now a joint cathedral with Brighton. The styles used were those current in the Victorian age, ie adapted Gothic or, in many cases, for reasons of close contact with Rome, Italianate or Baroque. Many of the newly-founded abbeys built large churches, such as Brompton Oratory (Gribble, 1878) and its companion in Birmingham, Farm Street, London, Jesuit (Scoles, 1844–9) with important contents, Farnborough (Ha), another Sainte

Chapelle type, with tombs of Napoleon III and his empress in the crypt and Brangwyn's Stations of the Cross, and St Joseph's, Highgate. Most monastery, seminary, or school chapels are relatively small and modest (eg St John's Seminary, Wonersh). Roman Catholic parish churches vary in interest. Some, like the Italian church in Clerkenwell, London, are distinctive, and a very interesting one, now rebuilt, is Notre-Dame-de-France, Leicester Square (L A Boileau, 1868, in a panorama of 1791, with an iron-ribbed dome). Post-war churches have sometimes been very good, such as St Charles, Glasgow (1960). The current trend is towards round or approximately round churches, such as Liverpool and Clifton Cathedrals and local churches like Alton (Ha) or Guildford (Sy).

OTHER DENOMINATIONS

It is hard to place some of the buildings in this section, as they are strictly neither churches nor chapels. They are in no logical order.

The *Orthodox* churches have a few buildings in London and the larger cities. Part of the Anglican church at Walsingham (Nf) is adapted for Orthodox use.

Genuine chapels are the few founded by the *Moravians*, who set up colonies, with housing, chapel, and schools, in the mid 18th century. There are good examples at Fulneck, near Bradford (1748) and Ockbeck (Db) (1752). There was a Moravian chapel in Fetter Lane, London – a typically simple building, with pulpit in the middle of the east wall. There are a few *Lutheran* churches, such as the small but distinguished Danish Seamen's Church, Stepney (G Hauss and H Richter, 1959). Some redundant Anglican churches have been given over to the Lutherans. The Dutch Church at Austin Friars (*Calvinist*) has had to be rebuilt since the war. The French *Huguenots* have a church in Soho Square, London (where their main colony was in the late 17th century), which was rebuilt in 1893; there is another French Protestant church in Brighton, and the crypt of Canterbury Cathedral has been used for this purpose since the 16th century. The Swiss have a Protestant church in Endell Street, the Swedes off Marylebone Road, and so on. These form cultural and social centres for their people too.

The *Catholic Apostolic* church was founded by Edward Irving in the years from 1826 to 1835. The church was centred on an "apostolic" ministry, and its rituals included elements from Anglican, Orthodox, and Presbyterian traditions. It had several good buildings, of which two are important: that at Albury (Sy), financed by Henry Drummond in his park (Brooks, 1840) owes something to Pugin also, with much ornamental woodwork and stonework, a wide space in the chancel for ritual, and also the chapter-house of the sect; and the great London church of Christ the King, Gordon Square, by Raphael Brandon, 1853, now the University (Anglican) church – a vast Gothic church of cathedral-like proportions. The sect has practically died out, and the church at Albury has not been used since 1950.

The vigour of the *Salvation Army* is of a different order. The Army was founded in 1873 and adopted a quasi-military stance. Its chapels are combined with social centres, and are called citadels. They are usually battlemented and fortress-like, and are of doubtful architectural value. That at Aberdeen (1893–6) has been described as in "debased Balmoral baronial"; it has four storeys, and a five-storey tower. That in Lincoln (1912) is typical, and examples can be found in the poorer districts of most big towns. But much modernisation has lately been carried out in the Army.

The *Temperance Hall* is another product of Victorian religion; there is a splendid example at Kirkby Stephen (Cb).

The smaller sects rarely have notable meeting places, and some are the traditional "tin chapels" of the villages and humbler urban districts. They include the Plymouth Brethren, Elim, the Assemblies of God, the Bible Christians (numerous in Cornwall), various Evangelical and Pentecostal groups, Jehovah's Witnesses, and a host of mission halls and, in the ports, missions to seamen. Ethnic communities too tend to have their own chapels.

The fringe Christian bodies have several striking buildings. The *Christian Scientists* can be found in most towns of any size, with buildings of early 20th-century character. The *Mormons* have an imposing temple at Newchapel (Sy) (1958). There are a few deserted churches of idiosyncratic and defunct sects, like that of the Agapemonites at Stamford Hill, London. *Masonic* halls look like small chapels, but several are in other hands and can only be recognised by their inscribed names. The central Masonic building in Queen Street, London, imposes itself, as do the buildings of the *YMCA*.

345

NON-CHRISTIAN RELIGIONS

No synagogues survive from the medieval settlement of the Jews in England, although it is known that the larger colonies at least, such as Lincoln and York, had them. The Jews were allowed back in the country, having been expelled in 1290, as a result of the mission by the Dutch rabbi Manasseh ben Israel to Cromwell in 1657.

The Jewish synagogue represents in miniature the form of the Temple at Jerusalem, itself an enlarged version of the ancient tabernacle. The faces of the congregation are turned towards Jerusalem. At the east end is the Ark, usually in an alcove or structure, with copies of the Pentateuch for reading from; near it hangs an ever-burning lamp. On a raised platform in the middle is the place of the reader or preacher. Women and men were normally separated by a low partition, but since the last century women have often been seated upstairs in a gallery and the men downstairs. There were once two early post-Cromwellian synagogues in London, but that at Dukes Place, Aldgate (1722, rebuilt 1790) was destroyed in World War II. The survivor, the oldest synagogue in England, is in Bevis Marks; this was the synagogue of the Spanish-Portuguese Jews (Sephardim) and was closely inspired by the Baroque synagogue at Amsterdam. It was built by Joseph Avis, a Quaker, in 1701, and replaced one in Creechurch Lane (1657). Outside London, Portsmouth had a synagogue in 1746, but this was rebuilt on a different site in 1936;

the cemetery is the oldest still in use (1749). The community at Exeter dates from 1728, its synagogue from 1763, and its cemetery from 1757.

The vast majority of synagogues date from the 19th century. They are in all styles except Gothic (eg the Italianate North London Synagogue of 1868). They are rectangular, often square, with a wide vestibule from which a staircase ascends to the women's gallery; in the wall opposite the entrance is a recess with the ark, and in front of it a rostrum. Typical examples are at Leeds (Belgrave Street, 1860), Birmingham (1856), and Manchester (Cheetham Hill Road, 1857). Manchester is a good example of a Jewish district, where there are many synagogues of all complexions; similar districts exist in Leeds (Chapeltown) and London (Stamford Hill, Golders Green, and formerly Whitechapel).

The various forms of Jewry have very similar synagogues, whether they are Orthodox or Independent Orthodox (Sephardim), members of the United Synagogue, formed under an Act of 1870 (Ashkenazim, from northern, central, and eastern Europe), Liberal, or Reformed.

Other religions also have centres here, such as the *Islamic* mosque at Woking (1889). There are over a million Moslems in Britain, with some 300 mosques; a central mosque has been built in Regent's Park, London. There is a Zen "Pagoda of Peace" at Willen, Milton Keynes, and there are many Hindu, Sikh, and Buddhist meeting places. A monumental Hindu temple has just been built at Neasden (Ln). The first Jain temple was built in Leicester in 1986.

The Styles of Architecture

In looking at a building, whether a church, castle, or house, even something quite humble, it is necessary for full understanding to have some grasp of the history of architecture itself. This at least enables one to place a building, or a part of it, into its broad historical setting, even if it needs more knowledge to go into fine detail. What follows makes no claim to be exhaustive. It should be treated merely as an aide-memoire, and is no substitute for the many good books on the subject.

CLASSICAL

Although most Roman buildings in this country are only fragmentary, the influence of Roman architecture, direct or indirect, has been so powerful at several periods since that one must begin there.

Well before the time of the Roman occupation of Britain, their architecture had two main threads: the native, largely Etruscan system of rugged construction based on thick piers between round-arched openings, vaulted roofs, and domes; and the Greek, based on beams supported on columns. The arch and pier construction is well known through monuments like the aqueducts, eg the Pont du Gard. Openings may be square as well as round (usually semicircular). An important Roman innovation was the use of concrete (a mixture of stone and lime), which was easy to make and use anywhere. This was used in domes (as at the Pantheon in Rome, a staggering example by any standard), cross and barrel vaults, eg at Hadrian's villa, and even walls, which could be faced with brick or stone. Walls were generally built of squared stones, as in Hadrian's Wall, sometimes with courses of bricks or tiles, eg in the walls at Silchester or Verulamium. Walls might be plastered and painted (Lullingstone); floors were often of *opus signinum*, a mixture of cement and crushed brick, which could be covered with plain cubes of brick (*tesserae*) or mosaics of coloured cubes. Both floors and walls could be covered with stone or marble, and patterned brickwork was used. Roofs were usually low-pitched wooden frames covered with tiles.

The Greek element consisted of three styles of column: Doric, a fluted shaft with plain rounded capital and no base; Ionic, a fluted shaft, slenderer than the Doric, with base, and capital with curving ornament (volute) based on a ram's horns; and Corinthian, with fluted shaft, base, and capital with ornament modelled on acanthus leaves. To these the Romans added three more: Roman Doric, with base; Tuscan, a variety of Doric, but with plain shaft, and base; and Composite, with fluted shaft, base, and capital combining the motifs of the Ionic and Corinthian (see **238**). Both Greeks and Romans used these styles (orders) in a definite sequence, with Doric or Tuscan on the ground floor, Ionic on the first floor, and Corinthian on the second. So the colonnades of fora or the courtyards of villas (eg Fishbourne) would normally be in Tuscan style. The Romans regularly used the Greek columns in a wholly unGreek way, by applying them as pilasters to their own pier and arch construction, and thus using them as ornament, not as carrying members; this is clearly seen in the Colosseum, and is common everywhere. The general effect of all this is of mass, often heavy and oppressive, and of immense strength, not of lightness and space.

ROMANESQUE

From the end of the Roman Empire in the 5th century until the beginnings of Gothic in the late 12th, the prevailing architecture in western Europe was the Romanesque, based partly on the late Roman and partly on the Byzantine of the Eastern Empire. In Britain the Romanesque took two forms, Anglo-Saxon and Anglo-Norman.

Saxon

The Saxons brought from the forest country of northern Europe the practice of building in wood. Most of their domestic buildings, even great royal palaces like that at Yeavering (Nd), and their early churches, were timber-framed. Walls were often clad or filled in with split logs standing vertically on a sleeper beam; a wall in this construction survives at the church of Greensted (Ex) (see **239**). Stone

347

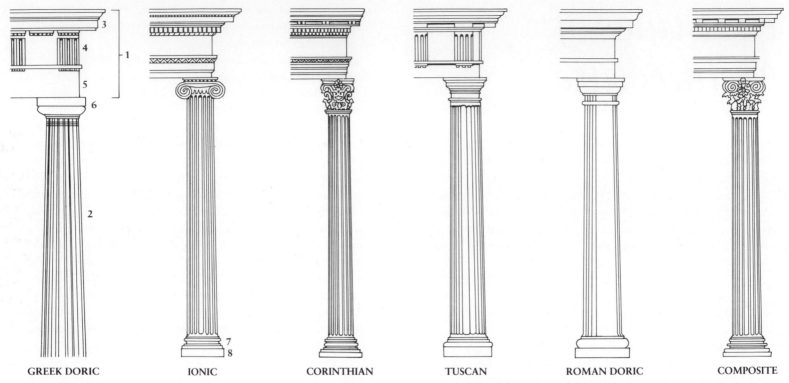

GREEK DORIC   IONIC   CORINTHIAN   TUSCAN   ROMAN DORIC   COMPOSITE

238 *The classical orders of architecture. Numbered details are: 1, entablature; 2, column (fluted); 3, cornice; 4, frieze; 5, architrave; 6, capital; 7, base; 8, plinth.*

churches began to be built by 670; indeed, churches are the only Saxon stone buildings to survive. Although most rural parishes were already well-established in 1066, most of the 400 surviving stone churches with Anglo-Saxon fabric are 11th century.

The main features of the architecture are: fabric of squared rubble or ashlar; short, stumpy piers with square capitals; round arches of one order only; narrow windows with round or triangular heads, and splayed openings to get the maximum light; roofs usually with simple barrel or groined vaults (eg in the mid 7th century crypts at Hexham, Ripon, or Repton); arches may have roll mouldings (eg the chancel arch at Wittering (Nh), late 10th century); through-stone work at doorways; height great in relation to the width (average 1:2); externally, long and short work (alternate upright and horizontal stones in the quoins); quoins sometimes of hewn stone; string courses; pilaster strips (based on wood building), often arranged in panelling; blind arcading in strips, round or triangular; baluster shafts in belfry windows; plinth round the base of the church (reminiscent of a wooden sleeper beam). Splendid examples of towers with these features are at Earls Barton (Nh) (see **240**), second half 10th century, Barton-upon-Humber (Hu) (see **241**), late 10th century, and Barnack (Nh) (see **242**) *c* 1000.

There have been disagreements among scholars on the dating of some of these features, but the work of H M Taylor has shed much light. It is beginning to be apparent that certain features must be late, although no sharp division can be made between an early period (say 650 to 850) and a late (say 850 to 1050). Moreover, dating is partly dependent on the plan and its elements. But early features include barrel vaults, height in relation to width (see **246**), single-splay windows (see **243**). Through-stone work in doorways occurs at all periods, as does the plinth. Long and short work goes back to the early 8th century at least (eg at Escomb (Nd)). Double-splay windows are late (see **244**), as are double windows (see **245**). Rubble may be earlier than ashlar, but this depends on the quality of the stone available.

239 *The nave at Greensted (Ex), c 845, has walls of upright logs.*

240 *The church tower at Earls Barton (Nh) shows many typical features of Anglo-Saxon architecture, such as strip-work on the walls (derived from timber frames), long and short work on the quoins, and narrow doors and windows. 241–6 show other features of Anglo-Saxon style.*

241 *Barton-upon-Humber church (Hu) has a triangular-headed doorway.*

242 *Barnack church (Nh) has a characteristic round-headed doorway.*

Carolingian influence from the mid 9th century should make a distinction possible. One foreign feature unmistakeably late is the Rhenish helm tower roof, occurring at Sompting (Sx) and perhaps once elsewhere also. This is an early 11th-century import (see **247**).

Doubts have arisen recently, however, about the age of this unusual spire. Investigation in 1984 showed that the lower part of the tower is late Saxon, and the upper early Romanesque. Both sections were plastered inside at an early stage, and the wooden framework of the spire runs over the top of the plaster. Radiocarbon dating of

350

243 *Anglo-Saxon single-splay windows.*

245 *Anglo-Saxon double windows.*

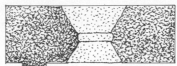

244 *Anglo-Saxon double-splay window.*

the timbers produced dates in the 12th to 14th centuries; further excavation in 1988–9 established that the lower part of the tower was originally part of the Anglo-Saxon nave; the tower was built up to at least the present belfry floor level, at the end of the 11th century. The topmost part was added later, *c* 1310, when the helm spire was rebuilt in its present form. The spire may have been rebuilt in 1762, using old timbers (see *Current Archaeology* 114, 1989). The matter is not yet resolved, but research continues. Sompting, for reference, also has triangular windows, pilasters, hewn stone quoins, and string course. Circular openings may be late Saxon or early Norman, as may also be herringbone masonry. Towers are usually at the west end, but some (eg Barton-on-Humber) are central.

The regional variations in Saxon churches seem to be due to the different kingdoms; eg there is only one long and short

246 *Escomb church (Nd) has a typical high narrow nave and chancel arch.*

quoining in Northumbria (Whittington (Nd)). Hood-mouldings are a Northumbrian type. Jarrow has the only double-splayed windows in Northumbria, which are of ashlar and are found otherwise only in the south-west; elsewhere double-splayed windows are of rubble.

Norman (1060s to 1180s)

The medieval periods overlap. The Norman style had already been adopted in England before the conquest, as in Edward the Confessor's Westminster Abbey and Harold's Waltham Abbey; and although the style persisted to about 1190, the Gothic had already appeared

351

in France in 1140, at St Denis, and in England in abbeys like Roche, 1165, and at Fountains perhaps as early as 1135.

The effect of Norman architecture is one of solidity and permanence. In fact, the impact of the Normans was so massive, and in effect so sudden, that the Romanesque they used should be regarded as an aspect of Norman civilisation and as a mark of the detachment of England

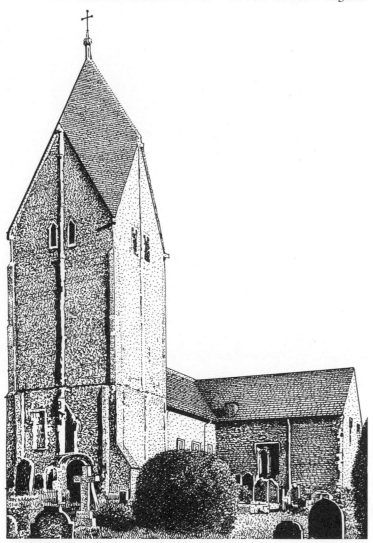

247 *The "Rhenish helm" roof of the tower of Sompting church (Sx). This is a rare type in this country, and is of Saxon origin.*

from the culture of northern Europe, and of its reorientation to and absorption into the world of the ultimate descendants of the Roman Empire. In some ways Anglo-Saxon architecture is not a curtain-raiser but a dead end – cut short, like so much else in England, by the Norman conquest.

As soon as they arrived the Normans began to build castles and churches on a scale absolutely as well as relatively vast, unmistakable symbols of dominance, power, and permanence. The origins of this architecture and of the architects were directly in France. Arcades of round arches are carried on massive piers, cylindrical, polygonal, or compound. Walls are thick (frequently 4ft (1.2m)), and usually made of rubble faced with ashlar. Vaults are barrel or groined quadripartite; larger spans at first had wooden roofs, but at Durham in 1128–33 appeared the first ribbed high vault in Europe, resting on arches concealed under the aisle roofs. There were broad flat buttresses outside, but they had little work to do, with the thick walls. Windows are of one light, flanked by blind arcading. Towers are squat, often with pyramidal roofs (eg Southwell). Two phases can be distinguished: the early, in the 11th century, with simple mouldings and crocket foliage on the capitals, which went with a continental-type apse or chevet east end; the second phase, from 1100, was more ornate, with rich decoration, eg patterns of chevrons (zig-zag), beakhead, cable, billet, nailhead, etc (see **248**). Doorways had lavish carving, often recessed in three orders, and with carved tympanum (eg Malmesbury). Capitals were carved, there was blind arcading on the walls, and rows of heads and animals on the corbels and gables outside (eg Kilpeck (He)). This went with the English square east end, double transepts, and Lady Chapels. Roofs were timber at first, steeply pitched, with flat ceilings beneath. Later, stone barrel or tunnel vaulting was used, developing into groined vaults. The oldest surviving roof of the nave of a parish church in the country is that of Kempley (Gl), which is Romanesque, perhaps early 12th century, although partly altered in the 17th. Rows of heads or grotesques are common at the tops of walls, on corbels supporting the roof. Triforia and clerestories appear in the larger churches. The culmination of the Norman style in England is Durham Cathedral, which illustrates most of its features, though its vaulting looks forward too.

Other buildings beside churches were built of stone in this period – castles, monasteries, and even quite small houses (eg those at Lincoln) – and the same principles were followed.

248 *Romsey Abbey (Ha) offers a fine example of Norman architecture. The north transept, on the right, dates from 1120–40, as does the round pillar in the nave (left); the next four bays of the nave are from 1150–80. The different decorative schemes can be clearly seen.*

GOTHIC

The achievement of the later 12th and 13th centuries was to transform this heavy and sometimes plodding Romanesque into a marvel of lightness and flexibility. The first moves were made in France, but the English contribution was not negligible. Emphasis was on the vertical, and the general tendency was towards thinner walls and columns (with the development of an ingenious apparatus for taking the thrust), and a corresponding increase in the size of windows, and thus more light (see **249**). Clear stages can be distinguished.

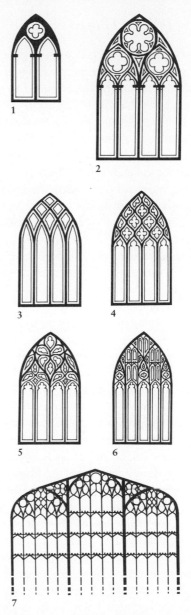

249 *Medieval window tracery: 1, plate tracery (earliest Gothic), 1175–c 1250; 2, geometrical (bar) tracery (Early English), c 1180–1300; 3, intersecting tracery, c 1300; 4, reticulated tracery (Decorated), c 1300–c 1350; 5, curvilinear tracery (Decorated); 6, early Perpendicular, c 1450–c 1580; 7, panel tracery (Perpendicular) c 1450–c 1580.*

Early English (1180s to 1280s)

This is sharply distinguished from the Norman style by the pointed arch. There has been much controversy on the origin of this; it could have been suggested by the construction of vaults, by the intersection of round arches in arcades (like those at St Bartholomew's, London), or it could have been imported from the Middle East during the Crusades. A combination of these is also possible. The pointed arch allowed the construction of rectangular vaults which were stable, thus giving extra support for the high vault. Ribs concentrated the thrust of the vaults. Flying buttresses (oversailing the aisles) or buttresses concealed in the aisle roofs took the thrust of the high vault over the aisles to vertical wall buttresses, and along them to the ground. Directing the thrust along certain lines at points spread along the walls, instead of allowing it to be generalised in the walls, enabled the spaces between the thrust lines to be opened out as windows. The use of stained glass then (see page 506) became feasible. The so-called Oxford corner came in in the early 13th century; this was a buttress set diagonally on the corner, instead of two buttresses continuing the two walls at the corner.

The columns supporting the pointed arcades were made of clustered shafts, which may be detached – Purbeck marble was a favourite material for some of these, for symbolic reasons, in the 13th century; the shafts were later merged with the main column. Capitals were carved with stylised foliage; mouldings on the edges of arches etc were bold, and were sometimes emphasised by dog-tooth decoration. (The value of mouldings is now being recognised for the light they can throw on dating, art history, designers and their movements, etc.) Walls may be covered with blind arcading or diaper patterns. Windows usually have pairs of lights, or three, under a single dripstone. There are windows of seven-light lancets at Ockham (Sy) and Blakeney (Nf). At first the lights were separate all the way up, but later the spandrels at the top were opened out to form plate tracery which in turn developed into geometrical bar tracery. Roofs are high-pitched, and towers are often finished off with spires, sometimes with broaches at the base (pyramidal structures to link the square base with an eg octagonal spire). Many of these features occur also in castles and houses, but of course in castles the problems were different, as large windows were not aimed at.

Decorated (1290s to 1370s)

This not only has more and wider-spread decoration, but new effects of light and shade, surface detail, and space. Arcades are wider, and columns taller and more slender, with all shafts engaged. Vaults have extra ribs, some structural (tiercerons), others purely ornamental (liernes), with carved bosses at the intersections. Walls are thinner and windows larger. The tracery now flows (as bars, not plates) in curving patterns, some based on ogee curves, some quite free, or in the shape of leaves etc. Towers have parapets and pinnacles, and spires crockets. Walls are freely decorated, both inside and out, with blind ogee tracery, statues (often in niches), and a profusion of naturalistic carving (eg the Leaves of Southwell); ball-flower is a common motif. Lichfield is a good general example.

Perpendicular (1380s to 1550s)

This is a purely English thing, and is a uniquely English contribution to European culture, like the 18th-century landscaped parks. It seems to have been the creation of a master mason of Norwich, William Ramsey, about 1330, but did not become current until later in the century.

On the Continent the Decorated (Flamboyant) continued until the Renaissance. Ruskin did not like the Perpendicular, but its skilful blending of the vertical and horizontal reflects an important aspect of English art (see above, page 275). It began in the late 14th century, eg at Gloucester and in the work of Henry Yevele at Westminster and Canterbury. The windows are wide and the arch at their tops is flattened; the tracery goes right to the top in straight (perpendicular) lines, cut by transverse bars. The ultimate achievement on this line is St Mary Redcliffe at Bristol, which is a cage of glass, the walls between the windows being insignificant. Pier shafts merge into moulded columns. Vault ribs multiply, and finally fan vaulting appears (eg at Gloucester (see **250**) and at Sherborne). Buttresses are very important, to counter the greater space of windows, and can have pinnacles. Roofs are lower-pitched, covered with lead more often than tiles, and can have low parapets, panelled or pierced. Towers can be ornate, and masterpieces of grace and balance occur in some regions (like Somerset). Mouldings are shallow, often in panelling or bands

251 *Fan vaulting – Henry VII's chapel, Westminster Abbey; the apogee of the style (1503–12).*

the transverse arches and not from the side walls (eg at Henry VII's chapel at Westminster (see **251**)). The new Renaissance ideas are represented by superficial ornament of Italianate type. Arches and window heads are generally still more flattened.

POST-MEDIEVAL

Up to now the main area for the study of architectural styles has been churches (where after all the problems were mainly worked out); castles and the few remaining medieval stone domestic buildings of course incorporate the same principles and styles, but on a much reduced scale. With the Renaissance and the growing prosperity of the middle classes during the 16th century, the position is gradually reversed, and we have to look primarily at domestic buildings, large and small, to see the development of architecture. Churches are now only one of the forms of building, although, owing to their prominence in the landscape or townscape, and their specialised nature, they are still conspicuous. A church may be described as a very stylised architectural expression of a highly specialised function, but the post-Reformation church had less or no need for many features essential to the medieval. Some Georgian churches

250 *Fan vaulting – Gloucester Cathedral (Abbey) cloisters; the earliest form of this style 1381–1412.*

round arches; ornament is also flat, tablet flowers and heraldic motifs being common. Roofs, when of timber, can be very complicated, with hammer-beam construction, carved angels, etc (eg March).

The Perpendicular, and with it Gothic architecture in England, reached its final phase under the earlier Tudors (1485–1550s). Fan vaulting now has pendants, where the main vault springs from

355

are almost domestic buildings outside, and halls inside; Victorian Gothic ones are positively not so, and many of the latter seem indeed to have missed the point. Traditionalism taken as far as the Victorians did can become meaningless.

Renaissance

Italy in the 15th century had rediscovered the classical world, and this had a revolutionary impact on literature, art, and architecture, as well as on science and philosophy. France took it in through Francis I's campaigns in Italy in the early 16th century, and the new learning reached England soon after through both France and the Low Countries. Apart from the superficial elements in Tudor architecture and monumental sculpture, the full impact was not felt in architecture until the 1550s.

Elizabethan (1558–1603)

In Italy the new ideas went back to the principles laid down by the Roman architect Vitruvius, and were developed by a line of geniuses including Bramante and Michelangelo and ending with Palladio. These men sought to express certain principles of mathematical and philosophical proportion. The result was a highly technical and self-conscious approach, which was too formal for English tastes. In England the new ideas were applied to, or blended with, the Tudor Perpendicular, and the ideal proportions were not always adhered to. This was also the period of the Great Rebuilding (see pages 211–12), and although the great houses might have tried to achieve a European standard (with varying success), the smaller houses inevitably reached a very English homely compromise.

The result was a composite style deriving from the native Tudor, with straight-headed windows mullioned and transomed, often with dripstones (hood-moulds), bay windows, triangular gables, the early 16th-century chateau style of France (Chambord etc), with the triumphal arch motif at doorways, three superimposed orders, and a triangular pediment (the orders were not always correctly applied), and decoration from the Low Countries, such as strapwork and Dutch gables (pattern books were used for these, a new medium of ideas). Great houses like Wollaton, Longleat, or Montacute give an idea of this phase.

Jacobean (1603–25)

The great houses of this period continue the Elizabethan style, but are less exuberant and less bizarre (eg Hatfield, Blickling, Temple Newsam). Facades are now more often of brick, though stone is still used. Windows are smaller, and wall areas larger. Windows are often reduced to four lights, and can have segmental or triangular pediments. Skylines are less fussy. Grand staircases are a feature, derived from Italian and Spanish models, with balusters and newel posts, carved and surmounted by figures.

Early Stuart or First Palladian (1625–50)

We are now entering an age dominated by individual architects. The age of Charles I is that of Inigo Jones (1573–1652), the first English architect in the modern sense. Jones studied the work of Palladio in Italy, and put his ideas into practice in England at a time when houses were still being built in the native hotch-potch. It was a revolution, the beginning of a new age, and the end of the Middle Ages in architecture. Jones's earliest works, the Queen's House at Greenwich (1616) and the Banqueting Hall in Whitehall (1619), must have stood out as something strange, fresh, and momentous. The effect was that of neatness and simplicity. The lines are horizontal, the roof unbroken by gables and turrets, but having instead a continuous balustraded cornice. The windows are smaller, narrower, mathematically proportioned, and sized according to the importance of the floor. Ornament is sparse, and the elevation symmetrical. The main rooms are on the first floor (*piano nobile*), and the ground floor is finished with rustication. There may be a pillared feature in the centre. Inside, the rooms are compact and again carefully proportioned, arranged round a central hall which may be a cube or double cube. The overall plan is square or rectangular. The interior decoration is lavish, with panels and high relief (often depicting fruit or flowers); fireplaces are prominent, and may be "architectural" with columns and broken pediments. All this contrasts with the plain exterior, whose main ornaments are the alternate triangular and segmental pediments over the windows and the frieze of masks and swags under the cornice.

Jones also introduced ideas of town planning, eg his piazza at Covent Garden. His town houses were of a type followed throughout the

Georgian period – narrow (necessarily) houses of brick with stone dressings, with plain windows again reflecting the social status of the floor, and straight roof with cornice.

Later Stuart (1650–1700)

This is the age of Wren (1632–1723). Wren continued the classical architecture of Jones, but his public buildings show French influence also, and his private houses Dutch ones. This mixture was a kind of Baroque, but with a strongly English flavour. He introduced the use of Portland stone to London. Wren's great chance came with the Great Fire of London in 1666, after which he had to rebuild St Paul's and over 50 City churches. These show enormous originality and variety. They are basically preaching boxes, usually plain and simple (within the limits of the style), but their steeples, no two alike, show every architectural device and motif; they have been described as Gothic spires in classical forms. Wren used the naturalistic wood-carving of Grinling Gibbons, the wrought-iron work of Tijou, the mural painting of Thornhill, and the sculpture of Colley Cibber.

The town houses of this period, which includes the "Queen Anne", show strong Dutch influence. Windows are of sash type; doorways have pediments or small canopies, supported by columns or pilasters. Roofs are steep and hipped; above the cornice is often an attic. Stone dressings are still used, now often with long and short work round the windows. The main rooms are not always on the first floor. Interiors are panelled.

EARLY MODERN AND MODERN

Georgian

This is a period with a succession of styles, all emphasising an aspect of the classical tradition.

BAROQUE (1690S–1720S)

Wren's last building, Greenwich Hospital, pushed English architecture over into the full Baroque, although still with an English flavour.

Baroque may be described as a classical architecture emotionalised. It sought its effects by over-emphasising. Its columns were doubled or twisted, its decoration and sculpture overripe and monumental. It distorted the formal proportions, and used curves where earlier architects would have used straight lines. Its houses were extended or strung out in rows of receding blocks, with courtyards, and had turrets and domes. Its churches recalled the Gothic, but in classical idiom. Its exponents were a group of brilliant men, Hawksmoor (All Souls, Oxford; Christchurch, Spitalfields), Vanbrugh (Blenheim; Castle Howard), and Gibbs (St Mary-le-Strand) being the greatest.

PALLADIANISM (1720–60)

The Baroque was succeeded by a reversion to Palladianism, and a new admiration for Inigo Jones. The leaders were Paine (Kedleston), Leoni (Clandon), and Kent (Horse Guards; Holkham). Some houses followed the model of the Italian Palladian villas (Chiswick; Mereworth), but some, like Holkham, had a central block with wings. The architecture was on the whole dull, and the interiors could be tasteless, with heavy mouldings, fireplaces, and doorways, and much plasterwork. Panelling was now pine instead of oak, and wall-hangings could be silk or damask, although Chinese wallpaper was coming in. Gardens and grounds were moving from the formal French styles to the free English landscaping.

The style was watered down in the second half of the century, as in Chambers' Somerset House, which has French elements. But a new aspect appeared, in the work of Adam (1760–1800). Robert Adam (1728–92), the most important of the Adam brothers, still worked in a broadly Italian style, but effected a revolution in the interiors. He created a new style here, which spread throughout the country to houses of all kinds. Adam revived the Roman technique of stucco, and used this for all kinds of ornament and for whole schemes like ceilings. His effects are delicate and not heavy. He liked curves (an unPalladian thing), and used alcoves and apses, often with screens of columns (as in the library at Kenwood). Marks of this style are marble or pine fireplaces, doorways with webbed fanlights, tall windows with narrow glazing bars and three panes in a width, and pilasters on the wall of a terrace or crescent, binding the row together (eg John Wood's unified Royal Crescent at Bath). The Royal Society of Arts in London gives a good idea of the Adam style.

Another influence at this period was Chinoiserie, a fanciful adaptation of Chinese, or supposed Chinese, motifs to furniture (Chippendale), or interior decoration (Claydon; the Pavilion at Brighton; Kew Pagoda).

Regency (1800–37)

Classicism continued until the accession of Victoria. The Adam spirit of lightness was still there, but given a Greek instead of a Roman turn. Stucco was used widely outside as well as in. Coade stone ornament is found on doorways, windows, etc (Bedford Square). Windows were still tall and narrow, with plain surrounds. Bays were popular, and wrought iron was used freely for balconies and canopies, and for railings and other details. Doorways could be round-headed. Roofs were low-pitched, and could have projecting eaves. Decoration had Greek overtones, like the key pattern. Nash's Regent's Park terraces are masterpieces of this style. A Romantic streak also appeared, in such things as "cottages ornés"; exotic styles were now possible.

Victorian (1837–1900)

Architecture now scattered in all directions. The dominant note of this period was revivalism, beginning with Greek (British Museum; Birmingham Town Hall; St George's Hall, Liverpool). This was followed by a neo-Renaissance (Reform Club), and finally by the Gothic, a fashion which became universal, in season and out; it grew out of nostalgia for the medieval village. It was not only applied to churches, but to stations, town halls, and any kind of building (Law Courts; St Pancras; Keble College, Oxford). The scale of buildings increased.

An important aspect of Victorian architecture was its functional buildings, like warehouses, mills, and bridges. Engineering was a factor here, and some of the finest achievements of the age are in this area (eg the work of Telford and Brunel). Cast iron was now applied to building – frames for mills etc – and glass could now be used on a large scale (Crystal Palace). Private houses were at first eclectic in style, but towards the end of the century a notable improvement took place under the civilising influence of thinkers like William Morris and architects like Philip Webb (The Red House, 1859). Webb led the way to Voysey, Shaw, and Lutyens.

Terrace housing was still standard for the workers, and architecturally there is not much to be said for it. Webb's principles eventually found their way into the housing in the garden cities and new suburbs, but terraces persisted.

20th Century

The real break with the past which has taken place in the last 60 or 70 years is not primarily due to changes in taste or preference for a different style, but to changed materials and methods of construction. The use of steel, concrete, glass, and latterly a wide variety of materials has determined the form of buildings. The result is therefore hardly a style, but the inevitable outcome of a process. Mass production and prefabrication are part of this picture. Theories of town planning have led to high-rise blocks as well as to the open layout of new town centres and residential areas. The function of the architect has changed with the new situation, and he cannot carry all the blame for what has happened.

SCOTTISH ARCHITECTURAL STYLES

Scotland has a very different architectural history from England. In the 12th and 13th centuries Scotland formed one cultural province with England, and hence has buildings in the Norman and Early English styles. But from the 14th century the paths diverged, and the main influences in Scotland were those of France and the Low Countries. Churches as well as castles now had battlements, step gables, pack-saddle roofs, and heavy ribbed vaults. In the 15th century, instead of the Perpendicular, which Scotland almost entirely missed, the Decorated was developed, as in France, into a kind of Flamboyant. There can indeed be nothing more flamboyant than Roslin (1446)! Other good examples are Lincluden chancel (1409–24) and much of Melrose, including the wonderful and profuse carving. The Renaissance touched Scotland in all kinds of details and in some major buildings, including castles and houses. The Renaissance wing at Caerlaverock has strong French overtones (see **252**).

But the most distinctively Scottish achievement, and the only thing which can be called a national style, is the Scottish baronial. This is the style of castle building adopted by the now more prosperous and better-educated castle owners of the later 16th and earlier 17th century. Its main features are the turrets with gabletted or pointed roofs, windows corbelled out, "corbie (crow)-stepped" gables, pinnacles, corbelled cornices, dormers in the steep roofs (often highly decorated with classical motifs), and spouts often ornamental and not functional. The lower part of the building was left bare, and the whole weight of the fanciful treatment was lavished on the upper parts (eg Amisfield Tower (Df)). Most of the best examples are in the eastern counties from Aberdeenshire to Angus, like Craigevar (see **253**) and Glamis. The tower houses are also very Scots, simple square towers, usually plain, with the living rooms on the first and upper floors, and the ground floor a vaulted store or stable. They are strictly functional, being designed for the border raiding conditions of the 15th to the 17th centuries, and so spill over into England.

Town houses are usually plain and simple, but with gables and some of the features of larger houses; there are also some local traits like the chimney-gables of Haddington.

Scotland missed many of the new movements which took England by storm in the 17th and earlier 18th centuries, from Inigo Jones on; but with Adam she came into line, and there are good examples of all styles thereafter. Adam shows in great houses like Mellerstain or Pollok. The Greek revival is strong in Glasgow, which later became one of the great centres of the various Victorian styles. At the turn of the

252 *Renaissance block, Caerlaverock Castle (Df). This 16th-century wing makes a civilised contrast to the forbidding masses of the medieval castle.*

253 *The Scottish Baronial style, Craigievar (Ab). This 16th- and 17th-century style is an exuberant and "romantic" concentration of medieval architectural features.*

20th century Glasgow shows the finest collection of Art Nouveau buildings in Britain, under the influence of Charles Rennie Mackintosh (eg the School of Art).

Finally, a distinctively Scottish style, if humbler, is that of the small single-storey house with dormers, often double-fronted, of the 19th and early 20th century. It is in fact this as much as anything else which tells one when the border has been crossed.

WALES

The most characteristic Welsh contribution to British architecture is the nonconformist chapel of the late 18th and 19th centuries. These buildings are naive and often grotesque, and are the product of local builders, using illustrated catalogues, not of architects. They are local and vary with their districts. In some the windows are emphasised, in others the emphasis is on the contrasting colours of brick or stone. (For more about chapels see pages 340–2.)

ARCHITECTURAL TIME-LAG

This is allied to cultural lag, but has social and economic aspects also. The dates given above for the architectural periods are roughly right only for the Lowland Zone of Britain. But styles, particularly in vernacular buildings (and in furniture and other objects) tended to continue in fashion in the Highland Zone after they had gone out of fashion in the lowlands. This lag can be as much as a century. Thus, farmhouses in Yorkshire which would be quite at home in the early 17th century, if not the 16th, were still being built well into the 18th, with prominent gabled porches and mullioned windows with dripstones. No doubt such houses, as well as satisfying their occupants aesthetically, also suited their way of life and fitted in with their habits of farming and feeding.

This lag in fact occurs at all periods in the Highland Zone; an early example is the survival of late Bronze Age traits into the Iron Age, no doubt for the same kind of reasons.

There are examples in greater buildings also, not only in the north. One can in fact suspect that some are due to purely personal taste – some people prefer to be surrounded by familiar, even "old-fashioned", things. Thus, Abbot's Hospital at Guildford, built in 1623 and with one of the finest brick gatehouses in the country, is surprisingly reminiscent of buildings of over a century before, eg the gatehouse of Trinity College, Cambridge. It seems to be a conscious throwback. Some apparent examples of this are more doubtful, and may be coincidences. Thus, in the tower at Fountains Abbey the great Perpendicular windows have tall pointed arches, quite unlike the flattened arches of normal windows of their time (early 16th century). They recall, disconcertingly, the pointed arcade in the nave, which dates perhaps from 1135, except that the latter arches have flattened sides. The pointed Tudor windows in the retrochoir at Peterborough are even more Early English-looking. Dating a building needs to be approached with caution!

Castles and Military Works

CASTLES

Castles are a very conspicuous feature of Britain, in both town and country, and directly reflect our history and the history of warfare. We are not here concerned with prehistoric hillforts, or Roman forts or walled towns, except in so far as they were used by later peoples. Again, in the Highland Zone, small stone "forts", such as duns and artificial timber and brushwood islands in lakes or swamps ("crannogs"), continued to be inhabited or used into the Middle Ages, and in some cases even to the 17th century. And some Iron Age hillforts were reoccupied after the Romans left; a well-known example is South Cadbury in Somerset, where buildings and remains of the late 5th and early 6th centuries indicated use by a cavalry commander of Arthurian type. The site was later, in the early 11th century, a small Saxon town. Promontory forts on the Welsh and Cornish coasts and inland strongholds in Wales (like Degannwy), of primitive types, were also used in post-Roman times, and pottery and other artefact from the Mediterranean area have been found in them.

But castles proper are a Lowland Zone phenomenon, spreading from there to other parts. The first fortress worth the name seems to have been that at Athelney (So), built by Alfred in 878 in his campaign against the Danes. This was merely an enclosure inside an earth bank, probably palisaded. As the next stage in the war, Alfred and his son, Edward the Elder, built a series of fortified towns. These are the Burghal Hidage forts (see pages 159–61), planted round the borders of Wessex, on the coasts, and on the rivers used by the Vikings. These were followed by another series for the defence of Mercia and the frontier of the Danelaw. They had a variety of defences: some merely had earth banks, with palisades; at some the banks were faced with stone (Cricklade, Lydford, Wareham); some used repaired Roman walls (London, Colchester); some had stone walls (Towcester).

But these Saxon *burhs* were fortified towns rather than genuine castles, owing to the Saxon system of communal defence by the local people. This lack of real castles was going to be bad for the Saxons when the Normans came.

The origin of private castles is in fact not easy to pin down. They appeared in the Rhineland and Flanders in the 9th and early 10th century, and in France by 862. The Normans were building stone towers about 920, and the Counts of Anjou after 975. Earth mottes in the Low Countries appeared when dwelling mounds (often merely to keep the farmhouse out of wet ground) were raised for greater safety. (In Ireland the Normans did the same to native raths.) The Danes who, in their earlier invasions of England in the late 9th century, had had no sense of fortress strategy, had acquired some by AD 1000. In Denmark itself the invasion fleets camped in great circular embanked forts, like Firkat or Trelleborg, containing wooden boat-shaped houses for each ship's crew. The low-lying Iron Age fort at Warham St Mary (Nf) is reminiscent of these, and may have been adapted or used by the Danes. They certainly built earthworks at the siege of London in 1016. There is some evidence for defended Saxon houses (see below).

Castles were important in Normandy from 1035, against troubles on the southern borders, and from 1044 there were castles in Maine against a northern push by Anjou, each commanded by a Vicomte appointed by the Count. By 1061 castles were so plentiful in Normandy that they had to be controlled by licence. Edward the Confessor was brought up at the Norman court, and some Normans came back with him in 1042; some Sussex towns were given to the Abbey of Fécamp, and his Norman brother-in-law Rolf became Earl of Hereford. By 1051 castles of Norman type had been built in Herefordshire, but it is not easy to see now what work in them is pre-conquest. The ringwork (circular banked enclosure) at Dover was until recently thought to be Harold's, but has now been shown to be late 12th century, although there is a bank and ditch which could go back to the conquest years. But in general no certain pre-conquest castle can be identified in England. Any such seem to have been built by Normans or under direct Norman influence, and the castle in England before 1066 is not an English thing. In fact, a contemporary historian, Ordericus Vitalis, blamed the defeat of the English on the fact that castles had not been adopted by them. But the evidence is not firm enough to be dogmatic; thus, at Sulgrave (Nh) the late Saxon timber hall was surrounded by a bank and ditch, and this was succeeded by a Norman ringwork; and at Goltho (Li) a motte inside a ringwork which may date from as early as *c* AD 1000 was built over the site of the earlier Saxon manor house, at a date still undecided.

The first Norman castles, which were simple bases for attack and defence in the actual years of the conquest, were *ringworks*. These were banks of earth with outside ditch, usually with V-shaped section, enclosing the necessary buildings, the hall, well, kitchen, sleeping quarters, stables, smithy, armoury, and perhaps a chapel. This enclosure, the *bailey*, could be round, oval, or triangular, depending on the arrangement of the buildings and the lie of the ground. William's campaign in 1066–67 involved the building of a few initial forts, in places like Pevensey, Hastings, Dover, Canterbury, Wallingford, Berkhampstead, and London. Traces of some of these, as at Dover, remain. Then from 1067–70, holding castles were laid down, mostly by William's deputies like Odo and FitzOsbern, in the areas under their control, such as the lower Severn (Berkeley, Monmouth, Chepstow) and in Hampshire and Kent, where ringworks are plentiful. William also built castles round the edges of his new territories: Exeter, 1067; to contain the north, Nottingham, Warwick, York, Lincoln, Huntingdon, Cambridge, 1068; and, in 1069, Chester, Stafford, and

Worcester. By 1071 there were castles in most parts of England, usually on hills overlooking towns. Sometimes whole quarters of the Saxon towns were cleared to make way for them, as at York, Lincoln, Norwich, and Oxford. By 1087 there was a fairly even spread south of the Chester–Lincoln line, and a few from Lincoln to Newcastle. The Welsh border was thick with them, and there were a lot on the east and south-east coasts.

Quite early on, probably by 1070, the simple ringwork was found to need a watch tower to make it more effective. This was raised on a

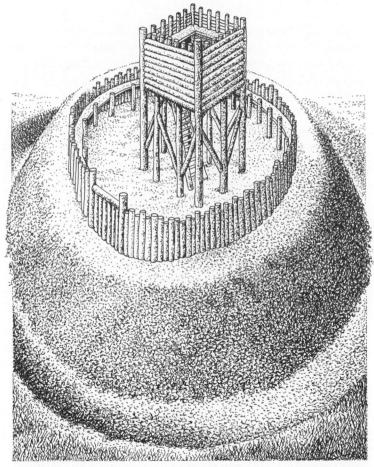

254 *The Bayeux Tapestry (finished by 1077) gives a vivid picture of Norman troops (or impressed men) throwing up a motte at Hastings during the invasion of 1066. This motte is surmounted by a wooden building, a watch-tower or small stronghold.*

255 *The early Norman motte at Abinger (Sy), excavated in 1949, was the first to confirm the picture given by the Bayeux Tapestry (see 254). This excavation revealed the wooden tower inside a fence, later built in stone as shell keeps.*

mound, or *motte*, inside the bailey, and often to one side of it. The motte top had its own fence and gate, and was reached by a bridge or a gangway up the slope. The Bayeaux tapestry (finished by 1077) shows such a motte, with its wooden tower and its own separate ditch (a frequent feature) (see **254**). In spite of this and other evidence, it was not until a motte was excavated in 1949 by Brian Hope-Taylor, at Abinger (Sy), that the accuracy of the picture was fully appreciated. The Abinger motte had all the classical features – ditch, square wooden tower, and fence of strong posts with struts to anchor it (see **255**).

Mottes are usually round, but can be oval or angular, high or low. High and very impressive examples are those at York, Thetford, and Tonbridge. Many of the mottes on the Welsh borders are little more than platforms. The tops can be flat or dished. Baileys can be circular, oval, triangular, quadrilateral, lobed, polygonal, or subdivided. The motte can be central to the bailey, with its own ditch, inside but close to the bank, astride the bank (as at Littledean (Gl)), or outside the bank.

While all mottes are not Norman (they went on being built for some centuries), their distribution does broadly reflect the Norman campaigns. Thus, the greatest numbers are on the Welsh borders and in south-west Wales (where storming and rebuilding were frequent). There is a fair sprinkling up the centre of England and north of London. They extend into southern Scotland (the Mote of Urr (Kb) is a particularly fine example), and there are a few in eastern Scotland.

In Scotland, mottes have a different distribution from castles, and are absent from the Lothians. Ringworks are the normal early castle in south-east Scotland, the Paisley region, and eg Rothesay; this may reflect a local preference. Some mottes in this area are square, and some are scarped from natural features. Some ringworks were built to protect a besieging force, like Corfe.

There are a few aberrant forms of mottes, such as the ring motte, which is a bank with outside ditch (sometimes wet), with no gap in it, enclosing a flat circular space (eg The Crump, Berden (Ex)); a recently discovered type shows from the air only as a system of ditches, a circular one with an enclosure attached – any banks must have been very low.

During the 1070s the wooden towers and other buildings in the more important and permanent castles began to be replaced on stone footings or completely in stone. Where the tower on the motte was so replaced, the result was a *shell keep* (see **256**). Examples are Cardiff (1081), and Carisbrooke, Durham, Kilpeck (He), and Lincoln (1120s–30s); the spectacular four-lobed one at York, Clifford's Tower (see **257**, **258**, and **259**) is late 12th century.

256 *Shell keep – Framlingham (Su), late 12th century. The shell keep was a replacement in stone of the wooden fence on the earliest mottes.*

257 *A shell keep on a motte – Clifford's Tower, York, 1245–59.*

But the motte was sometimes abandoned and a separate tower built to replace it, the *keep*. Saxon gentry had lived in halls, with flanking rooms for sleeping, cooking, etc, and this continued after the conquest. The stone keep was only a manor house on its end, with guardrooms, storerooms, etc on the ground floor, strongroom and prison below, hall for business, justice, great occasions etc on the first floor, and the lord's private quarters above. Similarly, a tower block of flats today is really

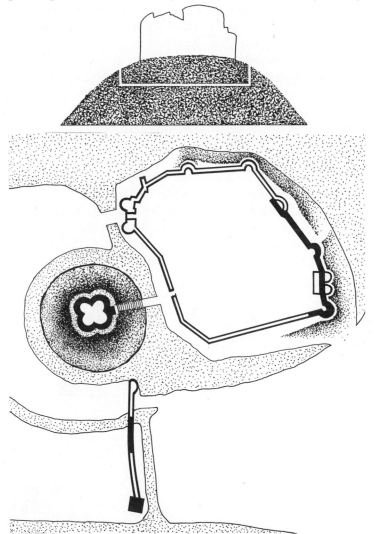

258–9 *Clifford's Tower, York: 258 section; 259 plan in relation to outer bailey.*

a street set on end. The gates of keep and bailey might be in stone before the rampart itself. They were protected by towers, galleries, movable doors, bridges, or by outworks (*barbicans*).

Major quarries for building stone were owned by the king or by a monastery; centres were Barnack, Maidstone, and Quarr. Many castles in southern England were built of Caen stone from Normandy, as water transport was cheaper than land. The stones were usually about a foot cube, split or sawn. Walls were usually ashlar (shaped stone) with rubble core. Sand, lime, iron, and lead were dug, burnt, or worked as near the site as possible; materials such as Roman bricks were reused if handy. Lead piping was used, and glass by the 12th century. The average rate of building a tower was 10–12ft (3–3.6m) a season. Half the cost of a castle went into materials (of which half was carriage), half into finishing and erecting.

The Normans built their main permanent castles between the 1070s and 1138 – London, 1078, Colchester, 1083, both based on the idea of a Carolingian palace; Rochester 1087, Corfe, Ludlow, Richmond, Canterbury, 1089–97. Rufus extended Norman influence into the north of England, Scotland and Wales, with castles at Carlisle, 1092, Edinburgh, 1093 (rebuilt 1175), Cardiff, Carmarthen, Cardigan, 1093–94, Rhuddlan, 1075. Many castles were of course altered, improved, or enlarged through the centuries, and the early work is sometimes not easy to sort out from the later. It has been suggested (by Eric Talbot in 1974) that several small thick-walled towers in northern Scotland, like Cubbie Roo's Castle on Wyre (Or), may have Scandinavian origins.

The great square keeps of these castles were larger in area than height (see **260**). Henry I went in for tall towers, and either built new ones or raised old ones. Examples are Corfe (early 12th century, to supplement Wareham), Gloucester, 1108–9, Portchester (where the heightening can be clearly seen above the old pilasters, and from the different form of windows), and Rochester, 1123–38.

The anarchy in Stephen's reign brought forth a crop of new castles of all kinds: Farnham (rebuilt), Taunton, Wolvesey, Bishops Waltham, etc. At Guildford the present square keep was built (with characteristic herringbone masonry) over a shell wall and partly down one side of the motte. There were also siege castles, like Wallingford, and some other buildings were fortified, like St Mary's Church, Lincoln, and Wilton nunnery. There is a clear area of about ten miles radius round Cambridge guarded by castles (Caxton, Burwell, etc). Round

Leicester there is a demilitarised zone of about 15 miles radius, with castles round the edge every ten miles or so: Coventry, Hartshill, Ravenstone, Donnington, Belvoir, Oakham (with its magnificent hall), and Rockingham.

When Henry II acceded in 1154 baronial castles outnumbered royal ones by five to one, and he set about reducing this discrepancy. He favoured rectangular keeps, and soon polygonal ones. The first great castles in the north had rectangular keeps: Appleby, Brough, and Bowes (1157), Newcastle (1170), Scarborough (1158–69). But the later series had very original designs of keep: Orford, 1166–68, is cylindrical within and multangular without; Chilham, 1171–74, is

octagonal, Oxford, 1173, decagonal, Tickhill, 1179–82, 11-sided. Perhaps the masterpiece is Conisbrough, 1178, cylindrical with six prominent buttresses, like a toothed wheel (see **261**).

From now to the end of John's reign in 1216 there was much experimentation, both in internal buildings and in fortifications. Ideas were coming in from the Crusades and from Europe. The domestic buildings were frequently rebuilt or altered, so early *halls* are few. But the type before 1160 was long and narrow, as at Chepstow, Monmouth, or Richmond. After 1160 halls were wider and shorter, as at Christchurch (with its chimney), Framlingham, and Grosmont

260 *Square keep of Henry I's type – Castle Hedingham (Ex), c 1135.*

261 *A keep of Henry II's reign – Conisbrough (SY), c 1180–1190. This is a fine example of a circular keep.*

(another chimney, but from a rebuilding in 1330). Early *chapels* are rare, but survive at Dover, Hereford, Thetford, and Ludlow (with round nave). The southern Welsh marches were rich in variety: at Tretower (Br) there is a polygonal shell with hall block attached of 1150–75, but inside this is a circular "juliet" tower of 1230–40. There are cylinders at Longtown and Skenfrith, and walls, towers, and enclosures of unusual form at White Castle, Morgraig, and Coity. There are round keeps at Pembroke (1189) and New Buckenham (Nf); these should not be confused with the simple round towers on mottes, as at Caldicot (Mo), by 1216, or Barnard Castle. Mottes were still being built, as at Rhayader, 1177–94, or Dingestow, 1182. The four-lobed shell keep at York was rebuilt in 1190. Oxford has a stepped keep, and Farnham a motte tower built up with the mound.

The long stable reign of Henry III needed little castle building, and is a good place to take stock. The contrast between the Anglo-Saxon timbered hall and the Norman castle cannot be too strongly stressed. Castles were a function of feudalism, the delegation of authority from the king. They were essentially seats of government, either at county or quite local level, or had some national strategic function (like Durham, a bulwark against the Scots). Their normal life was peaceful, a coming and going of functionaries, merchants, ecclesiastics, and officers; they were the place for justice, business, and social functions. Only rarely would they be involved in warfare, and this side, although perhaps the first that comes to mind when visiting one, should not be overstressed. Castles died out when the central power was able to manage all aspects of government effectively, and were anachronistic by the mid 14th century. They were replaced by great houses, castle-wise at first, but later not. From Henry II's reign a licence was needed to build a castle or to fortify a private house ("crenellate"). A castle or manor chapel could grow into a parish church, and are often side by side.

During the first half of the 13th century, the bank and palisades of every important castle had been replaced by a wall. This led to a diminution of the importance of the keep; the castle became *keepless*, a collection of buildings inside the wall, which had towers at intervals for more effective defence and an increasingly important *gatehouse*. These "castles of enceinte" lasted as the main type until the end of effective castle building in the second half of the 14th century. The gatehouse was developed to include the keep and the lord's house; in turn it was replaced in the late 14th century by the separate stone hall house, and became important again in the 16th century. White Castle (Mo) represents the point, soon after 1200, where the keep is merged with the gatehouse. Fully developed examples are Manorbier, Framlingham, which has a long history, beginning with a Saxon fort, followed by a motte and bailey, then by an enceinte with 13 towers, and Barnwell, 1266, rectangular, with two cluster towers – adjoining is an earlier motte and bailey and a later Elizabethan mansion. Bodiam, 1385, is one of the very last old-style castles, built to counter a scare of invasion from France; this is square with corner towers, inner court, gatehouse, and moat, and is not unlike Bolton (NY), 1379, although this is rectangular; Farleigh Hungerford (So) was also built in 1383 to meet the same scare.

The keepless castles went out of fashion in the late 14th century. Meanwhile a new type had arisen, the *concentric*, in which again the keep is replaced by a massive gatehouse, combining keep, gatehouse, and lord's quarters, but which has two rings of walls. This type was adopted by Edward I for some of his castles in Wales, through his very talented architect, James of St George. The idea came from Syria and the Levant (as at Le Krak des Chevaliers), and ultimately from the Byzantine Empire. Carcassonne was the first example in the west. The Tower of London is a complete example in this country (Henry III and Edward I). The keep-gatehouse is, however, an English invention.

Edward's first castle in Wales, Flint, 1277, is an exception to the new type, and is unique. It has a rectangular enclosure with corner towers, one of which is a keep with its own moat; there is an entrenched forecourt linked to the palisaded earthwork defences of the (planned) town. Rhuddlan, the next, is concentric (1277–82). Conway, 1283–92, and Caernarvon, 1283–1323 (uncompleted), are not concentric but have mottes. Caernarvon was meant to be the Windsor of Wales; it has two baileys with a ring of tall towers. Harlech, 1285–91, is the apogee of the concentric type; Beaumaris, 1295–1321 (incomplete), is remarkable for its extreme symmetry, even to two keep-gatehouses, probably explained by its need to be vigilant on two sides (see **262** and **263**). Edward I built nine castles and supported the building of other (baronial) castles in strategic positions, such as Denbigh, 1282, with planned town, and Caerphilly, the finest concentric castle of all. The plan of this was not built all in one piece, but developed and improved; the central castle is like Harlech, but the most astonishing feature is the water defences with their retaining barrage; the water defences of Kenilworth are also impressive, and date from the early 13th century.

Dr A J Taylor has pointed out similarities between features of Edward I's castles in Wales and those in Savoy. Three castles in the Rhône valley (now in Switzerland), Saillon, Saxon, and La Bâtiaz, also dating from the later 13th century, have round arches (even then old-fashioned), which occur in north Wales. La Bâtiaz has a semicircular garderobe, a feature it shares with Harlech. The round towers in both series were built in a way not found elsewhere – the materials were brought up on a ramp which gradually rose round the outside of the tower as it was being built. Thus the putlog holes are not in horizontal rows round the walls, as they would be if ordinary scaffolding had been used, but climb up the walls in a spiral. Taylor has discovered that Edward I, who had family links with Savoy, brought castle builders over to help his works in Wales, and several of these men have been identified as working on castles in both areas.

The castles of the 15th century, when the feudalism in which the castle was an essential element was passing away, are few but interesting. In eastern England they are built in *brick*; they usually have inner courtyards, and often moats. That at Hull, in a town founded by Edward I, was rebuilt in the late 14th century; others are Caister (Nf), Herstmonceux (Sx), 1441, Tattershall (Li), 1443–46, Buckden (HP), and Oxburgh (Nf), 1482. The Wars of the Roses called forth a system known as "bastard feudalism", under which lords provided private armies which were housed in quarters in castles separate from those of the lord and his legitimate household. Several castles were adapted for this, such as Ashby-de la Zouch, 1474, with a tower house; Kirby Muxloe (Le), 1480, a brick quadrangle with corner towers, gatehouse, and moat; Raglan, 1432–45, walls and towers, 1450–60; and Thornbury (Gl), unfinished in 1512, which has two courts, and was the last castle built for serious defence.

After this a few great houses were built with castle-like features, largely for reasons of romantic prestige; these include Carew, Donnington, Cowdray (1533), and the last castle house of all, Wollaton (No), 1580–88.

Although only medieval at some remove, mention should be made of Castell Coch, in the Taff valley behind Cardiff (see **264**). This was a small and very ruinous 13th-century castle, restored (if not almost

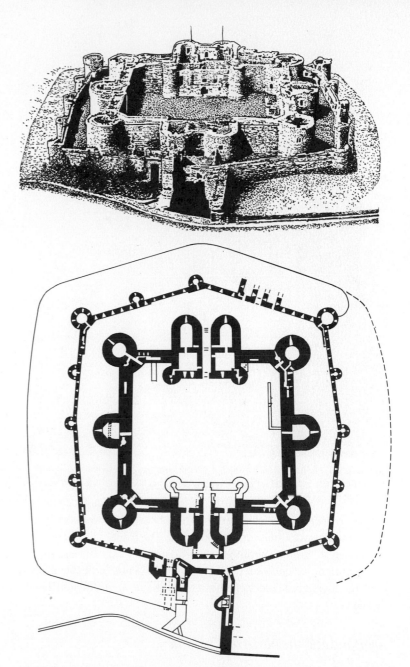

262–3 *A concentric castle of Edward I's type – Beaumaris (An), 1295–1300: 262 view and 263 plan.*

264 *Castell Coch, near Cardiff: a small 13th-century castle somewhat romantically restored (1870s) by Burges for the Marquis of Bute, but still conveying a compelling flavour of the original.*

entirely rebuilt) by William Burges in the 1870s. It now consists of three round towers and a small courtyard. The pointed roofs cannot be verified in Britain, although they existed abroad. The interiors are Victorian, violently so, but externally the whole probably gives a strong and not unfair idea of what a small medieval castle could have looked like.

Scotland and the north of England

The history of castles in Scotland takes a different course from England, reflecting different influences. At first, up to the late 13th

century, the Anglo-Norman presence or influence introduced the same kind of castles as in England, but from then on Scotland went its own way.

Castles were first mottes and baileys; a very fine example is the Mote of Urr (Kb). Towers on mottes appeared by the mid 12th century, as at Duffus (My), by 1151, which has half subsided down the slope under its own weight. Good stone keeps are those at Castle Sween, Knapdale, built by Magnus Barelegs in the manner of Colchester, and at Kisimul, Barra (*c*1200). The first stone castle in Scotland is Cubbie Roo's Castle, Wyre (Or), 1145. Castles of enceinte are represented by Dunstaffnage (early 13th century), Mingary (In), Tioran (Moidart), Inverlochy (In), Rothesay, and Dirleton (which has a clustered donjon – three towers round a court, *c* 1125. Bothwell has an impressive round keep in one corner of an enceinte. Kildrummy (Ab) has a keep-gatehouse.

In the 13th century a very distinctive Scottish type began to emerge, the *tower house*. There had been a few fortified halls, like Rait (Nn), in Edward I's reign, or Morton (Nithsdale); Hailes (EL) and Aydon Castle (Tyneside) are of the same type, but were later included in a walled courtyard; their plan is that of a T. Unsettled conditions and the threat of sudden attack led to the hall house being set on end to become a tower house, where the ground floor was kept for animals and the upper floors for the people. Dunnideer (Ab) was in existence by 1260; Yester (EL) is in the side of a motte, like Guildford; Drum (Ab) is also a good early tower. In the 14th century Lochleven (Kr) and Threave (Kb) dominate the scene; Dundonald (Ay) is a royal tower.

There are a few enceintes still in the 14th century, with keep-gatehouses and now reflecting the needs of "bastard feudalism", with separate quarters for the lord and his retainers; such are Tantallon (EL) and Doune (Pe). A perfect small late castle is Breachacha, Coll.

The later development of the Scottish castle shows increasing French influence. The Auld Alliance in 1168 against the Normans initiated this, and French influence appears already at Elgin in the early 13th century. The Anglo-Scottish wars cut the two countries off from each other, and the Norman barons left. So from the 14th century on, Scotland developed her own building styles, with a close eye on France and the Low Countries. Tower houses remained the favourite type until well into the 16th century. They pass through two stylistic phases. The *L-shaped tower* appears, eg at Craigmillar (Edinburgh) in 1374 (now surrounded by later additions – a curtain wall in

1427, chapel 15th century, house rebuilt in Renaissance style, 1661, pleasance, Charles I). David's Tower in Edinburgh Castle was of this form (1368–79), as is Preston Tower (ML), heightened 1626. Borthwick (ML), 1430, is a double L. The wing or "jam", which makes the L, may be square, as at Scalloway (Zd), or round, as at Pitfichie (Ab).

Ordinary castles of this period include Spynie (My), a 14th-century rectangular enclosure with three towers, hall, and chapel, and 15th-century gatehouse – tower house added *c* 1480; Ravenscraig (Fi), 1460, a promontory castle with two round towers, for defence against cannon; and the royal castles of Edinburgh, Stirling, and Linlithgow (1425–17th century – a square courtyard block).

The next phase of the tower houses is the *Z-shaped* castle of the 16th century, which is an L with a second tower or wing on the opposite corner. Some are strictly hall houses, like Drochil (Ps), with round towers, Noltland (Westray, Or), with square towers and a formidable array of ship-like oval firing ports, and Claypotts (Dundee). Towers of this type include Harthill (Ab) and Tolquhar (Ab), of two stages, 15th century and 1584–89.

This leads on to the well-known and romantic towers of the Borders, whose heyday was the 15th to 17th centuries. These are very numerous, and everyone has their favourite. Typical examples are Smailholm, Gilnockie, Kirkhope, and Newark. The endemic stock-raiding on both sides of the Border meant that the Scottish tower house province extended into the four northern counties of England. Here again the earliest fortified houses are halls, like Haughton, mid 13th century. Belsay Castle (Nd), *c* 1340, has wings; the present house adjoining it is 1614. Yanworth (Wd) is another. Warkworth has a tower house succeeding a bailey with hall and chapel, which itself succeeds a motte; the tower house is square, with square projections on each side, giving a complex plan. But the commonest are the small simple square towers, as on the Scottish side, like the Vicar's Pele, Corbridge, or the rectory at Embleton. The usual name, pele or peel, really means a palisaded enclosure, but has been transferred to the tower within it.

A late Scottish tower is Coxton (My), 1644, inhabited to 1708 (see **265**). Late castles, built in the late 16th and early 17th century, up to 1637, are in the *Scottish baronial* style, which is a blown-up tower house with fanciful ornament like turrets at the corners, high-pitched gables, etc. It ran to excess in the 19th century, for castle-like

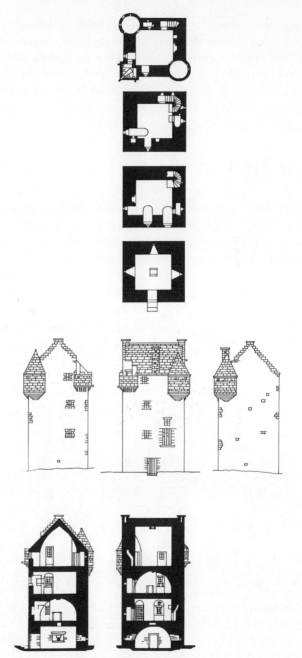

265 *A Scottish peel tower – Coxton Tower (My), 1644, inhabited until 1708. The ground floor is for storage, the higher floors for living.*

houses. The best examples are in Aberdeenshire, the Mearns, Angus, and Fife, and include Craigievar, Midmar, Fyvie, Glamis, Huntly, Edzell, and Crichton. Amisfield Tower (Df) is an example of *c* 1600. The very interesting and fine Bishop's Palace at Kirkwall dates from this period, as does the extraordinary Renaissance block at Caerlaverock. The Civil War cut short the Scottish national style, except for a few throwbacks like Hatton (ML).

FORTIFIED HOUSES

Although some of these have been mentioned already, there is more to be said. The larger Saxon houses were usually protected by a palisade, as were isolated farmhouses; these were sometimes, but not always, along the top of earthen banks, and there could be a ditch as well. Place-names like Stoke or Stockton refer to such stockades. A few of these banks can still be traced. A unique type of defence was excavated a few years ago at the Anglian royal palace at Yeavering (near Wooler (Nd)); this was a wooden wall supported by two rows of posts set in a trench; a gateway in this wall was flanked by two towers.

266 *Stokesay Castle (Sp) is the oldest and perhaps the finest example in England of a moated and fortified manor house – not a castle. The main range, of hall and solar, was built mainly between 1285 and 1305, but begun c 1240; the timber-framed gatehouse dates from 1570.*

Two defensible houses are recorded in Domesday Book (1086). These are at Eardisley (He), a squarish moated site with rounded corners, one occupied by a mound, and Clavering, which was similar but with no mound. There are fortified town houses in Norwich. A defensible building could be surrounded by a bank or wall, like the "barmkins" at tower houses in the north. If stone was used for a hall house, it was stronger than the usual timber-framing; there are medieval examples at Hemingford Grey (HP) and Boothby Pagnell (Li). Another way was to turn one's house into a sort of castle by adding towers and a gatehouse, and battlements ("crenellating"). The oldest and finest example of this is Stokesay – not a castle, but a fortified manor house; this has two towers, of 1115 and 1291, flanking a great hall of 1284; the timbered upper part of the gatehouse dates from 1570; there is a moat (see **266**).

A small but interesting group of defended houses is the *bastles* of the central part of the Scottish border. These are farmhouses, lower in the social scale than the tower houses, and are the only ones in Britain to have animals on the ground floor and humans above. The first comprehensive survey of them was published in 1971 by the Royal Commission on Ancient Monuments (H G Ramm, R W McDowall, and Eric Mercer: *Sheilings and Bastles*). They are usually rectangular, about 35x25ft (10.5x7.5m); they have two full storeys with steeply-pitched gables. The walls are of irregular stone blocks, packed with small chips in weak mortar, and about 4ft (1.2m) thick on the ground floor to *c* 3.5ft (1m) at first-floor level. There is a single narrow doorway in the middle of one of the gable walls and there are no windows on the ground floor, only slits. The first floor is entered by a doorway at one end of the long wall with the most southerly aspect; this was once reached by ladder, now by stone steps. Some had thatched roofs, but now all are slate. There are two types, one with timber floor to the upper storey, the other with stone barrel vault, like the peel-towers. Bastles are all in a strip 20 miles wide south of the border, except for a few in Roxburgh, north-east Cumberland, and western Northumberland. In date they range from say 1550 to 1650, but remained in occupation till the early 19th century. Some 50 certain examples survive, out of several hundreds: 5 in Cumberland, eg The Stonehouse, Naworth Park, Nether Denton, and 45 in Northumberland, like Hole, Bellingham; Whiteley Shield, West Allen; Gatehouse and Black Middens, Tarset; Woodhouses, Harbottle; and one built against the south gate of the Roman fort of Housesteads, with a drying kiln in a Roman guardroom. In addition, there are some 30 too fragmentary to be sure of, or houses in the bastle tradition but not really defensive.

Moats are a common feature of defended houses. They are a regular aspect of castles, unless the situation made them unnecessary. Some castle moats are very spectacular, like the deep rock-cut one at Goodrich (He) or the great square one at Bodiam. The water defences at Kenilworth and Caerphilly have already been mentioned.

The majority of moats were constructed between 1150 and 1400; they became standard for smaller houses (manor houses, granges, and lesser houses), particularly in heavy soils, in the 15th century, and the period of greatest occupation extends to the late 16th century. They are found in most counties of England. Some may have been meant as defences, but as the 15th century wore on it is clear that many were merely for prestige or in romantic reminiscence of castles and the castle class to which the owner would like to be thought to belong. Some of them, indeed, run round three sides of the house only. There may be a variety of reasons for them – defence, prestige, drainage, water to keep fish in or animals out, or just appearance. Protection against animals, brigands, or ill-wishers must have been powerful motives; people were more isolated than they are today. Other uses were to water stock and to act as a static water tank when most buildings were constructed of wood. Ducks, geese, and swans could be kept on them.

Moats are usually about 10ft (3m) deep and 20ft (6m) wide; they have vertical sides, often revetted with wood, stone, or brick. There may be a bank outside, but some have one inside. Most enclose square "islands", but some are oblong; and some, eg at Broughton Hall, Send (Sy), enclose an L-shaped space. Some have two or more islands.

The islands usually contain the dwelling house and some of its subsidiary elements, such as garden, orchard, and stables. In some cases the islands are separate, and in some only the subsidiary elements are moated; the house may be in a dry position, the other elements in a wet one – here drainage is clearly the motive for the moat. Some moats, if there are no remains of buildings inside them, may be mistaken for fishponds. Blickling Hall (Nf) (1620s) has a dry moat containing an ornamental garden, and succeeding the original medieval moat. The influence of moats on the development of courtyard plans in later manor houses needs further research, as does the question of the position of the main hall in relation to the bridge, and the latter's effect on the placing of other structures on the island.

The work of Alan Aberg and others, and of the Moated Sites (later Medieval Settlement) Research Group, has yielded important information on the significance and distribution of moats, and of the elements contained by them. Some 6,000 moats are thought to exist or to have existed. A high proportion of these is in eastern England; there are some 650 in Essex, 500 in Suffolk, 400 in Norfolk, and 300 in Lincolnshire; there is also a considerable concentration in Herefordshire, Worcestershire, and Warwickshire. Most are in the lowlands. The pattern is not uniform, and it is unlikely that moats were dug for the same reasons in all areas. For instance, at least 20 have been found in one extensive parish and royal manor in Warwickshire, Kings Norton, most of them related to free tenants who colonised the waste in the 12th and 13th centuries. In Essex too, moats seem to have been built in forested regions. But C C Taylor's analysis of Cambridgeshire (*The Landscape of Cambridgeshire*, Hodder & Stoughton, 1973) showed that the isolated moats – those away from the villages or hamlets – were in definite relation to the boulder clay. This might have been expected to have been densely forested when the moats were cut, but in fact the documentary evidence suggests that woodland had already been cleared from the boulder clay areas before the main moat-building period. A possible explanation is that these areas were taken up at a late stage by "colonisers".

Le Patourel's map of moats in Yorkshire (H E J le Patourel: *The Moated Sites of Yorkshire*, Society for Medieval Archaeology, Monograph 5, 1973) shows an almost complete agreement between the moats and the lowland parts of Yorkshire – the Vale of York and Holderness. It seems therefore as though, there, drainage must have been a major factor in deciding to have a moat. And indeed the attractive hypothesis has been put forward that moat-building was encouraged in England by the climatic deterioration of the later 13th century.

Clearly there is much more research to be done before the whole picture is fully understood. The Research Group is conducting a comparative study of moats in other countries, and this will no doubt give useful leads to the explanation of those in England. The merger with the Medieval Village Research Group initiated in 1986 has benefited both groups, in setting the field of each in a more complete context.

What was once regarded as the largest moat in England, the ditch, now filled in, round Fulham Palace in London, was excavated in

1972/3, and appeared to be a defensive ditch, with banks, round a hitherto unknown Roman village. There was a strategic crossing of the Thames here, where roads met; the site may even have been pre-Roman. The work may date from the later 4th century, and encloses 36.5 acres; its presence might explain why the Bishops of London took this site over in 705, and why the Danes chose Fulham to make camp.

(Details on moats will be found in F A Aberg, ed: *Medieval Moated Sites* (CBA Research Report 17, 1978), and the annual *Reports* of the Moated Sites Research Group.)

TOWN WALLS

These were normal in the Middle Ages for towns of any size, and not only for those of obvious strategic importance. Palisaded banks usually surrounded Saxon towns and villages; but the Saxons sometimes took advantage of Roman walls, which they repaired. An Anglian or very late Roman tower was discovered a few years ago in the walls at York. Medieval walls could also follow the Roman line, as at Gloucester

or Chichester. At York and London part of the circuit was the walls of a Roman fortress to which the town wall was later joined. The walls of York are on a bank, those of London have Roman lower courses and medieval work above. At Silchester (see **267**) the walls have lost most of their facing, but show clearly the interior rubble construction. When the town was on a new site, the walls were of course on a new line, as at Caernarvon. In some places the town walls are integral with those of the castle, as at Ludlow and Flint; or, as at Caernarvon, the town is closely guarded by the adjacent castle. The finest surviving circuits are those of York and Chester, but there are sizeable stretches at Oxford (in the gardens of New College) and Winchester. The line of former walls can often be followed by the course of modern streets, as in London (London Wall, Houndsditch), Nottingham, or Bristol (eg St Stephen's and St Nicholas streets); at Gloucester the curved

267 Roman town wall, Silchester: this has lost its facing, which enables the strengthening courses of harder stone to be visible.

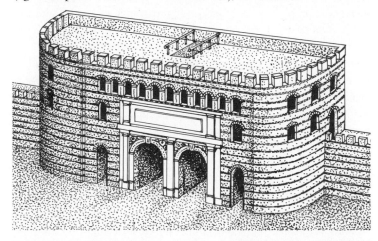

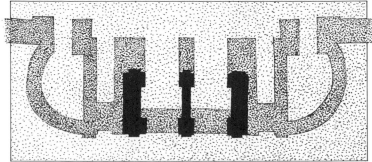

268–9 The Balkerne Gate, Colchester: a gate of the Roman colonia, incorporating an earlier monumental arch: 268 view; 269 plan.

south-east corner of the original Roman line is still visible in the modern street.

Gates are still to be seen in some numbers. Roman survivors are the Balkerne Gate at Colchester (see **268** and **269**) and the Newport Arch at Lincoln, but there are many fragmentary ones elsewhere. The finest complete ring of gates is that at York, the "Bars", some of which have outworks. Medieval gates still form needle's eyes for the camels of modern traffic, at places like Chepstow, Rye, and Winchelsea. Fine examples are the Bar at Southampton and the West Gate at Winchester (see **270**). Gates can be combined with other buildings, such as the chapel at Bristol (St John's, 14th century) or the Guildhall on the Stonebow at Lincoln (15th century).

In recent years doubts have been expressed whether town walls were entirely, or even primarily, defensive in intention, but rather built for prestige reasons or essentially for the control of egress of traders etc,

and the easier collection of market dues. But re-examination by T P Smith (1985) has shown that they were after all primarily defensive. Although some cases can be quoted of purely ornamental walls, such as the South Gate at King's Lynn, the Stonebow at Lincoln, or the North Bar at Beverley, these are all late (15th century). And admittedly some walls are poorly built, such as parts of the walls at Southampton and Great Yarmouth, but these were so built to avoid expense. Against this, most walls can be shown to have been built at times when strong defences were necessary or to counter invasion scares (eg Rye and Winchelsea); most walls have good military features. Some special cases can be cited, such as the barbicans added to bars at York (see **271**), or the boom towers on the rivers at York (Lendal Tower) or Norwich, where chains could be stretched across the river. Many walls are very high or thick, more than would be required for mere appearance, and some have ditches or outworks. All in all, the essentially defensive purpose of town walls is to be accepted.

More humble circuits, and direct descendants of the palisaded earth banks, are the *village enclosures*. Most of the survivors are related to castles, and are in fact banks running off from the bailey bank of the castle so that the whole forms one defensive complex. Such are those at Pleshey (Ex), Castle Acre and New Buckenham (Nf), and Lee (Bc); the latter contains two churches.

270 *West Gate, Winchester (13th-century, west face 14th); a typical town gate.*

271 *Walmgate Bar, York: the only surviving city gate to retain its barbican (and the only one in England); gate, 12th century, barbican 14th century, restored 17th and 19th centuries.*

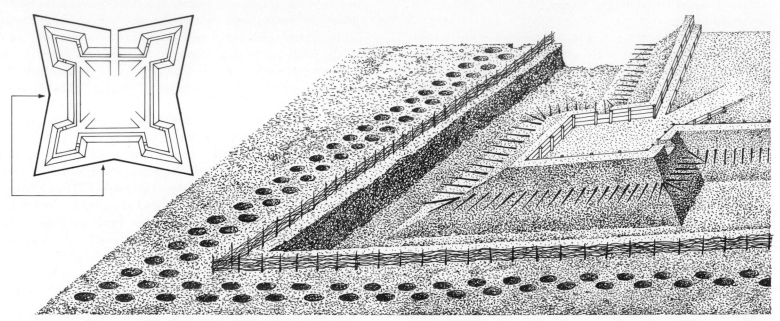

272 *The Queen's Sconce – an English Civil War defence work at Newark-on-Trent (from a model in Newark Museum).*

A wholly exceptional set of town walls is those of Berwick-on-Tweed. These are quite unlike the medieval pattern, and are a rare example in Britain of the Renaissance type later brought to perfection by Vauban, with pointed projections covering each other. They were begun in 1555 and the north front was completed in 1569; the rest is a later extension, not finished till 1747. They enclose a much smaller area than the medieval walls.

SIEGE WORKS

The wars of the Middle Ages have left few traces of *siegeworks*; most of them must have been portable or quite temporary, but there are some earthworks. Trenches or mounds survive at Wallingford, Corfe, Hereford, Bamburgh, Lincoln, Ludlow, and Arundel, from wars of Norman date; at Huntingdon is a motte just out of bowshot of the castle. At Berkhamsted there is a row of firing platforms built against the outer bank of the castle by the French in a siege in 1216. There are siege camps at Rackham Hill (Sx), 1102, and near Ely. The

Civil Wars left more marks. Many castles and houses were put in a state of defence, and several new works were built. These were of earth, sometimes revetted with stone; they have angular bastions and sharp corners. The defences of London have gone, but small sections remain of those of Bristol and Carmarthen. Forts (or "sconces", detached posts with bastions), exist at Dartmouth, and at Earith and Horsey Hill (HP). At Basing House (Ha) are three bastions; at Quarrendon (Bc) are trenches and gunposts – low earthworks with a ditch round all four sides, but a bank only on three; there are others at Skipton (NY) and Cornbury Park (Ox). One of the earthworks on Lansdown Hill, Bath, may be of this date. Some prehistoric hillforts were used by the rival armies, such as Oliver's Battery, near Winchester, a Romano-British enclosure reused by Cromwell in 1645, and Maumbury Rings at Dorchester (Do). There is a gun redoubt commanding Caerphilly Castle, based on earlier earthworks.

But the most important and extensive series of Civil War siegeworks in Britain is that at Newark-on-Trent. The town was a key Royalist garrison from 1642 until its surrender to the Scots in May 1646, after a siege from November 1645; during this time it suffered one assault

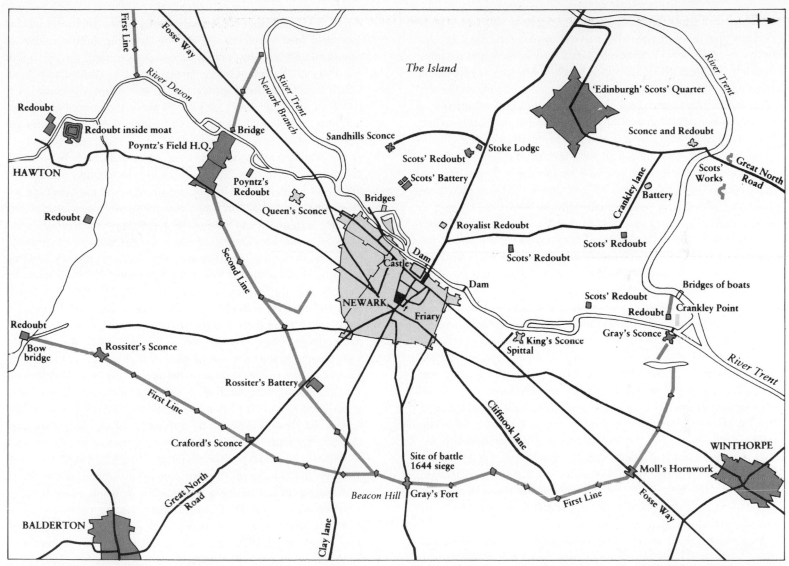

Map 14 *The Civil War fortifications of Newark-on-Trent. These works, which are well documented, reflect a long siege of the Royalist town by Parliamentary and Scots forces in 1645–6. The Royalist defences are shown in a light grey tint, and the Parliamentarian and Scots positions in a dark grey tint. Several remains of these works survive.*

and two sieges, and elaborate defences and siegeworks were built, from which the whole sequence can be followed (see **272** and **Map 14**). Much has gone of these earthworks, but much still survives. The Royalists built a new circuit of defences round the built-up area of the town, in 1642, as the medieval walls were obsolete and incomplete.

In 1643 this line was shown to be too weak, and was strengthened or replaced by a new one, with a sconce now gone. A large outpost, the Queen's Sconce, lay to the north, and there were several works on the Island in the Trent opposite the town. Several houses round the town were fortified. The besiegers linked up a ring of villages (which were fortified by rampart, ditch, and bastions) by forts and two lines of circumvallation, strengthened at intervals by redoubts. The Scots also built a headquarters ("Edinburgh"), and a few sconces and redoubts (small strongholds with no provision for flank defence). The surviving remains of all this are: Royalist – The Queen's Sconce, perhaps the best of its kind in the country, a sconce at Muskham Bridge, batteries at Crankley Lane and Wiverton Hall, and earthworks on Crankley Point; Parliamentarian – redoubt at Hawton (in medieval moat); Scots – the Sandhills Sconce, a flanked redoubt at Stoke Lodge, and redoubts near the brewery sports ground and on Crankley Point. There are also fragments of the Royalist town defences, and of the besiegers' village defences at Balderton, Coddington, Farndon, Winthorpe, as well as of the circumvallations and of 'Edinburgh'. The Royalist defences at local houses, like Belvoir, Shelford Manor, and Wiverton Hall, are unfortunately gone. This fascinating group of military works has been published in model detail by the Royal Commission on the Historical Monuments of England (1964).

By contrast, the defences of the two capitals in the war, Oxford (Royalist) and London (Parliamentarian), are much more elusive. At Oxford earthworks were thrown up at the outbreak of the war but were destroyed, at least in part, when the Parliament troops entered the city. On the King's entry in October 1642 a complete scheme was put in hand, of which a plan (by de Gomme, 1644) survives. These defences were dismantled in 1647. The scheme was a tight ring of heavily bastioned earthworks, three miles long, close outside the built-up area of the city. The line was constantly altered and reconstructed in the light of the latest theories. Two-thirds of it lay behind watermeadows which could be flooded at need. The system withstood three hard sieges before the final surrender. The Parliament side was based in a large fort on Headington Hill, flanked by long lines, with fortlets, on both sides, commanding the city.

Fragments of what survived the dismantling were drawn at various times, but most of such records are unpublished or lost. It does appear that the ditch sections developed during the war, from a narrow flat-bottomed type in 1642 to a wider rounded type in 1643 and a broad pointed-bottomed type in 1644. Only three small traces can now be seen: the boundary fence of the garden of Holywell Mill follows a tenaille line; there is a slight bank behind a house in Manor Road and under a building of the University OTC; and there is a low scarp between the Merton and Balliol cricket grounds, which makes

a turn by King's Mound House and turns back again, until west of Mansfield Road it is on the original line along the south boundary of Mansfield College – past here it turns again, to form the north-east boundary of Wadham College garden, as far as South Parks Road, where it ends; in the Wadham section the rampart is some 34 ft (10.2 m) wide and rises 13 ft (3.9 m) above the ground to the east and seven feet above the garden. The siegeworks at Headington have not survived.

The situation of London is even less satisfactory, because no complete plan survives. Parts are shown incidentally on various maps and plans, but the line of the whole system is uncertain for most of its length. No observation of a ditch section or a fort rampart has ever been made, and most of the system can be presumed buried for good under later uses of the terrain. An attempt to stimulate interest in the system, on the assumption that occasionally building work might momentarily reveal small portions, has been made by David Sturdy (in the *London Archaeologist*, 1975). The circuit ran, as at Oxford, closely round the built-up area, and had 14 fortified positions. Of these there is certainty over only three. Starting at the river-crossing 200yd (185m) east of Wapping Old Stairs (it is not known whether the river was blocked by a chain or commanded by a tower on the embankment), the bank ran to a fort or battery on Ratcliff Highway just south of St George's in the East; then along or close to Cannon Street Road to a fort on Whitechapel Road, just west of the London Hospital; then to a post at Cheshire Street just east of Brick Lane; then through Arnold Circus to one or perhaps two forts by Shoreditch Church commanding the Kingsland Road, the main route to the north; then probably just north of Old Street to a fort round the New River Head. The line is obscure here, as is the crossing of the Fleet, but it follows Great Ormond Street to a fort at Bedford House (now at the south side of Tavistock Square); it runs under the British Museum to a complex of forts etc between Great Russell Street and Wardour Street, commanding Tottenham Court Road and Oxford Street, main routes north and west; the line continued across Mayfair probably near Great Marlborough Street and Maddox Street; the next battery is "Oliver's Mount" at Mount Row, whence the line followed Farm Street and Waverton Street to a fort at Hyde Park Corner, not identified; it went under Buckingham Palace and reached the river just west of the Tate Gallery – here there was a fort, or a battery, near Vincent Square, and another across the river "at Vauxhall", not identified. The line is picked up again at the next fort, in the park beside the Imperial War Museum; it then runs to the Elephant and Castle (fort), and to the last fort, near the New Kent Road/Old Kent Road junction; between there and the river opposite Wapping it went close to Bermondsey Abbey. In all this circuit the only certain points are the forts at Bedford House, Mount Row, and the Imperial War Museum, and clearly fieldwork on the rest is urgent. From a military point of view, this line is not all satisfactory, and it changed hands twice in 1647. The medieval city walls, and the citizens' militia, may have been better defences in reality. The system was dismantled in 1647.

Small sections remain of the defences of Bristol and Carmarthen.

FORTS

As stated above, castles died out with the passing of feudalism. The need of the Tudors was for forts, mainly for coastal defence. Henry VIII, from 1537–40, built a series of forts along the south coast, following an invasion scare. They are thickest in the Thames estuary and the south-east, but go right along the coast, with a cluster round Southampton Water, as far as Devon (Dartmouth) and Cornwall (Fowey, St Mawes, Pendennis). The most sophisticated is the astonishing one at Deal (see **273**), which has a round tower with six semicircular bastions, inside six more larger bastions in a moat with gently scalloped sides, all like the petals of a sinister flower. A less complicated fort at Walmer was converted *c* 1730 into an official residence for the Lord Warden of the Cinque Ports. This south-eastern group stretches as far as Camber, near Winchelsea. The Armada scare of 1588 produced a few forts, or works like those inside the Roman fort at Pevensey.

Tilbury is an enlightening case, which repays a close look. It is one of a series of Henry VIII blockhouses along the Thames estuary; it was altered in 1588, redesigned in the late 17th century with angle-bastions, outworks, and two moats, and altered again at the end of the 18th century. It was finally rebuilt in the 1860s, by which time bastions had been replaced generally by a polygonal plan. Henry VIII's blockhouse had been removed before this. In the 1890s concrete gun positions were inserted. Tilbury thus reflects all the major theories

273 *Deal Castle; one of Henry VIII's more imaginative coastal defences.*

and periods of fort building since the early 16th century. Other Thames forts of the 1860s survive, such as Coalhouse, East Tilbury, still used, and Shornmead (Kt), ruined.

The defence of the Thames estuary was always a problem. Victor T C Smith (1975) has located five Tudor blockhouses round Gravesend, of which traces survive of one at Milton: these were D-shaped, with two storeys of brick on chalk foundations. A boom defence was added in 1588. When Tilbury fort was rebuilt *c* 1670, Gravesend blockhouse was converted into a magazine and a new gun terrace added. In 1778 another fort of irregular trace was added downstream. But all lacked command of the approaches until the whole system was remodelled in 1868–72.

Another very instructive site is Portsmouth, perhaps the most fortified town in Britain. The defences here fall into several periods:

1 The Round Tower dates from 1415, but is covered by a Henry VIII fort of 1538–40, the top of which has been altered. This is contemporary with the fort at Southsea, and with the group round the Solent (Netley, Cowes, Yarmouth (IW), Calshot, and Hurst). The Saluting Battery (a rectangular platform) dates from 1568.

2 Charles II, using the architect de Gomme, began a complete defensive circuit of the town, with angle-bastions, in 1665. The only stretch remaining is that on the south shore, the Long Curtain (altered in the 18th century), and the King's Bastion. The Dockyard Round Tower dates from 1683, and Frederick's Battery from 1688.

3 The 18th century saw, apart from some reworking of earlier works, Cumberland Fort at Eastney, perhaps the best 18th-century fort left in Britain. This was built in 1746 in the form of a five-cornered star, but was rebuilt in 1786 as a wide pentagon, with glacis beyond a dry moat, and one ravelin (outwork forming a salient angle outside the main ditch).

4 This was the precursor of "Palmerston's Follies", the forts along the heights at Gosport and Fareham, and the four circular island bastions in the Spithead (1860s to 1880s).

Scotland had its own series of forts in the 17th and 18th centuries. There were Cromwellian forts at Ayr, Leith, Perth, Aberdeen, Inverness, and Inverlochy, all now dismantled. But Fort Charlotte at Lerwick (Charles II, rebuilt 1781), a pentagonal fort, survives. Fort William, built in earth in 1655 and in stone under William III, has also gone. In the 18th century the ramparts at Edinburgh and Stirling were rebuilt, and Fort George near Inverness was built. After the 1745, Braemar and Corgarff were refortified.

OTHER MILITARY WORKS

The Napoleonic wars gave rise to two very distinctive works, the Martello towers and the naval telegraphs.

Martello towers (see **274**) were intended to provide concentrated fire on ships at sea, or repel an enemy landing, and were capable of withstanding a long siege. They derived from Mediterranean watch-towers, and specifically from a tower at Mortella Point, Corsica, which withstood a British land and sea siege in 1794. This was a massive tower, 40ft (12m) high, 45ft (13.5m) in diameter at the base, and with 15ft (4.5m) thick walls. It so impressed the authorities that, from 1796 to 1815, 194 such towers were built, at first in America, the Channel Islands, Ireland, and South Africa. From 1820 to 1870 more were built in the USA and Canada; none was built after 1873. Plans for building them in England took a long time, and it was not till 1805 that the first ones were started on the south coast. From

274 *Martello tower – Pevensey (Sx). These were gun-posts built between 1804 and 1812, at intervals along the coasts of southern Britain, Ireland, and Guernsey, to check a Napoleonic invasion (which in fact never happened).*

1805 to 1812, 103 were built, of which 43 remain. From 1805 to 1808, 73 were built from Folkestone to Beachy Head (Wish Tower), numbered 1 to 73, recorded over the door on a tablet, mostly in Roman numerals; no 74, at Seaford, was added in 1810. From 1808 to 1812, 28 were built along the east coast from St Osyth (Ex) to Aldeburgh (Su). The south coast towers are elliptical, the east coast ones ovoid, with steep batter on the sea side. The exception is the one at Slaghden, Aldeburgh, which is quatrefoil, like Walmer Castle. There is an impressive line of towers at Hythe and Dymchurch. Two more were built in Orkney from 1812–18, at Crookness and Hackness, guarding Longhope. There is a similar tower in Leith harbour. The English towers were 33ft (9.9m) high, with top diameter of 26ft (7.8m); the top had a 24-pounder gun and two 24-pound carronades; the ground floor was for magazine and stores, the middle floor for one officer and 24 men – the entrance to this was 20ft (6m) from the ground, by ladder; there was a solid central pillar.

During the Napoleonic wars the Admiralty found a need for very rapid communication with the main naval ports, and by 1796 had devised a system of *naval telegraph posts*, visible from each other, carrying a signalling apparatus. This was the Murray six-shutter system, consisting of a rigid frame in which were set square shutters in two rows of three (vertically); the shutters could be turned flat, and so invisible to the next station, by pulling on ropes (like bell-ringing). These frames could not be swivelled, so at junctions in the line there had to be two frames at the appropriate angle. The frames were erected on temporary wooden buildings, of which few traces, if any, probably remain. The lines were abandoned after the Peace of Amiens in 1802, but revived in 1803 when war broke out again, and continued until 1814. The door was kept open for a better system, and in 1798 Gamble's radiated telegraph was erected experimentally on the tower of Woolwich church. The final choice was Popham's semaphore (worked by winches), tried experimentally from London to Chatham in 1816 and adopted for the lines south of London in the 1820s. This was very efficient, and on a good day a message could be got from London to Portsmouth in less than a minute. The semaphore was mounted on the roof of a house, of which the standard type had a square tower with flat roof, and was whitewashed for visibility. Several of these survive, some in private occupation, as on Pewley Hill, Guildford. Another type was a bungalow, used at eg Older Hill, Midhurst, and a third type was a tall octagonal tower, of which

the only case seems to have been at Chatley Heath, Cobham. The sites are still known by names like Telegraph Hill.

The lines ran from London to Portsmouth, with a branch to Plymouth, to Chatham, with branches to Sheerness and Deal, and to Yarmouth. The routes were:

Chatham etc lines – 1796 (Murray system), Admiralty; 36 West Square, Southwark; New Cross Gate, Plow Garlic Hill; Shooter's Hill; Swanscombe; Gad's Hill, Shorne; Chatham Yard. At Gad's Hill a line branched off to Beacon Hill; Calham Hill; Tonge; Barrow Hill, Queenborough; Sheerness Yard (Boathouse roof). At Tonge a branch ran to Shotterden; Barham Downs; Betteshanger; Deal. The Popham experimental line in 1816 ran: Admiralty; West Square; New Cross; Red Hill, Chislehurst; Rowe Hill, Wilmington; Betsham; Gad's Hill; Chatham Yard. At Gad's Hill there was a branch to Beacon Hill; Calham Hill, where this line came to an end.

Portsmouth and Plymouth lines – 1796 (Murray), Admiralty; Lower Grosvenor Place or Little Chelsea, according to visibility; Putney Heath; Netley Heath; Hascombe; Blackdown; Harting Down; Portsdown; Portsmouth. This was soon changed to Admiralty; Chelsea Hospital, East Wing; Putney Heath; Cabbage Hill, Ashtead; Netley Heath; Hascombe; Romsell, Blackdown; Beacon Hill, South Harting; Portsdown Hill; Portsmouth, The Glacis. 1822 (Popham), Admiralty; Chelsea Military School; Putney Heath; Kingston Hill; Cooper's Hill, Esher; Chatley Heath, Cobham; Pewley Hill, Guildford; Bannicle Hill, Godalming; Haste Hill, Haslemere; Older Hill, Midhurst; Beacon Hill, Compton Downs; Camp Down, Bedhampton; Lumps Fort, Southsea; High Street, Portsmouth. The Plymouth line left the Portsmouth line at Beacon Hill (1806, Murray), for Chalton Down; Wickham; Town Hill, Southampton; Toot Hill, near Romsey; Bramshaw; Pistle Hill; Chalbury; Blandford Racecourse; Bell Hill, Belchalwell; Nettlecombe Tout; High Story; Toller Down; Lambert's Castle; Dalwood Common; St Cyres Hill; Rockbeare; Haldon Hill; Knighton; Manley; Ivybridge; Saltram; Mount Wise, Plymouth. The unfinished Popham line, 1829, left the Portsmouth line at Chatley Heath, for Worplesdon Glebe (in churchyard); Poyle Hill; River Hill, Binstead; Faringdon Common; Merifield; Cheesefoot; Farley Chamberlayne; Sherfield English; Woodfield Green.

Yarmouth line – 1808 (Murray), Admiralty; Chelsea Hospital, West Wing; Hampstead, Platt's Lane; Woodcock Hill; St Albans; Dunstable; Lilley Hoo; Baldock; Royston; Gog Magog Hills; Kings Chair, near Newmarket; Icklingham; Barnham; East Harling; Carleton Rode; Wreningham; Mousehold Hill; Yarmouth, on tower of South Gate.

The last message was sent on the Portsmouth line on 31 December 1847.

Another series of military works is the *"forts"* along the North Downs. In 1888 a scheme for the defence of London was drawn up, against an invasion prospect hard to visualise now, and this included a defence line from Guildford to the Darent, then to the Thames at Dartford, and on the north bank to North Weald in Essex. The line was to consist of entrenched positions which were in fact never dug;

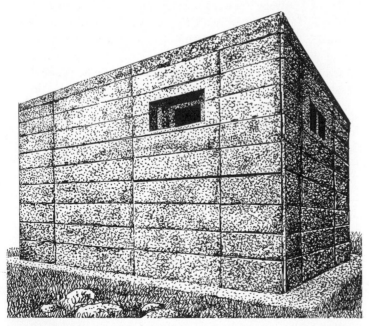

275 *Second world war concrete pillbox (near Dover): several types of these still survive in large numbers right up to the Northern Isles.*

380

but a series of thirteen storehouses to support them was actually built (from about 1895–7), and these can still be traced. Some of them are in private hands, and are worth a visit. They are not strictly forts, but were commonly called such from the beginning. They consist of massive earth banks surrounded by a moat faced with concrete. There are two at Guildford (Henley Grove and Pewley Hill), and others at Boxhill, Betchworth, Reigate, Westerham, Farningham, and elsewhere.

Barracks are notoriously unlovely buildings, but are prominent features of the towns that have them. There are a few old ones of distinction, such as those at Berwick-on-Tweed (1719, possibly by Vanbrugh). Wellington Barracks in London, 1834, has Doric touches. Most of them are Victorian, and many are bleak indeed (eg Devizes). A 19th-century conceit was to make them look like castles, as at Stoughton, Guildford. Most of those at Aldershot are being replaced by blocks of contemporary design, and modern ones are very different from the 19th-century ones. In Scotland fortified barracks were built in the Highlands between the 1715 and the 1745. These include Inversnaid (Sg), Fort Augustus, Bernera, and Ruthven in Badenoch (In); this dates from 1719, but was burnt in 1746, and its remains are very imposing.

Parade grounds can be historic, like those at the military colleges and that of the Honourable Artillery Company in City Road, London, 1735. Laffan's Plain has been an essential part of the atmosphere of Aldershot since 1854. Incidentally, Aldershot is unique as an entirely military town, complete with all the apparatus of armies since they went there in 1854, including hospital, garrison churches (of a style which has affected Victorian churches for miles around), and buildings of all kinds, few very inspired. Even when Aldershot is entirely modernised, it will still have a special atmosphere. A more interesting garrison church is that at Portsmouth, 1212–20, restored by Street, 1866.

Arsenals also have their character. The king of these is Woolwich, which was one of the prides of the Victorian age. There are still many buildings from the early phases; it was founded in 1716, as a Brass Gun Factory, and Vanbrugh's building for this, 1717, survives, as does the Model Room of 1719 and the entrance to the Gun Boring Factory of between 1719 and 1739. The next series of buildings, also in yellow brick, date from the first half of the 19th century. Some of these are magnificent timber-framed sheds.

Dockyards, too, still retain some relics of former processes. Portsmouth, Devonport, and Chatham have the best of these, and at Chatham the huge sheds where ship designs could be laid out full scale have been preserved as historical monuments.

Finally, *minor traces* of the military presence may just be touched on. These include the earthworks left by training or threats of war – trenches dug by 19th-century militia (eg on Farley Heath (Sy), where they at first confused the investigation of a Celtic temple by looking like its boundary ditches), or mid 20th-century Home Guards (air photographs of Battersea Park show parts of the park thickly scored with old trenches, gun-posts, etc); gunposts or radar-posts, circular hollows in the ground, can look like game-shooting butts in open or moorland country; practice rifle or gunnery ranges sometimes survive as straight banks of earth, which in sandy country may now be more or less decayed (as on Puttenham Common (Sy)); tank-traps are wide ditches across country, now filled in with flints or gravel, which can look like Roman roads; tank-tracks in soft land can leave deep ruts, or expose wide areas of subsoil; tank obstacles (concrete "teeth") have in some cases been left undisturbed (there are some in the woods in Stoke Park, Guildford); craters of practice bombs (1914–18) and real bombs (1939–45) still pock fields; pillboxes (see **275**) are so resistant to removal that they are now a subject of study and classification – they are found along the coasts, or inland, right up to the Northern Isles, and are of several shapes, polygonal, rectangular, circular, etc, built of concrete, brick, or a mixture, and some are even disguised as summer houses etc; the protective banks of magazines are sometimes found without their original buildings; linear ditches in open country, such as downland, were cut to prevent the landing of aircraft; some minor mounds or hollows can still be very hard to explain. Traces of wartime airfields still survive in level farmland.

Public Buildings

CENTRAL AND LOCAL GOVERNMENT BUILDINGS

Central government

Departmental headquarters are, in the main, concentrated in the Whitehall area of London, for proximity to Parliament. The *Houses of Parliament* itself, on a magnificent riverside site, was rebuilt after a disastrous fire in 1834 by Barry and Pugin (1840–50). The symmetry of its design, with the Lords one end and the Commons the other, and particularly the balance of the immense facade, is classical in spirit, but Pugin's details are Perpendicular, and the two are inseparable. In Pevsner's words, "the result is the most splendid Neo-Gothic public building in any country". The building incorporates the medieval hall of the old Palace of Westminster, built in 1097, but rebuilt, with Yevele's astounding timber roof, in 1399.

276 *The Banqueting House, Whitehall, London (Inigo Jones, 1619). This building, the only part of James I's new palace to be completed, and the Queen's House at Greenwich, introduced Palladian architecture into Britain, and had far-reaching effects.*

Whitehall itself is lined with some remarkable buildings: the Admiralty (Ripley, 1722–6), with Robert Adam's screen of 1759–61 in front of it; the Paymaster-General's and Scottish Office (Lane, 1732–3); the Horse Guards (Kent, 1745–8); the (old) Treasury and Privy Council (a complex building, combining early 16th-century work with Kent's of 1733–6, and Soane's and Barry's of 1845). South of this are the Home and Foreign Office block (Scott, 1868–73) and the (old) Ministry of Health and (present) Treasury block (Brydon, 1898–1900). On the east side of the street are the War Office (Young, 1898–1907); the Ministry of Defence (Harris, 1935); and Inigo Jones' Banqueting Hall (1619–25) of Charles I's projected new palace (see **276**). This all makes a remarkable, indeed unique, assemblage, completed at the south end by the Houses of Parliament, Westminster Abbey and St Margaret's church, and the Middlesex Guildhall.

Other government departments occupy office blocks of various dates and sizes, such as the Department of Trade and Industry in Victoria Street. Two older buildings lie further away. Somerset House (Chambers, 1776–80) was built to house a number of departments and learned societies, and extended by the New Wing for the Inland Revenue and by the East Wing for King's College; Somerset House and Greenwich Hospital have been described as the finest classical buildings in the country. The other building is the Custom House (Laing, 1813–17 and Smirke, 1825, but replacing earlier buildings). The great General Post Office (1870 on) is another huge building.

The other two British capitals, Edinburgh (with St Andrew's House) and Cardiff, each have central headquarters. Many departments also have offices of headquarters character in the great cities, to deal with regional matters; some have dispersed offices in widely scattered places, such as Newcastle, Basingstoke, Swansea, or Crawley. There are also local offices of social departments in most towns of any size – employment exchanges, Health and Social Security offices, etc – and of course post offices and telephone exchanges. The architecture of these latter two between the wars was in a characteristic neo-Georgian style. The Inland Revenue also has local offices, as has the Customs and Excise; the latter has some notable buildings at the ports, such as that at King's Lynn (1683) (see **277**).

The buildings of the government research establishments, such as the National Physical Laboratory at Teddington, the Royal Aerospace Establishment at Farnborough, or the National Engineering Laboratory at East Kilbride, are not in general very notable, except where they encapsulate an old house or an early building. The defence establishments in fact have buildings of greater interest, such as the dockyards at Portsmouth and Chatham (with long ship-halls and ropewalks, specialised buildings, dry-docks, etc), the arsenals, such as Woolwich, and the barrack centres, such as Aldershot. Most of these have 17th- and 18th-century, as well as Napoleonic, buildings.

Another class of public building is the *judicial*. London has the two main *Law Courts*: Street's Gothic fantasy in the Strand (1866–82), with its cavernous hall (or *salle des pas perdus*) and the Central Criminal Courts, the Old Bailey (Mountford, 1900–7). The great cities also have assize courts, such as that at Manchester (Waterhouse, 1859–64). Towns of any size have modest local crown (county) and magistrates' courts (eg Southwark); several have been built in recent years, eg at Guildford and Alton.

In Edinburgh the Court of Session and High Court occupy the old Parliament House of 1632–40.

Assize and high courts are accompanied by *judges' lodgings*, where judges could stay when on circuit. Distinguished examples are at York (18th-century, now a hotel) and Nottingham (now the County Record Office).

A very distinctive component of the British legal system are the *Inns of Court*, groups of buildings, many of them Georgian or earlier, providing both facilities for training barristers and barristers' chambers, with hall, chapel, and library. These are grouped near each other in London, the main survivors being the Inner and Middle Temple, Lincoln's Inn, and Gray's Inn.

The judicial system also contains the *prisons*. Few if any traces remain of the notorious early prisons, such as the Bridewell, the Marshalsea, the Clink, Newgate, etc, which were replaced from the later 18th century by buildings first on the Panopticon principle, or radial wings with an observation post in the centre (eg Millbank, 1813–21, now demolished) and later by galleried blocks (eg Walton, Liverpool, 1848–55; Strangeways, Manchester, 1866–8). "Open" prisons are a 20th-century development, eg Ford (Sx).

There are still remains of a few *local prisons* from before the large national ones just mentioned, eg that at King's Lynn (1784), or that for Stannary prisoners at Lydford (Dv). Castles had dungeons. Small village *lock-ups* also survive, as at Bradford-on-Avon (Wi) (adapted from a medieval bridge chapel) or Lingfield (Sy) (a cage, 1773). Many

villages still keep their *stocks* (eg Odiham (Ha)). The sites of *gallows* can be found all over the country, often on hills or prominent places which can sometimes be identified from place-names (eg Gibbet Hill, Galley (= gallows) Hill). A well-known reconstruction is that at Combe (Bk), on the ridge near Inkpen Beacon.

277 *Customs House – King's Lynn (Nf), 1683: originally a merchants' exchange.*

Town and city halls

Few towns in Britain, except London, reached any significant size until well into the 18th century; they used their *guildhalls*, if they had them, as the seats of their local government. Indeed, the town council was usually itself representative of the trade guilds. Examples are Norwich (1407–13, rebuilt 1535) and York (1447–53). London, always several times larger than the next largest towns, had by 1700 some half million inhabitants. Even here the great Gothic Guildhall of *c* 1410–40 is still the centre of the City's government.

278 *Manchester Town Hall – Waterhouse, 1868: a notable expression of Victorian civic pride.*

The 19th century saw the building, in all towns of any size, of town and city halls, as monumental as the local authorities could afford. At first these might be modest classical buildings, such as Hansom's in Birmingham (1832) or Elmes' and Cockerell's St George's Hall in Liverpool (1840), both necessarily supplemented later by huge office blocks. Leeds Town Hall (Brodrick, 1853–8) was integrated from the beginning, a pattern thereafter normal. These vast buildings indeed give local character to the great cities, such as Manchester (see **278**) (Waterhouse, 1868–77), Glasgow (Young, 1883–8), or Bradford (1873), leading on to 20th-century examples such as Nottingham (Howitt, 1927–9), Norwich (James and Pierce, 1932–8), Cardiff (Lanchester and Rickards, 1904, the centrepiece of an impressive collection of public buildings), or Southampton (Webber, 1932–9). Some cities also provided the Lord Mayor with an official residence, or Mansion House, such as York (1725–6) and London (1739–53). The mayor of Winchester has a house next to the Guildhall.

The Municipal Reform Act of 1835 set up *boroughs* as local administrative units, which necessitated every town of any size (even some quite small ones) having its own town hall. Middlesbrough and Tremadoc are good early examples. The trend became a rush after the Local Government Act of 1888, which set up County Councils (including the London County Council and the London Boroughs), followed shortly by Urban and Rural District Councils. All these bodies needed council chambers and municipal offices.

The town halls of London Boroughs, indeed, are as large as those of other places of their size; it is not always easy to remember, for instance, that Southwark has a population as large as Leicester's, with a great social variety as well. Some boroughs, under the reorganisation of 1974, absorbed others and contain more than one town hall (thus Hackney and Stoke Newington).

The wide range of town halls defies description, but interesting anomalies occur. Thus, Newtown (IW), a town founded in 1256, was destroyed by the French in 1377 and never succeeded as a town thereafter. But it hung on to its borough status until the disenfranchisement of 1832, and possesses a town hall (1699) which can only have been symbolic (see **279**). Ripley (NY) was rebuilt as a model estate village from 1827, a process culminating in a building of 1854 bearing the sculpted words "Hôtel de Ville". Ripley, although having a market cross and once three inns, seems in fact never to have been a borough.

The *county halls* are usually prominent features of the county towns, such as Hampshire's at Winchester, or West Sussex's at Chichester. The monumental County Hall in London, on its splendid riverside site, is of course exceptionally large (it has been found fresh uses following the abolition of the Greater London Council); the Middlesex Guildhall in Westminster served a county with no county town. There are county halls which precede the 1888 Act, to provide for administrative functions. Such include the Shire Hall in Nottingham (1770).

HOSPITALS

Provision of hospitals in the Roman Empire was taken over in the 4th century by the Christian monasteries, and in the Middle Ages every monastery had its infirmary, where not only the members of the house could be cared for when sick or injured, but other people as well. Remains of these infirmaries can be seen at many monastic sites. Thus at Fountains the infirmary is a large long room of nave and aisles, with chapel attached. Besides these, a few specific hospitals were founded in the towns by religious bodies, for example St Bartholomew's at Rochester (1078), and St Giles-in-the-Fields, London (1118), both for lepers, and St Bartholomew's, London (1123), a general hospital. St Thomas's was run by the Augustinian priory in Southwark from the late 12th century, and Bethlehem ("Bedlam"), for the insane, was founded in 1247. The suppression of the monasteries in 1536–40 cut short this valuable social service, and no new hospitals were founded for nearly 200 years.

The upsurge began again in the 18th century; Westminster Hospital was founded in 1719, Guy's in 1725, the Edinburgh Royal Infirmary in 1730, St George's in 1733, York and the London in 1740, Exeter in 1741, and Bath in 1742, to name only a few. There were specialised hospitals too: Queen Charlotte's Lying-in Hospital dates from 1739, and Tuke founded the Retreat at York in 1796 in order to give the insane more humane treatment than they got at Bedlam and its like. Since then a wide range of specialised hospitals has grown up, most of them from the mid 19th century.

Although modernisation of hospitals is proceeding as fast as possible, there are still many survivals of earlier phases. Guy's has retained some of its former atmosphere, with its arcaded courtyard

and its chapel. The Imperial War Museum in Lambeth Road occupies part of the Bethlehem Hospital buildings, transferred here from the City in 1812. The Lying-in Hospital in York Road (London SE1) is a rare example of a small hospital of its period; it is now closed, but the building is still there. St Thomas's moved from near what is now Southwark Cathedral across Borough High Street after the Dissolution, and some of its 18th-century buildings survive; wards can be seen behind the Post Office, and the chapel became the chapter house of the cathedral. But the most interesting survival is an operating theatre now approached from the chapel, which gives a grim reminder of conditions up to the mid 19th century; there is nothing like it outside Bologna and Uppsala. St Thomas's moved to its present site on the Albert Embankment in 1868; here it was laid out in seven four-storied blocks linked by arcades. This arrangement was for reasons of hygiene, and Florence Nightingale was connected with it. Some of these blocks still survive among the new tower blocks, which

279 *Late 17th-century town hall, Newtown (IW): this town was chartered in 1256, but failed, and is now a mere handful of houses, with traces of a street-grid; the town hall was built in the hope of reviving the town, but to no effect.*

of course have quite different internal layouts. There are fashions, or theories, in hospital building, and most of them reflect earlier ideas, even excluding those which had to use old workhouses. Thus, the rotunda was a feature of the earlier 19th century; perhaps the most famous is that in Dublin, but good examples in Britain are the military hospital at Aldershot and the Devonshire at Buxton. The county hospitals of the 19th century and the cottage hospitals of the late 19th and early 20th are also distinctive types. The first cottage hospital, at Cranleigh (Sy), set up in 1859 in a 15th-century house, still survives.

(An interesting account of the organisation and life of a medieval hospital is given in Margaret Wade Labarge: *Women in Medieval Life* (Hamish Hamilton 1986).)

Medieval hospitals, apart from the infirmaries of the monastic houses, catered for the sick, aged, and poor generally. Most were secular, but a considerable number were run by canons or sisters of some religious order or establishment. Most, in fact, of the religious orders ran hospitals, particularly the Augustinian Canons and the Trinitarians, and some orders, like those of St Lazarus, St Thomas the Martyr of Acon,

and St Mary of Bethlehem, existed chiefly for hospital management. There was a particular need for specialised hospitals for *lepers*. Leprosy seems to have evolved in the eastern Mediterranean area in the 2nd century BC, and was brought to Britain by the Romans. The earliest case found so far is a burial in the cemetery at Poundbury in Dorset, dating from about AD 350, and excavated in 1974. Leprosy took root in the English climate, and was a serious scourge until the mid 14th century, when it declined. Lazarhouses can be found in many old towns and villages. Many of them became ordinary hospitals during the 14th century. The chapel of St Mary Magdalene at Ripon represents a leper hospital built outside the town. This contains a "low-side" window (one coming down to very near the ground), which has been taken as a window at which the lepers could watch the services from outside the church. Although this theory is not accepted by all, it fits this case plausibly.

Bubonic plague was another terror of the medieval world (see pages 25–6 for a full discussion). The major outbreaks were really too much for the social resources, but in some places *pest houses* were set aside for the victims. There is one in the churchyard at Odiham (Ha). A very good example is that at Shalford, near Guildford (Sy). This is now a cottage in a recent suburban road (Pilgrims Way) but once stood isolated away from the village, beyond the common fields which

280 *Almshouse – St Cross, Winchester: this was founded in 1136 by Bishop Henry of Blois, and extended by Cardinal Beaufort in 1445, who built this range, of individual houses with prominent chimneys.*

stretched along the east side of the road to Guildford. This isolation can still be imagined. Some churchyards have flat stones on which food could be put for sufferers from plague and other contagious diseases (*plague stones*). That at Eyam (Db) is well known, and there is one at Alford (Li). (*Dole stones*, such as that at Norton Malreward (So) or Shipley (Sx), are also flat stones or tables, but were places where charities were distributed.) The "Watch Elm", on the road from Bridgwater to Bawdrip (So), was a "frontier" for necessary trade during the Plague of 1665. Many of the dead in outbreaks of plague were hastily buried in mass graves outside the towns, and the sites of some of these *plague pits* are known. One good example, never built over, is Charterhouse Square in London. An extreme case of (understandable) public panic is that of the village of Sandhurst (Kt), which is now half a mile from the church. The villagers fled from the plague pit by the church in 1349 and rebuilt their homes in a healthier place.

There are over 2,000 *almshouses* in Britain, housing some 30,000 people. Most towns have one, and many quite small villages. Some are for people from a particular place or district, some for men or women only, some for certain categories or occupations. Many of them are excellent examples of the domestic architecture of the time they were founded (or rebuilt), and some have exceptional features of interest.

They seem to have been first founded by the Knights of the Hospital of Jerusalem, and hence the medieval ones were commonly known as hospitals (a term which therefore did not connote the care of the sick). St John's at Canterbury was founded in 1084. Early almshouses were mostly founded by clerics, but from the 15th century increasingly by laymen. St Cross, Winchester (see **280**) was founded by Henry de Blois in 1135–6 for 13 poor brethren, and another house for "noble poverty" added by Cardinal Beaufort in 1446. The result is a very fine and complete establishment, with two courtyards, refectory, kitchen, master's house, church, and garden (with fishpond). St Mary's, Chichester (see **281** and **282**), founded by 1229, has occupied since the later 13th century buildings on the site of the Greyfriars' monastery; this consists of a large aisled hall, with the (female) occupants' "flatlets" along both sides of it and a chapel at the end. It is unique in Britain, and only a house at Lübeck compares with it. Later houses of note are: Ewelme (Ox), 15th century; Abbot's Hospital, Guildford, for 12 men and 8 women, built in 1619–22 in Jacobean brickwork, with a magnificent "Tudor" gatehouse (see **283** and

284); Leycester's Hospital, Warwick, 1571, in 14th/15th-century buildings; Beamsley (WY), 1593, for women, circular, with seven rooms round a chapel; and Morden College, Blackheath (London), for "decayed Turkey merchants", 1695, probably by Wren.

In the Middle Ages alms were given to the poor by the Church, a social service which ceased abruptly at the Dissolution of the monasteries in 1536–40. Provision for the poor was a serious problem for the rest of the 16th century, and various measures were passed making relief, in its different forms for different needs, the responsibility of the parishes. In 1601 the Poor Law Act authorised parishes to build *poorhouses* for the incapacitated poor. The parishes grappled unevenly with the poor for another 200 years, until the Poor Law Act of 1834 discontinued "outdoor" relief, and thus made all poor go into *workhouses*. The separate small houses run by each parish were replaced by larger houses maintained by "unions" of several parishes. These were built and maintained on the minimum of money; they looked like barracks, and conditions in them were spartan in the extreme. Some of them had separate wards for young, old, men, and

281 *St Mary's Hospital, Chichester, c 1290–1300, but founded c 1158.*

387

282 *St Mary's Hospital, Chichester (interior). An aisled hall with chapel at one end, and rooms along the aisle for the almshouse residents; a unique survival for Britain, comparable only to the hospitals in Beaune and Lübeck.*

women; "casual" wards catered for tramps. They were not unnaturally hated by the poor, and the growth of Friendly Societies in the 19th century is largely due to fear of the workhouse. A report in 1909 spelt the gradual end of workhouses, but their provision, building,

388

283 *The imposing brick gatehouse of Abbot's Hospital, Guildford (almshouse, 1619), in the style of an earlier generation.*

and management were still included in the consolidating Poor Law Act of 1930. They were not finally abolished until the National Assistance Act of 1948, which found other, more humane ways of meeting social needs.

After the Act of 1834, the small parish poorhouses were usually converted into dwellings, inns, etc, and it is intriguing to try to identify them. For example, the early 18th-century poorhouse of Peaslake (Sy) is now represented by two cottages, as is that at Selborne (Ha). The union workhouses, being larger, were converted into hospitals, factories, etc, and are easier to recognise. One such forms the older nucleus of St Luke's Hospital at Guildford, and a very clear example is at Easebourne, by Midhurst (Sx), converted into flats. The former workhouse at Alton (Ha), 1792 (see **285**), is a particularly fine building.

284 Almshouse – Abbot's Hospital, Guildford, interior of courtyard.

EDUCATION BUILDINGS

Schools

Throughout the earlier Middle Ages, education was dominated by the Church. Parish priests taught small groups of boys, often in their churches, while private chaplains acted as tutors in the great houses. Schools in a recognisable sense were run by monasteries, cathedrals, and collegiate churches, to produce the clerics and civil servants (frequently the same people) on whom the Church and State depended. Some of these schools survive, although they were refounded in the Reformation: thus, King's School, Canterbury was founded around 600, King's, Rochester in 604, and St Peter's, York in 627, with Warwick and Ely in the 10th century, Wells Cathedral School in 1180, and Norwich in 1250. The curriculum was based on the "seven liberal arts", the *Trivium* – dialectic, rhetoric, and grammar, and the *Quadrivium* – arithmetic, music, geometry, and astronomy. The language used was Latin, not vernacular; Latin was essential for international relations, both public and ecclesiastical, and for administration and the law. Greek was taught in a few schools. The schools in which these subjects were taught became known as *grammar schools*. The nobility and gentry had a different system, in which boys were attached as pages or squires to noble houses

285 Workhouse – Alton (Ha), 1793: a handsome example. Each "union" of parishes had a workhouse for the unemployed and the (generally elderly) poor. Work was expected; conditions were spartan, and sometimes bad; the system was universally hated.

and given a training geared to courtly and military activities, with less academic content.

In addition, during the 15th century a variety of small schools was set up by guilds in the towns (eg Stratford-on-Avon), by hospitals (eg Christ's Hospital), by chantries (eg Wotton-under-Edge, 1348), or by gentry or merchants in lieu of gifts to monasteries. At Ewelme (Ox), a unique combination of church, almshouse, and (elementary) school, of 1436–50, still survives. Chantry schools were numerous, and might be either of grammar school status, or "song schools" (elementary). They were conducted by the local chantry priest, normally in the church porch or in a chapel inside the church. At Lurgeshall (Sx), a 16th-century lean-to gallery attached to the south aisle, used first as a meeting place after services, was joined to the porch in 1622 for use as a school. At the abolition of the chantries under the Chantries Acts of Henry VIII and Edward VI, there were 259 of these schools, of which 140 were grammar schools; the total number of grammar schools before the Reformation was some 300. G M Trevelyan points out that many of these schools were of high quality, aimed at producing educated laymen as well as priests. By the end of the 15th century the nobility and their retinues and protégés were on the decline, while the gentry and the burghers (products of the grammar schools and the merchants' offices) were rising. Trevelyan concludes that "Grammar Schools were not, as used to be thought, the result of the English Reformation; they were its cause".

The most influential of the late medieval grammar schools were those at Winchester, founded by Bishop William of Wykeham in 1382, and Eton, founded by Henry VI in 1440. Both were linked to university colleges, Winchester to New College, Oxford, Eton to King's College,

Cambridge. Both retain their original buildings – scholars' court, classrooms, hall, chapel, library, kitchen, brewhouse, etc. The foundation of Winchester provided for 70 "poor and needy scholars", that of Eton for 25 "poor scholars and anyone else who wished to come". They were national, not local, from the first. The quality of these schools led to a demand for other boys to pay to live and be taught by masters in their houses, a practice which spread to other schools and eventually, by the 18th century, gave rise to the *public school* system, drawing boys from a wider than local range.

The 16th century saw a ferment in education and in the founding of schools. The Renaissance, combined with the Reformation, the needs of the mercantile state, and the rise of the middle class, opened up education throughout the post-medieval society. But, as Foster Watson points out, the influence of the Protestant clergy was strong, replacing the control of the Church in medieval schools, and an important factor in Tudor and 17th-century schools was the need to spread the new Protestant theology and outlook; many schools, such as Oakham and Uppingham, were founded by clergy exiled under Mary.

286 *A Tudor grammar school – the Royal Grammar School, Guildford, founded 1508; this building 1552.*

All these factors induced radical changes in the curriculum. Colet's St Paul's (1509) led the way by placing more emphasis on Greek and less on the medieval subjects; Wolsey in his school at Ipswich (of which the gatehouse survives) provided for Latin, ancient history, and "grammar" (the critical study of texts); Cranmer, at Canterbury, proposed Latin, Greek, Hebrew, French, and Science. Room was also allowed for physical pursuits of national importance such as archery. The 17th century added, particularly in the sea ports and mercantile cities, mathematics and navigation.

There was a tendency for the newer schools to base their practices on older ones; thus, Manchester Grammar School (1515) and Merchant Taylors' (1561) followed the methods used in the school at Banbury; Sevenoaks and St Saviour's followed St Paul's. Many 16th-century schools were founded by merchants, eg Tonbridge 1551, Rugby 1567, Bedford 1562, Oundle 1545, Holt 1548, or by yeomen, eg Harrow 1571. Even a few girls' schools were set up, eg Christ's Hospital 1552 and The Red Maids, Bristol, 1634; several were founded in the 18th century.

Those of the ancient medieval schools which had survived into the 16th century were refounded on the new lines. Some of the new schools themselves were "refounded" by Edward VI to increase their prestige in this area (eg Guildford 1509, refounded 1553 (see **286**)), and Elizabeth encouraged the founding of many new schools. Some schools were in pairs, "Classical" and "English" (Grammar and Elementary), often on the same site. Most old towns have remains, in the form of complete buildings, such as the impressive courtyard at Guildford, or the buildings at Stamford, Grantham, and Stratford-on-Avon, or fragments of their old schools. Some, like Sherborne, occupy former monastic buildings.

After the Restoration in 1660 the grammar schools went into a decline which lasted until the 19th century. This was largely due to their slowness in adapting their curricula to the changing needs of the times, which led to the growing popularity of other types of school. Prominent among these were the *Dissenting Academies*, schools set up by nonconformists to cater for the commercial needs of those barred from access via the universities to the professions. They were essentially grammar schools, but also taught languages and science, and were the soundest schools of the 18th century.

Meanwhile the upper classes were reacting against the grammar schools by adopting private tutors for their sons and the Grand Tour, although Winchester, Eton, and Westminster retained their hold on the aristocracy. The girls were taught at home, if at all.

Another type of new school, at a lower level, was the *charity school*. The Society for the Promotion of Christian Knowledge (SPCK), founded in 1698, was energetic in founding hundreds of these schools – over 1,600 by 1729. Money for these was raised from shopkeepers, artisans, and other local people; clothing was provided. They were very influential in Wales. In addition, there was a variety of private, unendowed grammar and commercial schools, and also parish (vestry) elementary schools.

Meanwhile, a few of the older grammar schools had been able to maintain their position, in the form of *public schools*, partly day and partly boarding, and these rose to the top of the ladder by the mid 19th century, becoming the cradle of the English ruling classes and those wealthy bourgeois who wished to join them. Some of the old city grammar schools, like Manchester, retained their high standards and came through this difficult period. The dissenting academies had by then correspondingly petered out.

The public schools were the subject of a regulatory enquiry – the Royal Commission in 1864. As a result the management of nine "great schools" was regulated under the Public Schools Act of 1868, and these nine (all old grammar schools) have retained pre-eminence (they are Winchester 1382, Eton 1440, St Paul's 1512, Shrewsbury 1552, Westminster 1559 (but originating in a medieval monastic foundation), Merchant Taylors' 1560, Rugby 1567, Harrow 1571, and Charterhouse 1611. The popularity of the public schools in the Victorian age was reflected in the foundation of several new ones, such as Cheltenham 1841, Marlborough 1843, Lancing 1848, Clifton 1862, Cranleigh 1863. The Grammar Schools Act of 1840 had already liberalised the curriculum and regulated the position of the staff.

In the elementary field the masses were largely illiterate until the introduction of Sunday schools in 1780, in spite of the charity schools and the efforts of village dames. In 1818 Brougham's Royal Commission enquired "concerning Charities in England, for the Education of the Poor"; the various elementary schools were finally rationalised under the Education Act of 1870, which set up school boards and recognised the church schools (which still exist). Older elementary schools in inner cities can still be found bearing inscriptions like "School Board for London".

An interlude in elementary education was the monitorial system (also known as the Lancaster or Madras system), sponsored by the National Society in the 1820s, which ran "National Schools" in which older pupils – monitors – taught the rest. This had disadvantages and was replaced by the Pupil Teacher system in 1857.

A miscellany of new schools appeared in the 19th and earlier 20th centuries. These include the private preparatory schools (eg Summer Fields, Cheam, and The Dragon School, Oxford) and private schools for all ages, often taking both sexes at the preparatory level. The cathedrals have choir schools, eg St Paul's (with a new building), Chichester (1497, in probably the hall house of one of the cathedral canons), Winchester (in a medieval building), and York (revived in 1903 in the 1833 building of St Peter's school). A few girls' schools were founded before the mid 19th century, eg Queen Anne's, Caversham (1698), North London Collegiate (1850), and Cheltenham Ladies' College (1853), but many were set up after the Act of 1869: thus, the schools of the Girls' Public Day School Trust and of the Church Schools Company in the 1880s, and important foundations like Wycombe Abbey 1896, St Swithun's 1884, Roedean 1885, and St Paul's 1904. Girls are now taken into the sixth forms of many boys' public schools, with separate boarding houses, and some schools are going completely coeducational.

The non-established churches necessarily set up their own schools – the nonconformists at Mill Hill 1807 and Caterham 1811, and the Roman Catholics at Downside 1607, Stonyhurst 1794, Ampleforth 1802, and Douai 1903. The Quakers have six schools, including Ackworth 1779 (in a Foundling Hospital of 1758), Bootham 1823 (in a building of 1796), and The Mount 1831; many smaller ones, either fully run by the Society of Friends or strongly influenced by them, no longer exist (eg Kinmuck (Ab) 1681 and Wigton (Cu)), or have lost some or much of their Quaker character (eg Polam Hall, Darlington). There are also "progressive" schools, not in the mainstream, such as Dartington Hall and Bedales.

The Endowed Schools Act of 1869 dealt with the rest of the grammar schools; schemes for their administration were drawn up by Special Commissioners, then, in 1874, control was transferred to the Charity Commissioners, and in 1899 to the Board of Education. This Act also provided for girls' schools, and widened the curriculum to include languages, science, and mathematics. Under the Education Act of 1902 the Board Schools were replaced by county and borough

287 *The general classroom of an old school – St Olave's Grammar School, Southwark, (this building, 1835–49): it was a common practice in such schools for several classes to be conducted in one room simultaneously (from a contemporary print).*

primary and secondary schools; new grammar schools were set up; some grammar schools adopted "voluntary-aided" status, receiving funds from local authorities (these schools were absorbed into the state system), while some became grant-aided, their funds (apart from their endowments) coming direct from the Department of Education and Science, then later became independent.

The next major step was the Education Act of 1944, which made far-reaching changes; within the state system fees were abolished and all pupils were maintained by local authorities. Comprehensive schools replaced the former secondary schools in 1965, but many grammar schools continued. The latest developments are the Sixth Form Colleges, hiving off the tops of the county secondary and comprehensive schools, and now the City Technology Colleges, partly sponsored by industry, of which the first was opened in Nottingham in 1989.

The examination system has changed many times, and further changes have either recently been made or are in contemplation.

There has been much building of new secondary and comprehensive schools since the war, including some distinguished buildings on new sites (thus St Olave's and St Saviour's Grammar School (1562 and 1571) moved from Southwark to Orpington in 1968). The

planning of schools has been adapted to meet changing attitudes. The early schools tended to have one large room in which all classes were taught (the "school hall" type (see **287**)); by the late 19th century the "central hall" plan was adopted, with classrooms opening off a hall; in the early 20th century came the "pavilion" type, with classrooms along a corridor; this was followed in the 1920s–1930s by the "quadrangle" type, which has classrooms on two sides, a hall at one end, and specialist rooms at the other.

In Wales the system is basically the same, but there are few public schools. In Scotland also the local grammar school (or "academy"), followed by the regional university, has been the traditional educational pattern, although recently some universities have attracted more English students. Some of the Scottish upper classes have tended to send their sons to Oxford or Cambridge. From the Reformation on, standards have been high in Scottish schools, and the curriculum wider than in England.

Higher education

This has given rise to some of the most splendid buildings in the country, and a brief sketch is not out of place here.

The medieval *universities* of western Europe originated in the great cathedral schools of the early Middle Ages, such as those of York, Lincoln, Paris, Tours, Auxerre, and Bologna. Bede had already, in the 8th century, set up schools at the monasteries of Wearmouth and Jarrow; one of his disciples, Archbishop Egbert of York, founded a school at York, in which his disciple Alcuin took the lead. This was not a loose gathering of scholars but an organised community, with an important library of religious and classical works. Alcuin took over in 767, but in 782 joined Charlemagne's entourage and ran the palace school at Aachen. In 796 he became abbot of St Martin's at Tours and died in 804, leaving Tours to become a great centre of scholarship. The school at York continued during the next century and had enormous influence, until the cultural life of the north of England was disrupted by the Danes. But it was in Alcuin's schools that teachers were trained and the medieval curriculum – the seven liberal arts (the Trivium and Quadrivium, see above) – was developed.

The formal crystallisation of the greater schools into universities (in Christopher Brookes' lapidary words) and the foundation of universities with special academic privileges took place in the late 12th and early 13th centuries. Among the cathedral and monastic schools, that of Oxford drew ahead in the 12th century and achieved legal recognition in *c* 1170, only a few years later than its model, Paris (*c* 1150). In 1167 English students in Paris left there and came to Oxford, not only stimulating Oxford as a centre of learning but probably indicating that it had already been one for some time. The students lodged in houses or inns (at their own cost), each with its own adult Principal (most students were teenagers); this custom of lodging in separate houses, thus on separate staircases, has been perpetuated at Oxford and Cambridge to this day, as opposed to rooms along corridors as at other universities. The row of medieval houses at Worcester College, Oxford, is a survivor of this early phase; it represents part of the late 13th-century Gloucester Hall, founded by the Benedictine abbeys. This hall was taken over by Gloucester College in 1560, and subsumed into Worcester in 1714 (see **288**). The coats of arms over the doors signify that each house was maintained by a different diocese for the use of its own scholars. The students soon acquired halls where they lived and dined (eg the Hostel of St John, Cambridge, 1135, under Augustinian canons); teaching was done by teachers in the town, who set up their own individual schools.

In 1209, after a fracas with the town, some students moved to Cambridge and set up a similar university there. In 1214 the Papal Legate reinstated the rights of Oxford, with privileges which increased over the years. In 1221 the friars arrived, and raised the level of teaching.

By the later 13th century colleges based on the model which had evolved in the university of Paris – in much the same form in which they have continued to the present – began to be set up in Oxford and Cambridge, but, as Richard Hunt points out, before *c* 1450 these had little influence over the university, in contrast to their power and dominance from the 16th to the 19th centuries. The colleges at both universities had (and to a great extent still have) considerable autonomy as against the university itself. They were independent foundations, owning their own property (and some were, and are, very wealthy); their functions were residence and tuition (although some of their academic staff have university appointments), in preparation for degrees etc granted by the university. The latter's function was examination, ceremonial and the provision of a central library, and science and engineering facilities. The relationship between the university and the college is of course necessarily close.

The college buildings are laid out in a standard form, with quadrangles (called courts at Cambridge) containing hall, chapel, library, teaching rooms, and living quarters; some, like New College and Magdalen, have cloisters as well. The first was University College at Oxford, though its Statutes were not granted until 1280; Balliol was set up in 1260, but obtained its charter later; Merton acquired its site, buildings, and charter by 1274, and has retained its founder's original buildings, including a library. By 1300 more colleges and halls followed, including Gloucester in 1283 (since absorbed into Worcester). During the 14th century four more were founded – Exeter, Oriel, Queen's, and New College (which retains its original buildings of 1379, as well as an angle of the city wall in its garden, and an ornamental mount). Lincoln followed in 1427, All Souls in 1437.

At Cambridge the first was Peterhouse, 1284. This moved to a suppressed monastery in 1309 and got its statutes in 1338, based on those of Merton, Oxford; both were non-monastic in character, that is, students did not have to become clerics, friars, or monks.

288 *This row of houses at Worcester College, Oxford, represents "mansions" for students founded by Benedictine abbeys in the late 13th century, as Gloucester Hall. This hall became part of Gloucester College in 1560, which was absorbed by Worcester College in 1714. The row of houses is a unique reminder of medieval university practice.*

Michaelhouse (later incorporated into Trinity) followed in 1324 and Clare in 1326. The rest of the 14th century saw Pembroke, 1347, Gonville (later Gonville and Caius), 1348, Trinity Hall, 1350, and Corpus Christi, 1352. These last two were set up to train clergy to replace the losses in the Black Death. Corpus has a complete original court; Peterhouse continued an earlier college-type community, and has a hall of 1286. Jesus occupies the buildings of a medieval convent. King's in 1441 completes the medieval series. Fewer Cambridge colleges were founded by clerics than at Oxford. There were also hostels for poor students, who learned a more limited range of subjects.

In about 1300, students of Brazen Nose Hall, Oxford, dissatisfied with aspects of the University's teaching or discipline, left Oxford in a body, and settled in Stamford (which seems to have been an educational centre of some kind). They were joined by students from Cambridge. They took with them the bronze lion's head knocker which gave their hall its name, and a replica of this can be seen on the gateway to their premises in St Mary Street, Stamford, since the original was returned to Oxford in 1890. The students returned to Oxford in 1335. Brasenose College, which succeeded their Hall, was founded in 1509.

Both universities have many later buildings of distinction, such as Queen's and St John's at Oxford (with its important garden), and, at Cambridge, St John's and Trinity gatehouses, the Wren library at Trinity and the Pepys library at Magdalene, King's chapel, and St John's Combination Room. There has recently been another wave of building, some of which is interesting and even distinguished, such as, at Oxford, the new buildings at Wolfson, St Catherine's (Arne Jacobsen 1960s), St John's (1958–60), Wadham (1953), Exeter (1964), Keble (Ahrends et al 1971–6), St Hugh's, or, at Cambridge, Churchill (Sheppard and Robson 1960), Clare's new buildings, Fitzwilliam College (Lasdun 1966).

But Oxford and Cambridge are not all colleges; the university itself has its central buildings of all periods, eg, at Oxford, the Bodleian (1480, 1602 etc, and a new building by Gilbert Scott (1935) and the Law Library of the 1960s), the Radcliffe Camera (formerly the Physics Library, Gibbs 1739), Wren's Sheldonian theatre, the old Ashmolean Museum (now the Museum of the History of Science, 1679–83), the new Ashmolean (Cockerell, 1840s), Ruskin's University Museum (1850s), and Nicholas Stone's gateway to the Botanic Gardens, c 1630

(the gardens are the oldest botanic gardens in England, 1621). Cambridge has the Senate House (Gibbs, 1722–30), the Library, and the Fitzwilliam Museum (Cockerell, 1837–47).

Indeed, the university quarters of both cities are treasure houses of architecture of all periods, with unsurpassed townscapes. They are unique.

In Scotland, university education followed a different pattern, with the universities modelled closely on that of Paris; the students lived in lodgings or at home. Until recent years the universities tended to be regional. St Andrew's was the first, founded in 1412 (St Salvator's College (1450) united in 1747 with St Leonard's (1512); St Mary's followed in 1538). Glasgow came next, in 1451 (the present imposing building, with its lofty tower and dominant site (and the Hunterian Museum), was built by Gilbert Scott in the 1870s (tower 1886). Aberdeen's history is exceptional: King's College was founded in 1495, modelled on Paris and Bologna, for a total of 36 staff and students. Some of its original Chairs still continue, such as that of Medicine (1497), the oldest medical Chair in the English-speaking world. Original buildings still in use include the chapel and the Crown Tower, with the spire supported on flying buttresses, a companion to those at St Giles, Edinburgh, and Newcastle-upon-Tyne cathedral. The 16th-century Reformers tried to destroy the college, and these difficulties led to the foundation of Marischal College in 1583. The two colleges were not united until 1860, with the result that, until Durham was founded in 1832, Aberdeen had two independent degree-granting universities, the same number as England! The present buildings of Marischal College are by Archibald Simpson, 1836–45, with the granite front, Mitchell Hall, and tower added in 1906. The last Scottish university under the *ancien régime* was Edinburgh, 1583. Its fine classical buildings are by Adam, 1789, and Playfair, 1834.

The English universities were, as Trevelyan points out, both orthodox and unadventurous until the New Learning of the 16th century transformed the intellectual scene. But the religious ferment of the 16th and 17th centuries again acted against them, by increasing state controls and progressive exclusions of Roman Catholics and nonconformists, who had to make arrangements for their own education and advancement outside the national system (see above). This impoverishment led to a decline, and even decadence, in the 18th century, in spite of a measure of academic freedom. Internal reforms and the raising of standards began in the late 18th century and continued until the modernisation measures of 1871, after which non-Anglicans could be admitted and dons were no longer obliged to be unmarried. London and the few Victorian universities were not under these disadvantages.

Meanwhile, the growing population and prosperity following the Napoleonic wars led to a demand for more university education. The first of the new foundations was Durham, 1832, endowed from the revenues of the prince-bishops (by then largely coal royalties). This was set up on Oxbridge lines, with residential colleges, and had an Anglican character. The castle became University College, and the others were housed in buildings of different ages on the promontory occupied by the cathedral and other ecclesiastical buildings. The university has since spread across the river and north and east of the town. The Senate House occupies the Old Shire Hall.

The University of London was founded in 1836, as an examining and degree-granting body. In fact two major colleges had already been founded, University College in 1826, by Jeremy Bentham and others, with no religious requirements (the impressive classical building is by Wilkins, 1827–9), and King's College, 1828, set up as an Anglican counterblast to "that Godless institution in Gower Street"; it occupies a wing of Somerset House, added by Smirke in 1829. As the university developed it acquired other institutions, and is now a vast federation of some 40 colleges and research institutes, although the effect has been blurred recently by mergers; eg the world-famous Institute of Archaeology has been incorporated into University College. Besides King's and UCL, it also contains centres of excellence such as Imperial College, Queen Mary College, and the London School of Economics. Its buildings include the Senate House (which also contains the great library), the last major building to be faced with stone (Charles Holden, 1932), and, in a more exotic vein, the astonishing Royal Holloway and Bedford New College at Egham, based on Chambord (W H Crossland, 1879–87).

The major London colleges now have direct access to the sources of state funding; and in 1994 the Senate of London University agreed that the major colleges should be authorised to grant degrees of the University on their students, to make appointments to University Chairs and Readerships, and to confer University titles on members of their staffs.

The next wave of university foundation arose from the colleges (some of them with a technical emphasis) founded by private benefactors in the great Victorian industrial cities. Thus the Victoria University, 1888, combined Owens College, Manchester (1851), the Yorkshire College of Science, Leeds (1874), and the University College, Liverpool (1881); in 1904 the University of Manchester was set up (including the Institute of Science and Technology, 1824), while Liverpool and Leeds became separate universities in 1903 and 1904, the latter incorporating the Leeds School of Medicine (1831). At Newcastle-upon-Tyne, the College of Medicine (1834) merged with Armstrong College (engineering) (1871), to become King's College, Durham in 1937; this became the University of Newcastle-upon-Tyne in 1963. At Southampton, Hartley College (1862) became a University College (in connection with London) in 1902, and a separate university in 1952. This was a pattern followed at Exeter and Hull also. The University of Wales was set up in 1893, linking four regional colleges, an institute of science and technology, and, recently, Lampeter as well. Reading became a university in 1926.

A later wave of foundation took place in the 1960s, when 16 new universities were set up in England and four in Scotland. Some of these grew out of technical colleges. Many of them have extensive campuses with scattered buildings, ornamental lakes, etc. The quality of the buildings varies from the utilitarian to the distinguished (eg Spence's at Sussex, or Lasdun's at East Anglia). Some also occupy an older building, such as the Tudor Heslington Hall at York.

Higher technological education is another important sector. Apart from institutions like the Loughborough Institute of Technology (1909; now a university) and technology-oriented universities like Surrey (which evolved out of Battersea Polytechnic), a number of *polytechnics* have been founded during this century, though the oldest, the "Regent Poly", until recently the Polytechnic of Central London, was founded in 1838. There are 30 of these; some were Colleges of Advanced Technology until the 1960s. Their courses end in degrees or diplomas. Most of them have now, since 1992, become full universities. In addition, there are a large number of colleges of higher education, covering a wide variety of subjects including teacher training and arts and crafts; their courses end in degrees granted by a university or by the Council for National Academic Awards. Such is King Alfred's College, Winchester. The College of Ripon and York St John is now part of the University of Leeds. Some of these were formerly teachers' training colleges or theological colleges; some, like Bath, incorporate a local college of art, and others, like the West Surrey

College of Art and Design, Farnham, or St Martin's School of Art, are purely art colleges. The music colleges come into this category (the Royal Academy of Music, the Royal College of Music, etc).

There are also specialised training schools run by the professional institutions for, eg, accountancy, architecture, drama (eg the Royal Academy of Dramatic Art), engineering, surveying and estate management, printing, etc. The once independent medical schools have been absorbed into their local universities. Solicitors are trained by the Law Society, and barristers at the *Inns of Court*. The latter are unique institutions combining hall, chapel, library, and teaching rooms, with barristers' chambers. The Inns seem to have been founded in the 14th century, and contain buildings of many periods, with fine Georgian squares and ranges (eg at Gray's and Lincoln's Inn) and halls such as the Middle Temple.

Finally, the theological colleges may be mentioned. Some of these, of all denominations, form part of universities (eg King's College, London), but many, including most of those of the Church of England (eg Cuddesdon, or Salisbury and Wells) are independent of the universities, but have courses leading to degrees. Lincoln Theological College occupies an 18th-century hospital built by Carr of York, and the wards are still visible under their new uses. An interesting group is the Selly Oak Colleges in Birmingham, where Quaker, Methodist, and intra-religionist studies are carried on in separate buildings but with a central library. The Quaker college, Woodbrooke, occupies a former home of the Cadburys. (Lincoln and salisbury have recently been closed.)

MUSEUMS AND ART GALLERIES

The great private collections, from Renaissance times, were influenced by classical tastes and the Grand Tour, and included pictures as well as statuary and a wide variety of *objets d'art*, some of doubtful importance. The separation of pictures came later. Many great country houses, such as Chatsworth or Petworth, have incomparable collections of this kind, and by far one of the most interesting survivals of an 18th-century collector's house, filled with his books, pictures, and objects, is Sir John Soane's museum in London.

The Royal Society, founded in 1660, stimulated serious and scientific collecting and led to the beginning of public collections. So the collections of the two John Tradescants, inherited by Elias Ashmole in 1662, passed to Oxford University in 1679–83. But, apart from a few cases like this, and the British Museum itself, museums are essentially a 19th-century movement. The heyday of museum founding in the big towns was the 1820s, and another stimulus was provided by the Great Exhibition of 1851.

The British Museum was founded in 1753, under an Act enabling it to house the libraries and collections of Hans Sloane, Cotton, and Harley, and the royal library (see "Libraries", below). It opened in Montague House in 1759, and for a long time contained natural history collections as well as books and antiquities; the Natural History Museum did not get a separate building until 1880. The present buildings began to be assembled in 1823, with the great room for George III's library in 1827, the classical front in 1852, and the Reading Room in 1857. The Victoria and Albert and the Science Museums were founded in 1852; the Museum of Practical Geology, later the Geological Museum, begun in 1841, was in a charming Victorian building in Jermyn Street from 1851 until it moved to its present site in 1935. Outside London, the Ashmolean comes first in 1683, followed by the Fitzwilliam at Cambridge in 1816, Leeds in 1818, Manchester in 1821, and Norwich in 1825. In Edinburgh the National Museum of Antiquities dates from 1781 and the Royal Scottish from 1812. The National Museum of Wales was set up in 1927. Most of these are conspicuous buildings in the taste of their periods.

The separate art galleries begin with the National Gallery in 1824, followed by the National Portrait Gallery in 1857 and the Tate in 1897, though the Tate houses earlier bequests. The great provincial galleries cluster at the end of the 19th century: Edinburgh 1850–8, Glasgow 1856, Birmingham 1867, Liverpool 1877, Manchester 1882, Leeds 1888. There were some 750 museums and galleries in Britain in 1964, and some 2,300 in 1987.

Below the national level, they can be divided between county, local, and specialised. County museums usually house a wide collection of antiquities, often superbly set out (as at Devizes), bygones, local industries, art, natural history, and relics of great men. A good general example is that at Dorchester (Do), which ranges from prehistory to Thomas Hardy and is partly housed in a Victorian iron and glass hall.

Local museums carry the same kind of collections, but on a smaller scale. The specialised museums range from great formerly private collections of pictures and art objects, like the Wallace Collection or Waddesdon, to small site museums like those at Richborough (Kt) or the group along Hadrian's Wall – Chesters, Corbridge, Housesteads, Vindolanda. Transport is well catered for: ships (the National Maritime Museum, the Maritime Museums at Exeter and Liverpool (Albert Dock), the Victory and Mary Rose at Portsmouth, the Cutty Sark at Greenwich, Buckler's Hard); railways (the National Railway Museum, York); road transport (tramways at Crich (Db), motors at Beaulieu (Ha)); the Transport Museum at Covent Garden; canals (Stoke Bruerne (Nh)). Industry is represented at Birmingham, Ironbridge Gorge, Beamish, and Morwellham, down to single sites like the Abbeydale Mill at Sheffield, or many wind and watermills; pottery is to be found at Stoke-on-Trent and the Wedgwood collection at Etruria (firms' museums are important for the technology of a particular product); there are museums of coalmining, fisheries, and many other industries. The history of medicine is shown at the Wellcome Museum in London, and the history of science at Oxford. There are planetaria. There are imaginative restorations of old mills, warehouses, etc, such as Styal (Ch), "Wigan Pier", or Albert Dock, Liverpool.

Earlier methods of farming are demonstrated at eg Botley (Ha) and Cogges (Ox); the whole history of farming is reflected in the Museum of English Rural Life at Reading. The past life of a whole area is exemplified by, eg, the Ryedale Folk Museum at Hutton-le-Hole (NY), and past houses by the Weald and Downland Open Air Museum, Singleton (Sx), or the Avoncroft Museum of Buildings, near Bromsgrove (Wo). St Fagan's near Cardiff is the British prototype of the open air museum, following Scandinavian models, as is the Castle Museum, York, with its reconstruction of an urban street. There are museums of costume, such as that in the Assembly Rooms at Bath. There is Madame Tussaud's, with waxworks. Cathedrals have their museums, such as that at Durham or the Treasury at Ripon; the Crypt at York reflects the history of the Minster site since Roman times. Another specialised type is the houses of the great, like those of Wellington, Dickens, or Carlyle in London, Burns at Dumfries, Jane Austen at Chawton, or Gilbert White at Selborne. Somewhat related to these are the one-man galleries such as Stanley Spencer's at Cookham or G F Watts' at Compton (Sy). Music is shown at Fenton House, Hampstead.

There are small collections of this, that, and the other; the variety is enormous, and often the interest and value equally so. Modern arrangements and display techniques enable everyone to assimilate the relevance of the past with enjoyment. This has been amply demonstrated by the advances in presentation made in the last few years which have resulted in a new kind of museum. The Museum of London is a milestone along this road, as is, more recently, the biological display at the Natural History Museum in London. The fascinating museum in the Roman baths at Bath, and the restored naval dock building at Chatham, where the public can try their hand at crafts, are among these; but the runaway success of the Jorvik Centre at York (opened in 1984) has amply justified a radically new approach. This is a joint venture of the York Archaeological Trust and consummate publicity; it displays the excavations of the Viking site at Coppergate, but sets these in the context of the Viking city. One descends through time to the Viking streets, reconstructed with people, sounds, voices, and smells, and passes through them to the excavations, then to the post-excavation work, and finally to a museum and shop. This has clearly touched the public imagination, and further museums on similar lines have opened in Edinburgh, Oxford, and Canterbury. Museums will never be the same again.

LIBRARIES

The first libraries of any note in post-Roman Britain were those of monasteries. Few exceeded 500 or 600 books; a thousand was very large, and most were quite small. They were kept in cupboards or cases in the cloister or a room off it. By the later Middle Ages some large monastic churches built special rooms for their books; examples can still be seen at Canterbury, Durham, and Winchester; at Gloucester the carrels or working alcoves survive.

The great churches with colleges of secular canons also had libraries; York built one against the south transept, and it is now housed in the chapel of the former palace of the Archbishops; Lincoln's medieval library was burnt in 1609, but was rebuilt by Wren in 1674; Ripon's was refounded in 1624. At Hereford the books are still chained to reading desks. At other places, including some country churches, chained books can also be seen. A good example is the old grammar school library at Guildford (1573).

At the Dissolution the monastic libraries were dispersed and bought piecemeal by private individuals, such as Robert Cotton, whose collection was left to the nation in 1702 and eventually became part of the British Museum in 1753.

Another important group of early libraries is those of the Oxford and Cambridge colleges. Many of these go back to medieval times, but have been enlarged through the centuries and mostly have more recent buildings. Two superb examples are those of Merton College, Oxford, 1371–8, the first "Renaissance" library in England, where the books are on shelves instead of in presses, and Magdalene College, Cambridge, c 1679, where the books are still as arranged by Pepys. The nucleus of a library of national calibre is Duke Humphrey's library at Oxford (1430–90); its building was restored by Bodley in 1602 and recently restored again, and this gives a fascinating idea of what an early major library was like.

Until the 18th century most libraries were still private or set up for limited groups of people. Thus the owners of country houses collected books on history, antiquities, and literature, to complement their experiences on the Grand Tour; there are many fine examples to be seen, such as those at Kenwood, London, or Blickling Hall (Nf) (the collection of Sir Richard Ellys, who died in 1742, which includes a large number of books printed before 1500). Parochial libraries also existed, such as those at Grantham (1598, still with some chained books), Langley Marish (Bc) (1623), and Wimborne Minster (Do). Chetham's, Manchester, 1653, is a rare example of an early town library, still housed in its old collegiate building. The great learned societies built up impressive collections in their special fields, some of which are of unique importance; these include the Royal Society (1660), the Society of Antiquaries (1717), the Royal Institution (1799), the Royal Society of Medicine (1805), and the Royal Geographical Society (1830). There are also specialised libraries, not always large but sometimes unique, such as that at Lambeth Palace, Dr William's library (nonconformist), and the Library of the Religious Society of Friends.

Subscription libraries, that is libraries open to all on payment of a fee, began in the 18th century and were very popular in the 19th and early 20th centuries. Early examples are that founded by Allan Ramsay in Edinburgh in 1725, and that of Cawthorne and Hutt in London, 1740; the famous Mudie's was founded in 1842, with branches all over the country, and lasted till well into the present century. By the end of the 18th century the big cities had private subscription libraries, such as the Liverpool Lyceum, the Leeds Library, and the Portico, Manchester, 1804; the London Library was founded in 1841. Aimed at working people, for self-education, were the mechanics' institutes, begun in Glasgow in 1800 and numbering over 400 in 1849; closely allied were the miners' libraries of south Wales, only recently dispersed, and Ramsey's institute at Leadhills (Lk). Some of these institutes still survive, essentially in the form of subscription libraries, such as that in Guildford. The Prince Consort's library at Aldershot was found in 1860.

By the mid 19th century the demand for free libraries for all became overwhelming, and a Public Library Act in 1850 enabled municipalities to spend rates on them. The first towns to adopt the Act were Brighton and Norwich, but the first actual library to be set up was that at Manchester (1852); this grew to be the largest municipal library in the country and the present enormous reading room was built in 1934. Westminster followed in 1857; by 1889 there were 155, and by 1919 some 450. A great impetus was given in the years between the wars by the trusts set up by Passmore Edwards and Andrew Carnegie, and the county libraries were set up with Carnegie help. The oldest public libraries in Scotland are Kirkwall, 1683, and Innerpeffray (Pe), 1691.

The apex of the system is the national libraries. The British Museum was set up under an Act of 1753, enabling the state to house the Sloane, Cotton, and Harley collections of books and manuscripts, together with the royal library (Edward IV to George II – greatly enlarged by the collection of George III). It was opened in Montague House in 1759, and the present buildings date from 1823 and later (the famous domed reading room is of 1857). The library contains some eight and a half million books, and has grown partly by the compulsory deposit of publications under the Copyright Acts from 1711 onwards. It also runs a Newspaper Library at Colindale.

The other national libraries benefiting from compulsory deposition are those of Oxford (Bodleian) and Cambridge universities, the National Library of Scotland (developed from the library of the Faculty of Advocates (1682), the National Library of Wales (1907), and Trinity College, Dublin. There are also several important state libraries for special purposes, such as the Science Library (now partly merged with the National Lending Library for Science and Technology at Boston Spa), the Patent Office library, and that of the Victoria and

Albert Museum. The British Library, combining that of the British Museum with other state libraries, was set up in 1973, and is being housed in new premises at St Pancras.

The university libraries are also important, such as that at London and its colleges. They, with other public bodies, support the National Central Library, the national centre for the loan of books through other libraries; it draws on some 21 million books all over the country. Some of the great libraries in Manchester, including the unique John Rylands Library (1900), form part of the university group of libraries.

Some government departments have important reference and research collections, such as the Foreign Office (with the famous India Office Library) and the Ministry of Defence (with the old War Office Library). Some clubs have distinguished collections, such as the Athenaeum. There are important county or local collections, like the William Salt Library at Stafford. Mention must finally be made of the record offices and archives maintained by counties and dioceses, and of the Public Record Office (1851). But libraries, big and small, are now a ubiquitous feature of modern life.

THEATRES

Theatres are a familiar feature of modern life and of the urban scene; but the theatre has a very long history, and traces of earlier phases survive. A brief background will set the stage (this draws for its main lines on the analysis by Richard Southern).

Drama arose from ancient religious ritual and seasonal enactments, and at that stage was closely allied to dance and mime, but used costume or masks. Very remote and diluted survivals of these pagan practices are still alive in the form of "wild men", masked performances like the Padstow Horse and the Welsh Mari Lwyd, the dance-centred Horn Dance at Abbot's Bromley (St) (see page 297), and particularly the Mummers, of which a good example is practised at Marshfield (Gl). The mummers enact a whole drama of death and resurrection (the yearly transition from winter to spring), and use both words and actions. All these were performed in the open, sometimes from house to house, sometimes along the village street or market place. In fact, the repetition of the mummers' play at successive street corners may have given rise to the use of a wagon in medieval plays. Some of these plays were performed in circular areas in the street, which again may

be an ancient feature. The comic or everyday elements in these plays arose to associate the people with the ritual drama, and because ordinary people could not live long on the high level of the gods and spirits.

While remaining at the level of folklore in this country, in the classical world these primitive rituals developed into high literature and stylised performance in special buildings at great religious festivals. The Greek theatre, with its complex stage and supporting rooms facing a tiered semicircular auditorium, was brought to Britain by the Romans (see **289**). Four of these theatres are known, at St Albans, Colchester, Canterbury, and Brough (the latter recorded in an inscription only), but others may await discovery. Only that at St Albans is complete (see **290**), and this gives a good idea of the sophisticated classical building which a prosperous Roman town was able to support. There was nothing else remotely like it until the 17th century.

But this was an alien intrusion into the cultural history of Britain, and after the Romans left organised religious theatrical festivals did not reappear until the 13th century, the age of the Gothic cathedrals and of the intensification of Christianity in Europe. In that century the old spring dramas began to be set in the context of real life, and a variety of plays grew up, religious epics (moralities), mysteries, saints' plays, and secular dramas. These were performed in the open air or in churches, and in some areas special structures called *rounds* were built. These were circular "places" with fenced banks round them, a raised floor inside, and booths or scaffolds ("tents") for the performances

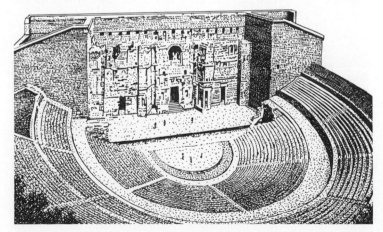

289 *Roman theatre – Orange, France, early 1st century AD: this remarkably complete survival preserves its permanent stage scenery building.*

round the edge; they could alternatively have an earth bank with outside ditch, sometimes filled with water to keep out non-payers; the banks could be terraced for seats, sometimes in wood, sometimes stone. Examples can be seen in Cornwall (Perran; St Just in Penwith), Wales (Llanidan), and Lincolnshire. Other forms involved "tents" scattered over a town square, or lined into a row on a long raised stage, or mounted on wheels and used independently (the York, Towneley (Wakefield), and Chester cycles used these "pageant-wagons"). These wagons were permanent settings for one scene only. Professional actors come in at this point, by the early 14th century.

By the 15th century there were regular performing companies, giving "interludes" – short plays with small casts and single themes, with intimate dialogue and human characterisation, before small audiences, and often indoors. These gave rise to the modern type of play. By the early 16th century these plays were being given at the screens (kitchen) end of halls of great houses. This setting provided two doors for entrances, and by 1559 a stage was built between the doors, often with a central scenery "house" on it. The earliest certain use of stage scenery was in Christ's Hall (later College) at Cambridge, 1551. In parallel with the interludes, maskings and mummings took place at court, with scenery. By the mid 16th century companies were regularly playing at court with portable scenery – painted canvas screens representing a city, a castle, a country house, a mount, or a prison. Some of these "houses" may have been out in the hall itself, not on the stage. This period saw the beginnings of moveable scenery.

The increasing complication of the companies' requirements led to the need for permanent theatre buildings which could house a place of entrance, a background, a raised stage, a dressing room, a property store, and an upper level. The booth stage had been in use since 1542 at latest, but James Burbage, leader of the Earl of Leicester's Men, was the first to build a specific wooden playhouse to house all these things, and for *public* audiences. This was The Theatre in Shoreditch, 1576. This was followed by several others, including the famous Globe, on Bankside, 1598/9, reconstructed on a different site 1992–5. The Hope, Bankside, 1614, was a mixed playhouse and bearbaiting arena. These theatres had a stage etc inside a three-storey square or round house; the galleries went all round, behind the stage, and the central space was unroofed (see **291**). This was reminiscent of the

291 *The Swan theatre, London, 1596. This is the only known contemporary representation of an Elizabethan theatre – the type Shakespeare called a "wooden O", like the Rose and the Globe (from an old print).*

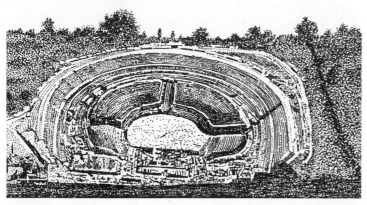

290 *Roman theatre, Verulamium, c 150–4th century. A British example of the type, less complete than that at Orange.*

performances from carts in the courtyards of galleried inns, such as the George at Southwark (see **352**, page 468), where performances still take place. There had been private house theatres, eg at Blackfriars, before 1574 (see **292**).

In parallel with this, the stage for spectacle (as opposed to plays) – masques, on the line of development to opera – was beginning. This originated in court performances, in Italy in the late 15th century, in England in the 16th. Inigo Jones was designing costumes and scenery for these between 1605 and 1640, eg for Ben Jonson's *Masque of Queenes* at Whitehall in 1609, resulting in the "House of Fame", which had a low stage. In 1635, Jones used shutters to change the scene and made a complete theatre for this, with framed scene on stage, a space in front, with a seat for royalty, and the audience round the sides and back. All theatres were closed in 1649; but a few open-air

private theatres remained in use, such as those at Crowhurst (Sy) and Saltram, near Plymouth, *c* 1750. In a garden at Weybridge is a mound on which performances were given to an audience seated in front of it; this is associated with Fanny Kemble and Mrs Siddons (late 18th century). Travelling troupes with portable theatres continued to operate during the 18th and 19th centuries.

Open-air theatres became a feature of great houses in the 18th century, drawing on Roman or Italian Renaissance inspiration. A fine example is that at Claremont (Sy), where Bridgeman (1726) cut tiers into a hillside beside the lake; another is the interesting type of a flat grassy oval arena, enclosed by an arrangement of graduated evergreen shrubs and trees, as at Painshill (Sy) (early 1740s), which is being replanted. More recent examples are the open-air theatres in Regent's Park, London, and at Polesden Lacey (Sy); some schools, such as Bradfield College, have open-air theatres of Greek type.

A new epoch in the theatre opened with the Restoration, drawing on Italian scenery systems and opera houses of the late 16th century, via a French compromise, and leading to a specifically English adaptation to English conditions and traditions. The Italian perspective stage, with its frame, had to be seen from in front, so the audience had to be closely grouped in front of it, preferably raked; the galleries, no longer behind the stage as well, were divided into boxes (see **293**). The French adapted this stage to contain different elements for use

292 *Burbage's second Blackfriars theatre, London, 1597: a hall type, but with seats all round the stage.*

293 *The Schouwburg, Amsterdam – Jacob van Comper 1638, based on Palladio's Teatro Olimpico in Vincenza. This has a permanent stage setting, with no proscenium arch (from an old print).*

401

294 *Drury Lane Theatre, London, in 1808: this is the 1794 building, burnt down in 1809; it has a proscenium arch, and curtains, and was used by Garrick (from an old print).*

295 *The Haymarket Theatre, London (1880), as remodelled by the Bancrofts.*

in different scenes. In England there had been a complete break, and a new start had to be made in 1660. Patents for new theatres were given to Thomas Killigrew and William Davenant; each took over private tennis courts, and so ended the Elizabethan tradition of open playhouses. Killigrew, at Gibbon's tennis court, Vere Street (Theatre

Royal, Clare Market), used a platform stage; Davenant, at Lisle's tennis court (Duke's Theatre, Lincoln's Inn Fields), used a scenic stage. After vicissitudes and new theatres, both companies united at the Theatre Royal, Drury Lane, in 1682; this had been designed by Wren in 1674. This was of the present "intimate" type. The small provincial theatres of the 18th century were based on Wren's Drury Lane (which was rebuilt very large, with five tiers, by Henry Holland in 1794) (see 294).

In 1705 Vanbrugh built an Opera House in the Haymarket, now, much altered and rebuilt, Her Majesty's Theatre. In 1714 a new theatre was built in Lincoln's Inn Fields, and in 1732 another in Covent Garden, which led to the present Opera House. In 1720 the New or Little Theatre (now the Theatre Royal) was built in the Haymarket (see 295): its Nash front dates from 1821. In 1729 a theatre was built in Goodman's Yard, by the Tower; after that there was a long gap until the 1760s and 1770s, which saw the Lyceum, Astley's, the Pantheon, the King's Concert Rooms (or Regency), the Royal Circus, and the Royalty. Bath, Bristol (1766), and King's Lynn got theatres at this time, and by the 1780s and 1790s most towns had one. King's Lynn built a complete theatre in the medieval St George's Guildhall in 1766 (no longer there). That at Richmond (NY) alone survives of this period (1788) (see 296). Harrogate also had one in 1788 (replacing one in

296 *The Georgian theatre, Richmond (NY): this was restored in 1963 (from an old print c 1820).*

298 Theatre in the round – the Victoria, Stoke-on-Trent, 1960s.

297 The Stratford (Ontario) Festival Theatre, which inspired the Chichester Festival Theatre, and pioneered a new concept.

a barn by the Granby Hotel, 1769), and this can still be seen as part of the houses in Church Square. The forestage shrinks in these little theatres, resulting in more entrances in the wings. The theatre reached its present form with Wyatt's Adelphi in 1858, with pit (important in the early 19th century) and stalls; the first tier of boxes has become a circle.

The 19th century saw the development of the theatre as a place of illusion and unreality; the 20th century returned to the representation of the real world. The theatre itself was the subject of experiment. The proscenium was abolished. The Cambridge Festival Theatre, 1926, had no frame – the audience was in direct contact with the players. Other movements included the Little and Art Theatres, the open stage (open on three sides), as at Chichester (see **297**), and theatre in the round with no stage at all (see **298**), just an arena, as at the Pembroke, Croydon. The theatre at Southampton University, 1961, combines an open stage with a picture-frame. The tradition of theatres in the halls of private houses was revived at Glyndebourne (where a separate private opera house has now been built) and Dartington. There are also a few "Greek" theatres for the performance of classical plays, such as that at Bradfield College (Bk). Examples of most of the types referred to can still be enjoyed, but several gems of their kind have been demolished in recent years, such as the

Lyric, Hammersmith (working from 1890 to 1965), and the Granville, Walham Green; some theatres have been converted to other uses. On the other hand, the Tyne Theatre and Opera House, Newcastle (formerly the Stoll), with its Victorian theatre machinery, was restored in 1986.

Music halls, partly originating from fairground shows in the mid 19th century, partly from entertainments in pubs, were a specialised kind of theatre, and had a vigorous life of their own. Famous examples include the City Varieties at Leeds, Collins Music Hall at Islington, the Old Bedford, Camden Town, (1861, present form 1899), the Octagon, Bolton, and the Players' Theatre, Charing Cross. Wilton's Music Hall (1859), the oldest survivor, has recently been restored, as has the Hackney Empire. A recent feature of this world is the "alternative theatre", small venues for the performance of busking, pub-type entertainment, or productions (cf the "Fringe" at the Edinburgh Festival), some of which are still carried out in pubs and working-men's clubs.

CINEMAS

These are essentially a phenomenon of the 20th century, although cinematography as such reached a viable state during the 19th. The first regular public film show was in 1905, and by 1914 there was a cinema in every large town. They reached their zenith between the wars, and were ubiquitous. They ranged from the small suburban "Roxy", charging only a few pence for entry and so intimate that they were known as "flea-pits", to luxury houses like the Curzon and the Palace (see **299**). The first super-cinema in London was the Pavilion at Shepherds Bush, 1923. Sound arrived in 1926; the Davis Theatre, Croydon, was among the first with sound, and was designed on American lines (1928). They could be very big – the Gaumont Palace, Hammersmith (1932) had a balcony seating 2,000. The Odeons of the 1930s were conceived as a complete stylistic entity, down to the ashtrays, so are an important source for Art Deco design; some still survive, as at Chingford (Ex). Cinemas suffered a reduction in numbers after the introduction of television, and many were converted to other uses (such as bingo, factories, or warehouses) or were rebuilt on smaller lines (eg the Gaumont, Haymarket, replaced by the Odeon in 1962). Some had already taken an opposite course, such as the Philharmonic Hall, Islington, 1860, now a cinema.

AMPHITHEATRES AND STADIA

Many Roman towns in Britain, probably most of any size, had amphitheatres for public games and spectacles. Most of these were close outside the walls of the town; they had excavated arenas, the earth from which was piled up to form the banks on which the seating was laid. Some took advantage of natural slopes, while some were faced with stone, like that at Caerleon (Mo), but Britain had none of the special stone buildings like the Colosseum at Rome or the amphitheatre at Arles. The imposing one at Maumbury Rings, Dorchester (Do) was an early Bronze Age henge adapted by the Romans (and used again in the Civil Wars as an artillery battery). The scale varies with the size of the place; that at Caerleon has an arena 200 x 150 ft (60 x 45 m) and could seat about 6,000 people. The mining town of Charterhouse-on-Mendip has a small earthen oval one. That at Silchester (Ha) was excavated and cleared in 1984–6. Conspicuous earthen banks remain of the large amphitheatre at Cirencester. In 1985 traces of an amphitheatre were discovered in front of the Guildhall in London; this is just outside the south-east

299 *Palace Picture Pavilion, Blackpool, c 1910, demolished 1961: theatrical decor in the cinema.*

corner of the Roman Cripplegate fort. Excavations are still going on, but it is clear that the structure was built in timber from AD 54 to 77, before being replaced in stone in *c* AD 120; it continued in use until at least the late 4th century. The site was used for a variety of purposes until modern times, and is of great archaeological importance; it is hoped that a museum can be established in part of it. A reminiscence of the Roman theatre or amphitheatre is probably to be found at Yeavering (Nd), where the Anglian palace had a wedge-shaped building (so far unique in Britain) which was a sort of segment of a theatre with tiers of seats facing the "chairman", presumably the king presiding over the tribal assembly.

There were no successors to the Roman buildings until quite recent times, when mass spectator sports like cricket and football needed special grounds. The nearest analogy is perhaps the *stadium*, for athletics, games, and other activities, sometimes on a scale large enough to take the Olympic Games. The best example is probably that at Wembley (a good sample of large-scale architecture of the early 20th century – built for the British Empire Exhibition of 1924–5). From here we may be led in two directions: to specialised arenas, such as those for dog-racing or motor-racing (eg Brooklands, Weybridge (1907), of which sections of the concrete banking can still be seen), or Brand's Hatch, the successors to the Roman chariot racecourses like the Circus Maximus in Rome or the smaller one now represented

300 *The Assembly Rooms at York – Lord Burlington, 1730, based on a Roman basilica. Most towns of any size had assembly rooms in the 18th century, where much of the social life of the town took place.*

by the Piazza Navona), an extension of which is the road circuit like that for motor cycles in the Isle of Man; and to *exhibition halls*, such as Olympia, Earls Court, or the Agricultural Hall (1861–2). A famous exhibition and entertainment hall was the Egyptian Hall in Piccadilly, London, which lasted from 1811/12 to 1905. Here a wide variety of events took place, including the first moving panorama (1843); later it was used by Maskelyne and his partners for conjuring shows.

CONCERT HALLS

The first room to be built in Europe solely for music was the Old Music Room in Holywell Street, Oxford (1748). But for a long time music continued to be performed in churches, private houses, and in places of the assembly room type (see below). It was the growth of leisure, wealth, and population, and also of the size of orchestras and choirs, that led to the provision of special concert buildings in the big cities and larger resorts, beginning in the mid 19th century. Birmingham Town Hall, 1832, had been used for concerts from the start, but other

places built separate halls – Liverpool (St George's Hall, 1839–47), followed by Leeds (Town Hall, 1853–8) and Manchester (Free Trade Hall, 1856, rebuilt). London's Albert Hall, a cross between the Colosseum and a bandstand, dates from 1867–71. The much-loved Queen's Hall was destroyed in the war, but its place has been taken by several notable complexes, such as the Festival Hall and the Barbican in London. Improvements in acoustic technology (not available to the Albert Hall), combined with modern design, have indeed produced some very fine halls, such as the Fairfield at Croydon. Some towns, such as Guildford, have multi-purpose halls as general civic entertainment centres. The converse of the concert hall is the *bandstand* in the public parks. Many of these are Victorian, and some are delightful and fanciful pieces of graceful ironwork.

ASSEMBLY ROOMS

Assembly rooms for dancing, gambling, and music were a feature of prosperous Georgian towns and resorts. The most famous is that at Bath, built in 1771 but restored in 1963 after destruction in the war. They range from this to quite small ones such as the Adam-style Atheneum at Bury St Edmunds. One of the more distinguished is that at York built by Lord Burlington in 1732–6 in the style of a classical basilica (see **300**). Many still survive as ballrooms or dining-rooms in old hotels, such as the Dolphin at Southampton (1751) or the George at Rye (1818).

DANCING

Dancing is a very ancient practice in all countries, and derives from prehistoric religious and fertility rituals. From this point of view it is part of folklore. It can be processional, that is the assembly of the people at a sacred place where dances were enacted to encourage the growth of animals and crops, to make rain, or to symbolise some mythological situation. For example, processions of dancing people converged on St Martha's Hill near Guildford (Sy) on Good Friday, and there performed energetic fertility dances. From this background emerged the country and Morris dances which were a feature of English rural life until recent times, with only a very nominal connection with Christianity. Scottish dancing has a similar pedigree, but combines this with the commemoration of persons and events.

These dances were carried out in the open, sometimes on the village greens but often at special places like moots, or at ancient sacred places like circles or barrows, at mazes, on hills, or round churches. There were also a few specially made dancing floors, such as the flat round mound with a low rim of earth round it at King's Caple (He). A reminder of dancing on the village green is the *maypole*. Several of these survive (eg at Aldborough, Nun Monkton, and – very fine – Barwick-in-Elmet – all Yorkshire), but the actual pole has in most cases been renewed. Large stones with central hole lying on a green may be maypole bases.

Country dancing was taken up as a social activity in the court and great houses in the later Middle Ages, and was a favourite pastime in Tudor times. The halls and long galleries of the great houses made

301 *Statue of William III, Petersfield – John Cleere, 1757. Statues were often placed in town squares as focal points.*

ideal locations. By the 16th century the old country dances were supplemented by formal dances of foreign origin, like jigs, courantes, and allemandes (and the Inns of Court in London had some special ones of their own). By the late 17th century these were largely superseded by other (French) dances, the gavotte and the minuet, but all these formal dances continued to be danced in places like Bath, where Beau Nash imposed rigid codes on the dancers.

Dancing again changed its character after the French Revolution, and at Almack's Assembly Rooms in London new dances were introduced (the waltz in 1812, the quadrille in 1815, and the lancers in 1817). Ballroom dancing stagnated in Victorian times, but there was a sharp revival in the 20th century, under the influence of negro and native dance forms and music from America (eg the jazz and rag movements). Thus, the foxtrot and onestep were introduced about 1912, and the tango in 1911/12; the Charleston appeared in 1926, the rumba in 1930, swing in 1937, and several forms were developed post-war. To meet the demand between the wars special dance-halls were built, the *palais-de-danse*, and dancing has become an integral part of contemporary culture. Meanwhile the old country and Scottish dancing has detached itself from its folkloric origins, and continues as a social pastime.

STATUES AND MEMORIALS

Most towns, and many villages, have some, and London is particularly rich in them. In one sense they may be seen as debris washed ashore by the tide of the centuries, voices speaking of the personages and events of the past, in contemporary accents. But as well as witnesses of history, some monuments have artistic merit too; some will remain curiosities.

Among such wealth and variety, preferences must be personal. The following somewhat random selection includes some masterpieces and some which are less distinguished but have other claims to interest (monuments in churches are not included here – see page 314). Among *notable people* the equestrian Charles I in Whitehall (Le Sueur, 1633) and William III at Petersfield (1724) (see **301**) stand out. King Alfred at Winchester (Hamo Thorneycroft) is perhaps more prominent than important, as is Queen Boudicca (Boadicea) on Victoria Embankment (Thomas Thorneycroft, 1850s); both are unauthentic as portraits. Queen Victoria has several memorials, apart from that in the Mall (1903); they include statues at Wolverhampton and Hull (this one surmounting a public convenience). Others include Churchill in Parliament Square, Foch in Grosvenor Gardens, and Marx in Highgate Cemetery.

Some monuments are not likenesses but artistic gestures, like the Eros in Piccadilly Circus, commemorating the 7th Earl of Shaftesbury (Alfred Gilbert 1893, the first aluminium statue in London), or Epstein's Rima in Hyde Park (to W H Hudson, 1925). There are also works of art with no commemorative connection, such as the cast of Rodin's Burghers of Calais on Millbank, Westmacott's Achilles in Park Lane (1822), or Watts' Physical Energy in Hyde Park. Contemporary works of art include the Elizabeth Frink Horseman in Winchester, the Barbara Hepworth in Holborn, and the Henry Moore at Harlow New Town. Piazzas, shopping malls, and town centres are increasingly being dignified by such works.

War memorials, mostly to the dead in the First and Second World Wars, are of course ubiquitous, often in churchyards but sometimes in the town or village streets. Lutyens' Cenotaph in Whitehall stands for them all, as do the Memorials at Edinburgh and Cardiff for Scotland and Wales. Institutions also have their own memorials, as Christ Church, Oxford, or Winchester College, or firms, railways, or regiments.

A particular, and touching, series of memorials are the *Eleanor Crosses*, erected to mark the stages in the cortège of Queen Eleanor of Castile from Lincoln to Westminster in 1290. Only three originals remain, those at Geddington (Nh) (see **227**, page 330), Northampton (Hardingstone), and Waltham Cross (Ht). That at Charing Cross is a copy.

Another form of monument is the *column*. These occur not only in towns but on prominent hills and landscaped parks. London has three of note: Wren's Monument (1671–7), on the spot where the Great Fire of 1666 broke out; the Duke of York's Column (Wyatt and Westmacott, 1834); and Nelson's Column (Railton and Baily, 1838–43). Outside London the Victory

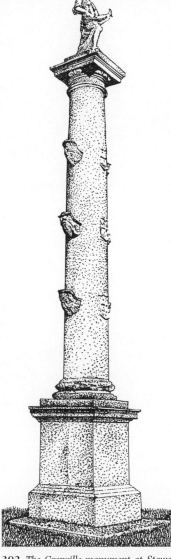

302 *The Grenville monument at Stowe (1748): the prow and anchors reflect the death of a naval officer.*

Column at Woodstock (1730, to commemorate Marlborough's battles) is typical, as is the Grenville monument at Stowe (see **302**). Cleopatra's Needle on the Victoria Embankment in London is a thing apart – it dates from about 1475 BC, and was erected in London in 1878, after a chequered history.

Curiosities include Peter Pan in Kensington Gardens, the Quadriga on Constitution Arch (Adrian Jones, 1912, showing Peace descending on four horses held by a boy), and the Burton memorial in the Roman Catholic cemetery at Mortlake (this is a concrete Arab tent with a crucifix over the door, built by Lady Burton for Sir Richard and herself – he died in 1890); cemeteries, such as Kensal Green or the Glasgow Necropolis, are rich in curiosities. Sir Sidney Waterlow, in Waterlow Park and Palace Street (1901), is the only statue with umbrella and hat. The Albert Memorial (George Gilbert Scott, 1872) verges on the curiosity.

An ubiquitous series of memorials are the *commemorative plaques* on the houses of distinguished people, such as Dickens in Doughty Street, Carlyle in Cheyne Walk, Jane Austen at Winchester, or Mary Russell Mitford at Alresford. These add greatly to the interest of visiting a town.

Scotland has several distinctive monuments: that to Prince Charles Edward, at his landing place at Glenfinnan on Loch Shiel (Ar) in 1745; the Memorial to the dead in the Napoleonic Wars on Calton Hill, Edinburgh (1822), which was left unfinished when funds ran out; the (highly incongruous in its setting) statue to James Hogg, the "Ettrick Shepherd", at St Mary's Loch (Sk); the Scott Memorial in Princes Street, Edinburgh (1840); the Wallace monument near Stirling (1869); and, at the other extreme, the memorial to the faithful dog, "Greyfriars Bobby", in Greyfriars Churchyard, Edinburgh.

A range of memorials peculiar to Scotland are those to the Covenanters of the 17th century. These are gravestones and other memorials commemorating the "martyrs" who were killed between 1679 and 1688, often in circumstances of extreme savagery, in their defence of the self-determination of the Presbyterian Church, following the Covenant of 1638, which respected the integrity of the Reformation tradition. There are a large number of these memorials, mostly in the south of Scotland; some of them were cut or recut by Robert Paterson, the "Old Mortality" of Scott. Typical is the gravestone, with long inscription, at Lesmahagow (Lk) of David Steel, 1686, who was shot by Crichton in front of his farmhouse, Nether Skellyhill, where a memorial records the event. The Covenanters' or Martyrs' Memorial at Greyfriars, Edinburgh (where the Covenant was signed), stands for the whole episode.

Communications and Trade

ROADS AND TRACKS

Prehistoric

No doubt human beings made tracks from their first occupation of Britain. Christopher Taylor has made the stimulating suggestion that some prehistoric trackways may have originally been animal tracks, made by wild cattle migrating from upland moors to maritime grasslands along "natural" routes. These routes arc broad bands, not narrow lines, only narrowing at fords or in valleys, like later prehistoric and even early medieval ways. Routes joined and crossed, so by Mesolithic times there was a complex of such "zones of communication".

By the later Mesolithic, *c* 6000 BC, fire was used, as it was by American Indians and Australian Aborigines, to create grazing land, break up the forest cover, and increase open areas. A new pattern of trackways evolved, based on the new pasture areas, and away from the old migration routes. New routes also developed for trade or exchange, eg of salt against implements or luxuries; thus, Portland chert is found from Surrey to Cornwall, brown flint from east coast boulder clay occurs in the western Weald, and perforated pebble tools in quartzite are widely distributed in southern England (see W F Rankine in *Archaeological News Letter*, 1951, 1952; and The Mesolithic of southern England (*Surrey Archaeological Society Research Paper* 4, 1956). Later routes often grew out of such movements.

The Neolithic and later farmers, settled instead of nomadic, needed tracks from farmstead to fields, fields to pasture, farm to farm, village to village, and to the social, economic, or power centres such as the "causewayed camps" or the later hillforts or oppida. Few of these are now visible – some may be under modern lanes or roads; but local lanes are met with in prehistoric field systems (eg at Park Brow, Sompting (Sx)), and can be seen more clearly from the air.

A specialised, and vivid, case is that of the wooden tracks across wetlands, as in the Somerset Levels or the Fens, which have come to light through excavation.

There were also major routes for long-distance trade between the local units represented by the hillforts and the *oppida*. That such routes were a reality is shown by the wide distribution in lowland Britain of, eg, stone axes of Cumbrian, Welsh, or Cornish origin, and by the presence of Irish gold in Wessex. A route can be demonstrated from Cornwall and Devon to Wiltshire and then along the North Downs (the Pilgrims' Way) into Kent. From Wessex the Icknield Way runs along the Chilterns into Norfolk. The route known as the "Jurassic Way", from the Mendips by the Cotswolds along the limestone belt of Northamptonshire to the Lincoln Edge and so to East Yorkshire, is less narrowly defined by prehistoric sites and finds than it formerly appeared to be; but there seems a strong probability that this was indeed a recognised route. In the north, Rombalds Way links the Lancashire coast, via the Ribble valley, through the Aire Gap, along the moorlands south of the Wharfe, across the Vale of York by the morainic ridges at York or Escrick, and so to the Wolds. Prehistoric ports such as Hengistbury (Do) needed access routes. There are many other such routes.

The present status of these ancient routes is of course complex: the Icknield Way begins as the Ridgeway in Berkshire, while from Luton to Thetford it is represented by main roads, and then by lanes, bridleways, and minor roads to Wells-next-the-Sea. A lane from Edgefield to Saxthorpe (Nf) may indicate the former existence of feeder routes. The Pilgrims' Way along the North Downs into Kent is partly a major road, from Farnham to Guildford, and partly paths, green lanes, farm tracks, and 18th- and 19th-century access roads; it also has a parallel lower way at the foot of the Downs on drier soil, used in the winter or wet weather (as has the Icknield Way along the Chilterns). So these great routes, although still generally on the same tracks, have broken up and changed in detail, which, with changing economic patterns, is only to be expected. Much of the maze of rural ways had a better chance of continuing through Roman times and even beyond.

Roman

In the 30 years or so after the conquest of AD 43 the Romans laid down a new road system, sometimes making use of earlier routes but mostly ignoring them, most Roman towns and forts being on new sites. As

409

Taylor concisely puts it, these roads were made "to link the towns, speed military traffic, move exports, send messages and transport new industrial products". The military use was the earliest; roads were needed to move troops and supplies between the Channel (Richborough, Dover, and Lympne) and London, Colchester, and the legionary fortresses, and for control of conquered areas. A provisional frontier was established on the line from Exeter through Ilchester, Bath, Gloucester, Cirencester, Leicester, and Lincoln – the Fosse Way, still largely used by modern roads. A second phase of conquest involved the relocation of the legionary fortresses further out – from Lincoln to York, from Wroxeter to Chester, from Gloucester to Caerleon. Economic factors necessitated a further network, linking the cantonal capitals and the centres of industry or imperial enterprises. The roads followed the development of the province. By the 70s the initial pattern had been completed, and in AD 79 the Romans turned to the north and reached the Clyde–Forth line by 82; during this campaign alone over 60 forts were built, and over 1,300 miles (2,080km) of road. The history of the final northern frontier of the Empire, beginning on the Tyne–Solway line, moving to the Forth–Clyde, and falling back to the permanent line of Hadrian's Wall by the mid 2nd century, is another story.

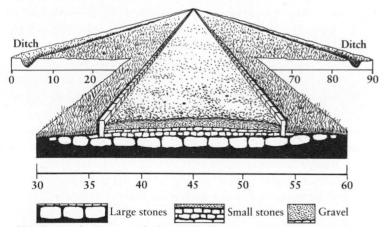

303 *Section of a Roman road. These roads differed according to local availability of material, but normally consisted of three layers, eg large stones, small stones, and a surface of gravel or flat stones; or, in chalk country, chalk rubble, flints, and gravel. The layers were from 2–3 to 6–12in (50–75 to 150–300mm) thick; the width was up to 30 ft (9.25m) on main roads, less on minor roads – main roads had side ditches c 84 ft (25.8m) apart.*

These major Roman roads, of which the OS map of Roman Britain gives a vivid picture, have often been likened to modern motorways, and in many ways (*mutatis mutandis*) the comparison is apt. In any case the planning, organisation, and effort involved were quite phenomenal.

The "economic" roads were also built by the army, and are hard to distinguish from the purely military ones. They radiated from the cantonal capitals, such as Silchester, and they linked major industrial centres, such as the lead mines of the Mendips and the Pennines, or the potteries along the Nene, into the network, and with the ports. The iron industry of the Weald was served by three major roads from London to the coast. The total length of specially laid roads was at least 8,000 miles (12,800km), and may in fact reach 10,000 (16,000km), all laid in the first hundred years of the Province.

Below the major roads in the hierarchy was a dense system of local roads, serving farms, villages, temples, etc, and linking these with major roads or market towns. Detailed studies of such roads have been made by I D Margary for the Weald, and The Viatores for the south-east Midlands. No village or farm was more than six or seven miles (9.16–11.2km) from an engineered road. The Iron Age ways persisted, with the addition of new lanes and tracks to new Roman farms, villas, hamlets, villages, and small towns. Some of these still exist (eg in the centuriated areas of Essex and Sussex), and others can be traced by air photography, and even on the ground. Many minor roads, if curved, reflect pre-Roman land boundaries or roads. The Roman Icknield Way follows the course of the prehistoric one, but not on the same line.

The "official" roads were laid as straight as possible, but deviated where the terrain dictated. In practice they were laid out in straight stretches between sighting points, and sometimes were forced to go round a natural obstacle (such as at Chute on the Winchester–Cunetio road, or in the Ebble valley on the Salisbury–Dorchester road). Margary demonstrates sharp deviations on the London–Lewes road, and other roads in the Weald. Sarn Helen in Wales is a good example of a Roman road winding through difficult terrain. Directions were kept accurately over long distances, even if deviated from, (eg the Fosse Way, or Stane Street, where from London to the Dorking gap the road is exactly aligned on Chichester, deviating to take advantage of the gap, but regaining Chichester in three straight stretches). Hilly country could involve cuttings, and marshy places were crossed on embankments or causeways of piles and timber; eg the Roman road east of Wellington (Sp) is laid on oak logs.

The roadway was made in layers mixed with earth, usually large stones at the bottom of an excavated bed, then smaller stones, then a surface layer of gravel, flints, or other local material; this was supported by kerbs or stones at the sides, with pegs to fix the metalling at intervals inside it (see **303**). In the north the road was often paved with slabs. The raised mound or *agger* on which the road was laid was wider than the metalled part; the *agger* could be some 30ft (9m) wide, and the roadway 17 or 18ft (5–5.4m). Outside the *agger* were verges, and the whole road was delimited by V-shaped ditches up to 90ft (27m) apart. When well preserved, such a road is conspicuous. But minor roads were less elaborate, although some in the Weald are metalled with iron slag from the local furnaces. Not only were local materials usually used, but the road was laid in stretches by different military units, and variations occur.

Roman roads can often be traced by the help of large-scale maps, and are sometimes marked by hedges, or may form parish or estate boundaries. Examples of paved stretches can be seen at Wade's Causeway, Wheeldale Moor (NY), Holtye (Sx), Blackstone Edge (SY); or Blackpool Bridge, Forest of Dean (Gl). The paving on the old road at Henley (Sx) is often regarded as Roman, but is more likely to be 17th century, although the road itself is very probably Roman (see **304**) (see I D Margary, *Roman Ways in the Weald* (Phoenix 1949)). Some Roman roads are overlaid by modern ones, as along Hadrian's Wall or north of Lincoln or Cirencester, and if the modern road deviates, the Roman one can often be seen continuing its straight line. Barns etc built on the dry, firm road can give a clue to its existence. Medieval houses, eg Kemp Town Manor House (Sx), or whole villages were sometimes built on Roman roads, which provided ready-made foundations. In the former Roman towns whole streets were built on the Roman street grid, and therefore the Saxon or later grid is to one side of the Roman, as in Winchester or Chichester, leaving only the main streets of the former city on the Roman lines. Place-names in "street" – Streat, Streatley, Streatham, etc – give a clue to the existence of a Roman road.

Roman roads crossed rivers by fords, natural or constructed, eg Iden Green, Benenden (Kt), by culverts, by bridges, either wooden or stone, by causeways, or by ferries (eg Severn and Humber). Bridge abutments are still visible at, eg, Chesters (Nd) or Piercebridge (Du) (see below).

Saxon

Little is known of the roads of the Dark Ages and early Saxon period, which was settled by scattered farmsteads and hamlets – villages and open fields came later. The old Roman system collapsed in the course of the 5th century; most main roads probably fell out of use, except for short stretches for local traffic, and in any case lack of repairs would have hastened the deterioration. Bridges broke down and were not rebuilt, surfaces disintegrated. Rivers and local tracks were probably the incomers' main ways. The Roman local network, and the Romano-British fields (themselves often continuing the prehistoric ones), must have been used in early and middle Saxon times. Some of the tracks in these fields persist today.

In the Highland Zone and the Celtic west, many lanes and tracks must be pre-Roman, as is the pattern of scattered farms and hamlets (eg in Anglesey, or the Hartland area of Devon).

Nucleated villages and open fields took shape in late Saxon times, 10th/11th centuries, which led to a new or modified road pattern in

304 *17th/18th century roadway on the line of a Roman road – Henley (Sx).*

the areas most affected – people not only had to have access to their fields, but to the village church, manor court, and cornmill – and to longer-distance routes, as Saxon kingdoms grew larger and England became finally unified. The new towns clearly needed new roads.

The main roads were known as *herepath* or *straet*. Herepaths, or harrow-ways (Harrogate is a form of this), meant military ways, but the word is of uncertain meaning, and some instances of it may derive from a word meaning "muddy", while others may link with *hearg*, a sacred place (eg Harrow (Mx)). Straet meant a constructed road or an old Roman road refurbished and reused (eg in Streatham); but it may only mean any Roman road, whether used or not, just as herepath may only mean an old trackway.

Other long-distance roads include the *saltways*, radiating from Droitwich and Northwich.

Many of the new towns, eg Stamford or Winchester, used Roman roads with modifications due to changes in the importance of towns, the development of new towns, or the unsuitability of stretches of Roman roads which had gone out of repair. But Tamworth, for example, developed a new road system, not using the Roman Watling Street. The roads serving the new nucleated villages related to the new open fields are still in use, subject to stretches declining to tracks and footpaths and to alterations caused by later buildings etc. The system can often be reconstructed over a larger area. Taylor instances the Cambridgeshire–Essex border, where the Anglo-Saxon villages were on east–west roads not geared into the present north–south system; the old roads remain, but at a lower status.

Medieval and post-medieval

The road pattern at 1066 has basically remained unchanged, except for some new roads in certain areas, such as round the Industrial Revolution towns, turnpikes and enclosure roads, deviations round parks, bypasses, motorways, local alterations, and many roads no longer in use. The medieval situation can often be reconstructed by careful study of large-scale maps, Gough's map of 1360, and manorial and other documents. Accounts of medieval royal progresses enable long-distance routes to be traced.

Medieval roads are of course often on the same line as modern roads – indeed, a centralised system was developed, radiating from London – but some cross them and go in and out of bypassed villages; many villages were bypassed in the 18th and 19th centuries. These often show as disused tracks or hollow-ways. Where Roman roads fell out of use, the villages along them (but not actually on them – the Saxons did not always build new villages on Roman roads) might be linked by a new, parallel lane. Taylor instances a good example between Alconbury and Wansford (Ca); here the Roman road came back into use later. The shape and growth of villages sometimes reveal changes in the use of roads; eg Stilton (Ca) was on an east–west road when a north–south Roman road became disused, but it later developed along the Roman road when this came back into use. Caxton (Ca) was actually resited to a new (Roman) road for the benefit of a new market on it. Taylor indeed says that "at least half of all medieval villages show some alteration in their basic plans as a result of variations in the importance of their local road systems". Some towns failed because they were not on a good route system, eg Hindon (Wi). Some, like Bicester, diverted a Roman road to suit it, or, like St Ives (Ca) built a new causeway and bridge to its own market, bypassing Slepe on the old road. This phenomenon is not of course confined to Roman roads; Sherfield English (Ha), a medieval village on an old road, moved to a new 18th-century turnpike.

The building of a new road can sometimes have drastic effects on the countryside. When a turnpike was built from Pateley Bridge to Ripon (NY), the life of Upper Nidderdale was reoriented to Ripon, and the former links with the mother church and market at Kirkby Malzeard, and with Masham, sharply declined.

Disused roads sometimes decline in status or disappear altogether; but some continue as *green lanes*. Most counties have these, and they can yield useful clues to former patterns. Essex is particularly rich in them (eg Epping Long Green, Aimes Green, and the network north-east of Waltham Abbey). Some old lanes have become fossilised inside towns, eg Cross Lanes in Guildford, or, no longer green, Marylebone Lane in London, which winds because it follows the course of the Tyburn.

Unmetalled roads in heavy or wet conditions (or when not well kept up), particularly on slopes, could lead to *braiding*, as traffic became unable to continue on the original line and had to run parallel with it on less disturbed land. There are good examples at Chinnor (Ox), the old London–Oxford road descending the Chilterns, and Beacon Hill, Bulford (Wi). *Hollow-ways* are formed when an unmetalled road descends a hill in friable soil, such as greensand. Hooves and wheels, and frost, disintegrate the surface, which is then washed or blown away. The road surface can sink as much as 15ft (4.5m) below the surrounding land, though the Fosse Way at Windwhistle Hill (So) is 30ft (9m) deep, and some of these cuttings are quite spectacular. Rackham points out that a hollow-way of this magnitude takes at least 300 years to form. There are many good examples in Devon, Surrey, and Hampshire, eg round Selborne. A conspicuous example is the Holloway in London, where the Great North Road climbs the Northern Heights at Highgate, spanned by the Archway.

The drove roads (see pages 420–5) and *packhorse tracks* continued in use well into the 19th century. Examples of the latter include those in the Yorkshire Pennines, eg from Heptonstall to Hebden Bridge, for transport of cloth to the fulling mills, or round the marketing centres such as Halifax; or the paved one east of Harlech (Me) – the so-called Roman Steps. There are paved tracks across the Pennines, such as that from Todmorden to Burnley.

Military roads were built in Scotland after the 1715 and 1745 – from 1724 by General Wade. These are still good, but not so well laid out as were Roman roads, eg Perth to Fort George. The military road from Newcastle to Carlisle (after 1745) was later turnpiked. More recent military roads include the straight stretch from Longmoor to Liphook (Ha).

Turnpikes

The growth of population and traffic in the 16th century placed more burdens on the roads, and improvements to these created yet more traffic (as is still the case today). The Highways Act of 1555 laid upkeep of roads on the parishes, but this was not a success. The growth of carrier services (carts and packhorses) continued, and by the mid 17th century the roads were far from adequate. The breakthrough came in 1663 when a *turnpike* – a road maintained by tolls – was built at Wadesmill (Ht). Stage coaches had begun in 1657.

But even this idea was not adopted quickly, and it was not until 1706 that it caught on generally. New Acts were passed throughout the 18th century – 452 from 1760 to 1774 – and a general enabling Act in 1773. By 1800, 1,600 turnpikes were in operation; by 1838 there were some 22,000 miles of turnpikes, including 2,000 in Wales. This was their peak; in 1836, 700 mail coaches and 3,300 stage

coaches were in regular operation, but they were killed by the canals and later by the railways, and the last trust died in 1895. The major roads had to wait to be revived by the motor vehicle.

Most turnpike trusts ran only 20 or 30 miles of road, but maintenance was often primitive. Early mail coaches (they began in 1784) ran at eight miles an hour, but the speed increased by the later 18th century and put great strain on the turnpikes. Real improvement was not possible until John Metcalf (Blind Jack of Knaresborough) and J L McAdam built roads with solid foundations and compacted surfaces. By 1823 McAdam was advising 32 turnpike trusts, and his three sons were assisting 85 more. Coaches could now run at 10–11mph. Telford too built good roads in Scotland (after Wade's military ones); in the 1820s he rebuilt the London–Holyhead road, and his engineering can still be seen.

Turnpikes tended to fix one road out of several as the main route, and this led to the modern system. Villages on old roads were often bypassed, and a shorter route fixed. The Cambridge–Newmarket road (14 miles) is a good example. Village plans could be changed by turnpike roads, and even new villages created, eg Sherfield English (Ha).

Turnpike roads had several accompaniments. In general, they stimulated the rise of the coaching inns and of iron bridges, eg Smeaton's bridge at Amesbury (Wi), 1775. The tolls – the *raison d'être* of the trusts – were collected at gates across the road at intervals. The gatekeeper was provided with a *tollhouse* by the gate, which combined his dwelling with suitably-placed windows from which he could see the traffic. In 1840 there were about 8,000 tollhouses in England, some of which survive. Many are quite simple, but they have a tendency to be ornamental and "picturesque". Hexagonal, octagonal, and round ones are common. There are good examples just east of Marlborough (Wi) and just west of Alresford (Ha); specimens have been reerected at the Weald and Downland Museum, Singleton (Sx), and at the Ironbridge Gorge Museum (Blist's Hill) (Sp).

Mileposts and *direction posts* were set up, largely different for each trust. Direction posts, as opposed to milestones, originated in the Middle Ages and were erected somewhat at the whim of public bodies or private individuals. A similar idea is embodied in the stone pillars and crosses erected by monasteries to mark tracks across the moors, eg Fat Betty near Rosedale (NY), Lacon Cross near Ripon, or Bennett's Cross on Dartmoor. It was only in 1773 that they were made compulsory on highways. Examples from before this date are

Broadway Hill (Wo), 1669, and Hopton (Db), 1705. A signpost in Devon, Otterton Cross at Bicton, is in the form of an ornamental square pillar, surmounted by a cross, which commemorates five martyrs burnt at the stake here; it has no arms, the directions being on tablets on the sides (1743). The latter feature occurs also at Cranleigh (Sy). Local styles in relatively modern signposts can still be found in remote parts (see 305); in the Peak District they are raised on pedestals to keep the wording clear of the snow. Some old signposts in Scotland, north-east England, and Hampshire show distances in furlongs ($\frac{1}{8}$ mile (200m)). There is an interesting group in the southern Pennines called guide *stoops*, which are stone pillars showing directions on lanes in the woollen districts of Yorkshire, for cloth trade traffic; there are about a dozen in the Huddersfield district alone, dating from 1737 to 1761.

Mileposts make a rich study and there are still a large number to be seen, with a very wide measure of local variety. They were used by the Romans; most of the survivors of these are of course in museums, but a few are still *in situ*, such as the possible example 1 mile (1.6km) from Dorchester (Do), at Stinsford. Four in Cornwall are very near their original positions (eg Trethevey). The London Stone (Cannon Street), once thought to be the point from which the Romans took the mileage of their roads, is now held to be of unknown origin and purpose. They were not again used in Britain until the turnpike roads were built; a few roads had marks or stones from 1663 (Dover road) and 1708 (Great North Road), but genuine milestones were erected in the

305 *A multiple cast-iron signpost – Semley (Wi).*

1720s (Trumpington (Ca), 1727); an Act of 1744 made them compulsory on most roads, and another in 1766 extended their use to all.

Many stones of this period survive, and some have very pleasing layouts and lettering (White Stone (He), 1700; Henley-in-Arden (Ww), 1748, on a tablet in a wall). They range from the low painted stone ones of south-east Scotland and slate ones in north Wales to monumental white specimens, eg one near Ascot (Bk) and the "White Lady" stone at Thames Ditton (Sy) by the Orleans Inn near Esher (1767). Most are about 2ft (60cm) high. Some are of cast iron, like those on the Godalming–Dunsfold road (Sy), or plaques affixed to posts (New Forest area). Millestones continued to be erected throughout the 19th century, and their date can usually be deduced from the style and lettering. Spellings, in the earlier ones, can be wild; many were made by local craftsmen; abbreviations were common: Cor for Corbridge, or even just C; B for Bodmin; at Tickhill, Wor 10 Lon 157, for Worksop and London. There is an excellent series in Fife (see 306), of which the most typical have cast iron tops fixed to stones. In all, 148 complete milestones survive, 28 incomplete, and 11 wayside markers at road junctions (see Walter M Stephen in *Proceedings of the Society of Antiquaries of Scotland*, 100, 1967–8).

Sometimes a lot of knowledge was presumed; Sarum for Salisbury may be familiar, but Barum for Barnstaple is not, nor is Shaston for Shaftesbury! There is a series in Yorkshire where the mileage shown is the "customary" mile, which itself varies, but which is usually between $1\frac{1}{3}$ and 2 statute miles, no doubt to comfort the traveller. For example, a stone in Rudding Lane, near Harrogate, still in its original position, reads Knaresborough 2 miles, Spofforth 2 miles, Harrogate 1 mile, Leeds 9 miles; the actual mileages are 3, 3, 2, and 14. There were still recently over 50 such stones in the West Riding alone.

Lime trees were planted about 1700 as mileposts from Salisbury to Shaftesbury, and some still remain.

Other items of the 18th and 19th centuries are *mounting-stones* (not to be confused with *churn-stands*), *hitching-posts*, and *tethering-rings*. *Packing-stones*, to rest one's pack on while walking uphill, survive in hilly districts.

The *Enclosures* of the 17th to 19th centuries (see pages 72–5) necessitated new roads for the new fields, and constituted almost a new system in the affected areas, replacing the old ways leading to the open field strips. They are in straight stretches, with wide verges between hedges or walls, 30, 40, or even 60ft (9, 12, or 18m) apart. Villages, and even towns like Cambridge, were affected by these roads. The wide verges proved tempting to landless labourers, who built cottages on them; the hamlet of Stour Row (Do) is made up of such squatters' cottages. Along these roads, and on turnpikes, can be seen little hollows from which was dug road-metal for repairing the roads, and sometimes heaps of the metal itself.

20th century

The present system was virtually complete by the mid 19th century. In the early 20th century radical changes were induced by motor vehicles and increased traffic. The Ministry of Transport was set up in 1920. In 1930, the County Councils took over the roads, with the Ministry responsible for A roads in 1936. Much experiment took place to improve road surfaces. Development of the system was piecemeal; for instance, ribbon development along *bypasses* was uncontrolled until after the Second World War, eg the Kingston Bypass and the North Circular Road. A national policy for long-distance routes was only embarked on in the 1960s; it led to the construction of the *motorways* (including Birmingham's monumental "Spaghetti Junction"). The system is constantly being extended and upgraded. Thus the early bypass of Guildford and Godalming has been "improved", and a new road to replace that at Winchester has been constructed. A major recent scheme has been the construction of the London Orbital road, the M25. Ring roads, inner and outer, are features of many towns, and one-way systems have brought their own problems. But motor vehicles continue to increase (there were over 20 million motor licences in 1988, and the increase shows no sign of ending), and transport policy seems to take insufficient account of the potential of the railways and other public transport. More roads, as things are, can only mean still more traffic, more congestion, and more economic penalties, and no satisfactory solution appears to be in sight.

Minor ways

These are the routes which do not form part of the modern metalled road system (although some of them may for short stretches). They have become tracks or footpaths, where they survive at all. They are the ways which linked farm to farm, farm to barns or fields, village to common fields, manor to manor or to its farms, village to abbey, castle, or market. Sometimes a winding lane represents once separate stretches of road which joined each pair of a row of manors, hamlets, or villages.

Areas which have retained or regained a state of under-population, such as the Pennines or the South Downs, are rich grounds for the study of minor ways. For the Pennines the study by Arthur Raistrick (*Green Tracks in the Pennines*, 1962) is valuable. He finds, in the area between the Aire and the Tees, a large number of minor or

306 *Wayside marker, Fife – Newton of Balcormo. A local and very informative type.*

	MILES
ARNCROACH	$\frac{1}{2}$
BALDUTHO	$1\frac{1}{4}$
OVER KELLIE	$1\frac{1}{2}$
LINGO	$3\frac{1}{4}$
HIGHAM	$4\frac{1}{2}$
BELLISTON	$1\frac{1}{4}$
GIBLISTON	2
LATHALLAN	4
LARGOWARD	3
GILSTON	6
FALFIELD	$6\frac{1}{2}$
TEASSES	9
MONTRAVE	$10\frac{1}{2}$
PEAT INN	$5\frac{1}{2}$
GREIGSTON	$6\frac{1}{2}$
PITSCOTTIE	$9\frac{1}{4}$
CUPAR	$12\frac{1}{2}$
ST ANDREWS	10

	MILES
OVENSTONE	$\frac{3}{4}$
CARNBEE	$1\frac{1}{4}$
BALMUNTH	$2\frac{1}{4}$
LOCHTY	$2\frac{1}{4}$
KINGSMUIR	$3\frac{1}{4}$
DRUMRACK	4
DUNIMO	6
CARVENNOM	2
PITKIERIE	$2\frac{1}{2}$
GRANGEMUIR	2
PITTENWEEM	3
ANSTRUTHER	4
KILRENNY	5
LOCHTON	$5\frac{1}{2}$
WORMISTONE	$6\frac{1}{4}$
CAMBO	$7\frac{1}{2}$
CRAIL	$6\frac{1}{4}$
ST ANDREWS	10

scarcely-used ways (stretches of these are sometimes on the line of modern roads). There are prehistoric tracks, between settlements on the moor or fell edges or from settlements to their fields or pastures, and Roman roads, such as that from Aldborough to Manchester via Ilkley, which can be traced over Blubberhouses Moor. Later roads include peat roads from moor to village, and saltways, from south Lancashire and Cheshire over the Pennines, such as Saltergate west of Harrogate. Packhorse ways, with their narrow bridges (such as at Linton or Birstwith) are ubiquitous; they were greatly developed in monastic times, and continued in use into the 19th century – many are now green roads (Mastiles Lane from Kilnsey westwards over Malham Moor is a conspicuous example). They began as ways for driving sheep to and from winter and summer pastures, to shearing and lambing points etc; they were then used to cart wool to weavers and cloth to merchants, and later for other produce when by the 18th century they had become the main ways of commerce. They crossed the rivers by fords and by the distinctive high, narrow packhorse bridges (eg Birstwith, Nidderdale). Packhorse tracks can sometimes be seen accompanying modern roads, as from Dolwyddelan to Penmachno (Cn). Mules' Stepway, Exeter, is a pack-path from the harbour to the old town. Bewdley is an example of a transit port (on the Severn) at the end of packhorse routes. The Horse Paddock at Mallerstang (Wd) is an example of a halting place for packhorse trains (each packhorse carried about three hundredweight); Kendal was the packhorse centre for the north-west. There are also drove roads, either green or with wide verges, part of a countrywide system (see below), corpse roads, leading to a distant parish burial ground, as from Reeth to Kirkby Stephen (or, on the North York Moors, to Danby), and a variety of specialised tracks linking villages with old leadmines or coalpits, or these to each other or to the nearest green road for longer traffic; one such *coal road* runs from Middlesmoor in Nidderdale to Masham. Then there are the 18th/19th-century Enclosure roads, straight among the newly laid-out fields, with green verges. Finally there is the system of roads of major communication between villages and market towns and from towns to major centres; many of these were turnpiked in the 18th and 19th centuries, and properly surfaced.

These networks of minor roads in the uplands carried a much larger volume of traffic of all kinds, and *inns* grew up as resting and refreshment places at the highest points. One such is the Tan Hill inn, above the head of Swaledale, a nodal point of minor roads, including a corpse road to Grinton (used until the chapel of ease was built at Muker in 1850). Others are the Clapgate Inn at the head of Bilsdale and the Cat and Fiddle between Buxton and Macclesfield.

The South Downs in Sussex, thanks to their emptiness and relative freedom from arable farming (although this has changed greatly since the First World War), also contain a large number of old trackways of different types (the works of Hadrian Allcroft and Cecil Curwen are good guides to these). Some can be shown to be of Neolithic origin, such as that on Bow Hill, cut through by flint mines. Port's Road, running north from Portslade, has a double-lynchet section, a Roman terraceway, and in part is a parish boundary of at least 7th-century date. While the Ridgeway along the north edge of the Downs, for 50 miles from Beachy Head into Hampshire, is certainly prehistoric, the corresponding "Underhill Road" at the foot of the Downs is not in fact continuous, but represents local lanes linking Saxon manors: South Harting, East Harting, Elsted, Treyford, Didling, Bepton, Cocking, and, further east, Alfriston, Berwick, Alciston, Firle, or even earlier linkages. This contrasts with the dual ways along the North Downs (the Pilgrims' Way) and the Chilterns (the Icknield Way). There are similar lanes along the valleys of the Cuckmere, Ouse, Adur, and Arun. Bronze or Iron Age settlements, such as Park Brow, Sompting, have internal roads. The "Covered Ways" – sunken tracks between banks, or with a single bank – cross downland ridges, and have been interpreted as cattleways from valley to valley. Good examples are: the War Dyke, Arundel, a mile from Rewell Wood to the Arun through South Wood; Glatting Down (late Bronze Age), breached by Stane Street; and Harting Down, several, all breached by the Roman road and one by a barrow. The downland scarp was descended by flat terraceways, still conspicuous. These are mostly Roman, but a few may be earlier; they do not usually link up with Saxon roads or droves at the foot of the Downs. Good examples are at Bignor Hill (Stane Street), Harting (Miller's Walk), Steyning Round Hill, or Firle Beacon (the "Rabbit Walk"). In Hadrian Allcroft's view, the finest Roman terraceway, 20ft (6m) wide and metalled, is that on Streat Hill; and this replaces an earlier road which is still visible. There are also shepherds' tracks, and tracks used (but not necessarily made) by smugglers. In the New Forest, eg round Burley, there are tracks which seem to have been made by the carts and packhorses of smugglers, at the end of their journey from Lymington. Indeed, a very specialised minor way is the *smugglers'* cross-track (recorded by Eric Parker, the writer on

Surrey). There are a large number of tracks running north from the Channel across the Weald and the Greensand. But the interesting thing is the tracks running at right angles to these, and joining them up. Parker suggests they were to enable smugglers on the run to change tracks without being seen; he mentions examples in the Hambledon (Sy) district. Smugglers of course used any secluded track which led from the port or stretch of lonely coast to their inland disposal centres, and preferably those over wooded country with soft (quiet) going. Thus they used the old Peddar's Way from Norfolk to the south; and there is a Smugglers Road from the Hampshire coast through the New Forest to Romsey.

There are also, on the Downs, 18th/19th-century roads, now green lanes, such as that from (London) – Henfield–Shoreham – (Brighton), over Beeding Hill, replaced by a new road on an easier route.

The downland rivers, Cuckmere, Ouse, Adur, and Arun, were mainly crossed at fords, and roads can be traced leading to these, eg North Stoke and Warningcamp on the Arun.

The rise of Lewes altered the old road system, which was based on Roman roads; Lewes is not a Roman town. So a new medieval track was formed up Chapel Hill and along the ridge to Saxon Down and Glynde, together with a new crossing of the Ritch, by Mill Lane up Firle Borstal; to this ford came also the trail from Southerham by Ranscombe, itself superseded by the marsh road straight across to Beddingham.

Two other types of minor roads in Sussex are the *sea-lanes* – lanes leading from an inland village or manor to the nearest beach. There is a good series between Littlehampton and Worthing: Rustington, Angmering, East Preston, Kingston Gorse, Ferring, and Goring. There are also tracks to pastures in the Weald from manors outside the Weald, sometimes several miles away. These were mostly pannage for pigs or sources of timber, but other animals were also kept there. Many of them can be identified by names ending in *-fold* (for sheep or cattle – mainly in the western Weald), as at Dunsfold or Cowfold, or *-den* (for pigs – mainly in the eastern Weald), as at Tenterden or Rolvenden. Other diagnostic names such as Shipley (the sheep pasture) also occur. Tenterden was a manor dependent on Thanet, 40 miles away as the crow flies; the manor of Wye had pastures 20 miles away in Biddenden, Cranbrook, and Hawkhurst. Domesday records 48 denes, but many more are known to have existed. Further west, most of the places in *-fold* are on roads running north–south, to manors on the Wealden edge, eg Lickfold, Chiddingfold, Dunsfold, Alfold, Slinfold, Cowfold. Each of the long narrow strip parishes in Holmesdale, below the North Downs in Surrey, has a road leading up to the Downs for transhumance of sheep, and into the deep Weald to the swine pastures. Transverse *ridging* on farm tracks is caused by the passage of cattle.

Changes in the relative importance of villages or towns, and in local communication patterns, have frequently led to changes in the road systems. These can often be made out by scrutiny of the 1:25000 OS maps. The former roads survive as bridleways, tracks, or footpaths, sometimes with gaps. A good example is the country round Selborne (Ha), a hilly and very difficult area before the 19th century. Gilbert White records that in a bad winter Selborne was virtually cut off from Alton, the nearest town, four miles away. The present main road to Alton was not built until the 1830s. Before that travellers had to take the tracks from Grange Farm, by Nine Acres to Norton Farm, then to Hartley Maudit and West Worldham, and along Water Lane to Alton. Similarly, a route left the Winchester road (which then ran along a slight ridge through Froyle, until it was replaced by the present A31 on the lower land to the south) at Froyle, to go through Wyck to East Worldham, then into Binswood and Hartley Wood to Candovers Farm, where it climbed the hanger (since made easier by a new road from Oakhanger to West Worldham), then went via Wick Hill to Norton, on to Newton Valence and Priors Dean, from which Liss, or Hawkley and Petersfield, could be reached. Most of these cross-country routes are still negotiable, and give a vivid idea of the difficulties of travel before the 19th century (see **307**, facing page 504). Some of them are still viable for modern traffic, like the lane from Selborne to East Tisted and on to Ropley, Bishops Sutton, and New Alresford (with a detour round Rotherfield Park, formerly crossed by a track). The old road from Alton to Winchester, before the A31 was built, ran by Medstead, Bighton, Old Alresford, Abbotstone, and the Itchen valley to Kings Worthy.

In wet country or flooded areas ways were carried on *causeways*; these are common in the Fens, as at Stuntney or Aldreth (Ca) which are medieval – some carry modern lanes. At Kellaways (Wi) is a path carried on 64 arches (late 15th century) (see **308**). On soft ground paths can be paved. One from Crowhurst Place (Sy) to the church, one mile, was laid down in 1631; that between Ripley and Clint (NY) is probably 18th century; five ancient paved paths meet at the woodland church of Okewood (Sy). At West Grinstead church (Sx) is a paved path on a causeway. The Roman Steps in the Rhinogs in Merioneth, though certainly not Roman, seem to be a medieval packhorse track from Harlech to Bala (laid between 1300, when the castle was built, and the Black Death, 1350) when labour, and travelling, became scarce; the actual stones may have been replaced.

Footpaths, as a class, need no elaboration. Roads, tracks, paths, or boundaries sometimes make sudden deviations or loops round a now unseen obstacle; this may be worth searching for – it may be a barrow or other monument which predated the road, or a building, notable tree, etc.

A specialised type of minor road is that from monasteries to their outlying estates. It is worth looking at a small area, upper Nidderdale (NY), to appreciate this (see Bernard Jennings (ed): *A History of Nidderdale*, 1967). The upper dale, from the 12th century, was divided between Byland Abbey (west of the river, and the dalehead – Stonebeck Up and Stonebeck Down townships) and Fountains Abbey (east of the river from Thwaite to Brimham, and west of it from Bewerley to Dacre and Hampsthwaite). Some of the roads in this area were already old-established routeways by the 12th century, such as "Watling Street", from Aldborough to Ribchester, crossing the Nidd at Hampsthwaite, "Blackgate" from Greenhow (Roman lead-mines) to Fewston, joining Watling Street, and Grassington–Pateley Bridge–Ripon, with a branch to Kirkby Malzeard.

In addition to these, the monasteries also secured rights of passage from local manorial lords and developed a private road network

308 *Maud Heath's Causeway, Kellaways (Wi), 1474: this is a causeway from Wick Hill to Chippenham, four and a half miles (7.5km); part of this consists of a structure of 64 arches carrying a path along the road over marshy ground, to the bridge across the Avon.*

serving their granges. The Fountains roads included one from Cayton to Hampsthwaite and Cayton to Brimham, and from Dacre Grange to above Pateley Bridge, crossing the river to granges on their side up to Lofthouse, from where a branch ran to the Byland grange at Middlesmoor; from this road ran links to Kirkby Malzeard and Fountains. Byland had a road from Ramsgill on the west bank, joining the Fountains road near Brighouse. The two abbeys entered into agreements to use stretches of each other's roads. Parts of these roads can still be followed, eg from Holme House to Wath and from Heathfield, through Bewerley to Heyshaw and Dacre. Lacon Cross, near Sawley, may have marked a road to Fountains.

The *monastic tracks* across the moors were usually marked by crosses, as waymarks and as resting-places. Examples can be seen on the North York Moors, and for instance on the Long Causeway, from Whalley Abbey along the Pennine edge to Burnley, Hebden Bridge, and Halifax.

Miscellaneous features

The "rolling English road", *pace* G K Chesterton, is not due to the progress of drunks, but to going round the edges of the small, irregular fields of the ancient countryside. In the planned countryside the roads are often in straight zigzags, going round the furlongs of the open fields. The same effect is produced by the straight lanes in areas of Roman centuriation, as in south Essex or near Lewes. In the Fens there is a pattern of long parallel straight roads, determined by 17th-century drainage channels, but each block of Fen was unrelated to the next, and the main roads (where not medieval) had to be improvised, and are winding and inconsequent. Some narrow strip fields along roads are due to old wide roads being narrowed and the verges being taken into the farmland.

To the specialised ways mentioned above may be added routes originated or developed for specific trades or traffic: eg the Mariners' Way from Bideford to Totnes was for seamen joining ships; Irish gold on its way to France crossed Cornwall from Padstow to Fowey; tin was brought from Cornwall to Kent, and Mendip lead to Winchester; Derbyshire lead was carried to Southampton for Rouen, in exchange for dyes for Pennine cloth, up to the 15th century; coal and millstones followed regular routes, as did turkeys walking from Norfolk to

London. Many northern valleys, eg Weardale, Wharfedale, and Nidderdale, have pairs of roads, one each side of the river, but one is now usually more "main" than the other.

Before the turnpikes there were no proper roads to London between the Dover and Portsmouth roads – Sussex was really only accessible by sea. This is one of the reasons that rivers and canals developed in the Weald before the turnpikes (see P A L Vine: *London's Lost Route to the Sea* (David & Charles, 1965)).

Packhorses could carry about three hundredweight, and waggons (17th and 18th centuries) up to three tons on a reasonable road, but at an average speed of only 2 mph, and a four-wheeled cart required six or more horses. A canal boat could carry 40 tons. The packhorse tracks were used by "jaggers", who owned or managed a string of packhorses, "badgers" (cadgers in Scotland), smaller carriers, wholesale dealers in farm produce, etc, operating a team of horses under licence, as well as pedlars, peddars, or chapmen, and smugglers and highwaymen.

Road surfaces

Unmodernised road surfaces are of course becoming increasingly rare, but some may still be found. Roads on hills were often paved with stones from the 16th/17th centuries, eg that at Henley (Sx) referred to above; the effect of this is not unlike that of the Roman roads in the north, such as Wade's Causeway (NY). In the 18th and 19th centuries setts were commonly used (see **309**), particularly in industrial towns and ports, and eg in Edinburgh New Town, and Guildford (Sy). Granite was frequently used for this, and Haslingden (La) stone was used all over England. Cobbles are also found (see **310**), as at Elm Hill, Norwich.

The macadamised surface of 19th-century roads did not stand up well to the motor traffic which began at the end of the century, and from 1902 experiments were done to develop a more durable surface. Tar with gravel and other stone was tried, was in use by 1908, and was universal until the last war; the tar was at first boiled in kettles on the roadside, and brushed on by hand. Until 1925 the old turnpikes were given a top dressing of tar, and a variety of stone chips was used. Tarred wood blocks were used in many towns, including London, and

were only discontinued after the war. Bridge Street, Westminster, had a surfacing of rubber blocks. Experiments with asphalt and various aggregate mixes were tried; the motorways are surfaced with asphalt over concrete.

309 *A granite sett road surface – Princes Street, Norwich.*

310 *A cobbled road surface – Mermaid Street, Rye (Sx).*

Pavement surfaces survive in greater variety. Medieval stone paths still exist, and there are cobbled pavements at Walsingham (Nf). Some brick pavements survive, as at Tunbridge Wells, and these have come back into fashion. "York stone" was a favourite in the 18th and 19th centuries, and fine examples can be seen in Bath and in some of the London squares (eg Gordon Square). Very large flagstones exist (or

311 *Raised pavement – Godalming (Sy). These reflect the sinkage of a roadway on a slope, owing to traffic wear and weathering, leaving the footway remaining on the old ground level.*

used to) under the Arches at Charing Cross, London. Slate is also found. In the south-east of England local "marbles" (Bethersden and Sussex) can be found, also rippled sandstones and mudstones. Sheep or deer bones, set upright, still exist in a few places, eg at almshouses at Wantage (Ox). The courtyard at Raglan Castle (Po) is set in patterns of stones, and at Hepstonstall (WY) is a collection of paving types. Masons' marks can be seen on kerbstones, eg in Bloomsbury, London.

Raised pavements can be found in many old towns, eg the fine examples at Godalming (see **311**) and Haslemere (Sy). They seem to reflect the creation of a hollow-way, ie the sinking of the road surface on a slope, leaving the roadside houses higher than the roadway.

Droving and drove roads

The droving of cattle and sheep from the Highland Zone to the English markets was an important trade, and indeed feature of life, particularly during the 18th and early 19th centuries. It has left traces in the shape of the roads by which the animals were driven, the inns used by the drovers, and some of the collecting points, "trysts", and pastures on the way. The trade has been studied in detail for Scotland, the north of England and Wales, but much work still has to be done to elucidate its routes in the Lowland Zone of England.

The trade from Scotland was vast and highly organised. Raiding of cattle and sheep was endemic, serious, and widespread in Scotland up to the end of the 17th century. But droving coexisted with this as early as the mid 14th century, and an Act of 1369 allowed cattle to be sold to Englishmen, fixing customs dues for beasts leaving Scotland. By the early 16th century a regular, if spasmodic, trade existed, and also a regular traffic between Skye and the east of Scotland, and from Argyll to the Lowlands, a foretaste of later developments. The anarchic situation in the Borders was largely resolved by the end of the 16th century, and the Union of 1603 led to freer trade. But still much of the traffic evaded the Border dues. But in 1662, 18,574 beasts passed through Carlisle (and paid toll), and things improved after 1680 when the trade was fully recognised and encouraged.

Special drove roads were used in preference to highways, as being easier on the beasts' (and the dogs') feet, and providing some grazing on the way as well. The beasts were brought from the farms to local collecting centres, and driven off in herds of up to 300 animals, with one drover for 50 or 60. Some centres, like Muir of Ord (Ross), collected larger droves, and in the 19th century droves often consisted of thousands, and were miles long. It must have been a remarkable sight. Fewer than 200 beasts were not economic. The drovers sold local goods also, such as cloth and knitwear. Up to the mid 18th century the tracks were ill-defined, although Wade's roads (1723–40) followed some of them. In the Lowlands and Angus the routes were defined by "raiks", 50–100ft (15–30m) wide tracks with turf dykes on each side (eg Annam to Gretna, 1619; New Galloway to Dumfries, 1697). In some parts of the Highlands drovers, sledge, and foot traffic all used the same routes. Drove roads are in "streams", diverging and converging with the terrain.

The growing use of metalled roads led to the *shoeing* of the cattle. The Welsh drovers had to do this also, and in Sussex cattle shoeing went on into the 20th century. Geese and turkeys were also "shod" with pitch and sand; in the 18th century 150,000 turkeys were driven to London from East Anglia each year, starting in August and taking three months. Cattle shoes were separate, broad plates for each side, with three wide-headed nails. Shoeing was done at the points where the drovers reached areas of metalled roads, such as Dingwall. There were shoe industries at several places, such as Bala, Grassington, and near Boroughbridge.

The droves did about 10 or 12 miles a day. They made for overnight *resting places* or "stances", which had food and water. These are green hollows or open stretches, mostly now forgotten, but some still to be made out, eg Shiel Bridge and Kinlochleven. Bridges on the roads were avoided, where they existed; rivers were forded. The droving season in the Highlands was from May or early June to the end of October. Drovers seldom slept under a roof, and they lived on porridge and black pudding. There were few inns anyway until the 19th century, when the use of ordinary roads was usual. That at Kingshouse on the Moor of Rannoch is a good example of an 18th-century one.

The drovers bought the cattle for eventual resale, often on credit. Their bills were payable at financial centres like Crieff and later Falkirk. The Scottish banks took advantage of this trade, and had branches along the routes; the Royal Bank of Scotland (founded 1727) developed a cash credit system. There were of course ferries, dues, tolls, etc to set against profits, and such things as cattle plagues (eg a severe outbreak in 1747), but some of the drovers (like Cameron of Corrieshalloch) did very well. Most of the beasts were small animals, and over four years old.

Trysts were markets established by agreement between buyers and sellers; fairs were established by burghs or the Crown. Both were called markets, but the larger ones became known as trysts. Crieff was the great centre from the end of the 17th century to about 1770, when it became hemmed in by land enclosures and lost its place to Falkirk. In 1723, 30,000 beasts were handled at Crieff. Falkirk began after 1707, at Polmont. From about 1770 to 1785 the tryst was held at the Roman fort on the Antonine Wall, Rough Castle, and then moved to Stenhousemuir, where it remained till the end of the 19th century. The trysts were held in August, September, and October; in 1812 the October tryst handled some 25–40,000 cattle and 25,000 sheep. There were local markets along the routes, such as Portree and Broadford (Skye), Kilmichael Glassary (Ar), Doune, Dumbarton, Hawick, and Dumfries (the next largest to Falkirk).

The Scottish drove roads were grouped in five systems, four of them converging on Falkirk, the fifth covering the south-west. Plotted on a map, and looked at from south to north, they seem like great trees, with their trunks on Crieff and Falkirk and their roots pointed away towards England.

1. North-west (islands)	Outer Hebrides–Skye (Uig and Dunvegan), then ferry Kyle Rhea–Bernera, also Barra to Kilchoan
(mainland)	by Glen Shiel–Fort Augustus–Dalwhinnie–Trinafour–Amulree–Crieff–Stirling–Falkirk; by Glen Garry–Spean Bridge–Killin–Comrie–Crieff (to 1770)–Doune (Stirling) (after 1770); by Arisaig/Kilchoan–Fort William/Corran–Kingshouse–Tyndrum (Crieff/Doune)
2. Argyll	Tiree–Coll–Mull:[1] Dervaig–Ballart–Stronbuy–Glen Aros–Salen; Glen Forsa–Lussa–Grass Point (see **313**), then ferry to Kerrera–Oban–Tyndrum–Crieff/Falkirk; Jura–Keills/Craignish–Inveraray–Balloch/Aberfoyle–Falkirk
3. North	Caithness/Sutherland–Bonar Bridge–Dingwall–Muir of Ord (for Lewis–Poolewe/Aultbea/Gruinard/Ullapool); then either by

1 Mull is of great interest in that a complete drove route can still be made out at Croag on the west coast is a specially-built *cattle port*, with ramp from the water for the cattle to leave the boats.

Inverness–Aviemore–Dunkeld–Amulree (Crieff), or Fort Augustus (via Strath Glass)–Dalwhinnie–Trinfour–Amulree, etc

4. East   via Braemar, Ballater or Banchory–Brechin/Glen Clova/Glen Isla–Blairgowrie–Dunkeld–Amulree

5. South   Ireland via Portpatrick; Galloway[1] (Wigtown/Newton Stewart via Gatehouse/New Galloway–Dumfries–Gretna–Carlisle

Falkirk–Cauldstaneslap–Peebles (see **312**), then Dryhope–Buccleuch–Mosspaul–Carlisle, or Selkirk–Hawick–North/South Tyne, or Romanno Bridge–Broughton–Lockerbie–Gretna

South of the Scottish border there were four routes:

1. West   Carlisle–Penrith–Kirkby Lonsdale–Settle, Skipton, Bingley, and Doncaster

2.   Carlisle–Penrith–Kirkby Stephen/Hawes–Wharfedale, Pad Gate–Wetherby to join the eastern route

3. East   Hawick–Riccarton–Larriston Fells–Gilsland/Birdoswald–Alston and Appleby–Hawes, or east via Bowes and Askrigg–Wharfedale[2]

4.   Hawick–Falstone and Allenheads–Barnard Castle Scotch Corner

Carter Bar–Otterburn–Newcastle

Carter Bar–Stagshaw Bank (Corbridge)–Wolsingham and Piercebridge–Scotch Corner, Catterick (where a branch came in from Appleby over Tan Hill – a famous drovers' inn – Reeth and Richmond), Boroughbridge (where the branch from Askrigg by Middleham, Masham and Ripon came in), then on to Wetherby and Doncaster

Stagshaw Bank–Durham–Yarm–Hambleton Hills–Scotch Corner (Oldstead)–Malton; then by Coxwold and Crayke–York

---

1   Galloway was a great breeding area, hence the vast areas of walled enclosures in Kirkcudbrightshire.

2   Craven was a great fattening area, eg round Malham, where a good stretch of route can be seen at Mastiles Lane (see **314**); many Scotch beasts were bought by Craven farmers at Malham fair.

After these complicated wanderings all over the mountainous north, the drovers left Doncaster along one route to the south, via Gainsborough, Newark, Grantham, and Peterborough to Stevenage and Barnet, where was one of the great cattle fairs for the London region.

Most of the Scottish cattle went to the south-east of England eventually. By 1707 at least 30,000 cattle were crossing into England each year; after that the trade steadily increased, as the population of England increased. In 1732 Smithfield handled 76,000 beasts, in 1794 109,000. But many went to the industrial areas, and many were bought by the army and navy (in 1805 the main naval ports alone took some 16,000). East Anglia was a fattening area, not only for Scots beasts, but for Wales and south-west England also; its centre was the great fair at St Faith's near Norwich, which ran from 17 October for several weeks. Barnet fair also took cattle from all directions. St Ives in Huntingdonshire was a town which owed its existence to a fair.

Welsh drovers were active from at least 1312. Their financial methods were different from those of the Scottish drovers. They usually received the cattle on trust for the farmers, paying for them on return from the markets in England. They were also used as agents by people wishing to transfer money to London or pay debts there, or even to handle official funds. These transactions gave rise to some of the Welsh banks, such as the Black Ox Bank of Llandovery, 1799. By the end of the 18th century 30,000 beasts were driven each year from south Wales alone.

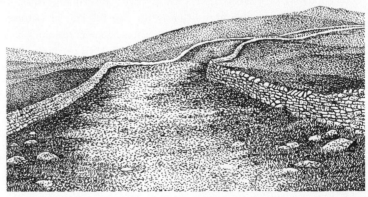

312 *Drove road, south of Peebles: typical of its kind, with wide verges for the animals' benefit.*

313 *Drovers' harbour – Grass Point, Mull: cattle from Coll and Tiree were shipped to Mull and driven across the island to Grass Point, from where they were taken to Kerrera and thence to Oban and the mainland; the harbour had a jetty, and a ramp for the cattle.*

North Wales	Whitchurch/Wrexham–Weston Heath, then either Brownhills (for Northampton–Wisbech–Swaffham–Dereham–Norwich)–Sutton Coldfield–Berkswell; or Wolverhampton–Wednesbury (connecting with routes from Llangollen, Oswestry, Shrewsbury, Montgomery and Bishops Castle) and Berkswell
Welsh Road	Kenilworth–Southam–Buckingham–Aylesbury–Amersham–Beaconsfield
	Builth Wells–Leominster–Worcester (for Evesham, Winchcombe, Cleeve Hill, Northleach and Lechlade to Wantage, Goring, Reading, Guildford, and then to the fattening grounds in Kent and the Romney Marshes, by Dorking or Horsham
	Goring–Maidenhead and Hounslow–Kent

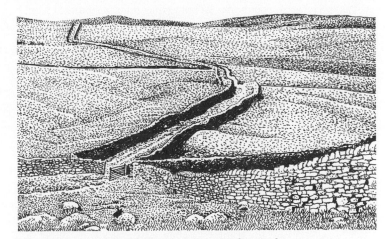

314 *Mastiles Lane, Wharfedale (NY); an important drove road.*

Builth–Hereford–Ledbury, Upton-on-Severn, Bredon Hill, Broadway–Banbury and Northampton Builth–Newent and Gloucester, Cirencester, Cricklade and onto the Berkshire Ridgeway

Brecon–Abergavenny–Monmouth–Arlingham–Bagendon–Lechlade–Abingdon–High Wycombe–Beaconsfield–Uxbridge and Hillingdon–London

315 *A drovers' inn at Stockbridge (Ha), which catered for Welsh drovers. The Welsh inscription means: "Seasoned hay, tasty pastures, good beer, comfortable beds".*

| | Brecon–Newport (connecting with Carmarthen), crossing the Severn either at Beachley/Aust or Blackrock/Redwick, then Chipping Sodbury–Chippenham–Avebury (the end of a southern loop from Redwick to Bristol and Bath)–Marlborough–Newbury and onto the Ridgeway |
| East Anglia | Peddar's Way: Hunstanton southwards
Icknield Way: Chilterns–Newmarket
Norwich–Long Stratton or Bungay and Harleston–Hoxne/Scole; then to Pakenham–Bury St Edmunds–Harleston–Sudbury (where a branch from Newmarket joined), Halstead, Braintree, Chelmsford, Brentwood, Romford, then either Wanstead and Old Ford, or Stratford, London |

The use of prehistoric trackways (Icknield Way, Peddar's Way, Ridgeway, etc) is of great interest; they were not always direct, but offered space and wayside grazing. The Drift on the borders of Leicestershire and Lincolnshire was also used, and, in the Scottish borders, Clennell Street and the Roman Crakemuir Road from Newstead to Eskdalemuir. Inn names and minor place-names should be looked at closely: there are Drovers' Arms at Boroughbridge and Wetherby, A Drover's Call between Gainsborough and Lincoln, and a Highland Laddie at Nottingham and at St Faith's near Norwich. Some of the Bulls and Black Bulls also probably recall their use by drovers. Local names such as Scotgate, Scot Lane, and Scotch Corner in Yorkshire are also significant. Names like Sheep Down and Cow Down, beside the Icknield Way, or Droveway Hill near the Ridgeway, refer to droving, as do the Cowdowns in Wiltshire and Dorset. There is an inscription in Welsh on a former drovers' inn at Stockbridge (Ha) (see **315**).

By 1800 about 100,000 cattle were driven from Scotland to England, The improvement of farming methods after 1760 had enabled them to be bred further north. The peak of the trade was in the last quarter of the 18th century. The decline of Crieff, as has been said above, was due to enclosure. But other factors now came in to affect the trade as a whole. New roads reduced wayside grazing; night grazing of cattle was reduced, or charged for, as sheep-runs got larger and more important. Shooting and deer-stalking, in the 19th century, also limited the passage of cattle. The use of steamships, after 1798 and particularly from 1820 to 1840, led to a marked change in the method of movement of cattle. Better farming produced fatter beasts not suited to droving. So sea transport was used more widely in the 19th century, and after about 1860 rail as well (in 1889 the Highland Railway moved a quarter of a million sheep). Falkirk was still important, and in 1827 130,000 cattle and 200,000 sheep changed hands there. Professional salesmen and auctioneers began to act early in the 19th century. The trade declined sharply after 1870, and in 1880 only 15,000 cattle and 20,000 sheep were at the October tryst. Falkirk was over by the 1890s. The last Skye drove passed about 1906.

In the early 19th century, sheep were as important as cattle. Sheep-farming developed greatly in the 18th century and spread into the Highlands. From then sheep replaced men, and their villages. In the 19th century sheep were driven as well as cattle. In 1812 40,000 were sold at Falkirk, and in 1818 150,000 at Inverness. In 1836 75,000 changed hands at Falkirk, and by mid century 200,000 (more than cattle). From then on the use of railways led to the decline of sheep-droving. Sheep-farming reached its peak about 1870, and has since declined generally.

The trade in sheep necessitated huge markets and collecting centres, of which Lairg in Sutherland and Weyhill near Andover in Hampshire are conspicuous; East Ilsley (Bk) was another, averaging 400,000 sheep a year, many of them from Wales. Good stretches of droveway, part of the Weyhill system, can still be seen in Hampshire, eg at Abbotstone.

Pigs were moved from the Midlands and Hampshire, particularly in the 17th century.

River crossing

FORDS

Bridges were not built on minor roads or over minor rivers, and fords were therefore very common, as the many place-names ending in -ford show; on many rivers they can still sometimes be seen close by the bridge that superseded them, as at Low Bridge, Knaresborough (NY), where the lanes leading down to the ford are still there, although blind now. At Eynsford (Kt) the ford and narrow bridge, side by side, are both in use. Most fords are merely broad shallow places, but some are metalled like the road and a few are paved. Recognisably Roman fords are still very rare, but occur at Iden Green (Kt) and Kempston (Bd); the latter was made of stone slabs, cemented, and partly held in place by rows of oak piles, 17.8ft (5.5m) apart, on the outside edges of the paved way, with one or two posts in the centre also, presumably to separate the traffic lanes. Pre-Roman fords existed, and there were several on the Thames; Julius Caesar used one at Brentford in 55 BC, which was marked by lines of stakes (the Cowey Stakes).

Causeways were laid at all periods to cross marshy ground, like the Neolithic/Iron Age ones in the Somerset Levels and similar ones in the Fens. In the Middle Ages they were often of stone, forming paved paths, as at West Grinstead (Sx). A causeway was laid c 1150 from Arundel Bridge to Lyminster, 700yd (646m) across the former estuary of the Arun; the priory of Pynham was founded to build and maintain this. Another medieval example is Maud Heath's Causeway, Kellaways, near Chippenham (Wi) (1474), which has 64 arches to carry a path along the road (see **308**, page 418).

Stepping stones are an alternative to a primitive type of bridge in shallow water. Good examples are at Bolton Abbey (NY), Stanhope (Du), Ambleside (Cb), and Studley Royal, near Ripon (18th century). A set over the Wylye in Wilton Park (Wi), raised on timber frames, is 19th century; those below Box Hill (Sy) are modern.

316 *A clapper bridge.*

BRIDGES

Primitive early bridges of rope or wood have not survived, but a few stone slab ones still exist – single span (clam) or multiple span (clapper) (see **316**). Post Bridge, Dartmoor (Dv) is a clapper bridge of four large granite slabs resting on two piers and two abutments of rough rocks, unmortared. A clam spans the Wallabrook, a tributary of the Teign (Dv), and there is a clapper at Teignhead (Dv), a clapper at Linton in Wharfedale (NY), both types at Wycoller (La), several in the Cotswolds, and the famous Tarr Steps over the Barle on Exmoor (So). Whether some of these were rebuilt, or even built, in (say) the 18th century is not important; the type is prehistoric, and some of these survivors may have a very long history.

Most *Roman* bridges were wooden, but a few important ones had wooden roadways on stone piers; a model of that at Corbridge (Nd) is in the museum there, and remains of the abutments of such a bridge, where Hadrian's Wall crossed the North Tyne, can still be seen at Chollerford not far away. Similar bridges stood where the Wall crosses the Irthing, and at Newcastle, London, Rochester, and elsewhere. At Piercebridge, where the main north road crosses the Tees, the south abutment, several piers, and the paved river bed were found in 1972, and make a spectacular monument. A few small bridges are built of stone arches of Roman type: that at Castle Combe (Wi) may be genuinely Roman; Harold's Bridge at Waltham Abbey (Ex) and one at Preston, if later (and Harold's Bridge may be 14th century), are certainly of Romanesque inspiration.

During the *Anglo-Saxon* period, probably only repairs to existing Roman bridges were carried out, and few if any new ones built.

In *medieval* times fords were still the usual method of crossing rivers. The first medieval bridges tended to be built at two points on a river, the lowest where a bridge could succeed and an inland port be established (London), and another at the lowest point which could be forded in all weathers (Wallingford). London Bridge has a long and complex history rather outside our scope; Wallingford had a bridge in the 13th century, now much rebuilt. Even important bridges were usually of timber, but began to be replaced by stone in the 13th century, eg Bristol, *c* 1250, and Chester, 1357; Stopham (Sx) was rebuilt in stone in 1423, had its centre arch raised in 1822 to let taller boats through, and has pointed cutwaters and refuges (see **317**); Congleton (Ch) was not rebuilt in stone till 1784; even in the 15th century timber bridges were still being built.

Medieval innovations were the ribbed arch, which saved material, and the road recess continuing the cutwater upward; the medieval cutwater is pointed, but this is less efficient than the round form introduced in the 18th century. Twizel Bridge (Nd) is a fine ribbed bridge, and many ribbed arches exist, some incorporated into later work or widening; High Bridge, Knaresborough (NY), for instance, shows three phases of building, which can be seen (from a boat) underneath its two arches. Good medieval bridges are too numerous to allow mention of more than a few, which are all variously characteristic: Radcot and New Bridges, above Oxford; Elvet Bridge, Durham; Chapel Bridge, St Ives (HP); Barnard Castle; Huntingdon; Dumfries; Ayr; Wadebridge, Bodmin, Bideford; Llangollen. Foundations and larger timbers of a Norman and 13th-century bridges have recently been found at Hemington (Le) on the Trent. Only the timber roof of

Lincoln Cathedral is a larger medieval structure. There is a group of 12 bridges (formerly more), some without parapets, on the Wey below Farnham (Sy), built by Waverley Abbey in the early 13th century (eg Eashing; Tilford). There are similar groups at Oseney (Ox) and near Maidstone (14th century).

Every medieval bridge had its cross, but these were mostly destroyed in the 16th and 17th centuries; many had chapels for the blessing of the traveller, for the collection of alms for maintaining the bridge, and even for regular services. The building and care of bridges were strongly religious activities. Wakefield (*c* 1358), Rotherham (1483), and St Ives (HP) (1426) still have their chapels (although Wakefield's is partly rebuilt); Bradford-on-Avon (Wi) has an oratory, used later

317 *A medieval bridge, with pointed cutwaters and refuges on the roadway – Stopham (Sx).*

318 *Bridge chapel or oratory – Bradford-on-Avon (Wi). It was later used as a lock-up and powder magazine; the roof was added in the 17th century.*

as a lock-up and powder-magazine, and with its roof altered in the 17th century (see **318**). A few bridges were fortified: Monnow Bridge, Monmouth, has a fine central tower gateway (see **319**); Warkworth (Nd) has a tower at one end. An unusual bridge is the (disused) Trinity Bridge at Croyland (Li), with three ways meeting in the middle (late 14th century). London Bridge had a chapel, houses, palace, and waterwheels (the present bridge dates from 1973). High Bridge, Lincoln, has houses dating from *c* 1540.

Packhorse bridges well repay searching for (see **320**). They date from the 14th to the 19th centuries and are common in the north, where roads suitable for wheeled traffic were few, and where large quantities of goods were carried over not always easy country. The West Riding and Lancashire have most (eg New Bridge, Birstwith, Nidderdale, rebuilt 1822), but many counties have a few (eg Coombe Bissett (Wi) and Eynsford (Kt), both medieval; and Stow (ML)). Packhorse bridges are very distinctive; they usually have one high single arch, with a passage the width of a pavement, not a road, and often have parapets as well. At Ashford-in-the-Water (Db) there is one with three arches (The Sheepwash Bridge), which has a sheep enclosure joined to it to make the sheep ford the river.

Renaissance to 18th-century bridges continued to be built in the medieval manner, eg St Neots (Ca), Berwick Old Bridge, 1611–24, Corbridge, 1674. The new styles of architecture began to be applied to bridges, however, before this; Palladian ideas involved wide arches of Roman type, lighter piers, and less depth between arch and crown and parapet; examples are Inigo Jones's bridge at Llanrwst (Gd), Lanercost (Cu), Barden Bridge (NY), and Clare College, Cambridge (1640 or earlier). From now on architects come by name into the story, such as William Edwards (Pontypridd bridge, 1750).

The landed proprietors built bridges widely on their estates, and many exquisite examples remain: Wilton Park (Wi), 1737; Blenheim, 1711 – only part of Vanbrugh's very elaborate plan; Kedleston (Db), *c* 1770 (Robert Adam); Chatsworth, 1762 (James Paine). Adam also built Aray Bridge, Inveraray, and Pulteney Bridge, Bath (1769). General Wade's military bridges in Scotland should not be overlooked (Aberfeldy, 1733).

The Thames has a fine set of 18th-century bridges, of which Chertsey (1785) and Henley (1786) may be mentioned. Smeaton and Mylne built many bridges at this time also, inaugurating the style of the later Industrial Revolution.

A new epoch, led by engineers, was brought in by the Iron Bridge at Coalbrookdale in 1779 (see **321**), and lasted till the Forth Bridge in 1890 (see **322**). The later ones, and the modern concrete bridges (the earliest is at Chewton near New Milton (Ha)), must be left out, but any study of bridges will inevitably lead on to them. The Iron Bridge, the first bridge in the world to be made almost wholly of iron, led to a revolution in civil engineering. Masonry of course continued in use, and bridges in the classical styles were made throughout the 19th century. Telford's canal bridges and aqueducts are dealt with in the canal section, but his Over Bridge, Gloucester, with its splayed arch, and his Dean Bridge, Edinburgh, may be referred to. He is perhaps best remembered for the Menai Bridge, an iron suspension bridge (1826, restored 1940). Brunel's Clifton suspension bridge, Bristol, was begun in 1836. The wooden swing bridge at Selby (*c* 1791) was an interesting survival, but was removed a few years ago. Recently some very large bridges have been built, such as the Forth, Severn, and Humber bridges. (Railway and canal bridges are dealt with on pages 432–3.)

319 *The fortified bridge at Monmouth.*

320 *A packhorse bridge, common where there were few roads suitable for wheeled traffic.*

INLAND WATERWAYS

Rivers

It is well known that rivers were used extensively up to at least the 17th century for moving heavy loads, such as building stone from the quarries to the building (eg from Barnack to Ely or Peterborough). Rivers and large streams which today would not be navigable were undoubtedly used; they ceased to be so partly because of silting and partly because of the lowering of the water table due to drainage and to the increasing use of water by a steadily rising population, quite apart from the effects of climatic changes.

But it should not be thought that transport of heavy goods was exclusively by water. The relatively higher cost of road transport (some five times as expensive in the period 1250–1450) did not always deter medieval people from using it, as Oliver Rackham (in *The History of the Countryside* (Dent 1986)) usefully reminds us. Building materials were not always of local origin, nor moved by water; the monks of Abingdon in the 12th century sent 12 ox wains 120 miles (193km) to north Wales to collect timber, even though suitable woodlands were passed on the way, as L F Salzman records (*Building in England down to 1540* (Oxford 1952)).

Yet rivers were certainly widely used, for people as well as goods, and there are many remains of medieval or even earlier river harbours in places which would not be navigable today, and many decayed ports on larger rivers. The earliest wooden waterfront yet known in Britain is at Egham, on the Thames, 8th century BC. West Grinstead (Sx), on the Adur, is an example of the former kind, with traces of wharves, and Torksey (Li), on the Trent, of the latter. Hedon (Hu) suffered silting of its river, and was killed as a port by Hull and Ravenserodd; remains of long narrow basins remain, although some have been filled in. Cricklade (Wi), on the upper Thames, was the river port for Corinium,

321 *The Iron Bridge, Coalbrookdale (Sp), the first iron bridge (cast iron) (Abraham Darby III, 1779). This part of the Severn valley is the birthplace of the Industrial Revolution.*

the Roman Cirencester. The Roman wharf and pool lay between the (later) High Bridge and causeway and the north wall of the late Saxon town; the Saxon and medieval port could have extended beyond this point to the north-west corner of the late Saxon town. Roman quays have come to light in many places, such as by the fortress at Caerleon, and near the pottery town at Castor (Ca). Bewdley, on the Severn, a medieval transshipment port at the end of packhorse tracks, still conveys the atmosphere of a river port, with quays.

Larger inland ports still retain wharves, warehouses, and some river traffic, such as Gloucester, Gainsborough, King's Lynn, Boston, or Norwich. Lincoln, where the Roman Car Dyke (from Waterbeach on the Cam near Cambridge, 73 miles (117km) away) meets the Foss Dyke (Lincoln to Torksey on the Trent) and the canalised Witham, still keeps much of the impressive Brayford Pool, the Roman harbour at the junction. Bristol had docks in the city centre, now partly filled in.

York was an important port from Roman times onward. Investigation of the waterfronts has not been easy, as many of them are covered by streets or listed buildings and opportunities to examine them have been few. But a detailed survey has now been made and sites of potential significance identified for possible future excavation. Roman riverside installations can be expected on the Ouse from Museum Gardens to St George's Fields (and potentially interesting sites may be available in Wellington Row and Coney Street), and on the Foss from Layerthorpe Bridge to the confluence. Anglian river fronts seem to be most likely in the Fishergate area on the Foss, but may exist along the Ouse also. Viking activity extended along the Ouse from Marygate downwards, as well as along the Foss. Medieval activity seems to have been on the Ouse, particularly below North Street, along Skeldergate (where a sequence of warehouses at City Mills has been found, and 12th/14th-century river walls) to Clementhorpe, and on the east bank along Coney Street and King's Staith. In the late 16th century the importance of York as a trading centre declined and was not revived until the 19th century, when wharves and warehouses were built along both the Ouse and the Foss.

322 *The Forth Bridge (Benjamin Baker and John Fowler, 1883–90) – North British Railway: this masterpiece was the first large bridge in the world to be built entirely of steel; it is more than 1.5 miles (2.27 km) long.*

Much effort has been devoted in recent years to the archaeology of waterfronts, with conspicuous success in London; many of the results of excavation here could no doubt be read across to other places. Investigations over several years by the Museum of London have greatly illumined the sequence: the port was developed soon after the Roman conquest of AD 43, and expanded from AD 70–80, when a timber-faced waterfront terrace, with integrated roads, drains, and buildings, was set up both east and west of the bridge. Several extensions were made to this nucleus in the 2nd and early 3rd centuries. All the quays were built on the intertidal foreshore, not in the deep water channel, so the ships using them had to be beached at low tide and floated off at high tide. Beaching is still carried out at fishing centres such as Hastings (Sx) or Beer (Dv), where no artificial harbour has been made. The mean high water spring or neap tide in London has been rising from *c* -9 ft 9in (-3m) OD to *c* +9 ft 9in (+3m) OD from 1500 BC to the present. The quays were of timber, in open box-like construction, supporting a planked platform, with warehouses behind. The 1st-century quays extended for about 670yd (620m); excavation has picked them up at Pudding Lane, St James Garlickhithe, and south of Cannon Street station. The Roman quays are well behind the present river wall (from 325 to 162 ft (100–50m)).

The middle Saxon port of London (Lundenwic) was west of the walled city (see pages 156–8), and boats were beached along the Strand. The late Saxon city was in the Roman walled area; at New Fresh Wharf (St Magnus House) a new waterfront has been discovered in front of the Roman one, which was used as the back of a bank of timber-based rubble. The bank seems to have been made to check erosion; the boats were beached in front of it. At the west end of the site, just below the bridge, was a large number of vertical stakes set into the foreshore; these have a parallel at the Viking port of Hedeby in Schleswig, and may either be a sort of groyne or part of a defensive work protecting the bridge.

Medieval London had a series of successive timber walls, each further into the river, to reclaim land progressively. The first new post-conquest wall dates from *c* 1150, followed by walls *c* 1270–90 (25m behind the present river wall), *c* 1330, *c* 1380, and culminating in a stone wall of *c* 1440, some 10m behind the present wall. There were also docks at Baynard's Castle and Queenhithe (which dates from at least the early 12th century – the first public lavatory in London stood here), above the bridge; Queenhithe declined in the 15th century as boats grew larger and docked below the bridge, at Billingsgate and Custom House. There was also an early dock (St Mary Overie's) in Southwark.

By the 15th century river *navigation* was becoming more difficult, and throughout the 16th efforts were made to clean and improve those rivers most used, and to make others navigable. The Exe was canalised as far as Exeter in 1566. By 1662, some 685 miles (1,100km) of river had been made navigable for traffic, together with serious attempts to drain the Fens. The Soar was made navigable in 1634, the Wey in 1653 to Guildford, and in 1762 to Godalming, the Itchen in 1710, the Kennet in 1723. The Wey has remains of old wharves and boatsheds, and, at Guildford, a 17th-century crane operated by a manpowered treadwheel; a similar crane, with two wheels, stands near the waterfront at Harwich. The navigations (rivers adapted for traffic) were carried out in three main spurts; several Acts were passed in 1662–5, again in 1697–1700, and again in 1719–21. By then some 1,160 miles (1,850km) of river were navigable, and only a narrow belt along the spine of England, and in central Wales and a few other small pockets, was more than 15 miles (24km) from the sea or from a navigable river. The pound-lock (as opposed to the flash-lock at weirs) had been introduced into England in Elizabeth's reign, and this made possible the use of rivers which mere dredging and cleaning could not fully open up.

Canals

But by the mid 18th century the Industrial Revolution was beginning to be felt, and with it a need for the transport of heavy goods and manufactures which could not be satisfied entirely by the rivers. The road system was improving and being greatly extended; but a horse could draw two tons in a cart, and from 50 to 100 tons in a barge. The rivers had therefore to be supplemented by a system of canals, linking the main centres of manufacture, and these with the sea. But the opportunity was not fully taken, as it was in France, the Low Countries, and Germany, and the railways, when they arrived in the 1830s, were able with little difficulty to kill the canals, which did not happen on the continent.

The size of boats used on the early navigations varied with the depth and width of the rivers and the traffic carried, and this affected the size of the canals, which were usually built to take a particular local traffic and in any case had differing types of country to run through. For hilly country, and to save building costs and water, many canals were built to take boats of about 30 tonnes, with locks only 6ft 6in (2 m) wide. This variation of size hampered the canals when they had to compete with the railways, and was one of the causes of their decline; frequent transshipment was uneconomic, and rebuilding was out of the question. The result is an incomplete system of relatively short lengths of various width and depth. The largest are the main canalised rivers (Severn, Trent, Weaver) and certain canals taking seagoing ships (Manchester Ship Canal, Gloucester and Berkeley, Caledonian, Crinan); next comes the bulk of the river navigations, and most canals north of the Trent and the Trent and Mersey Canal, with locks at least 12ft (3.7m) wide; after these are the "narrow" canals, with 7ft (2.13m) locks, which run in a band from south-east to north-west England (the Oxford, etc); finally, the tub-boat canals, now derelict, in Shropshire and the south-west, had boats 18ft–21ft (5.5–6.5m) long and about 5ft (1.5m) wide, usually working in trains and being raised to higher levels by inclined planes instead of locks. There was once a fifth class, the mine canals of the early days, such as the Duke of Bridgewater's at Worsley, which had nearly 42 miles (68km) underground.

The navigations and canals were designed to serve (and indeed they deeply influenced also) the pattern of trade of the years 1700–1850 (only two are later than this); this trade was the movement of coal and raw materials in industrial areas, and coal, limestone, road and building materials, and farm produce in rural areas. The Leeds and Liverpool still carries coal from the Yorkshire pits to canalside mills in the Aire valley; but in general this pattern has been broken. Modern canal traffic is in quite short hauls. But in 1840 the 4,250 miles (6,840km) of canal (of which about half are still open) and the 22,000 miles (35,400km) of turnpike road formed a coherent system, with a few tramroads and railways, and the coasting trade. The railway boom, which reached its height about 1845, eventually brought about the dislocation and final disruption of this balanced system.

The first canal in Britain was the Foss Dyke, built by the Romans; it runs from Torksey on the Trent to Lincoln, was restored in 1121, improved in 1782 and 1840, and is still in use (the Roman Car Dyke is also still in use as a land drain in the Fens). The next was the Exeter Canal (1566), from Countess Wear to Exeter, extended to near Topsham in 1677, and enlarged and lengthened to Turf in 1820–30.

Most rivers were navigable, but shipping was hindered by the frequent mills; boats had to pass through a movable section of a weir at each mill, and after the Civil War growing trade caused many rivers to be "improved". Locks were built to control the current. By the middle of the 18th century many smaller rivers had been so treated, and there were 1,930km of river passable for barges.

The Industrial Revolution greatly increased this demand; in 1759 the Duke of Bridgwater obtained an Act to build a canal from his coalmines at Worsley to Manchester. This was carried out by James Brindley (by 1761), who even got the canal over the Irwell by means of an aqueduct. This canal was extended to Runcorn on the Mersey. Brindley was much in demand by other canal promoters, and from 1761 to 1772 he planned, surveyed, and partly built a network of canals linking Trent and Mersey, together with the Coventry and Oxford, linking the Grand Trunk with the Thames, and others. About this time the Forth and Clyde canal was built and the Thames was linked to the Severn via Stroud. The mania was in full swing by 1792, and lasted till 1810; many towns subscribed to bring them into the system by branch canals, and more longer ones were cut – the Kennet and Avon, the Wilts and Berks, the Grand Junction (London to Braunston, with links to Leicester and the Trent, and with Birmingham), and two from Lancashire to Yorkshire. Passenger boats were run as well as freight, eg on the Lancaster and the Glasgow, Paisley and Ardrossan, and to Chester races as early as 1776. After a long gap the Manchester Ship Canal was built in 1894. A government enquiry in 1906 produced a valuable report which however was not implemented; in 1947 the British Transport Commission took over most waterways, with certain exceptions, including the Manchester Ship Canal, the River Thames, the Yorkshire Ouse, the Nene and Great Ouse system, and the waterways of East Anglia.

The first canals were based on existing rivers, with branches, bypasses, or links. The latter, which cross a watershed (eg Thames to Severn), have many locks, and a reservoir and pumping station at the top. Others are cross-country (Grand Junction), following a fairly direct line; some join an industrial region with a port (south Wales). Later, canals became straighter, and embankments, cuttings, tunnels, or aqueducts were needed (the Shropshire Union is a good example of this). The Leeds and Liverpool is a contour canal; the Oxford Canal was converted from a contour to a straight canal in 1829–34, and the old curves can still be seen. Similarly, a navigation, such as the Wey (to

Guildford 1653, to Godalming 1762), was based on cutting across the bends of the river, as well as on dredging and controlling what part of the river itself could be used. A 17th-century canal, with 12 locks and independent water supply, from near Stamford on the Welland to Market Deeping (22 miles, (13.5 km)), was rediscovered in 1958.

Subsidence produced problems, and many northern canals have their banks raised and strengthened at weak points. Towpaths were not used in early navigations (where men hauled the barges), but all canals which used horses have them. Horses are still used, for example, on the River Lea and the Birmingham and Fazeley canal. Distance posts at half-mile intervals can be seen on many canals. Basins and loading points had to be specially built, and Stourport is an example of a whole town created for the canals; many wharves can be seen, some disused, some in remote villages. At junctions, eg Braunston, a tollhouse and warehouse can be seen as well. Lock-houses are often of distinctive type on a particular canal, such as the "cottages" (c1770) on the Staffs and Worcs, the round houses on the Thames and Severn, and the classical bridge-houses on the Gloucester and Berkeley. More pretentious houses were built for the agents (managers of a stretch of canal); good examples are Lock House (1816) on the Wey and Arun at Alfold (Sy), or the house at the junction of the Erewash and the Nutbrook. Inns grew up for the canal workers, eg the Navigation Tavern at Mirfield (WY).

Canal bridges also can be characteristic and individual, not only road or accommodation bridges, but towpath crossings (roving bridges). Wooden bridges occur, and some swing or lift bridges; on the Stratford on Avon canal the roving bridges have a slit across them to take the towrope without unhitching it. Tunnels had to be built on some canals; their course above ground is often marked by a line of spoil-heaps, deposited above the tunnel from shafts. Standedge (5,414yds, (4,951m)) on the Huddersfield Narrow canal, and Sapperton (3,817yds, (3,490m)) on the Thames and Severn, are now disused; Strood (3,910yds, (3,575 m)) on the Thames and Medway is now used by the railway; the longest in use is the Blisworth (3,055yds, (2,794m)) on the Grand Union; Harecastle New (2,926yds, (2,676 m)) on the Trent and Mersey is accompanied by Brindley's old narrow tunnel, now disused. When a tunnel had no towpath, boats had to be poled along by pressing against the roof or sides (the marks are still there), or "legged" through, by men lying on top of the boat, or on planks at its sides.

Aqueducts were needed in some places, the greatest being Telford's masterpiece at Pontcysyllte over the Dee (*Shropshire Union*); those at Chirk, Marple, and near Bradford-on-Avon are also noteworthy, and there are many smaller ones of interest, including Telford's early iron one at Longdon-on-Tern (St) made of Coalbrookdale iron.

Canals are part of the water and drainage system of the country, and feeders and outlets are necessary. Differences of level are overcome by locks; most of these are of brick or stone, but at Beeston on the Shropshire Union is one of cast iron, with a bed of sand. Some have turf banks and timber framing (Kennet and Avon). Design of gates varies. Sometimes flights of locks had to be built, and spectacular examples can be seen at Devizes (Kennet and Avon), with 29 locks, and Tardebigge (Worcs and Birmingham), with 30. Where the locks adjoin, with common gates, they are known as staircases or risers (eg Northgate, Chester, and Bingley, on the Leeds and Liverpool, which has two groups of these). Inclined planes were built in a few places, where boats could be hauled up a slope to a higher level (Morwellham, Tavistock Canal, 236ft (72m); Hobbacott Down, Bude Canal; The Hay, Coalport). Vertical lifts were also used; the only survivor, the Anderton Lift on the Weaver navigation near Northwich (Ch), built in 1875, which has a lift of 50 ft (15.4 m), is under restoration, and will be back in operation by 1997.

It is a good plan to explore a stretch of live canal, then to trace a disused one. An accessible example of the first is the Regent's Canal in London (1820). In the stretch from Paddington to Islington can be seen a tunnel (Maida Hill, with poling scars), cuttings, basins, and branches, and "winding holes" for turning. Macclesfield Bridge in Regent's Park is a product of the Coalbrookdale Ironworks; it was blown up by accident, and the Doric iron columns were replaced with their best surviving sides outwards. Grooves worn by towropes can be seen on bridges, parapets, and walls (some canals have iron strips, rollers or wheels on these places); and there are horse-ramps along the towpath, so that horses which had fallen in could walk along in the water until they reached a ramp and could regain the towpath.

A clearly-traced disused canal is the Wey and Arun (1816, abandoned 1868). This leaves the Wey by the factories at Shalford south of Guildford, and runs nearly 19 miles (30km) to Newbridge. Its course, and some of its 23 locks, can be seen either as an empty, but very damp, wide ditch (eg at Birtley, near Bramley, where from a track just east of the railway a wet section also begins; also across

Run Common), or as rough and weedy, but still full of water (Birtley, and between Cranleigh and Loxwood).

The folk art of the old narrow boats is worth a mention – hand-painted sides, deck-houses, buckets, etc, with "roses and castles". Standardisation has nearly killed these, but a few can still be found. Incidentally, the word "navvy" recalls the men who dug the 18th-century navigations.

A related matter to canals is the isolated *dock* often for handling a particular commodity; a fine example is that at Bullo Pill, on the Severn near Newnham (Gl), build in the early 19th century for shipping coal from the Forest of Dean. That next to Battersea Church, London, is medieval in origin.

The roads and railways overtook the canals during the 19th century, and by 1880 they ceased to be of major importance. In some cases the railways took deliberate action to make a canal non-viable; but in some cases the general economic climate was to blame. For instance, the Wey and Arun survived until 1868, but at a low ebb, and only because it provided a through route from London to the sea. In the same area, the Basingstoke Canal failed (it was founded in 1788–94, and barely lasted until 1847) because the industries and agriculture in the south of England were declining. But again, it failed partly because none of the plans to continue it to the coast were carried out; there were abortive proposals to extend it to Andover, and on via the Test (1793), and again from Maidenhead to Reading (1790) and on to Winchester (1796), and yet again to extend the Wey Navigation from Godalming to Winchester (1807).

In recent years there has been a successful, and growing, movement towards using the canals for pleasure boats and recreation, and there is a lively trade in hiring narrow boats and smaller craft. On most canals commercial traffic has virtually ceased. As part of this movement, some canals have been, or are being, restored for use, mainly by local trusts using voluntary labour. Good examples are the Avon Canal in Warwickshire and the Basingstoke Canal.

RECLAMATION OF WETLANDS

Many, if not most, of our rivers, particularly in the Lowland Zone, are still liable to flood, and this was a major factor in determining where men with only primitive equipment could live. Moreover, the water table has been steadily falling, partly owing to drainage and partly to increased population, but before it did the problem for primitive humans was even more insoluble. The waterlogged areas also harboured liver-fluke and foot-rot; fortunately for early humans, lighter soils were also the best grazing areas. The Romans and Saxons tackled the problem, but the position then became complicated by the slow sinking of south-east England; even faster sinking of the Thames estuary has caused the mean sea level at London Bridge to be 11ft 6in (3.5m) above what it was in Roman times.

Taking the Thames at London as an example, although the Romans built a wall to contain the river, by medieval times the south bank was a vast sprawling marsh; Southwark was criss-crossed by drainage ditches, and even on the north bank the sites of the watergates of the great houses, well back against the terrace on which the Strand runs, show how much land the 19th-century embankment has reclaimed. Until well into the 19th century also the low-lying parts of the south bank could be used for little except market gardens; much of Bermondsey is below sea level.

The Roman works included the reclamation of part of the Fens (see below). Traces of sea wall (earthen embankments) have been found along the Essex coast at Barking, Dagenham, and Foulness, and in the west also, eg at Llantwit Major (Gl). In Kent, the Rhee Wall on Romney Marsh is probably Roman; reclamation south and west of it began in 774, and most of the area was "inned" by 1479, but not completed till 1661. The Somerset Levels, where trackways and platforms of timber had been laid over the marshes in Neolithic and Bronze Age times, may also have had Roman works; the drains or "rhines" there are at least medieval.

Serious reclamation was carried out by the Saxons and Scandinavians before the Norman conquest in the above areas, and also in Holderness and parts of Devon. In the Fens and Lincolnshire the "Roman Bank" was built, and a row of villages grew up on the dry edge; a similar line was that along the Sea Dyke from Tetney to Saltfleet. Many of these banks now carry roads, which wind along the old marsh line. More reclamation in the 12th and 13th centuries led to new "colony" villages and new cultivated land, out in front of the parent villages along the new coastline. The later (17th century) works in the Fens are in straight lines. The Essex coast from the Thames northward was progressively embanked from the 12th century; in

433

1531 "levels" or local authorities were set up to maintain the sea walls, of which there are now some 500km. By the 17th century a bank had been built along the south side of the Thames from Southwark to Greenwich; Canvey Island was reclaimed at this time.

Inland, too, drainage was carried out along the rivers, particularly by large landowners such as the monasteries. A good example of this, on a small scale, is the system of banks enclosing meadows along the Crimple Beck at Spofforth (NY), made by the priory.

It has been established that the Broads of East Anglia are not natural lakes but water-filled peat cuttings. Rise of water levels in the 14th–15th century flooded what had been a major local industry. The islands in Barton Broad are the remains of balks between the peat pits. The same events led to the embanking of the rivers which run beside (but not through) the Broads, by banks called *rodhams*.

In recent years much wetland has been brought into arable use by drainage. This has had a disastrous effect on wildlife, both animal and plant, and has brought the farmers into conflict with the conservationists. Some wetlands have however been preserved.

The Fens

The Fens are the low-lying lands which prolong the Wash inland as far as Peterborough. They are made up of clays and silts deposited by marine floods. In the north and west, roughly between the Welland and the Nene, these still form the soil; in the south and east, from Nene to Ouse, they are overlaid by thick layers of peat resulting from changes of relative land and sea levels and land subsidence since the Iron Age, which caused the rivers to slow up and flood the land, leaving it water-logged and choked with vegetation. The silt fens were reclaimed early, in Roman and Anglo-Saxon times, but the peat fens not until the 17th century. A piece of undrained natural fen can be seen at Wicken Fen (Ca). Drainage and other factors have caused the peat to shrink, which it is still doing. It is alkaline with only a few acid patches, unlike the strongly acid peat of the Pennines, formed in different conditions.

All the towns are on "islands" in the peat, except the two villages on rodhams; some islands carry only a single farmstead. Peat wastage caused by erosion, drainage, and intensive cultivation, has by now lowered the surface to Roman or even pre-Roman levels. Doors, once at ground level, can be seen high up in the walls of buildings. A cast iron pillar, Holme Post, was driven into the peat in 1851 so that its top was flush with the soil surface; it now stands 13ft (3. 9m) out of the ground. Holme Fen has lost 21ft (6.2m) in the past century. Stumps of old trees ("bog-oak") emerge from the peat. Roads have therefore had to be built up, or have stood out of the shrinking peat (eg Akeman Street). Faggot causeways were laid in the Bronze Age (eg Wicken promontory, at New Fordy Farm, which is 19.7ft (6m) wide with 7.9ft (2.4m) piles a yard (1m) apart, topped with 6in (15cm) of gravel and fascines). Roman roads (near Castor to Denver, Cambridge to Denver, and perhaps Ely–Soham–Colchester) used levees where possible, but where they crossed the peat they were laid on oak trunks and branches with stones; the metalling was wattles with gravel or gypsum. Medieval causeways were laid to abbeys and to the island on which Ely stands (eg Aldreth, early 12th century; Stuntney, 12th century; Hill Row).

Old watercourses are of several kinds: a dried-out canal, known as a *slade*, shows as parallel dark lines with whitish soil between – the banks carried peat and show dark, the course is chalky. A Roman example (probably) is at Stretham, and there is one from Reach to Upware. Old canals can also show as shallow depressions running across country (eg Colne Dyke). The pre-Roman courses of the Ouse and Nene have been altered by cuts, some Roman, some 17th century (like the Bedford Rivers). Some of the original courses dried up in the 17th century; they show as twin raised banks, often followed by parish boundaries (eg Doddington). Silt banks, otherwise known as *roddons* or *rodhams*, are caused by tidal action depositing silt up slow rivers; they show as a dark central line (the river course) with two lighter ones (the banks). Where rivers are wide there are two of these banks, joining into one upstream. They formed in the Iron Age and Roman period, as the result of land subsidence. They carry two Romano-British villages (eg Welney, occupied 1st–3rd centuries, abandoned in the late 3rd century, then reoccupied in the 4th – it has a triangular enclosure with double ditches), two Roman roads, the medieval village of Benwick, on the West Water, drove roads, and modern farms and houses. At Rodham Farm is a rodham 7.9ft (2.4m) high and 70yd (64m) wide, along a Roman channel. The old course of the Little Ouse runs 5 miles (8km) from Littleport to Old Decoy Farm; the Prickwillow Ouse east of Ely, a medieval cut in Caudle Fen, has two banks; the village of Prickwillow is built on this rodham. Old meres with chalky soil, due to their vegetation, stand out as platforms of soil above the shrunken peat (Willingham); Grunty Fen was a Bronze Age sacred lake, and has yielded votive deposits. Flag Fen (Peterborough) has yielded a complex Bronze Age site, consisting of a long alignment of *c* 1,000 oak posts continuing a Bronze Age droveway from Fengate to Northey; some 300 bronze artefacts – weapons and ornaments – were deposited among and to one side of the posts. The alignment crossed an artificial island in the fen, a platform built with some 1 million timbers, covering *c* 3.5 acres (1.4ha). The excavator, Francis Pryor, considers this complex – which was in use from *c* 1300–900 BC – to represent a religious or ritual centre to promote stability and continuity in a period of profound social and environmental change.

As for the Fen waterways, all but a few kilometres of each river are artificial. The origin of half the artificial waterways of the southern Fen is unknown, and dating is difficult. Some are undoubtedly Roman; the Car Dyke runs from the Cam at Waterbeach, via sections of river and dyke to Peterborough, then to the Witham at Lincoln, a distance of 72miles (117km). This is probably a transport canal, begun in the 1st century for the movement of corn to Lincoln; it was then extended by means of the Foss Dyke and the Trent to York, when the military centre shifted north. Other Roman dykes are assumed at Lark Slade, Reach Slade, and at Rodham Farm; the Colne Dyke may be part of the Car Dyke system. March Cut and Soham Lode may be Roman also. Cnut's Dyke is of uncertain age, but certainly pre-Norman (Saxon canals are known, such as the 1.2km cut through a bend of the Thames at Old Windsor). Conquest Lode is a boundary, and at least early 11th century. Several were cut in the Middle Ages, such as Monks Lode (late 12th century) and Old Podyke, 1223; Ely Cut may be monastic. Moreton's Leam is 15th century. Then followed the great drainage effort of the 17th century, largely sponsored by the Dukes of Bedford, and using Dutch engineers like Vermuyden. The Old Bedford River was cut in 1630 (River Delph), the New Bedford in 1650, to straighten the Ouse and drain the loop. This drainage led to peat wastage, and the use of windmills lowered the peat by 6mm a year; finally, steam and diesel pumps were used, with an effect of 10cm a year, to lift water into the now raised rivers. River banks had to be raised to maintain their levels, and these are now up to 6m above the Fen surface. There were once scores of windmills, mostly now replaced by power-driven wheels; the steam-pump at Stretham is noteworthy.

The land–sea levels are relatively the same now as in Roman times; the land rose until *c* AD 700, then sank to its present level. The Fens were higher and drier in Roman times, for the ends of Roman roads are now submerged in the Wash. The so-called Roman Bank is a Saxon sea wall, now 3.3–3.6m high; the land sank 2.4m from Roman to Norman times.

RAILWAYS

Wagonways are necessary, both inside mines and quarries and for getting the products to long-distance transport. In one sense they represent the prehistory of the railways, but they are also part of the history of mining.

The first reference to a wagonway is at Wollaton Hall, Nottingham, in 1597, followed by Broseley (Sp), 1606. The first widespread use was on Tyneside, from the 1660s, where a vast and complex network developed on both sides of the Tyne, leading from the collieries to staithes and loading places on the rivers. Many of these tracks can still be traced, but most of the staithes have been swept away by later developments. The early ways had square wooden frames or rails, laid on wooden sleepers; in the north-east the gauge was usually between four and five feet.

Some of these wagonways had to traverse difficult country, involving bridges. The first railway bridge in the world is still one of Britain's most spectacular industrial monuments. This is the Causey Arch (see **323**) a great stone single span, 103ft (3 m) across and 60ft (18.5m) high, on the trackway from Tanfield (Du) to the Tyne. It was built by 1725, and bears a date of 1727; it carried two 4ft (1.2m) wooden tracks. Other important 18th-century trackways include that at Prior Park, Bath, 1731 – 3' 9" (1.15m) gauge – serving the Combe Down quarries, and the Peak Forest Tramway of 1796, near Chapel-en-le-Frith, which has the oldest tramway tunnel in Britain.

Iron rails were introduced by the Coalbrookedale works in 1767. They were short – 3 to 4ft (0.92–1.23m) long – and L-shaped, pegged straight onto stone blocks, for use with flat-tyred wheels. L-shaped plateways continued to be used until into the 19th century. A large network of these developed in south Wales from 1800, and by 1824 over 400 miles (640km) were in use. The first railway for public use, the Surrey Iron Railway (1803–44), from Croydon to Wandsworth, with its extension, the Croydon, Merstham, and Godstone Railway (1805–43), used L-shaped rails on stone blocks. Blocks can still be seen in many places, such as impressive stretches leading from the granite quarries at Haytor (Dv) (1820 to 1850s) (see **324**).

Stephenson devised wrought- and cast-iron rails with bullhead section for flanged wheels from 1816 on, mounted above the blocks or sleepers in chairs, a practice which continued until recent years (modern welded rails have wide bases and are pegged straight onto the sleepers). Early examples include the Belvoir Castle railway (Le) (1815–1918), 4' 4½" (1.35m) gauge, stretches of which still survive. The oldest cast-iron railway bridge in the world is across the Afon Cynon at Aberdare, on an ironworks tramway (1811), of 4' 2"gauge. The multiplicity of gauges was not resolved until the advent of public steam railways – the Stockton and Darlington in 1825 (intended for freight) and the Liverpool and Manchester, 1830 (which took passengers also, from the beginning). These used the 4' 8½" gauge which became standard, although the Great Western Railway held out with its 7' "broad gauge" until 1892.

The motive power of the mine wagonways was of course horses until the 19th century (see **325**). Trevithick applied steam to

locomotives in 1804, but these were not a success and had to be used as stationary engines for inclines and pitheads. The first effective steam locomotive was used at Middleton Colliery in 1812. Narrow and standard gauge industrial railways are of course still in use, but are essentially railways, differing almost in kind from the earlier wagonways.

The application of steam power to a locomotive capable of running on rails and hauling laden wagons – by Richard Trevithick in 1804 – was the breakthrough which enabled the development of the wagonways into a countrywide network of *railways*. Long before the end of the century this network linked major and minor towns, taking in villages on the way, and gave a distinctive flavour to Victorian England. Passengers as well as freight could be carried all over the country, on regular services. Milk and mails, workers and commuters, building materials, coal to the factories, gasworks, and homes, fish to the cities, goods of all kinds could now be transported quickly. The economic and social face of the country was radically changed.

The physical face too. Tracks, stations, and sidings appeared in quite remote places; embankments, cuttings, bridges, and viaducts altered the appearance of the countryside; and the railway in cities sometimes created barriers and separated districts in a way only recently equalled by trunk roads, bypasses, and motorways.

Main lines had a different atmosphere from branch lines. They were laid out on a bigger scale, had larger stations, major engineering

323 *Causey Arch (Du) – the oldest railway (wagonway) bridge in the world, Ralph Wood, 1727.*

324 *Haytor Granite Tramway (Dv): a wagonway serving quarries, with shaped granite blocks instead of rails.*

works, larger locomotives, more comfortable coaches, and faster trains. But branch lines were often intimate, and fitted closely into the countryside.

The network which grew up, often capriciously and haphazardly, and often influenced locally by landowners who fought against the railway passing through their land, or towns which refused to have it, was laid out (as P J G Ransom points out) on the assumption that the alternative was the horse and cart or stagecoach. The network therefore retained its vitality until motor transport made the assumption irrelevant. Thereafter more and more drastic steps had to be taken to rationalise the system, and to keep it viable.

The history of railways in Britain (I lean heavily on the admirable summary of railway history by Jack Simmons in *The Railways of Britain* (1986) for this account) can therefore be divided into: the beginnings, 1807–25, 1830; the boom years of railway building, 1830s and 1840s; stability, 1850–1914; the grouping into four large companies, 1923; critical competition from road and air, during and

325 *Horse-drawn wagon on wagonway.*

after the Second World War; nationalisation, 1948, and rationalisation – radical changes to keep up with the competition, 1955–70 (Beeching's pruning, 1963; end of steam locomotives 1968); high-speed trains, 1980s.

Some 400 railways were built (by separate companies), and at the grouping in 1923 there were 123; a few small independents were left out of the grouping and out of nationalisation, and several still flourish. At its peak, in 1927, route mileage stood at 20,443; by 1980 this had been reduced to *c* 11,000, and passenger stations from over 7,000 to 2,362.

The beginnings

Railways in their modern sense grew up with the 19th century. Wagonways still continued in use for industry (indeed, they lasted from *c*1604 to 1968), and in the early years railways used a variety of locomotion, and indeed rails and stock. The first public railway, in that it could be hired to carry freight by anyone, was the Surrey Iron Railway (1803–46) with its offshoot the Croydon, Merstham, and Godstone (1805–38). This used plateways and horses for traction. The Oystermouth Railway (1807) carried passengers, but used horses. The Kilmarnock and Troon Railway (1818) also used horses. The breakthrough came with Stephenson's Stockton and Darlington Railway of 1825; this carried all traffic, but still with a variety of power – steam, horse, stationary engine. The Bowes Railway, strictly an industrial wagonway (1826), consisted of sections of inclined planes, and was operated by cable haulage. One section was worked commercially until 1974, and part of the line has been preserved. Some 25 new railways were authorised from 1826 to 1830 (including the Newcastle and Carlisle in 1829), culminating in the epoch-making Liverpool and Manchester of 1830, which finally demonstrated the possibilities and the viability of steam railways.

The boom years

This was followed (after a slow start, while investors sized up the prospects of the Liverpool and Manchester, and while various oppositions were overcome) by a feverish scramble to build railways all over the country, which lasted for 20 years. Fortunes were made or lost, and certain talented entrepreneurs like George Hudson emerged. The London and Birmingham got off the ground in 1833, as did the Grand Junction (Birmingham to Warrington, linking with the Liverpool and Manchester). Others soon followed: the London and Southampton (1834), the Great Western (London to Bristol) (1835). These four ran for 380 miles between them, and laid the foundation of the network of trunk lines out of London.

Fifteen hundred miles of new line were authorised in 1836–7, not all radiating from London but also connecting, eg, Birmingham with Leeds and Manchester with Sheffield; the Taff Vale line from Cardiff to Merthyr was very successful; and Glasgow and Edinburgh were joined in 1846.

All this looked impressive, but did not add up to a system. For long it remained an almost haphazard hotchpotch of independent companies, each with its own characteristics and atmosphere. They grew up where enterprise was strong and opposition weak. Some (like the Eastern Counties) were less successful than others. By 1843 there were over 2,000 miles of line. The Queen travelled by rail in 1842, and constantly thereafter.

There was serious "mania" in the mid 1840s. Most of Wales and Scotland and much of eastern England had no railways; there was a gap between Newcastle and Berwick. Rivalry between companies and lack of cooperation often went to extreme lengths of disservice to the public; in one case this forced an amalgamation of three companies into the Midland Railway in 1844. This was carried through by George Hudson, a ruthless entrepreneur who saw clearly the need to extend the network and fashion it into a useful and practical system covering all major points. By 1846 he controlled nearly half of England's railways; he left technicalities to others, and concentrated entirely on the financial and economic aspects. He understood the occasional necessity for amalgamation. That of the Midland was followed in 1846 by the London and North Western, and quickly by the Manchester, Sheffield, and Lincolnshire, and the Lancashire and Yorkshire. By 1849 Hudson controlled most of the major railways, except those to the south of London and the western route from London to Glasgow. His companies bitterly opposed the projected eastern route from London to York (the Great Northern), which had to struggle at vast expense from 1825 to 1846 to get its enabling Act through. This line was the rail equivalent of the Great North Road. A conspicuous

monument to Hudson can be seen in York (where he was Lord Mayor) – the original station, 1840, of the York and North Midland, later (1854) part of the North Eastern and now railway offices.

The inter-company rivalries led to cost cutting to the disadvantage of the third-class passengers, and a demand for more direct government control of the working of the railways. Gladstone's Act of 1844 did not achieve everything it aimed to do, but at least it prescribed minimum standards for the third class: at least one train a day, at a minimum speed of 12mph; carriages with seats and protection from the weather; and this at a fare of not more than a penny a mile. These provisions applied only to companies set up after the Act, but of course were followed by the others also. For the first time third-class passengers could travel faster, cheaper, and in greater comfort than on the old stagecoaches.

By the end of 1844 3,000 miles of new line were authorised, and in 1845–8 a further 9,000. In these years some 650 railway Acts were passed, and a similar number were in the pipeline. By 1854 nearly the whole of the system was complete in England, although Wales and Scotland still had far to go. But in England few towns of any size were not on a railway.

One problem of this uncontrolled explosion was the lack of standardisation of gauges. By the 1840s five different gauges were in use (apart from the many narrow-gauge lines): Scotch 4' 6" (1.35 m), New Scotch 5' 6" (1.65m); English 4' 8½" (1.435m); Blackwall and Eastern Counties 5' (1.5m); Great Western 7' (2.1m) – 6' 2" (1.85m) in Ireland. Ireland later adopted a standard of 5' 3" (1.575m). These anomalies were gradually ironed out, but not until 1892 was the Great Western brought into line with the standard of 4' 8½" (1.435m).

Stability

There followed a period of consolidation and stability lasting until the 1914–18 War. There were three amalgamations creating major railways dominating whole regions: the North Eastern in 1854, the Great Eastern in 1862, and the Caledonian in 1865–6; thereafter the broad pattern was set. Minor changes of course went on – small companies joined together or were absorbed by larger ones – and the total gradually decreased. Many companies lost independence and were leased or worked by neighbouring lines.

Gaps in Wales were filled in the 1850s and in Scotland by 1880. The Midland reached London in 1868 – at its conspicuous "Gothic" station at St Pancras – at first running to Derby, Leeds, and Bradford. It needed its own route to Scotland, independent of the LNWR, and in 1876 built the scenic Settle–Carlisle line. This was expensive, having 23 viaducts and cuttings in remote country, built manually; but it was forced into building this line by the machinations of its rivals. It is in fact one of the peaks of Victorian engineering.

In 1872 the Midland had third-class carriages on all trains; in 1874 it abolished the second class, and lowered first-class fares to the old second ($1\frac{1}{2}$d (0.6 p) a mile); in 1875 it provided upholstered carriages for the third class. Other railways soon had to follow the Midland, and the third class got corridors, lavatories, and restaurant cars – the Great Eastern leading the way. The 1860s saw the introduction of workmen's trains, and excursion trains ran from 1871 (when Bank Holidays were instituted). The attitude of the railways to cheap or suburban travel had a direct influence on the spread of suburbs; thus, London grew less on the north side than on the east, west, or south because of the reluctant attitude of the Great Northern and the Midland to suburban traffic. There was little new building after the 1870s, reflecting the national slump. The last new main line out of London – the Great Central, to Sheffield and Manchester – was opened in 1899, but could never compete with the LNWR, Midland, and Great Northern.

The 20th century saw growing competition from road transport, until in 1987 79% of UK freight went by road, as against 52% in France and 51% in Germany; the railways also suffered from internal problems. At first some railways toyed with light railways in rural districts, but this idea was soon ousted by the rapid development of motor buses. But bus services were not integrated with trains, and the railways lost out in the 1920s and 1930s. Trams in large towns, from 1905, creamed off rail passengers but encouraged the railways to electrify; suburban traffic declined (eg the Caledonian lines in Glasgow lost 30% from 1913 to 1922).

The railways were at the height of their prestige from 1890 to 1914. Nationalisation was in the air by the end of this period and received great impetus from the experience of state controls during the 1914–18 War. This war laid severe strains on the railways, such as those on the LSWR – not a robust line – which had to handle the vast army traffic through Southampton. In 1919 the Ministry of Transport was set up, and paid early attention to the railways. The Geddes plan led to the Railways Act of 1921, and to *grouping* on 1 January 1923.

Grouping

One hundred and twenty companies were merged into four, only minor lines and London's Underground being left out. The groups were very unequal, in resources as well as size. They were: the *Great Western*, which now included the Cambrian and other lines in Wales, and two in England; the *London Midland and Scottish*, consisting of the LNWR (which itself had in 1922 merged with the Lancashire and Yorkshire), the Midland, the Caledonian, the Glasgow and South-Western, and the Highland; the *London and North Eastern*, containing the Great Northern, Great Central, Great Eastern, North Eastern, North British, and Great North of Scotland; and the *Southern*, the LSWR, the London Brighton and South Coast, and the South Eastern and Chatham (which had already taken over the London Chatham and Dover).

The old companies were hard to knit together, since practices differed so much. Thus, in the LMS, the LNWR and the Midland were old rivals, but Midland ways eventually prevailed. The Southern developed electrification on a scale which made the London suburban system (extended to Portsmouth, Brighton, and Chatham by 1939) the world's largest electrified suburban system. This encouraged suburban house building.

Threats from roads

The threat from road transport had become serious in the 1920s, and fares were undercut by road charges in the 1930s. There were no general railway fare increases between 1920 and 1937. In response, over 1,200 miles of line were closed from 1923 to 1947. However, the railways improved their speeds (eg the GWR Cheltenham Flyer, 1932, running at over 70mph (112kmh); the LNER locomotive *Mallard* reached 126mph (198kmh) in 1938). The GWR developed automatic train control; the LMS standardised their equipment, and started UK air services; the Southern rebuilt stations (eg Surbiton), and ran a train ferry service from London to Paris. The London Passenger Transport Board was set up in 1933, covering road as well as rail services.

Nationalisation and rationalisation

The Second World War caused great damage to stock and track, and the next logical step was taken. Under the Transport Act of 1947 the railways were *nationalised* (from 1 January 1948) under the British Transport Commission. British Railways was divided into six Regions: Western – the former GWR; Southern – SR; London Midland – the LMS in England and Wales; Eastern and North Eastern – the LNER: and Scottish. Their first task was to repair the damages of the war, catch up with maintenance, and re-equip. The basic aim was that the railways should pay for themselves. The place of railways in the national life had to be thought out afresh. They needed to be free from commercial restrictions, to concentrate on what they were best suited to do, and to be brought up to mid 20th-century standards. The Transport Act of 1953 allowed them to adjust their charges and fix competitive freight rates. There was some decentralisation of control.

The closure of uneconomic lines went on: 2,944 miles (4,710 km) from 1948 to 1959, either to passengers or all traffic. Many stations were closed on lines otherwise open – these places were on bus routes – and trains could be speeded up between the new major points. More lines were electrified (eg the Manchester–Sheffield route via a new Woodhead tunnel). Modernisation and redevelopment plans were drawn up in 1955, providing for improvements to track and signalling, replacement of steam by electric or diesel, the modernisation of stock and stations, and the recasting of freight services (including the fitting of continuous brakes to all wagons). In this phase the main LMS line from London to Birmingham, Manchester, and Liverpool was electrified (1960–7); Euston was rebuilt (with the sad loss of the Great Hall and the Doric Arch (see **330**, page 446)), and New Street, Birmingham, was made into a great central junction for the whole country.

But the works were very costly: in 1952 there had been a surplus of £79m; in 1956 there was a deficit of £17m, in 1961 £87m, and in 1962 £104m. The effort to modernise had cost too much – too many types of diesel locomotive had been developed, the purchase of private wagons was over-expensive, the system was too large, and competition from road and air constantly increased. The Transport Act of 1962 abolished the British Transport Commission and set up a board for railways and one for London Transport; it relieved the railways of the interest on £1175m of accumulated debt and gave more freedom to fix charges, but insisted that the railways concentrate on services which could be run at a profit. Two reports by the new chairman of British Rail, Richard Beeching – *The Reshaping of British Railways* (1963) and *The Development of the Major Railway Trunk Routes* (1965) – dealt with these matters.

Half the passenger stations produced only 2% of the total passenger revenue, and half the freight stations only 3%. The reports analysed the social as well as the economic effects of economies. Beeching was succeeded in 1965 by Barbara Castle, who grant-aided "social" services. Route mileage fell by 30% from 1961 to 1968 and by 15% from 1969 to 1983. Staff fell from 543,000 in 1948 to 197,000 in 1972 and 155,000 in 1983. New measures were resisted by the railway staffs; 1982 there was a deficit of £109m.

However justified, the Beeching closures were, and still are, regretted by a large number of people, and not only on nostalgic grounds. They included innumerable branches and some main lines, such as the Sheffield–Manchester line via Woodhead and the Carlisle–Edinburgh line via Galashiels.

High-speed trains

The last steam train ran in 1968 (standard gauge). Electrification proceeded – to Glasgow in 1974, and by 1985 the Norwich line, and the main line to Leeds and Newcastle. The new Selby diversion line (14 miles (22.4 km), 1983) was the first new main line since 1910. High-speed trains (125 mph (198 kmh)) were introduced, from London to Swansea in 1976 and London to Edinburgh in 1978, and are now general on the main intercity routes. Stations were improved in the 1970s and 1980s, eg Stevenage and York.

The track was again improved and semaphore signals were replaced by colour lights – one box could replace 20 needed under the old system. Freight was now less important than passengers, and more than ever, with larger lorries, went by road. The railway hotels and ships were sold off (1982–4). British Rail (livery based on blue) regionalised its operations (eg Network South-East) in 1986.

But the future of the railways had never been considered as part of an integrated national transport policy. The first stretch of motorway was opened in 1958, and since then a network of 1,850 miles (2,960 km) has been laid down. This has vastly increased the number of cars on the roads and caused congestion in the inner cities on a scale which might react against road transport in favour of railways. In that event the loss of so many rail lines and branches will once again be an issue. One major challenge in the 1990s will be the Channel Tunnel, which will necessitate new approach lines to take 140mph (224kmh) trains, and new installations to handle trains, passengers, and freight. Meanwhile the re-privatisation of the railways began in 1994.

London's Underground

An interesting experiment was Cubitt's Atmospheric Railway (1845–6) from Forest Hill to West Croydon, on the London and Croydon Railway; this was soon abandoned for technical reasons. The first tube railway in the world was the cable-operated line from Tower Hill to Bermondsey (1870, closed after a few months). The first major line was the Metropolitan, begun in 1863. This was a "cut-and-cover" line, at first worked by steam and electrified by 1905, including the first colour light signals. The District followed, and the Inner Circle was completed in 1884. The "tubes" began with the City and South London in 1890; this was at first cable-operated but pioneered electricity underground. It was extended both ways, first to Hampstead, and became the Northern Line. Next was LSWR's Waterloo and City Line (1898). Other tubes followed: the Central, 1900; Bakerloo, 1906; Piccadilly, 1906; Northern, 1907. In 1913 all these lines combined. The Victoria line was built in 1968–70, the first since 1907; the Piccadilly was extended to Heathrow in 1977, and the Jubilee was completed in 1979. Drastic expansion of the system, to ease London's traffic problems, is under consideration.

Much modernisation of stations and stock has taken place. Early coaches were entered from open platforms at the ends, with iron lattice gates; they had wicker seats. The stations each had a different arrangement and pattern of coloured tiles, and a few remnants of these may still be found. There may also still be traces of disused stations, such as Dover Street and Down Street on the Piccadilly Line. Distinguished stations were built on the suburban extensions, such as Arnos Grove (see **326**) and Osterley.

The London underground railways, with their extensions into the outer suburbs and into the country, greatly encouraged subur-banhousing outside the central area, particularly in Middlesex,

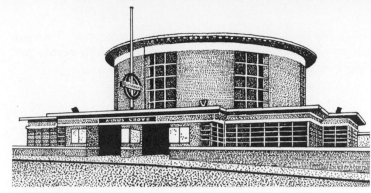

326 *One of London Underground's well-designed stations of the 1930s – Arnos Grove (Charles Holden).*

Hertfordshire, Essex, and Buckinghamshire. Indeed, the area once served by the Metropolitan railway became known as "Metroland" (from 1921).

A few other cities have somewhat similar systems. Glasgow got its subway in 1897 (4' (1.2 m) gauge, at first cable, electrified in 1935). The Liverpool overhead railway (1893) was the first electric urban railway in Britain outside London, and the first electric elevated railway in the world. It was closed in 1956, and was replaced by a new Merseyside system in 1978. The Tyne and Wear Metro (a light railway) was opened in 1984; this uses in part the Newcastle–North Shields line of 1839, the first provincial suburban railway in Europe. Back in London, the Docklands Light Railway was opened in 1987.

Narrow gauge and preserved railways

Several narrow gauge railways lie outside the nationalised system, and continue to provide services. These include the Ffestiniog railway (1' 1¹/₂" (33.75cm) gauge, 1863, for slate traffic, passengers 1865); the Talyllyn; the Snowdon; the Romney, Hythe and Dymchurch; the Ravenglass and Eskdale; the Isle of Man. They run on steam, and have features of great interest. The first electric railway in Britain was the Magnus Volk railway at Brighton (1883).

Since Beeching several abandoned branch lines have been reclaimed by private trusts and provide regular services, which have proved very popular. These include: the Bluebell Line (Sheffield Park to Horsted Keynes (Sx)); the Mid-Hants (Watercress line), Alton to Alresford; the Keighley and Worth Valley (WY); the Severn Valley; the Dart

441

Valley; the North Yorkshire Moors line; the West Somerset. There are also private ventures of preservation such as David Shepherd's East Somerset railway.

Specialised lines

These include the industrial lines from mines etc to river and sea ports, such as those in the coal valleys of south Wales, or in Co Durham. Major civil engineering works, such as the dams of reservoirs, sometimes justified the laying down of railways to transport men and materials. Such was that from Pateley Bridge (NY), continuing the branch line from Harrogate to Pateley along upper Nidderdale to the dams at Angram and Scar. This combined passenger stations also, as at Bouthwaite and Lofthouse. The line was built in 1907 and discontinued when Scar House reservoir was completed in 1936; Bouthwaite station has been converted to a dwelling, and the course of the track can still be followed.

Two light railways began at Brookwood Station (Sy); one went into the cemetery and had two stations there – funeral trains were run from a special bay at Waterloo. Remains of the track and buildings can be made out. The other left Brookwood at a bay on the upside of the station and ran to the rifle range at Bisley (with extensions to army camps). It was built in 1890 and closed in 1952. The bay at Brookwood can still be seen, and the remains of two bridges.

A miniature system developed round the Longmoor Military Railway in Hampshire, opened in 1908 for the training of Royal Engineers. From 1906 it was known as the Woolmer Instructional Military Railway, until it reverted to its original title. This ran round the military establishment at Longmoor, and had a spur linking it to the LSWR at Bordon, at the end of a branch from Bentley on the Winchester line. In 1933 another spur was laid southward to join the main SR line at Liss, and until after the Second World War this link from Bordon to Liss was much used. The Bordon branch was closed in 1966, and the LMR was discontinued in 1969. Much of the course of the track can still be followed, and a few details survive at Longmoor.

Oddments include the light railway along Southend Pier (Ex) and a pumping station at Starcross, Dawlish (Dv) for Brunel's atmospheric railway.

Urban tramways

The usefulness of railways along streets, for local transport, was realised in the 1880s, and a considerable mileage was laid down in London and other major cities. At first the trams were drawn by horses; the last in London ran in 1913. By the 1890s the tramways were electrified, mostly with overhead wires, but in the old London County Council area with a third rail in a slot. The trams reached their peak in 1924, but lost popularity (to buses) in the 1930s and had mostly ceased by the 1940s. In many towns the trams were replaced by trolley-buses before they were finally abandoned. Those in Glasgow and Sheffield lasted until the 1950s, and there are a few along the fronts of seaside resorts, for tourists, such as at Blackpool and Douglas; there is also the tramway from Douglas to Ramsey (IM). The Tyne and Wear Metro (opened in 1980) is a light railway centred on Newcastle. One of its two lines runs from Newcastle airport through the city to Jarrow and South Shields; the other follows the north bank of the Tyne to Tynemouth, then via Whitley Bay to Gosforth and back to Newcastle. This railway has an affinity to a tramway; the Docklands Light Railway in London is not dissimilar. Trams were revived in Manchester in 1991, in Sheffield in 1994, and other cities will follow.

Railway archaeology

The progressive standardisation under British Rail has meant the loss of a great deal of the working equipment of earlier phases of the railways. Much too of the smaller equipment has been sold off. A comprehensive collection is kept at the National Railway Museum in York, but this cannot have the same impact as seeing the items *in situ* and in use. Yet still a great deal remains, and in some respects the railways are a palimpsest, with Victorian as well as 20th-century layers.

Much railway building and architecture survive; in 1979 the railways had 43 scheduled ancient monuments, including the Penydarren Tramroad, on which Trevithick ran the first successful steam locomotive in 1804, and the Bowes Railway, operated by cable haulage since the 1820s, together with 511 listed buildings. A few formerly operational items still remain in sidings, stations, and along the tracks. The abandoned branches and other lines can still in many cases be followed (although the tracks have been removed), and their contours, cuttings, bridges, etc studied; the stations have mostly been diverted to other uses or demolished. Not all of these abandoned lines are the result of Beeching's actions in the 1960s; some were closed in the 1920s and 1930s, and some in the 19th century. They were the victims of changes in the patterns of travel, although the closure of some caused local hardship and may have been ill-judged.

The following are examples of remains deriving from before 1923, and which survive either whole or fragmentarily:

TRACK

The timber or stone blocks of the wagonways have already been mentioned. Metal rails, mounted in chairs and held firm with keys, were first used at the Lawson Main Colliery (Nd), in 1797. Early rails were of wrought iron, until replaced by steel in 1857. Fishplates were used to steady the joins in the 1850s. Stone blocks were still used on some of the early railways, but were soon replaced by wooden sleepers; Brunel's GWR used longitudinal timbers on the broad gauge. Concrete sleepers were brought in in the 1950s. Rails became heavier and longer, and by the 1880s a length of 60 ft (18.46 m) was common. After 1960 rails were welded together in lengths of 600 ft (184.5 m). Chairs were generally replaced by spikes or clamps (with a different rail section) in 1948, but the older type can still be seen on local and side lines (see 327).

SIGNALS

In the early days of railways a variety of signals was used – a red flag, or a board turned parallel to the track for the "off" position. A variant of the latter was the disc and crossbar, used on the Great Western from 1841 to 1869. These latter types are still used in France, or were till recently. In 1841 the London and Croydon adopted the semaphore, an arm used in three positions: horizontal for stop, halfway down for caution, vertical (in the post) for all clear. At night, lights were used: red for stop, green for caution, white for all clear. From the 1870s two arms were used, a stop signal with square end, and a distant signal with fishtail end. The Great Northern used an arm on a bracket, which fell clear of the post ("somersaulting"); the Great Eastern arm moved upwards and not downwards.

The "block" system, under which space not time intervals were used, and only one train was allowed in each section of line at a time, was introduced by the Yarmouth and Norwich in 1844. In the 1850s and 1860s "interlocking" was developed, whereby signals could not be moved in conflict with each other, and signals and points could be harmonised.

327 *Types of railway track: 1, L-section plate rail, spiked into a wooden plug in a stone block, for plain wheels (used on early wagonways and tramroads); 2, edge rail for flanged wheels, on a wooden sleeper; 3, bull-head rail with chair and key, spiked into a wooden sleeper; 4, flat-bottomed rail clipped to base plate on a wooden sleeper; 5, heavy flat-bottom rail with spring clips, on a concrete sleeper.*

443

Automatic signalling was used on the Liverpool Overhead Railway in 1893, and on the District line in 1906. Colour-light signals (red-yellow-green) replaced semaphores on the Underground system in 1953; on the main railways they were adopted in the 1920s and have now replaced semaphores on main lines.

Each railway had its own design of signal box and gantries, and a few of these can still be seen, even if now abandoned (see **328**).

CUTTINGS AND EMBANKMENTS

These were of course made manually, with picks and shovels, and trolleys on narrow-gauge tracks to take away the earth and stone, until earth-moving machinery became available. Early pictures and photographs give an idea of the vast toil, and the number of men, involved. A major line, the Settle–Carlisle on the Midland, was laid by hand as late as 1876; in 72 miles (115km) it has 17 viaducts, 12 tunnels, and innumerable cuttings and embankments.

In some cases earth removed from cuttings was not used to make embankments elsewhere, but piled up along the sides of the cuttings in ridges or mounds; such are the "bumps" at Pinner (Mx) on the old

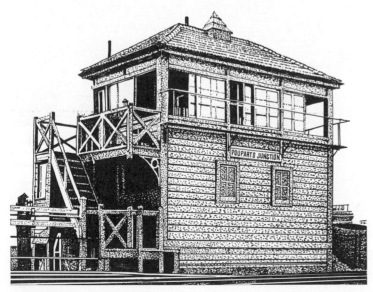

328 *Signal box – London Brighton and South Coast Railway, Battersea, 1911. Each railway had its own designs of buildings and equipment of all kinds.*

LNWR, or the mounds along the line west of Beaulieu Road (Ha) (LSWR). Some quarries for embankments may be filled by lakes, eg west of Weybridge (Sy) (LSWR).

There are some anomalies: the embankment at Shalford (Sy), leading towards the main Portsmouth line, was never used for track. The South Eastern Railway abandoned its design to get to Portsmouth, on agreement with the LSWR, who took the line through from Guildford (reached in 1845) via Godalming (once a terminal, 1849). The incredible cuttings in solid rock into Lime Street, Liverpool, from Edge Hill, made by hand in 1836, still astonish.

TUNNELS

Building the 19th-century railways necessitated hundreds of tunnels, most of them still in use. They were built by manual methods, with great hardship and considerable loss of life. The longer ones are notable engineering feats by any standard.

The longest tunnels include the Standedge, on the LNWR line from Manchester to Leeds (1850s): this is over 3 miles (4.8km) long. It surpassed the previous longest, the Woodhead tunnel (Sheffield Ashton and Manchester Railway, 1845); the original tunnel was doubled in 1848–52 and replaced in 1954 by a new double-line tunnel, itself closed in 1981. Box and Kilsby are two very long tunnels of the 1840s. The Severn tunnel, four miles 606yd (6.9 km) long, was completed in 1886, and is the longest main line tunnel in the country.

Many tunnels have elaborate entrances, sometimes at the insistence of local landowners. Box tunnel (Brunel) has a particularly imposing "classical" entrance, and some are castellated. Long tunnels built for steam traffic have ventilation shafts on the surface above, eg the castellated ones over the Chipping Sodbury tunnel (Gl). A tunnel abandoned and stranded in an urban setting is the Scotland Street tunnel in Edinburgh, which was once part of the line from Waverley to the north; it was superseded by a diversionary line in 1868, but its mouth can still be seen north of Scotland Street.

The longest tunnel in the world was the Northern line tube in London, from Morden to East Finchley, 17 miles (27.6km). These tube tunnels were made possible by the invention in 1890 of the "Greathead shield". They are of course now exceeded in length by the Channel Tunnel.

VIADUCTS

Even in the Lowland Zone of Britain, there is much country which is not flat or even gently undulating. Railway builders had to minimise the gradients, and when these became too steep or when it became impossible to follow the grain of the geology, the normal method of cuttings and embankments had to give place to viaducts. In the Highland Zone these are very frequent; in the 72 miles (115 km) between Settle and Carlisle there are 17 viaducts, including the great Ribblehead viaduct (1865) (see **329**)).

Many viaducts are short and insignificant; but some are very conspicuous, dominating a wide valley. Such are the Ouse viaduct just north of Haywards Heath, on the Brighton line (Rastrick, 1841, with end pavilions by Mocatta); it has 37 brick and stone arches. Other fine viaducts are Ballochmyle, near Mauchline (Ay) (Miller, 1848, with its great central arch), Digswell (Ht) (GNR, 1850), Stephenson's Royal Border Bridge, Berwick (1850), and Harringworth (Nh) (Midland, 1870s, 82 arches). Glenfinnan (1901) was the first to use concrete. Timber viaducts and bridges were used in the north of England and by Brunel on the Great Western, including a famous series in Devon and Cornwall, the last of which was not replaced until 1934. The first viaduct was that at Sankey (La), 1830.

Viaducts were sometimes, like tunnels, made "architectural", with pilasters, buttresses, parapets, and other features. Brunel's viaduct in Bath goes to extremes, with turrets and castellations.

BRIDGES

These are ubiquitous, and most of them are undistinguished; some, such as those to the Southern stations across the Thames in London, are positively ugly. The great variety of their size precludes any consistent pattern.

The oldest railway bridge is the Causey Arch, Tanfield (Du) (see **323**), built for a wooden tramroad in 1726; this is a remarkable monument, graceful and beautiful. The oldest iron railway bridge is on the Llwyd Coed tramroad near Aberdare (1811). A catalogue is unnecessary, but the great monumental works will always be memorable: Stephenson's Britannia Bridge over the Menai Straits (1851, of wrought-iron tubes, rebuilt after a fire in 1972, retaining the towers, and again altered in 1980); Brunel's Royal Albert Bridge at Saltash, over the Tamar (1859) the hybrid suspension bridge at Chepstow

329 *Ribblehead viaduct, Settle – Carlisle line, Midland Railway, 1875: a masterpiece on a line in difficult country, built by manual labour.*

(replaced in 1962) was a trial run for this; the rebuilt Tay Bridge (1887); and the stupendous Forth Bridge (Baker and Fowler 1890, using steel).

WORKING FEATURES

Sidings have become less important with the reduction of freight traffic and the effect of road transport. All stations had them, but most of those at small stations and on branch lines have been taken up. Local goods go by road, and coal is mainly sent to power stations. But some remain at mines and docks, eg the complex system for coal at Barry (SG). Much of the Midland's prosperity depended on their vast coal marshalling yard at Toton, near Long Eaton (No), funnelling the produce of the Notts and Derby coalfield.

Miscellaneous features include *water towers* for steam engines (a raised tank and movable pipe at the end of station platforms and in sidings); a *coaling plant* survives at Carnforth (La); *platelayers' huts* occur along the track, together with *lamp-stores*; several types of *level crossing* exist, with one or two gates, double or single or with poles or other barriers, and crossing-keepers' houses; *snow fences* are found in mountainous country, to prevent snow drifting onto the line.

LOCOMOTIVES AND ROLLING STOCK

These should be studied in the books, museums, and preserved railways. All the old railways had their needs and preferences, and their own designers, which resulted in a remarkable variety. Locomotives included passenger (express and local), freight, shunting and industrial, built-in units (steam and later electric and diesel), etc. Carriages too ranged from royal trains, mail coaches, sleepers, dining and buffet cars, to ordinary passenger stock. The Groups, and recently BR, have reduced the types and standardised progressively. *Wagons* too have always been in great variety, and pre-1923 many were privately

330 *The Euston Arch – Philip Hardwick, 1838; now unfortunately demolished. The symbolic gateway to the north-west (from a print of c 1850).*

331 *St Pancras Station, London, train shed, Midland Railway (W H Barlow, 1868): at the time this roof was the widest unsupported span in the world – 240ft (73.8m) (from a contemporary print).*

owned. Some of the old firms' names can occasionally be seen. *Liveries* are mentioned below.

Buildings

Stations naturally make the first impact on the casual traveller, and set the scene for what lies behind. Here again each company developed its own style. For the smaller stations a degree of uniformity for each railway, usually different for main and branch lines, crept in, but for major stations and terminals there was an element of prestige also.

The first major station was Brunel's Paddington (1835, with Digby Wyatt), designed for broad gauge and with a triple shed; the adjoining hotel, by Hardwick, was added in 1854. London Bridge followed in 1836, for the London and Greenwich and the London and Croydon Railways, later part of the London Chatham and Dover, and then of the South Eastern. London Bridge and Victoria are double stations, each covering the terminals of two lines, the different styles of which are still visible; these were the South Eastern and Chatham and the London Brighton and South Coast ("the Brighton side" at Victoria).

Hardwick's Euston (1837), with its magnificent Great Hall and Doric Arch (see **330**), was entirely recast in the 1960s. Waterloo was built in 1848, replacing the former terminal at Nine Elms (1838) which existed until recent years; but Waterloo has an Edwardian feel, in spite of much remodelling. Cubitt's King's Cross is a striking masterpiece in yellow brick. But externally as well as internally the most impressive London station is St Pancras. The railway part, with its magnificent single train shed, of 240ft (74m) span (see **331**), was built by Barlow in 1868 – it had wooden platforms until recently; the "Gothic" hotel was added to its front in 1873 by Gilbert Scott.

Outside London, Temple Meads in Bristol was built by Brunel in 1841 and remains an early railway monument, although now used for other purposes; the early history of the site is very complicated, owing to three railways meeting at different angles. Other distinguished stations include Newcastle Central (Dobson 1851), Glasgow Queen Street, 1842, with all-over roof added 1880, Birmingham New Street (Cooper 1854, altered), and York (Prosser 1877, with its exciting and majestic curve) (see **332**). The most imposing exterior is perhaps the very dignified classical Huddersfield (see **333**) (Pritchett 1848, for the Lancashire and Yorkshire and the LNWR jointly); Stoke-on-Trent has a fine "Tudor" front.

Major stations now disused as such include Manchester Central (1880), Glasgow St Enoch (1874–8), and Edinburgh Princes Street. Former Great Western stations such as Reading owe the great width between the platforms to the original need to take four tracks of broad gauge. A new terminal has been built at Waterloo, London, for the Eurostar service through the Channel Tunnel which began operation in 1994. This has a very elegant glass shed (Nicholas Grimshaw).

The variety of smaller stations precludes listing. The oldest still in use is Edge Hill, Liverpool (1836). Gravesend (Beazley 1849) has a pleasing classical front; Cambridge consists of one long platform (facing east into the Fens!). Local styles can be seen on branch lines, such as the "New Line" from Surbiton (rebuilt in 1937) to Guildford, eg Clandon and London Road, or minor main lines such as at Stamford or Wansford (Nh). Petersfield shows the LSWR style at its best; Lewes has a pleasant atmosphere. Reigate (1849) and Leatherhead (1867) are good Surrey examples. Disused stations have often been converted to other uses, such as dwellings (eg Baynards (Sy), Bouthwaite (NY); Lasham (Ha) is a coal depot; and so on.

The railways opened *hotels* at an early date, such as at Edinburgh Waverley, Perth, Dumfries, York, King's Cross, St Pancras, Charing Cross, Victoria, Liverpool Street, and some as holiday centres, such as Gleneagles. BR Transport Catering has a buffet or restaurant service at most stations of any size, and provides the meals and snacks on trains.

Other buildings include locomotive and carriage *sheds*, at points strategic to the services (eg Wimbledon or Farnham). A major locomotive shed, with turntable, was the Roundhouse at Camden Town, now disused. There are also *goods sheds*, for merchandise in transit, some taken over from canals and navigations. The larger railways maintained their own *works*, in which engines and rolling stock were built and repaired. These included such vast factories as Doncaster, Horwich, Swindon, Crewe, and Derby. Towns like Swindon and Crewe were virtually creations of the railways although incorporating older centres, and some towns, such as Woking, grew up round important junctions.

Diversification

From the early years, as well as hotels, railways went into *ferries* and *steamer services*, continuing to the present day with enterprises such as Sealink (sold off by BR in 1984) and MacBraynes Caledonian; the first railway steamships ran in 1845 from Dover and Folkestone. They

332 *York station, North-Eastern Railway (Prosser, 1877): built on a dramatic curve.*

333 *Huddersfield Station (JP Pritchett snr, 1848). This very dignified classical building was designed for the Huddersfield and Manchester Railway and Canal Company, but taken over before its completion by the Lancashire and Yorkshire and the London and North-Western Railways.*

also had *docks*, eg Barry, Southampton, and Harwich Parkeston Quay. They acquired *travel* firms like Thomas Cook, and had rights in Pullman cars. They ran *buses*.

Variety

Each of the 120 companies which survived to the Grouping of 1923 had developed its own style, and many had absorbed others on the way; in spite of British Railways standardisation much of this variety can still be seen. The changing details, of course, added greatly to the interest of a long journey until well after 1923.

The stations reflect this diversity very clearly, in the architecture and layout, and in details such as awnings, bargeboards, finials, cast-ironwork, railings, seats, drinking fountains, urinals, nameboards, and notices. But the disappearance of many of these details is rapid, apart from the hundreds of stations closed and dismantled since 1923.

The traveller also knew on which line he was by the design of engines and carriages. The class of engine varied with the type of train, and even the shape of the cab was peculiar to each railway. More obviously perhaps, the *livery* of the engines and carriages was distinctive, and made a long journey very colourful. Some companies had changed their liveries since their early days, but a very clear pattern existed in 1923 and took several years to be replaced by the colours of the four groups.

Many people will still remember the pre-1923 colours, and a number of examples survive in museums. Useful indications are given in the Science Museum books, *The Pre-Grouping Railways*, and in the many books dealing with each railway in detail. There is no space here to attempt a complete list, but the variety may be hinted at by recalling the various greens of the engines of the North Eastern, Great Northern, Great Western, LSWR, SECR, and some of the Scottish railways, as also the post-1923 Great Western, LNER, and Southern. Not only was each green different, but the engines were lined in different combinations of white, yellow, black, red, etc. The LNWR used black, and the Midland crimson lake was very distinctive. The Great Eastern, the Caledonian, and the Glasgow and South Western used blue, the North British deep orange, the Lancashire and Yorkshire black. The coaches were also distinctive: the North Eastern used dark brown with yellow linings, the Great Northern teak, the Lancashire and Yorkshire buff and dark brown, the LNWR white and purple-brown, the Great Western cream and chocolate, the Midland lake, the Highland red. It was always of interest to watch the activity in a large junction, such as York. The trains there were mostly in Great Northern, North Eastern, or North British colours, but occasionally a Lancashire and Yorkshire train would arrive, or even a Great Western.

Another, minor, source of variety was the *destination boards* on the carriages. Named trains merely carried their names above the carriage windows – *The Flying Scotsman*, *The Irish Mail*, the *Cornish Riviera*, *The Brighton Belle*. Lesser, but still major, trains showed the destinations – Paddington to Penzance, King's Cross to Leeds, King's Cross to Edinburgh and Aberdeen, London to Glasgow. These were perhaps not so informative as the square boards on the sides of the carriages, inscribed, usually in small letters, with a list of the stations called at, which were (and are) used on the Continent, but had a more immediate impact. And (although not a destination board) what

inscription over the windows of a carriage could have more impact and nostalgic allure than Compagnie Internationale des Wagons-Lits et des Grands Express Européens?

LETTER BOXES

The shape of pillar boxes has changed several times, enabling them to be dated. Although the postal service was widely used and the stamp had been introduced by Sir Rowland Hill in 1840, until 1846 the post was carried by bellmen with locked bags with a slit into which people put their letters when they had paid their penny. As a result of a request by the people of St Helier and a visit by Anthony Trollope, then an assistant postal surveyor, public boxes were introduced. Trollope proposed a box attached to a post, but Hill preferred a pillar box which he had seen in use on the Continent. The first British pillar boxes were therefore in the Channel Islands – four in Jersey in November 1852 and three in Guernsey in February 1853. These were hexagonal. The next was erected in Carlisle in October 1853. This type had forms with horizontal slit (the earliest) and with vertical slit with the VR and crown either above or below it.

London had its first boxes (six of them) in April 1855; these were square and squat, with a slit at the top, which was surmounted by a ball over willow leaf decoration (see **334**). They were followed by three in the town area and five in the rural area of Cheltenham in May 1855. In the next four years other types appeared, of which one was a handsome hexagonal box lavishly ornamented on all angles with scroll designs; this had a plain VR over a horizontal slit (1857). The provinces got a very handsome type in 1856, reminiscent of

334 *The first postbox (London, 1855).*

a Doric pillar, fluted, with a flattish top and POST OFFICE over a vertical slit (see **335**). These can still be seen in Warwick, Banbury, Christchurch, Birkenhead, and a few other places. A variant had a deeper plinth, and there was one variety, used in Birmingham, with a tall cap surmounted by a crown. These Doric pillars were set up from 1856–60.

In the absence of a national standard, designs were numerous. Cochranes of Dudley began producing round boxes in 1859, one of which had a crown on top. And even after a design for general use by J W Penfold was adopted in 1865, local varieties persisted. The Penfold box was tall and hexagonal, with an ornamental top (see **336**). It came into use in September 1866, and was made until 1879. About 100 still survive, in Buxton, Cardiff, Cambridge, Sheffield, and elsewhere, with five in north-west London. The Penfold box had four variations: high aperture with a flap, no flap but a bevelled edge, aperture lower and coat of arms above, and royal cipher and hours of collection plate reversed and time tablet brought from the side to the front. Sometimes the box was topped with an acorn.

The practice of painting boxes red began in 1874; before then there was a wide range of colours. The present cylindrical pillar box became standard in 1879, and there have been few changes since then, although there are still some varieties in detail, and of course the royal cipher or letters give a guide as to date (see **337**). A tall square form like a filing cabinet was brought in in 1968, and there are several kinds of wall box. In 1885 James Ludlow of Birmingham started to supply letter boxes which could be built into the walls of town sub-post offices. These were made of wood with a metal front. Before 1908 country sub-post offices had to provide a box at their own expense, and these were often made by the local carpenter or blacksmith in a variety of designs. One of these, little more than an enamel plate with Queen Victoria's cipher, survives at Alfold (Sy), and several others still exist. The design was standardised in 1912, when Ludlow became the sole supplier to country sub-post offices. These filled a hole right through the wall, and had a door both inside and outside the post office. They were made until 1965. There are also small boxes on posts.

335 *The first "pillar" box (1856).*

336 *The "Penfold" pillar box (1866).*

337 *The standard pillar box (1879).*

Some of the earlier types are rare and some no longer survive, but a surprising amount of variety can still be found. Makers' names often appear, such as Carron Ironworks. Letter boxes form the subject of lively research, and there is a Letterbox Study Group. The history is covered in Jean Ferrugia: *The Letter Box* (Centaur Press 1969).

GUILDS AND GUILDHALLS

Guilds were medieval associations of merchants or craftsmen; they exercised certain powers of control over the occupation they represented, and acted as friendly societies for their members. They flourished mainly in the towns, and their halls are still a prominent feature in many places. There were also religious *fraternities*, with social and benevolent objects; many bridges were maintained by such bodies. *Merchant* guilds began in the 9th century, for mainly religious and social purposes – relief for poor members, burial of the dead, and prayers for their souls. They had a patron saint and either the use of the nearest church or a chapel in the church. They organised processions and festivities. By the end of the 11th century economic functions were added to these; the guilds had privileges in the local market, and could engage in trade; non-members had to pay tolls and could operate only under restrictions. By the end of the 13th century such guilds operated in over 100 towns. (London had a different history – see below.)

During the 13th and 14th centuries the merchant guilds were largely superseded by *craft* guilds, each for a trade or group of trades. These had a monopoly of trade in their wares or services and discriminated against "foreigners" (any outsider); hence immigrants, such as the many craftsmen who came to England in the 16th century, had to live and work outside the cities. They regulated conditions of work, wages, terms of trading, etc; they also provided for the relief of distressed members and had some religious duties. In due course admission was only to sons and apprentices of members. Apprentices usually lived with masters (full members), and graduated to this rank after long training and proof of ability.

By the 16th/17th century there was a tendency to replace these guilds by large *companies* covering several trades each; thus, in Reading, all the trades were divided among five companies, in Ipswich into four, and in Devizes into three. There also grew up specialised large bodies, such as the Merchants of the Staple (13th century), who controlled the wool and cloth trades, and operated in several centres, the Merchant Adventurers (16th century), who traded with the Low Countries and northern Europe, and the great trading companies, such as the Baltic, the East India, and the Hudsons Bay (16th/17th centuries). A few Chartered Urban Guilds – Goldsmiths, Pewterers, Weavers – had special privileges.

The guilds declined during the 18th century, and their restrictive powers were abolished in 1835. They continued as social and charitable bodies, running schools, almshouses, etc; the City and Guilds Institute was founded in 1878 under this impetus.

In London there was a "Frithgild" in Saxon times, consisting of ten families who met regularly and maintained a fund for compensation in case of lawsuits against members. There was a "Knightengild" by the time of Edgar (mid 10th century), which had a territory, a soke, which gave its name to Portsoken Ward. These were for mutual defence. By the late 13th century trade guilds emerged, the earliest to be chartered being the Saddlers in 1272 and the Weavers about the same time, but probably existing before this date. The religious links of these guilds were strong; the Saddlers had a chapel in St Martin-le-Grand, and they maintained chantries, schools, almshouses, and bridges, and supported pageants and mystery plays. By the 16th century the guilds provided men for the army, loans for the exchequer, wheat to feed the poor, carts for cleansing the streets, equipment to fight fires, and settlers to colonise Ireland. Their social role was thus very important.

The guilds had royal charters and *liveries* (although some have none). The livery is only a small part of the membership (the rest are "yeomen"), but the court of assistants is co-opted from it, and this provides the wardens and master (though in the Ironmongers, the livery is the governing body). The members are "freemen". By the 15th century the issue of a freeman could be a member without being a craftsman, so the companies drifted away from their original purpose. They remained however monopolistic and protectionist. They owned land in or near the city, and grew very wealthy. Since Richard II's time (late 14th century) there have been Great Companies and Minor Companies. From that time to 1743 the Lord Mayor had to be a member of a Great Company. There are 12 Great Companies – Mercers, Grocers, Drapers, Fishmongers, Goldsmiths, Skinners, Merchant Taylors, Haberdashers, Salters, Ironmongers, Vintners, and

Clothworkers; 72 Companies are Minor, and 12 are extinct. The companies have a prescribed and numbered order of precedence. From 1375 to 1835 the livery of the companies had the sole municipal and parliamentary franchise. The whole living body (the Common Hall) elects the Sheriffs and the Lord Mayor. Most are now social and friendly societies, but the Fishmongers, Goldsmiths, and Gunmakers have retained their regulatory functions unbroken.

Many companies had their own *halls*, some of which often contained rich treasures of plate etc, of which some survive. Forty-four halls were lost in the Great Fire of 1666; only seven escaped, but little or nothing survives of the pre-Fire halls except the 14th-century crypt of the Merchant Taylors. Thirty-five companies had halls in 1939. They suffered great damage during the war, and only five late 17th-century halls remain intact or restored – Apothecaries, Innholders, Vintners, Tallow Chandlers, and Skinners; a few have fragmentary remains, like the Stationers and the Grocers.

A special class of London guild, that of the lawyers, was fortunate to have its halls, the *Inns of Court*, outside the range of the Great Fire, and much of these remain. In fact, they give as good an idea of

338 *The Cutlers' Guildhall, Thaxted (Ex), c 1400. A good instance of a guildhall later used as a town hall; the supreme example is the Guildhall in London.*

medieval collegiate buildings as anywhere outside Oxford and Cambridge. They have been added to through the centuries, and have a quite distinctive atmosphere. There were originally several, but the survivors are the Inner and Middle Temple, Lincoln's Inn, and Gray's Inn, with only fragments or sites of the others. They have halls, chapels, libraries, and courts or ranges of buildings.

The wide range of functions of the medieval guilds meant that in practice the local government was carried out by them. It was thus natural that the town hall should be known as the *guildhall*, and in earlier centuries they were the same. The guildhall in fact was where the guilds cooperated in the general affairs of the town. The Guildhall in London is a supreme example, comparable to the great halls of the continental cities. Some such hall existed at least by 1189, but the present building was begun in 1411, taking several decades to finish. Guildhalls are a familiar feature of most old towns; random examples are Thaxted (early 17th century) (see **338**) or Peterborough (1671).

There are many survivals of guildhalls outside London. The present Cutlers' Hall in Sheffield dates from 1832; the company was founded in 1624, and still has its function of granting trademarks to cutlery and plate. York has a Merchant Adventurers' Hall (1357–68) and also a Guildhall (1447–68, restored after war damage). Norwich has a Strangers' Hall, 15th century, a centre for immigrant weavers, and a Guildhall (1407–13, rebuilt 1535). Many towns have cloth halls, eg the Wool Hall at Lavenham (Su) (now the Swan Hotel; there is also a Guildhall here of 1529). Some cloth towns have Piece Halls where cloth was sold by the piece; the most splendid is that at Halifax, 1775, with 300 rooms round a vast square (see **386**, page 488).

Apprentices usually lived with their masters, but in large establishments a special house might be built for them; an example is at the model mill village of Styal (Ch), 1770s.

MARKET HALLS

Few places which had a market in the Middle Ages did not have a cross as its centre, to remind people of their religion, to inspire business morality, and to provide a collecting point for tolls. The earliest were shafts on steps, but the convenience of a roof over them was soon seen, to protect both traders and toll collectors. The roof then gradually

339 *A market hall of basic type – Pembridge (He).*

340 *Town (and market) Hall, Abingdon (Ox), c 1680: a fine example.*

took precedence over the cross, which might remain as a symbol on the roof or disappear altogether. Finally, an upper storey could be added, as offices for the traders' guild, the toll collectors, the weights and measures inspectors, or even the local authority. This development took place mostly during the 15th and 16th centuries.

The simplest form, with a cross and roof combined, can be seen at Cheddar (So), Woodstock (Ox), and Castle Combe (Wi). That at Bingley (WY) became too small, and a separate market hall was added next door in 1753. The next stage, the simple shed, might retain a vestigial cross inside in the form of a central pillar whose main function now was to support the roof, as at Oakham (Ru). Plain wooden sheds are found, as at Pembridge (He) (see **339**). In East Anglia some very elegant classical pavilions and temples were built in the 18th century, a long way from the idea of a cross; a fine example is at Swaffham (Nf) (1783). The most splendid pavilions are those at Salisbury, Malmesbury (both about 1490), and Chichester (1501) (see **228**, page 330); these are stone-built arched shelters like crowns of stone, rising on flying buttresses to a pinnacle, and ornately decorated.

Very many old towns still have a 17th- or 18th-century market hall or guildhall with an upper storey over a ground-floor shelter; the best is perhaps at Abingdon (Ox) (1677–80) (see **340**), but there are good examples at Dunster (So), Ross (He), Thaxted (Ex), Wymondham (Nf), Watlington (Ox), and Godalming (Sy) (1815). The last of this type is at Llandovery (Cm) (1858). The 18th and 19th centuries were the period of specialised market buildings, such as the corn exchanges (see **341**) which are still a feature of many country towns, eg Devizes (Wi). A plain and simple, but spacious, market hall is that at South Molton (Dv) (1863).

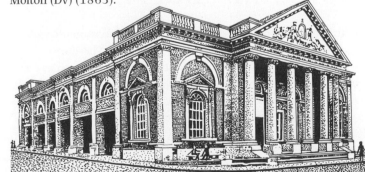

341 *Corn Exchange, Bury St Edmunds (Su) (Ellis and Woodward, 1836): a very satisfying example of a feature of most lowland country towns.*

London has several exchanges: the Royal Exchange (1568, rebuilt 1841) was originally a covered shopping precinct for foreign traders; the Stock Exchange has recently been rebuilt; the very interesting iron and glass coal exchange has been demolished; what is left of the hop exchange after a fire (in Southwark Street, 1866, with imposing entrance and iron gates) can still be seen. The London general markets are also interesting, like Leadenhall (1881) and the vast Smithfield (meat, 1866). Provincial cities usually have Victorian market halls, like the large round one at Leeds (1857, exterior 1904) and the fascinating one at Halifax (1895).

Horse repositories and selling rings (like Tattersalls and that at the Elephant and Castle in London) seem to have disappeared. But open-air cattle markets still survive, some, as at Guildford (Sy), with general stalls as well, but moved, like so many from the town centre (eg at Ipswich is a small square called Old Cattle Market).

Some of these are in quite small villages as survivals, eg Pannal (NY). There is a large sheep market at Lairg (Sd). General markets of stalls in special places, like the old Caledonian in London, have probably all gone now, but street markets (Leather Lane and Berwick Street, London) still continue, as do the weekly markets in streets and market places in most towns of any size.

An interesting relic of a former street market (discontinued by 1882) is at Hindon (Wi), where a band of cement along the front of two houses (High Steps and Barham) in the High Street was used for attaching lean-to roofs for market stalls.

SHOPS AND SHOPPING

Retail trade, the selling of the current necessities of life, is one of the main functions of towns and, at a simple level, of villages. There are numerous modern studies of this, mostly for the benefit of economists and town planners, and some narrower accounts, such as the lively books of Alison Adburgham on women's shops, eg *Shops and Shopping 1800–1914* (1964). A very useful general survey, from the historical point of view, was published in 1966 by Dorothy Davis (*A History of Shopping*).

In the Middle Ages the vast majority of the people were peasants, who were either wage labourers or smallholders. They had little surplus to buy things, and this was often what they could breed or catch. Their standard of living depended on what land they worked and what rights they had to pasture, cut fuel, catch fish, etc. Money was secondary to goods; the peasant indeed worked not simply for money, but (in Dorothy Davis' words) "so as to avoid as far as possible the need for money". But he had to have some, if only to pay taxes, and thus had to sell his surplus in the local market. But the peasant's negative attitude kept markets poor and crude outside London and a few large cities. Trade in the small market towns – usually no bigger than modern villages – was practically confined to market days. Today a town of 1,000 people has permanent shops; then, it was a collection of craftsmen rather than shopkeepers. On market days they put up their stalls. On other days they might go to other markets (at a price), or sell outside the church. There was a general prejudice against profit; middlemen were discouraged. Selling hours were regulated in the buyers' interests, so that all had an equal chance. Weights and measures were controlled, but there were many local variations; eg a "weigh" of cheeses was officially 168lb (75.6kg), but 256lb (115kg) in Suffolk, 336lb (151kg) in Essex, and at several other places 224lb (100.8kg). Another problem was coinage; silver got clipped and had to be weighed, not counted, and the smallest coin was a farthing when ale was a penny a gallon. Some foreign low coins were consequently in use. Bread and ale prices were fixed by local "assizes".

The baker, or the lord's oven, baked bread for everyone who had no oven. Brewing was casual and unorganised; many women did it, and in London in 1305 there were 1,300 brewers for under 50,000 people. Anyone who sold ale had to put out a bush as a sign. Meat was cheap and plentiful, although most people kept livestock of some sort, even in the heart of London. Fish, except on the coast, was salted, dried, or smoked, and there was a large trade in salt herrings (which indeed were sold by anyone). Cooks were another market trade, with ovens or open fires. Dairy produce was bought from farmers at the market. Firewood was sold by peasants.

A small market might only sell food and firewood, a big one would have leather, wood, and metal products as well. By the 14th century every town had at least one genuine retailer, a general store – even if he was called a mercer, grocer, or haberdasher. Leicester (population 3,000) had two or three. Clothes were usually secondhand. The general scene was more like an Eastern market than an English one.

Later in the Middle Ages the streets were regulated and traders assigned to specific areas or streets – hence the very common names like Bread Street, Cornmarket, etc. The shops were open, with shutters

342 *The Shambles, York: a medieval street with butchers' shops; a shamble is the shelf in front of the shop.*

343 *Cheap Street, Frome (So). This is a rare, perhaps unique, survival of a medieval shopping street, with central drainage channel (the trees are a modern embellishment).*

which let down to form counters. The Saxon word for these, which became the later "shamble" and meant a shelf, was often applied particularly to butchers' shops, as in York (see **342**), but originally could be used of any shop. Fishmongers and greengrocers often still retain the open front. It can be seen in a wider range of shops on the Continent. The narrow streets with these shops were not unlike souks. Sanitation in medieval towns was erratic, and shopping streets often had an open ditch or drain along them. A rare reminder of this is Cheap Street, Frome (So) (see **343**). Law and order was a problem. Nothing was packed or wrapped – buyers brought their own containers, except for barrelled goods. In general traders had to sell from stalls, not from shops. The streets were named not from the occupations of their residents but from those of the "foreign" (country) people who were allowed to pitch in the roadway to sell their produce, eg bakers from Stratford, once full of windmills, fishermen from the Thames etc, in London. Until recently many market places had permanent stalls with canvas awnings in bright colours or stripes. Nottingham had this until the market was moved, and Norwich still has it, opening a rare window onto the Middle Ages.

More durable goods, and a wider variety, were sold in *fairs*, which lasted days or weeks. By 1400 there were 30 or 40 annual fairs in the whole country. The biggest were international markets, where cloth or wool was sold in bulk, as well as foreign luxuries: glass and jewellery, silk and velvet, from Italy; Flemish linens and French wines; spices from the Levant, furs from the Baltic, tar from Norway; armour from Milan, horses from Spain. As well as bulk supplies of food, rushes, tallow, wax, salt, etc could be bought in quantities to last for months. These products were cheaper in bulk, and often better than at the local market. Stourbridge Fair, near Cambridge, indeed surpassed

London itself. The most important were St Giles' at Winchester, for wine and spice (14th century), St Luke's at Huntingdon, Stourbridge at Cambridge (luxury fabrics), and St Bartholomew's in London for English cloth (15th century). Other big ones were Boston, and Yarmouth for fish. Many were run by monasteries or churches; all needed royal permission. At the major fairs the booths were laid out regularly in "streets", some reserved for particular trades – Goldsmiths' Row etc. Prices were more or less stable before the Black Death. After that, slow inflation set in. Shortage of cash made house-keeping very difficult, even for the rich.

Retail trade took a modern turn in London in the late 16th and early 17th century; population expanded rapidly at that time, there were more wealthy people, and more luxury goods were available from abroad. So London had rapidly increasing purchasing power and demands. But prices doubled from 1543 to 1551, and then, after a short stability, doubled again from 1570 to 1620. Oliver Rackham; (in *The History of the Countryside* (1986)), has compiled a useful guide to price fluctuations since 1264. With a few brief rises and falls, the index remained at roughly 1 until just after 1500, when a steady rise began which is still continuing. Taking 1500 as 1, the index rose to 5 in 1600, remained in that area till 1750, rose to 15 by 1815, and dropped to 10 again by 1900. Since the Second World War the index has risen to 50 in 1960 (ten times the level of the 1630s), and to some 220 in 1984, and is still rising. Thus since the 1930s the value of money has fallen over twenty times.

These conditions led to the establishment of specialised retailers, *shops*. Retailers were both in the merchant (importing) class and craftsmen. The latter got their supplies from other craftsmen working at home (eg bookselling, which once was a sideline of printing, but to which printers became increasingly subordinate). The shopkeepers were middlemen, providing capital and enterprise and distribut-ing goods to the public. A few crafts went on selling direct, eg gunsmiths, musical instrument makers; and watchmakers. There were also specialist trades like tobacco, glass, and (later) tea, coffee, and china.

Food was closely supervised and the old medieval market system was reorganised. But the City fought against retail food shops, and preferred to stock and distribute food through recognised markets (Leadenhall, Billingsgate, etc). Country towns round London, eg Barnet or Leighton Buzzard, became collecting and reselling centres for livestock, corn, etc going into London, and grew rich on it. But retail shops were inevitable, and by the 1680s the markets had become free and wholesale.

The *London Markets*, a very distinctive institution in the period 1580–1666, comprised Smithfield (livestock), Leadenhall (poultry, meat, dairy produce, hardware, leather, cloth), Gracechurch Street (general), Eastcheap (meat), New Fish Street (fish), Southwark (general), Cornhill (the Stocks – meat and fish), Cheapside (general), St Nicholas (meat), Newgate (meal), Queen Victoria Street area (fish), Queenhythe, Bear Key, Billingsgate (open imports). Westminster had its own market in King Street, and between the two great landowners set up private markets at Clare Market (1650), Covent Garden (1651), Southampton Market (1662), St James' Market (1664), Hungerford Market (1680), etc. There were others at Spitalfields, Stepney, Rotherhithe, and Hoxton. After 1666 the central markets were reduced to four, in separate buildings: Smithfield, Leadenhall (the biggest in Europe), Honey Lane, and Paternoster Row; Queenhythe (corn), Billingsgate (fish), and the Stocks (fruit and vegetables) remained open, but wholesale.

Essex supplied most of London's cheese before the 17th century, but after then it came also from Gloucestershire, Wiltshire, and Cheshire. Mustard came from Tewkesbury, saffron from Essex. Grocers' shops existed all over the City in the 17th century, and overlapped with apothecaries and with chandlers (for soap and household stores). Beer and coal were separate trades. Food and fuel were very dear, and took the bulk of the expenditure of all except the very rich.

Outside food and fuel, shops of all kinds sprang up all over London and spread along Fleet Street and the Strand in the 17th century. By 1700 shops had taken their present form of glazed ground floors. The Royal Exchange was built by Sir Thomas Gresham in 1568 as a shopping precinct (with "pawne" or gallery) for foreign traders who had had to use Lombard Street up to then; this had lock-up shops, an innovation. The best shopping street in 1600 was Cheapside, lined with fine houses over rich shops; the south row was goldsmiths, the other side mostly silk mercers. Cheapside at its peak, *c*1300, had shops on the street front and bazaars behind – called *selds* – which were large structures where numerous traders stored, displayed, and sold their wares. These declined in the 15th century, and when trade picked up *c*1500 were not revived. By the 1620s the goldsmiths had moved west and a variety of trades replaced them. London Bridge too had some 40 retail shops on each side, most of them in some branch of the clothing trade.

Shoes were in the hands of aliens, in St Martins and Blackfriars. Cutlers congregated in Fleet Street, pawnbrokers and secondhand clothes dealers in Houndsditch and Long Lane (later in the 17th century they moved to Monmouth Street – "Rag Fair"). Glass got cheaper in the 17th century, and some shops sold nothing else. Ironmongers were in Lothbury, Lawrence Lane, and Thames Street, nails and chains in Leadenhall. Grocers and apothecaries were grouped in Bucklersbury. A New Exchange, after a bad start (1609), by Charing Cross, was active until the late 17th century, and there were two others. Wealth was moving west (St James's) in the 1680s.

Country towns fell far behind London for shops in the 17th century, but market trade increased. The wealthy shopped in markets over wide areas. Boston was a centre of French trade (wines etc) and Baltic iron; Stourbridge Fair was still important. Newcastle was a general trading port, and by the late 17th century had developed a variety of shops. Wine was perishable until the invention of the corkscrew in the 18th century – two-thirds of it came through London, and a lot through Boston, Hull, and Newcastle. Hexham sold saddles and horse furniture, Penrith boots and shoes. Linen came from Yorkshire, napkins from Lancashire. But the north still made most of its needs, and shops were consequently scarce; most money went on services and raw materials, not manufactured goods. Many people, eg woolbrokers or those who had to travel, did retailing as a sideline. Opening shops was restricted in old towns until 1835, but new towns like Manchester, Birmingham, and Leeds had less restriction. Markets and fairs grew less distinct from each other, and many new ones sprang up; eg in Essex the numbers rose from 19 to 28 in the 17th century.

Taverns, always popular, reached their peak after the Restoration, although coffee houses were spreading also. Taverns usually sold food as well as drink. They were centres of business and social life; Pepys mentions 105 over eight years of diary writing. They retained the form of private houses, with separate rooms. Coffee is first recorded at Oxford in 1648, and within 20 years coffee, tea, and chocolate were popular all over the country. By 1688 London had some 100 coffee shops, by 1710 at least 500. White's and Bocdle's coffee houses continued as clubs. In 1640 London had 211 licensed taverns, and in 1732, 652 inns and taverns and 551 coffee houses. Tobacco was expensive in the early 17th century. There were two

kinds, Spanish and colonial, which improved and stole the market by the end of the century in the form of a blend of Virginian and West Indian, with some English at first. The shops used two signs, the black ball of twist and the black boy. The clay pipe industry, later widespread, was at first centred round Bristol and Shrewsbury (see **344**). Barbers ceased to be general surgeons in the 16th century. Wigs came over from France in the Restoration, and were in vogue until the end of the 18th century.

By 1700 there were some 150 booksellers in London and 300 in other towns (most of the latter only as a sideline to stationery, pens, almanacs, tracts, bookbinding, etc). They congregated mostly round St Paul's; in 1666 there were 23 in St Paul's Churchyard alone. After 1666, law books went to the Temple and the Westminster Hall area, technical books to the Tower district, plays, poetry, and music to the Strand, while divinity and classics remained round St Paul's. Paternoster Row became filled with bookshops, which replaced fashion shops after the Fire; this, with Little Britain and Duck Lane, lasted as a centre for books until 1940. In the 17th century booksellers were publishers also, and the books were bound to order; many were financed by subscription. The growth of private libraries (like Pepys', later at Magdalene College, Cambridge, or Bishop Cosin's at Durham) led to a secondhand book trade. Big fairs had bookstalls, and that at Stourbridge was famous.

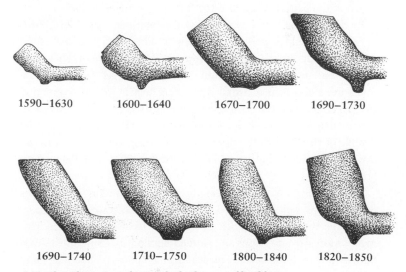

1590–1630   1600–1640   1670–1700   1690–1730

1690–1740   1710–1750   1800–1840   1820–1850

344 *Clay tobacco pipes, showing the development of bowl forms.*

A very useful survey has been made of traders in Norwich, which extends our knowledge to towns outside London (Ursula Priestly and Alayne Fenner: *Shops and Shopkeepers in Norwich 1660–1730* (University of East Anglia, Centre for East Anglian Studies, 1985)). Retail shops in the modern sense were unknown before the 17th century; craftsmen sold their wares on their premises or in the market, which also sold perishable goods from the countryside. By the early 17th century retail shops appeared in London and the larger towns, but these often dealt wholesale as well; shopkeepers began to stock goods not made by themselves, or actually imported. By the end of the century specialised shops appeared, catering for sophisticated or luxury demands. Most shops still had open fronts; glazed fronts were not universal until the late 18th century, and even later in many towns.

Priestly and Fenner's study of shops in Norwich describes the following trades: grocers; sellers of tea, coffee, and chocolate; confectioners and tobacconists; haberdashers of Small Wares; apothecaries; barbers and barber-surgeons; booksellers and publishers; ironmongers, tinmen, and cutlers; mercers, drapers, haberdashers, tailors, and milliners; pottery and china shops; florists and gardeners. Many of these shops kept other goods as well, such as tobacco. In addition there were the market stall traders and the inns, which often acted as centres of exchange and business. Thus, by 1700 much of the pattern familiar until quite recent times was already set.

By the 18th century shops were well established – the 17th century is the formative period, the 18th is "modern". Products were still not standardised, and prices were settled by argument. There was a lot of bad money in circulation, and foreign coins, bills, and local notes were also in use. Small sums were met by private coins and tokens; credit was universal. Cash sales at fixed prices became more general in the second half of the century, eg at James Lackington, "The Temple of the Muses", the first large-scale bookseller; the first to use this system was a haberdasher and draper, Flint and Palmer, on London Bridge.

In 1732 nearly a quarter of all the houses in London were taverns or food shops. London catered for visitors and country shopkeepers who came in to buy their stock, as well as for its own inhabitants. This meant a forest of shop signs and painted signboards. As shops changed hands the signs often became misleading (sometimes deliberately) and repetitious. Hanging signs were abolished in 1762, except for taverns and a few trades (see page 464). Many shops still had open fronts, and stalls and booths were still common. Plate-glass windows replaced crown and muff glass after 1773, and bow windows came in in the mid 18th century.

The biggest and best shops were now not in the City but the West End, eg in Oxford Street, which was lit by lamps in the 1780s. But the City was still full of shops. Furniture-makers were now prominent, and did interior decoration as well, employing upholsterers, carvers, gilders, glassmakers, etc. Table china, at first imported, was later made in English potteries (Chelsea, Worcester, Derby, Wedgwood). Wedgwood opened a London showroom in Grosvenor Square in 1765, and then a shop in Greek Street. Tea was sold in china shops (why did tea replace coffee in English taste until the quite recent spread of foreign travel?), and by apothecaries and coffee houses. Thomas Twining opened a teashop in the Strand, next to his coffee house, in 1713. Most of the coffee houses disappeared by the end of the century. All tea drunk before Victoria's reign was china tea. At least it was warm and safe – one had to boil the water. In 1722 the English bought an ounce a head a year, and by 1820 an ounce a head a week, while the drinking of beer was halved.

Grocers were important, and cheesemongers now sold all "provisions" – oilmen also sold provisions. Pastry cooks multiplied. Markets were still used for perishable food. Butter came from local farms ("Epping butter") and from the eastern counties ("Cambridge butter" was cheaper). Pork-butchers were a new trade. Quality declined and standards of hygiene were abysmal – uncovered milk, adulterated bread, etc. The alehouses were thickest in the poor quarters where wages were mostly below subsistence levels, and were universal providers. They let lodgings, ran benefit clubs, "employment agencies" etc, and a lot of people were in their debt. They were gradually brought under control after 1751. Eight million gallons of gin were consumed in 1750, only one million in 1800.

The main food suppliers of the poor in cities were the chandlers (general shops). Cellars were used for many trades, like cobblers, old clothes, old iron, and milk. Cookshops cooked for the poor (their own food), and sent out hot food. The south relied on secondhand clothes, the north made their own. This trade was centred in Rosemary Lane (Rag Fair), near the Tower, and Monmouth Street. Secondhand shops of all kinds abounded, and pawnshops. A lot of the goods sold in these were stolen; in 1796 there were over 3,000 known receivers in

London alone, most of them keeping open shop. So the poor did little to stimulate retail trade. Tallymen sold haberdashery and household goods. Debt was a constant threat. Street-selling and hawking were common occupations of the wives of the poor, some selling honest home-made goods, some buying cheap, some near-beggars. Some mended chairs or swept chimneys. Street cries were used by these people. These conditions lasted well into the 19th century.

Pedlars were known since at least the 14th century, selling every kind of portable goods, buying at the fairs and in London. Regular merchants objected to the competition. The 16th century lumped them in with the vast numbers of thieves and vagabonds on the roads, and damaged their reputation. But from the late 16th century they could enlarge their stock (from leather items, small metal goods, narrow woven goods, and toys), with tobacco, broadsheets, etc. In the 18th century they dealt in contraband as well. Some became respectable shopkeepers, and the breed has still not quite died out; indeed, there are still street traders selling goods on the pavements. In the 16th century there were picturesque pedlars, licensed to sell glassware direct from the glasshouses in the Weald etc, which they carried round in open baskets (see **399**, page 509). But in the 18th century a new man appeared, the *wholesale* travelling dealer, with *packhorse*, who took goods from the new factories direct to shopkeepers (the "Manchester Man"). There was also a *retail* trader, selling textiles on credit (the "Scotch Draper"), going on foot – these were a great boon to the working people. They were not unlike the London tallymen, but more honest, and they had the support of the manufacturers. They were eventually superseded by shops, in Victoria's reign, although a few still exist.

Up to about 1850 markets sold nearly all local food outside London. Today over half the shops in Britain are food shops. As late as 1873 there remained 1,500 private slaughterhouses in London alone. The wholesale trade became more highly organised, particularly in drapery. Some firms went from retail to wholesale, eg Twinings and Allen & Hanburys. Advertising and price tickets came in. Many drapers aimed at rapid turnover of stocks, and held frequent sales and "salvaged stocks", and pushed lines which hung fire at reduced prices. All this increased demand. Big shops paid employees little, and living-in and long hours were common. The use of gaslight did not improve these long hours. Drapers and haberdashers catered for home clothes-making, but tailors and shoemakers retained their direct links with the consumer. Milk also was still sold direct by cowkeepers, of which there were 700 in London in the 1880s (some survived to well between the wars). There were over 13,000 hawkers in London in the 1850s.

Shops differed between regions and localities; in big towns, some streets catered only for the upper and growing middle classes. In small towns and villages markets and fairs went on. Cheapjacks sold from the backs of carts. But shops were increasing everywhere. Even a village hardly big enough to have a shop at all would have a shoemaker, a pub, and a grocer/draper, although the range of goods sold is enormously greater today. But the wages and standards of the working and lower middle classes were rising, and consumption and production rose with them. So did credit and debt (and pawnshops). Truck (the payment of wages in kind), although not an unmixed evil at first, was going out.

In the past hundred years the process of retail selling has got much simpler and less skilled, while the organisation of retail trade has got much more complicated. Mass production has led to standardised goods, and pricing and advertising are in the hands of the manufacturers. Many chains of shops sell only one maker's goods, or lines of branded and advertised goods. Chain stores and large shops are increasing – one in five now in Britain, doing over half the total trade (unlike any other country). These have taken over the best sites in the main streets. They are cooperatives, multiple stores, department stores, bazaar-type stores (now supermarkets), and recently hypermarkets. The origins of most of these lie in the 19th century.

Cooperatives mushroomed after 1844 (beginning in Rochdale), but have a local pattern and are weakest in the big cities. Vertical integration (wholesale and retail) and the branch system turned them from utopian, self-supporting communities to retail trading. Branches were set up (eg in Rochdale in 1856) for the convenience of customers, but proved to be very profitable. The two Wholesale Societies enabled the movement to succeed, and develop modern methods of distribution.

When businessmen took up large-scale retailing, the whole trade was transformed. In the 1870s the grocery trade began to change, with multiple branch shops (Lipton in Glasgow 1872; by 1890 he had 70 shops in London and in 1898 245 in the country; there were also the Home and Colonial and the Maypole Dairy Company, which by

1913 was selling a third of all the margarine). Some of these chains grew their own tea and owned their own butter factories, creameries, etc. These chains, and small shops also, had to cater for the widening tastes of their working-class customers. They spread until the first war, but slowed down after 1918, coming up against intelligent competition from smaller shops. Manufactured goods were the key to this, and all classes now buy the same kinds and brands of goods of all types.

By the 1970s a quarter of all the groceries in Britain were sold by the big multiples and another quarter by the cooperatives; of the rest, some was sold in supermarkets and departmental stores and some by independent grocers (who are declining). Grocery now equals all the food trades together. There is now a tendency to diversify – grocers sell bread, tights, cigarettes, paperbacks, records, cards, etc; bakers sell sweets and butter. Self-service is widespread. New packaging and methods of preparation (dehydration etc) and refrigeration are accelerating this trend. So is the growing ownership of refrigerators and freezers in homes. All this undermines the purpose of specialised shops, and general self-service food shops have become the rule.

In non-food trades there has been since the 1880s the same spread of *multiple networks*, and also the development of the *department store*. Multiples succeeded in footwear, men's clothes, chemists' goods, and sewing machines, in the distribution of newspapers etc, and in hardware and tobacco. Since the first war they have also entered the field of women's fashion. The department store was a French invention (Bon Marché and Louvre in the 1860s). In London in the 1860s and 1870s several were started – Debenhams, Swan and Edgar, Dickens and Jones, Marshall & Snelgrove, Shoolbreds, Harrods (all expansions of existing shops), and new ones like Whiteleys, Army and Navy, and the Civil Service Stores. In the north stores like Lewis of Liverpool, Kendal Milne of Manchester, and John Anderson of Glasgow also appeared. These all expanded as fast as they could. They catered for middle-class customers, and had an air of luxury and leisure, or at least of comfort. They had central positions, and new building methods enabled them to have huge multi-storey palaces, vast windows, gas-lighting, lifts, and cash tubes or "railways". They rose with the rise of the white-collar worker. They offered the new products of industry, and a wide choice. One could furnish and equip a whole house in one shop, and see at the same time a lot of things one hadn't had before. Prices were clearly marked. These stores helped to mould the tastes of the rising middle class, and also introduced them to the new concept of obsolescence. Each had its own atmosphere.

Department stores ceased to expand between the wars, and new rivals appeared in the women's and children's clothing area – *mass production multiples*, which soon outstripped the department stores in that area. The *bazaar* type of shop (Woolworths, Marks & Spencers) gained ground fast. There are now 1,500 variety chainstores in Britain, catering for the mass market and with the minimum of personal service. In 1957, 5.8% of all shopping was done in department stores and 5.4% in variety chain stores; another 3% is now done in *mail-order* houses (Littlewoods, for example, which runs both types of store). *Discount* stores have not caught on, as they have in the USA, but advanced methods of self-service have (eg in the shoe and clothes area). Of every 20 shops, three belong to the big organisations, three to local firms with several branches, and 14 are independent small shops. These figures are changing, with a movement away from the small shops. Efficiency varies. A new feature between the wars was the local shopping row or area, in suburbs or housing estates (scattered shops were not allowed in housing estates after 1918). Their advantage and strength is psychological – service and neighbourliness. But economically they are an anachronism. Retail trade areas need to be planned, and transport and parking taken into account.

The psychology of shopping is receiving close attention now. The current phenomenon is the demise of the traditional High Street and its kind of shop. By 1980 few old-style grocers were left. Shops are being concentrated into shopping centres and precincts. Chains are selling mass produced goods and frozen foods. These centres cannot be in High Streets, because of the need for access, deliveries, parking, public transport, etc. A quarter of grocers and confectioners have vanished since 1961, and the old all-purpose corner shops are going too. But Asian shops in bed-sitter areas, and specialised middle-class shops, are thriving, off the expensive streets. Indeed, some of these streets are so full of trendy shops and restaurants that there is no room for "ordinary" shops at all. In some areas shortage of a full range of shops is an obstacle to leading a full life in the neighbourhood of one's home, and local authorities may have to intervene on behalf of the elderly.

The argument over out-of-town hypermarkets continues; not all planners agree with them. They can cut the cost of distribution by some 20%, but against that is the extra cost to the shopper of getting there. They could well affect town centre trade; they certainly affect the small shops. A lot of bad and large town centres have already been built, some of them out of a desire to outdo the town next door. The required size has not in all cases been accurately estimated, planning has been deficient, and amenities poor. A current planning trend is towards making centres more "local", more "community shopping" centres.

Shopping centres, precincts, or malls began in rebuilt cities like Coventry and in the New Towns (Harlow has an open or piazza type). They do well in medium-sized towns, and some have architectural merit, such as Peterborough, Ealing, or Milton Keynes. In some towns, like Farnham (Sy), old yards and alleys or groups of old houses have been restored and converted to shopping precincts. A major example is Covent Garden in London. More than 500 shopping centres were planned in 1987, of which 300 are in existing shopping areas. In addition some 200 megastores were planned (see below). The population trend away from big cities means that market and country towns are the growth points. Shopping centres on the fringes of old towns could indeed help to save the historic centres. In 1973 there were 43 superstores and hypermarkets; in 1983 there were 257, and in 1993, 776.

Pedestrianisation of streets in cities is another practice, and this can be well seen in Sauchiehall Street, Glasgow, or in Chichester. Major city centre remodelling is exemplified by the Bull Ring scheme in Birmingham, but here not all the planning problems thrown up by such a scheme were solved and this area is now being replanned.

In the country, specialist farm shops have developed, selling fresh produce and, recently, organically-grown and additive-free produce too. Garden centres have multiplied lately too. Another phenomenon at the smaller end of the spectrum is the growing number of individual small traders (sometimes housewives) making food or clothing etc and taking it to local shops or to private customers direct.

The latest, perhaps the ultimate, phase of the shopping revolution is the *megacentre*. These offer every kind of shopping service in one complex (and under one roof), and go further, providing leisure and sports facilities, cinema, restaurants, even a chapel. Families can spend the whole day there. There is one near Edinburgh (Cameron Toll).

345 *A Georgian shop-front – Artillery Lane, London E1, c 1757.*

There are at present four in England – the largest, the MetroCentre at Gateshead; Lakeside at Grays (Ex); Sheffield and Dudley (this is affecting shops in central Birmingham). (For useful background on earlier stages see Kenneth Hudson: *The Archaeology of the Consumer Society* (Heinemann 1983).)

Of course not all older shop buildings have been replaced in modern planning, and a wide range of earlier types can be seen everywhere. Stalls may well have changed least; it is probable that a stall in a market place today would be entirely recognisable to a man of the 14th century, although the naphtha flares used for 100 years until the 1920s have given way to electricity. Open shops are still used by fishmongers and greengrocers. The famous Shambles at York, although heavily restored, still has features of interest. Several old shops have survived intact, and are valuable witnesses to their types (see **345** and **346**). London has several: in St James's Street are Berry Bros and Rudd (wines, 17th century) and Locks (hats, 1759); in Haymarket, Fribourg and Treyer's old shop front still survives (18th century, tobacco); 19th-century examples are Paxton & Whitfield, Jermyn Street (cheese), and James Smith & Son, New Oxford Street (1867, umbrellas). Others can be found. Outside London, one might mention

346 *Early 19th-century shopfront – Stonegate, York.*

the chemist's shop in Knaresborough market place (early 17th century), and T & T Clark, Theological and Law Publishers, 38 George Street, Edinburgh (1780s).

A large number of fine shop fronts from the 18th and early 19th centuries survive in many parts of the country. Most old market towns have some. The fronts can be architecturally formal or quite fanciful, with carved wood or plaster work. There are large collections, in great variety, in Ripon, Rye, and Bury St Edmunds, to mention only three of the more productive places. By the 1830s, apart from the change in architectural tastes, shop fronts sometimes used plate glass and gas lighting – Smiths in New Oxford Street is a case in point. Shops in spas or resorts, and in some suburban high streets, are more likely to have kept their scale than in the bigger cities, but even this is changing fast. Some once very famous shops have gone, like Pugh's Mourning Warehouse in Regent Street, a resort of the Victorians, and some specialised shops catering for a vanished world, like Jay's, New Oxford Street (servants' clothing and uniforms), went well within living memory. The balance of whole streets has changed; Oxford Street, once catering for the middle class, has given that function over to Regent Street, while Bond Street still looks to the upper-class trade, if not now more to the tourist. There are still a few shops which retain the scale,

decor, and atmosphere of the early period of the department store; of these, Harrods holds a high place, and should be looked at closely for its monumental nature as a great store as well as for the range it sells.

Arcades

Protecting shoppers from the weather was not a common idea until the 19th century, but there are a few earlier examples. In Italy many cities have streets arcaded at ground level, as have the market places of 13th-century bastide towns in south-west France. In Britain wind and rain is more of a problem than sun, but the idea could well have reached us from France. For instance in some Scottish towns there are arcaded houses dating from the time of the Auld Alliance; good examples are at Elgin, where also the cathedral shows strong French influence. The best-known examples in England are the Rows at Chester, which are certainly medieval. These, however, are at first-floor level, perhaps because the street level, when the houses were built, was encumbered by Roman ruins (see page 240).

Early examples are scarce, but the idea came in again in the 17th century in a more academic form. Such is Inigo Jones' "Piazza" at Covent Garden in London (1631–5), which had shops under arcades all round; only a small piece of this is left, and that rebuilt. The idea for this came perhaps from the square at Leghorn or from the Place des Vosges in Paris (1605).

The idea of a whole pedestrian shopping street under cover was developed in the 19th century. The first was the Royal Opera Arcade in London (1816–18) (see **347**), stimulated perhaps by the Palais Royal in Paris (1786) or at least by French models. It was closely followed by the Burlington Arcade (1819), still the most famous. Thereafter arcades were built not only in the wealthy cities and resorts, but took particular root in the northern industrial cities. They were, for example, and to some extent still are a conspicuous feature of Leeds (eg Thornton's, 1878; County, 1898 (see **348**)). Many of these are fine and florid examples of Victorian iron and glass architecture. Their descendants are flourishing again as covered shopping centres and precincts in the new developments (see Margaret MacKeith: *Shopping Arcades 1817–1939* (Mansell 1985)).

347 *The Royal Opera Arcade, London (Nash and Repton, 1816–18): the first of its kind.*

348 *County Arcade, Leeds (1898): a good late Victorian example.*

Shop signs

In the Middle Ages, when houses were not numbered and few could read, most traders distinguished their premises by signs or devices. These were either signboards with painted devices, or effigy signs carved in the round. After the Great Fire many houses put up stone signs let into the wall under the first-floor windows, rather than swinging signboards.

Shop signs showed either the trade (eg the barber's pole) or the location (at the Sun and Bible in Giltspur Street, or the Eagle in Paternoster Row). There was a lot of duplication, with consequent confusion, and many accidents were caused by signs falling on passers-by. Numbering of houses and general literacy led to a decline in the use of these signs by the 18th century, and in 1762 they were abolished, except for a few trade signs, such as the barber's pole, the three balls of the pawnbrokers, and the pestle and mortar of the chemists (see **349**). In Scotland, where this Act did not run, more signs remained in use, such as a figure of a man dressed as a Highlander, advertising snuff (good example in Perth). But some still survive, although all are fast disappearing now. Cornhill in London

463

has several, some of them revivals; among these is the famous emblem of the Greshams, the grasshopper. Some have taken on a more general significance, like the scales of Justice (as that on top of the Old Bailey), which was once one of the trade emblems of the scale-makers.

Figureheads of ships were sometimes used, and when wooden ships died out the figurehead carvers turned also to fairground carvings for the steam-driven fairgrounds which came in in the 1870s.

A very distinctive sign is the oil jar or half jar, usually standing over the shop front. These are of western Mediterranean origin, and are associated with the 18th/19th-century import of second or third quality olive oil. They are mostly confined to the greater London area, where 22 were known at March 1975, although nearly as many are known to have disappeared. There are also examples at High Wycombe (Bc), Gillingham (Kt), Maidstone (Kt), and Ramsgate (Kt), and it is always possible that more may turn up. Similar jars in Plymouth and Edinburgh seem to have been used not by oilmen but by tobacconists. Chemists' windows had large glass jars of coloured water.

Inn signs

An idea of the enormous variety of medieval signs can be got from the inn signs, which are still in use. These are of the same types as shop signs, that is either painted boards or effigies in the round. Whereas in the Middle Ages any trader could have a sign, after 1393 all inns had to have them, so that the inspectors of the quality and measures of ale could recognise the alehouses. Inn signs have continued in use, while shop signs barely survive. There has in fact been a recent recrudescence of inn signs, and many new ones have been painted or modelled by good artists. But in general inn signs are examples of folk art.

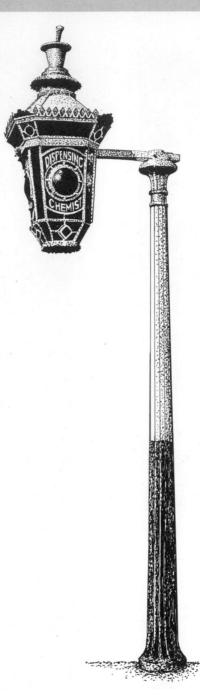

349 *A chemist's lamp sign, surmounted by a pestle and mortar – Milford (Sy).*

Inn signs touch on many facets of national life. Monastic hostels or inns at pilgrimage centres naturally had religious symbols, such as the George and Pilgrims at Glastonbury. But many ordinary inns used religious signs too, like the Angel or the Lamb; and the Crusades provided the Saracen's Head, or the Trip to Jerusalem in Nottingham. Royal symbols were always popular, if only to stress the political innocence of the house. In fact, the Crown and the King's Head are probably the commonest signs. Royal badges were also used, such as the White Hart of Richard II or the Red Lion of John of Gaunt. Badges and arms of great or local landowners are also common. Animals are another favourite, although some of these are also personal badges (Bear, Swan, Eagle). The White Horse is a Hanoverian symbol, but can also refer to the Saxon kings or to the hill figures cut in the chalk. An ingenious theory by S G Wildman suggests that the Black Horse, commonest in the Chilterns, Somerset, and the south-west Midlands, commemorates the victories of Arthur over the Saxons. Travel is another subject: Travellers' Rest, the Three Horseshoes, the Packhorse; and there are many railway and canal names. Trade and sport are also common subjects, as are great events and famous people; and there is a wealth of comic or out of the way names. Some old names are garbled, like the Elephant and Castle from the Infanta of Castile, the Cat and Wheel from the Catherine Wheel, or the Goat and Compasses from God Encompass Us.

The actual signs are often very interesting works. The Castle in Battersea has a sign which is a masterpiece of its kind. Some are of specialised interest, like the Masonic Arms at Gatehouse of Fleet (Kb). The King's Head in Southwark uses a 16th-century bust as its sign. The King's Arms (Newcomen Street, also in Southwark) has a carved royal arms brought from the 1742 London Bridge. A variant type is the picture made of tiles, like the Intrepid Fox in Soho or the one in coloured tiles (Victorian) at the Duchess of

Devonshire in Stoke Newington, London. Finally, there is the sign which crosses the street on a beam (a type discouraged after the Fire), such as the Swan at Waltham Cross.

Village signs

Self-conscious villages have recently taken to putting their own ornate name signs at their entrances. A handsome one is that at Thursley (Sy). Millstones are also used by some places, and in the early 20th century the (Automobile Association) put up distinctive yellow and black signs all over the country (see **350**, facing page 504).

COINS

Coins turn up everywhere, both singly and in hoards, not only on archaeological sites but in long-cultivated gardens, fields, and foreshores. (Items so found belong of course to the landowner unless other arrangements have been made.) They are good indicators of the economic life at the time they were struck.

Coins were made from blanks cut with shears out of sheet silver etc, or (after the 16th century) sliced from bar. The blank was placed on the obverse die (the head), which was fixed into a block of wood; the reverse (tail) die was then placed above it, and struck several times with a hammer. The product of this primitive method was naturally not always perfect. The dies of early Anglo-Saxon coins were engraved freehand, but from the 9th century punches were used, each punch making a line, dot, crescent, letter, etc. From 1279 the punches made a larger part of the design, and from 1878 the punch carried the whole design.

Clipping, forging, and illegal minting were rife in the Middle Ages, problems which were not successfully overcome until the introduction of mass production by machine, which could make coins of uniform standard and a fluted or lettered edge which was harder to clip or imitate. This was called *milling*. A screw-press was tried for a short time from 1561–72, and then from 1633. Charles II decided to go over to milled coinage completely from 1662. Hammered coins continued in use side by side with milled, and were finally withdrawn in 1696, the cost of this being met by the Window Tax (see page 200). The blanks were now cut from bar, and the edges grained or lettered. Power was applied to the process by Boulton and Watt in 1774 (Boulton and Watt made coins for the East India Company and for colonial and foreign governments, as well as tokens, and set up the Soho (Birmingham) mint in 1788). Boulton was asked to make copper coins for the British government in 1797 (distinctive penny and twopenny pieces, still to be found). The Royal Mint was powered in 1805–10, and Boulton's machinery for it was not superseded (by belt-driven presses) until 1881–2.

The making of coins was introduced into this country by the Iron Age tribes who settled here from north-east France in the late 2nd century BC. These were of gold, with "Celtic" designs deriving ultimately from staters of Philip of Macedon. They are found in the Belgic areas in south-east England, and in areas under Belgic influence; other coins came from north-west France by trade. In adjacent areas further inland wealth was hoarded by way of *currency bars*, long pieces of iron shaped like swords or spits. Coins of speculum (a tin-bronze alloy) are found along the Thames valley. Silver and bronze coins were also made after *c* 30 BC, but these are rare. When southern Britain came under Roman rule in AD 43 the coins of the Roman Empire became the universal currency, and remained so for the whole period of nearly 400 years during which Britain was a Roman province. Roman coins came here in vast quantities and are still plentiful, particularly the small bronze ones. Besides currency, coins were made by the Romans as media of political propaganda, and, as well as a good head of the Emperor, carry designs showing current events in a light favourable to the Empire. They are therefore of great historical interest. In the 3rd century London became an Imperial mint. In the late 3rd to 5th centuries economic difficulties led to the making of copies of Gallic coins, some of them very small.

Anglo-Saxon coin types, from the 5th century, were based on Roman types or copies of them. At first a *sceatta* of copper was used, then in the 6th century local types were struck at different mints. By the end of the 7th century the silver penny emerged, and this held the field for 400 years. Coins of the kings of all England begin with Edgar (959–75). From 975 the mint was shown. The reverse of the silver penny was a cross; from 1180 a Short Cross appeared and in 1247 the Long Cross (its arms reaching to the edges of the coin to discourage clipping).

A gold penny was struck in 1275, and from then on higher denominations appear, like the groat; there were also a farthing and a halfpenny in 1279. There was a gold florin and a gold noble (6s 8d) in

1344; but the penny was still the normal coin in everyday use. Coin was generally insufficient for the needs of trading throughout the Middle Ages, and coins of other countries also circulated. These show also the extent of English trade, like the Byzantine and Arab coins which occur in Saxon contexts.

The sovereign and the shilling came in with the Tudors: a gold sovereign in 1489, and a silver shilling in 1504, with a portrait of the king. There were many mints, and some debasement, in Henry VIII's reign; Edward VI tried to rationalise the situation and issued several fine coins, including a silver shilling and a silver crown in 1551. But the situation was still unstable when Elizabeth came to the throne, and she recalled the coins of Edward VI and Mary in 1561 and made a fresh start. James I initiated small copper coins (Lord Harington's farthings), which led to the later bronze coinage. Britannia (modelled on the Duchess of Richmond) appeared in 1672. The coinage was fully established and stabilised by 1642. The Civil War led to Welsh silver and melted-down plate being used, and gave rise to hoarding (hoards were collected and hidden in times of national disturbance and uncertainty, such as the Wars of the Roses and the Civil War). Siege pieces were also struck in beleaguered towns.

After 1649 English was used instead of Latin on coins, and the value stated. There was a constant series of values from 1662 to 1816–17. In 1696 hammered coins were called in (see above), and from then on the head was turned round with each reign. From 1760 to 1816 little except guineas was struck (the "spade" guinea in 1787). The lack of silver coins was made up by overprinting Spanish 8-reals (dollars). The denominations were constant from 1816 to the present metric series. A splendid George and Dragon, by Pistrucci, was used from 1817. Copper pennies, halfpennies, and farthings were struck from 1797, and a large twopenny, the "cartwheel" in 1797 only.

Victoria introduced a new silver florin in 1849. She used three main heads, the young one in 1837, the older in 1887–93, and the old in 1893. These were designed by members of the Wyon family, a brilliant family who were responsible for most of the coinage and a large number of medals and plaques, from George II to Victoria. From 1946 cupro-nickel was used; in this series the hexagonal threepence became popular. In 1969 the new metric series was brought in, including the seven-sided 50p. Maundy money has always been of silver.

Pieces allied to coins include jettons, tokens, and medals. *Medals* are not only decorations, but commemorate a wide variety of events, people, and institutions. *Jettons* are counters used for calculating in the Middle Ages. They were used on chequerboards (hence the "Exchequer"), being moved in different ways for adding and subtracting. The first English ones appear in 1280, actual coins being used before then. They were of brass and based on existing coins. Most are pierced, to distinguish them from coins. About 1440 French jettons came into use, and continued until the late 16th century. Flemish counters, made largely at Tournai, were also used here in the 14th and 15th centuries. In the 16th century also, jettons made at Nuremburg are very common; they have interesting classical, biblical, etc designs.

Traders' *tokens* were struck partly to supplement small coins in times when these were short or for use by workers in the employers' own shops. They bear devices or topical mottoes, and are important indications of social history. They appear at three periods: 1648–72, during and after the Civil War; from 1784–97, when coin was short; and again from 1812–16. Various other related pieces include plastic tokens for the London and Birmingham trams, metal ones for the Liverpool buses and trams, metal ferry tokens, slot-machine tokens, railway Directors' passes, hop-pickers' tokens, and Scottish Communion tokens.

TREASURE TROVE

It is imperative to bear in mind the potential importance of any archaeological find in its context, and that disturbance or removal may destroy irreplaceable evidence. Moreover, the ownership of finds must be respected.

The material of which a found object is made has a direct bearing on the subsequent course of action. In some countries no objects of any kind may be kept by the finder without the permission of the relevant authorities; but in England and Wales this limitation only applies to objects wholly or mainly made of gold or silver. The Treasure Trove Act of 1887, which repeated very old practice, provides that such objects must be reported to the local coroner (see below), whose duty it is to determine whether the objects are treasure trove. For this purpose the owner or his heirs must be unknown, and the objects must have been deliberately buried with the intention of recovery (the legal principle of *animus revertendi*). This is of course often not easy to determine, but if it is, the British Museum (or in Wales the National

Museum, and in Northern Ireland the Ministry of Finance), or a local museum, acquires the objects on behalf of the Crown, and the finder is rewarded with the full market value, or sometimes with some or all the objects.

If there is no element of hiding, eg coins found on the surface of the soil, the items will probably not be treasure trove, but will be the property of the owner of the land. Similarly, objects deposited (usually publicly), in a grave, or given to the gods (eg thrown into a sacred lake), were not expected to be recovered, and belong to the ground landlord. A conspicuous example of the former case is the rich treasure in the Anglo-Saxon ship burial at Sutton Hoo (Su), which was adjudged the property of the landowner – the fact that she gave the treasure to the nation does not of course alter the decision.

In Scotland the situation is quite different. Here, objects do not have to be hidden, nor intended to be recovered. *All* finds are treasure trove, and all treasure trove, whether gold or silver or not, belongs to the Crown. The Procurator Fiscal, without the intervention of a coroner, takes possession, and the National Museum of Antiquities values the finds, and disposes of them at its discretion.

Whatever the nature of the finds, they, their find-spots and the circumstances of their discovery, should always be reported promptly to the police, or to a local museum or archaeological society, who will ensure that appropriate action is taken.

It is appreciated that these arrangements have disadvantages, and fresh legislation is before Parliament. This Treasure Bill (which applies only to England and Wales) abolishes treasure trove, and introduces a new concept of treasure, which is defined as including any coin which is at least 300 years old and forms part of the same find as one or more coins any of which is more than 300 years old. Objects older than such coins will be treasure if they contain more than 5% of gold or silver. Objects part of the same find, such as a pottery container and other associated objects, are also classed as treasure. The finds must be reported within 14 days, and the coroner (who acts without a jury) identifies the owner and occupier of the land, and notifies the find to them. They and the finder may share the value of the items, but the finder would usually be given the full value. A museum may claim some or all of the finds. Items from wrecks are not included in the Bill. This new Bill is clearly of limited application, and there is still a case for comprehensive legislation covering all objects of archaeological, historical and cultural importance.

INNS AND HOTELS

Inns or lodgings were provided along the Roman roads, for officials travelling in the public service (*mansiones* or *praetoria*), and in the main towns. Some of these inns, as at Silchester and Caerwent, were quite large. One has recently been excavated, and is accessible, at the civil town attached to the fort at Vindolanda, near Haltwhistle in Northumberland. Small inns, *tabernae*, also existed.

After the Romans left Britain it was well into the Middle Ages before inns were maintained again. These were the hospices or guest houses of the monasteries, where invited guests, travellers, or pilgrims could stay. The accommodation was simple, often spartan. Travellers could also, at most such places, get free "doles" of bread and ale, as is still done at the hospital of St Cross, Winchester. Guest houses can be seen at most abbeys, such as that at Fountains. In some cases the abbey had a hospice at a market town or pilgrimage centre, or at key points along roads or river banks. Examples are the George at Stamford, the King's Head at Aylesbury (used by Henry VI in 1440), the New Inn, Gloucester (built by Gloucester Abbey before 1455), and the George and Pilgrim at Glastonbury (1470) (see **351**). Private inns also grew up at these centres in the later Middle Ages. The oldest such inn in England is the Trip to Jerusalem at Nottingham (early 12th century), with its name a reminder of the Crusades. Many begun in the 14th and 15th centuries still continue (although Chaucer's Tabard has been rebuilt); such are the George at Norton St Philip (So), 1397, begun as a hospice of Hinton Charterhouse, the Star, Alfriston (Sx), the King's Head, Horsham (1411), the Spread Eagle, Midhurst (1430), and the Mermaid at Rye (early 16th century).

Inns before the 12th or 13th century were perhaps indistinguishable from large dwelling houses. But in later medieval times two types can be distinguished: the *courtyard* type, where the main buildings are ranged round a courtyard, and the *block or gatehouse* type, which has a yard at the back reached through a gateway or passage, the principal rooms being in the street block. Examples of the former are the Golden Cross, Oxford, the New Inn at Gloucester, and the George in Southwark (see **352**), and of the latter the George, Norton St Philip, and the George, Stamford (see W A Pantin, "Medieval Inns", in E M Jope (ed): *Studies in Building History* (1961)).

The English inns of the 16th to the 19th century reached a high standard, and had a European reputation. They developed into

467

coaching inns, a regular feature of all country towns of any size, which can still be recognised by the wide entrance to one side of the house, leading to the stableyard. Some still have inscriptions dating from their coaching days, eg the Angel, Guildford (see **353**), and the Foley Arms, Malvern. Famous examples are the George in Southwark (with its galleries), the Feathers at Ludlow, the Maid's Head at Norwich, and the Red Lion at Colchester. At some towns, like Grantham on the Great North Road, inns such as the Angel were a major factor in the prosperity of the town. Some grew so prosperous that they rebuilt

351 *A monastic inn – Glastonbury (So).*

352 *The George Inn, Southwark: the last galleried inn in England. Its courtyard was used as a theatre in Tudor times.*

themselves in full Georgian style, like the White Hart at Salisbury or the Dolphin at Southampton. Many became the social centres for their towns. Thus, at Croydon, the Crown catered for the coaching traffic but the Greyhound (*c* 1493) accommodated a great deal of the social, economic, and political life of the town. Centres like this usually had a range of rooms for meetings or private meals, and often an assembly room or ballroom as well. At the same time there were of course a lot of smaller houses, the local pubs.

Angus McInnes (in *The English Town, 1660–1760* (Historical Association 1980)) makes the interesting point that in this period, when population, wealth, and demand were all increasing, the market areas of towns could get so congested that more and more business was done privately outside these areas. Inns were set up to cater for such trading. For instance, Northampton, which had 5,000 people in the mid 18th century, had 60 inns and over 100 alehouses. Indeed, sometimes a market moved to the proximity of an inn!

Inns were also to be found at points on the roads, outside the towns. Some were in very remote places and served as travellers' rests for packmen, drovers, etc; there are several in Yorkshire and Derbyshire, at ridge-tops, or crossroads. Some of these are the highest inns in England, like the Tan Hill and the Clap Gate in Yorkshire, and the Cat and Fiddle near Buxton. A similar one in Scotland is the Mosspaul between Hawick and Langholm. A good example of an old inn at a crossroads (where five roads meet in quiet country) is at Sandtoft, near Epworth (Li). Inns are a regular feature of the canals, and later of the railways. An interesting case is the Tram Inn near Hereford, on the tramway (completed in 1829) which brought coal to Hereford from the mines between Abergavenny and Blaenavon.

Inns passed through a distinctive phase in the Victorian era. Up to the 19th century they looked like private houses, except for their signs (see page 464). With the spread of literacy the name was added to the old sign, or replaced it, and the name of the supplying brewer also began to be shown. Pubs then adopted the new shopfronts, with plate glass and gas lighting, stone balustrades, big lamps, and illuminated clocks. Up to the 1830s, the *gin palace* survived from the 18th century – a famous London one was Thompson and Fearon's, Holborn, 1829–31. The duty on beer was abolished in 1830, and any ratepayer could then sell it for on or off consumption in his own house without a licence; this led to 24,000 new *beerhouses* by the end of 1830, and 46,000 by 1836. The public bar was at first in the kitchen

of the beerhouse, which had a partitioned-off store or "taproom" in it. Genteeler customers used the "parlour". When the kitchen became private, the public bar was called the taproom. Gradual specialisations of building, layout, and equipment took place; but the rural pub remained primitive throughout the century. By the 1850s there were three grades of rooms – the bar-room (standing), the taproom (sitting), and the parlour; there were various names in different areas, such as public bar, private bar, saloon bar, lounge. The classes were thus separated. Glasses replaced pewter pots at the end of the century.

Tastes in beer changed in the 19th century. The 18th-century worker had drunk "entire" (a beer brewed to imitate the customary

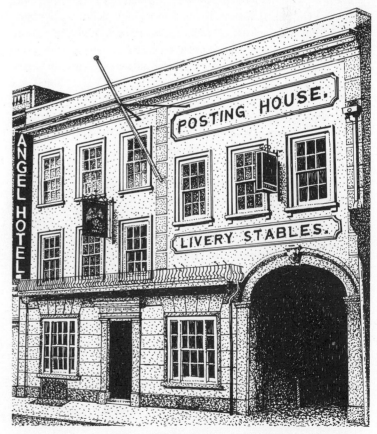

353 *Coaching inn – Guildford (Sy). The Angel is an ancient inn on the London to Portsmouth road; it has 13th-century cellars, but has been much altered.*

blend of beers drawn from different casks), or porter (a dark brown bitter from charred or browned malt; stout is a stronger, darker version of this). The upper classes preferred pale ale, and this seeped into the mass market after 1845, when repeal of the duties on glass encouraged the bottling of beer, and the decline of pewter tankards. Burton benefited from the demand for light ales. India pale ale was made for export to the Empire. Porter dropped from three-quarters of the market in 1863 to a quarter in 1899. The workers turned to mild ale, the saloon bar to bitter (the draught equivalent of bottled pale ale). The off-licence trade dates from 1860, under an Act allowing sale of wine in bottles without a justices' licence. Blended Scotch whisky also began in the 1860s, and challenged Irish by the 1880s.

Pre-Victorian public houses were divided into inns (providing rooms for travellers), taverns (to dine and wine), alehouses (for beer), and ginshops (for spirits). The change of name to hotel, restaurant, and public house was accompanied by certain changes of function. *Hotels* began in the Napoleonic Wars for officers on leave; they were run, or cooked for, by French refugees. By the 1830s "hotel" was used by most coaching inns and, later, railway hotels. A print of 1828 shows the Angel, Islington, calling itself "Inn, Tavern and Hotel, for Gentlemen and their Families", a neat illustration of the precise use of these words at that time. Taverns were replaced by cafés and then restaurants (both French words), for non-English food; and these pioneered the admittance of women. Blackwall and Greenwich, and other Thames-side towns, had waterside taverns for both sexes, providing whitebait and fish dinners. The Ship at Greenwich (to 1908) was very fashionable, as well as the Trafalgar (1837 to 1915, restored 1965). At a lower level were the "dining rooms", of which there were at least 250 in London in 1851; dinner was midday for clerks, evening for principals. Famous restaurants included Gatti's and the Café Royal, 1863, Kettner's 1867, Pagani's 1871. Speirs and Ponds' Criterion and Gaiety were very popular; others were the

Holborn Restaurant, Simpson's, and Evans'. There were suburban restaurants also, like the Star and Garter at Putney.

Many suburban taverns had *pleasure gardens*, like the Red House at Battersea. Cockfighting (The Old Fighting Cocks at St Albans – an inn said to date from 795 – may well have been a cockpit) and (from 1849) ratting took place, and, at a higher level, promenade concerts (as at the Crown and Anchor, Strand, 1840s). *Music halls* were the off-shoot of 18th-century public houses which offered entertainment (the Eagle, City Road, had pavilions as well as gardens). "Saloon theatres" flourished from the 1830s (eg the Duke's Arms, Lambeth). There were 23 in London by the early 1860s, 35 major ones in 1892, catering for 45,000 people nightly.

The architecture of pubs became distinctive and representative of their function of refreshment and recreation. The Castle at Ross, 1838, has romantic gables and bargeboards; the Swiss Cottage, Finchley Road, c 1840, is a "chalet". The Italian style was favoured in the 1850s, eg the Balmoral Castle, Pimlico, 1856. Gothic revival and composite styles appeared, and Second Empire (White Horse, Tottenham Court Road, 1875). Pubs on the new estates were dignified and "respectable", eg the Drapers' Arms, Barnsbury, 1843 (stucco classical). By the 1880s (the apogee of the Victorian pub), there were elaborate and ornate fronts and interiors, with polished wood, brass, glass, and mirrors (eg the Red Lion, Duke of York Street, St James's); the prevailing colour for decoration was a "masculine" brown. Glass and mirrors received a high degree of decoration – cut, etched, gilded, back-painted. Embossed wallpapers and plastered ceilings were popular, as

354 *St Pancras Station, London, the hotel (Sir George Gilbert Scott, 1865–73): a masterpiece of Victorian Gothic.*

was the architectural use of mahogany (Prince Alfred, Maida Vale). Any unmodernised survivors of these interiors are well worth tracking down.

Meanwhile the coaching inns were replaced by "station hotels", "railway taverns", etc, such as the Three Nuns, Aldgate, for the Metropolitan Railway, 1878. They can still be found in country towns. Big corner-site pubs, like the Archway Tavern, Highgate (rebuilt 1886), or the Elephant and Castle (London, SE1), appeared. After 1869, when free trade in ale was stopped, there was a gradual extension of ownership by brewers. The number of pubs declined from 1899 to 1904, under an Act to compensate for closure.

At the turn of the century distinguished architects took a hand in designing pubs, like the Tabard, Bedford Park (Norman Shaw, 1880) and the Wentworth Arms, Elmesthorpe (Li) (Voysey, 1895). A good Edwardian example is The Vines, Lime Street, Liverpool. Art Nouveau is seen, as at the Queen's, Crouch End (north London), 1901. But most are examples of popular architecture, cheerfully vulgar, and remained the "locals" of the ordinary man. The widespread "modernisation" (and standardisation) since the last war is not all benefit.

Hotels developed on their own, separate from pubs. The great railway hotels like St Pancras (now offices) (see **354**), Victoria, or Charing Cross in London, or those in the big cities like Manchester, Liverpool, and Leeds, are monuments of Victorian architecture. But they cover a wide range of size, amenities, and social levels, from the Ritz, Claridges, and Browns to the small seaside boarding house, from the luxury "expenses" type through the great golfing hotels and converted country houses to remote fishing inns. At the larger seaside resorts, like Brighton, they make an overwhelming impact, and partly determine the character of the town. With the current growth and importance of tourism, and the increasing use of hotels for conferences and company meetings, large standardised hotels, such as the Viking and the Post House at York, have been built all over the country in the past 20 years.

SOCIAL CENTRES, CLUBS, AND SOCIETIES

The normal centre of social life throughout the Middle Ages, and until well into the 19th century, was the parish church. Indeed, fixed pews were not usual until the 17th century so as to leave free space for activities other than services, which were attended standing, except for the infirm, who sat or leant along the walls. Here took place parish events, business meetings, private celebrations, markets, guild meetings, schools. Most of these activities were later to take place in separate buildings (*parish* or *church halls*, *market halls*, rooms built adjacent to the church, *dance halls*, *schools*, etc).

Inns and *hotels* also, particularly if near a market place, were used for business, for political meetings, and by local societies; and, when a large enough room was provided, for balls and concerts. The prestigious Society of Antiquaries of London began life in rooms at the Bear in the Strand (1707–8) and later (1717–6) at the Mitre, Fleet Street. By the 18th century *assembly rooms* for the latter purpose, which became the social centres for the local gentry, were provided in hotels (eg the Dolphin at Southampton or the George at Rye), or specially built, eg the Assembly Rooms at Bath (Wood the Younger, 1769–71), those at York (Lord Burlington 1732–6), or the Athenaeum at Bury St Edmunds (1789, possibly by Robert Adam).

The importation of tea and coffee by the East India Company in the 1660s led to a new social phenomenon, the *coffee house*, which became the normal haunt of the wealthier classes, particularly in London, until the mid 18th century, when some of them developed into *clubs* (with limited membership). In Queen Anne's reign nearly 500 are recorded in London. Coffee houses were not only social centres but places where news was exchanged and newspapers could be read. Important ones included Lloyd's in the City and the Windsor at Charing Cross; Garraway's (1669–1872) was a centre for auctions.

The clubhouses of London form a unique group of buildings, many of them of considerable architectural distinction. The oldest is White's, in St James's Street. This was founded in 1693 as White's Chocolate House, on the site now occupied by Boodle's. It moved across the street in 1697 and became a club (ie with restricted membership) in 1736. The present building dates from 1755, but was largely rebuilt by Wyatt in 1787; the bow window, where Beau Brummell held "court", is of 1811. Other early clubs are Boodle's, 1762, and Brooks's, 1764. The great age of club foundation was that of George IV and William IV, reflecting a social pattern. Men of the upper and increasingly the professional and business classes wished to spend their evenings with their fellows, without their wives. This practice lasted till the First World War and even beyond, although women have for many years penetrated the formerly closed world of the clubs. The club therefore had to represent, symbolically, the gentleman's home, or at least to provide him with the standards and services to which he was accustomed at home. It was however conceded that many club members could not afford, or had not the space for, the libraries and cellars kept by the clubs, which provided them accordingly (the Athenaeum, for example, has a large and important library). Each club tends to attract a particular kind of member, and some explicitly prefer to recruit their own kind; in any case, each has its own characteristic atmosphere.

The great clubs of the Regency and after include: the United Services (1815 to 1976, in a Nash building), set up to cater for officers after the Napoleonic Wars; the Travellers' (1819, Barry); the Athenaeum (1824, building by Decimus Burton (see **355**); this caters for literature, the arts, science, the church and the law, and other professions, and has counted a surprising number of distinguished men among its members); the United Oxford and Cambridge (1830, Smirke); the Garrick (1831), theatrical and literary; the Carlton (1832), Conservative; the Reform (1832, Barry), Liberal; the Savile (1868), arts; the Savage (1857), arts, science, law. The East India Company officials and officers founded two clubs for men on leave or in retirement: the Oriental (1824) and the East India (1849), now an amalgam of several clubs. There are also clubs for officers (eg the Cavalry, the RAF, or the Royal Aldershot Officers' Club (1858)), the Press, racing, etc.

Many towns outside London have similar clubs, of which a few date from the same years as the great London clubs, eg The New Club, Edinburgh, 1787, the Athenaeum, Liverpool, 1797, the Western Club, Glasgow, 1825, The Club, Sheffield, 1843, the Leeds Club, 1850, the Manchester Club, 1867, and the Birmingham Club, 1872.

Another group of institutions is the *learned societies* whose object is to further and publish research in their fields. The senior is the Royal Society (1660), which covers science in general. There is an important group occupying Victorian premises in Burlington House: the Society of Antiquaries (1707), the Royal Academy of Arts (1768), the Linnean Society (1788), for botany, the Royal Astronomical Society (1820), and the Geological Society (1807). Others include the British Academy (1901), the Royal Anthropological Institute (1843), the Royal Geographical Society (1830), and the Royal Society of Arts (1754). There is in fact a society covering most subjects with any

academic content, and most of them have a social element. Outside London there are the Royal Photographic Society (1853, now at Bath), the Royal Society of Edinburgh (1783), the Royal Scottish Academy (1826), the Society of Antiquaries of Scotland (1780), the Society of Antiquaries of Newcastle-upon-Tyne, the Royal Cambrian Academy of Art (Conwy, 1881), and the somewhat anomalous Gentlemen's Society of Spalding (1710). But this list merely touches the fringe of a vast and varied category.

There are also the *professional institutions*, each presiding over the standards, entry, and welfare of a professional body, eg the Law Society, for solicitors, the Royal Institute of British Architects (1834), the Royal College of Surgeons (1800), the Royal College of Physicians (1518), and the various engineering institutions. Any town can show a varied list of societies, some (like the county archaeological societies) having their own premises, others merely occupying a hired room for meetings.

At a different social level from the great clubs there are the local political social clubs, the working men's clubs, the British Legion, etc, which are a feature of most towns of any size.

The term "social centre" has perhaps also to be applied to casinos and night clubs. Exhibition halls, function rooms, and sports centres are dealt with on pages 404–6.

355 *The Athenaeum, London (Decimus Burton, 1829): a plain building, in spite of its frieze and Athene's statue, which belies the grander interior; the top storey is a later addition.*

Crafts

RURAL CRAFTS

These are crafts requiring only the simplest of equipment: some need only portable tools, others a few items of fixed equipment – nothing in the way of powered machinery, with the exception of carpentry (and this is not entirely rural). Some have been forced out of existence by mechanisation, mass production, or obsolescence; but many continue to fill a need or meet a fashionable demand, and are still carried on.

Woodland crafts need the simplest equipment, often only a chopping-block or jig, which may be of a special form. These crafts include the making of gate and wattle *hurdles*, still used for sheep-pens and in much demand for gardens. The latter use coppiced hazel, the former chestnut and ash. *Walking-sticks* are still made, eg at Wormley (Sy), of ash or chestnut. *Gardening* and *farming implements*, such as rakes, scythe-snaiths, forks, etc, were made of coppiced ash; hafts, helves, yokes, shovels, peels, and flails were of "standard" wood because of their dimensions. Yokes were of hornbeam, oak, or beech; shovels and peels of beech; hafts of ash; flails had a handle of ash, and the swinging arm, the "swingle", was of crab or holly. *Besoms* were made from birch twigs from the crowns of a seven-year plantation. These were carefully stacked by the besom-maker until they were used in the spring; unwanted twigs were used as kindling or oven firewood. Bundling the twigs for the broom-head required skill. The bundle was bound with thin strips of wood, which had advantages over wire. The handles were ash, lime, or hazel. Besoms were made in large quantities in Surrey in the 19th century; the "broom-squires" of Hindhead lived in some 60 cottages on the common and in the spectacular valley called the Devil's Punchbowl. Three of these cottages survive, but have been altered. Besoms are still made at Liphook and Tadley (Ha).

A conspicuous craft for which there is still a continuous demand, if less than formerly, is *thatching*. This has a local and an individual aspect. It can be done with long straw, combed wheat, Norfolk reed, and, in remoter parts, heather. A local form of thatching in the south Midlands is "bundle thatch", which consists of bundles of faggots bound with withies and laid over cross-beams, with thatch on top. This can be seen at Cogges Farm Museum, Witney (Ox). The thatcher binds an underlayer of material to the rafters, and pegs an upper layer onto this. The pattern on the roof ridge is the thatcher's personal signature. Hayricks were protected by thatching, and were finished off by a prominent bundle of straw. But stooking and rickmaking were killed by combine harvesting (see **95**, page 193).

The bundles of straw on the pinnacles or gables of ricks were ornamental, but the *corn dolly* was of folkloric, and ultimately religious, significance. After sowing and after harvest symbolic figures made of straw were carried in procession round the fields, the first to ensure a good harvest, the second to give thanks for one. Thus the figures represented the Earth Mother or the Corn Goddess in origin, however much they were demythologised later. Corn dollies took local forms, but most of them bore some (even if remote) relation to the basic idea. Thus there was a Mother Earth, a Suffolk Horseshoe, a Vale of Pickering Chalice, a Staffordshire Knot, the Horn of Plenty, the Essex Terret, etc. The Kern Baby (representing the goddess, and sometimes made from the last sheaf of corn to be cut), presided over the harvest ("mell") supper, and was sometimes also put in the church. Corn dollies are now made for ornament and decoration (see **356–362**).

Before we leave the fields, a craft now greatly restricted is *hedge-laying*. This is a winter task, every 10 or 15 years, when a hedge has got ragged and unkempt, or irregular. Some of the old stems are kept, the others cut out. The stems which are to form the basis of the hedge for the next few years are cut near the base, but not right through. They are then bent over at an angle, often 45°, and secured with stakes every yard. Strips or "edders" of willow or hazel are woven in along the top and round the stakes, to hold all together. There are regional styles of hedge-laying, which is said to have originated during the Enclosures in the hunting country of Leicestershire, to keep the hedges tidy. In the Midland style ("bullock fencing") the laid stems are pushed over so that the new stems can grow up freely. In the "arable style" of the east Midlands, the laid stems are held directly over the stools, and the new shoots come up through the old (see **13**, page 76). In the Welsh borders ("sheep fencing") the hedge is packed with dead wood. In Wiltshire and Dorset no stakes or edders are used, and the laid stems are spread out.

473

Hedge-layers use a distinctive tool for cutting and trimming the stems – the billhook, of which there are some 40 different local forms. The Leicestershire and Yorkshire types, which are closely related, are those most widely used. The layers also need an axe, a rake, a spade and mattock, and a mallet. Hedges are kept trim between layings with a "slasher", a curved blade on a long handle.

Charcoal-burning is another traditional woodland craft (see **363–5**). A shallow circle ("pan") is scooped in the ground, 19.5–29.25ft (6–9m) in diameter; within this lengths of coppice wood up to 4.5in (12cm) in diameter ("cords") are stacked round a triangular central hole or flue ("tunnel"). The wood is stacked vertically against this, and

when the heap is wide enough it is "roofed" by sloping pieces of wood laid on top. Gaps are filled by smaller pieces. The heap is then thatched with any vegetation to hand, and covered with fine earth free of stones. The heap is fired from the top by dropping live charcoal embers down the central hole, which is then sealed with turf and earth. Once alight, the kiln may take three days to burn through and must be watched day and night. Burning is controlled by small holes in the heap. When

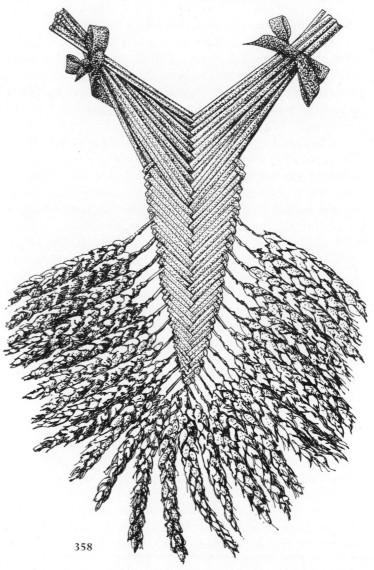

356

357

358

356–62 *Corn dollies are small figures made of straw, originating in prehistoric harvest rites; they include also stack ornaments with no ritual origin. They have regional forms; a few are shown here: 356 Traditional; 357 Cambridgeshire bell; 358 Welsh fan; 359 Yorkshire lantern; 360 Staffordshire knot; 361 Suffolk horseshoe; 362 Essex terret.*

ready, the fire is put out with water, the covering is removed, and the charcoal spread out, sorted, and sifted. The next kiln meanwhile has been prepared ready to fire, to ensure continuous production.

The sites of such kilns can be found in wooded areas, such as the Weald, Epping Forest, or the Forest of Dean; they show as low circular banks of burnt earth. They may also be turned up by the plough in former woodland. The charcoal-burners and their families had to live alongside their kilns; they made small huts, with turf and sacking over a pole frame. Reconstructions of the kilns and a hut are displayed at the Weald and Downland Museum, Singleton (Sx) (see **363–5**).

Charcoal has many uses, such as filters for gas and water, artists' pencils, and fuel for barbecues, but is now made, on a declining scale, in iron kilns, which may be seen at work, eg west of Sedlescombe (Sx). There are industrial uses also, and important by-products such as acetic acid, tar, and wood spirit. Ovens and retorts on a factory scale have been devised for their production.

Baskets are a very ancient woodland product, being made essentially of withies from willow (osier). This is now grown in dense plantations and coppiced annually. Most English willow comes from Somerset, but some is grown in Essex, the Kennet valley, and in the Midlands and north; but large numbers of baskets are now imported. The withies are stripped of bark and several grades of rod are used. Cane is also used. The woven texture is known as wickerwork. The tools required are few, being bodkins, shears, knives for cutting and trimming, a cleaver, and a driving iron.

The basket is built up from the base, the worker sitting with a large board on his lap. There is a wide variety of weaving

patterns, sometimes several in one basket. There is a great variety of baskets, in form, design, and use. Specialised forms of basketry include lobster and crab pots (which are started not at the base but at the neck), eel traps (Fens and Severn), and salmon traps (Severn), which are long frames of hazel rods, bound by withies. The potato baskets or "spelks" of Furness, Yorkshire, Monmouth, and Cardigan are also woven on a hazel frame, but those of Furness are not woven with willow but with "spale-oak", strips or bands of oak made pliable by boiling.

Sussex trugs, still made at Hurstmonceux, are miniature boats of seven or nine thin willow boards, soaked and steamed to shape, and set clinker-fashion (overlapping) longitudinally. They are held in a frame of ash or chestnut, and strengthened with cross-braces. Some have handles, and some feet. They are made in several sizes for different purposes in gardening or agriculture.

Crates for the transport of pottery are related to baskets, although with stouter bases and uprights.

Another object remotely linked to basketry is the *coracle*. The Irish curragh, still in use along the west coast of Ireland, although classed

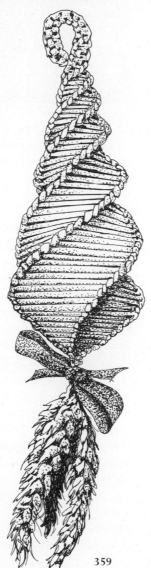

359

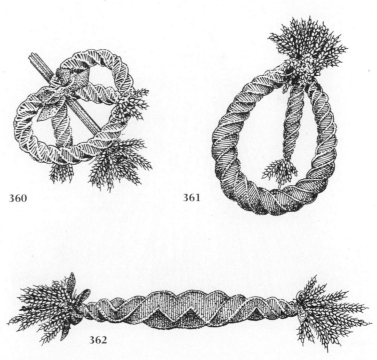

360

361

362

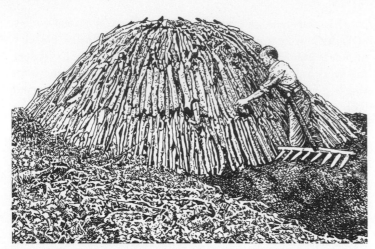

365

363–5 *Charcoal burning: 363 building the clamp; 364 erecting a sleeping hut; 365 the burners' camp, showing two clamps, a living hut, and an (unfinished) sleeping hut – Weald and Downland Museum, Singleton (Sx).*

364

as a coracle, is only remotely related to the British coracle, as James Hornell points out; it has a pointed prow and square stern and is derived from plank-built boats, although it was covered with hide, and now with canvas. It is also built gunwale first, and not, like the British coracle, bottom first.

The British coracle is older, and derives from the same common source as the coracles of Iraq, India, and Tibet. Coracles are recorded by the Romans as being used in Britain. They were in fact at that time used widely, on rivers and round the coasts, but have in recent centuries been steadily restricted to only a few rivers. Up to the end of the 19th century they were used on the Severn, Wye, Usk, Monnow, Lugg, and Dee, but now only on the Teifi and Towy in south-west Wales, with a few on the Taf and Cleddau. They may best be seen at Cenarth and Cilgerran on the Teifi, and at Carmarthen on the Towy (see **366** and **367**).

The British coracles have rounded ends and are light enough to carry. They are made of wickerwork; their covering was oxhide or horsehide until the late 16th century, then tarred or pitched flannel until *c* 1870, and now canvas or calico. There are several local variants. The Teifi coracles have frames made of cleft willow rods, the longitudinal ones crossed and interwoven by transverse rods. There are bands of plaited hazel withies as strengthening, and plaited hazel gunwales. The Towy type uses sawn ash laths instead of the cleft willow. There is a Scottish type, used on the Spey until the end of the 18th century, made of basketry; a few of these survived in the Hebrides until into the 20th century. The Boyne curragh is the only Irish coracle similar to the Welsh ones.

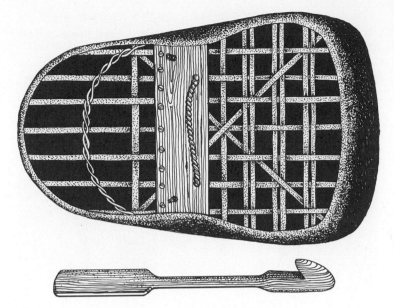

367

366–7 *Coracle of river Teifi type, with plan.*

Another branch of woodland crafts is based on bulk timber and planks rather than rods. *Planks* are used for fencing, clapboard, shingles, cooperage, wheelbarrows, furniture, etc. (But fences may also be made of other materials, such as reeds in East Anglia.) Baulks, beams, and blocks were used in building and shipbuilding, and smaller sections in gates, post and rail fencing, ploughs, harrows, wheels, wagons, etc. For all this suitable trees have to be selected, felled, and the wood seasoned if necessary. Felling, once done with an axe, and later by cross-cut saw, is now done by chain-saws. The trunks, once trimmed, were cut into planks or beams by *pit-sawing* (see **368**), where the timber was suspended over a narrow pit deep enough for

a man (the "bottom-sawyer") to stand and handle the lower end of a long saw, controlled at the higher end by the "top-sawyer". A few pits survive, though not in use, and most rural museums (eg Singleton) can show one. This work is now done by powered saws, such as a circular saw using a bench. (Details of pit-sawing are well set out in James Arnold's *Shell Book of Country Crafts* (John Baker 1968)). Some wood has to be cloven, not sawn. It is instructive to see the various processes in an estate sawmill and timber yard, such as that at Albury (Sy) or Herriard (Ha).

Wood for *furniture* has to be seasoned, sometimes for many years, and stacks can be seen in timber yards and furniture shops, such as that at Thompsons of Kilburn (NY). Furniture-making needs a considerable range of tools – planes, spokeshaves, saws, adzes, chisels, gouges, braces and bits, templates, squares, etc, as well as benches and vices. Chair-making is a special division of furniture-making; the legs are turned by a different craftsman – the "bodger" – from the man who makes the seats and backs (the primitive pole-lathe (see **369**) is still used, although rarely, for this, as for turning small objects). Lathes, usually wheel-lathes, are required also for hollow-ware – bowls etc. Chair-making in the Chilterns, centred on High Wycombe, altered the landscape in the 18th and

477

19th centuries, by the planting of miles of beechwoods which are still a feature. Chair seats, of cane and rush, are still made at High Wycombe, but now only in one factory.

Ladder-making, for builders and fruit-pickers, is another specialised craft, although metal ladders have largely replaced wooden ones.

The village carpenter made a variety of things, such as coffins, cowls for oasts, etc, as well as articles for the house.

Five-bar gates are traditionally made of oak, formerly cleft, now sawn, although softer woods are often used. The gateposts have one end thick and unshaped to keep them steady in the ground. Gateposts are often of stone in the Highland Zone. The gates are braced both sides with strips of wood of the same thickness as the bars, usually in a V on one side and an inverted V on the other, although there are regional variants.

A highly skilled craft based on the use of wood is *coopering*, the making of barrels and casks. The main users of oak casks were the breweries, but rising costs and chemical reactions with the beer have led to the almost universal use of metal casks for beer. Wooden casks are still in use for butter, tallow, apples, etc, and coopers also make certain kinds of measure and sieve. A large number of tools of special shapes is required.

Making a cask involves four stages: dressing, the preparation and shaping of the staves from butt oak; raising, the initial assembling of the staves in the truss hoops; heading, the shaping of the "heads" which form the ends of the cask; gathering, fixing the hoops. One of the staves is pierced by a bung-hole. These processes demand total precision if the cask is to hold liquids.

368 *Pit-sawing: the vertical saw is worked by a "top-sawyer" and a "bottom'-sawyer".*

369 *A pole lathe in operation: the piece to be turned is rotated by a cord wound round it, fixed at one end to a treadle and, at the other to a springy pole, anchored at its far end.*

Another craft combining wood and metal is *wheelwrighting*, again one of considerable skill and precision. A cart or carriage wheel consists of a nave (hub), the spokes, the felloes (sections of the rim), the iron tyre, nave hoops, and the "box" (the iron tube through the nave which forms the bearing for the axle). The nave is made of elm (cast-iron hubs were made from 1846), the spokes of cleft heart of oak, the felloes of ash, elm, or beech. When the wooden parts have been shaped and assembled, the wheel is laid on a metal plate for the tyre (hoop) to be put on (see **370**). The tyre is red-hot when forced onto the rim, then drenched with water to shrink it tight on. The fit and extent of shrinkage has to be exact, or the wheel will either fall apart or break up. Another kind of tyre has separate strakes nailed onto the felloes.

The *carts and wagons* (see **371** and **372**) for which these wheels were made were a picturesque class, with much local variation. A cart has two wheels, and is a very ancient form of transport. Most carts could be tipped to discharge their contents (muck, roots, stones, coal, building materials, etc). Dung carts (also used for harvest) had to be very strong, and needed heavy floor and sides. The boards of the floor ran parallel to the sides, for ease of raking out the contents. Some carts had floors made with "summers", longitudinal members which were often cross-boarded. "Scotch carts", a name first applied to factory-made carts from Scotland imported mainly into East Anglia, had plank sides, an arched frontboard, and was made to tip. Their decoration

might include "eyes", a very primitive device to see a safe way ahead and to ward off the evil eye. Tradesmen's vehicles were lighter than farm carts, and had springs.

Wagons, having four wheels, seem to have been introduced from Holland into eastern England in the 16th century. They spread throughout the arable regions of Britain, but did not catch on in hilly or pastoral areas. Wagons had a standard underframe, whose origins go back to the Bronze Age. The normal gauge of 4ft 8$\frac{1}{2}$in, taken over as the standard gauge by the railways, also has a prehistoric (even Neolithic) origin. The forecarriage, which swivels to turn the wagon, is made with various locks – a quarter, a half, three-quarters, and full; the first two were not suitable for drawing behind a tractor (when tractors superseded wagons). Wagon floors were built with summers for extra strength. The wheels were dished and slanted outwards, to take the strain of turning and jolting.

371 *A Yorkshire wagon.*

370 *Wheelwrighting; lowering the tyre onto the wheel.*

372 *All-purpose cart.*

The body of a wagon varied with the district. Details of these variants are conveniently summarised by John Vince in his *Discovering Carts and Wagons* (Shire 1970). He distinguishes two main forms: the *box wagon*, which has a simple rectangular elevation, and the *hoop-raved wagon*, in which the rave, or upper member, is curved up over the rear wheels. The box wagon in some areas, such as Lincolnshire and East Anglia, and Sussex, Surrey, and Kent, has the ends higher than the middle. Some variants have "outraves", boards attached to the raves to increase the wagon's capacity. The lines of the Derbyshire wagon are uncompromisingly straight. The Kentish wagon has a unique undercarriage arrangement. The hoop-raved wagon was common in the south Midlands, south, and west. The body is shallow. There are also *boat-wagons* in which the sides slope outwards, *barge-wagons*, the planks of whose sides were bolted together, timber-wagons, drays, water-carts, tumbrils, hermaphrodites, etc.

Carts and wagons were painted in bright colours, in a scheme peculiar to each county or district. For example Lincolnshire used red or prussian blue, Yorkshire brown or red for the body and red for the undercarriage, East Anglia blue (or stone in Norfolk) for the body and red for the underframe, Buckinghamshire yellow, with scarlet wheels and undercarriage The shapes of these carts and wagons were as distinctive as the colour schemes (see **373–8**, facing page 290).

Tractors superseded carts and wagons after the Second World War. Wagons survived in use until the 1950s, and carts until the 1970s. Most museums in the country, or those concerned with rural life, have carts and wagons to show. The best collection is at the Museum of English Rural Life, University of Reading.

The *blacksmith* was an essential element in rural life, and one of the most important members of the community. Not only did he shoe horses, but he made wrought ironwork of every kind, making and repairing tools and implements, often to the particular requirements of the customer, parts of gates and wagons, hoops for wheels and casks, crooks, fire-irons, etc, as well as ornamental work. He had to be a man of great ingenuity and resource. A summary of the development of horseshoes is given by James Arnold in *The Shell Book of Country Crafts* (John Baker 1968) (and see pages 531–2).

Miscellaneous crafts are as follows, *Millwrighting* combined carpentry, masonry, and metalwork. It involved erecting the frame (of a windmill) and cladding it; making and setting the sails; providing the internal arrangements (machinery, which included making and setting the cogs of the driving wheels, making the bins, chutes, etc); dressing the millstones; making the wheel (of a watermill). Up to the 19th century the moving parts were of wood, but by the early 19th century more and more metal was used, and the waterwheel was made of cast iron, and no longer locally. *Clog-making* was carried out till recently in Wales and the north-west. *Flint-knapping* was needed for guns (this craft survived at Brandon (Sf) until recently), and flint-trimming for walls. *Hornwork* includes a variety of small objects, such as spoons, combs, shoehorns, handles, rings, etc. This is still carried out at eg Kendal, and at Hermitage in Scotland. *Rickmaking* has been superseded by the combine harvester, but was once important. The rick was built on a foundation of planks or baulks, and the sheaves were laid on this, pointing to the centre. The whole was thatched. *Scything* is more an art than a craft, and requires great skill and exactitude, in the swinging and the honing.

The *gypsies* have their own crafts, which include peg and wooden flower making, containers for plants, walking-sticks, and other woodland products. They made "bender-tents" (see **379**) of bent rods covered with canvas. Their craftsmanship culminates in the splendid *caravans*, which are of distinctive design, and ornamented with freehand painting (see **381–2**, facing page 291). Only a handful of Romanies remain in this exacting craft, among whom is the inspired Peter Ingram of Selborne (Ha). The "rose and castle" painted decoration on narrowboats and their buckets is related to Romany art.

Dew-ponds may be included in an account of rural crafts, as they are entirely artificial. They occur on high ground mainly of

379 *Romany bender tents, so called because they are formed with bent poles covered with canvas.*

chalk or limestone, in southern England, although there are some in Derbyshire. They are reputed never to dry up, but are not fed by springs. It is possible that the nursery rhyme of Jack and Jill, who went *up* the hill to fetch a pail of water, refers to dew-ponds.

The name dew-ponds is misleading, and does not occur before 1877. In south-east England they are often known as mist-ponds or cloud-ponds. Ralph Whitlock (*Guardian Weekly*, 30 April 1989) has discovered that George III's pond-maker was a Mr Dew, and this may be the origin of the word. Studies of their operation, such as those by Edward A Martin (*c* 1910) and by Whitlock, show beyond doubt that dew plays a quite negligible part in the water supply; in any case dew, as the condensation of heat from the earth, rises, and does not fall. Condensation of moisture in the air at nightfall would not be sufficient either. Martin concludes that the ponds are fed by rain, mist, fog, or cloud. Whitlock concurs, and stresses that if the ponds have wide margins the rain retained will adequately exceed the evaporation from the actual pond surface.

To retain water the ponds must have carefully laid bases. Martin lists several alternative formulae: layers of clay and straw; broken chalk or rubble, straw, lime-tempered clay; stones, clay rammed; stones, puddled clay, straw; chalk puddle; lime-tempered clay; broken chalk, straw, quicklime, clay; and chalky rubble, straw, clay with fine lime. The effectiveness of straw in maintaining an even temperature has been questioned, but the puddled waterproof bottom is essential.

Much attention has been given to the antiquity of dew-ponds, but their Neolithic, or even Iron Age, origin, although plausible, has not been established, and the problem of where the inhabitants of prehistoric hillforts or upland settlements got their water remains unsolved. Most ponds are quite recent, but some may well date from the 16th century. Walter Johnson, in *Folk Memory*, quotes a record of a perpetual hilltop pond at Brabourne (Kt), from 1738. A good and well-known example is close to Chanctonbury Ring on the South Downs.

Industries

TEXTILES

Wool

For many centuries wool, and woollen cloth, was the principal industry of England, until overtaken by cotton in the 19th century. Up to the mid 14th century wool itself was the main export, and from then to the mid 18th woollen cloth. The industry has left a large number of relics of its earlier stages.

Raw wool is the main basis of the woollen textile industry – short staple for *fine woollens*, which are made from yarns in which the fibres lie in all directions, and long staple for *worsteds*, which require yarns in which the fibres lie parallel. The *low* woollen trade uses reworked waste; *felt* is not woven, but is made under heat and compression. Fibres other than wool can also be blended with wool, such as cashmere or mohair (produced by Angora goats), camel, or man-made fibres, any of which are also used alone.

Wool goes through several processes in the course of being made into cloth, not all of which are mechanised. It has first to be *sorted*, each fleece being divided by hand into its various qualities. It is then *scoured* in detergent to remove dirt and extract the lanolin, which is used in soap, cosmetics, ointments, and polishes. Scouring was formerly done in the fulling mills, where cloth steeped in urine or covered with hog's dung was beaten. When clean the wool can be *blended*, different qualities or colours being put together. It is then *carded*, passed through a machine (originally designed by Arkwright for cotton) which has revolving cylinders closely set with wire teeth, which tease the wool into a fine web of intermingled fibres; this web is then *condensed*, divided into loose threads (*slivers*). Carding was done from the 14th century by working the wool between two hand-held boards or cards set with wire hooks. The Romans used hedgehogs, and thistle and teazle heads were used until recent times; teazles are still grown in Somerset. *Scribbling*, the first stage of carding, was later used in Yorkshire instead of carding.

Worsted material, on the other hand, is straightened, washed, and dried after scouring, and put through a *combing* machine (invented by Cartwright in 1792, and developed by Noble and others from 1846 and 1856), which replaced hand-held combs. This machine separates the short fibres (*noils*) from the long fibres (*tops*), which are required for worsted (the noils have other uses). The recent *semi-worsted system* eliminates combing, which has not however been entirely superseded in the industry.

The slivers are then *spun*. Spinning was at first done by distaff and spindle, and later (from the 16th century) by spinning-wheel. But this process was mechanised during the 18th century, wool often following the lead of cotton (see below). The leading machines were Hargreaves' spinning jenny (1764), Arkwright's water-frame (1769), and Crompton's mule (1779). These were adapted and improved throughout the next century; Arkwright's frame was developed into the ring-frame (Thorp 1828), which became widely used after 1850, and is still in use.

The spun thread can now be *woven*. Cloth has been made eg in Egypt since the Neolithic. Evidence is lacking for the British Neolithic, but exists for the Bronze Age and is plentiful from the Iron Age onwards. Prehistoric looms are commonly of the *vertical warp-weighted* type, with two uprights sloping backwards and joined by a cross beam which could revolve. The warp was held taut by weights of stone or baked clay (cylindrical in the Bronze Age, triangular in the Iron Age, pyramidal in Roman times, annular (ring-shaped) in early Saxon times, bun-shaped in late Saxon times). A simplified explanation of the working of such looms is given by John Peter Wild in his Shire book *Textiles in Archaeology*. The cloth made on these looms forms at the top, and is beaten tight with a comb. This type was still in use in Scandinavia in the 1950s. The Romans used a *two-beam* vertical loom instead of the warp-weighted type, which however returned in Saxon times.

In the 13th century the *horizontal* loom was developed, which had heddles raised by treadles for opening the shed, a reed for beating up the weft, and a shuttle for carrying the weft across. This principle has persisted ever since. There are also small specialised looms for braid etc; *tablet-weaving* is another textile technique.

The 18th century saw the mechanisation of this process, although hand looms were in use until the 1880s and are still used in craft weaving today. Kay's fly shuttle (1733) began the new phase (although this took nearly a century to catch on), followed by Cartwright's power loom in 1785 (again, hand looms were not completely superseded in the trade for another century). The Jacquard system of punched cards which controlled the order of raising the warp threads, to vary the pattern, was introduced in the 1820s. The shuttle has been superseded by modern technological advances.

The woven cloth still has to be *finished*, with the object of stabilising the cloth so that it keeps its shape and feel, and to give it the appropriate surface. Except for worsted, which has to have a smooth surface, most cloths need to be thickened by *fulling*. This was originally done by soaking the cloth in a pit or vat in a mixture of Fuller's Earth and various cleansers, such as wood ashes, and treading (walking) them in. Remains of fulling pits can be seen, eg at Langrish House near Petersfield (Ha). By the late 12th century this process had been mechanised, and the human foot replaced by wooden stocks powered by water. The fulling mills eventually became centres for the industry, taking in other processes as well. Fulling stocks were replaced by a rotary milling machine (Dyer, 1833) using weighted rollers; the process is now carried out at high speed. The piece of cloth when fulled was dried by stretching it on *tenterhooks* on a tenter frame or rack, at first in the open air, later in heated rooms. Names like Racks Close (Guildford) reflect this, and tenter frames are still in use at Otterburn Mill (Nd). At Slaidburn (La) are the remains of a walk-mill, early potash pits, and tenter banks.

The cloth still has to acquire the right surface, and this is done by *raising the nap*, with teazles or wire cards, and *cropping* the nap with shears (now done by machines with spiral blades on a cylinder, like a lawnmower). At some point in the finishing process the cloth is *dyed* as necessary. The original natural dyes (madder, woad, indigo, etc) were largely replaced from the 1860s by synthetic (aniline) dyes. Former dyeing vats can be seen, eg at Pitt Whyte, Uplyme (Dv).

Woollen cloth

Woollen cloth has been found in prehistoric contexts, and from Roman Britain. Various weaves were used – tabby, basket, or twill and their variants; patterning was practised, and a range of dyes used. The making of cloth has in fact been continuous from the early Bronze Age onwards.

In the later Middle Ages, from the 12th to the mid 14th century, the emphasis in wool production lay in the export of raw wool rather than the production of cloth. By 1350, 51 grades of wool were produced in England – the best from Shropshire, Herefordshire, and the Cotswolds. Much of this went to Flanders (centred on Ghent), where cloth of all kinds was made, including the finest, and some went to Italy. The cloth in turn was exported all over Europe, either by sea or via the great fairs, eg those in Champagne. In England the wool was handled in fairs such as Stourbridge, Cambridge, and St Giles' at Winchester. Middlemen (*broggers*) collected the wool and sold it to export merchants at local fairs such at Northleach. London handled some 40% of the country's raw wool exports, and Southampton 10%. The quality was controlled by means of the *staple*; exports were only allowed from "staple" towns. The staple was moved from Winchester to London after the Black Death, and fixed at Calais from 1390 to 1558, after which it ceased to be important.

Cloth was of course made here throughout the Middle Ages, at first mostly in the towns (eg Beverley, Lincoln, Stamford, Northampton, with russets and cheap cloths in London, Winchester, Colchester, Oxford, etc). But trade and crafts in the towns were dominated by the guilds, and when the fulling mill was invented, in the late 13th century, the cloth industry began to move out of the towns into those parts of the country which had a ready water supply to drive the mills, such as the Cotswolds and Somerset. An early example is at Leonard Stanley (Gl), where there is a ground-floor weaving room with two storage rooms above, which opened out of the principal bedchamber of the 15th-century mercer's house attached.

Many small places grew as the weavers joined the spinners and fullers in the country, eg Frome, Shepton Mallet, etc. London replaced Bristol as the main exporting centre in the late 14th century; it preferred to deal with a few middlemen, rather than hundreds of weavers. The fulling mills therefore became comprehensive centres – they collected the wool, handed it out to the spinners, then gave the yarn to the weavers, who would then bring the cloth back to be fulled and finished. When finished it went to the merchants in London. But the "cottage industry" character of the trade lasted, at least so far as weaving was concerned, until the later 19th century.

East Anglia made worsteds, which did not need fulling, and this area became important particularly after Flemish weavers were allowed to settle there in the mid 14th century. Edward III, wishing to stimulate

English clothmaking, invited Flemish weavers, fullers, and dyers in the 1330s. At the same time the output of wool was increased, partly by the Cistercian abbeys in their granges, partly by enclosure after the Black Death in response to the shortage of labour and desertion of villages. So from *c* 1340 to *c* 1550 the exports of raw wool declined and the manufacture of cloth increased, with a cross-over point of *c* 1430. This is the age of the great "wool churches" of East Anglia and the west of England. The commercial centre of the trade from the late 14th century was London, in the hands of the Merchant Adventurers (York had a similar body) and the Hansards. The Hansa, which had rights of harbourage just above Custom House, was expelled in 1580, and the Adventurers then had a monopoly until 1688.

The shift to the countryside made spinning and weaving a domestic industry, although by the 16th century few towns in England had no cloth industry at all, and factories began in a tentative way as early as the 16th century (eg at Newbury and Osney). York and Beverley were overtaken by the West Riding (which had plentiful water power), and by the 17th century the industry was firmly located in the areas with water power, mostly the Cotswolds and the west of England (Somerset, west Wiltshire), the southern Pennines (Halifax, Huddersfield, etc), the Lake District (Kendal; Kendal cloth was regularly transported to Southampton in the 16th century for export – a month-long round trip), Surrey and

382 *A typical early woollen mill – Langfield (WY), 1832. Buildings like this, on rivers or canals, are familiar sights in the textile districts.*

Hampshire (Winchester, Southampton, Guildford, Godalming), Scotland (Borders, Ayrshire, Elgin, Harris), and Wales. The largely enclosed East Midlands supplied the long-fibre wool for the "new draperies" of East Anglia: they produced wool but not cloth.

In 1500 (based on John Patten: *Pre-Industrial England* (1979)), fine woollens were made in the Cotswolds and Somerset, medium woollens in West Yorkshire and Lancashire, and worsteds in the Norwich area. Broadcloths and kerseys (coarser, heavier, thinner cloths than worsted, made from short-staple wool) came from the Midlands, Suffolk, the west of England (Gloucester-Wiltshire-Somerset), the south-east, West Yorkshire, and the south-west. West Yorkshire and the south-west also made "dozens" and "straights". East Yorkshire made coverlets and broadcloths, Lancashire and the Lake District made "cottons", "friezes", and rugs, and West Yorkshire made "penistones".

By 1700 the "new draperies" had spread: shalloons, serges, and tammies in Yorkshire and the Midlands; bays, says, and penistones in Suffolk; "stuffs" in Norwich, and shalloons and druggets in the south. Yorkshire still concentrated on the heavier "old draperies", while the south-west made Spanish medleys and serges. The "new draperies" came from Italy via Flanders – they used distaff, not wheel, for spinning, and the cloth was pressed, not fulled. (For definitions of these cloths, see "Glossary".)

In the 18th century cloth was made in most parts of England; "homespun" was made everywhere, but centres of specialisation arose: broadcloths at Worcester, plush and horse-clothing at Banbury, blankets at Witney, and various textiles at Shrewsbury, Kidderminster, Reading, etc. The worsted industry of Norwich, in spite of cheap labour, eventually moved to West Yorkshire, where Huddersfield and Halifax became important centres by the mid 18th century. Cloth-making was essentially a domestic – "putting-out" – industry until it became a factory industry in the late 18th century; but domestic production continued well into the 19th.

The woollen industry gradually centred during the 17th and 18th centuries in a few areas, in particular the Cotswolds, the West Riding, and the eastern Scottish Borders. The greatest concentration was that in the West Riding, where physical and geographical conditions were ideal (by 1770 half of Britain's cloth exports was made here). The land was Millstone Grit, which had plentiful supplies of soft water; the grit area was contiguous to an area of Lower Coal Measures, which were less bleak and provided iron (for machinery) and coal (for power). The towns which had most potential, and which grew and prospered, were those on the edge of both formations, which could command not only the resources of the Coal Measures, but the pastures of the Grit. Their parishes were very large, containing villages and scattered farms and settlements (often medieval enclosures of waste). They became markets for these wide areas, and often developed their own textile specialities. The main places so situated were Halifax, Huddersfield (both cloth towns), Bradford (the raw wool centre), and Leeds (made-up clothing), on the Yorkshire side; and Rochdale, Bury, Burnley, and Colne in Lancashire.

The inhabitants of the scattered upland farms tended to combine weaving with smallholding. In the late 18th century, when carding and spinning machines were invented for cotton, the fulling mills took on these processes as well as fulling. The old hilltop villages continued to weave and manufacture. The merchants lived in larger houses in the uplands, and controlled the movement of yarn, cloth, etc; they sometimes added warehouses and factories to their houses (eg Lumb, Almondbury). The development of Lumb is instructive (see W B Crump and Gertrude Ghorbal: *History of the Huddersfield Woollen Industry*). The 17th-century house was long and low, with long upper (weavers') windows and a cottage at one end. A laithe, with barn, mistal, and stable, indicated the part-time farming. In the 18th century, as the woollen side grew, the clothier owner added to the house a warehouse, or "takin'-in place", and a shed for a dyehouse ("lead-house").

This pattern can still be clearly seen. Thus there are a number of merchants' "halls" around Halifax; Heptonstall was a village of weavers, and their long-light windows still survive (see **142**, page 249), as does the packhorse track down to the mills on the Calder at Hebden Bridge. Similar examples are Sowerby and Sowerby Bridge, Almondbury and Huddersfield, Holme and Holme Bridge and Holmfirth, and Rastrick and Brighouse. The concentration of mills along the rivers and streams led to ribbon development, the growth of the main towns, and the build-up of a conurbation. The old road system was replaced by new turnpikes and roads along the valleys.

As well as the mills along the rivers, other industries played a part. Wire-drawing, for carding, had been done at Barnsley since the 17th century, but later took place round Halifax and Brighouse. Iron, for machinery and tools, came from Low Moor from the end of the 18th century. Coal activated the first power loom in 1830.

There was a rapid and drastic transformation after 1760. The workers now lived round the mills (see **382**), as the woollen industry became factory-based instead of domestic (although the Yorkshire weavers remained independent of the clothiers for longer than those in the south of England). The process was inexorable – an urban population, an industrial class, grew up, divorced from the land. Hand labour was progressively replaced by powered machinery, and after 1800 by steam-driven machines. Wheelwrights and blacksmiths were replaced by engineers, machine tool mechanics, etc. The clothiers' houses in the uplands could, with steam, become mills or manufactories; the fulling mills in the valleys became at first scribbling, then spinning mills. Wire for the cards was often made in these mills also. In the later 19th century the merchant-manufacturers finally brought all departments into one powered mill, against the opposition of the small croppers and clothiers. These all-purpose mills are still a feature of the area (see **383**, **384**, and **385**).

The machines invented in Lancashire and Derbyshire for cotton were taken over or adapted by the Yorkshire woollen industry: eg Kay's flying shuttle, 1733, used for wool in Yorkshire 1763; Hargreaves' spinning jenny, 1765 (for wool 1776); Arkwright's carding engine, 1775 (wool 1780), and the Slubbing Billy; Crompton's mule (1779). Steam-powered machinery met with serious opposition from the domestic workers, and much machine-breaking took place, eg shearing-frames smashed by Luddites in 1812.

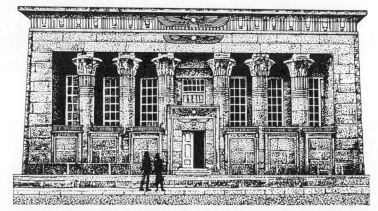

383 *Warehouse and offices in Egyptian style – Marshall's Mill, Holbeck, Leeds, 1842–43. Industrial offices were frequently elaborate, and some even exotic, for reasons of prestige.*

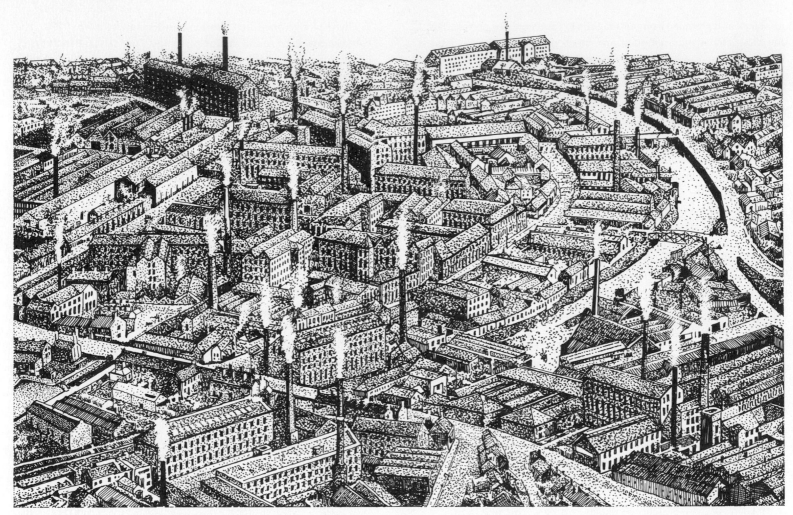

384 *Woollen and worsted mills, Huddersfield: this area was developed for milling in the mid 19th century, and remains a chilling reminder of the impact of industry on a townscape.*

By the end of the 18th century wool of a finer quality was used, brought in from the west and south of England and from Spain and Saxony; new "fancy" cloths began to be made, such as kerseymere (a mixture of kersey and cashmere).

The centres of the domestic industry were the cloth halls in the market towns. There the weavers could bring their pieces of finished cloth for sale to the merchants and clothiers. Early forerunners were, eg, the medieval Wool Hall at Lavenham (Sf), now incorporated in the Swan Hotel, and the Wool House at Southampton (14th century), with the Weigh House in French Street; Winchester had a Cloth Hall in the Brooks area. In Yorkshire they began in the early 18th century: Wakefield by 1710; Leeds 1711, replaced by the White Cloth Hall of 1775, which had an open court round a single-storey building, with gatehouse and cupola (this now survives only in part); Huddersfield had an oval building (1766, demolished 1930); Bradford and Colne also had one. The most magnificent survivor – one of the finest buildings in the country – is the Piece Hall at Halifax, 1775 (see **386**). This is a two-storey, colonnaded building round a large rectangular space (needed for carts, packhorses, and stalls); on the two floors are some 300 rooms where the transactions took place. These cloth halls were not used by the merchant-manufacturers themselves for their own products, nor by the fancy trade (who needed privacy to avoid being copied), but by the domestic weavers, nearly 500 of whom are recorded as using the Huddersfield hall in 1830. This important trade – 50,000 people lived on the woollen industry centred on Huddersfield in 1801 – was ended by the power loom in the 1870s, when the domestic industry was finally absorbed into the mills.

The fancy trade developed on the Coal Measures, where steam power was available (plain woollens being made on the Millstone Grit). Ten thousand looms were at work in 1825, making waistcoatings, cords, and sarsenets, using mixtures of wool, worsted, cotton, and silk. The Jacquard system was introduced into Halifax's damask trade in 1827, and a few years later in Huddersfield. The latter's fancy trade reputation was established by the Great Exhibition of 1851, since when fancy woollens and worsteds have remained Huddersfield's speciality. Leeds, which bought up the Halifax and Huddersfield cloth and made it up into garments, was also the market for the woad and teazles grown round Selby (teazles for the south of England trade came from Somerset). Dyeing tended to be concentrated, as at Painswick (Gl) and Bradford-on-Avon (Wi).

The pattern of the industry is now, broadly: worsted and raw wool, Bradford; ready-made clothing, Leeds; hunting cloths, Stroud-Nailsworth; cloths, west of England; tweeds, Cheviots, and Borders, Harris (hand-made); flannel, Newtown, Welshpool; textile machinery, Huddersfield.

There are also several minor sections of the woollen industry: *mungo* and the better quality *shoddy*, made from waste material and used in the 19th century for uniforms and other coarse cloths, was centred in Dewsbury and Batley (WY); *blankets* are still made at

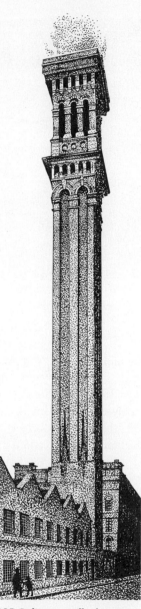

385 *Italianate mill chimney – Manningham Mills, Bradford, 1870–71: one of many Victorian styles of factory chimney. Some, like this one, were intended to attract the eye and advertise the product.*

Witney (Ox); *carpets*, of which there are several kinds, were made on the draw-loom at Kidderminster from 1735, and in the 1820s the Jacquard system was applied to make Brussels-type carpets. The Brussels power-loom was adapted for the manufacture of Wilton carpets in the 1860s; this mechanised the raising and cutting of the piles. In 1876 a machine was developed for making the Axminster pile. These three towns still make their carpets, but the huge Crossley mills at Halifax have ceased to operate.

Tapestry is a specialised form of carpet, with two warps and the colour variation being produced in the weft threads only. It has been made in Europe since the 14th century, at first in the Low Countries (eg Brussels and Tournai), and from the 17th century in France (eg Gobelins, Aubusson, Beauvais). Tapestry was made in Soho and at Mortlake (Sy) from 1619 to the 1640s, but has left no remains; William Morris sought to revive it at Merton Abbey in 1877.

Felt is made from woollen fibres by means of heat, moisture, pressure, and vibration, which causes the threads to lock together in mats of various densities. Felt-making for hats was a flourishing industry in the 17th and 18th centuries, centred on Luton; in the 19th century felt was used in carpets, in Leeds and later Rossendale. Industrial felt has a wide range of uses today.

The museums of the woollen industry are listed in "Sites and Museums" (see page 577)

The area pattern can be seen at Heptonstall–Hebden Bridge, and Almondbury–Huddersfield. The Piece Hall, Halifax, is magnificent. Stanley Mill, Stonehouse (Gl), 1813, can be visited, and there are several working mills in Wales and Yorkshire (see Colum Giles and Ian H Goodall: *Yorkshire Textile Mills 1770–1930* (HMSO for RCHME and The West Yorkshire Archaeology Service, 1992). Houses include the clothier's home, Lumb, Almondbury, and weavers' houses in Heptonstall and many places in the former West Riding.

386 *The Piece Hall, Halifax – Thomas Bradley 1779. This was the most monumental of the similar halls built in the Yorkshire woollen towns in the 18th century; it consists of a vast square surrounded by 315 rooms, where weavers could bring their "pieces" of cloth to the manufacturers, for onward sale. The system was superseded when cloth was woven in mills.*

Cotton

The cotton industry changed the face of the north-west of England, and dominated British industry for 200 years. It had a meteoric rise in the mid 18th century, and an equally sharp decline in the 20th. Its period of growth ran from 1770 to 1840; by 1850 cotton employed one-fortieth of the population of Britain. From 1803 to 1938 (the years of "King Cotton") it overtook wool as an export from Britain, being then overtaken by machinery. Its peak was 1912–13, after which it declined sharply; by 1958 cotton goods were being imported.

Cotton was introduced into East Anglia from the Levant in small quantities in the 16th century, and was used in the making of *fustian*, cloth with a cotton weft and linen warp. By 1600 it had reached Lancashire, where the conditions were more suitable. In the mid 18th century the application of powered machinery changed the character of the industry, which thus ceased to be domestic ahead of other textiles.

The processes of manufacture are similar to those of wool, but cotton fibres are shorter and finer, and more liable to snap. So, although the woollen mills of the West Riding might have been suitable for cotton, it was found that damp, rainy areas were better, and cotton developed in Lancashire and in the Pennine foothills, and

also round Paisley. The coalfield later enabled steam power to be used instead of water. This Lancashire–south Derbyshire–west Yorkshire–north-east Cheshire area achieved a remarkable concentration and organisation. Liverpool was the port of entry of raw cotton and of the export of finished goods, while Manchester was the marketing centre. Spinning was done in Derbyshire (Cromford and Belper), and in Lancashire round Bolton, Bury, Rochdale, Oldham, and Ashton. Weaving was done in Preston, Clitheroe, Accrington, Blackburn, and Burnley. Rossendale worked up waste from both sides of the industry. In all these places mills, often impressive or exotic, are prominent relics. Indeed, to a large extent the whole south-east Lancashire conurbation, with its mills, uninspiring workers' housing, but brave public buildings, is a creation of and monument to cotton. Many of the mills have been demolished or converted to engineering, chemicals, and other industry, but the bones of the urban landscape remain.

Cheshire produces salt, which is used for chemicals, dyes, bleaches, and soaps, all needed for textiles (Northwich, Middlewich, and Winsford – salt; Port Sunlight, Widnes, and Runcorn – chemicals and soap).

By 1800 all the factory processes were in use, together with steam power, and Eli Whitney's saw gin, which enabled raw cotton to be exported from the USA just as West Indian supplies were becoming inadequate, as Chris Aspin (*The Cotton Industry*, Shire 1981) points out. Cheap American cotton enabled Lancashire to sell all over the world, including India itself – the first industry to make the whole world its market. The decline since 1913 was due to competition from India and the Far East, and also from man-made fibres. Bolton is still the centre for fine spinning, but it now includes rayon and other artificial fibres.

Cotton has to be disentangled, cleaned, blended, and made into ropes of parallel fibres (*roving*), before it can be spun into yarn. When picked by hand and loosely baled it was easy to handle, but once mechanically harvested and baled (late 18th century) it had to be *willowed* and *scutched* to clean it. The resultant *lap* of tufts is then *carded* (Arkwright invented a machine for this in 1775), then *drafted* into parallel fibres, in a loose rope called a *sliver*.

The sliver is now *spun*. Paul and Wyatt attempted to mechanise this process in 1738, but this was not a success. Hargreaves did however succeed in 1765 with his *spinning jenny* ("jenny" means machine), which was based on the principle of the cottage hand-wheel (the Jersey wheel). Arkwright developed his *water-driven frame* at Cromford in 1771, which produced a strong warp yarn, with the jennies making the weft. These two machines were combined in Crompton's *mule* (1779); this was made "self-acting" by Roberts in the 1830s. It was perfected by 1885, and replaced by ring-spinning only in the 1950s. The latter is now challenged by the "open-end" spinning machine of the 1970s.

The yarn is now ready for *weaving*. Although Kay invented the *flying shuttle* in 1733, this was for some time used more for wool than for cotton. The real breakthrough for cotton was Cartwright's power-loom of 1785–7, perfected by others by 1842. The shuttle is now nearly obsolete. The cloth when woven has to be *finished*. This involves *bleaching*, *dyeing*, and (where required) *calico printing*. Mercerisation was adopted in 1850 to give lustre; Perkins applied aniline dyes in 1856. Printing was done by Bell's cylinder (1785); screen printing is widely used today. The Macintosh rainwear process (in which the cloth is impregnated with rubber dissolved with naphtha) dates from 1824.

Outside the area mentioned above, Nottingham was also a cotton-spinning centre in the 1760s when, owing to the lack of water power (horses had to be used), the industry moved to Derby-

387 *Masson Mill, Cromford (Db), 1783: a major part of Richard Arkwright's cotton spinning complex.*

shire (Cromford, later Matlock, Bakewell, Belper, Milford, etc). The complexes at Cromford and Belper are conspicuously fine; Cromford has Arkwright's mills (see **387**) of 1771 and 1777 (partly burnt 1890), and others, as well as a complete company town, with workers' housing, inn, and Arkwright's own house. Belper has the massive Strutt mills of 1803, and workers' housing. There were a few water-powered mills in Nottinghamshire, such as Mansfield and Sutton in Ashfield (1770s), and Pleasley (Hollins', 1784). Steam-power sent the industry back to Nottinghamshire, which had coal (eg Papplewick). Another major site is that of Styal (Ch), where the National Trust has restored a mill (adapted to both spinning and weaving), workers' housing, institute, apprentice hostel, etc.

The Greater Manchester Textile Mills Survey has been preparing a RCHME volume on the buildings of the textile industry; 2,434 mill sites have been identified on maps, of which 1,012 have been found to be extant in 1985–6; 90 selected sites are being surveyed and recorded. The most impressive group of early mills so revealed is at Ancoats. Of these, McConnel and Kennedy's (1818–1912) features the widest chronological range of fireproof mill architecture in Greater Manchester. Murray's Mills (1798–1806) have a unique variety of structures, built round a square canal basin linked to the Rochdale Canal by a tunnel. Peel's, at the Burns, Bury (1790s, cotton, water-powered, later steam; converted late 19th century to cotton bleaching, closed 1930) has a 131ft (40m) chimney stack, a mill wall retaining part of the mill pond dam, and the workers' back-to-backs. Excavation has revealed the wheel pits, ponds, leats, and tunnels.

There are many mills in the south-east Lancashire–south Derbyshire complex (see "Sites and Museums" page 577), and indeed the industrial landscape generally is worth studying. *Museums* include the Science Museum, London, the Greater

Flax and linen

Flax was used widely in the ancient world, from Neolithic times on, as a textile source. At first its tough stems were used in windbreaks or fish-traps; when these rotted the usable fibres were revealed. Linen reached Europe via the Roman Empire.

The conversion of flax fibres to linen cloth is long and complex, involving a large number of processes. The plant has first to be *pulled* by hand, not cut, and *bundled* to dry. It has then to be *retted* to get the fibres out. This can be done either by laying the plants out on grass in rows (*dew-retting*), which takes 20–30 days, or by soaking in pools or gently flowing soft water for 10–14 days, or in *lint-holes* dug in boggy ground (*water-retting*). Special *tanks* are now used. The seeds are saved for linseed and linseed oil. The retted plants are then dried and stored, ready for *dressing*. This involves *breaking* by beating with a mallet or bat, *scutching* with bat or blade to remove the broken straw, and *hackling* – combing to clean and remove the short fibres (*tow*), and align the long fibres (*line*). The line is made into bundles (*stricks*) for *spinning*.

Spinning involves drawing out the fibres from the bundle (*drafting* the *rovings*), twisting them into continuous yarn, and winding on the yarn to stop it untwisting. Originally the yarn was wound on round the shaft below the spindlewhorl, but in Europe the *spindle* had the *whorl* at the bottom end and a separate *distaff* was held in the other hand to support the fibres. In the later 15th century the flyer *spinning-wheel* was introduced (this differed from the wheel used for wool and from the Jersey wheel used for cotton). A treadle was added in the early 17th century. The wheels could be either vertical or horizontal. The distaff was at first held under the right arm, but in later wheels was fixed to or fitted into the wheel. Two-handed wheels were used in Scotland from the 17th century. A *reel* was used to wind off the full bobbin into a *hank*.

Flax spinning was mechanised in 1790 by Matthew Murray, but his machine only coped with coarser counts – finer counts had to be hand-spun till well into the 19th century (and much fine yarn was imported from Holland and Germany). In 1814 Philippe de Girard, in France, patented a wet spinning machine; this was improved by James Kay (1825) who used hot water in a trough, softening the gummy matter and enabling the fibres to be drafted into fine count yarns. Open-end spinning, as with cotton, is not used for flax.

The yarns could now be *woven*, using at first the simple hand-looms used for other textiles. Following the Crusades, the weaving of silk damask was introduced into Europe, using a wide and complicated *draw-loom*. This technique was applied to linen, and was introduced into Scotland from the Low Countries in the early 18th century (Edinburgh and Dunfermline). The Jacquard technique was applied in the 1820s. The loom used since the mid 20th century is the *rapier* type, which replaces shuttles by flexible rods, and greatly increases output.

The cloth when made has to be finished. This consists of *bleaching*, which has four stages: *steeping*; *bucking* (boiling in lye (alkalised water)); *grassing* or *crofting* (laying out on grass, a practice which continued until the 1930s); and *souring* (soaking in weak acid). The cloth is then *beetled* – pounded, now by machine, to close the cloth, which can, finally, be *dyed*.

Linen was made widely in north-west Europe, from northern France to Denmark; indeed, cambric takes its name from Cambrai, and lawn perhaps from Laon, while damask originated in Damascus. In Britain its main centres were Ulster and eastern Scotland, with some coarse linen being made in Yorkshire (Leeds and Barnsley). There is evidence also for a widespread linen industry in the north-west, contemporary with and often linked to the 12th- and 13th-century demesne woollen industry. At Newton (La) are remains of flax-retting ponds, and raised banks to dry the retted flax or hemp. Flax has been grown in England, but not since c 1960. In the 17th and 18th centuries wool was dominant in England, so linen was encouraged in Scotland and Ireland (it was a domestic industry until the late 18th century). It is still made in Ireland, but in Scotland now only at Arbroath.

In Scotland fine linen was made at Dunfermline (Fi), and coarser grades at Arbroath, Dundee (where there were close links with the jute industry), and Kinghorn (Fi). At all these places, and at eg Blairgowrie and Bridge of Dean (Pe), mills and warehouses of the 18th and early 19th centuries can be seen.

The coarser forms of flax (tow), jute (like flax but coarser), and hemp were made into *canvas* and *duck*, for sailcloth (and now for awnings, tents, luggage, etc) and for coarse cloths for wagon covers, grain bags, and sacks; hemp was best for ropes and cordage. In the mid 19th century *linoleum* was invented, and Kirkcaldy (Fi) became a major centre for its manufacture. Linoleum is a cement of linseed oil, resins, and cork, on a base of jute canvas; floorcloth or *oilcloth* is a cloth made from linen tow, sized and printed.

Linen was extensively replaced by cotton at the end of the 18th century (early bobbin lace was made from linen yarn). Linen sheets are now a luxury, but drying-up cloths and table mats are still made of linen. Flax is not elastic like wool, so creases and pleats readily; research goes on into crease-resistant linen. Linen conducts heat well, and is cool; although it is now only 2% of the world's textile production, it is still important.

(See "Sites and Museums" page 577.)

Hemp

Hemp has many of the properties of flax, but is coarser and heavier to work. The crop is cut, not pulled. It is then soaked to rot away the core, and beaten to separate the fibres (*bast*).

Hemp has been the primary material for *ropes* throughout history, although since the 19th century jute and coir have also been used and (from the late 19th century) Manila "hemp" and sisal also, which are rougher but cheaper. Jute is also used for cordage, string, and nets (with manufacturing centres in Dundee, London, and Belfast), and coir for ropes, matting, and padding.

Yarns were made by twisting fibres together by means of a spindlewhorl held in the hand, and later on a spinning-wheel. *Twine* is two or more yarns twisted together. It was also found convenient to make yarns, twine, and ropes in *walks*. These are long sheds, sometimes with storage on an upper floor. The yarns were twisted by a man carrying the supply of fibres, walking backwards from a wheel (the *jack*) which had rotating hooks on its rim. The machines which replaced this method work on the same principle.

Medieval centres of ropemaking were Bridport (Do) (since at least the early 13th century) and Newcastle-upon-Tyne. From *c* 1700 the naval dockyards (Chatham, Portsmouth, and Devonport) made their own ropes, and the rope-walks there are spectacular; that at Chatham is a quarter of a mile long, and has the longest tiled roof in Britain; that at Portsmouth is not much shorter. Other smaller ones survive, or did till recently, eg Heathfield near Pateley Bridge (NY), Bilston (St), Cambridge, Dover (open air), Hawes (NY) (still in use), and Bridport (closed 1970). Bridport indeed is instructive: the narrow alleys leading off the main street were used until recently for making rope and twine; in the cottages along them, and in eg South Street, where some still survive, the women and children made nets. The wide pavements in the main streets enabled nets to be *fitted* (see below) in front of the cottages. A very good account of this Bridport industry is given in Anthony Sanctuary's book in the Shire series.

Nets were originally – from ancient Egyptian times – made from flax, later from cotton, but now from nylon (since the 1930s), polyethylene and polythene (1950s), and polypropylene (1960s). These artificial fibres have more stretch than natural fibres, but great strength and resistance to bacterial rotting. Nets for fishing and sport were made by hand, using threads of various thicknesses, with appropriate knots. A netmaking machine was invented in 1812 in Scotland, and used from the 1820s (the *jumper*, which had a number of springs which were compressed by jumping on a foot-treadle). M Zang invented a multi-shuttle machine in the 1890s. These machines made slip knots. Power-driven jumpers (Mons machines) were made in France for herring nets. Improved Zang machines are in use today.

The sheets of net "cloth" have to be shaped by hand to meet the particular requirements (*fitting*): the first stage is to cut the sheet, the second to join the major pieces, the third to cut the individual article, and the fourth selvedge the final net. Most nets have then to be attached to a frame (wood, metal, or rope – *rigging*). Netmaking in Bridport was done by outworkers in their cottages, twine supplied; in 1900 there were 15 family firms making yarn, twine, rope, and nets, while by 1945 there were two groups, who combined in 1963.

Silk

This industry, somewhat unlikely for Britain, developed here by the 15th century to meet demands for luxury cloth. The British climate is too cold to breed silkworms successfully, although many attempts were made, and many mulberry trees planted, until well into the 17th century. Today the Lullingstone Silk Farm near Yeovil is a rare case of success. But, like cotton, the raw material had basically to be imported – at different times from the Far East, from Persia and India, from Italy and France, and from Brazil.

In the later 16th century immigrants arrived from France and the Low Countries who gave a great impetus to the industry. They settled in Spitalfields (London), Norwich, and elsewhere; by the 1570s Norwich was producing bombazine, a cloth with a silk warp and a worsted weft. Again, after 1685, there was another influx from France, and a range of cloths, including brocades and velvets, was now produced. Output increased by some 20 times from 1664 to 1713.

Before this date silk was a domestic industry. The workers carried out throwing and weaving in upper rooms with long windows on both sides (like the woollen and knitwear workers), and these can still be seen in Spitalfields and elsewhere. But changes were taking place. In 1702 Thomas Cotchett built a mill for throwing at Derby; this idea was taken up by John and Thomas Lombe, who used Italian throwing machines, and built at Derby the first successful powered factory in England in 1721. Other mills were built using water power – Macclesfield in 1743, Stockport in 1752, Congleton in 1755, feeding weaving mills at Spitalfields, Manchester, and Norwich. But the seed was sown, and from the 1760s the domestic workers lost out; by 1825 the industry had left London for East Anglia and the north-west. Derby had 12 mills in 1789 and 17 by 1840; some can be seen near the Markeaton Brook. During the earlier 19th century the industry spread into Nottinghamshire, eg to Nottingham itself, and Maythorne near Southwell, where are the remains of a self-contained industrial community – two mills and housing. Part of a large mill at Beeston (1826–1902) still survives.

The industry went into decline from the 1860s, although some silk weaving, for crepes (gauze-like fabrics with wrinkled surface), hand-kerchiefs, ties, etc remained in Macclesfield, Congleton, and Leek, and in West Yorkshire for velvets, plushes, and mixed goods (silk with cotton or wool), into the 1980s. But artificial silk like *rayon* (cellulose acetates) from the early 20th century, and *nylon* (synthetic chemical fibres, acrylic, Terylene, etc), invented by Dupont in 1939, completed the change. These fibres are made and woven at several factories in the UK, mainly those of Courtaulds, Braintree, and ICI. Now there is little silk throwing in Britain, and no spinning; weaving, both powered and hand, is still carried on on a small scale in the north-west, East Anglia, and Essex.

The processes of silk manufacture are complex. The cocoons are placed in warm water to soften and free the threads; two groups of threads are gathered together and wound onto reels; the skeins are then colour-coded for the qualities and number of threads, and placed in groups of three (a *moss*) – twelve form a *book*. *Throwing* can then take place, involving winding, cleaning, spinning, and doubling (spinning in this context involves giving a twist to the threads differing with their end-use; in the waste silk industry spinning means joining short staples together). Doubling is joining two, three, or four twisted threads together. Spinning and doubling were combined on one machine in 1851. The doubled warp threads now have to be twisted again, in the opposite direction, producing a strong rope-like thread (*organzine*). Thomas Lombe enabled organzine to be produced in England by importing Italian throwing machines (a 13th-century invention) to his silk mill at Derby in 1721. Several improved machines followed, until modern ones can operate at 12,000 rpm. These processes yield up to 50% waste material, which can be processed for use in cheaper fabrics. Silk waste processes are complex; the mills concerned had all closed by 1971.

The final process is *weaving*. The *draw-loom* was introduced by Flemish weavers in 1567; originally a boy sat on top of it and drew up the heddles, which carried the warp threads, in order to make the pattern. This was heavy work, as there could be up to 600 threads to the inch in a fine fabric, and several heddles could be in play at once. Attempts were made to make the process automatic, and finally the Jacquard system of punched cards was evolved (1804) and replaced the boy. It was in use in Britain by the 1820s.

Power-looms were first used by Courtauld in 1830. The speed of action was greatly increased by the *rapier loom*, used in Britain from the end of the Second World War. *Ribbons* are made on the *needle-loom*. (See "Sites and Museums", page 577.)

Knitting and lace

The archaeology of the hosiery and knitwear industry differs in many respects from that of other textile industries.

Knitting is not known before *c* AD 300, and did not reach Britain until the 15th century. Clothes had been woven since the Neolithic, and even in the Middle Ages woven cloth was used for hose. The demand for knitted fabric arose in the 16th century, to meet a change in male fashion (doublets and hose) which required cloth which would not wrinkle. Knitted stockings were made from the mid 16th century, from silk imported from France and Spain, and there was a growing trade throughout the century in silk knitwear to meet upper-class demand.

Lower down the social scale, stockings were made of wool for most people, and worsted by the end of the century; by the 17th century the hand-knitters were making 33 types of stocking, mainly in the Pennines, as a supplement to low farming wages. By the late 17th century England was exporting these products.

But hand-knitting was slow and laborious, and mechanisation would allow whole rows to be knitted at once. In 1589 William Lee, reputedly a clergyman of Calverton near Nottingham, invented a mechanical *knitting-frame*, a decisive invention which has dominated the textile industry of Nottinghamshire and Leicestershire ever since (both counties needed a dual economy when much land was enclosed for sheep, and fewer men were employed in farming). Lee's frame had problems with patents, but was improved by his brother and its use established in England by 1630, at first in London (where Spitalfields was a centre of silk-weaving). By 1657 a Company of Framework Knitters was set up in London. The later 17th century saw an increased demand for cheaper hosiery, so there was a concurrent growth of the industry in the East Midlands from 1670, at Leicester using worsted, at Nottingham with cotton, 1730, and at Derby with silk. By the 1770s Nottingham was the centre of the cotton hosiery industry, in the most innovative area in the world. But in the 1780s the cotton spinning industry moved to Yorkshire, and later to Lancashire. By 1782 there were some 20,000 stocking-frames in England.

Jedediah Strutt, with his Derby rib frame of 1758, had enabled ribbed hosiery to be made, by adapting the Lee machine, and there were several other innovations in the 18th century. Brunel's machine of 1816 produced a tube of fabric, while in the 1840s the power-driven circular frame came into use. Power was applied to the flat frame (for fully-fashioned work), and William Cotton (at Loughborough, 1864) invented a machine adapted to make a dozen or more hose at once, and to knit fashioned garments of all kinds. In 1887 the Americans adapted the powered sewing-machine to mechanise the seaming of knitted garments.

Stockings were at first knitted flat, and shaped and seamed to fit the leg. The change of men's fashion in the early 19th century to trousers

and socks had a bad effect on the stocking industry, which did not revive until the demand for women's stockings in the 20th century. Meanwhile the Griswold sock machine was introduced in the late 1840s. This was small and light, and could be operated by women. The redundant men – highly skilled – were absorbed into new industries in the area.

It was not the introduction of power that ended the domestic industry (as with the Pennine weavers), but the introduction in the late 18th century of machines too large to fit into the worker's home – "wide frames". These had therefore to be housed in workshops, which were vulnerable to Luddite wreckers, particularly active in 1811–12. Yet the wide frame allowed a variety of garments to be made when the demand for stockings fell, and initiated the modern knitwear industry. Its use became more general by the 1830s. An adaptation of the frame enabled net, and later lace, to be made (see below).

Lee's frame was of very considerable ingenuity, and its working cannot be described here (details are given in Marilyn Palmer's *Framework Knitting*). The earlier narrow frame had some 2,000 parts, the wide frame 4,000; subsidiary industries grew up to make needles, sinkers, boxes, and printing. A bearded needle was used until 1847, when it was replaced by the latch needle (invented by Matthew Townshend), which enabled power to be applied. The principles on which Lee's frame operates are still basically unchanged. But it was heavy to work, and its use was a male industry; the women of the family mended and made up, the children reeled the yarn.

The knitting industry, in its domestic phase, was organised by merchants or master hosiers, who kept the yarn in hanks in warehouses and let it out to the knitters (the yarn was spun by spinners also employed by the hosier). The knitter collected the yarn and delivered the finished goods to the warehouse in exchange for more. He was totally dependent on the hosier or the middleman, and, unless he owned his frame (few did), was charged a variety of rentals and other deductions from his earnings, which were scandalously low.

The cottage knitters therefore tended to live within reasonable reach of the "putting-out" centres of Leicester, Loughborough, Nottingham, Belper, and Sutton-in-Ashfield, with smaller centres at Derby, Ruddington, Shepshed, and Hinckley. It is in these places, and in the villages round them, that the visible remains of the industry are to be found. Other centres developed in Gloucestershire, Surrey (Godalming), and southern Scotland (Hawick and Dumfries).

Many knitters, like the weavers of the Pennines, inserted special windows into their cottages to increase the light – long horizontal windows or continuous rows, sometimes with sliding sash. Where possible, the room where the frame was had light on both sides, and a lack of inner walls or partitions. Such adaptations must have been common, but still most framework knitters were too poor to make them; those we see must be the survivors of a minority.

Marilyn Palmer (whose work is the main basis of this section) has defined the stages of the industry, of which she distinguishes four:

1 *Adaptations of existing houses*: Hinckley was called the "Cradle and Home of the Hosiery Trade', since William Iliffe set up a frame here in 1640. An adapted timber-frame house survives in Lower Bond Street, but the interior has been altered. Sutton Bonington (No) has the earliest dated house with inserted long windows; the house is dated 1661, but the windows (on two floors) may date only from the early 18th century.

2 *Purpose-built housing*: The hosiers did not normally provide this, but some knitters built their own house, or had it built by speculators or middlemen. Such houses had the work-rooms on the ground or second floor, with bedrooms on the first floor. Later, terraces were built with the top floors open along the row, for steam power. In Calverton (see **388**), where the industry began, ground-floor workshops seem to have been the norm (eg Windles Square, 1834): a pair of such cottages here was built as late as 1857. In north Northamptonshire and south Leicestershire similar houses may have been built for the boot and shoe industry, which remained domestic longer than hosiery, even taking over the latter's premises in some cases.

Topshops were used for hosiery, lace, and ribbon and fabric weaving (eg in Hucknall). These were three-storey houses, with the workshops on the middle floor and the attics used for yarn storage; but variations in the uses of the floors exist. The workplaces were kept separate from the living rooms as far as possible.

3 *Frameshops* (see **389** and **390**): The introduction of wide frames necessitated setting them up in workshops separate from the knitters' cottages. In 1845 Ruddington (No) had 330 frames, of which 226 were wide. These were crammed tightly into workshops, in rows along the windows, with a narrow gangway between them. The workshops had the long windows now, not the cottages.

388 *Knitters' housing – Calverton (No). The ground-floor workshops have large windows in both sides of the terrace.*

389 *Framework knitters' workshop (frameshop) – Ruddington (No), 1829. This complex also contains housing for the knitters.*

An excellent example is in Chapel Street, Ruddington (now a museum), which has two two-storey workshops, a short row of cottages, and outbuildings (mid 19th century). At Bushloe End, Wigston (Le) is a mid 19th-century frame-shop (now a museum) on the ground floor; the upper floor had yarn winders and Griswold (sock) machines. The associated cottages had a shop on the first floor, probably for mending and making up.

4   *Factories*: Steam power was not applied to knitting until the 1830s, and was not widespread until the latch needle was invented in 1847. Frame rents were abolished in 1874, and the Education Acts (1876 and others) took children away from the family working unit. These two measures broke up the domestic industry, which nevertheless in fact lasted till well into the 20th century in rural areas, and workers' housing had been improving since the 1880s. The last stockinger's shop in Calverton did not in fact close until 1955. (Other domestic industries which lasted till the late 19th or early 20th century include lace (Nottinghamshire), ribbon-weaving (Coventry), wool- and worsted-weaving (Pennines), nails and chains (West Midlands), boots and shoes (Northamptonshire, Leicestershire). Early factories can be seen at Hinckley and Leicester (eg Corah's, between Burley's Way and John Street – 1865, with later buildings) and more recent ones, eg I and R Morley, Nottingham (1877).

Lace, which is found in Egyptian tombs, is of two types: *bobbin lace* made on a hard cushion or pillow with threads weighted by wood or bone bobbins, and *needle lace* made with a needle and thread. Both types seem to have reached England from the Low Countries in the later 16th century. Bobbin lace became a domestic industry and was concentrated in two areas – the south-east Midlands (Bedfordshire, Buckinghamshire, and Northamptonshire, eg Olney) and the south-west (Devon, Dorset, and Somerset, eg Honiton). Some 120,000 people were engaged in this in the early 19th century. Cottages were not adapted; the lacemaker sat in her doorway when the weather was suitable – light indoors was by way of a lamp or candle shining through a glass globe filled with water and aqua fortis (which magnified the light).

Needle lace, an industry virtually local to Nottingham, grew out of framework knitting, by the adaptation of the knitting frame to make net, in imitation of hand-made net. This had small areas of embroidered pattern applied by hand. The demand for machine-made net grew in the 1760s and 1770s, when the hosiery industry had surplus labour; many attempts were made to devise a satisfactory machine, until John Rogers succeeded with an adapted frame in 1786. By 1810 there were some 1,500–1,800 point-net machines in Nottingham, employing some 15,000 people. Some houses were adapted for lacemaking, as in the hosiery industry.

The final break with the hosiery industry came in 1808, when John Heathcote devised a mesh net machine which was independent of the knitting frame – his "twist net" was not knitted. Nottingham boomed when Heathcote's patent ran out in 1823; a population of *c* 10,000 in 1750 rapidly rose to 50,000 in 1830 while the city boundaries remained the same, creating hopeless poverty and slums. John Leavers improved the twist net machine in 1813, and Jacquard cards were applied to this in 1841. Patterns could now be made on one machine, which made the hand embroiderers ("runners") redundant. John Livesey invented a curtain lace machine in 1846. Steam power could now be applied to lacemaking machinery, and by 1865 95% had been converted and factories then replaced small workshops.

From the 1880s most lace was made outside Nottingham, where land and wages were lower (eg in Long Eaton and Beeston), but

390 *Ruddington frameshop (interior). The knitting frames were packed tightly together in the workshop.*

495

Nottingham remained the commercial and marketing centre. A quarter devoted to the finishing and warehousing of lace grew up from the earlier 19th century in Nottingham – the *Lace Market*, an area of narrow streets round the old parish church of St Mary, on the hilltop which was the site of the Anglo-Saxon town. This may be compared, *mutatis mutandis*, with the gun and jewellery quarters of Birmingham, but there are differences of organisation and practice. In Nottingham there was, and is, no central market or selling point – each firm sells its own products, which are finished and warehoused on the premises. Particularly fine examples of Lace Market buildings are the Birkins building in Broadway and the Adams, Page and Co building in Stoney Street, which contains a chapel for the workforce (both by T C Hine, 1853–5). A museum for the area has been set up in a disused Unitarian chapel in High Pavement (the Lace Hall). The industry still employs 5,000 people in Nottingham and Long Eaton.

(See "Sites and Museums", page 577.)

LEATHER

Leather has been made from at least Mesolithic times, and has a variety of uses. It is not, however, clear when and where the complex processes of its manufacture were invented. Leather is the central layer of the skin, between the epidermis, to which the hair or wool is attached, and the layer of fat or flesh below. These have to be scraped off (and this is an obvious use for flint scrapers in prehistoric times; since Roman times the skins have been scraped over a convex sloping board with a two-handled blunt knife), and the skin must then be *cured* to make it usable. Various methods were used for this, including salting, sun-drying, smoking, and working in fats, alum, or alum and salt. Treatment with alum, or *tawing*, was still used in medieval times, and has certain applications today. The most important process is *tanning*, soaking in a solution of tannin, extracted from oak bark or oak galls by crushing. Tanning is done in permanent stone pits – the hides are passed from one to another, from a weak to strong concentration of bark. The whole process takes about a year, so many pits are required. Lighter skins, such as sheep, are tanned by other, shorter methods, including the use of alum, and in vats, not pits. The earliest medieval tanning pits found in Britain are those at Rievaulx Abbey (NY), 12th/13th century. The tanyard at Meaux Abbey (Hu) still survives in part. Tanning pits are often excavated on medieval sites, as at Winchester. Watch for street names like Tanner Street or Tanhouse Yard.

The hides are then hung in sheds or special drying rooms to dry, then passed to the currier to be *finished*. Finishing varies with the product, and includes oiling, stretching, and polishing: sole leather was hammered, harness leather curried (impregnated with grease while still damp after tanning), and Morocco leather (goatskin) and willow calf were rubbed. Colouring was got from kermes oak insects (red), copperas (black), or vegetable dyes.

Leather was used in the Middle Ages for clothing, shoes, buckets, balls, sheaths, gloves, saddlery, bottles and jugs, luggage, bookbinding, shields, and defensive armour. Cordovan, or Spanish leather, was made from moufflon skin, and imitated in goatskin all over Europe. The *cordwainer* made shoes, with no heels until the late 16th century, and high boots even later. Cheaper footwear was made from oxhide. Excavations on Roman and medieval sites (eg York and Leicester) have yielded large quantities of leather footwear and other goods. In the 16th and 17th centuries, the repertory was extended to chair seats, furnishings, upholstery, and screens; and leather waterpipes appeared in the late 17th century. In the 19th century much leather was used for machine belting.

Leather crafts tend to be individual crafts, but they are now largely mechanised and the industry is now factory-based. In medieval times each household often made its own shoes. The 17th century demand for standard military footwear, which led to bulk orders in Northampton from 1642, initiated an organised industry, but boots and shoes were partly a cottage (outwork) industry in rural Northamptonshire even into the 20th century. Over a sixth of the *c* 30,000 male and 12,000 female boot- and shoemakers in 1900 worked at home or on their own account. Northamptonshire shoemaking was divided into processes by the mid 19th century, each process being "put out", returned to the employer, and "put out" for another process, often to different cottages, and so on till finished. The village bootmaker, on the other hand, carried out the whole job. Outworking was reduced in 1894, but only finally came to an end after the First World War. In Leicestershire the workshop houses of the knitwear workers, with long ranges of window, are often indistinguishable from those of the shoemakers; indeed, some were used first for one craft, then for the other.

Oak bark for tanning became scarcer in the 19th century, so chrome salts were imported instead and a leather industry grew in the ports (Liverpool, Bristol, London), which retained the heavy leather industry (shoe soles, machine belting). At the same time mineral tannage helped to revive the inland industries hit by the bark shortage. Northampton developed into the main inland centre in the later 19th century. Other important centres were Stafford and Norwich (late 18th–19th centuries), Wiltshire, and Somerset; gloves were made in this area, at Westbury, Yeovil, Taunton, and Sherborne (Do), using non-local skins after the early 19th century, and boots and shoes are now concentrated at Street. In 1850 one-third of all leather came from Surrey, mainly from Godalming, Chiddingfold, and Bermondsey (now London), with parchment from Carshalton and Hackworth. London is still an important centre for leather. The Leather Market in Bermondsey (Western Street) was founded in 1879 to serve the local tanning industry. Skins were handled here in medieval times, and from 1700 on it was a major leatherworking centre, some of which still survives.

Massive footwear imports have caused a decline in the British industry in recent years (since the 1950s). There were 349 firms active in the major centres in 1965, against 482 ten years earlier. These were mainly in London (36), Norwich (22), Northamptonshire (11 – mainly Rushden, Wellingborough, and Northampton), Leicestershire (112), and Lancashire (Rossendale, 38). Minor centres are Bristol, Kingswood, Street, Kendal, Leeds, Stafford, and Stone. The ports still make soles, but belting has moved to Yorkshire, Lancashire, and the Midlands. The shoe factories have been rationalised to meet the reduced demand (in 1985, two-thirds of the shoes in the shops were imports), and are now only assemblers.

Shoemaking in the Middle Ages, although widespread, was centred particularly in the cities and market towns and round the royal castles, from at least the 12th century. Oxford had a cordwainers guild in 1131, London by 1160, and Northampton by c 1200. Shoes were also sold at the great fairs. Measurements were standardised in 1305. By the 16th century the welted shoe came in, and heels in the 1590s. There was an industrial structure of modern type by the 1640s (as in other industries, eg glass). Northampton specialised in men's footwear, London in women's (with Oxford, York, and Bristol). Stafford and Norwich became important in the later 15th century. By the mid 18th century warehouses stocked and sold shoes of many makes, relying largely on a domestic industry of outworkers.

French imports hit the English trade from the 1820s, until the English makers copied them. Strong American influence in the 1850s led to the building of new single-storey factories. In the 1920s Northamptonshire turned to women's fashion shoes, but was affected by the slump in 1929, and from c 1935 by cheap exports from eastern Europe and more recently from Italy and Asia. The number of firms declined from the 1950s, partly for trade reasons, partly through amalgamations.

Mechanisation of the industry began early in the 19th century, with eg Brunel's sole-rivetting machine in 1810 (rivets had in fact been used by the Romans). This was followed by Preston's pegging machine (1833) and the Singer sewing machine of 1856. The first factories in Northampton (those of Isaac, Campbell & Co, and Moses Mansfield) were set up in 1857; they have three storeys and a semi-basement. Such factories were necessary to take the big Lyman Blake machine for stitching on soles (1864), which was steam-driven. The use of machines enabled the industry to grow in other towns, eg Leicester. From the 1860s to the 1890s all the hand processes were mechanised.

Yet domestic craft shoemaking continued, and there has been a reaction towards hand sewing and simple machines. Small workshops at the ends of cottage gardens can be seen, eg at Long Buckby (Nh). The half-moon knife, used in Egypt in the early 2nd millennium BC, is still in use.

Twentieth-century developments have included the direct moulding machine (of sole to upper), 1950, and the use of plastics and synthetic leathers from the late 1960s, which spread very rapidly, but with a reaction back to leather in the 1980s.

(See "Sites and Museums", page 577.)

POTTERY

Pottery has been made in this country for over 6,000 years, and is an essential feature of settled life. It serves or has served for food storage, preparation, cooking, and eating off, for containing cremated ashes or to accompany inhumations, more recently for ornament and prestige, and for specialised uses too, in medicine, industry, and science. So ubiquitous is it, so varied in form, material, making, and decoration, and so durable, even when broken into sherds, that it is one of the archaeologist's main diagnostic tools for unravelling the past. Yet the remains of pottery-making are far less visible than the pots themselves, and most of them have to be excavated.

Crude pottery can be made in a bonfire (which can reach some 700°C), as it still is in parts of Africa, but for better quality ware higher temperatures are required – 1150°C for stoneware and 1350°C for porcelain – which necessitates enclosed kilns and controlled firing. There seems to be little evidence for prehistoric kilns, although they certainly existed, but quite a lot for the Roman period.

Pottery was made all over Roman Britain – in fact, pottery is made wherever there is suitable clay. In 1956 85 Romano-British kilns were known and some 20 potteries or areas of intensive pottery-making. These latter included Alice Holt/Farnham (coarse ware), Water Newton/Castor (coarse and Castor ware) in the Nene valley near Peterborough where over 200 kilns have been found, the New Forest (colour-coated and stamped wares), round Oxford (colour-coated wares), Dorset (black-burnished ware), Yorkshire (Malton, Crambeck, Throlam), and many other centres. In addition to these industrial-scale centres there was much local manufacture; pottery was made near Roman forts to supply them and their *vici* or towns, eg round Lincoln or at Housesteads (Nd). At Holt (Du) there was a legionary pottery and tilery with a battery of kilns. Samian ware (glossy red-coated pottery, often decorated in relief) mostly came from Gaul, but some was made here, eg at Colchester, and Sandford (Ox).

Early pottery-making techniques and kiln types

Romano-British pottery-making has been studied intensively. The elegant work of Heywood Sumner in the New Forest is still memorable. The Alice Holt industry may be taken as an example. This was investigated by Major A G Wade from 1926 to 1949, in the 1950s by the Alice Holt Pottery Research Group, and from 1971 by the Alice Holt Survey Group (a general survey of the various excavations is contained in M A B Lyne and R S Jeffries: *The Alice Holt/ Farnham Roman Pottery Industry* (CBA Research Report 30, 1979). Eighty-two pottery dumps, some with kilns, were found in the Forest, with others at Malthouse Farm (7), Baigents Bridge (1), Tilford (1), and Farnham (12). The kilns were of the *double-flued updraught* type. Updraught kilns are the commonest, if not the only, Roman type, with one or two hearths and a flue to the chamber, which has a pedestal or perforated floor, of clay firebars or tiles; the pots were stacked on this and covered with turf, straw, and clay on a framework of branches. Such kilns have been reconstructed and fired, with good results. A kiln was excavated by A J Clark in 1947 at Overwey, Tilford, and then interpreted as a horizontal type, with no superimposed chamber but a chamber at flue level. This and similar kilns at Snailslynch and "Mr Langham's" have now been reinterpreted as updraught; updraught kilns can be used as horizontal by blocking off one flue. At Highgate (London), another important production centre, the kilns were updraught, with single hearth, a clay pedestal, and buttresses on the outside wall to hold firebars across to the pedestal (*London Archaeologist* 1, 2, spring 1969; 2, 1, 1972). Pots could also be fired in an open-topped oven; there is no evidence for clamps at this period (except possibly for tile-making, as at Ashtead (Sy)).

There is no space here to describe the very numerous kinds of pottery made in prehistoric and Roman (or indeed later) times; these can be studied in books (see "Further Reading", page 600), and are well presented in most museums of any size.

Neolithic and Bronze Age pottery in Britain was hand-built, not thrown and turned on a wheel; for large pots the coil technique was often used. The wheel was introduced in the later Iron Age (2nd century BC). The wheel was at first slow, hand-turned, and later kicked, even into the Middle Ages. The treadle, as applied to the lathe, which enabled a fast and steady motion, was in use in Roman times. (Samian ware was moulded.) When the Romans left Britain the use of the wheel lapsed, and early and middle Saxon pottery is hand-formed. From the late Saxon period on, the wheel was again used.

Medieval kilns could be of various forms, and could be altered during their lives; the pottery was determined not by the shape of the kiln, but by the method of firing and the degree of oxidisation. Kilns were all basically *updraught*: a *single-flue* type was used in the pre-conquest period for wheel-thrown pottery, and up to the 13th century (eg Olney Hyde); this was superseded by the *double-flue* type, with two flues side by side (as at Lyveden) or on opposite sides (as at Laverstock); the *multi-flue* type was used in the Midlands and northern England from the 13th century (eg Nuneaton, Harefield Lane, late 14th–early 15th century) to use all winds. All three types occur at once at Chilvers Coton, near Nuneaton. A multi-flue kiln is reconstructed at Stoke-on-Trent museum. The ovens were round or horseshoe-shaped. Most kilns could be open-topped – not permanently domed, but capped during firing with peat or turves laid on a tile base and bonded with clay. Large multi-flued kilns were, however, domed. Clamps are sometimes found, some for making kiln furniture. The pots were stacked upside down on a raised floor.

The fires were lit in the flues; the stoke-pits were for fresh fuel and to hold ashes cleared out of the flues. Some double- or multi-flue kilns have no internal structure – the pots were stacked on the floor, inverted. Firing went up to 1000°C in about 12 hours; wastage was high, due to underfiring or overfiring, bursting through moisture or too much temper, or from imperfect glazing. Moulds were not used; pots were usually thrown (eg at Lyveden in the 14th/15th centuries), but some at Lyveden in the early 13th century were hand-made and trued up on a turntable. Thrown bodies could be finished with coil necks. Lead glazes were used; coloured slip or figures were added as ornament.

The medieval industry was small-scale, producing mostly earthenware, sometimes with quite limited distribution. In the middle Anglo-Saxon period pottery was made widely throughout most of lowland England: the main centres were Ipswich (hard grey, some gritty, made on a slow wheel), Whitby (soft sandy), Maxey (hand-made), and the London area (including grass-tempered and shelly). In the Saxo-Norman period (850–1150), the main centres were Thetford (hard grey sandy, with local variations), St Neots (rough, with crushed shell), Stamford (fine off-white, also sandy coarse ware), Torksey (rough sandy), Lincoln (hard sandy), York (very hard and gritty – pimply), Nottingham (brown sandy, with glaze splashed on), and Winchester (hard sandy brown, with various colour glazes). There were several other centres with merely local distribution. Most of this pottery was made in single-flue kilns with pedestals. Pottery was imported from the Rhineland and northern France also.

During the later Middle Ages most pottery was made in the countryside by peasants a with special skill (as at Lyveden); a few towns, however, had an artisan class which included potters, although for many of these pottery-making could be part-time or seasonal. But 54 out of the 62 sites excavated from 1956 to 1980 were in the countryside. Stamford continued in production till the end of the 13th century, but from then on production was scattered and regional. Distinctive types include the white wares of Surrey. Pottery was also imported (through Southampton, London, and other ports) from south-west France (including "Saintonge ware").

Kilns should not be seen in isolation but in their context: kilns or groups of kilns were associated with specific places, such as those at Laverstock (late 13th to early 14th centuries) supplying Clarendon Palace and Salisbury. Lyveden (Nh) (early 13th to early 14th centuries), which was the archaeological breakthrough in understanding medieval pottery techniques, may represent peasant craft production with a limited marketing area. Tiles, at least at first (13th century), were made in bulk for a specific contract, eg a palace or major church; by the 14th century factories were set up for commercial sale.

Excavation has shown that a medieval pottery consisted of: kilns; a workshop for potting, making glazes and slips, glazing, and pugging; stores for materials and finished pots; a clay storage pit; a puddling pit; a waste dump; a fuel store or stack (on stones); and a covered area for drying pots. Larger kilns were in use in the 14th to 16th centuries, allowing increased output.

Foreign influences in the 16th century, together with greatly increased demand, changed the whole nature and scale of the industry. The lead-glazed earthenwares of the Middle Ages gave place to tin-glazed earthenware (maiolica and delft), salt-glazed stoneware, and slipwares, through the porcelains and the varied developments of the 18th century, to the high-quality mass production of the 19th and 20th centuries, culminating in the revival of the hand-made craft tradition but at an altogether higher level of sophistication. From this has emerged the great range of creative studio pottery, some of it of oriental or African inspiration (see below).

Maiolica and stoneware were imported into England in the early 16th century, but were not made here till later. There was an influx of skilled craftsmen, of various trades, mainly from Germany and the Low Countries, in the mid 16th century, and from France in the 1570s. Large numbers settled in Norwich and round London, where they could not carry on their crafts in the City, so lived in the outskirts, particularly in Southwark. Rhoda Edwards ("London Potters c 1570–1710", *Journal of Ceramic History* 6, 1974) has traced no fewer than 25 potteries in the London area, of which four were north of the river. The other 21 were close to the south bank, from Woolwich to Mortlake; Southwark and Lambeth had seven each.

Earthenware and slipware were made in London until into the 18th century, beginning in Greenwich about 1540. Tin-glaze may have begun in 1540, but there is no firm evidence until 1568 in Norwich and 1571 in London. Stoneware may have begun by 1580 and there is some evidence for a date of 1614; Dwight's famous factory at Fulham, still to be seen, dates from 1672. The kilns were 8–10ft square, arched at the top, and wood-fired; the pots were packed in close. (A report of a recent excavation of such a kiln is Brian Bloice: *Norfolk House, Lambeth: Excavations at a Delftware Kiln Site*, 1968 (*Post-Medieval Archaeology* 5, 1971).) More recently still, an important Delftware pottery has been found at Platform Wharf, Rotherhithe (*c* 1638–62) during excavations on a royal palace by the Museum of London in 1986/87 (see *The London Archaeologist* 5, 15, 1988).

By the late 17th century the kilns began to be enclosed in a tall building called a *hovel*, narrowing at the top to form a chimney to control the draught and send it upwards. This soon developed into the *bottle oven* (see **391**), which became characteristic of pottery manufacture until recent years. The furnace itself, inside the bottle, was domed and reverberatory, so *saggars* were used; these are refractory clay containers in which the pots are packed to protect them from direct heat. The use of saggars also enabled the risky practice of placing small fragile vessels inside larger or more robust ones to be discontinued. Smaller, *muffle*, kilns were used for the final, or enamel, firing. Bricks, tiles, and sanitary ware were made in down-draught *beehive* kilns, sometimes also in bottles (see page 504). Calcining kilns too were often built like bottle ovens (see below).

In the 19th century the bottles were often enclosed in the buildings of the pot-banks, so that only the tops could be seen. But

391 *Bottle ovens – Etruria (St), 19th-century: once a ubiquitous sight in the Potteries.*

the townscape of the Potteries (the Six Towns of Burslem, Tunstall, Hanley, Stoke-on-Trent, Longton, and Fenton) was till recently determined by scores of bottles, under a pall of smoke.

In the early 20th century some down-draught bottle ovens were built, with a chimneystack alongside. This was an attempt to increase the efficiency of the firing process; several earlier improvements had been made, including Hoffman's continuous circular kiln of 1858. But since the Second War a decisive departure from the long tradition was taken, the gas-fired continuous horizontal *tunnel* kiln; this uses a conveyor belt, and does away with batch production. The bottles suddenly became obsolete in the 1950s, and few are now left. But enough remain to reflect, however faintly, the former character of the Potteries.

From the 18th century the pottery industry was largely concentrated in the Six Towns in Staffordshire because of the presence of suitable clay. At first this was quarried next to each pottery. As each section was worked out the quarry was backfilled with kiln-waste – pottery sherds and broken saggars (*shraff*). Much of this land later became built on. It is one of the most intriguing experiences in industrial archaeology to look down a hole in the road in the Six Towns and find it filled nearly to the surface with broken pottery, and to realise that much of this considerable conurbation is in fact built on the waste of the industry which created its prosperity. Many of the late 18th- and early 19th-century potteries were built beside canals, the normal means of transport at the time.

The Potteries are a conspicuous and informative centre of the industry, still operative in a highly sophisticated form. Firms have merged or in some cases changed their image, or broadened it; all have remodelled their premises and plant in the light of current technology. They have to operate in a highly competitive market worldwide.

Pottery types

It is outside our scope to describe in detail the various types of ware; these should be sought in the relevant books, eg David M Wilson: *The Archaeology of Anglo-Saxon England* (1976); K J Barton: *Pottery in England* (1975); W B Honey: *English Pottery and Porcelain* (1969). (See also "Further Reading", page 600.) The earlier wares showed local differences (see above). But from the later 15th century the situation changed radically; in addition to the profusion of domestic types, and a spread of the coarse, brown and red "Cistercian" wares, salt-glazed stoneware began to be imported from Germany and the Low Countries, which led to far-reaching changes later. During the 16th century pottery became urban and highly industrialised. Immigrant workers in all crafts, including potters, came to England by the mid century, with profound effects. A lively industry in tin-glazed earthenware (maiolica and delft) was set up from the 1540s; London became the main centre for this, and, in the later 17th century (from *c* 1684), for stoneware as well. Slipware was popular in the 17th and early 18th century, at first with slip heavily applied (Toft), later all-over and combed. By the later 17th century Burslem was growing, thanks to its rich source of suitable clay, and the Potteries became the scene, throughout the 18th century, not only of large-scale manufacture of domestic earthenware but of the long search for a realistic substitute for Chinese porcelain. This search led to several beautiful forms of *soft-paste* (having a formula similar to glass), but the final breakthrough did not come until the 1740s, when William Cookworthy of Plymouth first used kaolin – the Cornish china-clay – and petuntse – Cornish stone – and succeeded in producing a genuine *hard-paste* (Cookworthy's patent is 1768). But the Potteries specialised in *bone china*, a body similar to hard-paste porcelain, but containing 50% of crushed bone ash.

Salt-glazed stoneware with a white body was developed in the Potteries in the 1720s. John Astbury, about 1720, had invented a substitute for hard-paste porcelain which brought this within reach of a wider market, and laid the foundation for the prosperity of the Potteries. This salt-glazed ware, white throughout, and hard and translucent, depended on white-burning clay imported from outside Staffordshire, to which was added crushed and calcined flint (one part of flint to four of clay) which increased the hardness of the clay; silica is an important constituent of glazes too. The flints were first calcined in a kiln, and then crushed to a very fine powder in a special mill. The mill consisted of a heavy stone wheel, set vertically, and rotating in a trough (not unlike a Normandy apple-press). A good example at Cheddleton (St) has been restored, but they existed in Leeds, London, Co Durham, and elsewhere. An unusual type is found near Kirkcaldy (Fi), where at Balwearie and Hole, on the Tiel Burn, are the remains of flint mills in which the flints were crushed by four large stone blocks pushed round on top of them by wooden paddles. These date from the 1740s and 1750s. The white earthenware of Whieldon and later Wedgwood was based on china clay, ball clay, crushed flint, and Cornish stone.

Other centres developed their own specialities, some of which determined the character of 19th- and even 20th-century pottery. These included Bristol, Swansea, Sunderland (lustre and transfer-printing), Leeds (a fine light creamware), Liverpool (transfer-printing), Chelsea and Bow in London (soft-paste), Fulham (stoneware), Lambeth, Derby, Plymouth, Poole, Worcester, Lowestoft, Rockingham, and Coalport. This list of course sums up many of the famous names in figure as well as domestic pottery.

The early 19th century saw the popularity of *ironstone*; much statuary (figure) pottery and fine tableware was produced throughout the century, and by the end craft and studio pottery, characteristic of the 20th century, was coming in. This owed much of its stimulus to William Morris and his revival of medieval craftsmanship, followed by William de Morgan (tiles) and the Arts and Crafts movement; but equally powerful was the Japanese influence of Bernard Leach and his successors, and the African and "English peasant" influences of Michael Cardew. This studio pottery is now firmly established, and necessarily uses basic equipment and techniques (Leach indeed used wood-fired kilns).

Bernard Leach has been followed by his son David; other influential 20th-century potters include William Staite Murray (decorated vases), Lucie Rie, Hans Coper, Katherine Pleydell-Bouverie, Alan Caiger-Smith, Henry Hammond, Paul Barron, and Eric James Mellon. Examples of their works can be seen in museums. Potters of the younger generation include Julian King-Salter, Phil Rogers, Bernard Charles, and Peter Hayes. Influential designers include Keith Murray, and decorators such as Susie Cooper had a wide following in the 1920s and 1930s.

19th and 20th-century pottery-making techniques and kiln types

The basic techniques of pottery-making have hardly changed in principle. The clay is dug and left in heaps to weather. It is then made into a slip by mixing with water in a tank, and *puddled* or trodden, or stirred with paddles or (from the later 19th century) pounded in a *blunger*. When temper (material added to the clay to give it body) was used, it was added at this stage; temper was standard from prehistoric and Roman times into the Middle Ages – first shell, chalk, or grass, later sand, stones, grog (crushed pottery), or crushed flint. It was less used after the 15th century, but grog and flint continued to be used until the 19th century. The slip is then dried in a *sun-pan* (a stone-lined pit) and left to evaporate (there is a sun-pan at Wetheriggs Country Pottery, Penrith (Cu)); the drying could be speeded by passing hot air under the tank. From the mid 19th century the slip was passed through a *filter press* instead of being evaporated. The slip is made into balls and left till wanted. The balls of clay then have to be *wedged* (cut up and the pieces slapped hard against each other, to expel the air), either by hand or, after the 1820s, in mechanical *pugmills*.

The prepared clay is then built up into pots, using different methods. Prehistoric pottery was made by the *lump* method (hand-shaping) or built up in *coils*. From *c* 100 BC the *wheel* enabled clay to be thrown and raised under rotary motion; the previous turntable was then speeded up, at first as a kick-wheel and later worked by treadle or a power source. The clay can be made into *slabs* or *bats* and pressed into *moulds*, or sand- or slip-*cast*. Moulds were made of clay until *c* 1770, when plaster of Paris took its place. At this stage handles, spouts, etc are added, and the pot trimmed or *fettled*; pottery figures etc are assembled. The "green" pot must then be left to dry, either in the open air or in a gentle heat, until "leather-hard". Underglaze decoration, if used, is added at this stage, and decoration such as sgraffito or incision.

The pot is then *biscuit*, or first, fired. Some wares need to be fired once only (such as bricks, pipes, quarry tiles, salt-glazed stoneware, saggars, statuary porcelain, terracotta (unless glazed), and garden pottery (eg that of G F Watts)); in the 17th and 18th centuries green ware had lead glaze applied in dust form. But most pottery needs two firings. From the 16th century saggars – refractory clay containers – were used to separate the pots. Flatwares were bedded in flint to prevent warping, and figures were propped up to avoid sagging. Biscuit firing reaches 1000–1150°C, and temperature has to be controlled by dampers and regulating holes, using cones and other indicating devices. Stoneware needs firing to *c* 1280°C.

After biscuit firing the pots can be decorated – painted or transfer-printed (after *c* 1750) and *glazed*, normally by dipping, and often nowadays by spraying. Lead glazes, once normal, are no longer used. The glazed pots then need to be fired again (the *short* firing) to *c* 1080°C;

they are separated in the saggars by props (stilts, spurs, and thimbles) to prevent them sticking to each other. This is normally the final process, but if *on-glaze* decoration is required, enamel colours are applied at this stage, and the pot is refired at a lower temperature (500–800°C) to fix the enamel. This process can be repeated for different colours. Enamel firing was done in a smaller *muffle kiln*, not in the large bottle oven. As stated above, the bottle kilns have been replaced by *tunnel kilns*, which save time in placing, waiting for the oven to cool, and drawing. Specialised pottery, such as tiles, bricks, saggars, electrical porcelain, and sanitary ware, is, since the mid 19th century, made from *powdered clay*; these types of pottery are made in brick-type kilns.

(See "Sites and Museums", pages 577–8.)

BRICKS

(Bricks and tiles as building materials are dealt with on pages 190–4 and 197, encaustic tiles on page 185, and mathematical tiles on page 191.)

The manufacture of bricks shows a steady evolution. L S Harley (1974) describes six stages of development:

1 hand-moulding (used for prehistoric sun-dried bricks and for Iron Age salt evaporation pans – "briquetage")

2 "butter-pat" moulding (used in Britain until the late Middle Ages)

3 the "pastry" method – a sheet of clay cut up with a spade (used for Roman tiles, and Saxon and early medieval "great bricks")

4a moulded in a frame, dried in a shed, and fired in a clamp or kiln (13th–20th century) – these could have frogs (see below)

4b moulded on straw or sand in a frame, and left to dry *in situ* (12th–13th century "great bricks")

5 extruded and cut by wire (*c* 1855 on – no frog unless re-pressed)

6 mechanically pressed – various forms, including frog and name or trademark

The *frog*, a depression in the upper face of the brick to assist in keying the mortar, came into use in the 1690s, when it was a slot scooped by a finger. In the earlier 18th century a piece of wood was used, and resulted in a deeper and wider frog. By the later 18th century the frog was on average 1in (2.5cm) wide and 4 or 5in (10 or 12.5cm) long. In the early 19th century the slot was rectangular, sometimes with rounded corners, and some 6" x 2$\frac{1}{2}$" x $\frac{1}{2}$–1" (15 x 6.25 x 1.25–2.5cm) deep – this type is still used on handmade bricks. From about 1830 the frog had a triangular section, often with the maker's name or mark.

Some churches in Essex and eastern England incorporate thin red tiles, which may be Roman from a nearby villa etc or may, like some at Brixworth (Nh), be Saxon. Brickmaking began again in East Anglia in the early 13th century, with a large brick called a "great brick". This was in use until the early 16th century. Coggeshall Abbey (Ex) used "great bricks" in 1148–67 and sold them to 16 other churches. They were entirely superseded, if not at once, by the *Flemish* bricks from which all later bricks derive. These were imported from the Low Countries in the mid 13th century (Little Wenham Hall (So) has them *c* 1260–80); they appear at King's Lynn by *c* 1275 and at Hull by the end of the century. They came in two sizes, 9–10$\frac{1}{2}$" x 5–6$\frac{1}{2}$" x 1$\frac{1}{2}$"–2" (22.5–26.25 x 12.5–16.25 x 3.75–5cm); and 9" x 4$\frac{1}{2}$" x 2" (22.5 x 11.25 x 5cm). P J Drury (1981) sees them as linked at first to the Hanseatic trading area; they are found in Hansa towns on both sides of the North Sea, in Britain in all the major ports from Scarborough to Southampton, including York and London, and at Bristol. The other influence was the wool trade with Flanders, which peaked in the late 13th to early 14th century; wool was exported from England, bricks imported. But the demand in England soon outstripped this supply, and they began to be made in England (eg at Writtle (Ex) in 1427), though the 15th-century kilns were often operated by Flemings. Drury suggests a link here between the decline in wool exports in favour of English cloth production, in which Flemings were much involved, and the rise of English brickmaking in eastern England largely in the hands of Flemings and Germans. Essex and Kent were the main centres of brick production.

Very little survives of the earlier phases of brickmaking, but several early kilns have been excavated, such as the late 12th-century updraught tile kiln discovered in the centre of Farnham (Sy) in 1985; obsolete and disused kilns can sometimes be found in long-established or derelict brickworks. Hand-moulding methods can be seen in some brickworks.

Brickworks were usually sited next to a source of suitable clay, and many have such quarries still in use. The clay was stacked over the winter to weather, and kneaded with bare feet in the spring. The *pugmill*, a machine in which the clay could be kneaded by a spiral of horizontal knives, to force out air and reduce impurities, was probably invented by the Dutch in the 17th century. This could be operated by horses, and saved much labour. Various ingredients are added at this stage, such as crushed shale for pressed bricks, sand, manganese dioxide to control the colour, or barium carbonate to counter the effect of salts in the clay. The clay then went through a *pan mill*, where it was crushed by two heavy rollers and forced through perforations in a pan below; this could be a dry pan for hard clays and semi-dry pressing or wet for hand-moulding and soft-mud processes. Dry-ground clays were sifted on a piano-wire screen which retained oversize pieces for further grinding. A number of machines have been developed to refine these processes.

Simplifying, the clay could now be hand-moulded, moulded in frames, extruded and cut, or mechanically pressed. The bricks were then stacked under open sheds to dry and harden, and then fired. Up to the 18th century they were often fired in *clamps*, which were carefully made stacks of bricks, spaced to allow hot gases to circulate, and with fire channels in the base; these were covered with turf and old bricks, and fired. A temperature of up to 1150°C was necessary.

Besides clamps the Romans used an open-topped kiln in which the bricks were set out on the floor and covered with old bricks; two or three fire tunnels under the floor allowed the heat to rise through the bricks by way of slots in the floor. Wood was usually the fuel, but coal could be used instead, on grates. This type of kiln continued into the Middle Ages (eg that at Farnham – see above) and evolved into the *Suffolk* kiln. The last wood-fired Suffolk kiln was used at Ashburnham (Sx) until 1968, and a coal-fired Suffolk was operating near Lowestoft until 1982.

In the 18th century the *Scotch* updraught kiln was developed from the clamp, and this type is still in use, eg at Aldeburgh (Su) or Chesham (Bc). This is a squarish open-topped chamber, with a central wall to reduce cross-draughts. Along each side is a row of fireholes linked by covered channels. The spaces are filled with bricks to be fired, and covered over.

In north-east England the standard kiln was the *Newcastle* type, which had a long vaulted chamber. The smaller ones have fireholes at one end and a chimney at the other; larger ones have fireholes at each end and a central flue.

Downdraught kilns ("beehives") have domed or barrel roofs, with fireholes in the walls. The heat is directed by screens up to the roof, where it is reflected down onto the bricks, passing through them and out by way of a perforated floor to an outside chimney.

The multi-chamber kiln was a 19th-century invention, of which the best known variant is the *Hoffmann* kiln of 1856. This had a continuous annular gallery in which the bricks were set, divided into twelve or more chambers, each with a flue leading to a main flue and chimney. Hoffmann improved this in 1870 to a rectangular version, and there have been refinements since. The *transverse-arch* kiln grew out of this about 1890, with its *Staffordshire* form in 1904 which was in use until the mid 20th century. The *Belgian* kiln, with rows of grates, was patented in 1891, and could produce enough heat to make facings and firebricks. The French invented a *tunnel* kiln in 1751 for porcelain, of which several variants were tried (eg the Monnier top-fired type). The tunnel type was adopted in Britain only sparingly for bricks until the 1970s.

There is thus a variety of kilns in use or only recently superseded, and much can be learnt by visiting different brickworks. Some early kilns have been preserved, such as the bottle kiln at Nettlebed (Ox). Many brickworks closed in the 1960s owing to the wider use of concrete in building, and the remains of some of these survive. Massed brickworks can be visually impressive, eg the great London Brick Company complex at Fletton, south of Peterborough.

The colour, hardness, and consistency of a brick, of course, depend on the clay or clay mixture it was made from, the type of preparation of the clay (wet, dry, etc), and the degree of oxidisation in the firing. Thus blue bricks are made from an iron-rich clay from Staffordshire; yellow London stock bricks have ground chalk mixed with the clay and are made by the soft-mud process; Flettons, used for facings from 1882, have a high carbon content and are semi-dry before pressing – they are sandblasted to match other kinds of facing bricks; shale from the Coal Measures produces the hard, deep red bricks typical of the Midlands; Midhurst bricks are white; "rubbers", for window and doorway arches, were made from the 17th century to the 1980s of sandy red clay, well fired and hand-moulded; fireclays are made into firebricks and special shapes – low-grade fireclays are glazed for special effects. A fuller

list, and much useful background, is given in Martin Hammond: *Bricks and Brickmaking* (Shire 1981).

GLASS

Glass has long been one of the indispensable elements of our way of life, but is temperamental and difficult to make. The industry is a fascinating one in which most of the features are unique; the main lines of its history in Britain are well worth sketching here.

Glass is a strange material. Technically it is a supercooled liquid; its structure is amorphous and non-crystalline, which explains why a crack runs unchecked to the edge of the piece, and a blow results in cracks in all directions. The ingredients of glass, and the technique of glassmaking, remained virtually unchanged until new industrial processes were developed in the 17th and 18th centuries (see below). Traditionally, glass is made from silica (sand), which, in the past, had to be mixed with a flux such as soda or potash to bring the melting-point down from that of silica (c 1800°C) to a figure (1150–1500°C) which could be handled by the primitive furnaces available; lime was also required, and other ingredients could be added to produce special effects.

Manufacture involved several stages:

1   *Fritting*: the ingredients – soda was used as a flux in the ancient world, derived from natron or from the ash of maritime plants, such as barilla – were mixed and heated in a pottery crucible (*pot*) to about 7–800°C, a temperature too low to produce complete fusion and liquefaction but high enough to lead to granulation and a semi-vitreous condition (*frit*). The scum resulting from this was skimmed off, and lumps of it occur at glasshouse sites.

2   The residue, when cool, was broken up, placed in another pot, and mixed with *cullet*, broken glass, which helped fusion and reduced the cost of fuel and materials. This was heated to c 1200°C, when it melted. At this stage lime was added (but not in early Wealden glass, where enough lime was contained in the vegetable ash), as well as any other additives required (eg metallic oxides for colour – but see below for another method of obtaining colour).

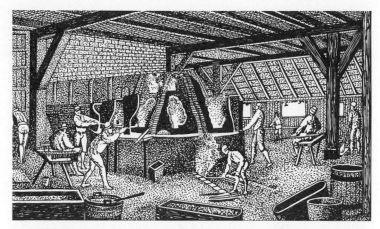

393 *Inside a glasshouse: we see the vertical furnace, with a man tending the fire, and others drawing glass from the second level, and two gaffers in their chairs crafting the glassware (from Diderot and d'Alembert's* Encyclopédie *of 1772).*

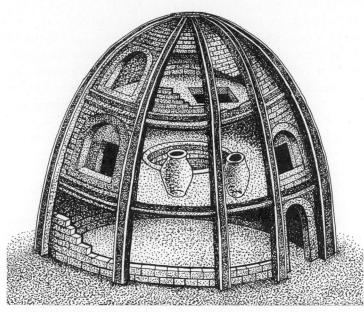

392 *Glass furnace of southern (Venetian) type: this is a vertical furnace in three stages – the fire at ground level, the glass-melting above (two pots (crucibles) can be seen), and lower-temperature processes (such as annealing) at the top.*

3   At the right consistency, "gobs" (lumps) of glass could then be "gathered" (taken out of the pot) on the end of a rod with a knob at the end (a *pontil*) or on a blow-pipe or *blowing-iron*; the gob could be worked up into window glass, vessel glass, etc.

4   When the product was made it had to be *annealed*, to eliminate differences of stress inside the glass, and avoid shattering. This was done by heating slowly in a separate oven, and cooling slowly.

Glass of a sort was known in Mesopotamia in the 3rd millennium BC, and to the Egyptians by about 2000 BC. By the 18th Dynasty (*c* 1500 BC) glass vessels were being made by the *core moulding* technique, in which a sand or clay core in the shape of the object was coated with glass and decorated or coloured as required, the core being picked out when the glass had cooled. This technique continued at eg Alexandria until into the Roman period.

The main line, however, was developed by the Syrians, who revolutionised the industry by inventing inflational *glass-blowing* in the later

1st century BC, an invention taken at once into the Roman world. Glass-blowing enabled glass articles to be plentiful and cheap, and the technology soon took root in Europe, including France, Germany, and even Britain, where several glassmaking centres are known. Several villas, as well as official buildings, had glass windows, and glass vessels were used in them. After the Romans left Britain the use of glass died out; but the Anglo-Saxons imported drinking vessels from the Continent, and some monasteries – eg Canterbury, Glastonbury, Jarrow, and Monkwearmouth – revived its use for windows. The two former set up glasshouses, and Bede records that the two latter sent for glassmakers from the Continent to make glass for them and to teach the English to do so (late 7th–early 8th century). But this did not lead to the establishment of a permanent industry. Glass was also made in Viking York and Lincoln.

The furnaces in which this glass was made, a type still the norm in the Mediterranean world, have been conveniently called the "southern" type by R J Charleston. These furnaces were round and beehive-shaped (see **392**); they had three tiers, the lowest for the fire, the middle for melting the glass (the crucibles stood on *sieges* – raised platforms or benches – inside holes in the outer wall 3ft (90cm) or so above the ground), and the upper tier for the lower temperature processes such as fritting, *pot-arching* (preheating the crucibles to prevent their cracking or bursting), and annealing (see **393**).

In the 11th and 12th centuries a new demand for glass arose for the castles and manor houses, and the churches, cathedrals, and abbeys, which sprang up all over Europe. This led to a spread of the industry north of the Alps, into central and western Europe, a movement which reached England in the first half of the 13th century, if not earlier. The increased demand outstripped the supply of soda from the Mediterranean, and the glassmakers turned to the ash of the products of the forests where they set up the new glasshouses – the beech and oakwood they burnt as fuel, and forest plants such as bracken. These yielded *potash* instead of soda as the flux.

It was found that coloured glass, wanted by the churches, could be made without the use of oxide additives, but, if beechwood was used as the fuel, by controlling the oxidisation of the firing. A wide range of colours could be obtained in this way. The method is described in a famous treatise by a monk, Theophilus – *De Diversibus Artibus*, written about 1110–40 (new translation by C R Dodwell, 1961). It was also found that the best form of furnace to facilitate control of oxidisation was one with a central straight fire-trench, with banks (sieges) each side for the pots to stand on and the fire at one or both ends of the trench. This type, with a rectangular and not circular plan, and with pots on one level only, therefore became the norm in central and western Europe (Charleston's "northern" type). Lower temperature processes were sometimes on the Continent (eg at Trestenshult, Sweden) carried out in lateral chambers joined to the main furnace, but in England, at least until the later 16th century, were done in separate small ovens.

The Forest industry, as it is called, concentrated in the areas where beech was most plentiful – Bohemia, parts of Germany, eastern and northern France and Belgium, and Normandy between Le Havre and Beauvais. England, as it happens, was at the northern limit of beech 1,000 years ago and, although beechwood was used when convenient, nearly all the medieval glasshouses were in virtually exclusively oak country, and burnt oakwood. A minute quantity of coloured glass, using additives, was made experimentally in the 15th and 16th centuries (eg at Chaleshurst (Sx)), but until the later 16th century English glass was just greenish, owing to the iron and other impurities in the sand, and throughout the Middle Ages English demands for coloured glass were met by imports from Normandy.

Syrian glassmakers settled in Italy under the Roman Empire, and their ideas and methods necessarily influenced early European glassmaking. But another wave of ideas reached Normandy as a result of the Crusades. For instance, *crown* glass had been invented in Syria about AD 700, together with specially designed furnaces for annealing it. Crown glass was made by blowing a sphere of glass, then cutting off the blowpipe, attaching a rod (*pontil*) to the other side, then spinning the sphere rapidly on the end of the rod until it opened out into a circular sheet with a thickening (the bull's-eye) in the centre where the sheet had been attached. This idea reached Normandy about 1200, and eventually England (see below). The other type of window glass, *muff* (a cylinder slit lengthwise and opened out), was made by the Romans and reached central Europe, including Lorraine, whence it came to England.

Glassmaking *crucibles* were of coil-made pottery, either bucket- or barrel-shaped, with open tops for ease of extracting the glass. They were of various sizes and thicknesses, of which the commonest held about a hundredweight of glass. Some appear to have been made at the glasshouses and fired in a melting furnace, not necessarily of local clay; but some seem to have been made elsewhere and brought to the glasshouses. The clays of Stourbridge and Dorset were suitable for crucibles. The rims were of various forms – flattened, rolled, pinched-in, etc – and each glasshouse had its distinctive rim or small group of rims. Breakages were not uncommon, and the main furnace at Blunden's Wood, Hambledon (Sy) had to be abandoned because its fire-trench became choked with molten glass spilt from the pots.

For well over a century after the Norman conquest the English requirements for glass had to be met by imports from Normandy. But in 1226 one Laurence Vitrearius is recorded as making glass in the Weald. This date is subject to different readings, and may be as late as the 1240s. From then on glass was made in a tight group of parishes in the Weald – Chiddingfold, Kirdford, Wisborough Green, Ewhurst, Alfold, Hambledon, Lurgashall, and Billingshurst, using local Weald clay for the furnaces, which were crude affairs made of rough stones embedded in clay, sand probably from Chiddingfold, Hambledon, or Lodsworth, and coppice wood and local plants for fuel and potash. This Norman-inspired industry is also found in Staffordshire, Cheshire (Vale Royal), and other places (eg for Salisbury Cathedral).

English Forest glass is divided into two phases: Early, from the mid 13th century to the 1560s; Late, from the 1560s to *c* 1615. Some 80 glasshouses are known in all, some 45 in the Weald, of which half are Early. No doubt others await discovery. The sites show on

350 *The Automobile Association (AA), in the early 20th century, put up distinctive yellow and black signs in towns and villages all over the country. A few can still be found. This one is in the Chalk Pits Museum at Amberley (Sx).*

307 *A hollow or sunken lane. Such lanes are common on slopes in sandstone country, particularly in southern England, and were caused by the continual wear of foot, horse and wheeled traffic, accentuated by rain and frost. Some have been surfaced as roads, and so fossilised; others, like this one at Selborne (Ha), are much as they have been for centuries.*

A tower windmill at Heckington (Li),
showing the machinery:

1, the sails;

2, revolving cap on

3, cogged curb, activated by

4, fan tails;

5, the brake wheel, which engages with

6, the wallower at the head of

7, the shaft, on which lower down is

8, the great spur wheel, which is geared to

9, the nuts which drive

10, the mill stones, which are fed from

11, hoppers and bins on the floor above;

12, the governor, which regulates the
speed at which the mill stones revolve.

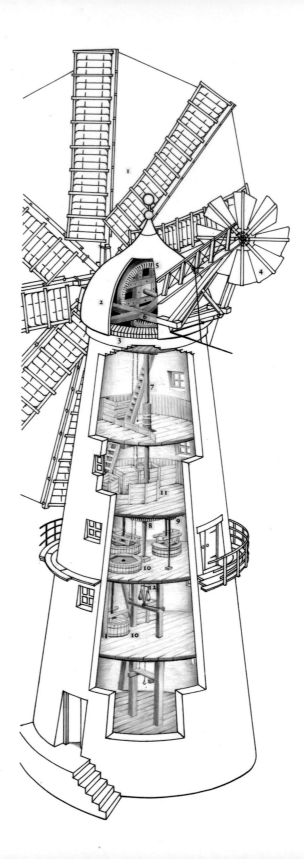

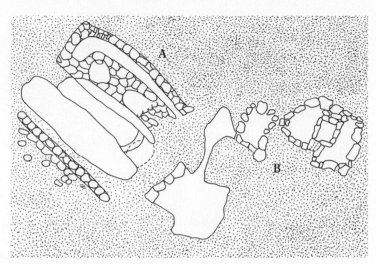

394 *Plan of a forest glasshouse of c 1330 – Blunden's Wood, Hambledon (Sy): this has a northern type furnace (horizontal, with central fire-trench and two banks (sieges) for the pots A; at B are separate small ovens for subsidiary processes.*

395 *A reconstruction (in the Pilkington Glass Museum at St Helen's) of the Blunden's Wood glasshouse: the roof would probably have been shingled (or tiled in late glasshouses), not thatched.*

the ground as low mounds, often on the edges of stream banks, with burnt soil and stones (in Late cases bricks and tiles as well), broken crucibles, and glass. The mounds cover the constituents of the glasshouses – one or more melting furnaces, subsidiary furnaces (mainly in the Early period), cullet heaps, and often a clay pit or pond. Bricks are found on Late sites, as are tiles from the roof of the shed which covered the furnaces; Early glasshouses were usually roofed with shingles. Glasshouses were rarely long-lived; the life of a furnace was about two years, and that of a crucible three months. Some glasshouses seem to have been worked seasonally, by men otherwise engaged in farming; but some were the sole trade of professional experts. The secrets of the craft were in the hands of quite a small number of families.

The fragmentary or disturbed nature of most sites inhibited full understanding of the Forest industry, although much is owed to the pioneer excavators such as S E Winbolt and the Rev T S Cooper; Hugh Kenyon's masterly summary of knowledge up to 1967 (*The Glass Industry of the Weald*) laid a solid foundation for later work. Since 1960 several sites have come to light which have enabled more complete excavation to be carried out (by eg David Crossley, Ruth Hurst Vose, Norman Bridgwater, Denis Ashurst, and Eric Wood), and this, together with economic studies such as those of Eleanor Godfrey

and David Crossley, technical studies like those of W E S Turner and R G Newton, and historical surveys of glass and furnaces such as those of D B Harden, R J Charleston, and Hugh Tait, have put understanding of the industry on a new level.

The first of the recent excavations was also that of the earliest glasshouse to be dated – Blunden's Wood, Hambledon (Sy), put at *c* AD 1330 by archaeomagnetism and the associated pottery (see **394** and **395**). This small glasshouse consisted of a main furnace of the usual northern type (see above), fired from both ends, two subsidiary ovens, one of them probably for annealing, and a cullet store. Blunden's Wood is typical of the Early phase. At Bagot's Park (St), David Crossley found no fewer than 14 furnaces scattered over a wide area. That selected for excavation was of the same type as at Blunden's Wood, with a smaller oven close by for annealing. This is dated *c* 1530.

The last of the Early glasshouses so far excavated is that at Knightons, Alfold (Sy), dated to the early 1550s (see **396**). This had a working furnace of the same medieval type, fired at one end only; this was soon replaced by another of the same type, in almost the same place. There was another similar furnace, used for fritting at least. The new feature at Knightons was a furnace with two square chambers side by side and linked together, for annealing crown sheets. It is indeed possible that this glasshouse was set up by workers from Normandy expressly to make crown, for which the demand was increasing. This type of annealing furnace has not been found elsewhere in England and may have reached Europe via the Crusades. Knightons also had a large cullet store, a pond for potash-making

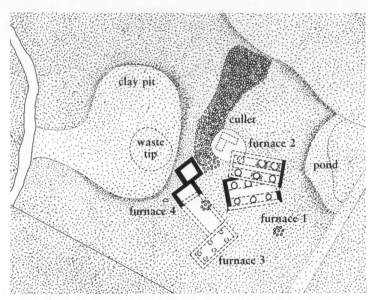

396 *Glasshouse at Knightons, Alfold (Sy), 1550s: a very complete site, at the transition between the Early and Late periods of Forest glass; the large melting furnace (furnace 1) was replaced by furnace 2 on an overlapping site; furnace 3 was connected to a two-chamber annealing furnace (furnace 4) designed to take crown sheets, and unique in Britain; the other features were well-developed.*

etc, and a claypit in which was a tip for furnace waste, which gave valuable evidence for the glass made there. Apart from crown, Knightons produced almost the full range of glassware in use at the time – bottles, drinking vessels, urinals, blood-letting vessels, hourglasses, linen-smoothers, plates and bowls, distilling apparatus. The remains of this site are displayed as a feature of the Forestry Commission's Trail in Sidney Wood. The Early type of furnace lingered into the Late period, and a complete example exists at Jamestown, Virginia, USA (1608), now restored as a working glasshouse.

In the 1560s demand, based on the rising prosperity of the middle classes and the beginnings of the Great Rebuilding, caused an increase in the number of glasshouses and attracted commercial interests. In 1567 an Antwerp entrepreneur, Jean Carré, set up a furnace at Fernfold (Sx), and in 1571 brought over Venetians to make soda-glass in London. The glass of the Early period had been yellowish-green, more or less opaque, and very subject to weathering; the glass of the Late period now beginning was harder, bluish-green, but clearer and more translucent than the Early, and did not weather so easily.

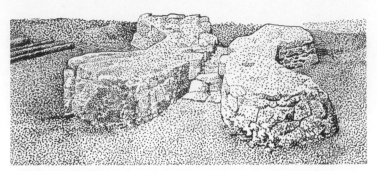

397 *The Rosedale glass furnace. This shows the furnace during reconstruction at the Ryedale Folk Museum, Hutton-le-Hole (NY).*

Two sites indeed, Sidney Wood (Sy) (c1610) and Woodchester (Gl) (c 1590–1615), produced glass of a very high quality. This improvement was partly due to improved furnaces; those of the Early period had been rough and very vulnerable. The Late furnaces were made of dressed stones or brick, and designed on geometrical lines, even if the principle of pot-banks on each side of a central fire-trench remained unchanged. Fernfold (Sx) and Bishop's Wood (St) are good examples. In the late 16th century another type of furnace came in, again with straight central trench, but with triangular "wings" at the four corners. This type became the norm for the remainder of the period; it appears at Buckholt (Ha) (1576) and the notable, if only because novel when excavated in the 1930s, example of Vann, Hambledon (Sy) (c 1580). Two such furnaces were excavated in the 1970s in North Yorkshire – Rosedale (see 397 and 398) and Hutton-le-Hole. Rosedale, which has been re-erected at the Ryedale Folk Museum at Hutton-le-Hole, had a small subsidiary oven for annealing muff window glass. The four wings of this type were used for the lower temperature processes, such as fritting, pot-arching, reheating the glass during making, and annealing. The commercial and distribution centre for the Early period in the Weald was Chiddingfold and for the Late period Wisborough Green (see 399).

By the 1610s the increasing demand for glass and iron in the Weald led to an acute shortage of coppice wood, used directly in glassmaking, and for charcoal in the iron industry. Timber was also needed for shipbuilding and houses. The iron industry, which produced armaments, carried the day, and in 1615 James I issued an edict prohibiting the use of wood by the Wealden glass industry. As

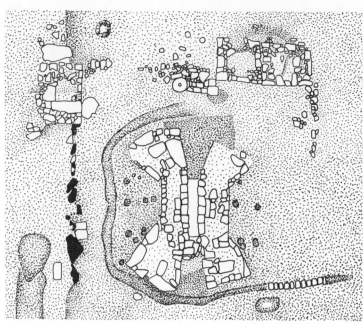

398 *Late period glasshouse, Rosedale (NY), late 16th century (plan): this has a "winged" type furnace, with wings projecting from the central section for lower-temperature processes, and a separate annealing furnace (top right).*

it happened, however, the use of coal in glass furnaces had been proved feasible in 1611, and by 1615 the glassmakers had mostly moved to London, and to coal-producing areas such as Stourbridge (which also had crucible clay), the Forest of Dean (eg St Weonard's, Newnham-on-Severn (where lumps of glass are built into walls), and Newent (1598–1638), and later to industrial centres such as Bristol, Sheffield, and Newcastle-upon-Tyne. The last Wealden glasshouse closed in 1618, and the Late period of Forest glassmaking expired with it.

Several glasshouses have been found of the early years of coal, such as Denton near Manchester and Kimmeridge (Do), which burnt coal in a winged furnace with long flues to increase the draught (1615–23). Coal-firing required not only flues but covered pots, to prevent the glass being discoloured by the fumes. The potash flux of the Forest industry was replaced by soda. The coal-fired industry was managed on fully commercial lines after Sir Robert Mansell took control of a monopoly in 1615.

399 *A 16th-century glass pedlar. Products of the glasshouses for domestic use (as opposed to window glass for large buildings) were sold at the door by pedlars – a perilous trade! This man is French (his cry was "Voirze (Verres) jolis"), but his counterpart could be seen in Britain too (from* Anciens Cris de Paris*).*

By the later 17th century the industry was well established and could now challenge Venice, which exported much quality glassware to England. In 1674 George Ravenscroft succeeded in making a clear glass by adding crushed flint; later, lead oxide was added. The resultant "crystal" enabled English glass to oust the Venetian and, during the 18th century, to equal Irish glass.

Furnace development continued, and by 1700 the large industrial glasshouse consisted of a *cone* of brick, containing a circular furnace with outlets all round (and corresponding "chairs", whose "gaffers", served by their teams, worked the glass into vessels etc), underground flues, and subsidiary ovens for pot-arching, annealing, etc round the outside wall. One such has been excavated at Gawber, near Barnsley (1730s), and cones survive at Catcliffe, in Sheffield (see **400**), Wordsley near Stourbridge (1795), Lemington near Newcastle-upon-Tyne, and Alloa in Scotland.

In 1773 the process of making plate glass was introduced from France, and the great Ravenhead casting hall at St Helen's (recently demolished), where the glass was cast and hand-polished, was one of the cathedrals of the Industrial Revolution. The use of plate glass, replacing small panes of crown or muff, enabled large shop windows to be made, which transformed retail commerce. Several improvements in plate glass manufacture took place in the 19th century, but the definitive breakthrough came with the perfecting of the "float" process by Pilkingtons in 1959. In this process the glass is floated in a continuous ribbon from the furnace along the surface of a bath of molten tin before entering the annealing chamber. This obviates distortion, and also the laborious grinding and polishing.

In the early 19th century the cone began to be replaced by a square or rectangular building housing one or two round working furnaces connected to a large central chimney, which also carried the fumes from subsidiary ovens. Annealing is now done by moving the glass through a long tunnel-like oven called a *lehr*, in which the temperature rises and falls as the glass goes through.

Optical glass was made in the early 17th century, but since the mid 19th century the scope and range of glassmaking has been greatly extended; many new uses have been found and much attention has been given to various compositions and their properties. Scientific glassware, and that for advanced equipment such as space and aviation components, can demand almost 100% silica, but is difficult to work. Plate and sheet glass, and that used for containers and lamp bulbs (made on machines developed in the 19th century), uses soda-lime-silica glass. Lead glass is used as "flint" glass for optical and other purposes and "crystal" for tableware. Borosilicate glasses are used for laboratory glassware and glass subject to high temperatures, such as "Pyrex"; aluminosilicate glass is even more resistant. Some optical glasses contain barium instead of lead; and a variety of ingredients, such as zinc, lithium, tellurium, vanadium, arsenic, and others, are used to meet special requirements. Toughened, laminated, and reinforced glasses have many applications, as have glass fibres.

The variety of forms and decoration of the traditional glassware – table, ornamental, and craft – cannot be listed in detail. Free blowing, mould-blowing, and moulding each has its place; decoration can be by adding, eg by trails, prunts, etc, or by taking away (cutting and engraving). Glass can be painted or enamelled; additives can produce lustre and other effects; cameo can be obtained by laying on a flash of a different colour and etching or cutting through it. Multi-colour effects can be got by "casing", moulding one colour inside another.

400 *Glass cone – Catcliffe, Sheffield, 1740: the oldest survivor in Europe of an important step in the history of glassmaking.*

Oxides can be poured on and allowed to run. Threads and twists can be inserted in stems, or in the walls of vessels; millefiori effects can be got by laying bundles of rods together. Wheel- and diamond-engraving are increasingly popular. The 19th century liked pressed glass, which gave raised or relief effects. Paperweights show a variety of ingenious inclusions, such as the waxed paper "flowerpots" etc inside green bottle glass made at Wakefield in the late 19th century; the millefiori paperweights of Clichy and Baccarat are notable, and Caithness and others are producing pleasing pieces now. Modern studio glass has achieved an astonishing range of effects and combinations of techniques, and has in the last ten years or so come of age, as pottery did in the late 19th century. Stained glass has a continually changing history.

Glass is indeed a most remarkable and versatile material. As well as having domestic, scientific, technical, and architectural applications, it also has a strong artistic and craft aspect. The vigour of the expression of this aspect can be appreciated from names such as Daum, Gallé, Tiffany, Dresser, Powell, Lalique, Marinot, Lindstrand, and Herman; there are also Piper, Reyntiens, and Brian Clarke (stained glass), Laurence Whistler and John Hutton (engraving), and pioneer factories like Kosta, Orrefors, and Holmegaard. Such talent is proliferating all over the world.

(See "Sites and Museums", page 578.)

QUARRIES

Quarries, for one material or another, are among the most ubiquitous remains of human activity, reflecting the breadth of demand and permanently affecting the environment, unless deliberately filled in. They preceded mines in cases where the material sought – slate, ore, etc – ran below the surface, but replaced mines where the material – sand, chalk, stone, etc – was itself part of the surface. In some cases quarries shade off into mines. They may begin as surface working, and then become mines either by way of pits, with galleries leading off to follow the seams, or of adits in a hillside leading to galleries (drifts or slants) along a seam, from an outcrop.

The first are the Neolithic *flint mines* (see **401**), of which the earliest are those in Sussex (Cissbury, Blackpatch, Harrow Hill, Findon, etc), which date from the early Neolithic (late 4th millennium BC). These show now as shallow pits. Their products were distributed widely in lowland England. They were followed in the late 3rd millennium BC by the more sophisticated mines at Grimes Graves, near Brandon in Norfolk, which supplied northern as well as southern England. Grimes Graves covers 93 acres of open land, centred on a low hill, and is closely covered with the remains of 350–500 galleried mines and many shallower opencast workings on the slopes. The flint occurs in tabular form in more or less horizontal thin bands (as can be seen eg in the cliffs at Brighton); two or more upper bands were not sought after, and the mining aimed at the good quality black band, the "floorstone". Contrary to what one might expect, the deep mines on the top of the hill were earlier than some of the shallow or opencast exploitation on the lower slopes, some of which appears to have sought nodules of flint rejected or overlooked by the deep miners; the seam in fact dies away from the hilltop. This working lasted until well into the second millennium BC. The opencast was also more ephemeral, and the flint from it was worked up into implements at working floors on the surface. Some of the opencast pits overlap.

Grimes Graves was investigated from 1914 to 1938, largely by A L Armstrong; his conclusions were reviewed in depth by the British Museum in an intensive campaign in 1972–6, using advanced

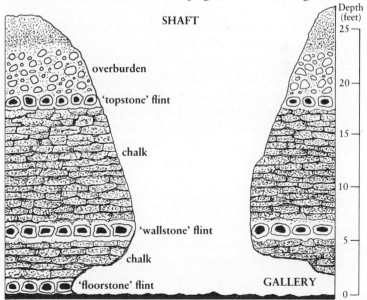

401 *Section of a Neolithic flint mine – based on Grimes Graves, near Brandon (Nf).*

methods and technology. This investigation, largely from the thorough excavation of the large Greenwell's Pit, showed that a large mine could be some 24 sq m at the top and could be 14m or so. The spoil was raised by means of ladders and plank stages in the shaft. When the floorstone was reached, galleries of c 1m high were dug along the seam, radiating from the base of the shaft and leaving thick undug areas for safety. The flint was got by means of red deer antler picks, and the galleries were lit by oil lamps. The galleries had niches or rooms in their walls, which were backfilled progressively when the gallery reached a safe length; the main shaft was finally itself backfilled, leaving only a shallow hollow with a low ring of chalk round it on the surface. From the air the whole minefield is a close mass of these hollows. Some pits were in two stages, if one level failed and had to be abandoned. This mining seems to have been seasonal. Not dissimilar procedures were used in mining for iron, copper, lead, etc up to quite recent times. Greenwell's Pit at Grimes Graves is open to the public.

In addition to the flint mines, igneous rock was also quarried in the Neolithic from several places in the Highland Zone and a few in the Midlands. Axes found all over the country have been examined petrologically, the type of rock determined, and in most cases the sources traced. The rocks have been analysed into 20 groups (and several ungrouped, such as jade), of which by far the most frequently found are those from West Cornwall (Group I – greenstone), Graig Lwyd in Caernarvonshire (Group VII – augite-granophyre), and Great Langdale in Cumberland (Group VI – a basic tuff or "ash"). Axes of these rocks are distributed widely from their sources: Group I is the dominant rock in most of southern and south-east England, Group VII over the northern half of Wales and in East Sussex, and Group VI in the whole of England as far as, roughly, the Thames.

The quarries for these axes are known – those in Great Langdale (four) are high up the mountainside and accessible only with difficulty. The ground is still littered with quarried stone and discarded rough-outs, which were taken to more accessible places several miles away to be worked up into axes (shaped, ground, and polished) and transported south. The four quarries are each accessible to different routes. Groups I and VI appear to have been in competition with each other, and each seems to be associated with different types of ceremonial monuments.

The Romans had a steady demand for stone, mostly for public buildings, town walls, and other defences, and quarried and transported it on a considerable scale. Exceptionally, building and decorative stone was imported from various parts of the Empire, as for the palace at Fishbourne (Chichester), but normally local stone was used. Many quarries remain, although without some positive indication such as Roman objects or inscriptions it is not of course easy to distinguish these from later quarries. But examples of Roman quarries include that linked by a track to the important villa at North Leigh (Ox), and the spectacular one which provided the building stone for the cantonal capital of *Isurium Brigantum* (Aldborough (NY)). This was "embellished" in the 18th century by having niches carved into its face containing classical busts and statuary. A major work such as Hadrian's Wall, built as quickly as possible, needed a long chain of quarries. In the central sector there is a line of them some half a mile south of the Wall; in the eastern sector a conspicuous example is at Fallowfield Fell, with inscriptions; at the western end are inscribed quarries, eg at Wetheral and The Gelt, near Brampton. Several inscriptions from other Wall quarries are in local museums. Roman York used large quantities of building stone from Tadcaster.

Other Roman stone quarries are on the oolite near Bath, on the sandstone between Bath and Bristol, in the Isle of Wight, Chilmark (Wi), near Swindon, and at Ham Hill (So). Rag was got from Barnack (Nh), "slates" from Collyweston, Easton, and Kirkby, and marble from Alwalton and Purbeck (Do). Hard sandstone for querns was got from the Pen Pits near Wincanton (So), Hunsbury (Nh), Faringdon (Ox), and Farnham and Godstone (Sy). The Pen Pits were also worked in the Iron Age, as were the Millstone Grit "edges" near Sheffield, such as Wharncliffe, where unfinished and broken querns can be seen, both beehive and flat disc types; the latter continued to be made at Wharncliffe until the 13th century, and until the 17th century at other Pennine sites. Kimmeridge shale was quarried in the Iron Age and by the Romans for furniture, floor tiles, and small objects.

Post-Roman quarrying was for building and roofing stone, and for surface deposits – clay, sand, gravel, and other materials covered by the term "extractive industries". It has left indelible marks on the countryside and, although some opencast workings have been filled in, in most cases its effects are permanent.

Medieval quarries were usually larger than Roman ones; there are many on the Jurassic belt. The great Norman castle and church building age led of course to an enormous demand for stone. At first much stone was imported from Normandy ("Caen stone"), but before long sources in England were opened up. These included Quarr in the Isle of Wight (whose name itself means "quarry"), and Taynton, near Burford (Ox), where quarries from the 11th century on have left a huge area of jumbled heaps of waste; 12th-century quarries are known at Box (Wi), where later, and at Corsham, vast mines of Bath stone were developed. Stone for the building of Salisbury Cathedral (early 13th century) came from Chilmark (Wi), for Exeter Cathedral from Beer (Dv), and for Peterborough from Barnack (Nh), where too there is a large area of "hills and holes" (see **402**). Purbeck and Corfe marble (hard and black, and taking a high polish) was in demand to vary the whiteness of the great churches. Clunch, a hard chalk, was used even for large buildings; an important source was Totternhoe in the Chilterns. In Guildford (Sy) Quarry Street indicates the clunch quarry and mine which was a source for the castle, St Mary's church, and other features in the town; the mine was then used as a wine and general store for the castle. Headington stone was used from the 15th century. These and other medieval quarries all over the country can still be seen, and few places in stone country are without small hollows and mounds from which the local churches and houses were built.

A special case of great interest is the 17km stretch of the Upper Greensand in Surrey, between Brockham near Dorking and Godstone. Here, in the parishes of Brockham, Betchworth, Buckland, Reigate, Gatton, Merstham, Chaldon (now Blechingley), and Godstone, are no fewer than 30 or 40 mines for hearthstone and firestone. Firestone is an easily worked sandstone, and was used freely for building in the Middle Ages and later, in London, Middlesex, south-west Essex, and north-east Surrey. It was known as "Reigate stone", and was used in Westminster Abbey and Windsor Castle as well as, later, in St Paul's. In the Middle Ages the main sources were Merstham and Chaldon, but mining continued into the 17th and 18th centuries at Reigate, Gatton, and Godstone as well. Similar stone, called "malmstone", was used in the western Weald from small quarries round Farnham and Selborne. When firestone mining declined in the mid 19th century, mines for hearthstone – a softer whitening and abrasive agent from higher in the Upper Greensand – were opened at Brockham, Betchworth, and Godstone. The last mines closed in the 1960s.

The mines consist of long parallel drifts and galleries in the rock, on the pillar and stall principle, with narrow connecting passages between the stalls joining the galleries. They are largely backfilled, and

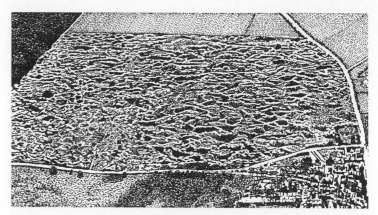

402 *Remains of medieval stone workings, "hills and holes" – Barnack (Ca).*

few indications remain on the surface. They are unusual in being entered not by adits into the hillsides but by pits sunk down to the stone beds level (some 33ft (10m) down), with galleries worked in from the pit floors. The land is closely honeycombed in this way for several miles. The mines have been intensively studied by several local groups, and much pioneering has been done by Paul Sowan.

The complex geology of the Weald can be used to illustrate the variety of materials which have been quarried since Roman times. The Wadhurst Clay country between Hastings and East Grinstead has been intensively exploited for ironstone, and hundreds of pits, many filled by ponds, survive. The Weald Clay yielded Horsham stone, used for paving and roofing in houses and churches over much of Sussex and Surrey, Bethersden or Sussex marble, clay for brickmaking, eg at Hambledon (Sy), and sand for glassmaking, near Chiddingfold. The various beds of the Lower Greensand have produced Kentish rag and hassock from the Hythe beds, Bargate stone from the Bargate beds (eg round Godalming), Fuller's earth from the Sandgate beds (Nutfield), and sand from the Folkestone beds. The Gault produces clay for brickmaking (eg at Selborne). The Upper Greensand is referred to above. Finally the Chalk – lower, middle, and upper – has been extensively quarried for lime, and conspicuous scars still remain on both the North and South Downs, eg Brockham, Dorking, Amberley, Lewes. This is of course a simplification.

Stones quarried since medieval times include *marble*, got from Purbeck (Do), Frosterley (Du), Ashford (Db), Dent (NY), Ashburton (Dv), and the Hopton Wood crinoidal limestone (Db). These usually occur in very narrow seams among limestone rocks, often worked by a series of small quarries; the stone was then sledged to a water-powered mill, for sawing and polishing. *Gypsum* is a soft rock (anhydrite) occurring in nodules or "balls", which were sawn into slabs after hardening. From the 14th century it was quarried near Derby, at Chellaston and Aston, and used – as *alabaster* – for statuary, tombs, fireplaces, etc. It is also quarried in the Vale of Eden, and mined at Billingham (Cl), on a large scale, for plaster of Paris and sulphur. *Grindstones* and *millstones* were made from Millstone Grit, eg at Hathersage (Db) and north of Sheffield.

Alum, used from medieval times in vegetable dyes as a mordant, is produced by the treatment of alum-bearing shales from the Lias. It had to be imported until in 1595 alum shale was discovered in north Yorkshire, on the coast from Whitby to the northern edge of the North York Moors, and inland as far as Guisborough. This area remained the source until the mid 19th century. The outcrops were quarried near the edge of the cliffs; the shale was broken small and calcined with brushwood and coal, in heaps – some very large – on the quarry floor. The calcined shale was then put into tanks in the quarry floor and leached. After leaching the spent shale was tipped over the cliff and the liquid was put in lead or iron evaporating pans, mixed with ammonia or potash, and heated over coal fires. The alum crystallised on the pan, leaving a liquor containing iron sulphate (copperas), which was recovered separately. The remains of these alum quarries and works, and of the waste tips, can still be seen; and at Sandsend near Whitby are the remains of an alum port, with wharf, tracks, and buildings.

In the mid 19th century other alum shales were found, at Campsie and Hurlet near Glasgow, and at Newton Heath near Manchester (where the Pendleton works became the largest producer in the world). The evaporation at the Scottish works was done by a different method from that in Yorkshire – a stone cistern was covered by a brick arch and fired like a furnace with a hearth at one end and a chimney at the other; remains of these survive. Whitby *jet*, so popular for "jewellery" and small objects, particularly among the Victorians, was collected – from Roman times – and not quarried.

York stone, a sandstone from the Coal Measures which can be split into slabs, comes from quarries south of Leeds and Bradford and round Halifax (eg Park Spring, Farnley). This stone has been used for paving, coping, sills, and steps since the 18th century. It is not, however, suitable for roofing, for which, until slates came into use, stones like Horsham, Collyweston, and Stonesfield were used. Stonesfield "slates" are a good example, and have been the subject of careful studies. They are not in fact slate in the strict sense, being limestone from the base of the Great Oolite (Jurassic) and split along the bedding plane, whereas the rock properly called slate (eg the Welsh) is metamorphic and splits along compression lines. Taynton stone, used for building, comes from higher in the Great Oolite. Stonesfield slates are found in buildings widely in west Oxfordshire and in the Oxford colleges. There are many other kinds of stone slates in the Cotswolds, used from Roman times onwards, but the characteristic of Stonesfield slates (and also of Collyweston slates from Northamptonshire) is that they were *frosted*. The stone is only found in a very limited area some two to two-and-a-half miles by one mile round Stonesfield village. It occurs in chunks or in rounded masses called "potlids", both forms being known as *pendle*. The pendle, which had a natural water content – the *sap*, was dug in the autumn and left out in the winter, when frosts made it easier to split into thin plates. The advantage of frosting seems to have been realised only in the late 16th century, which fortunately fitted in with the Great Rebuilding and enabled a big demand to be met. The heyday of the industry was the 18th and 19th centuries, and it came to an end in 1909.

In the 18th century the slate was got by opencast, adits, and shallow mines, in the 19th by mine shafts with basal galleries. The industry was probably replaced by the cheaper Welsh slates, which were also easier to lay. The stone was stored underground until the weather was cold enough – it was essential not to lose the sap – and was spread in the fields and wetted to let the frost act. The resulting slabs could then be split with a hammer and trimmed into finished slates. The waste from this work results in *chipping banks*, near the mine shafts. The slaters worked under a wicker or straw shelter. The slates were made in sizes, each with names, which resemble those used for other Cotswold (unfrosted) slates; a different set of names is used for Collyweston slates, and the Welsh names are completely different again. M A Aston lists 44 known workings, of which Spratts Barn is the only one now accessible.

Slate is a mudstone or shale metamorphosed under great pressure to a hard, even, and durable rock, highly suitable for roofing and also used for tombstones, paving, and billiard tables. It can be grey, black, blue, green, brown, or purple. It is split along compression lines, and can be quite fine and thin. Slate was used by the Romans and from the 12th century, but it was in great demand from the end of the 18th century to cope with the explosion of building in the industrial towns. Nearness of the deposits to sea transport was a factor in this. Slate occurs in Devon and Cornwall (eg Delabole, worked since the 16th century), north Wales (Bethesda (Penrhyn), Llanberis (Dinorwic), Nantlle and Blaenau Ffestiniog), Cumberland (Broughton), and Argyll (Ballachulish and Easdale).

Slate is usually quarried, and some of these quarries are enormous, as are the tips of waste. Quarrying is done by terraces or benches. But at Blaenau Ffestiniog the slate dips, and has to be got out in vast caverns. The depth of the workings necessitates systems of hoists, ropeways, and tramways. Some slate can be levered out, but blasting is necessary in most cases to dislodge large pieces of rock, which can then be reduced by plugs and feathers. Splitting is highly skilled and still done mostly by hand. The slates, which can be as thin as 4mm, are then trimmed to sizes which are given names of the female aristocracy, from princesses and duchesses down to ladies, small ladies, doubles, and singles. The industry, which declined after the First World War, picked up in the 1970s and found a new market for the cladding of buildings.

The quarrying of stone was done on a large scale in the 18th and 19th centuries, and reached its peak in the late 19th. There has been a decline in the 20th century, and now only a few stone quarries are left, although there is still a demand for natural stone. The word "quarry" refers to the production of "squared" stone for architectural or sculptural work, but is now applied also to workings for broken stone, and to diggings for clay, sand, gravel, etc.

The *limestones* of the Jurassic belt have been worked since Roman times, and some quarries were important in the Middle Ages: these include Ham Hill (So), Weldon (Nh), and Ketton and Clipsham (Le). The Isle of Portland (Do) was intensively worked, and by 1839 there were 56 quarries there, some of them run by the State using convict labour, for major works. Portland stone was used by Wren in St Paul's, and had a new vogue in the rebuilding of London after the Second World War. The usable beds were buried under up to 60ft of overlying rocks, which were blasted or broken up with wedges. The rocks used were the Roach, a hard shelly limestone for heavy engineering works, the Whitbed, the white oolite for building, and the Curf, for interior work. The blocks were detached by cutting a groove at the joints;

into this were inserted iron wedges (*plugs*) between thin iron plates (*feathers*) – the plugs were hammered in and the block would come away. Nowadays a row of holes is drilled to take the plugs; blasting can only be used if the rock is hard enough to come away in useable pieces or if indeed broken stone is the objective. Other important limestone quarries are at Ancaster (Li) and near Bath. Here the overburden is so thick that the Bath stone was mined underground. The huge mines at Corsham and Box, with massive pillars of rock, are very impressive. Mining here, begun in Roman times, has all but finished, but mines at Monks Park and Combe Down are still operating.

Sandstone is similarly quarried, eg the Pennant stone round Bristol and in south Wales, the red stones of Shropshire and Cheshire, white and red at Mansfield, and the white Craigleith stone used in Edinburgh. The millstone and grindstone quarries of the Sheffield area have already been mentioned.

The *granite* of Aberdeen and Peterhead was extensively used in the 19th century in London and elsewhere, for paving, road setts, monuments, and major works such as the Thames Embankments. Other major sources are Mull, Shap (Cu), Haytor (Dv), and Penryn (Co). Granite is naturally difficult to quarry and work up, but many of the former laborious methods have been replaced by mechanical processes such as compressed air drills and recently the thermal lance for detaching blocks, diamond-tipped and wire saws, radial polishers, etc; others stones have also benefited from such equipment.

Similarly, transport in quarries, once by sledges, was made easier by the use of tramways; cranes were once simple wooden derricks or shearlegs. Blocks were lifted by means of a two-pronged caliper or "*lewis*", and the lewis-holes in the stone to take the prongs can often be seen, eg on the Roman bridge at Chesters (Nd). Hoists were sometimes worked by horse and capstan. Stone is normally shaped and dressed, and sometimes carved as well, at the quarry. The masons do this at *banker* places under open sheds; old bankers can be found in disused quarries. "Freemasons" were those who worked "freestone" – stone which could be cut in any direction. Toolmarks indicate the tools and methods used. Loading places and staithes may also survive.

Quarrying for broken or crushed stone involves different techniques. Quarries are in open pits and worked in benches; blasting is used to get down large masses of rock. The stone is needed for roadstone, railway ballast, aggregates, and setts. Sites are usually handy for canal, railway, or sea transport; there are conspicuous ones at Bonawe and Furnace in Argyll, Penmaenmawr and Yr Eifl (Cn), and Penlee and St Keverne (Co). This type of quarry has special plant for crushing, grading, and screening.

Carboniferous limestone is worked on a large scale round Buxton and Wirksworth (Db) and near Grassington (NY); it is used for cement and chemicals, and as a flux for steelmaking. Some limestones were burnt for lime, and kilns can be seen at some quarries and also in the countryside or at ports, eg the impressive row at Beadnell (Nd); those round the coast, as at Gwbert and Mwnt (Cd) or Buck's Mills, near Bideford (Dv), served a local coasting trade.

The great chalk quarries on the North and South Downs also produced lime, mostly for cement and mortar (eg Brockham, which has a row of kilns, Merstham, and Amberley). But there are a large number of small chalk and marl pits, such as those on Noar Hill, Selborne (Ha). It was cheaper to cart the chalk than fuel and water, so the kilns which converted the chalk into lime for the fields were on the farms which needed it; thus, in the Weald,they are on the sands or clays (eg Hambledon (Sy)), not on the chalk downs.

The Lowland Zone, and particularly the valleys of the great rivers – Thames, Trent, Welland – are scarred by vast open pits for the extraction of sand, gravel, and clay. These use mechanical excavators and draglines. Little can be done with these when they are worked out – they destroy not only the agricultural land but any archaeological remains that were there. Some have filled with water, some have been turned into centres for water sports, and many stay derelict. But the demand persists, for sand and gravel for the construction industry, for clay for pottery and brickmaking. An average of 3,500 acres are in fact quarried annually. Special iron-free sands are wanted for glassmaking, such as those from Morvern (Ar) and St Helens (La). China clay, worked in Cornwall, where its intractable waste tips disfigure the landscape, needs special treatment – it is washed down into the quarry with hydraulic jets, made into slurry, and pumped to the surface for treatment.

Small shallow pits can often be seen along roads; these were for material for repairing the road or, in some cases, for making it. The sizeable pond by the railway just west of Weybridge station (Sy) represents the material taken out to make the embankment. Another special type of quarry, in the north of England particularly, is the following of an outcrop of roadstone, or a dyke, across country;

this leaves a long continuous trench which can be mistaken for a leadmining "rake" (example on Sleights Moor (NY)).

(See "Sites and Museums", page 578.)

COAL

Coal, in great variety, is very plentiful in Britain and, with iron, enabled Britain to lead the world into the Industrial Revolution. It is found (except for a small deposit of Jurassic age at Brora in Sutherland) in rocks of Carboniferous age. The central valley of Scotland has Lower Carboniferous coal deposits, which now form the coalfields of Ayrshire, Central (Lanark, Stirling, Clackmannan), Midlothian, and Fife. South of the Southern Uplands a great area of Coal Measures (Upper Carboniferous) once stretched unbroken to the Midlands of England and most of Wales. Another belt of higher land once separated this from the southern coal-bearing belt, from south Wales to Kent and on to northern France. Subsequent earth movements, and later deposits over the Coal Measures, have broken up this once continuous field into small islands of (accessible) coal-bearing rocks, forming the present coalfields. These are in Cumberland, Northumberland and Durham (this field continues under the sea, and is worked up to 4 miles (6.4km) out), West and South Yorkshire, with Nottinghamshire and Derbyshire (this is one great field, which continues east at more or less workable depths, and whose eastern edge is unknown – but within the last 20 years a deep (model) mine was opened near Selby), and Lancashire and Cheshire. South of these are small isolated fields, in north-east Wales, north Staffordshire, Shropshire, south Staffordshire (mining in the old Black Country has ceased), Warwickshire, and Leicestershire. The southern group consists of south Wales (with a narrow extension in south Pembrokeshire), the Forest of Dean (nearly extinct), Somerset, and east Kent. Deep mining is the rule in these fields, except the Forest of Dean, but some opencast mining was done during the War, and some still is, particularly in Northumberland – opencast is more efficient and economical than deep mining.

Until the recent mine closures, nearly half the total output came from the Yorkshire, Notts, and Derby coalfields, some 16% from Northumberland and Durham, and about 10% from south Wales. Most coal now goes for steelmaking and power stations. Much used to go to make gas (from 1805), but hardly any does now, with the advent of North Sea gas and natural gas shipped from North Africa, so local gasworks are rarities.

The quality and type of coal varies widely; thus anthracite is found in south Wales, metallurgical coal in south Wales and Durham, domestic "bright" coal in Yorkshire (strong and medium caking), and weak to non-caking coal in Nottinghamshire and the Midlands. Recently, major deposits of lignite have been found by Lough Neagh in Ulster.

Coal-getting was a "cottage industry" until the 1850s, and this continued on a reducing scale until the 1950s, and even now it persists in the Forest of Dean. Output from the mines peaked in 1913, when 290 million tons were raised. Output at this level declined thereafter, and the impetus was spent by the end of World War II. Mechanisation was then accelerated, suspended in the 1970s, and resumed on a larger scale in the 1980s. The output of a pit is now some 50 times that in the 19th century. But coal-mining became too capital-intensive to be economical, and the industry may be reverting to the level of the 1950s. There has in fact been a rundown of pits since the 1840s, and closures have accelerated in the last 2–3 years. (In 1990 there were some 80 pits, but only 20 or 30 remain operative now.) The fields in Scotland, Northumberland and Durham, south Wales, and Kent have now gone; a few pits are left in Yorkshire and Notts/Derby, and these are likely to survive. The closures have had devastating effects on the associated mining communities.

Coal was used by the Romans for metalworking and domestic purposes, and they appear to have got it from opencast or shallow pit workings in Cheshire, Flintshire, Dean, and Northumberland. The first major evidence comes from the 13th/14th centuries, in the form of "coalpits" (probably just surface digging on outcrops or river banks), then *bellpits*, and opencast. Bellpits leave surface remains – depressions with circular banks. The coal so dug was called "pit-coal" and, when sent down from the Tyne to London by sea, "sea-coal". By the 15th/16th centuries pits were deeper, with galleries radiating from them into the seams. *Drift* mines could also be driven into a seam from its outcrop; if the seam dipped the drift became a *slant*. The galleries had columns of coal left at intervals to support the roof – *pillar and stall* working. Props were used later, but any shallow mines could cause subsidence in the ground above, sometimes in a pattern which reflected the stalls beneath.

Whims or gins (horse-turned capstans) were used to wind into deep pits, using baskets. From the 17th century wagonways were laid down to bring the coal to the loading points, in the mines and on the surface (see below).

In the 18th century increasing demand led to deeper mines still, which were made possible by the application of steam power to winding and drainage from the 1710s; the oldest such plant on its original site is at Elsecar (SY), 1787–1923. The deep pits necessitated permanent pithead buildings. Cages were used after the 1840s. Most of these earlier buildings have been replaced or destroyed, but a few abandoned mines survive. The vast waste tips have unfortunately not yet all been cleared away. Two fine examples of specially designed coal ports are Seaton Sluice (Du) (1670s) and Seaham (Du) (1830s). 18th/19th-century pits and shafts can still be found in the Pennines; some of these are winding shafts to ventilate galleries. Ventilation was carried out until machinery could be used, by fire and draught.

At Worsley (La), drainage and transport were combined in a network of canals (46 miles (74km) by 1840), linked to the Bridgewater Canal. Steam pumping has been replaced by electric pumps. Pillar and stall working went on up to the 1950s, but from the 1860s *longwall* mining was introduced, associated with mechanical coal-cutting. By the 20th century the easiest seams had been worked out or the coal was harder to get, and many pits have been closed on economic grounds. The new deep pits (eg Selby) are expensive to build and run.

An important social byproduct of coalmining are the colliery villages and mining towns, of which those in the valleys of south Wales and in Durham have become notorious. But in the 18th and 19th centuries there was no alternative to building houses, schools, institutes, churches, and shops round the workplace. The profound effect of these, not only on the countryside but on the people isolated within them, was not appreciated until relatively recently.

In the days when burning coal was the normal method of heating a home or office, or powering a factory, every station, even remote country ones, had a coalyard and siding. Here coal of different grades was stored in open bins, where it could be bagged in hundredweight sacks and put on open carts for delivery. These yards are fewer now, but remains of disused ones can still be seen.

(See "Sites and Museums", page 578).

City of London coal duties boundary marks

These marks are usually known as "wine and coal posts" (see **403**). To help the City of London recover after the Great Fire of 1666 it was authorised to collect duties on all coals brought into the port and the surrounding district. This right, fixed at different levels as time went on, was only cancelled in 1889 and finally ceased in 1890. The duties were used for rebuilding, including St Paul's, the Guildhall, the markets and prisons, and later the embankments, Blackfriars Bridge, Holborn Viaduct, and the major sewerage scheme in the 1860s which greatly helped to wipe out cholera.

Coal was originally brought to London by sea, and later by rail and canal as well. Duty on seaborne coal was collected prior to unloading; but the canal had a collecting point (first at Watford, later at Rickmansworth), and the railways had to collect on all coal passing boundary marks set up by the City. Under the London Coal Duties Act of 1851 the marks were set up 20 miles (32km) from the GPO in London wherever any railway, canal, or road crossed this limit. In 1861 the area was amended by the London Coal and Wine Duties Continuance Act to coincide with the Metropolitan Police District. The 1851 boundary marks were moved to the new line and many new ones added. Much of this boundary is now followed by that of the (former) GLC. This move accounts for the inconsistency of the Act shown on some of the posts.

By 1890 about 265 marks had been set up, of which some 215 have been traced. Hillingdon has 21, and is the only borough to have all five types; Croydon has 12, Bromley 22, and there are several in the Ashtead-Epsom area. There were five types:

1 obelisks some 15ft high beside railways – 1837–50 in stone with the City coat-of-arms in cast-iron; 1851 onwards in stone or iron

2 cast-iron obelisks about 4–5 ft high beside railways

3 thick stone obelisks 4–6 ft high beside canals and navigable waterways

4 square ornamental cast-iron posts 3–5 ft high, beside roads, bridle-paths, etc

5 cast-iron plate 9in square on river bridges on county boundaries.

403 *A "wine and coal" post. These posts were set up, under an Act of 1861, at the boundary of the Metropolitan Police District, where it crossed roads, railways, and canals; the Act levied a duty on coal and wine brought into London, the money being used for the improvement of the metropolis.*

TIN

The prehistoric bronze industry depended on two then not very common metals, copper and tin. There were very few sources of tin available to the ancient world – Anatolia, Bohemia, and Spain among them – but Cornwall was one of the most important. Tin has been mined there until almost the present day. The earliest dateable working is at Redmore near St Austell, which is Iron Age, but there must have been a large number. Four sites are known to be of Roman date: Boscarne on the Bodmin Moors, Carnon in Feock, Treloy in St Columb Major, and Carnanton in Mawgan in Pyder. The industry slumped after the 1st century AD, being overtaken by Spanish tin; but sources of stream-tin there were exhausted by the 3rd century AD, and the Cornish mines were reactivated. The industry had another heyday in the Middle Ages, when Dartmoor was as important as Cornwall.

Tin was needed for bronze, an alloy 90% copper and 10% tin, and from Roman times also for pewter; Roman pewter had 70% tin to 30% lead, but medieval pewter had less tin.

The principal ore of tin is cassiterite, an oxide occurring in the form of black pebbles in the alluvial deposits round the granite blocks of Devon and Cornwall, and in lodes in the granite itself. It is thus found in and round Dartmoor, on Bodmin Moor, round Redruth, in Penwith (where St Just was a great centre, with many remains, eg at Botallack), and Scilly (see **404**).

The medieval industry was closely controlled, and the tin had to be checked and cleared at *stannary towns*. In Cornwall these were Bodmin, Lostwithiel (both replaced by Penzance when the industry moved west), Liskeard, Truro, and Helston. Dartmoor was divided into four

404 *This partly ruined engine house at the Cornish Levant tin-mine at Geevor, Pendean, provided the power for working pumps and other processes, and operated from 1840 to 1990.*

stannary districts from at least the 14th century, based on Chagford, Ashburton, Plympton, and Tavistock.

The well-preserved remains on Dartmoor have recently been studied by Tom Greeves and others, and illuminate the phases of the industry. Opencast excavations and shafts, as well as leats, can be seen in almost every valley. Most remains date from 1400–1700 – the peak of the industry was in the early 16th century – but sites range from prehistoric to 1930.

The first phase, from the 12th century, is that of *streamworks*, surface working of alluvium. These show as waste heaps, gullies, and shafts, and are plentiful in the Plym and Erme valleys. The heaps often occur in parallel or concentric ridges, with a retaining wall. By the 15th century lode tin was got by *opencast* working – linear gulleys up to 200m long by 20m wide by 10m deep, running mainly east–west, following the lodes. These *beamworks* mostly date before 1650. By the 16th century mining had to go deeper, by way of vertical *shafts* and *adits* (horizontal tunnels); most of these are late 18th/19th century. There is a line of such shafts at Eylesbarrow Mine, where there is also a blast and a reverberatory furnace of 1822–31.

Once dug, the ore had to be crushed and concentrated before smelting. This was done in *knocking mills*, powered by waterwheels. Smelting was done in blast furnaces in *blowing mills*, eg the remains at Nosworthy or Fishlake Foot, or round St Just. The ore was crushed by water-powered *stamps* on large stones, which were

replaced when too much worn and left lying about. Outside the mill were settling pits (*buddles*). The fuel was peat charcoal. The molten tin was moulded into ingots (as can be seen at eg Teignhead Farm). After 1750 the tin from the crushing or *stamping* was largely sent away to be smelted. Most of the finished tin was transported to London by sea from Exeter, Morwellham, Plymouth, and the Cornish ports.

The blowing house, developed from the 13th century, had so much of an advantage over the earlier simple kilns that it obviated the need for tin to be smelted twice. Good examples of complete 19th-century installations are Wheal Cumpston mine, Holne (Dv) or Wheal Castle lodes and mines, St Just. Some 30 mills from before 1700 on Dartmoor have visible remains; over 40 sites are known from before 1740 in the Erme, Plym, and Meavy valleys, and there have been over 100 mines on the Moor since 1800.

LEAD

Lead is one of the easiest metals to smelt, with a melting point lower than most other metals. Its poisonous properties were not realised until quite recent times, but it still has important uses. In the late Bronze Age it was used as part of the bronze alloy; in Roman times it was used for water-pipes, cisterns, baths, roofing, and for food preparation vessels; it was also used in paints and even cosmetics. Cumulative lead poisoning is regarded as a factor in the decline of the Roman Empire. After reduced demand during the Middle Ages, lead was again used extensively from the 16th century for roofing, rainwater goods, piping, and shot; in the 18th and 19th centuries it was needed also for paints, crystal glass (lead oxide additive), pottery glazes (even for food storage vessels), and even food additives; in the 20th century it has been used for electricity cables, batteries, and as an additive to petrol.

In the 18th century Britain was the world's leading producer of lead, but in the 20th century leadmining has been greatly reduced and most of Britain's needs are now imported. Although lead was mined only in small quantities, over a million tons were got from 1750 to 1850, and over three million tons from 1850 to 1950. But since then lead has been almost entirely a by-product of the mining of fluorspar (a flux for the steel industry) in Derbyshire and Weardale; Irish production has, however, soared, as new sources have been discovered, including one at Navan on the largest lead ore body in Europe.

Leads ores occur in veins in Carboniferous rocks. They tend to come in clusters or groups, *mining fields*, surrounded by less rich fringes. The main fields are in the Mendips (Charterhouse), Derbyshire, Yorkshire (Grassington-Greenhow area, and Swaledale), the northern Pennines (Alston Moor-Allenheads), Cumbria (Keswick), Lanarkshire (Leadhills and Wanlockhead), Devon and Cornwall (eg Bere Alston), several areas in Wales (Flintshire, Shropshire borders, Glamorgan, and west Wales), and the Isle of Man (Laxey).

The principal ore is *galena*. Being a sulphide, this has to be roasted to produce an oxide for direct smelting, but lead is easier than copper in this respect as the two processes can be carried out in the same furnace; the sulphide, as it roasts, reacts with the unroasted part progressively in a "double decomposition reaction", resulting in lead at the bottom of the furnace. A medieval furnace (*bole*) was circular, with stone walls pierced to admit draught, with a floor of clay, and with a channel to the outside to allow the lead to run out and form a pig. Seventeenth-century boles could be 5ft (1.5m) high. They were either mounted on platforms to enable them to be turned, so that the workers were not exposed to the poisonous fumes, or were built on hillsides. Bellows would not be needed for boles 5ft (1.5m) high.

The Romans undoubtedly had their eyes on the silver and lead produced in Britain, and lost no time in exploiting it after the conquest in AD 43. Some mines may have been in state hands, but many continued to be operated by natives, no doubt under Roman control. Up to 100 lead pigs have been found from leadmines, bearing official Roman stamps, the earliest being from the Mendips in AD 47. It is not possible, however, to be certain whether a given working is prehistoric or Roman, but Roman workings are definitely known in the Mendips, east Wales, Derbyshire, and Yorkshire. Roman mines were, as with other metals, either opencast or by way of adits, shafts, and levels, and drifts following the veins. Hushes (rushes of water from temporary dams) were used to wash the topsoil away to find ore deposits. As with gold, veins contained mostly gangue (worthless soil in which ore is found), and a galena content of 10% was rich but rare.

The Saxon and medieval lead industry seems to have been concentrated in Somerset and Derbyshire (Wirksworth and Ashbourne). The northern Pennines (Alston) are first recorded in the 12th century, and the Swaledale and Nidderdale mines were also active in this period (the latter worked by Fountains and Byland abbeys). A new phase began when Elizabeth I brought over Germans to reorganise metal mining generally in England; they worked ores at Keswick in 1565, using a new rectangular and shallow "ore hearth" furnace.

The growing demand by the end of the 17th century led to undertakings on a major commercial scale. Several companies were formed, of which the most important was the "Corporation of the Governor and Company for smelting down lead with Pitcoal and Seacoal", generally, and understandably, known as the London Lead Company, or, just as often, the Quaker Lead Company, as it was founded by prominent Quakers such as Edward Wright. It was formed in 1704 out of a fusion of the Ryton Company (1692, working by 1697) and the Welsh Company (the Royal Mines Copper), 1692. It developed the mining fields in Flintshire and Alston Moor, and expanded into the Pennines and Derbyshire. In Wales it operated from 1701 to 1790 at Gadlis (Fl) and Halkyn Mountain, with smelt mills at Bagillt. Silver was important in this field. In the northern field the London Lead Co had mines at Tyne Head (1704), Blanchland (1708–1808), Alston Moor (1734, with Nenthead as the centre for 150 years), Whitfield in West Allendale, and Egglestone (1753). Silver, refined in reverberatory furnaces, was supplied to the Royal Mint from Gadlis and Ryton; the ore richest in silver came from Clargill, Tyne Head – 36oz per ton of lead. In Derbyshire the Company operated at Wensley and Winster near Ashover (1720–92), but this ore was poor in silver. Ores were worked at Wanlockhead and Leadhills from 1710 to 1727, and there were other ventures in Ayrshire, in the Isle of Man (Laxey), and in the Yorkshire Dales.

The Company developed machinery for drainage and transport, using engines built by Darby at Coalbrookdale by 1748, sharing in Brindley's canals (Chesterfield 1771, Leeds–Liverpool 1768), and laying roads, such as that up East Allendale (linking with the Blackett and Beaumont – also Quakers – mines at Allenheads), with a branch to Nenthead and one into Weardale. Efforts were made to minimise the effects on the workers of the poisonous fumes from smelting, and in 1778 the method was adopted of laying a long flue from the smelter (or from several smelters) up a hillside to a tall chimney at the top. This not only condensed and got rid of the fumes, but provided excellent draught as well. The first such chimney, which is the oldest industrial chimney in the world, was at Stonedge, near Chesterfield, in 1778; others are at Egglestone, Stanhope, and Malham, and several others still exist. During its long life the London Lead Company applied its Quaker principles to improving working conditions and provided housing, lodgings for miners, cooperative shops, planned villages, schools, churches, and chapels. The Company ceased working in 1905. The Alston Moor mines continued to work until 1963. Today probably the best example of a planned mining village is Leadhills (La), which has terraces on a hillside with central green (on which stands a bell for calling workers to the mines), church, inn, and library.

The landscape of leadmining is very distinctive and has an unmistakeable atmosphere. There is still much to be seen of it, particularly in the Pennines where the former mining population has ebbed away, leaving acres of spoilheaps, hushes, "rakes" (trenches following a vein near the surface), pits, and adits, eg near Allenheads, Grassington, or Greenhow. Ruins of smeltmills can be found, as at Malham, and chimneys, eg in Swaledale. At Killhope, near Nenthead, is a very impressive ore-crushing mill, with waterwheel (see **405**). The enormous overshot Lady Isabella waterwheel at the Laxey mine (IM) (1854), now restored, is unforgettable. It is 72ft (21.6m) in diameter, and operated distant pumps by means of long flat rods.

COPPER

At first in its own right, and then as a major constituent of *bronze*, copper was the principal metal of the ancient world for some 4,000 years, and still has important uses. The ores are of two kinds: *oxides* and carbonates in surface deposits, easy to get and requiring simple smelting only, and *sulphides*, in deep veins needing mining, and having to be roasted as well as smelted. The oxide sources were naturally used first, until they ran out in the 3rd millennium BC. Ore deposits are mainly found under *gossans*, iron-rich surface deposits over sulphide veins. The iron oxides were used as fluxes to smelt copper and lead ores. Carbonates lay just below the gossans, and sulphides below these – secondary above and primary, less rich, below. The upper levels had various admixtures owing to leaching.

Copper ores are found in the Near East (eg Maden in eastern Turkey and Timna in Sinai), the Mediterranean (Cyprus, the Cyclades, Laurion near Athens, Sardinia (worked after 1100 BC),

405 *The great wheel of the pumping station of the Killhope lead-crushing mill in Weardale (Du).*

Corsica, northern Italy, southern France, and Spain (north-west and eg Rio Tinto)), in south-east Europe, Bohemia, the Alps, and the Harz, and in western and northern Britain and Ireland. Copper metallurgy was developed, perhaps independently, in the Near East and in the Balkans by 4500 BC, and in Spain by *c* 4000 BC. Sulphide ores were worked from *c* 3000 BC. For Britain the dates are later: copper artefacts began here about 2500 BC deriving largely from Irish sources, and bronze about 2000 BC, continuing until the introduction of iron about 600 BC.

British sources of copper are set out in the table; they show a similar pattern to lead, but quite different from iron.

Scotland	Shetland, Orkney, Caithness (Wick), Ross, Argyll, Loch Ness, Loch Tay, Perthshire, Glenesk, Ochils, Edinburgh (Calton Hill), Lammermuirs, Leadhills, south-west Scotland
Wales	Great Orme's Head, Anglesey, Plymlimmon
England	Keswick, Coniston, Alston Moor, Richmond, Cheshire (Alderley Edge), Derbyshire and Staffordshire, Shropshire (Llanymynech), Devon (Bere Alston), Cornwall (Mullion and Callington, Camborne–St Just area)

In Roman times and earlier, sources of copper ores were small and isolated. Pre-Roman workings have been found at South Molton (Dv), Alderley Edge (Ch), Parys Mountain (An), Great Orme (Ca), and Cwmystwyth (Cd), apart from Ireland. Ancient and Roman workings are hard to find intact, or to date, but Roman workings are on a larger scale than prehistoric ones. The Romans used adits, rarely deep mines. In any case, outcrops and surface sources are either worked out and no longer visible or are covered up or destroyed by later workings (as are those on Parys Mountain).

Oxide ores were frequently admixed with other metals or near-metals, such as tin, lead, silver, aluminium, antimony, bismuth, and arsenic. It was discovered at an early stage that arsenic increases the hardness of copper, and most Copper and early Bronze Age artefacts are either from 99% pure copper or have high (up to 7%) arsenic content. Tin-bronze (usually 10% tin/90% copper) took over from arsenical bronzes after 2000 BC (Wessex-middle Bronze Age). Late Bronze Age artefacts have low (under 1%) arsenic, being made from deep sulphide ores which have low arsenic content, but often have added lead (average 5%, but higher values are found).

The Romans often used copper-silver alloys, and copper-tin-lead. The high cost of tin in the Middle Ages encouraged the use of *brass* (latten), with up to 30% *zinc*, and memorial brasses are normally made of this. Up to the 18th century brass was made by mixing zinc ore (calamine) with copper and charcoal, with two raises of temperature, yielding a 20% zinc alloy. Modern brass used for working contains 10–30% zinc, and that for casting usually 40%.

T K Derry and Trevor I Williams (in *A Short History of Technology*, OUP 1960) give a vivid account of the complex process of making copper from the difficult sulphide ores in the 19th century. The ore was first roasted for 12–24 hours, and cooled with water; it was then melted with slag from a later stage, granulated in a water tank, calcined at a gradually rising temperature, melted again with more slag, and run out to form pigs. The pigs were heated with free access of air in a melting furnace to produce "blister" copper; to produce "tough pitch" copper suitable for manufacture, the blister copper had to be melted again to remove any remaining slag; the final product was toughened by throwing charcoal or anthracite on it, and stirring with a greenwood pole.

Copper has many uses, such as for coins, for sheathing ships (replaced in 1832 by Muntz's metal, three parts copper to two of zinc),

and for Sheffield Plate (developed by Thomas Bolsover in 1742 for making buttons and later used for ornamental tableware). Its high conductivity led to its use in great quantity for electric wire. Copper is in fact second only to iron in importance.

Mining of all metals was encouraged in the 16th and 17th centuries and expanded in the Industrial Revolution, when Parys Mountain, in the 1780s, was the largest copper mine in the world. Up to the mid 19th century Britain was in fact the world's leading producer of metals; at that time Devon and Cornwall were the dominant sources, although copper was not mined there until *c* 1700. But in the 20th century Britain was overtaken and now has to import ores. In 1800 three-quarters of the world's copper was smelted in south Wales, and in 1850 Swansea was still the centre of the world's copper industry. But, of 600 furnaces there in 1860, the last ceased in 1921. Lancashire was also a centre for copper-smelting.

Remains of mining still exist. Intensive copper mining in the Lake District began in 1565 when Germans were brought over to develop copper production in the area of Keswick, Coniston, Coldbeck, and Grasmere. The Keswick mines were pointlessly destroyed in 1651, since when the industry went through slumps and booms. By 1870 some 2,000 men and boys were employed, but there was then a steady decline, to 500 in 1890 and 6 in 1970, all in the barytes mine at Force Crag. The decline was accelerated by conservationist pressures. Copper was mined in the Quantocks from the late 18th century to *c* 1850, and there are two ruined engine houses near Nether Stowey. In Cwmystwyth (closed 1921) there are many remains, including hushes from a reservoir at Graig Fawr (17th century). Cornwall has many spectacular remains (mostly from 1700–1870) round Camborne and Redruth – engine houses, pumping stations, chimneys, smelters, etc, eg at Dolcoath, where tin was mined as well as copper, or at East Pool. An instructive example is Morwellham (Dv), on the Tamar above Plymouth. Here there is a restored port for the Tavistock Canal and the copper mines of the Devon Great Consols company. The features include docks and quays (tin was also exported from here), a manganese ore-crusher and waterwheel pit (there were once 33 waterwheels), inclined planes, copper-ore chutes, the Tavistock Canal, limekilns, and remains of a local railway. Morwellham's copper peak was from 1844 to 1865. The arsenic in the copper ores was also important, and by the 1880s Morwellham was producing half the world's arsenic.

SILVER

In Britain silver is mainly found in the sulphide ores of lead (galena etc) and in other non-ferrous ores, in particular copper ores. Some ores contain small quantities of gold as well as silver.

Silver is separated from the lead by the process of *cupellation*. The ore has to be roasted to get rid of some of the sulphur and then heated to a higher temperature with charcoal, which further reduces the sulphur content and leaves a lead-silver alloy at the bottom of the furnace. This alloy is then melted in a *cupel* (crucible) and a blast of air blown on it. This oxidises the lead (to litharge, which is either absorbed in the hearth or skimmed off), leaving the silver. The cupel had a clay base, lined with bone ash, and the charge and charcoal were covered with clay or tiles. This principle is still used.

The process of extraction of silver from copper-silver ores, or silver containing copper, is even more difficult. Here, the copper is oxidised and the silver released from it is dissolved in lead; this is then oxidised in its turn, leaving pure silver behind. Lead must be added frequently to take up the silver from the copper. Complex Roman cupellation charges have been found at eg Silchester, Wroxeter, and Hengistbury, containing lead, copper, galena, and oxides of copper and lead. In Roman times and later, silver was extracted from copper ores from Devon and Cornwall.

Silver was exported from Britain in the Iron Age (one port being Hengistbury (Do), which handled silver from copper ores). The lead and silver mines were intensively exploited by the Romans, and pigs of Roman lead have been found in Yorkshire (Wharfedale, Nidderdale, and Swaledale), Derbyshire, Flintshire, Shropshire, the Mendips, and Glamorgan. They are stamped EX ARG (short for EX ARGENTARIIS), "from the silver works"; the Romans seem to have regarded lead as a byproduct of silver, rather than the reverse. Ingots of Roman silver have also been found.

Silver continues to be extracted from lead ores, and after the Roman sources just mentioned medieval mines were opened in Devon, in the north Pennines, and near Keswick; in more recent times sources have been tapped in west Wales, the Isle of Man (Laxey, a rich source, yielding 30–40oz per ton of lead), and Scotland (Leadhills and Strontian). Recent yields have been less than 6oz per ton of lead, except in Devon and Cornwall (40oz, once 100–130) and the Isle of Man; the Mendips, in 1875, were yielding 137oz/ton, but in Roman times

a mine in Glamorgan was producing 170oz/ton. Silver also occurs in a native state but in deep veins (eg there was a silver mine at Hilderston near Linlithgow until 1873) (see, eg, R F Tylecote: *Metallurgy in Archaeology* (Arnold 1962)).

GOLD

Much of the prehistoric gold found in Britain came from the Wicklow Mountains in Ireland (gold also occurs in the Sperin Mountains of Co Tyrone, and since 1987 a very large deposit has been suspected near the village of Gortin), but gold also occurs in Britain itself – in Wales at Dolaucothi (Cm) and Dolgellau (Me), and in Scotland in a belt from Leadhills/Wanlockhead (Lk) to Linlithgow, and in Helmsdale (Sd), with a few sites elsewhere. The gold occurs in nuggets and dust in streams and in adjacent surface levels. Most of these sites have long since been worked out; but an interesting more recent one is in the Tweedsmuirs in Selkirkshire, at Glengaber, a tributary burn of the Megget Water. Here, for 1.5km or so along the burn, can be seen the embanked channels through which the burn was diverted for washing the gravel and the mounds of worked-over rock and soil. These workings are of uncertain date, but fall between the 17th and 19th centuries.

The gold workings at Dolaucothi were operated in prehistoric times by shallow pits dug into quartz veins on high ground. But the Roman workings here are surprisingly sophisticated. When the mines were reopened in the 1930s they cut into a system of Roman galleries (not fully explored) reaching 220m below the present floor of the main opencast. The roof was shored up by stacks of waste rubble held rigid by layers of brushwood. In these galleries was found part of a drainage wheel and other Roman objects. The next phase was that known as Opencast C, which is associated with a leat and aqueduct system bringing water 8–10 miles, ending in tanks at the mine. When opencast working became burdensome, adits and galleries were sunk into the ore body. A stone with hollowed scoops at this mine may be a multiple mould for ingots. (For Dolaucothi see P R Lewis and G D B Jones in *Antiquaries Journal* 49, 1969.) The gold near Dolgellau is still worked and produces wedding rings for the royal family.

The stream ore was crushed and washed and the gold dust melted in a crucible in a charcoal fire with bellows. In Scotland the surface gold in the Leadhills area was exhausted by 1575, and was then extracted from lead and copper ores by cupellation (as was silver from lead). British gold is usually found mixed with silver as well as copper and lead, and complete purification was not easy until recent times. The silver content is likely to be over 1%, and may be up to 12.5%. An alloy of the latter kind is electrum, which can be made to look like gold and was used for coinage in the Iron Age (a mint of that period has been excavated at Hengistbury Head (Do)) and for many purposes in the Middle Ages. Electrum was also a deliberate alloy. Most prehistoric gold objects, such as the Snettisham hoard, are alloyed; the processes of separation of silver and copper from gold were too complicated. But a few later objects, such as the Scottish Crown of the 1540s, are probably of natural gold. Objects with over 90% gold or with over 5% copper are likely to be Roman or later. Non-metallic impurities such as quartz or ferric hydroxide would be removed by melting, so objects containing these are probably made from beaten natural gold rather than from remelted gold.

IRON AND STEEL

Since its introduction into Britain about 600 BC, iron has become one of the most ubiquitous materials in our civilisation. It takes three forms: *wrought iron*, which contains no, or practically no, carbon, and is malleable; *cast iron*, which contains up to 5% carbon, is brittle and non-malleable, but can be moulded, filed, drilled, and ground; and *steel*, which contains up to 1.5% carbon (usually less than 1%), and can be forged or cast.

Wrought iron is the basic product of simple smelting of ore with charcoal. This was done in the Iron Age in a *bowl furnace*, a scoop in the ground; an upright *shaft* (*domed*) furnace, which made the handling easier and increased the quantity of iron produced, was introduced in the early 1st century AD. The heat was maintained, and the carbon removed from the iron, by burning it out by oxygen with bellows, through a clay tube (the *tuyère*) low down in the furnace wall. The iron collected at the bottom of the furnace in a small lump or *bloom*; the furnace is therefore called a *bloomery*. The bloom was hammered to consolidate it and to remove any remaining carbon, and could then be reheated and worked up by the smith into the form desired. If the ratio of charcoal to ore is increased beyond 1 to 1, a good quality *steel* is made.

The demand for greater quantities of iron led to progressive increases in the size of the furnace throughout the Middle Ages, until in the mid 15th century in Europe it ceased to be manageable by the former hand methods, and necessitated blowing by water power. The final stage of this development was the invention of the *blast furnace*, which was introduced into Britain in 1496 (at Newbridge (Sx)). The ore and charcoal were fed in from the top, as in the much smaller bloomery, and a powerful blast of air was fed lower down by two water-powered bellows. The molten iron collected at the bottom and ran out into moulds sunk in sand or loam outside the furnace. This was *cast iron* – the ingots could be massive *sows* or rows of smaller *pigs*. These could be reheated and cast into shapes, but could not be forged. The bowl and shaft furnaces were quickly superseded by the blast furnace, but charcoal continued to be used as the fuel.

The uses of cast iron were at once evident, and the immediate demand was for armaments; the first guns in England to be cast (and not made of wrought iron rods bound together, as are the guns in the *Mary Rose*), were made at Newbridge in 1509, and cannonballs were also cast. But a wide range of domestic and architectural ironwork was made as well, and by the later 17th century the demand was such that the supplies of charcoal were insufficient. Coal could not be used, as it contained sulphur which adversely affected the iron. The breakthrough, and the beginning of a new phase (in fact of the Industrial Revolution itself), came with the use of coke in 1709 by Abraham Darby I, at Coalbrookdale (Sp) (where the original furnace can be seen (see **406**)).

If cast iron were to be forged – and the demand for wrought iron remained strong – it had to be converted into wrought iron. This involved a process called *finery*, in which a pig was heated in a separate hearth in a hot blast from bellows, to eliminate the carbon. The iron then dropped into a bath of molten slag, to prevent it absorbing more carbon. When enough was collected, it was hammered to remove any entrapped slag; it was then reheated in a *chafery* hearth and made into bars etc, for sale to blacksmiths.

Blast furnaces needed a *pond* to work an overshot waterwheel. A pond could only hold two or three days' supply of water before the level fell too low, so had to be supplemented by a *pen-pond* higher up the stream. There needed to be a *spillway* at one side of the *bay* (dam); the *tail-race* – the spent water from the wheel – could be used by the workers. The water from the pond flowed along a *launder* – a wooden channel – from the bay to the wheel. Other methods were the *valley-side leat*, from a weir or bay higher up the valley (eg at Cowden Lower Furnace (Kt)), and an embanked river (eg Hasted (Kt)), where the whole river was rerouted. Ponds, or their bays, are common sights in iron districts, but remains of the furnace or forge buildings themselves are very few. Blast furnaces were at the lowest point of the bay; remains of the loading ramp sometimes survive. Good examples of bays and ponds can be seen in St Leonard's Forest and Knepp (Sx); there are remains of a wheelhouse at Ashburnham (Sx).

Slag can still be found at these sites. Slag is the non-iron material in the ore – clays, sands, etc; after melting in the furnace it was tapped off, like the iron, and was difficult to dispose of; much was used in Roman and medieval times as road metal, and today it goes into tarmac, railway ballast, etc. Bloomery slag is black (blue-black when broken). Cinder is also found, looking like coke. Blast furnace slag is glassy, owing to the silica in the ore, blackish to green to creamy yellow, and shiny and smooth when broken; green is the commonest colour. This slag is aerated if from an early site, solid if more recent. Conversion forges can be recognised by *forge bottoms* – circular dished masses of slag, the waste from the firing. Fragments of cannon and other moulds turn up on casting sites.

Iron was almost certainly worked in the Forest of Dean in pre-Roman times, probably by the Dobunni of Gloucestershire. Their shallow workings cannot be distinguished from Roman ones, known as "scowles", eg at Bream or west of Coleford. Weston-under-Penyard was a Roman ironworking town (Ariconium), which may have continued a pre-Roman centre. Blackened earth in the fields at this site reflect this industry (see Cyril Hart: *Archaeology in Dean* (Bellows, Gloucester, 1967)).

Thirteen sites are known in the Weald from pre-Roman times, eg Garden Hill, Footlands, Sedlescombe, and Crowhurst Park. There are also indications of pre-Roman smithing and forging (not necessarily of smelting) at hillforts such as Saxonbury and Hascombe.

Sixty-seven Roman sites are known in the Weald. Their distribution is partly coastal (eg Beauport Park, Battle), partly in the High Weald (eg Great Cansiron, Holtye, Bardown, Wadhurst). The western sites seem to have been under civilian management, the eastern sites under the direct control of the Fleet (*Classis Britannica*), whose stamped tiles have been found on the sites. Some sites have sizeable remains

(pits, furnace sites, slag, and refuse), eg Bardown, Beaufort Park, Great Cansiron, Broadfields, Crawley, Chitcombe, Brede, Crowhurst Park, Crowhurst, Footlands, Sedlescombe.

By this time there were some ten unpowered bloomeries in the High Weald, and seven powered bloomeries or forges (eg Chingley). Some bloomeries survived until the mid 16th century in the Weald, the late 16th century in the Midlands and north, and even into the 18th century in north Lancashire.

The Wealden industry reached its maximum size in the late 16th century; in 1548 there were 53 works (eg Panningridge), and in 1574 52 furnaces and 58 forges. The products were ordnance, pig iron, and bar iron. By 1653 there were 36 furnaces and 45 forges; ordnance was made until the success of the Carron works in 1775; pig production declined in the 17th century, and bar in the 18th. But a trade in cast items (firebacks, grave-slabs, rollers, pipes, etc) developed in the 17th century, with increasing skills in mould-making and founding. The extensive remains at Chingley, from which much has been learnt, are now submerged under a reservoir.

A field survey was carried out in 1976 by the Wealden Iron Research Group to assess the situation and density of bloomery sites, in an area of

406 *Abraham Darby's iron furnace, Coalbrookdale (Sp). Here coke was first applied in iron founding, 1709. This furnace was built in 1658 and enlarged or rebuilt in 1777.*

70 square miles (182 sq km) including Crowborough, Eridge, Mayfield, and Heathfield in Sussex. This area contained 246 sites – 3.5 per square mile. There is no way of distinguishing medieval from earlier bloomery slag, but from surviving pottery 40 sites could be dated; of these two were Iron Age, 33 Romano-British, and five medieval (see C F Tebbutt in *Sussex Archaeological Collections* 119, 1981). Some 500 bloomery sites are now known in the Weald, but many more remain to be found. Tylecote points out that it is not easy to distinguish early smelting sites from smithing sites. Place-names often give a clue (as they do to glassmaking or lime-burning sites also), such as Blacklands (though some names in "Black" refer to surface water, not coal or fire), Cinder Mead, Abinger Hammer, Furnace Pond, Forge Field, Smithy Close, etc.

Some 170 water-powered sites are known in the Weald alone. Water power was in fact used in the final stages of the bloomery period, and Schubert lists 11 sites before 1450. Charcoal continued to be used long after the application of coke in 1709: Ashburnham (Sx) continued until 1813 (and perhaps to c 1820); Trosnant (Mo) closed in 1831, Duddon Bridge (Cu) c 1866, and Newland (La) not till 1891. (Schubert again provides a valuable list of charcoal blast furnaces.) Steam power superseded water progressively from 1784.

Iron ore occurs in several forms and is widespread in Britain, except in the northern Home Counties. The main types are as follows: *Carbonate* ores (clay ironstone) are found as nodules in the Weald, in the Coal Measures, and along the Jurassic scarp from Cleveland to Oxfordshire (especially Northamptonshire, Rutland, and Lincolnshire). The main seam in the Weald lies at the bottom of the Wadhurst Clay, but there are outcrops further west in the Weald Clay, and another near Crawley; the Ashdown Sand and Tunbridge Wells Sand also contain deposits. The main ironworking area in the Weald thus lies between the Medway in the north, Horsham in the west, Cranbrook in the east, and the coast from Bexhill to Rye, with a second area west of this, including Petworth, Haslemere, Cranleigh, and Fernhurst. *Haematite* ores (oxides) occur in west Cumberland and Furness, and *limonite* ores (mainly crystalline oxides) in the Forest of Dean and south Wales. Ores of all these types are also found where deposits of lead, copper, etc occur, eg at Leadhills (Lk). Ores are also found in the Coal Measures of the Central Valley of Scotland, and Argyll and Lanarkshire. Another source of iron is *bog-iron* or *iron pan*, not a rock but a deposit caused by leaching of iron salts to an impervious level in the soil, usually 8–18in below the surface. This occurs in northern and western Britain, and in the Lower Greensand of the Weald. Many of these sources were worked in Anglo-Saxon times and by the Cistercians (eg in the Pennines). The only ores of present importance are the Jurassic ones of Cleveland, south Humberside, south Lincolnshire, and Northamptonshire, and the haematites of Cumberland and Llanharry (Gl).

The ores are usually in seams which outcrop in valley sides or where tilted strata emerge. They were got till recently by shallow workings, "minepits" (or "bell-pits", up to 30ft deep), or opencast. Some opencast pits in the Weald can be mistaken for marlpits; minepits show as depressions up to 20ft across and up to 5ft deep, the pit proper having been backfilled. Minepits are commonest in the blast furnace period, followed by deep mining since the 18th century. Ore-digging, wood-cutting, and charcoaling were small-scale operations up to the 19th century, and seem to have been largely done by individuals (as coal is got in the Forest of Dean to this day).

The iron of the Coal Measures (from Derbyshire to Scotland) was worked out by about 1820. The Jurassic ores were then tackled, from Cleveland to the East Midlands and the Cotswolds; these were not so rich, but easy to get. From the mid 19th century the Jurassic ores were got by mining in Cleveland and by opencast in the East Midlands. The waste was dumped in ridges until well into the 20th century (see **407**); opencast areas are now restored to farming use – but not to the small fields, hedges, and trees which were there before!

Charcoal, the fuel of the iron industry until the 18th century (and even later in some places), was made for smelting and domestic use from at least Roman times. (For details of charcoal-burning see "Crafts", page 474.)

B K Herbert has calculated that, on the assumed basis that the ratio of ore to charcoal in the bloomery was 1:1, only 10% of the weight of roasted ore became wrought iron. Thus, with an assumed iron output of 20lb a day, 200lb of charcoal a day would be required. A kiln of charcoal 20ft (6m) across yielded some 8,000lb (3.5 tonnes), and would therefore last some 40 days. In the blast furnace period efficiency was 50%, so two tonnes of charcoal would be needed to make one tonne of cast iron, and the charcoal kiln would only last for two days. This, coupled with the increasing demand for iron (for armaments and domestic products), put a severe strain on the supply of coppice wood, which was also used as direct fuel by the glass industry. So in 1615 James I issued an edict prohibiting the use of such wood for glassmaking (it so happened however that coal-firing was applied to glassmaking in 1611, and that this industry was already leaving the Weald for the coal-producing areas). But charcoal continued to be used in the Wealden iron industry until as late as 1820.

Developments since 1709 include Abraham Darby I's discovery that coke could be used instead of charcoal, which not only by-passed the by then acute shortage of charcoal but obviated the contamination of the iron by the sulphur contained in untreated coal. This discovery, although successful, took a long time to spread; by 1788, out of 77 blast furnaces in England and Wales, 53 were coke-fired but 24 still used charcoal. In one case – Backbarrow – charcoal lingered till 1921, but generally it went out with the 18th century.

Another advance was made in 1784 by Henry Cort, this time to improve the conversion of cast iron to wrought iron. Cort used a reverberatory furnace in which the iron and coal were in separate compartments, thus keeping the sulphur away from the iron. The decarburisation was done by drawing atmospheric air across the iron by the draught from a chimney stack. The iron was stirred with a bar to increase the reaction of air and carbon, and the process was thus known as *puddling*.

From 1784, when Newcomen and Watt enabled steam power to be applied to pumping machinery and to drive hammers, rolling mills, etc, the iron industry became independent of water power, and could expand in convenient areas, such as south Wales and particularly the Black Country (where it had been since the 17th century), which had ore, coal, clay, and limestone; Britain became for a time the biggest iron producer in the world. By 1823 there were 237 blast furnaces in Britain. Much effort went into improving the technology, particularly in the conversion of cast iron to wrought iron.

A long-standing problem with iron was the difficulty, by simple hammering, of making long thin rods suitable for blacksmiths and nailmakers. This was solved in principle by the *slitting* mill, worked by water power, and introduced into Britain from the continent in 1590. A piece of iron was hammered into a flat strip, then passed between two rollers to flatten and extend it, then through rotating disc cutters, which "slit" it into rods. The *rolling* mill itself was progressively improved – by John Hanbury in 1720, who widened the rolls, and by Henry Cort in 1783, who designed grooved rolls, enabling shaped bars to be produced. The number and direction of

407 *Spoil heaps of iron mines – Bentley Grange, Emley (SY). These were monastic workings of Byland Abbey, 12th–16th centuries.*

rotation of the rolls – "two-high" or "three-high", reversing or continuous – was also varied, and by 1862 a wide range of effects could be produced.

Cort's "dry" puddling process was refined in 1816 by Joseph Hall, who used an oxygen-rich material, such as slag, to line the furnace. This increased the oxygen intake and speeded up the decarburisation; it was known as *wet puddling* or pig boiling, because the iron boiled during the process. Preheating the air blown into the furnace (Neilson 1828) also saved fuel and increased output, and this idea was refined by recycling the waste gases from the blast furnace (see below).

In an attempt to improve further the conversion of cast iron into wrought, Henry Bessemer (1856) invented a process which in fact resulted in a metal closely akin to wrought iron – *steel* – but which was more versatile, cheaper, and quicker to produce. Bessemer blew cold air through molten cast iron; this not only burnt out the carbon very rapidly but raised the temperature at the same time, so decarburising more thoroughly. No fuel was needed, as the cast iron could be tapped straight out of the blast furnace into the converter. A puddling furnace made some 5cwt of wrought iron in two hours; a Bessemer converter made several tons (eventually over 30) in half an hour. Wrought iron was handled in lumps of 1cwt but steel could be cast straight out of the converter into ingots of several tons each. This was of course revolutionary, at once enabled large structures etc to be made, and spelt the end of wrought iron, industrial-scale production of which ceased in 1976. Cast iron is still produced, but steel production continues to increase.

At the same time (from 1856), another method of making steel was being developed – the *open-hearth* process, which early in the 20th century overtook Bessemer steel in quantity produced. This process, initiated by Frederick Siemens, followed by Cowper, the Martins, and Talbot, used hot waste gases to preheat incoming fuel and air; scrap iron and low-grade coal could be used. Thomas and Gilchrist (1875) used limestone in the walls of the converter and in the charge, which enabled phosphoric ores to be used (opening up new vast sources of ore) and at the same time resulted in basic slag, which could be used as a fertiliser. The alloying of steel with metals such as nickel, tungsten, manganese, cobalt, and chromium, from the 1860s, also increased the uses of steel. All these new processes enabled a vast expansion of railways, shipping, buildings, and machinery to get under way from the 1870s (see below). The Bessemer and open-hearth processes are now being superseded by a continuous process.

No bloomeries survive, although some are excavated from time to time. Reconstructions have been made and fired, in museums or by bodies such as the Wealden Iron Research Group. There are however several 17th- and 18th-century blast furnaces which can be visited: the Ironbridge Gorge Museum has Abraham Darby's furnace of 1709, and a 19th-century range also (at Blist's Hill). At Blaenavon (Gl), five blast furnaces of *c* 1790 are preserved, and at Bonawe (Ar) there is one of 1753. Some 30 other sites have remains to show, more or less complete, eg Duddon Bridge (Cu) or Moira (Le) (see **408**). The romantically-sited banks of blast furnaces at Consett (Du) and Corby (Nh), the inspiration of many artists, have now been demolished. Furnace and hammer ponds, and their associated remains (usually very fragmentary), are mentioned above.

The village *smithy* is almost a thing of the past, although a few still exist. Certainly the buildings of many remain, or are indicated by names such as The Old Forge. One such stands on the green at Chiddingfold (Sy). To see a blacksmith in action one should go to a firm making wrought ironwork. Some museums, such as the Weald and Downland, have working smithies; the Avoncroft Museum of Buildings has a chain shop, and there is a needle-making shop at Redditch. Abbeydale Mill at Sheffield, and Sticklepath Mill near Okehampton (Dv) are more elaborate examples, with water power, of edge tool and general smithing. For heavier work and casting it is necessary to visit a foundry or engineering works.

Wrought ironwork

Wrought ironwork is partly the expression of the skill and imagination of the local blacksmith, and reflects the changes in popular tastes and methods through the centuries; but it is also a minor art form in itself, sharing in its own way the artistic influences of its day (such as the Scandinavian aspect of English art in the 11th century, or the Baroque in the late 17th). It remained in ordinary use until it was superseded by the cheaper and more plentiful cast iron in the 18th century, resulting from changes in the method of iron production.

The earliest examples are hinges on church doors dating from the mid 11th century, of which some were reused in the next century in Norman buildings. These are wide crescent-shaped straps, with a horizontal bar inside the crescent, made to support the massive plank doors. The oldest are at Stillingfleet, near York, and Staplehurst in Kent (see **409**). Both these doors also have ironwork decoration

408 *Blast furnace – Moira (Le), c 1800. The furnace is on the right. The adjoining building is the foundry; the materials for the furnace were transported across the bridge on the left through the upper floor of this building.*

representing Scandinavian pagan myths. Crescent hinges continue into the 13th century; their development may be seen from the form of the ends of the straps. The first phase, to *c* 1125, ends in snakes' heads; the second, *c* 1125–75, has delicate curled tendrils (Old Woking (Sy), Peterchurch (He)); the third, *c* 1175–1250, finish in flowers, leaves, or other forms (see **410**). A major example of the first phase is at Little Hormead (Ht) and of the second at Durham Cathedral.

The third phase foreshadowed the Gothic style, which became mature by 1250. Whole doors were covered with arabesques springing from the hinges (eg Merton College, Oxford, Leighton Buzzard (Be)). After 1300 such ironwork was replaced by elaborate woodwork. Punched work is common throughout this period, and pieces were joined by welding. Screens were also made, and some survive in Winchester Cathedral. Ironwork was also used on chests and cupboards.

Entirely new methods and styles reached England from Italy soon after 1300. Patterns were now geometric (trellises etc, derived ultimately from Islamic art), or architectural. The new technique, called "locksmith's work", replaced the former hot working by cold working, treating the iron as though it was wood. Once the bars were made, they were cut and sawn, filed and drilled; main members were morticed and tenoned together, and joints rivetted. Thin sheet iron was used, pierced or cut into ornamental designs. Examples are the choir gates at Canterbury and the screen at Lincoln. By the 15th century this style had reached a remarkable peak, as in the screen to Edward

409 *Ironwork on a church door, c 1050, with ships, fish, and sea monsters – Staplehurst (Kt).*

410 *Ironwork on door, with a regular pattern based on vegetation – York Minster, c 1275.*

411 *Wrought iron gates – Hampton Court, Jean Tijou, 1690.*

IV's tomb at Windsor (John Tresilian, 1483). Tomb railings were in vogue from the 13th to the late 17th century, but only some 50 survive out of hundreds, eg the Black Prince's tomb, Canterbury, *c* 1375, Thame (Ox), 1502, West Tanfield (NY), 1630. Locks and doorplates also survive in the locksmith style.

Apart from tomb railings, little ornamental ironwork comes from the years from 1483 to 1688, possibly because of lack of patronage for it. But during the 17th century great houses began to use iron gates to screen their forecourts without blocking the view, and with changes in garden design gates and screens were set up there also. Among the few examples are the screen at Cowdray House, Midhurst (Sx), *c* 1600, the Sheldonian Theatre, Oxford, and gates at Groombridge Place (Kt), Ham House (Sy), 1670s, and Traquair (Ps). Staircase balustrades and balconies began to appear, as at Guildford Guildhall, 1683.

The Baroque style was introduced into England by William III, who brought over a French worker, Daniel Marot, in 1686. This style was a balanced blend of linear members and scrolls with leaves and flowers of sheet iron to provide mass. Another Frenchman, Jean Tijou, worked at Chatsworth in 1688 and at Hampton Court in 1690 (see **411**), and had enormous influence. He excelled at repoussé work, of which much can still be seen in St Paul's. Tijou had many successors in England, but most of these worked with a more English restraint and solidity. Some of these are Thomas Robinson (New College, Oxford, 1711), John Gardom (Castle Howard and Chatsworth), Robert Bakewell

412 *Robert Bakewell's "Cage" – a wrought-iron garden arbour at Melbourne Hall (Db), 1706–11. A fine example of its period.*

(eg the Cage at Melbourne (Db), 1711 (see **412**), Radcliffe Camera, Oxford, 1744), John Warren (Clare College, Cambridge, 1715), William Edney (St Mary Redcliffe, Bristol, 1710), and Robert Davies (Chirk, 1719, and other places in Wales). There is a very fine bracket for the inn sign at The Ship at Mere (Wi), possibly by Kingston Avery, between 1730 and 1763.

Chinese influence lightened the Baroque and added asymmetry, but by the time this style was in vogue here Gothic was coming back and much work after 1750 combines the two (eg at Strawberry Hill (Mx)).

439 *Papplewick pumping station (interior). This pumping station, part of Nottingham's water supply, is a fine example of the flamboyant and "architectural" Victorian engineering (1883–5); the beam engines were built by James Watts & Co.*

455 *The Needles lighthouse (IW) designed by James Walker, 1858. A typical 19th-century form, shown here before the top of the lighthouse was altered for a helicopter pad. It is now automatic.*

413 *Handrails at a hotel doorway, of a design which adds a piquancy to the generic word – Rutland Arms, Bakewell (Db). A very graceful achievement.*

Chinese latticework, extensively used by Chippendale, can be seen everywhere, dating from after about 1765. Robert Adam brought in the Neo-Classical style in 1758, and this became a strong competitor. But by the end of the 18th century wrought iron had become three times as expensive as cast, and its days were over.

There was a revival of craftsmanship in the 1860s and architects reverted to wrought iron, such as at the Law Courts in London and Cardiff Castle. These pieces of work are generally heavier and less simple than their medieval models. The Art Nouveau phase used wrought iron also. It has of course persisted for rural and domestic use, such as gates of small houses and for items like brackets and frames for inn signs. It continued into the present century for farming and craft purposes like gate hinges, horseshoes, and craftsmens' tools. Some street furniture survives from before the influx of cast iron (see 413).

A specialised use of wrought iron is for *weathervanes* and *weathercocks*. There were weathercocks in England by the 8th century. The cock is a symbol of vigilance and of the supremacy of the Church. The oldest to survive is at Ottery St Mary (Dv) (1335), and there is a very fine one at Winchcombe (Gl). Many have no cardinal pointers, but the church is itself oriented east–west, so this is not necessary. Vanes derive from medieval armorial pennants, and only owners of these could use them (dovecotes were also limited to manorial lords). Wind pointers

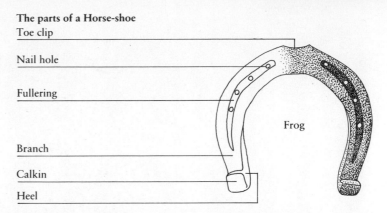

The parts of a Horse-shoe
Toe clip
Nail hole
Fullering
Frog
Branch
Calkin
Heel

414 *The parts of a horseshoe.*

were added later, and compass letters later still. The oldest of this type is at Etchingham Church (Sx) (1387). A great variety of devices can be found, such as the gilded fish at Charmouth (Do) (a Christian symbol), the ship on Rochester Town Hall (17th century), and birds and animals of all kinds. Sporting subjects, like fox and hounds, became popular in the 19th century. Norfolk is rich in vanes.

Horseshoes (see 414) were until well into this century among the commonest products of the blacksmith; they can still be picked up in the countryside, and are seen fixed to walls and doors of farm buildings and cottages, where they once had the function of protecting those within. They have varied in shape over the centuries, which enables a rough dating to be made (see 415). Gordon Ward (*Hull Museum Publications*, 205 (1939)) classified horseshoes into four groups:

1 *Celtic and Romano-British*: these have edges bulging round the nail-holes and fiddle-key nails (the wavy edge is found until the 13th century)
2 *Medieval and packhorse* (to mid 16th century or later): these have no countersinking, fullering (the groove in which the nails are sunk), or clips (the sharp point rising in front of the hoof)
3 *Renaissance and keyhole* (1550–1800): these have fullering, but no clips
4 *Modern*: these have clips

Later shoes do not generally taper so much along the branches, and 18th-century shoes often have keyhole openings. Nail-holes are

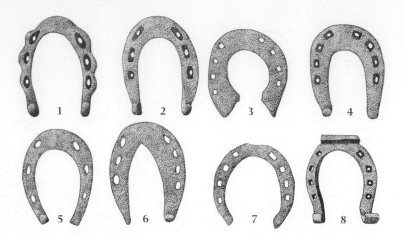

417 *A cast-iron fireback – phoenix in flames, 16th-century, made from Wealden iron (Lewes Museum).*

415 *The changing forms of the horseshoe: 1, Wavy rim (Celtic, Saxon and early Norman); 2, Norman (12th–13th century); 3, Keyhole (early 17th–late 18th century; 4, Tongue (late 17th–early 19th century); 5, Dove (13th–15th century); 6, Guildhall (late 13th–16th century); 7, Toe-clip rim (19th–20th century); 8, Bar-clip draught (19th–20th century).*

usually rectangular (to take hand-made nails), but some are round. There may be two, three, or four nails on each branch; in general, the more the later. Indeed, a horse-shoe found at a glasshouse site at Blunden's Wood, Hambledon (Sy), dated to *c* 1330, seems to have had only three nails, one at the bow and a larger one in the middle of each branch. Early shoes may have wide bows and tapering branches, and are often thin. There is a remarkable collection of dated horseshoes at Oakham Castle (Ru).

Bullock-shoes are in two parts, to fit cloven hooves. Shoes have also been made for other animals, and for large birds (see **416**). (See also R W Murray: "Dating Old English Horseshoes" (*Journal of the British Archaeological Association*, third series 2, 1937).)

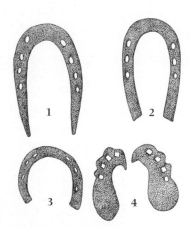

416 *Shoes for other animals: 1, mule-shoe; 2, donkey-shoe; 3, pony-shoe; 4, ox-shoe.*

Cast ironwork

The products of the Wealden iron industry were principally armaments (guns and cannonballs), grave-slabs and crosses, and domestic products, including firebacks. The first gun was cast (with wrought iron chamber) in 1509, and entirely in cast iron in 1514; from 1543 guns were cast with a core in the mould. Medieval guns of wrought iron were made with bars or plates bound with hoops. It was later found that guns were stronger if cast solid and bored, but the Wealden ironmasters were reluctant to do this, and the trade went to the Carron Company of Falkirk (founded in 1759), and the Wealden industry – still using charcoal – died by 1820.

Firebacks (see **417**) and firedogs were also made in quantity in the Weald. Firebacks were cast, with a variety of patterns – heraldic, floral, etc. Some were moulded with separate movable stamps. There are extensive collections at Petworth, Lewes, and the Victoria & Albert Museum. Grave-slabs were cast with lettering and various devices; there are some 80 in the Weald, ranging from 1537 to 1711, of which 33 are at Wadhurst church. They were succeeded by cast iron crosses and "headstones", of which many survive.

The Quaker firm of Darby at Coalbrookdale, being unwilling to make armaments, made a variety of domestic wares – cauldrons, pots and pans, boot-scrapers, seats, fountains, lamps, etc – an excellent collection of which is displayed at the Museum of Iron at Coalbrookdale. During the 18th century this firm innovated widely: from the 1720s iron cylinders for steam engines, in 1729 iron wheels for railway wagons, iron rails in 1767. Iron plates for ships were made from 1787. Other distinguished ironmasters and engineers worked at or with Coalbrookdale – John Wilkinson, Richard and William Reynolds, Charles Bage, and others. Thomas Telford designed the iron aqueduct at Longdon-on-Tern (1796) and Richard Trevithick built his steam locomotive (1804) in cooperation with this seminal group. Bage built the first cast iron-framed building, the Ditherington flax mill in Shrewsbury (1796–7). The culmination of the work of the Darby dynasty is arguably the first iron bridge in the world, the Iron Bridge over the Severn at Coalbrookdale (1779); this is still in use, and still excites admiration.

The Iron Bridge has five ribs, each a near semicircular arch with a span of 100ft, and a rise of 45ft. Each rib was cast in two pieces. The spandrels are filled with two parallel ribs linked to the main arches by decorative braces; a ring of iron steadies and decorates each corner, and against the stone piers on the river bank are "gothic" ogee arches. The bridge is covered with iron plates which support the roadway, and finished with simple but elegant balustrades. It has the austere grace of high art (see **321**, page 428).

The industry went on to produce machinery, buildings, bridges, railways, and ships throughout the 19th century, and the material successes of the Industrial Revolution are impossible to imagine without it.

Nineteenth-century machinery was often conceived in architectural terms, and many large pieces, such as pumping engines, are embellished with cast iron Doric columns, "gothic" features, and the like. The concept was applied in an extreme form to printing presses, which lent themselves to fanciful excrescences like eagles or dragons. Buildings too did not escape this tendency, and even cotton mills could have members in which the functional was disguised. There still survives ornamental ironwork on eg railway stations (such as Great Malvern or Kettering), which comes today as a possibly not unwelcome aesthetic surprise.

That cast iron could lend itself to the monumental is shown by conspicuous examples such as Telford's Pont Cysyllte canal aqueduct (1805), Rennie's Southwark Bridge (1819), or Stephenson's Britannia Tubular Bridge over the Menai Straits (1850). Brunel's ship the *Great Eastern* (1854–8) is another Victorian triumph – 32,000 tons, 692ft long – even though she was not an economic success and ended up laying cables. The first iron warship in the world (now on view at Portsmouth) was *HMS Warrior*, built in 1860. The great railway stations still excite awe – Barlow's St Pancras (1868), with its great 240ft span single roof; Newcastle Central (Dobson, 1855); Bristol Temple Meads, which reflects the range of Victorian station architecture from Brunel's wooden shed of 1840 to Digby Wyatt's iron and glass roof of 1878; and the astonishing curving vistas at York (Prosser, 1877). In another field, Paxton's Crystal Palace, built for the Great Exhibition of 1851 and burnt down in 1936, was the world's first important prefabricated building; it was built with pulleys and without scaffolding. It was entirely functional, only to be succeeded by late Victorian ornateness, such as in market halls (eg Halifax) or arcades; buildings like the now regrettably demolished London Coal Exchange (1846–9) are in the same tradition, as is Smithfield Market, London (1866), and other markets. The widespread adoption of architectural simplicity had to await the 20th century.

From the early cast iron-framed buildings, such as the flax mill at Shrewsbury (1796) and Strutt's cotton mill at Belper (1797), the use of cast iron members became the norm for large buildings and can be seen in most factories, mills, and warehouses built until late in the 19th century; after that date, steel and reinforced concrete enabled even bigger frames to be built.

Cast iron, more or less ornate, lent itself to use for smaller objects like gates, railings, balconies, canopies, and street furniture. Some of these could be light and graceful, but in general cast iron gives a heavier impression than wrought iron. Cases in point are the great gates exhibited by Coalbrookdale at the Exhibition of 1862, and Queen's Gate in Kensington Gardens (1857). But cast iron is essentially an urban phenomenon, wrought iron a rural one. So cast iron reflected the aesthetic fashions of urban building and decoration; thus it has been said that stucco and cast iron are the marks of the Regency. Certainly, the great late Georgian and Regency centres, such as Bath, Edinburgh, Cheltenham, Brighton, and parts of London, are still full of such cast ironwork (see **418**).

The first cast iron railings seem to be those round St Paul's, made

418 *Regency ironwork – Scarborough (NY). Ironwork, both wrought and cast, showed great variety and invention in the Georgian and Regency periods.*

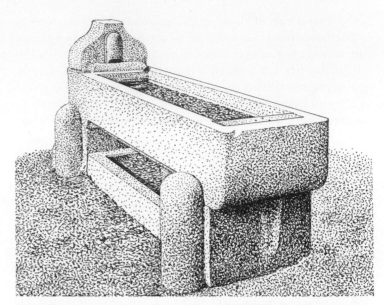

419 *A horse-trough, with water for dogs too: a much needed amenity before the motor car – West Horsley (Sy).*

in 1710–14 at Lamberhurst in the Weald, and not to the taste of Wren. The finials of railings are very varied – spears, crowns, urns, fleurs-de-lys, etc – but again after the Regency they can be heavy and clumsy. The railings themselves may be balustrades, or of "filled-in" designs, which also applies to balconies. These designs include the "Heart and Honeysuckle", used by Robert Adam at the Adelphi in 1774 (cast by Carron), which is very widespread and has several derivative forms, the "Chinese" (the Chippendale style), and the "Greek Key". Amina Chatwin has, for Cheltenham, discerned three periods of design: Early, 1800–20 (but it began in the 1770s in other places); Middle, 1820s and 1830s; Late, after 1840 (ornate and heavy). These periods can often give useful clues to the dating of the houses themselves. With railings go minor items such as torch-extinguishers, lamp-holders, and foot-scrapers.

Street furniture consists of bollards and bollasters, lamp-posts, sign-posts, traffic signs, fountains, horse troughs (see 419), clock towers, pumps and standpipes, manhole and coalhole covers, seats, letter boxes, telephone boxes, urinals, street names, boundary marks, insurance (fire) marks, gratings, drain-covers, sandbins, hitching posts, milestones, public notices, and much else. One cannot indeed imagine a complete list. Some of these are not wholly of cast iron, or, like fire marks, were sometimes of other materials (lead, copper, brass, tinplate, stone, wood, etc), but most were naturally in cast iron. Bollards were sometimes made from gun-moulds, and some are actually surplus guns (eg at Newcomen Street, Southwark (see 420)); Cambridge has a wide range. Clock towers are often in extreme and, to present taste, horrendous designs, such as the Victorian ones in Birmingham. That at Newnham-on-Severn (Gl) contains a chiming clock. Fountains lend themselves to fantastic figures. Street-names can be very tasteful and elegant, like those in Bath. Birmingham has a fine set of ornamental names, some fixed to walls, some on little posts. Iron urinals are a dying breed; there was, at least till recently, a circular one in the (old) Cattle Market by the Castle in Norwich. That inscribed Public Urinal No 1, in an alley off Lamb's Conduit Street, London, regrettably disappeared some years ago, apparently unrecorded. Letter boxes are dealt with on pages 449–51. Coalhole covers are frequently of very fine openwork design (see 421 and 422), and some carry their makers' names; some

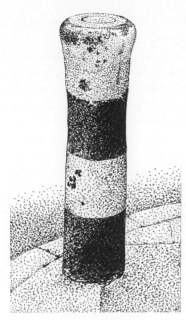

420 *Street bollard made from an actual gun barrel (Southwark).*

have the name of the trader outside whose shop they are – eg Thomas, Hair Cutter, in Duke Street, St James's (if this is still there). Such items are collectable. There is an interesting parish pump in St Paul's Churchyard, inscribed "St Faith's Parish, erected 1819", and others in Queen Square and Bedford Row. A few iron signposts still survive. Lamp-posts and lamp-brackets come in wide variety, as do gateposts, canal and railway items, and dock and industrial machinery and equipment. The characteristic iron clothes-posts in the back gardens of Edinburgh and other Scottish towns should not be overlooked.

Greenhouses and conservatories usually had iron frames, up to the largest, such as those at Syon or Chatsworth or the Palm House at Kew (Burton 1844–8, which now (1985–87) has stainless steel substituted for its wrought iron glazing bars). Shelters at former tram stops are sometimes of iron, as are some cabmen's shelters and those on sea fronts. In Piccadilly, London, is an iron porter's rest (1861). Hitching-posts for horses, and tethering-rings, can still be found. Dorset bridges bear engaging iron notices promising transportation for life for damaging the bridge (see **423**). Other iron items include staircases, window frames and glazing bars, lift-gates, various architectural details, shop fronts (eg Regency Square, Brighton, and Asprey's, Bond Street, London), piers, bandstands, pipework, even chimneys. Domestic items include fireplaces, spits, stoves and ovens (note the splendid Gurney stoves in some cathedrals, eg Ely and Peterborough), and a vast range of utensils and tools, as well as bedsteads, furniture, and window, door, and gate fittings. There is no point here in trying to be comprehensive; Raymond Lister's book (*Decorative Cast Ironwork in Great Britain*, Bell 1960) comes near it.

421–2 *Coalhole covers – London. These often carried the maker's name, or some other device.*

Enamelled cast iron, invented in Germany in the 1760s, was brought to England by the end of the 18th century, and had a lasting use for saucepans, baths, etc.

422

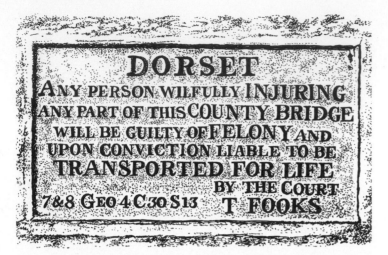

423 *Dorset bridge plaque, 1827. A surprisingly drastic penalty by modern standards.*

Of course much street furniture is not made of cast iron, or may be of a mixture of materials. Thus many milestones are indeed of stone, but equally many are of cast iron. The stone obelisk at Cranleigh (Sy), which commemorates the London to Horsham and Brighton turnpike (1794), incorporates a drinking-fountain and has cast iron plaques giving the distances to various places, including Windsor and Brighton. Bollards and bollasters are often of stone or wood, as are notice boards. Signposts may be wood or iron, or both. Inn and shop signs are usually wooden, but their brackets are often iron.

The first *wireworks* in Britain operated by water power was at Tintern (Mo) (1566–7). Small square-sectioned iron bars were heated in a furnace and "strained" (elongated) by a light and fast water-powered hammer. The elongated rods were cut into lengths and rounded with hand hammers; they were then drawn through a "draw-plate" pierced with holes. This process was repeated until the desired size of wire was reached. The best and finest wire was made from Osmond iron, derived from special ores containing manganese, and was very tough and ductile. This was made until the 18th century in south-east Wales and the Forest of Dean. *Nails* and *needles* were made by hand from thin rods or wire until about 1830, after which they were machine-made, and later were made of steel. Hammered handmade nails can still be seen in old timbers. The processes of making needles are displayed at the National Needle Museum at Redditch (Wo). Nail- and needlemaking were centred to the south-west of Birmingham.

Chain-making was another specialised craft, involving cutting bars of requisite sizes into short lengths, bending these under heat into a U-shape, then reheating and flattening the ends, which were then hammered together and finally shaped. The process can be seen at the Mushroom Green Museum at Brierly Hill (St) and at the Avoncroft Museum of Buildings at Bromsgrove (Wo) (which also has a nail shop). *Anchors* were also forged from bar.

Cast iron *anvils* were still being made into the 18th century, but were subject to cracking under the prolonged hammering needed to make steel cutlery and so on. In the late 16th and early 17th century a method of making more lasting anvils was invented in the Forest of Dean. The anvils were made of scrap iron and slag, and the surface was coated with a thick layer of steel welded on. Special anvil forges developed in the late 17th century.

Steelwork

Steel had been used for cutting and edge tools for centuries. The steel was made by carburising bars of wrought iron in various ways or by heating iron with charcoal in crucibles, resulting in "wootz" steel, which originated in south India and had been used by the Romans. This method was known in England in the 17th century, and developed by Benjamin Huntsman in the 1740s at Sheffield. Using this steel, Sheffield became the centre of *cutlery* making, and by 1787 at least six firms were using the crucible process, which became standard.

Before the Huntsman crucible and the Bessemer and Siemens-Martin processes of the 1850s, "shear" steel suitable for edge tools (which could be ground to make a durable cutting edge) was made by hammering the heated bars of iron coated with charcoal. The elongated bars were then folded in half and forge-welded together. The water-powered tilt-hammer enabled bundles of such "blister" steel bars to be welded and then to be drawn out into bars of shear steel, which could be made into cutting tools. This process can be seen at the Sticklepath Foundry in Devon, which made agricultural and industrial edge tools from 1814 to 1960, and at Abbeydale Forge in Sheffield. The discovery of *stainless steel* – an alloy with 20% chromium and 10% nickel, discovered in 1913 – led to a transformation of medical, scientific, and domestic cutlery and utensils.

536

The cheap production of large quantities of steel resulting from the new processes of the 1850s led to a leap forward in the use of steel for construction, ships, railways, and machinery, on a scale which practically constituted a new phase of the Industrial Revolution. By the 1890s steel had generally replaced cast iron. The last major construction in iron may have been the Eiffel Tower of 1889.

The new Bessemer and open-hearth steels were "mild", and not suitable for edge tools; but they were highly suitable for large constructions. Larger and heavily-armoured (and armed) ships could now be built, as well as larger armaments, thousands of miles of railways, huge bridges (such as the Forth Bridge of 1890), and high-rise buildings; the first large steel-framed building in London was the Ritz Hotel, 1904. Larger and more powerful steam locomotives and other engines, and steam turbines (pioneered by Charles Parsons in 1884), were now possible, and heavier machine tools and industrial plant and equipment. The size of the castings for some of these items remains impressive, and of course the list of such products could be indefinitely extended.

Iron and steel, which took off instantly in late prehistoric times, have been progressively more central in our lives ever since – even in the light metal, plastic, and electronic phase of the Industrial Revolution in which we now are – and have determined many of the key features of our civilisation to a degree which makes it, at the point we have reached, seem unlikely that we shall be able to continue a recognisable Western way of life without them.

(See "Sites and Museums", page 578.)

SALT AND SALTWAYS

Salt has been recognised as a vital commodity since prehistoric times. It had early been discovered that bodily exertion reduced the salts in the body, which had to be replaced, and that cooking removed the salts from food. In fact the requirement for salt by the human body is very small, and some primitive diets provided all that was needed. But there was satisfaction in actually tasting salt and adding it to food. It was also found that salt was a preservative of flesh; enormous quantities were used throughout the Middle Ages to salt meat and fish, so that these could be kept longer and be transported from their sources of supply. For instance, the 13th/14th-century curing industry of the Baltic used 2,400 tons of salt to 13,000 tons of fish in a good year. Salt was also used in other processes, such as pottery glazes.

Salt was got in two ways; either by the evaporation of brine, from sea water or saline springs, or by the mining of rock salt. In warm climates the sun could be used unaided for evaporation. But in Britain and elsewhere in northern Europe it had to be assisted. By the Iron Age a technique had been evolved. Sea or saline water, led along collecting channels, was, after settling, evaporated in shallow pans or hollows in the ground. The brine could then be poured into vessels and heated, or poured over hot stone, clay, or brick. The wet salt then had to be dried and made into cakes; this was done in clay pans. The broken pans, reddened by the charcoal or turf fires used for the heating and drying, constitute the "briquetage" found on saltmaking sites, mixed with ash and blackened earth. The Red Hills of the Essex coast, long a puzzle, are the remains of Iron Age and later salterns.

By Roman times shallow iron pans were used, heated over coal-fired furnaces. The undried salt was put into wooden moulds which were dried in a hot room; the salt was then crushed. In medieval times iron, latten, and lead pans were used, but the used of briquetage had never died out.

As each ground got silted up, new ones had to be embanked nearer the sea and the old ones became pasture, which also absorbed much of the burnt matter. In some places the whole system can be made out, such as at Marsh Chapel (Li) and in Essex and Kent. At Black Haven (Li) the curving enclosure banks and the blackened patches can be seen not only on the coast but up to 15 miles inland, where the sea has receded. At Seasalter (Kt) long oval mounds of clay represent the breached remains of a medieval sea wall, used for a time as a saltern. Roman salterns were at Colchester and on the Blackwater near Maldon, in the Fenlands, in Lincolnshire, and in Cornwall and Somerset; there are Iron Age ones also in Dorset. In the Middle Ages salterns are also found in Kent and Sussex, near Lymington (Ha), and in Cheshire and Lancashire; there were a few round the Tees in the 14th/15th centuries and round the Wear and Tyne by the 17th. The Domesday survey records 1,195 *salinae* along the coasts between Lincolnshire and Cornwall, the major concentrations being in Sussex (294) and Norfolk. Brittany was producing salt of better quality by the 14th century, and English production was reduced. But saltmaking went on until the mid 19th century in some places (eg Hampshire).

Saltmining took place at two places in England: round Nantwich in Cheshire, and at Droitwich in Worcestershire. There are vast medieval workings under both towns. At Droitwich springs come through the deposits to produce a saline spa important since Roman times. Brine pumping succeeded mining in the 18th/19th centuries in Cheshire as the workings collapsed.

The salt industry developed a widespread network of roads, leading all over the country from the salterns and the mines, to get the salt to the markets and the ports; of course, many salterns were close to the fishing ports anyway. Some of these are no doubt older tracks, but many are special to the trade. Some have been followed through, but much work remains to be done in most parts of the country. Few areas have been studied in the intensive way that Arthur Raistrick has done for the Pennines. In this area tracks can be followed from Lancashire and Cheshire across to Yorkshire. For instance, the road from Skipton by Bolton Bridge and Blubberhouses to Knaresborough (known locally as the Skipton road), is a saltway; it follows for part of its course a Roman road over the moors. Such roads can be picked out by place-names such as Saltergate (or, as for a branch of this road down the Washburn valley to Otley, Psaltergate). There are other signs, such as inns called Salt Box, Salters Arms, etc. There is a similar road (also called in one place Saltergate) from Whitby to Pickering, and one from Sunderland into Yorkshire.

H P R Finberg has mapped a network (*The Agrarian History of England and Wales* vol I, II, AD 43–1042, CUP 1972) radiating from Droitwich. These roads went from there to Birmingham, Warwick, and Princes Risborough (where there was a royal manor entitled to be supplied from the royal mines) via Stratford, or, by another route, via Chipping Campden and Chipping Norton, Bampton, Lechlade, Old Sodbury, Ross-on-Wye, Wellington, Leominster and Kidderminster. Another road went from Droitwich to Lincolnshire, entering that county at Saltby. This network is considered to have played an important part in the Anglo-Saxon road system.

The armed forces consumed vast and increasing amounts of salted meat up to the end of the Napoleonic Wars. The end of this diet was foreshadowed in 1813 by the introduction of meat in cans, and the need for salt was finally abolished by the use of refrigeration. In 1879 the first frozen cargo of meat was shipped from Australia. These developments had a serious effect on the cattle-droving trade (see page 421).

LIME

Limeworks are a familiar feature of the chalk downs end of the limestone belts. They are usually backed by huge quarries, create noise, and shed fine white dust over the countryside; near towns, as at Buxton, this can be a serious nuisance. They are large enough to be landmarks, like that at Chinnor in the Chilterns.

They produce three main primary materials:

1 *Lime* is made by burning chalk (or limestone) at about 900°C in a kiln to convert it into *quicklime*. The chalk is mainly calcium carbonate, with various impurities; heating resolves it into carbon dioxide gas and calcium oxide (the quicklime). The stone is burnt in kilns usually close to the quarry; if not sold away as lump lime it is then ground and hydrated in plants adjacent to the quarry. Ground lime is also sold away. For both agricultural and building purposes ground quicklime is *slaked*, that is covered with water; it combines with the water, generating heat, to form slaked lime, which is mainly calcium hydroxide. Under specially controlled conditions a purified powder can be made called hydrated lime; hydration (or slaking) is usually done on site, but hydrated lime can be sold away and used after mixing with water. Sand is mixed with slaked or hydrated lime to produce *mortar*. When excess water is used, the slaked lime in suspension in the water is *milk of lime*; when this is allowed to stand it thickens into *lime putty*, used for mortar and plastering.

2 Another main product, using chalk as a raw material, is *cement*, which depends for its properties on the types and proportions of clays, earths, or gravels with which the chalk is mixed. They are crushed together in a wet mill and calcined into a mass which is ground into a fine powder. Quality improved throughout the early 19th century, under the influence of men like Vicat and Frost, and in 1824 Joseph Aspdin patented a cement of modern type ("Portland" cement). But the first fully reliable cement was not produced until 1845, by I C Johnson at Swanscombe. *Reinforced concrete*, patented by W B Wilkinson in 1854, was the final stage in this long development.

3 The third product of chalk is *whiting*. This is finely divided calcium carbonate, used in gesso, paints, putty, etc. No chemical process is involved; the chalk is merely ground in water, the fine material is separated by sedimentation, and the settled sediment dried and powdered. Normally in this process the chalk was broken up and crushed in a wash mill (a circular floor) by rollers drawn round a central upright. The resulting "slurry" was transferred, or flowed, into an artificial pond, where the coarser material sank to the bottom. At intervals, say once a year in the summer, the pond was allowed to dry; the fine material was dug out, dried, and broken to powder, perhaps in the same mill. The coarser pieces were usually left in the pond.

The plant in a limeworks can be visualised from the above account. The kilns were high up-draught structures (see below), and in a large works could be in banks or connected rows. The great works at Merstham (Sy) had a bank of eight. A disused bank can be seen at Betchworth (Sy). At Merstham, in 1962, an installation consisting of a pond adjacent to a circular floor with a central brick posthole-type structure was excavated by the writer. This was not easy to interpret, but may have been specially built to produce the large quantities of mortar required for the brick railway tunnel nearby (in the 1840s). Incidentally, the Merstham works made mortar and cement for many large buildings in London, including Rennie's London Bridge. (For a useful survey see R A Collins: "Chalk Quarrying in Surrey *c* 1800–1914" (*Surrey Archaeological Collections*, 66 (1969).)

Another aspect of lime production is represented by the large number of single, isolated kilns to be seen in the countryside. These were for making agricultural lime for spreading on the land as a sweetening agent and to replace losses, a regular practice in the 18th and 19th centuries. Although to be found in most parts of the country, the distribution of limekilns shows some odd anomalies, and would repay further study. But in general it seems that they were located where the need was greatest, and in the farmlands where the lime was required. They also had to be close to a supply of fuel (usually wood) and water. It was always cheaper to transport the raw material (the chalk) than the fuel, as was also the case in the rural iron and glass industries. A study was made in 1960, by D J Robinson and R U Cooke, of the kilns in the country round Dorking in Surrey (see *Surrey Archaeological Collections*, 59 (1962)). This showed that in fact none of the kilns located were on the chalk downs; a few were on the greensand, but the majority were on the Weald clays. Each kiln seems to have served several farmers, unless the farm was large enough to need one on its own; groups of kilns close together may be explained by defects in one or more of the group. The kilns were mostly on north–south roads, that is in contact with a chalk quarry on the downs, or were on a feeder track from such a road. Some, as Eric Parker pointed out, stood at the junction of several tracks, for easy access to several farms. Besides coppice timber, furze was grown in special areas for kindling the fires. Kilns may also be looked for on common land or on road verges. Disintegrated kilns can sometimes be identified as such by the presence of chalk round about, on soils where this is a foreign material.

A few medieval kilns are known, such as that at Ogmore Castle (Gl), 13th/14th century, and a 12th-century one found in 1973 at Bedford Castle. But most date from the 17th century onward; indeed, most are in fact probably 19th century. Mass production of lime and changed methods of agriculture led to the abandonment of the local kilns by early in the 20th century.

The kilns in Surrey, and probably in the south of England generally, are small up-draught structures, usually built into a slope. Their form can be illustrated by a perfect example opposite the church at Hambledon (Sy). This consists of a wedge-shaped mound of earth in which is the vertical kiln proper, a circular brick chamber some 4ft (1.2m) wide at the top, tapering to 2' 6" (76cm) at the bottom, and about 8 ft (2.4m) high. Lime-burning involved the direct contact of the fuel and the chalk, unlike pottery, glass, bricks, or hops etc, where the products were kept in a separate oven away from the fire. The hearth was at the end of a short brick tunnel, 4 ft (1.2m) long, emerging at an arch 2ft 6in (76cm) high and wide. The front has a containing stone facade, slightly concave, some 20ft (6m) wide by 8ft (2.4m) high. The top of the kiln is level with the slope behind it, so that direct access is possible to the top for loading and unloading the chalk and lime. The purpose of the tunnel to the hearth is for draught. Such kilns sometimes have external buttresses to prevent or correct slipping on the slope.

In the Highland Zone the kilns are of a different pattern, the reason for which is not obvious. Here they are often free-standing, although some are against slopes; they are much higher than the southern

424 *The door of a late 18th-century limekiln – Lindisfarne (Nd).*

425 *A coastal limekiln. These are common all round the coasts, the coal for firing them, and often the limestone as well, being brought by sea. This one is at Gwbert (Cd); the adjacent mounds are spoil-heaps from limestone quarrying.*

the south Wales coast, such as at Gwbert (Cd) (see **425**). Similarly, there is a spectacular row on the quay at Beadnell (Nd) (see **426**).

To supply north Devon (a sandstone and gritstone area) with lime, limestone and coal (culm) were brought into Appledore and Bideford from south Wales; the lower Torridge had 16 lime kilns in the 18th century. Kilns were also built at suitable anchorages along the coast. For instance, there are three at Bucks Mills, two of which may be 16th century; the other is very large and fine, and was built in 1760.

ones, and have prominent tall arches for draught instead of the small low tunnel. Where they are not against a slope they have an earth "tail" built on one side for access to the top. There are some excellent examples in Northumberland (see **424**) and Yorkshire, such as one on the roadside above Kettlewell (NY) and one just north of the road by the Dike Hill signal tower on Hadrian's Wall. Not far from this one, at West Grindledikes, is one with three arches.

Coal was used for firing Highland Zone kilns wherever it was economic to do so. This accounts for the frequency of kilns along the coast, using coal brought by sea. Thus there are many kilns along

426 *Limekilns – Beadnell (Nd).*

540

Coal from the many small pits on the northern moors was also used and transported to the kilns by regular "lime roads" or "coal roads" which can still be traced across the moors. One such runs from Kirkby Malzeard into Nidderdale (at Middlesmoor). R W Moore has described the roads in the moorland behind Whitby. There were four of these, from Hutton-le-Hole to Castleton and Danby, from Cropton to Egton, from Newton Dale and Pickering to Goathland, and from Lockton to the lower Esk valley and Whitby. In the 1830s (it is recorded) a farmer of Danby would set off in the morning with an empty wagon to the Rosedale Head coalpits. Leaving the empty wagon at the pits, he would take on a wagon left there the previous day and now loaded with coal; this would be taken on to Hutton-le-Hole for unloading, where he would pick up a third wagon loaded with lime. This he would take home for unloading in preparation for another day. The farmer paid for the coal at Rosedale Head; in receiving the lime at Hutton he was given a small sum with it in exchange for the coal. In this way (and this is no doubt typical of many northern farmers) he brought 40 wagonloads of lime, each weighing 1/2 ton, on 40 consecutive days, for use on his farm or those of his neighbours. This traffic declined by the middle of the century, as better quality lime was imported by sea to Whitby from Sunderland and Flamborough.

Clues to the discovery of limekilns can often be got from local names, such as Kiln Field, Copse, Lane, etc. Names containing Furze are also likely to refer to local limemaking.

MILLING

Watermills

Water and wind were the only sources of mechanical power until well into the 18th century. Waterwheels were used in Roman Britain and increasingly from Saxon times on; the first record seems to be in 762 at Dover. In Domesday (1086), 9,250 manors were recorded, of which 3,463 had 5,624 mills, each catering for some 250 people; mills were manorial property, and tenants had to use them. During the Middle Ages they were mainly used for grain-grinding, fulling, and drainage, but they became adapted to a wide range of processes from the 16th century on.

Cornmills

Like a windmill, a water-driven cornmill has three storeys – the top floor for the grain bins, the middle (or stone) floor for the stones, and the ground floor for the reception and bagging of the flour. The waterwheel is at this level. The waterwheel is connected by its axle, which passes through the wall, to a large cogged *pit wheel* fixed to the axle close to the main shaft, and turning with the waterwheel. The pit wheel engages with a smaller cogged wheel, the *wallower*, on the main shaft, which rises vertically into the stone floor above. On the main shaft, at stone floor level, is fixed the cogged *great spur wheel*, from which drives are taken off to actuate the millstones and the hoist for raising the grain to the top floor. The stones may be actuated either from above or from below through the floor, from a lower spur wheel on the main shaft at ground floor level. The gearing is arranged so as to increase the speed of the stones to 10 to 15 times that of the waterwheel. The gear wheels were originally wooden, but became replaced by iron in the early 19th century. But the cogs are still sometimes of wood (frequently pear), for greater resilience. The corn is fed to the stones and the flour descends to the ground floor, entirely by gravity.

The waterwheel may be either *overshot*, where the water is led along a wooden trough from the millpond to strike the buckets of the wheel just past its highest point, turning the wheel by the weight of water, or *undershot*, where the water flows against the bottom of the wheel, striking flat paddles or "floats" (see **427**). The two types of wheel of course revolve in different directions. An overshot wheel, which can only be used where it is possible to create a millpond, with a fall at the dam ("bay") of 8–10ft (2.4–3m), is twice as efficient as an undershot wheel. The latter type was normal in hilly country with deep valleys, where the stream itself could be used as it was, without weirs and dams, which were costly to build and maintain. There was also a *breast-shot* type, where the water struck below the top of the wheel.

If the stream was too shallow or too slow, a *millpond* had to be made by damming the stream just above the mill, creating a head of water. When the mill was not working the stream flowed from the pond past the mill by way of a leat, controlled by a sluice; this could be shut off and the water directed at the wheel, by another sluice at the wheel. The great ponds in the Weald, made for driving the bellows and hammers of the iron industry, are still impressive, eg those in

St Leonard's Forest, near Horsham, or Knappmill Pond, near Shipley. Some cornmills are still in use, as at Headley (Ha) or Calthorpe (IW). Even quite small streams could have mills, as at Selborne (Ha).

Other uses

The Wandle, surprisingly, was one of the most industrialised rivers in Britain, having in its heyday some 200 mills between Croydon and Wandsworth. In 1610 it had at least 24 cornmills and a number of others, including mills for snuff grinding, papermaking, gunpowder, copper and brassware (stamping and rolling), leather-dressing, cloth-fulling, hemp-spinning, bleaching, and calico printing; this last mill had in 1724 an undershot iron wheel with four sets of spokes and hubs, and in 1885 it became the famous Liberty works. The Stroud area of Gloucestershire had a similar number, mostly in the woollen industry. Kent had a large number of papermills. The streams of the Bradford area, the dales of West Yorkshire, Lancashire, and Derbyshire, and the Water of Leith at Edinburgh were also intensively used.

The Weald of Kent and Sussex had some 160 iron forges and furnaces, driven by waterwheels, of which none remains. Abbeydale Mill in Sheffield and Sticklepath Mill near Okehampton (Dv) illustrate the use of water power in forges. The cotton and woollen industries used water power for driving the looms, for scribbling (carding and slubbing), spinning, and fulling. Flax was scutched (bruised to extract the fibres) by water power; a flax mill at Foster Beck, near Pateley Bridge (NY), had an overshot wheel of 1864, 36ft (11m) in diameter. Hemp and silk mills also used water power. Other uses include sawmills and slate processing.

A major use was in mining, where water power was used to raise water (draining) or to raise the mined ore, coal, etc to the surface. The finest example is the famous Isabella Wheel at Laxey (IM), an over-shot wheel 71ft (21.3m) in diameter (1854), used to pump water from a leadmine (see **428**). This has been spectacularly restored to working order.

Raising water is indeed a major use of waterwheels. A wooden wheel was installed in one of the narrow arches of Old London Bridge in 1581/2 to pump Thames water to supply the City. This was destroyed in the Great Fire of 1666; by 1737 there were four wheels, and in 1767 one at the Southwark end of the bridge as well. In 1817 one wheel

was replaced by an iron one. By 1821 four million gallons of water a day were being pumped to 10,000 customers. In 1822 the building of the new bridge brought this system to an end and London's supply was transferred to the New River.

Waterwheels were also used in ornamental parks. At Painshill, Cobham (Sy) there is an iron Bramah wheel, of the 1830s, 36ft (11m) in diameter, which lifts water from the river Mole to flow in a channel carried on a brick aqueduct to the top of the Cascade and thence into the Lake (see **429**). This is one of the first examples of cast iron in gardens.

427 *Undershot waterwheel – Mapledurham (Ox).*

Apples and roots were crushed by stones mounted vertically and running "on edge" round a circular vat; this method was also used for extracting oil from linseed and rape, and for ore and flint-crushing, eg at Cheddleton (St). Water power was also adapted on farms for chopping and slicing roots, chaff-cutting, and even for threshing.

Waterwheels were superseded by steam power during the 18th century – as in the Cornish tin mines, by beam engines. Mills went over either to steam or to water-driven turbines. These were invented in France in 1827 and used a jet of water against blades, which produced much higher powers and speeds than waterwheels. A MacAdam turbine from Catteshall Mill, Farncombe (Sy) (paper) has been scheduled as an ancient monument and restored. There is a turbine *in situ* at Hatch Mill, Godalming, installed only in 1940.

Horizontal watermills

The very distinctive type of watermill with a horizontal wheel seems to have been invented somewhere in Asia Minor or the Levant in the late first millennium BC. It took root all over the Mediterranean world and from there, in the mid first millennium AD, found its way to Scandinavia. From Scandinavia it reached the Norse dependencies in Scotland, and perhaps also Ireland, although the shape of blade is different in the Irish mills, and these may have come direct from south-west Europe. There is no satisfactory evidence that this type of mill was used in the rest of Scotland, or in England and Wales.

As used in the Norse parts of Britain, the horizontal mill consisted

428 *The Great Laxey Wheel ("Lady Isabella"), Isle of Man. This was built in 1864, and is 71 ft (21.3m), in diameter; it is used to drain leadmines. A supreme achievement of its class.*

429 *Bramah waterwheel (32 ft, 9.8m in diameter) – Painshill (Sy), 1830s. It was used to raise water from the river Mole to the ornamental lake in the park.*

of a vertical shaft of wood or iron, in which were set a number of straight blades or paddles, usually at an angle, to be at right angles to the wooden trough which led the water to the wheel. The simplest type had 4–12 blades, but there was another type with up to 20, strengthened by a "shroud" or rim round the ends of the blades. The mill was enclosed in a simple building of two stories. The shaft went up through the floor and was fixed to the upper millstone, which therefore rotated over the stationary lower stone. Grain was fed onto the upper stone by means of a hopper suspended from the rafters. The controls of the gap between the stones, and stopping and starting, are of the simplest. Mills of this type were used in Scotland (where in 1814 Sir Walter Scott reported some 500) – Orkney, Caithness, Sutherland, and the Hebrides. They are also recorded in the Isle of Man. The Irish mills had spoon-shaped blades, and a few of these got to Scotland.

There was no millpond; a stream was used direct. Traces remain of several of these mills in remote places in this area. One has been restored and is accessible – the Click Mill at Dounby, on Orkney Mainland (see **430**). This gives an excellent idea of what, until living memory, was the standard mill over the whole of northern Scotland, but it happens to be a variant, in that it has two sets of blades on the shaft. None is still in use.

Although in recent centuries mills of this type were confined to the more remote parts of the Highland Zone, they had a wider distribution in the early Middle Ages. There must have been many in use in Anglo-Saxon England, of which two have been located and excavated. One of these was discovered in 1971 at the Mercian royal mill at Tamworth (St), dating from the 8th century. At Old Windsor (Bk) there was a 9th-century mill with three vertical

430 *A horizontal watermill – Click Mill, Dounby, Orkney.*

shafts working in parallel; this was destroyed by Vikings and replaced by a Tamworth-type mill, which remained in use until the early 11th century.

Millstones

Millstones were replaced for grinding corn by rollers in the bulk milling processes of the 19th century, but are still used in small mills, mainly for smaller-scale processes such as grinding animal feed, but also for "stone-ground" flours. They are rounds of stone, 4–6in (10–15cm) thick, with a standard diameter of 4ft (1.2m) (see **431**). They are used in pairs, the bottom stone (the bed stone) fixed and the top or runner stone rotating upon it, driven either by a shaft from below (usual in watermills) or from above (in windmills). The grain is fed through a "shoe" in the centre of the upper stone, and is gradually led from the centre to the edges by means of the pattern of grooves cut in the stones; from there it falls off and is collected. The normal pattern of grooves is in groups of three (harps), one long one running slightly askew from centre to edge and two shorter ones parallel to it. The long ones are called furrows, the shorter ones stitching; the higher spaces between the grooves are the "lands". Turning at 125 or even 160 revolutions a minute for eight hours a day, the pattern soon wears and has to be frequently recut. This is done with a "bill", a cutting tool resembling a double-ended wedge. Replacing the upper stone the right distance from the lower is a tricky business.

The stone preferred for grinding corn was the French burr, a hard freshwater quartz from the Paris basin; this was so popular that it continued to be imported even during the Napoleonic Wars. It was quarried in small pieces and the millstone built up in sections backed with plaster of Paris and bound with an iron hoop like a cartwheel. Another hard stone was the blue German or cullin (from Cologne). Niedermendig lava from the Rhineland was used for querns in Roman and Iron Age times. British stones were softer and mostly used for grist work, grinding barley, oats, peas, beans, etc. They came from Anglesey, and particularly from Derbyshire – these were the "Peak" stones, of Millstone Grit, cut to size from rough-hewn blanks. Remains of these can still be seen under the

431 *Millstone, showing the traditional pattern of grooves.*

scars east of Hathersage. They were also used for edge-runners, vertically-mounted stones for crushing apples, dyewoods, etc, and for cutlery grinding at Sheffield.

Stones wore out or developed faults, and discarded ones can be seen all over the country, leaning against walls or set in pavements. In some areas, eg North Yorkshire, they are used to carry the names of villages, and they are set up, very happily and appropriately, where roads enter the Peak District National Park.

Flint mills

The use of ground flint in the pottery industry led to a specialised form of watermill. There were many in the north of England, of which the mill at Cheddleton (St) between Leek and Longton has been restored.

Flint was recognised by Astbury in 1720 as a useful agent for whitening earthenware and to make the clay more refractory to withstand higher firing temperatures, instead of the sand used till then. Astbury used ground flint in a white slip to wash the insides of his buff-coloured wares; Daniel Bird was probably the first to recognise the correct proportion (about 35%) to yield a satisfactory earthenware body. The dust caused in the grinding process was so dangerous that Thomas Benson took out a patent in 1726 to grind flint in water.

The North Mill at Cheddleton was built, probably by Brindley, in 1756–65, specially to grind flint. When the canal was opened the supply of flint was increased, and the older South Mill was converted for flint-grinding between 1780 and 1820, when the pottery industry expanded very rapidly. The mills were working till 1963.

Flints were imported from the south and east coasts of England and sent up the canals into the pottery areas. They were unloaded at the flint mills and fed into kilns, in layers between layers of coal. There they were calcined for three or four days to shatter then and make them easier to grind. From the kilns they were carried in wagons on a plateway to the mill, hoisted to the top floor, and charged onto a pan, with water. The pan was paved with chert stones, and heavy chert runners were driven round the pan by cast iron arms. After being ground for 24 hours the slop flint was run off into a wash tub for thorough mixing with water before passing to the settling ark. Here the flint settled and the clear water was drawn off. At the right point the remaining slop was dried in a kiln, and when dry sent by canal to the potteries.

Tidemills

An interesting variant of the stream-driven watermill is the tidemill. These grew up at suitable places round the coast, particularly in the south-west (eg Carew and Pembroke in Wales, and Pomphlett in Devon), parts of the south coast (Emsworth, Beaulieu, Eling, and Birdham), and in Essex and Suffolk (Thornington, Stambridge, and Woodbridge). They are also found well inland on tidal rivers, such as the three at Bromley-by-Bow in east London. Twenty-three were recorded in 1938, of which ten were still using the tides. But since then all have ceased to do so, and where remaining as mills at all use other sources of power.

The tidemill at Woodbridge was restored in 1974, and shows how these mills worked. This mill is also of interest in being probably the earliest recorded tidemill in Britain (1170) and the last to give up (1957, when the wheel-shaft broke). The wheel was not turned, as is sometimes thought, by the incoming tide, but by the controlled flow from a pond behind the mill. In fact, most tidemills were built a few miles up shallow creeks, not at their mouths. The pond was made with earth banks high enough to hold the tidal water, and varied greatly in size; that at St Osyth's (Ex) was over 30 acres (12ha), that at Birdham 13 acres (5.2ha), but at Woodbridge on 7 acres (3ha) (this one has been converted into a yacht marina). There were two sets of gates in the bank: one, opened by the incoming tide, which filled the pond, and held the gates closed as the tide fell; the other, a pair of sluice gates just behind the wheel. These were in the mill race; one could be raised or lowered vertically to shut off the water or let it flow against the wheel, while the other was close to the wheel; if lowered the water flowed over it (when the other gate was raised) and struck the wheel halfway up (breast-shot), and if raised as well the water flowed along the bed of the race and the wheel was undershot. The mill worked for about two hours on each side of low tide, making the miller's working day very irregular. The present building at Woodbridge is not medieval but probably early 18th century; it has timbers of pitch-pine, probably imported from the Baltic, and there are traces of what may be a predecessor near the entrance of the present yacht harbour.

A recent adaptation of the tidemill is the *barrage* across a tidal water for the production of hydroelectric power. France (the Rance estuary) and Canada have barrages in operation; in Britain various studies have been made and a comprehensive one was launched in 1987. Possible sites are the Bristol Channel and the Mersey.

Horse-driven cornmills

A few examples are known of the use of horses to drive cornmills with conventional millstones, that is replacing the usual water or wind-power by horsepower. Cider mills, with upright runners, were often driven by horses, either direct or through cog and run gearing; these methods gave rise to the substitution of millstones for the runners. The mills at Woburn Park Farm (Bd) and Great Tew (Ox), both early 19th century, were cases where the horse-wheel is equivalent to the great spur wheel of a watermill, and in which the horse-wheel engaged with the stone nuts and drove the millstones. If the wheel made four revolutions a minute the nuts would convert this to some 80 per minute, a speed at which, although low, corn-grinding can just be done. The geared system occurs at Woolley Park (Bk), where the horse-wheel is on the ground floor and connected by gearing to a frame on the first floor, on which two pairs of wheels are driven (at 115rpm). This mill can still be seen. At Mill Farm, Eversholt (Bd) is a somewhat similar machine dating from about 1875, but dismantled (it has been re-erected at the Museum of Milling, Billing (Nh)). The principle was used to drive a pump at the Weevil Brewery, Gosport (Ha) (1812). That there may have been other such mills is suggested by the street-name Horsemill Square at Knaresborough (NY).

Treadmills and horse-wheels

The *treadmill* proper is a large wooden wheel, mounted vertically and turned by men or animals walking round inside; the power was transmitted to a drum or shaft and used for various purposes. The smallest are the roasting spits, used in inns and great houses from the late medieval period to the 17th century, and in some cases even into the 19th, and turned by a dog. An example survives at the George Inn, Lacock (Wi). Human power was used by the Romans to work scoop-wheels for the drainage of mines, for cranes, and for milling. In Britain they were used in the Middle Ages and up to the 18th century, mostly for cranes and hoists. There is a crane by the river Wey at Guildford (Sy) and one with two wheels at Harwich (Ex); neither of these is in its original position, owing to remodelling of the wharves. Hoists survive in, eg, Beverley Minster and Canterbury Cathedral. Most, particularly those made from the 15th to the 17th century, were powered by donkeys. These were generally for raising water from wells, and are mostly on the chalk where the wells had to be deep. Important examples accessible to the public are at Carisbrooke Castle (IW), Greys Court, near Henley (Ox), and Burton Agnes (Hu); several others are still in place, eg at Saddlescombe (Sx). That at the Weald and Downland Museum at Singleton (Sx) (from Catherington (Ha)) is smaller than these, and may have been worked by a man or boy (see **432**); a similar wheel survives at The Milbury's (formerly the Fox and Hounds) at Beauworth (Ha). Many of these wheels remained in use until the end of the 19th century.

Donkeys were used by the Greeks and Romans to drive *horizontal* wheels, for purposes like ore-crushing at mines and corn-grinding. The latter were replaced by waterwheels in the 4th century. In the Middle Ages oxen could be used, but by the 16th century horses were used to turn wheels in Britain. These were wooden, until the 19th century, when iron was used. These drove the machinery in three ways: *direct-drive* for crushing mills, eg bark, chalk, clay, ores, apples for cider, stone, and for butter churning – the axles were generally of a short type west of Severn and a long type east of Severn; *rope-winding* was used for raising coal, ore, or water from mines, and earth from canal and railway tunnels (through shafts) – the mine application lasted from the 16th to the mid 19th century, and in the 17th century drainage of the Fens was carried out in this way, using scoop-wheels, chain-pumps, or buckets; *gear-turning* was used for threshing or working farm machinery.

Nineteenth-century iron wheels still exist, eg at Patching and Billingshurst (Sx). There is an iron pugmill (for preparing clay for making bricks etc) at Ashburnham (Sx).

Horse-wheels ("gins" in England, "whims" in Scotland) were usually housed in special sheds (*gin-houses*), attached to the barn

432 *Treadwheel, for raising water from a well, or similar tasks. This one, from Catherington (Ha), is in the Weald and Downland Open Air Museum. It is too small to be driven by a donkey, and was probably worked by a man or boy (early 17th century).*

or building in which was the actual machinery and the supply of material. They are commonest in north-east England and east Scotland, but there are many also in south-west Scotland and south-west England. They also occur in the Midlands, the north-west, and in Sussex; recent research is finding them to be quite widespread. Cast iron wheels standing in the open air were used in the Western Isles, the Highlands, Orkney, central Scotland, southern England, the Midlands, the north-west, and Yorkshire. These needed no shed and could be moved if the farmer changed farms. There are examples at the Ryedale Folk Museum at Hutton-le-Hole (NY) and at the Weald and Downland Museum.

The most intensive research has been carried out on the gin-houses of the north-east of England, where they are probably most plentiful. Over 200 have been traced or recorded in the North York Moors and south Tees-side, and over 500 "gin gans" are recorded in Northumberland. This proliferation is due to the invention of an improved threshing machine, by Andrew Meikle of Clackmannanshire, which was first installed at Phantassie in East Lothian in 1787. By 1807 there were 350 in use in East Lothian alone, and the device spread to all the corn counties of Scotland and into northern England; it reached Nunnington in North Yorkshire in 1790. Most of them were built by 1853, and the last between 1878 and 1886. They were later used for turnip- and straw-chopping as well. The wheel was really a wooden frame, fixed to a wood or iron upright shaft. It took its shape from the number of horses – two, three, four, or six (there is a wheel for six at Sawley Hall, near Ripon) – which would drive it. The frame was bolted to a ring-gear (or sometimes, and particularly in Tyneside, to a cog and rung), which drove a shaft leading to the threshing machine in the adjacent barn, which was itself geared to run at 1,000 revolutions per minute.

The sheds are of three types: *square*, mostly stone-built, and enclosed; *five- or six-sided* with central roof couple – the commonest form – mostly open but some with the spaces between the pillars filled in later; or *pyramid-roofed*, open, one side common to the barn wall – this is a very local type and a good example, semicircular, is at Grange Farm, Cowesby (NY). All these project from the side of the barns like apses, except that those in Fife are almost detached. Gin-houses can still be seen in many parts of the country, for instance in Sussex one at Redford (for a pugmill), Arundel (for crushing linseed), and at Patching (for a pump).

Windmills

The type of windmill in use in northern Europe is the "western" type, with horizontal axle, which may have been inspired by the Vitruvian waterwheel used in the Roman world from the late 1st century BC. There is another, unrelated, "eastern" type, invented in Persia in the 7th century AD, which has a vertical axle; this seems to derive from the Greek or Norse watermill (see page 543). The first mention of the western type is in a Norman deed of *c* 1180, and there is no reason to think that it was invented much earlier. They appear in England by 1185. By the end of the 13th century these windmills were common throughout northern Europe, including Britain.

The main uses of windmills were corn-grinding and water-pumping. They generated much the same power as watermills – 5–10 horsepower. Windmills and watermills were the only mechanical power sources until well into the Industrial Revolution, when both were superseded by steam from the late 18th century, and by roller milling in the 19th; a very wide range of applications was found for water power. Several thousand windmills once existed, and there are still some 2,000 derelict mills, with fewer than 100 working or able to work. They are mostly in the Lowland Zone of Britain – the drier, corn-growing areas – with large numbers on the east coast, Sussex and Kent, and the Fylde of Lancashire; 80% are in eastern England. There was a group in the Fens used for drainage.

The earliest type of windmill was the *postmill*, where the whole structure revolves round a central post, machinery, sails, and all. The post rises from a ground frame of two intersecting beams (cross-trees), usually resting on four piers of brick or stone and steadied by braces (quarter-bars). Instead of resting on piers, early mills especially were often sunk into slots in a circular mound; these mounds, now looking like hot cross buns but with a ditch from which the earth to make them was dug can be found near deserted villages, or on lanes in medieval ridge and furrow. If raised on piers, the space so formed was enclosed by a wall – the round-house – which gave storage space. The main post supported a beam, the crown-tree, from which the superstructure was hung. This contained three floors, and was weatherboarded for lightness. The topmost floor contained the grain bins and the hoist for lifting the sacks to that level; the windshaft from the sails also came in here. The middle floor held the millstones, sometimes two pairs; the lower floor was for the reception and bagging of the flour.

The stones are driven (the upper one turns, the lower is fixed) through geared shafting by the sails; these at first were canvas-covered and had to be adjusted by hand to match varying wind strengths. About 1770 the spring sail was introduced, which had a series of shutters controlled by the action of the wind against springs; an almost fully automatic type was introduced in 1807, where the shutters were preset by means of a weighted rod, to a given limit of closing. The whole superstructure had to be turned to bring the sails into the wind, and until the mid 18th century this was done manually by a tail-pole projecting over the round-house – a very arduous job. This needed constant attention to catch variations of wind, and in 1745 a "fantail" was introduced which enabled the wind itself to move the tail-pole, by means of a small fan at the end of the pole at right angles to the sails, which, by gearing, moved a carriage rotating, often on a track, on the ground round the base of the mill (see **433**, facing page 507).

In the late 14th century another type of windmill appeared, the *tower mill*. This consists of a round tower built of stone or brick, which was both stronger than the wooden postmill, and obviated the need for massive timbers. A variety of this type, where all or most of the tower is wooden, usually octagonal, is called a *smock mill*. These tower mills have a moveable cap which carries the sails and avoids the necessity to turn the whole superstructure. At first the cap was turned by means of a long pole operated from a platform round the tower, but later a fantail was fitted for automatic action. Caps vary regionally: in Norfolk they are like an upturned boat, in west Suffolk and Cambridgeshire they are conical or dome-shaped. Most windmills have four sails (and if there are now two these are the survivors of four); but five, six, and even eight were sometimes used. The speed of revolution varied with the wind, but the rate of rotation of the stones was regulated by governors. Both directions of rotation were used, and the length and area of the sails varied quite widely; they could be up to 13yd (12m) long.

There are several mills, either working or in working order, which give the feel of this very specialised plant and way of life. No post-mills built before the 17th century survive, but that at Bourn (Ca) (before 1636) has a powerful personality; it has no round-house. Perhaps the epitome of the type is that at Saxstead Green, near Framlingham (Su) (18th century, but succeeding earlier mills since before 1309); its round-house has been heightened). The postmill at Outwood (Sy) (1665) is still working, or was till very recently. A rare variant, a hollow postmill, where the shaft passes down through the post, stands on Wimbledon Common (1817). Tower mills are well represented in Norfolk, such as Billingford near Scole (1860), or Berney Arms, Braydon Water (for drainage, *c* 1864). There is a small drainage mill at Wicken (Ca), among many in the Fens. The smock mill at Cranbrook (Kt) is notable, as is that at Upminster (Ex).

Windmills were not often used to drive farm machinery; wind is fitful, mills are costly, and farms are not by preference built in windy spots. The architect J C Loudon (1833) illustrates a windmill built as an integral part of farm buildings, but this was intended to grind flour as soon as the corn was threshed in the barn. Wind power was indeed used in Northumberland not only for corn-grinding but for threshing, but this use was not general. However, at West Blatchington (Sx) is a barn surmounted by a windmill (1833); this operated a threshing machine in one section of the barn and two chaff-cutters in the other. This arrangement appears to be unique.

Horizontal windmills

There is a less familiar type of windmill using horizontal sails or vanes. This idea has exercised inventors for centuries, and a large number of variants has been tried. There are small forms, from Tibetan prayer wheels to toys and advertising devices, but the principle can be applied to full-scale milling. These mills have been classified (by Greville Bathe in 1948) as turbines with unshrouded blades; articulated wind wheels; shrouded wind wheels; horizontal windmills of China; horizontal sail mills; windmills of the Great Plains; turbine shutter mills; horizontal draft mills of Persia; draft machines; modern horizontal windmills; and rotating signs.

Some of these classes have been tried out in Britain, although it is not clear whether any survive, except as parts or models in museums. A hinged vane wheel stood on Mitcham Common in the early 19th century; this had a feathering type of vane. There was also at this period an articulated mill in the south of Scotland. The shrouded wheel type occurred on a water tank at Hornsea station (Hu) (early 20th century). Walter Blith, in 1652, describes mills with four scroll-shaped wooden sails. The turbine shutter type appears at Margate, *c* 1790, Sheerness, 1797, and Battersea, 1788. Draft machines include John Braithwaite's Smoke Jack of 1795.

There are a few undefined examples, merely described as horizontal mills. Of one, at Pashley near Eastbourne, recorded in 1752, foundations remain. Others have been reported from Lichfield (invented by Erasmus Darwin and seen by James Watt in 1779), Audley End, Dunbar, and Lambeth. But as experiments with these ideas began in the 16th century at least, there must once have been very many more than these.

PAPERMAKING

This industry was widespread, particularly in the south of England, from the 16th century to the late 19th, after which it became concentrated in large factories. It required a plentiful supply of iron-free water, and proximity to sizeable towns as sources of rags. Few watermills were built specially for papermaking; the norm was to occupy a mill which had been used for another purpose, such as corn-milling or fulling. Papermills are therefore small-scale and not distinctive.

The process was simple, if laborious, and the output usually modest. The rags were cleaned and boiled then pulped, often by water-driven hammers. The pulp was mixed with water in a vat, where additives such as china clay could be added. The "vat man" then lifted out some pulp on a mould consisting of a wire screen in a wooden frame ("deckle"). This was drained, the deckle removed, and the pulp fibres turned, on a bed of woollen felt, by the "couch man". The sheet was then transferred to a screw press to remove any excess water, and was hung in a loft to dry, pressed, given a coat of size, and then dried and pressed once more. A watermark could be produced by incorporating a figure of wire into the mould.

The time consumption and limited output of this process led to its mechanisation. A machine invented in France in the 1790s was developed in England by Henri and Sealy Fourdrinier, and built by Bryan Donkin at Bermondsey from 1803. This machine followed the hand processes in sequence, and its successors are still based on it. As in other industries, water power was succeeded by steam, and later by electricity, during the 19th century. A method of using wood pulp instead of rags was invented by Matthias Koops at Neckinger Mill, Bermondsey, in 1800. Esparto grass was imported from c1860, and barges containing this were familiar sights on the Thames near where the National Theatre now stands before the Second World War.

The first papermill in England was established at Hertford in 1488; the industry grew steadily throughout the Home Counties, attracted by London as a source of rags and as a market for the paper. Buckinghamshire and Kent were particularly important, but Surrey and Hampshire also had a thriving industry.

The industry in Surrey (which, before 1974, included much of London south of the Thames) has recently been studied by Alan Crocker (see, eg, *Surrey History* IV/1, 1990), and may be taken as typical. Surrey had 38 mills in all, with a maximum of 17 working at any one time. The decline of the cloth industry in the 17th century led to many fulling mills becoming available for other uses, and papermakers took advantage of this as London grew. The first Surrey mill was at Stoke-next-Guildford, 1636 (this ceased in 1869). Others followed on the Wey, Mole, Tillingbourne, Hogsmill, and Wandle, and a windmill was used in Southwark. By 1750 there were 16 sites; steam power became common after 1800. The numbers declined after 1850 and by 1900 only four were left. At Carshalton (1744–1806) paper was still being made by hand. The last mill, Catteshall (near Godalming), closed in 1928.

Catteshall mill was run by the Sweetapple family from 1661 to 1865, then by the Spicers to the 1890s; in this period – in 1873 – a Fourneyron water turbine was installed, the oldest of the few which survive and the largest of its type ever built – this has been conserved. From 1907 to 1928 Catteshall was run by the Reeds, who, in 1922, built at Aylesford (Kt) what was then the largest papermill in Europe. Another example of long-running family ownership is that of Sickle Mill, Haslemere, 1735–1850, by the Simmons family.

In Hampshire the mill at Laverstoke is of interest. Here Henri Portal made the first watermarked paper in 1712. The mill was built in 1719, but was rebuilt in 1881. The Portals made Bank of England notes here from 1724 for over 200 years. Papermaking ceased here in 1963. The earliest mill in Hampshire was at Warnford, c 1618, built specially for paper; it was destroyed in 1952.

North Wiltshire had papermills along the By Brook, and there were a few in Somerset, Devon, and Cornwall. The largest mills in the south and west are now round Bristol, built from the mid 19th century, eg the Golden Valley Mill at Bitton. Paper was also made further north, eg at the King's Mills, Castle Donington (Le) from 1680 till well into the 19th century. In Scotland, in 1868, there were 57 papermills, of which 22 were in Midlothian, eg St Leonards, Lasswade (late 18th century to 1966), or Valleyfield, near Loanhead, 18th century.

GUNPOWDER

The ingredients of gunpowder are saltpetre, charcoal, and sulphur, usually in the proportion of 75:15:10 for firearms and 70:15:15 for blasting. The saltpetre was made from animal matter mixed with earth, lime, and ashes; the animal matter was mostly pigeons' dung, collected from the large number of dovecotes all over the country (which, in times of war, were compelled to supply it for this purpose). But the supply was inadequate and the process slow and unsavoury, and much saltpetre was imported (from Italy, India, etc). Sulphur had to be imported from Italy, and charcoal was made locally but required a plentiful supply of timber (alder and dogwood being specially favoured; dogwood was planted for this, and the remnants of these plantations can still be seen, eg in Surrey). The gunpowder mills thus had to be within reach of a seaport and of suitable woodland. They also had to have water power on the spot to drive the mills, and waterways to float the powder safely from process to process within the works.

The processes involved preparing the ingredients, mixing them in proper proportions in a mixing machine, and "incorporating" them in a mill with heavy stone or iron runners revolving on a bed with water, thus making a uniform substance with ingredients properly distributed in it; this was done by hand, with pestle and mortar, up to the 17th century. The result was then ground to various specifications for different purposes, broken down, pressed into cakes (between plates by hydraulic rams), and granulated by a machine with gunmetal teeth. The powder was then polished with Spanish graphite in revolving tubs, finished, by stoving or drying on racks heated by steam pipes, and finally flasked, cased, and packed. This complicated sequence required a large number of specialised buildings, spread over a considerable area, and employed a variety of hands, men and women. Thus the Faversham mills, at their height, employed nearly 400 men, almost a quarter of the male population of the town.

Gunpowder was probably first made in Europe in the 13th century, but for a long time England imported her requirements. The earliest works were at Rotherhithe (by 1555, but may have been started by Bermondsey Abbey in or before 1536), Faversham (by 1558), and Long Ditton (by 1561). Gunpowder was also made in Surrey. In 1588 there was a mill near Ewell, transferred to Godstone in 1613, and to Chilworth in 1626. Some ironworks, eg Frith Wood, near

Northchapel (Sx), had their own gunpowder works for the armament side of their business. Their product became known as *black powder*, to distinguish it from new, smokeless types of powder developed in the 1880s. Modern high explosives and propellants, using cellulose, glycerine, and other organic compounds, were developed for blasting in the 1860s and for ballistic use in the 1890s. Black powder was made until 1977.

Gunpowder manufacture was at first concentrated in south-east England (16th and 17th centuries), particularly in Surrey, the Lea Valley in Essex, and round Faversham in Kent. The industry spread to north Somerset in the 18th century, and later to north-west England. In Scotland it began in the late 18th century (south-west of Edinburgh, from Kent), reached Argyll in the 1830s from Glasgow and ultimately from Cumberland (eg the important works at Melfort), and reached Ayrshire (Ardeer, 1872 to 1977) from Faversham.

The Chilworth works have been investigated in the last few years by the Surrey Industrial History Group, and much of the history of the site has been pieced together. The works were founded by the East India Company in 1626, and passed through a series of ownerships until they closed in 1920. In the late 17th century there were 16 or 18 powder mills, but by 1728 the works had declined to four or five powder mills, coal and brimstone mill, charcoal house, corning house, saltpetre houses, and boiling and stove plot. The late 19th century and First War buildings which replaced these are mostly ruinous, but can still be seen, with remains of the machinery. By the end of the life of the works there were separate factories for gunpowder, smokeless powder, and cordite. The village street consists of rows of cottages built for the workers.

Faversham, being a seaport and near the naval base at Chatham, survived and prospered under private ownership. About 1760 the works were nationalised, becoming the Royal Powder Mills. Areas of mills were spread all over the town, with major groups at Home Mills (with St Ann's, Chart, King's), Oare Marsh and Abbey works, and others nearby at Harty Ferry, Uplees, and other places. In 1900 there were 26 mills in the Home Works alone. These works were sold to a private firm in 1825, and other sales followed. The long history came to an end in 1934. Chart Mill has been restored.

The best example extant of the specialised landscape produced by a gunpowder works is at the former Explosives Research and Development Establishment of the Ministry of Defence at Waltham

Abbey (now part of the Royal Armament Research and Development Establishment). This was a private firm from 1665 until nationalisation as the Royal Gunpowder Factory in 1787, which continued until 1945. The black powder mills were destroyed in the Second World War, but guncotton was produced experimentally in the 1860s, and the factory later produced modern propellants. After 1945 it became a research establishment. It is on the Lea Navigation, and has developed a series of channels, fed by the Lea system, for water power and non-friction transport. No early mills survive, but examples of the special boats do, and some pleasant semicircular iron footbridges over the canals. Process and storage houses, well earthed, are scattered about the site, away from the mills on the waterways and buried in woods of poplar, to absorb blast. The whole scene has an atmosphere of its own, quite unique for industrial sites. It is not normally open to the public.

INDUSTRIAL ARCHAEOLOGY

The investigation of the buildings and relics of superseded industrial processes constitutes the basis for *industrial archaeology*, an activity which assumed its present form in the early 1960s. This investigation may be by way of the excavation of dilapidated buildings or of the sites of former buildings, survey and measurement of existing remains, study of obsolete machinery and processes, and analysis of firms' records. A considerable literature on these aspects now exists, and several periodicals. There is a vigorous network of local societies supporting the largely amateur practitioners of the subject; there are also some specialised national societies, such as the Newcomen Society and the Railway and Canal Historical Society. Gazetteers of industrial monuments have been published for most counties. Valuable back-up is given by museums, from the Science Museum in London and the great provincial industrial museums such as those in Birmingham and Manchester, or museums like Ironbridge Gorge, Beamish, the Museum of English Rural Life, or the National Railway Museum. There are also a large number of specialised or site museums, such as those devoted to pottery, glass, or mining, or preserved monuments like pumping stations or forges. Interest is also taken by the economic history departments of universities. The National Trust, English Heritage etc conserve their own industrial monuments, such as Styal Mill. Indeed, a system has evolved for industrial archaeology separate from, but parallel to, that originating in the 19th century for archaeology in the traditional sense.

Public Utilities and Other Industries

WATER

The Romans had elaborate water supply systems to their towns, sometimes involving bringing water across country for considerable distances. Thus there was an aqueduct to Lincoln from the north, and at Dorchester there was not only an aqueduct but a conduit to dispose of surplus water. These were supplemented by cisterns, reservoirs, and, where necessary, pumps to raise water to a higher level. There were street fountains, and water was piped into larger houses. Wells were also used.

Medieval water supplies were less sophisticated, relying essentially on wells and rivers. Some of the great monasteries had impressive systems, such as Canterbury with its cistern houses (see **434** and **435**) and Winchester with its streams. By 1236 London's population had increased to the point where water had to be brought in lead pipes from the Tyburn to the City, and in 1245 there was a conduit house in Cheapside, taking water from Piccadilly, nearly two miles away. Thereafter many such systems were laid down, and by 1600 there were some 16 conduits. The first pumped supply was in 1581, from London Bridge. In 1606 and 1607 Acts were obtained by Sir Hugh Myddleton for the construction of a canal (the New River) from Amwell near Hertford into London (Clerkenwell), which was completed in 1613. This was a private venture, and the water had to be paid for. The system, in spite of changes, still exists. After the Great Fire in 1666 several companies sprang up and the public conduits declined. Iron mains were used from 1746, but remains of old wood and lead piping still turn up in road works.

Most of the companies still used unfiltered water from the Thames, and the extent of pollution from sewage and industrial waste became a serious health hazard. Cholera epidemics continued until 1868. Various attempts were made to improve the chaotic situation, and from 1852 water had to be drawn from above Teddington. But not until

1902 was the Metropolitan Water Board formed to take over the task of supplying clean, unlimited water to all. The great reservoirs round London (Staines, Lea Valley, etc) postdate this reform. Regional water authorities were set up in 1974. The London Water Ring Main was opened in 1994 at Ashford (Mx); it is a huge tunnel, big enough to take a vehicle, designed to carry half of London's water.

Other cities solved their problems by damming streams and forming reservoirs, such as Thirlmere (Manchester), Loch Katrine (Glasgow), Cwm Elan (Birmingham), and Nidderdale (Bradford).

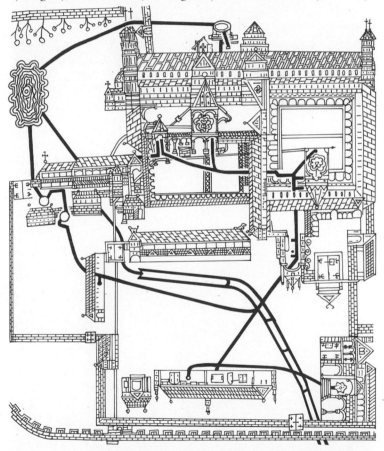

434 *A unique medieval plan of the monastery at Canterbury (Christ Church), showing its water supply, c 1153 (black lines). This begins with a spring or well (at the top of the diagram), from which one line runs to a cistern-tower and to buildings beyond, and another to a fishpond (on the left), from where the other lines serve other monastic buildings and, beyond them, St Augustine's Abbey.*

These are impressive monuments. More recently similar works in lowland areas have resulted in large lakes, with leisure uses as well as water supply, eg in Rutland, and recent projects in Derbyshire and Devon.

Victorian pumping stations tended to be highly ornate, and an impressive example is Papplewick, near Nottingham (see **436** (below) and **437**, facing page 530). A good Edwardian example is at Twyford (Ha). But all relics of former water supplies are worth noting, down to the village fountains and pumps (see **438**, **439**, and **440**, such as that at Holmbury St Mary (Sy)). Selborne (Ha), for instance, relied till the 1890s on a spring, the Wellhead, led onto the village street through an iron screen called the Lion's Mouth (see **441**). Then a ram was installed at the spring, leading part of the flow up the hill to a cistern, from which several standpipes throughout the village were supplied. These were in use until the 1950s; piped water reached the village in the 1930s, but some houses were not connected till later. Remains of this system are still visible.

435 *A cistern tower at Canterbury Cathedral, part of the water supply system of the monastery (1160).*

436 *Pumping station – Papplewick (No).*

SEWAGE DISPOSAL

Roman towns and permanent fortresses had adequate sewers, into which public and private privies discharged. Those at York were recently excavated (see **442**). But since then, and until well into the 19th century, sewage was removed from the towns to the country by men with carts to be used as fertiliser. Medieval towns had constant trouble with refuse, offal, dead dogs, etc in the streets, in open drains, and in the town ditch (cf Houndsditch in London). A traveller to Paris, and no doubt London too, could smell the city before he could see it. Castle garderobes normally discharged direct into the moat.

438 *Victorian fountain – Wallingford (Ox). The Victorians loved ornate fountains and clock towers.*

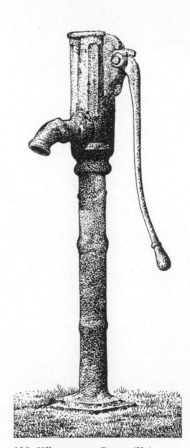

439 *Village pump – Barton (Hu).*

440 *Village pump – Leyburn (NY).*

441 *A public fountain: – the Lion's Mouth, Selborne (Ha). This was put up in 1879, the sole water supply for the village; in 1893 water from the same source was diverted to standpipes along the village roads. These sources served the village until piped water arrived in 1934. The Lion's Mouth is still used in emergency.*

The 15th-century farmhouse, "Bayleaf", re-erected at the Weald and Downland Museum, has its privy projecting from the house over the farmyard. A monastery like Fountains was fortunate to be able to build its reredorter over a flowing river (see **443**). Conditions in the enclosed, overcrowded courts of the urban slums may be gauged (at comfortable arm's length) from books like Dorothy Marshall: *Industrial England 1776–1851* (Routledge Kegan Paul, 1973).

London made attempts after the Fire of 1666 to keep the streets reasonably clean, but it was not until the cholera outbreaks of the 19th century that the problem was tackled in a massive and heroic way, creating a system of sewers which are still in use. A tangle of inadequate covered ditches and sewers was replaced (1855–75) by a planned system of feeder sewers linked to main outfall sewers along both banks of the Thames (see **Map 15**). The engineer (Sir Joseph Bazalgette) who conceived this plan linked it with two embankments to contain the river, the Victoria on the north side from Blackfriars to Vauxhall, and the Albert from Waterloo to Vauxhall on the south. The main sewer on the north bank discharged into the river

442 *Roman sewer – Church Street, York. This formed part of the sanitation and water supply system of the legionary fortress.*

at Barking (Abbey Mills) and that on the south at Crossness, where fine steam beam pumps survive.

Cities without major (and tidal) rivers had to treat their sewage before it went into local rivers, and sewage farms were set up. Disposal of domestic and industrial waste is another problem, and alternatives to landfill continue to be sought.

GAS

Coal gas for lighting was explored as early as the late 16th century, but seems to have been first used for lighting a room about 1760.

Researches were made in France from 1791 (by Lebon), but not until 1792 was gas lighting used on a larger scale. This was by William Murdock in the Redruth factory of Boulton and Watt in 1792, and in 1802 in their Soho factory in Birmingham. In London the Lyceum Theatre was gas-lit in 1804, and Pall Mall in 1807. The London Gas Light & Coke Company was set up in 1812, and by 1842 most of London's main streets were gas-lit. By then every town of any size had its gasworks, with their characteristic and unconcealable gasholders. The numbers of these diminished after nationalisation in 1949, but some 700 are still in use. Most of them date from 1880–1910. Oil gas was tried, but coal gas was cheaper and had coke as a useful by-product.

Gasholders came into use in the early years of the 19th century, and were rigid. Under a regulation of 1813 they had to be encased in solid buildings, for safety, but it has been pointed out that, in the event of an explosion, the bricks or stones of the building would have acted as dangerous missiles! An example is the building at Saltisford (Ww), with two brick towers. The familiar telescopic form was adopted in Leeds in 1826 and in London (Vauxhall) in 1834. In 1832, for safety and reliability, the container cylinders of this form were guided up inside a frame of vertical columns (eg at Fulham). There are some spectacular examples of this type, eg the matching interlocking cluster at King's Cross or the group of seven (once eight) at Bromley-by-Bow (1870–5). The spiral-guided design was invented in 1887 (eg Northwich).

Although the gasholder was originated by Lavoisier in 1782, its real father was Samuel Clegg, who designed many variants, including gasometers which measured the gas used. The gasworks at Fakenham (Nf) can be seen as a unit, but its gasholders are its most significant remains.

Since the Second World War oil gas has been used and pumped into a national grid, with the more recent addition of natural gas from the North Sea.

ELECTRICITY

The first power stations for public supply were at Holborn Viaduct and Brighton in 1882. But there had been small generators for lighthouses and some street lighting from the 1850s. For instance, Westminster Bridge was lit by electricity in 1858, with wider use in London by

443 *Monastic sewer – Paisley Abbey, late 14th, early 15th century.*

1880. Outside London, Godalming was lit in 1881. There was a complete system at Deptford in 1889. By 1900 most towns of any size had a power station and some had several, eg to run lighting, trams, the Underground, etc separately.

This development was facilitated by Parsons' steam turbine (1884). Most large generating stations are still run on steam, whether coal-fired or nuclear, except for a few water-powered stations in mountain areas, eg Fort William. The cooling towers of these stations are conspicuous, eg Ferrybridge, Didcot, and Rugeley, and have been a regrettable feature of the landscape since the early 1920s. Only riverside stations with a ready source of water, such as Bankside and Battersea (both superseded), can dispense with these towers. Nuclear power stations, eg Berkeley, Dungeness, and Eastriggs, also use steam turbines to convert the heat from the reactors to electric current.

The power is distributed over the country by way of the national grid, filtered through substations. The land-lines of the grid are supported by pylons, which do nothing for the landscape but can sometimes be spectacular. For instance a line crosses the Thames at Dagenham, on pylons 487ft (146m) high, with a span of 3,060ft (918m).

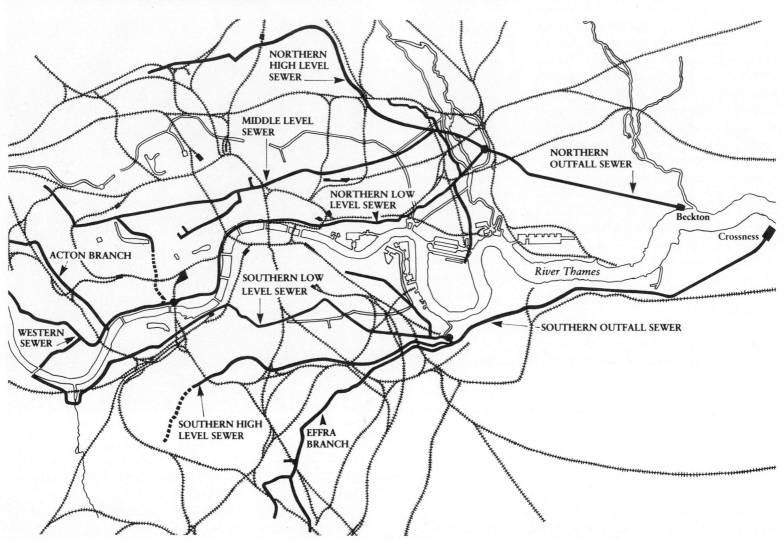

Map 15 *Sir Joseph Bazalgette's sewers and embankments of London. By the mid 19th century the sanitation of London had got out of hand. After serious cholera outbreaks, Bazalgette devised a system of sewers and pumping stations, completed in 1875. He also built the Victoria, Albert, and Chelsea Embankments to control the Thames.*

POSTS AND TELEPHONES

The early history and apparatus of these services should be sought in museums; recent changes have been rapid. Post-boxes have survived in variety, covering design changes over 150 years (see pages 449–51), and telephone boxes have changed also. The distinctive neo-Georgian post offices of the inter-war years are still to be found. Perhaps the most conspicuous monument of the postal service is the vast Mount Pleasant sorting office in London, which handles some three million letters a day. This is served by the unique Post Office railway, a tube opened in 1927 from Paddington to Whitechapel. It carries up to 50,000 bags of mail each day. Another prominent London landmark is the 620ft (186m) high Post Office Tower (now called, since British Telecom became independent of the Post Office, the British Telecom Tower); this handles VHF material such as radio, television, and telephone calls. It was built in 1964 and is 580ft (174m) high, or 620ft (186m) with its mast and aerial.

CIVIL AVIATION

This is a 20th-century phenomenon, following Orville Wright's flight in 1903. Commercial services began in the 1920s, not only by aircraft but by airships, whose hangars at Cardington (Bd) still survive. Very little remains of the factories in which the early (propellor) aircraft and engines were built, nor of the airfields from which they flew, nor of the town terminals. Growing demand and military needs dictated the development to jet aircraft, jumbo jets, and Concorde, but this necessitated the replacement of the early airfields. Thus Croydon has only fragments of its terminal buildings, and Shoreham (Sx) gives the best idea, with its airfield with no hard runways and its terminal resembling a golf club. But the very remote "local" airfields are still far less sophisticated than Heathrow or Gatwick. And less than 20 years ago the far north had airfields like Papa Westray (Or), with a terminal like a large garden shed

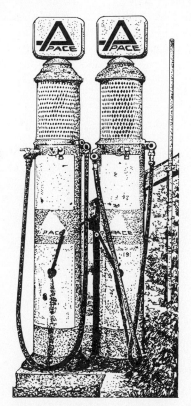

444 *Early 20th-century petrol pumps – Selborne (Ha).*

on the edge of a grass field. 1950s, manufacture is represented by the Brabazon hangar at Bristol. And there are still remains of abandoned RAF airfields, with overgrown concrete runways and Nissen huts.

The history of aviation should be seen in museums such as the Science Museum in London and RAF museums such as Hendon and Biggleswade.

OTHER INDUSTRIES

Only brief notes will be given here. In general a factory is a factory, even if it has changed its function or fallen out of use, although many factories incorporate older buildings. The archaeology of the industry is more often in the equipment, machinery, and processes (eg **444**), which, if they survive at all, will more usually be in museums.

Vehicles

An interesting relic is Brooklands, Weybridge, where part of the steeply-embanked testing track (1906, later used as a racing circuit) has been preserved. There is also here the Clubhouse, Members' Restaurant, and Barnes Wallis's office.

What is probably the oldest surviving purpose-built multi-storey car factory in Britain, erected in 1901 for Dennis Brothers (originally makers of cycles, later of cars until 1913, then of specialist vehicles like fire-engines) is also in Surrey, Rodborough Buildings at Guildford. The firm also built an estate of 102 workers' houses in 1933.

Oil

The great refineries at Fawley and Grangemouth and the storage installation at Milford Haven are not yet industrial archaeology, but are conspicuously part of the landscape, as is, for example, the chemical works at ICI Billingham.

Broadcasting

The original building for the first radio station (1922), 2LO, at Savoy Hill, still exists, although no longer in BBC hands. The Alexandra Palace is a somewhat incongruous centre for broadcasting, having been built for exhibitions and entertainments. Broadcasting House (1932), however, still serves its original purpose.

Newspapers

Fleet Street has ceased to be the centre for the national press; some papers have gone to west London, others to Wapping. The *Daily Express*, with its distinctive black glass and chrome building (the first curtain wall building in London, built by Ellis, Clarke, and Williams, 1931) was the last major paper to leave the Street, moving to Blackfriars Road in 1988.

Various

The drastic redevelopment of the City of London, halted only by the recession of 1990, which created buildings such as the new Stock Exchange, Lloyds, and NatWest, has left little coherent of the Victorian City.

Some important buildings have been destroyed, eg Firestone, Brentford, 1920s, or emasculated, eg Carreras, Mornington Crescent, once "Egyptian"; the Hoover building at Perivale, 1932–3, has become a supermarket.

The *clothing* industry had its monuments. Burton's enormous factory at Hudson Road, Leeds (1920s), the largest clothing factory in Europe, is no longer manufacturing. The "Moorish" block at Park Square, Leeds – Barran's clothing factory and warehouse, 1879, and one of the country's best exotics – is no longer used for its original purpose. But "Italianate" and other 19th-century chimneys can still be seen in cotton mills and, eg, at Surbiton waterworks.

This subject is inexhaustible, but a longer list of industries is unnecessary here. The books listed under "Industrial Archaeology" in "Further Reading" should be consulted.

The Coast

This book is necessarily almost exclusively concerned with inland matters – town and country. But we live on an island, and the seaboard is of vital importance to us. Moreover, the presence of the sea gives rise to a lot of features not found inland, and these must be outlined here.

HARBOURS AND PORTS

The coast is dominated, or at least punctuated, by resort towns (mostly 18th-century or later), fishing harbours, and commercial ports. Resort towns are dealt with on page 166. Both fishing and seaborne trade begin well back in prehistory. Finds of prehistoric boats have been made at many places round the coast and up the rivers. The Channel was well used, as far west as Cornwall, but without harbour works in the later sense; no doubt boats were beached. One major Iron Age port has been identified at Hengistbury Head, on Christchurch harbour in Dorset; imports through it were carried well inland, along the rivers.

The Romans made harbour works at their ports of entry – Dover, Lympne, and Richborough – and elaborate *waterfronts* at their river ports – London and York. These were walls of solid timbers, serving as quays and wharves. They were replaced at intervals further out into the river, as land was reclaimed. Such a sequence has been excavated at Miles Lane and Pudding Lane, by London Bridge. The quays were lined with warehouses and perhaps market buildings.

Similar waterfronts were built in London in medieval times, and moved forward into the river periodically. In addition, the inlet of Queenhithe was used as a dock and quays from late Saxon times to the 15th century, when it was superseded by Billingsgate. But in London the Pool was used as the harbour until well into the 19th century. The Hansa merchants had a depot there, and Dutch eel-boats berthed by the Custom House until the Second World War.

Anglo-Saxon and medieval waterfronts have been excavated at other ports too, including Ipswich, Southampton, York, and Kingston-on-Thames. To waterfronts of this embankment type must be added a variety of structures where ships could berth, load, and unload – quays, berths, wharves, staithes, jetties, piers, and landing-stages. Piers indeed were originally built to allow pleasure steamers to reach seaside resorts, and landing-stages are still the normal points of arrival and departure in the Scottish Highlands and Islands.

The growth of population and trade during the Middle Ages, and particularly from the 15th century, led to a variety of *ports*, some of which grew into major installations. The East coast ports handled most of the Baltic trade (cf the Hansa warehouse at King's Lynn, 1428 to 1751). The Tyne ports specialised in a coastal trade with London and the south in coal. London had a virtual monopoly of trade with the Low Countries, competing for centuries with Antwerp and in the 17th century with Amsterdam. London dominated the cloth trade in the 15th century, the Mediterranean trade in the 16th, and the colonial trade in the 17th and 18th, although here Bristol, Liverpool, and Glasgow were also important. In the 18th century indeed trade spread round the English ports. Thus in 1582, the main ports were London, Newcastle (coal), Yarmouth (fisheries, particularly herrings) and Grimsby (once the biggest fishing port in the world); in 1702 the list included London, Bristol, Newcastle, Yarmouth, Liverpool, and Whitby. Medieval Southampton had an important trade with south-west France, importing wine and pottery.

Harbours, which developed generally after the mid 17th century, can be classified in a broad way according to their situation, which may influence the form and layout of the port: *coastal* ("pier ports", with piers built out into the sea, enclosing the working area) include Dover, Peterhead, Whitehaven (the most complex system), Lyme Regis, and Ayr. The Scottish coast has a large number of small pier ports, many designed by Telford, such as Crail. *Estuary* ports include Leith, Grimsby, Southampton, Cardiff, and Liverpool. Southampton and Liverpool, besides having docks, are linear, with long lines of berths for ocean liners and shipping. The supreme *river* port is London, but these include Hull, Newcastle, Norwich (medieval), Exeter, Manchester (the Ship Canal, 1894), Glasgow, Goole, Boston, King's Lynn, and minor ports such as Gainsborough, and many medieval river quays at places no longer navigable. *River-mouth* ports include Aberdeen, Sunderland, Whitby, Newhaven, Littlehampton, and Weymouth, where the port is protected by piers.

Specialised ports have specialised equipment and installations. Thus fishing ports like Peterhead, Ullapool, Grimsby, Hull, Ayr, Fleetwood, and Plymouth have fish markets, curing and smoking

445 *These tall, narrow wooden buildings on the sea's edge at Hastings (Sx) are netshops. The type may date back to the 16th century, and they were built to permit nets to be stored at full length.*

446 *Bucklers Hard (Ha) was set up as a shipbuilding yard in 1749 by Henry Adam. His house, where he lived until 1806, is at the lower end of the right-hand row of houses. Buckler's Hard consists of a wide street of shipbuilders' cottages, and an inn of 1793 (top of left-hand row); stocks of timber and other materials were stored in the street, and remains of slipways can be seen in the river.*

booths (eg Arbroath), processing plants (eg Lerwick), (former) saltings (eg Lymington). Hastings, where the fishermen pull their boats up onto a steep shingle beach, has a row of wooden *netshops* in which nets can be stored hanging (see **445**). These are tall narrow buildings 8ft (2.5m) square and three storeys high; the concept seems to date from the 16th century. At Tollesbury (Ex) is a row of wooden buildings on stilts built about 1900 for the winter storage of sailing gear from the great J-class yachts moored there.

Coal ports, such as Tyneside, Sunderland (16th–17th centuries), and Seaham (1830s), have coal staithes, coal drops, and railways from the mines. Seaton Sluice is a "model" coal port, built in the 1670s and replanned in the 1750s. Cardiff, with Penarth and Barry, is a coal port on a wider scale, developed from 1870 to 1914, with rail links to the Valleys. Goole has unique barge hoists. Some ports were planned, or have developed, for shipbuilding, such as Glasgow, Sunderland, or Barrow; Buckler's Hard (Ha) (see **446**) is a minor 18th-century village devoted to building, in its only street, wooden ships for the Navy. Oil ports, such as Fawley, Grangemouth, Sullom Voe, or Milford Haven,

have storage tanks and refineries. Naval ports, eg Portsmouth, Chatham, and Devonport, have highly specialised buildings such as sail-lofts, planning-lofts, rope-walks, and dry docks. Ferry ports have roll-on roll-off facilities.

DOCKS

London, by reason of its size and volume of trade, is a special case where the history of *docks* can be followed. Up to the 17th century traffic mainly used the Pool, being loaded and unloaded by lighters; docks were virtually small inlets in the river banks, such as Queenhithe, Billingsgate, the mouth of the Fleet, and St Mary Overie in Southwark. But as the port spread below the Tower docks

447 *Warehouse – St Katherine's Dock, London, Telford 1825–8; a characteristic example.*

(enclosed areas of water) were constructed on the low-lying land along the river. The first such wet dock was at Blackwall (1660), for East Indiamen; this became later part of Brunswick Dock. The Howland Dock (1697–1700) was also for laying up ships, afloat. Daniel Defoe, soon after 1700, records three wet docks, 22 dry docks for ship repairs, and 33 shipyards for building merchant ships. The first enclosed dock was opened in 1802, the West India. This was followed by the London, 1805, the East India, 1805, the Surrey, 1807, St Katharine's (Telford,

448 *Dry dock – Portsmouth naval dockyard (c 1800); shaped to give easy access to the hulls of wooden ships.*

449 *19th-century river warehouses – Guildford (Sy).*

1828) (see **447**), West India South, 1829, Royal Victoria, 1855, Millwall, 1868, Royal Albert, 1880, and King George V, 1921 – an enormous area, now obsolete and largely built over. In the 1920s docks and quays were built at Tilbury, to attract ocean liners to the port of London; but this was only partly successful.

The Sea Mills dock at Bristol was built in 1710, those at Liverpool from 1715 to 1836, and those at Portsmouth from 1691 to 1803 (see **448**).

Early docks had no *warehouses*, but 19th-century docks did. Those at St Katharine's, London, and Albert Dock, Liverpool, have been restored and put to other uses. Warehouses at river ports (eg Gainsborough or Guildford (see **449**)) began in medieval, even Roman, times. Those at Boston date from the 13th century. The magnificent series in London is rapidly disappearing.

Dock designers favoured either long and narrow docks (such as Albert Dock, Hull) or with internal piers, giving "branches" (Telford's idea – these exist at Liverpool and, for a time, existed in London).

Port installations include bollards and capstans, dredgers, and cranes – 17th-century treadmill cranes survive at Guildford and Harwich but the simple crane with wooden jib is now. *Custom Houses* are prominent features and some, eg King's Lynn, 1682, are architecturally distinguished. The first custom house in London was built in 1275, and was replaced several times until the present building of 1717–25 (T Ripley). *Buoys* mark channels off the ports; some have bells or sirens as well as lights.

LIGHTHOUSES

Lighthouses were first built in Britain by the Romans. There are two high octagonal towers at Dover (see **450**), made to take an open fire or beacon on their tops to guide ships into the harbour. The next oldest is the early 14th-century one on Chale Down (IW) (St Catherine's Oratory (see **451**)).

Some were maintained by monasteries, such as the Chapel of the Fire at Holy Island, a small building in which a fire was kept lit to shine through the windows. The 15th-century east tower of Blakeney Church (Nf) seems to have been used as a beacon (see **452**). Fire towers on the Roman model were common in the 17th century and many survive, such as Tynemouth (*c* 1608), Isle of Man (1636), St Agnes (1680); there are two fine ones on the Farne Islands. The first waveswept tower, the Eddystone, was built in 1695–8, but the present lighthouse there is not the original. St Catherine's (IW) was built in 1780, and Bell Rock in 1807–10. Reflectors to increase the power of the light were first used in the Mersey about 1763, and from then on lighthouses develop into what we have today (see **453**, facing page 531). Lighthouse crews have been phased out as the lights have been made automatic.

Land lighthouses or *beacons* were also used to guide travellers through forests or difficult country. These could be tops of church towers adapted, as at Monken Hadley (Ht) or All Saints Pavement, York; or they might be specially built towers, round or square with a lantern at the top (see **454**). One built about 1770 survives on Lincoln Heath (Dunston Pillar, beside the Lincoln-Sleaford road); when no longer needed the lantern was replaced by a statue of George III.

OTHER COASTAL FEATURES

Look-out posts, often on towers, are similar buildings. The Plummer Tower in Croft Street, Newcastle-upon-Tyne (13th century), is a

450 *Roman lighthouse – Dover.*

451 *Medieval lighthouse – St Catherine's Oratory, Chale Down (IW), early 14th century; traces are visible of the room occupied by the monk who tended the light.*

restored survivor of 24 such towers in the district. A round stone tower on Caldy Island, Bristol Channel, with a deep embrasure, may have been a beacon or look-out.

Coastguards have their own stations, with look-out posts, cottages, and stepped posts for training in the use of breeches buoys. *Lifeboat stations* are sheds for the lifeboat, with a slipway into the water.

Sea walls have to be maintained along vulnerable stretches of coast, and groynes or breakwaters have to be built on beaches with strong lateral tides, to minimise drifting of sand or shingle along the beach.

Limekilns on the coast represent 18th- and 19th-century limeburning for spreading on the land. They were at points where the stone was quarried, the product being shipped away or carted to the farms. There was a flourishing lime industry in south-west Wales (eg Solva (Pb) and Gwbert (Cd)) and north Devon (eg Buck's Mills). There is a spectacular group of three on the quay at Beadnell (Nd); they date from *c* 1789 to *c* 1801, and were in use until at least 1841 (see pages 538–41).

452 *Beacon tower – Blakeney (Nf). Coastal churches often have a high tower as a landmark for sailors; this one is unusual in having a separate tall tower for a light.*

454 *Happisburgh church (Sf), with its disproportionately tall tower, a "landmark" to guide ships at sea.*

Coastal defences – forts, Martello towers, etc – are dealt with on pages 377–81. Maritime activity may have an influence on *town plans*. For instance at Great Yarmouth there are successive streets following the shore line, linked by narrow passages (rows). At Stromness (Or) the main street follows closely to the shoreline, and has a series of jetties, each with cottages, leading off it.

Fish-farms, such as the oyster beds of Whitstable and Colchester, go back to Roman times; but in recent years lobsters have been farmed in Orkney and salmon on the Scottish sea lochs.

A very much untapped archaeological resource is the enormous number of *wrecks* along the 6,000 miles (9,600 km) of the British coastline – some 40,000 at a recent count, ranging from the *Mary Rose* (1545) to small prehistoric boats. Only a few of these have been investigated.

Rescue Archaeology

The threat to historic buildings and archaeological sites was totally transformed by World War II. Bomb damage called for reconstruction and often radical replanning, sometimes on a very large scale, and this was compounded by new building methods and commercial and industrial reorientation. Roads and car parks, estates of new dwellings, both low and high rise, and New Towns, sterilised wide areas, not only of urban land, but of open country. Town centres took on a new look – shopping precincts, supermarkets, stores, new public buildings of all kinds, mostly on a greatly increased scale from pre-war standards. Towns of all kinds were affected, from historic city centres to quite small market towns. In all this rapid development little thought was given to the historic and archaeological potential lying in the path of the advancing rebuilding; for the planners and developers the rate of advance was paramount. By the end of the 1950s some towns had little left to preserve or even investigate. Throughout the 1960s public consciousness began to become alive to the threat to their heritage, and tentative steps were taken. A sense arose that time was running out, and urgent action was needed if anything of significance was to be saved. Already too much had gone for ever.

The problem was compounded in two ways. The first was the rapid change inherent in the life of any town; for instance, in 1947 it was suggested that a quarter of all buildings in the City of London were rebuilt on average in a span of 30 years. By 1908, 80% of the buildings which existed in 1855 had been rebuilt, and about 20% of those existing in 1905 had been rebuilt by 1939. Later buildings destroy more archaeological evidence too, by deep foundations. The second was the nature of the rebuilding and replanning itself, which destroyed more evidence than straight rebuilding of a war-damaged house would have done. The new buildings were usually on a larger scale than the old, and obliterated ancient property boundaries. New roads cut across the old town plans, street lines, and plot layouts.

Individual excavations and observation of building sites had, of course, taken place in the city centres, but this was not enough.

By the late 1950s the pressure from the archaeologists began to be coordinated and organised, and thus increasingly effective. The Council for British Archaeology, under its Secretary (later its President), Professor Maurice Barley, got things going nationally. Professor Grimes' spectacular excavations of the Cripplegate Roman fort in London, and the discovery of the Temple of Mithras, and Professor Biddle's well-publicised work over ten years (1961–71) at Winchester focused public attention sharply, and prepared the ground for further advance. The CBA was campaigning for a nationwide survey of historic towns, bringing out their archaeological potential and needs and the threat facing them. This emerged first in a seminal book by C. M. Heighway: *The Erosion of History* (1972), in which some 200 towns were listed as needing urgent attention. This was followed closely by *The Future of London's Past* (1973), which explored the enormous threat to London itself. This came just when the Corporation of London was grappling with the problem of organising an effective archaeological service in the city, and played a significant part in the setting up of a well-funded unit attached to the then Guildhall Museum and the London Museum (later to form part of the Museum of London). Much apathy and even opposition had to be overcome, but gradually many developers came round to accepting the idea of archaeological work in advance of the bulldozers, and even eventually to agreeing to a clause in their contracts giving the archaeologists the right to be there. Many developers now actively support archaeology on their sites, in financial and other ways.

In parallel with Winchester, a formal archaeological committee had been set up for Southwark in 1962, extended to Lambeth in 1976, and was properly funded from 1972. The prestigious York Archaeological Trust was founded in 1972; similar bodies exist in other towns, such as Oxford, Canterbury, Chester, Lincoln, and Bath. But not all towns of prime historic importance are covered in this way. The fact remains, and must rankle, that in most cases these efforts came too late to save all that should have been saved, and in some cases major centres have been lost altogether.

The wave of discontent among archaeologists created by cases such as the destruction by insensitive development of the historic centre of Worcester led to the formation, in 1971, of a body called RESCUE: the Trust for British Archaeology. The first trustees were Martin Biddle, Charles Thomas, Peter Fowler, and Philip Barker. This body is still active in making the public aware of the destruction of our archaeological heritage, and in increasing public knowledge and appreciation of archaeology. It seeks to increase the funding and effort allotted to rescue excavation and its publication, and to improving the level of conservation, study, and display of sites and finds. It also encourages the raising of standards of training of archaeologists, and the improvement of protective legislation and its implementation, and it seeks closer cooperation with central and local government and with developers and private interests. In some of these objects it runs in consonance with the Council for British Archaeology, the Society of Antiquaries, the Institute of Field Archaeologists, and other bodies.

There are just over 1,500 towns in England, Scotland, and Wales. Of these some 900 were towns before 1750, and of these, some 600 are being redeveloped or are under threat. In fewer than 200 has rescue or research excavation been done, or is in progress, and only in some 20–30 cases is this work satisfactorily based and funded. In England only five areas of archaeological importance have been "designated" under the Act, and only about 12,000 sites have been scheduled – some 2% of known sites.

By 1979 there were 155 full-time rescue organisations in the country, and some 1600 archaeologists were employed in them; there are fewer now. Courses in archaeology at the universities, both for professionals and amateurs, and covering degrees or diplomas in fieldwork and laboratory back-up, have multiplied, and the first professional institution for archaeology, the Institute of Field Archaeologists, was set up in 1982. Many of the full-time rescue organisations have few permanent staff, some only consisting of one person; only some 40–50 can be called "units". Of the people employed in rescue archaeology, only some 40% have any job security; indeed, most of them are either temporary or on *ad hoc* contracts. Some 25 universities offer courses in archaeology, of varying emphasis and specialisation. A survey for the years 1976–8 showed that 57% of single honours graduates, 35% of dual honours, and 60% of post-graduates, stayed in archaeology after graduation. Of the 222 single honours graduates over the three years, 74 were employed in rescue archaeology, 40 in museum, conservation, academic, or inspection work, and the rest in postgraduate research or other archaeological work. By mid 1993 the membership of the Institute of Field Archaeologists stood at 1,100, and this figure continues to rise. 58% of rescue funds are spent in towns and 42% in rural areas.

The bulk of the funding for the units was initially provided by the Department of the Environment, under the control of its Inspectorate of Ancient Monuments. Funding was at first by way of block grants, but latterly by separate projects. A growing proportion of the funds is now coming from local authorities and from a variety of private sources, including the developers themselves (see below).

In April 1984 the care of monuments in state charge was taken over from the DoE's Inspectorate of Ancient Monuments by a new body, the Historic Buildings and Monuments Commission for England (English Heritage). This new body thus acquired the management of some 400 ancient sites and monuments (prehistoric, Roman, and later), castles, abbeys, houses, and a variety of other structures. Its responsibility included the recommendation to DoE of the scheduling of sites and the listing of buildings. It also took over the Ancient Monuments Laboratory of the DoE, and assumed responsibility for funding rescue archaeology in England (although only a tenth of its funds are spent on this). Arrangements in Scotland remained unchanged (the Historic Buildings and Monuments Directorate of the Scottish Development Department), but for Wales, Welsh Historic Monuments (Cadw) has been set up, assisted by the Inspectorate and four Regional Trusts. The Royal Commission on the Historical Monuments of England (RCHME) took over the DoE Air Photographs Library in 1984, and now holds the national air photographic archive. The RCHME took over in 1986 the Greater London Council Survey of London, the National Monuments Record, and the archaeological work of the Ordnance Survey. The other functions of the Historic Buildings Division of the former Greater London Council went to English Heritage.

Rescue archaeology in London was rationalised in 1983. The DoE began to bow out in favour of the GLC, and the London units were combined in a joint service, parallel to the existing unit for the City, as part of the Museum of London (except for an area in east London under the control of the Passmore Edwards Museum). English Heritage took over the funding in 1984.

The emphasis outside the towns is somewhat different. Here the main threats are from roadworks, modern agriculture and forestry, gravelworking, etc. The RCHME led the way in pinpointing these threats in a book which had wide influence – *A Matter of Time* (1960) – which dealt mainly with gravelworking in the Trent and Thames valleys. Many counties set up their own archaeological offices, to survey and evaluate the sites under threat and to encourage their conservation and study. There are now 32 of these, and nine observers associated with counties. Most of these are individual posts, but some 10–15 have attached units. A county unit may not always be run by the county council, but by a separate body (as in Oxfordshire). Here again, this kind of organisation is weaker in Scotland and Wales.

The Government contribution to rescue archaeology in England in 1986/87 was £5.9 million, which included £4 million for nearly 300 projects and post-excavation work (the processing of finds, publication etc), and funds for storage, and for the scientific study of the environment, health, diet, clothing, crafts etc of excavated sites. The distribution of this money was however uneven as between the units concerned, and it represented only about two-fifths of the sum the units considered necessary. The grant for 1987/88 was over £7 million. The grant for work in Scotland, by the Scottish Development Department, was £400,000 in 1986/87, and that for Wales was even less. Of the total, England takes some 85%, Scotland 9.5%, and Wales 5%, and the latter two represent underfunding, although considerable distinguished work has been done in both countries. Funding from local authorities increased after 1978.

The situation changed radically in November 1990, when the DoE issued a *Planning Policy Guidance* note, no 16 (PPG16), entitled *Archaeology and Planning*, the implications of which, for archaeology, are still being finally worked out. PPG16 stresses the national value and irreplaceability of archaeology, and presumes in favour of preservation when archaeological deposits are threatened by development. It provides for evaluation and assessment of the site before development, and for the cost of archaeological work to be borne by the developer. Archaeology thus has an officially recognised place in the development process.

The archaeological structure has been reshaped; evaluation of the potential of a site is carried out by "consultants"; if excavation is to follow, this is done, for the developers, after competitive tender, by a "contractor". Conservation and management of the project is the responsibility of "curators". The contractors may be regional trusts (eg York or Wessex), county or district units (eg London), local societies, or independent firms. Some units have found it possible to combine two or more of these functions, eg to act as contractor to developers, carry out work for local authorities, and act as curator of the archaeological resources of the locality. In spite of predictable teething troubles, this new structure is likely to persist, in its broad lines, for some time to come.

The measure of the change in financial support for rescue archaeology can be shown by comparing the figures for 1978–79 and 1990–91:

1978–79	£		
central government	2,800,000		
MSC	1,238,000		
local authorities	1,098,000		
developers or "business"	58,000		
other	506,000	total	£5,700,000

1990–91			
national heritage bodies	9,427,000		
local authorities	5,450,000		
developers	15,570,000		
other	640,000	total	£31,090,000

Presentation of the results to the public and to the specialists is another problem. In general, publication is difficult to adapt to the requirements of the ordinary reader. Exhibition has been more successful, and some recent museum displays are quite spectacular; one may cite the Museum of London, the new display at Bath, and, perhaps the apogee, the Jorvik Centre at York. A recent landmark was the exhibition at the British Museum in 1986/87 – *Archaeology in Britain since 1945*. The public are being kept informed of the progress and results of rescue archaeology by press reports, journals such as *Current Archaeology* and *Antiquity*, museum displays, open days, training digs, lectures, symposia, etc, and public awareness and interest is steadily increasing. In spite of the recent upheavals in government funding, and in the roles of some of the largest local authorities, the outlook for rescue archaeology is not all bleak; and the results of its work so far have materially increased our knowledge and understanding of our past.

Sites and Museums

The following is a brief list of sites (**S**) and museums (**M**) containing material of significant relevance to the topics dealt with in this book. It is necessarily far from exhaustive, and many more entries – but for the exigencies of space – might well have been included.

Some museums (and not only those in private ownership) have limited seasons or times of opening, particularly in remote or holiday areas, and it is therefore as well to check in advance. Detailed information can be found in books such as *The Times Museums and Galleries Passport Guide* (published annually), or the HMSO regional series, *Exploring Museums*, eg South-west Eng-land (1989), Scotland (1990), East Anglia (1993). *The National Trust Handbook* is valuable for the buildings and gardens in their care, as is *Guide to English Heritage Properties*, and the annual *Gar-dens of England & Wales* supplements these. Many of the Shire handbooks on crafts and industries contain pertinent lists. Some subjects, such as buildings or gardens, cannot be appreciated or understood from museums alone, and need to be visited if their character is to be savoured and absorbed.

The sites listed here are similarly only the small tip of a very large iceberg; many sites well worth visiting have, for reasons of space, had to be left out. But the use of good guides, such as the Blue Guides, and the "Further Reading" section, as well as the text of this book itself, will often help to fill out the picture. Sites are usually in private hands, and permission should be sought to visit them, and the country code on closing gates, keeping to paths and leaving no litter, strictly observed. Many key sites have museums associated with them, and the lists do not always make this clear.

The lists follow the sequence of the contents of this book.

The Personality of Britain

General

S *U-shaped glacial valleys* – Buttermere (Cu), Llanberis (Gd), Littondale (NY), Glencoe (Hi), Wasdale Head (Cu).
Raised beaches – Boxgrove (Sx), Brighton (Sx). Scotland, cg Stonehaven to Fraserburgh; Kirkcudbright; Stranraer (100ft, 30m)
Raised beaches of glacial lake – "Parallel Roads" of Glenroy (Hi).
River terraces – Thames: Ambersham (200ft, 60m), Swanscombe (100ft, 32m), Fairmile (Sy); Taplow (60ft, 18m); Spey valley (Gr).
Moraines: terminal – Tal-y-Llyn (Me), Loch Skene (Df); *lateral* – upper Nidderdale (NY).
Drumlins – between Settle and Skipton (NY), Vale of Eden (Cu), south and central Scotland.
Fossil forests – Victoria Park, Glasgow; Swansea, beach; the Fens; Lulworth Cove (Do).

M *Early man* - Natural History Museum (Ln).
Structure and glaciations – Geological Museum, London.

POPULATION/ DEMOGRAPHY

S Pest house, Odiham (Ha).

M *Diseases* – Wellcome Museum of the History of Medicine at the SM.
Foreign Contributions – Museum of London.

The Land

THE COUNTRYSIDE

S *Ancient countryside* – Essex, Herefordshire, Devon, Cornwall.
Planned countryside – Cambridgeshire, Leicestershire.
Ancient woodland – Glen Trool (Kb); Bow Hill (Sx); Ebernoe Common (Sx).
Wood pasture – Binswood (Ha), Groton (Su), Hatfield Forest (Ex).

FARMING

M Butser Ancient Farm, Chalton (Ha); W&D; MERL
County museums of rural life – Museum of Lincolnshire Rural Life, Lincoln; Museum of East Anglian Rural Life, Stowmarket (Su); WFM (also crafts); Old Kiln Museum and Rural Life Centre, Tilford (Sy); Ryedale Folk Museum, Hutton-le-Hole (NY); Countryside Museum, Breamore (Ha); Manor Farm, Burlesdon Ha); Cogges Manor Farm Museum, Witney (Ox); Coates Agricultural Museum, Swindon (Wi); Wye College Museum of Agriculture, Ashford (Kt); Acton Scott Working Farm, Church Stretton (Sp); Scottish Agricultural Museum, Edinburgh; Gwent Rural Life Museum, Usk (Gw); Museum of Kent Rural Life, Cobtree, Maidstone (Kt); Norfolk Rural Life Museum, Gressenhall, Dereham (Nf); South of England Museum of Agricultural Heritage, Tenterden (Kt); Highland Folk Museum, Kingussie (Hi); North of England Open Air Museum, Beamish, Stanley (Du); Yorkshire Museum of Farming, Marton, York; late Medieval farming – Markenfield Hall, near Ripon (NY); 18th and 19th-century model buildings, Holkham Hall (Nf); Buscot (Ox).

FIELD SYSTEMS

S *Prehistoric/Romano-British* – Grassington (NY); Wessex, eg Bishopstone North (Wi); Cottenham (Ca); Dartmoor reaves, eg Dartmeet system, Holme Moor (Dv).
Medieval open fields – remains, Laxton (No); Braunton (Dv); Axholme (Li); West Runton (Nf); Westcote (Gl); Portland (Do).
Ridge and furrow, mostly in central belt – eg Padbury (Bc); Crimscote (Ww); Ilmington (Ww); many in Northamptonshire and Leicestershire.
Cultivation terraces – Thorpe West Field, Wharfedale (NY).
Enclosures – Raunds (Nh); Croydon (Ca);

Slawston (Le); Yorkshire dales.
Hedges – Meikleour (Pe), ornamental.
Walls – Derbyshire; Yorkshire dales;
Kirkcudbrightshire.

M Drystane Dyking Centre, Ruskie, Thornhill (Df).

S *Watermeadows* – eg Hampshire rivers, Test;
Liphook (Ha) area.

FARMING EQUIPMENT

M MERL; tractor collection – Stocksfield (Nd);
National Tractor Musuem, Winchester.

FARM BUILDINGS

S *Tithe barns* – Great Coxwell (Ox); Tisbury (Wi); Bradford-on-Avon (Wi).
Model buldings – Holkham Hall (Nf); Windsor Great Park (Bk); Buscot (Ox).

M W&D; North of England Open Air Museum, Beamish (Du); WFM; Ryedale Folk Museum, Hutton-le-Hole (NY); Yorkshire Museum of Farming, Marton (NY); Avoncroft Musueum of Buildings, Bromsgrove (Wo).

S *Brewing and Distilling: maltings* – Farnham (Sy); *brew houses* – Selborne (Ha); Traquair, Innerleithen (Pb); *brewery townscape* – Burton on Trent (St); *oasts* – impressive range, Beltring (Kt).

M Old Kiln Museum, Tilford (Sy); Curtis Museum, Alton (Ha); Heritage Brewery Museum, Burton on Trent (St); Stamford Steam Brewery Museum (Li); Farnham Museum (Sy).

S *Dovecotes* – Albury (Sy); Garway (He); Bisham Abbey, Marlow (Bk); Glamis (Ag); Phantassie (EL).

The Village

THE SHAPE OF VILLAGES

S *Two row* – Appleton-le-Moors (NY); Castle Bolton (NY).
Greens – Matching Green (Ex); Wisborough Green (Sx); East Witton (NY); Milburn (Wd); Dunsfold, Forest Green (both Sy).

Planned – Fochabers (My), Tomintoul (Ba); Middridge (Du), Milburn (Wd).

SHRUNKEN, SHIFTED AND DESERTED VILLAGES

S Abbotstone (Ha); Hound Tor (Dv); Wharram Percy (NY); Theddingworth (Le); Great Stretton (Le); Barton Blount (Db) – more than 3,000 are known.
Scottish clearances – Rosal, Strathnaver (Sd); Auliston, Morvern (Ar); Auchnashiel, Glen Shiel (Hi).

THE FORM OF PARISHES

S *Strip parishes* – North Downs; Chilterns; Lincoln Edge; Dingwall; Logie Easter; Alness (long parishes from low to high ground taking in a variety of soils etc).

Parks, Gardens, and Sports

HUNTING

S *Deerparks, Forests and chases* — Slindon (Sx); Staverton (Su); Magdalen Deer Park, Oxford.
Warrens and pillow mounds – High Beech (Ex); Hutton Nab, Hutton-le-Hole (NY); Steeple Langford Cowdow (Wi); Llanfihangel nant Melan (Ra); Llanelwedd (Ra).
Fishing – Minehead (SO), medieval fish-weirs; *fishponds* – Alresford (Ha); Bishop's Waltham (Ha); Frensham (Sy) – these are the Bishop of Winchester's, 13th century; Harrington (Nh).

M WFM.

S *Fowling: decoy ponds* – Mickle Mere, East Wretham (Nf); Abbotsbury (Do).

GARDENS AND AMENITY PARKS

S *General* – Westbury on Severn (Gl), Dutch water garden; Ham House (Ln), 17th century; Albury (Sy) – 17th century; Wallington (Nd), 18th century; Hackwood (Ha), 17th–18th century; Basing House (Ha), c 1600 restored; Hampton Court.
16th–17th century – Winchester Castle,

Queen Eleanor's Garden, restored; Tudor House, Southampton, restored.
19th–20th century – Jekyll/Lutyens, Hestercombe (So); Hidcote (Gl); Marsh Court (Ha); Folly Farm, Sulhampstead (Bk); Manor House, Upton Grey (Ha).
Others – Nymans (Sx); Sissinghurst (Kt); Savill Gardens, Windsor (Bk); Leonardslee (Sx); Exbury (Ha) – rhododendrons; Mottisfont (Ha) – roses; Cotehele (Co).
Landscaped parks – Petworth (Sx); Stowe (Bc); Painshill (Sy); Blenheim (Ox); Studley Royal (NY); Castle Howard (NY); Chatsworth (Db); Stourhead (Wi); Longleat (Wi).

M Museum of Garden History, St Mary's, Lambeth (Ln).

S *Garden features : topiary* – Packwood (Ww); Levens Hall (Wd), also first ha-ha, 1694; *Tudor Pavilions* – Montacute (So); *arbour* – Melbourne (Db); *Tudor mount* – New College, Oxford; *Terrace* – Albury (Sy); *cascades, greenhouses* – Chatsworth (Db).
Follies – Out of very many – The Pineapple, Dunmore (Ce); Brighton Pavilion; Witley (Sy), Welbeck (No) – rooms under lakes; Stowe (Bc); Painshill (Sy) – variety of structures (eg grottoes, sham ruins, hermitage, etc.); Claremont (Sy) – belvedere; Oxenford (Sy) – barn in form of medieval chapel; Farley Mount (Ha) – pyramid; Dallington (Sx) – "Sugarloaf"; Penrice Wall, Gower (WG); Bladon Castle, Newton Solney (Db).
Mazes and Labyrinths – Breamore (Ha); Wing (Ru); Saffron Walden (Ex); Hampton Court; Alkborough (Li).
Hill Figures – White Horse, Uffington (Ox); Giant, Cerne Abbas (Do); Giant, Wilmington (Sx); White Cross, Bledlow (Ox); Whiteleaf Cross (Ox).

THE ROYAL PARKS

S Windsor (Bk); London Parks – Hyde Park, Kensington Gardens, St James's Park, Green Park, Regent's Park, Greenwich Park, Richmond Park, Hampton Court/Bushey.

OPEN SPACES

S *Ancient Forest and Woodpasture* – Hatfield Forest (Ex); Binswood (Ha); Bradgate Park (Le); Sutton Coldfield Park (WM); Epping Forest (Ex); New Forest (Ha).
City of London Open Spaces – Epping Forest, Hainault Forest (Ex); Burnham Beeches (Bk).

URBAN PARKS

S *London, non-royal* – Hampstead Heath, Battersea Park, Victoria Park, Dulwich Park, Finsbury Park, etc.
Outside London – Roundhay, Leeds; People's Park, Halifax; Cathay's and Bute, Cardiff; Queen's, Manchester.

SPECIALISED PARKS AND GARDENS

S *Botanic Gardens* – Oxford; Chelsea Physic Garden (Ln); Edinburgh; Glasgow; St Andrews; Sheffield; Ventnor (IW); Royal Botanic Gardens, Kew and Wakehurst (Sx); Royal Horticultural Society, Wisley (Sy); Northern Horticultural Society, Harlow Car, Harrogate (NY);
Arboretums – Winkworth (Sy); Westonbirt (Gl); Hilliers, Ampfield (Ha); Scone (Pe); Bedgebury pinetum (Kt).
Zoos – London/Whipsnade (Bc); Edinburgh; Bristol; Marwell (Ha); Jersey (CI).

COMMONS

S Wimbledon, Clapham, Wandsworth etc (Ln); Southampton; Bristol, Clifton Down; Harrogate, Stray; Newcastle-upon-Tyne, Town Moor; Bath, High and Low Common (with Royal Victoria Park); Cambridge, Midsummer Common; Oxford, Meadows.

NATIONAL PARKS

S Dartmoor Dv); Exmoor (So & Dv); North York Moors (NY); Peak (Db); Yorkshire Dales (NY); Lake District (Cu); Snowdonia; Brecon Beacons.

SPORTS AND GAMES

S *Cricket* – Lord's Cricket Ground (Ln); The Oval (Ln); Headingley, Leeds; Old Trafford, Manchester; Edgbaston, Birmingham; Trent Bridge Nottingham. Halfpenny Down Hambledon (Ha).
M MCC Museum, Lord's
S *Football* – Wembley Stadium (Ln); Old Trafford, Manchester; Arsenal (Ln); Cardiff Arms Park; Ibrox, Glasgow.
Rugby Union – Twickenham (Ln).
Tennis – Wimbledon (Ln).
Golf – St Andrew's (Fi); Gleneagles (Ta); Wentworth (Sy)
Horse-racing – Epsom (Sy); Ascot (Bk); Doncaster (SY); Aintree (La); Newmarket (Su); Sandown Park, Esher (Sy).

The Evolution of Towns

PREHISTORIC

S *Oppida* – Stanwick (NY); Danebury (Ha).
M Museum of the Iron Age, Andover (Ha).

ROMAN TOWNS

S *Lay out visible* – Winchester; Chichester; Gloucester; York; *exposed sites* – Silchester (Ha); Verulamium (Ht).
M Reading Museum (Silchester material) (Bk); BM; Museum of London; Corinium Museum, Cirencester (Gl); Yorkshire Museum, York.

ANGLO-SAXON TOWNS

S *Wics* – London (Strand area); Hamwih, Southampton; York; Lincoln (Wigford); Ipswich.
Burhs – Cricklade (Wi); Wallingford (Ox); Lydford (Dv); Wareham (Do).
Late Anglo-Saxon town plans – Winchester; Chichester (inside Roman walls and using main streets).

THE DANELAW

S The Five Boroughs of the Danelaw were Stamford, Nottingham, Derby, Leicester and Lincoln.

MEDIEVAL TOWNS

S New Winchelsea (Sx).
M reconstructed medieval village, Cosmeston, Penarth (SG).

SPECIALISED TOWNS

S *Pilgrimage* – Canterbury, Glastonbury (So); Walsingham (NF).
University – Oxford, Cambridge.
Dominant activity – racehorses, Lambourn (Bk); Newmarket (Su).
Single industry – The Potteries: Stoke-on-Trent and adjacent towns.
Gun and jewellery quarters – Birmingham.

RESORT TOWNS

S Brighton; Blackpool; Scarborough; Weymouth; Southend.

SPAS

S Bath; Harrogate; Cheltenham; Leamington (Ww); Buxton (Db); *traces of former spas* at eg Epsom (Sy).
M Roman Baths Museum, Bath.

THE CINQUE PORTS

S Dover (Kt); Sandwich (Kt); Walmer (Kt); Deal (Kt); Hythe (Kt); New Romney (Sx); Hastings (Sx); Rye (Sx); Winchelsea (Sx).

TOWNS IN WALES

S *Medieval* – Caernarfon (Gd).

TOWNS IN SCOTLAND

M Auchindrain Old Highland Township (Ar).
S *Medieval burghs* – Edinburgh (Old Town and Canongate); Stirling; St Andrew's; Perth; Haddington (Lo).
18th century – Edinburgh (New Town); Fochabers (My); Halkirk (Cs); Glasgow.

Houses

THE MEDIEVAL BUILDING INDUSTRY

S *Masons' marks* – Lincoln Cathedral; Salisbury Cathedral; Dundas canal aqueduct, Bath; Westminster Abbey.
Medieval tiles – Winchester Cathedral; Westminster Abbey;

M BM

S *Mathematical tiles* – Canterbury; Brighton; Guildford House, Guildford (Sy); Lamb House, Rye (Sx).

S *Protective devices: galleting* – Dunsfold Church (Sy); walls etc in western Weald; *brickwork* – Hampton Court; Layer Marney (Ex); *17th century brickwork* – High Street, Godalming (Sy).

BUILDING MATERIALS/ BUILDING FEATURES

S *Roofs* – Westminster Hall (Ln).
Chimneys – medieval: St Cross, Winchester; Vicar's Close, Wells; *Tudor* – Hampton Court.
Coade Stone – Bedford Square (Ln).
Timber – Little Moreton Hall (Ch).
Weatherboarding – common in Kent and Essex (eg Tenterden).
Doors – Chichester; York.
Pargeting – Saffron Walden (Ex); Newport (Ex).

VERNACULAR HOUSES

M W&D; Avoncroft Museum of Buildings, Bromsgrove (Wo).

PRE-CONQUEST HOUSES

M *Prehistoric* – Butser Ancient Farm, Chalton (Ha); Yorvik Viking Centre, York

S *Timber* – Little Moreton Hall (Ch).
Roman villas – Chedworth (Gl); Bignor (Sx); Littlecote (Wi); Fishbourne (Sx); Lullingstone (Kt); Rockbourne (Ha)
Anglo-Saxon Houses – West Stow (Su).
Viking Houses – Jarlshof (Zd); Birsay (Or); The Braaid (IM).

M Jorvik Viking Centre, York.

POST-CONQUEST HOUSES – RURAL

S *Longhouses* – Mostly in the south-west, north-west and Yorkshire, eg Shilston, Throwleigh (Dv); Charity Farm, Osmington (Do); Ona Ash, Kirkoswald (Cu); Heights, Wharfedale (NY).
Wealden Houses – Common in south-east England, notably in Kent, eg Marden, Pattenden, Goudhurst; Smarden House, Smarden; northern example, Goodramgate, York.

M W&D; for Bayleaf – Chiddingstone (Kt).

S *Aisled halls* – Fyfield Hall (Ex); group round Halifax, eg High Bentley, Shelf (WY); St Mary's Hospital, Chichester (Sx).
First-floor halls – Boothby Pagnell (Li); Charleston Manor House (Sx); Christchurch Castle (Do); Markenfield Hall, nr Ripon (NY).
Tower houses and peles – Nappa (Nd); Staward Pele, Allendale (Nd); Corbridge (Nd); Embleton vicarage (Nd); Mortham rectory (Nd); Neidpath (Ps); Smailholm Tower (Rx); Branxholm Tower (Rx).
Black house – Arnol, Lewis (WI).
Great Houses: medieval and Tudor – Haddon Hall (Db); Burghley (Ca); Longleat (Wi); Montacute (So); Wollaton (No); *early 17th century* – Knole (Kt); *medieval to 17th century* – Hatfield (Ht); *late 17th-18th century* – Chatsworth (Db); Castle Howard (NY); Blenheim (Ox); Chiswick (Ln); Petworth (Sx); Stowe (Bc); Clandon (Sy); Uppark (Sx).
Ice Houses – Croome Court (Wo); Morden Hall (Ln); Hatchlands, East Clandon (Sy); Barrells Hall, Ullenhall (Ww).

POST CONQUEST HOUSES – URBAN

S *Norman* – Bury St Edmunds; Jew's House and Jew's Court, Lincoln.
Medieval – numerous examples in eg York, including the restored Barley Hall, off Stonegate; The Chester Rows (Ch).
Terrace houses – Nash terrace houses, Regent's Park (Ln); Georgian and Regency terraces, squares, crescents, etc, in eg London, Edinburgh, Glasgow, Bath, Brighton, Clifton (Av), Cheltenham.
Workers' houses – back-to-backs, Leeds; up-and-down houses, Hebden Bridge (WY).
Occupational houses : *weavers'* – Heptonstall (WY); Spitalfields (Ln); *knitters* – Calverton (No).
Model villages – New Lanark (Lk); Saltaire (WY); Bournville (WM); Port Sunlight (Ch); New Earswick (York).
Garden cities – Letchworth (Ht), Welwyn (Ht), Stevenage (Ht); Hampstead Garden Suburb (Ln).
New towns – Milton Keynes (Bc); Harlow (Ex); Crawley (Sx); Washington (Du); Cumbernauld (Sg).

The Church

RELIGIOUS PREHISTORY

S *Centres with circles, henges, standing stones, tombs, etc* – Avebury/ Silbury area (Wi); Stonehenge area (Wi); Thornborough area (NY); Penwith area (Co); Kilmartin area (Ar); Callanish (WI); Orkney; Camster area (Cs); Clava (In); inscribed stone – Routing Linn (Nd).

THE GREATER CHURCHES

S Most, if not all, have features of importance: Winchester, Lincoln, York, Peterborough, Ely, Norwich, Durham, Wells, Exeter, Salisbury, Lichfield, Canterbury, Chichester, Hereford, Worcester; Coventry (new); London, St Paul's; Southwark, Southwell, Ripon, Portsmouth, Westminster Abbey, Beverley, Selby, Romsey, Hexham, Christchurch, Tewkesbury, Wimborne, St George's Windsor, St Cross Winchester, King's College, Cambridge. *Wales* - St David's, Llandaff; *Scotland* – Glasgow, Kirkwall; St Andrew's, Elgin (ruins).
Bishops' palaces – Wolvesey, Winchester (medieval ruins and 17th century); Wells

(moated); Bishop Auckland (Du); Southwell (No), Bishops Waltham (Ha) (ruins); Lincoln.

MONASTIC HOUSES

S *Monasteries* – Fountains Abbey (NY); Kirkstall (WY); Rievaulx (NY); Battle (Sx); Tintern (Mo); Glastonbury (So); Mount Grace, Carthusian (NY).
Wales – Strata Florida (Dy); Valle Crucis (Cw); Llanthony (Gw); St Dogmael's (Dy).
Scotland – Whithorn (Wg); Sweetheart (Df); Dundrennan (Df); Melrose, Jedburgh, Dryburgh (Rx); Iona.
Granges and tithe barns – Tisbury (Wi); many of Fountains and Byland, in Nidderdale (NY), eg Bouthwaite, Ramsgill; *tithe barns* – Great Coxwell (Ox); Bradford on Avon (Wi); Tisbury (Wi); Coggeshall (Ex).
Dissolution conversions – Fountains Hall (NY), built from stones of abbey; St Osyth (Ex); Forde (Do); Newstead (No); Sherborne (Do), school.

PARISH CHURCHES

S Among a great many others, the following have features of exceptional interest – Ewelme (Ox); Lavenham (Su); Mells (So); All Saints North Street, York; Compton (Sy); Bosham (Sx); Ottery St Mary (Dv); Patrington (Hu); Ashbourne (Db); Wellingborough (Nh); Brixworth (Nh); Repton (Db), crypt: London, Christ Church, Spitalfields; All Saints Margaret Street; St Stephens, Walbrook; St Bartholomew the Great; Temple: Thaxted (Ex); St Mary Redcliffe, Bristol; East Meon (Ha); Cirencester (Gl); Fairford (Gl); Bradford-on-Avon (Wi); Deerhurst (Gl); Stow (Li); Escomb (Du); Greensted (Ex); St Mary, Whitby (NY); Minstead (Ha); Brookland (Kt, belfry); Lastingham (NY); Warwick; Blythburgh, Southwold (Su); Kilpeck (He), sheela-na-gig; Barnack, Earl's Barton; St Mary, Nottingham.
Wales – Pennant Melangell (Po); Clynnog

Fawr (Gd); Nash (Gw); Llanbadarn Fawr (Dy); Llantwit Major (Gm).
Holy wells : Roman – Conventina's, Carrawburgh (Nd); *medieval* – Holywell (Ft); St Non's, St David's (Pe); St Anne's, Stoke (Dv); St Beuno's, Clynnog Fawr (Cn); St Cybi's, Llangybi (Cn); St Ann's, Malvern (Wo); St Helen's, Thorp Arch (NY); St Ronan's, Innerleithen (Ps).
Round churches – Temple (Ln); Cambridge; Little Maplestead (Ex); Northampton; Ludlow Castle (Sp); related, Orphir (Or).
Round towers – Suffolk mainly, eg Mutford.

FITTINGS AND FURNISHINGS

S *Pews* – Holy Trinity, Goodramgate, York (also Laudian rails); Minstead (Ha); Warminghurst (Sx); bench ends, Dennington; Fressingfield (Su); Brent Knoll (So).
Stalls and misericords –Ripon (NY); Manchester; Beverley (Hu); Winchester; Cartmel Priory (Cu); Lancaster Priory (La); Ripple (Wo).
M *Bells* – Whitechapel Bell Foundry (Ln); Taylor's Bell Foundry, Loughborough (Le).
S *Stained glass* – York Minster; All Saints, North Street, York; Fairford (Gl).
M Stained Glass Museum, Ely Cathedral; V&A.
S *Pulpits* – Kenton (Dv); stone, Shorwell (IW); three-decker, Minstead (Ha), Molland (Dv); royal arms, West Grinstead (Sx).
Galleries – Whitby (NY).
Wall painting - Winchester Cathedral; Hardham (Sx); Chaldon (Sy); St Thomas, Salisbury; (secular) Longthorpe Tower, Peterborough (Ca);
Fonts: Tournai – Winchester, Lincoln; St Michael, Southampton, East Meon (Ha), Thornton Curtis (Li), St Peter's, Ipswich;
Seven Sacraments – Norfolk and Suffolk, eg East Dereham; Nettlecombe (So); *Aylesbury group* – *others*, Lenton (No); Southrop (Gl); Castle Frome (He).
Easter sepulchres –Crediton (Dv); Hawton (No)
Lavish interior – St Mary, Wellingborough

Oxford movement – All Saints, Margaret Street (Ln); Studley Royal (NY).

THE SYMBOLISM OF CHURCHES

S *Angel roofs* – March (Ca).

CHURCHYARDS

S *Hogbacks* – Gosforth (Cu), Brompton (NY), Lowther (Cu); Lythe (NY); Dewsbury (WY); Bexhill (Sx)
M *Hogbacks* – Meigle (Pe).
S *Hudds* – Odiham (Ha); Friskney (Li); Ivychurch (Kt).
Watchmen's huts – Crail (Fi); Wanstead (Ex)
Bedboard tombs – Yateley (Ha); Thursley (Sy).

CEMETERIES

S Highgate (Ln); Kensal Green (Ln); Brookwood (Sy); Liverpool; Lawnswood, Leeds; Necropolis, Glasgow; Dumfries (DG).

CROSSES

S Iona; Gosforth (Cu); Bewcastle (Cu); Govan (Glasgow); Isle of Man.
Eleanor crosses – Geddington (Nh); Hardingstone (Nh); Waltham Cross (Ht); Charing Cross (Ln, replica); *market crosses* – Chichester; Salisbury; Dunster (So); Swaffham (Nf); *mercat crosses* – Culross (Fi).
S *Pictish symbol stones* – Nairn (Nn); Aberlemno (Ta); Sueno's Stone, Forres (My);
M *Pictish symbol stones* – Meigle (Pe); Glamis (Ta); St Vigean's (Ta); Royal Museum of Scotland, Edinburgh.

CHURCHES IN THE LANDSCAPE

S *Chantries* – Winchester Cathedral; Ewelme (Ox); Fotheringay (Nh); St Alban's Cathedral
Private chapels – St George's, Windsor.

NONCONFORMIST CHAPELS

S *Congregational/United Reformed* – Horningsham (Wi); City Temple (Ln).
Unitarian –Bury St Edmunds (Su); York (Greek Cross); Friars Street, Ipswich; Norwich

(octagon); Mill Hill Chapel, Leeds; *Methodist* – City Road, (Ln); Bristol; Heptonstall (WY) (octagon); Yarm (Cl); *Baptist*, Tewkesbury (Gl); Winchester; *Catholic Apostolic*, Christ the King (Ln), later the University of London church; Albury (Sy).

FRIENDS' (QUAKER) MEETING HOUSES

S Hertford; Brant Broughton (Li); Brigflatts, Sedbergh (Cu); Jordans (Ht); Farfield (WY); Come to Good, Kea (Co); Godalming (Sy).

THE WELSH CHAPEL

S Ubiquitous; but some stand out, either for their architecture or their dominant situation, eg Maesteg (GM); Mount Pleasant, Swansea; Treveca, near Talgarth (Po).

THE CHURCH OF SCOTLAND

S *Round Towers* – Brechin (Ag); Abernethy (Fi).
Parish churches – St Andrew's, Edinburgh (oval); Leuchars (Fi); St Rule, St Andrew's; Reilig Oran, Iona; Stirling; Crail (Fi); Haddington; Roslin (Lo).
T-plan – Duddington; Monymusk; Durisdeer (Du).
in England – Pont Street (Ln).

ROMAN CATHOLIC CHURCHES

Westminster Cathedral; Southwark Cathedral; Liverpool Cathedral; St Ethelreda's (Ln); Slipper Chapel, Walsingham (Nf); Brompton Oratory (Ln); Farnborough Abbey (Ha); Notre-Dame de France, Leicester Square (Ln).

OTHER DENOMINATIONS

S *French Protestant* – Soho Square, London
Swiss Protestant – Endell Street, London
Dutch – Austin Friars (Ln)

NON-CHRISTIAN RELIGIONS

S *Synagogues* – Bevis Marks (Ln).
Mosques – Woking (Sy); Regent's Park (Ln);

Whitechapel (Ln).
Buddhist temples – Eskdalemuir (Df); Chithurst (Sx).
Hindu temple – Neasden (Mx).

The Styles of Architecture

CLASSICAL

S *Of Greek/Roman inspiration* – British Museum; St George's Hall, Liverpool; St Pancras church (Ln); Glasgow, Wellington Church, St George's in the Fields; The Grange, Northington (Ha); Hereford Shire Hall.

ROMANESQUE

S *Saxon* – Greensted (Ex); Escomb (Du); Bradford-on-Avon (Wi); Earls Barton (Nh); Barnack (Nh); Brixworth (Nh); Barton upon Humber (Hu); Deerhurst (Gl).
Crypts – Ripon, Hexham, Repton.
Norman – Durham; St Albans; St Bartholomew's (Ln); Romsey; Selby; St Mary's, Guildford (Sy); Compton (Sy); Southwell (No).

GOTHIC

S *Early English* – Salisbury Cathedral.
Decorated – Lichfield Cathedral.
Perpendicular – Gloucester; Sherborne (Do); Westminster, Henry VII's Chapel; Christ Church College, Oxford; St Mary Redcliffe, Bristol.

POST MEDIEVAL

S *Renaissance and Elizabethan* – Montacute (So); Wollaton (No); Longleat (Wi).
Jacobean/ early Stuart or first Palladian/ Later Stuart – Banqueting House, Whitehall (Ln); Queen's House, Greenwich (Ln); Hatfield (Ht); Blickling (Nf); Temple Newsam, Leeds; .

EARLY MODERN

S *Baroque (1690s–1720s)* – St Paul's Cathedral, (Ln) and Wren churches; Greenwich Hospital (later the Royal Naval College).

Palladian (1720–60) – Kedleston (Db); Horse Guards (Ln); Holkham (Nf); Chiswick House (Ln); *Adam* – Kenwood (Ln); Royal Society of Arts (Ln); Royal Crescent, Bath; Edinburgh (New Town); Somerset House (Ln).

MODERN

S *Regency* – Bedford Square (Ln); Cheltenham. *Victorian* – Manchester Town Hall; Law Courts, London; St Pancras Station (Ln); Keble College, Oxford; *Ruskin/Morris movements* – The Red House, Eltham (Ln). *20th Century* – South Bank complex (Ln); Hoover factory, Perivale (Ln); Boots factory, Beeston (No); Lloyds building (Ln).

WALES

S See chapels.

SCOTLAND

S Roslin Chapel (Lo); Melrose Abbey (Bo); Caerlaverock Castle, 16th-century wing (Df); *baronial style* – Craigievar (Gr); Glamis (Ta); Fyvie (Gr); *18th-century* – Mellerstain (Bo); Pollok, Glasgow; *late 19th-century* – School of Art, Glasgow.

Castles and Military Works

S *Hillforts* – Maiden Castle (Do); Cissbury (Sx); The Caburn (Sx); Tre'r Ceiri (Cn); Yeavering (Nd); Dunadd (Ar).
Ringworks – Dover (Kt); Paisley area; Rothesay (Bu); Mote of Urr (Kb).
Mottes – Abinger (Sy); York; Thetford (Nf); Tonbridge (Kt); Welsh borders.
Keeps: Shell keeps – Cardiff; Durham; Kilpeck (He); Lincoln; Ludlow (Sp); *square keeps* – London, Colchester, Rochester, Ludlow (Sp).
Castles: tall towers – Corfe (Do); Gloucester; *polygonal towers* – Orford (Su); Conisborough (SY); *round towers* – Pembroke (Pb); *lobed towers* – York.
Castles of enceinte – Framlingham (Su); Bodiam (Sx).

Concentric – Rhuddlan (Fl); Harlech (Me); Caerphilly (MG).
Water defences – Caerphilly; Kenilworth (Ww); Leeds (Kt).
15th century – Tattershall (Li).
Scotland – Edinburgh; Stirling; Hermitage (Rx); Noltland castle, Westray (Or); Cubbie Roo's castle, Wyre (Or).
Moats – Ightham Mote (Kt); Goodrich castle (He); Bodiam castle (Sx); and some 3000 castles and houses.

FORTIFIED HOUSES

S Stokesay Castle (Sp).

TOWN WALLS

S York; Berwick on Tweed; Chester; (Roman) Silchester; Verulamium; Ludlow; Caernarfon
Town gates – Southampton; York; Winchester; Rye (Sx); Lincoln.
Siege works – Newark on Trent (No).

FORTS

S *Forts (early): prehistoric brochs* – Midhowe, Rousay (Or); Gurness (Or); Mousa (Zd); Clickhimin (Zd).
Roman walls: forts on Hadrian's Wall – Housesteads, Chesters, Vindolanda; *forts on the Antonine Wall* – Rough Castle (Sg).

M Roman Museum, Newcastle University; Tullie House Museum, Carlisle; *Museums at main Hadrian's Wall forts*, and at Corbridge (Nd); Hunterian Museum, Glasgow; BM; Museum of London.

S *Later forts: Henry VIII* – Southsea (Ha); Tilbury (Ex); Yarmouth (IW); *18th century* – Fort George (Nn); Fort Augustus (In); *Napoleonic* – Cumberland Fort, Eastney (Ha); Fort Nelson, Fareham (Ha); Fort Brockhurst, Gosport (Ha).
Martello towers – Folkestone; Beachy Head (Sx); Seaford (Sx); Slaghden, Aldeburgh (Su); Leith (ML).
Linear earthworks – Wansdyke (So/Wi); Offa's Dyke (Welsh Borders); Catrail Dyke (Sk/Rx).

OTHER MILITARY WORKS

S *Naval telegraphs* – Chatley Heath (Sy).
Barracks – Berwick on Tweed; Wellington Barracks (Ln).
Parade grounds – Hon Artillery Company (Ln); Horse Guards (Ln); Laffan's Plain, Aldershot (Ha).
Arsenals – Woolwich (Ln).
Dockyards - Portsmouth (M); Chatham (M).
Minor works: pill boxes – widespread.

Public Buildings

CENTRAL AND LOCAL GOVERNMENT

S *Central government* – The Houses of Parliament (Ln); Whitehall (Ln); Somerset House (Ln); Custom House (Ln); St Andrew's House, Edinburgh; the Record Office, Edinburgh.
Local government – Civic Centre, Cardiff;
Law Courts – Law Courts and Old Bailey (Ln).
Judge's lodgings - Nottingham; York (now a hotel); Lancaster (now a children's museum).
Prisons – Princetown (Dv).
Custom House, King's Lynn (Nf).

M Customs House, Lancaster (La).

S *Town and City Halls* – Manchester; Guildhall, London; Glasgow; Leeds; Nottingham; Bradford; civic centre, Southampton; Birmingham Town Hall

HOSPITALS

S St Thomas's (Ln), operating theatre (M); Buxton; cottage hospital, Cranleigh (Sy); St Bartholomew's and Guy's Hospitals (Ln).
Almshouses – Abbot's Hospital, Guildford (Sy); Warwick; St Mary's Hospital, Chichester; St Cross, Winchester; Beamsley (NY); Ewelme (Ox).
Workhouses – Easebourne, Midhurst (Sx); Alton (Ha).

EDUCATION BUILDINGS

S *Schools* – Winchester College; Eton College; Guildford Grammar School.

M *Higher education: universities* – Oxford; Cambridge; Durham; London; St Andrew's - all with individual constituent colleges, eg at London, University and King's Colleges: *modern campuses* – eg York, Exeter, Sussex (Brighton), East Anglia (Norwich), Nottingham, Lancaster.

MUSEUMS AND ART GALLERIES

M *Museums: London* – British Museum; Science Museum; Natural History Museum; Geological Museum; Victoria and Albert Museum; Museum of Mankind; *outside London* – Jorvik Viking Museum, York; Museum of English Rural Life, Reading University (Be); Weald and Downland Open Air Museum, Singleton (Sx); WFM; Ironbridge Gorge Museum (Sp).
Art Galleries : London – National Gallery; Tate Gallery; National Portrait Gallery; Hayward Gallery; Victoria and Albert Museum; *outside London* – Tate Gallery, St Ives; Tate Gallery and Walker Gallery, Liverpool; Leeds City Museum and Art Gallery; Museum of Modern Art and Asmolean Museum, Oxford; Fitzwilliam, Cambridge; Southampton; City Art Gallery and Whitworth Gallery, Manchester; Birmingham; Scottish National Gallery and Gallery of Modern Art, Edinburgh; the Burrell Collection, Pollok House and the Glasgow Art Gallery, Glasgow; National Museum, Cardiff.

LIBRARIES

S *National libraries* – British Library (Ln); National Library of Scotland; National Library of Wales, Aberystwyth; Public Record Office (Ln).
Regional libraries – Leeds City Library; Manchester City Library.
University libraries – Bodleian, Oxford (with Duke Humphrey's Library); *college libraries, Oxford* – Merton, Christ Church, Queen's; *college libraries, Cambridge* – Trinity, St John's, Magdalene; *London* – University and King's

College, London School of Economics; *university libraries* – eg Brotherton, Leeds. *Private libraries* – Royal Society, Society of Antiquaries, London Library, Dr Williams (Ln), Society of Friends (Ln and Woodbrooke, Birmingham); Chetham's and John Rylands, Manchester (University); Syon College (Ln); The Athenaeum (Ln); Kirkwall (Or); Innerpeffray (Pe). *Church libraries* – Lambeth Palace (Ln), Winchester, Durham, Lincoln, Canterbury.

THEATRES AND CINEMAS

S   *Roman* – Verulamium (Ht).
    Tudor – Globe (Ln); Rose (Ln).
    Eighteenth century – Haymarket (Ln): the Georgian Theatre, Richmond (NY).
    Nineteenth century – Drury Lane (Ln); Royal Opera House, Covent Garden (Ln); Old Vic (Ln); Grand Theatre Leeds; Nottingham, Theatre Royal; Manchester, Royal Exchange Theatre.
    Twentieth century – Shakespeare Memorial Theatre, Stratford on Avon (Ww); Chichester Festival Theatre; National Theatre and National Film Theatre (Ln); theatre in the round – Young Vic (Ln); Bristol, Theatre Royal (Old Vic).
    Music Halls – City Varieties, Leeds; Collins Music Hall, Islington (Ln); The Hackney Empire (Ln); Winter Gardens, Blackpool (La); Victoria Palace (Ln); Alhambra (Ln); Colosseum (Ln).
M   Theatre Museum, Covent Garden (Ln); Richmond (NY)

CINEMAS

S   Odeon, Leicester Square (Ln); Astoria (Ln); Chingford (Ex).

AMPHITHEATRES AND STADIA

S   Silchester (Ha); Caerleon (Gw), Roman

EXHIBITION HALLS

S   Olympia (Ln); Earls Court (Ln); Horticultural Halls (Ln); National Exhibition Centre, nr Stonebridge (WM).

CONCERT HALLS

Covent Garden Opera House (Ln); Glyndebourne (Sx); Dartington (Dv); Albert Hall (Ln); Royal Festival Hall complex (Ln).

ASSEMBLY ROOMS

Bath; York; Bury St Edmunds (Su); Devizes (Wi); and in some hotels, eg The George, Rye (Sx); The Dolphin, Southampton.

DANCING

Tower Ballroom, Blackpool (La).

STATUES AND MEMORIALS

S   The Cenotaph, Whitehall (Ln); Charles I, Whitehall (Ln); William III, Petersfield (Ha); Eros, Piccadilly Circus (Ln); Duke of York's Column (Ln) Albert Memorial (Ln); the Scott monument (Ed).

Communications and Trade

ROADS AND TRACKS

S   *Prehistoric* – Ridgeway/Icknield Way (Wessex to East Anglia; North Downs Way; Fosse Way; Rombalds Way (across Pennines through Aire Gap).
    Roman – system radiating from London, with cross links - much still followed by modern roads, eg Ermine Street (A1); Watling Street (A5), Fosse Way.
    Saxon – manorial lanes, eg Alfriston to Firle (Sx).
    Medieval and post-medieval –
    Turnpikes – toll houses at eg Marlborough (Wi), Alfresford (Ha), Selborne (Ha).
M   W&D; Ironbridge Gorge (Sp).
S   *General Wade's roads* – Fort Augustus (In).
    20th century – by-passes and motorways, eg M1; Spaghetti Junction, Birmingham; Petersfield (Ha); Bentley (Ha).
    Minor ways – hollow ways, on Surrey and Hampshire greensands, eg round Selborne.
    Road surfaces and miscellaneous features : surfaces – Guildford High Street (Sy); Rye (Sx); Elm Hill, Norwich; *raised pavements* – Godalming, Dorking and Haslemere (all Sy).
    Droving and drove roads – south of Peebles; Clennell Street-Crakemuir Road (Sk/Df); Mastiles Lane, Malham (NY); Abbotstone (Ha), on Weyhill route; The Drift (Le/Li).
    River crossing: fords – Geddington (Nh); *causeways* – Maud Heath's Causeway, Kellaways, Chippenham (Wi); *bridges:clapper and clam* – Post Bridge, Dartmoor (Dv); Linton (NY); Wycoller (La); Tarr Steps, Exmoor (So); *Roman or Romanesque* – Castle Combe (So); Waltham Abbey (Ex); Piercebridge (Du), Roman footings; *monastic bridges* – of Waverley Abbey (Sy), eg Eashing, Tilford; *medieval* – Dumfries, with fish weir; Bideford (Dv); Elvet Bridge, Durham; Twizel Bridge (Nd); High Bridge, Lincoln; Stopham (Sx); Croyland (Li), triple; *bridge chapels* – Wakefield (SY); Bradford on Avon (Wi); *fortified bridges* – Monmouth; Warkworth (Nd); *packhorse* – New Bridge, Birstwith (NY); Linton (NY); Ashford-in-the-Water (Db); *18th–20th century* – Palladian, Wilton (Wi), Stowe (Bc), Prior Park, Bath; Berwick Old Bridge; Clare College, Cambridge; Aray Bridge, Inverarary (Ar); Pulteney Bridge, Bath; Chertsey; Henley (Ox); General Wade's Bridges, eg Aberfeldy (Ta); Dorset bridges with damage warnings; *iron bridges* – The Iron Bridge (Sp); Menai Bridge (An); Clifton Suspension Bridge, Bristol; modern bridges, eg Humber, Severn

INLAND WATERWAYS

S   *Rivers and River Ports* – London, Norwich, Goole, Tyne ports, Glasgow, Bewdley (Wo), Bristol, Exeter, Morwellham (Dv), York.
    Canals: ports – Stourport (Wo); Birmingham; *tunnels* – Sapperton (Gl); Harecastle (WY); Braunston (Nh); Standedge (WY); Blisworth (Nh); *aqueducts* – Chirk and Pontcysyllte

(Cw); Longdon on Tern (Sp); Dundas and Avoncliffe (So); Barton Swing Bridge (La); *flights of locks* – Devizes (Wi), 29; Tardebigge (Wo), 30; Bingley (WY), 5; Banavie (Hi), 8; *inclined planes*, Blist's Hill (Sp); Morwellham (Dv); *lifts* – Anderton (Ch); *pumping engines* – Crofton (Wi); *agents' houses* – Alfold (Sy); Trent Lock (No/Db); *scenic* – Crinan canal (Ar); Caledonian Canal (Hi).

M The Canal Museum, Stoke Bruerne (Nh); National Waterways Museum, Gloucester; Ellesmere Port Boat Museum (Ch); Exeter Maritime Museum (Dv).

RECLAMATION OF WETLANDS

S *The Broads*– eg Hickling Broad and Horsey Mere (Nf).
The Fens – the fens proper are in Holland (Li), Norfolk and Cambridgeshire, eg Bedford Level; but there are other important *wetlands* – eg the Somerset Levels; the Flow Country, Caithness and Sutherland.

RAILWAYS

S *Wagonways* – Belvoir Castle (Le); Haytor tramway, Dartmoor (Dv); Cinderford (Gl); Cwmavon (Gm); Pontypool (Gm); Chapel Milton (Db).

M Ironbridge Gorge Museum (Sp).

S *Tramways* – Douglas (IM), Blackpool, Manchester, Sheffield, Newcastle.

M National Tramway Museum, Crich (Db).

S *Railways and railway features: viaducts and bridges* – Causey Arch (Du); Forth Bridge; Saltash Bridge (Dv/Co); Menai Bridge (Cn/An); Ouse Viaduct (Sx); Ribblehead (Cu).

M National Railway Museum, York; Didcot Railway Centre (Ox); GWR Museum, Swindon (Wi).

S *London's Underground* – 1930s stations – eg Arnos Grove.

M London Transport Museum, Covent Garden.

S *Narrow gauge and preserved railways* – Ffestiniog railway; the Talyllyn railway; the Snowdon railway; Ravenglass and Eskdale;

the Isle of Man railway.

S *Specialised lines* – London Post Office Railway. *Railway stations and other buildings*– St Pancras (Ln); Paddington (Ln): York; Huddersfield (WY); Bristol, Temple Meads; Stoke-on-Trent (St).

LETTERBOXES

S *Pillar box* – Warwick (1856); *Penfold* – (1866, copy) Haslemere (Sy).

GUILDS AND GUILDHALLS

S London; Thaxted (Ex); City Livery Company halls (Ln); Merchant Adventurers Hall, York; Cutlers' Hall, Sheffield.
Inns of court – Inner Temple, Middle Temple, Lincoln's Inn, Gray's Inn (Ln).

MARKET HALLS

S Smithfield (Ln); Oakham (Ru); Pembridge (He); Abingdon (Ox); Ross on Wye (He); Watlington (Ox).

SHOPS AND SHOPPING

S *Shopfronts* – Bury St Edmunds; Ripon; London, Haymarket, Artillery Lane;*arcades* – Royal Arcade (Ln); Burlington Arcade (Ln); County Arcade, Leeds.
Market places – Petersfield (Ha); Wickham (Ha); Thame (Ox), partly infilled; Masham (NY); Leyburn (NY).

INNS AND HOTELS

S *Monastic* – Glastonbury (So); *medieval* – The Trip to Jerusalem, Nottingham; *coaching inns* – Angel, Grantham; Saracen's Head, Southwell (No); King's Head, Aylesbury (Bc); George, Southwark; *drovers' inns* – Tan Hill, near Brough (Cu/Du/NY border).

SOCIAL CENTRES, CLUBS AND SOCIETIES

S *Assembly rooms* (see above);*clubs* – the

London clubs form a distinctive group, of which several are of architectural importance, eg Brooks', Boodle's, White's, Athenaeum, Travellers', Reform, Garrick. Other cities have similar institutions, eg Manchester, Glasgow, Leeds

COINS

M BM.

TREASURE TROVE

M BM (eg Mildenhall and Snettisham treasures; the Sutton Hoo treasure belonged to the landowner, and was presented to the BM).

Crafts

RURAL CRAFTS

S *Dewponds* – Chantonbury (Sx); Ditchling Beacon (Sx).

M WFM; W&D; MERL; Old Kiln Museum, Tilford (Sy); Romany Museum, Selborne (Ha).

Industries

TEXTILES

S *Wool* – Piece Hall, Halifax; *mills* – Huddersfield; Stroud area (Gl) – eg Stanley Mill.

M Tolson Memorial Museum, Huddersfield; WFM; Lavenham Guildhall (Su); most local museums in West Yorkshire; Museum of the Lancashire Textiule Industry, Rossendale (Fulling Mill); WFM (working woollen mill); see also the industrial museums at Leeds, Bradford and Halifax.

S *Cotton* – Masson Mill, Cromford (Db); Quarry Bank Mill, Styal (Ch).

M Museum of Lancashire Textile Industry, Rossendale (La); SM; Manchester Museum of Science and Industry; Bolton Steam Museum (La); SM; Greatrer Manchester Museum of Science and Industry.

S *Silk* – fragments of Lambe's Mill, Derby; complete mills at Bridge Street, Derby, also at Beeston,Station Road and at Southwell, Maythorne; *weavers' garrets* – Macclesfield, Spitalfields, etc..

M *Silk* – Macclesfield Museum, Paradise Mill and Roe Street (Ch); V&A; Whitchurch Silk Mill (Ha).

S *Linen and flax: wheel* – Foster Beck Mill, Pateley Bridge (NY); also Bridge of Dean (Pe); Dundee; Arbroath; Blairgowrie; *linoleum* – Kircaldy.

M Dumfermline District Museum; SM; V&A.

S *Rope-walks* – Chatham, Portsmouth, Hawes.

M *Rope and nets* – Bridport Museum (Do).

S *Knitting* – Ruddington (No); Calverton (No); Hinckley (Le).

M Leicestershire Museum of Technology, Leicester.

S *Lace* – Lace market, Nottingham.

M Lace Centre, Nottingham.

LEATHER

S Shoes – Bolham Mills, Retford; Clark's original factory at Street (So); the tannery at Gomshall

M Northampton Central Museum; Brideswell Museum; Norwich; Westfield Museum, Kettering (No); Newarke Houses Museum, Leicester.

POTTERY

S *The Potteries* – Stoke-on-Trent City Museum, Hanley (St); Worcester, Derby; Poole (Do); Doulton, Lambeth (Ln)Stoke-on-Trent City Museum, Hanley (St), a reconstructed multiple kiln.

M BM; V&A; Pitt-Rivers Museum, Oxford; Ashmolean Museum, Oxford; Fitzwilliam Museum, Cambridge; Wallace Collection (maiolica, Ln); Stoke-on-Trent Museum; *firms' museums, eg* Spode, Wedgwood, Minton; Gladstone Pottery Museum, Longton (St); Allen Gallery, Alton (Ha); Nottingham Castle Museum; *Flint mill* – Cheddleton (St).

BRICKS AND TILES

S *Bricks and tiles: brickworks* – Bursledon (Ha).

M Blists Hill Museum (Sp).

GLASS

S *Glass* – Site of 16th-century glasshouse, Knightons, Sidney Wood, Alfold (Sy); Caithness Glass, Wick (Ca); Dartington (Dv); *cones* – Stourbridge (Wo); Catcliffe, Sheffield.

M BM; V&A; Pilkington Glass Museum, St Helen's (La); Stourbridge Museum (Wo); Guildford and Haslemere Museums (Sy); Ryedale Folk Museum, Hutton-le-Hole (NY); the Laing Museum, Newcastle-upon-Tyne; the Royal Scottish Museum, Edinburgh; Fitwilliam Museum, Cambridge; Ashmolean Museum, Oxford; Manchester City and University Museums; *stained glass* – Ely; Burrell Collection, Glasgow; V&A and York Minster.

QUARRIES

S *Flint mines* – Grimes Graves, Thetford (Nf); Cissbury and Harrow Hill (Sx).

S *Slate* – Bethesda (Gd).

M Blaenau Ffestiniog Museum (Cn); Welsh Slate Museum, Llanberis (Gd).

S *Stone, querns* – Wharncliffe, Sheffield; Beer (Dv).

M Beer Museum (Dv);National Stone Centre, Warksworth (Db); Barnack, "Hills and Holes" (Ca); roofing "slate" – Stonesfield (Ox).

S *Chalk* – Amberley (Sx).

M Amberley Chalk Pits Museum; Brockham (Sy).

S *Limestone* – Buxton (Db); Threshfield (NY).

M Black Country Museum, Dudley (WM).

S *Firestone and hearthstone* – along North Downs from Brockham to Merstham (Sy). *Sand and gravel* – along rivers, eg Thames, Trent, Welland. *Granite* – Ballater; Kenmay; Bonaive (all Ab).

COAL

M Big Pit Mining Museum, Blaenavon (Gw); Mining Museum, University of Newcastle; Ironbridge Gorge, Blist's Hill (Sp); Beamish Open Air Museum (Du); Yorkshire Mining Museum, Wakefield; Mercer Museum, Clayton-le-Moors (La); Salford Science Museum; University Museum of Mining Engineering, and Museum of Sicence and Engineering, New castle-upon-Tyne; Chatterley Whitfield Mining Museum, near Tunstall, Stoke-on-Trent.

S *London "wine and coal post"* – Epsom Common (Sy).

COPPER

S Parys Mines, Amlwch (An); Great Orme, Llandudno (Gd); Morwellham (Dv).

TIN

S Carn Brea, Redruth, Camborne area, Cornwall, eg Wheal Peevor, Botallack; Levant Mine, St Just; also many sites on Dartmoor, eg Vitifer, nr Postbridge.

M Geevor Mine, Pendean (Co); Morwellham Quay Open Air Museum (Dv); Poldark Mine, Helston (Co); Beam Mine Engines, Pool (Co).

LEAD

S Alston/ Allenheads area (Nd); Grassington area (NY); Charterhouse on Mendip (So); Leadhills/Wanlockhead (Lk); *ore crushing mill* – Killhope (Du).

GOLD

S Dolaucothi (Cm); Dolgellau (Me); Glengaber (Sk).

SILVER

(product of the processing of lead; see above).

IRON AND STEEL

S *Hammer and furnace ponds* – in the Weald, eg Cowden (Kt); Imbhams (Sy); Knepp (Sx); St Leonard's Forest (Sx); Vachery Pond, Cranleigh (Sy); blast furnaces, Ebernoe (Sx); Moira (Le); Bonawe (Ar); Blaenavon (Gw);

bloomeries – mostly Roman: Beaufort Park, nr Battle (Sx); Chitcombe, Brede (Sx); Garden Hill, Hartfield (Sx); Bardown, Ticehurst (Sx).

M V&A; Ironbridge Gorge Museum (Sp); Sheffield City Museum; Abbeydale Indiustrial Hamlet, Sheffield.

S *Horseshoes* – Oakham Castle (Ru).
Ornamental ironwork – Tijou's gates, Hampton Court; Bakewell's Cage, Melbourne (Db).
Railings etc – London, Edinburgh, Brighton, Bath, Cheltenham.

M *Firebacks* – V&A; Petworth House (Sx); Anne of Cleve's House, Lewes (Sx).
Nails – Abbey House Museum, Kirkstall, Leeds.
Needles – Redditch Museum (Wo).

SALT AND SALTWAYS

S *Salterns* – Essex "Red Hills", eg nr Maldon (Ex); Bradwell (Ex); Lymington (Ha); Marsh Chapel and Bicker Haven (Li); *mines* – Nantwich (Ch); Droitwich (Wo).

M Droitwich Heritage Centre; Northwich Salt Museum.

LIME

S *Limekilns* – Beadnell (Nd); Gwbert (Cd); Solva (Pb); Buck's Mills (Dv), Hambledon (Sy), and numerous examples on the coast and inland.

MILLING

S *Water wheels* – Laxey (IM); Killhope (Du); Foster Beck, Pateley Bridge (NY);.
Water mills – Mapledurham (Ox); Calbourne (IW); Headley (Ha); *horizontal mills* – Click Mill, Dounby (Or).

M Haxted, nr Edenbridge (Kt).

S *Tide mills* – Woodbridge (Su); Eling (Ha).
Wind mills: postmills – Bourn (Ca); Saxstead Green (Su); Outwood (Sy); Lowfield Heath, Charlwood (Sy); *smock mills* – Cranbrook (Kt); Shipley (Sx); *tower mills* – Hickington (Li).
Animal powered machines: cranes – Harwich (Ex); Guildford (Sy); *wells* – Carisbrooke Castle (IW).

M W&D; WFM.

PAPER

S Many of the mils, eg in Surrey and Kent were built or adapted for paper, eg Chilworth; Postford; Farncombe (Sy); banknote–paper, Laverstoke (Ha).

GUNPOWDER

S Faversham (Kt); Chilworth (Sy), ruins.

INDUSTRIAL ARCHAEOLOGY

S See under various headings for *Industries*, etc.

M SM and the other museums of science and industry, eg Glasgow, Manchester, Birmingham, Newcastle-upon-Tyne. Some specialised museums are also relevant, eg Beamish Open Air Museum (Du); Ironbridge Gorge Museum (Sp); Amberley Chalk Pits Museum (Sx); National Railway Museum, York; National Canal Museum, Gloucester; Black Country Open Air Museum, Dudley (WM); Forncett Industrial Steam Museum, nr Thetford (Nf).

Public Utilities

WATER

S *Medieval systems* – Canterbury Cathedral; Winchester; Exeter.
Reservoirs – Staines (Mx); Cwm Elan (Ra); Scar and Angram, Nidderdale (NY); Thirlmere and Haweswater (both Cu).
Pumping stations – Papplewick (No); Ryhope (Du); Kew (Ln); Crofton (Wi).
Sewage system – London (Bazalgette, 1860s).

GAS

S *Gas holders* – a few still survive: King's Cross (Ln); Bromley by Bow (Ln).

M Fakenham Museum of Gas and Local History (Nf), unique non-working gasworks.

ELECTRICITY

S *Power stations* – Didcot (Ox); Ferrybridge (NY).
Hydro-electric – Tummel-Garry system (Ta).

AVIATION

S A few traces of Croydon airport remain; Brabazon hangar, Filton, Bristol; airship hangars, Cardington (Bd).

M Brooklands Museum, Weybridge (Sy); Newark Air Museum (No); RAF Museum, Hendon; SM.

MOTORS

M National Motor Museum, Beaulieu (Ha); Brooklands Museum, Weybridge (Sy).

The Coast

M *Waterfronts* – Museum of London.

S *Warehouses* – Gainsborough (Li); Boston (Li); Guildford (Sy).
Ports and harbours: Roman – Richborough (Kt); *modern* – London, Tilbury (Ex), Liverpool, Glasgow, Newcastle-upon-Tyne, Southampton; *medieval and small harbours* – Rye (Sx); Hedon (Hu); Seaton Sluice (Nd); Lyme Regis (Do); *Scottish fishing harbours* – Crail, Anstruther, Elie (Fi); Kirkwall (Or); Lerwick (Zd); Ullapool (Hi).

M Scottish Fisheries Museum, Anstruther (Fi); Museum of Spey salmon fisheries, Spey Bay (My); WFM.

S *Docks* – London, eg St Katherine's Dock; Liverpool; Gloucester; *naval docks* – Portsmouth, Chatham.
Lighthouses: Roman – Dover; *medieval* – St Catherine's Down (IW); *modern* – Needles (IW).

M *Shipbuilding yards* – Buckler's Hard (Ha).

S *Old ships* – Portsmouth (Ha), *Mary Rose, Victory, Warrior. Cutty Sark* (Ln); *Great Eastern*, Bristol.

M *General* – National Maritime Museum, Greenwich; Maritime Museum, Customs House, Lancaster (La); National Lifeboat Lifeboat Museum, Bristol; Merseyside Maritime Museum, Albert Dock, Liverpool; Exeter Maritime Museum.

Further Reading

The books and articles listed here are to a large extent those I have found particularly helpful in writing this book, and their inclusion is a grateful acknowledgment to their authors.

I have listed books primarily, but many subjects are covered in greater detail (or only) in articles in periodicals, and these have been referred to when this seemed appropriate. Some of the items are expensive or scarce, but a public or specialised library should be able to locate most of them.

I do not claim that all these items are the only authoritative or exhaustive sources for their subjects, but most of them carry their own bibliographies which will take the reader further. Many of the topics touched on in this book are far from static, and only the help of an expert in any given field will open up later developments.

The lists are organised by topics, in the order in which the topics occur in the book, and in narrative form rather than alphabetically. Comments are made on some items which may be helpful in the search for relevant background material. Where Harvard references occur in the text, full references are given here, under the relevant subject heading.

It will be apparent from these lists that considerably more research has been done relating to England than to Scotland, Wales or Britain generally. In the nature of things this is inevitable, as there are more physical remains in England and more has been written and published about them, but efforts have been made to minimise undue bias in the selection of items.

Archaeological Techniques and Prehistory

Although this is not a book about the techniques of archaeology, and says very little about prehistory, it may be thought desirable to list a few books which will fill out the general background to these topics. A recent general account of archaeology and its problems across the world is Colin Renfrew and Paul Bahn: *Archaeology: Theories, Methods and Practice* (Thames and Hudson 1991). There are many books on the archaeology of Britain; two valuable surveys are J V S Megaw and D D A Simpson et al: *Introduction to British Prehistory* (Leicester University Press 1979), well illustrated; and Timothy Darvill: *Prehistoric Britain* (Batsford 1987), with itemised bibliography.

The meaning of unfamiliar terms can conveniently be sought in Paul Bahn ed: *Collins Dictionary of Archaeology* (1992).

A useful background to life, particularly in the historic periods, is Asa Briggs: *A Social History of England* (Weidenfeld and Nicolson, new edition 1994).

Ordnance Maps

For detailed coverage, clarity and information there is no rival to the maps of the Ordnance Survey. For general touring the Travelmaster series is adequate (two Routeplanner maps at 1 inch to 10 miles, 1 cm to 6. 25 km), and 8 regional maps at 1 inch to 4 miles, 1 cm to 2. 5 km); there is also a Motoring Atlas of Great Britain at 1 inch to 3 miles.

For general coverage of smaller, but reasonably large, areas, the Landranger maps, at 1 1/4 inches to 1 miles, 2cm to 1 km, are indispensable; these cover the whole country. Certain areas, eg National Parks and AONBs, are covered by the Outdoor Leisure maps, at 1:25000 scale (2 1/2 inches to 1 mile, 4cm to 1 km) series. Other leisure areas are covered on the same scale by the Explorer series. The rest of the country is covered at this scale by the Pathfinder maps.

There are also specialised maps, of Ancient Britain, Roman Britain, Hadrian's Wall, Roman and Anglian York, Viking and Medieval York, Roman and Medieval Bath, Georgian Bath, Roman and Medieval Canterbury, and Londinium (Roman London). An earlier map of Monastic Britain is useful, and may still be found secondhand. A detailed Catalogue of all the Ordnance Survey maps, and an Index of Pathfinder, Outdoor Leisure, Explorer and Landranger series, are available free of charge.

Introduction

Material on the rate of change is published from time to time in the journals of bodies such as RESCUE, national and county conservation trusts, CPRE, the Woodland Trust, English Nature (the former Nature Conservancy Council (eg *Nature Conservation in Great Britain* (1984)), periodicals such as *Natural World*, and official statistics. See also G J Wainwright: *The Pressure of the Past* (*Proceedings of the Prehistoric Society* 50, 1984).

The Personality of Britain

THE TWO ZONES

Sir Cyril Fox: *The Personality of Britain* (Cardiff, National Museum of Wales 1932, 4th ed 1943).

THE STRUCTURE OF BRITAIN/ NATURAL RESOURCES

An invaluable comprehensive survey is Sir Dudley Stamp and S H Beaver: *The British Isles* (Longman 1933, 5th ed 1971); this covers fully the natural resources – minerals etc – as well as other aspects. Dudley Stamp's *Britain's Structure and Scenery* (Collins 1946, 1949) gives a very accessible account, as does A E Trueman's *Geology and Scenery in England and Wales* (Gollancz 1938, Penguin 1949). See now Richard Fortey's exciting and poetic *The Hidden Landscape* (Cape 1993). The Ordnance Survey Geological Map of the British Islands (25 miles to an inch, 3rd ed 1939) is useful for reference, but displays the solid geology only, and ignores the drift. Local details will be found in the series of British Regional Geology published by HMSO for the Institute of Geological Sciences (eg The Wealden District, 1935, 1965 ed), and in local geological guides issued by the Geologists' Association. See also volumes in Collins New Naturalist series, such as S W Wooldridge and Frederick Golding: *The Weald* (1953); K C Edwards et al: *The Peak District* (1962); L A Harvey and D St Leger Gordon: *Dartmoor*.

CLIMATE

Gordon Manley: *Climate and the British Scene* (Collins 1952, 1971); the books of H H Lamb are excellent guides, eg *Climate History and the Modern World* (Methuen 1982); an interesting special aspect is dealt with in Robert Raikes: *Water, Weather and Prehistory* (John Baker 1967, author 1984).

Glaciations and their effects

Frederick E Zeuner: *Dating the Past* (Methuen 1946, 1958) and Kenneth Oakley: *Frameworks for Dating Fossil Man* (Weidenfeld and Nicolson 1969 ed.) are still valuable, although overtaken in many respects; a useful more recent survey is John G Evans: *The Environment of Early Man in the British Isles* (Paul Elek 1975). General works on archaeology normally cover the glaciations, such as Colin Renfrew (ed): *British Prehistory* (Duckworth 1974); J V S Megaw and D D A Simpson: *Introduction to British Prehistory* (Leicester University Press 1979); Timothy Darvill: *Prehistoric Britain* (Batsford 1987); John Wymer: *The Palaeolithic Age* (Croom Helm 1982); and more specialised, Desmond Collins: *Palaeolithic Europe* (Tiverton, Clayhanger Books 1986).

VEGETATION

The works of Oliver Rackham are central here, eg *Trees and Woodland in the British Landscape* (Dent 1976); *The History of the Countryside* (Dent 1986); and his chapter in S R J Woodell: *The English Landscape* (OUP 1985). G F Peterken, in *Biological Conservation 6*, 1974, gives a list of ancient woodland indicator plants. For the general background, A G Tansley: *Britain's Green Mantle* (1968); and H Godwin: *The History of the British Flora* (1956).

LAND USE

There are useful statistics in the annual volumes *Britain 1991* etc (HMSO for Central Office of Information); in *The UK Environment* (HMSO for DoE 1992); and in *Countryside Survey* (HMSO 1993).

POPULATION

This is dealt with, in varying measure, in most books on social history, eg Asa Briggs: *Social History of England* (Weidenfeld and Nicolson 1983, revised ed 1994). Estimates differ, sometimes widely, but the following will build up a picture: J C Russell: *British Medieval Population* (1948), and *Late Ancient and Medieval Population* (Transactions of the American Philosophical Society 48, 1958); also *Medieval Regions and their Cities* (David and Charles 1972). For prehistoric and Roman: P J Fowler: *The Farming of Prehistoric Britain* (CUP 1971); A H A Hogg in Margaret Jessen and David Hill eds. *The Iron Age and Its Hillforts* (Southampton University 1971). Other relevant books include: John Patten in John Patten ed: *Pre-Industrial England* (1979); B H Slicher van Bath: *The Agrarian History of Western Europe, AD 500–1850* (1963); C M Cipolla ed: *The Fontana Economic History of Europe* (1972, 1974); Peter Clark and Paul Slack: *English Towns in Transition 1500–1750* (OUP 1976); W G Hoskins in Peter Clark: *The Early Modern Town* (Longman 1976). For particular places: Ben Weinreb and Christopher Hibbert: *The London Encyclopedia* (Macmillan 1983); Barbara Green and Rachel Young: *Norwich, the growth of a city* (Norwich Museums 1972); (Winchester) T B James in *Hampshire Field Club, Local History Newsletter*, ns 9, 1988.

DEMOGRAPHY

Roger Mols in *The Fontana Economic History of Europe* vol 2, 1, (Collins1972); also J C Russell in *The Fontana Economic History of Europe* vol 1, 1, (Collins1969); and André Armengaud in *The Fontana Economic History of Europe* vol 3, 1, (Collins1970). Peter Laslett: *The World We Have Lost* (Methuen 1965, 1968) presents this area most attractively. Pia Bennicke: *Palaeopathology of Danish Skeletons* (Copenhagen, Akademisk Forlag 1985); (health) Calvin Wells: *Bones, Bodies and Disease* (Thames and Hudson 1964); Steven Bassett ed: *Death in Towns AD 100–1600* (Leicester University Press 1993). For 19th-century health and conditions see eg Dorothy Marshall: *Industrial England 1776–1851* (RKP 1973, 1982): E G Mingay: *The Transformation of Britain 1830–1939* (RKP 1986).

Sources of population

Catherine Hills: *Blood of the British* (George Philip 1986).

The Black Death and its effects

Brief account in May McKisack: *The Fourteenth Century* (OUP 1959); full treatment in Philip Ziegler: *The Black Death* (Collins 1969); Robert S Gottfried: *The Black Death* (Macmillan 1983); and Rosemary Horrox, trans. and ed: *The Black Death* (Manchester University Press 1994). Medical details in *The Pest Anatomized* (Wellcome Institute 1985). For the black rat in Roman London see *The London Archaeologist* 4/14, 1984; for typhus, Hans Zinsser: *Rats, Lice and History* (Macmillan 1934, 1963); for anthrax, *Current Archaeology* 93, 1984.

Foreign contributions to British life

There are scattered references in social histories, eg Asa Briggs: *A Social History of England* (Weidenfeld and Nicolson 1994); general study, W Cunningham: *Alien Immigrants to England* (1897). For the French, see the *Proceedings of the Huguenot Society of London*; for the Flemish, Colin Nicolson: *Strangers to England 1100–1952* (Wayland 1974); for the Dutch, D W Davies: *Dutch Influences on English Culture 1558–1625* (New York 1964); David Ormrod: *The Dutch in London: the influence of an immigrant community 1550–1800* (HMSO for London Museum 1973); for the Jews, Cecil Roth: *A History of the Jews in England* (OUP 1964, 3rd ed); Stephen Brook: *The Club: Jews of Modern Britain* (Constable 1989); R B Dobson: *The Jews of Medieval York: the Massacre of March 1190* (University of York, *Borthwick Papers* 45, 1974); for the gypsies, Brian Vesey-Fitzgerald: *Gypsies of Britain* (David and Charles 1944, 1973).

THE NEW GEOGRAPHY

Many of the very significant developments in rural and urban geography in the last 30 years are set out, or drawn on, in a number of seminal books: M Chisholm: *Rural Settlement and Land Use* (Hutchinson 1962); Peter Haggett: *Locational Analysis in Human Geography* (Arnold 1965);

Arthur E Smailes: *The Geography of Towns* (Hutchinson 1953, 1966); James H Johnson: *Urban Geography* (Pergamon 1967, 1972); Ester Boserup, in *The Conditions of Agricultural Growth* (1965); Hugh D Clent: *Rural Geography* (Pergamon 1972); Peter J Ucko, Ruth Tringham and G W Dimbleby eds: *Man, Settlement and Urbanism* (Duckworth 1972); David L Clarke ed: *Models in Archaeology* (Methuen 1972); Colin Renfrew ed: *The Explanation of Culture Change* (Duckworth 1973); M W Beresford and J K St Joseph: *Medieval England: an Aerial Survey* (CUP 1958, 1979); A Lösch: *The Economics of Location* (1954); Eric Grant: *Central Places, Archaeology and History* (Sheffield University 1986); an early pioneer was W Christaller: *Die Zentralen Orte in Süddeutschland* (1933); Peter Haggett: *Geography: a modern synthesis* (Harper and Row, New York, 3rd ed 1983).

ENGLAND AS A MEDIEVAL REGION

Josiah Cox Russell: *Medieval Regions and their Cities* (David and Charles 1972).

SETTLEMENTS AND LAND DIVISIONS

Emrys Jones: *Towns and Cities* (OUP 1966); C M Heighway: *The Erosion of History* (CBA 1972).

Shires and smaller divisions

Sir Frank Stenton: *Anglo-Saxon England* (OUP 1943, 1971).

The Land

THE COUNTRYSIDE

W G Hoskins: *The Making of the English Landscape* (Hodder and Stoughton 1951) – this has become a classic; John Higgs: *The Land* (Studio Vista 1964); Leonard Cantor ed: *The English Medieval Landscape* (Croom Helm 1982); S R J Woodell ed: *The English Landscape* (OUP 1985); Richard Muir: *Shell Guide to Reading the Landscape* (Michael Joseph 1981); Oliver Rackham: *The History of the Countryside* (Dent 1986) – indispensable; Tom Williamson and

Liz Bellamy: *Property and Landscape* (George Philip 1987); R N Millman: *The Making of the Scottish Landscape* (Batsford 1975); J G Evans, Susan Limbrey, Henry Cleere (eds): *The Effect of Man on the Landscape: the Highland Zone* (CBA Research Report 11, 1975); Susan Limbrey and J G Evans: *The Effect of Man on the Landscape: the Lowland Zone* (CBA Research Report 21, 1978).

Ancient and planned countryside

Among many, Oliver Rackham: *The History of the Countryside* (Dent 1986), George Bourne: *Change in the Village* (Duckworth 1912); Robin Page: *The Decline of an English Village* (Davis-Poynter 1974, Ashford, Shedfield 1989).

PLACE-NAMES AND THE SETTLEMENT OF ENGLAND

The recent changes in this area are set out in J McNeill Dodgson in *Medieval Archaeology* 1966; Barrie Cox in *Journal of the English Place-Name Society* 5, 1973; Gillian Fellows Jensen: *Scandinavian Settlement Names in Yorkshire* (Copenhagen 1972); Margaret Gelling: "Recent work on English Place-names" (*The Local Historian* 11/1, 1974); see now Margaret Gelling's masterly *Place-Names in the Landscape* (Dent 1984); Joost Kuurman in *Journal of the English Place-Name Society* 7, 1975); Kenneth Cameron (ed): *Place-name Evidence for the Anglo-Saxon Invasion and Scandinavian Settlement* (English Place-Name Society 1975); W F H Nicolaisen: *Scottish Place-Names: Their Study and Significance* (1976). Earlier books on Scottish place-names include J B Johnston: *The Place-names of Scotland* (Edinburgh, Douglas 1892), and W J Watson: *The History of the Celtic Place-Names of Scotland* (Irish Academic Press 1926). See also P H Sawyer: Kings and Vikings: *Scandinavia and Europe AD 700–1100* (Methuen 1982).

(Standard books on place-names such as E Ekwall: *The Concise Oxford Dictionary of English Place-names* (OUP 1936, 1960), Kenneth Cameron: *English Place-names* (Batsford 1961, but see now his revised edition of 1988), most of the county volumes of the English Place-Name Society, and A H Smith: *English Place-Name Elements* (CUP 1956), although still very valuable and useful, do not embody the recent thinking.) Recent county studies which embody the new approach, include J McN Dodgson's chapter in Peter Brandon ed: *The South Saxons* (Phillimore 1978); R W Morris: *Yorkshire Through Place-Names* (David and Charles 1982); Richard Coates: *The Place-Names of Hampshire* (Batsford 1989). For field names, John Field: *English Field Names* (David and Charles 1972); for street names, John Wittich: *Discovering London Street Names* (Shire 1977); for York, R W Morris *op cit*; Adrian Room: *The Street Names of England* (Stamford, Paul Watkins 1992). A L F Rivet and C Smith: *The Placenames of Roman Britain* (Batsford 1981).

FARMING

An essential source is the Cambridge multi-volume survey, *The Agrarian History of England and Wales* (see below). Also B H Slicher van Bath: *The Agrarian History of Western Europe, AD 500–1950* (1963); M E Seebohm: *The Evolution of the English Farm* (Allen and Unwin 1927, revised ed 1952); Ralph Whitlock: *The English Farm* (Dent 1983); Alan Everitt: *Landscape and Community in England* (1985); John Higgs: *The Land* (Studio Vista 1964) gives a wide range of illustrations; Robert Trevor-Smith: *Life from the Land: The Growth of Farming in Western Europe* (Longman 1967). There is useful material in C T Smith: *An Historical Geography of Western Europe before 1800* (Longman 1967), particularly on agrarian structures and field systems, rural settlement, and the growth of towns.

Prehistoric

Peter Fowler: *The Farming of Prehistoric Britain* (CUP 1983), reprinted in revised form from Stuart Piggott ed: *The Agrarian History of England and Wales*, vol 1, i, Prehistoric (CUP 1981); Peter Reynolds: *Ancient Farming* (Shire 1987); Peter J Reynolds: *Iron-Age Farm* (British Museum Publications 1979); R Mercer ed: *Farming Practice in British Prehistory* (Edinburgh University Press 1981).

Roman

H P R Finberg ed: *The Agrarian History of England and Wales* vol 1, ii, AD 43–1042 (CUP 1972); for Roman villas and State farming see eg Peter Salway: *Roman Britain* (OUP 1981).

Medieval

H P R Finberg as above, and volumes 2 and 3 of the same series.

16th–18th Centuries

Joan Thirsk ed: *The Agrarian History of England and Wales*, vol 4, 1500–1640 (CUP 1967, 1984) – this contains important sections on rural housing in England (by M W Barley), and in Wales (by Peter Smith); Joan Thirsk: *England's Agricultural Regions and Agrarian History 1500–1750* (Macmillan for Economic History Society 1987) – the latest refinement of this topic; E Kerridge: *The Agricultural Revolution* (Allen and Unwin 1967); G E Mingay: *The Agricultural Revolution: Changes in Agriculture 1650–1880* (Black 1977); Mark Overton in A R H Baker and D Gregory eds: *Explorations in Historical Geography* (CUP 1984); Mildred Campbell: *The English Yeoman* (Yale 1942, Merlin 1960); Paul Bairoch: "Agriculture and the Industrial Revolution 1700–1914" in C M Cipolla ed: *The Fontana Economic History of Europe*, vol 3, section 8 (Collins 1969); E L Jones ed: *Agriculture and Economic Growth in England 1650–1815* (1967).

19th century

C A Jewell ed: Victorian Farming (Winchester, Barry Shurlock 1975) – an edition of extracts from Henry Stephen: *The Book of the Farm* (3rd ed 1876), which gives a vivid insight into the detail of 19th-century farming practices; P J Perry: *British Farming in the Great Depression 1870–1914* (David and Charles 1974), with valuable bibliography; Roy Brigden: *Victorian Farms* (Crowood Press 1986); chapter by Joan Thirsk in Jerome Blum ed: *Our Forgotten Past* (Thames and Hudson 1982); John Vince: *Old Farms* (John Murray 1987); John Addy: *The Agrarian Revolution* (Longman 1964).

20th century

For post-war developments, Tristram Beresford: *We Plough the Fields* (Penguin 1975); Howard Newby: *Green and Pleasant Land?* (Penguin 1980, Wildwood House 1985) and his *Country Life* (Weidenfeld and Nicolson 1987, Cardinal 1988); M H R Soper and E S Carter: *Modern Farming and the Countryside* (Association of Agriculture 1985, with addendum 1987) – this deals usefully with the interaction of farming and conservation. G E Mingay ed *The Rural Idyll* (RKP 1984) also for the 19th century.

Rural life and conditions

A good feel for the lives of country people of all kinds is given in G E and K R Fussell: *The English Countryman AD 1500–1900* (Andrew Melrose 1955, reissued by Orbis 1981, by Bloomsbury Books 1985); also their *The English Countrywoman*. An important study of pre-industrial England is Peter Laslett: *The World We Have Lost* (Methuen 1965, 1971). B Rowland Parker: *The Common Stream* (Collins 1975, Paladin 1976) is also stimulating. Also Pamela Horn: *Labouring Life in the Victorian Countryside* (Gill and Macmillan, Dublin 1976, Alan Sutton, Gloucester 1987) – this gives a very thorough insight; Richard Heath: *The English Peasant (1871–1875)* ed Keith Dockray as *The Victorian Peasant* (Alan Sutton 1989); H S Bennett: *Life on the English Manor (1150–1400)* (CUP 1937, Alan Sutton 1987); J L and B T Hammond: *The Village Labourer 1760–1832* (1911, reissued by Alan Sutton 1987); Alan Armstrong: *Farmworkers in England and Wales (1770–1980)* (Iowa State University Press 1988); Sadie Ward et al: *Seasons of Change* (Allen and Unwin 1982). There are many excellent regional studies such as Gertrude Jekyll: *Old West Surrey* (Longman, Green and Co 1904, reprinted by Kohler and Coombes, Dorking 1978); Marie Hartley and Joan Ingilby: *Life and Tradition in the Yorkshire Dales* (Dent 1968) and *Life in the Moorlands of N E Yorkshire* (Dent 1972); J H Bettey: *Rural Life in Wessex 1500–1900* (Moonraker Press

1977, Alan Sutton 1989); J Geraint Jenkins: *Life and Tradition in Rural Wales* (Alan Sutton 1976); see also Ann Cripps ed: *The Countryman Rescuing the Past* (David and Charles 1976). Personal statements include Richard Jefferies: *Hodge and his Masters* (1880, reprinted by Quartet Books 1979); Flora Thompson: *Lark Rise to Candleford* (OUP 1939, 1941, 1943, one vol 1945, Penguin 1973) – based on life in the 1880s and 1890s; H Rider Haggard: *A Farmer's Year* (Longman 1899, repub. Century Hutchinson 1987); George Ewart Evans: *Ask the Fellows Who Cut the Hay* (Faber 1956), and *The Horse in the Furrow* (Faber 1960); Shaun Payne and Richard Pailthorpe eds. *Barclay Wills' The Downland Shepherds* (Alan Sutton 1989). William Cobbett's *Rural Rides* (1820s) still have much of interest. A delightful approach to 16th century farming practice is given, in cheerful doggerel, by Thomas Tusser, in *Five Hundreth Pointes of Good Husbandrie* (1573, expanded from shorter version of 1557). There are several studies of contemporary people, such as Mary Chamberlain: *Fenwomen* (Virago 1975); Charles Kightly: *Country Voices* (Thames and Hudson 1984); Phoebe Somers: *A Time There Was* (Alan Sutton/Weald and Downland Museum 1993). The theory and practice of oral history is elaborated in Paul Thompson: *The Voice of the Past* (OUP 1978).

FIELD SYSTEMS

Pre-Saxon Field Systems

H C Bowen: *Ancient Fields* (British Association nd c1960); Christopher Taylor: *Fields in the English Landscape* (Dent 1975); "brickwork" patterns, Derrick Riley in *Current Archaeology* 66, 1979; P J Fowler: *The Farming of Prehistoric Britain* (CUP 1983); Nigel Harvey: *Fields, Hedges and Ditches* (Shire 1976). Reaves etc, Andrew Fleming in *Proceedings of the Prehistoric Society* 44, 1978 and 49, 1983; and *The Dartmoor Reaves* (Batsford 1988); Richard Bradley, Roy Entwistle and Frances Raymond: *Prehistoric land divisions on Salisbury Plain* (EH Archaeological Report no 2, 1994) .

Anglo-Saxon field systems

For Anglo-Saxon farming, Peter J Fowler in David Wilson (ed): *The Archaeology of Anglo-Saxon England* (Methuen 1976).

Medieval and later field systems

W. G Hoskins: *Provincial England* (Macmillan 1963) and *Fieldwork in Local History* (Faber 1967); Maurice Beresford: *History on the Ground* (Alan Sutton 1984); Christopher Taylor: *Village and Farmstead* (George Philip 1983); Richard and Nina Muir: *Fields* (Macmillan 1989); Leonard Cantor (ed): *The English Medieval Landscape* (Croom Helm 1982); Oliver Rackham: *The History of the Countryside* (Dent 1986).

Pre-enclosure field systems

The classic is F Seebohm: *The English Village Community* (1883, 1915); his view was successfully challenged by H L Gray: *English Field Systems* (1918), and C S and C S Orwin: *The Open Fields* (1938); see now A R H Baker and R A Butlin eds: *Studies of Field Systems in the British Isles* (1973); Robert A D Dodgshon: *The Origin of British Field Systems: an Interpretation* (Academic Press 1980); R T Rowley (ed): *The Origins of Open-Field Agriculture* (Croom Helm 1981); Warren O Ault: *Open-Field Farming in Medieval England* (Allen and Unwin 1972) – village by-laws etc); Robert F Hartley in *The Medieval Earthworks of Rutland* (Leicestershire Museums Service Archaeological Report 7,1983); David Hall: *The Open Fields of Northamptonshire* (Northants Heritage 1993); V Beckett: *A History of Laxton* (Blackwell 1980).

Enclosures

These are dealt with in most books on agricultural, social and economic history, but see also W G Hoskins: *Local History in England* (Longman 1972 ed); Maurice Beresford: *History on the Ground* (Alan Sutton 1984); Asa Briggs: *A Social History of England* (Weidenfeld and Nicolson 1994); Ralph Whitlock: *The English Farm* (Dent 1983); Joan Thirsk: *Tudor Enclosures* (Historical Association 1958); W E Tate: *The English Village Community and the Enclosure Movements* (Gollancz 1967); F Seebohm: *The English Village Community* (1883, 1915); David Hall: *Medieval Fields* (Shire 1982); Richard and Nina Muir: *Fields* (Macmillan 1989); V Beckett: *A History of Laxton* (Blackwell 1980). Also relevant are W G Hoskins and L Dudley Stamp: *The Common Lands of England and Wales* (Collins 1963); G Slater: *The English Peasantry and the Enclosure of Common Fields* (1907, reprinted New York 1968); J A Yelling: *Common Field and Enclosure in England 1450–1850* (Macmillan 1977).

Field boundaries

Hedges – The pioneer for dating is W G Hoskins in *Fieldwork in Local History* (Faber 1967); the major study is E Pollard, M D Hooper and N W Moore: *Hedges* (Collins 1974); see also *Hedges and Local History* (National Council of Social Service 1971); Nigel Harvey: *Fields, Hedges and Ditches* (Shire 1976). A useful study of mixed hedges (planted as such) is by Christopher Currie and A Scivier in *The London Archaeologist* 5/10, 1987. The case against Hooper's Rule is set out in Richard and Nina Muir: *Hedgerows: Their History and Wildlife* (Michael Joseph 1987). For local studies see eg W W Baird and J R Tarrant: *Hedgerow Destruction in Norfolk 1946–1970* (Centre of East Anglian Studies 1973); H E Jean Le Patourel, Moira H Long and May E Pickles: *Yorkshire Boundaries* (Yorkshire Archaeological Society 1993).

Drystone walls – F Rainsford-Hannay: *Dry Stone Walling* (1947, 3rd ed 1966); Lawrence Garner: *Dry Stone Walls* (Shire 1984); Arthur Raistrick: *Pennine Walls* (Clapham, Dalesman 1946); Robin Callander: *Drystane Dyking in Deeside* (1982); A J Brooks (ed): *Dry Stone Walling* (British Trust for Conservation Volunteers 1977) – a technical manual. There are useful chapters on both hedges and walls in Oliver Rackham: *The History of the Countryside* (Dent 1986).

Watermeadows

The sources are brief and very scattered, but see eg *Hampshire's Countryside Heritage: Rivers and Wetlands* (Hampshire County Council 1984).

Transhumance

Much research has been done into this, but the literature is scattered, and the clearest picture is found in French sources. A useful summary of continental types is given in F Braudel: *The Mediterranean* (1949, 1966 – English edition Collins 1972, vol 1). Detailed studies for France, eg Marie Mauron: *La Transhumance du pays d'Arles aux grandes Alpes* (1952); Gabriel et Pierre-François Fournier: *La Vie pastorale dans les montagnes du centre de la France* (Bulletin historique et scientifique de l'Auvergne, no 676, 1983); for marking and social aspects, *L'Archaeologie de la France rurale* (Paris, Belin 1986). Archaeological aspects, *World Archaeology* 15, 1, 1983. For England, a useful account of medieval monastic sheep-farming is Bryan Waites: *Moorland and Vale-land farming in north-east Yorkshire* (University of York, Borthwick Papers no 32, 1967); see also Christopher Taylor: *Roads and Tracks in Britain* (Dent 1979). For transhumance in Wales, see "In the hills of summer" (*The Countryman* 100, 4, 1955).

FARMING EQUIPMENT

Nigel Harvey: *The Industrial Archaeology of Farming in England and Wales* (Batsford 1980); G E Fussell: *The Farmer's Tools, AD 1500–1900* (Andrew Melrose 1952, Orbis 1981); G E Fussell: *Farming Techniques from Prehistoric to Modern Times* (Pergamon 1966); Michael Partridge: *Early Agricultural Machinery and Farm Tools Through the Ages* (both Osprey 1973); Jonathan Brown: *Farm Machinery 1750–1945* (Batsford 1989), and *Farm Tools and Techniques* (Batsford 1993); C A Jewell (ed): *Victorian Farming* (Winchester, Barry Shurlock, 1975). Other useful surveys, Sian Rees: *Ancient Agricultural Implements* (Shire 1981); John Vince: *Old Farm Tools* (Shire 1974); Roy Brigden: *Harvesting Machinery* (Shire); *The Agricultural Gallery* (Welsh Folk Museum 1976); John Vince: *Vintage Farm Machinery* (Shire 1979); John Vince: *Discovering Carts and Wagons* (Shire 1970); John Higgs: *The Land* (Studio Vista 1964); Roy Brigden: *Victorian Farms* (Crowood Press 1986); and

Ploughs and Ploughing (Shire), also *Agricultural Hand Tools* (Shire 1983). Important papers include Charles L Cawood: "The History and Development of Farm Tractors" (*Industrial Archaeology* 7, 3 and 4, 1970); and John R Gray: "An Industrial Farm Estate" (*Industrial Archaeology* 8, 2, 1971 (Buscot)). S E Rees: *Agricultural Implements in Prehistoric and Roman Britain* (BAR 69, 1979, 2 parts).

FARM BUILDINGS

Prehistoric and Roman

For "four-posters" see Peter J Reynolds: *Iron-Age Farm* (British Museum Publications 1979); Barry Cunliffe: *Danebury* (Batsford 1983). For Roman villas, A L F Rivet (ed): *The Roman Villa in Britain* (RKP 1969); S S. Frere: *Britannia* (RKP 1987 ed). For Littlecote, *Current Archaeology* 80, 1971. A valuable insight based on villas in northern France is in Roger Agache: *Détection Aërienne* (Amiens, *Bulletin Société Préhistorique du Nord*, 7, 1970). Saxon and medieval, P Rahtz in David M Wilson (ed): *The Archaeology of Anglo-Saxon England* (Methuen 1976, CUP 1981); J Chapelot and R Fossier: *Le village et la maison au Moyen Age* (Hachette, Paris 1980; trans H Cleere as *Village and Town in the Middle Ages*, Batsford 1985); for Gomeldon, M W Beresford and J G Hurst: *Deserted Medieval Villages* (Lutterworth 1971); for Raunds, *Current Archaeology* 106, 1987.

Post-medieval

The most comprehensive recent source is R W Brunskill: *Traditional Farm Buildings of Britain* (Gollancz 1982); see also Nigel Harvey: *A History of Farm Buildings in England and Wales* (1970) and *The Industrial Archaeology of Farming in England and Wales* (Batsford 1980). J E C Peters: *Discovering Traditional Farm Buildings* (Shire 1981) is a useful summary; a good local study is A Raistrick: *Buildings in the Yorkshire Dales* (Dalesman 1976). Farm buildings are also dealt with, more or less fully, in most books on farms, such as Martin S Briggs: *The English Farmhouse* (Batsford 1953), or M E Seebohm: *The Evolution of the English Farm*

(Allen and Unwin 1952 ed); John Weller: *History of the Farmstead* (Faber 1982); R L Brown: *The English Country Cottage* (Hale 1979). Both Brunskill and Harvey give valuable bibliographies. For Scotland, Robert Naismith: *Buildings of the Scottish Countryside* (Gollancz 1985); for Wales, P Smith: *Houses of the Welsh Countryside*. For factory farms, T Beresford: *We Plough the Fields* (Penguin 1975); Ralph Whitlock: *The English Farm* (Dent 1983). Malcolm Kirk: *The Barn: Silent Spaces* (Thames and Hudson 1994). Bill Laws and Andrew Butler: *Old English Farmhouses* (Collins and Brown 1992).

Gins and Ginhouses – Frank Atkinson: "The Horse as a Source of Rotary Power" (*Transactions of the Newcomen Society* 33, 1960–61); Hugo Brunner and J Kenneth Major: "Water Raising by Animal Power" (*Industrial Archaeology* 9, 1972); Anne and John K Harrison: "The Horse Wheel in North Yorkshire" (*Industrial Archaeology* 10, 1973); Bruce Walker in *Scottish Archaeological Forum* 8, 1977; J Kenneth Major: *Animal-Powered Machines* (Shire 1985).

Beekeeping – Eva Crane: *The Archaeology of Beekeeping* (Duckworth 1983); A M Foster: *Bee Boles and Bee Houses* (Shire 1988).

Farmhouses – Martin S Briggs: *The English Farmhouse* (Batsford 1953); M W Barley: *The English Farmhouse and Cottage* (Routledge and Kegan Paul, 1961).

Planned farmsteads

Early sources – Arthur Young: *Six Months Tour in the North of England* (1770); John P Raw: *Ferme Ornée or Rural Improvements* (1800); Charles Waistell: *Designs for Farm Buildings* (1827); J C Loudon: *Encyclopedia of Cottage, Farm and Villa Architecture* (1833); R Stephens: *The Book of the Farm* (1871). For Buscot, John R Gray in *Industrial Archaeology* 8, 1971.

Recent sources – C T Smith: *An Historical Geography of Western Europe before 1800* (Longman 1967); Harold Bonnett: *Farming with Steam* (Shire 1974); Bruce Walker: "The Influence of Fixed Farming Machinery on Farm Building Design in

Eastern Scotland in the late 18th and 19th Centuries" (*Scottish Archaeological Forum* 8, 1977); John Weller: *History of the Farmstead* (Faber 1982).

Oasts, maltings and whisky kilns

For beer, ale and hops, H S Corran: *A History of Brewing* (David and Charles); Maurice Lovett: *Brewing and Breweries* (Shire 1981); Richard Filmer: *Hops and Hop-Picking* (Shire 1982); G Jones and J Bell: *Oast Houses in Sussex and Kent*. For Scottish brewing and distilling, John Brett: *The Industrial Archaeology of Scotland* (David and Charles 1967).

Dovecotes

A O Cooke: *A Book of Dovecotes* (T N Fowlis 1920); Peter and Jean Hansell: *Dovecotes* (Shire 1988); Peter and Jean Hansell: *A Dovecote Heritage* (Millstream 1992); Tim Buxbaum: *The Scottish Doocot* (Shire 1987). A useful local study is Alan Whitworth: "Yorkshire Dovecotes and Pigeon Lofts: a preliminary survey" (*Yorkshire Archaeological Journal* 65, 1993).

The Village

The works of Brian K Roberts are central here, particularly *Rural Settlement in Britain* (Dawson, Folkestone; Archon, Hamden, Conn, 1977); *Village Plans* (Shire 1982); *The Making of the English Village* (Longman 1987); see also Trevor Rowley: *Villages in the Landscape* (Dent 1978); Jean Chapelot and Robert Fossier: *Le village et la maison au Moyen Age* (Hachette, Paris 1980; trans. H Cleere as *Village and Town in the Middle Ages*, Batsford 1985); Christopher Taylor: *Village and Farmstead* (George Philip 1983). An important survey of current views is Della Hooke (ed): *Medieval Villages* (Oxford University Committee for Archaeology Monograph no 5, 1985); as is "The Origins of the Midland Village" (*Economic History Society, Leicester Conference papers* 1992). Other useful works include Ann Ellison: "Villages Survey" (*CRAAGS Occasional Paper* no 1, 1976) – summary of problems; E M Yates: "The Evolution of the English Village" (*Geographical Journal* 14, 2, 1982);

Leonard Cantor (ed): *The English Medieval Landscape* (Croom Helm 1982); F G Emmison: *Some Types of Common-Field Parish* (National Council of Social Service for *Standing Conference of Local History*, 1965); Tom Williamson and Liz Bellamy: *Property and Landscape* (George Philip 1987). Still of interest is Thomas Sharp: *The Anatomy of the Village* (Penguin 1946). For Roman villages, Robin Hanley: *Villages in Roman Britain* (Shire 1987). "Current thinking in Medieval Rural Settlement and Towns" (*Medieval Settlement Research Group Annual Report* 8, 1993). Victorian Rural Life, David Souden: *The Victorian Village* (Collins and Brown 1991).

THE SHAPE OF VILLAGES

For the importation theory of nucleated villages, Harry Thorpe: "The Green Village in its European Setting", in Alan Small (ed): *The Fourth Viking Congress* 1965). Classical surveys are those of W G Hoskins: *The Making of the English Landscape* (Hodder and Stoughton 1955), *Local History in England* (Longman 1959, 1972) and *Provincial England* (Macmillan 1963). Hoskins has also edited a county series, of which Christopher Taylor: *Dorset* (Hodder and Stoughton 1970) may be given as a valuable example; see also Maurice Beresford: *History on the Ground* (Lutterworth 1957, Alan Sutton 1984). Technical aspects of fieldwork are dealt with in W G Hoskins: *Fieldwork in Local History* (Faber 1967); Michael Aston and Trevor Rowley: *Landscape Archaeology* (David and Charles 1974); Christopher Taylor: *Fieldwork in Medieval Archaeology* (Batsford 1974).

SHRUNKEN, SHIFTED AND DESERTED VILLAGES

Maurice Beresford: *The Lost Villages of England* (Lutterworth 1954) – the pioneer work, followed and partly superseded by Maurice Beresford and John G Hurst eds: *Deserted Medieval Villages* (Lutterworth 1971); Trevor Rowley and John Wood: *Deserted Villages* (Shire 1982); Richard Muir: *Lost Villages of Britain* (Michael Joseph 1982) and his *The English Village* (Thames and Hudson 1980); Maurice Beresford and John Hurst: *Wharram Percy: Deserted Medieval Village* (Batsford/EH 1990).

THE FORM OF PARISHES

For Surrey parishes, E M Yates in *Field Studies* 1, 3, 1961. For Withington, H P R Finberg in *The Agrarian History of England and Wales*, vol 1, ii (CUP 1972).

Roman Estates – Peter Salway: *Roman Britain* (OUP 1981); Ann Goodier in *Medieval Archaeology* 28, 1984. For strip parishes, John P Steane: *The Northamptonshire Landscape* (Hodder and Stoughton 1974).

Breckland – Oliver Rackham: *The History of the Countryside* (Dent 1986).

Parks, Gardens, and Sports

HUNTING

Deerparks, Forests, and Chases

Ralph Whitlock: *Historic Forests of England* (1979); Leonard Cantor (ed): *The English Medieval Landscape* (Croom Helm 1982); Raymond Grant: *The Royal Forests of England* (Alan Sutton 1991).

Warrens

J. Simpson: *The Wild Rabbit* (Pawson and Braisford, Sheffield, 3rd ed 1908); O G S Crawford and A Keiller: *Wessex from the Air* (1928); A Harris and D A Spratt: "The Rabbit Warrens of the Tabular Hills, North Yorkshire" (*Yorkshire Archaeological Journal* 63, 1991 (see also A Harris in *Yorkshire Archaeological Journal* 42, 1970).

Fishing

Edward Roberts: "The Bishop of Winchester's Fishponds in Hampshire, 1150–1400" (*Proceedings of the Hampshire Field Club* 42, 1986).

Fowling

Sir R Payne-Gallwey: *The Book of Duck Decoys* (1886).

GARDENS AND AMENITY PARKS

General

Susan Lasdun: *The English Park* (André Deutsch 1991); Hugh Prince: *Parks in England* (IOW, Pinhorns 1967) – a gazetteer. Many books on garden history impinge on the amenity park, but garden history is well covered in the following: Barry Cunliffe: *Fishbourne: A Roman Palace and Its Garden* (Thames and Hudson 1971); John Harvey: *Medieval Gardens* (Batsford 1981); for the restoration of the medieval garden at Winchester Castle see Sylvia Landsberg in Gill Hedley and Adrian Rance: *Pleasure Grounds* (Horndean, Milestone Publications 1987); David Jacques: *Georgian Gardens* (Batsford 1983); Brent Elliott: *Victorian Gardens* (Batsford 1986); Julia S Berrell: *The Garden: an Illustrated History* (Penguin 1966, 1978); Miles Hadfield: *A History of British Gardens* (Hamlyn 1969); Richard Bisgrove: *The National Trust Book of the English Garden* (Viking 1990, Penguin 1992); Christopher Thacker: *The Genius of Gardening* (Weidenfeld and Nicolson 1993). Short but useful: Christopher Taylor: *The Archaeology of Gardens* (Shire 1983); John Anthony: *Discovering Period Gardens* (Shire 1972); Margaret Baker: *Discovering Topiary* (Shire 1969); Miles Hadfield: *The English Landscape Garden* (Shire 1977): Betty Massingham: *Gertrude Jekyll* (Shire 1975). See also Gertrude Jekyll: *A Gardener's Testament* (ed Francis Jekyll and G C Taylor, Country Life 1937, Macmillan 1984). Brown: *Garden Archaeology* (CBA Research Report 78); Geoffrey Dimbleby: *Plants and Archaeology* (John Baker 1967, Granada 1978); P Hobhouse: *Plants in Garden History* (Pavilion 1992); E B MacDougall (ed): *Ancient Roman Gardens* (Dumbarton Oaks Colloquium on the History of Landscape Architecture no VII, 1981); E B MacDougall (ed): *Ancient Roman Villa Gardens* (Dumbarton Oaks Colloquium on the History of Landscape Architecture no X, 1987).

Follies

Barbara Jones: *Follies and Grottoes* (Constable 1953, 1974); Gwyn Headley and Wim Meulenkamp:

Follies (Cape 1986, 1990); also Sir Hugh Casson: *Follies* (Chatto and Windus for The National Benzole Co Ltd, 1963).

Mazes

W H Matthews: *Mazes and Labyrinths* (Longmans, Green and Co, 1972); Jeff Saward: *The Caerdroia Field Guide* (1987); John Kraft: *The Goddess in the Labyrinth* (Åbo Akademi 1985).

THE ROYAL PARKS

Richard Church: *The Royal Parks of London* (HMSO 1956, 1967, 1993).

OPEN SPACES

William Addison: *Epping Forest* (Dent 1945); Georgina Green: *Epping Forest through the Ages* (1982). For Hatfield Forest (Ex): Oliver Rackham: *The Last Forest* (Dent 1989).

URBAN PARKS

May Woods and Arete Warren: *Glass Houses* (Aurum Press 1988).

SPECIALISED PARKS

Botanic and Zoological Gardens and Amusement Parks

Adequate local guides are published; but for Kew and the London zoo see also Ben Weinreb and Christopher Hibbert (eds): *The London Encyclopedia* (Macmillan 1983) – this latter book also covers the London amusement parks, such as Vauxhall and Ranelagh; see also Douglas Taylor: "West Riding Amusement Parks and Gardens" (*Yorkshire Archaeological Journal* 58, 1986).

COMMONS

L Dudley Stamp and W G Hoskins: *The Common Lands of England and Wales* (Collins 1963); (footpaths) *Rights of Way: Law and Practice* (Open Spaces Society).

NATIONAL PARKS

These issue substantial guides; see also Frank Noble: *The Shell Book of Offa's Dyke Path* (The Queen Anne Press 1969); M Gelling (ed): *Offa's Dyke Reviewed by Frank Noble* (British Archaeological Reports British Series 114, 1983).

SPORTS AND GAMES

Brian Jewell: *Sports and Games: History and Origins* (Midas 1977); Iorwerth Peate: *Denbigh Cockpit and Cockfighting in Wales* (St Fagans Museum handbook 1970). Alan Delgado: *Victorian Entertainment* (David and Charles 1971).

The Evolution of Towns

The Function of Towns/ Urban Morphology

Two classics, Lewis Mumford: *The Culture of Cities* (1938), and *The City in History* (Secker and Warburg 1961, Penguin 1966); Joseph Rykwert: *The Idea of a Town* (Faber 1976); Helen Rosenau: *The Ideal City* (RKP 1959, Methuen 1983); Arthur E Smailes: *The Geography of Towns* (Hutchinson 1953, 1966); Maurice Ash: *A Guide to the Structure of London* (Bath, Adams and Dart 1972).

Prehistoric Urbanism – Peter J Ucko, Ruth Tringham and G W Dimbleby (eds): *Man, Settlement and Urbanism* (Duckworth 1972); Barry Cunliffe and Trevor Rowley (eds): *Oppida in Barbarian Europe* (British Archaeological Reports Supplementary Series 11, 1976); Peter S Wells: *Farms, Villages and Cities* (Cornell University Press 1984); Richard Hingley: *Rural Settlement in Roman Britain* (Seaby 1991). Françoise Audouze and Olivier Büchsenschütz: *Towns, Villages and Countryside of Celtic Europe* (Batsford 1991).

ROMAN TOWNS

John Wacher: *The Towns of Roman Britain* (Batsford 1978, 1995); J S Wacher (ed): *The Civitas Capitals of Roman Britain* (Leicester University Press 1966), John Wacher and Barry C Burnham: *The "Small Towns" of Roman Britain* (Batsford 1990); Warwick Rodwell and Trevor Rowley (eds): *Small Towns of Roman Britain* (BAR 15, 1975); Guy de la Bédoyère: *Roman Towns in Britain* (Batsford/EH 1992). There is a useful *mise-à-point* in Ian Longworth and John Cherry (eds): *Archaeology in Britain since 1945* (BM Publications 1986). For the principles of Roman town planning, Joseph Rykwert: *The Idea of a Town* (Faber 1976); Francis Grew and Brian Hobley: *Roman Urban Topography in Britain and the Western Empire* (CBA Research Report 59, 1985); Pierre Grimal: *Les Villes Romaines* (Presses Universitaires de France 1954) is a useful study of evolution and influences; translated and edited by G Michael Woloch as *Roman Cities* (University of Wisconsin Press 1983).

Excavations – The urban excavations in specific places are published in journals such as *Britannia*, *Interim* (York), *The London Archaeologist* and *Current Archaeology*, or in series of fascicules at an academic level. For London, Ralph Merrifield: *London, City of the Romans* (Batsford 1983); Brian Hobley: *Roman and Saxon London: a Reappraisal* (Museum of London 1986, with full bibliography); Dominic Perring: *Roman London: the archaeology of London* (Seaby 1991); Gustav Milne: *Roman London* (Batsford 1995). For Silchester, George Boon: *Silchester: the Roman Town of Calleva* (1974); Michael Fulford: *Antiquaries Journal* 65, 1985 (forum and basilica), Britannia Monograph 5, 1984 (defences etc), Britannia Monograph 10, 1989 (amphitheatre). For York, Patrick Ottaway: *Roman York* (Batsford/EH 1993); P V Addyman and V E Black (eds): *Archaeological Papers from York* (York Archaeological Trust 1984); recent excavations are published in a continuing series by CBA and the York Archaeological Trust. For Bath, Barry Cunliffe: *Roman Bath Discovered* (Routledge and Kegan Paul 1971, 1984). For Exeter, Paul T Bidwell: *Roman Exeter: Fortress and Town* (Exeter Museum 1980). For Colchester, M R Hull: *Roman Colchester* (Society of Antiquaries 1958); Philip Crummy: *In Search of Colchester's Past* (Colchester Archaeological Trust, 3rd ed 1986). St Albans, R E M Wheeler: *Verulamium: a Belgic and two Roman Cities* (Society of Antiquaries 1936); S S Frere: *Verulamium Excavations* (Society of Antiquaries 1972, 1983, 1984). Winchester: Martin Biddle et al, excavation reports in *Antiquaries Journal* 44, 1964 to 55, 1975; vol 3 of *Winchester Studies*; convenient summary, *The*

Study of Winchester (OUP 1984, from *Proceedings of the British Academy* 69, 1983). Canterbury, S S. Frere: *Roman Canterbury*. For an important study of a *vicus*, Robin Birley: *Vindolanda* (Thames and Hudson 1977).

THE ANGLO-SAXON TOWN

Richard Hodges: *Dark Age Economics: the origins of towns and trade AD 600–1000* (Duckworth 1982) – includes *wics* and *emporia*; Martin Biddle, "Towns" in David M Wilson (ed): *The Archaeology of Anglo-Saxon England* (Methuen 1976, CUP 1981); Martin Biddle: "The Evolution of Towns before 1066" in M W Barley (ed): *The Plans and Topography of Medieval Towns in England and Wales* (CBA Research Report 14, 1975); Jeremy Haslam (ed): *Anglo-Saxon Towns in Southern England* (Phillimore 1984); Alan Vince: *Saxon London* (Seaby 1990).

Middle Saxon Towns and the wics

M. W Barley (ed): *European Towns* (Academic Press 1977); for Northampton, John H Williams, Michael Shaw and Varian Denham: *Middle Saxon Palaces at Northampton* (Northampton Development Corporation, Archaeological monograph 4, 1985); see also *Current Archaeology* 85, 1982. *Wics Lundenwic*, M Biddle in *Popular Archaeology* July 1984; A Vince in *Current Archaeology* 93, 1984; Tim Tatton-Brown: "The Topography of Anglo-Saxon London" (*Antiquity* LX, 1986); *Hamwih*: P V Addyman and D H Hill: "Saxon Southampton: a Review of the Evidence" (*Proceedings of the Hampshire Field Club* XXV, 1968 and XXVI, 1969); M F Garner et al: "Middle Saxon Evidence at Cook Street, Southampton" (*Proceedings of the Hants Field Club* 49, 1993); A D Morton (ed): *Excavations at Hamwih* vol 1 (CBA Research Report 84, 1992) – excavations 1946–83, excluding Six Dials and Melbourne Street; brief account in *Saxon Southampton* (Southampton Archaeological Research Committee 1975); Middle Saxon Norwich is coming to light north of the river, in the Magdalen Street–Fishergate area, *Digging Deeper* (Norwich Museum Service 1987); for York, Richard Kemp in *Interim* 10/4, 1985; 11/3, 1986; 11/4, 1986/87.

Late Saxon and the burhs

Martin Biddle and David Hill: "Late Saxon Planned Towns" (*Antiquaries Journal* 51, 1971); C A Ralegh Radford: "The Pre-Conquest Boroughs of England" (*Proceedings of the British Academy* LXIV, 1978, printed separately by OUP, 1980); Jeremy Haslam: *Early Medieval Towns in Britain. 700–1140* (Shire 1985). For specific places see, eg C A R Radford: "Excavations at Cricklade 1948–63" (*Wiltshire Archaeological Magazine* 67, 1972); Martin Biddle: "The Study of Winchester" (*Proceedings of the British Academy* LXIX, 1983, and printed separately by OUP,1984).

THE DANELAW

Helen Clarke and Björn Ambrosiani: *Towns in the Viking Age* (Leicester University Press 1991).

MEDIEVAL TOWNS

Maurice Beresford: *New Towns of the Middle Ages* (Lutterworth 1967, Alan Sutton 1988) – a vital source; Maurice Beresford and H P R Finberg: *English Medieval Boroughs: a Handlist* (David and Charles 1973); Peter Clark (ed): *The Early Medieval Town* (Longman 1976); Richard Holt and Gervase Rosser (eds): *The Medieval Town, 1200–1540* (Longman 1990); Colin Platt: *The English Medieval Town* (Secker and Warburg 1976); Jeremy Haslam: *Early Medieval Towns in Britain* (Shire 1985); Brian Paul Hindle: *Medieval Town Plans 700–1140* (Shire 1990); M W Barley (ed): *The Plans and Topography of Medieval Towns in England and Wales* (CBA Research Report 14, 1975); John Schofield and David Palliser with Charlotte Harding: *Recent Archaeological Research in English Towns* (CBA 1981); Eric Grant (ed): *Central Places: Archaeology and History* (Sheffield University 1986). For London, Christopher Brooke and Gillian Keir: *London 800–1216: the Shaping of a City* (Secker and Warburg 1976); John Schofield: *The Building of London, from the Conquest to the Great Fire* (British Museum Publications 1984). John Schofield and Alan Vince: *Medieval Towns* (Leicester University Press 1994).

SPECIALISED TOWNS

Jonathan Brown: *The English Market Town* (Crowood, Ramsbury, 1986); Russell Chamberlin: *The National Trust, The English Country Town* (Webb and Bowes 1983); still valuable are Christopher Hobhouse: *Oxford* (Batsford 1939), and John Steegman: *Cambridge* (Batsford 1940, 1941–2); see now Christopher Brooke and Roger Highfield: *Oxford and Cambridge* (CUP 1988); George Scott-Moncrieff: *Edinburgh* (Batsford 1947); Alan Massie: *Edinburgh* (Sinclair-Stevenson 1994).

Resort Towns – Colin and Rose Bell: *City Fathers* (Cresset 1969); Sarah Howell: *The Seaside* (Studio Vista); Pat Hodgson: *The Changing Seaside* (Hove, Wayland 1979); S M Adamson: *Seaside Piers* (1977).

SPAS

R L P and Dorothy M Jowitt: *Discovering Spas* (Shire 1971); Peter J Neville Havins: *The Spas of England* (Hale 1976). Bath is well covered, eg Barry Cunliffe: *Roman Bath Discovered* (Routledge and Kegan Paul1971), and *The City of Bath* (Alan Sutton 1990); John Haddon: *Bath* (Batsford 1973); Diana Winsor: *The Dream of Bath* (Bath, Trade and Travel Publications 1980) – a well-illustrated account.

THE CINQUE PORTS

Donald F Jessup: *The Cinque Ports* (Batsford 1952); C E Whitney: *Discovering the Cinque Ports* (Shire); Margaret Brentnall: *The Cinque Ports and Romney Marsh* (John Gifford 1972, 1980).

TOWNS IN WALES

Harold Carter: *The Towns of Wales* (1965); Ian Soulsby: *The Towns of Medieval Wales* (Phillimore 1983).

THE GEOGRAPHY OF TOWNS IN SCOTLAND

Grace Meiklejohn: *The Geography of Towns in Scotland* (1927); Robert J Naismith: *The Story of Scotland's Towns* (Edinburgh, John Donald 1989); Jeremy W R Whitehead and Khan Alauddin: "The

Town Plans of Scotland: some preliminary considerations" (*Scottish Geographical Magazine* 85, 1969).

STREET NAMES

See above under *Place-names*.

THE TOWNSCAPE

General – Thomas Sharp: *The Anatomy of the Village* (Penguin 1946); Ewart Johns: *British Townscapes* (Arnold 1965); Kurt Rowland: *The Shape of Towns* (Ginn 1966); Geoffrey Martin: *The Town* (Vista 1961); Sir John Summerson: *Georgian London* (Pleiades 1945, Penguin 1962); Michael Aston and James Bond: *The Landscape of Towns* (Dent 1976); Kerry Downes: *The Georgian Cities of Britain* (Phaidon 1979); David W Lloyd: *The Making of English Towns* (Gollancz 1984, 1992); Colin McWilliam: *Scottish Townscape* (Collins 1975).

Post-medieval – C W Chalklin: *The Provincial Towns of Georgian England* (Arnold 1974); Peter Clark and Paul Slack: *English Towns in Transition, 1500–1700* (OUP 1976); Angus McInnes: *The English Town, 1660–1760* (Historical Association 1980); Peter Clark (ed): *Country Towns in Pre-industrial England* (Leicester University Press 1981); Michael Lynch (ed): *The Early Modern Town in Scotland* (Croom Helm, 1987); Patrick Ottaway: *Archaeology in British Towns* (RKP 1992) – synthesis of the past 25 years of urban archaeology. Also Robert E Dickinson: *The West European City* (Routledge and Kegan Paul 1951, 1961, 1967); and *City and Region* (Routledge and Kegan Paul 1964); D Burtenshaw, M Bateman and G J Ashworth: *The City in West Europe* (Chichester, John Wiley 1981). Asa Briggs: *Victorian Cities* (Penguin 1968).

Suburbs – David C Thomas: *Suburbia* (MacGibbon and Kee 1972); Arthur M Edwards: *The Design of Suburbia* (Pembridge Press 1981); F M C Thompson (ed): *The Rise of Suburbia* (Leicester University Press 1982); Nick Taylor: *The Village in the City*.

Houses

The monumental work of Sir Nikolaus Pevsner et al: *The Buildings of England* (Penguin), in multi-volume series by counties – companion volumes for Wales and Scotland in progress – is indispensable. See also T W West: *Discovering English Architecture* (Shire 1979); David Iredale: *This Old House* (Shire).

THE MEDIEVAL BUILDING INDUSTRY

L F Salzman: *Building in England Down to 1540* (OUP 1952); John Harvey: *The Master-Builders* (Thames and Hudson 1971); John Harvey: *The Medieval Architect* (Wayland 1972); E M Jope (ed): *Studies in Building History* (Odhams 1961).

Masons' marks

G T Hemsley, record of over 1000 marks in Lincoln Cathedral; T B Parks, list of marks in Lincolnshire churches, (see Eric Thornley: *Masons' Marks* (Lincolnshire Old Churches Trust, 21st Annual Report 1973)); R O C Spring: *The Masons' Marks of Salisbury Cathedral* (1980).

Medieval tiles

Elizabeth Eames: *Catalogue of Medieval Lead-glazed Earthenware Tiles in the British Museum* (British Museum Publications 1980); Elizabeth S Eames: *Medieval Tiles: A Handbook* (British Museum Publications 1968); Elizabeth S Eames: *English Tilers* (British Museum Publications 1992).

Delft and later tiles

Rhoda Edwards in *Journal of Ceramic History* 6, 1974.

Reuse of materials and buildings

Maurice Howard in *The Early Tudor Country House* (Philips 1987) – monastic conversions.

Protective devices on buildings

Ralph Merrifield: *The Archaeology of Ritual and Magic* (Batsford 1987).

Weathervanes – Patricia and Philip Mockridge: *Weathervanes* (Shire).

Sheela-na-gigs – Anthony Weir and James Jerman: *Images of Lust* (Batsford 1986).

Celtic heads – Sidney Jackson: *Celtic and other stone heads* (published by the author, Shipley, 1973).

Galleting – W R Trotter in *Transactions of the Ancient Monuments Society* 33, 1989.

Witch posts – Marie Hartley and Joan Ingilby: *Life in the Moorlands of North East Yorkshire* (Dent 1972).

Corn dollies – M Lambeth: *Discovering Corn Dollies* (Shire 1974).

BUILDING MATERIALS

General – Norman Davey: *A History of Building Materials* (Phoenix House, 1961); Alec Clifton-Taylor: *The Pattern of English Building* (Batsford 1972, 1987); John and Jane Penoyre: *Houses in the Landscape* (Faber 1978).

Wall Materials

Brick – R W Brunskill and Alec Clifton-Taylor: *English Brickwork* (Ward Lock 1977); Nathaniel Lloyd: *A History of English Brickwork* (H G Montgomery 1928); Martin Hammond: *Bricks and Brickmaking* (Shire); L S Harley: "A Typology of Brick" (*Journal of the British Archaeological Association* 38, 1974); R W Brunskill: *Brick Building in Britain* (Gollancz 1990); A Plumridge and W Meulenkamp: *Brickwork: Architecture and Design* (Studio 1993).

Mathematical tiles – T P Smith et al: *Mathematical Tiles* (Ewell Symposium notes 1981);

Cob – John McCann: *Clay and Cob Building* (Shire 1983).

Timber – R W Brunskill: *Timber building in Britain* (Gollancz 1985, 1994).

Stone – see *General* above, also Alec Clifton-Taylor and A S Ireson: *English Stone Building* (Gollancz 1983); Rosemary Leach: *An Investigation into the use of Purbeck Marble in Medieval England* (published by the author, Crediton 1978).

Roofing Materials

Thatch – see *Crafts*, below.

Tiles – see *Building materials: General* above.

Other Materials

Iron – Raymond Lister: *Decorative Wrought Ironwork in Great Britain* (Bell 1957); G J Hollister-Short: *Discovering Wrought Iron* (Shire 1970);

Raymond Lister: *Decorative Cast Ironwork in Great Britain* (Bell 1960); Jacqueline Fearn: *Cast Iron* (Shire); Amina Chatwin: *Cheltenham's Ornamental Ironwork* (published by the author, Cheltenham 1974).

Coade stone – Ben Weinreb and Christopher Hibbert (eds): *The London Encyclopedia* (Macmillan 1983)

Wood – Oliver Rackham: *Trees and Woodlands in the British Landscape* (Dent 1976); Oliver Rackham in Kathleen Riddick (ed): *Archaeological Approaches to Medieval Europe* (Kalamazoo, *Studies in Medieval Culture* 18, 1985).

Sources of Building Materials

John and Jane Penoyre: *Houses in the Landscape* (Faber 1978); Norman Davey: *Building Stones of England and Wales* (National Council of Social Service for the *Standing Conference for Local History* 1976); E M Jope in *Medieval Archaeology* 6, 1964; R J Brown: *The English Country Cottage* (Hale 1979); Robert Naismith: *Buildings of the Scottish Countryside* (Gollancz 1985).

BUILDING FEATURES AND DETAILS

A Clifton-Taylor: *The Pattern of English Building* (Batsford 1972, 1987).

Chimneys and smoke bays

Margaret Wood: *The English Medieval House* (Bracken 1965); Valentine Fletcher: *Chimney Pots and Stacks* (Centaur 1993, reprint); Joan Harding in John Warren (ed): *Wealden Buildings* (Coach Publications, Horsham, for Wealden Buildings Study Group 1990).

Doorways

Francis W Steer: *A Selection of Chichester Doorways* (Chichester City Council, the Chichester Papers 18, 1961); Alexander Stuart Gray and John Sambrook: *Fanlights* (A and C Black 1990) – covers Georgian doorways also.

VERNACULAR BUILDING

R W Brunskill: *Illustrated Handbook of Vernacular Architecture* (Faber 1970); R W Brunskill: *Houses* (Collins 1982); Eric Mercer: *English Vernacular Houses* (HMSO for RCHME, 1975); Richard Harris: *Discovering Timber Framed Buildings* (Shire 1978); John Warren (ed): *Wealden Buildings* (Wealden Buildings Study Group 1990); John L Baker: *A Picture of Surrey* (Hale 1980); John L Baker: *A Picture of Hampshire* (Hale 1986); K W E Gravett: *Timber and Brick Building in Kent* (Phillimore 1971); Joan Harding: *Four Centuries of Charlwood Houses: Medieval to 1840* (Charlwood Society 1976); J T Smith: "Timber-framed Building in England" (*Archaeological Journal* XXII, 1966); J T Smith in *Archaeological Journal* 31, 1974; J T Smith: "Cruck Construction: A Survey of the Problems" (*Medieval Archaeology* 6 1964); N W Alcock: *Cruck Construction* (CBA Research Report 42, 1981); Jean Chapelot and Robert Fossier: *Le village et la maison au Moyen Age* (Paris, Hachette 1980, trans Henry Cleere as *Village and Town in the Middle Ages*, Batsford 1985); Julian Munby in Gwyn Meirion Jones and Michael Jones (ed): *Manorial Domestic Buildings in England and Northern France* (Society of Antiquaries 1993); R T Mason: *Framed Buildings of England* (Coachhouse Publications 1973).

Roofing of solid-wall houses

J. T Smith: "Medieval Roofs: a Classification" (*Medieval Archaeology* 115, 1959); N W Alcock and M W Barley: "Medieval Roofs with base crucks and short principals" (*Antiquaries' Journal* 52, 1972).

Crown posts – J M Fletcher and P S Spokes in *Medieval Archaeology* 6, 1964. Earthfast posts, used even into the 19th century – R A Meeson and O M Welch: "Earthfast Posts: the Persistence of Alternative Building Techniques" (*Vernacular Architecture* 24, 1993).

VERNACULAR HOUSES

General – R W Brunskill: *Illustrated Handbook of Vernacular Architecture* (Faber 1970).

Social classes and types of house

Sir Frank Stenton: *Anglo-Saxon England* (OUP 1971).

The Great Rebuilding

W G Hoskins: "The Rebuilding of England" (*Past and Present* November 1953, also in *Provincial England*, Macmillan 1963); R Machin: "The Great Rebuilding: A Reassessment" (*Past and Present* 77 1977); C Currie: "Time and Chance" (*Vernacular Architecture* 19, 1988); M H Johnson in *Oxford Journal of Archaeology* 12/1 1993; Colin Platt: *The Great Rebuildings of Tudor and Stuart England: revolutions in architectural taste* (University College London Press 1994).

End of the Vernacular

Christopher Powell: *Discovering Cottage Architecture* (Shire 1984).

PRE-CONQUEST HOUSES

Prehistoric

Ian Longworth and John Cherry (eds): *Archaeology in Britain since 1945* (British Museum Publications 1986); V G Childe: *Skara Brae* (1931); Hans-Ole Hansen: *I Built a Stone Age House* (Phoenix House 1962); Peter J Reynolds: *Iron-Age Farm* (British Museum Publications 1979); Malcolm L Reid: *Prehistoric Houses in Britain* (Shire 1994).

Roman

A L F Rivet: *The Roman Villa in Britain* (RKP 1969); John Percival: *The Roman Villa* (Batsford 1976); Keith Branigan and David Miles (eds): *The Economies of Romano-British Villas* (J. R Collis, University of Sheffield 1988); John Wacher: *The Towns of Roman Britain* (Batsford 1975, revised ed 1995); Guy de la Bédoyère: *Roman Towns in Britain* (Batsford/EH 1992); Guy de la Bédoyère: *Roman Villas and the Countryside* (Batsford/EH 1993); Guy de la Bédoyère: *The Buildings of Roman Britain* (Batsford/EH 1991) – reconstructions and construction techniques.

Anglo-Saxon

D M Wilson (ed): *The Archaeology of Anglo-Saxon England* (Methuen 1976, CUP 1981); P V Addyman: "The Anglo-Saxon House: a new review" (*Anglo-Saxon England* 1, 1972); Mary and Nigel

Kerr: *Anglo-Saxon Architecture* (Shire 1983); *Cowdery's Down* – Martin Millett in *Archaeological Journal* 140, 1983 and 141, 1984.

POST-CONQUEST HOUSES – RURAL HOUSES

Jean Chapelot and Robert Fossier: *Le village et la maison au Moyen Age* (Paris, Hachette 1980, trans Henry Cleere as *Village and Town in the Middle Ages*, (Batsford 1985)); John Hurst: "Rural Building in England and Wales: England" in H E Hallam (ed): *The Agrarian History of England and Wales II, 1042–1350* (CUP 1988); H E J Le Patourel: "Rural Building in England and Wales: England" in E Miller (ed): *The Agrarian History of England and Wales III, 1348–1500* (CUP 1991); M W Barley: "Rural Housing in England" and Peter Smith: "Rural Housing in Wales" in Joan Thirsk (ed): *The Agrarian History of England and Wales IV, 1500–1640* (CUP 1967)

Cottages

R G Brown: *The English Country Cottage* (Hale 1979); J M Proctor: *East Anglian Cottages* (Providence Press, Ely, 1979); Iorwerth C Peate: *The Welsh House* (Brython Press, Liverpool, 1940, 1946); P Smith: *Houses of the Welsh Countryside* (HMSO 1975, 1988); Robert Naismith: *Buildings of the Scottish Countryside* (Gollancz 1985); Crispin Paine and John Rhodes: *The Worker's Home* (Oxfordshire Museums Service 1979); Christopher Powell: *Discovering Cottage Architecture* (Shire 1984); L H Landin: *English Cottage Interiors* (Weidenfeld and Nicolson); *Guides* to the Weald and Downland Open Air Museum, Singleton.

Blackhouses – Alexander Fenton: *The Island Blackhouse* (HMSO Edinburgh 1978).

Small houses

Peter Eden: *Small Houses in England 1520–1820* (Historical Association 1969); J T Smith and E M Yates: *On the Dating of English Houses from External Evidence* (reprinted from *Field Studies*, 2, 5, 1968); Martin S Briggs: *The English Farmhouse* (Batsford 1953); M W Barley: *The English Farmhouse and Cottage* (Routledge and Kegan Paul1961); Andrew Henderson: *The Family House in England* (Phoenix House 1964); M W Barley: *The House and Home* (Vista 1963); F Lyndon Cave:*The Smaller English House* (1981); J and M Richards: *Timber-Framed Houses in the Scottish Countryside* (HMSO); John Woodforde: *Georgian Houses for All* (RKP 1978); J T Smith: "The Evolution of the English Peasant House to the Later 17th Century; the evidence of buildings" (*Journal of the British Archaeological Association*, XXXIII, 1970).

Longhouses – R W Brunskill: *Houses* (Collins 1982); P Smith: "The Longhouse and the Laithehouse" in Foster and Alcock (eds): *Culture and Environment* (1963).

Large houses

Margaret Wood: *The English Medieval House* (Bracken 1965); Gavin Stamp and André Goulancourt: *The English House 1860–1914* (Faber 1986); Gwyn Meirion-Jones and Michael Jones (eds): *Manorial Domestic Buildings in England and Northern France* (Society of Antiquaries 1994). (The categories cottage, small and large often overlap in these books.)

Great Houses

John Summerson: *Architecture in Britain 1530–1830* (Pelican History of Art 1953); Mark Girouard: *The Victorian Country House* (Yale University Press 1979); Mark Girouard: *Life in the English Country House* (Yale University Press 1978); R Dutton: *The English Country House* (Batsford 1949); H Fenwick: *Scottish Baronial Houses* (Hale 1986). An inside view is given in Alice Fairfax-Lucy (ed): *Mistress of Charlecote: Memories of Mary Elizabeth Lucy* [1880s] (Gollancz 1986). For monastic conversions, Maurice Howard: *The Early Tudor Country House* (Philips 1987). J Jackson-Stops: *Vanishing Houses of England* (1982); C W R Winter: *The Manor Houses of the Isle of Wight* (Wimborne, Dovecote Press, 1984).

Ice Storage

Monica Ellis: *Ice and Ice houses through the ages* (Southampton University Industrial Archaeology Group 1982) – with a gazetteer for Hampshire; Brian John: *The Ice Age, past and present* (1977); Alan Penny: *Icehouses in Dorset* (1963) and in *Proceedings of the Dorset Archaeological Society* 1965; F W B Yorke: *Ice-houses* (1955) – Warwickshire; Tom Cook in *Local History News* 11, 1986; Sylvia Beamon and Susan Roaf: *The Ice-Houses of Great Britain* (Routledge and Kegan Paul1988); Tim Buxbaum: *Ice houses* (Shire 1992); Ron Martin: "Ice Houses in Sussex" (*Sussex Industrial History* 24, 1994) – description of the three main types and gazetteer.

URBAN HOUSES

Medieval

M R G Conzen: *Alnwick, Northumberland, a study in town plan analysis* (*Transactions and Publications of the Institute of British Geographers* 27, 1960); John M Steane: *The Archaeology of Medieval England and Wales* (Croom Helm 1984); John Schofield: *The Building of London* (British Museum Publications 1984, 1992); John Schofield: *Medieval London Houses* (Yale University Press 1995) – c 1200–1666 with the topography; Michael Aston and James Bond: *The Landscape of Towns* (Dent 1976).

The Chester Rows

B E Harris et al: "Galleries which they call The Rows" (*Journal of the Chester Archaeological Society* 67, 1985).

Post-medieval (including the Industrial Revolution – workers' houses)

Stefan Muthesius: *The English Terraced House* (Yale University Press 1982); John Summerson: *Georgian London* (Penguin 1945, 1962); John Summerson: *John Nash: Architect to King George IV* (Allen and Unwin 1935, 1949); Colin McWilliam: *Scottish Townscape* (Collins 1975); C W Chalklin: *The Provincial Towns of Georgian England* (Arnold 1974); F Engels: *The Condition of the Working Class in England* (1845); Stanley D Chapman (ed): *The History of Working-class housing* (1971); J B Lowe:

Welsh Industrial Workers' Housing 1775–1875 (National Museum of Wales 1977); Malcolm I Thomis: *Old Nottingham* (David and Charles 1968); *Early Industrial Housing: the Trinity Area of Frome* (HMSO for RCHME 1981).

20th Century

Colin and Rose Bell: *City Fathers* (Cresset 1969); M Ash: *A Guide to the Structure of London* (Adams and Dart, Bath 1971); Ebenezer Howard: *Tomorrow: A Peaceful Path to Land Reform* (1898) – reissued in 1902 and again in 1946, as *Garden Cities of Tomorrow*; David C Thoms: *Suburbia* (Granada 1972); Arthur M Edwards: *The Design of Suburbia* (Pembridge Press 1981); F M L Thompson (ed): *The Rise of Suburbia* (Leicester University Press 1982); J B Cullingworth: *Town and Country Planning in Britain* (1972); Colin McWilliam: *Scottish Townscape* (Collins 1975); Robert J Naismith: *Buildings of the Scottish Countryside* (Gollancz 1985).

A few books now of historical interest – Ralph Tubbs: *Living in Cities* (Penguin 1942); Ralph Tubbs: *The Englishman Builds* (Penguin 1945); E J Carter and Ernö Goldfinger: *The County of London Plan* (Penguin 1943).

The Church

RELIGIOUS PREHISTORY

Prehistoric tombs and other monuments are described in books on archaeology eg J V S Megaw and D D A Simpson: *Introduction to British Prehistory* (Leicester University, Press 1979). See also Miranda Green: *Symbol and Image in Celtic Religious Art* (RKP 1989); Anne Ross: *Pagan Celtic Britain* (Routledge and Kegan Paul 1967); Ronald Hutton: *The Pagan Religions of the Ancient British Isles* (Blackwell 1991); Aubrey Burl: *The Stone Circles of the British Isles* (Yale University Press 1976) and *From Carnac to Callanish* (Yale University Press 1993) – stone rows and avenues. A Thom: *Megalithic Sites in Britain* (OUP 1967).

Roman Britain – For Roman temples etc, M J T Lewis: *Temples in Roman Britain* (CUP 1966); Ann Woodward: *Shrines and Sacrifice* (Batsford/EH 1992); Miranda J Green: *The Gods of Roman Britain* (Shire 1983); Ralph Merrifield: "Art and Religion in Roman London" in Julian Munby and Martin Henig: *Roman Life and Art in Britain* (BAR 41, 1977).

Christianity in Roman Britain

Jocelyn Toynbee: "Christianity in Roman Britain" (*Journal of the British Archaeological Association* 16, 1953) – the groundbreaking survey; Charles Thomas: *Christianity in Roman Britain to AD 500* (Batsford 1981); M W Barley and R P C Hanson (eds): *Christianity in Britain 300–700* (Leicester University Press 1968); Richard Morris: *The Church in British Archaeology* (CBA Research Report 7, 1983) – useful general summary for all periods. Dorothy Watts: *Christians and Pagans in Roman Britain* (RKP 92); N Cookson: "The Christian Church in Roman Britain: a synthesis of archaeology" (*World Archaeology* 18/3, 1987).

CELTIC CHRISTIANITY

Charles Thomas: *The Early Christian Archaeology of North Britain* (OUP 1971); G W O Addleshaw: *The Pastoral Structure of the Celtic Church in Northern Britain* (Borthwick Papers no 43, York, 1973); Susan M Pearce (ed): *The Early Church in Western Britain and Ireland* (BAR 102, 1982); N Edwards and A Lane (eds): *The Early Church in Wales and the West* (Oxbow Monograph no 16, 1992).

The Element eccles in Place-names

Kenneth Cameron in M W Barley and R P C Hanson eds. *Christianity in Britain 300–700* (Leicester University Press 1968);

Scotland – G W S Barrow in *Scottish Studies* 27, 1983; for *cill* names in Scotland, W F H Nicolaisen: *Scottish Place-Names: their Study and Significance* (1976).

THE DEVELOPMENT OF THE PARISH

G W O Addleshaw: *The Beginning of the Parochial System* (St Anthony's Hall Publications no 3, York 1953, 1970); G W O Addleshaw: *The Development of the Parochial System from Charlemagne (763–814) to Urban II (1088–1099)* (St Anthony's Hall Publications no 6, York 1954, 1970); Katherine Barker: "The Early History of Sherborne", in Susan M Pearce (ed): *The Early Church in Western Britain and Ireland* (BAR 102, 1982).

Minsters – A Ralegh Radford: "Pre-Conquest Minster Churches" (*Archaeological Journal* 130, 1973); John Blair: *Early Medieval Surrey: Landholding, Church and Settlement before 1300* (Alan Sutton/Surrey Archaeological Society 1991) – covers settlement, minsters and churches in a small area; John Blain in Minsters and Parish Churches – *The Local Church in Transition 950–1200* (Oxford University Committee for Archaeology Monograph no 17, 1988).

Church records – David Iredale: *Discovering Your Family Tree* (Shire 1977); W G Hoskins: *Local History in England* (Longman 1972); and any book on genealogy.

THE PARISH AS RITUAL TERRITORY

Sir James George Frazer: *The Golden Bough* (one vol ed, Macmillan 1922, and later reprints); Charles Phythian-Adams: *Local History and Folklore – a new framework* (Standing Conference for Local History, 1975); Geoffrey Palmer and Noel Lloyd: *A Year of Festivals* (Frederick Warne 1972); Crichton Porteous: *The Beauty and Mystery of Well-Dressing* (Pilgrim Press 1949); Roy Christian: *Well-Dressing in Derbyshire* (Derbyshire Countryside Ltd, Derby 1987)

THE GREATER CHURCHES

Sir Nikolaus Pevsner (with others): *The Buildings of England* (Penguin) is indispensable, giving information not easily available elsewhere and valuable introductions. (Most counties now covered, Scotland and Wales in hand.) Nikolaus Pevsner: *The Englishness of English Art* (Architectural Press 1956, Penguin 1964); R J L Smith (ed): *A Guide to Cathedrals and Greater Churches* (published by the editor, Much Wenlock 1988, 1991); George Henderson: *Chartres* (Penguin 1968).

Cathedrals

J H Shrawley: *The Origins and Growth of Cathedral Foundations* (Lincoln Minster Pamphlets no 1, 1965); Kathleen Major: *Minster Yard* (Lincoln Minster Pamphlets Second Series no 7, 1974); C Wilson: *The Gothic Cathedrals: the Architecture of the Great Church* (Thames and Hudson 1992 ed); Herbert Felton and John Harvey: *The English Cathedrals* (Batsford 1950, 1956); David Pepin: *Discovering Cathedrals* (Shire 1971); Russell Chamberlin: *The English Cathedral* (Webb and Bower1987); R Morris: *Cathedrals and Abbeys of England and Wales* (Secker and Warburg 1984); A Clifton-Taylor: *The Cathedrals of England* (Thames and Hudson 1967); Nikolaus Pevsner and Priscilla Metcalf: *The Cathedrals of England* (Southern and Northern, Penguin 1985).

Historical and archaeological studies of individual cathedrals – G E Aylmer and Reginald Cant (eds): *A History of York Minster* (OUP 1977); Frederick Bussby: *Winchester Cathedral 1079–1979* (Southampton, Paul Cave Publications 1979); John Crook (ed): *Winchester Cathedral: Nine Hundred Years* (Phillimore 1993); Dorothy Owen (ed): *A History of Lincoln Minster* (CUP 1994); Philip Barker et al: *A Short Architectural History of Worcester Cathedral* (Worcester Cathedral Publications 1994); Mary Hobbs (ed): *Chichester Cathedral: An Historical Survey* (Phillimore 1994); Thomas Cocke and Peter Kidson: *Salisbury Cathedral: Perspectives on the architectural history* (HMSO for RCHME 1993) – first of three books on the cathedral – the next will deal with monuments, fittings, and glass; *The History of Canterbury Cathedral* (OUP 1995); Helen Henderson: *Cathedrals of France* (Methuen 1929); Martin Biddle: *The Study of Winchester* (*Proceedings of the British Academy* LXIX 1983, and issued separately by OUP) – has full relevant bibliography.

MONASTIC HOUSES

Ordnance Survey map of Monastic Britain (N and S sheets; 2nd ed 1955, 1954); Alan Phillips: *Some Monasteries of Yorkshire* (HMSO 1973); Colin Platt: *The Abbeys and Priories of Medieval England* (Secker and Warburg 1984); Glyn Coppack: *Fountains Abbey* (Batsford/EH 1993) – also for granges; *Kirkstall Abbey: The Guest House* (Wakefield, West Yorkshire Archaeology Service 1987); Geoffrey N Wright: *Discovering Abbeys and Priories* (Shire 1969); F H Crossley: *The English Abbey* (Batsford 1935); C H Lawrence: *Medieval Monasticism* (Longman 1984); M R James: *Abbeys* (Great Western Railway 1925); Michael Aston: *Monasteries* (Batsford 1993); Bernard Jennings (ed): *A History of Nidderdale* (The Advertiser Press, Huddersfield 1967); Bryan Waites: *Moorland and Vale-land Farming in North East Yorkshire* (University of York, *Borthwick Papers*, no 32, 1967); Colin Platt: *The Monastic Grange in Medieval England* (Secker and Warburg 1970); G R Anderson; *The Abbeys of Scotland* (J Clarke); R Cooper: *Abbeys and Priories of Wales* (Davies 1992); J Patrick Greene: *Medieval Monasteries* (Leicester University Press 1992).

THE PARISH CHURCHES

J Charles Fox and Charles Bradley Ford: *The Parish Churches of England* (Batsford 1935); Sir John Betjeman: *Parish Churches of England and Wales* (Collins 1958, 1980); Mervyn Blatch: *Parish Churches of England* (Blandford Press 1974); Lawrence E Jones: *The Observer's Book of Old English Churches* (Warne 1969); John Harries: *Discovering Churches* (Shire 1972); Colin Platt: *The Parish Churches of Medieval England* (Secker and Warburg 1981); Richard Morris: "The Church in the Countryside" in (ed): *Medieval Villages* (Oxford University Committee for Archaeology Monograph no 5, 1985); Elizabeth and Wayland Young: *London's Churches* (Grafton 1986); Mervyn Blatch: *A Guide to London's Churches* (Constable 1978); Richard Morris: *Churches in the Landscape* (Dent 1989).

Siting – see Richard Morris: *op cit.*

Orientation – Gilbert White: *The Antiquities of Selborne* (1788). Dedications – see R Morris: *op cit.*

Folklore – Geoffrey Palmer and Noel Lloyd: *A Year of Festivals* (Warne 1972); C Phythian-Adams: *Local History and Folklore* (Bedford Square 1975).

Sheela-na-gigs – Anthony Keir and James Jerman: *Images of Lust* (Batsford 1986).

Green Men – William Anderson and Clive Hicks: *Green Man* (HarperCollins 1990); Ronald Hutton: *The Rise and Fall of Merry England* (OUP 1994).

Holy Wells – R C Hope: *The Legendary Lore of the Holy Wells of England* (Elliot Stock 1893); Francis Jones: *The Holy Wells of Wales* (1954, University of Wales Press 1992); Roy Christian: *Well-dressing in Derbyshire* (Derbyshire Countryside Ltd, Derby 1987).

The Shape of the Church – J C Cox and C B Ford: *The Parish Churches of England* (Batsford 1935); Warwick Rodwell: *The Archaeology of the English Church* (Batsford 1981).

Sompting – Fred Aldsworth in *Current Archaeology* 99, 1986.

Local styles – Sir William Addison: *Local Styles of the English Parish Church* (Batsford 1982); M O Whiffen: *Stuart and Georgian Churches: The Architecture of the Church of England outside London 1603–1837* (Batsford 1947); Alec Clifton-Taylor: *English Parish Churches as Works of Art* (Batsford 1974, 1986).

Wren towers and spires – Gerald Cobb: *The Old Churches of London* (Batsford 1941/2).

Fittings and Furnishings – Eric R Delderfield: *A Guide to Church Furniture* (David and Charles 1966); J C D Smith: *A Guide to Church Woodcarvings* (David and Charles 1974); M D Anderson: *History and Imagery in British Churches* (John Murray 1971); Christopher Howkins: *Discovering Church Furniture* (Shire 1969); C A Hewett: *Church Carpentry* (Phillimore 1982); and *English Cathedral and Monastic Carpentry* (Phillimore 1985); Francis Bond: *Fonts and Font Covers* (1908, 1985); G L Remnant: *A Catalogue of Misericords in Great Britain* (OUP 1969); Charles Tracy: *English Gothic Choir Stalls* (The Boydell Press 1989, 1990).

Windows – John Harries: *Discovering Stained Glass* (Shire 1968); Painton Cowen: *Rose Windows* (Thames and Hudson, 1979); Painton Cowen: *A Guide to Stained Glass in Britain* (Thames and Hudson, 1985); Catherine Brisac: *A Thousand Years of Stained Glass* (Macdonald 1986); Sarah Crewe:

Stained Glass in England 1180–1540 (HMSO for RCHME 1987); Peter Gibson: *Stained Glass in York*; Y Delaporte: *L'Art du vitrail aux XIIe et XIIIe Siècles* (Houvet, Chartres 1963) – useful introduction, based on Chartres.

Symbolism – Painton Cowen: *Rose Windows* (Thames and Hudson, 1979).

Bells – John Camp: *Discovering Bells and Bellringing* (Shire 1968).

Fonts – C S Drake: "The Distribution of Tournai Fonts" (*Art Journal LXXIII*, 1993); Francis Bond: *Fonts and Font Covers* (1908, 1985).

Memorials – Katharine A Esdaile: *English Church Monuments 1510–1840* (Batsford 1946); B Kemp: *English Church Monuments* (1980); Malcolm Cook: *Discovering Brasses and Brass-rubbings* (Shire 1971).

Wall paintings – E Clive Rouse: *Discovering Wall Paintings* (Shire 1968, 1971, 1980), expanded as *Medieval Wall Paintings* (Shire 1991).

Churchyards

Frederick Burgess: *English Churchyard Memorials* (Lutterworth Press 1963); Warwick Rodwell: *The Archaeology of the English Church* (Batsford 1981); Maurice Beresford and John Hurst: *Wharram Percy: Deserted Medieval Village* (Batsford/EH 1990); Mark Child: *Discovering Churchyards* (Shire 1982); P A Rahtz: "Grave Orientation" (*Archaeological Journal*. 135, 1978); Brian Bailey: *Churchyards of England and Wales* (Hale 1987, Magna 1994); C St J H Daniel: *Sundials on Walls* (National Maritime Museum Monographs and Reports no 28, 1978); "Surrey Cast Iron Gravestones" (*Surrey Industrial History Group Bulletin*, 64 1991); R M Willetts: "Pre-Industrial Cast-iron Graveslabs" (*Wealden Iron* 2nd series 8, 1988: 9, 1989: 14, 1994) (J S Hodgkinson); Llangar – Ron Shoesmith in *Arch Cambrensis* 129, 1980; Spitalfields –*The Spitalfields Project* (CBA Research Report 1993) vol 1, archaeology: Jez Reeve and Max Adams, vol 2, anthropology: Theya Molleson et al; J M Lilley, G Stroud, D R Brothwell and M H Williamson: "The Jewish Burial Ground at Jewbury" (*The Archaeology of York* 12/3, CBA/YAT 1994); J Jones: *How to Record Graveyards* (CBA 1976, 1979, 1993); Bo Gräslund in *PPS* 60, 1994, is an important and profound analysis of prehistoric tombs in relation to beliefs in the soul.

Cemeteries

Hugh Meller: *London Cemeteries: An Illustrated Guide and Gazetteer* (Avebury Publishing Company,1981, Gregg International 1985); J S Curl: *The Victorian Celebration of Death* (1972); John Morley: Death, *Heaven and the Victorians*; Howard Colvin: *Architecture and the After-Life* (Yale University Press 1992); John Gay and Felix Barker: *Highgate Cemetery: Victorian Valhalla* (John Murray 1984); Julian Litten: *The English Way of Death* (Robert Hale 1991); R Reece (ed): *Burial in the Roman World* (CBA Research Report 22, 1977).

Crosses

Aymer Vallance: *Old Crosses and Lychgates* (Batsford 1920); George H Haines: *Discovering Crosses* (Shire 1969); Richard Bailey: *Viking Age Sculpture in Northern England* (Collins 1980); G Baldwin Brown: *The Arts in Early England vol VI, part II: Anglo-Saxon Sculpture* (Murray 1937); W G Black: *The Scots Mercat Cross* (1928); James Lang: "Corpus of Hogback Tombstones" (*Anglo-Saxon Studies 3*, 1988); T D Kendrick: *Late Saxon and Viking Art* (1949).

Picts – Anna Ritchie: *Picts* (HMSO for HBM, 1989); Anthony Jackson: *The Symbol Stones of Pictland* (1988); Stewart Cruden: *The Early Christian and Pictish Monuments of Scotland* (HMSO Edinburgh 1964).

Churches in the Landscape – Richard Morris: *Churches in the Landscape* (Dent 1989), a key book.

THE ARCHAEOLOGY OF CHURCHES

P V Addyman and R Morris (eds): *The Archaeological Study of Churches* (CBA Research Report 13, 1976); Warwick Rodwell: *The Archaeology of the English Church* (Batsford 1981); Richard Morris: *The Church in British Archaeology* (CBA Research Report 47, 1983); Warwick Rodwell: *Church Archaeology* (Batsford/EH 1989); Richard N Bailey, Eric Cambridge and H Denis Briggs: *Dowsing and Church Archaeology* (Intercept 1988).

THE NONCONFORMIST CHAPEL

Kenneth Lindley: *Chapels and Meeting Houses* (John Baker 1969); David A Barton: *Discovering Chapels and Meeting Houses* (Shire 1975); John Hibbs: *The Country Chapel* (David and Charles 1988); Christopher F Stell: *An Inventory of Nonconformist Chapels and Meeting Houses in Central England* (HMSO for RCHME, 1986), Christopher F Stell: *An Inventory of Nonconformist Chapels and Meeting Houses in the South-West of England* (HMSO for RCHME, 1991), Christopher F Stell: *An Inventory of Nonconformist Chapels and Meeting Houses in the North of England* (HMSO for RCHME, 1994) – a comprehensive survey up to 1800, selective after that date.

FRIENDS (QUAKER) MEETING HOUSES

Herbert Lidbetter: *The Friends Meeting House* (William Sessions, York 1961); David M Butler: "Local Variations in Quaker meeting-houses" in David Blamires, Jeremy Greenwood and Alex Ken, (eds): *A Quaker Miscellany for Edward H Milligan* (David Blamires, Manchester, 1985).

THE WELSH CHAPEL

Anthony Jones: *Welsh Chapels* (National Museum of Wales).

THE CHURCH IN SCOTLAND

W Douglas Simpson: *The Ancient Stones of Scotland* (Hale 1965); Stewart Cruden: *Scottish Medieval Churches* (John Donald, Edinburgh 1986); George Hay: *The Architecture of Scottish Post-Reformation Churches 1560–1843* (1957); Ian G Lindsay: *The Scottish Parish Kirk* (The Saint Andrew Press, Edinburgh 1960); Mike Salter: *The Old Parish Churches of Scotland* (Malvern, Folly Publications 1994).

The Styles of Architecture

Mortimer Wheeler: *Roman Art and Architecture* (Thames and Hudson 1964); John Harvey: *English Medieval Architects* (Sutton, revised ed 1987) – biographical dictionary to 1550; John Harvey: *The Master Builders: Architecture in the Middle Ages* (Thames and Hudson 1971); John Fleming, Hugh Honour, Nikolaus Pevsner: *The Penguin Dictionary of Architecture* (Penguin 1966, 1972); David Watkin: *A History of Western Architecture* (Barrie and Jenkins 1986); James Stevens Curl: *Classical Architecture* (Batsford 1992) (from Graeco-Roman times to today); Mary and Nigel Kerr: *Anglo Saxon Architecture* (Shire 1983); H M and J Taylor: *Anglo-Saxon Architecture* (1965); Jack Bowyer: *The Evolution of Church Building* (Granada 1977); Mark Child: *Discovering Church Architecture* (Shire 1976); T W West: *Discovering English Architecture* (Shire 1979); W Douglas Simpson: *The Ancient Stones of Scotland* (Hale 1965).

Castles and Military Works

Prehistoric

Hillforts are dealt with in books on prehistory and the Iron Age. Specific books which are still of value are: Margaret Jesson and David Hill (eds): *The Iron Age and its Hill-Forts* (University of Southampton, Monograph Series no 1, 1971); J Forde-Johnston: *Hillforts of the Iron Age in England and Wales* (Liverpool University Press 1976); A H Hogg: *Hillforts of Britain* (Hart-Davies 1975). Also Leslie Alcock: *"By South Cadbury is that Camelot. . . "* (Thames and Hudson 1972); Barry Cunliffe: *Danebury* (Batsford 1983).

Roman forts – Specific books include David J Breeze and Brian Dobson: *Hadrian's Wall* (Allen Lane, Penguin 1976); Stephen Johnson: *Hadrian's Wall* (Batsford/EH 1994); James Crow: *Housesteads* (Batsford/EH 1995); Patrick Ottaway: *Roman York* (Batsford/EH 1993); Robin Birley: *Vindolanda* (Thames and Hudson 1977).

CASTLES

Q Hughes: *Military Architecture: The Art of Defence from Earliest Times to the Atlantic Wall* (Beaufort, 2nd ed 1991); Brian K Davison: "The Origins of the Castle in England" (*Archaeological Journal* 124, 1968); Brian Hope-Taylor: "The excavation of a motte at Abinger in Surrey" (*Archaeological Journal* CVII, 1952); and in R L S Bruce-Mitford (ed): *Recent Archaeological excavations in Britain* (Routledge and Kegan Paul 1956); Joseph Decaëns: "De la Motte au Château de Pierre dans le Nord-Ouest de la France" in Gwyn Meirion-Jones and Michael Jones: *Manorial Domestic Buildings in England and Northern France* (Society of Antiquaries, *Occasional Papers* no 15, 1993); A J Taylor: "The Castle of St Georges d'Espéranche" (*Antiquaries Journal* XXXIII, 1953) – Savoyan influence. Brian K Davison: *The Observer's Book of Castles* (Warne 1979); R Allen Brown: *English Castles* (Batsford 1954, 1976); D J Cathcart King: *The Castle in England and Wales* (Croom Helm 1988); M W Thompson: *The Rise of the Castle* (CUP 1991); and *The Decline of the Castle* (CUP 1987); Derek F Renn: *Norman Castles in Britain* (1968); Tom McNeill: *Castles* (Batsford/EH 1992); Robert Higham and Philip Barker: *Timber Castles* (Batsford 1992); Steward Cruden: *The Scottish Castle* (1960); W Douglas Simpson: *The Ancient Stones of Scotland* (Hale 1965); M Salter: *The Castles of South West Scotland* (Malvern, Folly 1993); A J Taylor: "Castle-Building in Wales in the late thirteenth century" in E M Jope (ed): *Studies in Building History* (Odhams 1961) – reorganisation of the works.

Fortified Houses

Margaret Wood: *The English Medieval House* (Bracken 1965); H G Ramm, R W McDowell and Eric Mercer: *Sheilings and Bastles* (HMSO for RCHME 1971).

Moats – F A Aberg ed: *Medieval Moated Sites* (CBA Research Report 17, 1978) and Annual Reports of the Moated Sites Research Group, and (later) the Medieval Settlement Research Group; H E Jean Le Patourel: *The Moated Sites of Yorkshire* (Society of Medieval Archaeology, Monograph no 5 1973);

C C Taylor: *Cambridgeshire* (Hodder and Stoughton 1973); D Wilson: *Moated Sites* (Shire 1985); J P Green: "Moated Haystacks" (*Landscape Archaeology* 4, 1972); Harold Mytum (ed): *Bibliography of Moated Sites* (Moated Sites Research Group 1982 – updated at intervals in Annual Reports).

Siege works

Newark on Trent: The Civil War Siegeworks (HMSO for RCHME, 1964); (London) David Sturdy in *The London Archaeologist 2*, 1975.

Forts

Henry VIII and the development of coastal defence (HMSO 1976); Martin Brice: *Forts and Fortresses* (Facts on File, OUP 1990).

Other Military Works

Martello Towers – M Brice: *op cit.*

Naval Telegraphs – Geoffrey Wilson: *The Old Telegraphs* (Phillimore 1976); T W Holmes: *The Semaphore* (A H Stockwell Ltd 1983).

North Downs Storehouses – Victor Smith: "The London Mobilisation Centres" (*The London Archaeologist 2/10*, 1975)

Pill Boxes – M Brice, *op cit*; *20th-Century Defences in Britain – An Introductory Guide* (CBA 1995)

Public Buildings

Nikolaus Pevsner: *A History of Building Types* (Thames and Hudson 1976) covers Government buildings, town halls, theatres, libraries, museums, hospitals, prisons, hotels, exchanges and banks, warehouses and offices, railway stations, market halls etc, shops and factories; and has a formidable bibliography.

Asa Briggs: *Victorian Cities* (Odhams 1963, Penguin 1968) for Manchester, Leeds, Birmingham, Middlesborough and London.

Prisons – John M Steane: *The Archaeology of Medieval England and Wales* (Croom Helm 1984).

HOSPITALS

Margaret Wade Lebarge: *Women in Medieval Life*

(Hamish Hamilton 1986); F N L Poynter (ed): *The Evolution of Hospitals in Britain* (1964); R M Clay: *The Medieval Hospitals of England* (1909); P H Cullum: *Cremetts and Corrodies: Care of the Poor and Sick at St Leonard's Hospital, York, in the Middle Ages* (University of York, *Borthwick Papers* no 79, 1991); Nicholas Orme and Margaret Webster: *The English Hospital 1070–1570* (1995).

Almshouses

B Bailey: *Almshouses* (Hale 1988); W H Godfrey: *The English Almshouse with Some Account of Its Predecessor, the Medieval Hospital* (Faber 1955); Brian Howson: *Houses of Noble Poverty: A History of the English Almshouse* (Bellevue Books, Sunbury, 1993).

EDUCATION BUILDINGS

Schools

There is much useful background in G M Trevelyan: *English Social History* (Longman 1945). Classic presentations are contained in the work of A F Leach: eg *The Schools of Medieval England* (1915); *English Schools at the Reformation: Winchester College*; and articles on individual schools in eg *Victoria County History* and *Yorkshire Archaeological Journal*. The summary in Foster Watson: *The Old Grammar Schools* (CUP 1916) is still of value. Details of one school and its complex foundation and growth in R C Carrington: *Two Schools* [St Olave's and St Saviour's Grammar School] (St Olave's School, Southwark, 1971). But every school has its history, and some, like Winchester, have many.

Higher Education

For the origins and development of medieval universities, there are brief accounts in Sir Frank Stenton: *Anglo-Saxon England* (OUP 1971 ed); R Fossier (ed): *The Cambridge Illustrated History of the Middle Ages Vol 1, 350–950* (CUP 1989); and a fuller study in J Marenbon: *From the Circle of Alcuin to the School of Auxerre* (CUP 1981). For the curriculum etc, Christopher Brooke, *The Twelfth Century Renaissance* (Thames and Hudson 1969);

for the medieval universities generally, Richard Hunt in Joan Evans (ed): *The Flowering of the Middle Ages* (Thames and Hudson 1966). George Holmes (ed): *The Oxford Illustrated History of Medieval Europe* (OUP 1988), also has stimulating material on education, and a useful bibliography. of the many books on Oxford, Christopher Hobhouse: *Oxford* (Batsford 1939) is still useful. Not only does it deal with the history and architecture, but captures the city and university at the end of an era, enabling the subsequent changes to be put more readily in context. A similarly useful companion to this is John Steegmann's *Cambridge* (Batsford 1940). The latest study is Christopher Brooke and Roger Highfield: *Oxford and Cambridge* (CUP 1988).

The RCHM vols, *The City of Oxford* (HMSO 1939) and *The City of Cambridge* (HMSO 1959, reissued in 2 vols 1988) cover the architecture to 1850 in impressive detail. Cambridge is also covered in a classic study: Robert Willis and John Willis Clark: *The Architectural History of the University of Cambridge* (1886, now reprinted by CUP 1988).

The uniquely complex "federal" university of London is described in Negley Harte: *The University of London 1836–1986* (Athlone Press 1986); and see eg Gordon Huelin: *King's College London 1828–1978* (King's College London 1978).

MUSEUMS AND ART GALLERIES

A S Witlin: *The Museum, its history and its tasks in education* (1949, 1970, 1974); Sir David Wilson (ed): *The Collections of the British Museum* (British Museum Publications 1989).

LIBRARIES

F Wormald and C E Wright (eds): *The English Library Before 1700* (Athlone Press 1958).

THEATRES

The Oxford Companion to the Theatre (OUP 1951, 1983); Simon Tidworth: *Theatres, an illustrated history* (1973).

CINEMAS

Kenneth Hudson: *The Archaeology of the Consumer*

Society (Heinemann 1983); C W Ceram: *The Archaeology of the Cinema* (Thames and Hudson 1965).

AMPHITHEATRES AND STADIA

For the Roman amphitheatre in London discovered in 1983 see *Current Archaeology* 137, 1994.

STATUES AND MEMORIALS

W J Strachan: *Open Air Sculpture in Britain* (1984); Sir Hugh Casson (ed): *Monuments* (Chatto and Windus for the National Benzole Co, 1963). 1983. Lists of the memorials and statues of London are given in Ben Weinreb and Christopher Hibbert (eds): *The London Encyclopaedia* (Macmillan 1983). Fuller treatment (up to its date) in C S Cooper: *Outdoor Monuments of London* (1928), and Godfrey Thompson: *London Statues* (Dent 1971); also Margaret Baker: *London Statues and Monuments* (Shire 1968, 1992). See also Martin Hall: *The Blue Plaque Guide to London Homes* (1976).

The Covenanters' graves and memorials are movingly described in J H Thomson: *The Martyr Graves of Scotland* (ed Matthew Hutchison – Oliphant, Anderson and Ferranti, c 1905). Arthur Byron: *London Statues* (Constable 1981); J Darke: *The Monument Guide to England and Wales* (Macdonald 1991).

Communications and Trade

ROADS AND TRACKS

The most comprehensive recent study, which is indeed indispensable, is Christopher Taylor: *Roads and Tracks of Britain* (Dent 1979). More traditional studies include Hermann Schreiber: *The History of Roads* (Barrie and Rockliff 1961); Geoffrey Boumphrey: *British Roads* (Nelson 1939); Sir William Addison: *The Old Roads of England* (Batsford 1980); Jane Oliver: *The Ancient Roads of England* (Cassell 1936); suggestive chapters in Oliver Rackham: *History of the Countryside* (Dent 1986) and by B P Hindle in Leonard Cantor (ed): *The English Medieval Landscape* (Croom Helm 1982).

Prehistoric

W F Rankine in *Archaeological Newsletter* 4. 4. 1951, 4. 10. 1952; W F Rankine: *The Mesolithic of Southern England* (Surrey Archaeological Soc iety Research Paper 4, 1956); Ian Longworth and John Cherry (eds): *Archaeology in Britain since 1945* (British Museum Publications 1986).

Roman and later

Ordnance Survey: Map of Roman Britain; I D Margary: *Roman Roads in Britain* (Baker, 1973 ed), and I D Margary: *Roman Ways in the Weald* (Phoenix House 1948); The Viatores: *Roman Roads in the South-East Midlands* (1964); B Bury: *A Lost Roman Road – Bath to Poole* (1963); Wilfred Hooper: "The Pilgrims' Way and its supposed Pilgrim Use" (*Surrey Archaeological Collections* 34, 1936); Brian Paul Hindle: *Medieval Roads* (Shire 1982); A Raistrick: *Green Tracks on the Pennines* (Dalesman 1962); A H Allcroft: *Downland Pathways* (Methuen 2nd ed 1924). See also E C Curwen: *Prehistoric Sussex* (Homeland Association, 2nd ed, 1930); J Crofts: *Packhorse, Waggons and Post: Land Carriage and Communications under the Tudors and Stuarts* (Routledge and Kegan Paul 1967).

Monastic roads – B Jennings: *The History of Nidderdale* (Huddersfield, Advertiser Press 1967).

Turnpikes

See summary chapter in Jack Simmons: *Transport* (Studio Vista 1962); Geoffrey Wright: *Turnpike Roads* (Shire).

Minor ways

C Cochrane: *The Lost Roads of Wessex* (David and Charles 1969); Shirley Toulson: *Lost Trade Routes* (Shire 1983).

Droving and Drove Roads

K J Bonser: *The Drovers* (Macmillan 1970); A R B Haldane: *The Drove Roads of Scotland* (Nelson 1952); Fay Godwin and Shirley Toulson: *The Drovers' Roads of Wales* (Wildwood 1977).

River Crossing

Bridges – Eric de Maré: *The Bridges of Britain* (1956); G Bernard Wood: *Bridges in Britain* (Cassell, 1970); and the regional studies of A Jervoise: *The Ancient Bridges of the North [etc] of England*. For the Wey bridges see Derek Renn in *Surrey Archaeological Society Research* vol no 1, 1974.

INLAND WATERWAYS

Rivers

Oliver Rackham: *The History of the Countryside* (Dent 1986); L F Salzman: *Building in England down to 1540* (OUP 1952).

Waterfronts – For waterfronts and river ports, see eg J M Steane: *The Archaeology of Medieval England and Wales* (Croom Helm 1984); Gustav Milne: *The Port of Roman London* (Batsford 1985); John Schofield and Tony Dyson: *Archaeology of the City of London* (Museum of London 1980); G Milne and B Hobley: *Waterfront Archaeology in Britain and Northern Europe* (CBA Research Report 41, 1981); P V Addyman et al: *The Waterfronts of York* (York Archaeological Trust 1988).

Canals

Hugh McKnight: *The Shell Book of Inland Waterways* (David and Charles 1975); P J G Ransom: *The Archaeology of Canals* (World's Work 1980); Charles Hadfield: *British Canals* (David and Charles, 4th ed, 1969) is very valuable. Peter L Smith: *Canal Architecture* (Shire 1986). Charles Hadfield has compiled a series of regional studies, eg *The Canals of the West Midlands* (David and Charles 1966), and has edited a series of studies of individual canals, such as Peter Stevenson: *The Nutbrook Canal, Derbyshire* (David and Charles 1970), or P A L Vine's *London's Lost Route to the Sea* (David and Charles 1965).

RECLAMATION OF WETLANDS

A K Astbury: *The Black Fens* (1958); Dorothy Summers: *The Great Level* (David and Charles 1976); C W Phillips (ed): *The Fenland in Roman Times* (Royal Geographical Society Research Series 6, 1970); Francis Pryor: *Flag Fen* (Batsford/EH 1991); *Current Archaeology* 137, 1994. David Hall and John Coles: *Fenland Survey* (English Heritage Archaeological Report no 1 1994).

Romney Marsh – see Anne Roper: *The Gifts of the Sea – Romney Marsh* (Ashford, Birling, 1984).

Somerset – J M Coles and B J Orme: *Prehistory of the Somerset Levels* (Somerset Levels Project 1980); Bryony and John Coles: *Sweet Track to Glastonbury* (Thames and Hudson 1986). Bryony Coles (ed): *The Wetland Revolution in Prehistory* (Prehistoric Society/Wetland Archaeology Research Project 1992).

The Broads – J M Lambert et al: *The Making of the Broads* (Royal Geographical Society/Murray 1960).

RAILWAYS

The Beginnings

Wagonways – B Baxter: *Stone Blocks and Iron Rails* (David and Charles 1966); A Raistrick: *Industrial Archaeology* (Eyre Methuen 1972, Paladin 1973); Brian Bracegirdle (ed): *The Archaeology of the Industrial Revolution* (Heinemann 1973); P J G Ransom: *The Archaeology of Railways* (World's Work 1981). For the Surrey Iron Railway and other Surrey plateways, see C E Lee in *Transactions of the Newcomen Society* 21, 1941; C E C Townsend in *Transactions of the Newcomen Society* 27, 1958; Bruce E Osborne in *Proceedings of Croydon Natural History and Scientific Society* 17, 1982; and Derek A Bayliss: *Retracing the First Public Railway* (Living History Publications, *Local Guide* no 4, 1985 ed).

General – The range and number of books on railways is vast, and one wonders how it is possible to find new facts to publish. Thus, George Ottley: *Bibliography of British Railway History* (HMSO 1983) includes over 7900 items; this is a reprint of the 1965 edition – but the 1988 supplement brought the items up to 12,956 and they still come out! For the history, I have here drawn heavily on Jack Simmon's excellent account, *The Railways of Britain* (Macmillan, 1986 ed.) which has a notable bibliography. Other key books include P J G Ransom: *The Archaeology of Railways* (World's Work, 1981); Christine Heap and John van Riemsdijk: *The Pre-Grouping Railways* (HMSO for

Science Museum, three parts, 1972, 1980 and 1985); M R Bonavia: *The Four Great Railways* (1980); Richard (Lord) Beeching: *The Reshaping of British Railways* (1963), and *The Development of the Major Railway Trunk Routes* (1965); David Carter: *The Longmoor Military Railway* (David and Charles 1974).

Stations and buildings – C W Meeks: *The Railway Station: an Architectural History* (1957); G Biddle: *Victorian Stations* (David and Charles 1973); Jeffrey Richards and John M Mackenzie: *The Railway Station: A Social History* (OUP 1986); F G Cockman: *Railway Architecture* (Shire).

Relevant periodicals include: *The Railway Magazine* (1897 onwards); *Transactions of the Newcomen Society* (1920 onwards); *The Journal of Transport History* (1953 on); the *Journal of the Railway and Canal Historical Society* (1955 on); the *Industrial Archaeology Review*.

LETTER BOXES

Jean Farrugia: *The Letter Box* (Centaur 1969); Martin Robinson: *Old Letter Boxes* (Shire 1987).

GUILDS AND GUILDHALLS

Ben Weinreb and Christopher Hibbert (eds): *The London Encyclopedia* (Macmillan 1983).

Inns of Court and Inns of Chancery – see *The London Encyclopedia* (Macmillan 1983).

MARKET HALLS

London Markets

See *The London Encyclopedia* (Macmillan 1983).

SHOPS AND SHOPPING

Dorothy Davis: *A History of Shopping* (1966); Alison Adburgham: *Shops and Shopping 1800–1914* (Barrie and Jenkins 1964, 1989); Ursula Priestly and Alayne Fenner: *Shops and Shopkeepers in Norwich 1660–1730* (University of East Anglia 1985); Margaret MacKeith: *Shopping Arcades 1877–1939* (Mansell 1985); Alan Powers: *Shopfronts* (Chatto and Windus 1989); Jonathan Brown and Sadie Ward: *The Village Shop* (Rural Development Commission 1990); Kenneth

Hudson: *The Archaeology of the Consumer Society* (Heineman 1983); Nikolaus Pevsner: *A History of Building Types* (Thames and Hudson 1976). For price fluctuations since 1264, see Oliver Rackham: *The History of the Countryside* (Dent 1986). (Fairs) C Walford: *Fairs, Past and Present* (Elliott Stock 1883).

Markets – also *The London Encyclopedia* (Macmillan 1983) William Addison: *English Fairs and Markets* (1953).

Shop signs

Ambrose Heal: *The Signboards of Old London Shops* (1947) – mainly 17th and 18th centuries; John Ashdown: "The Oil Jar as a London Shop Sign" (*London Archaeologist* 2/7 1974, 2/10 1975).

Inn signs

R F Delderfield: *Introduction to Inn Signs* (David and Charles 1969); Dominic Rotheroe: *London Inn Signs* (Shire); Cadbury Lamb and Gordon Wright: *Discovering Inn Signs* (Shire 1968).

COINS

A useful general introduction is Philip Grierson: *Numismatics* (OUP 1975). See also R A G Carson: *Coins, Ancient, Medieval and Modern* (2nd ed., 1970); H A and P Seaby: *Coins of England and the United Kingdom* (12th ed 1973, but continuing). For the pre-Roman coinage: D F Allen: "The origins of coinage in Britain: a reappraisal" in S S Frere (ed): *Problems of the Iron Age in Southern Britain* (University London Institute of Archaeology Occasional Paper 11, 1961). J R S Whiting: *Trade Tokens* (David and Charles 1971); M Dickinson: *Seventeenth-Century Tokens of the British Isles* (Seaby 1986).

INNS AND HOTELS

There are many books on inns; a still useful one is the National Trust book – Richard Keverne: *Tales of Old Inns* (Collins 1939). Also Peter Clark: *The English Alehouse: a Social History 1200–1830* (Longman 1983); Thomas Burke: *The English Inn* (Jenkins 1930, 1947); W A Pantin: "Medieval Inns" in E M Jope (ed): *Studies in Building History*

(Odhams 1961); Angus McInnes in *The English Town 1660–1760* (Historical Association 1980); A Oswald: *Clay Pipes for the Archaeologist* (BAR 14, 1975).

Hotels – Nikolaus Pevsner: *A History of Building Types* (Thames and Hudson 1976).

SOCIAL CENTRES, CLUBS AND SOCIETIES

Clubs

Anthony Lejeune and Malcolm Lewis: *The Gentlemen's Clubs of London* (Bracken Books 1979, republished by Studio Editions 1984). Several clubs have their own histories, eg The Athenaeum: *Club and Social Life in London 1824–1974* (Heinemann 1975).

Learned societies

Joan Evans: *A History of the Society of Antiquaries* (OUP for Society of Antiquaries 1956).

Crafts

There is a large number of books on rural crafts; useful ones are James Arnold: *The Shell Book of Country Crafts* (John Baker 1968) and John Norwood: *Craftsmen at Work* (John Baker 1977) which gives much fine detail.

Carts and wagons – James Arnold: *The Farm Waggons of England and Wales* (John Baker 1969); John Vince: *Discovering Carts and Wagons* (Shire 1970).

Wheelwrighting – Two classics are George Sturt (George Bourne): *The Wheelwright's Shop* (CUP 1922 ed) and George Ewart Evans: *The Horse in the Furrow* (Faber 1960). See also Jocelyn Bailey: *The Village Wheelwright and Carpenter* (Shire 1975).

Blacksmithing and Horseshoes – Jocelyn Bailey: *The Village Blacksmith* (Shire 1977); Ivan G Sparkes: *Old Horseshoes* (Shire 1976); see also T H McClough: *The Horseshoes of Oakham Castle* (Leicester Museums 1978).

Coopering – K Kilby: *The Village Cooper* (1977); *Charcoal Burning* – D W Kelly: *Charcoal and Charcoal Burning* (1986).

Farm Tools – John Vince: *Old Farm Tools* (1974); Roy Brigden: *Agricultural Hand Tools* (1983).

Thatching – Jacqueline Fearn: *Thatch and Thatching* (Shire 1976); Judy E Nash: *Thatchers and Thatching* (Batsford 1992); M Billet: *Thatching and Thatched Buildings* (Hale, 1988 ed.)

Corn Dollies – M Lambeth: *Discovering Corn Dollies* (Shire).

Dew-ponds – Edward A Martin: *Dew Ponds* (T Werner Laurie c 1910); G and A Hubbard: *Neolithic Dewponds and Cattleways* (Longman 1905, 3rd ed 1916); Ralph Whitlock in *Guardian Weekly* 30 April 1989.

Drystone walling – see under *Building Materials*

Hedge-laying – E Pollard, M D Hooper, N W Moore: *Hedges* (Collins 1974)

Basketry – Dorothy Wright: *The Complete Book of Baskets and Basketry* (David and Charles 1977, 1992).

Gypsy crafts – Brian Vesey-FitzGerald: *Gypsies of Britain* (Chapman and Hall 1944, David and Charles 1973); C H Ward-Jackson and D E Harvey: *The English Gypsy Caravan* (David and Charles 1986 ed); D J Smith: *Discovering Horse-drawn Caravans* (Shire 1981). See also John Vince: *Discovering Carts and Wagons* (Shire 1970).

Coracles – James Hornell: *Water Transport* (CUP 1946, David and Charles 1970).

Books on bygones are relevant also – Gertrude Jekyll: *Old West Surrey* (1904, re-issued by Kohler and Coombes, Dorking 1978); Ann Cripps (ed) *The Countryman Rescuing the Past* (David and Charles 1973); J Geraint Jenkins: *Life and Tradition in Rural Wales* (Dent 1976); there is much valuable material in Marie Hartley and Joan Ingilby: *Life and Tradition in the Yorkshire Dales* (Dent 1968) and *Life in the Moorlands of North-East Yorkshire* (Dent 1972).

Industries

For the industrialisation of Britain see T S Ashton: *The Industrial Revolution 1760–1830* (OUP 1948 and 1962); Dorothy Marshall: *Industrial England 1776–1851* (Routledge and Kegan Paul 1973);

J D Chambers: *The Workshop of the World (1820–1880)* (OUP 1961); G E Mingay: *The Transformation of Britain 1830–1939* (RKP 1986); T K Derry and Trevor J Williams: *A Short History of Technology* (OUP 1960).

TEXTILES

Wool

There are of course numerous accounts of the woollen cloth industry. A full account is E Lipson: *The History of the Woollen and Worsted Industries* (3rd ed., Black 1950). A basic summary is in Chris Aspin: *The Woollen Industry* (Shire 1982). A brief general view is in John Patten: *Pre-Industrial England* (Dawson 1979). Local studies include: for the West of England, Kenneth Hudson: *The Industrial Archaeology of Southern England* (David and Charles 1965); J de L Mann: *The Cloth Industry in the West of England from 1640 to 1880* (1987 ed); Jennifer Tann: *Gloucestershire Woollen Mills* (Augustus Kelly 1967). For Kendal, M Davies-Shiel: *Wool is my Bread* (published by the author 1975) – this gives a simple account of an important centre of the industry to 1575, with lists of the types of cloth made. For West Yorkshire, W B Crump and Gertrude Ghorbal: *History of the Huddersfield Woollen Industry* (Tolson Memorial Museum Handbook IX, 1935) – a solid and valuable account, from which I have drawn heavily. For prehistoric textiles, A S Henshall in *Proceedings of the Prehistoric Society* 16, 1950; John Peter Wild: *Textiles in Archaeology* (Shire 1988); Colum Giles and Ian H Goodall: *Yorkshire Textile Mills, 1770–1930* (HMSO (RCHME and WYAS) 1992); R A Innes: *The Halifax Piece Hall* (Calderdale Museums Service 1975).

Cotton

Chris Aspin: *The Cotton Industry* (Shire 1981); David Smith: *The Industrial Archaeology of the East Midlands* (David and Charles 1965); D Bythel: *The Handloom Weavers: a study in the English cotton industry during the Industrial Revolution* (CUP 1969).

Flax and Linen

Patricia Baines: *Flax and Linen* (Shire 1985); Wallace Clark: *Linen on the Green* (Universities Press, Belfast, 1982); John Butt: *The Industrial Archaeology of Scotland* (David and Charles 1967).

Hemp

Anthony Sanctuary: *Rope, Twine and Net Making* (Shire 1980)

Silk

A very adequate brief account is given by Sarah Bush in *The Silk Industry* (Shire 1987). See also David Smith: *The Industrial Archaeology of the East Midlands* (David and Charles 1965).

Knitting and Lace

Knitting – W Felkin: *A History of the Machine-Wrought Hosiery and Lace Manufactures* (Longman 1867, reprinted David and Charles 1967); F A Wells: *The British Hosiery and Knitwear Industry* (Allen and Unwin 1972 ed.). Marilyn Palmer: *Framework Knitting* (Shire 1984). Houses and Workplaces: *The Framework Knitters of the East Midlands* (Leicestershire Industrial History Society Bulletin 11, 1988). Useful chapter in David Smith: *The Industrial Archaeology of the East Midlands* (David and Charles 1965).

Lace – Jeffery Hopewell: *Pillow Lace and Bobbins* (Shire 1975). Margaret Simeon: *The History of Lace* (Stainer and Bell 1979). *The Story of Nottingham Lace* (Lace Hall, Nottingham, 1988) – brief but useful account. A detailed local study is *Ruddington 120 Years Ago: The Framework Knitters* (Ruddington Local History and Amenity Society, Working Group, no 1, 1971).

There are useful details on all textiles in John Peter Wild: *Textiles in Archaeology* (Shire 1988).

LEATHER

A brief but very adequate and well-illustrated account is June Swann: *Shoemaking* (Shire 1986) – this has a short bibliography. Details of excavated Roman and medieval leather goods will be found in excavation reports and in monographs such as Clare E Allin: *The Medieval Leather Industry of Leicester* (Leicestershire Museums *Archaeological Report* no 3, 1981); S Thomas: *Medieval Footwear from Coventry* (Coventry Museums 1980); F Grew and M de Neergaard: *Shoes and pattens* (HMSO 1988: Medieval finds from excavations in London, 2); or in histories of costume.

POTTERY

Pottery Types

Prehistoric Pottery – any comprehensive book on British archaeology, eg J V S Megan and D D A Simpson: *Introduction to British Prehistory* (Leicester University Press 1979).

Roman Pottery – the following are useful: Vivien G Swan: *Pottery in Roman Britain* (Shire 1975); for coarse ware see Graham Webster (ed): *Romano-British Coarse Pottery, a student's guide*; the chapter in R G Collingwood and Ian Richmond: *The Archaeology of Roman Britain* (1969), with references; J P Gillam: "Types of Roman coarse pottery vessels in Northern Britain" (Archaeological Archive 1957, and separate revised ed Oriel Press, 1968); A Detsicas (ed): *Current Research in Romano-British Coarse Pottery* (CBA Research Report 10, 1973); (Overwey) A J Clark in *Surrey Archaeological Collections* 51, 1950; M A B Lyne and R S Jefferies: *The Alice Holt/Farnham Roman Pottery Industry* (CBA Research Report 30, 1979). Vivien G Swan: *The Pottery Kilns of Roman Britain* (HMSO, RCHM Supplementary Series 5, 1984). For Highgate, Harvey Sheldon in *London Archaeologist* 1, 2 Spring 1969; *London Archaeologist* 2. 1. 1972; for Brockley Hill London *Archaeologist* 7/9 1994. The excavation reports of the York Archaeological Trust (the *Archaeology of York* series) include several containing valuable surveys of pottery: eg Holdsworth: "Selected Pottery Groups AD 650–1780" (*Fascicule* 16/1 1978); Perrin: "Roman Pottery from the Colonia: Skeldergate and Bishophill" (*Fascicule* 16/2 1981); Brooks: "Medieval and Later Pottery from Aldwark and other sites" (*Fascicule* 16/3 1987); Perrin: "Roman Pottery from the Colonia: Tanner Row and

Rougier Street" (*Fascicule* 16/4 1990); Ailsa Mainman: "The Anglo-Scandinavian Pottery from 16–22 Coppergate" (*Fascicule* 16/5 1990); Mainman: "The Pottery from 46–54 Fishergate" (*Fascicule* 16/6 1993); Monaghan: "Roman Pottery from the Fortress: 9 Blake Street" (*Fascicule* 16/7 1993).

Anglo-Saxon Pottery – David M Wilson (ed): *The Archaeology of Anglo-Saxon England* (Methuen 1976, CUP 1981); J N L Myres: *Anglo-Saxon Pottery and the Settlement of England* (Oup 1969); J N L Myres: *Corpus of Anglo-Saxon Pottery of the Pagan Period* (CUP 1977); V I Evison: *A Corpus of Wheel-thrown Pottery in Anglo Saxon Graves* (1979); *Anglo-Saxon Pottery: A Symposium* (CBA Research Report 4, 1959).

Medieval Pottery – S A Moorhouse: "The Medieval Pottery Industry" in D W Crossley (ed): *Medieval Industry* (CBA Research Report 40, 1981) – good bibliography. Organisation of medieval pottery industry, see H E J Le Patourel in *Medieval Archaeology* 12, 1960; for kilns, see section in Helen Clarke: *The Archaeology of Medieval England* (British Museum Publications 1987), or in John M Steane: *The Archaeology of Medieval England and Wales* (Croom Helm 1984). A comprehensive recent survey is M R McCarthy and C M Brooks: *Medieval Pottery in Britain AD900–1600* (Leicester University Press 1988).

Post-Medieval Pottery – Rhoda Edwards: *London Potters 1570–1710* (*Journal of Ceramic History* 6, 1974). For Norfolk House, Lambeth see Brian Bloice in *Post-Medieval Archaeology* 5, 1971). For Platform Wharf, Rotherhithe, see *London Archaeologist* 5, 15 1988.

Post-Roman history and products – Basic books are George Savage: *Pottery Through the Ages* (Penguin 1959) and *Porcelain Through the Ages* (Penguin 1963 ed); W B Honey: *English Pottery and Porcelain* (Black, 6th ed revised by R J Charleston 1969); K J Barton: *Pottery in England* (1975); G A Godden: *British Pottery and Porcelain: an Illustrated Encyclopedia* (Magna, 2nd ed, 1992).

Manufacture – David Sekers: *The Potteries* (Shire 1981).

Pottery-making Techniques

Among very many books on the subject, Bernard Leach: *A Potter's Book* (Faber 1946) remains a classic; also David Outerbridge (ed): *The Potter's Challenge* (Souvenir 1976), with list of museums; Tony Birks: *The Potter's Companion* (Collins 1974); Dora M Billington: *The Technique of Pottery* (Batsford 1962); Kenneth Clark: *Practical Pottery and Ceramics* (Studio Vista 1964); Malcolm Haslam: *Pottery* (Orbis 1972); Jolyon Hofsted: *Pottery* (Pan 1972).

BRICKS AND TILES

Bricks – Norman Davey: *A History of Building Materials* (Phoenix 1961); L S Harley: "A Typology of Brick" (*Journal of the British Archaeological Association* xxxviii, 1974); Nathaniel Lloyd: *A History of English Brickwork* (H G Montgomery 1928); Alec Clifton-Taylor: *English Brickwork* (Ward Lock 1977); P J Drury in D W Crossley: *Medieval Industry* (CBA Research Report 40, 1981); Martin Hammond; *Bricks and Brickmaking* (Shire 1981) for processes and kilns.

Tiles – Elizabeth S Eames: *Medieval Tiles: A Handbook* (British Museum Publications 1968); and *English Tilers* (British Museum Publications 1992).

GLASS

The main lines of glass history are set out in W A Thorpe: *English Glass* (Black, 1961 ed.); E Barrington Haynes: *Glass through the Ages* (Penguin, 1959 ed); Ada Polak: *Glass – its tradition and its makers* (Putnam's, New York, 1975); Dan Klein and Ward Lloyd (eds): *The History of Glass* (Orbis 1984); Roger Dodsworth: *Glass and Glassmaking* (Shire 1982); Eleanor S Godfrey: *The Development of English Glassmaking 1560–1640* (OUP 1975); R J Charleston: *English Glass and the glass used in England, circa 400–1940* (Allen and Unwin 1986). For the early history, Anita Engle: *Ancient Glass in its Context* (Readings in Glass History no 10, 1978); and see Theophilus: *De Diversibus Artibus* (c1110–1140 – new translation by C R Dodwell 1961).

Techniques and Archaeology – Ruth Hurst Vose: *Glass* (The Connoisseur, 1975); F J Terence Maloney: *Glass in the Modern World* (Alders 1967); Susan Frank: *Glass and Archaeology* (Academic Press 1982).

Window Glass – D B Harden in E M Jope (ed): *Studies in Building History* (Odhams 1961). The surveys by D B Harden are also key sources: "Ancient Glass I: Roman" (*Archaeological Journal* cxxvi, 1970); "Ancient Glass III: Post-Roman" (*Archaeological Journal* cxxviii, 1972); "Medieval glass in the west" (*Proceedings of the 8th International Congress on Glass*, 1968); "Anglo-Saxon and Later Medieval Glass in Britain: some Recent Developments" (*Medieval Archaeology* 22, 1978). Also J R Hunter "The medieval glass industry", in D W Crossley (ed): *Medieval Industry* (CBA Research Report 40, 1981).

Specific sites – G H Kenyon: *The Glass Industry of the Weald* (Leicester University Press 1967); Blunden's Wood: E S Wood in *Surrey Archaeological Collections* lxii, 1965 and *Post-Medieval Archaeology* 7, 1973; Knightons: E S Wood in *Surrey Archaeological Collections* lxxiii, 1982; Bagots Park: D W Crossley in *Post-Medieval Archaeology* 1, 1967; Rosedale, D W Crossley and F A Aberg in *Post-Medieval Archaeology* 6, 1972; Gawber, Denis Ashurst in *Post-Medieval Archaeology* 4, 1970. Also Robert J Charleston in *Journal of Glass Studies* 20, 1978; David Crossley: "The Wealden Glass Industry Re-visited" (*Industrial Archaeology Review* XVII, 1, 1994).

Coloured Glass – R G Newton in *Glass Technology* 19, 1978; 20, 1980, and 25, 1984.

Stained Glass – Catherine Brisac: *A Thousand Years of Stained Glass* (Macdonald 1986); Peter Gibson: *The stained and painted glass of York Minster* (Jarrold 1979); John Haines: *Discovering Stained Glass* (Shire 1968); Painton Cowan: *Rose Windows* (Thames and Hudson 1979).

Craft Glass – G Bernard Hughes: *English, Scottish and Irish Table Glass* (Bramhall House, New York, 1956); D B Harden et al: *Masterpieces of Glass* (British Museum 1980, re-presented by Robert J Charleston: *Masterpieces of Glass* (Harry N

Abrams, New York, for Corning Museum of Glass, 1980); Hugh Tait: *The Golden Age of Venetian Glass* (British Museum 1979); Geoffrey Beard: *Modern Glass* (Studio Vista/Dutton 1968); *New Glass* (Corning Museum, New York, 1979); Ray Flavell and Claude Smale: *Studio Glassmaking* (Van Nostrand Reinhold, New York 1974).

A useful handlist of societies, museums and publications is in Brigit Harry: *Glass* (BBC 1985)

QUARRIES

Useful information about quarries in relation to the geology will be found in the British Regional Geology series of the Geological Survey and Museum, eg *The Wealden District* (HMSO 1965).

General – Arthur Raistrick: *Industrial Archaeology* (Eyre Methuen 1972, Paladin 1973); Peter H Stanier: *Quarries and Quarrying* (Shire 1985).

Specific aspects – N Bezzant: *Out of the Rock* (Heinemann 1980) – Bath and Portland; J Lindsay: *A History of the North Wales Slate Industry* (David and Charles 1974); Merfyn Williams: *The Slate Industry* (Shire); A J Richards: *Slate Quarrying in Wales* (Carreg Gwalch 1995); Paul W Sowan: "Firestone and hearthstone mines in the upper Greensand of east Surrey" (*Proceedings of the Geological Association* 86 1975); M A Aston: *Stonesfield Slate* (Oxfordshire Museum Services Publication no 5, 1974). There is a good account of the Sussex flint mines in E Cecil Curwen: *Prehistoric Sussex* (Homeland Association 1930). For Grimes Graves see G de G Sieveking in Harriet Crawford (ed): *Subterranean Britain* (Baker 1979); R Mercer: *Grimes Graves, Norfolk, Excavations 1971–72* (HMSO 1981); and technical details in *Proceedings of the Prehistoric Society* 39, 1973. For stone axes see T H McK Clough and W A Cummins (eds): *Stone Axe Studies* (CBA Research Report 23, 1979); and for details of the petrological grouping and distribution of the axes see several reports in *Proceedings of the Prehistoric Society*, eg vols 17 (1951), 28 (1962), 38 (1972), 39 (1973), 40 (1974); for general comments see also eg J V S Megaw and D D A Simpson: *Introduction to British*

Prehistory (Leicester University Press 1979); Richard Bradley: *The social foundations of prehistoric Britain* (Longman 1984). For Roman quarries see J Collingwood Bruce (ed Charles Daniels): *Handbook to the Roman Wall* (Newcastle, Harold Hill 1978); Stuart Needham and Mark G Macklin: *Alluvial Archaeology in Britain* (Oxbow Monograph 27, 1992).

COAL

The geology of coal, and a description of the industry, will be found in Sir Dudley Stamp and S H Beaver: *The British Isles* (Longman 1963 and later eds). For the archaeology see eg Arthur Raistrick: *Industrial Archaeology* (Eyre Methuen 1972, Paladin 1973); Brian Bracegirdle (ed): *The Archaeology of the Industrial Revolution* (Heinemann 1973); Harriet Crawford (ed): *Subterranean Britain* (Baker 1979). Information on 18th- and 19th-century methods, equipment and economics is given in T J Taylor: *The Archaeology of the Coal Trade* (1858, reprinted 1971 by F Gresham, Newcastle). *Welsh Coal Mines* (National Museum of Wales 1976) gives a remarkable collection of photographs of mines and mining.

Wine and Coal Posts – Maurice Bawtree: "The City of London Coal Duties and their Boundary Marks" (*London Archaeologist* 1/2 Spring 1969).

TIN

H Harris: *The Industrial Archaeology of Dartmoor* (David and Charles 1968); Susan Pearce: *The Archaeology of South-West Britain* (Collins 1981); T A P Greeves in D W Crossley, (ed): *Medieval Industry* (CBA Research Report 40, 1981), and Tom Greeves in *Devon Archaeology* no 3, 1985. The 19th- and 20th-century industry is usefully introduced in R C Atkinson: *Tin and Tin Mining* (Shire 1985); also Bryan Earl: *Cornish Mining* (D Bradford Barton 1968) – tin and copper; D B Barton: *A History of Tin Mining and Smelting in Cornwall* (1989 ed).

LEAD

See books on industrial archaeology.

Early phases – R F Tylecote: *Metallurgy in*

Archaeology (Arnold 1962), and Harriet Crawford (ed): *Subterranean Britain* (Baker 1979).

London Lead Company – A Raistrick: *Quakers in Science and Industry* (Bannisdale 1950, new ed David and Charles 1968).

Local fields – A Raistrick: *Lead Mining in the Yorkshire Dales* (Dalesman 1972), or A Raistrick and B Jennings: *A History of Lead Mining in the Pennines* (Longman 1965). Lynn Willies: *Lead and Leadmining* (Shire 1982) has a useful bibliography and note on museums.

COPPER

R F Tylecote: *Metallurgy in Archaeology* (Arnold 1962); H Hamilton: *The English Copper and Brass Industry to 1800* (Longman 1926); T K Derry and Trevor I Williams: *A Short History of Technology* (OUP 1960); Harriet Crawford (ed): *Subterranean Britain* (Baker 1979); C J Williams: *Great Orme Mines* (Northern Mine Research Society, *British Mining* 52, 1995).

SILVER

R F Tylecote: *Metallurgy in Archaeology* (Arnold 1962).

GOLD

R F Tylecote: *Metallurgy in Archaeology* (Arnold 1962).

IRON AND STEEL

General – H R Schubert: *History of the British Iron and Steel Industry* (RKP 1957); R F Tylecote: *Metallurgy in Archaeology* (Arnold 1962), and *The Prehistory of Metallurgy in the British Isles* (Institute of Metals 1986).

18th Century – Arthur Raistrick: *Dynasty of Ironfounders* [the Darbys] (David and Charles 1970). W K V Gale: *Ironworking* (Shire 1981) – useful short account.

Wealden Iron Industry – The pioneer work on this is Ernest Straker: *Wealden Iron* (1931); this has been brought up to date in a masterly survey by H F Cleere and D W Crossley: *The Iron Industry of the Weald* (Leicester University Press 1985, revised ed Merton Priory Press 1995). A practical summary

is B K Herbert: *The Fieldwalker's Guide and an Introduction to the Iron Industries of the Weald* (1985, through the Wealden Iron Research Group, which publishes a *Bulletin*, and is the focus of these studies). For bloomery sites in the Weald, C F Tebbutt in *Sussex Archaeological Collections* 119, 1981. Philip Riden: *A Gazetteer of Charcoal-fired Blast Furnaces in Great Britain in use since 1660* (published by the author, University College, Cardiff, 1987).

Uses of Iron – Two books by Raymond Lister give useful accounts: *Decorative Wrought Ironwork in Great Britain* (Bell 1957), and *Decorative Cast Ironwork in Great Britain* (Bell 1960); the latter also gives a detailed account of the moulding and casting processes. A valuable local study is Amina Chatwin: *Cheltenham's Ornamental Ironwork* (1975). For an earlier stage, S B Hamilton: "The Structural Use of Iron in Antiquity" (*Transactions of the Newcomen Society* XXXI, 1957–58 and 1958–59).

Street furniture – Henry Aaron: *Street Furniture* (Shire 1980, brief, with no bibliography); Geoffrey Warren: *Vanishing Street Furniture* (David and Charles 1978); Henry Aaron: *Pillar to Post* (Warne 1982). John Vince: *Fire-Marks* (Shire 1973); Philip Davies: *Troughs and Drinking Fountains* (Chatto and Windus 1989). For horseshoes: Gordon Ward (Hull Museum Publications no 205, 1939); R W Murray: "Dating Old English Horseshoes" (*Journal of the British Archaeological Association* 3 series II, 1937); Ivan G Sparkes: *Old Horseshoes* (Shire 1976).

Histories of technology and books on industrial archaeology should also be consulted – eg T K Derry and Trevor I Williams: *A Short History of Technology* (OUP 1960). Also L T C Rolt: *Victorian Engineering* (Penguin 1970), and the chapter on Iron and Steel by W K V Gale in Brian Bracegirdle, (ed): *The Archaeology of the Industrial Revolution* (Heinemann 1973); Hugh Bodey: *Nailmaking* (Shire 1983); Peter Smithurst: *The Cutlery Industry* (Shire 1987); D W Kelley: *Charcoal and Charcoal-Burning* (Shire 1986); Lyn Armstrong: *Wood Colliers and Charcoal Burning* (Weald and Down-

land Museum); Catherine Clark: *Ironbridge Gorge* (Batsford/EH 1993).

SALT AND SALTWAYS

Information on salt-making is scattered in local journals, and in books on industrial and period archaeology, eg the brief account in John M Steane: *The Archaeology of Medieval England and Wales*. Useful introductions are P L Gouletquer: "The Development of Salt Making in Prehistoric Europe" (*Essex Journal* 1974); J Nenquin: *Salt: A study in Economic Prehistory* (de Tempel, Bruges, 1961).

LIME

Richard Williams: *Limekilns and Limeburning* (Shire 1989); R A Collins: "Chalk Quarrying in Surrey" (*Surrey Archaeological Collections* 66, 1969); K W E Gravett and E S Wood: "Merstham Limeworks" (*Surrey Archaeological Collections* 64, 1967); D J Robinson and R V Cooke in *Surrey Archaeological Collections* 59, 1962; Peter H Stanier: "Dorset Limekilns: a first survey" (*Proceedings Dorset Natural History and Archaeological Society* 115, 1993) – information on more than 300 sites.

MILLING

C P Skilton: *British Watermills and Windmills* (Collins 1947); Leslie Syson: *British Watermills* (1982 ed); P Wenham: *Watermills* (Hale 1989); Rex Wailes: *The English Windmill* (Routledge Kegan Paul 1954 and 1968); John Reynolds: *Windmills and Watermills* (Hugh Evelyn 1970); R J Brown: *Windmills of England* (Hale 1976); Rex Wailes: *Tide Mills*, parts I and II (SPAB); also, M A Weaver: *The Tide Mill*, Woodbridge (Friends of WTM 1974); David Luckhurst: *Monastic Watermills* (SPAB); Paul N Wilson: *Watermills with Horizontal Wheels* (SPAB 1960); Hugo Brunner and J Kenneth Major: *Water Raising by Animal Power* (1972, offprint from *Industrial Archaeology*); Anne and John K Harrison: "The Horse Wheel in North Yorkshire" (*Industrial Archaeology* 10, 1973); Brian Flint: *Windmills of East Anglia* (Pawsey, Ipswich 1973) – lists 64 mills in Norfolk, Suffolk, Cambridgeshire and Essex;

Rex Wailes' site guide to *Saxstead Mill* will be found helpful; Rex Wailes: "Horizontal windmills" (*Transactions of the Newcomen Society* XL 1967–8); John Vince: *Discovering Watermills* (Shire). Another helpful local book, geared to and issued by Haxted Mill, Edenbridge (Sx), is C E Woodrow, B K Herbert and C Smart: *A History of Water Mills, the Wealden Iron Industry and Geology of the South-East* (1979, 1987).

PAPERMAKING

R L Hills: *Papermaking in Britain 1488–1988* (Athlone Press 1988); D C Coleman: *The British Paper Industry 1495–1860* (OUP 1958); A H Shorter: *Paper Making In the British Isles* (David and Charles 1971); A and G Crocker: *Catteshall Mill* (Surrey Archaeological Society, Guildford 1981); Alan Crocker: *Paper Mills of the Tillingbourne* (Tabard Press, Oxshott, 1988); Alan Crocker and Martin Kane: *The Diaries of James Simmons* (Tabard Press, Oxshott 1990). There is a useful article on the Paper Mills of Surrey by Alan Crocker in *Surrey History* IV/1, 1990).

GUNPOWDER

Glenys Crocker: *Gunpowder Mills Gazetteer* (Society for the Protection of Ancient Buildings, Wind and Watermill Section, Occasional Publication no 2, 1988) – with bibliography.

Chilworth – Glenys Crocker: *Chilworth Gunpowder* (Guildford, Surrey Industrial History Group, 1984).

Faversham – A Percival: *The Faversham Gunpowder Industry and its Development* (Faversham Society, 1967, 3rd ed 1986).

Industrial Archaeology

An invaluable overview is T K Derry and Trevor I Williams: *A Short History of Technology* (OUP 1960). Of the many books devoted to industrial archaeology, three classics are: Kenneth Hudson: *Industrial Archaeology* (John Baker 1963); R A Buchanan: *Industrial Archaeology in Britain* (Penguin 1972); Arthur Raistrick: *Industrial Archaeology* (Eyre Methuen 1972 and Paladin 1973); also Neil Cossons: *The BP Book of Industrial Archaeology* (David and Charles 1975, 1993). The practical aspects are covered in J Kenneth Major: *Fieldwork in Industrial Archaeology* (Batsford 1975). Other general studies include: Brian Bracegirdle: *The Archaeology of the Industrial Revolution* (Heinemann 1973); Barrie Trinder: *The Making of the Industrial Landscape* (Dent 1982); Anthony Burton: *Industrial Archaeological Sites of Britain* (Weidenfeld and Nicolson 1977). A useful summary of a fast-changing scene is Kenneth Hudson: *The Archaeology of the Consumer Society* (Heinemann 1983).

Most counties have published lists of industrial sites and monuments, which should be sought in local libraries. A rather more elaborate example is Aubrey Wilson: *London's Industrial Heritage* (David and Charles 1967). The regional series published by David and Charles is indispensable for a broad overview: eg David Smith: *The Industrial Archaeology of the East Midlands* (1965); John Butt: *The Industrial Archaeology of Scotland* (1967).

Scotland – see L M Thoms (ed): "The Archaeology of Industrial Scotland" (*Scottish Archaeological Forum* 8 1977); and G D Hay and G P Stell: *Monuments of Industry* (HMSO for RCHM Scot 1986).

Wales – see C S Briggs (ed): *Welsh Industrial Heritage: a review* (CBA Research Report 79, 1992).

Many of the local groups issue informative newsletters, such as that of the Surrey Industrial History Group. The periodical *Industrial Archaeology* pioneered this field. The Association for Industrial Archaeology publishes the valuable *Industrial Archaeology Review*, as well as the quarterly *Industrial Archaeology News*. Specialised aspects are covered in the publications of the Newcomen Society, the Railway and Canal Historical Society, the Wind and Watermill group of the Society for the Protection of Ancient Buildings, among others.

Public Utilities and Other Industries

A brief account of public services is given in R A Buchanan: *Industrial Archaeology in Britain* (Penguin 1972). Kenneth Hudson's *The Archaeology of the Consumer Society* (Heinemann 1983) is a useful summary of a rapidly changing area. This also gives a brief bibliography of books on individual industries,

WATER

Ben Weinreb and Christopher Hibbert: *The London Encyclopedia* (Macmillan 1983) is useful for the New River and Bazalgette's sewerage system. For the latter see *Proceedings of the Institution of Civil Engineers* 24 (1864/65) and 54 (1877/78). For sanitation, L Wright: *Clean and Decent* (RKP 1960); Dorothy Marshall: *Industrial England 1776–1851* (RKP 1973).

Roman Water Supplies – John Wacher: *The Towns of Roman Britain* (Batsford 1975, 1995).

GAS

There is a useful article on gasholders by Marcus Binney in the *Independent Magazine*, 6 April 1991

ELECTRICITY

W T O'Dea: *The Social History of Lighting* (Macmillan 1958); Francis Haveron: *The Brilliant Ray* (Godalming Electricity Centenary Celebrations Committee, 1981).

POSTS AND TELEPHONES

G Stamp: *Telephone Boxes* (Chatto 1989).

The Coast

Keith Muckelroy: *Maritime Archaeology* (CUP 1978); F H Thomson (ed): "Archaeology and Coastal Change" (*Society of Antiquaries Occasional Paper* 1, 1980). See also the National Maritime Museum's publications.

Ships

George F Bass (ed): *A History of Seafaring* (Thames and Hudson 1972); James Hornell: *Water Transport* (David and Charles 1970); J du Platt Taylor and H Cleere: *Roman Shipping and Trade* (CBA Research Report no 24); Peter Marsden: *Ships of the Port of London, First to Eleventh Centuries* AD (English Heritage 1995) – this also covers the development of the port. Gillian Hutchinson: *Medieval Ships and Shipping* (Leicester University Press 1994) – all aspects of water transport for Britain 1066–1500); Christer Westerdahl (ed): *Crossroads in Ancient Shipbuilding* (Oxbow Monograph 40, 1994) – also deals with maritime archaeology.

Ports

Gordon Jackson: *The History and Archaeology of Ports* (World's Work, Kingswood 1983) – has a useful bibliography. Gustav Milne: *The Port of Roman London* (Batsford 1985); J Pudney: *London's Docks* (1975); R D Brown: *The Port of London* (1978); G Milne and B Hobley (eds): *Waterfront Archaeology in Britain and Northern Europe* (BAR 1981).

Fishing

Good, Jones and Ponsford: *Waterfront Archaeology* (CBA Research Report 74); Michael Aston (ed): *Medieval Fish, Fisheries and Fishponds in England* (BAR 182, 1988); Edward Roberts: "The Bishop of Winchester's Fishponds in Hampshire", 1150–1400 (*Proceedings of the Hampshire Field Club* 42, 1986); the Welsh Folk Museum, St Fagan's, issues a useful handbook on fishing boats and devices.

Lighthouses

D B Hague and R Christie: *Lighthouses, their Architecture, History and Archaeology* (Gomer 1975).

Rescue Archaeology

Influential pioneering works in this field were *A Matter of Time* (HMSO for RCHME 1960) – threats to river gravels; C M Heighway: *The Erosion of History* (CBA 1972); Martin Biddle and Daphne Hudson with Carolyn Heighway: *The Future of London's Past* (RESCUE 1973); Philip A Rahtz (ed): *Rescue Archaeology* (Penguin 1974). More recently, Martin Carver: *Underneath English Towns* (Batsford 1987): Harold Mytum and Karen Waugh (eds): *Rescue Archaeology – What's Next?* (University of York, Department of Archaeology, Monograph 6, 1987); very relevant is John Hunter and Ian Ralston (eds): *Archaeological Resource Management in the UK* (Alan Sutton/Institute of Field Archaeologists 1993). RESCUE and other bodies keep a close watch on threats to archaeological and historic sites, and publish reports and surveys in their newsletters or journals. Periodicals such as *Current Archaeology, The London Archaeologist, Interim* (York), and *Antiquity*, are also concerned with rescue archaeology, both urban and rural. *The Field Archaeologist* (published by the Institute of Field Archaeologists) reports new administrative and legal developments, as does *RESCUE News* (RESCUE). The source of recent changes is *Planning Policy Guidance Note* (PPG16), *Archaeology and Planning* (DoE1990), and a general explanation of the changes is in *Exploring our Past* (HBMCE (EH) 1991). The current legal situation is summarised in Paul Spoerry: *Archaeology and Legislation in Britain* (RESCUE 1991); also *Rescuing the Historic Environment* (RESCUE 1994). Martin Biddle: *What Future for British Archaeology?* (Oxbow Lecture no 1, Oxbow Books, OUP 1994) – destructiveness of piling.

Illustrations and Sources

In the course of preparing the illustrations for this book a great many sources were consulted, including material contained in the archives of specialised bodies such as the Museum of English Rural Life, as well as a wide variety of books. Grateful acknowledgement is made to these various and multiple sources here. Photographs or notes taken by the author or illustrator are indicated by the initials: ESW and RN.

MAPS

Map 1 The geological structure of Britain (Richard Fortey: *The Hidden Landscape* (Cape 1993/ ESW notes).

Map 2 Geology of the Weald (HMSO for the Institute of Geological Sciences, 1965 (Crown copyright), but simplified in the light of the W&D *Guide*, 1992).

Map 3 Sources of minerals in Britain (ESW).

Map 4 Anglo-Saxon and Celtic kingdoms and peoples in the 6th century AD (Kenneth Cameron: *English Placenames*, Batsford 1961 among others).

Map 5 The midland system of open fields (Leonard Cantor: *The Changing English Countryside 1400–1700*, RKP, 1987).

Map 6 English farming regions, 1640–1750 (Joan Thirsk: *England's Agricultural Regions and Agrarian History, 1550–1750*, Macmillan 1987).

Map 7 Enclosures of common fields by Act of Parliament (G Slater: *English Peasantry*, Constable, 1907/ MERL).

Map 8 The territorial divisions of Roman Britain (Sheppard Frere: *Britannia*, Routledge and Kegan Paul, 1987).

Map 9 Roman towns in southern Britain in Thiessen polygons (Ian Hodder in Andrew Sherratt (ed): *Cambridge Encyclopaedia of Archaeology*, CUP, 1980).

Map 10 Burghal Hidage towns and forts, AD 890–930 (Martin Biddle in David Wilson: *The Archaeology of Anglo-Saxon England*, Methuen 1976).

Map 11 Anglo-Saxon kingdoms in *c* AD900, with the Danelaw (Kenneth Cameron: *English Placenames*, Batsford, 1961/ *The Vikings in England*, Anglo-Danish Viking Project, 1981).

Map 12 The sources of building materials: walling (John and Jane Penoyre: *Houses in the Landscape*, Faber 1978)

Map 13 The sources of building materials: roofing (John and Jane Penoyre: *Houses in the Landscape*, Faber 1978).

Map 14 The Civil War fortifications of Newark-on-Trent (*Newark-on-Trent: the Civil War Siege Works*, HMSO 1964).

Map 15 Sir Joseph Bazalgette's sewers and embankments of London (*Proceedings of the Institution of Civil Engineers* vols 24 (1864–5) and 54 (1877–8), by courtesy of the Institution of Civil Engineers).

GRAPHS

Graphs 1–4 Climate history (H H Lamb: *Climate History and the Modern World*, Methuen, 1982).

ILLUSTRATIONS

1 The "Parallel Roads of Glenroy" (Eric Wood: *Field Guide to Archaeology in Britain*, Collins 1963/ Crown copyright).

2 Glacial river terraces (ESW notes).

3 A fair on the frozen Thames, 1683–4 (Sir Walter Bezant: *London in the 18th Century*, vol 6, 1903, from an old print).

4 Coppicing (Oliver Rackham: *A History of the Countryside*, Dent 1986).

5 Pollarding (Oliver Rackham: *A History of the Countryside*, Dent 1986).

6 Oriental porcelain (G A Godden: *Oriental Export Market Porcelain*, Granada 1979)

7 The origins of cultivated wheat (*Cambridge Encyclopaedia of Archaeology*, CUP, 1980).

8 A bow-ard (G E Fussell: *Farming Techniques from Prehistoric to Modern Times*, Pergamon 1966).

9 Threshing (MERL).

10 Prehistoric and Romano-British fields (P J Fowler: *The Farming of Prehistoric Britain*, CUP 1981).

11 Medieval cultivation terraces – Thorpe West Field (NY) (Arthur Raistrick: *The Pennine Dales*, Eyre and Spottiswoode, 1968).

12 Enclosure fields (Arthur Raistrick: *The Pennine Dales*, Eyre and Spottiswoode 1968).

13 Hedge-laying (E Pollard, M D Hooper, N W Moore: *Hedges*, Collins 1978/ *Hedging*, British Trust for Conservation Volunteers).

14 Drystone walling (Lawrence Garner: *Drystone Walls*, Shire 1984).

15 A sheep-creep (Arthur Raistrick).

16 A watermeadow (MERL).

17 A caschrom (G E Fussell: *The Farmer's Tools, AD 1500–1900*, Andrew Melrose 1952, Orbis 1981).

18 A Kentish turnwrist-plough (RN).

19 A seed-drill (MERL).

20 A threshing machine (ESW).

21 A Fordson tractor (MERL).

22 A horse gin (Pyne: *Microcosm*, 1808).

23 A field barn (M Hartley and J Ingilby: *Life and Tradition in the Yorkshire Dales*, Dent 1968).

24 A brick granary on staddles (Joy Peach in *Hampshire*, September 1992).

25 A wooden granary on staddles (ESW).

26 A pound – Dorking (Sy) (ESW).

27–9 Beeboles: pointed; round-headed; square-topped (Eva Crane: *The Archaeology of Beekeeping*, Duckworth 1983).

30 Probably the oldest grain silo in England (Nigel Harvey: *The Industrial Archaeology of Farming*, Batsford 1980).

31 Model farm (MERL/Nigel Harvey: *The Industrial Archaeology of Farming*, Batsford 1980).

32 The first concrete farm building (Nigel Harvey: *The Industrial Archaeology of Farming*, Batsford 1980).

33 Oasts (MERL).

34 Maltings (ESW).

35–6 Exterior and interior of dovecote – Kinwarton (Ww) (Robin Felden and Rosemary Joekes (eds): *The National Trust Guide*, Cape 1973, 1980 ed).

37 A special Scottish type of "doocot" ((ESW).

38–9 Village plan elements: 1 and 2 (Brian Roberts: *The Making of the English Village*, Longman 1987).

40 The radial type of village – Beaumont (from a map of 1867 in Brian Roberts: *The Making of the English Village*, Longman 1987).

41 A very basic form of village – Wasdale Head (Cu) (from a map of 1862 in Brian Roberts: *The Making of the English Village*, Longman 1987).

42 Agglomerated village – Braithwaite (Cu) (from a map of 1866 in Brian Roberts: *The Making of the English Village*, Longman 1987).

43 Agglomerated village – Cardington (Sp) (from a map of 1883 in Brian Roberts: *The Making of the English Village*, Longman 1987).

44 Basic medieval village (Brian Roberts: *Village Plans*, Shire 1982).

45 A German Rundling (from a map of 1843 in Brian Roberts: *The Making of the English Village*, Longman 1987).

46 A regular two-row village – Appleton-le-Moors (NY) (from a map of 1895 in Brian Roberts: *The Making of the English Village*, Longman 1987).

47 A regular two-row street green village – Middridge (Du) (from a map of c 1844 in Brian Roberts: *The Making of the English Village*, Longman 1987).

48 Swaffham Bulbeck (Ca) (Trevor Rowley: *Villages in the Landscape*, Dent 1978).

49 A regular grid village – Aberchirder (Ba) (from a map of 1868 in Brian Roberts: *The Making of the English Village*, Longman 1987).

50 Cottenham (Ca) (Christopher Taylor: *Village and Farmstead*, George Philip 1983).

51 Pockley (NY) – the early medieval village (Christopher Taylor: *Village and Farmstead*, George Philip 1983).

52 Pockley (NY) – the modern village (Christopher Taylor: *Village and Farmstead*, George Philip 1983).

53 A medieval deserted village from the air (Trevor Rowley and John Wood: *Deserted Villages*, Shire 1982).

54 A decoy pond (Eric Wood: *Field Guide to Archaeology in Britain*, Collins 1963).

55 Roman garden at the palace at Fishbourne (Sx) (Judges of Hastings, postcard).

56 A medieval garden (13th century) recreated by Sylvia Landsberg in 1986 at Winchester Castle (Winchester Tourist Information Centre postcard/ ESW).

57 A garden in the style of *c* 1600, recreated at Basing House (Ha) by Elizabeth Banks 1989 (ESW).

58 The gardens of Westbury Court (Gl) (from an old print in Miles Hadfield: *The English Landscape Garden*, Shire 1977).

59 A ha-ha – Stowe (Bc) (ESW).

60 "Chinese" bridge, Painshill (Sy) (ESW).

61 "Capability" Brown's park layout for Packington (Ww) (from an old plan in Richard Bisgrove: *The National Trust Book of the English Garden*, Penguin 1992).

62 Greenhouse, Syon House (Ian Nairn: *Nairn's London*, Penguin 1966).

63 People's Park, Halifax (photograph, Calderdale libraries).

64 Plan of an Edwin Lutyens–Gertrude Jekyll garden, Folly Farm, Sulhamstead (Bk) (David Ottewill: *The Edwardian Garden*, Yale University Press 1989).

65 A formal Elizabethan garden – New College, Oxford (M Batey: *The Historic Gardens of Oxford and Cambridge*, from an old print).

66 Palladian Bridge, Stowe (Bc) (ESW).

67 Gilbert White's ha-ha at the Wakes, Selborne (Ha), 1761 (ESW).

68–9 Crinkle-crankle, view and plan (ESW).

70 Brighton Pavilion, 1815–22 (Keith Spence: *The Companion Guide to Kent and Sussex*, Hodder and Stoughton 1964).

71 The Pineapple, Dunmore Park (Sg), 1761 (Gwyn Headley and Wim Meulencamp: *Follies*, Cape 1986).

72 A maze of the Chartres type (*The Caerdroia Field Guide* 1987).

73 Plan of a labyrinth (*The Caerdroia Field Guide* 1987).

74 Palm House, Kew, 1844–8 (Nikolaus Pevsner: *A History of Building Types*, Thames and Hudson 1976).

75 Roman and medieval Lincoln (City of Lincoln Archaeological Service).

76 A Roman auxiliary fort – Chesters, on Hadrian's Wall (Nd) (R G Collingwood and Ian Richmond: *The Archaeology of Roman Britain*, Methuen 1969).

77 The Roman fort at Vindolanda (Nd) (Guy de la Bédoyère: *Roman Towns in Britain*, EH/Batsford 1992).

78 A Roman basilica and forum (Guy de la Bédoyère: *Roman Towns in Britain*, EH/Batsford 1992).

79 Plan of Silchester (Ha) (George C Boon: *The Roman Town Calleva Atrebatum at Silchester*, Calleva Museum 1972).

80 Plan of a Roman town reoccupied later – Chichester (*Official Guide* 1972).

81 Late Anglo-Saxon Winchester with the underlying Roman street grid (Colin Platt: *The English Medieval Town*, Secker and Warburg 1976).

82 A late Saxon *burh* – Wallingford (Ox) (Jeremy Haslam ed: *Anglo-Saxon Towns*, Phillimore 1984).

83 Medieval planted town, showing burgage plots – Wickham (Ha) (OS map 1:10560, SU51SE 1968/ with *Hampshire's Heritage*, Hampshire CC 1984).

84 New Winchelsea (Sx) as originally laid out (H Lovegrove: *Official Guide* 1973).

85 A medieval street – Low Petergate, York (*York, Historic Buildings in the Central Area*, HMSO for RCHME 1981).

86 A medieval building scene (John Harvey: *The Master Builders*, Thames and Hudson 1964).

87 Masons' marks (John Harvey: *The Master Builders*, Thames and Hudson 1964/ R O C Spring *Mason's Marks of Salisbury Cathedral*/ Fds of Salisbury Cathedral 1974/*Mason's Marks*: Lincs Old Churches Trust 1973).

88 Stonemason, Lincoln Cathedral (RN)

89 Carving a mason's mark ("banker's mark") (RN).

90 Sheela-na-gig – Kilpeck (He) (Anthony Weir and James Jerman: *Images of Lust*, Batsford 1986).

91 Galleting (garneting) in a wall – Dunsfold church (Sy) (ESW).

92 Common types of brickwork bonds (Norman Davey: *A History of Building Materials*, Phoenix House 1961).

93 17th-century ornamental brickwork – Godalming (Sy) (ESW).

94 Pargeting – Newport (Ex) (*Essex Homes 1066–1850*, Essex CC, Essex Record Office Publications no 30 1978).

95 Thatching with longstraw (MERL).

96 Coade stone on a doorway (J Summerson: *Georgian London*, Penguin 1945, 1962).

97 A 17th-century open fireplace (Marie Hartley and Joan Ingilby: *Life and Tradition in the Yorkshire Dales*, Dent 1968/ Gertrude Jekyll: *Old West Surrey* 1904; Kohler and Coombes, reprint 1978).

98 Tudor chimneys (HMSO postcard).

99 Adam style doorway (Francis W Steer: *A Selection of Chichester Doorways*, Chichester City Council, The Chichester Papers no 18).

100 Georgian doorcase – High Petergate, York, *c* 1779 (*York, Historic Buildings in the Central Area*, HMSO for RCHME 1981).

101 Box frame house construction (R W Brunskill: *Houses*, Collins 1982).

102 Cruck construction (Richard Harris: *Discovering Timber-framed Buildings*, Shire 1978).

103 Structure of a roof-truss in box-frame construction (Richard Harris: *Discovering Timber-framed Buildings*, Shire 1978).

104 Sstructure of jetties (Richard Harris: *Discovering Timber-Framed Buildings*, Shire 1978).

105 Roof-truss (Margaret Wood: *The English Medieval House*, Bracken Books 1965).

106 Plan of the neolithic village at Skara Brae (Or) (adapted from V Gordon Childe/ *Official Guide*, HMSO 1950.

107 Interior of Hut 7, Skara Brae (*Official Guide*, HMSO 1950).

108 Framework of a prehistoric round house (Peter J Reynolds: *The Iron-Age Farm*, BM Publications 1979).

109 The Pimperne house reconstructed

(Peter J Reynolds: *The Iron-Age Farm*, BM Publications 1979).

110–11 A broch and its associated village – Gurness (Or), plan and view (*Ancient Monuments of Orkney*, HMSO 1978).

112 The broch of Mousa (Zd) (Noel Fojut: *Guide to Prehistoric Shetland*, Shetland Times Ltd 1981).

113 Roman hypocaust system – Fishbourne (Frith, postcard).

114–16 The three types of Roman villas (A L F Rivet (ed): *The Roman Villa in Britain*, RKP 1969).

117 The facade of a Roman aisled building (from excavated evidence/ Anthony King in *Hampshire Field Club Newsletter* ns 13 1990).

118–19 Two forms of truss of an aisled hall (Richard Harris: *Discovering Timber-framed Buildings*, Shire 1978).

120 Footings of a Viking-age house – Birsay (Or) (Magnus Magnusson and Graham White (eds): *The Nature of Scotland*, Canongate Press 1991).

121 Plan of two Viking-age houses – Birsay (Or) (*Ancient Monuments of Orkney*, HMSO 1978).

122 A Scottish blackhouse – Kilmuir, Skye (Richard Muir: *Reading the Celtic Landscape*, Michael Joseph/Shell UK 1985).

123 Plan of a large Scottish blackhouse – Callanish (Richard Muir: *Reading the Celtic Landscape*, Michael Joseph for Shell UK 1985).

124 A longhouse, view and plan (R W Brunskill: *Houses*, Collins 1982).

125 A possible longhouse – Spout House, Bilsdale (NY) (Eric Mercer: *English Vernacular Houses*, HMSO for RCHME 1975).

126–27 A Wealden house – Bayleaf; view and plan (W&D *Guide Book* 1975, 1987).

128 Schematic view of a lobby-entrance house (R W Brunskill: *Vernacular Architecture*, Faber 1970)

129–30 A double-pile house, view and plan (Richard Harris: *Discovering Timber-framed Buildings*, Shire 1978).

131 A "first-floor hall" – Boothby Pagnell (R W Brunskill: *Houses*, Collins 1982).

132 A typical peel, or fortified house (RN).

133 Jew's House and Jew's Court, Lincoln (City of Lincoln Information Centre leaflet/ Lincoln Central Library leaflet).

134–5 The Chester Rows, view and section ("Galleries Which They Call, The

Rows", *Chester Archaeological Society* 67 1985).

136 A late Georgian house, West Street, Farnham (Sy) (ESW).

137 The 18th-century development of part of west London (John Summerson: *Georgian London*, Penguin 1945).

138 Cumberland Terrace, London (Nikolaus Pevsner: *London*, Penguin 1952).

139 The Circus, Bath (Diana Winsor: *The Dream of Bath*, Trade and Travel Publications 1980).

140 James Craig's plan for part of the first New Town of Edinburgh, 1767 (Colin McWilliam: *Scottish Townscape*, Collins 1975).

141 Back-to-back housing, Leeds (Stefan Mutesius: *The English Terraced House*, Yale University Press 1982).

142 Woollen weavers' houses, Heptonstall (WY) (ESW).

143 Shop with workshop over (W&D/ ESW).

144 A "picturesque" cottage in a "model village", Blaise Hamlet (Nikolaus Pevsner: *North Somerset and Bristol*, Penguin 1958).

145 New Lanark (La) (Kenneth Hudson: *Industrial History from the Air*, CUP 1984).

146–8 Saltaire – "model village"; Congregational church; the Institute (*Yorkshire Textile Mills 1770–1930*, (HMSO for RCHME/ WYAS 1992).

149 Plan of an earthen long barrow.

150 Megalithic tombs (Eric Wood: *Field Guide to Archaeology in Britain*, Collins 1963).

151 Late Neolithic stone circle at Callanish, Lewis (WI) (Magnus Magnusson and Graham White (Eds): *The Nature of Scotland*, Canongate 1991).

152 Callanish stone circle plan (Aubrey Burl: *The Stone Circles of the British Isles*, Yale University Press 1976).

153 Round Barrows (L V Grinsell: *The Ancient Burial Mounds of England*,Methuen 1936).

154 Praying figure in painted plaster, Lullingstone (Kt) (G W Meates in R L S Bruce-Mitford: *Recent Archaeological Excavations in Britain*, RKP 1956).

155 Head of Christ, mosaic from Hinton St Mary (Do) Roman villa (Ann Woodward: *Shrines and Sacrifice*, EH/Batsford 1992).

156 Chi-rho device – Roman wall-painting, Lullingstone villa (G W Meates in

R L S Bruce-Mitford: *Recent Archaeological Excavations in Britain*, RKP 1956).

157 Winchester Close, plan (Nikolaus Pevsner: *Hampshire*, Penguin 1967).

158–9 The Vicars' Close at Wells (So) (John M Steane: *The Archaeology of Medieval England and Wales*, Croom Helm 1984).

160 Plan of Salisbury Cathedral (Nikolaus Pevsner: *Wiltshire*, Penguin 1975).

161 Plan of Chartres Cathedral (George Henderson: *Chartres*, Penguin 1968).

162 A major Saxon church – St Augustine's, Canterbury (Bridget Cherry in D M Wilson (ed): *The Archaeology of Anglo-Saxon Engand*, CUP 1976).

163 Lincoln Cathedral – Norman west front (1072–92) (William Anderson and Clive Hicks: *Cathedrals in Britain and Ireland*, Macdonald and Jane's 1978).

164 Plan of Fountains Abbey (NY) (F H Crossley: *The English Abbey*, Batsford 1935).

165 Mount Grace Priory (NY) (F H Crossley: *The English Abbey*, Batsford 1935; Alan Sorrell postcard).

166 A monastic tithe barn at Great Coxwell (Ox), at a former grange of Beaulieu Abbey (Colin Platt: *Medieval England*, RKP 1978).

167 The 13th-century tithe barn at Tisbury (Wi), on a former grange of Shaftesbury nunnery (Do), exterior (Colin Platt: *Medieval England*, RKP 1978).

168 Tisbury tithe barn, interior (Colin Platt: *Medieval England*, RKP 1978).

169 Christ Church, Spitalfields (Ln) (Ian Nairn: *Nairn's London*, Penguin 1966).

170 Rudston church (NY) (M D Anderson: *History and Imagery in British Churches*, John Murray 1971/ Alec Clifton-Taylor: *English Parish Churches*, Batsford 1074).

171 The Abbots Bromley Horn Dance (St) (Geoffrey Palmer and Noel Lloyd: *A Year of Festivals*, Warne 1972).

172 The carved image of a Green Man – Llangwm (Mo) (William Anderson: *Green Man*, HarperCollins 1990).

173 Celtic head – Gloucester (Anne Ross: *Pagan Celtic Britain*, RKP 1967).

174–6 Celtic heads – Gigglestone, Wakefield; Boston Spa; Greetland, Halifax (WY) (Sidney Jackson: *Celtic and Other Stone Heads*, author 1973).

177 Celtic head set in a wall –Ramsgill (NY) (ESW).

178 Holy Well of simple type – St Non's Well, St David's (Pb) (W M Mendus postcard).

179 A well – Tissington (Db): **a**, before dressing; **b**, after dressing (Roy Christian: *Well-Dressing in Derbyshire*, Derbyshire Countryside Ltd 1987).

180–7 The development of a church in nine stages – St Peter's, Barton-upon Humber (Warwick Rodwell: *The Archaeology of the English Church*, Batsford 1981).

188 The 15th-century spire at Louth (Li) (William Addison: *Local Styles of the English Parish Church*, Batsford 1982).

189 Broach spire – Sleaford (Li) (RN).

190 A typical 14th-century broach spire – Olney (Bc) (William Adddison: *Local Styles of the English Parish Church*, Batsford 1982).

191 Parish church with three naves – Shorwell (IW) (J A Dixon, postcard PW86870).

192 The crown spire of King's College, Aberdeen (Cuthbert Graham: *Portrait of Aberdeen and Deeside*, Robert Hale 1972).

193 Misericord – Exeter Cathedral (J C D Smith: *A Guide to Church Woodcarvings*, David and Charles 1974).

194 A three-decker pulpit and box pews (Christopher Howkins: *Discovering Church Furniture*, Shire 1964).

195 A stone pulpit, *c* 1440, with a Jacobean wooden tester – Shorwell (IW) (ESW).

196 A Gurney "Tortoise" stove (ESW).

197 An Easter sepulchre – Crediton (Dv) (Eric R Delderfield: *Church Furniture*, David and Charles 1966).

198 Norman font (M D Anderson: *History and Imagery in British Churches*, John Murray 1971/ Alec Clifton-Taylor: *English Parish Churches*, Batsford 1974).

199 Font of black Tournai marble, Winchester Cathedral (Winchester Cathedral postcard (Judges)/ M D Anderson: *History and Imagery in British Churches*, John Murray 1971).

200 A Seven Sacraments font, East Dereham (Nf) (J Charles Cox and Charles Bradley Ford: *The Parish Churches of England*, Batsford 1935 1943 ed).

201 A 12th-century shrine, for the relics

of a saint – Pennant Melangell (Mg) (local guide/ photo in the *Independent* 26 July 93.

202 Wall paintings, Holy Sepulchre Chapel, Winchester Cathedral ((Frederick Bussby: *Winchester Cathedral 1079–1979*, Paul Cave 1979/ *Winchester Cathedral*, Pitkin Visitors Guide 1990).

203 Norman doorway, with tympanum – Kilpeck (He), (William Addison: *Local Styles of the English Parish Church*, Batsford 1982).

204 Sanctuary knocker, Durham Cathedral (RN).

205 Scratch-dial (mass-clock) on a Norman doorway – Martyr Worthy (Ha) (ESW).

206–7 The "Leaves of Southwell" and Green Man (Nikolaus Pevsner: *The Leaves of Southwell*, Penguin 1945).

208–9 Hogsbacks – Brompton (NY) and Gosforth (Cu) , with bear ends (Richard N Bailey: *Viking-Age Sculpture*, Collins 1980).

210 A bedboard tomb (Frederick Burgess: *English Churchyard Memorials*, Lutterworth 1963).

211 Multiple bedboard over a family grave – Yateley (Ha) (ESW).

212–14 Chest tomb, bale tomb, and table tomb (Frederick Burgess: *English Churchyard Memorials*, Lutterworth 1963).

215 Brick barrel graves – Froyle (Ha) (ESW).

216 Lychgate with coffin rest – Chiddingford (Sy) (Aymer Vallance: *Old Crosses and Lychgates*, Batsford 1920).

217 Hudd – Odiham (Ha) (ESW).

218 Pest house for isolating people with contagious diseases – Odiham (Ha) (ESW).

219 Highgate Cemetery, London (*Highgate Cemetery: Victorian Valhalla*, John Murray 1984).

220 Six types of cross (Eric Wood: *Field Guide to Archaeology in Britain*, Collins 1963).

221 The main letters of the Ogam alphabet (Eric Wood: *Field Guide to Archaeology in Britain*, Collins 1963).

222 Pictish symbol stones (A Ritchie: *Picts*, HMSO 1989).

223–6 Borre, Jellinge, Mammen and Ringerike (Richard N Bailey: *Viking-Age Sculpture*, Collins 1980).

227 Eleanor cross – Geddington (Nh) (ESW).

228 The City Cross, Chichester (1501): the

finest of its type (*City Guide* 1972).

229 Scottish mercat cross – Culross (Fi) (Colin McWilliam: *Scottish Townscape*, Collins 1975).

230 Chantry chapels, Winchester Cathedral (John Crook: *Pitkin's Guide to Winchester Cathedral* 1971).

231 Methodist chapel, Heptonstall (WY) (Simon Warner).

232 Nonconformist chapel – Horningsham (Wi) (John Hibbs: *The Country Chapel*, David and Charles 1988).

233 Old Meeting – Horningsham (Wi)(John Hibbs: *The Country Chapel*, David and Charles 1988).

234–5 A Quaker meeting house – Come to Good, Kea (Co) (John Hibbs: *The Country Chapel*, David and Charles 1988).

236 Welsh chapel – Maesteg (Kenneth Lindley: *Chapels and Meeting Houses*, John Baker 1969).

237 The apprentice Pillar, Rosslyn Chapel (Andrew Sinclair: *The Sword and the Grail*, Century 1993)

238 The classical orders of architecture (John Fleming et al: *Penguin Dictionary of Architecture* 1972)

239 The timber nave at Greensted (Ex), c 845 (Mary and Nigel Kerr: *Anglo-Saxon Architecture*, Shire 1983).

240 The church tower at Earls Barton (Nh) (Mary and Nigel Kerr: *Anglo-Saxon Architecture*, Shire 1983).

241 Barnack church (Nh), round-headed doorway (Mary and Nigel Kerr: *Anglo-Saxon Architecture*, Shire 1983).

242 Barton-on-Humber church (Hu), tri-angular-headed doorway (Mary and Nigel Kerr: *Anglo-Saxon Architecture*, Shire 1983).

243–5 Anglo-Saxon single-splay windows; double-splay windows; double windows (Mary and Nigel Kerr: *Anglo-Saxon Architecture*, Shire 1983).

246 Escomb church (Nd), high narrow nave and chancel arch (William Addison: *Local Styles of the English Parish Church*, Batsford 1982).

247 The "Rhenish helm" roof of the tower of Sompting church (Sx) (William Addison: *Local Styles of the English Parish Church*, Batsford 1982).

248 Romsey Abbey (Ha) (*Romsey Abbey*, English Life Publication 1988).

249 Medieval window tracery (John

Fleming et al: *Penguin Dictionary of Architecture* 1972)

250 Fan vaulting – Gloucester Cathedral (Abbey) cloisters (G B Nicholson: *England's Greater Churches*, Batsford 1949).

251 Fan vaulting – Henry VII's chapel, Westminster Abbey (G B Nicholson: *England's Greater Churches*, Batsford 1949).

252 Renaissance block, Caerlaverock Castle (W Douglas Simpson: *The Ancient Stones of Scotland*, Hale 1965).

253 The Scottish Baronial style, Craigievar (W Douglas Simpson: *The Ancient Stones of Scotland*, Hale 1965).

254 Norman troops (or impressed men) throwing up a motte at Hastings during the invasion of 1066 (from the Bayeux Tapestry).

255 The early Norman motte at Abinger (Sy) (Colin Platt: *Medieval England*, RKP 1978).

256 Shell keep – Framlingham (Su) (Colin Platt: *Medieval England*, RKP 1978).

257–9 A shell keep on a motte – Clifford's Tower, York, view, section and plan (R Allen Brown: *The Castle in England and Wales*, Croom Helm 1988).

260 Square keep of Henry I's type – Castle Hedingham (Ex) (*Essex Homes 1066–1850*, Essex CC, Essex Record Office Publications no 30 1978).

261 A keep of Henry II's reign – Conisborough (Sy), *c* 1180–1190 (R Allen Brown: *English Castles*, Batsford 1954).

262–3 A concentric castle of Edward I's type – Beaumaris (An) – view and plan (R Allen Brown: *English Castles*, Batsford 1954).

264 Castell Coch, near Cardiff (HMSO/ Aerofilms).

265 A Scottish peel tower (W Douglas Simpson: *The Ancient Stones of Scotland*, Hale 1965).

266 Stokesay Castle (Sp) (Colin Platt: *Medieval England*, RKP 1978).

267 Roman town wall, Silchester (ESW).

268–9 The Balkerne Gate, Colchester – view and plan (Philip Crummy: *In Search of Colchester's Past*, Colchester Archaeological Trust 1986).

270 West Gate, Winchester (ESW)

271 Walmgate Bar, York (Ronald Willis: *The Illustrated Portrait of York*, Robert Hale 1988).

272 The Queen's Sconce, Newark-on-Trent (from a model in Newark Museum).

273 Deal Castle (Kt) (D J Cathcart King: *The Castle in England and Wales*, Croom Helm 1988).

274 Martello tower – Pevensey (Sx) (Martin Brice: *Forts and Fortresses*, Facts on File, OUP 1990).

275 Second world war concrete pillbox (Martin Brice: *Forts and Fortresses*, Facts on File, OUP 1990).

276 The Banqueting House, Whitehall, London (Nikolaus Pevsner: *London*, Penguin 1952)

277 Customs House – King's Lynn (John Seymour: *The Companion Guide to East Anglia*, Collins 1970).

278 Manchester Town Hall (Nikolaus Pevsner: *South Lancashire*, Penguin 1969).

279 Town Hall, Newtown (IW) ESW).

280 Almshouse – St Cross (Jo Draper: *Hampshire: The Complete Guide*, Dovecote Press 1990).

281–2 St Mary's Hospital, Chichester, interior and exterior (local *Guide*).

283 Gatehouse of Abbot's Hospital, Guildford (ESW).

284 Almshouse – Abbot's Hospital, Guildford, interior of courtyard (ESW).

285 Workhouse – Alton (Ha) (ESW)

286 Royal Grammar School, Guildford, 1508 (ESW).

287 The general classroom of an old school – St Olave's Southwark (Ln) (from an old print in R C Carrington: *Two Schools* 1971).

288 Row of houses at Worcester College, Oxford (ESW).

289 Roman theatre – Orange, France (*The Oxford Companion to the Theatre*, OUP 1983).

290 Roman theatre, Verulamium (*The Oxford Companion to the Theatre*, OUP 1983).

291 The Swan theatre, London (from an old print/ *The Oxford Companion to the Theatre*, OUP 1983).

292 Burbage's second Blackfriars theatre, London, (*The Oxford Companion to the Theatre*, OUP 1983).

293 The Schouwburg, Amsterdam (from an old print/ *The Oxford Companion to the Theatre*, OUP 1983).

294 Drury Lane Theatre in 1808 (from an old print/ *The Oxford Companion to the Theatre*, OUP 1983).

295 The Haymarket Theatre, London (from an old print *c* 1820/ *The Oxford Companion to the Theatre*, OUP 1983).

296 The Georgian Theatre, Richmond (NY) (*The Oxford Companion to the Theatre*, OUP 1983).

297 The Stratford (Ontario) Festival Theatre,

which inspired the Chichester Festival Theatre (*The Oxford Companion to the Theatre*, OUP 1983).

298 Theatre in the round – the Victoria, Stoke-on-Trent 1960s (*The Oxford Companion to the Theatre*, OUP 1983).

299 Palace Picture Pavilion, Blackpool, *c* 1910(Iris Publishing Ltd, Peterborough).

300 The Assembly Rooms at York (John Summerson: *Architecture in Britain 1530–1830*, Penguin 1958).

301 Statue of William III, Petersfield (Ha) (ESW).

302 The Grenville monument at Stowe (1748) (ESW).

303 Section of a Roman road (Eric Wood: *Field Guide to Archaeology in Britain*, Collins 1963).

304 17th/18th century roadway on the line of a Roman road – Henley (Sx) (ESW).

305 Cast-iron signpost – Semley (Wi) (ESW).

306 Wayside marker, Fife – Newton of Balcormo (Walter M Stephen in *Proceedings of the Society of Antiquarians of Scotland*, 100 1967–8).

307 A hollow lane – Selborne (Ha) (ESW).

308 Maud Heath's Causeway, Kellaways (Wi) (Nikolaus Pevsner: *Wiltshire*, Penguin 1963).

309 A granite sett road surface – Princes Street, Norwich (National Trust *The English Country Town*, Webb and Bower 1983).

310 A cobbled road surface, Rye (Sx) (The National Trust: *The English Country Town*, Webb and Bower 1983).

311 Raised pavement – Godalming (Eric Wood: *Field Guide to Archaeology in Britain*, Collins 1963).

312 Drove road, south of Peebles (A R B Haldane: *The Drove Roads of Scotland*, David and Charles 1973).

313 Drovers' harbour – Grass Point, Mull (David Howitt).

314 Mastiles Lane, Wharfedale (NY) (Arthur Raistrick: *Green Tracks on the Pennines*, Dalesman 1962).

315 Drovers' inn at Stockbridge (Ha) (ESW).

316 A clapper bridge (Mustograph).

317 A medieval bridge – Stopham (Sx) (Mustograph).

318 Bridge chapel/oratory – Bradford-on-Avon (Courtney Dainton: *Clock Jacks and Bee Boles*, Phoenix House 1957).

319 The fortified bridge at Monmouth (J Salmon Ltd).

320 A packhorse bridge (G Bernard Wood:

Bridges in Britain, Cassell 1970).

321 The Iron Bridge, Coalbrookdale (Sp) (Iron Bridge, a pictorial souvenir, Ironbridge Gorge Museum).

322 The Forth Bridge (P J G Ransom: *The Archaeology of Railways*, World's Work 1981).

323 Causey Arch (Du) (Frank Atkinson: *Industrial Archaeology – Top Ten Sites in NE England*, 1971).

324 Haytor Granite Tramway (Dv) (Bertram Baxter: *Stone Blocks and Iron Rails*, David and Charles 1966/ R J Westlake: *View of Devon*, Hale 1977).

325 Horse-drawn wagon on a wagonway (Derek A Bayliss: *Retracing the First Public Railway*, author 1985).

326 Arnos Grove Underground station, London (London Transport Museum).

327 Types of railway track (ESW notes).

328 Signal box – London Brighton and South Coast Railway, Battersea (Jack Simmons: *The Railways of Britain*, Macmillan 1986).

329 Ribblehead viaduct (P J G Ransom: *The Archaeology of Railways*, World's Work 1981).

330 The Euston Arch (from an old print, *c* 1850).

331 St Pancras Station, London (Christine Heap and John van Riemsdijk: *The Pre-Grouping Railways*, Part 1, HMSO for the Science Museum 1972).

332 York station (Jack Simmons: *The Railways of Britain*, RKP 1961, 3rd ed Macmillan 1986).

333 Huddersfield Station (Jack Simmons: *The Railways of Britain*, RKP 1961, 1986).

334 The first postbox, London, 1855 (Martin Robinson: *Old Letter Boxes*, Shire 1987).

335–7 The first "pillar" box, "Penfold" and standard pillar boxes (1856) (Martin Robinson: *Old Letter Boxes*, Shire 1987).

338 The Cutlers' Guildhall, Thaxted (Ex) (*Towns of Essex*, Essex Record Office Publications no 57).

339 Market hall – Pembury (He) (ESW)

340 Town (and market) Hall, Abingdon (Ox) (David W Lloyd: *The Making of English Towns*, Gollancz 1984).

341 Corn Exchange – Bury St Edmunds (Su) (Borough of St Edmundsbury, *Official Guide* 1976).

342 The Shambles, York (Marie Hartley and Joan Ingilby: *Yorkshire Album*, Dent 1988).

343 Cheap Street, Frome (So) (ESW).

344 Clay tobacco pipes, showing the development of bowl forms (Eric Wood: *Field Guide to*

Archaeology in Britain, Collins 1963).

345 A Georgian shop front – Artillery Lane, (Ln) (Nikolaus Pevsner: *London*, Penguin 1952).

346 Early 19th-century shop front – Stonegate (*York, Historic Buildings in the Central Area* (HMSO for RCHME 1981), York.

347 The Royal Opera Arcade, London (*Survey of London* vol 30, St James 1960).

348 County Arcade, Leeds (David W Lloyd: *The Making of English Towns*, Gollancz 1984).

349 A chemist's lamp sign – Milford (ESW).

350 AA sign, Amberley Museum (ESW).

351 A monastic inn – Glastonbury (So) (The National Trust *The English Country Town*, Webb and Bower 1983).

352 The George Inn, Southwark (Russell Chamberlin: The National Trust *The English Country Town*, Webb and Bower 1983).

353 Coaching inn – Guildford (Sy) (ESW).

354 St Pancras Station, London, the hotel (Christine Heap and John van Riemsdijk: *The Pre-Grouping Railways*, Part 1, HMSO for Science Museum 1972).

355 The Athenaeum, London (Nikolaus Pevsner: *London*, Penguin 1952).

356–62 Corn dollies: Traditional; Cambridgeshire bell; Welsh fan; Yorkshire lantern; Staffordshire knot; Suffolk horse-shoe; Essex terret (M Lambeth: *Discovering Corn Dollies*, Shire 1974).

363–5 Charcoal burning (W&D/MERL).

366 Coracle of river Teifi type, view and plan (Dixon postcard/ James Hornell: *Water Transport*, David and Charles 1970).

368 Pit-sawing (MERL).

369 A pole lathe in operation (ESW).

370 Wheelwrighting; lowering the tyre onto the wheel (MERL).

371–8 A Yorkshire wagon; all-purpose cart; Berkshire wagon; Devonshire wagon; Dorset wagon; Huntingdonshire wagon; Sussex wagon; East Anglian wagon (all MERL).

379 Romany bender tent (postcard, Peter Ingram, Romany Museum, Selborne).

380 Romany (gypsy) caravan: bow top type (ESW photo in P Ingram's Yard, Selborne).

381 Romany (gypsy) caravan: Reading type (Hampshire Museum Service postcard).

382 Early woollen mill – Langfield (WY) (*Yorkshire Textile Mills 1770–1930* (HMSO/ WYAS 1992).

383 Warehouse and offices in Egyptian style – Marshall's Mill, Leeds (*Yorkshire Textile Mills 1770–1930*, HMSO/ WYAS 1992).

384 Woollen and worsted mills, Huddersfield (*Yorkshire Textile Mills 1770–1930*, (HMSO/ WYAS 1992).

385 Italianate mill chimney – Manningham Mills, Bradford (*Yorkshire Textile Mills 1770–1930*, (HMSO/ WYAS 1992).

386 The Piece Hall, Halifax (*Official Guide 1988/ Yorkshire Textile Mills 1770–1930*, HMSO/WYAS 1992).

387 Masson Mill, Cromford (Db) (N Pevsner: *A History of Building Types*, Thames and Hudson 1976).

388 Knitters' housing – Calverton (ESW).

389 Framework knitters' workshop (Marilyn Palmer: *Framework Knitting*, Shire 1984).

390 Ruddington frameshop, interior (Dorothy Shrimpton: "Ruddington Framework Knitters' Museum" in *Textile History*, 17, 2 1986).

391 Bottle ovens – Etruria (St) (Barrie Trinder: *The Making of the Industrial Landscape*, Dent 1982).

392 Glass furnace of southern (Venetian) type (Ruth Hurst: *Glass*, Collins 1980/ Johann Kunckel: *Ars Vitraria Experimentalis* 1679)

393 Inside a glasshouse (*La Verre*, Hachette 1960, from Diderot and d'Alembert's *Encyclopédie* of 1772)

394 Plan of a forest glasshouse of *c* 1330 – Blunden's Wood (Sy) (Eric Wood in *Surrey Archaeological Collections* LXII 1965).

395 A reconstruction of the Blunden's Wood glasshouse (Pilkington Glass Museum).

396 Glasshouse at Knightons, Alfold (Sy) (Eric S Wood in *Surrey Archaeological Collections* LXXIII 1982).

397 The Rosedale glass furnace, plan (D W Crossley).

398 Late period glasshouse, Rosedale (D W Crossley).

399 A 16th-century glass pedlar (from *Anciens Cris de Paris* in G H Kenyon: *The Glass Industry of the Weald*, Leicester University Press 1967).

400 Glass cone – Catcliffe, Sheffield (Arthur Raistrick: *Industrial Archaeology*, Eyre Methuen 1972).

401 Section of a neolithic flint mine – based on Grimes Graves, near Thetford (Nf) ((Eric Wood: *Field Guide to Archaeology in Britain*, Collins 1963).

402 Remains of medieval stone workings, "hills and holes" – Barnack (Ca) (M W Beresford and J K St Joseph: *Medieval England:*

An Aerial Survey, CUP 1958/Crown copyright).

403 A "wine and coal" post (Courtney Dainton: *Clock Jacks and Bee Boles*, Phoenix House 1957).

404 Partly ruined engine house at the Cornish Levant tin-mine – Geevor (*National Trust Magazine* no 68 1993).

405 The great wheel of Killhope lead-crushing mill in Weardale (Du) (ESW).

406 Abraham Darby's iron furnace, Coalbrookedale (SY) (Arthur Raistrick: *Dynasty of Ironfounders*, David and Charles 1970/ Brian Bracegirdle: *The Archaeology of the Industrial Revolution*, Heinemann 1973).

407 Spoil heaps of iron mines – Bentley Grange, Emley (Kenneth Hudson: *Industrial Archaeology from the Air*, CUP 1984).

408 Blast furnace – Moira (Le) (ESW).

409 Ironwork on a church door – Staplehurst (Kt) (G J Hollister-Short: *Discovering Wrought Iron*, Shire 1970).

410 Ironwork on door –York Minster (G J Hollister-Short: *Discovering Wrought Iron*, Shire 1970).

411 Wrought iron gates – Hampton Court (G J Hollister-Short: *Discovering Wrought Iron*, Shire 1970).

412 Robert Bakewell's "Cage" (Melbourne House Guide).

413 Handrails at a hotel doorway – Rutland Arms, Bakewell (Db) (ESW).

414–16 The parts of a horseshoe; the changing forms of the horseshoe; shoes for other animals (Ivan G Sparkes: *Old Horseshoes*, Shire 1976).

417 A cast-iron fireback (H R Schubert: *History of the British Iron and Steel Industry from c 450BC–AD1775/* John Every Bequest, Lewes Museum).

418 Regency ironwork – Scarborough (NY) (ESW).

419 A horse-trough – West Horsley (Sy) (ESW)

420 Bollard made from a gun barrel (ESW)

421–2 Coalhole covers – London (ESW).

423 Dorset bridge plaque (Henry Aaron: *Street Furniture*, Shire 1980).

424 The door of a late 18th-century limekiln – Lindisfarne (Nd) (RN).

425 A coastal limekiln – Gwbert (Cd) (Anthony Vickers).

426 Lime kilns – Beadnell (Nd) (RN).

427 Undershot waterwheel – Mapledurham (Ox) (ESW).

428 The Great Laxey Wheel (IM) (Kenneth Hudson: *Industrial Archaeology*, John Baker 1963).

429 Bramah waterwheel – Painshill (ESW).

430 A horizontal watermill – Click mill, Dounby, Orkney (RN).

431 Millstone, showing the traditional pattern of grooves (Eric Wood: *Field Guide to Archaeology in Britain*, Collins 1963/ Crown copyright).

432 Treadwheel, for raising water from a wall – Catherington (Ha) (W&D).

433 Heckington windmill (Li) (RN).

434 A unique medieval plan of the monastery at Canterbury (Joan Evans (ed): *The Flowering of the Middle Ages*, Thames and Hudson 1966).

435 Cistern tower – Canterbury Cathedral (*Canterbury Cathedral*, Pitkin Pictorials 1972).

436 Pumping station – Papplewick (ESW).

437 Papplewick pumping station (ESW).

438 Victorian fountain – Wallingford (ESW).

439 Village pump – Barton (Hu) (R Page: *The Decline of the English Village*, Ashford 1989).

440 Village pump – Leyburn (NY) (ESW).

441 A public fountain – the Lion's Mouth, Selborne (Ha) (Anne Mallinson Collection, Selborne).

442 Roman sewer – Church Street, York (*The Archaeology of York*, fascicule 3/1 1976).

443 Monastic sewer – Paisley Abbey (John Malden: in *Current Archaeology* 131 1992).

444 Early 20th-century petrol pumps – Selborne (Ha) (ESW).

445 Netshops – Hastings (Sx) (Peter West in the *Independent*, 6 August 1990).

446 Bucklers Hard (Ha) (site leaflet/ Pitkin postcard).

447 Warehouse – St Katherine's Dock (Ln) (Ian Nairn: *Nairn's London*, Penguin 1966).

448 Dry dock – Portsmouth (ESW).

449 19th-century river warehouses – Guildford (Sy) (ESW).

450 Roman lighthouse – Dover (R J A Wilson: *Roman Remains in Britain*, Constable 1988).

451 Medieval lighthouse – St Catherine's Oratory, Chale Down (IW) (ESW).

452 Beacon tower – Blakeney (Nf) (John Bethell: *The English Coast*, Weidenfeld 1993).

453 The Needles lighthouse (Isle of Wight *Official Guide* 1992, with OS Map, Landranger 196/Crown copyright).

454 Happisburgh church (Sf) (ESW).

Subjects